BLUE RIBBON

College Football Yearbook

Other sports titles from Brassey's

Blue Ribbon College Basketball Yearbook: 2001-02 Edition, edited by Chris Dortch

Playing Hurt: Evaluating and Treating the Warriors of the NFL, by Pierce E. Scranton, Jr., M.D.

Links Lore: Dramatic Moments and Forgotten Milestones from Golf's History, by Peter F. Stevens

Baseball Prospectus: 2001 Edition, by Joseph S. Sheehan et. al.

Jewish Sports Legends: Third Edition, by Joseph M. Siegman

At Speed: Up Close and Personal with the People, Places, and Fans of NASCAR, by Monte Dutton

Rebel with a Cause: A Season with NASCAR Star Tony Stewart, by Monte Dutton

The Most Wanted Series:
Football's Most Wanted: The Top 10 Book of the Great Game's Outrageous Characters, Fortunate Fumbles, and Other Oddities, by Floyd Conner

Golf's Most Wanted: The Top 10 Book of Outrageous Duffers, Deadly Divots, and Other Oddities, by Floyd Conner

Baseball's Most Wanted: The Top 10 Book of the National Pastime's Outrageous Offenders, Lucky Bounces, and Other Oddities, by Floyd Conner

Basketball's Most Wanted: The Top 10 Book of Hoop's Outrageous Dunkers, Incredible Buzzer-Beaters, and Other Oddities, by Floyd Conner

NASCAR's Most Wanted: The Top 10 Book of Outrageous Drivers, Wild Wrecks, and Other Oddities, by Jim McLaurin

Soccer's Most Wanted: The Top 10 Book of Clumsy Keepers, Clever Crosses, and Outlandish Oddities, by John Snyder

Wrestling's Most Wanted: The Top 10 Book of Pro-Wrestling's Outrageous Performers, Punishing Piledrivers, and Other Oddities, by Floyd Conner

College Football Yearbook

2001 Edition

Edited by Chris Dortch

Washington, D.C.

ISBN 1-57488-374-7

Printed in the United States of America.

Brassey's, Inc.
22841 Quicksilver Drive
Dulles, Virginia 20166

First Edition

10 9 8 7 6 5 4 3 2 1

FROM THE EDITOR

A year ago while doing publicity for the debut edition of *Blue Ribbon College Football Yearbook*, I elicited a few stunned reactions from talk show hosts and our loyal readers with a comment I made about the quality of our new publication.

"This is the best product *Blue Ribbon* has ever done," I said to anyone who would listen. "Bar none."

After such a bold statement, many of our friends in the electronic media, along with long-time fans of *Blue Ribbon College Basketball Yearbook*, thought I had been playing a little too much golf in the hot sun. Was this new venture better than our basketball book, which at that time was about to enter its 20th printing? Was it better than our popular NCAA Tournament edition?

Yes it was. And is.

Don't misunderstand. No one loves college basketball more than I. And after devoting the last 10 years of my life to our basketball yearbook, I've grown very fond of that publication, called the "Bible" of the sport by nearly everyone who reads it.

So what makes our football yearbook better than the Bible? Sheer volume.

Without a doubt, no publication has ever covered college basketball the way *Blue Ribbon* does. The book profiles every NCAA Division I team with a full story and gives the royal treatment to Top 40 teams, with stories of 4,000 words and up.

Certainly, that's as much college basketball info as anyone, even the most hardcore junkie, needs. In football, we take that times 10.

How? Our football edition focuses only on the 115 schools classified by the NCAA as Division I-A. With fewer schools to include than the basketball edition—last year the total was 318—the football book can expand its coverage. The average length of a *Blue Ribbon* football story is 4,500 words. Most are a lot longer.

Thus my contention that the football book is the best publication we've ever put out. We write more on Nebraska than most publications write about the entire Big 12. Our readers can learn so much more about their favorite teams—and their opponents—in the football book.

Lest I do our great team of writers an injustice by focusing only on the length of our stories, let me say this. The quality of our writing is first-rate. Our staff has a unique knack for getting great insider information and turning into readable copy.

A lot has happened since *Blue Ribbon College Football Yearbook* debuted last year. This year, we have entered into a publishing agreement with Brassey's, Inc. of Dulles, Va. Brassey's, which produces the excellent *Baseball Prospectus*, longs to become the premier publisher of sports annuals. After bringing *Blue Ribbon* yearbooks into the fold to join *Baseball Prospectus*, that lofty goal might have already been met.

Brassey's and its solid team of professionals brings a new dimension to *Blue Ribbon*. For the first time, our books will be marketed and promoted to a wide audience. The two yearbooks will be available in all major bookstores and their corresponding web sites or by calling two toll-free numbers. Those numbers: 800-775-2518 during normal business hours Monday through Friday, or 800-ALLBOOK 24 hours a day, seven days a week.

Blue Ribbon will be easier to purchase than ever, and Brassey's plans to sell a ton of them. It does my heart good to know that our books will be seen by an increasing number of readers.

Other changes are in store. At this writing, *Blue Ribbon* is negotiating a deal to offer several of our products on-line. We'll offer more details on that project soon.

In closing, I'd like to thank all the dedicated professionals who helped make this book a reality. That list includes my loyal and hard-working associate editors, Dave Link and Stan Crawley, and Brian Hinchman, our talented designer. I also want to thank Richard Billingsley, whose Top 25 poll, used to help determine the BCS rankings, is the basis for the rankings you'll find in *Blue Ribbon*. Visit Richard's web site (www.cfrc.com) for rankings past and present. You'll be amazed.

We think you'll also be amazed by the second edition of *Blue Ribbon College Football Yearbook*. It's the best publication we produce. Really.

Team Index

Conference Index

BLUE RIBBON MEDIA, LLC

PRESIDENT—Drew Maddux
EDITOR AND PUBLISHER—Chris Dortch
OPERATIONS MANAGER—Bryan Chance
ASSOCIATE EDITORS—Stan Crawley, Dave Link

EDITORIAL STAFF

ATLANTIC COAST—Mike Ashley, Dan Collins, Al Featherston, Tim Peeler, Bob Thomas
BIG EAST—Michael Bradley
BIG 12—Wendell Barnhouse, Blair Kerkhoff
BIG TEN—Bill Doherty, Patrick Donnelly, Michael Grant
CONFERENCE USA—Stan Crawley, Dave Link, Mike Strange
INDEPENDENTS—Steve Bradley, Bill Doherty, Mike Sorensen
MID-AMERICAN—Rob Cornelius
MOUNTAIN WEST—Mike Sorensen
PACIFIC-10—Jay Heater
SOUTHEASTERN—John Adams, Chris Low
SUN BELT—Stan Crawley
WESTERN ATHLETIC—Cody Monk

PRODUCTION

DESIGN—Brian Hinchman
PRINTING—Ambrose Printing, Nashville, Tenn.
RANKINGS—Richard Billingsley, College Football Research Center

Offensive Player of the Year

Ken Dorsey

Quarterback, Miami

The quarterback legacy at Miami is well established.

The Hurricanes breed quarterbacks the way MIT does engineers and Harvard does attorneys.

It's a fraternity that includes the likes of Jim Kelly, Vinny Testaverde, Bernie Kosar, Steve Walsh, Craig Erickson and Gino Torretta.

The latest entry is Ken Dorsey, who heads into this season as one of the top returning quarterbacks in the country, and as good a candidate as any for the Heisman Trophy.

His rise has been nothing short of meteoric, surprising even Dorsey. After all, the 6-5, 195-pound junior from Orinda, Calif., has played just one season as a full-time starter.

But his production, poise and smarts helped steer Miami to a No. 2 national ranking last season and a 37-20 whipping of Florida in the Sugar Bowl.

Above everything else, what Dorsey has done best is win. He's guided the Hurricanes to victories in 14 of his 15 starts.

"Ken became a very strong leader for us last year, and he needs to continue to develop as a leader," said first-year Miami head coach Larry Coker, who took over after Butch Davis left for the Cleveland Browns. "He will have the responsibility of bringing our young receivers along, much like the veteran receivers did during his early days as a starter. So you could say he's come full-circle."

Dorsey, who reminded Davis most of Kosar with his lanky frame and feel for the game, passed for 2,727 yards and 25 touchdowns last season, while throwing just five interceptions.

Closing the season with a flurry, Dorsey broke the school record for passes thrown without an interception. His totals for completions, completion percentage and yardage rank among the top 10 single-season performances by any Miami quarterback.

But gone are star receivers Santana Moss and Reggie Wayne. Returning senior Darryl Jones has shown plenty of promise, but it's clear that Dorsey's role will broaden substantially.

"I have to take more of a leadership role and be more vocal," Dorsey told USA Today. "Last year, a lot of that was left up to guys like Santana and Reggie, but now the younger guys are looking to me to fill that role. But I'm comfortable with it.

"I did it in high school, and in my position, it's something I'm expected to do."

—Chris Low

Blue Ribbon College Football Yearbook Offensive All-America Team

Quarterback

KEN DORSEY
Miami, 6-5, 210, Jr.

Running Backs

DAMIEN ANDERSON
Northwestern, 5-11, 204, Sr.

KEN SIMONTON
Oregon State, 5-8, 191, Sr.

T.J. DUCKETT
Michigan State, 6-2, 250, Jr.

Receivers

JABAR GAFFNEY
Florida, 6-1, 202, So.

ANTONIO BRYANT
Pittsburgh, 6-2, 185, Jr.

ROY WILLIAMS
Texas, 6-5, 210, So.

Tight End

TIM STRATTON
Purdue, 6-4, 258, Sr.

Offensive Line

TERRENCE METCALF
Ole Miss, 6-3, 315, Sr.

BRYANT MCKINNIE
Miami, 6-9, 330, Miami, Sr.

FRANK ROMERO
Oklahoma, 6-4, 286, Sr.

CHRIS GIBSON
Oregon State, 6-3, 279, Sr.

MIKE PEARSON
Florida, 6-7, 292, Jr.

Kicker

JONATHAN RUFFIN
Cincinnati, 5-10, 185, Jr.

Specialists

LATARENCE DUNBAR
TCU, 5-11, 192, Jr.

JULIUS JONES
Notre Dame, 5-10, 201, Jr.

Defensive Player of the Year

John Henderson

Defensive Lineman, Tennessee

Tennessee defensive tackle John Henderson was dominant as a junior, so much so that he evoked comparisons to another superstar defensive lineman from Big Orange Country, Reggie White.

But Henderson's teammate, offensive guard Fred Weary, says you ain't seen nothing yet.

"The thing about John is that what he did last year is just that, last year," Weary said. "He's going to push himself and push everybody else, too.

"It's going to be amazing to see how good he can be this year on that football field."

The 6-7, 295-pound Henderson was pretty amazing last season. He won the Outland Trophy as college football's top interior lineman and led the SEC with 12 sacks.

Opposing teams tried just about everything to slow him down, but Henderson was a one-man wrecking crew with his combination of size, strength, agility and improved technique.

"I don't know if there's a better football player in the country," South Carolina head coach Lou Holtz marveled toward the end of last season.

The mere fact that Henderson is back for his senior season is somewhat of a surprise. Draft analyst Mike Detillier thought Henderson would have gone in the top 10 picks of this year's NFL draft.

But by staying, Henderson's the odds-on favorite to be the top player selected overall in the 2002 draft by the expansion Houston Texans.

This spring, Texans general manager Charley Casserly was in Knoxville to get a closer look at Henderson during the Vols' spring workouts.

Henderson admits that at one point last season he thought he would probably bypass his senior season for the NFL.

"But as the season went on, some things started changing," said Henderson, who racked up his totals last season despite facing a steady stream of double teams.

"I thought about everything and not just football. I guess you could say that I saw the big picture. ... The next level is basically about money and business, and I wasn't ready for that."

Instead, he's ready for another college season of opposing offenses ganging up on him from every angle. But Henderson says that's OK.

"That's going to give [tackle cohort] Albert Haynesworth and our ends and linebackers a chance to destroy some people," said Henderson, who sat out his freshman season as a partial qualifier. "Teams are going to have to decide which way they want it."

—Chris Low

Blue Ribbon College Football Yearbook Defensive All-America Team

Linebackers

ROCKY CALMUS
Oklahoma, 6-3, 235, Sr.

LEVAR FISHER
N.C. State, 6-4, 229, Sr.

KALIMBA EDWARDS
South Carolina, 6-6, 260, Sr.

BEN TAYLOR
Virginia Tech, 6-2, 240, Sr.

Defensive Line

JOHN HENDERSON
Tennessee, 6-7, 290, Sr.

WENDELL BRYANT
Wisconsin, 6-4, 293, Sr.

JULIUS PEPPERS
North Carolina, 6-6, 270, Sr.

ALEX BROWN
Florida, 6-4, 262, Sr.

LARRY TRIPPLETT
Washington, 6-1, 300, Sr.

Defensive Backs

LITO SHEPPARD
Florida, 5-10, 194, Jr.

EDWARD REED
Miami, 6-0, 190, Sr.

MIKE DOSS
Ohio State, 5-11, 197, Jr.

ROY WILLIAMS
Oklahoma, 6-0, 221, Jr.

QUENTIN JAMMER
Texas, 5-11, 198, Sr.

PIG PRATHER
Mississippi State, 6-3, 191, Sr.

Punter

PRESTON GRUENING
Minnesota, 5-10, 204, Jr.

Specialists

ANDRE DAVIS
Virginia Tech, 6-1, 194, Sr.

AARON LOCKETT
Kansas State, 5-7, 165, Sr.

Blue Ribbon College Football Yearbook Preseason Top 25

1. Miami
2. Florida
3. Oklahoma
4. Nebraska
5. Texas
6. Tennessee
7. Florida State
8. Virginia Tech
9. UCLA
10. Georgia Tech
11. Oregon
12. Northwestern
13. Kansas State
14. Michigan
15. Mississippi State
16. Notre Dame
17. Wisconsin
18. Washington
19. LSU
20. Clemson
21. Southern Cal
22. Michigan State
23. South Carolina
24. Purdue
25. Georgia

ATLANTIC COAST

BLUE RIBBON FORECAST

1. Florida State
2. Georgia Tech
3. Clemson
4. North Carolina State
5. Maryland
6. Virginia
7. North Carolina
8. Wake Forest
9. Duke

ALL-CONFERENCE TEAM

OFFENSE

POS. PLAYER SCHOOL HT. WT. CL.

WR Kelly Campbell, Georgia Tech, 5-11, 170, Sr.
WR Atrews Bell, Florida State, 5-11, 201, Sr.
OL Brett Williams, Florida State, 6-6, 315, Jr.
OL Jermese Jones, Virginia, 6-6, 320, Sr.
C Kyle Young, Clemson, 6-3, 280, Sr.
OL Montrae Holland, Florida State, 6-3, 325, Jr.
OL Evan Routzahn, Virginia, 6-5, 303, Sr.
QB Woodrow Dantzler, Clemson, 5-11, 200, Sr.
RB Antwoine Womack, Virginia, 6-0, 215, Sr.
RB Travis Zachery, Clemson, 6-0, 190, Sr.
TE Willie Wright, N.C. State, 6-4, 226, Sr.

DEFENSE

POS. PLAYER SCHOOL HT. WT. CL.

DL Julius Peppers, North Carolina, 6-6, 270, Jr.
DL Greg Gathers, Jr. Georgia Tech, 6-1, 260, Jr.
DL Nick Rogers, Georgia Tech, 6-2, 255, Sr.
DL Darnell Dockett, Florida State, 6-4, 260, So.
LB Levar Fisher, N.C. State, 6-1, 229, Sr.
LB Chad Carson, Clemson, 6-3, 235, Sr.
LB Recardo Wimbush, Georgia Tech, 6-1, 218, Jr.
DB Chris Hope, Florida State, 6-0, 205, Sr.
DB Terrence Holt, N.C. State, 6-2, 199, Jr.
DB Brian Williams, N.C. State, 6-0, 200, Sr.
DB Errol Hood, North Carolina, 5-11, 195, Sr.

SPECIALISTS

POS. PLAYER SCHOOL HT. WT. CL.

PK Luke Manget, Georgia Tech, 5-9, 176, Jr.
P Brooks Barnard, Maryland, 6-2, 182, Jr.
RS John Stone, Wake Forest, 5-11, 180, Sr.

OFFENSIVE PLAYER OF THE YEAR

Woody Dantzler, QB, Clemson

DEFENSIVE PLAYER OF THE YEAR

Levar Fisher, LB, North Carolina State

NEWCOMER OF THE YEAR

Chris Rix, QB, Florida State

ACC NOTEBOOK

ACC coaches will no doubt be spending extra time in the film room this season. Eight of the nine league schools have new offensive coordinators: Marty Galbraith at N.C. State, Brad Scott at Clemson, Bill O'Brien at Georgia Tech, Jeff Bowden at Florida State, Charlie Taaffe at Maryland, Gary Tranquill at North Carolina, Bill Musgrave at Virginia and Troy Calhoun at Wake Forest. ... That turnover was caused in large part by turnover at the top. Four league schools have new head coaches: Ralph Friedgen at Maryland, Al Groh at Virginia, John Bunting at North Carolina and Jim Grobe at Wake Forest. ... Five ACC head coaches are working for their alma maters. In addition to Friedgen, Groh and Bunting, that list includes N.C. State's Chuck Amato and Duke's Carl Franks. ... The turnover among head coaches isn't unusual. Since Florida State joined the ACC in 1992, every team in the league but the Seminoles have changed coaches at least once. All but Georgia Tech and Virginia have changed twice. Only FSU's Bobby Bowden has remained comfortably at his job, and he doesn't appear to be going anywhere any time soon. ... In an effort to boost the league's overall strength of schedule, the ACC helped arrange for six of its schools to set up home-and-home series with Notre Dame over the next decade. Florida State, Georgia Tech, Virginia, Maryland, N.C. State and North Carolina all have at least two games scheduled against the Fighting Irish between 2002 and 2012. ... The ACC's top three rushers from 2000, and eight of the top 10, are due back this season. Both of the league's 1,000-yard rushers—Virginia's Antwoine Womack and Clemson's Travis Zachery—return for their senior seasons. In all, seven of the nine ACC teams return their leading rushers from a year ago. ... North Carolina will open its season with three consecutive road games for the first time since 1893. ... Clemson and North Carolina lead all ACC teams in returning lettermen with 54 and 53, respectively. Wake Forest returns a league-high 19 starters.

Clemson

LOCATION	Clemson, SC
CONFERENCE	Atlantic Coast
LAST SEASON	9-3 (.750)
CONFERENCE RECORD	6-2 (t-2nd)
OFFENSIVE STARTERS RETURNING	7
DEFENSIVE STARTERS RETURNING	4
NICKNAME	Tigers
COLORS	Orange & White
HOME FIELD	Memorial Stadium (81,473)
HEAD COACH	Tommy Bowden (W. Virginia '77)
RECORD AT SCHOOL	15-9 (2 years)
CAREER RECORD	33-13 (4 years)
ASSISTANTS	Brad Scott (South Florida '79)
	Offensive Coordinator/Tight Ends
	Mike O'Cain (Clemson '77)
	Quarterbacks
	Rick Stockstill (Florida State '81)
	Wide Receivers/Recruiting Coordinator
	Burton Burns (Nebraska '76)
	Running Backs
	Ron West (Clemson '79)
	Offensive Line
	Reggie Herring (Florida State '81)
	Defensive Coordinator/Linebackers
	Thielen Smith (LSU '77)
	Defensive Line
	Rodney Allison (Texas Tech '78)
	Defensive Ends
	Jack Hines (West Virginia '73)
	Defensive Backs
TEAM WINS (last 5 yrs.)	7-7-3-6-9
FINAL RANK (last 5 yrs.)	27-19-45-33-13
2000 FINISH	Lost to Virginia Tech in Gator Bowl.

COACH AND PROGRAM

In his first two years at Clemson, Tommy Bowden has done more than enough to get excitable Tiger fans back in the RVs, traveling from points far beyond for three-day tailgate parties and the chance to camp on campus.

Clemson won six games in Bowden's first year, despite playing against one of the toughest schedules in the nation. In Bowden's sophomore season, the Tigers won their first eight games and rose to No. 3 in the national polls in November, their highest spot in 16 years.

But then came disappointment, when Clemson lost three of its final four games, including a 41-20 whipping by Virginia Tech in the Gator Bowl.

Bowden could erase the memory of last season's letdown by posting another three-win improvement, going 12-0 and winning the school's second national championship exactly 20 years after Danny Ford led the Tigers to the first. After all, Florida State has to come to Memorial Stadium on Nov. 3, and it's about time that Daddy learned a lesson.

"They'd like that," Bowden said. "They'd probably like me to win one or two more than that."

However, with only 12 starters returning (only the deeper Seminoles have fewer), the younger Bowden knows his team isn't quite ready to start thinking about championships just yet, either in the ACC or the BCS.

"Beat Florida State?" Bowden said. "We can't beat Georgia Tech yet, much less Florida State. We have our work cut out for us."

Bowden has lost twice to the Yellow Jackets, who have a four-game winning streak over the Tigers and should again be Clemson's biggest obstacle in playing second fiddle to the Seminoles.

This year, Clemson's biggest holes are on defense, the Tigers' traditional strength dating back to the Ford era. They have only four returning starters on defense, thanks to a handful of early departures, some unexpected losses because of legal problems and the end of eligibility.

Gone is All-America linebacker Keith Adams, who left for the NFL after his junior year. Gone is All-ACC cornerback Alex Ardley, who was kicked off the team after an ugly confrontation on the field with an official and on the sideline with Bowden during the Gator Bowl. Gone is safety Robert Carswell, after four stellar years in the secondary. Gone are three-quarters of the defensive front.

"Defense is going to be a question mark simply because we don't have the experienced depth at all," Bowden said. "The first 11 we are going to put out there are going to be pretty good, but I am concerned about the inexperience and depth behind the first team."

Bowden feels good about his offense and his special teams. Why wouldn't he, with a healthy **Woody Dantzler** under center? The senior quarterback, used as a second tailback in Clemson's high-flying offense, was on pace to become the first player in Division I-A history to run for 1,000 yards and pass for 2,000 yards until he suffered a severe ankle injury in the eighth game of the season. He continued to play, but not like the Heisman Trophy candidate that he was billed to be. The Tigers, with Dantzler sharing time with backup **Willie Simmons**, lost three of their final four games: to Georgia Tech, Florida State and Virginia Tech.

Dantzler is healthy going into the season, but there are still two big questions on offense for the Tigers. First, who will take over for wide receiver Rod Gardner as the Tigers' primary go-to guy?

Bowden says Gardner, a first-round pick in the NFL draft, was the only player besides Dantzler to make a big play over the last two years.

There are several candidates for Gardner's old job, beginning with junior wide receiver **Kevin Youngblood**, who had a good spring, and sophomore **Jackie Robinson**, who tends to make as many bad plays as he does good ones. Tiger fans are banking on immediate production from four talented recruits—all from South Carolina high schools—who constitute one of the best hauls ever for receiving talent.

But Bowden isn't sure if all four of the freshmen will make it to school in the fall, and he's not sure just how good they will be if they get there. Recruiting analysts insist the class of **Roscoe Crosby** (6-3, 200), **Airese Currie** (5-11, 175), **Derrick Higgins** (6-2, 190) and **Tymere Zimmerman** (6-4, 195) were all among the best at that position in the nation last year.

The other question on offense is how the team adjusts to the loss of Bowden's offensive coordinator, Rich Rodriguez, who left to become the head coach at his alma mater, West Virginia. The Tigers had one of the most exciting attacks in the country and it will be up to former South Carolina head coach and Florida State assistant Brad Scott, who was elevated from tight ends coach, to keep things going.

Bowden also hired former N.C. State head coach Mike O'Cain as his team's quarterbacks coach, hoping O'Cain could teach Dantzler some basic option.

Meanwhile, Bowden had more to deal with this spring than just filling in the holes on his offense and defense. In April, three Tiger players were charged in a series of burglaries on campus. One of them was also alleged to be part of a campus counterfeiting ring.

Bowden kicked the three players—Paul White, Marcus Lewis and Tyrone Dickerson—off the team, but not before taking some heat from local media, who accused the younger Bowden of being as lenient as his father.

Ford was always faced with similar situations, though his run-ins with the NCAA finally caused his demise. Bowden shouldn't have to worry about that for now, as long as he can find a way to compete with Florida State and Georgia Tech.

2001 SCHEDULE

Sept.	1	Central Florida
	8	Wofford
	15	Duke
	22	Virginia
	29	@Georgia Tech
Oct.	13	@North Carolina State
	20	North Carolina
	27	@Wake Forest
Nov.	3	Florida State
	10	@Maryland
	17	@South Carolina

QUARTERBACKS

As much as he would like to see it, Bowden doesn't really think Dantzler (5-11, 200), a senior, will get the chance to win the Heisman Trophy.

Dantzler, a scurrying runner who could be Clemson's most dangerous rushing weapon, looked like a sure-fire candidate through the first seven games last season, when he was on pace to become the first player in college football history to rush for 1,000 yards and pass for 2,000 yards in the same season.

With the Tigers ranked in the top 10, Dantzler was averaging nearly 300 yards a game in total offense and was getting more attention than any player in the country. Then he got hurt. He suffered an upper ankle injury against North Carolina that didn't knock him out for the year, but pretty much ended his effectiveness as a runner, at least through the final three games of the regular season. He had surgery after the Tigers' loss to Virginia Tech to correct the problem, but missed all of spring practice while rehabilitating.

And therein lies the trouble with the offense that Bowden and Rodriguez developed while at Tulane and brought with them to Clemson. The quarterback is always a target. But Bowden doesn't plan to change anything, even with Scott taking over offensive coordinator responsibilities.

"We're going to do it again," Bowden said. "We'll run Woody at quarterback until he gets hurt and then roll the other guy in."

The "other guy" is the talented Simmons (6-1, 190), a sophomore who came in for Dantzler against the Tar Heels and threw four touchdown passes. He completed 10-of-18 passes in that game for 228 yards. With Dantzler hobbled, but still starting and sharing time with Simmons, the Tigers lost three of their final four games. But Simmons performed well enough during the season—his passing efficiency rating was one-tenth of a point higher than Dantzler's and he threw only three interceptions against eight touchdown passes—to give Bowden confidence in the young passer.

With Dantzler out of commission in the spring, Simmons got most of the repetitions, along with junior **Matt Schell** (6-2, 205), and Bowden believes his team is better prepared to handle an injury to its premier runner. So the coach is not going to let up now.

"It's not like we are going to sit back there and let him hold the ball with maximum protection," Bowden said. "Our style of offense leaves the quarterback open for some shots. That's why we need a good backup behind him."

No doubt, Dantzler is a premium weapon. In a 31-10 victory over Virginia, he rushed for 224 yards and passed for 154. He had four consecutive games in which he rushed for more than 100 yards and had at least 300 yards of total offense. That is believed to be a college football first.

For the season, Dantzler set 16 school records, including most yards rushing by a quarterback (1,024) and most touchdowns passing and rushing (24). But Bowden believes that trying to be too cautious with Dantzler would be devastating to the Tigers' attack.

Besides, Dantzler has usually been able to handle anything opponents have dished out.

"He's very quick, agile and durable," Bowden said. "He very seldom takes a flush hit. You usually hit him on the edges. It's not like we are lining him up in an I-formation and slamming him off-tackle. We spread the field and try to create as much green space as possible."

Bowen does expect a few new things offensively. He wants new quarterbacks coach Mike O'Cain to teach Dantzler and Simmons a few basic option tenets. O'Cain, a former Clemson quarterback, was head coach at N.C. State when the Wolfpack beat Florida State and was the offensive coordinator at North Carolina last year.

"We wanted to experiment with some option," Bowden said. "We'll dabble in that a little bit. We'll do a little bit more drop-back passing. We will try to be a little more unpredictable, but the overall philosophy will be the same."

RUNNING BACKS

For some reason, Bowden has never been a big fan of senior tailback **Travis Zachery** (6-0, 190), who rushed for 1,027 yards as a junior. The coach wants someone who is speedier and more productive at the position.

"I really thought that position should have been close to 1,300 or 1,400 yards," Bowden said. "He is hitting right about 1,000. We are looking for a guy who can get us about 1,500. Speed is a factor. We have adequate speed at running back, but nothing earth shattering."

Never mind that Zachery has led the Tigers in rushing the last two seasons and became in 2000 just the eighth back in school history to run for more than 1,000 yards. He led the ACC in scoring with 9.2 points a game, scored more touchdowns than any player in the league, lost the ACC rushing title to Virginia's Antwoine Womack by a mere 16 yards, was voted first-team All-ACC and was second on the team to Gardner with 29 receptions.

So when Zachery needed surgery to repair the broken ankle he suffered in the Gator Bowl, forcing him to miss spring practice, Bowden took the opportunity to give three underclassmen a strong look at tailback. The Tigers have their top six rushers returning this year.

The coach liked what he saw in sophomore **Keith Kelly** (6-0, 206), junior **Bernard Rambert** (6-0, 200) and sophomore **Chad Jasmin** (5-10, 214).

"All of them will press for more playing time," Bowden said. "It's good to have competition at every position, and we have that on offense. I want to make sure we don't have a 1,300-yard runner sitting on the bench."

Kelly, the gem of last year's recruiting class, might make the biggest challenge. He was third to Zachery and Dantzler with 243 yards in just six games as a freshman.

Rambert and Jasmin both got spot action last year. Rambert shared time with Kelly as Zachery's backup, while Jasmin was the backup to departed Terry Witherspoon at the little-used fullback position. He is listed as the starter there going into the fall.

WIDE RECEIVERS/TIGHT ENDS

All Bowden wants to do in preseason practice this fall is find someone who can do what Rod Gardner did throughout his career: make spectacular plays on a regular basis.

Of the five experienced receivers who return, none of them have a history of doing that, and that makes for a huge void in a big-play offense.

Gardner, picked in the first round of the NFL draft by the Washington Redskins, is the only 1,000-yard receiver in Clemson history. Last year he caught 51 passes for 956 yards and six touchdowns.

Bowden has high hopes for Youngblood (6-5, 210), a sophomore who had a strong spring.

"He's the only one who has made big plays on a consistent basis," Bowden said. "We need someone to step forward."

Youngblood, who attended the same Jacksonville, Fla., high school as Gardner, caught 13 passes last year, starting five games as part of the Tigers' receiving pool.

Senior **Matt Bailey** (6-4, 220) also started five games last year but was hampered late in the season with a torn tendon in his finger that forced him to miss four games. He is a steady but unspectacular receiver with mediocre speed.

Junior **Joe Don Reames** (5-10, 185) made big plays on special teams, but he averaged only 7.8 yards on his four catches last year. Robinson (6-1, 190), a junior, has big-play potential, but has been inconsistent throughout his career, causing Bowden no end of frustration.

Bowden liked the spring performance of redshirt freshman **Derrick Hamilton** (6-4, 190) and sophomore **Ronnie Thomas** (5-11, 190), who played last year as a freshman. Junior **J.J.**

McKelvey (6-4, 215) also participated in 12 games last year.

But Bowden's real hopes rest with four highly touted receivers—all from the state of South Carolina—who collectively might eventually be remembered as the best receiver class in ACC history. Three of the players—Crosby, Currie and Zimmerman—were prep All-Americans, while the fourth, Higgins (6-2, 190), had 80 catches his senior year in high school.

"Our high-caliber guys in this year's recruiting class are offensive skill guys," Bowden said. "So it wouldn't surprise me to see some true freshmen receivers perform early and be the guys who can make the big plays for us."

That vaunted cadre of receivers might not arrive in Clemson intact. In early June, Crosby was taken in the second round of the Major League Baseball draft by the Kansas City Royals. He was the 53rd pick overall. Crosby seemed intent on playing both sports, and because he wasn't drafted in the first round, he might not have to choose between a no-brainer signing bonus and a college football career.

There are also academic questions with Currie, which won't be answered until Clemson gets results from the NCAA Clearinghouse later this summer.

"We could very easily lose one to baseball and one to academics," Bowden said. "If that happens, we can survive, but those guys right now have bigger play potential than what we have here on campus. We can survive, but those guys would make it a little easier."

The Tigers are loaded at tight end, despite the transfer of Jason LeMay to Appalachian State. However, most of the talent is young with no game experience, which is why senior **Morgan Woodward** (6-0, 212) is listed as the starter going into the fall. He caught four passes for 89 yards and two touchdowns last year. But he will likely get competition from sophomore **Todd McClinton** (6-6, 275), ranked as the best prep tight end in the nation two years ago. He sat out last year as a partial qualifier.

OFFENSIVE LINE

When Bowden first arrived at Clemson, he had no returning starters on the offensive line, something that hadn't happened at Clemson since the 1940s. Those who were on campus were small by Division I-A standards. To hear Bowden tell it, you would think he was playing with a bunch of converted cornerbacks.

The truth is, Bowden likes having a small, agile line because the Tigers' offensive scheme calls for lots of downfield and wide-out movement. Bowden would have preferred players in the 275-285 range, instead of the 260 range, which is the weight **Akil Smith**, **T.J. Watkins**, **Will Merritt** and **Kyle Young** played at as sophomores two years ago. In five years as a head coach, Bowden has never had a 300-pound player up front on offense.

"Big guys who can't move just can't be very productive in our offense," Bowden said.

This year, however, the Tigers will have some size up front, including three potential 300-pounders, plus 13 players who have game experience, a far cry from what Bowden inherited when he got the job. Five of those letter winners have been starters at some point in their careers.

Left tackle Smith (6-4, 290), center Young (6-3, 280) and guard Watkins (6-3, 285) are much bigger as seniors than they were as sophomores.

"It takes some time for them to develop, gain some size and still be able to run the way we want them to," Bowden said. "I am probably the only guy in Division I-A that has never had a 300-pound lineman. We do so much running with the line, it makes it hard to have someone that big."

Merritt (6-3, 260) is still a little undersized for Bowden's tastes, and was pushed at right guard in the spring by sophomore **Greg Walker** (6-5, 315), who caught the coach's eye with his improvement. The two are listed as co-starters going into fall practice.

There were several other shakeups during the spring, with junior **Gary Byrd** (6-4, 290) listed as the starter over Smith at left tackle and junior college transfer **Derrick Brantley** (6-5, 287) winning the right tackle position. Byrd started 11 games in 1999, but sat out last after undergoing reconstructive knee surgery.

Redshirt freshman guard **Cedric Johnson** (6-4, 317) impressed Bowden during the spring, and the Tigers finally have some depth along the line at center with senior **Brian Outlaw** (6-2, 245) and at tackle with sophomore **Nate Gillespie** (6-3, 271).

Bowden, of course, likes to complain, but the Tigers ended the 2000 season ranked 10th in rushing offense and 23rd in passing efficiency. Opponents had only 29 sacks, but that may be because of Dantzler's elusiveness more than anything else.

The coach was troubled by the fact that the Tigers didn't gain more than 200 yards rushing in their final five games, after gaining well more than that when Dantzler was healthy in the first seven games. They particularly struggled against Florida State (95 yards) and in the Gator Bowl against Virginia Tech (season-low 88).

"In the games we lost," Bowden said, "an inability to run the ball had a lot to do with it. We need to run the ball against teams that have strong defenses if we are going to go to the next level. We are getting bigger and stronger, but we are still looking for that 300-pounder who can run."

Then again, isn't everybody?

2000 STATISTICS

Rushing offense	236.4	10
Passing offense	210.1	63
Total offense	446.5	10
Scoring offense	36.0	14
Net Punting	35.7	37
Punt returns	15.0	14
Kickoff returns	20.4	35
Rushing defense	101.8	18
Passing efficiency defense	110.1	38
Total defense	340.5	37
Scoring defense	18.7	18
Turnover margin	+5	34

Last column is ranking among Division I-A teams.

KICKERS

In his first two years at Clemson, Bowden knew he didn't have the experienced specialists the Tigers needed to truly challenge Florida State or even Georgia Tech. He enters this year with a little more confidence about his kicking game.

"The kicking game should be the best since I have been here," Bowden said. "But it hasn't been that great since I have been here, probably not up to what they have had here in the past."

Sophomore **Aaron Hunt** (5-11, 210) is firmly in place as the Tigers' place-kicker. He was ninth in scoring in the ACC last year, making eight of his 14 field-goal attempts and converting 43-of-45 PATs in the regular season. He kicked three field goals in the season-finale against arch rival South Carolina, including the 25-yard game-winner with three seconds remaining, and added two more field goals and extra points in the Gator Bowl. So half of the 10 field goals he made came in the final two games of the season.

It was an excellent debut for Hunt, a Tennessee native who arrived on campus with big expectations. He made eight of his nine attempts inside the 30-yard line. However, here's the rub: Hunt's longest field goal of the season was 31 yards and that came in the last game of the season.

So for him to be useful this year, when the Tigers need to score as many points as possible while the defense takes shape, he needs to improve his range.

Junior **Tony Lazzara** (5-9, 185), the starter two years ago as a freshman, has more range than Hunt, but is less consistent. He made his only field goal attempt last year and six of his eight PATs. He'll still handle all kickoffs. Last year, 17 of his 74 kickoffs went for touchbacks.

DEFENSIVE LINE

Twenty years ago, the Tigers won a national championship thanks to their great defense and a make-do offense. This year, as the school remembers its football apex two decades ago, the defense is the side of the ball that will have to make do all season long, especially along the defensive front.

The Tigers lose three starters from last year's team, which was third in the ACC and 18th in the nation against the run, allowing only 101.8 yards a game. Both tackles, Terry Jolly and Jason Holloman, are gone, as is defensive end Terry Bryant.

Fortunately for the Tigers, defensive coordinator Reggie Herring liberally used several other players for depth last year and they will team with returning starter **Nick Eason** (6-4, 265) to form the Tigers' first line of defense.

Eason, who had seven sacks and 11 tackles for loss last year as a defensive end, was voted the Tigers' defensive MVP last year, a remarkable selection considering the presence of All-America linebacker Keith Adams and three other first-team All-ACC players.

Eason missed the Gator Bowl after tearing his Achilles tendon in pre-bowl practice. He spent much of the spring rehabilitating, but is expected to be at 100 percent by the beginning of fall practice.

The likely starters at end will be junior **Bryant McNeal** (6-5, 235) and sophomore **Khaleed Vaughan** (6-4, 260), who had five sacks and six tackles for loss between them last year. They each started only one game, playing most of the season behind starters Eason and the departed Bryant.

Depth could be a concern after Bowden booted reserve end Marcus Lewis off the team because of his involvement in a burglary and counterfeiting scheme.

Sophomore **J.J. Howard** (6-3, 220) and junior **David Ellis** (6-1, 240) are listed as reserves.

Eason will be joined at tackle by senior **Jovon Bush** (6-5, 305), a talented but inconsistent player his first three years. He had 16 tackles in the regular season last year and four in the Gator Bowl.

Redshirt freshman **Donnell Washington** (6-6, 320) and sophomore **DeJuan Polk** (6-2, 265) will be counted on for depth.

LINEBACKERS

There is no doubt that the loss of All-America linebacker Adams, who opted to turn pro after his junior season, is critical for a thin Tiger defense. But as good as Adams was last year, linebacker **Chad Carson** (6-3, 235) might have been better.

Carson, a senior led the Tigers, was second in

the ACC and fourth in the nation with 13.3 tackles per game (a total of 156 in the regular season). He had double-figure tackles in 10 of Clemson's 12 games, including a career-high 22 against Georgia Tech. He also had 10 tackles for loss.

With so many new players on the field for the Tiger defense, he will be asked to carry a huge load, though that might not be necessary if the guys up front have a better year.

"He is our centerpiece guy," Bowden said. "He is our anchor."

One of two first-team Academic All-Americans on Clemson's roster (offensive lineman Young is the other), Carson will again be expected to make big plays in a slightly revamped defense that will technically have only two linebackers.

Senior **Altroy Bordick** (6-1, 215) and junior **Rodney Feaster** (6-0, 210) are the top two candidates at the other linebacker position, with junior **Rodney Thomas** (6-0, 215) listed as Carson's backup.

Bordick started once last year when he had a career-high 10 tackles against Wake Forest. But over the last three years, he has appeared in 29 games. Feaster was Adams' understudy last year, appearing in all 12 games and finishing the season with 25 tackles. Thomas was a special teams demon last year, setting a school record with 26 special teams tackles, accounting for more than half of his season total.

Senior **Braxton K. Williams** (6-2, 203) enters his third season as a starter, though his position has been changed to "star" safety in Herring's new scheme. It's a combination linebacker and safety that will let Williams roam free, especially in passing situations.

A durable but small player, Williams has never missed a game because of injury. But he better not falter: sophomore **John Leake** (6-2, 210) had an outstanding spring, highlighted by an interception he returned for a touchdown in the spring game.

Because he is of similar size and has similar speed as Williams, Leake won't likely win the job over a senior, but Bowden likes his playmaking ability and he will certainly see a lot of action this fall.

DEFENSIVE BACKS

If any current Tigers besides the wide receivers should be looking over their shoulders, it is the cornerbacks. Bowden has not been pleased with the performances of junior **Brian Mance** (5-11, 185) and sophomore **Kevin Johnson** (6-0, 185), both of whom were reserves last year.

Johnson played behind All-ACC cornerback Alex Ardley, who was dismissed from the team after an enraged outburst during the Gator Bowl. Ardley, who led the ACC with six interceptions, made himself available for the NFL draft, but was not picked.

Mance, meanwhile, made three starts during the season and was the top reserve the rest of the time. But Bowden isn't convinced the two can cut it enough for the Tigers to play man-to-man defense in the secondary, which puts tremendous pressure on the corners to cover top wide receivers on every play.

Clemson was sixth in the league last year in passing yards allowed. So this fall, Bowden will give a handful of freshmen hopefuls the chance to win a starting job. Look for redshirt freshman **Ryan Hemby** (5-10, 166) and incoming freshmen **Jamaal Fudge** (5-10, 180), **Travis Pugh** (6-1, 180) and **Tavaghn Monts** (6-2, 183) to challenge in the fall.

"If the best guy is a freshman, we'll put him on the field and let him play," Bowden said. "If not, it will force us to go to more zone than playing man-to-man. There are more running opportunities when you play zone. We would like to play man. If we don't have the players, we'll play zone and see if we can hold them inside or just score more points."

The safety position is a little more settled, thanks to senior strong safety **Charles Hafley** (6-1, 195) and junior free safety **Eric Meekins** (6-2, 190). Hafley started all 12 games last year and was the Tigers' most consistent player in the secondary. He had 106 tackles, six tackles for loss, two interceptions and eight pass breakups. He was third on the team in tackles and second in pass breakups, which included one in the end zone that preserved Clemson's win over N.C. State.

Redshirt freshman **Rony DeLusme** (6-2, 185) is Hafley's backup. Meekins played behind the departed Robert Carswell all last season, but he will probably be challenged by sophomore **Marcus Houskin** (6-0, 200), who had a great spring. The two enter the season bracketed as starters at the position.

PUNTERS

Coaches always hate when they have to find a new starter at either of the kicking positions. Face it: kickers are weird, extremely necessary and easy scapegoats when things go wrong.

But Bowden feels good about his replacement for the departed Jamie Somaini, who finished seventh in the ACC with a 39.3-yard average. That's because junior **Wynn Kopp** (5-9, 172) already has plenty of experience in big games. Kopp transferred from Georgia after the 1999 season and sat out last year under NCAA transfer rules. He had 82 punts in two years for the Bulldogs. His 36.9 net punting average in 1999 is better than any Clemson punter since 1995. Last year, Clemson's net punting was sixth in the ACC at 35.7 yards per kick.

SPECIAL TEAMS

The Tigers led the ACC in punt returns and were ranked 14th in the nation, thanks to the combination of Reames and Mance. Reames, who had 24 punt returns for the year, was fourth in the conference and 24th in the nation with a 12.2-yard average per return. Mance, who returned only six punts all year, had a spectacular 32-yard per return average, but that's due mostly to the 88-yard punt return for a touchdown he had against Georgia Tech, the fifth longest in school history.

Because both players return this year, Bowden expects big things from his punt return unit.

Reames and Mance were also contributors on kickoff returns, though Gardner led the team with eight returns. Mance had a team-best 26.8-yard average on his five returns, while Reames had a 22.6-yard average on seven returns. The Tigers were fifth in the league in returns, but third in the league in kickoff coverage, allowing only 20.0 yards per return.

Senior long snapper **Henry Owen** (5-11, 225) returns, as do sophomore holder **Jeff Scott** (6-1, 190) and junior place-kicker **Tony Lazzara** (5-9, 189).

RECRUITING CLASS

This year, no one broke through Bowden's defenses at the South Carolina border. Last year, the Tigers lost four big-time recruiting prospects to out-of-state schools, including two to Florida State.

"The objective from day one was to keep the in-state guys in state," Bowden said. "South Carolina is not a heavily populated state, but the players who are here are good. The objective is to keep them here."

Bowden and his staff traveled all over the state talking to high school coaches, the way Ford used to do. The extra effort paid off—13 South Carolinians signed with the Tigers. Bowden did pretty well outside the state, too, bringing in six players from Florida and three each from Georgia and North Carolina.

The four receivers and three tight ends fill obvious holes on the offense, and they probably will get immediate playing time.

"Our offense is attractive to skill guys," Bowden said.

All the defensive signees—Bowden brought in four defensive linemen and five defensive backs—will also get early looks.

Defensive back **Travis Pugh** (6-1, 180) and defensive linemen **Leo Reed** (6-4, 295) and **Charles Bennett** (6-4, 220) might be the best bets, but Reed may spend this season at prep school.

BLUE RIBBON ANALYSIS

OFFENSE	A-
SPECIAL TEAMS	B
DEFENSE	B
INTANGIBLES	B+

Bowden's long-term goal is to get the Tigers back to double-digit victories, which hasn't happened since Florida State joined the ACC. The Tigers had at least 10 victories four consecutive years from 1987-90 and have reached 10 victories seven times in school history.

"Getting there, that's the hard part," Bowden said. "Getting to that next level. There are things we need to do here at the university to get to that level and we are working on them."

Bowden is referring to improvements being made around Memorial Stadium, which includes a new field house, a new scoreboard and other amenities, including a new pedestal for Frank Howard's famous rock.

So, heading into his third season, Bowden knows it's up to his players to improve if they want to reach that next level.

"The players have to realize that if they want to get there, there is a lot more involved to what we are doing because we haven't got there yet," he said. "If we want to get there, they better crank it up a notch in the weight room and in the summer conditioning program and their work in August."

Despite an easy schedule that features four home games to start the season, the Tigers are probably at least a year away from reaching that double-digit plateau. But Clemson fans can rest assured that goal will be met.

(T.P.)

2000 RESULTS

The Citadel	W	38-0	1-0
Missouri	W	62-9	2-0
Wake Forest	W	55-7	3-0
Virginia	W	31-10	4-0
Duke	W	52-22	5-0
North Carolina State	W	34-24	6-0
Maryland	W	35-14	7-0
North Carolina	W	38-24	8-0
Georgia Tech	L	28-31	8-1
Florida State	L	7-54	8-2
South Carolina	W	16-14	9-2
Virginia Tech (Gator Bowl)	L	41-20	10-2

Duke

LOCATION	Durham, NC
CONFERENCE	Atlantic Coast
LAST SEASON	0-11 (.000)
CONFERENCE RECORD	0-8 (9th)
OFFENSIVE STARTERS RETURNING	7
DEFENSIVE STARTERS RETURNING	7
NICKNAME	Blue Devils
COLORS	Royal Blue & White
HOME FIELD	Wallace Wade Stadium (33,941)
HEAD COACH	Carl Franks (Duke '83)
RECORD AT SCHOOL	3-19 (2 years)
CAREER RECORD	3-19 (2 years)
ASSISTANTS	Bob Trott (North Carolina '76) Defensive Coordinator
	Jim Pry (Marshall '74) Quarterbacks
	Scott Brown (Adams State '74) Defensive Line
	Fred Chatham (North Carolina '74) Running Backs/Recruiting Coordinator
	Louis Clyburn (Duke '95) Tight Ends
	Dennis Creehan (Pittsburgh '77) Special Teams/Outside Linebackers
	Joe D'Allessandris (Western Carolina '79) Offensive Line
	Aubrey Hill (Florida '95) Receivers
	Brad Sherrod (Duke '93) Inside Linebackers
TEAM WINS (last 5 yrs.)	0-2-4-3-0
FINAL RANK (last 5 yrs.)	65-51-64-66-89
2000 FINISH	Lost to North Carolina in regular-season finale.

COACH AND PROGRAM

The contrast between Duke's two revenue sports was never more obvious than on the afternoon of March 31, 2001.

Just after noon that day, Carl Franks put the Blue Devil football team on display in front of a couple of hundred diehard fans at Wallace Wade Stadium who showed up for the team's annual spring scrimmage. A few hours later, in Minneapolis, Mike Krzyzewski's Blue Devil basketball team faced Maryland in an NCAA Tournament semifinal in front of 46,000 spectators and a national television audience.

Krzyzewski's squad rallied from a 22-point deficit to beat the Terps, then knocked out Arizona two nights later to win the school's third NCAA men's basketball championship in 11 years. Throw in the fact that Duke's cagers have played in the national championship game six times in the last 12 years and it's easy to make the case that Krzyzewski has the nation's best program in his sport.

Unfortunately, it's also possible to argue that Duke's football program is the nation's worst, at least in Division I-A. The Blue Devils have won just nine games in five years. They have twice finished 0-11 in that span. Duke has had just one winning season in the last 11 years and will open the 2001 season with a 12-game losing streak—the nation's longest.

But don't blame Franks for the mess Duke football has become. The Blue Devils, once the premier football program in the ACC, began sliding down hill when Bill Murray retired in 1966. A combination of neglected facilities, low coaching salaries and high academic demands—combined with a couple of questionable coaching hires—served to erode and eventually destroy the legacy that Wallace Wade, Eddie Cameron and Murray had bequeathed to the school.

Duke's only real gridiron success in the last 35 years came during two brief associations with former Florida Heisman Trophy winner Steve Spurrier. Former Blue Devil athletic director Tom Butters rescued Spurrier from the coaching trash heap in the early '80s, hiring him as Red Wilson's offensive coordinator. Later in the decade, he brought Spurrier back to Duke as head coach and in three seasons, the pass-happy Gator led Duke to 20 wins, a share of the 1989 ACC title and a bowl game.

Franks, who grew up in nearby Garner, N.C., (about a 30-minute drive from the Duke campus), was a third-string fullback when Spurrier first came to Duke as an assistant in 1981. Spurrier moved him to tight end, where Franks became an integral part of the wide-open passing game he built around quarterback Ben Bennett. Franks followed Spurrier to the USFL, then joined his staff when he returned to Duke as head coach. He followed Spurrier to Florida, where he helped build the powerhouse that won the 1996 national championship.

Obviously, Duke athletic director Joe Alleva was trying to recapture the magic that Spurrier had brought to Duke when he hired the then-38-year-old Blue Devil graduate to replace Fred Goldsmith (who was 10-39 after a miraculous 7-0 start in 1994) and to restore the school's fortunes.

"I'm fortunate to work at a place where people understand it takes time to build," Franks said. "I think this football team knows this program is headed in the right direction, that we're building a program."

Alleva warned Franks when he hired him that the 2000 season would be a rough one. Franks' inherited a fairly strong (by Duke standards) senior class, but after those veteran players left, there wasn't much left in the talent cupboard. The new coach would have to recruit the players to turn the program around. Last season's 0-11 record was the direct result of force-feeding the youngsters that Franks expects to win with this season ... or maybe the next.

"We played 23 freshmen and redshirt freshmen last year," Franks said. "They are the nucleus of our football team—and they are going to get better. They've had some game experience. They've had another year in the weight room, of being in a conditioning program, of physical maturity."

Clearly, he expects some progress this season.

"In terms of number of wins, I don't know what that translates into," he said. "Hopefully, we'll be in position to come out on top in most of the close games. The guys who did most of the playing [in 2000] were freshmen and redshirt freshmen. Now they're going to be sophomores and redshirt sophomores.

"It's not like they're seniors and redshirt seniors yet, but I think they're hungry. I think they've dedicated themselves to getting in great condition and getting stronger."

One tangible proof of that dedication was provided last spring by sophomore wide receiver **Reggie Love**. A heralded prospect out of Charlotte, N.C., the 6-4, 225-pound Love started four times as a freshman and caught eight passes for 101 yards and a touchdown. But he also joined the Duke basketball team as a walk-on and when starting center Carlos Boozer was sidelined with a broken foot in the next to the last game of the regular season, Love suddenly found himself playing significant minutes for the nation's top-rated basketball team.

Ironically, that happened just as Duke was opening spring football practice. Two years earlier, when quarterback **D. Bryant** was a little-used walk-on on another Blue Devil Final Four team, Bryant concentrated on basketball, making just a few token appearances on the football practice field.

Not Love.

"He'd go to basketball practice, then come out for football practice," Franks said. "He only missed about five practices all spring. I think it was very important for him to get out and practice with his teammates, because they saw that football was very important to him. Coming out after basketball practice wasn't easy to do."

Franks hopes that Love can inject some of the confidence and spirit that Krzyzewski's basketball team always displays into his young football team.

"It's special to be part of a national championship," Franks said. "He's the only national champion we've got. There is a lot of experience he can bring. It can help him motivate himself and his teammates."

Maybe Love can be the bridge between Duke's ultra-successful basketball program and the Blue Devils' struggling football team. Of course, before Franks' team can aspire to the heights that Krzyzewski's program has achieved, the Blue Devils need to achieve respectability—or at least mediocrity—first.

2001 SCHEDULE

Sept.	1	Florida State
	8	@Rice
	15	@Clemson
	22	Northwestern
	29	@Virginia
Oct.	6	Georgia Tech
	13	Wake Forest
	20	@Maryland
	27	Vanderbilt
Nov.	3	North Carolina State
	17	@North Carolina

QUARTERBACKS

If there was a bright spot to illuminate the doom of Duke's 2000 season, it would have to be the development of Bryant (6-3, 211), a junior, at quarterback. He came into his sophomore season as an unknown commodity and—after a rather painful growing process—emerged as a promising signal-caller.

Bryant was a prep All-American coming out of Cass Tech in Detroit, where he was hotly pursued by a majority of Big Ten powers because of his athleticism. He could have signed with Michigan State as a wide receiver or with Wisconsin as a defensive back. Instead, he picked Duke because former coach Fred Goldsmith promised him a chance to play quarterback.

But Bryant didn't make a very good impression on Franks, who arrived after his redshirt season. The "quarterback of the future" was playing basketball and didn't get much work in that first spring, when Franks was busy installing his "Airborne" offense. Worse, the attempt to combine football and basketball proved too much of an academic strain, forcing Bryant to sit out the fall of 1999. He spent the time working in a factory in Detroit—an experience that convinced him to make the most of his football opportunity.

He made enough of an impression in the spring of 2000 to convince Franks to give the young quarterback a chance the next fall. Duke started the year with two fifth-year seniors sharing the job, but Franks made sure that Bryant got most of the garbage time in a string of early blowouts. He saw enough that when Spencer Romine was injured at Vanderbilt, he installed

Bryant as his starter.

There wasn't an immediate payoff. Bryant struggled with Franks' complex passing game as Duke continued to lose big. But he made steady progress, increasing both his completion percentage and his passing yardage in six straight starts. He hit his peak in Duke's 10th game, a 35-31 loss to bowl-bound N.C. State, when he completed 23-of-36 passes for 310 yards and three touchdowns.

"He moved around and he made a lot of plays, plays other guys couldn't make," Franks said. "But even during that game, he still did things that when he looks back on it, he'll say, 'I could have been so much better.' That was all a learning experience for him. That's not a complaint. He was going to have to go through that."

Franks is hoping that Bryant, who finished with 1,448 yards passing, is now ready to provide the kind of quarterback play that his pass-oriented offense requires. He was delighted to see that Bryant continued to raise his level of play in the spring, earning the award as the team's most improved offensive player.

"D. Bryant is certainly the guy right now," Franks said. "He has the best delivery of the football. He's got a quick release. He throws a beautiful pass. He has the ability to help us open up the offense because of his athleticism. That should allow us to get in the shotgun more, maybe even add the option play and hopefully spread the field more."

Bryant is vital to Duke's hopes, basically because he's the only quarterback on the rosther who has ever taken a snap in a college game. Backing him up are two redshirt freshman—**Adam Smith** (6-5, 180) and **Chris Wispelway** (6-5, 200).

Smith played at the same California high school as Miami's Ken Dorsey and was judged to be almost a carbon copy of the Hurricanes' star. But Franks didn't see that on the practice field last fall.

"Something happened between the time we signed him and when he showed up here as a freshman," the Duke coach said. "His motion changed and he couldn't make the long throw. He couldn't get any velocity on it."

New Duke quarterback coach Jim Pry appears to have fixed the problem. Smith played well enough last spring to edge Wispelway for the second-team spot.

"He was the most improved quarterback we had," Franks said. "He worked his tail off."

But Franks doesn't rule out the chance that Wispelway, who led his New Jersey high school team to a perfect season and a state title, could move past Smith on the depth chart.

"He's a big, tall guy with a good release," he said. "We're trying to get him to be a little more demonstrative in his leadership."

Franks will go with just three quarterbacks this season after moving **Darryl Scott** to wide receiver.

RUNNING BACKS

Despite losing both starters to graduation, Duke's running game should improve as sophomore **Chris Douglas** (5-10, 178) gets more work.

Douglas led the Blue Devils in rushing and scoring last season, despite getting less carries than starter Duane Epperson. But the speedy back from Sherrill's Ford, N.C. averaged a yard more per carry than the player he was backing up and demonstrated an elusiveness that Duke hasn't seen in the backfield since the days of Mike Grayson. He broke off touchdown runs of 41 yards (versus Clemson), 45 yards (versus Florida State) and 69 yards (versus North Carolina). He finished the year with 503 yards on 110 carries.

"What we needed to do was get more muscle on him so he can make more plays," Franks said. "He's done that. I think he's going to carry the ball more."

Douglas is adept as a pass receiver (22 catches as a freshman) and as a kickoff returner (45th nationally with an average of 21.9 yards on 35 returns). Overall, he led all the nation's freshmen with 1,442 all-purpose yards, the ninth-best total in Duke history.

Franks plans to complement Douglas with sophomore **Alexander Wade** (6-0, 243), a bruising runner who was slowed last year by a bad shoulder.

"He's a big, strong man who had a really good spring," Franks said. "He's more of a running back than he is a fullback, although we've had to use him some at fullback."

Actually, Duke doesn't use a fullback very often. Franks prefers to go with a one-back set, although he often starts a wide receiver or a tight end in the backfield, then sends him in motion.

If there is a need for a blocking back, redshirt freshman **Zack Novak** (6-2, 235) is likely to get the nod.

But Franks is more anxious to find backup runners. He wants to see if sophomore **Brian Clemmons** (5-9, 197) can recover from a knee injury that forced him to sit out all last season and last spring.

The Duke coach may also give a couple of true freshmen a chance to contribute. **Brendan Dewan** (6-0, 197), who helped his Austin (Texas) Westlake team to the Texas 5-A championship game; **Cedric Dargan** (5-11, 184), who rushed for 1,500 yards as a senior at White Oak High in Jacksonville, N.C.; and **Jamin Pastore** (5-9, 198), an all-state quarterback running the option from Lisbon, Ohio, seem to have the best chance to contribute.

Duke averaged just 82.4 yards a game on the ground last season, which sounds bad, but includes more than 400 yards in quarterback sacks. If Franks can get a few more plays from Douglas and find another threat, the Blue Devils could mount a respectable ground game in 2000.

WIDE RECEIVERS/TIGHT ENDS

A successful passing game requires three consistent elements: good protection, a good passer and receivers who can run good routes and catch the ball.

Duke had problems with the first two parts of that equation last season—but nothing to compare to the third part. The Blue Devil receivers struggled to get open and when they did, they often dropped the ball. While the school didn't keep statistics on drops, a reporter who followed the team all year estimated that the Devils usually dropped between five and 10 passes a game.

Franks has addressed the problem in the off-season.

"The guys coming back, I think they're going to be better," he said. "They're out there on their own [in the off-season], catching over 100 balls a week. You can develop hands to a certain extent. We're going to try to maximize the training so that we're going to make the catches."

Lack of depth and experience may have played a part in last year's failures. Franks never had enough wide receivers to run the four- and five-receiver sets that his offense requires or to rotate the players who were there. He was forced to use several freshmen extensively and even the returning upperclassmen had never been more than backups in the past.

One exception to the rule was senior tight end **Mike Hart** (6-6, 246), who led the team with 31 catches for 540 yards. A big target with good speed and excellent hands, Hart was voted the team's MVP and earned second-team All-ACC honors. His backup, sophomore **Nick Brzezinski** (6-4, 240) also had a promising debut season with 12 catches for 177 yards. Indeed, the two big receivers were so much more reliable than Duke's wide receivers that Franks often used a two tight-end set as a passing formation.

The tight end position should only get stronger this season with the addition of redshirt freshman **Calen Powell** (6-5, 230), a superior athlete who competes in the decathlon for the track team.

Franks has plenty of good athletes at the wide receiver spot. He just needs for those athletes to prove that they can get open and catch the ball.

There's not a better athlete on the team—or a more promising prospect—Love. He has the combination of size, speed and strength to be an overpowering receiver. His freshman performance (eight catches for 101 yards) only hinted at that, but he demonstrated just what kind of athlete he is on the basketball court, where he stepped in when center Carlos Boozer was hurt and averaged 20 minutes a game as a backup center—twice matching up with North Carolina's 7-0, 270-pound Brendan Haywood in Blue Devil wins.

"It was great to see the energy he had on the basketball court," Franks said. "He's gotten stronger. I think that strength helped in basketball, when he had to go up against Haywood. It's going to help him run routes and catch the ball with guys hanging on him."

Franks is also counting on another big receiver with basketball ties: sophomore **Jeremy Battier** (6-5, 187), the younger brother of basketball All-American Shane Battier. He showed flashes of his talent in a freshman season marred by injuries, catching 12 passes for 78 yards.

Franks would like to balance his two tall receivers with some speed guys. His first option is senior **Kyle Moore** (5-11, 187), a player of eternal promise who has yet to deliver on the field. He did catch 17 passes for 280 yards and a team-high three touchdowns last season, but Franks was hoping for a lot more than that.

"Kyle Moore is a guy who has made some phenomenal catches in practice," Franks said. "Now he's got to carry it over into the game because he's the guy who gives us our best deep threat."

Moore and senior **Ben Erdeljac** (6-0, 198) offer the most experience. Erdeljac, who missed all of 1998 and most of 1999 with knee injuries, led Duke's wide receivers with 31 catches for 329 yards. He caught only one touchdown pass as a junior, but he also ran for a touchdown and threw for another.

Duke's four veteran wide receivers are not nearly enough to run the offense that Franks envisions. If the Blue Devils' passing game is going to take off, then several young players will have to make a major contribution.

Redshirt freshman **Khary Sharpe** (5-10, 165) is a former prep sprint champion who could provide a deep threat. Freshman **Senterrio Landrum** (5-9, 170), the son of former Major League baseball player Cedric Landrum, is also expected to make a contribution. Scott (6-3, 205), a freshman, came to Duke as a quarterback and worked out briefly as a defensive back last fall. But he returned to offense in the spring and after failing to challenge the top three quarterbacks on the depth chart, Scott was moved to wide receiver.

"I didn't feel his talents were those of a fourth-team player," Franks said. "He can be a contributing player on our football team right now—as a wide receiver."

The Duke coach may also dip into his latest recruiting class for wide receiver candidates. He has three newcomers with the raw talent to make an impact: **Ben Kittleson** (5-11, 172), the Kentucky prep 200-meter champion; **Mark Wigal** (5-10, 171), the West Virginia Player of the Year; and **Lance Johnson** (6-0, 184), a three-sport star at Hickory, N.C.

OFFENSIVE LINE

There's no question that Duke's offensive line has gotten progressively bigger in the last three years.

But has it gotten any better?

That's not an easy question to answer. For instance, the Blue Devils gave up an ACC-high 53 sacks in 2000—20 more than in 1999. However, Franks blames some of that on his inexperienced quarterback, who was frequently unable to get the Devils out of bad plays, especially in his first few games as a starter. As D. Bryant improved in that area, the pass protection began to look better.

The run blocking was clearly better in 2000 than in 1999. The average rush improved from 2.2 yards a carry to 2.4 yards and the average gain per game went up from 73.7 yards a game to 82.4 yards a game. In reality, the improvement was even better than the numbers indicate; Duke's rushing statistics were grossly distorted by more than 400 yards in sack yardage. Subtract those numbers and Duke's running game averaged more like 118 yards a game and 3.9 yards a carry.

Obviously, the Blue Devils still have a long way to go to threaten Nebraska's rushing statistics, but Franks believes his offensive front has made progress. It's one area where maturity and extra work in the weight room almost always pay off.

"I think we've gotten a lot, lot better," he said. "I think we're going to be a lot more durable and a lot stronger up front."

At least three key blockers come into the season healthier after undergoing off-season shoulder surgery. That should help senior guard **John Miller** (6-6, 333), who was voted the team's top offensive lineman last season despite playing all season with a bad shoulder. His running mate, sophomore guard **Daryl Lewis** (6-3, 323), also corrected a nagging problem and should be better. And freshman tackle **Christian Mitchell** (6-6, 300), slated to play last year in his first season on campus, fixed the shoulder problem that kept him on the bench.

Mitchell is slated to replace three-year starter Wes White at right tackle. On the other side, Franks is set with sophomore **Drew Strojny** (6-7, 265), who started eight games as a freshman.

"Drew Strojny is a guy who has the ability to be as good an offensive lineman as we've ever had here," Franks said.

Senior **Shawn Lynch** (6-4, 270) started nine games as a sophomore guard in 1999, but was shifted to center last season where he backed up three-year starter Troy Andrew. Franks is comfortable with Lynch, one of his smartest and most experienced linemen, playing the position he describes as "quarterback of the offensive line."

There's not a lot of experience behind the starting unit. Sophomores **Rusty Wilson** (6-3, 296) and **Luke Bayer** (6-5, 278) have the most game experience and could back up a number of positions, while juniors **Drew Martin** (6-5, 297) and **Michael Connolly** (6-8, 320) offer size and maturity, if not a lot of playing experience. Franks may prefer to go with a pair of promising redshirt freshman instead: **Patrick Worsham** (6-6, 287) and **Dan Mooney** (6-5, 266).

Freshmen rarely make much of an impact on the offensive line, but Mitchell would have played in his first season, except for his injury. So it's possible that Franks could dip into his latest recruiting class for line help. **Jim Moravchik** (6-5, 287), a Wisconsin native who was pursued by most Big Ten schools, and **Ben Baker** (6-5, 290), a Californian coveted by a number of Pac-10 programs, appear to be the recruits with the best chance to make an immediate impact.

2000 STATISTICS

Rushing offense	82.4	106
Passing offense	198.5	71
Total offense	280.8	106
Scoring offense	14.1	110
Net Punting	39.6	6
Punt returns	7.9	79
Kickoff returns	22.3	15
Rushing defense	185.4	87
Passing efficiency defense	152.3	111
Total defense	457.7	113
Scoring defense	39.1	113
Turnover margin	-13	107

Last column is ranking among Division I-A teams.

KICKERS

Duke has had plenty of problems on the football field in the last decade, but finding kickers has not been one of them. When Tom Cochran, the best place-kicker in Duke history, graduated after the 1995 season, the Blue Devils merely replaced him with Sims Lenhardt, who was even better.

And when Lenhardt finished his remarkable four-year run after the 1999 season, **Brent Garber** (6-1, 185) was on hand to take his place. Now, it's too early to anoint Garber as Lenhardt's superior—or even equal—but after completing a solid freshman season, the Thomasville, Ga., sophomore has a chance to build a special career. His leg is stronger than Lenhardt's, which already makes him a superior kickoff man.

"He's got a tremendously strong leg," Franks said. "Sometimes the best kickoff coverage is a touchback."

Garber hit 16-of-18 extra points as a freshman and seven of 12 field goals, including seven of eight inside 50 yards.

"We let him attempt some pretty long field goals," Franks said. "He's got to learn to kick the long ones the same as the 20- and 30-yarders. His leg is strong enough that he doesn't have to over kick."

Garber did hit from 47 yards out against Georgia Tech. He also added a 42-yard field goal against Maryland and a 41-yarder against Wake Forest.

Walk-on **Heath Freeman** (5-9, 170) is listed as Garber's backup.

DEFENSIVE LINE

Considering Duke's difficulty in finding superior defensive linemen—the Blue Devils have produced just one first team All-ACC defensive tackle in 20 years—last season's inexperienced unit turned in a surprisingly competent job.

Nobody's comparing the Devils' front three to the Steel Curtain or the Purple People Eaters, but the unit could have been worse—it could have been the disaster area that Duke's secondary became.

Instead, seniors **Tryan Grissom** (6-4, 273) and **Charles Porter** (6-4, 249) laid the groundwork for a defensive front that Franks believes will be even more solid and aggressive this season.

"That's still an area where we don't have much depth," the Duke coach said.

Grissom, who started 10-of-11 games last season and played a remarkable 666 snaps, provides an anchor at one tackle. On the other side is Porter, who is coming off a spotty junior season but impressed Franks with a strong off-season performance.

"He has renewed enthusiasm," Franks said. "He's had his ups and downs in his career. He's a passionate young man. He just has to learn how to channel it."

The two veteran tackles combined for 47 tackles and 12 tackles for loss last season. Porter even caught Northwestern quarterback Damien Anderson in the end zone for a safety.

Sophomore **Shawn Johnson** (6-5, 257) is challenging Grissom for a starting job after recording 23 tackles, including four for loss, as a freshman. Whether he starts or not, his presence is important for Duke's depth.

"He needs to play well if we're to have a strong front," Franks said.

Lining up between the two tackles will be junior nose guard **Jeff Lonergan** (6-2, 269), who finished fast last year, recording three sacks in Duke's last three games. He'll be backed up by sophomore **Matt Zielinski** (6-2, 255), who saw action as a linebacker in six games last season before suffering a knee injury that forced him to miss the rest of the season and all of spring practice. Converted offensive lineman **Greg Dufala** (6-3, 279) is also available in the middle.

Franks will also take a look at a couple of freshmen who showed promise in the spring: **Drew Ciepcielinski** (6-5, 221) and **Joe Boniewicz** (6-4, 245). Any other help will have to come from his latest recruiting class. **David Gutshall** (6-4, 225), rated one of the top 10 prospects from South Carolina, and **Demetrius Warrick** (6-6, 237), a *SuperPrep* All-American from Delaware, appear to be the most ready to contribute right away.

LINEBACKERS

Duke's youth was nowhere more evident last year than at linebacker, where a number of first-year players were forced to learn on the job.

None learned faster or better than sophomore **Ryan Fowler** (6-3, 223) who found himself in the starting lineup less than a month after arriving on campus. Instead of redshirting or playing a supporting role as a freshman, he became a seven-game starter who led the team in tackles (87), tackles for loss (13) and sacks (seven). He had his best games against the best competition: 12 tackles and two sacks against Florida State and 11 tackles against Clemson.

"Linebackers generally do have the most tackles," Fowler said. "I'm in a position where a lot of plays come my way. I get to roam around a lot."

While it's true that Duke's defensive scheme protects the linebackers—asking them to make the majority of the tackles—it's hard to attribute Fowler's freshman success to that factor alone.

"He's got good speed," Franks said. "He plays hard. He gets good leverage ... he knows how to use his hands well. He stays on his feet. He's going to continue to get better. He needs to improve his footwork. He needs to improve his tackling—as many plays as he made, he could have made even more last year."

Franks has switched Fowler from inside to outside, where he can put his quickness and instincts to better use. He'll be on the opposite side of the line from senior **Nate Krill** (6-8, 248), who missed last season with a shoulder problem. Krill, one of the most heralded recruits ever to sign at Duke, has been hampered by injuries throughout his career. But he brings experience (60 tackles and 3.5 sacks in his first three seasons) and a strong, physical presence to a hybrid position that's sort of a cross between a linebacker and a defensive end. His return should give freshman **Cory Broadnax** (6-4, 250) time to develop as a backup. Broadnax is an exciting prospect whose development was slowed by a severe knee injury in his junior year of high school. It bothered him as a senior, but after a redshirt season at Duke, he's healthy and appears ready to fulfill his earlier promise.

That's also something that 24-year-old freshman **Jim Scharrer** (6-4, 233) is hoping to do. The onetime prep All-American was offered scholarships by Penn State, Ohio State and Notre Dame when he came out of high school. But Scharrer decided to sign a pro baseball contract instead. After spending six fruitless years in the Atlanta Braves' farm system, the Erie, Pa., product is trying to pick up his football career where he left it. He showed Franks enough last spring enough to win a starting job at inside linebacker.

"There wasn't much of an adjustment after six years of playing baseball," Franks said. "He's a very physical player. He gives us size and speed."

Scharrer's unexpected arrival helps Duke compensate for the loss of three-year starter Todd DeLamielleure, who opted to transfer when his father—former NFL star Joe DeLamielleure – was dismissed as Duke's tight end coach.

The other inside spot belongs to junior **Jamyon Small** (6-1, 212), who started at outside linebacker a year ago and finished with 50 tackles.

Sophomores **J.T. Cape** (6-4, 199) and **Kurt Miller** (6-0, 218) will provide the backup duty inside. Cape has a lot of promise, especially if he can add some weight to his lanky frame. He played in nine games last season as a true freshman, recording 21 tackles and two sacks. Miller is a bit undersized, but plays aggressively. Junior **Jason Davis** (6-3, 220) adds depth after recording 35 tackles last season.

Franks will also take a look at several other young linebackers, including freshmen **Chad Rice** (6-3, 205) and **Paul Pugsley** (6-3, 211) and junior **Akil Ross** (6-1, 216), who missed last season with a shoulder injury.

DEFENSIVE BACKS

An 0-11 team is obviously the sum total of a lot of problem areas. But if Franks had to designate one position as his biggest nightmare, he wouldn't hesitate to point the finger at his inept secondary.

"The secondary is one of the most vulnerable areas on our football team," he said.

Duke allowed opponents to complete 63.7 percent of their passes for an average of 272.4 yards a game. The Blue Devil secondary came up with eight interceptions, but surrendered 21 touchdown passes. Duke's cornerbacks were credited with just seven pass breakups in 11 games. The safeties managed four.

Franks can only hope that maturity will help his younger defenders improve. He also has high hopes that the addition of junior **B.J. Hill** (5-11, 206) at strong safety will provide a solid anchor for his secondary.

The problem is that Hill has never played a game at that position. He was recruited out of Detroit Renaissance High School to play safety, but a rash of injuries at running back forced former coach Fred Goldsmith to switch Hill to tailback three weeks before the 1998 opener.

All Hill did was rush for 121 yards in his first college game and 798 yards in his freshman season. He was off to another good year as a sophomore when he suffered a knee injury so severe that it sidelined him for the rest of the 1999 season and all of 2000.

Hill is one of the best athletes on the team. If healthy—and Franks believes he'll be at 100 percent by the start of the season—then Hill appears to have the tools to be a superior safety. He'll team with senior cornerback **Ronnie Hamilton** (5-8, 178) to provide some stability to a unit that will otherwise be in a state of flux. Hamilton isn't an All-ACC caliber corner, but he's a three-year starter and the best the Blue Devils have. He finished last season with two interceptions and six pass breakups.

In the long run, youngsters such as sophomores **Terrell Smith** (5-11, 170) and **Temo George** (5-9, 173) could be better. Both saw action last year before suffering season-ending injuries. Freshman **Kenneth Stanford** (5-9, 170) also shows promise after redshirting last season.

The kids will push converted wide receiver **Jeff Phillips** (6-3, 180) and **Derrick Lee** (5-11, 195)—the two players who shared the starting job a year ago—for the playing time at the corner opposite Hamilton. Phillips and Lee are juniors.

At free safety, Franks returns 11-game starter **Josh Kreider** (6-1, 208), a junior, and sophomore backup **Anthony Roberts** (6-3, 201). While they have plenty of experience, both must improve to make Duke competitive.

"Josh led the team in takeaways, but he's got to make more tackles," Franks said. "Anthony has got to be more physical."

Don't be surprised to see the Devils continue experimenting in the secondary, either shifting over receivers (as Phillips was shifted at midseason last year) or trying out recruits such as safety **Alex Green** (6-2, 180), the top-rated prospect in this year's class, or cornerback **John-Paul Kimbrough** (5-11, 181), a speedster who put up some impressive numbers at a small school in Hendersonville, N.C.

PUNTERS

Franks has to replace All-ACC punter Brian Morton, who finished his career with more punting yards than any player in ACC history. It won't be easy making up for his average of 45.2 yards a kick.

But just as place-kicker Brent Garber spent a redshirt year preparing to replace Sims Lenhardt, redshirt freshman **Trey McDonald** (6-2, 210) is primed to take over for Morton.

"He has the physical tools," Franks said. "But he's a freshman. He's got to do it with the bullets flying at him."

If McDonald does falter, Garber is prepared to add punting to his repertoire.

SPECIAL TEAMS

Duke's special teams have been a strength despite the team's poor record over the last few years. Overall, the Blue Devil kickers have been excellent, coverage has been solid and the return teams have been above average.

In fact, Duke's special teams have been so good that it cost Franks his special teams coordinator in the off-season. Assistant coach Joe DeForest was lured away by Oklahoma State, leaving newcomer Dennis Creehan to coordinate Duke's special teams.

He inherits most of the players who did such a good job last season. Running back Douglas and wide receiver Moore averaged almost 23 yards a kickoff return between them. In addition, cornerback Stanford, who teamed with Douglas on Duke's 4 x 100 relay team, will get a chance to show off his speed.

Cornerback Hamilton will get the first shot at returning punts. He had an 84-yard touchdown return against Florida State last season. Wide receiver Erdeljac is also available. He's not much of a threat to break one, but he's a remarkably reliable punt catcher.

Duke's secret weapon in the kicking game is sophomore long snapper **Seth Carter** (6-1, 223), who was recruited specifically to handle snaps on punts, field goals and extra points. He performed all three duties flawlessly as a freshman.

RECRUITING CLASS

Franks is a realist. After coaching at Florida under Steve Spurrier, he understands that even the best coach has to have talent to win. As a Duke graduate, he understands the limitations that the Blue Devils have to operate under in recruiting. Not only does Duke have the stiffest academic requirements in the ACC, but the coach also has to overcome three decades of mediocrity, which has led to lukewarm support from the community.

But Franks is confident that he can overcome those limitations and find the talent he needs to be successful at Duke. He argues that the $24 million football complex that is going up alongside Wade Stadium is evidence of the school's commitment to rebuilding Duke's football reputation.

"We've gotten better athletically and we've gotten better speed-wise," Franks said. "I think our recruiting went pretty well. I think it will continue to go well because of the football building."

Franks said he had three major priorities in this year's class: adding depth on the defensive line, more size at linebacker and some big-play wide receivers.

He landed four defensive line prospects, including two with national reputations. Gutshall, from Spartanburg, S.C., was rated one of South Carolina's top prospects and was pursued by most ACC programs. Warrick, of Wilmington, Del., picked Duke over Notre Dame and several top Eastern programs.

Franks got four linebackers, the most intriguing of which is 24-year-old Scharrer, a former prep All-American who signed with Duke after playing six years of minor league baseball. He should make an immediate impact after arriving last winter and earning a starting job last spring. **Micah Harris** (6-4, 227), an all-state player from Ohio, also has a chance to contribute.

Franks brought in three wide receivers, although a couple of his prospects at that position were actually running backs in high school. Wigal was the West Virginia Player of the Year after rushing for 1,810 yards and 41 touchdowns as a senior at Morgantown High School. Kittleson also did more running than catching at Oldham County (Ky.) High school, but Franks plans to convert the Kentucky 200-meter sprint champion to wide receiver.

Duke landed some promising players at other positions, too. The Blue Devils scoured the country to find prospects able to meet the school's tough academic standards. The search even went beyond the borders of the USA as Franks ventured into Canada to sign tight end **Chris Best** (6-5, 252) from Calgary.

Duke landed three players from Texas, found prominent offensive linemen in California and Wisconsin and plucked promising prospects from Maryland, Delaware, West Virginia, Kentucky, New York and Georgia. The 22-man class contains just four prospects from North Carolina.

Franks' class may not be rated very high by the recruiting services, but the Blue Devil coach is convinced he's continuing to upgrade Duke's talent to the point where the Devils can move out the lower echelons of the ACC.

BLUE RIBBON ANALYSIS

OFFENSE	C-
SPECIAL TEAMS	B+
DEFENSE	C-
INTANGIBLES	B

Duke will enter the season with the nation's longest losing streak—12 games. It's vital for the Blue Devils to end that streak early. The longer it grows, the more ignominy accumulates and the harder it will be for Franks to break the cycle of defeat.

Franks wants to use the streak as motivation. But he also concedes that there's a mental hump that his team must surmount. The Devils had three excellent changes to win last season, but lost all three games in the final minutes. This year Duke must not only get close, but also win—at least two or three times.

There's reason for some optimism. The Blue Devils will be older and more experienced in 2001. After a year of turmoil at the quarterback spot, Bryant appears ready to solidify the single most important position in Franks' offensive scheme. There's also reason to expect better play at running back (where Douglas could be a star), on the offensive line and along the defensive front.

But all of that will be for naught if Duke can't show significant improvement at wide receiver and in the defensive backfield. There is little evidence over the course of last season that the Blue Devils were improving in those areas. Before Duke can get better, receivers such as Love and Battier have to put their physical gifts to good use. And young defenders such as Smith and Stanford have to prove that they are better than the veterans who have failed to do the job in recent years.

Until Franks' receivers prove they can get open and catch the ball with any degree of consistency and his secondary defenders prove they can cover opposing receivers, Duke will continue to struggle.

Realistically, Franks can't be asked to turn the program around in his third season. The Blue Devil program was too far down when he arrived to revive quickly. But this is the season that his program should begin to show progress. This is the season that will demonstrate whether Franks is on the right track or if he's just treading water.

(A.F.)

2000 RESULTS

East Carolina	L	0-38	0-1
Northwestern	L	5-38	0-2
Virginia	L	10-26	0-3
Vanderbilt	L	7-26	0-4
Clemson	L	22-52	0-5
Florida State	L	14-63	0-6
Georgia Tech	L	10-45	0-7
Maryland	L	9-20	0-8
Wake Forest	L	26-28	0-9
North Carolina State	L	31-35	0-10
North Carolina	L	21-59	0-11

Florida State

LOCATION	**Tallahassee, FL**
CONFERENCE	**Atlantic Coast**
LAST SEASON	**10-2 (.833)**
CONFERENCE RECORD	**8-0 (1st)**
OFFENSIVE STARTERS RETURNING	**4**
DEFENSIVE STARTERS RETURNING	**4**
NICKNAME	**Seminoles**
COLORS	**Garnet & Gold**
HOME FIELD	**Doak Campbell Stadium (80,000)**
HEAD COACH	**Bobby Bowden (Howard College '53)**
RECORD AT SCHOOL	**242-55-4 (25 years)**
CAREER RECORD	**314-87-4 (35 years)**
ASSISTANTS	
	Mickey Andrews (Alabama '64) Defensive Coordinator/Secondary
	Jim Gladden (William Jewell '62) Defensive Ends
	Billy Sexton (Florida State '74) Running Backs
	Jimmy Heggins (Florida State '78) Offensive Line
	Jeff Bowden (Florida State '83) Offensive Coordinator/Wide Receivers
	Odell Haggins (Florida State '93) Defensive Tackles
	John Lilly (Guilford '90) Tight Ends/Recruiting Coordinator
	Joe Kines (Jacksonville State '65) Linebackers
	Daryl Dickey (Tennessee '85) Quarterbacks
TEAM WINS (last 5 yrs.)	**11-11-11-12-11**
FINAL RANK (last 5 yrs.)	**2-3-2-1-3**
2000 FINISH	**Lost to Oklahoma in Orange Bowl.**

COACH AND PROGRAM

The year 2001 has not been kind to Bobby Bowden and his Florida State football program, beginning with a startling 13-2 Orange Bowl loss to Oklahoma and continuing six weeks later by the tragic death of freshman linebacker Devaughn Darling during the team's off-season conditioning program.

Mix in the loss of 25 seniors who left as the winningest class in program history—after playing for three national championships—and longtime offensive coordinator Mark Richt's departure to become Georgia's head coach and the Seminoles' immediate future becomes a topic of conversation.

Is the dynasty that Bowden built—14 consecutive 10-win seasons and top four (or five, depending on the poll of preference) finishes—beginning to show cracks within its infrastructure?

Under any other coach, those indicators would be undeniable, but Bowden hardly falls into the "any other" category. Nine wins removed from Paul "Bear" Bryant's mark as the winningest coach in Division I-A history with 323 career victories—though he still trails Penn State's Joe Paterno by seven—Bowden forges ahead in a manner that belies his 71-plus years.

"We've been in this situation before," Bowden said. "I'd say we were no better off in 1990 than we are now, and we were no better off in 1994 than we are now. "

The record will show that the Seminole teams of '90 and '94 responded to similar graduation losses by finishing 10-2 and 10-1-1, respectively, capping their seasons with bowl victories over Penn State and Florida.

Florida State's track record of reloading notwithstanding, Bowden and his staff rolled up their sleeves last spring, helping the team work through an emotionally charged period in the wake of Darling's death. While sensitive to the team's mental state, practices were every bit as grueling as before and perhaps the most important 20 days for the program over the last decade.

"I think the kids are back on track," Bowden said coming out of spring practice. "I thought they responded pretty well under the circumstances."

The circumstances leading up to the Seminoles' 2001 season are indeed unique. No other FSU team over the last 14 seasons has lost more starters (15) in addition to Heisman Trophy-winning quarterback Chris Weinke, the first three-year starter at that position in Bowden's 25 seasons with the Seminoles.

And though FSU emerged from the spring unsettled on a quarterback and desperately needing several members of its top-rated recruiting class to emerge as instant contributors in the fall, Bowden said it will be "business as usual" when the 'Noles take the field to face Duke in the season opener.

One of Bowden's greatest attributes through the years has been his ability to adapt to changing times. Unfortunately, that adaptability hasn't carried over quite as successfully on the sidelines, particularly during the bowl season. From 1982-1995 Florida State was unbeaten in 14 consecutive bowl appearances; including 11 straight victories to close the run.

That streak has been followed by three bowl losses in the last five seasons, none more confounding than the Orange Bowl loss to the Sooners. In suffering their second setback in three consecutive appearances in the Bowl Championship Series' national championship game, the Seminoles appeared ill prepared mentally and physically to meet the challenge of a well-schemed opponent.

If nothing else, the most recent failure forced Bowden to reassess his program. In the wake of Weinke's departure, and with so many personnel voids to be filled, spring practice took on a different look. Emphasis was once again placed on developing a more physical running game, and teaching the basics became the main staples for practice consumption.

Richt's departure—one year after popular defensive coach Chuck Amato left for North Carolina State—forced the retooling of Bowden's staff. Receivers coach Jeff Bowden, Bobby's youngest son, takes over the offensive coordinator duties for Richt while retaining his duties as the wideouts tutor. Former Tennessee quarterback Daryl Dickey, a one-time FSU graduate assistant, was brought in to coach the quarterbacks and provide some fresh ideas to a system that likely needed some tweaking. Dave Van Halanger, Bowden's strength coach for 18 seasons, left with Richt for Georgia and was succeeded by Jon Jost, who not coincidentally cut his professional teeth at Nebraska.

In summation, the loss of personnel and the shuffling of assistant coaches mark the most dramatic change in the program since the 1993 national championship season. That's when the 'Noles lost Heisman winner Charlie Ward and nearly two dozen players to graduation and early exits to the NFL, plus three top assistant coaches.

How the Seminoles will respond to the changes is anyone's guess. The personnel, while largely untested in many key areas, remains a collection representative of the top high school talent Bowden has been bringing to Tallahassee for almost 20 years.

The schedule, however, has its share of potential problem spots. While there is no denying Florida State's dominance of the Atlantic Coast Conference over the last nine seasons—to the tune of a 70-2 record—Georgia Tech and Clemson appear to be making inroads in their attempts to close the gap on the 'Noles. FSU plays host to the Yellow Jackets in week three, but must travel to face Tommy Bowden's Tigers in early November. Add an October home date against Miami, which ended FSU's 17-game winning streak last season, and the season finale at Florida, and it's easily the stiffest regular season test the 'Noles will face since the onset of the dynasty in 1987.

With a nation watching to see if the dynasty crumbles, Bowden may be facing one of the toughest challenges of his FSU tenure.

2001 SCHEDULE

Sept.	1	@Duke
	8	UAB
	15	Georgia Tech
	22	@North Carolina
	29	Wake Forest
Oct.	13	Miami
	20	@Virginia
	27	Maryland
Nov.	3	@Clemson
	10	North Carolina State
	17	@Florida

QUARTERBACKS

The first snap of the 2001 season will go to a player that has never been under center in a college football game before. Freshman **Chris Rix** (6-4, 215) and junior **Anquan Boldin** (6-2, 205), FSU's second leading wide receiver last season, represent life AW (after Weinke). Unlike the last AW era (after Ward), there is no Danny Kanell waiting in the wings.

While the experience factor will be sorely missed, that might not be an altogether bad thing. For the first time since Ward's departure, the Seminoles will have a bonafide running threat at quarterback; a nice fit given the current national trend.

"It will be [an asset], because I think they will be able to create," said Dickey, the first-year quarterbacks coach. "You see great point guards on basketball courts, they get out and create. As these two individuals mature in this position, I think they'll become more confident in their ability to get out and create."

Of course, they will never be able to match the maturity the 28-year-old Weinke utilized en route to becoming the most prolific passer in program and ACC history.

Rix and Boldin, each blessed with 4.5 40-yard dash speed, were thrust into the battle for the starting job in the spring after junior Jared Jones was dismissed for violating team rules. While Rix had been preparing himself for the opportunity to take over the reins from Weinke, Boldin was recruited into the battle by the coaching staff shortly after Jones' dismissal.

A *Parade* All-American high school quarterback, Boldin is the all-time total yardage leader in Florida high school history. Though he was heavily recruited as a quarterback, Boldin requested a move to receiver just three days after arriving on campus in 1999. Over the last two seasons he's recorded 53 receptions for 775 yards and eight touchdowns. More importantly, his game experience gave him a slight edge over Rix heading into spring drills.

"Under the circumstances, I felt it was my obligation to go back [to quarterback]," Boldin said. "Playing receiver can be both an advantage and disadvantage. It helped me a lot in terms of knowing and understanding the offense. But I hadn't thrown a football in two years, so I knew that I was going to have to work even harder [in spring drills]. It's going to be a matter of getting back in the groove. But it's something I am really looking forward to."

Boldin got the better of the battle early on in the spring, but Rix—who worked almost exclusively with the first-team offense—appeared to pull ahead coming out of the spring game. They head into August two-a-day drills with Rix running ahead of Boldin.

"They both showed they can do it [in spring practice] and we can build on that," said Bowden, who is hopeful the continued competition will push both players. "They're the real deal with everything to learn. On a 100 percent scale, they're only at about 20 [percent] because of the inexperience, but at least they showed they can do it."

Though the two contenders share similar assets—mobility, strong arms—Rix carries himself in a confident manner that belies his 19 years, while Boldin is far more reserved.

"I've gone from a back seat role to a driver role; one of the guys who was handed the keys to drive this Ferrari," Rix said. "I had my [learner's] permit last year and now I'm getting my license."

That's not to say Boldin isn't confident that he can make up what little ground separates him from Rix. In the spring game, both players avoided the mistakes that often come with inexperience, despite playing behind an inexperienced offensive line and without many of the playmaking receivers, who were out with injuries.

"I think it's good for the team that neither one of us are making those mistakes," Boldin said. "If we were, the coaches would probably be shaking right now. It's good to see both of us improve because the more we improve, the better off this team will be."

Regardless which player emerges, it's quite possible both will play this season. Bowden said he would not move Boldin back to receiver, even if Rix is able to get a permanent foothold on the job. That's because the lack of experience behind the two contenders: three freshmen who won't put on a uniform until the first of August.

FSU signed three quarterbacks in its stellar recruiting class, headed by All-American Joe Mauer (6-4, 205), who hails from Cretin-Derham Hall in St. Paul, Minn., the same school that turned out Weinke more than a decade earlier and also produced baseball great Paul Molitor. But the hometown Minnesota Twins might have ended Mauer's college football career before it began, making him the No. 1 pick in the Major League Baseball draft on June 5. Mauer, a left-handed hitting catcher, was regarded as one of the nation's top baseball prospects.

The Twins had been negotiating with USC pitcher Mark Prior in hopes of making him the top pick, but when those talks stalled, they settled on Mauer. "This is a natural for the Minnesota Twins," general manager Terry Ryan told the Associated Press. "[Mauer] just happens to be from St. Paul the year we're picking No. 1."

As the top pick, Mauer will command a lucrative signing bonus. So Seminole fans better not count on him showing up in Tallahassee.

The two-sport theme also applies to **Adrian McPherson** (6-3, 178), who was selected Florida's Mr. Football and Mr. Basketball after starring at Bradenton (Fla.) Southeast, the same school that produced Peter Warrick. McPherson is expected to contribute immediately as a walk-on with the basketball squad, but if Mauer does not enroll, he will probably get the longest look as the No. 3 quarterback.

Rounding out the incoming trio is **Matt Henshaw** (6-4, 208), a drop-back type passer who the coaching staff has said will almost certainly redshirt his freshman season. Henshaw, who attended Brentwood (Tenn.) High School, is the son of former FSU assistant George Henshaw, now an assistant for the Tennessee Titans. Last season, the younger Henshaw completed 57 percent of his passes for 2,173 yards and 15 touchdowns.

RUNNING BACKS

There is no mistaking the importance the coaching staff has placed on the running game for the 2001 season. Not only does the inexperience at quarterback dictate a shift away from the pass-first philosophy that has prevailed the last two seasons, the desire to become more physical up front has clearly been an emphasis heading into the season.

While the Seminoles' rushing attack improved measurably in 2000—from 83rd to 34th nationally—FSU must replace its No. 3 all-time rusher in tailback Travis Minor (3,218 yards).

By most accounts the duties will be handled in a by-committee fashion among at least a trio of returning players.

Senior **Davy Ford** (5-11, 188), the fastest and most experienced player of the group, has 118 career carries and 572 yards to his credit. A sprinter who has overcome a pair of reconstructive knee surgeries, Ford provides the potential outside threat the 'Noles have lacked since Warrick Dunn's graduation.

Fourth on the team with 239 yards last season, Ford missed the final three games after suffering a broken collarbone against Wake Forest. His history of physical troubles is just another reason the coaching staff is reluctant to go with a single tailback.

Junior **Nick Maddox** (6-0, 190) actually emerged from spring drills as the No. 1 tailback. Maddox's slicing, cutback style provides the 'Noles with a distinct change of pace and his athletic ability appears well suited for third-down situations.

Maddox's value as a pass receiver should only be enhanced by his experience last season at wide receiver. That was a move he made in order to help a team that was short on bodies in the early going because of injuries. Maddox had seven receptions for 135 yards (19.3 yards per catch), but also rushed for 70 yards on seven carries in some mop-up action at tailback.

If there was a disappointment in the spring it was the ankle injury that prevented sophomore **Greg Jones** (6-1, 235) from getting the repetitions the coaches had hoped for. A prototype power back with breakaway speed, Jones provided a glimpse of his immense potential when he rushed for 266 yards on 41 carries, highlighted by a 78-yard performance against N.C. State.

Collectively, the trio of returning tailbacks has accumulated enough career rushing yardage—1,019 for an impressive 5.5 yard average—to give every indication it can ease the loss of Minor.

The addition of freshman **Eric Shelton** (6-2, 230), a *Parade* and *USA Today* All-American from Bryan Station High School in Lexington, Ky., provides ample depth. Shelton rushed for 4,970 yards and 59 touchdowns in his career. He averaged 10 yards per carry.

It's unclear how the fullback's role will evolve given the new offensive wrinkles installed, but the Seminoles are not lacking for experience at the position.

Senior fullback **William McCray** (6-0, 225), when healthy, has been productive on the goal line and coming out of the backfield as a receiver. McCray has battled injuries throughout his career, including an Achilles strain that limited him over the final four games, though he still managed to lead the team with eight rushing touchdowns last season.

Sophomore **Randy Golightly** (6-2, 237) and senior **Chad Maeder** (6-3, 240), neither of whom has McCray's running ability, are capable blockers who have willingly accepted that role in extensive relief action.

WIDE RECEIVERS/TIGHT ENDS

A year ago the Seminoles were bemoaning the prospect of replacing the 1-2 punch provided by wide receivers Peter Warrick and Ron Dugans, and out of the blue emerged Marvin Minnis, who put up All-American worthy statistics (63 receptions, 1,340 yards, 11 touchdowns).

The coaching staff is hopeful the 2001 receiving corps can produce a similar story line, given the fact that the top three pass catchers—Minnis, Minor (42 receptions) and Boldin (41)—are no longer available.

It's hard to imagine how senior flanker **Atrews Bell** (5-11, 201) can possibly improve his impeccable production over the last two seasons. Bell, a one-time walk-on, has clearly been FSU's most efficient pass catcher in terms of touchdown production, with a reception to touchdown ratio of 1:3.8.

Though he lacks the blazing speed of some his teammates, Bell turned 37 receptions into 10 touchdowns last season and is easily the most accomplished returnee. He caught at least one pass in all 13 games and provided the lone offensive bright spot in the Orange Bowl with seven receptions for 137 yards, despite playing with a tender hamstring.

Senior split ends **Robert Morgan** (6-0, 180) and **Javon Walker** (6-3, 190) have flashed playmaking signs, but have been limited by injury. Morgan, widely regarded as the most sure-handed of FSU's receivers, collected 19 receptions for 366 yards and three touchdowns in a breakout season, despite missing the final three games due to injury.

Injuries also took a toll on Walker, a heralded junior college transfer who caught eight passes for 70 yards and a touchdown in his debut against BYU last season. Walker's production fell off dramatically after he suffered an ankle sprain while hauling in a 63-yard touchdown reception at Georgia Tech in the second game.

The coaching staff is still waiting for junior **Talman Gardner** (6-2, 195) to fulfill his potential. Blessed with size and sprinter's speed, Gardner has battled bad hands and a myriad of minor injuries throughout his career. Those problems have limited him to 19 career receptions.

Beyond the four returnees there remain many questions. Sophomore **Devard Darling** (6-3, 195) faces an uncertain future following the unexplained death of his twin brother Devaughn. School officials are taking precautionary measures to insure Darling's healthy before he's cleared to play.

The overall lack of depth certainly opens the door for a pair of talented freshmen—**Craphonso Thorpe** (6-2, 185) and **P.K. Sam** (6-3, 185)—to emerge as early contributors. As high school seniors each eclipsed 1,000 receiving yards. Thorpe, from Tallahassee's Lincoln High School, was a second-team *USA Today* All-American. He caught 64 balls as a senior. Sam, a first-team all-state pick from Buford (Ga.) High School, averaged 27.4 yards per catch and was also a state hurdles champion.

FSU's tight end situation is muddled at best. Senior **Carver Donaldson** (6-6, 245) and junior **Patrick Hughes** (6-5, 245) both pass the look test but have been less than productive throughout their careers, with one career reception each.

OFFENSIVE LINE

Aside from the quarterback position, no unit will be under greater scrutiny that the Seminoles' offensive line, which despite the loss of four key contributors from one of the best units in school history, remains the focal point of the offense.

Initially, depth is a serious concern along the offensive front, where only six returning scholarship players have seen any measurable playing time.

Junior split tackle **Brett Williams** (6-6, 315), a third-year starter and an All-ACC performer for a second consecutive season, is the lone returnee guaranteed a spot in the starting lineup. Upon his arrival at FSU, Williams was an accomplished run blocker with room to grow as a pass protector. Having mastered the art of holding rush ends at bay, Williams should feel much more comfortable as the Seminoles prepare to gear up for the run once again.

The split guard position will go to junior college transfer **Milford Brown** (6-4, 315), who arrived after an All-American season at East Mississippi Junior College in January, just in time to jump into the mix during spring drills. The coaching staff is hopeful that Brown—athletic and naturally strong—will pan out as well as the last junior college offensive line pickup the 'Noles made—Walter Jones, who was a first-round NFL draft choice by Seattle.

Line coach Jimmy Heggins has been waiting two years for junior center **Antoine Mirambeau** (6-4, 280) to be ready to play. Now they have no other option. Mirambeau is the team's strongest player, bench-pressing more than 500 pounds, but has virtually no experience calling out blocking assignments.

Up to this point junior tight guard **Montrae Holland** (6-3, 325) has yet to live up to his promise. Holland was expected to be the full-time starter last season but an ankle injury prevented him from cracking the lineup until mid-October. A road grading run blocker, Holland sat out the entire spring after undergoing relatively minor knee cartilage surgery. His health is imperative to the unit's success.

Junior **Otis Duhart** (6-4, 290), who started in Holland's absence over the first five games, must be ready to fill in at a moment's notice. Duhart also provides the unit with some much-needed versatility—he's capable of handling tackle or center duties in spot action.

Junior tight tackle **Todd Williams** (6-6, 305), a gifted, free spirit, will earn his first starting assignment come opening day. Blessed with outstanding feet and a mean streak, the bookend to Brett Williams could emerge as a star with some seasoning.

Beyond the six front-line players, junior guard **Ronald Boldin** (6-5, 291) and freshmen tackles **Ray Willis** (6-6, 270) and **Alex Barron** (6-6, 290) provide depth. Boldin—who has been tried at virtually every interior line position on both sides of the football—and Willis received valuable playing time in the spring.

So too did junior **Rian Cason** (6-4, 285), a converted defensive tackle who was moved across the line to shore up deficiencies.

Though highly unlikely, any one of the six freshmen signees could emerge as a backup if they are capable of getting a grasp on the offense in the early stages of two-a-day practice.

2000 STATISTICS

Rushing offense	165.0	35
Passing offense	384.0	1
Total offense	549.0	1
Scoring offense	42.4	3
Net Punting	34.7	54
Punt returns	10.5	40
Kickoff returns	19.7	55
Rushing defense	73.9	2
Passing efficiency defense	91.7	5
Total defense	277.0	7
Scoring defense	10.2	2
Turnover margin	+12	16

Last column is ranking among Division I-A teams.

KICKERS

After a seven-year run of steady production from Scott Bentley and Sebastian Janikowski, Seminole fans were forced to live through yet another kicking calamity in 2000. When walk-on Matt Munyon pushed a game-winning 49-yard field goal attempt outside the crossbars on the final play at Miami, Wide Right III was in the books.

In short, the kicking game was disastrous from start to finish as the Seminoles used three different players in an attempt to find the cure to what ailed the team.

Sophomore **Brett Cimorelli** (6-4, 220), signed a year ago as the heir to Janikowski, battled through a myriad of minor injuries that kept him on the bench early in the season to win the job down the stretch.

Cimorelli was 6-of-9 on field goal attempts, not counting a horrible shank of a 30-yarder in the Orange Bowl, and converted on 23-of-24 point-after tries.

Cimorelli's job status in tenuous at best. Unsatisfied with his performance, the 'Noles signed freshman **Xavier Beitia** (5-10, 180) in the spring. Beitia, who was good on all nine field goal attempts inside 50 yards and 31-of-32 on PATs as a senior at Jesuit High School in Tampa, will get a legitimate shot at unseating Cimorelli in the fall.

Also in the mix is sophomore **Jesse Stein** (6-0, 200), a walk-on transfer from the Air Force Academy who sat out last season.

Cimorelli and Stein handled almost all of the kicking in the spring after Munyon was dismissed from the team and junior **Chance Gwaltney** (5-10, 175) turned his full attention to the punting job. Still, any one of the four could end up handling the kickoff responsibilities, an area where FSU has long been spoiled.

Given the uncertainty surrounding the offense, the 'Noles can ill-afford to have a repeat of the 2000 season, when Cimorelli, Gwaltney and Munyon were a combined 14-of-24 on field goal attempts and missed seven PATs.

DEFENSIVE LINE

The greatest defensive concern entering the 2000 season was replacing the interior duo of Corey Simon and Jerry Johnson, who piled up 150 tackles, including 30 for losses and five sacks, a year earlier. A trio of freshmen were assigned to the task and performed more than admirably.

Sophomores **Darnell Dockett** (6-4, 260), **Jeff Womble** (6-3, 295) and **Kevin Emanuel** (6-4, 260) more than made amends in their first season, combining for 158 stops, including 37 for loss to go with 10 sacks. Dockett emerged as the budding star of the group. A high-energy player with an insatiable appetite for high-speed collisions, he earned All-ACC honors after registering 66 tackles, including a team-leading 18 for losses to go with seven sacks.

Their emergence was even more significant when the 'Noles lost their most experienced interior backup to an ankle injury at the start of the season. Junior **Chris Woods** (6-3, 268) should be ready to go after ankle surgery that kept him out of spring drills. Woods should slide immediately into the hole in the three-player rotation created by Emanuel's move to defensive end, his natural position.

The depth at tackle will be further enhanced by freshman **Travis Johnson** (6-5, 240), one of the nation's prized high school talents who earned a medical hardship after suffering a shoulder injury a week into last season.

Junior **Tony Benford** (6-4, 270), who came on late in the season to provide solid relief work, gives FSU a five-deep rotation that is clearly the team's defensive strength.

FSU's history of turning out first-round NFL draft picks at defensive end will probably be postponed for at least a season after the departure of Jamal Reynolds and David Warren. The position is entirely manned by underclassmen who have yet to produce the kind of consistent pass rush the Seminoles are accustomed to receiving.

Junior **Alonzo Jackson** (6-4, 255), who had five sacks and six tackles for loss as part of a three-man end rotation last season, will finally have the opportunity to shine in an extended role. Long and lean, Jackson has the ability to disrupt, by deflecting passes and getting to the quarterback. Emanuel didn't have quite the impact at end throughout the spring the coaches had hoped for after sliding him over from tackle, but should improve significantly as he regains the quickness he exhibited upon his arrival at FSU.

The most imposing player in terms of pressuring the quarterback this past spring was junior **O.J. Jackson** (6-2, 235). With lightning-bolt quickness and speed to chase down plays from behind, Jackson was virtually unblockable. While undersized for every-down duties, Jackson should provide quite a lift in certain passing situations.

Senior **Eric Powell** (6-4, 270) and sophomore **Charles Howard** (6-4, 245) are expected to push the aforementioned trio for playing time. Powell was something of a disappointment as a junior college transfer last season; he never seemed to grasp the Seminoles' scheme as a defensive tackle, prompting the move outside. Still, he is one of the Seminoles' most impressive physical specimens and the hope is those talents will be realized by cutting him loose from the corner.

Howard saw spot duty as a freshman and was a key special teams contributor. A relentless worker with a high threshold for pain, he played effectively through a myriad of minor injuries.

The wild card in the defensive front mix is freshman **Eric Moore** (6-4, 235), who failed to qualify after signing with the Seminoles in 2000 but has been cleared to join the team in the fall. The top-rated high school linebacker in Florida as a senior, Moore was slotted for a move to end. It's possible that the coaching staff will work him both places early on as they determine the greatest need area.

LINEBACKERS

This is one of the positions hit hardest by graduation, and the Seminoles must find replacements for drafted outside linebacker Tommy Polley and Brian Allen, who combined for nearly 600 career tackles as multi-year starters.

Linebackers coach Joe Kines, however, has a great anchor in senior middle linebacker **Bradley Jennings** (6-3, 230), who has waited three seasons for the opportunity to emerge from the long shadow cast by his running mates. A two-year starter, Jennings shared the team lead with 102 stops last season and has 196 in two years, living up to his nickname, "Monster."

Jennings emerged as one of the team leaders in the wake of linebacker Devaughn Darling's shocking death in February; a pleasant surprise considering his quiet demeanor. Darling, who was slotted as the prospective starter on the strong side, will be replaced by sophomore **Michael Boulware** (6-3, 205). The brother of former FSU All-American end and NFL All-Pro linebacker Pete Boulware, he will have to rely on exceptional speed to make up for his lack of size and strength. Primarily a special teams player, Boulware logged 21 stops as a reserve last season.

Sophomore weak-side linebacker **Kendyll Pope** (6-2, 212) gained significant playing time last season while backing up Polley. Playing in all 12 regular season games, Pope was ninth on the team with 52 tackles. A rangy player, he is expected to significantly improve on his big-play numbers with extended work after managing an interception, two pass breakups and a quarterback hurry last season.

Junior middle linebacker **Jerel Hudson** (6-3, 240) represents the only experienced backup among the linebacking corps. Hudson has a nose for the football, but is especially suspect against the pass, which will probably limit his repetitions behind Jennings.

Sophomore **Allen Augustin** (6-1, 224), a former walk-on, enjoyed an outstanding spring backing up at both outside positions. Extremely bright with a good sense for the game, Augustin could see significant time spelling Pope and Boulware in addition to starring on special teams.

The lack of depth at linebacker will provide several newcomers with the opportunity to jump into the competition early on. Freshman **Ray Piquion** (6-0, 215), who enrolled in January to take part in spring drills, will have a leg up on incoming freshmen **Willie Jones** (6-1, 200) and **Marcello Church** (6-1, 190).

DEFENSIVE BACKS

Graduation gutted the Seminoles' secondary, leaving defensive coordinator/secondary coach Mickey Andrews with the tall task of quickly preparing a group of largely untested defensive backs for battle.

The Seminoles appear sturdiest at the two safety positions, where senior free safety **Chris Hope** (6-0, 205) is set to emerge as a bonafide All-America candidate. Hope opted to return for his final season rather than declare for the draft after finishing fourth in tackles with 83, to go along with eight pass breakups and a pair of interceptions. Hope's improved pass defense last season provided the 'Noles with a big lift, but he's best known as one of the team's most ferocious hitters and a stalwart in run support.

Joining Hope on the last line of defense is senior rover **Abdual Howard** (6-0, 200), a career backup who has played virtually everywhere in the secondary. Playing in 11 games last season, Howard had 33 stops, five pass breakups and an interception, spelling third-year starter and first-round NFL draft choice Derrick Gibson.

FSU is particularly thin behind the starting safeties. Senior free safety **Gennaro Jackson** (6-0, 190) has seen most of his action on special teams. So too has sophomore **Yohance Buchanan** (6-1, 205). Freshman **Claudius Osei** (6-0, 200) is slated to back up Howard at the rover position.

The cornerback positions will probably go to a pair of players who have never made a career start, because of the graduation of four-year starter Tay Cody and Clevan Thomas. Cody's spot will be particularly difficult to replace after his monster senior season that included 82 tackles, six interceptions and 12 pass breakups, the most outstanding numbers by a corner since LeRoy Butler.

Rail-thin junior left corner **Malcolm Tatum** (6-1, 170) saw action in only five regular season games last season after suffering a broken back vertebrae. Tatum, however, played well in extended Orange Bowl action after Cody was injured.

Sophomore **Stanford Samuels** (5-10, 180) is listed as the projected starter on the right side after contributing 23 tackles and four pass breakups in nine games worth of backup work. Samuels, who returned from reconstructive knee surgery last season, may be the team's most fundamentally sound corner, though he lacks the size and speed of some teammates.

Don't be surprised if Andrews doesn't baptize a talented group of newcomers by fire at the corners.

Freshman **Bryant McFadden** (6-0, 185) is a highly acclaimed cover corner who will push Tatum on the left side. He sat out last season with a neck injury that went undetected, foiling Andrews' hope of getting him ready for this season.

Sophomore **Rufus Brown** (5-9, 175) and freshman **Leroy Smith** (5-10, 175) are the backups on the right side, but could be pushed aside if freshman signee **Dominic Robinson** (6-1, 192) is he's as good as advertised.

Regardless, the Seminoles will be hard-pressed to match last season's pass defense, which ranked fifth nationally in efficiency, collecting 19 interceptions while allowing just seven passing touchdowns.

PUNTERS

Over the last four seasons the Seminoles have been able to count on Keith Cottrell's reliable leg to punt them clear of trouble on those rare times when the offense was backed up deep. Cottrell averaged better than 40 yards a punt throughout his career and suffered only two blocks.

Junior **Chance Gwaltney**, who shared the place-kicking duties last season, is listed first among three contenders for the starting job. Gwaltney's experience is limited—three career attempts for a 39-yard average—and his leg strength is nowhere near Cottrell's, though he does punt the ball relatively high.

Gwaltney held off freshman walk-on **Eric Resta** (6-0, 200) in spring competition, but may also be tested by freshman signee **Kyler Hall** (6-1, 183), a defensive back by trade who averaged more than 43 yards per punt as a high school senior.

Given the uncertainties surrounding the effectiveness of the offense, the punting game could potentially become a trouble spot for the 'Noles, who have had to punt only 92 times the last two seasons.

SPECIAL TEAMS

Spoiled by years of success on special teams, the Seminoles were pedestrian at best in this area last season, including their well-documented kicking game woes. Fortunately, those shortcomings were easily overlooked, largely because the 'Noles led the nation in total offense.

With the offensive overhaul, FSU may not be able to afford anything less than a return of stellar—read dangerous—return units.

FSU tried five different players as the primary kickoff return specialists and no one stood out. Fortunately, they only had the opportunity to return 26 kickoffs for a dismal average of 19.7 yards.

Junior wide receiver Gardner is the most experienced of the returnees, but his 21.9-yard average for a team-high eight returns wasn't overwhelming for a player with his sprinter speed. Likewise the punt return numbers weren't particularly potent. Three different players shared that load, but two of them won't return those duties, leaving junior tailback Maddox (18 returns, 10.6

average) as the most accomplished.

The dearth of return talent will lead to numerous opportunities for a trio of incoming freshmen. Running back **Willie Reid** (5-10, 175) was an accomplished punt returner in high school, while wide receiver Thorpe has returned 12 punts or kickoffs for touchdowns over the last two seasons. Wide receiver Sam is also an option.

Perhaps the only settled position on the special teams units belongs to sophomore long snapper **Brian Sawyer** (6-3, 250), who handled all of those duties last season with just one errant snap.

RECRUITING CLASS

While on one hand the loss of 25 seniors to graduation is cause for concern for the immediate future, it also allowed the coaching staff to go out and reel in its largest signing class in more than a decade. Not surprisingly, the Seminoles scored high marks in all of the recruiting polls as Bowden closed with a flourish once again.

Not only did FSU address its needs, it landed more than its share of top-rated players. Particularly bountiful was the haul of seven offensive linemen led by junior college transfer Brown and freshmen **Ron Lunford** (6-5, 324), **Eric Broe** (6-6, 290), **Matt Heinz** (6-5, 260), **Andrew Henry-Kennon** (6-4, 285) and **Blake Williams** (6-4, 270), the brother of starting tackle Brett Williams.

The thin secondary corps was aided by the addition of cornerback Robinson, and safeties **Jerome Carter** (6-0, 208) and **Gerard Ross** (6-2,190).

Additional need-based freshmen signees include kicker Beitia, tight end **Justin Tomerlin** (6-5, 240), linebackers Church, Jones and **B.J. Dean** (5-11, 235), and most notably a trio of quarterbacks—Mauer, McPherson and Henshaw.

Robinson, a late addition to the class from California, represents the continued reach FSU has on the national scene. Though the class is predominantly made up of Florida and Georgia prep standouts the 'Noles plucked two players from California, two from Alabama and one each from Louisiana, Minnesota, Tennessee and Kentucky.

Mauer, Shelton and Robinson earned *Parade* and *USA Today* first-team All-America honors, with Mauer voted national player of the year.

BLUE RIBBON ANALYSIS

OFFENSE	B-
SPECIAL TEAMS	C-
DEFENSE	A-
INTANGIBLES	A

With only eight returning starters, a fourth consecutive appearance in the BCS national championship game would appear to be a reach for Bowden's Seminoles. It has been a long time since a glance at FSU's schedule provoked conversation of four potential losses.

Substantial graduation losses aside, what the Seminoles sorely lack is a core group of vocal leaders, something recent teams haven't had to worry about given the presence of players like Weinke and Allen.

That, however, is not to say there has been a tremendous drop in talent. On the contrary, Bowden's team is as stacked as usual. The only difference is there are far more players lacking experience who will be thrust into significant roles.

Of course the biggest concern comes at quarterback, where Weinke's leadership and Heisman Trophy-winning numbers will not even be remotely approached. The offense, capable of scoring from any point on the field and matching any opponent, must find a way to replace the 6,739 yards and 49 touchdowns that the trio of Weinke, Minor and Minnis accumulated last season.

Couple that was some offensive changes in terms of scheme, as well as a new coordinator, and the potential for problems in easily identifiable. That will put an additional burden on a defense that may be susceptible to the pass, given the lack of a proven pass rusher and an untested secondary.

Fortunately, Andrews is one of the best when it comes to not only teaching, but adjusting on the fly. FSU's odd-year schedule, with November trips to Clemson and Florida looming large, isn't the most conducive for a team with so many unanswered questions. Fortunately, the schedule's front end is loaded with teams the 'Noles should handle, save a Sept. 15 home date against improving Georgia Tech. That should provide the team with some much-needed confidence and experience before October opens with a visit from Miami, followed by a trip to Virginia.

As for the intangibles, no one can match Florida State's nation-leading 52-game home unbeaten streak. FSU will also benefit from its veteran staff, given the changing faces in the Atlantic Coast Conference, where there are four new coaches and nine new offensive coordinators (counting FSU).

What remains to be seen is how motivated the 'Noles will be to make amends for last season's Orange Bowl collapse. All of those uncertainties lead to a season that will probably be scrutinized closer than any other by Seminole fans looking for the slightest hint that the dynasty may finally be crumbling.

(B.T.)

2000 RESULTS

Brigham Young	W	29-3	1-0
Georgia Tech	W	26-21	2-0
North Carolina	W	63-14	3-0
Louisville	W	31-0	4-0
Maryland	W	59-7	5-0
Miami	L	24-27	5-1
Duke	W	63-14	6-1
Virginia	W	37-3	7-1
North Carolina State	W	58-14	8-1
Clemson	W	54-7	9-1
Wake Forest	W	35-6	10-1
Florida	W	30-7	11-1
Oklahoma (Orange Bowl)	L	2-13	11-2

Georgia Tech

LOCATION	**Atlanta, GA**
CONFERENCE	**Atlantic Coast**
LAST SEASON	**9-3 (.750)**
CONFERENCE RECORD	**6-2 (t-2nd)**
OFFENSIVE STARTERS RETURNING	**7**
DEFENSIVE STARTERS RETURNING	**9**
NICKNAME	**Yellow Jackets**
COLORS	**Old Gold & White**
HOME FIELD	**Grant Field (46,000)**
HEAD COACH	**George O'Leary (New Hampshire '68)**
RECORD AT SCHOOL	**45-28 (6 years)**
CAREER RECORD	**45-28 (6 years)**
ASSISTANTS	**Bill O'Brien (Brown '92)**
	Offensive Coordinator/Quarterbacks
	Geoff Collins (Western Carolina '94
	Tight Ends
	David Kelly (Furman '79)
	Wide Receivers
	Mac McWhorter (Georgia '74)
	Offensive Line
	Ted Roof (Georgia Tech '87)
	Defensive Coordinator/Linebackers
	Peter McCarty (Massachusetts '78)
	Defensive Line
	Lance Thompson (The Citadel '87)
	Defensive Ends/Recruiting Coordinator
	Danny Crossman (Pittsburgh '90)
	Defensive Backs/Special Teams
TEAM WINS (last 5 yrs.)	**5-7-10-8-9**
FINAL RANK (last 5 yrs.)	**49-24-12-21-17**
2000 FINISH	**Lost to LSU in Peach Bowl.**

COACH AND PROGRAM

For someone who has the second-most established program in the ACC, Georgia Tech coach George O'Leary still has a few questions to answer as he begins his seventh year in Atlanta.

There is no doubt that the Yellow Jackets, who have played in four consecutive bowl games and won at least eight games the last three years, have been the most consistent challenger to Florida State since North Carolina made a run in 1996 and '97. They even tied the Seminoles for the ACC title in 1998.

But that was with Ralph Friedgen, Tech's mastermind offensive coordinator, calling the plays. Friedgen is gone now, leaving in December to take the top job at his alma mater, ACC rival Maryland.

And ever since, O'Leary has been bombarded with questions about how that departure will affect his team, even though every other team in the league except for Duke also has a new offensive coordinator.

"Ralph's been around for a long time," O'Leary said. "As far as coordinators go, I don't think there's much better in the country."

To replace him, O'Leary promoted Bill O'Brien, a seven-year veteran of the staff who spent the last three years coaching the running backs. It was a rather controversial choice—at 31, O'Brien is one of the youngest offensive coordinators in Division I-A.

And it's a challenging role. O'Brien pretty much knew from the time he accepted the job that filling the mountainous Friedgen's shoes would be about as difficult as filling his pants. It didn't help that in the first game of the Post-Ralph era, the heavily favored Yellow Jackets lost, 28-14, to LSU in the Peach Bowl. The offense sputtered along with only 317 yards in total offense and the Jackets, who were second in the nation in turnover margin last year, committed six turnovers.

"I know you are going to be judged on what was the last thing you did," O'Brien said. "We played our worst game of the year that game. I understood that when I came out of that locker room, I was going to be blamed."

O'Leary tried to deflect criticism from his young coordinator in the spring, accepting the blame for the team's sloppy play.

"It's the head coach's job to make sure they are not doing the sloppy things that get you beat," O'Leary told the *Macon Telegraph.* "I take the blame for that. I thought a lot of people put undo pressure on him. And Billy probably put more pressure on himself than he should have.

"As I said to Billy, 'The only thing you have to worry about is what I think.' "

O'Leary says he didn't hire O'Brien to be an exact replica of Friedgen, whose creative offenses uses multiple formations and sets. O'Leary fully expects there to be changes in the Yellow Jacket offense this season, if only because the personnel is different.

"I told Billy that you have to be your own self,"

O'Leary told the *Telegraph.* We have to have the ability to play two-back, three-back, but every team is different.

"He's made some changes, which I think have been good. I think more importantly, he has to feel he's in charge of the offense and has to run it the way he feels necessary because he's judged by how many points he puts on the board."

Under Friedgen, that was a lot of points. The Yellow Jackets were first in the nation in total offense and second in scoring in 1999 when Joe Hamilton was the starting quarterback. Last year, the Jackets were 36th in total offense and 18th in scoring with senior **George Godsey** (6-2, 205) at the controls.

"Last year, we sat down and limited what George could do because he couldn't do everything that Joe did," O'Leary said. "But what he did, he did well. And that's the secret. It's the same thing with this team. It might not be the same as last year, but you don't fix what's not broken."

There's a lot for O'Leary to be excited about. He has the most starters (18) returning of any team in the ACC. His defense, the Achilles heel of his best teams, looks to be the team's biggest strength. He has an established quarterback and perhaps the best receiving corps in the league.

The down side is that Godsey is still recovering from a major knee injury he suffered in the Peach Bowl. He did not participate in spring practice and the Yellow Jackets don't have an experienced backup to replace him, though sophomore **Andy Hall** beat out redshirt freshman **Mark Logan** as the No. 2 quarterback.

"George Godsey missing the spring was a bad thing for him but a good thing for our football team," O'Leary said. "We had to go with the guys that we had, and they got a lot of repetitions. More pressure was put on them to get it done and get it done right because there wasn't someone waiting in the wings."

Whoever plays quarterback will have a basketful of skill players to get the ball to, from senior All-America wide receiver **Kelly Campbell** to tailback Joe Burns. The offensive line is a little shaky after losing two four-year starters.

So the key question for the Yellow Jackets is whether O'Brien's offense can churn out the points and production Friedgen's did. If that doesn't happen, O'Leary won't be able to deflect derogatory comments for long.

2001 SCHEDULE

Aug.	26	Syracuse (Kickoff Classic)
Sept.	1	The Citadel
	8	@Navy
	15	@Florida State
	29	Clemson
Oct.	6	@Duke
	13	Maryland
	20	North Carolina State
Nov.	1	North Carolina
	10	@Virginia
	17	@Wake Forest
	24	Georgia

QUARTERBACKS

Who knew Godsey would be so valuable? Entering his senior year, Godsey is the centerpiece of an offense that hopes to develop a different identity. That's a big leap for someone who started last season as simply "The Guy who Replaced Joe Hamilton."

Godsey isn't the spectacular playmaker Hamilton was, but he put up incredible numbers right up until he suffered a severe knee injury in the Peach Bowl. His surgery and rehabilitation on his left knee kept him from participating in spring practice, but he was there every day as a student coach for Hall (6-2, 195) and Logan (5-11, 195) as they battled to win the backup job.

Godsey was one of the biggest surprises in the ACC last year, as he went from a little known reserve to the talk of Atlanta with his accurate passes. He completed 222-of-349 passes for 2,906 yards, earning a spot on the All-ACC second team.

It was the second-best season, statistically, in Georgia Tech history. Not bad for a guy who entered last season having thrown only 36 passes in his first two years on campus.

But the injury threw a scare into O'Leary and new offensive coordinator O'Brien. Neither Hall nor Logan has any real game experience and the Jackets might be out of luck if Godsey's knee isn't completely healed by the time the season-opener against Syracuse rolls around.

O'Leary doesn't think that will be the case, though he doesn't want to push his top passer.

"He's way ahead of schedule," O'Leary said. "I see too many guys try to come back too soon and all of a sudden they're hampered for the rest of the season."

So, with Godsey watching every step of the way, Hall and Logan went to war in the spring, hoping to win the job as Godsey's back up. Hall, who lost out last season to Godsey for the starting job, edged Logan for the No. 2 spot by being more consistent and less skittish. With Godsey's knee still healing, Hall's importance can't be underestimated going into the fall.

"Andy showed a lot more maturity and poise than he did last year," O'Leary said. "Obviously, he has the athletic talent. We tried to put a lot of pressure on him because that is where he needs the most work, and I thought he had a good spring."

Logan still needs time to mature, the coach said.

"He is probably where Andy Hall was last year," O'Leary said. "At times, when he knows what he is doing, he shows poise and can make plays, but there are too many uncertainties right now. He got better this spring."

Reports from spring practice are that neither Godsey, Hall nor Logan was the best quarterback on campus. That title belonged to Tennessee transfer A.J. Suggs (6-4, 220), who must sit out this season under NCAA transfer rules. He's a pure passer who might already have a hand up on next year's starting job. He'll have two years of eligibility remaining.

RUNNING BACKS

For the last three years, the Yellow Jackets have had a hive-full of running backs. This year, the only difference is that all of last season's backs return with another year of experience behind them.

The premier player is junior Burns (5-10, 205), even though he only saw one week of action in the spring. He took the rest of the time off to concentrate on academics. O'Leary emphasized that Burns is not in academic trouble, but that he needed to spend some time catching up.

"Joe didn't have to show me much on the football field, and I wanted to see what the other guys were doing," O'Leary said in the spring.

Burns is the most versatile back in Tech's offense. He not only rushed for 908 yards and 12 touchdowns, he also was the third-leading receiver on the team with 26 catches for 242 yards and one touchdown. He had his best day of last season against North Carolina, rushing for 123 yards and tying the school record with four touchdowns, three rushing and one receiving.

But the Jacket offense may ask the workhorse Burns to do too much. He had nearly four times as many carries as the next tailback and, given that he's already missed most of one season because of an injury, O'Leary wanted to develop some depth at the position.

Undersized junior **Sidney Ford** (5-9, 205), who had the team's best yards-per-carry average at 5.0, got plenty of repetitions and ended up second on the post-spring depth chart.

But the player who was most productive was redshirt freshman **Jimmy Dixon** (6-1, 200), a highly regarded back out of Texas who sat out last season.

"I thought Jimmy Dixon emerged back there," O'Leary told the *Telegraph.* "And he is a guy that's going to push other guys for playing time."

One guy pushed out of the way, seemingly, is former starter **Sean Gregory** (6-0, 211), a senior who is listed fourth on the depth chart. Gregory, Tech's leading rusher in 1999 when the two players in front of him were injured, rushed for a team-high 837 yards and 13 touchdowns, which ranks third in school history for a single season.

Last year, however, Gregory was the team's second-leading rusher with 291 yards on 63 carries, as Burns took over the position once again.

At fullback, the Jackets will have to find a replacement for the steady Eddie Wilder, who rarely ever touched the ball but always found a way to help the team. He was an excellent blocker.

The starting position, almost by default, goes to senior **Ross Mitchell** (6-2, 242), who is also a good blocker but has little experience touching the ball. But there are some young players who could push him for playing time and Burns will probably get some time there in some of Tech's more interesting formations.

Redshirt freshman **Jonathan Jackson** (6-2, 225) came to Tech from Florida, where he was ranked among the top 50 players in the state as a high school senior. Jackson impressed coaches during the spring.

Sophomore **Brian Camp** (6-1, 235) spent two years as a quarterback before moving to fullback in the spring.

WIDE RECEIVERS/TIGHT ENDS

Assuming Godsey is able to stand upright and an inexperienced offensive line can protect him, there will be plenty of targets to throw to in Georgia Tech's complex offensive system, starting with two-time All-ACC pick Campbell (5-11, 170). The senior from Atlanta is the best receiver in the league and one of the top players in the country. He has already set the school record for touchdown receptions in a year with 21 and needs only 27 catches and 92 receiving yards to break Harvey Middleton's school marks in those categories.

Those records, the opportunity to help the Yellow Jackets win a national championship and a possible run for the Heisman Trophy are three reasons Campbell cited in his decision to return to school. He could have gone into the NFL draft, like former teammate Dez White did the year before, but the undersized Campbell might still need to convince pro scouts he can play against the best players in the country. He was projected to be no higher than a third-round pick.

"I felt I needed an extra year," he said in making his decision, "and I want to take this team to a national championship.

"When I came here, my eyes weren't on breaking records. Now that I have started breaking them, that is in my mind. I have goals set. I want to break all the records. I'll have the opportunity to win the Heisman."

Campbell had a spectacular junior season,

catching 59 passes for 963 yards and 10 touchdowns. He also carried the ball four times for 87 yards and two touchdowns and averaged 24.3 yards on 26 kickoff returns. His 1,682 all-purpose yards was the second-highest total in school history. His biggest day of the year came at Clemson, when the Yellow Jackets upset the No. 5 Tigers, 31-28. Campbell tied the school record with 14 receptions for 209 yards, including a 48-yard touchdown reception in the fourth quarter.

There are many other options for Godsey to go to. Juniors **Kerry Watkins** (5-11, 186) and **Will Glover** (5-10, 178) and sophomore **Nate Curry** (5-10, 186) all had at least 20 catches last year and sophomore **Jonathan Smith** (5-10, 175) was an effective player who had a good spring.

Watkins might be the team's second-best big-play receiver, though he has been inconsistent at times. He dropped a pass that could have helped the Yellow Jackets beat N.C. State in overtime, but was the hero of the Clemson game when he caught the game-winner with just seven seconds remaining.

Watkins was third on the team with 26 receptions, but his 18.5-yard-per-catch average was the best on the team. Glover was a reliable target whose 29 catches were second to Campbell on the team. But he is less of a big-play threat and more of a possession receiver whose career average is 10.2 yards per catch.

Heading into the fall, the flashy Curry is listed as the other starter at wide receiver. Curry was one of 11 freshmen who played last year, and he kept getting better as the season went along. Of his 22 receptions, 16 came in the final four games for 227 yards.

"The receiver corps is good, and the competition is only going to make everyone better," O'Leary said.

All four tight ends return, starting with senior **Russell Matvay** (6-4, 245), who caught 20 passes for 199 yards last year. Sophomore **John Paul Foschi** (6-4, 268) was another of 11 freshmen to play for the Jackets last year.

Junior **Will Heller** (6-6, 255) and junior **Brian Lee** (6-5, 245) are primarily used as blockers, though Heller did catch five passes for 60 yards and Lee caught the game-winning touchdown against Central Florida.

The lone newcomer at the position is redshirt freshman **Darius Williams** (6-6, 248), who may get a chance to contribute in Tech's multiple-formation sets.

O'Leary was not pleased with the way his veteran tight ends performed in the spring and will be looking for more production in the fall.

OFFENSIVE LINE

Over the years, the Jackets have done the best job in the ACC of maintaining consistency on the offensive front, no matter who moved on. This year, however, offensive line coach Mac McWhorter must replace a pair of four-year starters in All-America tackle Chris Brown and All-ACC guard Brent Key. The line allowed an ACC-low 16 sacks last year. Only 14 of those sacks were allowed by the starting five.

The Yellow Jackets recruit this position heavily and O'Leary has confidence in his newcomers.

"It's not rebuilding the offensive line, it's replacing," O'Leary said. "I think we filled our needs in the spring, and the line has a chance to be good. We still need to work on building depth over there, but I am happy with the first five."

At guard, junior **Raymond Roberts-Blake** (6-2, 273) returns after a solid first season as a starter at left guard, while sophomore **Hugh Reilly** (6-4, 279) won the starting job at right guard in the spring by impressing the coaches.

Sophomore **Clay Hartley** (6-4, 280) and junior **Tim Brown** (6-2, 295) both saw relief and special teams action last year and will be utilized in reserve roles this year. Senior **Brian Meager** (6-5, 275) hasn't played the last two seasons because of a broken ankle, but should be available as a reserve.

At tackle, sophomore **John Bennett** (6-5, 290) was a freshman All-American last year, starting all 12 games. Senior **Jason Kemble** (6-4, 299) has played behind Brown for the last three years, but will have to fend off redshirt freshman **Leon Robinson** (6-4, 290) to keep the starting position.

Junior college transfer **Garren Findlay** (6-5, 290) will back up Bennett, because redshirt freshman **Jeremy Phillips** (6-7, 295) suffered a knee injury during the spring and will not play this year. Junior walk-on **Will Hardy** (6-4, 285) is also available.

At center, senior **David Schmidgall** (6-2, 272) enters his second year as a starter. He was a steady addition to the line last year and will have to be a leader this year. He'll also have to be durable, because freshman **Gavin Tarquino** (6-3, 265), Schmidgall's projected backup, suffered torn knee ligaments in spring practice and will probably be lost for the season.

Tarquino was a 2001 signee who enrolled at Tech in January so he could participate in spring drills. Schmidgall's new backup will be junior walk-on **Beau Cleland** (6-3, 250).

2000 STATISTICS

Rushing offense	164.3	36
Passing offense	271.1	17
Total offense	435.4	16
Scoring offense	33.8	18
Net Punting	37.6	18
Punt returns	9.3	58
Kickoff returns	23.5	6
Rushing defense	94.5	13
Passing efficiency defense	126.6	86
Total defense	379.6	70
Scoring defense	19.0	22
Turnover margin	+18	2

Last column is ranking among Division I-A teams.

KICKERS

Here's an area where O'Leary has no concerns. Junior **Luke Manget** (5-9, 176) is one of the nation's best place-kickers, entering this season as a front-runner for the Lou Groza Award.

Manget led all ACC kickers and was third overall in scoring with 74 points, which was actually down four field goals from his freshman year, when he had a school-record 86 points on a team that led the nation in total offense and was second in scoring.

Manget has never missed an extra point in his two years as Tech's place-kicker. He has converted 91 consecutive PATs and is only two away from the ACC record held by former Maryland kicker Jess Atkinson. He has made 23-of-32 field-goal attempts, including game-winners against Clemson, North Carolina and Georgia. Manget is practically perfect on short kicks. He has made 18 of his 21 attempts inside the 40-yard-line. He is less reliable from beyond that distance, making five of his 10 attempts outside of 40 yards.

DEFENSIVE LINE

The Yellow Jacket defense is hardly a laughingstock any more.

Remember 1997? The Yellow Jackets had a good enough offense to compete with any team in the country, but was last in the ACC in total defense, giving up an embarrassing 429 yards per game. Even in 1998, when Tech tied Florida State for the ACC championship and finished the season 10-2, it was eighth in the league in total defense, allowing nearly 400 yards per game.

O'Leary made changes in his staff and now former Jacket linebacker Ted Roof is in his third year as defensive coordinator. Under Roof's direction, those formerly frightening numbers have improved dramatically.

Last year, with six sophomores and freshmen in the starting lineup, the Yellow Jackets continued their steady improvement, ranking 13th in the nation in rushing defense and second in the nation in turnover margin. They still gave up more passing yards than any other team in the ACC, but Roof hopes some experience in the secondary and more pressure from the front line will improve those numbers, too.

He certainly has the defensive ends to build around. Junior **Greg Gathers** (6-1, 260) is one of the premier players in the country. He finished third in the nation last year with 13 sacks, while adding 20 tackles for loss, an interception and a fumble return for a touchdown. His partner, senior **Nick Rogers** (6-2, 255) wasn't far behind, making 13 tackles for loss and getting nine sacks.

There is not much experience depth behind them, though sophomore **Hobie Holiday** (6-3, 255) was a high school All-American who moved from linebacker to end midway through last season. He should get enough time on the field that will help him be a standout player next season.

Redshirt freshman **Chirod Williams** (6-4, 245) impressed coaches with his performance in the spring and moved up the depth chart behind Rogers. Williams has the height and quickness to become an outstanding pass rusher and should get several opportunities this fall.

"We are not where we need to be yet, but we have a lot of young players who can run and enjoy hitting people," O'Leary said.

Up front, O'Leary was disappointed with the performance of his tackles. Senior **Merrix Watson** (6-3, 290), a three-year starter, missed spring practice with knee and back injuries and O'Leary hoped someone in a group of five players would step up and distinguish himself. That didn't really happen.

Watson has more starts than any player on Tech's defense and has been a steady, though unspectacular performer throughout his career, during which he has 17 1/2 tackles for loss and 4 1/2 sacks. He sat out in the spring after undergoing minor knee and back surgeries, but should be at full strength in the fall.

In Watson's absence, O'Leary had hoped someone else would step up and make a strong statement about winning the other starting tackle position. Junior **Gary Johnson** (6-1, 275) came away listed as the starter, but O'Leary is open to looking at other options.

"There's no one dominant player inside, but collectively they've got to go out and give us some good downs," O'Leary said.

His choices include junior **Fred Wright** (6-4, 270), redshirt freshman **Alfred Malone** (6-4, 285), sophomore **Reggie Koon** (6-4, 295) and junior **Casey Loesch** (6-3, 285).

In the spring, Wright moved over from defensive end, where he played behind Gathers and Rogers his first two years on campus. Malone made a similar move two years ago but has yet to distinguish himself. Koon saw limited action as a freshman last fall, mostly coming in on short-yardage situations.

Loesch, a transfer from South Florida, is in his first year of eligibility.

LINEBACKERS

Sometimes recruiting pays off in a hurry. Three years ago, the Yellow Jackets were clearly desperate to get some big-time talent on defense and now they have it. No position is more loaded than linebacker.

The Yellow Jackets likely have never had a trio of young starters as good as junior **Recardo Wimbush** (6-1, 218), sophomore **Daryl Smith** (6-2, 225) and sophomore **Ather Brown** (6-3, 220). Add in sophomores **Keyaron Fox** (6-3, 220), **Anthony Lawston** (6-3, 220) and **Sterling Green**, and Tech looks like it can be dominant at this position for years to come.

However, the Jackets lost two veteran players to injuries that ended their careers. Matt Miller was a one-time starter who never fully recovered from a knee injury he suffered at the end of the 1998 season. Cody Price, a transfer from Arizona State, played mostly on special teams last year, but was bothered by a foot injury.

Wimbush has been a starter since the day he arrived on campus as a freshman. He became the first freshman to lead the Jackets in tackles with 91 hits in 1999 and was second on the team with 94 tackles last year. He has 17 tackles for loss in his career, three sacks, two fumble recoveries and two interceptions.

Smith became the second freshman to lead the Jackets in tackles in 2000, amassing 90 hits after taking over the starting middle linebacker position in the third game of the season, when it became obvious that Miller was not his former self. He was selected a freshman All-American at the end of the season.

Brown started every game last season as a redshirt freshman, but he could get pushed by Fox this fall. The speedy Fox, who missed three games last year with a broken arm, had a great spring and will get plenty of playing time.

Lawston is Smith's backup at middle linebacker and Green, a former safety who moved to linebacker in the spring, plays one of the outside positions.

The Jackets signed four freshmen linebackers and, as O'Leary has proven in the last two years, are not afraid to use them. **Gerris Bowers-Wilkerson** (6-3, 215), a top 20 player in the state of California, might be the best of the litter.

Tabugbo Anyansi (6-1, 210), a native of Nigeria, didn't play football until his junior year of high school in Mableton, Ga., but he graduated as one of the best prospects in the state.

DEFENSIVE BACKS

O'Leary is ready to try anything to improve his team's pass coverage, including shaking up his coaching staff. When former defensive backs coach Paul Ferraro left to become the defensive coordinator at Rutgers, O'Leary moved Danny Crossman from defensive ends to the secondary.

Crossman has a big job ahead of him, considering his thin corps of cornerbacks, but he found reason to be optimistic this spring because of better competition.

Notre Dame transfer **Albert Poree** (5-10, 190), a sophomore who spent only one season in South Bend, won one of the starting cornerback positions, allowing Crossman to move senior **Chris Young** (6-0, 207) back to strong safety, where he feels more comfortable. Young played the final five games last year at cornerback.

"I think Poree is a kid who would have started at Notre Dame last year and he was on our scout team," O'Leary said. "I think he's a great football player and an excellent tackler with great foot speed."

He is also brimming with confidence. When asked by a reporter from the *Atlanta Journal-Constitution* if there is a receiver he can't cover, Poree said: "If there is, I haven't met him yet."

Junior **Marvious Hester** (5-11, 170), a part-time starter the last two seasons, has a tenuous hold on the starting cornerback job. He is a big-play guy who returned an interception 50 yards for a touchdown against Florida State, but he's never been consistent enough for O'Leary.

That's why sophomore **Jonathan Cox** (5-10, 185), who started five games last year, will continue to push Hester in the fall.

Junior **Kelly Rhino** (5-7, 179) is speedy enough to help on special teams and will play some at cornerback.

There is much more experience at safety, where junior **Jeremy Muyres** (6-3, 205) returns after winning second-team All-ACC honors last year. Muyres had four interceptions and 12 pass break ups as a sophomore.

Young is big and can be a brutal hitter, so playing him at cornerback wasn't the best career move for him. But he moved over to cover Clemson's Rod Gardner in Tech's 31-28 victory and played great, holding Gardner to only three catches for 27 yards. He also forced Gardner to fumble on a key play and had an interception on the final play of the game. But he's better as an enforcer, as long as somebody can hold down the corners.

When Young moved to corner, junior **Cory Collins** (5-11, 180) took over at strong safety. He started five games and made 44 tackles and will get plenty of opportunity to contribute this year. Sophomore **Tony Hollings** (5-10, 203) can play either at corner or safety and senior **Marty O'Leary** (5-11, 178), the youngest son of the head coach, returns this season after missing all of last year with a knee injury.

PUNTERS

Two-time academic All-American Dan Dyke (6-0, 184) returns for his third year as Tech's punter, with hopes of returning to his freshman form. In 1999, Dyke averaged 43.8 yards per kick and 40.4 yards in net punting. As a sophomore, those numbers dipped slightly to 41.8/37.7 yards. However, 13 of his 34 punts were inside the 20-yard line.

Of course, he may just have gotten winded the second time around. In his first year, he punted only 30 times in 11 games. Last year, he had 34 kicks in nine games.

Dyke is a walk-on who attends Tech on the school's highest academic scholarship, but he doesn't always say the smartest things. He poked fun at O'Leary in a newspaper article last fall and was benched for the season opener against Central Florida.

He regained his starting job, but junior **Chris Morehouse** (6-1, 200), a former Division III All-American at Albright College, gave the coach reason to keep disciplining Dyke. Morehouse will continue to push Dyke this season.

SPECIAL TEAMS

It stands to reason that a guy who was a special teams specialist in the NFL would run a successful outfit as a coach. Georgia Tech assistant Danny Crossman played professional football for three years and knows the importance of special teams.

Maybe that's why the Yellow Jackets were sixth in the nation in kickoff returns (23.5 yards), 18th in net punting and first in the ACC in kickoff return coverage (16.4 yards allowed).

Campbell was 18th in the nation in kickoff return yardage, Dyke was 25th in punting and Manget was 25th in field goals per game.

Junior Kelley Rhino averaged 9.1 yards on punt returns.

Crossman's philosophy is fairly simple: he finds five- to eight guys on the team who he wants to be on most of the special teams and gives them a chance to shine.

"On average, it's a chance for a player to be in on between 28 and 40 plays per game," Crossman told the *Atlanta Journal-Constitution*. "And it's a one-shot deal. There are no first and second downs on special teams."

This year, all of Tech's primary specialists return, right down to senior long-snapper **Alex Tetterton** (5-10, 229), who begins his third year as a starter at that position.

RECRUITING CLASS

The loss of Friedgen certainly didn't hurt Georgia Tech on national signing day, when O'Leary brought in a banner crop of 24 players from 11 different states. He called it the best class he's ever recruited. Most national analysts agreed, putting the Yellow Jackets among the top 15 classes in the country.

Of course, no coach in the history of college football ever signed a bad recruit (to hear them tell it). But there were some antsy people around Atlanta when Friedgen left and the Yellow Jackets stunk up the Peach Bowl.

"I am anxious to see what they can do," O'Leary said. "I think this class is as talented and as athletic as any class that we've brought in, but that remains to be seen."

With two more Thursday night ESPN games planned for this year—bringing the school up to a record 13 Thursday appearances—and a season-opener against Syracuse in the Kickoff Classic, the Yellow Jackets won't lack for national exposure this year. This year's class includes players from California, Colorado, Utah, Texas, Ohio and Minnesota.

"We have always been a big in-state team," Friedgen said on signing day. "I think you need to recruit your state very well to succeed. Once you address certain areas, you have to go out of state. We have recruited California and Texas and were received very well."

The primary emphasis in this class was up front, where the Yellow Jackets signed six offensive linemen and five defensive linemen. Interestingly, the Jackets signed three more quarterbacks, with two giving commitments after Friedgen left. They will join Hall, Suggs and Logan at the position next year.

Damarius Bilbo (6-3, 200) is the most highly regarded of the three new passers on campus, throwing for 3,034 yards and 31 touchdowns as a senior. But, like Clemson's Roscoe Crosby, Bilbo's baseball potential could keep him from ever playing college football.

So two more quarterbacks were signed for insurance, and they are certainly athletic enough to help in other areas if they don't remain under center.

O'Leary isn't shy about using players from his signing class. Last year, he used 11 freshmen.

BLUE RIBBON ANALYSIS

OFFENSE	B
SPECIAL TEAMS	A
DEFENSE	A-
INTANGIBLES	B+

The Yellow Jackets will know early whether they will challenge Florida State's ACC dominance. The Seminoles, under massive reconstruction this year, play host to the Yellow Jackets on Sept. 15 and Tech loyalists hope that O'Leary is right when he says that the Jackets are closer than ever to matching the Seminoles athlete-for-athlete.

The Jackets have been within a touchdown of the Seminoles the last two years. Could this be the year?

"That's a tough chore," O'Leary said. "A lot of things have to happen right."

That's one of the reasons O'Leary agreed to play Syracuse in the Kickoff Classic. He wanted his team to face strong but beatable competition before going against the Seminoles and season-opening games against The Citadel and Navy didn't really seem like the best preparation.

However, the Jackets' next game after Florida State is Clemson, a team that has Tech in its sights. O'Leary should know before September is over whether his team will challenge for the ACC title.

But the well-established coach—he's been at his school more than twice as long as any ACC coach except Bobby Bowden—is optimistic that his team can compete with the best teams in the country.

"I think we have a chance to be a good team," O'Leary said. "I really do. As I tell the kids all the time, you're either going to get better or worse. You're never the same. And I thought we got better in the spring."

(T.P.)

2000 RESULTS

Central Florida	W	21-17	1-0
Florida State	L	21-26	1-1
Navy	W	40-13	2-1
North Carolina State	L	23-30	2-2
North Carolina	W	42-28	3-2
Wake Forest	W	52-20	4-2
Duke	W	45-10	5-2
Clemson	W	31-38	6-2
Virginia	W	35-0	7-2
Maryland	W	35-22	8-2
Georgia	W	27-15	9-2
LSU (Peach Bowl)	L	14-28	9-3

Maryland

LOCATION	**College Park, MD**
CONFERENCE	**Atlantic Coast**
LAST SEASON	**5-6 (.454)**
CONFERENCE RECORD	**3-5 (t-6th)**
OFFENSIVE STARTERS RETURNING	**8**
DEFENSIVE STARTERS RETURNING	**8**
NICKNAME	**Terrapins**
COLORS	**Red, Black & Gold**
HOME FIELD	**Byrd Stadium (48,055)**
HEAD COACH	**Ralph Friedgen (Maryland '69)**
RECORD AT SCHOOL	**First Year**
CAREER RECORD	**First Year**
ASSISTANTS	

Charlie Taaffe (Sienna College '75)
Offensive Coordinator
Gary Blackney (Connecticut '67)
Defensive Coordinator
Tom Brattan (Delaware '72)
Offensive Line
James Franklin (East Stroudsburg '95)
Wide Receivers
Mike Locksley (Towson '92)
Running Backs
Ray Rychleski (Millersville '79)
Special Teams Coordinator
Rod Sharpless (Maryland '75)
Linebackers
Al Seamonson (Wisconsin '82)
Outside Linebackers/Special Teams
Dave Sollazzo (The Citadel '77)
Defensive Line

TEAM WINS (last 5 yrs.)	**5-2-3-5-5**
FINAL RANK (last 5 yrs.)	**50-59-54-38-35**
2000 FINISH	**Lost to Virginia in regular-season finale.**

COACH AND PROGRAM

A jolly fat man appeared in College Park this winter with lots of packages. Offensive packages, that is. Multiple sets. A pro-style passing attack. A proven option game.

The new big man on campus was Ralph Friedgen, a 1969 Maryland graduate and an offensive trendsetter who has struck fear in the hearts of college and pro defenses and restaurant buffet lines for years. "Fridge" is a rookie head coach 33 years into his career and he's chomping at the bit to run his own show—especially at his alma mater.

The 54-year-old Friedgen has said he wants his presence to "be a uniting force for all Maryland people and return the program to where we feel it should be—as one of the outstanding programs in the country."

Good luck, Ralph.

The Terrapins have posted only one winning season since 1985. And 1985 was now four coaches ago at Maryland. The last three coaches, Ron Vanderlinden, Mark Duffner and Joe Krivak, combined for an average of less than four victories per season.

Vanderlinden, now on hollowed ground as the linebackers coach at Penn State, had back-to-back five-win seasons, the second best such mark over this forgettable stretch in Terrapin history. But that wasn't good enough for athletic director Debbie Yow, or more precisely, for the steadily dwindling and restless contingent of fans in Byrd Stadium.

Yow had given Vandy an extension just a season ago when that first five-win campaign seemed like the launching pad to future success. Last year's five-win effort, though, was more like an implosion on the pad when the Terrapins tried to lift off.

Injuries in the offensive line dashed tailback LaMont Jordan's Heisman campaign. Indecision at quarterback seemed to unhinge the whole season and the defense—Vanderlinden's calling card—was slapped around on the land and through the air week after week.

It didn't go unnoticed in the Maryland locker room the last four years that Georgia Tech hadn't scored less than 30 points against the Terps in each meeting. Heck, if the NCAA played "make-it-take-it," the Maryland defense might still be on the field.

As soon as it was announced in late November that Vanderlinden was out, some of the Maryland players even queried Yow about "that offensive coordinator at Georgia Tech." Yow was way ahead of them, knowing Friedgen was a popular alum and the architect of Bobby Ross' offenses during Maryland's last run of bowl teams in the early '80s.

Friedgen followed Ross to Georgia Tech and added a national championship to his resume in 1990. He was running Ross' offense at San Diego, too, when the Chargers went to the Super Bowl in 1994.

Friedgen missed the college game, though, and in 1997 he returned to Georgia Tech to run the offensive line and serve as coordinator for George O'Leary. In 1999, he won the Frank Broyles Award as the top assistant coach in the nation, and the last three years, his offense has averaged 36.7 points and 444 yards per game. Tech was 27-8 over that span.

Those are the kind of numbers Yow wanted to market in Maryland and see if the Terrapins could refill storied Byrd Stadium. Battling for a piece of the sports dollar pie in the tough Washington-Baltimore Metro area, Terrapin football has been knocked off the charts in recent years in attendance and media attention.

The program needed a boost and there's nobody in the Metro area with a bad word for "Fridge." He's a personable, sincere guy and obviously, one heck of a football mind. His first spring practice was brutal for the players who were used to a more laid-back approach, but they've seen the results at Georgia Tech and have first-hand knowledge after two five-win seasons about just how hard it is to turn the corner and establish a winning program.

So can Friedgen do what the last three Maryland coaches couldn't? Can he return Maryland football to the top of the ACC, and capture the imagination of a sports market that hasn't had much reason to pay attention to Saturdays in Byrd? Can "Fridge" stock up on players from the rich local talent pool?

There are more questions in College Park this season than answers, but at least fans are talking Maryland football after a lackluster 2000 season. Friedgen probably doesn't have the parts to put his whole game into action this season, but the allure of his big-time offense could keep fans and recruits interested.

And he could look a lot more like Santa Claus if he delivers a bowl berth at Maryland for the first time since 1990.

2001 SCHEDULE

Sept.	1	North Carolina
	8	Eastern Michigan
	15	West Virginia
	22	@Wake Forest
Oct.	6	Virginia
	11	@Georgia Tech
	20	Duke
	27	@Florida State
Nov.	3	Troy State
	10	Clemson
	17	@North Carolina State

QUARTERBACKS

A trouble spot for several years, the quarterback position at Maryland—the same one that sent Boomer Esiason, Frank Reich, Neil O'Donnell, Scott Zolak and Scott Milanovich to the NFL—looks like one of the most solid portions of Friedgen's first Terrapin team.

Incumbent **Shaun Hill** (6-3, 235) got the keys to the offense early last season when sophomore starter Calvin McCall faltered. Hill, a transfer from Hutchinson (Kansas) Community College, won friends and games with his hard-nosed style.

Now a senior, Hill is learning his third different offense in as many years, but no one will out-work him for the job and no one will play any harder when given a chance. Hill's finest hour came late last season when he returned from a shoulder separation to come off the bench for McCall with the Terps trailing North Carolina State, 21-6, at the half.

Hill completed 15-of-24 passes for 137 yards and two touchdowns to engineer an overtime upset, his 1-yard run providing the winning score. On the season, the burly quarterback completed 73-of-126 passes for 778 yards, six touchdowns and four interceptions. And while he's not Boomer Esiason, he can get the job done.

Hill has surprised Friedgen with his ability to

run the option, although Hill's approach to running is more like that of a fullback than that of a quarterback. He's not afraid to put his head down and plow over defenders.

That tough trait makes it a necessity that Maryland has depth at quarterback, and the Terps do. Friedgen recruited redshirt sophomore **LaTrez Harrison** (6-3, 223) at Georgia Tech, and Harrison has all the tools to be a star. Likewise, no quarterback was more impressive in the spring workouts than redshirt freshman **Chris Kelley** (6-2, 198), a local product from Germantown's Seneca Valley High School.

Harrison, from Atlanta, Ga., redshirted last year with McCall and Hill battling atop the depth chart. The year off might have helped more if he weren't in a new offense this season, but he's the prototype Friedgen quarterback—much more mobile than Hill, downright elusive in fact, and with a cannon for an arm.

Harrison has two career starts under his belt but has completed just 5-of-24 passes for 30 yards and three interceptions. For the second straight year, though, he raised eyebrows in the spring game with a long touchdown pass to **Guilian Gary**; this year it was a 57-yard strike. Playing with both the first- and second teams, Harrison was 10-for-16 for 165 yards. But in addition to the spectacular touchdown, he threw an ill-advised interception to the flat that was returned for a score.

Harrison also had a 13-yard scramble in the game, no mean feat because it was "touch" on the quarterbacks instead of tackle. In fact, he is so dangerous on the naked bootleg and in option situations, the inventive Friedgen may be eyeing more ways to get him in the game.

Kelley, going through his first collegiate practices, was one of the surprises of the spring. He seemed to pick up the offense quickly, and there isn't a Terrapin fan in the Metro area not thrilled with the promise of a local product leading the team.

Perhaps capitalizing on that interest, Friedgen often pointed out during spring practice how well Kelley was playing. "Shaun Hill has the job but he doesn't have an insurmountable lead over Chris Kelley," said the coach. "What Chris has done in just 13 or 14 college practices has been impressive."

Kelley missed all of last season after tearing the ACL in his left knee in a summer all-star game. He has a good combination of physical skills to go with a remarkable poise for such an inexperienced player. Barring disaster, he will have time to master the offense and run it in the future, though he looked rusty in the spring game.

His 8-for-19 passing performance for 72 yards included two interceptions and was easily the least impressive of the three candidates. Of course, he got the least snaps with the first team offense, too.

"He has a lot of poise for a young kid and that's the thing that has really impressed me," Friedgen said. "He doesn't get flustered, even when I get on him and I get on him to see if I can fluster him. That's a real plus for him. He has a very strong arm and a quick release."

Friedgen hasn't said as much, but the feeling is he will use more than one quarterback. He has an eye on the future and he just likes to cross up defenses. Vanderlinden tried to be deceptive about his signal-caller last year, but it just seemed to further unsettle an already delicate balance on offense. He virtually antagonized the media with a perceived uncertainty about the issue that could have played a factor in his ultimate downfall.

Friedgen won't spend a whole lot of time worrying about that aspect with the media. He has proven to be his own man over the years and his track record of success speaks for itself. While Vandy had a growingly testy relationship with the media, Friedgen has openly complained there weren't enough media attending spring practice.

At those practices, Kelley and Harrison moved up on the depth chart when McCall, who would have been a junior, had his basketball season extended by the Terrapins' Final Four run. The 6-3, 210-pound McCall missed the opening of practice and Friedgen dropped him to fourth string. Shortly thereafter, McCall told Friedgen of his intentions to quit football to pursue basketball full time. Friedgen didn't blink at the odd decision but saw that McCall's football scholarship was changed to a basketball grant. A two-year starter in football, McCall is at best the 10th man on the basketball team.

"We want players who want to be out there playing football," said Friedgen early in the spring in a veiled reference to McCall. "We want guys who bring their lunch pail and go to work. That's the only way to be successful."

Friedgen and offensive coordinator/quarterbacks coach Charlie Taaffe had just the three scholarship quarterbacks during the spring. They'll welcome two freshman walk-ons, **Shai Ward** (6-1, 195) of Sandy Springs, Md., and **Brian Ramey** (6-0, 185) of Upper Arlington Ohio, this fall.

RUNNING BACKS

For four consecutive seasons, LaMont Jordan carried the load—and the ball—in the Maryland offense. Jordan set school records for career yards (4,147), attempts (807), 100-yard games (18) and all-purpose yards and attempts (4,960 yard in 889 handles). He had the most career yards of any back in the ACC in the last 20 years and he's got a dizzying array of season- and single-game records, too. Now he's also got a contract with the New York Jets.

When Hill turns around to hand off to a running back this season, he'll have behind him a group of returnees who accounted for exactly 21 yards on 10 carries last year. Steady blocking fullback Matt Kalapinski and backup tailback Mukala Sikyala also departed with Jordan.

Senior **Marc Riley** (6-3, 225) is battling redshirt sophomore **Bruce Perry** (5-9, 190) for the workload at tailback. Riley had all of six carries for 15 yards last year, while Perry redshirted after an impressive freshman season. Caddying for Jordan in 1999, Perry averaged 6.5 yards per rush, carrying 30 times for 195 yards.

The two candidates' running styles couldn't be more dissimilar. Riley is a bruiser who likes to run over opponents and Perry is a speedy scatback. The steadier Riley, more of a "north-south runner," held the upper hand through much of the spring practices but Perry came on late and shined in the spring game. He had 60 yards on nine carries, while Riley had 22 yards on six attempts.

"I like both of them," Friedgen said. "We've got a real change of pace since their styles are so different."

Friedgen is a major proponent of that north-south running. Part of earning a reputation as a play-calling genius is to "stay on schedule with down and distance," he said. "Sometimes a 2- or 3-yard run when it looked like you were going to lose yardage is a great play and it keeps you on schedule. Our guys have to understand that. They think they can score a touchdown every time they touch the ball and half the time they lose five yards. That kills drives."

Friedgen's oft-stated need for speed would seem to give Perry an edge but don't be surprised to see Perry lined up on a wing for reverses or misdirection plays. He'll also be a target for screen passes to spring him. Riley will probably get most of his work out of the I-formation, and could be great in short yardage situations.

Junior **Chris Downs** (5-8, 189) sat out all of last year after transferring from Valley Forge (Pa.) College, where he rushed for 2,013 yards and 23 touchdowns in two years. He had 12 rushes for 33 yards in the spring game, and speedy freshman **Chris Parson** (5-10, 180) had eight carries for 48 yards, including a 16-yard dash.

Parson, who enrolled at Maryland this winter and went through spring practices, was a heavily recruited four-year starter at Newark (Del.) Academy. Even with the likes of Syracuse, Michigan and Nebraska, courting him though, he's not the prize of the backfield-recruiting haul.

That title would belong to **Jason Crawford** (6-2, 215) of Forestville. Md. Crawford is big, strong and fast (4.5 in the 40-yard dash) and he got an extra year of seasoning at Fork Union (Va.) Military Academy, where he split time with two other backs headed to Division I-A this fall—Raymond Kirkley (Pittsburgh) and Leshon Peoples (Indiana).

Crawford committed to Maryland a year ago out of Parkdale High School, but then on signing day, signed with North Carolina. After rushing for 1,310 yards and 18 touchdowns at Parkdale, though, Crawford fumbled the ball academically and ended up at Fork Union. A year later, he finally signed with Maryland.

"I see Crawford playing [this year]," Friedgen said. "I get really excited when I think of all the ways we can use him in our offense. We spread people out and that makes everyone think I'm looking for scatbacks, but if you look at our track record at Georgia Tech, we've had a lot of success with big backs.

"We're going to get our best players on the field."

Friedgen smiles at the thought of defenses spread out to stop the pass while Crawford bangs it up inside. The big back can also catch passes, another must in the new offense.

Catching balls is also a strong suit for **Mario Merrills** (5-10,180) of Columbia, one of the fastest prospects in Maryland. Merrills was clocked at 4.37 in the 40, and rushed for 1,743 yards and 21 touchdowns at Wilde Lake High. He'll get a close look this fall, too, and could be involved in some of that wingback chicanery Friedgen loves to spring on unsuspecting defenses.

At fullback, the playing situation seems clearer cut. Sophomore **James Lynch**, all 5-11 and 261 pounds of him, is back as the favorite to replace 36-game starter Kalapinski. He saw action last year, particularly in short-yardage and goal line situations, and demonstrated remarkably quick feet for a big man. The only question about him is his weight, which has ballooned to 280 in the past, making him a one-man Lynch Mob.

Junior special teams standout **Chad Killian** (6-2, 256) has become a Friedgen favorite with his hard work and attention to detail, and at his size, he doesn't get lost in an elevator, either. Sophomore **Bernie Fiddler** (6-1, 241), originally recruited as a linebacker, is also on hand.

The fullbacks didn't get much work in the old offense, and it's unlikely, with Friedgen's predilection for speed and multiple wideouts, they'll get much work in the new system. Look for the guys with the scarred helmets (from blocking) when you try to pick out the Terrapin fullbacks.

WIDE RECEIVERS/TIGHT ENDS

To hear veteran Gary describe the new system from the wide receivers' perspective is to understand the definition of a complex offense.

"It's so much more to learn than before," said Gary (6-0, 187). "I used to line up in a 5-to-7 yard range, now the receivers have to line up in an exact spot depending on where the ball is and what hash mark I'm closest to.

"Before the ball is snapped, I have to read the linebacker and the safety and make a call based on their formation and then we have to make another read once the ball is snapped and adapt our route based on what we see."

Not surprisingly, the wide receivers had difficulty in the spring with those nuances. Still, senior Gary is destined for stardom this year no matter the offense. He had six catches for 95 yards, including that 57-yard great-catch-and-run from Harrison, in the spring.

Last season, he led the team with 40 receptions, 568 receiving yards and seven touchdown catches. He's one of the toughest Terps and has led the team in punt returns the last three years. He caught Fridge's eye last season when he had three touchdown catches against Georgia Tech.

The other receiver spot is wide open, and Friedgen is hoping that trend continues during games. Junior **Scooter Monroe** (6-1, 185) started 10 times last year and had 14 catches. He's got speed and makes the big catches in traffic, now if he would just make all the routine ones, too. Monroe has been moved to the "Z" receiver slot behind Gary, but he'll see lots of duty somewhere in Friedgen's packages.

Redshirt freshman **Rob Abiamiri** (6-3, 213) emerged as the "X" receiver starter in the spring based on his speed and ability to stretch defenses. But he's unproven. Sophomore **Jafar Williams** (6-2, 193) averaged 12.3 yards on his nine catches last year, and he'll push for playing time, too.

Receiver is one of the Terps' deepest positions thanks to the emergence of Abiamiri and fellow redshirt freshmen **Steve Suter** (5-9, 186) this spring. The cat-quick Suter is a near carbon copy of graduated Jason Hatala. Suter is the fastest Terp, and Friedgen and Taaffe have already drawn up lots of plays—inside screens, reverses, options—to get the ball in his hands in open space.

Two more redshirt freshmen, **Maurice Shanks** (6-4, 184) and **Ike Roberts** (5-11, 168) are also available. Shanks, a highly recruited, sure-handed receiver, was making waves before a broken toe sidelined him in the spring. Little-used senior **Daryl Whitmer** (6-0, 183) is also in the mix after appearing in 10 games last season, mostly on special teams.

Friedgen had enough confidence in his returnees that he didn't recruit any freshmen at the position.

Like receiver, tight end will be one of the squad's deepest positions. Sophomore **Jeff Dugan** (6-4, 263) was second on the team last year with 25 receptions and he accounted for 319 yards in the passing game. With good speed for a big man, Dugan is an emerging star in the ACC, but he can't rest on his laurels with the depth Maryland boasts at tight end.

Senior **Matt Murphy** (6-3, 261), who has also played some defensive end, impressed the new coaching staff this winter with his strength and athleticism. He has yet to catch a pass in his career, though, and his hands are suspect. Senior **Eric James** (6-2, 263) has caught six passes each of the last two years, including three for touchdowns in 1999.

The glut of talent allowed Maryland to run some three tight end formations last year in short-yardage situations, and the depth just got deeper, to borrow a Yogi Berraism. Redshirt freshman **Ryan Flynn** (6-4, 238) is pushing for playing time this season, too, and he has a great combination of size and ability.

Freshman **Derek Miller** (6-8, 240) fits into that category as well, only more so. Friedgen said the Terps just couldn't pass up the chance to sign him this year but he needs work on his run blocking. He should eventually flesh out to 260 pounds.

OFFENSIVE LINE

The quick history lesson on recent Maryland football fortunes is all about the offensive line. The group came together in 1999, punished opposing defenses to the tune of an ACC-leading 234 yards rushing per game, controlled the ball and kept the defense off the field. The result was a feel-good 5-6 mark and a just miss of a bowl berth.

Last year, with a couple of starters lost to graduation, injuries hit and the unit never got on track. Neither did Jordan. He finished with 920 yards, the defense was exposed, the Terps again finished 5-6, and Vanderlinden was cleaning out his office when the season was over.

So it's not overstating matters heading into 2001 to say much of Maryland's chances for success rest on the front five. And Fridge, a former Terrapin offensive lineman himself, took an immediate liking to the group.

"I think we're blessed in this area, and if you have to have only one area like that, this is a good place for it to be," the coach said. "It takes the longest to develop linemen and if we had to go out and recruit prospects to fill holes, we'd be a long ways away from being successful."

The centerpiece is senior **Melvin Fowler** (6-3, 292), who Friedgen thinks is ready to be all-conference. Smart and quick, Fowler at center anchors what could be a great unit, if everyone is healthy.

"He's such an intelligent football player and once he learns more of what I want, he's going to be even better," Friedgen said.

Junior **Todd Wike** (6-3, 295) at left guard and sophomore **Lamar Bryant** (6-3, 307) at right guard flank Fowler. Wike, a battler, has started 21 consecutive games. Bryant started six of the last seven games last year as a freshman, moving in when nagging injuries finally undid Bob Krantz' season. (Krantz gave up football this winter because of a chronic neck injury.)

Bryant is big and agile and still learning. He could be the building block for the unit soon, though, and he has the chance to play on Sundays when his college career is over—if he can eliminate mistakes.

Matt Crawford (6-6, 311) and sophomore backup **Eric Dumas** (6-6, 300) were both injured as spring practices ended, but they'll probably regain the tackle jobs in the fall.

Their absence gave a couple of younger players, redshirt freshmen **Lou Lombardo** (6-6, 301) subbing for Dumas at left tackle, and **C.J. Brooks** (6-5, 304) in for Crawford on the right side, a chance to gain experience.

Crawford, a junior, had his string of 20 consecutive starts snapped last season when he suffered an ACL injury in his left knee that required surgery. He missed all of spring workouts. Dumas broke his left foot near the end of spring. He was the heir apparent for graduated Tim Howard at the vital left tackle spot (which guards the right-handed quarterback's blind side). Dumas played in five games, and the previous coaching staff regularly lamented not using him more.

Friedgen likes Lombardo and Brooks, calling them, "big, strong kids who like to play football." Brooks, the coach stressed, is athletic enough to play on the left side, if needed. Offensive line coach Tom Bratton also inherited the Terrapin offensive line insurance policy—senior **Chris Snader** (6-5, 293), who can play practically anywhere on the line and has in the past.

Brandon Miller (6-2, 296) is a redshirt sophomore who backs Fowler at center, and redshirt freshman **Kyle Schmitt** (6-5, 298), a prize of last year's recruiting class, can play center or guard.

Sophomore **Ed Tyler** (6-3, 300) and redshirt freshman **Reggie Kemp** (6-4, 332) round out the returning linemen.

Friedgen has said he likes to have 17 or 18 offensive linemen in his program to give the younger ones time to develop and he added five "wide-bodies" in his first recruiting class. Winston-Salem's **Russell Bonham** (6-4, 339), generally regarded the top offensive lineman out of North Carolina last year, is the top prospect, but **Raheem Lewis** (6-3, 335) has a big upside (in addition to a big backside), especially as a guard, where his size will be an anomaly.

The talkative Lewis of District Heights, Md., is nicknamed "Radio" for his non-stop gab and should become a locker room favorite. His coaches say he is already one of the program's top recruiters.

Tim Donovan (6-6, 316) of Crofton, Md., impressed coaches with his quick feet and could be a lucky find as a "late-bloomer." **Matt Powell** (6-4, 315) of Fort Washington, Md., and **Jason Holman** (6-2, 270) of Midlothian, Va., are the new coaching staff's first projects up front. Powell had six "pancake" blocks last season and while Holman ruins the average size statistic of this year's newcomers, coaches love his agility. He'll redshirt and get a shot at center next year.

2000 STATISTICS

Rushing offense	124.1	79
Passing offense	211.1	59
Total offense	335.2	81
Scoring offense	22.5	78
Net Punting	37.9	14
Punt returns	5.1	108
Kickoff returns	19.1	73
Rushing defense	186.1	89
Passing efficiency defense	134.1	97
Total defense	440.0	107
Scoring defense	25.8	63
Turnover margin	+3	46

Last column is ranking among Division I-A teams.

KICKERS

Someone's going to have to fill graduated Brian Kopka's kicking shoes, and the leading candidates are senior **Vedad Siljikovic** (6-2, 218) and redshirt freshman **Nick Novak** (6-0, 186).

The two were even through much of the spring, though Siljikovic kicked a 38-yard field goal in the spring game and Novak had a PAT blocked. Siljikovic has more experience, particularly after punting 13 times last season as a "pooch" punter.

DEFENSIVE LINE

The Maryland defense gave up so many big pass plays last season fans didn't even notice opponents averaged 186 yards rushing per game and 4.1 yards per carry against the Terrapin ground defense. A good portion of those big pass plays came from Maryland's inability to pressure opposing quarterbacks.

And those problems all start up front. Now take away the unit's best player, hulking Kris Jenkins, who was the first Terp taken in the NFL draft (second round, Carolina Panthers), and the forecast doesn't look much better this season. Maryland is undersized and depth shy on the defensive line and somebody better blossom like Jenkins did last year or Friedgen may not be able to get his high-octane offense on the field.

Senior nose tackle **Charles Hill** (6-2, 292) played well alongside Jenkins in the middle. Hill had a career-best 43 tackles, including three sacks and six tackles for loss. He's the most experienced of the returnees and he'll need to anchor the middle and keep blockers off the linebackers.

"I have concerns there," Friedgen said. "I think some of the guys are playing to their capabilities. My concern is if we don't play low we'll get blown off the line and we'll get in the way of our linebackers."

Sophomore defensive tackle **C.J. Feldheim** (6-3, 263) is trying to fill the huge shoes left by Jenkins at defensive tackle. He came on strong in the second half of last season, appearing in four of the last five games as a freshman. His play was so impressive that coaches moved junior **William Shime** (6-4, 265) to back Hill at nose tackle.

Another possibility in the middle is sophomore **Landon Jones** (6-4, 256), who has battled nagging foot problems so far in his college career. He got three starts last year at end but defensive line coach Dave Sollazzo hopes he can bulk up and bring more experience to the middle.

Fourth-year junior **Durrand Roundtreee** (6-3, 250) is back at defensive end. Roundtree started five games at the spot last season but was often overpowered in the running game. Redshirt sophomore **Scott Smith** (6-4, 259) took over the position the last two games after returning from a back injury, but Roundtree won the spot back in the spring. Scott has quickness but needs to regain some of the weight and strength he lost while injured.

Redshirt freshman **Kevin Eli** (6-4, 253) is another possibility at end. The former *PrepStar* All-American's athleticism had him working first at the hybrid rush linebacker position. If he can make the transition to the more traditional end, it will give the front a lift.

Sophomore **Tosin Abari** (6-0, 245), a walk-on who appeared in two games last year, is also available at nose guard.

The real key to this unit's success could be how fast at least one new freshman can contribute.

Maryland product **Randy Starks** (6-5, 290) was rated the eighth-best defensive lineman in the country by *SuperPrep* and the top defensive line prospect in the state by recruiting analyst Tom Lemming. He's got the size and tools to remind folks of Jenkins, and the Terps need him to play this fall.

Akil Patterson (6-3, 260) of Frederick, Md., and **Will Ferguson** (6-3, 255) of Bethesda, are less heralded but either could play into a role with a good fall camp.

LINEBACKERS

Of all the new assistant coaches, inside linebackers coach Rod Sharpless and outside linebackers coach Al Seamonson were dealt the best hands.

The linebacking corps, even without two-year starter Marlon Moye-Moore, who may not be with the team because of a brush with the law last year, remains the strength of the Maryland defense. Defensive coordinator Gary Blackney has been busy installing a more aggressive scheme to take advantage of the size, speed, experience and play-making ability of this group.

Senior **Aaron Thompson** (6-1, 234) is back to anchor the strong side. An acknowledged team leader, he has started every game of his college career and is the team's returning leader with 6 1/2 sacks and three forced fumbles. His numbers weren't as impressive as a year before, but teams consciously made an effort to avoid his side.

Junior **E.J. Henderson** (6-2, 238) is the emerging star in the middle. He took over for injured Kevin Bishop last year and led the team in tackles (109) and ranked second in tackles for loss (13), despite missing the Clemson game with a sprained knee. He came back to post double-figure tackles in four of the last five games and catch the eye of opposing offensive coordinators.

"It's a rare situation to take over a team you just game-planned for and one of the things I had noticed was E.J. Henderson," said Friedgen. "He was great tackle-to-tackle but I had no idea the range he has. This guy can run and he's physical and he's nasty. I really like the guy."

Sophomore **Leon Joe** (6-1, 217) came out of spring the weak-side linebacker. The suspension of Moye-Moore and a shoulder injury to senior **Reggie Lewis** (6-0, 233) cleared the way for Joe, who has worked hard to improve his strength.

The embarrassment of riches at the linebacker spots includes sophomore **Leroy Ambush** (6-1, 220) and freshman **Ricardo Dickerson** (6-3, 238) behind Thompson. Ambush, in addition to having such a marvelous name for a linebacker, has experience after playing in nine games. He's a standout on special teams.

Dickerson, from Hyattsville, Md., has a little experience, too, after enrolling at Maryland this winter and going through spring practice. Coaches love his speed.

Seniors **Monte Graves** (6-0, 238) and **Kevin Bishop** (6-2, 233) back up Henderson. Graves is a special teams standout who got into every game last season. Bishop, after a brilliant 1999 season when he was third on the team in tackles, has been slowed by injuries to both knees.

Redshirt freshman **Kenneth Jerry** (6-2, 217) lends depth on the weak-side with walk-on sophomore **Andrew Henley** (5-10, 210). Henley's stock went up after he made two interceptions in the spring game, returning one 48 yards for a score. He may get a chance to help on special teams but it's hard to imagine him working into the mix with so many older players ahead of him.

Maurice Smith (6-0, 210) is an undersized freshman from Waldorf, Md., who obviously needs to put on weight but caught Friedgen's eyes with his hard-hitting style at Westlake High School, where he was a teammate of Starks.

The rush linebacker position, which plays more like a down lineman, is in good hands. **Mike Whaley** (6-1, 233) started every game last season, and earned third-team Freshman All-America honors from *The Sporting News*. He was third on the squad with sacks (five) and tackles for loss (12).

Fifth-year senior **Ryan Swift** (6-1, 238) battled hamstring and ankle injuries last year, playing in just three games. He backed up Thompson on the strong side his first two seasons but was moved to rush end last year and expected to push for a starting job until injuries and Whaley's often-spectacular play derailed him.

Redshirt freshmen **Jon Condo** (6-3, 232) and **Jamahl Cochran** (6-0, 243) are also trying to break in behind Whaley. The previous coaching staff loved Condo's potential and Cochran has added 23 pounds since the beginning of last season.

DEFENSIVE BACKS

The most maligned part of last season's squad, the secondary, returns six of the top eight players. Maryland yielded 253.9 yards per game through the friendly skies and several young players got a baptism under fire.

Tony Okanlawon (5-11, 186) started every game last season and **Curome Cox** (6-1, 185) all but two. Okanlawon, a senior, and Cox, a sophomore, learned some hard lessons, but they're each a year older and wiser.

Blackney has them in more "press" coverages, moving up to battle receivers off the line. They'll probably be exposed more in single coverage as the Terrapins try to be more aggressive with blitzes.

Friedgen has singled out Okanlawon, Cox and sophomore backup corner **Dennard Wilson** (5-11, 183) for praise and he thinks they're up to the challenge. More pressure on the passer will solve a lot of their ills.

The safeties are solid with senior **Tony Jackson** (6-1, 209) on the strong side and senior **Randall Jones** (6-2, 233) stepping into Shawn Forte's vacated free safety spot. Jackson was third on the team with 101 tackles and earned All-ACC honors in his first injury-free season.

Jones, who came to Maryland as a quarterback, has shown a penchant for the big play. He had a 100-yard interception return in one spring scrimmage. His backup, junior **Tyrone Stewart** (6-0, 199), missed most of the spring with a bad hamstring that gave coaches a good look at two youngsters, redshirt freshman **Curtis Williams** (6-2, 192) and junior transfer **(Towson) Madieu Williams** (6-1, 185).

There's been talk of moving the speedy Williams to wide receiver.

Senior **Rod Littles** (5-11, 204) will see lots of duty behind Jackson, and is an aggressive hitter, though he needs to improve his coverage. Redshirt freshman **Raymond Custis** (5-8, 180) rounds out the safeties.

Highly regarded Rovel Hamilton, who played some as a freshman last year, left the program. But his spot behind Okanlawon has been ably filled by incoming freshman **Domonique Foxworth** (5-11, 175) of Randallstown, Md. Foxworth, one of three freshmen who enrolled early and went through spring workouts, was rated the sixth-best defensive back in the nation by *PrepStar*.

Another freshman, safety **Marcus Wimbush** (5-11, 180) of Washington, D.C., was rated the 13th best defensive back in the country by SuperPrep.

Junior transfer **Jamal Chase** (6-1, 190) from Lackawanna (Pa.) Junior College and freshman **Gerrick McPhearson** (5-11, 185) of Columbia, Md., are also in this year's recruiting crop.

Sophomore corner Andrew Smith, Jr., who played in nine games and started one, was suspended this spring for his involvement in the same incident that has sidelined Moye-Moore.

PUNTERS

It's a sad testament that a highlight of Maryland's 2000 season was the punting of **Brooks Barnard** (6-2, 182).

The junior, a transfer from Oklahoma who wants to be a meteorologist, put enough footballs into the stratosphere to rank fourth in the nation with a 44.7 yards per punt average last year. Friedgen said Barnard could be even better if he improves his mechanics.

Between Barnard's booming punts and Kopka's kickoffs for touchbacks, the Terrapins often enjoyed a field position advantage.

SPECIAL TEAMS

One of Friedgen's first hires was special teams coordinator Ray Rychleski, and in fact, he has two coaches (Seamonson is the other) overseeing special teams. The first thing Friedgen's first team worked on this spring was kicking and punting.

Tell you anything about Fridge's emphasis on this phase of the game?

He's got a lot of pieces from last year to build around. Gary was the primary punt returner with 13 for a 5.0 average, and he averaged 23 yards on his four kickoff returns. Monroe had 10 kickoff returns for a 14.5 average, the second most runbacks behind the graduated Sikyala (16 for a 22.8 average).

It's hard to imagine the speedy Suter won't figure in here somewhere, too. Fact is, though, Fridge put off working on kickoff returns until the fall, and then a fast freshman might even work into the mix.

Sophomore **Jimmy Connolly** (6-5, 211) is back after filling in late last year as long-snapper. He stepped in and did well, but his lack of girth is a concern. Barnard is the primary holder on placements, backed by the sure-handed Suter.

RECRUITING CLASS

Considering the coaching change, Maryland had a great recruiting year, and seems to already be off to a fast start for next season. Much of the credit goes to running backs coach Mike Locksley, who serves as recruiting coordinator.

Friedgen quickly—and accurately—realized he needed to retain Locksley from Vanderlinden's staff, and the first payoff was the salvaging of this recruiting season. Thirteen of the 18 signees were committed to Maryland before Friedgen's hiring, and Locksley kept them in the fold.

Starks, Foxworth, Wimbush and Crawford were not only considered big-time prospects; they were big-time prospects at positions Maryland needed the most help.

If the Terps had landed Pittsburgh defensive tackle Troy Banner, a last minute commit to Pittsburgh, this class would have been near perfect. Fridge would have loved a junior college defensive tackle, too, but as he pointed out, everyone would love more help at that position.

The best thing about this class was the success the Terps enjoyed in their own backyard. Thirteen of their 18 signees were from either Maryland or Washington, D.C., including Merrills, the Gatorade Maryland Player of the Year. This program can get fat and happy keeping the best area players home every year.

"I think we can get all the players we need within a five-hour radius [of College Park]," Friedgen said. "We want Maryland kids to come to Maryland. We won't ignore the other areas like Florida, but this is where our bread is buttered."

BLUE RIBBON ANALYSIS

OFFENSE	C+
SPECIAL TEAMS	B
DEFENSE	D+
INTANGIBLES	B+

Friedgen certainly seems primed for his shot at this head-coaching thing. The question is whether he has the players to immediately translate those best-laid plans into wins.

Quite simply, on both sides of the ball, it's what's up front that counts. Fridge needs his offensive line healthy, which would be a change from last season in College Park. The line has the potential to be big and dominating, and that could take the heat off unproven running backs and quarterback Hill, who is running his third offense in as many seasons.

No one will outwork this staff or this team. The pace of practice shocked players this spring, but they're so hungry for a winning season they've bought into the work ethic.

Best case scenario: Fridge's fireworks on offense spark the team to that elusive six wins and a bowl bid. It's possible. The Terps have seven home games next year, including the first three at home—an excellent chance to build some early confidence and momentum.

The flip side of this scenario begins with the defensive line. Undersized and not deep, the line can ill-afford injuries. Even healthy, the unit has question marks against the run and the pass. Read all the hype about Friedgen's offensive heroics but believe the real key to this season is what Blackney does with the defense.

Growing pains are likely as new systems are incorporated on both sides of the ball. Of course, N.C. State made that transition work last year in the ACC, so there is precedent. The more you hear about Friedgen's offense, though, the more you worry he needs a couple of seasons to get his personnel in place.

He certainly needed more practices than the 15 allotted by the NCAA in the spring. Friedgen didn't get all of his playbook in, and it's hard to imagine, with new freshmen in the mix in the fall, the Terps will have all the nuances down by the Sept. 1 opener against North Carolina.

That game looms large for two new coaching staffs, as does game three at home against West Virginia. Figure a win over Eastern Michigan in the second game and those other two games shape the direction of the Terps' season.

No matter how things shake out next season, the offensive mind of Friedgen should make it worth watching, and the fans will give him a pass for a season in his efforts to return Maryland to the ranks of the bowl bound.

Their patience—and Fridge's in waiting for this head-coaching job —should be rewarded soon.

(M.A.)

2000 RESULTS

Temple	W	17-10	1-0
West Virginia	L	17-30	1-1
Middle Tennessee	W	45-27	2-1
Florida State	L	7-59	2-2
Virginia	L	23-31	2-3
Clemson	L	14-35	2-4
Wake Forest	W	37-7	3-4
Duke	W	20-9	4-4
North Carolina State	W	35-28	5-4
North Carolina	L	10-13	5-5
Georgia Tech	L	22-35	5-6

North Carolina

LOCATION	**Chapel Hill, NC**
CONFERENCE	**Atlantic Coast**
LAST SEASON	**6-5 (.545)**
CONFERENCE RECORD	**3-5 (t-6th)**
OFFENSIVE STARTERS RETURNING	**7**
DEFENSIVE STARTERS RETURNING	**7**
NICKNAME	**Tar Heels**
COLORS	**Light Blue & White**
HOME FIELD	**Kenan Stadium (52,000)**
HEAD COACH	**John Bunting (N. Carolina '72)**
RECORD AT SCHOOL	**First Year**
CAREER RECORD	**First Year**
ASSISTANTS	

Gunter Brewer (Wake Forest '87)
Wide Receivers
Rod Broadway (North Carolina '78)
Defensive Tackles
Ken Browning (Guilford '68)
Tight Ends/Recruiting Coordinator
Robbie Caldwell (Furman '76)
Offensive Line
Dave Huxtable (Eastern Illinois '79)
Linebackers/Special Teams Coordinator
Jon Tenuta (Virginia '81)
Defensive Coordinator/Defensive Backs
Gary Tranquill (Wittenberg '62)
Offensive Coordinator/Quarterbacks

TEAM WINS (last 5 yrs.)	**10-11-7-3-6**
FINAL RANK (last 5 yrs.)	**9-6-34-63-29**
2000 FINISH	**Beat Duke in regular-season finale.**

COACH AND PROGRAM

If nothing else, new North Carolina coach John Bunting will make sure his team is more intense this season than it was a year ago.

The Tar Heels may not be better—because of a brutal schedule that includes three consecutive road games to start the season—but the former NFL linebacker will chew straight through the helmet of anybody he doesn't think is tough enough.

"When I got here, I saw a team that lacked confidence," Bunting said. "The reason they lack confidence, I think, is that they don't really understand how tough it is to play this game day in and day out, play after play after play.

"I think they were complacent in some places. I think there were times during the spring when things didn't go well, our team would just kind of give in. That is going to change. The only way for that to change is for our off-season strength and conditioning to get better. In a very short time, we have been able to show these kids how much stronger and how much better condition they can be in. Now, they are more confident."

Bunting played at UNC in the 1970s under Bill Dooley, and went on to have a 13-year career as a linebacker for the Philadelphia Eagles. When his playing days were over, Bunting started his coaching career at Division III Glassboro State (now Rowan College), first as an assistant and for three years as the head coach.

In 1993, he jumped to the NFL as an assistant coach for Marty Schottenheimer with the Kansas City Chiefs, and later was co-defensive coordinator of the St. Louis Rams during their unlikely run to the 2000 Super Bowl championship. He was hired from the New Orleans Saints last December, becoming the ACC's fifth current head coach to lead his alma mater.

For a guy who has no Division I-A coaching experience, making the transition to the college game was difficult for Bunting. He hired a staff with 184 years of college coaching experience, including veterans Gary Tranquill as his offensive coordinator and John Tenuta as defensive coordinator.

Tranquill has 39 years of college experience, most recently at Virginia. Tenuta spent the last six seasons as Ohio State's defensive coordinator. For continuity, Bunting kept three members of Torbush's staff: offensive line coach Robbie Caldwell, defensive line coach Ken Browning and wide receivers coach Gunter Brewer.

Bunting made it through recruiting, signing 22 players in his first class. It wasn't spectacular, but it was a pretty good haul in a transitional year.

Spring practice was scheduled late, to ensure that two-sport stars **Ronald Curry** and **Julius Peppers** would be able to participate, and Bunting spent much of his time inspiring a new self-respect into the sagging program, mainly with uniform-soaking workouts.

"We've got a lot of catching up to do in the hard-work department," Bunting said before spring practice began.

The players bought into his tough-as-concrete

sales pitch and headed into the summer dedicated to getting stronger and tougher. What Bunting didn't understand is how his beloved alma mater, with a great academic reputation and some of the best football facilities in the country, could get in such mediocre shape. Just listen to what he told the *ACC Area Sports Journal* about the Tar Heels' chances against Florida State, a team UNC hoped to challenge just a few short years ago.

"It's obvious, we're not going to beat the Florida States with the talent level that is here," he said. "You can't do it, I don't think anybody could. If Knute Rockne came back, I don't think he could take this group and beat Florida State."

Over the last three years, the Heels lost the edge it once had, when Mack Brown led UNC to back-to-back Top 10 finishes in 1996 and '97. When Brown bolted for Texas after the '97 season, defensive coordinator Carl Torbush was elevated to head coach after a failed run at then-Georgia coach Jim Donnan.

Torbush, a career assistant whose only other head coaching job was on the Division I-AA level, was known as one of the best defensive coaches in the country. But as a head coach, he had his shortcomings—especially in the area of hiring assistants—and his program never got off the ground.

UNC athletics director Dick Baddour was ready to fire Torbush after the 1999 season, but held off after the Tar Heels won their final two games over rivals N.C. State and Duke to finish 3-8. But soon after the 2000 team finished its 6-5 season, Baddour decided it was time to let Torbush go. He did it with an ace up his sleeve. The school had been contacted earlier in the fall by the agent of Virginia Tech coach Frank Beamer, who was constantly banging heads with his athletic department administration and was looking for some leverage.

By most accounts in North Carolina, Baddour had an agreement with Beamer, but not a signed contract, when Beamer left Chapel Hill in early December to return to Blacksburg, Va. Baddour expected him to return as the Tar Heels' next head coach. It never happened. Beamer got a raise for his assistant coaches and some promises from the Virginia Tech administration and he pulled a Roy Williams, leaving Baddour and the Tar Heels scrambling for a career candidate.

Baddour barely knew who Bunting was before Beamer pulled out, but after spending more than a week interviewing other candidates, then getting assurances from some of the best people in the NFL, Baddour hired Bunting on Dec. 11.

Bunting spent many of his 16-hour workdays cleaning up messes. He wanted to renew relationships with former players, who he did not think were warmly embraced by former coaching staffs. He had to handle some disciplinary problems and some injuries, including a degenerative condition that ended the career of his starting fullback and a knee injury that will keep one of his starting defensive linemen out this season.

There are problems that will have to be settled in the fall, specifically along the offensive line, which has only one returning starter, and the defensive front, which is thin after Peppers.

But Bunting isn't afraid of challenges, which is why he agreed to add a 12th game to the Tar Heels' schedule, a season-opener against defending national champion Oklahoma in Norman in the Hispanic College Fund Classic, followed by road games at Maryland and Texas. It's the first time since 1893 that UNC has opened the season with three consecutive road games.

Under Brown, the Tar Heels were successful, but they rarely played against real competition. That's certainly not Bunting's philosophy.

"Some people think I am crazy for playing them, but I think it is important," Bunting said. "My thinking is to help a young offensive line get a game under its belt before we open the conference schedule against Maryland.

"It gives us an extra game on the schedule and an extra week of practice, especially for those young linemen and young defensive players. If I am a player, that is a tremendous incentive for me to get ready to play. It's on national television, against the defending national champion. What football player in America doesn't want to do that?"

It's a new era in Chapel Hill, one that will take a tougher kind of Tar Heel.

2001 SCHEDULE

Aug.	25	@Oklahoma (Hispanic Classic)
Sept.	1	@Maryland
	8	@Texas
	15	SMU
	22	Florida State
	29	@North Carolina State
Oct.	6	East Carolina
	13	Virginia
	20	@Clemson
Nov.	1	@Georgia Tech
	10	Wake Forest
	17	Duke

QUARTERBACKS

Bunting has two problems with his quarterback, senior Curry (6-2, 200). The first is how little protection the multi-talented, two-sport athlete got from his offensive line last year. He was sacked 35 times in 2000—which is not an inordinately large number considering the fact that North Carolina's defense had an ACC-leading 53—but he was forced out of the pocket too many times.

Bunting's second problem with Curry is what he did once he was forced out. Usually, Curry would just improvise, make something up as he went along. It was exactly what made him one of the greatest high school players ever. But that kind of thing won't cut it with Bunting this year. He wants Curry to have a plan the next time he leaves the comfort of his protection.

"I don't want him to improvise," Bunting said. "I want him to know what to do. If the throw is there, take it. Don't wait, take it."

Curry, who is on the verge of breaking Jason Stanicek's school records in passing yardage and total offense, won't be easy to break. He's been doing those things instinctively for years.

It will be up to new offensive coordinator and quarterbacks coach Gary Tranquill (Curry's third position coach in three years) to teach the talented player about his options and how to take advantage of them.

"I don't think there is anybody better than Tranquill at helping him learn to make the right decisions," Bunting said. "We are going to be aggressive. We are not going to hold Ronald back from running the ball. But what we are not going to do is let him sit back there and improvise, running backwards or throwing the ball down field and hoping someone will catch it. That is not going to help us."

In a 39-year-career that includes two stops at ACC rival Virginia with a four-year stint at Michigan State under Nick Saban in between, Tranquill turned three Cavalier quarterbacks into All-ACC selections (Scott Secules, Shawn Moore and Matt Blundin). He also worked with Bernie Kosar and Vinnie Testaverde during a three-year foray into the NFL.

Curry, the starting point guard on the Tar Heel basketball team, didn't get much work with Tranquill in the spring, even though Bunting delayed the start of his first spring practice to accommodate Curry and Peppers. He will certainly be inundated with information in the fall.

"We have great skill people," Bunting said, referring to his wideouts and tailbacks. "We need to develop some instinct with those receivers so we can make some big plays. This is a big year for Ronald and it is a big year for us with him at the helm.

"In most football games, production is generally dependent on the quarterback being productive back there."

It's hard to question the productivity of the Tar Heels' offensive most valuable player. Last year, he set the single-season record for total offense at 2,676 yards, including 2,325 passing yards and 351 rushing yards. He threw 11 touchdown passes and ran for six more scores. But he also had 12 interceptions and was caught behind the line of scrimmage too many times. Bunting is just asking for a little more consistency.

"Gary is going to be able to put Ronald in position to make a lot of plays," Bunting said. "What I don't want is Curry out there trying to re-invent plays as the play develops.

"Gary is a great teacher. He got Ronald to focus on various parts of the field, depending on what the situation is."

As long as Curry stays healthy, the Tar Heels won't get much out of his backup quarterbacks. Junior **Luke Huard** (6-4, 220) is the top reserve, but two redshirt freshmen will get a lot of reps throughout the season in practice. **Darian Durant** (6-1, 215) and **Aaron Leak** (6-3, 215) were both highly regarded recruits coming out of high school.

RUNNING BACKS

Bunting was pleasantly surprised to discover the talent he had at tailback, with three speedy sophomores on the squad: **Brandon Russell** (5-11, 185), **Willie Parker** (5-10, 200) and **Andre Williams** (6-0, 215).

Russell started the first eight games at tailback last year, becoming the first UNC freshman to start at tailback since the legendary Charlie Justice in 1946. He led the team in rushing with 508 yards on 145 carries and scored three touchdowns. He was the third consecutive freshman to lead the Heels in rushing. Russell also had 11 catches out of the backfield.

However, like Curry and Peppers, Russell saw limited action in the spring because of his two-sport status. Russell was a reserve outfielder on the baseball team, hitting .206 with no home runs and 10 RBI in 44 games.

Parker was the hit of last spring and the preseason. He won the starting position at tailback, only to lose it a week before the season opener when he injured his back. He played sparingly throughout the season, but ended strong, averaging more than five yards a carry in the final four games. He regained his starting job for the final three games of the season, rushing for 158 yards on 21 carries against Maryland.

Williams was third on the depth chart, finishing the season with 165 yards on 39 carries. Junior walk-on **Michael Harris** (5-10, 200) is also an option.

The Tar Heels were already critically thin at fullback, even before it was determined that senior Anthony Saunders' career was over because of a shoulder injury.

The only returning options are sophomore **James Faison** (6-0, 220) and redshirt freshman **Madison Hedgecock** (6-3, 235). Faison is a walk-on who became one of the team's best blocking backs late last season. He started the last game against Duke, carrying the ball three times for seven yards. His best game came against Virginia, when he had a career-long 16-yard run.

Hedgecock ran for nearly 1,800 yards as a high school senior, but sat out last season as a redshirt.

Bunting also moved former linebacker **Kitwana Jones** (6-0, 220) to the offensive side of the ball in the spring and was pleased with how quickly he picked up the position. It appears to be a permanent move.

"He is really a devastating lead blocker," Bunting said.

WIDE RECEIVERS/TIGHT ENDS

Because his team won't be able to grind it out up front, Bunting hopes to use Curry and a veteran corps of receivers to make big plays, put a lot of points on the board, and hope that the defense can hold on.

"We have big-play people," Bunting said.

The Tar Heels certainly have big-play potential among the receivers, starting with junior **Bosley Allen** (6-1, 200). The group is led by senior **Kory Bailey** (6-3, 187), a consistent contributor in his first three years on campus. In all, six of the Tar Heels' top seven receivers return this season.

Allen is an exciting player with game-breaking speed, which he uses on offense and as a record-setting punt returner. He caught 40 passes for 634 yards last year and set the school record with 421 return yards on 28 attempts.

"It excites me a lot that they have so much confidence in us as receivers," Allen said after the UNC spring game. "A lot of people have doubted us, saying North Carolina's a running school with defense mixed in. But we know what we can do, and we'll get to show it."

Bailey is hardly the game-breaker Allen is, but he's durable and consistent. He enters the season ninth in school history in career receptions with 95 catches for 1,331 yards and eight touchdowns. Last year, he had 32 catches for 550 yards and two touchdowns.

Junior **Sam Aiken** (6-2, 190) was third on the team with 29 catches for 410 yards. Three of his catches went for more than 40 yards and he twice had at least five catches in a game.

Sophomore **Jamal Jones** (5-11, 200) led the team with his 19.2 yards per catch. Three of his 15 catches on the year went for more than 50 yards, including the first reception of his career, a 55-yard touchdown pass from Curry against Tulsa.

Senior **Danny Davis** (6-0, 190), sophomore **Isaiah Robinson** (6-0, 190) and junior **Chesley Borders** (6-0, 180) all have experience and should be able to provide quality depth. But Tranquill believes that wide receiver is the easiest place on offense for a freshman to play, and he'll take long looks at his strong crop of freshmen receivers—**Danny Rumley** (6-4, 215), **Derrele Mitchell** (6-3, 190), **Jarwarski Pollock** (5-8, 175), **Chris Curry** (5-11, 185), and **Chris Hawkins** (5-11, 185).

The tight end position has been turned over to Kenny Browning, the defensive coordinator under Torbush last year and the defensive ends coach for the last seven years. It's a position where the Tar Heels desperately need some help, with the loss of seniors Alge Crumpler and Dauntae Finger, both of whom were drafted by the NFL.

Senior **Doug Brown** (6-4, 245) was clearly the best blocking tight end during the spring, Browning said, and he does have some ability to catch the ball. But Brown is certainly not the weapon that the combination of Crumpler and Finger provided the last two years.

Junior **Zach Hilton** (6-6, 255) has good hands, as does walk-on **Kevin Sergent** (6-3, 225). Former linebacker **Richard Moore** (6-2, 235) worked out at fullback and tight end and could contribute at either position next year.

"We are not as fast as I want us to be at the tight end position," Bunting said. "But they are tough, and Doug Brown is my best finishing blocker on the offense. I was really excited about learning that."

Bunting could look to a pair of freshmen, **Brian Chacos** (6-5, 253) and **Chase Page** (6-5, 250), to challenge for playing time in the fall. Chacos, the son of former UNC player Andy Chacos, is perhaps the most talented player in Bunting's first recruiting class.

The Heels might have gotten a bonus in mid June, when former Kentucky tight end **Bobby Blizzard** elected to transfer to North Carolina. Blizzard (6-7, 246), who caught 23 passes last year, could be ruled eligible right away if the NCAA penalizes Kentucky for alleged recruiting violations. If Kentucky is barred from a bowl game for two years, Blizzard, a junior, would be eligible immediately. Otherwise, he'd have to sit out this season.

Blizzard is a former high school teammate of Ron Curry.

OFFENSIVE LINE

It must have been fun sitting outside Bunting's office in the spring, listening through the door as he watched game tapes and screamed at the screen. He would then come outside and find someone to scream at.

"Anybody can tell you that I would come out of there just sick watching Ronald Curry get hit, watching Ronald Curry trying to run for his life and watching the running game have very little ability to get started," Bunting said. "It was just tough to watch."

It may not be any better this year.

The Tar Heels have to replace three starters, and have almost exclusively underclassmen to fill the holes. Senior center **Adam Metts** (6-0, 270) and junior **Isaac Morford** (6-3, 300) started all 11 games last year and will certainly be expected to guide the youthful players who will surround them this fall. Morford played guard last season, but was moved to center to back up Metts in the spring.

Bunting likes two sophomore tackles—**Jeb Terry** (6-5, 280) and **Greg Woofter** (6-5, 265), who were brought in three years ago to help with this very problem. Apparently, they have matured and are ready to contribute.

Terry, who played on the defensive line in 1999, sat out all last season with an ankle injury.

Junior **Bryant Malloy** (6-3, 310), who started six games at tackled in 2000, is also an option, but he did not compete in spring practice because of charges stemming from a domestic battery incident. He was later reinstated to the team. However, Bunting is not likely to be lenient with anyone who causes problems for his program.

At right guard, sophomore **Jupiter Wilson** (6-2, 300) has the edge over junior **Don Peters** (6-2, 305) and sophomore **David Stevenson** (6-3, 315) as the starter.

Among the reserves are sophomore center **Marcus Wilson** (6-2, 270), redshirt freshman center **Skip Seagraves** (6-5, 250), sophomore tackle **Brandon Lugabihl** (6-6, 300) and redshirt freshmen tackles **Justin Barton** (6-6, 290) and **Willie McNeill** (6-5, 280).

Bunting knew he needed to get his young players some experience, so he asked his most promising players to double their workload in spring practice.

"Those guys were always working," Bunting said. "They were getting double the reps, which is hard on the coaching staff because it makes it hard to coach. But that's what we needed."

The Tar Heels will need it even more when they open the season against an experienced Sooner defense, which may give Bunting a whole need reason to get sick thinking about his young offensive line.

2000 STATISTICS

Rushing offense	148.5	55
Passing offense	222.6	48
Total offense	371.1	58
Scoring offense	24.5	66
Net Punting	31.5	94
Punt returns	13.1	18
Kickoff returns	18.0	89
Rushing defense	103.5	19
Passing efficiency defense	125.5	80
Total defense	327.5	30
Scoring defense	25.8	63
Turnover margin	-12	104

Last column is ranking among Division I-A teams.

KICKERS

One position Bunting won't have to fret about is place-kicker. Senior **Jeff Reed** (6-0, 200), a fourth-year walk-on, turned into one of the most reliable place-kickers in the ACC last year.

In his first year as a starter, Reed earned second-team All-ACC honors by making 16-of-20 field goals and all 30 of his PATs. Not bad for someone who had never kicked in a college game before.

Reed ended up as one of 20 semifinalists for the Lou Groza Award, given annually to the best place-kicker in the nation. He finished the season ranked fourth in scoring in the ACC, with more than seven points per game on a team that was fifth in the league in scoring offense.

Bunting demands excellence from his kickers and he restructured how kickers participate in practice. Instead of working out on their own they are part of the regular practice, working out with a member of the strength and conditioning staff.

"We stay busy," Reed told UNC writer Lee Pace. "It's more like a game situation. We have to have our heads in it all the time."

DEFENSIVE LINE

The best tactic Bunting could think of to improve his team's poor offensive line was to make it work overtime in blocking the Tar Heels' veteran defensive ends—junior All-American Peppers (6-6, 270) and senior **Joey Evans** (6-5, 255).

Peppers is perhaps the premier end in college football. He led the nation last year with 15 sacks and set the school record with 24 tackles for loss. He finished one sack short of the UNC single-season record set by a guy named Lawrence Taylor.

Peppers, like Taylor, is a monster on the football field, but he got just as much attention as the sixth man on the Tar Heels' nationally ranked basketball team.

If you think trying to block Peppers is tough, try taking a charge on him. He is certainly the centerpiece of a veteran defensive line that the Tar Heels will have to use to make up for a lack of depth at linebacker with production from the ends.

Redshirt freshman **Jermicus Banks** (6-3, 247) and sophomore **Isaac Mooring** (6-3, 257) arrived on campus together last fall and will back up Peppers and Evans. Other options at ends include sophomore **Tony Pigford** (6-3, 220) and redshirt freshman **Larry Jessup** (6-6, 230).

"My philosophy is that you have to win up front," Bunting said.

At tackle, the Tar Heels suffered a blow in the spring when senior **Anthony Perkins** (6-5, 260) suffered a knee injury that will prevent him from playing this fall. Perkins—who of course is called "Psycho" by his teammates—is a former walk-on who earned a starting position and scholarship last year. He started every game and had two sacks and four tackles for loss among his 46 tackles.

He will be replaced in the lineup by sophomore **Will Chapman** (6-4, 271), with help from junior **Eric Davis** (6-3, 263). Chapman, like Perkins, is a former walk-on who has earned a scholarship. He and Davis both played in every game last year as reserves.

The premier player up front is senior **Ryan Sims** (6-4, 295), who didn't get as much attention as Peppers but was a key reason the Tar Heels led the ACC with 53 sacks. He had 56 total tackles last year, including six sacks and nine tackles for loss. He's been a big contributor since his freshman season and a starter for the last two years.

Sims' back up is redshirt freshman **Jonas Seawright** (6-6, 306). Others at the position are redshirt freshman **Isaac Montgomery** (6-5, 285) and sophomores **Dontl Coats** (6-3, 290) and **Darryl Grant** (6-2, 270).

Bunting is a big believer in winning battles up front, which is why he is so disappointed in the offensive line and so optimistic about the defensive line. With Peppers and Sims leading the way, who wouldn't be?

"Peppers and Sims are NFL players, and in a sport where you have to win the battles in the trenches, that's a pretty good place to start," Bunting said. "I was very impressed with Sims, because it was obvious that he was one of those who was working very hard before we got here."

LINEBACKERS

Even when Bunting was playing for the Tar Heels, the linebacker position was UNC's pride and joy. Over the years, plenty of other linebackers of distinction have come through the program, and under Torbush's guidance, they were the reason UNC had dominating defenses throughout the 1990s.

All of a sudden, however, that deep pool has suddenly dried up, now that Sedrick Hodge and Brandon Spoon, a pair of three-year starters, have taken their games to the NFL.

This year, as Bunting turns the linebacking corps over to Dave Huxtable, the Tar Heels are as thin on experience as they have been since the early days of Mack Brown.

Three of the players on the post-spring depth chart are former walk-ons—junior middle linebacker **Robert Harris** (6-1, 230), senior backup middle linebacker **Sean Williams** (6-1, 218) and senior strong-side linebacker **David Thornton** (6-2, 222). Both Thornton and Harris were listed as starters coming out of spring practice, though that will probably change in preseason practice.

"If not starters, I think they will be really good backups," Bunting said.

Bunting believes there is some surprising talent in the group, which he has a particular affinity for because he is a legacy at the position.

"I would say we are better than you think we are at linebacker," Bunting said. "I actually think that's where we have the most depth on defense. "There are some skilled guys who are on the verge of playing."

Senior **Merceda Perry** (6-5, 253) is a potential NFL player, but he is recovering from an ankle injury that forced him to miss nine games last season. Perry started 10-of-11 games in 1999, when he finished second on the team in tackles with 83 total hits.

"I think he is the key guy for us at linebacker," Bunting said. "When he plays healthy, he can be terrific."

Senior **Quincy Monk** (6-3, 235) stepped into Perry's starting position after Perry's injury, finishing fourth on the team with 76 tackles. He had six tackles for loss and two sacks in his nine games as a starter.

"I think he is going to have a banner year," Bunting said. "I think he is going to be an All-ACC choice and I think he is going to be a draft pick."

Redshirt freshman **Clarence Gaddy** (6-4, 210) was one of UNC's premier recruits two years ago, and he will join redshirt freshman **Devllen Bullard** (6-1, 215) and junior **Malcolm Stewart** (6-3, 225) as backups at the position.

Freshman **Doug Justice** (6-3, 215), who was recruited by Florida and Michigan, is the best newcomer at the position and could help out immediately.

DEFENSIVE BACKS

With three-of-four starters returning, the Tar Heels are set in the secondary, with a couple of adjustments. UNC is so deep, in fact, Bunting signed only one defensive back in his first recruiting class.

In the spring, junior **DeFonte Coleman** (6-1, 215) moved from strong safety, where he started the final eight games of the season, to free safety.

Coleman was third on the team with 78 tackles last year and added an interception and two pass break-ups. For his efforts, he was selected the team's most improved player.

His move clears the way for senior **Billy-Dee Greenwood** (6-2, 185) to take over the strong safety position, where he started three games last year before losing the starting job to Coleman. Greenwood started all 12 games at free safety as a sophomore.

The two veterans could be pushed, however, by two young players who have impressed the new coaching staff. Sophomore **Dexter Reid** (5-11, 180) and redshirt freshman **JoVon Lewis** (6-1, 181) are both talented players who arrived on campus last fall.

Reid was one of only a handful of freshmen to play last year, and he made an impact with 69 tackles, one interception and six pass deflections. He had his best game against Clemson, making 13 tackles with two tackles for loss and a sack of Willie Simmons. Lewis was impressive during the spring and will probably play a lot this fall.

Other candidates at safety include junior **Marcus Jones** (6-2, 205), junior **Adam Holland** (6-0, 180) and redshirt freshman **Bryant Macklin** (6-0, 195).

The Tar Heels are set at cornerback with two of the most talented cover players in the league. Senior **Errol Hood** (5-11, 195) and junior **Michael Waddell** (5-11, 170) each broke up 12 passes last year. Hood, entering his third year as a starter, intercepted two passes, the most on the team. Waddell is one of, if not the, fastest players in the ACC. He was timed at 4.21 seconds in the 40-yard dash by new strength and conditioning coach Jeff Connors, but he is still having a difficult time converting that speed into coverage. Last year was his first on the squad, after sitting out for one year for academic reasons. He started all 11 games and had 42 tackles on the year, with one interception.

The coaching staff also feels good about junior **Kevin Knight** (5-8, 175), who has experience as a starter and as a special teams contributor, and sophomore **Derrick Johnson** (5-9, 187). Both played liberally last year and will be counted on as top reserves this year.

Sophomore **Justin Browne** (5-9, 175) and junior **Ronald Brewer** (5-6, 155) are also options.

Bunting's only signee in the secondary is **Ronnie Bryant** (6-1, 196) of nearby Durham.

PUNTERS

Last year, Torbush had to change punters a couple of times, because of ineffectiveness and illness. Both sophomore **Blake Ferguson** (6-0, 170) and walk-on **John Lafferty** (5-10, 180) return and are looking to improve on less-than-impressive numbers from last year.

Lafferty began the season as a starter, but that lasted only one game. Ferguson took over punting duties for the next five games, until he was replaced again by Lafferty. But Lafferty developed mononucleosis, and Ferguson ended the season as the starter.

Ferguson had the better statistics, averaging 36.9 yards on 40 punts. Lafferty had half as many attempts, averaging 35.4 yards per kick and dropping six of his 20 punts inside the 20.

However, the Tar Heels had the worst net punting average in the ACC (and were 94th among I-A teams), getting only 31.5 yards per kick. That was three yards less than the eighth-place team in the league. Ferguson will be the starter, but Bunting hopes Lafferty's presence will push him to better production.

SPECIAL TEAMS

To Bunting, special teams aren't just an emphasis. They are an obsession, something he inherited from former boss Dick Vermiel.

Bunting hired veteran defensive coach Dave Huxtable from Oklahoma State to train his linebackers and coordinate his special teams. Huxtable, who had two different stints at nearby East Carolina and spent five years at ACC rival Georgia Tech, has a reputation for building strong special teams.

"We have to win the kicking game," Bunting said. "We have to do that especially this year to have a chance to break even. We have to control it."

So the Tar Heels spent extra time in the spring working on punt coverage at the goal line, on having stability in the snapper-punter exchange and on blocking punts.

Bunting should feel comfortable with his return specialists. Junior Bosley Allen was one of the most exciting punt returners in the ACC last year, setting a school record with 421 punt return yards. He also scored two touchdowns on punts, a 78-yarder against Wake Forest and a 63-yarder against Duke. He was second to N.C. State's Koren Robinson in the ACC with a 15.0-yard average.

However, the Tar Heels need some help in kickoff returns. They were last in the ACC in that category last year, averaging 18.0 yards per return last year. Huxtable hopes to find one consistent player to handle those duties, which were spread among eight different players last year. Aiken had the most returns, bringing back 18 kicks for 365 yards. He also returned two punts. He ranked eighth in the ACC with a 20.3-yard average. Allen also brought back five kicks last season for a 17.0-yard average, while junior Kevin Knight returned 10 kicks and had a 15.5-yard average.

RECRUITING CLASS

Since 1988, when Mack Brown replaced Dick Crum and rekindled UNC's relationship with North Carolina high schools, the Tar Heels have tried to dominate in-state recruiting. Brown, the consummate salesman, spent much of his off-season time traveling the state and getting to know the coaches. He even hired one of the most successful high school coaches in the state, Durham Northern High coach Ken Browning, as an assistant.

Torbush continued the emphasis on in-state recruiting, and eventually elevated Browning to defensive coordinator. It's no surprise, then, that Bunting kept Browning on the staff, to maintain the relationship with the state's high school coaches for recruiting purposes. Of the 22 players in Bunting's first recruiting class, 13 are from North Carolina.

However, unlike Brown's heyday, the Tar Heels didn't get a high percentage of the state's best players, as N.C. State lured a few players to Raleigh, East Carolina brought some to Greenville and Clemson, Virginia, Tennessee and Maryland all raided the state for a few top recruits.

Torbush had a start on recruiting before he was fired, with 12 commitments listed before December. Some of them would have never made it to school, but the nine or 10 players that were still committed to playing for the Tar Heels represented a decent foundation.

The best players among the recruits are defensive end **Jocques Dumas** (6-8, 220), tailback **Jacque Lewis** (5-11, 187), wide receiver Danny Rumley, linebacker Justice and tight end Brian Chacos.

Dumas, who committed to the Tar Heels last summer, has drawn immediate comparisons to Peppers, because of his explosive ability off the line. He had 133 tackles and 10 tackles for loss as a high school senior. But he needs to add some bulk, while maintaining his speed, meaning he'll be spending more time in the weight room over the next year or so than he will on the football field.

Lewis, from the remote eastern coastal town of Elizabeth City, was considered one of the best players in the state last year. However, he flew below the radar of most recruiting analysts because he lived so far from the state's biggest towns. He proved he could play with the best players in North and South Carolina, earning the offensive most valuable player award at the Shrine Bowl All-Star Game.

Because the Tar Heels are thin on experienced tight ends, Chacos may get an early chance to play for UNC, just like his dad Andy did in the early 1970s.

Despite the short amount of time he had to recruit, Bunting was pleased with what he was able to piece together in his first class.

"We have a lot of athletes," Bunting said. "I thought we needed to improve our team speed, and we did that. I thought we had some position-specific needs, and we addressed those."

BLUE RIBBON ANALYSIS

OFFENSE	C
SPECIAL TEAMS	B-
DEFENSE	B
INTANGIBLES	B-

Bunting won't admit it, but it is pretty obvious that he's not counting on a great debut season. He may even be writing it off until he can get his own system with his own kind of players into positions across the board.

He talks about winning with a tricked-up offense that includes multiple formations, lots of quarterback rollouts and bootlegs and a heavy reliance on talented skill players to make big plays.

The Tar Heels should be solid on defense (except for the huge question at linebacker) and they are decent in special teams play, but Bunting knows his first team won't be able to line up and bowl people over.

"Are we going to be able to grind it out with a sophomore offensive line?" Bunting said. "Who are you kidding? That's asking for the impossible."

So why would he schedule a season-opening game at defending national champion Oklahoma? Bunting says it's because he wants to toughen up his weak offensive line for the ACC opener the next week at Maryland. But the outcome may also be demoralizing, consider the tough games that follow, including a third consecutive road game at Texas and a UNC reunion with Longhorns coach Mack Brown.

After the three road games and the home-opener against Southern Methodist, the Tar Heels play, in succession, Florida State, at N.C. State, East Carolina (the first meeting since 1981), Virginia, at Clemson and at Georgia Tech.

Bunting's initial team will be fortunate to enter November with more than two victories. So he seems willing to let this year's team take its lumps, so he can go through another recruiting season to fill some of the many holes he sees and another spring practice so he can toughen up the Tar Heels.

And who knows? If he gets more than four wins, next spring might not be so hard to live through.

(T.P.)

2000 RESULTS

Tulsa	W	30-9	1-0
Wake Forest	W	35-14	2-0
Florida State	L	14-63	2-1
Marshall	W	20-15	3-1
Georgia Tech	L	28-42	3-2
North Carolina State	L	20-38	3-3
Clemson	L	24-38	3-4
Virginia	L	6-17	3-5
Pittsburgh	W	20-17	4-5
Maryland	W	13-10	5-5
Duke	W	59-21	6-5

North Carolina State

LOCATION	**Raleigh, NC**
CONFERENCE	**Atlantic Coast**
LAST SEASON	**8-4 (.667)**
CONFERENCE RECORD	**4-4 (5th)**
OFFENSIVE STARTERS RETURNING	**7**
DEFENSIVE STARTERS RETURNING	**7**
NICKNAME	**Wolfpack**
COLORS	**Red & White**
HOME FIELD	**Carter-Finley Stadium (52,500)**
HEAD COACH	**Chuck Amato (N.C. State '69)**
RECORD AT SCHOOL	**8-4 (1 year)**
CAREER RECORD	**8-4 (1 year)**
ASSISTANTS	
	Marty Galbraith (Missouri Southern '72) **Offensive Coordinator**
	Doc Holliday (West Virginia '79) **Wide Receivers/Assistant Head Coach**
	Curt Cignetti (West Virginia '82) **Tight Ends**
	Mike Canales (Utah State '84) **Quarterbacks**
	Dick Portee (Eastern Illinois '65) **Running Backs**
	Buddy Green (N.C. State '76) **Defensive Coordinator**
	Cary Godette (East Carolina '77) **Defensive Line**
	Joe Pate (Alabama '68) **Linebackers/Special Teams**
	Chris Demarest (Northeastern '88) **Defensive Backs**
TEAM WINS (last 5 yrs.)	**3-6-7-6-8**
FINAL RANK (last 5 yrs.)	**54-21-40-46-47**
2000 FINISH	**Beat Minnesota in Micron PC.com Bowl.**

COACH AND PROGRAM

Chuck Amato knows just how thin an edge his team lived on last year, a season-long tight rope walk that resulted in a surprising eight victories and a fifth-place finish in the ACC.

Now, in his second season at his alma mater, Amato is the school's football version of Jim Valvano, a fast-talking, successful Italian who can make the farmers and engineers laugh while winning lots of close games.

But he also knows just how close his Wolfpack was from a disastrous debut that could have featured losses to Arkansas State, Wake Forest and Duke. The Wolfpack played in eight games that were decided by eight points or less, including a double-overtime victory over Arkansas State, an overtime victory over Georgia Tech and an overtime loss to Maryland.

The Pack needed fourth-quarter comebacks in six of its eight victories, including a spectacular rally to beat Minnesota, 38-30, in the Micron PC.com Bowl.

The biggest problem, it turns out, was that Amato's debut season might have been too successful. That's because three key components of that success cashed in, leaving the program with big holes to fill in the coach's sophomore effort.

The first to depart was All-America wide receiver Koren Robinson, a speedy threat to score a touchdown every time he touched the ball, either by pass, kickoff return or punt return. He caught 62 passes for 1,061 yards and seven touchdowns during his spectacular sophomore season, then opted to enter the NFL draft, where he was taken as the ninth pick in the first round by the Seattle Seahawks.

Not long afterward, hard-hitting strong safety Adrian Wilson decided to forego his senior season and enter the draft also. He was picked in the third round by the Arizona Cardinals.

Then, in February, Amato received what some people regard as an even bigger blow when Southern Cal hired away offensive coordinator Norm Chow after only one season in Raleigh. Chow was the architect of the Wolfpack offense, which Amato describes as a pure "pain in the butt" for defenses.

The offense utilizes multiple formations, from five wide receivers to two tight ends; throws a lot of short passes to players coming out of the backfield on multiple crossing patterns; and occasionally goes down field for the home-run play.

Chow, who spent nearly two decades at Brigham Young before following Amato to Raleigh, quickly taught the basic tenets to the Wolfpack's young quarterback, **Philip Rivers**, who graduated from high school early and arrived on campus in January, 2000, to get an early start to his football career.

Rivers, barely 18 when the season started, developed a quick bond with Robinson and the offense was an immediate success. The Wolfpack averaged 292.6 yards passing, the second-highest average in school history.

Rivers became the first freshman in ACC history to throw for more than 3,000 yards in his rookie season, finishing with 3,054 yards, 25 touchdown passes and only 10 interceptions. He easily became the third consecutive Wolfpack player to win ACC Rookie-of-the-Year honors, following tailback Ray Robinson in 1998 and wide receiver Koren Robinson (no relation) in '99.

If the Wolfpack has a fourth, it will probably be one of a slew of receivers Amato lured to campus who wanted to play in such a wide-open offense. But will the offense be the same without Chow? Amato bristles at the question.

"This is the North Carolina State offense," Amato said. "I made that perfectly clear to everybody when Norm Chow left. He did a great job in bringing all those personalities together in that offensive staff room and put the best from here and the best from there together, but in the final analysis it was our offense.

"There were things I wanted, being a defensive coach. I wanted a defense to have to adjust maybe once or twice before the ball was snapped."

Rivers, even with his stilted throwing motion, was able to keep defenses confused and get the ball in the hands of both Robinsons, who had 103 catches between them. He stayed healthy despite having a weak offensive line in front of him, and this year he's bigger, better and married.

All he needs is a few targets, which Amato hopes Rivers will find among a 30-player recruiting class that features some of Florida's speediest and most talented receivers.

Amato turned the offense over to offensive line coach Marty Galbraith, with instructions to run the offense just like Chow did last year. He hired Michael Canales from South Florida to be the quarterback coach, with strict instructions not to change Rivers' odd throwing motion.

"This is our offense," Amato said. "We will tweak it and change it however we need to this year, but it will be basically the same."

What won't be the same is the Wolfpack's home, Carter-Finley Stadium. After more than a decade of talk, the school finally broke ground on a renovation and expansion of the facility, which hasn't had a facelift since it opened in 1966. By the time the season begins, the stadium will have 6,000 permanent seats in the south end zone and a state-of-the-art video board in the north end zone.

By the time work is finished on the three-year, $100 million project—which includes a five-story football training center, new practice fields and many other bells and whistles on the sprawling off-campus site near the school's new basketball arena—Amato's program should be soaring.

2001 SCHEDULE

Sept.	1	Ohio
	6	Indiana
	22	@SMU
	29	North Carolina
Oct.	6	@Wake Forest
	11	Clemson
	20	@Georgia Tech
	27	Virginia
Nov.	3	@Duke
	10	@Florida State
	17	Maryland

QUARTERBACK

Rivers (6-5, 228) certainly doesn't lack for people to tell him what to do. In his 18 months on campus, he's worked under two offensive coordinators, two quarterback coaches, a head coach who says "don't change" every time they pass in the hallway and a father who moved to Raleigh for the express purpose of being able to watch game film and counsel his son over the family dinner table on his frequent visits home.

And in May, right after spring football and final exams were over, River hooked up with his most important coach of all when he married his high school sweetheart, Tiffany Goodwin.

Luckily, he takes instruction well.

"Last year, he was the only starting freshman quarterback in the nation that didn't shave," Amato said. "Now, he is the only married sophomore in the nation. And he still doesn't shave."

But Rivers can run a football team, as he proved last fall when he quickly learned Chow's complicated system and found a way to get the ball in the hands of his best teammates. Rivers set school records almost from the moment he stepped on the field as he earned the nickname "Young Man Rivers."

In his first game, he shattered an N.C. State freshman record with 397 passing yards, and broke it twice more during the season. Rivers broke the single-season passing record for a freshman in his fourth game and eventually eclipsed Duke's Ben Bennett for the ACC's freshman passing record. He was voted the league's rookie of the year, the third consecutive Wolfpack player to win that award.

Robinson was the team's star last year, with his game-breaking ability as a receiver, kickoff returner and punt returner. But early on it was obvious that Rivers quickly matured into the cornerstone of Amato's program, someone who promises to be around for four years with the ability to take the Wolfpack to unprecedented heights.

Rivers has an unorthodox throwing motion, one that new quarterbacks coach Michael Canales was not allowed to tinker with during the spring. It's a short-armed push, reminiscent of Florida's Danny Wuerfle. But Rivers was never a skittish freshman, overwhelmed by his instant success and sudden fame around campus. He was particularly good late in games last year. In the fourth quarter of the Pack's 11 regular-season games, he completed 65 of his 124 passes for 787 yards and eight touchdowns. He led the Pack on two scoring drives in the final period against Minnesota in the Micron PC.com Bowl.

This year, Rivers will be the biggest quarterback in the ACC, having added about 15 pounds during the off-season training program. Canales helped him improve his footwork in the pocket and Rivers will probably move around even more back there, with several different drops, rollouts and bootlegs.

"He is running them better," Amato said. "You have to take a quarterback and get him moving. The defensive linemen always know what their target is, and that makes their job easy. But if the bull's-eye keeps moving, it makes it harder."

Rivers has a competent backup in senior **Olin Hannum** (6-1, 196), one of the toughest players on the team. Hannum was Chow's insurance for Rivers, coming to Raleigh from a junior college in his native Utah, where he got more Division I scholarship offers in rodeo than he did in football.

Hannum found his way on to the field in some of the Wolfpack's stranger formations, lining up as a split receiver or in a split backfield. He caught four passes in six games, serving as an effective decoy.

Look for much of the same from Hannum this year, because Amato likes seeing his cowboy ride.

Amato has already found Rivers' successor in freshman Jay Davis (6-3, 190), one of 10 players the coach recruited from Florida. He's a record-setting passer who liked the Wolfpack's offensive style, and when he committed, a wave of receivers followed.

Davis thinks he can compete for the starting job in the fall, but it's unlikely, barring an injury, that anyone besides Rivers will be under center for much of the season.

"That shows you the kind of competitor he is," Amato said of Davis. "Sure, a lot of people wondered why he came here, with Philip in front of him. If it doesn't work out this fall, then he definitely wants to redshirt to put some distance between them."

RUNNING BACKS

The Wolfpack offensive scheme is so oriented toward throwing the ball there is barely any chance to run it. New offensive coordinator Marty Galbraith admits that the Wolfpack needs to be a little more balanced this year, which means senior **Ray Robinson** (5-10, 212) could have a big season.

Robinson, the 1998 ACC Rookie of the Year, was hampered by several injuries as a sophomore but made a strong comeback as a junior. He played in all 11 games and was second to Koren Robinson with 41 receptions for 366 yards.

He became a master of catching short swing passes from Rivers, sometimes turning them into long plays, like the 81-yard touchdown he scored at Clemson. But those short swing passes were also the Wolfpack's version of the option, plays they could run on first or second down that were almost assured of getting somewhere between four to eight yards.

Robinson, hampered by ankle and knee injuries in his sophomore season, showed that he could also be a threat running the ball. He had 139 yards in the season opener and rushed for more than 100 yards three times, including a school-record 40 rushes for 178 yards in the loss at Maryland.

But Robinson is really the only experienced running back returning to the lineup. Junior **K.J. Stone** (5-11, 190) had only eight carries for 24 yards last year as he recovered from a knee injury he suffered in 1999. He also suffered a new hip injury that kept him on the bench most of the season.

Junior **Carlos Doggett** (5-10, 212) played in only one game, and was hampered in the spring by a broken foot. The Wolfpack staff has high hopes for freshman **Tramain Hall** (5-11, 180), who arrived on campus in January and went through spring drills. Hall, highly recruited out of Deerfield Beach, Fla., can also play wide receiver, a position where the Wolfpack also needs help.

The Wolfpack offense doesn't really rely on ground production from its fullback, which is frequently replaced by a fourth wide receiver. Wolfpack fullbacks carried the ball only twice last season. However, Derek Roberts and Tramayne Simmons, both of whom have departed, combined for 27 catches.

This year, junior **Cotra Jackson** (5-11, 215) will likely be the starter, but he missed all of spring practice after sustaining severe facial injuries while trying to break up a fight in his hometown in Alabama.

Jackson played backup to Robinson last year, finishing second on the team with 174 rushing yards. He had 94 yards in the fourth quarter of the North Carolina game, helping the Wolfpack run out the clock and snap an eight-game losing streak to the Tar Heels.

Converted defensive lineman **Chance Moyer** (6-4, 230), a redshirt freshman, moved to fullback in the spring and will get an opportunity to contribute.

WIDE RECEIVERS/TIGHT ENDS

One of the best things about Rivers is that he speaks the truth. Probably, he's so young he doesn't know better. But the young quarterback thinks that the Wolfpack will have a better receiving corps this year, even without Robinson and the departed Eric Leak. That's because Rivers will have many options to choose from, thanks to Amato's emphasis on bringing in young receivers in this year's recruiting class.

"I think our receivers as a whole will be better," Rivers said after the annual spring game. "Not that last year we didn't spread it around, because we did, but everybody was so concerned about stopping Koren. This year, we'll have some good wide receivers.

"The ball will probably get spread around more this year and I think that will be good for us because the defense will have to cover the whole field."

Amato agrees, thanks to a deep and talented recruiting class that featured five freshmen receivers—**Dovonte Edwards** (6-0, 180), **Sterling Hicks** (6-1, 165), Tramain Hall (see above), **Chris Murray** (6-4, 194) and **Fred Span** (6-1, 175).

All but Edwards, a two-sport star from nearby Chapel Hill High School who plans to walk on to the N.C. State basketball team, are from the football diamond mines of Florida. All are supposed to be fast.

"We are going to have to find out what they can do," Amato said. "On paper, they are fast. They may get here in the fall and our clocks might be slower than the ones they had in high school.

"Then there is the factor of whether they can take what I give them, how will they handle that and how will they mature. But they have a lot of good things going for them."

Hall, like Rivers last year, arrived on campus in January so he could get a head start on learning the system by participating in spring practice as both a running back and wide receiver. However, he was injured much of the spring and did not participate in the Red-White Game in April.

The newcomers will push a handful of returning receivers—junior **Bryan Peterson** (5-10, 187) and sophomores **Andy Bertrand** (6-1, 191), **Jericho Cotchery** (6-2, 183) and **Troy Graham** (6-2, 188).

Peterson had decent numbers last year (28 catches, 394 yards, three touchdowns), but he was fifth on the team behind Koren Robinson, running back Ray Robinson, departed senior Eric Leak and tight end Willie Wright in receptions.

Translation: Peterson isn't exactly an experienced go-to guy. But he's the closest thing the Pack has going into the season, at least until Amato decides which of his many young receivers have the best chance to contribute early.

"We will have to find other ways to get the big play at this point," Amato said. "I think these youngsters we have coming in, one or two of them will have to come up. We have a lot to look at."

Senior tight end **Willie Wright** (6-4, 226) has some of the most reliable hands in the ACC, Amato thinks. Last year Wright tied Duke's Mike Hart with the most receptions by an ACC tight end with 31. He should be an even bigger weapon this year.

The Wolfpack offense frequently uses double tight ends, so senior **Andy Vandeveer** (6-4, 245) and junior blocking specialist **Joe Gray** (6-4, 253) will both get plenty of action.

OFFENSIVE LINE

With a program cornerstone like Rivers, it's no wonder that Amato is concerned about his underperforming offensive line, which lost its biggest and best player, massive tackle Jarvis Borum, to graduation. But four starters return, along with two part-time starters who missed most of last year with injuries.

Amato expects perfect protection for his young prodigy.

Sophomore **Chris Colmer** (6-5, 292) has been handed the ultimate responsibility of guarding Rivers' blind side. Colmer, who started all 12 games at right tackle last year despite a nagging ankle injury, will take over Borum's spot at left tackle.

At left guard, senior **William Brown** (6-2, 265) is solidly entrenched as the starter, with junior **Joe Lardino** (6-3, 279) and **Travis Brinson** (6-3, 257) as backups.

Junior **Scott Kooistra** (6-6, 300) missed most of last season with a knee injury but will return to reclaim his starting position at right guard. That will probably mean a shift for senior **Reggie Poole** (6-2, 312) to right tackle after he started 11 games at guard last year.

At center, offensive line coach Marty Galbraith has an interesting choice. Junior **Derek Green** (6-3, 264) took over for senior **Keegan Weir** (6-5, 258) after Weir's second consecutive season-ending injury in the season opener. Green started the final 11 games of the season and developed into a solid blocker.

Weir petitioned for a sixth season from the NCAA and will play. Both Green and Weir will get competition from freshman **Brandon Moore** (6-3, 290), who enrolled early in school and was on hand for spring practice.

Galbraith does have more depth available with juniors **Tim Turner** (6-6, 301) and senior **Matt Broel** (6-5, 298) available to fill in at tackle. But Amato has reasons for concern.

"The offensive line has to stay healthy," he said.

2000 STATISTICS

Rushing offense	103.8	96
Passing offense	292.5	15
Total offense	396.4	41
Scoring offense	31.0	32
Net Punting	34.3	65
Punt returns	13.5	16
Kickoff returns	22.7	9
Rushing defense	191.0	92
Passing efficiency defense	117.2	52
Total defense	375.5	66
Scoring defense	28.0	78
Turnover margin	+4	37

Last column is ranking among Division I-A teams.

KICKERS

Sophomore **Austin Herbert** (6-1, 204) thinks he can do it all, and Amato plans to let him. Last year as a freshman, Herbert punted and kicked off, leaving the place kicking duties to departed senior Kent Passingham, who was surprisingly effective in his final year.

Herbert spent most of the spring working on kicking field goals, and Amato gave him several chances in the spring game to prove himself. Herbert converted three of those chances, making field goals from 46, 36 and 32 yards. Perhaps his most impressive kick, however, was a 53-yard attempt that had plenty of distance, but sailed wide right—two words that make an old Florida State guy like Amato cringe. But the several thousand fans in attendance appreciated the effort.

"The kid got a standing ovation for going wide right," Amato said. "Those people have a lot to learn about going wide right.

"[But] at least we know he is a spring gamer. Whether that will carry over to the fall, I don't know."

Herbert was perhaps the second most important recruit of Amato's first class. The Cary native set the North Carolina high school record with 37 field goals during his prep career. He hit a career-long 50-yarder as a senior.

If Amato needs a replacement, he can turn to sophomore **Adam Kiker** (6-0, 178), a walk-on who kicked one field goal during the spring game.

DEFENSIVE LINE

Amato hopes three junior college linemen will help improve the Wolfpack's pressure up front. State was fifth in the ACC with a total of 32 sacks last season. Defensive ends **Brian Jamison** (seven) and **Corey Smith** (six) lead the team in sacks. Linebacker **Levar Fisher** had five.

Jamison (6-1, 224) was moved in the spring to join Fisher (6-1, 229) at linebacker, but Smith (6-2, 245) returns at one defensive end, where he hopes to continue his climb up the school records in tackles for loss. His 22 tackles for loss in three years ranks eighth in school history.

But who will play the other end? Junior **George Anderson** (6-0, 236) missed most of last season and all of the spring with a leg injury. He should be back in the fall, but the competition will probably be intense. Junior **Drew Wimsatt** (6-4, 244) returns after missing most of last season after back surgery.

To shore up the position, Amato brought in a pair of ends from Los Angeles Valley College in California. **Terrance Chapman** (6-4, 240) had 90 tackles, 12 sacks and 18 tackles for loss at the school last year, while **Shawn Price** (6-2, 235) had 62 tackles, and 16 sacks. Both were selected junior college All-Americans by Rivals.com and both picked the Wolfpack over Miami and other well-established programs.

Amato had recruited Price in high school while still at Florida State and was eager to bring him to Raleigh.

"His up-field speed is awfully fast," the coach said. "How he is going to play the run is another story. He is a strong kid and Chapman is really only about a step behind him."

At tackle, the Pack loses Jeff Fisher, but has a handful of options, starting with senior **Darius Bryant** (6-1, 287), the strongest player on the team, junior **Shane Riggs** (6-3, 269) and sophomores **Sean Locklear** (6-3, 290) and **Ricky Fowler** (6-2, 286). Riggs and Locklear played the end and tackle positions at times last year.

Junior college transfer **Terrance Martin** (6-4, 290) will also look for playing time.

LINEBACKERS

With a bona fide All-American returning, the Wolfpack would seemingly be in good shape at this position. But Fisher, a senior who led the nation in tackles last year with 166, can't make every tackle on the field, though it seems that way at times. The 2000 ACC Defensive Player of the Year was all over the place for the Wolfpack, despite playing with a badly damaged shoulder that he had surgically repaired in the off-season.

However, because of the graduation of senior Clayton White, the legal trouble of junior Corey Lyons and the decision by Edrick Smith to leave the team, the Wolfpack is dangerously thin at linebacker.

That's why Amato moved Jamison to linebacker in the spring to play in the middle and on the outside. The coach was thrilled with the results, especially after Jamison had a team-high eight tackles in the spring game.

"He can cover some ground," Amato said. "I think he is a natural there and I think I think it has given him a breath of fresh air."

Jamison has Fisher's desire to be in on every play, which could make them a fearsome tandem when they finally get to play together.

Fisher immediately became one of Amato's favorite players for the way he went after the ball. But the coach expects the senior All-American to be more consistent this year. Despite the gaudy total of hits, Amato thought Fisher missed too many tackles last year. But that's a relatively minor criticism.

"You like having a guy like him on the team," Amato said. "You like to point at him and tell other guys 'Look at him go.' "

Junior **Dantonio Burnette** (5-10, 228) was second on the team in tackles with 105 while filling in for the injured White at middle linebacker. Sophomore **Roger Pollard** (6-1, 212) was the only freshman to see action at linebacker last year, but most of his time was spent on special teams.

In the spring, junior **Quenton Allen** (6-2, 201) was moved from safety to outside linebacker to help give the Wolfpack some depth, but that is still one of Amato's major concerns.

"We can't lose any linebackers," Amato said. ""We are very, very thin there."

There are four linebackers among the incoming freshmen—**Freddie Aughtry-Lindsay** (6-3, 215), **Kennie Covington** (6-2, 238), **Avery Gibson** (6-3, 210) and **Patrick Thomas** (6-2, 210). At least two of them will get the chance to play this year.

DEFENSIVE BACKS

The secondary is one of the few places where the Wolfpack has some depth and is already stockpiling talent for later on. Three starters return from last year. The only one missing is hard-hitting strong safety Adrian Wilson, who was taken by the Arizona Cardinals in the third round of the NFL draft after he decided to forego his final year of eligibility.

But the Pack has several talented players ready to join junior **Terrence Holt** (6-2, 199), the younger brother of Wolfpack All-American Torry Holt, who has turned into a big-play specialist on defense. Holt, a second-team All-ACC pick last year, blocked three kicks, broke up six passes and had an interception. His backup is junior **Rod Johnson** (5-9, 175).

Wilson will be missed, but several players will be given the chance to take over the rover position. Junior **Julius Patterson** (5-10, 180), a nickel back most of last year who had two interceptions, will get a shot as starter, but sophomore **Quenton Allen** (6-2, 196) and freshman **J.J. Jones** (5-11, 175) are also candidates for the vacancy.

Allen worked out at linebacker during the spring and Jones is still trying to trim off the rust that collected while taking last year off from football. Jones was too old to play in his final season at Scotland County (N.C.) High School, so he worked out with the team instead.

The Wolfpack's strength is at cornerback, where senior **Brian Williams** (6-0, 200) returns for his third year as a starter. At the other corner, sophomore **J.J. Washington** (5-7, 180) should be healthy after suffering a season-ending knee injury midway through last season. Sophomore **James Walker** (6-0, 183) took over the position and played better than he did early in the season.

Amato will also look at a handful of fast freshmen to help in pass coverage. **Greg Golden** (5-11, 182), **Marcus Hudson** (6-2, 180) and **Andre Maddox** (6-0, 180) all came from football-rich Florida and could be ready to play immediately.

PUNTERS

Herbert, a top-notch place-kicker in high school, eased his way into the kicking game as the Pack's starting punter all last year. He handled the responsibilities well, but finished eighth among ACC punters with a 37.7 average.

The Wolfpack was eighth among ACC teams in net punting. However, Herbert had only one punt blocked and he landed 15 of his 46 kicks inside the 20. He came on strong at the end of the season, averaging a season-best 43 yards against Duke, thanks in part to a career-long 59-yard punt.

Herbert didn't work much on punting during the spring. Instead he concentrated on his place kicking skills. He should mature into the position this season.

SPECIAL TEAMS

Koren Robinson was more than just a receiver. He was second in the ACC in kickoff returns (25.3 yards) and first in punt returns (15.6 yards), boosting him into 10th in the nation in all-purpose yardage last year. His speed and elusiveness made him difficult to catch, and allowed the Wolfpack to have some of the most productive special teams in the nation.

So how are Amato and his staff going to replace that productivity? With several choices. Patterson, Peterson, Williams and Cotchery, each had chances to return punts while Robinson took a well-deserved breather.

They will get more this season, as will Washington and perhaps Bertrand. Golden, who returned eight punts and two kickoffs for touchdowns during his prep career, will also get a look.

Patterson and Ray Robinson are the only returning players that had a kickoff return last year, getting nine between them for an average of 20.3 yards per return. Amato will look at the same list of players to help there.

Sophomore **Danny Young** (6-4, 225), the final player signed in Amato's first recruiting class, won the long-snapper position in preseason practice and will continue his steady work there this year.

RECRUITING CLASS

On signing day, Amato sat in front of a roomful of media and popped a bottle of faux champagne on what many analysts consider one of the best recruiting classes in school history.

It was certainly one of the largest. Amato, hired two days after Florida State won its second national championship, got a late start on his first recruiting class and signed only 18 players, even though he could have gone to the NCAA limit of 25. So this year, he mined the familiar recruiting fields of Florida and lured a dozen of the best players in North Carolina to Raleigh, getting a total of 30 new players on campus this fall by working the NCAA rules to his advantage.

Five of the newcomers, including West Virginia transfer **Sean Berton** (6-5, 255), a senior, arrived on campus in January, just like Rivers did last year. The NCAA counts those recruits among the 2000 class, leaving Amato with a full 25 spots for players arriving in the fall.

Amato took advantage of his team's week-long stay in Florida for the Micron PC.com Bowl, opening the doors to the Wolfpack's practices and making sure all the top recruits knew the practice schedule. Short of the playing in the Orange Bowl, playing in the Micron PC.com Bowl was the best possible postseason scenario for Amato, who recruited South Florida for 17 years for Florida State.

It didn't hurt that one of Amato's top assistants, Doc Holliday, also recruited the area for nearly two decades at West Virginia. It gave him a chance to show off his new program to his buddies in the high school ranks, and it gave the players a chance to see Amato's dedication to success.

"You can't put a price tag on what that is worth," Amato said.

In the end, 10 Floridians signed up.

Overall, Amato said the only thing he needed in this particular signing class was "everything." But he clearly went after players who could help him at wide receiver, as previously noted. Hall and Murray are supposed to be the gems; Hall because of his speed and Murray because of his size and speed.

The coach also knew he needed immediate help along the defensive front, which is why he brought in three junior college transfers—Chapman, Price and Martin.

Chapman and Price were teammates at Los Angeles Valley College. Chapman had 24 sacks and 33 tackles for losses in his two seasons there, while Price had 32 sacks and 37 tackles for losses.

Amato also found speed for his defensive backfield with Golden, Jones, Hudson and Maddox. They will get a chance to prove themselves immediately, with two likely to play this fall and the other two being redshirted.

The recruiting class also included five offensive linemen, all of whom are 6-3 or taller.

The Wolfpack received national acclaim for making in-roads in Florida, and Amato's second recruiting class was ranked among the Top 25 in the nation by most analysts.

BLUE RIBBON ANALYSIS

OFFENSE	B+
SPECIAL TEAMS	C
DEFENSE	B-
INTANGIBLES	B+

When Dick Sheridan arrived at N.C. State in 1986, he won eight games in his first season, thanks to a handful of fourth-quarter comebacks and a few miraculous finishes. Amato's debut season was practically identical.

Sheridan went on to become one of the most successful coaches in school history, taking the Wolfpack to six bowls in seven years and compiling a 52-29-3 record. He retired for health reasons before the 1993 season.

Sheridan's only losing season came in his second year, when his team took a step backwards with a 4-7 season. Will Amato have a similar sophomore slump?

It's doubtful, if only because the Pack's non-conference schedule should provide the opportunity for three wins, assuming Rivers can find someone to catch the ball in the season-opening Thursday night games against Indiana and Ohio University.

The Wolfpack doesn't have nearly the depth necessary to challenge either Clemson or Georgia Tech as Florida State's top challenger. But if Amato has a few more recruiting classes like this year's, the Pack won't be too far behind, especially when all the new facilities are in place.

The coach, with a much more enjoyable personality than the droll and controlling Sheridan, has already whipped up a frenzy among the Wolfpack boosters, who are hungry to build a program that will dominate the state's ACC teams and eventually compete with the Tigers, Yellow Jackets and even the Seminoles.

What the coach and his team need to do this year is be less exciting. Sure, it's nice to win games with fourth-quarter comebacks, but the Wolfpack frequently played down to its competition, nearly losing to Duke and Wake Forest and falling in overtime to Maryland, a team it should have beaten.

This year, Amato would be happier to grind out a few impressive wins without all the beat-skipping heroics. Besides, there's no one like Koren Robinson around who has a history of making those kinds of plays.

(T.P.)

2000 RESULTS

Arkansas State	W	38-31	1-0
Indiana	W	41-38	2-0
SMU	W	41-0	3-0
Georgia Tech	W	30-23	4-0
Clemson	L	27-34	4-1
North Carolina	W	38-30	5-1
Florida State	L	14-58	5-2
Maryland	L	28-35	5-3
Duke	W	35-31	6-3
Virginia	L	17-24	6-4
Wake Forest	W	32-14	7-4
Minnesota (Micron Bowl)	W	38-30	8-4

Virginia

LOCATION	**Charlottesville, VA**
CONFERENCE	**Atlantic Coast**
LAST SEASON	**6-6 (.500)**
CONFERENCE RECORD	**5-3 (4th)**
OFFENSIVE STARTERS RETURNING	**5**
DEFENSIVE STARTERS RETURNING	**6**
NICKNAME	**Cavaliers**
COLORS	**Orange & Blue**
HOME FIELD	**Scott Stadium (61,500)**
HEAD COACH	**Al Groh (Virginia '67)**
RECORD AT SCHOOL	**First Year**
CAREER RECORD	**26-40 (6 years)**
ASSISTANTS	**Dan Rocco (Wake Forest '84) Assistant Head Coach/ Linebackers/Recruiting Coordinator; Al Golden (Penn State '91) Defensive Coordinator; Bill Musgrave (Oregon '90) Offensive Coordinator/Quarterbacks/Tight Ends; Corwin Brown (Michigan '93) Special Teams; Mike Groh (Virginia '95) Wide Receivers; Mike London (Richmond '83) Defensive Line; Bob Prince (Cal Poly-Pomona '78) Defensive Backs; Ron Prince (Appalachian State '92) Offensive Line; Kevin Ross (Navy '88) Running Backs**
TEAM WINS (last 5 yrs.)	**7-7-9-7-6**
FINAL RANK (last 5 yrs.)	**21-26-17-36-36**
2000 FINISH	**Lost to Georgia in Jeep O'ahu Bowl.**

COACH AND PROGRAM

Just when folks were ready to write off Virginia football as irrelevant on the national scene, the Cavaliers go out and get an NFL coach to leave his pro gig and set up shop in Charlottesville.

Al Groh, who coached in two Super Bowls under Bill Parcells and was 9-7 last year as head coach of the New York Jets, is back at his alma mater. And pro coaches don't leave head jobs like that unless they're certain they can do something special on the college level.

Something special happened in Charlottesville the last 19 years as coach George Welsh took a perennial doormat to the upper echelon of the Atlantic Coast Conference and became the ACC's all-time winningest coach. Once a national gridiron laughingstock, the Cavs played in 12 bowl games and posted 14 consecutive seasons finishing .500 or better under Welsh.

But Virginia stumbled to a 6-6 mark last season, on the heels of a 7-5 record in 1999, when that season ended with an embarrassing 63-21 shellacking to Illinois in the Micron PC.com Bowl. Meanwhile just down the road that year, arch rival Virginia Tech played for the national championship.

Cavalier fans, in their dress shirts and pressed khakis, were as upset as when they ran out of pate' at the tailgate party. A growing discontent caught up with Welsh in the Wahoo Nation and arguably, Virginia's somewhat sagging football fortunes are directly linked to a lessened commitment to recruiting the last few years.

That can happen when a staff has been in place for 19 years at one stop. The perception, real or not, was that the UVA coaching staff was out of touch with today's high school athlete and that Welsh wasn't amenable to changes in his philosophies.

We may never know, because true to his coaching demeanor during his best seasons, Welsh went quietly, allowing for a smooth transition in the program he built. More refreshingly, the old coach is apparently welcome back at the sparkling new football offices and facilities the new coach inherited. Groh has welcomed Welsh to remain a part of the program, and the new coach has even grander ideas about continuing the links with Welsh's successes.

"We'd like to play in the last game of the college season [for the national championship]," Groh said. "When we do, we want to have former players down on the sideline encouraging the team, just as we see with some of the teams now that are on the top rung of college football."

For UVA to attract Groh is a feather in the Cavalier mascot's chapeau. He's now a proven commodity as a motivator and evaluator of talent at the highest level, and he's got experience in the college game, too. He was head coach at Wake Forest from 1981-86, and he has also been an offensive coordinator at South Carolina (1988) and a defensive coordinator at Texas Tech (1980).

But more than those credentials, Groh brings a prestige in his connection to the pros, and more importantly, a vitality that the program may have been missing the last few years. His younger coaching staff has already connected with the returning players and promises to be more effective in bringing more proven high school talent to Charlottesville.

Players are excited about working under a coaching staff that knows exactly what it takes to play pro football. The offense and defense will have more of a pro look to their schemes, and chances are, that characteristic will attract more players with pro potential.

And for those who don't think the caliber of Cavalier football has dropped off, for the first time since 1996, just one Virginia player (tight end Billy Baber) was selected in the NFL draft. The day spring practice ended, recruiting again became job one in Charlottesville.

"What we have to do is forget about the Xs and Os and nuts and bolts of football," Groh said, "and for the next month or five weeks devote ourselves entirely to the recruiting process."

Groh was the perfect choice to alleviate the worry of Welsh's departure. There was a perception that Virginia football had to take a downward spiral after the most successful run in school history, but Groh, it would seem, has the potential to take Virginia to another rung on that college football ladder.

He may not have all the pieces—on the field or in a schedule that includes non-conference games at Wisconsin and against Penn State—to be immediately successful this year. But Cavalier fans better start stocking up the pate' and Virginia bourbon because the tailgate parties the next few years could be a lot of fun in Charlottesville.

2001 SCHEDULE

Aug.	25	Wisconsin (Eddie Robinson Classic)
Sept.	1	Richmond
	13	Penn State
	22	@Clemson
	29	Duke
Oct.	6	@Maryland
	13	@North Carolina
	20	Florida State
	27	@North Carolina State
Nov.	3	Wake Forest
	10	Georgia Tech
	17	Virginia Tech

QUARTERBACKS

Groh's first season at the helm on the Cavalier sideline may well be defined in how the veteran coach sorts out the burgeoning quarterback controversy he inherits. Sophomores **Bryson Spinner** and **Matt Schaub** were the story line last spring just battling for *backup* duties behind senior Dan Ellis.

This year, the talented duo are battling for the starting job, and it's a question Groh will deal with every day until he selects a starter prior to the Aug. 25 opener at Wisconsin. So just what are you looking for in a quarterback in your system, coach?

"There are eventually really only two things that are the key criteria for quarterbacks," Groh said, "and that is: Does the guy get his team in the end zone? And can he get it there more than the quarterback on the other team?"

Spinner (6-2, 225) eventually emerged as the winner when Ellis was out with a hamstring injury last year. He played in six games but completed just 41 percent of his passes (25-of-61) and was sacked nine times. The prototype mobile, athletic quarterback, Spinner seems to sometimes struggle in the passing game and that may not be the best fit in offensive coordinator Bill Musgrave's pro-style attack.

The dimension that excites fans and coaches, though, is his ability to make something happen when the play breaks down ala Michael Vick or Donovan McNabb or even former UVA star Aaron Brooks. Spinner rushed for 93 yards last season (minus the yards lost to sacks). His 61-yard run against North Carolina State was the longest jaunt for a Virginia quarterback since 1964.

Shaub (6-5, 222) looks the part of the more traditional "drop back" passer but has surprising athleticism and is certainly the more picturesque passer. In spot duty last year, he completed 7-of-8 attempts for 50 yards during the regular season, and then hit 6-of-10 passes for 47 yards more in mop-up duty in the O'ahu Bowl against Georgia.

Spinner played considerably more over the course of the season, but that doesn't mean much now under a new regime. He also had the upper hand in Virginia's open spring practice when he completed 11-of-18 passes for 125 yards and two touchdowns. Schaub was just 4-for-16 for 49 yards on a day clearly dominated by Virginia's defense. Groh stressed he will not make a decision based on one practice.

"I think they both had their plays, and they both had some I wish they hadn't tried," the coach said of the open practice, attended by 2,200 curious fans. "I'm not going to allow myself to think that way, because with these young players, you've got to spread it out over a period of time. A lot of it now is going to be handling game situations, leadership, making the team respond to him."

Part of that pro football mentality could mean Groh and Musgrave will settle on the candidate who simply makes the fewest mistakes.

"Bobby Dodd—who was a great Hall of Fame coach and one who had many good quarterbacks—said once that before he tries to figure out which quarterback he has that can hurt the other team the most, he tries to figure out the one that could hurt his team the most," the defensive-minded Groh said.

"They're a lot more similar than most people think," junior receiver **Billy McMullen** said of the quarterbacks. "Bryson can get outside of the pocket and can hurt a defense and Matt can stand in there and pick apart a defense. But Matt can run and Bryson can pass, too."

Groh broke down tape of both quarterbacks this winter, and came away impressed when he finally saw them throw in practice. And he's not tipping his hand about who will see the bulk of duty come fall.

"I think if we have two good players, we'll play two players," he said. "I think if that's what you need to do and have the wherewithal to do that, I'm not opposed to doing that."

The Cavs seem set at this position if the top spot sorts itself out. Behind the two sophomores, redshirt freshman **Billy Schweitzer** (6-3, 200) of Alexandria, Va., looks like another top prospect with a strong arm. Proof of that lies in the fact he drew offers from more pass-happy programs like Kentucky, Marshall and Boston College.

Another redshirt freshman, walk-on **Henry de Lauréal** (6-3, 195) of New Orleans, La., lends additional depth to a position at Virginia that has sent Brooks, Shawn Moore, Don Majkowski, and Scott Secules to the NFL during the Welsh years. Brooks, Matt Blundin and Bobby Goodman all led the ACC in passing in the '90s.

A couple of big-name quarterbacks got away from the Cavaliers in recruiting, as a result of the coaching change. **Marques Hagans** (5-10, 196) of Hampton, Va., and **Heath Miller** (6-4, 225) of Honaker, Va., signed, but they certainly won't play on offense this year. Hagans has also been projected at defensive back and Miller has the size to get a trial at linebacker, if needed.

RUNNING BACKS

In recent years, running back has eclipsed quarterback at Virginia as the glamour position. A Cavalier tailback has led the ACC in rushing for three consecutive seasons, four of the last five years and seven times since 1985.

Tiki Barber did it in 1995, and Thomas Jones did it in back-to-back years in 1998 and 1999. In 2000, senior **Antoine Womack** (6-0, 215) took the ball and ran. He racked up 1,028 yards (93.5 yards per game) last season as a junior.

A dynamic combination of power and speed, Womack had four 100-yard games, including a career-high 180 against Wake Forest. He was the only Cavalier to earn first team All-ACC honors and showed little effect of taking a leave of absence from football the previous year.

He picked up where he left off in Groh's open spring scrimmage, powering for 91 yards and three scores on just 14 carries.

"He listens and wants to know, and then, most particularly, he goes out and tries to do those things that have been pointed out to him," Groh said of Womack. "He's hungry for information and he's hungry for knowledge, because it's become apparent to me that he wants to be the best."

In his first individual meeting with his talented tailback, Groh stressed to Womack the workload he might expect in his offense.

"I had a back last year (Curtis Martin) who had 70 catches and 316 carries," Groh said. "You've got to have a lot of stamina to do that and you can't start developing that July 15. I told him, 'That's the way you've got to train.' "

Like the quarterback spot, tailback is a deep position for the Cavaliers. Sophomore **Arlen Harris** (5-11, 205) sat out most of the spring practices to concentrate on academics, but running backs coach Kevin Ross is counting on him this fall. Harris had 25 carries for 101 yards last season, a solid 4.0 per carry average, and coaches like the way he hits the hole. He began last season as the starter at tailback, but a knee injury shelved him after three games and opened the door for Womack.

Harris' absence from many of the spring workouts gave redshirt freshmen **Marquis Weeks** (5-11, 196) and **Brandon Isaiah** (6-0, 213) more work, and that will prove beneficial in the long run. Weeks in particular was impressive enough to allow senior **Tyree Foreman** (5-11, 224) and big **Jon Ward** (6-0, 222), a sophomore, to move to fullback full time instead of splitting time at the two positions like last year.

"Weeks is a developing player and he's got a lot of work in the spring," Groh said. "He's been getting better every day and he has taken to coaching well and made improvements."

Blocking fullback Pat Washington, who helped open all those holes for the ACC's leading rushers the last three years, graduated. Foreman looks like the heir apparent with Groh moving John Duckett back to linebacker.

Both Foreman and Ward have a little experience at fullback, though that hasn't meant much in the past. A year ago, Washington had all of two carries. And he was the starter.

Foreman is certainly a better fit in the new offense than Duckett. Groh and Ross, the son of former college and NFL coach Bobby Ross, are trying to convince the converted tailback the change will help him. They point to Jets fullback Richie Anderson, who caught 88 passes and went to the Pro Bowl last season. Anderson is Foreman's cousin.

"Tyree has some of the same skills; it must be in the genes," Groh said. "The fullback position here now is a multi-dimensional job requiring a very versatile player."

Foreman fits the bill. He was second on the team last year with 397 yards rushing on a gaudy 5.5 yards per carry average. He also caught three passes that totaled to 77 yards, a 25.7 per catch average. Foreman's knack for picking up needed short yardage was critical for the team last year, and he'll fit into the offense somewhere prominently this season.

Ward, though not a proven blocker or receiver, is a powerful, bruising runner. He gained 74 yards in five games but would have seemed an excellent redshirt candidate considering his potential.

Walk-on redshirt freshmen **Trae Tolliver** (5-9, 200) and **Ben Vincent** (6-0, 226) are also available at fullback.

Incoming freshman **Alvin Pearman**, a 5-10, 192-pound tailback from Charlotte, N.C., was one of the gems of a thin recruiting class. He rushed for 2,148 yards and scored 28 touchdowns last season but had committed to Virginia early, and the rating services seemed to forget about him as his rankings began dropping.

The top college recruiters didn't forget him. After Welsh retired, Pearman visted Notre Dame, North Carolina, Northwestern and Clemson before deciding to stay with the Cavaliers. He'll probably redshirt unless his 4.4 speed fills the team's void on kick returns.

WIDE RECEIVERS/TIGHT ENDS

Whoever is throwing the football, he will have a talented and experienced group of wideouts on the receiving end.

McMullen (6-4, 202), a junior, headlines the returnees after catching 30 passes for 541 yards and three scores last season. His size and penchant for big plays, particularly over smaller cornerbacks, draws comparisons to former Cav receiver Herman Moore.

McMullen already ranks 20th in school history with 1,024 receiving yards and he should get even more balls thrown his way this fall.

McMullen led the team in receptions and receiving yardage last season. He had eight catches for 189 yards against Duke in one memorable game but was sometimes plagued by drops. He did catch the coach's eye this spring, though. Groh said McMullen was "probably having one of the better spring practices" on the team during workouts.

The rest of the Virginia air force isn't so clear-cut. If junior **James Johnson** doesn't return, four of the Cavs' top five receivers from a year ago are gone. Johnson (6-1, 189) missed spring practices because of "family business and illness," and his return this fall was uncertain.

If Johnson doesn't return, fellow junior **Tavon Mason** (5-11, 181) is ready to step in, as is sophomore **Michael McGrew** (6-2, 184). Groh singled them out over "a whole cast of others" vying for the job in the spring.

The speedy Mason caught eight passes for 124 yards (15.5 average) last year, and showed flashes of immense potential. He's one of the fastest players on the team. McGrew caught two passes in eight games, and was another likely redshirt candidate who wasn't redshirted. He's the only other receiving returnee who has caught a pass. He caught four more for 58 yards and a touchdown in the spring open practice.

Unproven sophomore **Sharif Rosales-Webb** (6-1, 198), and redshirt freshmen **Jeremiah Chambliss** (5-10, 162), **John Monahan** (5-11, 197) and **Scott Penwell** (6-4, 201) are also available. Juniors **Keith Kobrya** (6-1, 192) and **Todd Estrin** (6-3, 200) and sophomore converted defensive back **Ryan Sawyer** (6-2, 195) round out the receiving corps from the spring.

Of the incoming freshman prospects, **Scott Robinson** (6-0, 170) of Neshanic Station, N.J., might offer the biggest challenge for playing time, He was rated the No. 14 prospect in New Jersey by *SuperPrep*.

Ottawa Anderson (5-11, 183) of Norfolk, Va., and **Jermaine Hardy** (5-10, 200) of Roanoke, Va., should also get their first look at receiver, but neither is expected to contribute right away.

At tight end, senior **Chris Luzar** (6-7, 250) will take over for Baber and do well. He caught nine passes for 149 yards last season, including six receptions against Florida State. His size makes him an NFL prospect, and he certainly has good hands. He's a sculpting major in the art department.

The rest of the tight ends with game experience are all walk-ons, junior **Marcus Martin** (6-5, 234), and sophomore **Kase Luzar** (6-2, 215), Chris' younger brother. Redshirt freshman **Zac**

Yarbrough (6-4, 251) was the only other scholarship tight end this spring, but they'll get more help this fall.

Tyree Spinner (6-7, 250), the younger brother of quarterback Bryson, is destined for stardom—somewhere, whether it's tight end, defensive end or on the basketball court. **Patrick Estes** (6-7, 240) of Richmond, Va., is another incoming freshman with similar size. **Mawase Falana** (6-3, 270) of St. Petersburg, Fla., is another candidate, though he may be better suited for defense.

OFFENSIVE LINE

Groh and offensive line coach Ron Prince welcome back a veteran unit up front, anchored by three returning senior starters. In fact, counting Luzar at tight end, The Cavaliers will have five fifth-year seniors starting in the line.

Senior tackle **Jermese Jones** (6-6, 320) anchored the left side last year but he has moved to the right side to make way for sophomore **Kevin Bailey** (6-6, 295). Jones came back strong from an ankle and foot injury in 1999, and played one of his best games against Florida State's Jamal Reynolds, holding the All-American end to just three tackles and no sacks.

That means Bailey, who was selected the team's outstanding freshman last year, must really be something special to unseat Jones. While that assertion may be true, Groh said it was simply a matter of expediency. Some day the athletic Bailey was destined to play the left side (the quarterback's blindside) so why not this year?

Bailey will line up alongside second-team All-ACC guard **Josh Lawson** (6-5, 295), who has started 29 games the last three seasons. The senior joins classmate and right guard **Evan Routzhan** (6-5, 303) as two of only five linemen in Virginia history to start in three bowl games.

Senior **Jared Woodson** (6-6, 282), who began last season at left guard, was felled in the third game with a neck injury that ended his season. He moved over to center in the spring, a position he had played in the past.

Sophomore **Jay Green** (6-2, 280) and redshirt freshman **Mark Farrington** (6-2, 264) are also available at center. Sophomores **Ben Carber** (6-1, 305) and former defensive lineman **Micah Kimball** (6-4, 284) and redshirt freshman **Joe Holt** (6-4, 290) lend depth at the guard position.

Junior **Mike Mullins** (6-8, 297) was all set to battle Bailey for the job at right tackle before Jones moved over. Other tackle candidates include redshirt freshman **Tom Howell** (6-4, 278) and junior walk-on **Drew Nelson** (6-6, 282).

Among the incoming freshmen, **Robert Jenkins** (6-4, 280) of the Bronx, N.Y., and Milford (Conn.) Academy, is the most highly touted. **Brian Barthelmes** (6-7, 255) of Garrettsville, Ohio, looks like he has the potential to get even bigger, and **Elton Brown** (6-4, 315) of Hampton, Va., is another lineman sought by a lot of colleges.

"I think we have a lot of players who can play," said Groh of his linemen. "One of the things that we look for in an offensive lineman is an ability to consistently win against the man he's blocking."

2000 STATISTICS

Rushing offense	163.7	37
Passing offense	195.5	75
Total offense	359.2	68
Scoring offense	20.7	86
Net Punting	39.6	5
Punt returns	5.5	106
Kickoff returns	19.8	37
Rushing defense	184.5	86
Passing efficiency defense	123.9	76
Total defense	421.9	98
Scoring defense	23.2	47
Turnover margin	+2	51

Last column is ranking among Division I-A teams.

KICKERS

Senior **David Greene** (5-10, 180) took over the kicking job last year and turned in a brilliant performance. He connected on 11-of-15 field-goal attempts (73.3 percent) and was the only player in the ACC with more than one field goal of at least 48 yards (he had two).

Greene also used that strong right leg to boot 30-of-49 kickoffs into the end zone, 18 of them resulting in touchbacks. He was 27-for-28 in his extra-point attempts.

The kicking job is Greene's again, but junior **Andy Dugger** (6-3, 192), and redshirt freshmen **Sean Johnson** (6-1, 180) and **Bryan Smith** (5-10, 143) are also on hand to boot balls in practice. Dugger was the primary holder in spring practices, too.

Sophomore **Ryan Childress** (6-0, 197) is the long-snapper, but he may have to fend off a challenge from junior **Heath Boucek** (6-3, 240).

DEFENSIVE LINE

Virginia had some offensive problems last season when Ellis went down, but the last few years, when fans have complained loudest, it was usually about the defense. Opponents scored more than 31 points in the Cavaliers' six losses last season.

A now familiar pattern continued as Virginia was outscored 69-26 in the fourth quarter of games. Foes converted 44.6 percent of their third downs against Virginia, and the Cavs sacked quarterbacks just 15 times all season.

"In this day and age, you better be able to hit the quarterback," Groh said. "And if you don't, it makes it hard to win. Now whether that means you rush two, three, four, five, six, seven or more. Whatever you do to make it difficult for the quarterback to perform at a high level, you have to do that because right now this is a quarterback-driven game.

"If those quarterbacks can go out and play to the top level of their ability, they in themselves can make it hard for you to win. So you have to make it hard for them."

To that end, defensive line coach Mike London has four starters back from last year, though he and defensive coordinator Al Golden are designing some new schemes to make them more productive.

Senior **Ljubomir Stamenich** (6-3, 250) is a two-year starter at end and has been the team's most effective pass rusher the last two years. He led the team with four sacks last season. Senior **Darryl Sanders** (6-3, 268) returns at the other end where he turned in a career-best 44 tackles and tied for second on the team with two sacks.

At tackle, two more seniors return, **Monsanto Pope** (6-4, 282) and **George Stanley** (6-2, 292). Pope came back from a knee injury in 1999, to post 33 tackles and two sacks. Stanley was having a good season before an ankle injury knocked him out of the last three games. He had 26 tackles prior to the injury.

Questions abound behind the starting front four. Most of the reserves are young and unproven now that end Merrill Robertson has moved to linebacker. Junior defensive end "**Boo" Battle** (6-4, 253) has battled injuries throughout his career (ankle, back) and has yet to prove he can consistently contribute.

Sophomore **Terrell Ricks** (6-5, 265) can play end or tackle but he saw limited action in eight games last year. Junior **Colin McWeeny** (6-4, 275) lettered his first two seasons and should continue to provide help at tackle if he's over nagging back problems. Sophomore **Larry Simmons** (6-3, 275) had two sacks among his nine tackles last fall, and could have a future.

Sophomore **Andrew Hoffman** (6-4, 259) was pressed into duty as a freshman but saw his playing time decrease as the season progressed. Redshirt freshmen **Chris Canty** (6-6, 246) and **Marcus Hardy** (6-3, 219) are both highly regarded prospects but don't have any experience. Junior **Butch Jefferson** (6-4, 288) and sophomore **Justin Walker** (6-2, 278) round out the defensive line returnees.

This area was a point of emphasis in Groh's first recruiting class, and despite the late start, he may have picked up some help. Defensive end **Brendan Schmidt** (6-3, 265) of Arlington, Va., who played at DeMatha in Maryland, was rated the No. 9 prospect in Maryland by *SuperPrep*, and he has the tools to contribute if he's ready for the college game.

Defensive end **Darryl Blackstock** (6-5, 225) had 29 sacks last season at state champion Heritage High School in Newport News, Va., so he'll merit a look, too, if he makes grades. If not, he'll head to prep school.

Matt Stone (6-3, 235) of Boca Raton, Fla., is also headed into the fold, and don't forget Estes, Falana and Tyree Spinner, all tight ends, who could switch over to defense if needed.

LINEBACKERS

The strength of the defense the last two years, Virginia's linebacking corps lost all three starters to graduation but there's a long list of candidates to step into the open spots on the depth chart and the open holes in the line during a game.

One candidate already made a name for himself with a sterling performance in Virginia's open spring practice. Sophomore **Raymond Mann** (6-1, 220) was pressed into service at defensive end last fall and seemed like a player without a natural position when he tallied 11 tackles.

In the open spring practice, he roamed sideline to sideline and seemed involved in nearly every play, wreaking havoc on the offense out of the new 3-4 defensive alignment.

"I don't know what the question was [about his position], but he looked like a damn good linebacker to me," Groh said. "I think we've got a spot for him in this system in which he can use his skills."

The speedy Mann received the Rock Weir Award as Virginia's most improved defensive player this spring. And much of his competition for that honor may have come from his fellow linebackers, all trying to fill the void left by the graduation of Yubrenal Isabelle, Byron Thweatt and Donny Green, the team's top three tacklers last season.

Junior **Angelo Crowell** (6-1, 224) is the leading returning tackler with 87 stops, and he seems to have nailed down a starting berth alongside Mann, junior **Merrill Robertson** (6-1, 250) and senior **John Duckett** (6-1, 226).

Crowell and Duckett, converted from fullback this spring, man the middle. Duckett was Virginia's fourth linebacker in1998, then sat out the 1999 season for personal reasons and returned last year, only to move to fullback. He's quickly taken to the move back to defense.

"He seems to have a sense for where's the ball's going," Groh said. "He's a very high-motor-player. Plus, he's outstanding on special teams."

The speedy Robertson is also making a transition, after playing well last year as a defensive end with 34 tackles in spot duty. He began his career as a fullback, but seems another natural fit at linebacker, where apparently many of Virginia's best athletes will surface under the new coaching staff.

It's no coincidence so many fast players and players with pass rush experience are moving to linebacker. It's just another tip-off of how aggressive the Cavs should be this fall blitzing and showing varying packages. They worked on blitzing every single day of the spring.

Another converted defensive end, **Antonio Mayfield** (6-3, 215), rejoined the team after an academic suspension last season. And redshirt freshman **Dennis Haley** (6-1, 219) is expected back in the fall from arthroscopic knee surgery. The athletic Haley was pushing for a starting job before the injury and the move of Duckett back to defense.

Sophomore **Stan Norfleet** (6-3, 236) missed all of last season with a knee injury, and he's moving into the linebacking corps after working at defensive end. Senior **Earl Sims** (6-1, 228) was coming back from an abdominal injury, but he was practicing this spring.

Holdovers from last year include fifth-year senior **Scooter Clark** (6-1, 220), sophomore reserves **Rich Bedesem** (6-1, 236), **Beau Dickerson** (6-3, 222) and **Sam Sangobowale** (6-0, 223) and red-shirt freshman walk-on **Jon Thompson** (6-2, 210).

With so many linebackers already in the mix, it's hard to imagine a freshman breaking in this year. **Melvin Massy** (6-3, 235) of Newport News, Va., is the biggest and best of the lot, choosing Virginia over Syracuse. **Alexander Hall** (6-1, 227) of Corpus Christi, Tex., and **Bryan White** (6-1, 230) of Knoxville, Tenn., are also joining the program.

DEFENSIVE BACKS

When the 2001 season opens, whatever duo emerges as the Cavaliers' starting cornerbacks, they will mark the third different set the last three years. Last year's starters, Tim Spruill and converted receiver Ahmad Hawkins, have graduated and that leaves the job wide open—something Groh and secondary coach Bob Price hope opposing receivers won't be.

The safety positions look solid with junior starters **Jerton Evans** (5-11, 195) and **Shernard Newby** (6-1, 208) both back. A jarring tackler, Evans led Virginia defensive backs with 50 tackles last year while Newby had 45 stops.

The duo will be pushed by the return of former freshman All-American **Chris Williams** (6-3, 190), a junior who is back from academic suspension. Williams quickly made a name for himself with the new coaching staff with his work on special teams, and Groh has said he likes him more and more each time he watches him play in the secondary.

Fifth-year senior **Devon Simmons** (5-11, 200) came back from a year off last season to play in every game and average 4.2 tackles per contest. A ferocious tackler, he will push for time at safety, or he may get a chance at cornerback this fall.

Sophomore **Almondo Curry** (5-8, 168) also played well at safety this spring and came up with a big fumble recovery and long return in the open practice. The starting cornerbacks that day—sophomores **Art Thomas** (6-2, 203) and **Jamaine Winborne** (5-10, 199)—looked good, though they were certainly working against routes they had seen all spring.

Curry, Thomas and Winborne all prepped a year at Fork Union (Va.) Military Academy before coming to Virginia last fall. They saw action on special teams but very few plays in the secondary.

Besides Simmons, Curry could also figure in the mix at corner, as will junior **Rashad Roberson** (5-11, 186), who started three games last fall, and redshirt freshman **Jay Dorsey** (6-2, 180).

"Cornerback is a relatively inexperienced group, but like at linebacker I see good young talent," Groh said. "A lot of playing cornerback is about personality and attitude as much as anything."

PUNTERS

The punting chores are again in good hands, or on good feet, as the case may be.

Senior punter **Mike Abrams** (6-4, 224) averaged 42.6 yards per kick last season. Many of his kicks were so high and so effective that Virginia ranked fifth in the nation in net punting with a 39.6 average.

Sophomore **Bryce Coffee** (5-11, 173), a left-footed punter, is the only competition for Abrams' job this fall.

SPECIAL TEAMS

Twenty-seven years into his coaching career, Welsh hired his first special teams coach last year. Talk about "old school."

Groh came aboard with one, Corwin Brown, a former special teams standout himself with the Patriots, Jets and Lions of the NFL. Now the Cavs are one of the few programs in the country with a coach devoted entirely to that aspect of the game.

Quality kickers have masked many ills on the Cavalier special teams the last several years but Groh is counting on big improvement.

"Special teams play is very important in the success of any team," he said. "There may be times when we need a big play from our special teams and I want them prepared to make that play. I also will not hesitate to use first-line players on special teams if I think that will put us in the best position to succeed."

Everyone who returned a kickoff for Virginia is back this year: Mason (16 returns for a 21.6 average), Thomas (18 for 18.7), Womack (4 for 24.2) and Duckett (2 for 5.5). Harris, Weeks and McGrew could also see some return duty, and Groh has hinted about putting a new freshman back there, possibly Pearman.

James Johnson had all but two of Virginia's punt returns last season and he averaged 5.8 yards on his 20 attempts. If he doesn't return in the fall, Harris might get more duty. He had one return for 15 yards last season, after ranking second in the ACC in 1999, with a 12.4 average.

RECRUITING CLASS

Groh and his staff got such a late start recruiting this season it's hard to count this year against them. Recruiting was certainly one of the major areas that got Welsh in trouble with fans the last few years, so who could expect this crop to be a banner one?

Pearman, Schmidt and Jenkins are all great prospects but this class wasn't as deep in talent as Virginia probably needed. Late signee Blackstock helped, and his signing along with that of Massy and Brown, all of the greater Virginia Beach area, gave the Cavs a handful of the Top 25 prospects in the state.

Under the circumstances, the class is not bad. But if this program is going to do what Groh wants it to do, Virginia will have to do much better in the immediate future. The coach has a sign above the desk in his office, "Coaches with schemes but not talent become the coaches of unimportant teams."

"What should be a paramount thing in your mind is the acquisition and development of talent," Groh said. "If you have a choice of drawing up another coverage of blitz or another pass pattern or working on the acquisition of talent, that little credo helps make the decision."

Yet Groh has surrounded himself with a young staff, heavy on knowledge of the pro game but relatively inexperienced in collegiate recruiting. Assistant head coach Dan Rocco is the recruiting coordinator, and like the other young coaches on the staff, he's a go-getter. In fact, there's a school of thought the staff is young enough recruiting may become an in-house competition for the coaches—a far cry from the laid-back days under Welsh.

BLUE RIBBON ANALYSIS

OFFENSE	B-
SPECIAL TEAMS	C
DEFENSE	C+
INTANGIBLES	B+

There's a chance—if the quarterbacking situation works out—that the Cavaliers could be a lot better this year than they were last season. Problem is, it's hard seeing that improvement showing up in the record.

The Aug. 25 opener at Wisconsin is a killer for a team learning a new system, and the Sept. 13 home date with Penn State looks tough, too. Figure the Cavs lose those two and beat Richmond on Sept. 1, they're 1-2 heading to Clemson Sept. 22, and the season already seems in jeopardy.

Unless they beat somebody they're not supposed to—Florida State, Georgia Tech or Virginia Tech—that's six losses and that's if they beat everybody else they should or realistically could.

Groh, his staff and players aren't thinking that way, though. They spent so much time getting to know one another over the winter and into the spring, they're still having a "love-in" heading to fall practices.

"The new staff has a lot of young guys who are very enthusiastic and can relate to us more," quarterback candidate Schaub said. "They're running around and screaming, and that translates into high intensity on the practice field."

It's a nice story line, but the fact is Welsh was finally run out of his job because there are problems with this team. The defense certainly looked ahead of the offense in the spring and if the defense can make some improvements, Virginia could break the score-a-lot-of-points-and-still-lose malaise of recent years.

Groh plans on reinventing the squad as a more defense-oriented, smash-mouth team. They'll emphasize forcing mistakes by opponents, limiting their own, and making plays in the kicking game. Groh was on the sideline for a lot of Bill Parcells' wins using that proven formula.

It may be just the anecdote to eventually return the Cavaliers near the top of the ACC, just not this year or even next. The new coaching staff's first job is to re-stock the team with more talent, and they've got the coaching credentials and the facilities to get that job done.

Next, they need to implement the new style of play. With so many high-octane offenses like Florida State, Clemson, Georgia Tech, N.C. State, and possibly Maryland in the conference, this defensive approach may just work if the Cavaliers can execute it.

Give the ball to Womack a ton, keep the chains moving and put pressure on the other team's quarterback. Six wins isn't out of the question and that would be a good start in the new era at Virginia.

Win one of those late home games with Florida State, Georgia Tech or Virginia Tech, and that'll really be one to Groh on.

(M.A.)

2000 RESULTS

Brigham Young	L	35-38	0-1
Richmond	W	34-6	1-1
Duke	W	26-10	2-1
Clemson	L	10-31	2-2
Wake Forest	W	27-10	3-2
Maryland	W	31-23	4-2
Florida State	L	3-37	4-3
North Carolina	W	17-6	5-3
Georgia Tech	L	0-35	5-4
North Carolina State	W	24-17	6-4
Virginia Tech	L	21-42	6-5
Georgia (O'ahu Bowl)	L	14-37	6-6

Wake Forest

LOCATION	Winston-Salem, NC
CONFERENCE	Atlantic Coast
LAST SEASON	2-9 (.182)
CONFERENCE RECORD	1-7 (8th)
OFFENSIVE STARTERS RETURNING	10
DEFENSIVE STARTERS RETURNING	9
NICKNAME	Demon Deacons
COLORS	Black & Gold
HOME FIELD	Grove Stadium (33,941)
HEAD COACH	Jim Grobe (Virginia '75)
RECORD AT SCHOOL	First Year
CAREER RECORD	33-33-1 (6 years)
ASSISTANTS	Troy Calhoun (Air Force '89) Offensive Coordinator/Quarterbacks Dean Hood (Ohio Wesleyan '86) Defensive Coordinator/Secondary Keith Henry (Catawba '89) Outside Linebackers Brad Lambert (Kansas State '87) Inside Linebackers Steed Lobotzke (Air Force '92) Centers/Offensive Guards Ray McCartney (Guilford '80) Recruiting Coordinator/Defensive Line Billy Mitchell (East Carolina '72) Assistant Head Coach/Running Backs/Kickers Jeff Mullen (Wittenberg '90) Tight Ends/Offensive Tackles Kevin Sherman (Ferrum '92) Receivers
TEAM WINS (last 5 yrs.)	3-5-3-7-2
FINAL RANK (last 5 yrs.)	66-45-48-26-85
2000 FINISH	Lost to North Carolina State in regular-season finale.

COACH AND PROGRAM

Holly Grobe said her husband Jim is not one to discourage easily.

"One of his favorite sayings is "You just keep chopping wood," she said. "So you just keep doing what you're doing and eventually it will pay off."

As head coach at Wake Forest, Jim Grobe had better have a sharp blade and a strong back. Because the stand of timber he agreed to tackle when he accepted his new position in December, 2000, may be college football's ultimate old growth forest.

Indeed, it may be said that the Deacons peaked in football in 1892, when they finished 4-0-1. Over the next century, Wake Forest won 347 games, lost 542, tied 31 and enjoyed just 28 winning seasons. Since the ACC formed in 1953, the Deacons have won 91 conference games, lost 233, tied 10, managed only 10 winning seasons and finished above break-even in conference play just six times.

Only Kent State—known unfortunately for a disaster off the field as well as on—has a lower all-time winning percentage among NCAA Division I-A programs. And of the nine ACC programs, eight have all-time winning percentages above .500. Wake Forest's all-time percentage, conversely, is .395.

Many factors have contributed to Wake Forest's ineptitude on the football field, but for the most part poor coaching has not been the problem. Jim Caldwell, Grobe's predecessor, proved overmatched during his eight years, as his 26-63 record would attest. And Chuck Mills was even worse, compiling an 11-43-1 mark from 1973-77.

But the three coaches between Mills and Caldwell were John Mackovic, Al Groh and Bill Dooley.

"I look back on it and I say, 'Gosh, Cal Stoll and John Mackovic and Al Groh and Bill Dooley,' " said Gene Hooks, a former athletics director at Wake Forest. "We had good coaches.

"It's a hard job. I don't want to say anything to discourage the situation. What I want to say is it's a really hard job and Wake Forest is in it for the long haul and I just hope that Jim can be successful."

So why did Jim Grobe, born and raised in Huntington, W.Va., educated at Ferrum Junior College and the University of Virginia (Class of '75) and mentored in his chosen profession by coach Fisher DeBerry of the Air Force Academy, agree to accept such a challenge?

Apparently, some people just like challenges.

"Everybody keeps telling me it's going to take awhile," Grobe said. "And I'm not stupid. I know that's a possibility. But that's not the mentality we've got.

"I think by nature I'm a pretty patient person. But we're not going to approach this situation with patience. We're going to try to win right away."

Athletics director Ron Wellman chose Grobe because of Grobe's experience with downtrodden teams. When Grobe took over at Ohio University in 1994, the Bobcats were coming off an 0-11 season and were ranked last among the NCAA's Division I-A teams.

In six seasons under Grobe, Ohio finished 2-8-1, 6-6, 5-6, 5-6 and 7-4. The Bobcats also finished with a winning conference record five straight seasons.

"Ohio University was one of the worst programs in the country when Jim went there," Wellman said. "And for him to turn it around as quickly as he did, you certainly notice that as an administrator."

Grobe, though steeped in option football from his days at Air Force and Ohio, has said he will tailor his scheme at Wake Forest to best utilize the existing talent. Throughout spring practices the Deacons operated mostly from a one-back set, but Grobe said the final decision on base formation wouldn't be made until the summer months.

"The one thing I can promise you is we will not be a jack of all trades," Grobe said in April. "We are not going to go out and be a gimmicky football team on either side of the ball.

"We're going to have a thought of what we're going to be doing, and we're going to be good at it. We're going to limit what we do and try to do a few things very well. It would make me feel better if I could tell you what that's going to be, but I just don't know right now."

Defensively, the Deacons will operate from a 3-4 formation, a departure from the 4-3 deployed by Caldwell.

Grobe's challenge is massive, but he's not tackling it alone. Of his nine assistants at Ohio, one, Brian Knorr, succeeded him as head coach and the other eight followed him to Wake Forest. That already gives him a distinct advantage over Caldwell, who in his eight years struggled to assemble and maintain a competent staff.

It also speaks to the respect and admiration Grobe commands from those know him best.

"That not only says something for him that he brought everybody, it says something for him that we all wanted to come," said Dean Hood, the Deacons' defensive coordinator. "There are a lot of guys on our staff now who have been offered jobs over the years. A lot of guys. And for more money and quote-unquote higher jobs in better conferences than the Mid-American Conference. And we have stayed with coach Grobe.

"It's not just the quality of life, though that's important. It's the fact that you believe in the man. You believe in what he stands for."

The question has often been asked of Wake Forest football, why even try? The obvious answer is that to protect their coveted membership in the ACC—and be able to compete in one of the nation's best basketball conferences—the Deacons must play football. That's the catch.

But Wellman, for one, insists that what has always been doesn't have to always be. There's a formula to be found for winning football at Wake Forest, he said, and he's convinced that it starts with Grobe.

Wellman is certainly not the man to tell that Wake Forest can never win in football.

"That's bogus," Wellman said. "That is just absolutely bogus. It can be done at Wake Forest and it will be done at Wake Forest. We aren't that far away. We really aren't.

"It's just a matter of getting a few more good kids, a few more great athletes and the right type of approach to coaching and we'll get over this hump. I'm absolutely convinced of that."

2001 SCHEDULE

Sept.	1	@East Carolina
	8	Appalachian State
	15	Northern Illinois
	22	Maryland
	29	@Florida State
Oct.	6	North Carolina State
	13	@Duke
	27	Clemson
Nov.	3	@Virginia
	10	@North Carolina
	17	Georgia Tech

QUARTERBACKS

The quarterback who was to lead Wake Forest out of the college football wilderness to the promised land was spotted at practice a couple of times during the spring. He was standing along the wall where spectators, like curious birds, gather to watch the drills. He had never met Grobe. His days at Wake Forest were numbered. Having already announced his intentions to transfer to the University of Tennessee, C.J. Leak was just completing his spring classes before departing Wake Forest for good.

Widely hailed as the most coveted recruit to ever sign with Wake Forest, Leak never started a game that ended in a Deacon victory. After spending his freshman season as an apprentice to senior Ben Sankey, Leak started the first three games of 2000 before a massive knee injury suffered in the second half of a 55-7debacle at Clemson ended his season and threatened his career.

Before being carried off the field, Leak completed 30-of-70 passes for 341 yards. Two of his passes resulted in interceptions, none in touchdowns. Though the offensive line was still very much a work in progress, it was hard not to reach the conclusion that Leak—the high school All-American who had spurned the likes of Notre Dame, Penn State and Syracuse to sign with Wake Forest—was vastly overrated.

So by the time Leak announced he would leave Wake Forest—in the aftermath of the school's decision to fire Caldwell—no one seemed inclined to beg him to stay. The two quarterbacks thrown into the breach after Leak's injury, freshman **Anthony Young** (6-3, 190) and sophomore **James MacPherson** (6-2, 197), both performed better. For all the problems the Deacons encountered in their 2-9 season, quarterback play really was not one of them.

Young, recruited as a wide receiver, is a marvelous open-field runner and MacPherson, though considerably shorter than the 6-2 listed on the roster, is a hard-nosed competitor with an impressive passing touch. Young finished second on the team with 455 yards rushing and was responsible for four of the Deacons' five longest plays —a 66-yard run against North Carolina State, a 56-yard run against Navy, a 55-yard run against Clemson and a 53-yard run against Virginia. MacPherson, meanwhile, completed 113-of-207 passes (55 percent) for 1,324 yards and three touchdowns.

Young and MacPherson continued their battle for the starting position through spring drills and Grobe said the final decision might not be made until a week or two before the Sept. 1 opener at East Carolina. But Grobe did say he wants to settle on one front-line quarterback, as opposed to alternating the two as Caldwell did over the final eight games of 2000.

"I think you need to develop a personality and an identity and we need somebody to take charge of the offense," Grobe said. "It's hard to do that if you're floating quarterbacks back and forth. My guess is we'll settle on one and he'll be the guy unless he can't get it done. And then we'll go to plan B.

"And of course if we can't get it from either one of them, we're not afraid to play a freshman. I don't want to do that, but the way we run our program is the best players play —period."

There were grumblings that Leak received special treatment while at Wake Forest. A condition he set on coming to Wake Forest was that he could wear No. 12, and Caldwell's staff accommodated Leak by switching veteran cornerback Adrian Duncan from No. 12 to No. 7. And while the parents of other players stood outside the locker room after a game, Leak's father, Curtis, would walk past and into the inner sanctum for Caldwell's post-game address.

Grobe's philosophy could not be more different. So determined is Grobe to treat all his players alike that he refuses to adorn his quarterbacks in the red practice jerseys that signify no contact.

"I want our quarterbacks to have the same mentality our offensive linemen have," Grobe said. "They've got to be just as tough as anybody else. With us running the option and those kinds of things, they're going to get tagged a little bit. And I think our quarterbacks right now have a good mentality.

"If you're going to be a quarterback who comes to play at Wake Forest, you'd better not be just concerned about having your socks nice and neat or your wrist bands just perfect. You'd better have a little bit of a blood and guts mentality."

The Deacons survived spring drills with just two quarterbacks. Grobe indicated that come fall, the third-team spot will probably be manned by an incoming freshman. The leading candidate would probably be **Nick Smith** (6-1, 185), an impressive athlete who led his Centreville High team to the Virginia championship.

RUNNING BACKS

Before he decides which running backs he plans to use, Grobe first must decide on an offensive formation to deploy. The Deacons experimented throughout the spring, but spent most of their time in a one-back set. The player who stands to be most affected is **Ovie Mughelli**, a 6-2, 248-pound junior fullback who is one of the most powerful players on the team.

Striving to get Mughelli on the field as much as possible, Grobe actually had him line up at tight end in various formations. Though a fearsome blocker, Mughelli must prove he has the speed and quickness to be the featured back in a one-back set. A season ago, he gained 128 yards on 40 carries.

The returning starter is **Tarence Williams**, a 5-10, 178-pound junior who gained 661 yards on 130 carries and led the Deacons with seven touchdowns. He has breakaway speed, as he proved with a 72-yard touchdown run against Duke, and is more durable than his size might suggest. But a one-back set, paradoxically, demands that a team have more than one back, for no one player can stand up to the punishment that comes from carrying the football 35-40 times a game.

Two candidates, junior **Jamie Scott** and redshirt freshman **Tyrek White**, have been moved to linebacker. So Williams' chief competition should come from sophomore **Fred Staton** (6-0, 200), a widely heralded recruit two years ago who gained just 126 yards on 39 carries last season.

Nick Burney, a 6-3, 215-pound sophomore, is listed third-team tailback and **Trevor Harris**, a 6-2, 210-pound redshirt freshman, is listed as second-team fullback.

WIDE RECEIVERS/TIGHT ENDS

Week after week, over the last couple of seasons, Caldwell vowed that he would have to find a way to get the ball in the hands of senior **John Stone** (5-11, 180). Yet he rarely succeeded.

Stone, one of the fastest players in the ACC who won the conference championship in the 100 meters and 200 meters in 1999, caught 12 passes last season for 146 yards and a carried 10 times from scrimmage for 74 yards. Opponents had to breathe a sigh of relief every time the Deacons threw the ball to someone other than Stone.

If nothing else, the Deacons' first spring game under Grobe signaled a new day for Stone. Featured as both a runner and receiver, Stone caught three passes and ran six times for a total of 118 yards and two touchdowns. Grobe, realizing that his resources are limited at Wake Forest, is determined not to squander one of Stone's abilities.

The decision by Jimmy Caldwell, who would have been a senior, not to play for the man who succeeded his father has left the Deacons a bit thin in the wide receiving corps. But with senior **Ira Williams** (6-2, 206), junior **Fabian Davis** (5-11, 173) and senior **Jax Langfried** (5-8, 172) returning, the talent level isn't dangerously low. Williams had 45 catches for 495 yards, Davis 33 for 596 and Langfried 10 for 114.

Expect to see plenty of freshman **Jason Anderson** (6-3, 180), who should benefit from Caldwell's decision to redshirt him last season. As a senior at Butler High School in Charlotte in 1999, Anderson caught 55 passes for 954 yards and 14 touchdowns.

"One of the groups that has stood out a little bit has been our receivers—not only foot quickness and ability, but their work ethic has been pretty good," Grobe said. "We've got to find a way to get those guys the football."

Although Caldwell's offense rarely utilized the tight end as a receiver, junior **Ray Thomas** (6-4, 246) finished with 18 catches last season for 184 yards. Just as fullback **Ovie Mughelli** (6-2, 248) lined up some at tight end during the spring, Thomas found himself occasionally at fullback as Grobe endeavored to get his best players on the field.

Thomas' backups at tight end, sophomore **Josh Warren** (6-4, 252) and redshirt freshman **Jerome Nichols** (6-2, 255), have yet to distinguish themselves.

OFFENSIVE LINE

For the eight years he was at Wake Forest, Caldwell touted his players as "bigger, stronger and faster" than any to have played at the school. He repeated the phrase so often it began to sound like a mantra. Unfortunately for the Deacons, and eventually Caldwell himself, he could never translate those supposed off-the-field improvements to the field.

Before he coached his first game at Wake Forest, Grobe made it clear that he's not interested in his players being bigger than their predecessors. In fact, in the offensive line, where the Deacons routinely averaged 300 pounds a man, the reverse is true.

"We're just too big," Grobe said. " Don't get me wrong. If our guys are big and agile, I don't worry about it. But our guys are big and stiff, so we've asked them to get their weight down. Very rarely is there a need for kids to be over 300 pounds."

Grobe will build his first offensive line around two senior All-ACC candidates, center **Vince Azzolina** (6-4, 301) and guard **Michael Collins** (6-6, 318). Both have been fixtures on the offensive line since their freshman seasons. Azzolina has started 24 games in a row, though Collins' streak of consecutive stars was interrupted by arthroscopic knee surgery that kept him out of two games in 2000.

Collins, after starting for three seasons at left tackle, will move to guard for his senior season.

Senior guard **Michael Moosbrugger** (6-7, 296) also has good experience after starting all 11 games in 2000. Junior **Tim Bennett** (6-4, 289) was also in the lineup at both guard and tackle last season when his health permitted, but missed four games with an injured shoulder and two more with a sprained knee. He will get the first crack at starting at right tackle, and **Tyson Clabo**, a 6-6, 295-pound sophomore who played in 10 games last season, emerged from spring drills as the starter at left tackle.

The starting lineup may be shaken up, however, if junior **Blake Henry** (6-6, 294) is able to return from a knee injury that hampered his 2000 season and kept him out of spring drills. Henry, a guard who can also play tackle, transferred to Wake Forest before last season from Northwestern.

Otherwise, the most experienced lineman is senior **Seth Houk** (6-3, 306), who started the final seven games last season. Houk is one of the few junior college transfers on the roster, having transferred to Wake Forest before last season from Garden City (Kansas) Community College.

Two linemen moved to defense by Caldwell's staff, junior **Masanori Toguchi** (6-3, 290) and sophomore **Chad Rebar** (6-3, 295) have been moved back to offense and will supply depth. Another reserve will be sophomore **Mark Moroz**

(6-4, 261), recently moved to tackle from tight end.

2000 STATISTICS

Rushing offense	150.2	54
Passing offense	175.8	88
Total offense	326.0	83
Scoring offense	16.5	101
Net Punting	36.0	33
Punt returns	4.9	109
Kickoff returns	21.6	20
Rushing defense	205.5	100
Passing efficiency defense	142.7	104
Total defense	432.9	102
Scoring defense	32.9	97
Turnover margin	-9	97

Last column is ranking among Division I-A teams.

KICKERS

There's thunder in the foot of **Tyler Ashe** (5-11, 177), a senior place-kicker who has handled kickoffs for three straight seasons. But thunder is unpredictable, and accordingly, Ashe was anything but automatic last fall in his first season as the regular kicker.

Though he successfully converted 22-of-23 extra-point attempts—including the last 19—Ashe was just 5-for-10 on field-goal tries. He missed twice in three tries from inside 30 yards. So the great promise that was afforded Ashe when he signed with the Deacons after his all-state career at Shelby (N.C.) High School has yet to be realized.

Ashe was a tremendous weapon as a kickoff specialist his sophomore season, when he booted 43-of-55 kickoffs either into or through the end zone. Of those 43, 32 resulted in touchbacks. His power ebbed somewhat last season, however, when only 15 of his 38 attempts were downed in the end zone.

The backups are two redshirt freshman walk-ons, **Andrew Shelton** (6-0, 185) and **Billy Cobb** (6-2, 188). Shelton also punts and Cobb is listed as a reserve wide receiver.

DEFENSIVE LINE

A perennial problem for Wake Forest is finding players with the speed and size to play defensive line. Florida State usually stocks its roster with seven-to-10 such candidates. The Deacons, in a good year, are lucky to have five.

One of Grobe's first moves was to reduce the need for defensive linemen by 25 percent. Whereas his predecessor, Caldwell, ran a 4-3 defense, Grobe has already installed a 3-4. But instead of using his defensive linemen to occupy blockers and thus free up linebackers to make tackles, Grobe's scheme requires the defensive linemen to make plays. At least that's the plan.

Juniors **Calvin Pace** (6-6, 256) and **Roderick Stephen** (6-4, 242) emerged from spring drills as the starters at defensive end, but the Deacon defensive lineman with the most experience is senior **Nate Bolling** (6-4, 272). A free spirit, Bolling initially resisted the no-nonsense, highly regimented system installed by Grobe and his staff. A month or two after Grobe arrived, Bolling appeared headed out the door.

Grobe calls recalcitrant players "knotheads." Upon arrival, he found the team's No. 1 "knothead" to be Bolling.

"In winter workouts and at the start of spring practice I wouldn't have given a nickel for him, and in fact I wanted to get rid of him," Grobe said. "Right now we're proud of him because he's doing the things he needs to do."

Bolling's decision to get with the program is one of the most positive developments of Grobe's early days at Wake Forest. Aggressive and fearless, Bolling had 52 tackles in 10 games last season. Only linebackers **Marquis Hopkins** and Nick Bender and defensive end Bryan Ray had more.

But for the Deacons to have the necessary depth at defensive end, they will need considerable contributions from untested players such as redshirt freshmen **Joe Salsich** (6-4, 245), **Cardell Richardson** (6-2, 240), and **Jacob Perry** (6-5, 238).

Grobe's first candidate to man the pivotal nose tackle position is junior **Montique Sharpe** (6-3, 272), a gifted athlete who, in the opinion of Grobe, needs to get tougher. The only backup listed at the conclusion of spring was senior **Matt Myers** (6-2, 235), who in his career has played fullback and defensive end.

"I think we've got some good kids up front," Grobe said. "The hardest things to find are corners and defensive linemen. I think we're pretty solid on the corners and I think our defensive linemen run pretty well. Now, how tough are they? How physical are they going to be? How tenacious are they going to be? I can't tell you that. But I can tell you they move really well."

LINEBACKERS

The best part of switching from a 4-3 to a 3-4 defense is the need for one less defensive lineman. The worst part is the need for another inside linebacker. And coming out of his first spring at Wake Forest, Grobe was still casting for the part.

One inside linebacker is Hopkins (6-2, 236), a senior who led the Deacons last season with 100 tackles. The two other leading candidates for playing time, sophomores **Dion Williams** (6-1, 235) and **Kellen Brantley** (6-3, 238), had 26 and 27, respectively.

To boost the numbers, Scott (6-0, 211) has been moved to inside linebacker from running back.

"We've got some real problems at inside linebacker, not only from the standpoint that we need two or three guys to step up and show us they can play," Grobe said. "But we've also got problems depth-wise there. We've always felt that we need five guys to roll them in and out and keep them fresh and healthy.

"It may involve us actually moving some outside linebackers to inside linebacker, and then possibly even looking at some of our safeties as outside linebackers."

The leading candidate to move inside would be senior **Ed Kargbookorogie** (6-3, 219), but Grobe is resisting the move because Kargbookorogie, who had 27 tackles last season, is far better suited physically and temperamentally for the outside.

"I think the 3-4 defense is geared toward Kargbo," Grobe said. "I think he's got good feet. He's a tough guy. He likes to fly around."

Though most of the other outside linebackers lack experience, Grobe is excited about the existing talent level. Redshirt freshman **R.D. Montgomery** (6-6, 235) has the size and foot speed to disrupt offenses on the corner. Others on the depth chart are senior **Tehran Carpenter** (6-3, 204), who has been bumped up from safety, and two converted redshirt freshmen running backs in **Mike Hamlar** (6-2, 200) and White (6-2, 212).

"Tyrek White's a good move for us," Grobe said. "I think he's a really good outside linebacker.

"I think we've got some crazy edge players for us right now. They're not going to have to worry too much about 'What foot do I step with?' They're just going to have to pin their ears back and play."

DEFENSIVE BACKS

Sophomore **Quintin Williams** (6-2, 185) has the ability to be a future star at cornerback. Senior **Adrian Duncan** (6-1, 192), started 10 games at cornerback last year, picked off two passes and finished seventh on the team with 46 tackles. Senior **Michael Clinkscale** (6-1, 194) started 10 games at safety last season and finished sixth on the team with 47 tackles.

Senior cornerback **Chris Justice** (5-10, 194), junior safety **Walter Simmons** (6-0, 196) and sophomore safety **Obi Chukwumah** (6-2, 196) have also started since arriving at Wake Forest.

So what are two redshirt freshmen, cornerback **Marcus McGruder** (5-9, 180) and strong safety **Warren Braxton** (6-0, 195) doing at first team on the spring depth chart? Either Grobe was tremendously impressed by the abilities of McGruder and Braxton or quite unimpressed by the abilities and attitudes of the veterans. Most probably, it was a combination of the two.

Duncan, for one, was in and out of Caldwell's doghouse his previous three seasons at Wake Forest. But he has proven he has the speed and toughness to play college cornerback.

Williams has the look of a special player, the kind with the instincts and ability coaches covet. In his first season, as a true freshman, he started six games, picked off two passes, broke up another, forced a fumble and amassed 31 tackles.

Chukwumah emerged from spring practices as the starter at free safety. Depth at the Deacons' deepest positions is expected from safeties Simmons, Clinkscale and redshirt freshman **Caron Bracey** (6-0, 197) and cornerbacks Justice, **Ricky Perez** (6-1, 181), **Elliott Ivey** (6-0, 197), and **Eric King** (6-9, 180).

King, though a freshman, enrolled in January and participated in spring drills. Ivey is a junior and Perez a sophomore.

PUNTERS

Junior **Matt Brennie** (6-2, 188) held up underneath his massive workload pretty well last season, averaging 42 yards on his 63 punts. The performance represented quite an improvement from his freshman season, when he averaged 36.6 yards on 53 punts and, along the way, lost his starting position to quarterback MacPherson.

Brennie finished the season ranked No. 4 in the ACC and No. 20 nationally in yards per punt. He had 13 punts travel at least 50 yards. His best game came against North Carolina, when he averaged 46.5 yards on 11 punts, booted a career-long 56-yarder and kicked three inside the 20-yard line.

If Brennie falters, MacPherson has proven he can handle the job. As a freshman, he averaged 45 yards on six punts.

SPECIAL TEAMS

Early last season, Wake Forest's best offensive play seemed to be to allow the other team to score and have to kick off. Stone, a former ACC champ in the 100 and 200 meters, returned a kickoff 88 yards against Appalachian State for the Deacons' first touchdown of the season and averaged 30.5 yards per return over the first three games.

Beginning with the fourth game, against Virginia, opponents did a better job covering kickoffs and Stone eventually finished No. 14 in the nation with 24.7 yards a return. He did finish the season with a bang, averaging 30.5 yards in two returns against North Carolina State.

Duncan and Davis shared the punt return duties last season, with Duncan averaging 4.5 yards on 13 returns and Davis averaging 6 yards on six punts.

RECRUITING CLASS

Grobe and his staff signed a class that included six linemen, four linebackers, three defensive backs, two quarterbacks, two wide receivers and two running backs.

The 2001 signees are from eight states. Florida and North Carolina lead the way with four each, and there are three signees from Virginia. Grobe used his Ohio connections to sign two recruits from that state.

Recruits also come from Tennessee, Maryland, New Jersey, and Texas.

Grobe wanted to place an emphasis on recruiting North Carolina players.

"Our first thought is to bring in kids who can win at Wake Forest and help us compete for championships and go to bowl games," Grobe said. "With that said, we will always want to take as many kids from in-state as we possibly can. We want to compete in the state of North Carolina. The kids we have coming in here from in-state can all play. We don't take anybody just to be able to say we're taking kids from North Carolina. If we take them, we feel like they can come here and win for us."

One such player is **Goryal Scales**, a 6-0, 265-pound defensive lineman from Winston-Salem Carver. Scales, a first-team All-North Carolina pick, was selected to play in the Shrine Bowl of the Carolinas All-Star game after making 97 tackles his senior year. He had 12 sacks and five fumble recoveries. A physical specimen, Scales bench-presses 400 pounds and squats 650.

"When we watched Goryal on film, he's the perfect defensive lineman for our scheme," Grobe said. "We like to move our linemen around a lot and make offensive linemen hit moving targets. This kid is one who's going to be special. He's a guy who can play sideline to sideline. A lot of schools would look at him and say he's not tall enough. For us, we feel like he's the perfect size because he'll be a pad under pad type guy. He's the kind of lineman that will drive offensive linemen in this conference crazy. Not only that, but he's a wonderful kid."

Four high school state championships and six state finalists are represented by recruits in the 2001 class. There are eight all-state picks as well as the Virginia Offensive Player of the Year, quarterback Smith of Centreville High School in Sterling, Va. Smith is a two-way threat. Last season, he completed 80-of-138 passes (57.9 percent) for 1,329 yards and 16 touchdowns. He also ran for 1,494 yards and 26 touchdowns.

"I think we have helped ourselves with this recruiting class," Grobe said. "I am pleased that we were able to find some quality kids in such a short amount of time. Sometimes it's easy to make mistakes in the first year of transition and we were careful not to just add numbers to the roster. We feel that all of the players in this class will fit into our scheme very well."

In addition to Smith, Florida stars **Cornelius Birgs** (5-10, 198), a running back out of Boyd Anderson High School in Ft. Lauderdale, Fla., and quarterback **Cory Randolph** (6-1, 180), from Columbia High School in Lake City, Fla. are also talented additions to Wake's offense. Both were all-state picks.

Another first-team All-Florida pick, **Dominic Anderson** (6-0, 190) of St. Thomas Aquinas High School in Hollywood, Fla., joins the roster as a running back. **Greg Adkins** (6-3, 265) of Lakeland, Fla., **Craig Jones** (6-1, 280) of Garland, Texas and center **Kreg Rotthoff** (6-3, 275) of Massillon, Ohio add depth on the Deacons' offensive line.

BLUE RIBBON ANALYSIS

OFFENSE	C-
SPECIAL TEAMS	B
DEFENSE	D+
INTANGIBLES	B

Blessed with 19 returning starters, the Deacons will be one of the most experienced teams in the ACC. But how those veterans will respond to a new coaching staff will determine the fate of Grobe's first season as Wake Forest's head coach.

If Caldwell had a strength as a coach, it was the ability to identify and attract talented players often overlooked by other programs. The Deacons have had their share of good players over the last few seasons, but were consistently guilty of underachieving.

Grobe's charge is to convince his players they can win, and then give them the direction and organization to do so. Down-to-earth, self-effacing, but demanding, Grobe has made a strong impression on everyone—from media to fan base to players—in his first months at Wake Forest. There's a sense that he's a man who knows what he's doing —and he's got a full, well-acquainted staff on hand to help him get it done.

But ultimately the question is not whether Jim Grobe can turn Wake Forest into a consistent winner. The question is, can anybody?

(D.C.)

2000 RESULTS

Appalachian State	L	16-20	0-1
North Carolina	L	14-35	0-2
Clemson	L	7-55	0-3
Virginia	L	10-27	0-4
Vanderbilt	L	10-17	0-5
Georgia Tech	L	20-52	0-6
Maryland	L	7-37	0-7
Duke	W	28-26	1-7
Florida State	L	6-35	1-8
Navy	W	49-26	2-8
North Carolina State	L	14-32	2-9

Boston College

LOCATION	**Chestnut Hill, MA**
CONFERENCE	**Big East**
LAST SEASON	**7-5 (.583)**
CONFERENCE RECORD	**3-4 (t-5th)**
OFFENSIVE STARTERS RETURNING	**6**
DEFENSIVE STARTERS RETURNING	**8**
NICKNAME	**Eagles**
COLORS	**Maroon & Gold**
HOME FIELD	**Alumni Stadium (45,000)**
HEAD COACH	**Tom O'Brien (Navy '71)**
RECORD AT SCHOOL	**23-23 (4 years)**
CAREER RECORD	**23-23 (4 years)**

ASSISTANTS

Jerry Petercuskie (Boston College '75)
Assistant Head Coach/Special Teams
Dana Bible (Cincinnati '76)
Offensive Coordinator/QBs/Receivers
Don Horton (Wittenberg '82)
Tight Ends
David Magazu (Springfield '80)
Offensive Line
Bill McGovern (Holy Cross '85)
Linebackers
Bob Shoop (Yale '88)
Defensive Backfield
Frank Spaziani (Penn State '69)
Defensive Coordinator
Jason Swepson (Boston College '92)
Running Backs
Keith Willis (Northeastern '82)
Defensive Line

TEAM WINS (last 5 yrs.)	**5-4-4-8-7**
FINAL RANK (last 5 yrs.)	**64-67-60-31-39**
2000 FINISH	**Beat Arizona State in Aloha Bowl**

COACH AND PROGRAM

When we last caught up with Tom O'Brien, he was trying to quell expectations. Boston College fans, thrilled with his team's eight-win 1999 season, were expecting more of the same in 2000. They figured the corner had been turned. The building was done. The program was ready for some sustained success.

Most coaches run from the perception that good times are nigh and that prosperity is just around the corner. They need that for job security, of course, but they would prefer if the only people who noticed were their athletic directors and recruits, who would then flock in blue-chip droves to their campuses.

O'Brien said how teams that win in the third year of a coach's tenure often stumble the next season. He offered some evidence that it could happen in Chestnut Hill, Mass., because the Eagles had lost some big-time players (Chris Hovan, Frank Chamberlin) from their defensive front seven, and that the best recipe for success did not include a defense that resembled the French army. It didn't help that BC wasn't even able to reach the NCAA-mandated scholarship limit of 85, thanks to graduation and attrition.

While other schools on their schedule had 85, plus a couple dozen walk-ons, at their disposal, the Eagles were just trying to meet the minimum. Depth, as O'Brien said, would be at a premium throughout the lineup.

So, 2000 dawned with Boston College fans curious as to whether their heroes would take the next step toward what would eventually be sustained success and Big East contention, or whether '99 was something of an early arrival and shouldn't be confused with true prosperity.

Guess what? O'Brien has to deal with the same stuff this year. His Eagles didn't duplicate the eight wins of 1999, but they won seven, including a resounding 31-17 win over Arizona State in the Aloha Bowl. Even the previous year's edition, for all its regular-season success, couldn't boast a postseason triumph. It was waxed, 62-28, by Colorado in the Insight.com Bowl.

So, there it is. Boston College has won 15 games, including a bowl, the last two years. Things look like they're rolling in the right direction. The Eagles successfully replaced their lost defensive stalwarts. They uncorked an offense that scored 40 or more points four times. They demonstrated depth and an improved overall talent level. Sounds like sustained success to us. How about you coach?

"I think we're almost to that point," O'Brien said. "This year will prove whether we are. Our biggest losses are up front on offense. If we replace those guys and have a good offensive line, then we'll have a pretty good football team."

The question at hand is whether the Eagles will get past the "very good" stage. One of the problems they have had during the last few seasons is that there is always one large question mark heading into the season. Last year, it was up front on defense. This season, it's the offensive line. What needs to happen—and can't always be accomplished in four seasons—is a constant replenishment. If the big guns go, then

BIG EAST

BLUE RIBBON FORECAST

1. Miami
2. Virginia Tech
3. Pittsburgh
4. Syracuse
5. Boston College
6. West Virginia
7. Temple
8. Rutgers

ALL-CONFERENCE TEAM

OFFENSE

POS. PLAYER SCHOOL HT. WT. CL.

WR Antonio Bryant, Pittsburgh, 6-2, 185, Jr.
WR Andre Davis, Virginia Tech, 6-1, 194, Sr.
OL Joaquin Gonzalez, Miami, 6-5, 290, Sr.
OL Martin Bilba, Miami, 6-4, 300, Sr.
C Dan Koppen, Boston College, 6-3, 288, Sr.
OL Brad Knell, West Virginia, 6-5, 290, Sr.
OL Bryant McKinnie, Miami, 6-9, 335, Sr.
QB Ken Dorsey, Miami, 6-5, 200, Jr.
RB William Green, Boston College, 6-1, 215, Jr.
RB Lee Suggs, Virginia Tech, 6-0, 204, Sr.
TE Jeremy Shockey, Miami, 6-6, 236, Jr.

DEFENSE

POS. PLAYER SCHOOL HT. WT. CL.

DL Dwight Freeney, Syracuse, 6-1, 250, Sr.
DL Bryan Knight, Pittsburgh, 6-2, 230, Sr.
DL David Pugh, Virginia Tech, 6-3, 271, Sr.
DL Chad Beasley, Virginia Tech, 6-5, 292, Sr.
LB Ben Taylor, Virginia Tech, 6-2, 235, Sr.
LB Clifton Smith, Syracuse, 6-2, 249, Jr.
LB Gerald Hayes, Pittsburgh, 6-3, 240, Jr.
DB Edward Reed, Miami, 6-1, 198, Sr.
DB Mike Rumph, Miami, 6-2, 190, Sr.
DB Ramon Walker, Pittsburgh, 6-0, 195, Jr.
DB Ronyell Whitaker, Virginia Tech, 5-9, 192, Jr.

SPECIALISTS

POS. PLAYER SCHOOL HT. WT. CL.

PK Carter Warley, Virginia Tech, 5-11, 184, So.
P Freddie Capshaw, Miami, 5-11, 190, Jr.
RS Andre Davis, Virginia Tech, 6-1, 194, Sr.

OFFENSIVE PLAYER OF THE YEAR

Ken Dorsey, QB, Miami

DEFENSIVE PLAYER OF THE YEAR

Dwight Freeney, DL, Syracuse

NEWCOMER OF THE YEAR

Andrew Williams, DL, Miami

BIG EAST NOTEBOOK

The Big East was unable to escape a ride on the coaching carousel and introduces three new coaches this year, Miami's Larry Coker, West Virginia's Rich Rodriguez and Rutgers' Greg Schiano. The place many figured would be needing a new boss was Virginia Tech, because Frank Beamer was mentioned prominently for the Alabama position. But Beamer re-upped in Blacksburg and will probably stay put for the rest of his coaching days. Then again... Despite protestations to the contrary, Temple will be playing its last year of football in the Big East. The league's presidents voted to oust the Owls last winter, citing poor attendance, sub-par facilities and continued poor play as their reasons. The real culprit could have been Temple's membership in the Atlantic 10 for everything else. It seems as if the Big East wanted to keep its schools pure. ... The Big East will be scrambling for another guaranteed bowl berth in the wake of the June 12 decision by the Music City Bowl to use one of its guaranteed spots on a Big Ten team. That could be a double hit for the Big East, because other bowls with tie-ins to the conference can choose Notre Dame over another league team. That wasn't a problem last year, when the Irish earned a BCS berth, but it could cost a full-time Big East team an invite this season. ... The league will try again to have one of its members play in a preseason game, when Syracuse faces Georgia Tech in the Kickoff Classic in East Rutherford, N.J., on Aug. 26. You'll remember that Virginia Tech was scheduled to play Georgia Tech in the BCA Classic last Aug. 27, but an ugly electrical storm forced the game to be canceled. ... Miami and Virginia Tech have moved their game to Dec. 1 so that ABC can televise the game. Because the Big East does not have a championship game—like the SEC, Big 12 and MAC—this could well fill the bill.

the new guys step in, often more effectively. There was some evidence of that last year, when the defense absorbed the losses and moved on—to a point. Opponents averaged 4.9 yards per carry against the Eagles, which was even better than BC's impressive 4.8-yard figure. But the Eagles were good enough to win seven games, and that's important, when one considers that BC won that many in Dan Henning's first year with the program (1994) and then proceeded to stumble to a total of nine the next two seasons.

Boston College is making progress, but it remains behind the better Big East teams. Miami and Virginia Tech are clearly the league's class, and the Eagles are in a cluster with Syracuse, Pittsburgh and West Virginia behind the two leaders. With Greg Schiano pledging a resurgence at Rutgers, it is a critical time for the Boston College program, because those middle-of-the-pack teams are all jockeying for a place at the table with (or ahead of) the Hokies and 'Canes, and there is only so much room. If BC doesn't move quickly, it could find itself behind three or four schools. That wouldn't preclude a postseason invitation, but it sure wouldn't be bringing the big BCS candy, either. Remember that four of last year's seven wins came outside the confines of the Big East, where BC went 3-4. That was good for a tie for fifth with West Virginia—which is under new management these days because 3-4 finishes weren't too appealing to its fan base.

O'Brien certainly isn't in trouble, but he understands the urgency. An ex-Marine with a decidedly all-business attitude, he isn't about to let his team take some steps backward, even if he doesn't offer a ringing promise of grandiose 2001 success. And he sees the progress. This year's spring drills featured good competition at most positions.

"At a lot of spots, there was either no clear-cut starter or a lot of guys the same," he said. "We had some competition, and we have some guys who can play and want to do it."

BC has some talent on offense, even if its line is shaky. Tailback **William Green** gained 1,164 yards and scored 14 times last year. Wide-out **Dedrick Dewalt** averaged 17.8 yards on his 38 catches last year and has true defense-stretching potential. And O'Brien is confident that junior **Brian St. Pierre** is a worthy heir to Tim Hasselbeck, a two-year starter. The defense is still young, but players like middle linebacker **Scott Bradley** and corners **Lenny Walls** and **Will Poole** have the potential to be standouts.

BC hasn't been to three straight bowl games since the Doug Flutie era in the mid-1980s. A reprise of those days would establish this team as a perennial achiever and answer O'Brien's immediate questions. That doesn't mean he won't be back with a fresh set next year. That's just the way he is.

2001 SCHEDULE

Sept.	1	West Virginia
	8	@Stanford
	22	@Navy
	29	Army
Oct.	6	Temple
	13	@Virginia Tech
	20	Pittsburgh
	27	Notre Dame
Nov.	10	Miami
	17	@Rutgers
	24	@Syracuse

QUARTERBACKS

Hasselbeck graduated with the sixth most passing yards and fifth-highest touchdown total in school history. He was also the man who led the team's attack to the two bowl games. That's not bad for a couple years' work.

Now, it's up to St. Pierre (6-4, 213). Though the record books are not filled with the names of great passers with French surnames, O'Brien has every reason to believe St. Pierre will do the job for his Eagles. He completed 47-of-77 passes for 543 yards and four scores last year and has one start under his belt, which came last year at Notre Dame. In that game, a 28-16 Irish victory, St. Pierre was a solid 15-of-29 for 172 yards, a pair of scores and two interceptions. The previous week, against Temple, he replaced the injured Hasselbeck and completed 11-of-16 for 155 yards and a score. He had mop-up duty in wins over Army, Navy and Connecticut and showed himself to be a good pocket passer.

"He had an excellent spring," O'Brien said. "He learned a lot, having to play against Notre Dame last year. It's his football team now. He has to take it and run with it. The offense will be similar to the one we ran with Tim, because (St. Pierre) has good mobility."

St. Pierre certainly came to BC with a good resume. He was selected the Massachusetts Player of the Year as a senior and left St. John's Prep in Danvers with nearly every school passing record. After redshirting in '98, he saw time in nine games the following season, including a start against Pittsburgh, when Hasselbeck injured his shoulder. He completed 9-of-15 passes for 115 yards and a score and ran seven times for 62 yards.

St. Pierre has the tools and pretty good experience for someone who sat behind a two-year starter. Now, he has to deliver every week.

While O'Brien felt comfortable using St. Pierre during the last two seasons, he won't enter summer camp with the same easy feeling about his backup situation. He had hoped to find a backup during the spring, but an injury to redshirt freshman **Eric Boatwright** (6-3, 223) limited him to just five practices, and sophomore **Kevin Kiley** (6-3, 217) didn't distinguish himself.

Expect Boatwright to earn the spot, although a pair of incoming freshmen, **Ray Henderson** (6-3, 195), from Cresskill (N.J.) High School, and **Quinton Porter** (6-5, 190), from Portland (Me.) High School, will try to make a good impression.

RUNNING BACKS

Last season, the Eagles pounded and flashed their way to 201.0 rushing yards per game, not quite Oklahoma, circa 1977, but not bad in today's pass-happy climate. They used a two-pronged weapon, Green and Cedric Washington, who has since graduated. Now, it's Green's show, and the 6-1, 215-pound junior has a chance at some pretty big numbers. But that doesn't mean he's going to get 300 carries.

O'Brien enjoyed using the Green/Washington tandem last year, and he wants some backup support for his main man this season. To that end, a pair of sophomores, **Derrick Knight** (5-9, 192) and **Greg Toal** (5-11, 217), will vie for significant time as the No. 2 ball carrier.

Both can handle the inside stuff, although Toal is a little better between the tackles. A wild card, incoming freshman **Brandon Brokaw** (6-3, 225), from Morrisville (Pa.) High School, who gained 568 yards in his first two games last year, could have an immediate impact.

"He has a lot of what Green has," O'Brien said. "If he's as good as Green, we'll have to play him, because he won't be around more than three years."

For now, Green is the man. He had four 100-plus yard games last year and topped 200 on a pair of occasions, against Connecticut (19-225, three scores) and Rutgers (22-223, three touchdowns). A first-team all-Big East choice, Green can burst through people in tight quarters and then run to daylight. Though not the greatest receiver around, he does have potential. The Eagles are in great shape, as long as he stays healthy.

The fullback spot is an ongoing struggle between 6-2, 229-pound senior **Ryan Utzler** and sophomore **J.P. Comella** (6-0, 233). Although Utzler is the incumbent, O'Brien has made clear his main criteria for the job.

"Both can catch the ball, but the better blocker will have the job."

Stay tuned.

WIDE RECEIVERS/TIGHT ENDS

An experienced crop of wideouts should make St. Pierre's transition a little easier. Boston College may not have the kind of overpowering depth and speed that will make other defenses quake, but it does have talent and enough burst to make its passing game multi-dimensional and capable of hitting the home run.

The main man is senior **Dedrick Dewalt** (5-9, 180), who led the team with 38 catches and averaged a strong 17.8 yards per catch. Dewalt scored eight times, including twice on plays of 75 yards or longer. Dewalt has the potential to catch 60 passes, but it depends on a couple of things. One is whether St. Pierre shines and is able to find him enough. The other depends on him. Though he had three games of more than 100 receiving yards, Dewalt also had some duds, mostly against teams that were able to control him at the line of scrimmage more and keep him from flowing freely downfield.

If Dewalt can get himself clearance better and more often, he'll become an all-star-caliber player.

"He's as close to a game-breaker as we've had since we've been here," O'Brien said.

Expect the other starter to be **Jamal Burke** (6-1, 207), a junior who caught 26 passes last year and scored three times. After starting slowly and making just four catches in the Eagles' first three games, Burke became a steady target and had some signature performances. He caught three balls for 107 yards against Connecticut, including a 58-yarder. He had five catches for 74 yards against Temple. Though in Dewalt's shadow somewhat, Burke has the size, strength and enough speed to become a good second target and give St. Pierre a physical presence on the outside and over the middle.

The backup situation is strong, too, and it's possible that senior **Ryan Read** (6-0, 183) could blossom into a big-time threat. Last season was Read's first for BC; he transferred from Navy after the 1998 season. He is blessed with tremendous speed and proved it in the Aloha Bowl by catching a 40-yard scoring pass. Read may not catch 35 balls, but you can bet he'll make a handful of big plays.

"Read can get deep," O'Brien said. "He improved as much or more than anybody during the spring. He's comfortable now."

The other top reserve is senior **DuJuan Daniels** (5-11, 184), who caught 15 passes last year, while 6-2, 201-pound junior **Keith Hemmings**, who caught eight balls last year, will also see time. Redshirt freshman **Joel Hazard** (5-9, 171) had a strong spring and will push Hemmings and Daniels.

The tight end situation is not as bright as the outside. All three of the Eagles' top performers at the position from last year are gone, leaving BC with a pair of defensive emigres as its leading candidates. Actually, sophomore **Sean Ryan** (6-5, 266) and junior **Frank Misurelli** (6-4, 257) began their Boston College careers as tight ends but were switched to defensive end last year, because of the program's dearth of experience at the position.

Ryan actually started six games last year, and made 29 tackles, while Misurelli started twice.

"They acclimated themselves to the tight end position during the spring, and each proved he can block and catch," said O'Brien, who didn't seem too concerned that two relative newcomers would be manning the spot.

OFFENSIVE LINE

The Eagles have some work to do here in replacing a trio of starters, but it's not as if O'Brien doesn't have any good news up front.

Junior center **Dan Koppen** (6-3, 288) was a second-team All-Big East selection last year, his first as a regular in the middle. Smart and quick, Koppen makes sound pre-snap calls and has the potential to be a first-rate center.

"He had the benefit of being between two good guards (Paul Zukauskas and Paul LaQuerre) last year," O'Brien said. "Now, he's the person who has to provide leadership."

The other returning regular is senior tackle **Marc Colombo** (6-8, 303), who handles the right side and has the size and athletic ability to be a first-rate road-grader. Colombo started all 12 games last year but now—like Koppen—he won't have the benefit of lining up to a stalwart at guard, or an experienced tight end. He must become a leader and a consistent standout.

"He can be an excellent offensive lineman," O'Brien said.

The left guard spot, which was LaQuerre's domain, should go to 6-4, 282-pound senior **John Richardson**, who started three times last year, including in the Aloha Bowl. But O'Brien doesn't sound so sold on the upperclassman.

"He has the edge in experience, but more than anything else, no one else has distinguished himself there," O'Brien said.

That could open the door for redshirt freshman **Chris Snee** (6-3, 285). There is no clear-cut choice yet to replace Zukauskas, a first-team All-Big East choice and a first-team All-American as voted by the American Football Coaches Association.

The battle, which was joined by junior **Mark Parateau** (6-5, 287) and sophomore **Augie Hoffman** (6-3, 308) during spring drills, will continue into summer practices. Hoffman started one game last year, while Parateau has seen backup duty.

Sophomore **Leo Bell** (6-8, 297) is the top candidate to replace second-team All-Big East choice Michael Cook at the left tackle position, although O'Brien has faith in sophomore **Frank Wilpert** (6-5, 289) as well. Although neither is expected to be an all-star this season, either player has the talent to be solid. Snee, who has added 20 pounds since the end of last season, has plenty of potential.

Although the Eagles don't have the experience they had on last year's line, this edition should be good enough to propel a strong running game and give St. Pierre enough time to throw. Should it come together more than that, BC could have an extremely dangerous offense.

2000 STATISTICS

Rushing offense	201.0	20
Passing offense	213.9	57
Total offense	414.9	29
Scoring offense	31.5	25
Net Punting	34.1	72
Punt returns	9.0	67
Kickoff returns	18.6	81
Rushing defense	212.5	107
Passing efficiency defense	105.3	24
Total defense	380.7	73
Scoring defense	23.6	51
Turnover margin	+11	10

Last column is ranking among Division I-A teams.

KICKERS

Heading into last season, it looked like **Sandro Sciortino** (5-10, 200) had a line on the placement job, but that position went to Mike Sutphin, who proved to be a reliable, albeit limited, performer. Sutphin made 12-of-14 kicks, but his longest was 43 yards, not exactly the perfect situation. Sciortino, a sophomore, has the leg to be a big-time kicker, but he needs to improve his confidence and consistency.

"He's an outstanding kicker," O'Brien said.

Sciortino handled the Eagles' kickoffs last year and does have a big foot. But if he doesn't do the job, O'Brien could well turn to junior punter **Kevin McMyler** (6-1, 195), who handled some placement work during the spring.

DEFENSIVE LINE

An indication that this area is in good shape came when O'Brien was able to shift Ryan and Misurelli to tight end to fill that need. A year ago, he was looking for conscripts. Now, he believes he has what could eventually become a dominating line. The big question mark is experience on the inside. While there is talent and potential available, the Eagles will still be going primarily with second and third-year players at tackle.

The starters should be sophomores **Keith**

Leavitt (6-6, 312) and **Tom Martin** (6-4, 271). Martin started five games last year, including the bowl win over Arizona State. He made 28 tackles, four of which came in enemy backfields, and showed the potential to be a disruptive force inside.

"Martin stepped it up versus Arizona State and continued through the spring," O'Brien said. "He has a good mix of quickness and power."

Leavitt was a 10-game starter last year and was sixth on the team with 49 tackles, five of which were for loss. He came to BC as a highly touted recruit (he was ranked among the top 10 in New England by *SuperPrep*) and has shown the potential to be a great run-stuffer inside.

Expect sophomores **Justin Hinds** (6-3, 288) and **Doug Goodwin** (6-1, 279) to be their primary backups, although redshirt freshman **Anthony Crosson** (6-3, 288), perhaps last year's most heralded recruit, will push for time.

The end situation is even better, thanks to the return of 6-4, 294-pound senior **Antonio Garay**, who missed all but one series of the 2000 season with a torn knee ligament. Although O'Brien acknowledges that Garay had some rust during spring drills, the fact that he was able to compete in the NCAA wrestling championships (he advanced to a quarterfinal) demonstrates that the knee is pretty strong.

"He moved into Hovan's spot last year and can be that kind of player," O'Brien said, referring to the former BC All-American.

The other end spot will be fought for by senior **Sean Guthrie** (6-4, 248) and junior **Derric Rossy** (6-3, 247). Guthrie started all 11 games last year and made 37 tackles, including a team-high eight for loss. He should see the majority of snaps there, but Rossy (31 tackles) will get onto the field for plenty of action.

One youngster worth watching is redshirt freshman **Phillip Mettling** (6-2, 275).

"Guthrie and Rossy have played a lot of football for us," O'Brien said. "This has gone from a position that was trouble for us to one that has some depth."

LINEBACKERS

This is another strong spot for the Eagles, because experience abounds. Nowhere is that more evident than at middle linebacker, where three players will see action.

Gone is Ryan Burch, who started 10 games last year and made 62 tackles, third on the team. Senior **Andy Romanowsky** (6-2, 228) was a one-game regular last season and made 30 tackles, but he can't be certain that the spot is his, thanks to the continued emergence of junior **Vinny Ciurciu** (6-0, 238), a Clemson transfer who impressed on the scout team last year.

"He had an excellent spring," O'Brien said of Ciurciu. "He has all the qualities you like in a middle linebacker. He can cover, run and tackle."

Expect the strong side to be manned by 6-1, 221-pound senior **Scott Bradley**, who missed the last half of the 2000 season with a knee injury. Bradley did start five games and made 25 tackles and showed that he was healthy during spring drills. O'Brien is counting on Bradley to be a big part of the defense this season and that is quite possible, given his 1999 performance.

Bradley made 59 stops that year, including eight for loss, and had five sacks. He has the potential to be a major contributor this year. He'll be backed up by junior **Jerome Ledbetter** (6-1, 226), who missed all but two games last season with a knee injury. He has the potential to make big plays for the Eagles but must stay healthy. He missed a good portion of the 1999 season with a bum shoulder.

The weak-side battle between sophomore **John Ott** (6-2, 216) and junior **Curtis Bolden** (6-1, 220) could rage throughout the season. Although Bolden is believed to have a small edge coming out of spring drills, Ott isn't going away.

"Bolden is a little quicker and better in the open field," O'Brien said. "But Ott is bigger. It might depend on who we're playing."

Bolden started all 12 games last year and made 45 stops, while Ott had 50 tackles. Although they have talent and experience, they also have to contend with junior **Marco Williams** (6-0, 208), who has excellent speed and was a regular in six games last year.

As we said, this is a deep group that can give O'Brien considerable options, depending on what team the Eagles play. If everybody stays healthy, Boston College can count on plenty of production from this area.

DEFENSIVE BACKS

BC is in good shape here, too, although there may not be as much depth as there is among the linebackers. There is still experience and talent. Both starting cornerbacks return, as does junior free safety **Ralph Parent** (6-2, 210). And though the strong safety position is open, O'Brien has three solid candidates for work there.

When O'Brien says that senior **Lenny Walls** (6-4, 191) and sophomore Will Poole are "probably the best corner tandem we've had here at BC in a while," he isn't exaggerating. Walls came to Chestnut Hill last year after helping City College of San Francisco to a 12-0 record. His impact was immediate. He led the team in interceptions with six and deflected 11 passes, also tops on the team. He also made 42 tackles and had four sacks.

Walls is big, can run and doesn't mind contact. He goes after the ball well and is a valuable weapon to have in a conference that boasts plenty of wideout talent.

His partner isn't too bad, either. Poole began last year behind Jonathan Ordway on the corner but ended up starting nine games and amassing 75 tackles—second on the team. Like Walls a bigger corner, Poole is physical and covers well.

Unfortunately for BC, Poole was suspended in late May for the 2001-02 academic year. The reason for the suspension was not announced.

The third corner should be junior special teams standout **Trevor White** (5-8, 181), while redshirt freshman **Peter Shean** (5-9, 169) can be expected to play in nickel and dime situations.

Parent started all 12 games last year and had 56 tackles and three interceptions. His eight stops and two interceptions against Syracuse earned him the Big East Co-Defensive Player-of-the-Week honor. Parent made seven stops against Notre Dame and West Virginia. Experienced, strong and quick, Parent is an excellent center fielder.

Junior **Doug Bessette** (5-11, 202) emerged from spring drills as the top strong safety, but he has some company. O'Brien reports that redshirt freshman **T.J. Stancil** (6-1, 192) is learning the defense well.

"He looks like he can play," O'Brien said.

Meanwhile, sophomore **Paul Cook** (5-11, 192) has made the switch from free safety to the strong spot and has shown potential. Expect sophomore **Brian Flores** (5-11, 204) to back up Parent.

PUNTERS

McMyler did a good job last year and should be one of the league's best in 2001. His 39.7-yard average wasn't spectacular, but it was solid. More impressive were his combination of fair catches and balls put inside opposing teams' 20-yard lines.

McMyler dropped 17-of-63 kicks within 20 yards of the other goal line and had 19 punts fair-caught. He does, however, have to work on his hang time somewhat; rivals were able to average 15.4 yards per return.

SPECIAL TEAMS

This was something of a mixed bag for the Eagles last year. The aforementioned trouble stopping enemy punt returners must be corrected. Not only did they post an embarrassing average; they also returned three for touchdowns. That can't be repeated.

BC must also improve its kickoff coverage. Although the opposing average of 21.6 wasn't overwhelming and there were no scores, anything more than 20 yards is generally unacceptable. The expected increase in depth this year should help the Eagles' special teams.

Dewalt did a fair job returning punts, averaging 9.0 yards and scoring once, but he needs to improve his consistency. The kickoff situation is in pretty good shape, thanks to Daniels (20.0 average) and Green (22.1). Each has the speed to go the distance, although neither did make it to the end zone last year. Green, however, did return a kick 84 yards, against Army.

RECRUITING CLASS

It is a testament to the Eagles' improved depth and overall talent that although they brought in a strong recruiting class—perhaps one of their best in many years—not many of the newcomers will have the opportunity to contribute this year.

The exception could be Brokaw, who has the size and breakaway speed to get some carries behind Green. The others will have to wait, not that they won't be making things happen soon. One of the areas which received a boost was the offensive line, which welcomes **Chris Hathy** (6-4, 305), from Mount Lebanon High School in Pittsburgh, Pa., **Pat Ross** (6-3, 265), from St. Xavier High School in Cincinnati, and **Jeremy Trueblood** (6-7, 270), from Cathedral High School in Indianapolis.

Boston College picked up some speed in the defensive backfield by landing **Jazzmen Williams** (5-9, 175) from Sutherland High School in Pittsford, N.Y., a highly touted corner, and **Larry Lester** (5-8, 175), from Piscataway (N.J.) High School, both of whom were all-purpose machines during their prep days.

Expect **Quinton Porter** (6-5, 190), from Portland (Maine) High School, and **Ray Henderson** (6-3, 195), from Cresskill (N.J.) High School to be in the race for quarterback time in a couple years.

Look for linebacker **Patrick McShane** (6-1, 195), from Catholic High School in Joliet, Ill., and tackle **Tim Bulman** (6-3, 270), from Boston (Mass.) High School, to make impacts on the defense in the near future.

BLUE RIBBON ANALYSIS

OFFENSE	B
SPECIAL TEAMS	C+
DEFENSE	B+
INTANGIBLES	B+

O'Brien is right to consider this year something of an acid test for his program. If the Eagles make it to a third consecutive bowl game, fans should consider them more than just one-hit wonders and adjust their expectations skyward.

It's unlikely BC will ever mount a consistent charge toward a BCS berth, but there is no reason to believe that the team cannot someday vie for the Big East championship. If Boston College can win seven or eight games this year, that "someday" shouldn't be too far in the distance.

Unlike last season, before which O'Brien worried about the Eagle defense, it is the BC offense which merits concern. The installation of St. Pierre, despite his noteworthy experience in 2000, brings a slew of questions. And the rebuilt offensive line, which must find a way to be strong up the middle again, could cause the team's trademark ground game to struggle, at least early on. The bad news is that Boston College doesn't have the luxury of an easy path, which will allow it to ease its new offensive pieces into the puzzle.

The Eagles open with a visit from West Virginia in an early league game that neither team wants. Seven days later, BC will be in Palo Alto to play Stanford, which should be improved from last year's mediocre finish. If the defense and ground game arrive on time, that tough stretch could result in a 2-0 start and considerable momentum. Misfire out of the gate, and BC might find itself 0-2 and struggling to reach the six wins necessary for inclusion in the postseason party.

St. Pierre should be all right, provided his decisions are sound. He has the arm and legs to be a productive quarterback in the multiple BC system. If he can eliminate some of the mistakes that hurt him last year, the Eagles have lots of potential.

Green could approach 1,500 yards, even if his backups get a chance. He has the speed and power necessary to be a standout.

Boston College's defense should be excellent. The Eagles have plenty of depth and experience along the front seven, even if some of the players are chronologically young. They have played and succeeded. The secondary is also in good shape, especially if Bessette can handle the strong safety responsibilities.

The good news is that O'Brien has some options if that doesn't happen. Boston College has potential this year—no doubt about it. Even though the top of the Big East isn't available, a third-place finish and eight wins are definitely within reach.

The key —after the tough start, of course—will come in October and early November, when the Eagles play home games against Pittsburgh, Notre Dame and Miami in a four-week stretch. Win one (or more) of those, and the Eagles are on their way. Even if that doesn't happen, O'Brien and his program are making strides and getting closer to the goal of consistent production and success. Of course, next year we'll hear all about how hard it is to keep it going, when the expectations mount. Then again, that's not the worst problem to have.

(M.B.)

2000 RESULTS

West Virginia	L	14-34	0-1
Army	W	55-17	1-1
Navy	W	48-7	2-1
Virginia Tech	L	34-48	2-2
Connecticut	W	55-3	3-2
Syracuse	W	20-13	4-2
Pittsburgh	L	26-42	4-3
Rutgers	W	42-13	5-3
Temple	W	31-3	6-3
Notre Dame	L	16-28	6-4
Miami	L	6-52	6-5
Arizona St. (Aloha Bowl)	W	31-17	7-5

Miami

LOCATION Coral Gables, FL
CONFERENCE Big East
LAST SEASON 11-1 (.917)
CONFERENCE RECORD 7-0 (1st)
OFFENSIVE STARTERS RETURNING 6
DEFENSIVE STARTERS RETURNING 8
NICKNAME Hurricanes
COLORS Orange & Green
HOME FIELD Orange Bowl (72,319)
HEAD COACH Larry Coker (NE Okla. St. '70)
RECORD AT SCHOOL First Year
CAREER RECORD First Year
ASSISTANTS Rob Chudzinski (Miami '90)
Offensive Coordinator/Tight Ends
Randy Shannon (Miami '89)
Defensive Coordinator
Vernon Hargreaves (Connecticut '84)
Linebackers
Curtis Johnson (Idaho '85)
Wide Receivers
Art Kehoe (Miami '82)
Offensive Line
Greg Mark (Miami '89)
Defensive Line
Don Soldinger (Memphis '68)
Running Backs
Mark Stoops (Iowa '89)
Defensive Backs
Dan Werner (Western Michigan '83)
Quarterbacks
TEAM WINS (last 5 yrs.) 9-5-9-9-11
FINAL RANK (last 5 yrs.) 14-48-21-13-2
2000 FINISH Beat Florida in Sugar Bowl.

COACH AND PROGRAM

Anybody who doesn't think Larry Coker isn't the right person to continue Miami's post-probation prosperity need only consider how he acted after athletic director Paul Dee selected him interim head coach, in the wake of Butch Davis' I-don't-want-to-go-but-look-at-all-the money-and-control-they're-throwing-at-me defection to the Cleveland Browns.

Instead of worrying about whether Barry Alvarez was going to take the job, or if Dee would search high and low for a big name, Coker acted like The Man from day one. He told his assistants to keep calm and not start looking for real estate agents. He told the players that he would be back, and even if he weren't, somebody equally talented would be taking over. He told recruits that Miami was still going to play fun, aggressive, winning football. His hold on the job may have been tenuous, at best, but his actions screamed that he wasn't going anywhere. Now, that's the kind of swagger that Miami loves.

The school that brought you Jerome Brown in fatigues before to the '87 Fiesta Bowl and an avalanche of penalty yards in the '91 Cotton Bowl was being led by a man who had never been a head coach before. Still, he felt right at home adding his name to the lineage of sideline bosses that began with Howard Schnellenberger and continued on with Jimmy Johnson, Dennis Erickson and Butch Davis.

It's a wonder somebody didn't throw a flag for unsportsmanlike contact or excessive celebration.

"When I was named interim coach, I felt I was the best person for the job," Coker said. "I thought I was going to get the job. Even though history didn't prove that to be the norm, I felt good. I met with my assistants and told them I felt that I would get the job and to recruit like we were going to be here."

Coker was right. He did get the job. He might not have been Dee's first (or fourth) choice, but the career assistant has been handed the keys to one of the nation's best-known football teams and has been asked to carry on. Because Miami won 11 games last year and deserved a berth in the BCS title game, thanks to its Oct. 7 win over Florida State, that is quite a chore.

Five years ago, the Hurricanes were rocked by probation and were reeling under the weight of scholarship sanctions and the perception that they were not only arrogant but also out of control. The good-time carrying on of the late '80s and early '90s had been replaced by hard time in the NCAA penitentiary.

Davis told everyone who would listen about his team's woes. Few people were sympathetic.

Last year, the Orange-and-Green Death Star was fully operational once again. Miami's defense was bloodthirsty. Its offense could hit teams with speed or with power. And though the 'Canes still celebrated a little louder than most, they were not the poster children for bad manners that their predecessors had been. Davis had shown Miami that it was possible to win big with a team that didn't embarrass the school or insult its opponents. That was huge.

But through the entire 2000 season, Davis was the subject of rumors. First, the new Houston entry in the NFL was going to hire him away from Coral Gables. Then, Alabama was going to money-whip him into running to Tuscaloosa. Cleveland finally got him, but not after a long series of denials by Davis and a late departure that jeopardized the team's recruiting.

While Davis insisted that he was not stringing the Hurricanes along, rather holding out for more control over the Browns' football operations, his leaving left Miami in a tough spot. The program was enjoying the kind of prosperity it did in the old days and had generated enough momentum to make prominent players crave the chance to play for the 'Canes.

But without a coach, it would be hard to convince recruits to come to town. When Dee finally decided to make Coker the full-time boss, he and his staff had all of four days to close some high-powered deals.

"There was no great joy when I got the job," Coker said. "I told our staff, 'Let's go and save this recruiting class.' "

Coker and his assistants, which include six holdovers from Davis' 2000 staff, did indeed save the class, losing only one player who had committed to the Hurricanes and adding three more blue-chip types. It showed the value of continuity and the program's reputation among top high school players.

And it showed that while Coker may not be the most recognizable name in America, he knew how to deliver under pressure. He will get a chance to do it again this season, because Hurricane fans figure that last year's 11-win season was just a warm-up. Forget about the schedule, which includes non-conference games with Florida State, Washington and Penn State. Nobody cares that the Big East schedule features trips to Virginia Tech, Boston College and Pittsburgh. Miami is back, and even if the 'Canes had to play every member of the AFC Central, fans would be expecting big things.

"The expectations here are unrealistic, off the charts, but that's OK," Coker said. "But we did lose four first-round draft choices, and sometimes you miss guys like that.

"But players come to Miami to play the kind of schedule we have. If I didn't want that, I shouldn't have taken the job. We're excited and looking forward to opening the season at Penn State and that Washington is coming to our place."

Fans know about the Nittany Lions and Huskies. But not a lot of them know about Coker, who spent five seasons as offensive coordinator and quarterbacks coach at Miami. He was also offensive coordinator at Oklahoma, Oklahoma State and Tulsa and coached quarterbacks at Ohio State. He knows how to teach that part of the game, and that's big, especially at Miami, where big point totals are expected. But Coker hasn't been a head coach since his days at Clarmore High School in Oklahoma, and there are worries he might not be up to the job.

Of course, none of those concerns are his. He has always thought Larry Coker was the best man for the Miami head coaching job, and that's not about to change, no matter how high the expectations are or how demanding the schedule is. Hurricane fans have to love that.

2001 SCHEDULE

Sept.	1	@Penn State
	8	Rutgers
	15	Washington
	27	@Pittsburgh
Oct.	6	Troy State
	13	@Florida State
	25	West Virginia
Nov.	3	Temple
	10	@Boston College
	17	Syracuse
Dec.	1	@Virginia Tech

QUARTERBACKS

With just three regular-season starts on his resume, **Ken Dorsey** stepped under center last year and elicited comparisons to former Miami standout Bernie Kosar. Not bad.

The skinny (6-5, 200) junior now must become more than just a prodigy-in-training. Dorsey needs to blossom into a team leader, capable of overcoming the losses of wideouts Santana Moss and Reggie Wayne and still keeping the Miami attack crackling along.

"It's somewhat of a reversal for him," Coker said. "Last off-season and the summer before we started, Santana and Reggie helped bring Ken along. They helped make him look good. Now, he's got to bring [receivers] **Andre Johnson**, **Jason Geathers**, **Kevin Beard** and **Daryl Jones** along."

Dorsey is good enough to do it. In fact, he could well be the nation's best quarterback by season's end. Dorsey is *Blue Ribbon*'s preseason offensive player of the year.

A year ago, Dorsey completed 58.4 percent of his passes last year for 2,737 yards, 25 touchdowns and an impressively low interception number—five. He was extremely poised and accurate. He played well in big games and proved that he was not too fragile to last an entire season.

Dorsey was outstanding in the win over Florida State, completing 27-of-42 passes for 328 yards and a pair of scores. More importantly, he led the Hurricanes on drives late in the game, answering the Seminoles' attacks. He was extremely productive against Virginia Tech, completing 11-of-23 for 283 yards and three scores.

This season, look for Dorsey to be more vocal as a leader. He has added about 15 pounds to his lithe frame and understands how important it is for him to be durable. His teammates have also noticed his commitment.

"He did a great job in the weight room, and should be a more physical player," Coker said. "He'll never be a John Elway-looking guy. That's not him. But he's much, much stronger. He earned respect from his teammates, too, for working so hard."

Last spring, the Hurricanes were so thin at quarterback that they had to use wide receiver **Ethenic Sands** at the position, reprising his days as an option quarterback. Sands is back at split end, and redshirt freshman **Derrick Crudup** (6-1, 202) is Dorsey's backup. Crudup is obviously raw, but Coker has faith that he can become a reliable backup.

Crudup's biggest challenge is continuing his adjustment to the Miami offense. He played in an option attack at Deerfield Beach (Fla.) High School, and while he completed 75 percent of his passes for more than 1,500 yards as a senior, Crudup has work to do to become a steady, consistent passer.

"Derrick is a talented athlete," Coker said. "He can pass and run and has quick feet. He has a good release. He just has to develop into a good quarterback for our style of play. Ken had great high school training for our offense. Derrick didn't. He made progress during the spring, but the summer will be the key for him.

"I feel comfortable Derrick can get there. We didn't expect Ken Dorsey to start as a freshman, but he did and won three games for us, allowing us to get to a New Year's Day bowl. So, it can be done."

RUNNING BACKS

Coker doesn't try to hide his enthusiasm for this bunch.

"This is probably the best group of running backs I've been around, as far as sheer numbers go," Coker said.

He won't get an argument here. The Hurricanes are loaded, so much so that a newcomer like freshman **Frank Gore** (5-10, 190) from Coral Gables (Fla.) High School, who rushed for 2,953 yards and 34 touchdowns last year, will be redshirted and will even have trouble finding time the season or two after that. That's how deep Miami is at the halfback and fullback spots.

Miami can load up with the big fellas, unleash some pure speed or smack opponents with backs who bring a little (or, in the case of redshirt freshman **Willis McGahee**, a lot) of both. Even without James Jackson, who gained 1,006 yards last year and scored 11 times, Miami should have a ground attack capable of taking considerable pressure off the new crop of receivers.

The halfback spot should be the most interesting, because Coker has three front-line backs, each capable of being an every-down player. Junior **Clinton Portis** (5-11, 195) came out of spring drills atop the depth chart. Although he missed three games last year with a foot injury, Portis still gained 485 yards and scored a pair of touchdowns. His most impressive work, however, came in the Sugar Bowl, against Florida, when he relieved an injured Jackson and rushed for 94 second-half yards against the SEC champions.

Portis is fast and has a penchant for breaking long runs. Witness his 82-yard touchdown bolt against McNeese State. And Portis has a pretty good track record. He gained 838 yards as a freshman in '99. He has good hands and can turn short passes into big gains.

"I don't know what to say about Portis," Coker said. "All he does is gain a lot of yards."

Portis will get his carries, but so will 6-2, 205-pound sophomore **Jarrett Payton**, who gained 262 yards in a reserve role in 1999 but redshirted last year. He missed spring drills after ripping open his foot on some coral, an injury that nobody has to worry about in the Big Ten, but Coker has been impressed with Sweetness' son and expects him to be quite a weapon.

Then there's McGahee. He redshirted last year and is now 100 percent after missing part of his senior prep season with a knee injury. Still, the 6-1, 225-pounder gained 677 yards in just five games in 1999 and has the rare blend of speed and power that reminds some Miami coaches and fans of former 'Cane standout Edgerrin James.

Expect to see senior **Najeh Davenport** (6-2, 245) playing fullback, even if his time to date has been spent at the other backfield position. Coker used **D.J. Williams** there last year, but Williams has been switched to outside linebacker, so there is an opening.

Rather than use promising, but raw, redshirt freshman **Kyle Cobia** (6-2, 231) or career reserve **Nick Nettles**, a 6-2, 250-pound junior, Coker may go with Davenport, who gained 308 yards last year and can make opposing linebackers sad if they meet him at the point of attack. One of the most powerful physical specimens on the team, Davenport is fast and strong and now completely recovered from the serious knee injury he sustained in 1999.

WIDE RECEIVERS/TIGHT ENDS

We start with what Miami lost, and it was plenty. Moss and Wayne combined to catch 86 passes, score 15 touchdowns and average just about 17.0 yards per catch. Moss was the nation's best punt returner, as evidenced by his sick, 18.2-yard average and four touchdowns, while Wayne left Miami as the school's career leader in receptions and receiving yardage. The NFL thought enough of the two of them to make each a first-round draft choice. The Jets took Moss with the 16th pick, while Indianapolis spent the 30th choice on Wayne.

"We were spoiled last year," Coker said. "Our offense is about consistency, and we like to have someone make that 6-yard catch, so we can go second-and-four. If somebody doesn't catch that ball, then the defense is going to blitz. Last year, if you blitzed, we threw an 80-yard touchdown pass to Santana Moss. This year, I don't know what's going to happen in those situations."

Enough about the past. The Hurricanes move on, and it's a good bet Dorsey won't be throwing to a bunch of mannequins. That doesn't mean there is a lot of game experience out there. Leading the way is 5-10, 190-pound senior Jones, who made 12 catches last year and averaged a strong 15.1 yards per reception. A two-time Big East 100-meter dash champion, Jones averaged 24.1 yards on seven punt returns and brought one back for a score. He caught four passes for 81 yards against McNeese State in last year's opener and had a pair of receptions in the Sugar Bowl against Florida.

"He has experience and great speed, but he has to become consistent," Coker said. "He has some work to do, but he has made some plays before."

Opposite him is sophomore Johnson (6-3, 220), who has the chance to be a great one. Johnson caught three passes last year, including a 32-yard touchdown against McNeese. He also averaged 20.1 yards returning kicks and showed a burst that will make him dangerous. Add in his speed and substantial athletic ability, and Miami has itself quite a weapon.

"He has a chance to be really good," Coker said. "He's so big, and though he missed some of the spring with a pulled quad, he came back and practiced the last week and made some nice plays in the spring game."

Sands, a 6-0, 177-pound junior, may have stunted his development as a wideout some last spring by working at quarterback, but that kind of unselfish, team play is hard to find. Sands completed 9-of-13 passes last year for 174 yards and a touchdown as Dorsey's reserve last year, pretty good numbers. But he's back at receiver this season, where his speed will help the 'Canes.

Sands is also pretty valuable with the clippers. Every Thursday, he gives the team haircuts, a ritual that has become as important to the 'Canes' pre-game preparation as any practice.

"He is a natural receiver," Coker said. "He adjusts to the ball well, and I think the time he spent at quarterback will help him at receiver. He's more knowledgeable about what these guys have to do."

Expect Geathers, a 6-3, 215-pound sophomore, and Cobia to find their way into the rotation, and don't be surprised if freshman **Kellen Winslow II** (yes, the son of that Kellen Winslow) makes an impact. Winslow (6-5, 210), from Scripps Ranch High School in San Diego, Calif., caught 45 passes and scored nine times last year.

Also expected to see playing time is Beard, a 6-2, 175 sophomore.

The Hurricanes have one of the nation's best pass-catching tight ends. Junior **Jeremy Shockey** (6-6, 236) snared 21 balls last year, including a 13-yard throw that clinched the 27-24 win over Florida State. Shockey has great instincts, soft hands and enough speed to break long ones up the middle. Shockey joined the 'Canes last summer after one year at Northeast Oklahoma Junior College and made a quick adjustment to big-time ball. One can only imagine how talented he will be this year, with a season's experience.

"He's outstanding," Coker said. "He looked as good as any offensive player we had last year. The thing that separates him from other tight ends I've been around is that he can separate from coverage. He's also tough after the catch, and he wants to get better at blocking."

Backing up Shockey is 6-4, 240-pound senior **Robert Williams**, although Winslow may get some time at the spot.

OFFENSIVE LINE

The Hurricanes return four starters from this unit, and all of them have the chance to receive high Big East honors. It all starts with senior tackles **Bryant McKinnie** (6-9, 335) and **Joaquin Gonzalez** (6-5, 290), both of whom were first-team all-conference last year, and each of whom is favored to repeat in 2001.

This time last year, we were all gushing over Gonzalez, with good reason. But the funny thing is that McKinnie—on *Blue Ribbon*'s preseason All-America team—may well be ahead of Gonzalez in the long run. His decision to return for his senior year sets him up to be a coveted commodity come draft time next April. He's huge, has a gigantic wingspan and requires opposing ends to pack a change of clothing if they're thinking about going around him.

"He's a freak," Coker said, with awe. "He has no body fat, is a great athlete, can run and has a great arm span. His top end is sky-high. He is potentially a great player."

Gonzalez is pretty good, too. A roughhouse type who can clear plenty of room on the right side for the 'Cane running backs, Gonzalez is also an excellent pass protector. He's also smart. Gonzalez came to Miami on an academic scholarship and earned a football free ride. He won't be waiting too long by the phone on draft day, either.

"He is more physical than he has ever been," Coker said. "He is bigger than he's ever been, too. He plays so hard that he allows himself to get it done."

Carlos Joseph, a 6-6, 322-pound redshirt freshman, is McKinnie's heir apparent at left tackle, and he has the potential to be a great one. Junior **Joe Fantigrasi** (6-4, 270) and sophomore **Joe McGrath** (6-5, 288) will fight it out behind Gonzalez.

Coker calls 6-4, 300-pound senior right guard **Martin Bibla**, "maybe our best college lineman."

That's high praise, with McKinnie and Gonzalez around, but Bibla is a physical run-blocking specialist who can handle pass protection too. Few work harder. Mountainous sophomore **Vernon Carey** (6-5, 363) backs him up.

The center spot belongs to 6-3, 293-pound junior **Brett Romberg**, who moved over from left guard last spring and became a leader. Romberg has the chance to be one of the nation's premier centers this year.

"He sticks his head in there and just mauls," Coker said. "He's an athletic, tough kid."

Romberg's backup is senior **Scott Puckett** (6-3, 283), who could move to left guard, if neither of a pair of juniors, **Sherko Haji-Rassouli** (6-6, 326) or **Ed Wilkins** (6-4, 318), distinguishes himself. Coker couldn't identify one of them as a starter in June, and each had better work hard before fall practice or Puckett could slide over as Miami attempts to put its best five linemen out there.

2000 STATISTICS

Rushing offense	194.8	23
Passing offense	266.0	22
Total offense	460.8	5
Scoring offense	42.6	2
Net Punting	39.0	9
Punt returns	17.8	3
Kickoff returns	22.7	12
Rushing defense	112.8	26
Passing efficiency defense	95.8	8
Total defense	333.5	34
Scoring defense	15.5	5
Turnover margin	+12	6

Last column is ranking among Division I-A teams.

KICKERS

The Hurricanes have a good one here in 6-3, 214-pound junior **Todd Sievers**, who just needs some consistency and good health to emerge as a front-line kicker. Sievers suffered two concussions last year and was diagnosed with diabetes but still made 11-of-17 field goals, including 10-of-11 from inside 40 yards. He also had the rather interesting distinction of making a pair of 50-yard extra points, against Boston College and Florida, after post-touchdown celebrations got out of hand.

"He kicked a 60-yard field goal in high school, so he has the leg," Coker said. "He can become one of the best kickers in the nation. My goal is to make sure that if we get the ball inside the 30, we're a threat to score."

Sievers has a big enough leg to handle the kickoffs, as evidenced by the four touchbacks he registered on seven tries against Virginia Tech.

Freshman **Mark Gent** (6-3, 203) from St. Thomas Aquinas High School in Ft. Lauderdale, Fla., who signed with the 'Canes in February of 2000 but didn't enroll until last January, will back him up. A first-team all-stater in '99, Gent was 29-of-35 in career field goal tries and registered touchbacks on 60 percent of his kickoff tries.

DEFENSIVE LINE

Coker can remember a time, back in the late 1980s, when the Miami backup (backup!) defensive tackles were Russell Maryland and Cortez Kennedy. How's that for depth? While the Hurricanes aren't close to that level, they will have a strong front four with plenty in reserve. In the hot Florida sun, that is imperative.

"Our depth there is better than it has been in a long time," Coker said. "We have players who can get up field. They're aggressive and fast."

Leading the way is junior tackle **William Joseph** (6-5, 297), who made 49 tackles last year, his second as a starter. Joseph didn't get much press last year, largely because of the other standouts on the Miami defense, namely Damione Lewis and Dan Morgan, but he is a rising star with considerable potential and all-star notices likely awaiting him. Joseph is strong and quick and can get into opposing backfields, particularly against the run. While Joseph needs to improve his pass-rushing skills, he is a skilled tackle with a bright future.

Junior **Matt Walters** (6-5, 263) should take Lewis' spot. He played in all 12 games last year and made 27 tackles, four of which came for losses. He also had two sacks. He isn't an overpowering player, but he works hard and has good quickness. Walters is also no slouch in the classroom; he is majoring in mechanical engineering.

"He played well last year and is having a great off-season," Coker said.

Their primary backups will be sophomore **Santonio Thomas** (6-4, 296) and redshirt freshman **Vince Wilfork** (6-1, 338). Wilfork is a prodigy who should develop into a dominant player down the road.

The ends belong to junior **Jamaal Green** (6-3, 257) and senior **Cornelius Green** (6-4, 250). They are not related, but they do give the Hurricanes a strong pair of bookends capable of making plays in opposing backfields.

Cornelius Green started five games last year, after coming to town from Kilgore (Texas) Junior College. He had 27 tackles, seven of which came behind the line, and three sacks. He was last year's defensive rookie of the year, and anybody who saw his 10-tackle performance against Temple understands why. He has only one year left in Coral Gables, but it could be a big one.

Jamaal Green started all nine games in which he participated last year and helped a line that had been hit hard by injuries. He had three tackles for loss against Virginia Tech and six stops against Syracuse. Green is fast and strong and has the endurance to stay on the field a long time. Like Joseph and Cornelius Green, he is a rising star.

Behind the Greens are juniors **Andrew Williams** (6-4, 260) from Hinds (Miss.) Community College and Hillborough High School in Tampa, Fla., and **Jerome McDougle** (6-4, 270). Williams enrolled in January after a huge career at Hinds that included 20 sacks last year alone. A great pure pass rusher, he needs only to improve against the run to challenge for serious playing time.

McDougle is another Hinds product who sat out last year as a redshirt after a circuitous route to Coral Gables. He had 12 sacks in '99 at Hinds, one year after sitting out a season at Pittsburg (Kansas) State. He signed out of high school with Maryland. Got all that? Miami doesn't care if you do. It just wants to turn McDougle loose on enemy quarterbacks.

LINEBACKERS

The loss of Morgan, who made 138 tackles last year and garnered just about every all-America honor available, leaves a huge hole in the second line of defense. But the next star is rising on the horizon and should be taking his place among the pantheon of great Miami linebackers within the next season or two.

Butch Davis used Williams at fullback last year, primarily to get the 6-2, 244-pound prodigy on the field. Now, the sophomore is back at outside linebacker. Though Coker and his staff flirted with switching Williams to the middle, particularly after **Jonathan Vilma** missed the spring with a knee injury suffered in a jet-ski accident (another problem they don't worry about too much in Columbus or Ann Arbor), Williams will handle the weak side and is ready to rock.

"He's so explosive, and he changes direction so well," Coker said. "He's a special player who makes great plays. We had a toss to the tailback in the spring that looked like it was going to be a good play. He tackled the guy for a 1-yard loss from the other side of the field. Like Morgan, you need to know where Williams is all the time."

Williams was *USA Today*'s 1999 Defensive Player of the Year. His senior year was so good it would have been ripped by critics had it been part of a movie script. Williams rushed for 1,974 yards and made 123 tackles at De La Salle (Calif.) High School and was rumored to have called all the plays, lined the field, painted the goal posts and called every coin toss right all year. Timed at 4.45 as a prep senior, Williams is a fully armed weapon who should challenge for all-league honors from week one.

Vilma's knee injury gave the Miami coaches an opportunity to evaluate further junior **Howard Clark** (6-1, 224), who started eight games last year and made 60 tackles. He got better as the 2000 campaign moved along, a fact evidenced by his eight tackles and interception against Boston College in the regular-season finale.

Also stepping up was 6-2, 215-pound junior **Ken Dangerfield**, who started one game last year and made 12 of his 20 tackles against McNeese State. Dangerfield played the strong side last year but could be in the middle this time.

Vilma, a 6-2, 220-pound sophomore, played in all 12 games last year and made 38 tackles. He was quick to pick up the defense and was extremely valuable as Morgan's backup. If healthy, he could develop into a standout.

The strong spot will most likely go to 6-2, 225-pound senior **Chris Campbell**, a three-year starter who combines speed and tremendous athletic ability. But Campbell missed spring drills after twisting his knee in off-season conditioning. Campbell was huge in the win over Florida, making six tackles, breaking up two passes and stopping one ball carrier in the backfield.

Another sideline-to-sideline player, Campbell is a force against the pass and run.

Backing him up is sophomore **Jarrell Weaver** (6-3, 210), who has made the switch from defensive end and had 22 tackles last year in limited action. He was a strong special teams player and showed an ability to get to the quarterback. Weaver has added some bulk during the last year, but he needs to get bigger to become an every-down player.

Another outside linebacker is 6-2, 215-pound sophomore **Darrell McGlover**, who was primarily a special teams player last year.

DEFENSIVE BACKS

The trend continues in the secondary, where the Hurricanes are loaded with experienced players and all-star candidates. Three starters return from a unit that picked off 23 passes last year and allowed enemy quarterbacks to complete just 50.5 percent of their throws.

Even though first-team all-Big East safety Al Blades is gone, a pair of first-teamers is back, beginning with 6-1, 198-pound senior free safety **Edward Reed**. All he did last year was pick off eight passes, break up 23 others and make 59 tackles. That earned him first-team All-America honors and the fear of just about every offensive coordinator in the nation. Reed is on *Blue Ribbon*'s preseason All-America team.

"When Reed was on the scout team (in 1997), you could tell he was special, even as a freshman," Coker said. "He would bait quarterbacks and then close quickly on their throws. He's a physical player, and we're lucky to have him for another year."

Senior **James Lewis** (5-11, 196) is slated to take Blades' place. Lewis saw action in all 12 games last year, made 26 tackles and broke up four passes. Lewis has extensive experience as Blades' understudy and is now ready to step into the featured role. Backing him up is junior **James Scott** (6-2, 193), who has a world of potential that he has shown at times on special teams and running the ball. If he becomes consistent, he could stand out.

The cornerbacks are excellent as well. Leading the way is 6-2, 190-pound senior **Mike Rumph**, another first-team All-Big East choice. Though last year his tackles dropped from 75 to 41 and his interception total dwindled from four to one, Rumph remains quite a specimen. He is big and strong yet retains the speed necessary to hang with anybody he faces.

Rumph teams with 5-11, 182-pound junior **Phillip Buchanon**, who took over the other side last year when Leonard Myers was hurt and showed excellent instincts. He picked off two passes last year and added another in the Sugar Bowl that helped preserve the Hurricanes' win.

"In our defensive scheme, you need to have good corners, and Buchanon and Rumph give you that," Coker said. "Buchanon is real special, and so is Rumph. He's physical."

The main nickel back should b 5-11, 186-pound senior **Markese Fitzgerald**, who has seen plenty of reserve work during his career at Miami and has also started 13 games. He picked off two passes last year. The other corner in the rotation is 6-1, 182-pound sophomore **Alfonso Marshall**.

PUNTERS

Coker offered this post-spring assessment of junior punter **Freddie Capshaw** (5-11, 190): "The ball exploded off his foot."

Not bad, huh?

Capshaw averaged 43.2 yards per boot last year, a nice improvement from his '99 average of 39.7. Although Capshaw put only seven of his 49 punts inside opposing 20-yard lines and had 12 touchbacks, he was quite a weapon and could change field position quickly for the 'Canes. An example came during the Sugar Bowl, when he pinned Florida deep in its territory in the fourth period, helping to set up a late touchdown. Capshaw led the Big East in punting average last year and is primed for a big season.

SPECIAL TEAMS

With the abundance of speed and athletic ability on the Hurricanes' roster, one might expect them to be every bit as formidable as Virginia Tech in the punt and kick-blocking departments. Sometimes, however, teams don't live up to expectations. Miami blocked only one kick last year, a figure that Coker understands must improve.

"I'd like to see our special teams back to where they were in the past," he said. "We're getting the types of players who should be able to run and block kicks."

That's for sure. The deep Hurricane roster and the influx of outstanding prep talent the last couple years should give Miami plenty of candidates for its coverage teams.

Not that the Hurricanes suffered in those departments last year. Rivals averaged just 7.4 yards bringing back punts and 17.5 on kicks. Those are great numbers. If Miami adds more blocked kicks, it will be extremely dangerous.

The return game looks good, despite the loss of Moss. Jones has the capacity to break long ones on punts or kicks, while Andre Johnson and Buchanon could also be dangerous. Look out also for Beard.

RECRUITING CLASS

The Hurricanes landed another great class, despite Davis' departure. Most analysts had Miami rated among their top 10, with the main ingredient in the group of newcomers being—you guessed it—speed.

We have already mentioned some of the fresh faces, studs like Gore, Winslow and Gent. Let's meet the rest.

Miami may have landed the nation's best linebacking prospect when **Leon Williams** (6-4, 220) from Canarsie High School in Brooklyn, N.Y., signed on. He will be joined on the second line of defense by **Roger McIntosh** (6-3, 220) from Gaffney (S.C.) High School.

The defensive line adds **Orien Harris** (6-4, 280) from Newark (Del.) High School. His brother, Kwame, is at Stanford. Harris is quick and nasty—perfect for Miami. Also expected to fortify the defensive front is **Jeff Littlejohn** (6-3, 282) from Gaffney (S.C.) High School. He was a teammate of McIntosh's.

The offensive front adds three big-time horses—**Robert Bergman** (6-5, 275) from Bakersfield (Calif.) High School, **Randy Boxill** (6-5, 300) from Sanaluces High School in Lantana, Fla., and and **Rashad Butler** (6-5, 290) from Dwyer High School in Palm Beach Gardens, Fla.

And *Parade* all-America choice **Antrel Rolle** (6-1, 205) from South Dade High School in Homestead, Fla., is expected to be a future star at safety, while **Jovonn Ward** (6-0, 195) from Northwestern High School in Miami, Fla., also has a bright future in the secondary.

BLUE RIBBON ANALYSIS

OFFENSE	A-
SPECIAL TEAMS	B+
DEFENSE	A
INTANGIBLES	B

OK, so it would be crazy to pick the Hurricanes the preseason No. 1 team, thanks to the extremely difficult schedule, the new wide receivers and Coker's inexperience as a head coach. But take a good look around that roster and try to imagine this team losing any more than a game or two—including a bowl.

Miami has all-league talent all over the place, in bunches. Dorsey, Gonzalez, McKinnie, Joseph, Williams, Rumph, Reed, Buchanon and Capshaw could all end up on the first team. That's remarkable. It's also one hell of a foundation.

Miami has fought long and hard to get to the point where its roster includes enough talent to insert new faces as needed, and now the pipeline is producing big-timers every year. Morgan leaves, and in steps Clark or Vilma. Miami loses Blades, and Lewis steps up. And so on.

Sure, there are questions. Can the receivers deliver? Will the middle linebackers make plays, and can the other linebackers pick up the slack, because Morgan is gone? What will Coker do when times get tough? They are legitimate concerns, but they are all wiped away by the answers elsewhere.

Dorsey could well win a Heisman, provided his targets do their jobs. But he won't have to throw for 3,000 yards for Miami to be successful—the ground game will be so dominant, behind that great line. The defensive front seven is quick and filled with playmakers, while the secondary should be good for close to 20 interceptions.

There is speed all over the special teams, and Sievers and Capshaw have first-rate legs.

Coker picks up quite a loaded gun for his first year as boss. Miami has the potential to do big things—even win it all. That schedule is formidable, and games in State College, Tallahassee and Blacksburg will be extra tough. But the talent is there, in droves. Last year, we said that Miami was back. This year, the 'Canes are *Blue Ribbon*'s preseason No. 1.

It's clear that the Hurricanes aren't going anywhere, even if their former coach did.

(M.B.)

2000 RESULTS

McNeese State	W	61-14	1-0
Washington	L	29-34	1-1
West Virginia	W	47-10	2-1
Rutgers	W	64-6	3-1
Florida State	W	27-24	4-1
Temple	W	45-17	5-1
Louisiana Tech	W	42-31	6-1
Virginia Tech	W	41-21	7-1
Pittsburgh	W	35-7	8-1
Syracuse	W	36-0	9-1
Boston College	W	52-6	10-1
Florida	W	37-20	11-1

Pittsburgh

LOCATION	**Pittsburgh, PA**
CONFERENCE	**Big East**
LAST SEASON	**7-5 (.583)**
CONFERENCE RECORD	**4-3 (3rd)**
OFFENSIVE STARTERS RETURNING	**6**
DEFENSIVE STARTERS RETURNING	**10**
NICKNAME	**Panthers**
COLORS	**Blue & Gold**
HOME FIELD	**North Shore Stadium (65,000)**
HEAD COACH	**Walt Harris (Pacific '68)**
RECORD AT SCHOOL	**20-26 (4 years)**
CAREER RECORD	**31-50 (7 years)**
ASSISTANTS	**Bob Junko (Tulsa '69)**
	Assistant Head Coach/Defensive Tackles
	J.D. Brookhart (Colorado State '88)
	Offensive Coordinator/Receivers
	Paul Rhoads (Missouri Western '89)
	Defensive Coordinator/Secondary
	David Blackwell (East Carolina '94)
	Linebackers
	Curtis Bray (Pittsburgh '92)
	Defensive Ends
	Bryan Deal (Heidelberg '80)
	Recruiting Coordinator/Specialists
	Tom Freeman (San Diego State '69)
	Run Game Coordinator/Offensive Line
	Bob Ligashesky (Indiana, Pa. '85)
	Tight Ends/Special Teams Coordinator
	Shawn Simms (Bowling Green '86)
	Running Backs
TEAM WINS (last 5 yrs.)	**4-6-2-5-7**
FINAL RANK (last 5 yrs.)	**77-64-78-58-32**
2000 FINISH	**Lost to Iowa State in Insight.Com Bowl.**

COACH AND PROGRAM

It's kind of hard to blame Pittsburgh for throwing a net over Walt Harris during last season's coaching feeding frenzy. For a while there, it seemed as if every I-A school except for Florida State and Oklahoma was looking for a new boss. The mid-major stars were moving up. The broadcast guys were getting fresh starts. Old and new pro coaches were heading back to school.

Moving vans were backing up to four bedroom homes in college towns all across the country. Relocation was the name of the game.

Not for Harris. When Ohio State politely asked Pittsburgh athletic director Steve Pederson if it could ask Harris a few questions to measure his level of interest in the vacant Buckeye spot, Pederson was not too hospitable. Last summer, Pederson had tied Harris into a lucrative contract through the '06 season, and he wasn't about to let any other school try to ruin that marriage. Pittsburgh was on the way up, and the Panthers wanted Harris to keep the program heading skyward.

"Ohio State called, and Pitt denied them permission," Harris said matter-of-factly. "The other fact was that a lot of people thought, 'Why would [Harris] go to Ohio State, when Pittsburgh is a better job for me and my family?' With what the coaching staff has done here, and what the university has done, this is a better job."

We're not going to launch a full-fledged case against Harris' reasoning. We will just say that anything Pittsburgh has, Ohio State has more of: More tradition. More seats in its refurbished stadium. More TV exposure. Oh, and more pressure. Just ask John Cooper about that. Cooper's team won eight games last year and played in a New Year's Day bowl game. Pitt was 7-5 and lost to Iowa State in the Insight.com "classic." Cooper was fired. Harris is a blue-and-gold Panther god.

While the media put the pieces together and assumed that a former Buckeye assistant would eat light bulbs for the chance to coach the Scarlet and Gray, Harris had other ideas. He decided that continuing Pitt's resurgence in a new stadium, with a one-year old gaudy football practice and training facility on campus and a roster that for the first time in a long while includes some real depth and win-now I-A talent, wasn't such a bad idea.

"Our football complex opened [last] Aug. 1," Harris said. "It's scary how nice and classy it is. I have a view of our four practice fields, and you can see the hills of western Pennsylvania in the distance. The river is on one side. The furniture in the offices is nice. I can tell by what the recruits say when they come here. They haven't seen anything like it anywhere else."

That new stadium is pretty cool, too. And unlike teams that share a field with a professional team, this one is almost as much the Panthers' as it is the Steelers'. When the city put up the dough for the sports palace, it did so with the expressed intention of making it something that wouldn't just be the province of one team, 10 times a year.

When you're throwing out in the neighborhood of $300 million, you're looking for some return on the investment, beyond two handfuls of dates. That's why Pitt won't be a second-class citizen in its own home. Sure, it would be nice to have a 65,000-seat stadium on campus, within walking distance for all the frat boys and co-eds, but if you can't have that, a state-of-the-art home just a 20-minute ride away is a fine consolation prize.

Last year, we told you how excited Harris was about the number of bathrooms in the new stadium, a total that far outstrips what was available in creaking Pitt Stadium. This year, we can fill in some of the finer strokes and talk about the view of the Pittsburgh skyline, the enormous video replay board, the quality of seating—even for those unfortunate enough to find themselves in the upper deck—the grass field, the number of available concession and souvenir stands and the high-end amenities, like luxury suites and club seats. The Panthers are moving rapidly into the 21st century in all areas, and Harris is happy to be a part of the progress—and happy that the Panthers are not being viewed as Saturday afternoon interlopers by the Steelers.

"There are three identifying marks on the stadium—on the scoreboard, on the outside gates and on the seats," Harris said. "Each will have our insignia and the Steelers' emblem. They're letting us share deeply in the stadium."

It's probably a good idea, because the present-day fortunes of the two teams are somewhat divergent. The Steelers find themselves struggling to stay close to the big boys in what has become the NFL's best division. Pitt, on the other hand, is clearly on the rise, as last year's bowl season proved.

It's a progression that ought to continue this year, thanks to the return of 16 starters and both specialists. Pitt's two lines will be bigger, older and deeper. And there is some star power, as well, thanks to the returns of Biletnikoff -winning wide receiver **Antonio Bryant**, standout defensive end **Bryan Knight** and fierce-hitting safety **Ramon Walker**.

Things look good, but not perfect. Pitt has no proven ball carriers on the roster. None. And those lines may look better, but there are still some questions and problems with injuries. And though the Panthers are on the rise, they remain a step (at least) behind Virginia Tech and Miami. Or is that Miami and Virginia Tech? We'll see on Dec. 1.

Then there is that small concern of the burgeoning attack pack in the Big East. Boston College has played in two straight bowls. Syracuse remains formidable. And West Virginia is certain to improve under new coach Rich Rodriguez. There isn't a lot of room for error.

That's why it was so important for Pitt to keep Harris. New practice fields and stadiums dazzle recruits, but coaches put it all together on the field. Harris has been doing that for four seasons, and his efforts may just be ready to pay off in a big way. Last year, there were some huge steps taken.

The thumping of Penn State was significant, even if the Nittany Lions were playing at a diminished capacity. Beating Boston College was big, and just making it to a bowl was a landmark, even if a special teams gaffe and key late turnover prevented Pitt from making a big comeback. The stage is set for big things, and Harris might not be upset that he stuck around.

2001 SCHEDULE

Sept.	1	East Tennessee State
	8	South Florida
	15	UAB
	27	Miami
Oct.	6	@Notre Dame
	13	Syracuse
	20	@Boston College
	27	@Temple
Nov.	3	Virginia Tech
	10	@Rutgers
	24	@West Virginia

QUARTERBACKS

There aren't too many programs around the country that could lose a starter who threw for more than 2,000 yards and possibly feel better about their fortunes at the position. This time last year, the Panthers were counting heavily on 6-4, 205-pound senior **David Priestley**, an Ohio State transfer who had flashed bits of brilliance during the '99 season.

Although Harris is notoriously hard on his quarterbacks, he believed Priestley had all the tools to be a top-flight signal caller. But Priestley didn't make a complete recovery from off-season shoulder surgery and was unable to grab the starting job away from John Turman. Now, the spot is Priestley's. Or, it will be, provided he can make it through the whole season healthy.

Priestley played in eight games last year and made one start—against Bowling Green. He completed 55.3 percent of his 103 passes, for 829 yards, five scores and four interceptions. Although he didn't have a performance that matched his 407-yard outburst against Virginia Tech in '99, Priestley did throw for 183 yards and two scores against Kent State and 154 yards and the team's lone score against Temple.

Priestley does have a big arm and pretty good wheels. He no doubt understands Harris' system, after three full years in it (one sitting out as a transfer and two on the field) and has the size and experience to be a good one. Now, it's time for him to stay healthy and deliver.

"He had a very, very solid spring, and he ought to be a very good football player," said Harris, who came about as close to gushing as he could. "His 407 yards against Virginia Tech was one of the five best performances I've seen. They knocked his butt off, but he didn't quit.

"Priestley is the most knowledgeable quarterback I've coached in the last six years. He's been in the system now almost four years, and that experience is hard to defeat. David has some very good abilities, and he understands his situation."

Priestley won't be taking all the snaps, no matter how healthy he remains. That's because 6-3, 215-pound sophomore **Rod Rutherford** is moving steadily from an intriguing prospect to a full-fledged quarterback weapon. A great runner and improving passer who also caught two passes for 82 yards and a score last year, Rutherford is the Panthers' future under center and presents an interesting situation for Harris, who hasn't had a quarterback like him before. Though Stanley Jackson at OSU was similar, he didn't have Rutherford's size or cannon arm. By this time next year, the Panthers could be unleashing quite a weapon on the Big East.

The big question about Rutherford, and the one he will ultimately have to answer favorably to get playing time beyond just a cameo role, is whether he can mature into a full-fledged quarterback, rather than just an athletic curiosity. That's what Harris wants to see.

"He has unique abilities," Harris said. "He has to improve in all phases of the game. When he's out running, he's a threat. He's a big guy who's fast. He can run through people. Last year, he played 47 plays as a third-string quarterback. I don't think anybody else in the nation used their third-stringer that much.

"We're going to play Rod regardless of David's situation. We're hoping he continues to grow and mature."

This year's third teamer is likely to be redshirt freshman **Pat Hoderny** (6-6, 220), who threw for more than 3,200 yards during his final two seasons at McDowell High School in Erie, Pa. A classic drop-back passer, Hoderny won't see 47 plays worth of action, barring injury, but has potential.

RUNNING BACKS

Things look pretty good all over the Pitt roster—except for here. The losses of leading rusher Kevan Barlow (1,053 yards, eight touchdowns) and backup Nick Goings (296) have left the Panthers in what would appear to be dire straits. Neither of the two top players listed on the depth chart—**Mike Jemison** and **Malcolm Postell**—has ever carried the ball in real action. That makes sense—Postell is a redshirt freshmen, and Jemison arrived at mid-year and participated in spring drills. Harris understands his situation but doesn't seem too concerned.

"At least we have some possibilities at tailback," Harris said. "It's sort of the same as our offensive line, where we are also young. But you don't need as much experience to play running back as you do to play offensive line. You have to take some snaps, read the defense and be a football player."

Jemison (5-11, 215) and Postell (6-1, 210) both have glowing prep resumes. Postell gained 1,658 yards and scored 232 points as a senior at Keyport (N.J.) High School, while Jemison amassed nearly 5,000 career yards at Greencastle-Antrim High School in western Pennsylvania. Harris sees that each could become a contributor, but realizes that it will take some time.

"Postell has talent, but he was a little confused with things like pass protection," Harris said. "Jemison has good running ability. Both need great summers. They have to get stronger, faster and smarter."

The fullback position is completely different, from an experience point of view. **Lou Polite**, a 6-0, 240-pound sophomore, returns after starting last year. A bruising blocker who can also handle the short-yardage work, Polite surprised many by going wire-to-wire as a first stringer last year. His biggest game was an eight-carry, 43-yard, one-touchdown effort against Rutgers.

What made Polite's performance so impressive was that many people believed sophomore **Dustin Picciotti** (6-3, 250) would come in and grab the position by the throat. A powerful player with good speed, excellent hands and a warrior's mentality, Picciotti was a star at mighty Central Bucks West High School in suburban Philadelphia and one of the nation's most highly-regarded prospects in 2000. His adjustment to the big time, however, has been slow.

"He's trying to understand the difference between high school and college," Harris said. "He has good ability, size and strength."

Don't be surprised to see both Picciotti and Polite in the backfield at the same time, in a jumbo configuration designed to bring 500 pounds of pain to opponents.

WIDE RECEIVERS/TIGHT ENDS

There is no such question about the wideouts, thanks to the return of Bryant, a 6-2, 185-pound junior who had a smashing 2000 season. Bryant led the nation with 130.2 receiving yards per game, caught 68 balls, scored 11 times and averaged a whopping 19.1 yards per reception—and he didn't even play in Pitt's opener last year.

The All-American didn't record double-figure catches in any one game, but he did show steady production and had some huge yardage outputs, including a pair of 200-yard plus efforts. He was outstanding in the Insight.com Bowl, catching five balls for 155 yards and a pair of scores.

Bryant is a rare talent with amazing speed. It doesn't appear possible to overthrow him. He proved that against Iowa State, when he scored on catches of 72 and 44 yards. The 44-yarder was particularly impressive, because Bryant caught a ball that few in the stadium—including the Cyclone defender—figured he could reach.

"Antonio is a great football player," Harris said. "Our offensive system has developed seven first-round draft choices over the years, and he's with all of them. He's an intense, passionate football player.

"I don't know what his exact speed is, but he has football speed. John [Turman] never overthrew him. When the ball's in the air, he goes and gets it."

The big challenge for Bryant this season is to improve his performance in the face of what should almost certainly be extremely close attention. Last year, Bryant was able to see some single-coverage situations, thanks to the presence of Latef Grim, who caught 39 passes. Grim is gone, and no one on the current depth chart has the kind of proven ability needed to keep the double- and triple-teams away from Bryant.

That's not to say there aren't some intriguing candidates. Junior **Lamar Slade** (6-4, 205) caught 11 balls last year and scored twice.

"He has the most consistent hands of all the guys," Harris said. "He has to be more detailed in his route running." Another intriguing prospect is 6-3, 215-pound senior **R.J. English**, who had knee surgery late last year but averaged 21.7 yards on the 15 catches he made during eight games. English also scored three times. He caught two passes for 128 yards, including an 80-yarder, against Kent and had a huge, 8-yard scoring reception that forced overtime against Syracuse.

"He's a big, strong, dynamite player," Harris said. "If he's healthy—and he'll start running in June—he'll help us. He knows what he's doing."

There are plenty of candidates for the fourth receiver spot. Senior **Darcey Levy** (6-2, 215), who came to Pitt last year from Notre Dame, via Front Range (Colo.) Community College, has made the switch from tailback and has great speed.

Another newcomer to the receiving corps is junior **Robb Butler** (6-0, 200), a former Panther corner who was an all-state pass catcher in high school. And don't forget redshirt freshman **Donny Patrick** (6-2, 205), who caught 209 passes during his career at Hazleton (Pa.) High School and was a three-time all-state performer.

The tight end position is solid, thanks to the return of 6-7, 280-pound senior blocking demon **Mike Bosnic** and sophomore **Kris Wilson** (6-3, 230), who has the potential to be a valuable up-the-middle receiver. Harris would love it if each of the players borrowed the other's stronger traits.

"Bosnic has to become a better route runner and pass catcher, and Wilson has to become stronger and a better blocker," Harris said. "Wilson has tremendous talent. We used him as one of our four wide receivers last year. He can really run. We're looking for him to become an every-down player."

OFFENSIVE LINE

By this time next year, Harris should be crowing about his offensive line, because the Panthers will return every player of note from the unit. But this is 2001, and Pittsburgh wants to score points now. That means the linemen must get and stay healthy for an entire season. Two starters must be replaced, and quality depth must be found from among several relatively untested performers.

"Nobody is set," Harris said. "It's all in progress. We have to improve there, get more strength and get the players to watch more tape to learn."

Pitt has only been able to recruit quality linemen these last couple seasons, but it has not been easy. In fact, the Panthers moved two defensive front men to the other side of the ball this year to get some depth.

"Linemen win championships, and the great programs get the linemen," Harris said. "For a while, we were moving offensive linemen to defense. Now, we're moving them back. Players like **Dan LaCarte** and **Penny Semaia** are one and a half- to two years behind where they would have been, if they had stayed put. Experience is everything. But we won't graduate anybody this year, and that will help us—finally."

Expect to see junior **Bryan Anderson** (6-5, 305) at either right guard or center. He started last year at both spots, and his final placement will depend on two other Panthers. The first is junior **Chad Reed** (6-3, 280), a fine prospect who has struggled with shoulder surgery. If healthy, he'll handle the pivot, with Anderson at guard.

Then again, should redshirt freshman **Rob Petitti** (6-6, 320) continue to emerge, perhaps Anderson will play left guard.

"Our best prospect of all is Petitti," Harris said. "He's big and likes to play. He can move and likes to hit people. He's working to be good."

Another candidate in the middle is redshirt freshman **Justin Belarski** (6-3, 270), who is undersized and needs to grow. Right now, sophomore **Jon Schall** (6-4, 295) is the top candidate at left guard, but Semaia, a 6-5, 315-pound sophomore, has a lot of potential and could find his way into the starting lineup, should he re-acclimate himself to the position quickly.

Junior **Khiawatha Downey** (6-4, 305) returns at right tackle and has the potential to be a pretty good road grader. His backup should be junior **Joe Manganello** (6-4, 295).

The other side could be manned by sophomore **Matt Morgan** (6-7, 290), who is hoping to take over for graduated starter Mark Browne, although sophomore LaCarte (6-4, 280) could mount quite a challenge, particularly if he adds some muscle during the off-season.

2000 STATISTICS

Rushing offense	129.6	76
Passing offense	269.5	18
Total offense	399.1	39
Scoring offense	24.3	67
Net Punting	33.2	79
Punt returns	8.4	73
Kickoff returns	20.3	42
Rushing defense	99.7	17
Passing efficiency defense	109.1	35
Total defense	325.7	29
Scoring defense	19.1	22
Turnover margin	-11	101

Last column is ranking among Division I-A teams.

KICKERS

There is only one person worth knowing in this category, 6-2, 210-pound senior **Nick Lotz**, who has the potential to be one of the nation's best, provided he improves his consistency. Last year, he struggled from 30-39 yards, making just 5-of-8. That's odd, because he was perfect on his two tries from 40 or longer, including a 48-yarder. Lotz made 10-of-15 kicks last year, after converting 13-of-17 in '99.

"Nick got better in the spring," Harris said. "It's Nick's job, and he should be an outstanding player for us."

Lotz has a big leg and is quite a weapon on kickoffs, helping the Panthers hold enemy returners at bay. His backup is redshirt freshman **J.B. Gibboney** (5-9, 165), a walk-on.

DEFENSIVE LINE

Harris was extremely concerned about this group last year, but it surprised him, leading the Big East with 35 sacks and surrendering just 99.7 rushing yards per game. Even more impressive was the 2.6 yards per carry average the Panthers allowed.

That performance convinced Harris that it was time to free the offensive line exiles. He might regret that situation if the unit's injury list doesn't shorten. One person on whom Harris knows he can depend is senior end Knight (6-2, 230), who had 74 tackles, with an amazing 26 coming behind the line. That was a Big East record. Knight led the Panthers and was second in the league with 11 1/2 sacks, four of which came against Bowling Green. A former wide receiver who has bulked himself up, Knight is fast and dangerous off the edge.

"He is a big-time football player every day," Harris said.

Knight will be backed up by sophomore **Claude Harriott** (6-4, 235), who made 22 tackles in 2000 and has a bright future.

The other end spot should be handled by 6-4, 255-pound junior **Ryan Smith**, who missed spring practice after back surgery. He had 56 tackles, including eight behind the line, last year. If healthy, he teams with Knight to give the Panthers a pair of formidable ends. If not, expect rugged junior **Brian Guzek** (6-2, 245) to step up. He's not as fast as Smith, but he has a high-revving motor.

The tackle situation has potential—if everyone is healthy. Senior **Joe Conlin** (6-5, 280) had 44 tackles last year but has had problems with his shoulder. When available, he's a tough drain plug who can fight off double teams and make the plays. The other tackle is sophomore **Darrell McMurray** (6-4, 295), who was recruited to play offense but has made a successful switch to the other side.

"He'll provide a spark," Harris said.

A pair of redshirt freshmen, **Dan Stephens** (6-2, 270) and **Vince Crochunis** (6-4, 270), will also be in the rotation.

LINEBACKERS

The big story in this area is the emergence of senior **Brandon Williams** (6-0, 225), who has finally settled in at a position. For those who don't remember, Williams came to Pitt as a highly regarded running back and was expected to pile up the 1,000-yard seasons. That never happened, and he became something of a nomad within the program, switching from role to role before settling in at weak-side linebacker.

"I'm excited he found a spot," Harris said. "It's not his fault he had all those accolades [coming out of high school]. He tried to be the best football player he could be. He can run and make plays."

Williams will team with 6-1, 225-pound junior **Brian Beinecke** on the weak side. Beinecke made 52 tackles last year, with seven of them coming behind the line. He also had three sacks.

"He was all over the highlight tape last year," Harris said.

The two should give the Panthers plenty of pop and production on that side.

The middle could be interesting, too. Although senior **Ryan Gonsales** (6-2, 245) was listed as the starter coming out of spring drills, he could lose his position to junior **Gerald Hayes** (6-3, 240). Although Gonsales made 57 tackles last year, Harris wasn't happy with the leadership he provided and wants to see the senior put everything together this year.

"He went through a maturing experience last fall, and he didn't handle some situations very well," Harris said.

Hayes led the Panthers in tackles with 104 last year, including 10 behind enemy lines. A second-team All-Big East performer, Hayes could become a big-time player this year, either in the middle or on the strong side, where he wreaked havoc last year.

If Hayes makes the switch to the middle, look for 6-2, 245-pound sophomore **Lewis Moore** to work on the strong side. A special-teams standout last season, Moore is aggressive and quick. He just needs experience to become a major contributor.

Also vying for time in what is one of the league's deepest linebacking brigades is 6-2, 235-pound senior **Amir Purifoy**, who started in the middle last year and made 81 tackles, second on the team. His presence gives Harris and his defensive staff many different options and will allow the Panthers to tailor their personnel more to opponents' strengths.

DEFENSIVE BACKS

Harris is blunt when he describes Walker's 2000 season: "He didn't have as good a year as he did the year before," Harris said.

Fair enough, but there were some mitigating circumstances, like a knee injury that limited the 6-0, 195-pound junior to just seven games. But anybody who saw Pitt's bowl game knows what Walker can do. He had 15 tackles and forced two fumbles in a spectacular performance that could well be a harbinger of this year. If he's healthy, the hard-hitting Walker will be a major force in the league and could well earn first-team All-Big East honors.

He will be backed up by sophomore **Corey Humphries** (6-2, 205), who in Walker's absence made 34 tackles and started four times last year.

Senior **Mark Ponko** (5-10, 200) is the leading candidate at strong safety. He's backed up by **Gary Urschler**, a 5-10, 195-pound junior. Though neither is overwhelmingly fast or strong, each works extra hard to get it done.

"They're not extremely athletic, but they're quick, smart and give you everything in their tanks," Harris said.

They could also be pushed by **Tyrone Gilliard** (5-11, 175) from Valley Forge (Pa.) Military Academy and Princeton (W.Va.) High School. Gilliard is a mid-year signee who participated in spring drills.

"He has a chance," Harris said. "He likes to play, but time will tell."

The Panthers' cornerback situation wasn't great last year, but it should be improved this time. Especially worth watching is junior **Shawn Robinson** (6-1, 180), who was yo-yoed between wideout and the secondary before settling at the corner last year. All he did was pick off six passes. Now comfortable and experienced, he should provide considerable production.

The other side is sophomore **Shawntae Spencer** (6-2, 170), who made 45 tackles and picked off two passes last year. Expect to see sophomore **William Ferguson** (5-10, 185) and **Torrie Cox**, a 5-10, 185 junior with exceptional athletic ability, in the nickel and dime mix. Given his many options, it's no surprise Harris is optimistic about this area.

"I feel 100 percent better about the secondary this year," he said.

PUNTERS

The Panthers return both punters from last year, but the job appears to belong to sophomore **Andy Lee** (6-2, 195), who took over for **Jay Junko** during the final four games of 2000 and the bowl game. The key for Lee is to find the consistency that allows him to produce every time he punts. He averaged 39.2 yards per boot last year and has some strong performances, like his 42.6-yard average on five boots against West Virginia, and his 40.4-yard consistency on eight kicks, at Miami.

But he also had some games where he was below average, something that must be erased.

"We worked extremely hard on special teams during the spring," Harris said. "Andy needs to step up and be as good as he can be down after down."

Junko, a 6-4, 210-pound junior, averaged a mediocre 34.1 yards on 21 kicks. He started the year fairly well and did average 39.7 yards on three boots at Bowling Green, but he staggered after that, bottoming out with an average of 27.0 yards against Boston College and Virginia Tech, and is expected to be a reserve this year.

SPECIAL TEAMS

The Panthers are in pretty good shape here, thanks to good coverage units—a byproduct of the team's enhanced depth—and some fine speed in the return game. Bryant averaged 11.3 yards on 16 punt returns last year and is a threat to go long, while Rutherford, Levy and Cox have the speed to make big plays bringing back kicks.

Pitt blocked only one punt last year, a figure that must increase, although the Panthers didn't have any of their tries swatted away. And Pittsburgh did an excellent job in coverage, limiting rivals to 7.7 yards on punt returns and an average of 18.7 on kickoffs.

RECRUITING CLASS

The Panthers did a good job in this area, adding talent all over the roster, particularly at the skill positions and at linebacker.

Expect **Joe Dipre** (6-4, 241) from Cathedral Prep in Erie, Pa., and **Monroe Weekley** (6-3, 252) from Aliquippa (Pa.) High School to be future standouts at linebacker. Each is big and fast.

The running back coffers were fortified by the signings of **Marcus Furman** (5-8, 172) from Connellsville (Pa.) High School, James Johnson (6-1, 220) from H.D. Woodson High School in Capitol Heights, Md., and **Tim Murphy** (5-10, 230) from John R. Buchtel High School in Akron, Ohio. All three will get a look this year. Add in Jemison, who took part in spring drills, and you have a pretty formidable class.

Dale Williams (6-5, 290) from Cathedral Prep in Erie, Pa., is the best of three new offensive linemen, while **Thomas Smith** (6-4, 245) from Suitland High School in Capitol Heights, Md., and **Craig Akins** (6-6, 295) from Webster (N.Y.) High School are future contributors along the offensive front.

Erik Gill (6-5, 245) from Belle Vernon (Pa.) High School, is an outstanding tight end prospect, and **Bernad Lay** (6-1, 184) from Aliquippa (Pa.) High School has the talent to make an impact in the defensive backfield quickly.

BLUE RIBBON ANALYSIS

OFFENSE	B
SPECIAL TEAMS	B-
DEFENSE	B+
INTANGIBLES	B+

Even if Harris had wanted to shop his services around some after last season, he might have come back to Pittsburgh, if only to see how the story is going to turn out. With so much new construction around the program—on and off the field—it's almost impossible not to turn to the end of the book.

Harris has authored an impressive turnaround on the Hill, and it's time for a new chapter. We don't know if those pages include a return to national prominence, because the Panthers still have some mighty big questions. The biggest is along the offensive front, where there is talent and promise but not a lot of experience. It makes sense for Harris to worry about that group, because his young running backs will need some help. If the line isn't healthy and/or reliable, the Panther ground game could stagger.

That won't help quarterback Priestley much. He has talent, experience and knowledge, but if defenses know he's going to pass all the time, they'll load up and try to pound him. That's not the best thing for an injury-prone passer.

There are plenty of good things in Pittsburgh, though. Bryant is an outstanding receiver, and you can count on Harris to find many ways to get him the ball. The defense has plenty of front-line performers and good depth. In fact, the whole program's overall depth is much improved. That's perhaps the best part of the story. Pittsburgh isn't just loading up for one year. It's aiming for some stability.

The Panthers should be good for at least six wins this year, a total which could swell to eight or even nine if the line gets it together and Priestley is healthy. In a Big East that is rapidly improving, that would be quite an accomplishment. Pitt has a chance to be quite good again, and Harris ought to hang around long enough to enjoy it—no matter who calls.

(M.B.)

2000 RESULTS

Kent State	W	30-7	1-0
Bowling Green	W	34-16	2-0
Penn State	W	12-0	3-0
Rutgers	W	29-17	4-0
Syracuse	L	17-24	4-1
Boston College	W	42-26	5-1
Virginia Tech	L	34-37	5-2
North Carolina	L	17-20	5-3
Miami	L	7-35	5-4
Temple	W	7-0	6-4
West Virginia	W	38-28	7-4
Iowa St. (Insight.com)	L	29-37	7-5

Rutgers

LOCATION	**New Brunswick, NJ**
CONFERENCE	**Big East**
LAST SEASON	**3-8 (.273)**
CONFERENCE RECORD	**0-7 (8th)**
OFFENSIVE STARTERS RETURNING	**6**
DEFENSIVE STARTERS RETURNING	**7**
NICKNAME	**Scarlet Knights**
COLORS	**Red & White**
HOME FIELD	**Rutgers Stadium (41,500)**
HEAD COACH	**David Schiano (Bucknell '88)**
RECORD AT SCHOOL	**First Year**
CAREER RECORD	**First Year**
ASSISTANTS	**Bill Cubit (Delaware '75)** **Offensive Coordinator** **Paul Ferraro (Springfield '82)** **Defensive Coordinator** **Mike Miello (Rhode Island '66)** **Recruiting Coordinator/Running Backs** **Ben Albert (Massachusetts '95)** **Defensive Line** **Mario Cristobal (Miami '93)** **Offensive Tackles/Tight Ends** **Mark D'Onofrio (Penn State '92)** **Linebackers** **Darrell Hazell (Muskingum '86)** **Wide Receivers** **Scott Lakatos (Western Connecticut '88)** **Defensive Backs** **Joe Susan (Delaware '76)** **Offensive Line**
TEAM WINS (last 5 yrs.)	**2-0-5-1-3**
FINAL RANK (last 5 yrs.)	**87-92-73-98-88**
2000 FINISH	**Lost to Syracuse in regular-season finale.**

COACH AND PROGRAM

Now, it's up to one of their own. After wandering through the wilderness under the unsteady hand of West Coast offense-meister Terry Shea, Rutgers has turned to former Miami defensive coordinator and (most importantly) New Jersey native Greg Schiano to bring respectability and prosperity to the program. It's a big job. Some might say it's an impossible job.

Just not Schiano. The 34-year old is brimming with optimism, which either makes him crazy or incredibly sure of himself. Anybody who has paid close attention to the Rutgers program the last 20 years realizes that it is just a step or two ahead of the miserable standards set by perennial NCAA dogs Kansas State and Oregon State before they became powerhouses under other coaches who were brimming with optimism.

If the Wildcats and Beavers could make it to double-figure win seasons and BCS games, why can't the Knights?

That's what Schiano wants to know. From the moment he took over, on Dec. 2, one month to the day that athletic director Bob Mulcahy served Shea with his walking papers, Schiano has not talked about winning games. He has promised to win championships. He doesn't want to bring the Knights to just any bowl. He wants them playing in the BCS finale. Now, that kind of attitude might just land him in the laughing academy, to borrow a phrase from Tony Soprano, who incidentally filmed a promotional commercial with Schiano in a show of Jersey solidarity. But Schiano doesn't think so. He's not the kind of guy who looks for negatives. And when he sees them, he tries to change them around.

That's the kind of spirit the Knights need. That and a few dozen big-time football players. Schiano promises to get those, too. He didn't do too bad a job of it in his first recruiting class, convincing six all-state players to stay home and then grabbing a few speed guys from south Florida, his old stomping grounds.

It's no secret that New Jersey is filled with talent every year. It's also no secret that other programs around the country treat the Garden State as if it were a shopping mall. Need a great back? Just grab one. Quarterback, anyone? Here are three from which to choose. If Schiano can convince the best players in the state to join his team each year, then the Knights will be good. Just imagine what it would have been like in New Brunswick had Ron Dayne stayed home. And how good would the Rutgers offense look this season with Chris Simms at quarterback, or even Matt LoVecchio. That's just for starters. There are big-time players all over the country with Jersey roots, and it's a safe bet that only a small percentage of them even visited Rutgers, much less seriously considered the school.

Schiano believes that will change. Believes it has already changed. He brought a lot of Jersey guys onto his staff. He has improved relationships with the state's 300-plus high school coaches. He is tracking underclassmen, to make sure they know Rutgers is interested and interested early. This year's haul was pretty good. Schiano expects to do much better in the coming years, a belief that will pay off big on the field, should it become reality.

"I think everybody in New Jersey wants this to be a power," he said. "They want to have their own national power. They want to have a place where they go visit, where they say, 'Hey, I'm going to visit national champion Rutgers football.' Now, are they skeptical? I don't know if everybody understands the history totally, and there's some scar tissue from the past, but I think what we need to build upon with these guys is we're them. I'm them. I coached in high school here. I played in high school here. My family's here."

Schiano has come home, and he pledges to stick around for a while, not just turn the Knights around and then bolt for a better job. He's telling the recruits the same thing. Stay home and make Rutgers a winner. Commit to the program. Meanwhile, Schiano is trying to change the program's culture. It began during the off-season, with a conditioning program that had two goals: first to get everybody in great shape and second to change the losing attitude that had permeated the program. Both were accomplished.

Rutgers lost more than 2000 pounds of "goo," as the Knight coaches call it, an average of about 40 pounds per man. And by the end of spring practice, Schiano could see a more aggressive, confident team. It's hard to tell whether that will make a difference Sept. 8 at Miami, but it's a good first step.

Schiano plans to take many more steps during the next few years. Recruiting will improve. Wins will come. He promises championships. It's hard to spend any time with him and not believe it.

Schiano does not approach football with a zealot's enthusiasm, rather the direct confidence of a man who has experienced success before. His resume is pretty impressive. Make that very impressive. He spent time at Penn State. He coordinated the defense at Miami. He was with the Chicago Bears for three seasons. He even spent a season as a graduate assistant at Rutgers in 1989. Even though he's 34. Even though he hasn't coached a game as a full-fledged boss at any level, Schiano is clearly in charge at Rutgers. It's his program. It's his future. And he believes it's going to be bright.

The facilities, including a $6.1 million addition to the school's football complex, are up to par with the rest of the league. Now, it's up to Schiano to attract and develop the talent. He's confident it can be done.

"I thought if the university was committed to winning championships, then this job could be the best job in the country," Schiano said. "But if they're not, it was just going to remain as it was. And I didn't know that they were.

"But when I came up for an interview and met with Bob Mulcahy, I had a list of about 30 things I thought we needed to do here to turn this place around and make it a championship program—not just win enough games to get to a bowl game.

"They had already thought of most of them, and the ones they hadn't thought of, they were no problem."

2001 SCHEDULE

Aug.	30	@Buffalo
Sept.	8	@Miami
	15	California
	22	Virginia Tech
	29	Connecticut
Oct.	6	Syracuse
	13	@Temple
	20	Navy
Nov.	3	@West Virginia
	10	Pittsburgh
	17	Boston College

QUARTERBACKS

This cannot be considered a strength for the Knights. Gone is Mike McMahon, who despite completing just 49.7 percent of his throws last year (for 2,157 yards, 18 scores and 17 interceptions) was still picked in the fifth round of the NFL draft by the Detroit Lions.

His departure leaves the Knights with junior **Chad Schwenk** (6-2, 200) as the main man under center. In five games last year, Schwenk completed 45.3 percent of 75 passes for 330 yards, just one touchdown and four interceptions. His career numbers are a little better: 106-of-200 for 1,175 yards, four touchdowns and nine interceptions.

Schwenk is a perfect backup. He doesn't make awful decisions, but he doesn't make many things happen, either. But he's the best they have at Rutgers right now, at least among those who have some experience. That's not necessarily good news for a program that can't point to a dominant ground attack, either. Schwenk has a fair arm and is pretty mobile. He must become more accurate and consistent in order to help the Knights win.

"I really wanted someone to jump out and take hold of the position better than they did," Schiano said. "Chad is not overly talented at one thing, but he's a smart gamer. You can find ways to win with a guy like that. But it will be wide open this summer."

It's not as if Schwenk had a lot of competition in the spring. Running second is 6-2, 215-pound junior **Ted Trump**, a walk-on who came to school to play on the baseball team. He didn't attempt a pass last year.

The player the Knights were hoping would emerge during the spring was redshirt freshman **Chris Dapolito** (6-3, 215), who had a fine career at Jersey's Matawan High School.

Dapolito completed 102-of-196 passes for 1,793 yards and 15 scores as a senior and was expected to be the man on whom the Knights could rely for big things. He still might make them happen, but he has yet to prove he can be a starter yet. In fairness to Dapolito, Schwenk has seen considerable game action, but he isn't a front-line Big East quarterback.

Anybody watching Rutgers practice this year should keep a close eye on a pair of freshmen—**Chris Baker** (6-4, 200) from Marist High School in Jersey City, N.J., and **Ryan Cubit** (6-3, 195) from David Hickman High School in Columbia, Mo.

Cubit is the son of new Rutgers offensive coordinator Bill Cubit. He had committed to play at Clemson before his father moved north after being swept out at the University of Missouri with the rest of former coach Larry Smith's staff.

Cubit is accurate and strong and can run. Baker has a lot of the same qualities and showed the ability to run and pass well last year at Marist. Both have the ability to play down the road, provided they can get past Dapolito.

RUNNING BACKS

The Knights bring back a pair of starters here, including leading rusher **Dennis Thomas**, a 6-1, 225-pound senior. If Thomas can pick up where he left off at the end of last year, when he rushed for 331 yards in Rutgers' final three games, the Knights will be in good shape. Thomas gained 115 yards against West Virginia during the binge and had 127 the next week against Notre Dame. He closed the year by gaining 89 yards against Syracuse.

Thomas isn't a speedster, but he is consistent and has good hands. Last year, he caught 21 passes, fourth on the team. In the game against West Virginia, he had seven catches for 91 yards.

"Thomas has some talent, and at times this spring he looked real good; at other times, he didn't look so good," Schiano said. "To be a great back, you can't have off days."

Expect 6-2, 240-pound senior **Seth Stanton** to begin the year as the main fullback. He works hard, contributes mightily on special teams and can block. But it shouldn't be a surprise to anybody if he is supplanted—and quickly —by freshman **Rikki Cook** (6-1, 235) from Montclair (N.J.) High School. Cook was generally considered the best offensive player in the state last year and is the prize catch of Schiano's first recruiting class. He had committed to Virginia, but began to waver when coach George Welsh decided to retire.

Schiano jumped at the opportunity to pitch Cook, and was able to convince him that playing in front of friends and family in Jersey was a good thing. Last year, Cook gained 2,152 yards and scored 28 times. He could well be a T.J. Duckett/Ron Dayne type halfback/fullback hybrid who can handle all the duties of both positions.

Cook has enough speed to blow past defenders, as evidenced by his nine scoring runs of greater than 40 yards. He's a hard worker, dedicated lifter and somebody who should make an immediate impact.

"I think he can be real good," Schiano said. "You never know when you make the change from high school to college, but he's a big back who can run. I don't care if you're playing little league, anybody who gains 2,000 yards is doing something."

Other backs of note are 6-0, 195-pound senior halfback **Jason Ohene**, who gained 304 yards last year and caught 10 passes and senior **Ravon Anderson** (5-10, 195), who joined the Knights last year after transferring from North Carolina. Two more freshmen, **Marcus Jones** (6-0, 195) from St. Augustine (Fla.) High School and **Clarence Pittman** (5-10, 185) from Northwestern High School in Miami, Fla., could make some noise early.

Jones gained 1,769 yards last year and averaged 10 yards a carry to earn 5A (second-largest classification) all-state honors. Pittman also topped the 1,700-yard mark and scored 23 times. Both have good speed and the ability to knock some people over.

WIDE RECEIVERS/TIGHT ENDS

You will notice that most descriptions of these positions in *Blue Ribbon* begin with the wideouts, but Rutgers is a little different. The Knights' corps of receivers is relatively ordinary, thanks to the graduation of big producers Errol Johnson (46 catches) and Walter King (26).

The man here lines up at tight end. Although senior **L.J. Smith** (6-4, 225) sat out during the spring to work on his grades and to fight a minor injury, he will be ready come fall and should give Rutgers a big weapon in the passing game. Smith caught 34 passes for 374 yards and scored once last year. He's a big, strong target who has added about 15 pounds of muscle to his frame but still has a graceful gait and soft hands.

Smith should be able to get up the seam for the Knights, while still providing a safety net for Schwenk in the short zones. He caught six balls for 51 yards and his lone score against Villanova, had five catches against Temple and caught four balls on two other occasions. He's one of the best in the league.

Smith is backed up by senior **Rob Ring** (6-4, 250), who doesn't have Smith's pass-catching abilities but is a good blocker.

Even though senior **Delrico Fletcher** (6-1, 200) caught just six passes last year, he came out of spring drills as the starter at split end. Fletcher missed the '98 and '99 seasons concentrating on academics and rehabbing injuries, so this year marks the first season he can gather some momentum on the field. He's quick and athletic and could have a breakout season, provided he stays healthy and hits the books.

His partner in the starting lineup is junior **Antoine Lovelace** (6-2, 185), who last year caught four passes for a 19.5-yard average. Like Fletcher, Lovelace has all the tools to make an impact. He could be even more dangerous, thanks to his speed. He has nine career receptions, and three have been for touchdowns, so there is some potential there.

"I think Lovelace has a chance to be a big-play guy," Schiano said. "Fletcher just outworks people. He's a leader and was our most consistent guy there this spring."

The primary backups are junior **Aaron Martin** (6-4, 205) and senior **David Stringer** (6-0, 205). Martin averaged 18.8 yards on 13 catches last year and is a big target, while Stringer, who became eligible last year after transferring from North Carolina State, caught 12 passes and scored three times.

Josh Hobbs, a 6-2, 205-pound junior who had 17 receptions last year, will also be a factor, although he sat out spring drills because of some disciplinary problems. That hampered his ability to make a good first impression, but he'll no doubt work his way into the rotation come fall.

No description of any position at Rutgers this year would be complete without mentioning some of the freshmen. A pair of Florida products, **Jerry Andre** (6-1, 175) from Miami Lakes High School in Hialeah and **Tres Moses** (5-10, 180) from Atlantic Community High School in Delray Beach, bring the speed Rutgers needs to make defenses drop off the line. Moses averaged an eye-popping 23.7 yards on his 38 receptions last year and scored 15 times, while Andre caught 19 balls and averaged 24.4 yards on each.

OFFENSIVE LINE

The Scarlet Knight coaches spent a lot of time during the spring trying to find the right combination up front. It still remains to be seen whether they were successful. The Knights retain four starters from last year's line, with all-Big East guard Rich Mazza the only loss.

One of the holdovers was supposed to be 6-4, 280-pound center Jeremy Womack, who started all 11 games last year after making the move from guard. But he isn't with the team any more, having decided to leave when Schiano took over.

There is some experience along the line. Senior left guard **Travis Mills** (6-3, 305) was last year's starter at right guard, but he had to sit out the last seven games when it was determined that Rutgers had misapplied an NCAA rule in Mills' earlier transfer to the school from Garden City (Kansas) Community College. Mills is eligible now and should be a mainstay.

His fellow starting guard is 6-5, 300-pound junior **Brian Duffy**, a tough player who added 15 pounds of bulk during the off-season and could become a good one. In reserve are junior **Trohn Carswell** (6-5, 288) and sophomore **Jacob Garner** (6-6, 276).

The middle belongs to senior **Mike Esposito** (6-4, 291), for now. He took over for Mills at right guard for the end of the 2000 season and showed some promise. His biggest success may have come during the off-season, when he trimmed nearly 25 pounds from his frame. That should make him a more agile pivot, something that will no doubt help in pass protection. He's backed up by sophomore **Mike Williamson** (6-5, 289).

"Espo has certain limitations, but he'll outwork you," Schiano said.

One fixture is senior left tackle **Howard Blackwood** (6-4, 301), who started nine games last year and has the potential to be a good one. He bulked up considerably during the off-season, adding those 25 pounds that Esposito lost. He has the potential to be a good back side bodyguard for Schwenk.

On the right side, sophomore **Krzystof Kaczorowski** (6-6, 280) has plenty of potential and substantial room for growth. His trouble could be that he's undersized for a position that often goes to a behemoth. Expect to see Carswell and sophomore **Rob Dinsmore** (6-5, 276) in the rotation at tackle.

Don't be surprised to see a freshman find his way into the mix somewhere along the line, even if it's harder for players that young to work well up front. The Knights need talent. Among three newcomers, **Mike Clancy** (6-4, 290), from Toms River (N.J.) North High School, has the best shot to make an immediate impact. Also expected to be in the picture by early fall is 6-5, 320-pound sophomore guard **Rich McManis**, who is still recovering from a knee injury.

"Our problem with the line is zero depth," Schiano said.

2000 STATISTICS

Rushing offense	105.5	94
Passing offense	228.9	39
Total offense	334.5	82
Scoring offense	21.2	85
Net Punting	30.5	104
Punt returns	9.8	50
Kickoff returns	18.7	80
Rushing defense	222.2	111
Passing efficiency defense	129.8	93
Total defense	423.4	100
Scoring defense	36.3	108
Turnover margin	-7	93

Last column is ranking among Division I-A teams.

KICKERS

The Knights need senior **Steve Barone** (5-11, 170) to find some consistency after a 2000 season that featured trouble every time he attempted a placement longer than 29 yards. Barone was 6-of-13 for the season and was a combined 4-of-10 from 30 yards or longer. Distance isn't the problem. Barone needs to upgrade his accuracy. He has the potential to be solid, as evidenced by the 41-yarder and 40-yarder he made in '99 and the 51-yard kick he drilled against Navy in '98.

His backup is sophomore walk-on **Ryan Sands** (6-0, 225), who has yet to try a kick in game competition.

DEFENSIVE LINE

When Schiano was at Miami, he had the luxury of quick, big, aggressive linemen who got up field and disrupted enemy attacks. It was almost easy for the linebackers to make plays with all the commotion the front four created.

That's something Schiano wants to recreate in New Brunswick. He is an attacking coach by nature, despite his measured personality, and he will be looking to turn people loose along the defensive line. The question is whether the Knights have anybody who can create some havoc.

There are some familiar names up front, although no one should get comfortable, not with freshmen **Davon Clark** (6-4, 285) from Paterson (N.J.) Catholic High School and **Ryan Neill** (6-3, 225) from Wayne Hills (N.J.) coming in. Both could play right away.

Among the holdovers, the most interesting player is senior **Torrance Heggie** (6-5, 230), who has been moved from rush linebacker to left end. Heggie played the last part of the 2000 season with a painful groin injury but still made 64 tackles, 10 of which came behind the line, and posted five sacks. He's quick and has the size to make some plays. He also has a large wingspan that makes him a capable pass blocker. Heggie enters his second year at Rutgers, after transferring from Ventura (Calif.) Junior College.

The other end is senior **Will Burnett** (6-4, 275), who registered three sacks in seven games last year before suffering a season-ending knee injury. Now healthy, he has the potential to stand out, thanks to a good combination of size, speed and strength. If he can last a full year, Burnett could be a surprise.

Senior **Marcus Perry** (6-1, 271) made 24 tackles last year and started five games. He provides some pretty good depth at end. Also in the mix is sophomore Jeff Olsen (6-6, 276), who added 30 pounds of muscle to his substantial frame. He blocked two kicks last year against Syracuse.

The Knights are not huge inside, and that could be a problem. It sure was last year, when opponents averaged 4.3 yards per carry against Rutgers and scored 37 ground touchdowns.

Senior **Greg Pyszczymuka** (6-2, 264) started 10 games last year and made 39 tackles, and senior **Bill Tulloch** (6-3, 268) had 2 1/2 sacks last season. Neither is all-league caliber, but their experience gives them a chance to be solid performers.

Their primary reserves are sophomores **Ron Jenerette** (6-4, 278) and **Marty Pyszczymuka** (6-2, 262), both of whom saw limited action last year. It's possible that Clark, an aggressive all-state choice, could find his way into the mix, too.

"Between the Pyszczymuka brothers, I hope we can get one good player," Schiano said. "They're not every-down guys, because they're not that big."

LINEBACKERS

If the shoulders, knees and transcripts are healed among this bunch, Rutgers could be in pretty good shape here.

"The linebackers are the strength of our team," Schiano said. "We've got some depth there."

We start with junior middle man **Raheem Orr** (6-4, 240), who made it through spring drills without any academic incidents, a good sign, because he missed the last two seasons concentrating on the books. Orr smacked people around last year as a member of the scout team and would like to bring that nastiness to the varsity this season. If he's available, he provides a big upgrade for the defense.

If Orr doesn't go, sophomore **Jeremy Campbell** (6-2, 225) will get a look. He has potential but no experience.

"Orr can be a dominant player in this league," Schiano said.

It looked like junior **Brian Bender** (6-2, 228) was on his way to a pretty good season last fall, after registering 11 tackles in week two against Buffalo. But a shoulder injury sustained in practice ended his year after only four games. He's back on the outside and has the quickness to make plays sideline-to-sideline.

His counterpart on the other side is 5-11, 220-pound junior **Gary Brackett**, a former walk-on who plays tough and makes plenty of tackles. Brackett had 40 stops last year, and while he won't overwhelm anybody with speed or size, he gives plenty of effort. Schiano likes those guys.

Junior **Nate Leonard** (6-1, 225) started the first four games of '00 on the inside and averaged

7 1/2 tackles per contest, before tearing his ACL. He's back but will begin summer camp as a reserve. He does, however, have potential and can get to the ball, if healthy. He has also been plagued by shoulder trouble during his time at Rutgers. Another outside candidate is sophomore **Bill Hambrecht** (6-2, 227), who made 40 tackles last year and has some quickness.

The newcomers to watch here are **Cedric Brown** (6-2, 240) from Hackensack (N.J.) High School, who made 17 tackles for loss last year, **Piana Lukabu** (6-3, 215) from Colonia (N.J.) High School, who was a two-way prep terror, and **Ishmael Medley** (5-11, 230) from Hun School/Elizabeth (N.J.) High School, a big-time hitter.

DEFENSIVE BACKS

Three starters return here, but the staff did some shaking and baking during the spring, and there will be a few faces in new places this year.

The cornerbacks return to their customary positions. Juniors **Brandon Haw** (6-0, 180) and **DeWayne Thompson** (5-9, 185) started last year but need to be more productive. The tandem accounted for just one interception (Thompson's) all year. That can't happen again. If the Knights are to pressure the pocket with the front seven, they need corners who can press cover.

Expect to see senior **Tony Berry** (6-1, 190) as the primary nickel back, with **Nate Jones**, a 5-10, 170-pound sophomore, in on the dime package.

Schiano and his staff are no doubt excited to see what freshman **Eddie Grimes** (6-0, 170), from Hialeah (Fla.) Senior High School, can do. He's a hitter who can also lock down receivers.

Another Florida speedster arriving in late summer is **Jarvis Johnson** (5-11, 190) from South Dade High School in Homestead. Both could help.

"I think we've got three good corners in Thompson, Haw and Berry," Schiano said. "But it doesn't matter how good your secondary is if you can't get a pass rush."

Senior **Tarell Freeney** (6-0, 200) started at linebacker last year and made 82 tackles. Schiano moved him to strong safety for this year, where he earned a starting berth in '99 before tearing a knee ligament, and Freeney is now running second team, behind junior **Nate Colon** (5-11, 190). Colon started eight times last year and made 48 tackles. He's a big hitter who can get to the ball. Starting at free safety should be junior **Shawn Seabrooks** (5-10, 190), who had 57 stops last year.

Senior **Ben Martin** (6-0, 205) will back him up. Freeney made 82 tackles as a linebacker last year and knows how to get to the ball. He will see plenty of time.

PUNTERS

Rutgers describes junior **Mike Barr** (6-3, 225) as "steady," and we guess that's so. But a "steady" average of 36.2 yards isn't going to get it done on a winning team. Although Barr has a great physique and played linebacker in high school, he doesn't have the ability to knock them high and deep. On a team that could struggle offensively, Barr must step up and pin some rivals back deep in their territory.

It's not like the Knights have much of a choice. Junior walk-on **Todd Domlas** (6-2, 240), Sands and sophomore **Andrew Carton** (6-2, 185), another non-scholarship player, have zero punts between them. Dapolito punted in high school and could get a look, if times get particularly tough.

SPECIAL TEAMS

Rutgers fans had to smile when Schiano said he would be overseeing the special teams personally. The Knights had four punts and a placement try blocked last year. That can't happen again.

As Schiano and his staff recruit more talented players, the Knights should be able to prevent repeats. And they should be able to create some special-teams mayhem of their own. Rutgers blocked a pair of punts last year, but that can improve, too, particularly if Schiano decides to use starters on the special teams, a la Virginia Tech and Miami.

The return crew returns en masse, beginning with Thomas, who averaged a strong 22.4 yards bringing back kickoffs last year. Stringer is another return man with the ability to crack one open. Junior **Sean Carty** (6-0, 185) had a 10.1-yard average returning punts last year, and that's good enough. Fletcher was not so strong, averaging 6.4 yards.

While Schiano would like to see his special teams swat away a few more kicks and punts, he would be happier if the enemy return yardage shrank. Rutgers allowed 23.1 yards on kicks and 9.8 on punts. Those numbers must improve, especially if the kickers and punters aren't going to be sending missiles into orbit.

RECRUITING CLASS

Some might laugh when the Knights crow about their "Top-50" class, but considering where Rutgers has been, that's a pretty good start, particularly for a staff that had just two months to sell itself.

Just about all the main players have been mentioned already, but a few warrant further review. Cook is the gem of the bunch, and his decision to commit paved the way for several other in-state performers who believed the talented fullback validated Schiano and his staff.

Quarterbacks Baker and Cubit have potential, quick feet and good size, while new targets Andre and Moses have the chance to be big-play types. Jones can be a productive ball carrier and Clancy looks to be a future standout along the offensive line, while Clark has a bright future on the other side of the ball.

Schiano used his south Florida connections to grab some much-needed speed in the defensive backfield—Grimes and Johnson. Linebackers Brown, Lukabu and Medley won't have to wait too long for a chance to play. Schiano wants to lock down New Jersey and harvest speed in south Florida, and this class was a good start toward that ultimate goal.

BLUE RIBBON ANALYSIS

OFFENSE	C
SPECIAL TEAMS	C
DEFENSE	B-
INTANGIBLES	A-

The decision to hire Schiano was great one by Mulcahy. Even though he doesn't have the name recognition of some of the other candidates out there, and he hasn't been a head coach before, the 34-year old has all the ingredients (and then some) to lead the Knights to prosperity.

Even if you don't believe in Schiano's championship declarations, it's impossible not to believe that he can make Rutgers respectable—at worst.

The key is how much of the Jersey talent he can grab each year. Even though this year's crop is good, there were some big-timers that got away. In fairness to Schiano, many of those were gone before he got started. But the fact remains that Rutgers must keep players like them home in the future, in order to move from a team that chases a low-level berth to one that can play with the better teams in the league.

Trouble is, with schools like Boston College, Pittsburgh and West Virginia on the rise, and Miami and Virginia Tech already at the top, it's going to be a difficult climb. Schiano, however, seems to be the perfect Sherpa to guide the program up the mountain.

Just don't expect a whole lot this year. Rutgers will play harder, more exciting and smarter football. That's a given. Whether that translates to wins, particularly in conference, is another story. The quarterback situation is shaky, the offensive line needs work, and there are precious few playmakers on offense. The defense will be better, but the front four lacks a monster capable of mandating a double team every play.

If Rutgers somehow makes it to five wins this year, Schiano deserves serious coach-of-the-year consideration. But he's not looking for that kind of acclaim. He's thinking big, and that means the big picture. If Rutgers plays right and hard this year and eliminates some of its historical gaffes, he will be happy—for now.

The long-term goal is clear: keep 'em home and teach 'em to win. Do that, and there could be some real success surrounding Rutgers football for the first time in decades. Hey, if Kansas State and Oregon State did it, why can't Rutgers? That's Schiano's question, and he thinks he has the answer.

(M.B.)

2000 RESULTS

Villanova	W	34-21	1-0
Buffalo	W	59-0	2-0
Virginia Tech	L	0-49	2-1
Pittsburgh	L	17-29	2-2
Miami	L	6-64	2-3
Temple	L	14-48	2-4
Navy	W	28-21	3-4
Boston College	L	13-42	3-5
West Virginia	L	24-31	3-6
Notre Dame	L	17-45	3-7
Syracuse	L	21-49	3-8

Syracuse

LOCATION	**Syracuse, NY**
CONFERENCE	**Big East**
LAST SEASON	**6-5 (.545)**
CONFERENCE RECORD	**4-3 (t-3rd)**
OFFENSIVE STARTERS RETURNING	**8**
DEFENSIVE STARTERS RETURNING	**6**
NICKNAME	**Orangemen**
COLORS	**Orange & Blue**
HOME FIELD	**Carrier Dome (49,550)**
HEAD COACH	**Paul Pasqualini (Penn St. '72)**
RECORD AT SCHOOL	**81-36-1 (10 years)**
CAREER RECORD	**115-53-1 (15 years)**

ASSISTANTS

Jerry Azzinaro (American International '81), Defensive Line/Recruiting Coordinator
Steve Bush (Southern Connecticut '81) Quarterbacks
George DeLeone (Connecticut '70) Offensive Coordinator/Offensive Line
Steve Dunlap (West Virginia '76) Linebackers
Dennis Goldman (Southern Connecticut '71) Wide Receivers
Chris Rippon (Southern Connecticut '82),

Defensive Coordinator
Brian Stewart (Northern Arizona '85)
Defensive Backs
David Walker (Syracuse '93)
Running Backs
Chris White (Colby '90)
Tight Ends/Special Teams Coordinator

TEAM WINS (last 5 yrs.)	**9-9-8-7-6**
FINAL RANK (last 5 yrs.)	**18-29-27-51-37**
2000 FINISH	**Beat Rutgers in regular-season finale.**

COACH AND PROGRAM

Coaches always say that they don't make their schedules. How else would Colorado have ended up with last year's death march (Colorado State, at USC, Washington, Kansas State, at Texas A&M)? You can't tell us Gary Barnett wanted to start the year like that. And Bob Davie can't be too happy that his Fighting Irish have road trips to Nebraska, Texas A&M and Purdue in their first four weeks, with a visit from Michigan State added, just for fun. But that's the way it goes. Line 'em up and play 'em.

That's Paul Pasqualoni's mantra, even if the above "Team Wins (last five years)" category doesn't exactly indicate any real degree of happiness with a schedule that isn't exactly constructed with a reversal of fortune in mind.

You get the impression that the close-cropped 'Cuse coach might have ambled into athletic director Jake Crouthamel's office and asked whether he was trying to get rid of his sideline boss, after 10 years of service.

Take a close look.

Syracuse plays both Tennessee and Auburn. Its non-conference "easy" games are visits from perennial bowl participant East Carolina and Central Florida, which beat Alabama last year. In Tuscaloosa. Worse still, Syracuse visits Miami and Virginia Tech, the Big East's two best teams.

But it's not all Crouthamel's fault, or even the league's. Pasqualoni can blame his players, too. In addition to the aforementioned killers, Syracuse will meet Georgia Tech in the Kickoff Classic in August. The Yellow Jackets return a host of starters and have one of the nation's emerging stars in quarterback George Godsey. Maybe the Orange players are in with Crouthamel in trying to get rid of Pasqualoni. Somebody call Oliver Stone. It looks like we have one heckuva conspiracy theory here.

Then again, maybe not. The Orangemen didn't go to a bowl game last year, so they wanted to do a little something special for the start of the 2001 campaign. Because there are 24 players on the Syracuse roster from New Jersey, it's only natural that they might want to play in their home state, before family and friends. Don't think that fact wasn't lost on the Kickoff Classic folks, who no doubt envisioned fat ticket sales to the Orange folks. (An aside: it also might help, although there is no concrete proof, that New Jersey has towns named "Orange" and "South Orange.") Whatever the case, don't think for a second that Pasqualoni was out stumping for a trip to East Rutherford.

"We have an unbelievably tough schedule, and I was trying to talk them out of it," he said. "I told them we were going to Tennessee [Sept. 1], so we already had a big opener. But I don't worry about the schedule. I coach every day, and I enjoy the kids in the program. They're a good group of kids."

By this time, there are probably some Syracuse fans who would not like to see Pasqualoni coaching every day. The Orangemen didn't play in a bowl last year, despite their 6-5 record. It had to be particularly galling to watch Syracuse lose to Cincinnati and absorb a 17-point beating from East Carolina. Even though Syracuse finished 4-3 in the Big East, tied for third, it continued to slip from its once-lofty perch. Pasqualoni deserves considerable credit for following popular coach Dick MacPherson and authoring a winning percentage of 68.8, quite a strong number.

But that doesn't mean he isn't feeling some heat. Today's college football world doesn't reward past success, unless you are a living legend, like Joe Paterno. Then, it's OK to finish 5-7. There are enough true believers to carry your name into battle and fight off the critics. But Pasqualoni doesn't have that, and that makes the 2001 season a vital one. Winning six or seven games might be enough for him to hang onto his job, but it won't endear him to the masses, either. Although Pasqualoni points out with pride —and rightly so—that 13 of the 22 seniors on this year's roster have already graduated, the hard, cold facts are that diplomas don't bring in bowl revenues and don't secure TV appearances. Wins do, and the Orangemen need to accumulate more than six this year.

That could happen, although the schedule doesn't make it seem too likely. Tennessee is probably going to be a top 10 team. Auburn is still dangerous, even if running back Rudi Johnson left a year early. East Carolina and Central Florida are potential wins, but don't go looking for deep backups or walk-ons to get any playing time against the Pirates and Golden Knights. Those games should be pretty close. As for the Big East, well, devoted readers of this publication will know that there aren't too many layups around the circuit anymore, now that Temple has its beak pointed in the right direction, and Greg Schiano is in the process of turning Rutgers into a full-fledged Division I-A school.

So, what will the Orangemen do? A lot depends on the quarterback spot. In fact, the whole season may well depend on whether Pasqualoni can get quality, consistent production from either **Troy Nunes** or **Robin Anderson**.

Perhaps he will have to turn to touted freshman **Cecil Howard**. Whatever the case, it's time for somebody to step up and carry on the recent tradition of fine 'Cuse quarterbacks that has included Don McPherson, Marvin Graves and Donovan McNabb, to name a few. With so many offensive linemen returning, a passel of skill position performers that should provide plenty of thrills and a defense that needs a little help along the front seven but certainly has potential, Syracuse has everything else to be good. Good enough to beat Tennessee, Auburn, Miami or Virginia Tech? Maybe not. But 8-4 wouldn't be so bad, particularly after last year.

Pasqualoni may not like that schedule, but it could help lower the expectations a little bit and set him up for some success. At least that's the glass-is-half-full version. You can imagine the other side, even if Pasqualoni doesn't want to.

2001 SCHEDULE

Aug.	26	Georgia Tech (Kick-Off Classic)
Sept.	1	@Tennessee
	8	Central Florida
	15	East Carolina
	22	Auburn
Oct.	6	@Rutgers
	13	@Pittsburgh
	20	Temple
	27	@Virginia Tech
Nov.	10	West Virginia
	17	@Miami
	24	Boston College

QUARTERBACKS

There are plenty of candidates for the starting job here, but like the 2000 presidential election, none of them might be particularly right for the job. Somebody has to play under center, but Pasqualoni has no idea whether he will be able to hand the controls to one person full-time, or if he will have to rotate two or even three players throughout the whole season. You can bet that won't be a recipe for success.

Right now, it appears as if Nunes, a 6-2, 185-pound junior, is the frontrunner, although his lead is precarious, at best. Nunes relieved Anderson in the season finale against Rutgers last year and completed 5-of-7 passes for 94 yards and scored once on the ground in a 49-21 win that featured 42 second-half points by the Orangemen.

Nunes completed 94-of-154 passes for 1,366 yards, eight scores and 14 interceptions last year. He threw for 221 yards and a touchdown against Cincinnati and 279 yards and a pair of scores in the overtime win against Pittsburgh. Nunes has a pretty good arm, but he isn't always as accurate as Pasqualoni would like. He also isn't that dangerous a runner, as evidenced by his 1.4-yard average per carry in 2000.

"Troy had some very good games last year," Pasqualoni said. "He had an exceptional game against Brigham Young (10-for-11, 228 yards, two touchdowns) and played well against Pittsburgh. He had some inconsistencies, too. His Boston College game was not a good performance (9-for-22, 134 yards). The biggest priority in selecting a quarterback is production. It's not who looks good or throws the ball faster or harder."

Anderson started the last four games of the 2000 season, but he faltered early against Rutgers and was pulled. The 6-1, 242-pound sophomore completed 42-of-91 passes (46.2 percent) for 512 yards and two scores but tossed five interceptions. His biggest game was an 18-for-33 performance against West Virginia that included 203 yards, two touchdowns and 64 yards rushing in a 31-27 win in Morgantown. Not bad for a freshman's first start. But Anderson didn't do so well after that, and Pasqualoni replaced him with Nunes against the Scarlet Knights.

"That was a lights-out performance against West Virginia," Pasqualoni said. "But he didn't play well after that. Robin is a great athlete, but he needs to be more consistent and productive."

Anderson may be better suited for the Orangemen's multiple offense, but Nunes is a steadier hand on the throttle—usually. Both had better be on the lookout for Howard (6-2, 215) from McKeesport (Pa.) Area High School, whom Tom Lemming rated the fourth-best quarterback prospect in the country. He rushed for 1,383 yards and 18 touchdowns as a senior but attempted only 49 passes all year, completing but 18, for 302 yards.

"He's an awfully good athlete, but he's a true freshman," Pasqualoni said. "It's difficult for a true freshman to come in and practice only 29 times and play."

None of the aforementioned quarterbacks will have to worry about senior Madei Williams, who saw extremely limited action last year. Williams, who didn't come out first or second on the depth chart, decided to transfer to Southern Illinois, a Division I-AA school. NCAA rules allow him to play right away for the Salukis, so Williams will close his college career in the action, rather than on the sideline.

RUNNING BACKS

There is no shortage of candidates here,

either, beginning with senior **James Mungro** (5-9, 215), who rushed for 797 yards last year while splitting time with Dee Brown (1,031), who has graduated. Mungro averaged an impressive 6.9 yards per carry and scored seven touchdowns. He clearly has the talent to be a first-rate back, but he must be ready to play every down. He came to Syracuse as a highly regarded prospect and was expected to be a big-time performer almost immediately.

While his 1,699 career yards and 15 touchdowns are nothing to sneer at, there were many who believe that should be a one-year total, rather than a three-season cumulative.

Mungro has great speed and has the power to stick it up the middle. He rushed for 155 yards on 15 carries against Boston College, 136 yards and two scores in the win over Temple and 119 yards and two touchdowns against Brigham Young.

Unfortunately, he gained just 387 in the other seven games. (He missed the Buffalo game because of a violation of team policy.) Mungro could be an All-Big East-caliber back, but he must be ready to go every game.

"James had a good spring and needs to put himself in position to have a good summer camp," Pasqualoni said.

When Mungro doesn't get the ball, expect to see sophomore **Diamond Ferri** (5-10, 204) carrying it. He is even faster than Mungro and capable of big plays. All he needs is a little more experience and confidence. Ferri gained 101 yards on 20 carries last year, with a 49-yard, one-touchdown performance against Buffalo his high-water mark.

"He's very explosive, very fast and physically tough," Pasqualoni said.

Also in the mix are redshirt freshman **Walter Reyes** (5-11, 202) and junior **Barry Baker** (6-0, 195). Baker is an intriguing prospect. He played defense last year and missed the '99 season because of academic problems. As a high school player he scored 77 career touchdowns and rushed for 4,050 yards.

The fullback situation could be the best in the nation, as far as depth and versatility. It starts with sixth-year senior **Kyle Johnson** (6-1, 238), who earned an extra year of eligibility after breaking his fibula in the 2000 season-opener. He was redshirted way back in '96, played three more seasons—with a 157-yard, three-touchdown '99 campaign his best performance—and is now ready for full-time action after rehabbing his injured leg. He didn't do much during the spring, other than jog, but he is a good short-yardage runner and excellent blocker.

Junior **Chris Davis** goes 5-11, 230 and is described by Pasqualoni as "physically as gifted as any fullback we've had here."

Davis gained 86 yards and scored three times last year and should get a good chance to show off his talents. He had better be ready, because the Orangemen brought in yet another fullback this year, sophomore **Thump Belton** (6-0, 221). Belton took a circuitous route to Syracuse, moving from West Charlotte (N.C.) High School to Northeast Mississippi Community College to the Orange last winter. Belton rushed for 650 yards last year, after missing the '99 season with a knee injury.

"Thump is an excellent fullback, but we have to give him time to learn," Pasqualoni said.

WIDE RECEIVERS/TIGHT ENDS

Sometimes, it can be traumatic for a team to lose its top pass-catcher, but when that man (Pat Woodcock) made just 29 catches, the wound can mend more easily. Syracuse has a good stable of experienced receivers but needs its quarterbacks to become more adept at finding them.

Leading the way is 6-2, 186-pound senior **Malik Campbell**, a former quarterback and basketball player who has decided to concentrate full-time on wide receiver. He caught 26 balls last year and scored once. Expect Campbell to provide a strong possession weapon for the Orange. He isn't going to break too many loose, but he should be more productive than he was in 2000, if only because he is now devoted to one sport.

Starting opposite him could be senior **Maurice Jackson** (5-8, 169), who averaged 16.9 yards on 20 catches last year. Jackson has the speed to make trouble for opponents downfield and should team with explosive junior **David Tyree** (6-1, 197) to give the 'Cuse a couple of deep threats.

Though Tyree caught just 14 passes last year, he averaged 23.8 yards per reception and scored three times. Tyree also blocked three kicks. He caught two balls for 88 yards and a pair of scores against Pittsburgh and had a 40-yard reception against Temple. This could be the year Tyree shines.

He may have some company in sophomore **Johnnie Morant** (6-4, 218), who was expected to be an instant game-breaker last year but played in just three games and didn't catch a ball.

"Morant has a much better feel for what we expect him to do," Pasqualoni said.

An X factor could be redshirt freshman **Andre Fontenette** (6-1, 216), who has good size and impressed coaches during the spring.

The tight end spot belongs to returning senior starter **Graham Manley** (6-3, 255), who caught 11 passes last year but made a huge jump from his sophomore season. Manley is a good blocker who caught three passes on three different occasions last year. Backing him up are senior **Jeremie Frazier** (6-1, 246) and sophomore **Lenny Cusumano** (6-2, 242).

OFFENSIVE LINE

While there are plenty of familiar names along the rest of the offensive unit, this group is the most experienced en masse and should help some of the players who must step up this year do so. Although none of them received any All-Big East honors last year, the line will feature four senior starters and has a chance to be cohesive, thanks to the experience contained in it.

"With five returning players and four starters, we have a chance to have a good offense," Pasqualoni said.

The new starter is 6-5, 307-pound senior right tackle **Giovanni DeLoatch**, who played in eight games last year and started the season finale against Rutgers. The other bookend is 6-4, 296-pound senior **P.J. Alexander**, who switched to left tackle from center last spring and started the 10 games in which he played. Backing them up are redshirt freshman **Adam Terry** (6-7, 291) and sophomore **Kevin Sampson** (6-4, 277).

The middle belongs to sophomore **Nick Romeo** (6-1, 292), who started all 11 games last year after redshirting in '99. Romeo was a highly decorated prep performer who has the chance to become a standout. Backing him up is 6-2, 292-pound sophomore **Chris Buda**.

Two more seniors will be playing guard. **Sean O'Connor** (6-3, 293) is on the left, although he did play one game at left tackle last year. The right side belongs to **Joe Burton** (6-5, 287), who played both tackle and guard last year. Their main reserves are redshirt freshman **Matt Tarullo** (6-5, 311) and junior **Erik Kaloyanides** (6-4, 298).

Tarullo has an especially bright future at Syracuse.

2000 STATISTICS

Rushing offense	207.3	18
Passing offense	171.0	92
Total offense	378.3	52
Scoring offense	26.7	51
Net Punting	35.1	43
Punt returns	10.8	37
Kickoff returns	22.6	13
Rushing defense	135.8	42
Passing efficiency defense	100.1	14
Total defense	311.9	18
Scoring defense	19.3	23
Turnover margin	-6	87

Last column is ranking among Division I-A teams.

KICKERS

The Orangemen need some help here. Junior **Mike Shafer** (5-9, 180) took over the placement job last year and made just 7-of-20 field-goal attempts. And it's not like he was trying 55-yarders all the time, either.

Shafer missed 10 tries from 40 yards or closer last year, including a pair from inside the 30. If he doesn't improve quickly, he'll be giving up his job to redshirt freshman **Colin Barber** (6-1, 192).

Barber made 17-of-29 field goals during his career at Lexington (Ky.) Catholic High School and showed enough leg to put 50 percent of his kickoffs out of the end zone. Although he has no experience kicking at the college level, he couldn't do much worse than Shafer did last year.

If both falter, the Orange may turn to freshman **Justin Sujansky** (5-10, 210) from Valley Forge (Pa.) Military Academy via Upper St. Claire High School in Pittsburgh, Pa. Sujansky made 6-of-7 placement tries last year, including a 43-yarder, at VFMA. He tore his ACL as a senior at Upper St. Claire but made seven field goals as a junior.

DEFENSIVE LINE

No other area on the 'Cuse roster took a bigger hit than did the defensive front, which must replace three starters, including tackles Rick Simpkins and Eric Downing, who combined for 131 tackles, 14 of which came behind the line. Also gone is end Duke Pettijohn, who had 14 stops in enemy backfields, including 7.5 sacks.

But the one returnee is a prime-timer. Senior **Dwight Freeney** (6-1, 250) played in just seven games last year, missing the last four because of illness, but still had 13 sacks and 18 stops behind the line. Freeney was a unanimous selection to the first-team All-Big East unit and had some mammoth games. He piled up a school-record 4 1/2 sacks in a remarkable performance against Virginia Tech and had 2 1/2 sacks against BYU. Freeney is strong and fast and almost always commands a double team in passing situations.

The other end will be senior **Mark Holtzman** (6-4, 250), who started in place of Freeney in the last two games of 2000 and made 19 tackles. But he had better beware of 6-6, 256-pound sophomore **Josh Thomas**, who played in just two games last year—his first at Syracuse—but flashed star potential. Thomas had five tackles and a sack against Buffalo but broke a bone in his foot the next week, against Cincinnati, and was done for the year. He could be a good one.

Inside, expect a pair of sophomores to start. **Louis Gachelin** (6-1, 280) is the nose tackle, and **Christian Ferrara** (6-3, 278) will play the other tackle spot. Gachelin made 22 tackles and had 2 1/2 sacks last year and has excellent quickness off the ball, while Ferrara had 12 tackles last year and recovered a fumble. He started two games. Backing them up are redshirt freshman **Brian**

Hooper (6-1, 281) and 6-1, 259-pound senior **Sheldon King**.

LINEBACKERS

The Orangemen will certainly miss outside man Morlon Greenwood, who made 98 tackles a year ago, but two starters return on the second line of defense, and it appears there is some quality depth available.

Leading the way is 6-2, 249-pound junior **Clifton Smith**, a two-year starter who paced the Orange with 108 tackles last year, seven of which came for a loss. A first team All-Big East choice in 2000, Smith is quick and nasty and thrives on having his best games against 'Cuse's toughest opposition.

Last year, he had 18 stops against Miami and blocked an extra point. Smith amassed 14 tackles in the near-miss against Virginia Tech. Smith had 10 or more tackles six times last year and is on the verge of breaking into the national consciousness. Two players are vying for the top backup spot in the middle. Senior **Rodney Wells** (5-11, 235) had six tackles against Buffalo last year, while redshirt freshman **James Dumervil** (6-0, 234) has tremendous potential.

The other incumbent is 6-0, 225-pound senior outside man **J.R. Johnson**, who started seven games last year and finished with 60 tackles. He too was strong against VT, recording eight stops. His most productive game was an 11-tackle performance against Boston College. He had better watch out, however, for sophomore **Jameel Dumas** (6-2, 220), who started two games and made 15 tackles. He missed spring drills to work on his academics but has some big-time talent and potential.

"His first start last year, he earned a game ball," Pasqualoni said. "He can be an exceptional player."

Greenwood's spot will probably go to 6-3, 216-pound senior **Maurice Minter**, who had 11 tackles last year and was a strong special teams performer. Also expected to make an impact on the outside is 6-1, 228-pound sophomore **Rich Scanlon**, who had shoulder surgery during the off-season but has a bright future.

"He has a chance to be a good player here," Pasqualoni said.

Also in the mix outside are juniors **Jose Harris** (6-4, 236) and **Gerald Hall** (6-2, 217) and redshirt freshman **Greg Hanoian** (6-1, 232), who was a standout prep fullback but has made a good transition to defense. And look out for senior **Charles Burton** (6-1, 231), who has been moved to the outside spot after playing strong safety for three years. He can hit and find the ball.

DEFENSIVE BACKS

You can look at this area two ways. The pessimist sees a huge hole left by the departure of speedy cornerback Will Allen, the first-round pick of the New York Giants. The optimist would talk about the other three returning starters, including strong safety **Keeon Walker** and some talented corners.

Walker is a 5-10, 192-pound junior who was switched from running back to strong safety last spring and made a pretty impressive transition, piling up 85 tackles and recovering two fumbles. He had 14 stops against Cincinnati and 10 against Miami. He played so well Pasqualoni was induced to move Burton to linebacker.

"After making the transition last year, he has the chance to be a good player," Pasqualoni said.

Redshirt freshman **Jeremiah Mason** (6-3, 185) will be his primary backup.

The center-fielder spot goes to senior **Quentin Harris** (6-0, 216), who has started for two seasons now and played in 11 games as a freshman. Harris played in only nine games last year because of shoulder and knee troubles, and made 55 tackles. That was well below his total of 97 in 1999. He set a school record with a 91-yard fumble return for a touchdown against Buffalo and has good speed and instincts.

Junior **Maurice McClain** (6-1, 172), who started once last year, and redshirt freshman **O'Neil Scott** (6-0, 188) will back him up.

An interesting battle is shaping up at Allen's vacant corner spot between junior **Latroy Oliver** (5-8, 191) and senior **Will Hunter** (5-10, 185). Although the post-spring depth chart listed Hunter in the lead, Pasqualoni believes Oliver is a little ahead.

"Oliver is a good cover corner who is great on the stop-and-go," the coach said. "He's quick."

Hunter played in 11 games last year and started against Cincinnati. He finished with 27 tackles. Oliver also had a start last year and finished with 15 stops.

The other corner job belongs to senior **Willie Ford** (6-2, 199), a two-year starter with excellent size and good speed. Also in the picture are redshirt freshman **Jeremiah Mason** (6-3, 185), seniors **Jeremy Cooper** (6-0, 181) and **Andre Brinson** (5-8, 176) and sophomore **B.J. Darnell** (5-7, 176), who can move.

PUNTERS

Shafer may not have been the most accurate field goal kicker last year, but he did have a pretty good year punting the ball. Now entering his third season as the Orange's full-time man at that position, he has a chance to challenge for all-league honors, provided he can cut down on his blocks (two) and can get a little better at putting balls inside opponents' 20-yard lines.

Ten of Shafer's 51 punts fell inside opposing red zones, and 17 were fair-caught. That's not a bad overall percentage, and his punts were high enough that Syracuse coverage units were able to limit rivals to a 7.2-yard return average. Shafer averaged 40.9 yards per kick last year, a big improvement from the 38.4-yard average he managed as a freshman. He has a big leg and could be on the verge of becoming a standout in this area.

He's backed up, as he is on placements, by Barber, who averaged 41 yards per punt during his high school career and was selected all-state as a senior.

SPECIAL TEAMS

Just as the Syracuse kicking situation is something of a mixed bag, so too are the rest of the special teams inconsistent. The Orangemen blocked five kicks last year, with Tyree swatting away three. That's pretty good. In fact, it's very good. Problem is, Syracuse had six kicks of its own blocked. That's awful.

Shafer had three placement tries rejected, and three punts were batted down. Good teams don't let that happen. Heck, even some of the nation's lesser schools can do better than that.

The return situation is pretty good. Campbell and sophomore **Jamel Riddle** (5-7, 173) each averaged more than 10 yards per attempt bringing back punts. But the Orangemen will turn to Jackson and Mungro to return kicks. Neither has had much experience doing that. The good news is that Jackson has potential. He brought back four kicks last year and averaged 24.8 yards. He has the speed to go places, but his 5-8, 169-pound frame might not stand up well to some of the special-teams crazies he might encounter throughout the season.

The 'Cuse coverage units were sound last year and should be good again. The Orange allowed enemy punt returners to average just 7.2 yards per try, while rivals managed just 17.0 yards bringing back kicks. Good team speed and plenty of depth should make those groups good again.

RECRUITING CLASS

Four years ago, Syracuse couldn't land the player it really wanted, quarterback Michael Vick, and the recent history of the Big East took a turn for the Hokies. This February, Pasqualoni and his staff swung things back a little when Howard decided to play for the Orangemen. He was the Western Pennsylvania Interscholastic Athletic Association League Player of the Year. Rivals.com chose him a first-team All-American, and *SuperPrep* tabbed him the nation's eighth-best quarterback. Howard is an excellent runner, has good size and should be a fine fit in the 'Cuse system. Don't be surprised if he sees some time right away, although with Nunes and Anderson around, he could redshirt.

The other big-name recruit in this class is defensive back **Larry McClain** (5-10, 185) from Forestville (Md.) High School, who holds the Maryland state record with 34 career interceptions. A fine running back who gained 1,385 yards as a senior, McClain should be an excellent cover corner and ball hawk.

Steve Gregory (5-11, 170), from Curtis High School in Staten Island, N.Y., joins McClain in the secondary reinforcements, while Syracuse upgraded its offensive line future by signing **Jared Pierce** (6-6, 280) from St. Joseph's High School in Trumbull, Conn., and **Jason Greene** (6-5, 265) from Somerville (N.J.) High School.

Kader Drame (6-5, 280) from Wilbur Cross High School in New Haven, Conn., is a promising defensive tackle prospect.

BLUE RIBBON ANALYSIS

OFFENSE	B-
SPECIAL TEAMS	C+
DEFENSE	B-
INTANGIBLES	B

Although Pasqualoni's record of graduating a huge percentage of his players and his streak of 10 straight winning seasons is excellent, the Orangemen have slipped lately. There can be no doubt about that. Syracuse used to play for the Big East title every year. The last two seasons, 'Cuse has been playing to qualify for shaky, second-tier bowl games. It didn't even succeed in that mission last year.

So, while Pasqualoni doesn't need to break out the flame-retardant pants, he knows it's time to win, or else the Syracuse Nation will start to grumble louder than it already is. The trouble is, the 2001 schedule isn't exactly set up to facilitate a nine-win season. Those games against Georgia Tech, Tennessee and Auburn are potential killers, and the visits from East Carolina and Central Florida won't be easy, either. Pulling out a nine- or 10-win season won't be easy at all. In fact, seven triumphs could be hard to reach, too.

The key is the quarterback position. If Nunes or Anderson can play consistently and make use of the Orange's deep crop of receivers, Syracuse will score points. It could become a formidable team, thanks to a defense that should make big plays, and if the defensive line comes together around Freeney, pose some real problems for opponents.

Syracuse definitely has talent and depth

throughout its roster. That has never been the trouble. Because the Orange offense demands so much out of the quarterback, both running and passing, play at that position has become the key that often determines whether Syracuse will be successful. When McNabb and Graves were running the show, the Orange rolled. When there wasn't the necessary production under center, Syracuse struggled. Nunes and Anderson will get their chances, but Pasqualoni may have to turn to Howard. Whoever takes the snaps must be good, or Syracuse won't be.

(M.B.)

2000 RESULTS

Buffalo	W	63-7	1-0
Cincinnati	L	10-12	1-1
East Carolina	L	17-34	1-2
Brigham Young	W	42-14	2-2
Pittsburgh	W	24-17	3-2
Boston College	L	13-20	3-3
Virginia Tech	L	14-22	3-4
West Virginia	W	31-27	4-4
Temple	W	31-12	5-4
Miami	L	0-26	5-5
Rutgers	W	49-21	6-5

Temple

LOCATION Philadelphia, PA
CONFERENCE Big East
LAST SEASON 4-7 (.363)
CONFERENCE RECORD 1-7 (7th)
OFFENSIVE STARTERS RETURNING 10
DEFENSIVE STARTERS RETURNING 10
NICKNAME Owls
COLORS Cherry & White
HOME FIELD Veterans Stadium (66,592)
HEAD COACH Bobby Wallace (Miss. St. '76)
RECORD AT SCHOOL 8-25 (3 years)
CAREER RECORD 90-61-1 (13 years)
ASSISTANTS
Raymond Monica (North Alabama '90)
Assistant Head Coach/
Defensive Coordinator/Inside Linebackers
Charlie Fisher (Springfield '81)
Offensive Coordinator/Quarterbacks
Nick Rapone (Virginia Tech '78)
Defensive Backs
Rocky Hager (Minot State '74)
Tight Ends/Recruiting Coordinator
Spencer Prescott (Villanova '80)
Outside Linebackers
John Reagan (Syracuse '94)
Defensive Line
Blair Thomas (Penn State '89)
Running Backs
Mike Schad (Queen's '86)
Offensive Line
Rob Likens (Mississippi State '90)
Wide Receivers
TEAM WINS (last 5 yrs.) 1-3-2-2-4
FINAL RANK (last 5 yrs.) 80-77-89-85-75
2000 FINISH Lost to Pittsburgh in regular-season finale.

COACH AND PROGRAM

It would be hard to find another team in the country that could be so excited about a four-win season. But when Temple ended 2000 with a 7-0 near-miss against Pittsburgh, the Owl players and coaches had the kind of optimism usually reserved for a team which would be charging into its upcoming season after soaring to great heights.

Then again, everything is relative. Four wins at Michigan would be cause for a palace insurrection. At Temple, which hadn't won that many games since 1990 (really), a 4-7 mark served as a harbinger of great things to come. For the first time in a decade, the Owls weren't overwhelmed by the better teams on their schedule. They hung with West Virginia, Syracuse and Pitt. They showed spunk against Miami. For the first time in a long time, people in Philadelphia actually talked about Temple football in optimistic terms, rather than as the continuous butt of jokes.

With 20 starters scheduled to return and a schedule that might just produce the six wins necessary for bowl qualification, Temple appeared to be on the verge of a renaissance. In February, all that changed. In a move that staggered the Temple community, the Big East Conference announced that it would be severing its ties with the Owls. In effect, the other schools in the league had decided that they would rather move on with seven members—and wait until 2005 for Connecticut's arrival—than continue to associate with Temple, which was a member for football only.

The reasons for the break were simple. Temple had spent the last decade wobbling from season to season, playing before meager gatherings at cavernous Veterans Stadium, providing little or no real competition for other Big East members and siphoning off a couple million a year in bowl and TV monies. All this despite contributing little in the way of postseason revenue or broadcast attractiveness.

Compounding the situation were two conditions that hampered the Owls considerably. The first was the aforementioned football-only status. Unlike every other Big East member, the Owls had no other tie to the conference. Once Virginia Tech became a full-fledged Big East brother, in 2000, the Owls were on an island—and a dangerous one at that. Though Temple had tried to join the Big East in all sports a couple times during the '90s, it was always rebuffed. Now, it had precious little tying it to the conference.

Another problem was its 1999 decision to play Marshall—at Marshall. The Thundering Herd had been trying to get a game against Big East member West Virginia, the only other I-A team in the state, for years. The Mountaineers had resisted, not wanting to give the Herd any more legitimacy in a state which has precious few big-time prep recruits each year. Then the Owls consented to play Marshall, proving that, yes, a Big East member would schedule the Herd.

That was just what Marshall needed in its quest (which had moved on to the state legislature) to play WVU. As one might expect, the Mountaineer community was not happy. When your footing is precarious, it doesn't make sense to take chances. Temple did. That almost definitely cost the Owls any chance of getting West Virginia to back it in any membership vote.

The Temple community was appalled—for the most part. Many of the faculty, however, celebrated. If the Owls were kicked out of the Big East, they would certainly have to drop football, because it became clear that no other conference would be interested in them. During the last decade, Temple's football program had been a huge drain on the university's coffers.

Even once it started to get the full benefits of the Big East's TV and bowl packages, the program was losing money. Meanwhile, several academic programs had been cut because of insufficient funds. As one might expect, professors and staff university wide were not big football boosters.

Neither, many suspected, was new president David Adamany. He had come to Temple in late 2000 to replace Peter Liacouras, who had been a huge booster of Owl athletics and had made in the mid-1980s the now-infamous promise that Temple would be playing in the Sugar Bowl by the end of the decade.

Adamany had a reputation as a bottom-line guy who didn't care too much about athletics or anything else that didn't make money. When Temple received the heave-ho from the Big East, many in the Temple community thought Adamany was ready to pull the plug on the program.

Howard Gittis was not included in that group. The chairman of the school's Board of Trustees, Gittis was not about to let Temple football die. He called an emergency meeting of the board and made it clear that not only was Owl football going to live, it was going to thrive. Gittis, a high-powered lawyer for Revlon, convinced Board members not only to save the sport but also to buy nearly 20,000 season tickets. That assured the Owls that they would have more than 25,000 season seats sold—one of the league's criteria for the program's continued residence in the Big East.

But Gittis didn't stop there. He vowed to meet individually with each of the league presidents to make his case. Temple would sell tickets and fill the seats. The Owls were already more competitive and were getting better, thanks to Wallace. Temple would be joining the Eagles in a new stadium in 2003, under an arrangement similar to the one Pittsburgh would have with the Steelers. And, should none of that persuasion work, Gittis vowed litigation.

Temple would sue the Big East, saying the league gave Temple no clear deadline by which it had to meet the terms for membership and then dismissed the Owls without sufficient due process. It was a bold, aggressive plan of action.

As of early May, it hadn't resulted in any change. In a May 7 article in the Charleston (W. Va.) Gazette, West Virginia athletic director Ed Pastilong was quoted as having said, "Our league presidents discussed, reviewed and evaluated Temple for several years. When they were voting (to oust the Owls), they realized the importance of the vote. They cast their votes. It's unlikely that will be re-addressed."

So, the Owls head into what they had hoped would be a landmark season in a bad state of limbo. If, as Pastilong asserts, the Big East isn't going to let Temple back in, then Gittis' suit will more than likely result in a cash settlement—at best. That might help Temple live as an independent for a season or two, although that would be a horror show from scheduling and attendance standpoints. If there is no payoff, then the Owls would more than likely have to cease football operations, because they would be out the $2 million they get each year from the Big East and would be further in the red.

Because no other league appears interested (neither Conference USA nor the Mid-American Conference will consider adding Temple), it would be disastrous.

Yet coach Bobby Wallace and the players forge ahead, amidst the uncertainty. Wallace reports that spring practice featured excellent competition for jobs. None of the recruits in the large, 31-player crop of newcomers begged to be released from his letter-of-intent. None of the returning players of note have left North Broad Street. The future may be shaky, but the Owls are still Big East members and are preparing to compete as such.

"Everybody wants to know what our situation is in the Big East," Wallace said. "The only thing that we can tell them is what believe. We feel strongly that Howard Gittis and the board have been given the support needed to keep us in the

Big East for a period.

"We haven't given up hope that we will be in the Big East. We're telling recruits that we hope a decision will be made before next year's signing date and that they should keep us in their plans."

It doesn't matter to Wallace what predictions are being made or what Pastilong says. He can only put a team on the field and try to win games with it. Temple's non-conference schedule (Navy, Toledo, Connecticut and Bowling Green) could well produce four wins, particularly from a team with 20 starters returning. The Owls will have talent and good depth across the offensive front for the first time in years. Wallace wants to start the season today.

"We can only control what we can control," Wallace said. "Right now, I'm so excited for this football team and this season. We see the light at the end of the tunnel. We're going to take care of business on the field, and we have to have faith that good things will happen after that.

"The kids and coaches here are going to play 11 football games, hopefully 12. Our players are worried about beating Navy (in the Aug. 30 opener) and competing for positions. I don't want to downplay (what has happened with the Big East), but we all feel good about the season."

2001 SCHEDULE

Sept.	1	Navy
	8	Toledo
	15	Connecticut
	22	@Bowling Green
Oct.	6	@Boston College
	13	Rutgers
	20	@Syracuse
	27	Pittsburgh
Nov.	3	@Miami
	10	Virginia Tech
	17	@West Virginia

QUARTERBACKS

Even though **Devin Scott** shared part of last season under center with **Mike Frost** and even watched as Frost started three contests, the 6-1, 202-pound senior never really lost his status as the program's top quarterback.

When spring drills finally ended in April, Scott was again atop the depth chart, and Wallace was talking about redshirting Frost, who struggled mightily at times last year and finished with an awful 38.6 percent rate of completion.

Not that Scott was perfect. While he did complete 63 percent of his passes, Scott threw only five touchdown passes and had seven intercepted. He also averaged just 132.4 passing yards per game, not exactly a figure that would have 'em cheering at BYU. Not that Scott doesn't have potential. He has had some huge games during his career and can make things happen. He does, however, have problems with consistency, although a more effective offensive line would be a big help.

Last year, Scott completed 24-of-34 for 336 yards against Maryland and was 23-of-32 for 247 yards and two scores against Bowling Green. Neither was on par with his wild, 36-of-45 performance against Rutgers in 1999, during which he finished with 311 yards and six touchdowns. You get the point.

Scott can deliver, but he must become more efficient and get the ball into the end zone more if the Owls are to be more than just second-division also-rans this season. It would also be helpful if Scott were healthy. Concussions have dogged him during his time at Temple.

"It's Devin's job," Wallace said. "He had a sound spring, but we didn't let him get hit, because of the concussions. Staying healthy will start when we have an offensive line. He had some good games, but he looked bad at times, because we were overmatched up front. Any game we played well up front in, he did well. He brings leadership to us, because he's a senior."

Expect the backup job to go to senior **Mac DeVito** (5-11, 179), who has played quarterback and receiver, held for placements and returned punts. DeVito is an excellent runner but not much of a consistent pocket passer. Though he's long on experience and moxie, DeVito is not the man Temple fans want to see under center on a regular basis. Wallace isn't buying that—"I have all the confidence in the world in Mac," he said—but he wouldn't have recruited Frost from the junior-college ranks last year had he felt better about his quarterback situation.

Speaking of Frost, the 6-2, 226-pound senior fell to fourth on the depth chart in the spring, thanks to his inaccuracy. Redshirting him will allow the Temple coaches to work on his odd release and perhaps prepare him for regular action in 2002, that is if he can beat out redshirt freshman **Collin Hannigan** (6-5, 240), who has impressed Wallace with his steady play, despite an unconventional release. Another player in the quarterback derby this fall will be freshman **Mike McGann** (6-5, 195) from St. Joseph's Prep in Havertown, Pa., who led his high school to the Philadelphia Catholic League title and showed plenty of promise when he threw for 245 yards in the title game.

RUNNING BACKS

Tanardo Sharps' 2000 outburst was not predicted by anybody, even within the Temple community. After being part of one of the nation's most anemic ground attacks in '99, Sharps (5-11, 182) was expected to improve over his 184-yard total from his freshman season, but not go for 1,038 yards and 10 touchdowns. The junior was the Owls' first 1,000-yard rusher since 1987 and averaged a gaudy 5.2 yards per carry, impressive given the offensive line's inconsistent play.

Sharps started the season right, rushing for 180 yards and a score against Navy. Three weeks later, he erupted for 203 yards and a pair of touchdowns against Eastern Michigan. Sharps had three more 100-yard outbursts, against West Virginia (113), Rutgers (168) and Syracuse (104). It was a great year by the speedy back, who may not have the size to average 25 carries a game but certainly has the burst to make big plays and outrun some defenders, if he gets clear of the line of scrimmage.

"He gained 1,000 yards last year behind a pretty weak offensive line," Wallace said. "This year, we should be better than average up front, so he could be better. He's a great back, and I've been around great backs. I wouldn't trade him for anybody. He's consistent, gives great effort and has tremendous quickness and speed."

Last year this time, Temple fans were excited about freshman **Lawrence Wade** (6-0, 191), a highly touted recruit who had gained 5,710 yards during his career at Eastern Senior High School in Washington, D.C. By November, however, Wade had carried the ball just six times in nine games and had gained just 20 yards. Now, Wallace is talking about redshirting him, the better to let Wade gain some weight and strength.

That leaves the backup tailback's job in the hands of junior **Lester Trammer** (5-10, 193), who gained 178 yards and scored a touchdown last year. Trammer has quick feet, pretty good speed and can take a hit. Behind him is sophomore **Makonnen Fenton** (5-9, 186), who has yet to play a game at Temple after redshirting last year and sitting out the '99 season as a partial qualifier. Fenton is fast and sturdy and can handle work between the tackles.

"We have four really good backs," Wallace said.

The fullback spot is ably manned by a pair of experienced seniors, hulking **Harold Jackson** (6-2, 270) and **Jason McKie** (5-11, 239). Jackson is a bruising blocker who spent two years at North Carolina State, spent '99 at Lackawanna (Pa.) Junior College and then carried 14 times for 37 yards last year. He won't get much more action this year, but he will be asked to clear a path for Sharps, work he should be able to handle.

McKie is more athletic but isn't about to get too many more carries. He is, however, a big part of the Owl passing attack and caught 20 balls last year.

WIDE RECEIVERS/TIGHT ENDS

The Owls have plenty of experience returning at these spots, but it's not as if they're loaded with game-breakers. There is some speed, but it hasn't yet translated into a bunch of big plays. That could change this year, but at least Temple isn't wanting for targets.

Leading the list is senior **Greg Muckerson** (5-11, 190), who caught 41 balls last year and scored two touchdowns—tied for the team lead in receiving scores. Although Muckerson averaged just 11.9 yards per reception, he does have the nation's longest streak of games with a catch (22).

"That's shows exactly what he is," Wallace said. "He's dependable. He comes to play every game. He's made some great plays for us and is solid."

Muckerson showed that last year by posting six catches against Boston College and five versus five other opponents.

Lining up opposite him should be junior Za**mir Abdul-Hakim Cobb** (6-0, 173), who has changed his name from Charles to one reflecting his Islamic faith. Cobb caught 27 passes last year and scored twice and blends good speed with a penchant for acrobatic catches. What he needs this year is more consistency and better work deep.

Cobb did have some impressive performances last year. He had five receptions against West Virginia, including a 14-yard touchdown catch that gave the Owls a 24-23 fourth-quarter lead. He also had a touchdown reception against Virginia Tech, a one-handed beauty in the corner of the end zone.

The Owls are hoping junior **Sean Dillard** (5-9, 162) will be as strong this year as he was in last season's finale against Pittsburgh, when he snared 11 balls for 91 yards.

"He's got great speed and can be a big-play man for us," Wallace said.

Also in the picture is sophomore **Ikey Chuku** (6-3, 172), who improved considerably during the off-season and the spring. He averaged an impressive 17.3 yards on his 13 receptions last season. Junior **Terrence Stubbs** (6-1, 193) should see some time, along with junior **Krishan Lewis** (6-3, 211), who has the size and potential to be an excellent over-the-middle target.

"He had a great spring," Wallace said. "He has the ability to catch the ball better than any other receiver I've been around. He's got a great body, long arms and tremendous hands."

Kelly Nead (6-4, 240) jumped right to the head of the tight end class after transferring at mid-season to Temple from Ricks (Ind.) College. The junior caught 10 passes for 100 yards and a pair of scores last year. Wallace calls him "solid."

The backup role will be manned by senior

Chris Pitt (6-2, 239) or redshirt freshman **Jordan Witzel** (6-6, 236), who broke his ankle last year and missed the season. He has tremendous potential and needs just a little more heft and experience to become a big contributor.

OFFENSIVE LINE

Barring serious injury in another area, this could well be the key to the Temple season. Although the team has much more depth than it did last year, it must also find a combination that allows for maximum performance.

Owl quarterbacks were sacked 36 times last year, and though the team did increase its rushing totals considerably from '99, Temple backs still averaged an unspectacular 3.5 yards per carry.

"We played too many young people last year," Wallace said.

In order to fortify his line, Wallace imported five junior-college players, including three from Nassau Community College. It's hard to know whether any of them will start, but it's certain that several of the quintet—and perhaps even a freshman—will provide much-needed depth up front.

Four starters return, with tackle Mathias Nkwenti the only regular gone. He was taken in the fourth round of the NFL draft by Pittsburgh.

Expect junior **Vincent Gabriele** (6-5, 283) to handle the pivot. He was the first-ever player to commit to Wallace and his staff. Though the Owls have tried him at guard (and he is listed as a backup at strong guard), they like him better in the middle. Right now, **Jason Heilman**, a 6-3, 280-pound junior, is listed as his backup, but that could change when the newcomers arrive.

"They'll play, but I don't know where," Wallace said.

The guards are junior **Donny Klein** (6-2, 286), a returning starter, and sophomore **Joe Laudano** (6-2, 283), who started six times last year and has finally become a full-time lineman after struggling to stay svelte enough to play tight end.

Junior **Dave Yovanovits** (6-3, 295) is back at strong tackle and is a fixture on the line. He's backed up by 6-5, 321-pound sophomore **John Maxim**. Taking over for Nkwenti is junior **Damian Hendricks** (6-4, 278).

"He has really improved," Wallace said. "He has a lot of growing up to do, but he has realized what he has to do. He was recruited as a defensive lineman but has made the switch."

The Owls expect to redshirt one of the junior college imports—**Adam Boyd** (6-3, 295), from El Camino, Calif., College and Palos Verdes Pensinsula High School—but the others will likely see action. One or two might even start.

Perhaps the top newcomer is **Anthony Nembhard** (6-5, 300) from Nassau (N.Y.) Community College and Evander Childs High School in Harlem, N.Y. Nembhard was recruited by many schools coming out of high school but had to spend two years on Long Island. He has potential.

So does **Jason Heilman** (6-4, 280), from Mt. San Antonio (Calif.) Community College and West Covina High School in Anaheim, Calif. Wallace thinks Heilman could play center or quick tackle.

Also in the mix are **Anthony Bolden** (6-5, 295) from Nassau Community College and Baldwin High School in Freeport, N.Y., and **Scott Norris** (6-6, 295) from Nassau Community College and Monroe High School in Jamesburg, N.J.

And don't rule out an early contribution from massive freshman tackle **Yohance Perry** (6-5, 330) from Iona Prep in Mount Vernon, N.Y. Wallace is particularly high on the rookie.

2000 STATISTICS

Rushing offense	130.5	74
Passing offense	179.6	85
Total offense	310.2	99
Scoring offense	20.4	88
Net Punting	31.0	99
Punt returns	8.0	83
Kickoff returns	18.2	87
Rushing defense	136.8	43
Passing efficiency defense	122.3	69
Total defense	333.4	33
Scoring defense	24.5	55
Turnover margin	+3	46

Last column is ranking among Division I-A teams.

KICKERS

The Owls will again rely on junior **Cap Poklemba** (5-11, 175), who had a solid 2000, making 9-of-13 field goals and all but one of his 27point-after kicks.

The key for Poklemba is increased leg strength. His longest successful try last year was a mere 41 yards, and he made only 2-of-4 from 40 yards or longer. Wallace reports that Poklemba, who also doubles as a member of the Temple baseball team, had a good spring and showed more leg.

"He did an excellent job, particularly kicking off," Wallace said. "He was kicking them into the end zone all spring. He has great nerves. Nothing bothers him."

Poklemba's backup is junior **Jared Davis** (5-6, 133), younger brother of Owl defensive end **Jason Davis**, who outweighs him by more than 100 pounds and is eight inches taller.

The younger Davis was born two months premature but is now thriving. He shared in the kickoff duties last year with Poklemba and attempted (and made) one PAT. Davis was the Owls' primary kickoff man in '99 and actually made a pair of touchdown-saving tackles.

DEFENSIVE LINE

When Wallace says that all four of the Owls starters up front could "possibly make all-Big East," he isn't hyperbolizing. Temple has one of the league's top quartets and should be able to rotate in some solid reserves this year, making the line the strength of what should again be a fine defense.

Although senior tackle **Russell Newman** (6-2, 274) was the sole all-league honoree (second team) last year, the real horse on the Temple front is junior **Dan Klecko** (6-1, 264), who missed a good part of last year with a sprained knee that he followed up with a sprained ankle. Although Klecko gamely played in eight games and made seven of his 21 tackles behind the line, he was clearly a shell of his highly talented self for much of the season. Now completely healed, expect Klecko to be a full-time interior force once again and give the Owls much-needed push between the tackles.

Newman is just as effective and maybe quicker than Klecko. He had 47 tackles in 10 games last year, and 15 came in enemy backfields. He also had 5.5 sacks. A great story, Newman came to Temple as a walk-on, weighing just 220 pounds. Thanks to a huge work ethic and motor that wouldn't shift out of fifth gear, he worked himself into the starting lineup and all-league notice.

"We probably have the best pair of tackles in the league," Wallace said. "I'll be glad if they stay healthy and play together for 11 games."

Backing them up will be 6-2, 255-pound junior **Rob Sack** and sophomore **Taso Apostolidis** (6-0, 267). Sack made 40 tackles in 11 games last year and had nine stops behind the line.

Wallace reports that Apostolidis "benches 500 pounds." It's also possible that junior **Dominique Veney** (6-3, 280 from Valley Forge (Pa.)Military Academy and Washington, D.C., could find his way into the mix.

The end situation is in good shape, provided senior **Raheem Brock** (6-4, 257) was able to accrue the credits necessary to graduate this year and thereby regain the season of eligibility he lost as a partial qualifier. If he did, then the Owls have quite a weapon on the outside. Brock is fast and strong, and he had 11 tackles for loss and four sacks last year. He also recovered three fumbles and forced three more.

If Brock isn't available, look for senior **Jason Davis** (6-2, 244) to handle one end spot. Davis moved from linebacker to end before the 2000 season and brought speed to the outside. Expect him to be improved this year, thanks to increased bulk and experience at the other position.

The other end spot belongs to **Akeiff Staples**, a 6-3, 240-pound senior who is another converted linebacker. Staples posted 3.5 sacks and six tackles for loss in 2000 and should be counted on for some pressure on the passer this year. His backup is likely to be sophomore **J.D. Stanley** (6-4, 239), although a pair of sophomore transfers from New Mexico Military Institute, **Ismael Seals** (6-4, 258) and **Marques Coleman** (6-4, 215), could make an impact. Seals is particularly impressive and could be used as a pass rusher right away.

LINEBACKERS

The only significant hole in the Temple defense can be found here, thanks to the graduation of LeVar Talley, last year's top tackler (135). Wallace promises that he and his staff will move quickly during summer practices to establish some sort of hierarchy at the two positions.

At least he doesn't have to worry about the strong spot, which is manned by 6-2, 231-pound senior **Taylor Suman**, who was second to Talley in stops last year with 110, including seven behind the line. Suman isn't the fastest linebacker around, and he isn't overwhelmingly large, but he makes plays and should be well above 100 tackles again this year.

His backup, as of now, is junior **Terrance Belvin** (6-1, 222) from Dodge City (Kansas) Community College and Palmetto (Fla.) High School. The junior college import has excellent speed.

Coming out of spring practice, Talley's former weak-side spot was the province of junior college newcomer **J.D. Nichols** (6-1, 226) from Phoenix (Ariz.) College and Mountain Point High School in Phoenix. Nichols was an All-Arizona JUCO performer in 2000 and has good speed, even if he isn't the biggest player around.

Behind him is sophomore **Leon Gray** (6-1, 223), who played in nine games last year, primarily on special teams. Gray made 64 tackles in '98 and started six games. He is quick and athletic. But he had better be ready to work.

The Owls spent four scholarships on linebackers, including **Quintae McLean** (6-4, 258) from Lackawanna (Pa.) Junior College and India River High School in Virginia Beach, Va. McLean was an honorable-mention junior college All-America last year and has the perfect body to provide run support.

Three freshmen will also get a chance at a spot in the rotation. They are **Anthony DeGannes** (6-4, 220) from Hillside (N.J.) High School, **Donta Rajah** (6-2, 225) from Archbishop Carroll High School in Washington, D.C., and

Manuel Tapia (6-3, 225) from Niskayuna (N.Y.) High School.

DEFENSIVE BACKS

The Owls begin in good shape here and could have a special bunch, if a couple things go right. It beings with "Owl Back" **Chonn Lacey** (6-2, 218), a senior who plays the hybrid linebacker/safety position extremely well.

"He's the best athlete on the team," Wallace said. "He's smart, too."

Lacey is so valuable that the Owls plan to use him in some four-receiver sets on the other side of the ball. He made 67 tackles last year, 11 of which came in enemy backfields, and picked off three passes.

Backing him up is senior **Brian West** (5-11, 188), who hopes to be clear of his long-time shoulder problems this year.

The safeties are experienced and productive. Senior **Jamal Wallace** (6-0, 186) made 91 tackles last year, the third-best total on the team, while Wallace describes senior strong safety **Lafton Thompson** (6-2, 199) as a "solid, physical football player."

Thompson's 65 tackles and nine stops for loss would back up that assessment.

Speaking of backups, junior **Shawn Walker** (6-2, 183), who saw time exclusively on special teams but has good size and senior **Philip Shepard** (5-10, 182) are in reserve along the back line. Shepard was a starter at right corner last year but will be used primarily as a nickel back this year.

The rising star at corner is junior **Terrance Leftwich** (6-0, 169), who made 71 tackles last year and picked off four passes in his final five games. Leftwich made the switch from wide receiver last year and has plenty of potential.

"Halfway through last year, he got his confidence," Wallace said. "He could lead the league in interceptions this year, easily."

There could be some excitement at Shepard's old spot if 6-2, 207-pound senior **Dante Coles** is eligible. Coles has yet to play a down at Temple in two seasons, because of academic problems, but he flashed tremendous athletic ability as a prep at Conestoga (Pa.) High School and at Valley Forge Military Academy during the '98 season. Coles has great size and speed. He hawks the ball aggressively and can deliver a big-time blow.

"If he's eligible, he has a chance to be a special player," Wallace said.

If Coles doesn't go, expect sophomore **Yazid Jackson** (5-9, 166) to handle the right side. Jackson saw time in nine games last year as a nickel back. Providing support on the left corner is **Donnie Coleman** (5-10, 162), another sophomore.

PUNTERS

This is an area that needs some improvement. Even Wallace will admit that. The incumbent is junior **Garvin Ringwelski** (6-5, 224), who averaged only 37.4 yards per boot last year. While that wasn't awful, his other numbers were disturbing. Only four of his 55 kicks were fair caught, and only eight were inside opponents' 20-yard lines. Those numbers must improve if the Owls are to have any chances at an above-.500 record.

Ringwelski had some competition this spring from redshirt freshman walk-on **Mike McLaughlin** (6-1, 172), but he can't be counted upon because of his lack of experience.

"Going into the fall, we're worried about our offensive line, our linebackers and our punting," Wallace said. "Garvin did better last year, but he still hasn't reached his potential."

If Ringwelski and McLaughlin fail, it could fall to freshman **Jace Amore** (6-0, 180) from Elizabeth Forward Senior High School in Elizabeth, Pa. He had a 40.4-yard average as a prep senior and showed a big kickoff leg.

SPECIAL TEAMS

Because the Owls had only 67 scholarship players last year, they were unable to populate their special teams the way they wanted to or create competition for those spots. Now that they'll be up near 85, Wallace is excited, particularly because the team's depth at linebacker and defensive back will provide some much-needed depth on punt and kick teams.

Not that the return game doesn't need some help, too. DeVito, Lacey and Dillard are adequate at bringing back punts, but none is a game-breaker. And while Sharps is a reliable kick returner and has good outside speed, he averaged just 19.9 yards per return last year, with a long of 49. Cobb and Coles will get the chance to prove themselves in those areas.

Temple didn't allow too much yardage on enemy returns last year (9.7 on punts, 20.2 on kicks). But it needs to make more things happen, particularly in the kick-blocking department. The Owls blocked just one punt last year, hardly reminiscent of the marauding Virginia Tech coverage units.

RECRUITING CLASS

It's a big one, that's for sure. And it has some potential. The Owls piled up the junior college talent, the better to fill immediate needs and try to develop a winning personality as quickly as possible, but it's the freshmen who will make the biggest long-run impact.

Among the best are Perry, the big offensive lineman whom Wallace believes could play right away, McGann, who could figure in the quarterbacking picture in 2001, and DeGannes, who was a highly sought linebacker.

Other freshmen of impact are sure-handed tight end **Eric Carpenter** (6-5, 250) from Cedar Crest High School in Lebanon, Pa.; speedy defensive end **Michael Dollman** (6-3, 218) from Penn Hills (Pa.) High School; fleet wideout **Jamel Harris** (6-1, 190) from Red Bank High School in Shrewsburg, N.J.; and linebacker Manuel Tapia.

BLUE RIBBON ANALYSIS

OFFENSE	C+
SPECIAL TEAMS	C
DEFENSE	B
INTANGIBLES	C

Had the Big East not lowered the boom on the Owls in February, this season could have been viewed as a stepping stone to big things. And while Wallace finally has the momentum, depth and talent to chase six wins and bowl qualification, the entire program is operating in a state of limbo that could prove disastrous.

Even if Temple wins six or seven this year, is there any guarantee it will even be in the football business next year, given the difficult life of an independent?

It's too bad that the Owls were bounced from the Big East, because it finally appears they have their football act headed toward prosperity. There is a new football headquarters and practice field on campus. Temple will move into a new, state-of-the-art stadium in 2003. Wallace is clearly qualified to run a I-A program, and a winning program at that.

The talent level is rising. The non-conference schedule (Navy, Toledo, Connecticut, Bowling Green) is much more manageable than those in the past have been. And attendance has been rising slowly. Things look much better than they did during the dismal Ron Dickerson Era.

The fact of the matter is that Temple didn't have anything else to secure it to the Big East, so the league cut the Owls loose. Kansas State and Oregon State were full-fledged members of their conferences while their football teams stunk like old shoes. That's how they hung on to membership.

Temple doesn't play another game in another sport as a Big East member. It was easy for the presidents to cut the cord.

So, the Owls wait. And hope. And probably sue. It's unlikely that course will get them back in the Big East, but it could save their football program for a while. And, for once, it's worth saving. The offense still needs work, particularly if Scott can't stay healthy, but the line is improved, the backfield is stocked with proven performers, and there is some talent on the outside. The defense is even better, and if some of the newcomers (and Coles) contribute, it could improve on last year's national finish (33rd).

Temple could well win six games this year. It might even sneak in a seventh victory. But the Owls need a quick start to build momentum, or else they could get depressed about the program's state of affairs and begin to slide. That wouldn't help make an argument that Temple needs to continue as a football program, much less a Big East member. There is the chance for success this year and down the road, but there is little margin for error.

(M.B)

2000 RESULTS

Navy	W	17-6	1-0
Maryland	L	10-17	1-1
Bowling Green	W	31-14	2-1
Eastern Michigan	W	49-40	3-1
West Virginia	L	24-29	3-2
Virginia Tech	L	13-35	3-3
Rutgers	W	48-14	4-3
Miami	L	17-45	4-4
Boston College	L	3-31	4-5
Syracuse	L	12-31	4-6
Pittsburgh	L	0-7	4-7

Virginia Tech

LOCATION Blacksburg, VA
CONFERENCE Big East
LAST SEASON 11-1 (.917)
CONFERENCE RECORD 6-1 (2nd)
OFFENSIVE STARTERS RETURNING 6
DEFENSIVE STARTERS RETURNING 9
NICKNAME Hokies
COLORS Chicago Maroon & Burnt Orange
HOME FIELD Lane Stadium/Worsham Field (55,075)
HEAD COACH Frank Beamer (Va. Tech '69)
RECORD AT SCHOOL 99-61-2 (14 years)
CAREER RECORD 141-84-4 (20 years)
ASSISTANTS Billy Hite (North Carolina '74)
Assistant Head Coach/Running Backs
Rickey Bustle (Clemson '77)
Offensive Coordinator/Quarterbacks
Bud Foster (Murray State '81)
Defensive Coordinator/Inside Linebackers
Tony Ball (Chattanooga '81)
Wide Receivers
Jim Cavanaugh (William & Mary '70)

Strong Safeties/Outside Linebackers
Danny Pearman (Clemson '87)
Tight Ends/Offensive Tackles
Bryan Stinespring (James Madison '86)
Offensive Line
Lorenzo Ward (Alabama '90)
Defensive Backs
Charles Wiles (Murray State '87)
Defensive Line

TEAM WINS (last 5 yrs.) 10-7-9-11-11
FINAL RANK (last 5 yrs.) 11-53-23-3-4
2000 FINISH Beat Clemson in Gator Bowl.

COACH AND PROGRAM

Life is good in Blacksburg. Real good. The offers keep pouring in. The building projects roll on at a pace that would thrill any union boss. The wins are piling up. The stadium's getting bigger. The talent level is rising. The roster depth is better than ever.

It doesn't seem to bother anybody that Michael Vick isn't around anymore. That's because Frank Beamer is. In one of the biggest upsets of the off-season, the Virginia Tech coach decided not to take the Alabama job, even if everybody figured he would hitchhike naked to Tuscaloosa, for the honor and privilege of taking over one of America's most prestigious and tradition-bound programs.

The Crimson Tide establishment was even willing to part with its previous, er, fiscally conservative ways to get Beamer. It was the pinnacle: a rabid fan base, tremendous facilities and the opportunity to compete in the nation's top conference, the SEC. Layup. Slam dunk. Spike. Home run.

Beamer didn't go. Turns out he likes it at his alma mater. And, to be honest, what's not to like these days? Athletic director Jim Weaver came through with yet another pay hike, making Beamer part of the growing college coaches' millionaires club. He also made sure the Virginia Tech staff would stick around, even if they all received offers from other schools. And, as Beamer surveyed the landscape at his school, he couldn't help but like what he saw.

"There are good things happening here," Beamer said. "We'll have a new practice field we'll be moving onto in the fall. We're re-doing the stadium turf. We're adding stands in the south end zone. In two years, we'll have 11,000 more seats, including boxes and club seating. Then, we're going to add some new boxes on the press box side of the stadium. After that, another indoor facility is planned.

"We have a lot of exciting, good things happening. Things are really on the move. There's a lot of momentum, and I like being a part of it."

Beamer's decision to stick around Tech's campus surprised a lot of people, but it showed how the college landscape is changing. Thanks to the redistribution of prosperity, the game has become something of a Marxist affair, what with equal opportunity abounding and previously wallowing programs now piling up the wins and cash. Ten years ago, anybody who said Beamer would turn down Alabama for Virginia Tech or Dennis Erickson would stay at Oregon State rather than coach Southern California would be booked into a suite at the Laughing Academy.

Now, it makes perfect sense. Coaches can win anywhere now, thanks to TV revenues, scholarship limits and the conveniently short memories of college recruits. These days, "tradition" is what happened three years ago, not Bear Bryant or Anthony Davis or the Four Horsemen. You might as well be selling prospects on Peloponesian War heroes, if that's what you have in your arsenal. So, win a dozen games over four or five years, and you have high school players' attentions—such as they are.

That's why losing Vick is something of a good news/bad news situation for the Hokies. Nobody at Tech wanted him to go early to the NFL, because they knew the Hokies would be national title contenders—favorites, even—had he stuck around. But there is something to be said for producing the top pick in the NFL draft. People notice that. Eighteen-year-old high school seniors-to-be notice that. It's just another part of the sales pitch. You will be noticed at Tech. You will get Heisman Trophy consideration. You will get the chance to be a high draft pick. And you will win games. Lots of them.

Vick may be gone, but the Hokies have plenty left. And they're going to get plenty more. Whom did Cardinal O'Hara (Springfield, Pa.) running back Kevin Jones, perhaps the nation's top prospect, choose when it came down to Penn State and Virginia Tech? The Hokies. He didn't care about the 1982 national title or the '87 Fiesta Bowl, when the Nittany Lions picked off Vinny Testaverde six times. He cared about the here and now. And here and now, the Gobblers have it going on.

"There are only six other schools that have gone to eight straight bowl games," Beamer said. "When you're in that group, it makes it legitimate that you'll be a player, year-in and year-out. We talk about that all the time. Every year, we want to be knocking on the door for the Big East championship."

Beamer speaks about his program's prosperity and this year's prospects like a man who knows what he's doing. There is no false humility or bad-mouthing of his team. So what if he has to replace four starting offensive linemen?

The Hokies have been preparing for this situation and are ready with some top-quality newcomers. Vick's gone? It's a big loss, but so were the departures of Al Clark, Jim Druckenmiller, Maurice DeShazo and Will Furrer before him. Grant Noel is ready to step in. He doesn't have Vick's burst of speed or missile-launcher of an arm, but he's talented.

And what about that defense? Nine starters are back, but Beamer can't stop talking about all the reserves. It sounds like the Hokies could stock three bloodthirsty defenses.

You want to know why Beamer stayed? He likes to win. His whole staff is back, including trusted top aides Bud Foster (defensive coordinator) and Rickey Bustle, who directs the offense. That's huge, particularly at a time when assistants are job-hopping, in an attempt to better their situations and resumes for future shots at running a program.

Virginia Tech has also won 11 games two years in a row. That's pretty amazing, given its roots as a former largely anonymous independent. Tech heads into this year on the cusp of joining the big boys as a perennial power. It has already established itself as a school that will play in a bowl every year; now it wants to take the final step. Another double-digit win season and continued devotion by Beamer to his alma mater will establish Virginia Tech as more than just a nouveau riche power.

In the ever-changing world of college football, where old rules don't apply anymore, Virginia Tech is on the verge of really arriving. Win big without Vick, and we can see that the Hokies can withstand the loss of a marquee player and keep sailing along. We think it will happen. Beamer certainly agrees. If he didn't, he'd be in Tuscaloosa.

2001 SCHEDULE

Sept.	1	Connecticut
	8	Western Michigan
	22	@Rutgers
	29	Central Florida
Oct.	6	@West Virginia
	13	Boston College
	27	Syracuse
Nov.	3	@Pittsburgh
	10	@Temple
	17	@Virginia
Dec.	1	Miami

QUARTERBACKS

Ask Beamer about his quarterback situation, and he'll tell you about the rest of the team. He likes the Hokies' ground game. He believes the Virginia Tech offensive line will come around, even though it will have four new starters.

And then there's that defense. It should shut down most opponents and make it easier for the offense by requiring the Tech attack to produce fewer points. The message is clear: Grant Noel isn't Michael Vick, and he doesn't have to be. The 2001 Hokies won't need a magician under center.

"The first thing about Grant is that he has good people around him," Beamer said.

Whereas the Hokies counted heavily on Vick last year to make big plays and save the day, there can be no such reliance on Noel, who played in just three games last year as a third-string quarterback and attempted just 10 passes. A 6-1, 224-pounder who has spent three years in the program but enters the 2001 season with junior eligibility, resembles Vick somewhat in stature. He isn't that tall. He has good size and strength. But don't expect him to flash the same remarkable skills as Vick.

At the same time, Tech isn't about to alter its offense or change its philosophy for Noel. The Hokies will still run plenty. They'll throw out of rolls and boots. And they'll run the option. Beamer points out that Virginia Tech did that even when slow-footed Jim Druckenmiller was under center.

What will change is the team's insistence that its quarterback dominate the game and force opposing defenses to concoct wild strategies to contain him. Noel isn't going to make anybody do that. And he shouldn't have to. Virginia Tech has proven receivers, a big-time back in **Lee Suggs** and enough solid candidates up front to make sure Noel has sufficient time to throw, particularly against Virginia Tech's historically soft non-conference schedule, which features Connecticut, Western Michigan and Central Florida in September. Because of that, Noel seemed comfortable and in charge during the spring. The job is his, and he's acting that way.

"He did a lot of good things in spring practice," Beamer said. "He was very much in control and very confident. The players feel good when he's in the huddle. He's a good athlete. We tackled him in the spring game, and he took some hits and kept going.

"He has a feistiness and toughness. The one thing he has to do is get better at accurate throwing, time after time. Each time we scrimmaged, there was one play, where if he made a good throw, we would have had a big play. He has to get more accurate on his crossing patterns, so the players can catch it. But he did a lot of good things. He has enough skills for us to win a lot of football games with him."

Bustle, too, has confidence in Noel, despite his lack of game experience.

"Grant doesn't have a lot of experience from the standpoint of playing time, but he does have some wisdom from being around our offensive system for three years," Bustle said. "He's a guy who has shown he can make plays when things break down.

"Grant hasn't had much opportunity to work with the first team in the past. Now it's time to see what he can do—how he responds and plays—with our best people around him."

Redshirt freshman **Jason Davis** (6-1, 195) flashed plenty of potential during the spring game and could get some meaningful time this year, particularly if Noel struggles early. The biggest thing he needs to work on is his presence on the field. Davis has skills but doesn't yet have the swagger and ability to lead. That's a big thing that puts him behind Noel and could cost him the backup job, if one of three freshmen comes in and makes a big first impression.

"Jason made some good throws this spring," Beamer said. "But Grant looks poised in front of the football team, and Jason needs to work on that. He has to take charge of the team."

"This will be a new experience for Jason," Bustle said. "With Michael leaving early, Jason's timetable has accelerated and he must be up to the task. It will help that he came in last spring. He has a strong arm, now we need to see what kind of play-making ability he has."

The three freshmen have potential, but Tech does not like to use newcomers under center all that much. **Chris Clifton** (6-4, 200), from Deep Creek High School in Chesapeake, Va., was recruited originally by Beamer and his staff as a generic athlete, perhaps to be placed at receiver or the defensive backfield. But he played so well at quarterback during his senior year that he's back in the mix there.

Bryan Randall (6-2, 205), from Bruton High School in Williamsburg, Va., comes from the same part of Virginia as Vick, North Carolina quarterback/point guard Ronald Curry and Allen Iverson. Beamer says he's the top athlete in the state, and Randall's two seasons with 1,000 yards passing and throwing would back up that assertion.

Will Hunt (6-1, 205), from Springdale (Ark.) High School, isn't the smoothest player around, but he is tough and makes good decisions. He was listed as the top high school quarterback in Arkansas by *SuperPrep*.

The three rookie QBs may not contribute this year, but the future looks pretty sound at quarterback in Blacksburg.

RUNNING BACKS

It's a lot easier to debut a new quarterback when a tailback like Suggs is around. The 6-0, 204-pound junior had a tremendous 2001 season, rushing for 1,207 yards and an amazing 27 regular-season touchdowns (he added one in the Gator Bowl against Clemson), to help Virginia Tech to 2,975 yards, a Big East team record.

It was the second year in a row the Hokies had set a league mark for rushing yards. And while the losses of Vick, Andre Kendrick (547 yards, one giant Afro) and the aforementioned line starters would indicate Tech isn't headed for a repeat, there can be no doubt about the Hokies' commitment to the ground game, particularly with an inexperienced quarterback.

Suggs averaged 5.4 yards per carry and led the nation in scoring. He has the ability to break big runs and also has the power to work within the tackles. He carried the ball 20 times a game, not bad on a team that had so many weapons in the backfield.

His backup should be junior **Keith Burnell** (6-0, 202), who like Suggs mixes speed and strength. Burnell carried it 17 times last year but gained 111 yards and scored once. He shouldn't be too complacent, however, because if freshman Jones (6-1, 205), from Cardinal O'Hara High School in Chester, Pa., is eligible this fall, he could grab some immediate time. A rare blend of flat-out speed (he was the 2000 100- and 200-meter sprint champion in the Philadelphia Catholic League) and power, Jones was considered by some the nation's top recruit. If he's ready to play, Beamer will undoubtedly use him and could get some big returns on his investment.

The fullback spot belongs to senior **Jarrett Ferguson** (5-9, 222), who rushed for 215 yards and six touchdowns last season. His biggest value to the team, however, comes as a blocker. Suggs (or Kendrick) couldn't have had so much success last year without him.

"I don't know if there's a better fullback-tailback combination than Ferguson and Suggs," Beamer said.

Backing up Ferguson will be **Doug Easlick** (5-11, 228), a sophomore, and senior **Wayne Brigs** (5-10, 247). Neither was able to secure the second-string job during spring drills.

WIDE RECEIVERS/TIGHT ENDS

You won't find too many Smurf-like receivers on the Hokie roster. All four of Tech's top wideouts are taller than 6-0, with sophomore **Ernest Wilford** a robust 6-5, 211. Holy matchup problem, Big East!

"I like big receivers who can run," Beamer said. "**(Andre) Davis** and **(Emmett) Johnson** can flat run. That helps."

This time last year, we were wondering where Davis (6-1, 196) would go in the draft. His big sophomore season had convinced us that he was a prime candidate for an early exit to the NFL. But injuries and Vick's low completion percentage (54.0 percent) limited Davis' production and forced him to come back for his final year. The numbers weren't pretty. After averaging a remarkable 27.5 yards per catch during the magical 1999 season, Davis slipped to a 13.2-yard average on 24 receptions last year. He also scored just two times, after hitting the end zone on nine occasions in '99.

Part of it was injury-driven. Davis had a bad foot sprain that limited his running ability considerably. He also drew considerably more attention that he did the previous year, when he often galloped free in single coverage. He still has great speed, excellent open-field instincts and big-play potential. What he must do this year is become a reliable target on every down, in every situation, to help Noel and his own draft status.

"I think Davis is a guy who can help himself," Beamer said. "We've got to make sure he can get his hands on the ball. He can take a simple play and turn it into a great play."

Johnson (6-3, 206) is a senior who has many of the same qualities as Davis. He showed them last year, leading the team with 34 catches and scoring three times. His 16.9-yard average wasn't too shabby, either. It was quite a breakthrough year for Johnson, who had made just 10 catches in '99 and only 13 in his Virginia Tech career. Teams that concentrate on Davis too much will be burned by Johnson. In fact, it has come to the point where maybe Johnson deserves more attention than his teammate. Whatever the case, Tech is blessed with plenty of talent on the outside.

Wilford, a sophomore, and 6-0, 194-pound junior **Shawn Witten** are the primary backups. Wilford caught 12 balls last year, while Witten hauled in nine. Neither scored a touchdown nor showed any breathtaking speed, although they didn't have much chance. Wilford sat out the spring to recover from knee surgery but is expected to be fine for the season.

Several others, including junior **Terrell Parham** (6-0, 196), sophomore **Ron Moody** (6-1, 190) and redshirt freshman **Richard Johnson** (5-10, 189), will fight for time.

Tech is in good shape at tight end, where second-team All-Big East choice **Browning Wynn** (6-3, 232) and **Bob Slowikowski** (6-5, 247), both seniors, are ready for another strong season.

"They get after you and stay after you," Beamer said. "I like those two guys."

Wynn is the better receiver of the two, having caught eight passes last year, but neither is going to be used as a downfield threat. They're aggressive blockers who don't mind the dirty stuff.

"I have a tremendous amount of confidence in both Browning and Bob," said tight ends coach Danny Pearman. "They have done everything we have asked them to do to improve as players. Now, we need them to take on leadership roles."

Sophomore **Keith Willis** (6-5, 240) will also figure in the mix.

OFFENSIVE LINE

The lone holdover among the regulars up front is senior center **Steve DeMasi** (6-3, 278), who isn't the biggest pivot around but makes good calls, moves well and is a strong anchor. Of course, the Hokies would like to have a little more experience up front, but if you're going to be breaking in some new starters, it helps to have experience in the middle.

The Hokies made what they consider a critical move during the off-season, shifting sophomore **Jake Grove** (6-3, 272) from center to right guard. Grove had back problems last year, but he seemed fine during the spring and could develop into a top-flight lineman.

"If he stays healthy, he's going to be an excellent player," Beamer said.

Grove will still back up DeMasi, with either junior **Luke Owens** (6-3, 310) or redshirt freshman **James Miller** (6-5, 291) the top reserve at right guard.

On the left side, sophomore **Jacob Gibson** (6-4, 293) steps in, but he too, has some injury history. He missed part of the spring, but Beamer is confident he'll be all right this year. A fine athlete, Gibson just needs to add some strength to become a first-rate guard.

If he can't go, sophomore **Anthony Nelson** (6-3, 313) will step in.

Left tackle belongs to 6-4, 314-pound junior **Anthony Davis**, with junior **Tim Selmon** (6-5, 287) in reserve. Former tight end **Matt Wincek** (6-5, 284), a senior, is the main man on the right side, giving the Hokies an athletic presence there. He's backed up by 6-7, 320-pound redshirt freshman **Jon Dunn**, whom Beamer labels "a great prospect."

"Anthony and Matt are more than ready to step in and take over the tackle spots," offensive line coach Bryan Stinespring said. "Having them has been like having additional starters."

While the names aren't too familiar up front, the Hokies do have plenty of potential, provided everybody stays healthy.

"Any time you lose five seniors, four of whom were starters, you have to be concerned," Stinespring said. "We lost good players, as well as experience, but the cupboard isn't bare. We have a good nucleus coming back that mixes some proven players with some talented young players who haven't had the opportunity to prove themselves yet."

2000 STATISTICS

Rushing offense	270.5	5
Passing offense	155.9	100
Total offense	426.4	20
Scoring offense	40.3	5

Net Punting	32.6	87
Punt returns	18.2	1
Kickoff returns	18.9	77
Rushing defense	99.3	16
Passing efficiency defense	110.7	40
Total defense	323.6	27
Scoring defense	22.6	45
Turnover margin	+6	28

Last column is ranking among Division I-A teams.

KICKERS

Sophomore **Carter Warley** (5-11, 184) had a pretty good debut as the Hokies' placement specialist, making 7-of-9 kicks, including 6-of-8 from 30 yards and up, with a long of 47. The problem with him is a cranky back that forced him to stay out of spring drills.

"That worries me some," Beamer said. "He could only kick one day a week last year, other than game day, because of the back."

Warley has a big leg and is capable of drilling tries of 50 yards or so, but if his back continues to limit his availability, Beamer might have to go with junior **Jon Mollerup** (5-11, 202).

Mollerup saw junior varsity action the last two years but has potential. He doesn't have the same big leg as Warley and has never stepped onto the field in a real college game. That's not the best situation for a program that could need some kicking production while its new quarterback adjusts to bringing his team to the end zone.

DEFENSIVE LINE

Because senior starting tackles **Chad Beasley** (6-5, 292) and **David Pugh** (6-3, 271) missed spring drills while nursing injuries, the Hokies were able to develop depth. Most top-flight programs in the country—particularly those in Florida—are able to run at least two full defensive lines (and then some) out onto the turf, the better to keep the front-line troops rested for the fourth quarter.

As Beasley (surgery on both ankles) and Pugh (foot surgery) rehabbed, senior **Channing Reed** (6-2, 311) emerged as someone who can cause trouble in the middle.

"We started to notice him this spring," Beamer said. "He made a difference and disrupted some things."

Another potential contributor at tackle is sophomore **Kevin Lewis** (6-1, 280).

Their growth doesn't push Pugh and Beasley out of the first unit. Pugh was a first-team All-Big East choice last year, after making 57 tackles, including 12 for loss and five sacks. Quick and strong, he provides an excellent push up front and should spend plenty of time in enemy backfields this season.

Beasley was voted to the league's second team after posting 58 stops, eight of which came behind the line. They comprise an excellent tandem and should help the Hokies be even more stingy defensively this season.

"David and Chad are two of the best tackles not only in the conference, but in the country," defensive line coach Charley Wiles said. "They are the core for us up front and they're playmakers. They're two big kids who are athletic and make plays and that's huge on this level."

The end situation is just about as promising, thanks to the return of starters **Lamar Cobb** and **Nathaniel Adibi**. Cobb is a 6-2, 226-pound junior who made 47 tackles last year and trapped runners behind the line five times. He's quick and gets to the ball well.

Adibi might have an even brighter future, if his 2000 debut is any indication. Heralded by Beamer before the season as one to watch, Adibi made had five sacks and seven tackles behind the line. The sophomore goes 6-3, 253 and has the speed to create mayhem off the edge and the strength to handle the heavy lifting against the run. His challenge this year is to become more consistent, the key to greatness for him.

Don't expect a huge eruption from Adibi, because his backup, sophomore **Jim Davis** (6-4, 251) "keeps gets better and better," Beamer said. Behind Cobb is sophomore **Cols Colas** (6-0, 232), who is so quick that Beamer is invoking the name of a recent Tech great in comparison.

"He's the fastest guy on the line," Beamer said of Colas. "He reminds you of Corey Moore the way he comes off the corner. He's got speed."

"Jim probably made the most big plays for us at end last year and he has great potential," Wiles said. "Hopefully he'll develop better practice habits, mature and come on for us this year. Cols has a lot of ability, but he's still learning the position. On paper, Cols has it all, but he has to come on and play the game."

LINEBACKERS

Beamer was pleased to see his backup inside linebackers emerge throughout the spring, while senior inside starters **Jake Housewright** (6-3, 237) and **Ben Taylor** (6-2, 235) rehabbed injuries, but the coach definitely wants to see those two ready for action this fall. While Taylor is practically guaranteed to be back—the ankle on which he had surgery should be completely recovered—it's still anybody's guess whether Housewright can recover from the torn ACL he suffered in the Gator Bowl, against Clemson.

Taylor was a semifinalist for the Butkus Award last year, given annually to the nation's top linebacker, and led the team with 103 tackles, six of which came for loss. He also picked off two passes and was chosen first-team All-Big East. He's a tackling machine who is perfect for the Hokie system because he moves so well to the ball.

Housewright had 75 tackles last year, with four behind the line. He was finally healthy last season—for the first time during his tenure in Blacksburg—and showed it.

"Ben's a guy who I thought improved as the season went along," Foster said. "He's an exceptional football player and we have high expectations for him. It's disappointing that he's hurt, but it's allowed him to spend more time in the weight room.

"This last year for Jake was the first year he's been healthy. He showed steady improvement and played his best game in the Gator Bowl. I look for both him and Ben to be leaders for us and we're expecting big things from them."

But Housewright may not be ready to go (and he still has a redshirt year available). In that case, the Hokies will turn to senior **Brian Welch** (6-0, 232), who made 42 tackles last year in a reserve role, after making a full recovery from a '99 knee injury. He's strong and capable but not as big as Housewright, or Taylor, for that matter.

Though Welch took most of the first-team reps during the spring at Housewright's position, it's possible that a pair of younger players who impressed Beamer during practice could take over. Sophomore **Vegas Robinson** (6-0, 233) and red-shirt freshman **Mikal Baaqee** (5-10, 218) each got reps during the spring and showed potential.

"Vegas is a guy who I have a lot of hopes for," Foster said. He has good speed, is very physical and had a great winter. Now is the time for him to step it up and I think he's ready to rise to that challenge. Mikal is another guy who has a lot of ability. He has good speed and quickness. We just need to get him to where he understands the defense."

Outside, expect junior **T.J. Jackson** (6-1, 214) to slide into the starting spot vacated by Phillip Summers and Nick Sorensen, who split time there last year. Jackson saw action in just eight games last year and made eight stops.

He also was waylaid halfway through spring by a knee injury that shouldn't prohibit him from practicing in the summer. Behind him is sophomore **Deon Provitt** (6-1, 209), who needs only consistency to become a valuable contributor.

DEFENSIVE BACKS

Even though the Hokies lost second-team All-Big East rover Cory Bird to graduation, they should have a deep, talented and fast secondary. Don't worry about that. Taking over for Bird is senior **Kevin McCadam** (6-1, 219), who backed up at free safety last year and made 28 tackles.

"He has good size and speed, and he's a smart guy," Beamer said.

McCadam is so capable that he made a strong run at the free safety spot during preseason practice but suffered a high ankle sprain. His understudy is sophomore **Michael Crawford** (5-11, 205), who saw time on special teams last year.

Junior **Willie Pile** (6-3, 197), last year's regular free safety, returns to the spot after making 56 tackles and leading the team with six interceptions. He missed spring drills with shoulder surgery, giving junior **Billy Hardee** (5-11, 198) and redshirt freshman **Vincent Fuller** (6-1, 178) a chance at action, but the job is Pile's. That doesn't mean Beamer can't get excited about his reserve situation, particularly Fuller.

"He needs a little more size, but he can flat run," Beamer said. "He can flat find the ball."

Junior **Ronyell Whittaker** (5-9, 192), a second-team All-Big East choice who had 61 tackles and five interceptions, returns at the boundary corner and brings excellent coverage skills to the party.

"He can get tight with receivers, in their hip pockets," Beamer said.

"Ronyell knows he can play with anybody," defensive backs coach Lorenzo Ward said. "He had a tough assignment in the bowl game [Clemson's Rod Gardner] and he did a great job against him. There was a great size disadvantage and Ronyell held his own. The thing he needs to do now is evolve to the point where he understands the entire game of football."

Whittaker's partner will probably be senior **Larry Austin** (5-9, 187), who has recovered from a torn ACL and brings excellent speed to the outside.

The backup situation is excellent. All sophomore **Eric Green** (5-11, 177) did last year when pressed into service in relief of Austin was earn second-team freshman all-America honors from *The Sporting News*, after making 31 tackles, picking off four passes and knocking away 12 more.

Sophomore **Garnell Wilds** (5-11, 193) has the potential to be a strong cover man, although he too is recovering from a blown-out knee ligament.

PUNTERS

Although sophomore **Robert Peaslee** (6-0, 192) was the Hokies' main punter last year (Taylor also kicked three times), he lost his starting role during the spring to redshirt freshman **Vinnie Burns** (5-11, 177). Burns demonstrated a big leg during drills and needs only consistency in live action to solidify his status.

"The last 12 kicks I charted of his during the spring averaged 46.9 yards with a 4.0-second hang time," Beamer said. "If he can consistently do that, he'll help us greatly with field position."

Peaslee isn't going away, but he must get stronger and keep his punts aloft longer to reclaim his spot.

SPECIAL TEAMS

By now, everybody knows this is a Virginia Tech strength. In fact, the argument can be made that the Hokies have set the standard for special teams play nationwide. The previous quote by Beamer shows one of the reasons. He doesn't give the special teams over to someone else. He handles them.

And the Hokies' top athletes want a spot on them. Why not? Blocking kicks and returning them for scores is a lot of fun. Tech swatted away eight kicks and punts last year, a good start toward their goal of blocking more kicks than any other school for the second straight decade.

Tech's return game is excellent, too. That's thanks in large part to Davis, who averaged an impressive 22.0 yards bringing back punts—second in the nation behind Aaron Lockett of Kansas State and his 22.7 average—and scored three times. Not that Whittaker's 14.4-yard average on 17 returns was too shabby.

The loss of Andre Kendrick takes away last year's main kick returner, but Suggs, Whittaker, Davis and perhaps freshman Kevin Jones will do just fine.

Deep snapper **Ken Keister**, a 6-1, 229-pound junior returns, but he missed spring drills to recover from a knee injury, allowing redshirt freshman **Travis Conway** (6-3, 282) to take a shot at the position. Peaslee is back as the holder on placements.

RECRUITING CLASS

The Hokies had a strong class, and though it wasn't considered one of the top 10 in the country, it certainly will provide the program with enough size, speed and talent to sustain its recent run of success.

Jones is the plum. He finished second all-time in career rushing yards among Philadelphia backs with 5,878. He also won the first-ever High School Heisman Award for the Northeast region.

Randall was rated the fourth-best quarterback in the nation by *PrepStar* and the 15th-best player nationally by *SuperPrep*. He was also a great prep point guard and will be going out for coach Ricky Stokes' basketball team when the football season ends.

"Our recruiting continues to get better and better," Beamer said. "I think this class bears that out. When we look back at this group in five years, I believe it will have proven to be a highly successful class.

"... This class has everything—size, speed, quickness, good academics and versatility. There are a lot of players in this group who have the ability to contribute at more than one position."

Of the 22 players Virginia Tech signed, 13 were from the Hokies' talent-rich home state.

"If we can continue to recruit Virginia like this, we will remain a strong contender for the Big East title," Beamer said. "And if we win the Big East, that means we will compete for the national championship."

BLUE RIBBON ANALYSIS

OFFENSE	B
SPECIAL TEAMS	A-
DEFENSE	B+
INTANGIBLES	A

Michael Vick is gone, but the warning sirens are not wailing in Blacksburg. That's because Virginia Tech is not a program boosted to tremendous heights by the miraculous convergence of a few highly talented individuals—particularly Vick—and then left with the same average personnel as before. This is a program that has been built to sustain success, not chase it.

As a result, the 2001 season should be pretty darn successful. Were Vick around, Tech would likely be a top two or three inhabitant of every preseason ranking. Without him, Virginia is still a top-10 or 15 caliber club with higher aspirations, provided a few things come together.

The most obvious is the quarterback situation. Noel needs to be consistent and productive. He must show that he can lead a team, make good throws on a regular basis and mount at least two or three crucial drives throughout the season. That could bring the Hokies 10 regular-season wins, considering their soft non-conference schedule and the fact that most of the Big East is still a big step behind Beamers' Bunch in the talent department.

Noel has a fine running game at his disposal, plenty of proven targets, and if Beamer is to be believed, a good offensive wall.

Then there's the defense. It should be a bloodthirsty bunch, capable of stuffing opponents by land or air. It has big-play potential and the ability to generate good field position for an offense that will need some time to come together. It is fast and deep, and as always, opportunistic.

Throw in the traditionally strong Tech special teams, and you have the makings of a team that should finish first or second in the Big East standings and play in a significant bowl. That's just the way it goes in Blacksburg these days.

The Hokies aren't nouveau riche anymore. They're threatening to become part of the establishment, and that means piles of wins and bowl cash each season. Beamer may have never imagined such a situation when he took over at his alma mater, back in 1987, but the Hokies have arrived—and expect to keep moving on. Why else would Beamer still be around?

(M.B.)

2000 RESULTS

Akron	W	52-23	1-0
East Carolina	W	45-28	2-0
Rutgers	W	49-0	3-0
Boston College	W	48-34	4-0
Temple	W	35-13	5-0
West Virginia	W	48-20	6-0
Syracuse	W	22-14	7-0
Pittsburgh	W	37-34	8-0
Miami	L	21-41	8-1
Central Florida	W	44-21	9-1
Virginia	W	42-21	10-1
Clemson (Gator Bowl)	W	41-20	11-1

West Virginia

LOCATION	**Morgantown, WV**
CONFERENCE	**Big East**
LAST SEASON	**7-5 (.583)**
CONFERENCE RECORD	**3-4 (t-5th)**
OFFENSIVE STARTERS RETURNING	**5**
DEFENSIVE STARTERS RETURNING	**9**
NICKNAME	**Mountaineers**
COLORS	**Blue & Gold**
HOME FIELD	**Mountaineer (63,500)**
HEAD COACH	**Rick Rodriguez (West Va. '86)**
RECORD AT SCHOOL	**First Year**
CAREER RECORD	**47-44-2 (8 years)**
ASSISTANTS	
	Phil Elmassian (William & Mary '74)
	Defensive Coordinator/Defensive Backs
	Steve Bird (Eastern Kentucky '83)
	Wide Receivers
	Jeff Casteel (California, Pa. '84)
	Defensive Line
	Todd Graham (East Central Okla. '86)
	Linebackers
	Herb Hand (Hamilton College '90)
	T-Backs
	Calvin Magee (Southern '90)
	Running Backs
	Bill Stewart (Fairmont State '75)
	Quarterbacks/Special Teams
	Rick Trickett (Glenville State '73)
	Offensive Line
TEAM WINS (last 5 yrs.)	**8-7-8-4-7**
FINAL RANK (last 5 yrs.)	**26-47-25-52-31**
2000 FINISH	**Beat Mississippi in Music City Bowl.**

COACH AND PROGRAM

It had to be an odd experience for West Virginia players, during preparations for the Music City Bowl against Ole Miss, to have a pair of head coaches pacing the turf inside the school's Caperton Indoor Facility.

On the one hand there was Don Nehlen, venerable WVU institution and veteran of 21 seasons in Morgantown, who was preparing the Mountaineers for one final game before heading into a retirement filled with reminiscences and golf dates.

On the other was Rich Rodriguez, Nehlen's successor. A West Virginia alum, Rodriguez had come to town with a resume that screamed "OFFENSE!" and a reputation for invigorating programs with an exciting, wide-open style that filled the seats and padded the win column. There they were, on display,

West Virginia's past and its future. Rodriguez was there as an "observer," learning as much as he could about the program while Nehlen and his staff took one final team into battle. Underclassmen no doubt wanted to win the game over the Rebels, but they were certain to practice with an extra verve, because their new boss would be looking on. Perhaps that's why WVU smoked Ole Miss, 49-38, looking as imposing offensively as it had in years.

Maybe the players wanted to win one last one for Nehlen, who despite some fan grumblings to the contrary, was a popular fixture in the state for two decades. Or maybe Rodriguez had some input into the game plan, and that's why senior quarterback **Brad Lewis** threw for 318 yards and five touchdowns. Whatever the case, it was a fine exit for Nehlen, who not only went out a winner but snapped an eight-game postseason losing streak (dating back to 1986) in the process.

It was a nice, tidy wrap-up, and in many ways, it was overdue. While Nehlen did a fine job squiring the Mountaineers through the 1980s and even played for the 1988 national title against Notre Dame (WVU lost, 34-21), West Virginia had become increasingly irrelevant on the national scene during the last six years of the Nehlen regime. Its Big East status slipped dramatically, too, from that of a perennial contender to a middling pretender who hoped to gather the six needed wins to sneak into a minor bowl.

Nehlen supporters are right to point to the inherent disadvantages of coaching at the school, from the state's small population and dearth of top-flight football talent to its perceived backwater climate, hardly the type of drawing card necessary to convince out-of-towners to spend four years there. But football powers are sprouting up in all sorts of odd places these days, and it was increasingly difficult for the Nehlen camp to justify its troubles with the familiar arguments when schools from Blacksburg, Va., Manhattan, Kansas and Corvallis, Ore., were making giant strides with double-figure win totals and pricey bowl appearances.

In the grand scheme, West Virginia had gone from a successful regional player with occasional forays into the "Big Picture" to a mom-and-pop operation that was complaining about what it couldn't do more than trumpeting any sizeable accomplishments.

And so, Nehlen was replaced by Rodriguez, and a New Era began.

Like most fresh beginnings, there were several of the usual events. The off-season conditioning program was suitably Draconian, with considerable weight lost and plenty of vomiting. That's a given with any new coach. They want to find out if the players have a strong commitment to the program and have "what it takes" to compete at a high level.

There was a spring practice season filled with learning. There are new, more aggressive systems on both sides of the ball. West Virginia will use a no-huddle offense and a bring-'em-on defense that features plenty of blitzing from eight- and nine-man fronts. When it was all over, Rodriguez wasn't quite sure what he had, particularly on offense.

"It's hard to tell, because (Nehlen's and his) schemes are so different," Rodriguez said. "When you have some skills guys, like we do, it gives you a chance. Last year's offensive line was filled with so many seniors that we lost a lot of guys. It's not an empty cupboard up front, but we have a lot of young players, and they have to learn so many new things."

Rodriguez graduated from West Virginia in 1986 after an interesting career. He spent three seasons (1982-84) as a defensive back and two more as a student assistant before moving on. That he played for Nehlen could have made for something of a difficult transition, because the former coach certainly wasn't leaving after winning the BCS title game and riding into the West Virginia sunset as a conquering hero. But Rodriguez has shown the proper respect for his old coach, first by deferring to Nehlen during last year's bowl and then by saying all the "Right Things" when asked about the program's status.

"The transition was a smooth one, because I played here before and knew the support people and knew the university," Rodriguez said. "It's always easier to follow somebody that nobody liked. It's tougher to follow someone who has been so respected. It's tough to follow a legend. But there are things in place. We're not desperate."

The Mountaineers aren't that bad, but they have plenty of work to do if they want to break away from Boston College, Pittsburgh and Syracuse in the middle of the Big East pack, let alone join Miami and Virginia Tech atop the standings. The most important thing is to improve the school's recruiting efforts. Rodriguez expects his offense to do just that.

When offensive players see how much fun they can have, they'll want to take a look. During Rodriguez's two years at Clemson, the Tigers averaged 403 and 446.5 yards (10th nationally) with a balanced attack that showcased the Tigers' skill performers by giving them ample opportunities to succeed, rather than depending on them to make plays by themselves or—worse—forcing them to surrender to the tyranny of a rigid system.

That's something anybody could sell. Thanks to new coordinator Phil Elmassian, late of LSU and Wisconsin, the Mountaineers can make the same pitch to defensive prospects. Come to West Virginia and careen all over the field.

The results were evident on signing day. Last year's team had players from 14 different states and the District of Columbia, but six of those states were represented by just one player. Rodriguez's first class included players from eight states, including Texas, California, Alabama, Georgia and Massachusetts, which were not represented on the 2000 roster. It's clear that Rodriguez is intent on expanding the program's reach by targeting players throughout the Southeast—and beyond.

"It's easy for me to sell this area, and education and environment, because I'm from here (he grew up in Grant Town, W. Va.) and I played here," Rodriguez said. "We have to start attracting quality out-of-state guys."

Having coached at Clemson and played at West Virginia when the Mountaineers were capable of flexing some serious muscle, Rodriguez understands what goes into making a program more than just capable of eking out invitations to the Whothehellisthatdotcom Bowl. He wants the Mountaineers to be a major player.

That starts Sept. 1, at Boston College. Rodriguez is ready for the challenge. WVU fans were sure ready for a change.

2001 SCHEDULE

Sept.	1	@Boston College
	8	Ohio
	15	@Maryland
	22	Kent
Oct.	6	Virginia Tech
	13	@Notre Dame
	25	@Miami
Nov.	3	Rutgers
	10	@Syracuse
	17	Temple
	24	Pittsburgh

QUARTERBACKS

Lewis' Music City explosion was certainly a good audition for his new coach. He completed 15-of-21 passes and led the Mountaineers to scores on their first six possessions. It almost seemed too easy. Here was Lewis, who had thrown for all of 94 yards against Rutgers in an overtime near-miss, carving up an SEC team. Rodriguez had to be impressed—to a point.

In spring drills, Lewis (6-3, 220) was not a dominant quarterback. In fact, by the time the Mountaineers had completed their spring game, Rodriguez believed that redshirt freshman **Rasheed Marshall** (6-1, 185) was "closing fast" on Lewis. That's not the best endorsement for a senior incumbent. But Lewis has some issues that make him a candidate to struggle in Rodriguez's offense. He isn't the most accurate passer around. He completed just 50.4 percent of 244 passes last year. He also isn't that mobile. And though he threw just eight interceptions last year, Lewis had only 13 touchdown passes, and five of those came against Mississippi.

"He was outstanding in the bowl game," Rodriguez said. "He was poised, made the right decisions and executed the game plan. He did well, but he has a lot to learn. He only has one year left, and he has to be above and beyond everybody else."

Uh oh. Sounds like there will be a revolving door at quarterback in Morgantown this year. Rodriguez makes it clear that he will use whatever players at whatever positions to help West Virginia win. That's not only good news for Marshall, but for the two incoming freshman quarterbacks, **Danny Embick** (6-1, 207), from William T. Dwyer High School in Jupiter, Fla., and **Robert Johnson** (6-2, 210), from Americus (Ga.) High School.

While Rodriguez likes Lewis' experience, he also likes Marshall's potential.

"He has all the tools you want in a quarterback," Rodriguez said. "He can throw and run. He's a tough guy, and he's intelligent as well. He had an excellent spring. But he's never played before. You don't know how he'll react."

Embick has a pretty impressive resume. He was the first-team Class 5A all-state quarterback in Florida after throwing for 2,400 yards and 21 touchdowns. He also ran for 650 yards and 12 more scores. It's clear he has the skills Rodriguez likes. So does Johnson, who was the class AA player of the year in Georgia.

Though Rodriguez would no doubt like to redshirt his new quarterbacks, he won't hesitate to use one of them if he proves he can handle the workload. One thing the freshmen have in their favor is that neither Lewis nor Marshall has the luxury of spending a full season in Rodriguez's offense. In a way, all four are like newcomers.

RUNNING BACKS

The Mountaineers don't have any worries here. They return their top two rushers from last year—**Avon Cobourne** and **Cooper Rego**—and should also benefit from the services of sophomore **Quincy Wilson** (5-10, 215), who missed all of last year after tearing his ACL during spring drills.

Cobourne (5-9, 195), a junior, was excellent last year, gaining 1,018 yards despite missing two full games with a left foot sprain. The second-team All-Big East choice had a quartet of 100-yard rushing efforts, with a 166-yard outburst against Syracuse the most impressive. Although his total was 121 yards fewer than he posted during his freshman season, Cobourne was still dangerous. He has a great blend of strength and power, and you can bet he will improve on last year's meager five pass receptions.

"He learned the offense quickly," Rodriguez said. "He's very physical and has all the tools to run, catch and block. He emerged this spring as a leader."

Rego (5-10, 190), a senior, is an interesting player. He gained 591 yards last year and scored nine times and "has the most speed of all the backs," Rodriguez said. But he is clearly trapped behind Cobourne on the depth chart and could slip behind Wilson, should he come back completely from his knee surgery. The one-time Notre Dame blue-chipper is fast, but he doesn't have Cobourne's consistency. Meanwhile, Wilson could be a Cobourne with training wheels—and then some.

"He was a little tentative at first (during the spring), because he was testing the knee out, but during the second half, he became physical and showed that he's a guy we can count on," Rodriguez said. "He's the most physical of the backs."

Josh McMillen, a 6-2, 210-pound senior, will also see some action, albeit limited.

WIDE RECEIVERS/TIGHT ENDS

Rodriguez would like to have eight or nine capable receivers at his disposal, but the Mountaineers didn't make enough progress in that direction during the spring. Expect WVU to use four or five receivers at a time this year, if only to spread things out for Cobourne.

But the wideouts won't be mere ornamentation. They have to catch, also. At this point, WVU has two proven threats and plenty of candidates for action, with three freshmen also likely to get a look.

The team's primary deep threat will be 5-10, 165-pound senior **Antonio Brown**, who led the team with 51 catches last year and averaged an impressive 17.2 yards per reception. Brown was particularly impressive late in the year and had a total of 21 catches for 426 yards (20.3 average) and all three of his touchdowns in the final three games of 2000.

"He can stretch the field with his speed," Rodriguez said. "He made some big plays last year."

Rodriguez expects junior **Phil Braxton** (6-3, 200) to become the Mountaineers' main threat this year, even though Braxton caught just nine passes last year. There are a few reasons for Rodriguez's confidence in the third-year player. First, when Braxton did catch the ball, he made things happen, as evidenced by his 26.3 yards-per-catch average.

Then there's Rodriguez's recent affinity for larger receivers. At Clemson, he used Rod Gardner to great advantage. At Tulane, JuJuan Dawson was the Green Wave's top target.

"I like big, physical guys who can get to the ball," Rodriguez said.

The rest of the receiving picture is blurry. If the season started today, it is likely that senior **Shawn Terry** (6-3, 175) and junior **A.J. Nastasi** (6-0, 185) would be the main men behind Brown and Braxton. But a host of candidates, including seniors **Seth Abraham** (5-11, 175) and **Shawn Swindall** (5-9, 170) and redshirt freshmen **Harold Leath** (6-4, 190) and **Mike Page** (5-8, 165), will be vying for time.

A trio of freshmen—**Dee Alston** (6-0, 170) from Theodore (Ala.) High School, **Miquelle Henderson** (6-3, 192) from Theodore High School in Mobile, Ala. and **Keith Mills** (6-0, 190) from Garland (Texas) High School—will also try to crack the rotation. All have good speed.

The tight end position has been eliminated, per se, replaced by what Rodriguez calls the "T-back" spot. The players there can line up all over the place—in the backfield, on the wing, along the line and could even be split out on occasion. Heading into the summer practices, 6-4, 255-pound sophomore **Tory Johnson** is the early leader, with junior **Tim Frost** (6-4, 265) behind him.

"Johnson is the most athletic of the two," Rodriguez said. "He could play in the backfield and even carry the ball some."

OFFENSIVE LINE

The Mountaineers had four senior starters up front last year, and the fifth, guard **Brad Knell** was a fourth-year junior. This year's quintet will have no such experience. It will, however, be a quicker, leaner unit.

While at Tulane and Clemson, Rodriguez favored linemen who were lighter (usually 270-290 pounds) and able to run.

"I don't mind if our guys are 280 or 285 pounds, as long as they're in shape," Rodriguez said. "We block with angles, block down and kick out. We'll pull the center. We move around."

The West Virginia version of the streamlined Rodriguez front will be a little larger than his previous editions, but it won't have the same heaping serving of beef as many of its Mountaineer predecessors had. The biggest projected starter of the bunch is 295-pound sophomore tackle **Tim Brown**. No lineman on the spring roster weighed in at more than that.

Rodriguez has them leaner, but it is still questionable whether he will have the Mountaineers better up front. Not that last year was a gigantic success. WVU averaged a mere 3.4 yards per rush and was unable to bully its rivals. That's why Rodriguez favors the movable feast, in which his teams take advantage of spacing and angles to create room for backs and protection for the man under center. West Virginia will have to rely on that philosophy, because it is clear that there isn't a wealth of proven talent up front.

"We're not overloaded with NFL-caliber type guys," Rodriguez said. "Some of the guys are athletic. The rest are just players."

Rodriguez reports that Knell (6-5, 290), a senior, had the best spring of all the linemen.

"He's a good football player," Rodriguez said.

Rodriguez also feels pretty confident about junior tackle **Lance Nimmo** (6-6, 285), who had a solid spring. The aforementioned Brown (6-5, 295), a sophomore, has substantial potential, but he needs to get in better shape.

The days of WVU using zone blocking to open holes are over. Even the tackles have to move. Expect to see 6-4, 290-pound senior **Jason Brooks** in the other guard spot, provided he is focused. Brooks was a highly-regarded recruit from St. Ignatius High School in Cleveland who had to leave the University of Michigan two years ago, because of some off-field problems. He saw limited time last year and has a lot of talent, but he remains an unproven commodity.

The middle is manned by 6-2, 276-pound junior **Zach Dillow**—for now. A former walk-on, Dillow impressed the coaches somewhat in the spring, but Rodriguez doesn't rule out moving Knell to center and using 6-3, 295-pound junior **Roderick Smith** at guard. Look for redshirt freshman **Jeff Berk** (6-5, 285), whose quick feet have impressed Rodriguez, to see some time at both tackle spots.

2000 STATISTICS

Rushing offense	140.8	64
Passing offense	207.5	66
Total offense	348.3	73
Scoring offense	27.9	46
Net Punting	30.6	103
Punt returns	7.3	96
Kickoff returns	20.5	32
Rushing defense	146.5	53
Passing efficiency defense	121.4	66
Total defense	379.5	69
Scoring defense	29.5	84
Turnover margin	+7	23

Last column is ranking among Division I-A teams.

KICKERS

Gone is Jon Ohliger, who went from kickoff specialist to primary placement performer last season and made 8-of-14 field goals. His is not a huge loss; he converted only 2-of-7 tries longer than 40 yards.

Expect to see senior **Brenden Rauh** (5-9, 180) handling the point-after kicks and field goals in 2001. Rauh made all three of his attempts last year, with a long of 43 yards.

"He's accurate, but he doesn't have a booming leg,"

Rodriguez said.

The big foot belongs to 6-3, 205-pound sophomore **Todd James**, who will likely handle the kickoffs, but don't be surprised if he's called upon for some long-range tries.

DEFENSIVE LINE

Even though Rodriguez is concerned about team-wide depth on defense and says that the Mountaineers have about "eight or nine solid guys" on that side of the ball, the front wall is in pretty good shape, thanks to a relative abundance of experience, at least among the starters.

There have been some position changes, the better to create a faster, more aggressive unit. Both senior **Corey McIntyre** (6-0, 245) and junior **James Davis** (6-3, 215) have been switched from linebacker to defensive end, and McIntyre should start.

"We need speed off the edge, so that we can rush the passer," Rodriguez said. "He's got a big motor and enough speed to give us a good dimension on the outside."

McIntyre made 49 tackles last year as a backup middle linebacker, with eight stops against Idaho and seven against Rutgers his high-water marks. He also had an interception in the third quarter of the Music City Bowl that helped quell the Mississippi comeback, when the Rebels went to redshirt freshman quarterback Eli Manning.

The tackles should be 6-5, 275-pound junior **Jason Davis** and senior **Antwan Lake** (6-5, 285). Davis was a full-time starter at end last year and made 30 tackles, nine of which came behind the line. He had six tackles against Idaho and five solos against Maryland. Lake, meanwhile, started all nine games in which he saw action last year but was hampered by a sprained ankle that limited his effectiveness.

Lake finished with just 13 stops, after making 39 the year before. He is a strong player with some quickness who can get to the passer. He and Davis should both enjoy Elmassian's system, which prefers tackles to get upfield rather than merely occupy blockers so linebackers can make tackles.

The backup situation isn't so great, with redshirt freshman **Cecil Hagwood**, who checks in at a light 6-5, 235, available.

The other starting end is 6-4, 275-pound junior **David Upchurch**, who made 40 tackles as a nose guard last year. A weight room strongman who handled a lot of dirty work last year, Upchurch had eight tackles and two sacks against Idaho and seven stops in the near-miss against Syracuse. He has good size and speed, although he isn't a classic charger off the end. Neither is his backup, **Sedrick Lewis**, a junior who goes 6-2, 300. Last year, Lewis saw minimal time inside.

LINEBACKERS

Because Elmassian's system is basically a 4-2-5, this unit will have a different look this year. One thing that won't change will be the contribution of 6-1, 230-pound sophomore **Grant Wiley**, last year's Big East Rookie of the Year. Voted second-team freshman All-America by *The Sporting News*, Wiley finished 2000 with 94 tackles, 12th in the league, and 14 stops behind the line, seventh-best in the conference. He had three interceptions, including picks for scores against Idaho and Boston College.

Wiley had 13 tackles against Notre Dame and 10 against Pittsburgh. Even though Wiley broke his leg in the Music City Bowl, he was able to operate at half speed during spring drills and impressed Rodriguez with his play and attitude.

"He's an outstanding player," Rodriguez said. "He's all instincts and has great athletic ability. He also has a hard edge to him, a little bit of attitude. He doesn't just like to tackle you. He likes to put some pain into you."

The other incumbent is senior **Kyle Kayden** (6-3, 235), who made 109 tackles last year and stopped 13 enemy ball carriers behind the line. Kayden was a captain—only the third junior during Nehlen's tenure to earn that distinction—and had four double-digit tackle performances, including a 15-tackle game against (guess who?) Idaho. Kayden can play the middle or the strong side and brings excellent intensity to the

Mountaineer defense.

"He did some good things during the spring and has good leadership ability," Rodriguez said. "He's a pretty good athlete who can run well."

But Kayden is in a fight for his starting job with 6-4, 220-pound redshirt freshman **Adam Lehnortt**, who was one of the best prep linebackers in Pennsylvania in 1999 and who should be a key contributor down the line for the Mountaineers.

"He has an excellent future," Rodriguez said. "He'll push Kayden, because of his athletic ability." Also in the mix at linebacker is junior **Ben Collins** (5-11, 210), who played in all 12 games last year and made 14 tackles.

DEFENSIVE BACKS

The five-man secondary hybrid should give the Mountaineers increased flexibility in both running and passing situations, provided Elmassian can find the right people to handle the "Rover" and strong safety positions.

Were the season to start today, junior **Angel Estrada** (6-2, 190), a converted free safety, would handle the rover position, with last year's top tackler, senior **Shawn Hackett** (6-1, 195), manning the strong safety spot. Hackett had 115 stops last year, picked off two passes and recovered two fumbles. He needed little time to acclimate himself to I-A football, after joining WVU out of Lackawanna (Pa.) Junior College. Hackett had six double-digit tackle games, including a 14-stop effort in the win over Ole Miss. He returned an interception 41 yards for a score in his first-ever major-college game, against Boston College, and didn't slow down for a minute afterward.

"He's one of our best football players," Rodriguez said. "He's an all-around performer. He plays special teams and works hard every day. You could put him at rover, free safety, strong safety or linebacker, if needed."

Estrada didn't make a tackle last year, but as is often the case when a new coach comes to town, he moved from a backup free safety to the first-string rover position. The spot is a combination of strong safety and outside linebacker and requires a player who can provide strong run support (usually on the weak side) and also handle zone and man coverage assignments.

Its purpose is to allow the Mountaineers the opportunity to react to whatever formations an offense shows by having a player who can slide immediately into nickel coverage, while still being available to stop the run, should an opponent load up for a ground assault. Rodriguez believes Estrada has the size and speed to perform both tasks.

"He is a good athlete who showed the kind of athletic ability we need on the outside," Rodriguez said. "He's also physical."

Expect juniors **Arthur Harrison** (5-9, 185) and **Lewis Daniels** (6-1, 190) to fight it out for the backup rover position with junior **Ben Meighan** (6-1, 195). Meighan and Daniels were special teams performers last year.

The free safety spot belongs to senior **Rick Sherrod** (6-3, 195), who returns to the starting role after a fine 2000 season. Sherrod was third on the team with 106 tackles, picked off three passes, knocked down 12 others, recovered two fumbles and blocked a kick. He, like most of his defensive mates, had a huge game against Idaho, piling up 16 tackles. Sherrod is quick, covers a lot of ground and doesn't mind knocking people over.

"He's a big guy," Rodriguez said. "Our free safety is pretty involved in run support, and Rick's a good fit for us."

Depth is a problem at the free safety spot, although it's possible junior **O'Rondai Cox** (6-0, 180), who comes to WVU from South Carolina, via Butler (Pa.) Community College, could find his way into the mix there. He might also play some cornerback, although Rodriguez is relatively pleased with the Mountaineers' options there. Not that he was too thrilled heading into spring drills.

"That was a concern coming in," he said. "We didn't think they played as well as they should have last year. But they were a pleasant surprise. We think they learned some things, and we're better there than we thought we'd be."

One starter returns, and he's senior **Richard Bryant** (6-0, 165), who led the team with five interceptions last year. After seeing nickel duty in 1999, Bryant started from day one last season and had a pretty good year. He'll be teamed with sophomore **Lance Frazier** (5-10, 185), who started four games last year and picked off a pair of passes. The third man is 6-0, 175-pound sophomore **Brian King**, a nine-game regular last year who had 42 tackles and a interception.

Although the trio wasn't as productive last year as Rodriguez (or Nehlen) would have liked, they played well during the spring and have given the new coach some confidence.

"All three can cover," he said. "They did a good job with our wideouts. We did have a concern that they wouldn't tackle, but they did that in the spring."

Redshirt freshman **Joe Scritchfield** (5-10, 175) will try to get some time on the corner, too.

PUNTERS

The Mountaineers had expected to have some competition at this spot, but Zach Anglin, who punted nine times last year, for a 39.1-yard average, broke his leg this spring and will not play this season. That leaves the position to junior **Mark Fazzolari** (6-0, 185), who had a pretty good 2000 season and was selected second-team All-Big East. He averaged 41.2 yards on 62 punts and put 15 inside opposing teams' 20-yard lines. The bad news is that he had three blocked. Rodriguez doesn't want that happening again.

"We're trying to speed him up," Rodriguez said. "He's a talented guy who should be a solid punter for us."

Fazzolari did have his moments last year. He averaged 46.4 yards on eight kicks against Boston College and 47.0 on nine kicks against Idaho. Included was a 76-yard howitzer, which was the fourth-longest boot in WVU history. His 41.5-yard average was the top mark in the league in 1999.

SPECIAL TEAMS

The Mountaineers are in pretty good shape in the return game, thanks primarily to the return of Terry, who was one of the nation's most dangerous kickoff men in 2000. He averaged 28.8 yards on 29 returns and brought three back for touchdowns.

Although there is experience bringing back punts, that is an area the Mountaineers would like to improve upon. Antonio Brown has good speed, but he averaged a pedestrian 7.7 yards on his 27 tries, a figure that was inflated by a 69-yard return against Idaho. Take that away and he averaged just 5.3 yards. Expect to see Frazier bringing back more than the one punt he did last season.

The coverage picture must improve. Opponents averaged 14.6 yards on punts and 20.8 on kicks last year. That's way too much. WVU did block two punts last year but had four swatted away and had two kicks knocked back.

RECRUITING CLASS

The Mountaineers certainly didn't spend the weeks after signing day collecting accolades from the recruiting "experts" about their class. Their class couldn't be found in top 25s or even most top 50s. And none of their signees can be considered a true, everybody-wants-him blue-chip prospect. But that doesn't mean Rodriguez and his staff laid an egg.

Because Nehlen coached the bowl game, Rodriguez was left with about a month to get it all together, and that's not easy, especially when you're selling a school like West Virginia, which is something of an acquired taste. Give Rodriguez credit for the aforementioned far-flung characteristics of his class, and he did bring in a crop that included players at just about every position.

The top newcomers begin with linebacker **Shane Graham** (6-1, 218) from Allen (Texas) High School, who will be playing for his uncle, Todd Graham, WVU's new linebackers coach.

Expect to hear good things down the road from offensive lineman **Rod Olds** (6-3, 280) from Rutherford High School in Panama City, Fla., and **Josh Stewart** (6-6, 290) from University High School in Morgantown, W. Va., who could play on either line.

Defensive back **Brandon Hall** (5-11, 180) from Churchland High School in Suffolk, Va., has plenty of potential, as does defensive lineman **Ernest Hunter** (6-3, 260) from Lake Braddock High School in Burke, Va. And Rodriguez can't wait to see what he'll get under center from Embick and Johnson.

BLUE RIBBON ANALYSIS

OFFENSE	B
SPECIAL TEAMS	C+
DEFENSE	C+
INTANGIBLES	B+

The Mountaineers did a great job choosing Rodriguez, who would have surely copped another major-conference job by this time next year (if not sooner), had he not come back to Morgantown. His job now is to return WVU to its not-so-distant past, when the Mounties could be counted on for one good run up the rankings every four or five years.

That's a pretty good goal for Rodriguez, who no doubt has more grandiose plans. For now, he'll have to concentrate on making West Virginia a viable Big East player once again.

The Mountaineers have even slipped behind hated Pittsburgh, of all programs. The formula will be one that has been repeated all over the country. Expect WVU to play that wide-open offense, with lots of short passes and runs out of spread formations. The defense will boast quicker, hungrier athletes, who will be given the opportunity to make plays in one-on-one situations. It's a high-risk, high-reward strategy that should pay off, once the Mountaineer talent level rises.

As for 2001, expect a win total around six. WVU will run the ball effectively, thanks to its deep stable of backs, but the relative unreliability of the offensive line will prevent the team from being a ground juggernaut. Lewis has the potential to be a productive passer, but the question with him is whether he can do it every Saturday, particularly against a schedule that that includes road trips to Notre Dame, Miami and Syracuse.

If he grasps the offense well and makes good decisions, the Mountaineers will score points. That's the way it goes in Rodriguez's attack. If Lewis staggers, Rodriguez will go young.

West Virginia has some potential on defense,

particularly Wiley, Hackett and Sherrod. Expect them to have plenty of opportunities to shine, and look for West Virginia to create plenty of turnovers. It remains to be seen whether the Mountaineers will have the depth and talent to stand tall for 60 minutes against the better offenses they face.

Rodriguez is in a pretty good position, and there can be little question that he was the right pick for West Virginia. The Mountaineers have a bright future, but fans should refrain from expecting huge things right away. These things take time, even with a good coach in place.

(M.B.)

2000 RESULTS

Boston College	W	34-14	1-0
Maryland	W	30-17	2-0
Miami	L	10-47	2-1
Temple	W	29-24	3-1
Idaho	W	28-16	4-1
Virginia Tech	L	20-48	4-2
Notre Dame	L	28-42	4-3
Syracuse	L	27-31	4-4
Rutgers	W	31-24	5-4
East Carolina	W	42-24	6-4
Pittsburgh	L	28-38	6-5
Mississippi (Motor City)	W	49-38	7-5

Illinois

LOCATION	Champaign, IL
CONFERENCE	Big Ten
LAST SEASON	5-6 (.455)
CONFERENCE RECORD	2-6 (t-9th)
OFFENSIVE STARTERS RETURNING	8
DEFENSIVE STARTERS RETURNING	6
NICKNAME	Illini
COLORS	Orange & Blue
HOME FIELD	Memorial Stadium (70,900)
HEAD COACH	Ron Turner (Pacific '77)
RECORD AT SCHOOL	16-29 (4 years)
CAREER RECORD	23-33 (5 years)
ASSISTANTS	
	Mike Cassity (Kentucky '76) Defensive Coordinator
	Dan O'Dell (San Jose State '98) Quarterbacks
	Donnie Thompson (Connecticut '75) Defensive Line
	Jim Helms (Texas '67) Running Backs
	Harry Hiestand (East Stroudsburg '83) Offensive Line
	Robert Jackson (Northern Illinois '74) Wide Receivers/Recruiting Coordinator
	Osia Lewis (Oregon State '86) Linebackers
	Mike Mallory (Michigan '86) Defensive Backs
	Greg McMahon (Eastern Illinois '82) Special Teams
TEAM WINS (last 5 yrs.)	2-0-3-8-5
FINAL RANK (last 5 yrs.)	51-65-67-28-48
2000 FINISH	Lost to Northwestern in regular-season finale.

COACH AND PROGRAM

Like his older brother Norv (the new offensive coordinator of the San Diego Chargers), Illinois coach Ron Turner knows a thing or two about offense. Always has and always will, in fact.

After improving from 0-11 in 1997 to 3-8 in '98 , the Turner-led Illini more than matched that win total in '99, producing an 8-4 overall record with a 4-4 Big Ten Conference mark and the school's first winning season and bowl appearance since '94. The Illini's 63 points scored in the lop-sided 63-21 victory over Virginia in the Micronpc.com Bowl were the second most ever scored by a college team in NCAA bowl history.

The architect of the Orange and Blue's pro-style offense, Turner engineered the highest scoring offense in school history in '99, including five games with 40-plus scores. Illinois' 388 points last season surpassed the 1902 total of 380 scored in 13 games. Bolstering the best offensive numbers in Turner's three years, Illinois rushed for 2,082 yards and passed for 2,805 yards, resulting in a total offensive average of 407.3 yards a game. Last year, the Illini still averaged almost four touchdowns per game (26.7 points per game).

Before working his offensive magic in Champaign, Turner was a successful offensive coordinator in another part of the state of Illinois. In four seasons working with the Chicago Bears, Turner coordinated the offense that improved every season, breaking the club record for passing yards with 233 yards per game in '95 and producing a 1,000-yard receiver and rusher in the same season. The diversity of the Turner offense in Chicago found success under four different quarterbacks in Jim Harbaugh (1993), Steve Walsh (1994), Erik Kramer (1995) and Dave Krieg (1996). In '94, the Bears led the NFC Central Division for much of the regular season and defeated division rival Minnesota, 35-18, in a first-round playoff game.

Turner entered the professional ranks in '93 after a long and successful college coaching

BIG TEN

BLUE RIBBON FORECAST

1. Northwestern
2. Michigan
3. Wisconsin
4. Michigan State
5. Purdue
6. Ohio State
7. Illinois
8. Minnesota
9. Penn State
10. Iowa
11. Indiana

ALL-CONFERENCE TEAM

OFFENSE

POS. PLAYER SCHOOL HT. WT. CL.

WR Ron Johnson, Minnesota, 6-3, 216, Sr.
WR Marquise Walker, Michigan, 6-3, 212, Sr.
OL Adrien Clarke, Ohio State, 6-4, 325, So.
OL Leon Brockmeier, Northwestern, 6-7, 302, Sr.
C Luke Butkus, Illinois, 6-4, 287, Sr.
OL Jonathan Goodwin, Michigan, 6-4, 294 Sr.
OL Lance Clelland, Northwestern, 6-6, 317, Sr.
QB Zak Kustok, Northwestern, 6-1, 200, Sr.
RB Damien Anderson, Northwestern, 5-11, 204, Sr.
RB T.J. Duckett, Michigan State, 6-1, 252, Jr.
TE Tim Stratton, Purdue, 6-4, 258, Sr.

DEFENSE

POS. PLAYER SCHOOL HT. WT. CL.

DL Jake Frysinger, Michigan, 6-4, 290, Sr.
DL Wendell Bryant, Wisconsin, 6-4, 293, Sr.
DL Jimmy Kennedy, Penn State, 6-5, 335, Jr.
DL Akin Ayodele, Purdue, 6-3, 253, Sr.
LB Larry Foote, Michigan, 6-1, 228, Sr.
LB Josh Thornhill, Michigan State, 6-2, 234, Jr.
LB Napoleon Harris, Northwestern, 6-3, 243, Sr.
DB Todd Howard, Michigan, 5-10, 183, Sr.
DB Cedric Henry, Michigan State, 5-10, 180, Sr.
DB Mike Doss, Ohio State, 5-11, 197, Sr.
DB Mike Echols, Wisconsin, 5-10, 172, Sr.

SPECIALISTS

POS. PLAYER SCHOOL HT. WT. CL.

PK Dan Nystrom, Minnesota, 5-11, 194, Jr.
P Preston Gruening, Minnesota, 5-10, 204, Jr.
RS Kahlil Hill, Iowa, 6-3, 195, Sr.

OFFENSIVE PLAYER THE YEAR

Damien Anderson, RB, Northwestern

DEFENSIVE PLAYER OF THE YEAR

Wendell Bryant, DL, Wisconsin

NEWCOMER OF THE YEAR

Charles Rogers, WR, Michigan State

BIG TEN NOTEBOOK

Here are a couple of dates for Big Ten football fans to circle on their calendar: On Nov. 3, Ohio State travels to Minnesota. Who can forget how badly Golden Gophers coach Glen Mason wanted the top job at OSU (his alma mater) that eventually went to former Youngstown State coach Jim Tressel? The Nov. 17 Northwestern at Illinois game has been changed to Nov. 22. That's Thanksgiving Day, which might bring unprecedented exposure to what is becoming a hot rivalry. The game could well decide who will become the All-Big Ten quarterback. Will it be Northwestern's Zak Kustok or Illinois' Kurt Kittner? ... After going to the Sun Bowl in 1999 and the Micron PC.com Bowl in 2000, Minnesota has a chance this year to make three consecutive bowl trips for the first time in school history. ... Listed at just 238 pounds, Wisconsin senior Ben Herbert is probably the skinniest nose tackle in major Division I-A football. ... Although he's often overshadowed by the likes of Northwestern's Damien Anderson and Michigan State's T.J. Duckett, Iowa senior Ladell Betts is already third on his school's all-time rushing list with 2,626 career yards. He needs 1,530 more yards rushing to become the school's all-time leader. ... Indiana's Antwaan Randle-El is one of only two Division I-A players to score 200 points and pass for 200 points in his career. The other is former Michigan quarterback Rick Leach. ... The 2000 bowl season represented a major step backward for the Big Ten. The league went just 2-4 in bowl games after a 5-0 post-season mark in 1998 and a 5-2 record in 1999. ... Is imitation really the sincerest form of flattery, or do other Big Ten coaches want in on some of Northwestern's action? Northwestern was 3-8 in coach Randy Walker's first year (1999), but after installing a wide-open spread offense, last year's team shocked the nation, going 8-4 overall (6-2 in Big Ten play) and winning a share of the conference title. The Wildcats are favored to win the league championship again this season. Is it any surprise that Michigan State and Wisconsin are dabbling with the spread offense?

career. In '92, Turner was selected head coach at San Jose State. In just one season, Turner led a remarkable turnaround at SJSU, leading the Spartans to a 7-4 record and a second-place finish in the Big West Conference. Turner guided San Jose State to its best record in six years and directed a potent offense that churned out 400 yards per game while averaging 30 points per game, good for 15th in the nation.

Before that, Turner spent the previous 16 years as an assistant at the major college level. He earned the San Jose State post after coordinating the Stanford offense for three seasons under Dennis Green. Turner began his coaching career as a graduate assistant coach at the University of Pacific before becoming the receivers coach at Arizona, a post he held for two seasons (1978-79). After coaching the Arizona running backs in 1980, Turner joined Green the next year at Northwestern, where he spent two seasons as quarterbacks/receivers coach. At Northwestern, Turner helped turn the Wildcat offense into one of the most exciting in the Big Ten, tutoring NU quarterback Sandy Schwab to several school and Big Ten records. As an assistant at Northwestern, Turner also recruited all-time NU punt and kickoff return leader Steve Tasker, who went on to a long career in the NFL.

In '83, Turner became the quarterbacks coach at Pittsburgh, working with Panther quarterback John Congemi for two seasons. He joined the Ted Tollner staff at Southern California in 1985 in a similar role before he was elevated to offensive coordinator in '86, coaching '88 Heisman Trophy runner-up Rodney Peete.

In '87, new head coach Larry Smith retained Turner on the USC staff as receivers coach as the Trojans romped to the Pac-10 title. The following season, Turner moved to Texas A&M as the quarterbacks coach before moving to Stanford University in '89. With the Micronpc.com Bowl, Turner has been a part of eight bowl teams, including the '88 Rose Bowl team and the '91 Stanford Aloha Bowl squad.

The goal in '01 is to get Illinois back in the bowls—and perhaps get himself on the "hot" lists of coaches. After the Illini's sterling 1999 season, Ron Turner received a cluster of phone calls from NFL teams wondering if he was interested in a head-coaching job. Turner says his family loves Champaign and he has said more than once he would like to stay until all of his children are done with high school. That's at least a decade away.

Last year though, his phone stopped ringing. The reason? Turner's Illini squad finished with a 5-6 mark, which was particularly disappointing after the 8-4 record in 1999 and a 3-0 start in 2000. Scoring wasn't the problem, though. Sure, the Illini averaged just 26.7 points per game, down from 32.3 in 2000. But, on most Saturdays, nearly four touchdowns per game is enough scoring.

The problem was defense. The Illini allowed 232.5 rushing yards per game, the highest total allowed by any Big Ten team and 113th out of 114 teams. They were eighth in the conference in total defense (412.5 yards per game).

Those numbers and the 61 points allowed by the Illini in the 2000 season finale against Northwestern cost defensive coordinator Tim Kish his job. Unlike Kish (who preferred the bend-but-don't-break approach), the Illini's new defensive coordinator Mike Cassity uses more of an attacking, pit-bull approach to defense.

Cassity will install a scheme with some of the elements of the old Buddy Ryan "46" defense: A blitzing style of defense with seven or eight guys in the box mixed with lots of aggressive man-to-man coverage with big, physical cornerbacks on the outside. Cassity's staff includes some other new faces, including new defensive line coach Donnie Thompson, a longtime North Carolina assistant, and defensive backs coach Mike Mallory, whose dad Bill coached at Indiana.

"The biggest change that you'll see defensively is we're going to be much more aggressive," Turner said. "I feel good about our defense."

If he is saying the same thing by the time he sits down to Thanksgiving dinner, then Illinois will be going to a bowl game for Christmas. And Turner's phone figures to be ringing again.

2001 SCHEDULE

Sept.	1	@California
	8	Northern Illinois
	15	Louisville
	22	@Michigan
Oct.	6	Minnesota
	13	@Indiana
	20	Wisconsin
Nov.	3	@Purdue
	10	Penn State
	17	@Ohio State
	22	Northwestern

QUARTERBACKS

With the Big Ten's two Drews (former Michigan star Drew Henson and former Purdue passing whiz Drew Brees) now playing pro sports and Indiana's human highlight film Antwaan Randle-El moving to wide receiver, the race for first-team All-Big Ten quarterback in 2001 figures to be between Northwestern's Zak Kustok and Illinois senior **Kurt Kittner** (6-3, 212).

The potential is there for the Illini offense, with seven returning starters and one of the nation's best quarterbacks in Kittner, to be as explosive as it was in 1999, when it averaged a school-record 32.3 points per game. But they will need a return to form by Kittner, who was inconsistent last season. In fairness, Kittner's productivity was hurt by the fact that the Illini's ground game struggled and that a freak off-season leg injury to his go-to receiver **Brandon Lloyd** (6-2, 176) took away his best option.

Despite those obstacles and the fact that Kittner missed the season finale against Northwestern because of injury, Kittner still completed 58.2 percent of his passes (173-of-297) for 1,982 yards, 18 touchdowns and eight interceptions in 10 games. Kittner is an old-fashioned pocket passer who relies on his strong arm and his wits to beat opponents. He is a steady performer who has thrown a combined 42 touchdowns and just 13 interceptions in the past two seasons. With the speedy Lloyd back, Kittner figures to continue to post gaudy numbers.

"A lot of people have said that Kurt didn't have the year last year that he had the year before," Turner said. "That's hogwash. After looking at the film, you realize that he played just as well last year, but he didn't have Brandon Lloyd and that changes everything."

Look for Kittner to rebound in 2001. Sure, Illinois lost four-year starters at tackle (Marques Sullivan, a fifth-round pick of the Buffalo Bills) and guard (Ray Redziniak) along with sure-headed team leader Josh Whitman at tight end and rugged fullback Jameel Cook (a sixth round pick of the Tampa Bay Buccaneers). But it has all the rest of its skill players back, including Lloyd.

Kittner, too, is 100 percent healthy again after suffering a knee injury and a concussion in 2000. He completed 16-of-19 passes for 232 yards and three scores in the annual Orange and Blue spring game. Kittner isn't the most nimble quarterback on the planet, so it's up to the Illini to keep him upright and in one piece this year. If that happens, Kittner will pick opposing defenses apart and a bowl berth is probable. If not, there could be troubles again.

If all goes well, Kittner could find himself in the Heisman race—a fact that even blows Kittner away.

"When I was a freshman, nobody knew who I was," Kittner said. "Now people are always staring at me. It has changed a lot since I first got here."

Illini sports information personnel have begun a Heisman Trophy campaign designed to make sure Kittner is on everyone's mind when the season starts. Illinois will be mailing selected media outlets a package that includes a seven-minute videotape of Kittner highlights and clips that chronicle his career.

Kittner ranks fourth in Illinois career passing with 5,466 yards and second with 43 career touchdown passes. Jack Trudeau's school record for career touchdown passes (55) is within reach and Kittner is on pace to be second all-time to Trudeau in passing yards (8,725 career yards).

Turner thinks Kittner is the best quarterback in college football.

"There are very good ones out there with different styles," Turner said. "I wouldn't trade him for anyone in running the offense and being the quarterback."

The Heisman race blew wide open when quarterback Michael Vick left Virginia Tech early for the NFL and Michigan's Drew Henson traded in his shoulder pads to play minor league baseball.

"It would be a great honor," Kittner said. "I had mixed feelings in the beginning. I think it's great for me, the university and the team. It puts us on a national level, helps in getting new recruits and making Illinois a better team for years to come."

Who will be the Illini quarterback after Kittner is gone? Right now, sophomore **Dustin Ward** (6-3, 193), a hometown boy from Champaign, is No. 2 on the depth chart. When Kittner suffered a concussion in the Ohio State and then missed the season finale against Northwestern, Ward saw significant time. For the season, Ward completed 33-of-62 throws (53.2 percent) for 390 yards, four touchdowns and two interceptions.

Ward will be a serviceable backup and did nothing this spring to play his way out of the No. 2 spot. But one wonders if ultra-athletic sophomore **Christian Morton** (6-1, 180), a Randle El clone during his prep days in St. Louis, will be moved from cornerback back to quarterback in 2002.

Becoming a defensive player this spring wasn't an easy move for Morton to swallow. Last season, he became frustrated in his inability to move past Ward as the team's No. 2 quarterback. And this spring, it became more apparent he would continue at No. 3 when his passes sailed off course. Morton always has envisioned himself as a future NFL quarterback, and he can't be blamed for that after winning national honors for ringing up 40 touchdowns (26 throwing, 14 running) as St. Louis Riverview Gardens quarterback in '98.

He sat out his freshman season to work on academics, then resisted Turner's suggestion that he give wide receiver a try last season. But this year, Morton seems to have finally agreed that a change was best.

"I miss offense a little bit, but sometimes you have to make adjustments to get to the ultimate goal," he said. "And the ultimate goal for me is to get to the NFL and be successful."

For his part, Turner said he doesn't see Morton returning to quarterback. But that could change once Kittner is playing for pay.

"He [Morton] will play cornerback, return punts, return kicks and even get a few plays at wide receiver," said Turner. "He's smiling a lot, he's happy, he's making big plays and he's contributing."

With Morton is the jack-of-all-trades role, redshirt freshman **Mark Kornfield** (6-1, 192) will probably move into the No. 3 spot on the depth chart at quarterback.

Another youngster who will figure in the quarterback mix in either 2002 or 2003 is freshman **Matt Dlugolecki** (6-5, 220) from Coto De Caza, Calif. Dlugolecki was chosen the Best of the West by the *Long Beach Press-Telegram* after throwing for 1,307 yards and 17 touchdowns as a senior. He will probably redshirt in 2001, which will allow him plenty of time to learn Illinois' intricate pro-style offense.

RUNNING BACKS

Fullback Jameel Cook left school a year early for the NFL and will be sorely missed. Cook was the second Illini drafted as the 174th pick of the sixth round by the Tampa Bay Buccaneers. Cook switched to fullback midway through the '99 season to give Illinois another offensive threat out of the backfield, catching six touchdown passes in his career. He totaled 60 catches for 506 career receiving yards and 526 yards rushing with the Illini. He will back up yet another Big Ten tough guy (Mike Alstott) with the Bucs.

With Cook gone and junior backup **Carlos Lattimore** (6-1, 215) battling knee problems, sophomore **Carey Davis** (6-1, 218) takes over as the starter. He impressed the coaches this spring with his blocking and his hands. Davis will be spelled by Lattimore, if his knee gets stronger and doesn't require serious surgery.

If Lattimore is out, then sophomore **Brad Haywood** (6-1, 222) from football-rich Mt, Carmel, Ill. (the town that produced NFLers Donovan McNabb and Simeon Rice), will be Davis' backup. Lattimore, who had been shifted to linebacker, was moved back to fullback this spring.

The Illini have a nice one-two punch at tailback in shifty senior **Rocky Harvey** (5-9, 183) and powerful junior **Antoineo Harris** (6-1, 222). The duo combined for 1,455 yards and 10 touchdowns in 2000. Harvey is now eighth on the school's all-time rushing list and could inch his way into the top five with a productive senior season.

Harris was the Illini's top ground gainer last season with 772 yards on 192 carries (4.0 average) and seven rushing touchdowns. Harvey is more adept at running outside the tackles. He finished with 683 yards and three scores, averaging 5.6 yards per tote. Another plus is that Harvey has good hands. He caught 17 passes for 91 yards last season.

"It's thunder and lightening," Harvey said. "When we need speed, I go in, when we need power, Antoineo goes in, and that helps us."

Illinois' "Thunder and Lightning" duo of Harris and Harvey will miss the crunching lead blocks of Cook, but will run behind a better-than-average line that returns three starters.

The concern, though, is the lack of quality depth at tailback. But come fall, incoming freshmen **Abe Jones** (5-11, 179) and **Morris Virgil** (5-10, 185) will add depth and quickness. Jones rushed for a combined 3,380 yards in his final two years at Rolling Meadows (Ill.) High School, while Virgil rushed for 1,585 yards and 29 touchdowns as a prep senior right down the road from Illinois' campus at Urbana (Ill.) High.

WIDE RECEIVERS/TIGHT ENDS

The return of speedster Lloyd from a broken leg has brought wide smiles to faces of Turner and Kittner. The reason? Lloyd automatically makes this group better. Lloyd, who set school freshman receiving marks in '99 when he caught 30 balls for 511 yards, suffered a freak injury and missed all of last season.

Lloyd broke his left femur while jogging to catch up with some friends on campus when he stepped off the sidewalk and caught his left foot between a parking block and the pathway. Lloyd looked like his old self again this spring, catching a 47-yard pass from Kittner on the No. 1 offense's first play in the spring game.

Juniors **Greg Lewis** (40 catches, 544 yards, six touchdowns in '00) and **Aaron Moorehead** (30, 520 yards, four touchdowns), both former walk-ons, are also back. Both Lewis (6-0, 180) and Moorehead (6-3, 195) are more possession-type receivers who will be helped by the ability of Lloyd and sophomore **Dwayne Smith** (6-2, 195) to stretch the field with their speed.

Smith, listed as the team's No.1 split end (Lloyd is the first-team flanker), didn't get a real chance to display his skills last fall in his first season with Illinois, catching just eight passes. He opened many eyes this spring, catching four balls for 65 yards and a touchdown.

Also in the mix are tall junior split end **Walter Young** (6-5, 218) and redshirt freshman flanker **Ade Adeyemo** (6-0, 196). Young caught 27 balls for 403 yards (14.9 yards per catch) in '00 and is listed as the team's second-string split end, behind Young. Adeyemo is a former prep All-American out of Chicago who figures to see time when Turner goes to multiple wide receiver sets.

Senior **Brian Hodges** (6-4, 262) steps in for Josh Whitman as the team's starting tight end. Whitman, who caught 13 balls for 144 yards last season, is trying to make the Buffalo Bills as a free agent. But Turner likes Hodges, who caught eight balls for 69 yards last season. Sophomore **Kenny Boyle** (6-3, 240) and redshirt freshman **Anthony McClellan** (6-3, 238) are competing for the backup tight end role.

OFFENSIVE LINE

This unit suffered big losses in Sullivan and Redziniak, but does return three starters in senior center **Luke Butkus** (6-4, 290), senior left guard **Jay Kulaga** (6-5, 300) and junior right tackle **Tony Pashos** (6-6, 315).

Butkus, the nephew of former Illini great Dick Butkus, is being touted for more postseason honors after earning honorable-mention All-Big Ten notice last fall. Butkus possesses the same type of competitive nature as his uncle and will be an emotional leader up front. Butkus, as well as Kulaga and Pashos, all have the size to play pro ball someday.

But who will replace the two guys who have left Champaign and are currently in NFL camps? Sullivan, was a fifth-round pick of the Buffalo Bills, and Redziniak a free-agent signee of the New York Giants. Sullivan was a two-time, second-team All-Big Ten selection who protected Kittner's blind side and led the team with 71 knockdowns last fall, while Redziniak was a three-year fixture at guard. Both will be sorely missed.

Turner says junior **David Diehl** (6-5, 294) and sophomore **Sean Bubin** (6-7, 302) will continue to wage a spirited battle for Sullivan's tackle spot in August, while sophomore **Aaron Hodges** (6-5, 290) and redshirt freshman **Bucky Babcock** (6-4, 295) are dueling for the opening at guard.

"Babcock and Hodges are having a great battle," Turner said. "They really, really played well this past spring. I'm very pleased with the progress they are making. Babcock is just a freshman and Hodges is much improved. He has put on about 15 pounds and he's learning to play with that weight. His athleticism shows up. I think, in time, we'll have the most athletic offensive line since we've been here."

Three other redshirt freshmen—center **Duke Preston** (6-4, 290), left guard **Brian Koch** (6-3, 280) and right tackle **Clark Collins** (6-3, 285)—will be counted on as backups for Butkus, Kulaga and Pahos, respectively.

2000 STATISTICS

Rushing offense	162.7	39
Passing offense	217.2	55
Total offense	379.9	51
Scoring offense	26.7	53
Net Punting	36.3	29
Punt returns	12.1	24
Kickoff returns	17.4	99
Rushing defense	232.5	113
Passing efficiency defense	107.0	29
Total defense	412.5	93
Scoring defense	26.0	68
Turnover margin	-2	67

Last column is ranking among Division I-A teams.

KICKERS

Last season, Turner handed all three kicking duties to senior **Steve Fitts** (6-0, 201). He struggled, particularly with his place kicking, which led to Turner easing back on his expected duties for this season. Fitts definitely will punt in '01 and probably handle kickoff duties, but the battle for place kicking duties is open.

It was expected that sophomore **JJ Tubbs** (5-9, 160) would ease into the starting role. But Springfield native **Peter Christofilakos** (5-9, 166) completed a superb spring with a 41-yard field goal in the spring game and gave himself a chance to compete with Tubbs for the starting position later this summer.

"Kicker is very close," Turner said. "Peter Christofilakos really came on this spring and showed major improvement, and Tubbs is not backing down from the competition. They're both kicking really well. They're both doing enough to take the job."

One of the biggest concerns with Christofilakos last season dealt with the trajectory of his kicks. A former soccer player, Christofilakos' distance and accuracy on field goals was good, but his low trajectory made it easy for rushing lineman to block attempts. In the off-season, Illinois coaches designed a device for Christofilakos to practice with that simulated the height of a rusher. The improvement in his trajectory has been significant.

Freshman **Steve Weatherford** (6-4, 205) from Terre Haute, Ind., also is expected to compete for place-kicking duties when he arrives on campus this summer. A two-time all-stater at Terre Haute North High School, Weatherford made a 55-yard field goal and seven others from more than 40 yards last season. He also averaged 45.4 yards per punt as a high school senior.

DEFENSIVE LINE

This group was decimated by injuries and other factors last year. In all, the team lost five defensive linemen and as a result, was manhandled up front—giving up a Big Ten-worst 232.5 rushing yards per game.

Ultra-quick rush end Fred Wakefield (team-high nine sacks and 21 tackles for loss) is gone, but senior end **Terrell Washington** (eight sacks, 17 tackles for loss in '00) and senior tackle **Brandon Moore** (6-3, 280) are both experienced hands. Washington is a playmaker, as his eight sacks and 16 tackles for loss in 2000 prove.

Moore is entering his third year as a starter.

Illinois will need help from junior college transfer **Jamie Hanton** (6-4, 290), who was on campus early and participated in spring ball. He is currently down on the depth chart a bit at the other tackle spot, but he has skills. Last season at Chaffey (Calif.) College, Hanton registered 45 tackles and six sacks.

He will battle with exciting sophomore **Charles Gilstrap** (6-3, 290) and junior **Brett Kautter** (6-2, 275) for the starting nod. Further inside depth will be provided by sophomore **Jeff Ruffin** (6-4, 290).

Senior end **Robby Long** (6-3, 260) and sophomore end **Mike O'Brien** (6-6, 215), who missed all of 2000 with a stress fracture in his foot, are locked in a too-close-to-call battle to secure Wakefield's spot, while sophomore **Derrick Strong** (6-4, 250) is scheduled to back up Washington. Strong was voted the most improved defensive player in spring practice and will help bolster the Illini's shaky pass rush.

Promising sophomore end **Jemari Perry** (6-4, 220) was slowed by a bum knee in spring ball and was on crutches. His status in 2001 is uncertain.

LINEBACKERS

Linebacker is the least tested group on the team; five of last season's top six have exhausted their eligibility. Only junior **Jerry Schumacher** (6-3, 235) returns and while Turner likes the potential, he is naturally wary of newcomers. Defense, most agree, will make or break the Illini.

"We're really excited about the ability of this group, but we're concerned about the lack of experience," Turner said.

Schumacher, who led the team with 104 tackles a year ago, has shifted from outside to middle linebacker (where he replaces Robert Franklin, the Illini's top hit man last season with 109 tackles). Schumacher is one of two family members who are starring on Big Ten campuses (His sister Katie is an All-America volleyball player at Penn State). Schumacher is not the most athletic linebacker on the planet, but he has a nose for the football. His primary backup is redshirt freshman **Mike Gawelek** (6-2, 235).

"We're excited about Jerry Schumacher and the player he's going to be," Turner said. "Before he's through here, he's going to be one of the best linebackers in the country."

Redshirt freshman **Lamont Holden**, an athletic-looking 6-3, 225-pounder, and junior college transfer **Mario Ivy** (6-3, 225) are vying for the outside linebacker spot held for the last four years by Michael Young. Bet on Ivy getting the nod, because he's a little more seasoned after a stint at Ellsworth (Iowa) Junior College.

Ty Myers, a speedy 6-4, 222-pound sophomore, has taken over at the other outside linebacker spot. Myers had just two tackles in 2000. His backup will be sophomore **Joe Bevis** (6-0, 215)

DEFENSIVE BACKS

Cassity believes in playing the attack-style "46" defense that Buddy Ryan made famous with 1985 Super Bowl champion Chicago Bears. In order to play that aggressive scheme with seven or eight guys in the box, Cassity needs in-your-face cover corners.

Junior **Eugene Wilson** (5-11, 183), an honorable mention all-Big Ten pick last season after grabbing four interceptions, has secured one cornerback spot. The other starting spot will be manned by either converted quarterback Morton or **Mike Hall** (5-10, 175), a JUCO All-American from Bakersfield, Calif.

Right now, Morton has the upper hand. Once thought of as a Michael Vick-type quarterback, Morton is one of the team's best athletes. He might have an NFL future at corner with his combination of size and speed.

"My ultimate goal is to play in the NFL," Morton said after picking off a pass in the spring game. "My plan is to stay on defense and help this team win."

The key reserves at cornerback figure to be sophomore **Nana Agyeman** (6-2, 196), sophomore converted wide receiver **Jamaal Clark** (6-2. 190), senior **Anthony Hurd** (5-10, 189) and junior **Marc Jackson** (6-1, 201). Jackson moved from free safety to cornerback, although he was withheld from contact in the spring after shoulder surgery.

Safety is a position of strength with seniors **Muhammad Abdullah** (6-1, 202) and **Bobby Jackson** (6-1, 211), Marc's brother, both returning. They ranked No. 3 and No. 4 in tackles last season.

Feisty redshirt freshman **Kevin Anderson** (6-2, 195) will back up Jackson at strong safety, while Marc Jackson could always move back to free safety, if injuries occur or his experiment at cornerback is unsuccessful. Another possibility at free safety is well-decorated freshman **Chuck Moore** (6-4, 200), a *SuperPrep* All-American from El Grove (Ill.) High School.

PUNTERS

Turner believes that by relieving Fitts of some of the place kicking duties that he will return to his '99 form. In '99, Fitts was an honorable mention All-Big Ten performer, averaging 42.3 yards per punt. Last season, Fitts was a special teams Superman—handling the punting, place kicking and kickoff duties.

All of that added responsibility took its toll as Fitts' punting average dipped to a still-respectable 40.9 yards per punt. He figures to do even better in 2001 with a lighter workload.

Fitts' eventual replacement will be either redshirt freshman **Matt Minnes** (6-3, 223) or freshman **Steve Weatherford** (6-4, 205). Whoever boots the ball better in August, will be Fitts' understudy in '01 and then take over as the team's punter in '02.

SPECIAL TEAMS

Fitts will concentrate only on punting after an erratic season when he handled both the punting and place kicking duties. Spending less time working on his feet will make Fitts less tired. If the experiment works, Fitts should be the second-best punter in the Big Ten, behind Minnesota All-American Preston Gruening.

Who takes over the kicking duties from Fitts? Tubbs was the early leader, with Christofilakos and Weatherford in the mix.

It was expected that Tubbs (1-for-1 on field goals, 13-of-13 extra points in 2000) would ease into the starting role, but Christofilakos had a great spring and Weaetherford has an impressive resume.

"It's pretty simple for kicking," Turner said. "The ball either goes through the uprights or it doesn't. Some other positions maybe there is a little gray area you have to look at and make some judgments, but kicking is pretty simple to judge. The most accurate guy will get the job."

The other special teams jobs seem to be in good hands. Fitts will be the holder and punter. Morton will be the primary return man. He returned 27 kickoffs for 539 yards (19.9-yard average) and had eight punt returns for 195 yards, including an electrifying 80-yard touchdown return against Indiana. The long snapper will be one of two seniors, either **Mike Malczyk** (5-11, 232) or **Pat Rouse** (6-0, 227).

RECRUITING CLASS

Despite a lackluster year on the field, Illinois cleaned up in its home state as defensive backs **James Cooper** (5-11, 185) and Moore, running backs Jones and Morris, defensive end **Lionel Williams** (6-5, 240) and offensive tackle **Rob Needham** (6-6, 305) were all ranked among the top 25 high school players in Illinois.

Moore, a prep All-American safety, and the two running backs (Jones and Virgil) should contribute sooner rather than later.

Special teams coach Greg McMahon, who recruits Missouri for the Illini, earned his keep by getting commitments from six of the top 10 players in the city of St. Louis in linebackers **Matt Sinclair** (6-3, 225), **T.W. Norman** (6-3, 240) and **Antonio Mason** (6-0, 240); offensive lineman **Kyle Schnettgoecke** (6-4, 252); defensive lineman **Brian Schaefering** (6-5, 210); and wide receiver **Kenrick Jones** (6-3, 170). Of the St. Louis contingent, the speedy, ball-hawking Sinclair (135 tackles, two interceptions) seems the most ready to contribute immediately.

Speaking of immediate contributors, Turner went the quick-fix route along the defensive line, recruiting a junior college import at both defensive end in **Mario Ivy** (6-3, 225) from Ellsworth (Iowa) Junior College and at defensive tackle in **Jamie Hanton** (6-4, 290) from Chaffey (Calif.) College. Both will be on the two-deep right away.

BLUE RIBBON ANALYSIS

OFFENSE	B+
SPECIAL TEAMS	C+
DEFENSE	C
INTANGIBLES	C+

With the return of the speed demon Lloyd from a broken left leg that sidelined him for the entire 2000 season, Illinois might have the league's second-best collection of skill players, behind Big Ten preseason favorite Northwestern.

Illinois senior Kittner looked like Kurt Warner in '99, but slipped a bit in '00 because he was throwing primarily to two former walk-ons. With Lloyd and the maturation of fellow sophomore Smith, the receiving corps will be much improved. The one-two running punch of Harvey and Harris is killer and the offensive line returns three starters.

While scoring points won't be any trouble, stopping other teams might continue to be. A new coordinator in Cassity and a more aggressive scheme should help some, though. How much? It could mean another win or two in '01, which would spell a return to a minor bowl for '01. After a 5-6 record in '00, that would be reason enough to pop the champagne in Champaign.

(B.D.)

2000 RESULTS

Middle Tennessee	W	35-6	1-0
San Diego State	W	49-13	2-0
California	W	17-15	3-0
Michigan	L	31-35	3-1
Minnesota	L	10-44	3-2
Iowa	W	31-0	4-2
Penn State	L	25-39	4-3
Michigan State	L	10-14	4-4
Indiana	W	42-35	5-4
Ohio State	L	21-24	5-5
Northwestern	L	23-61	5-6

Indiana

LOCATION	**Bloomington, IN**
CONFERENCE	**Big Ten**
LAST SEASON	**3-8 (.272)**
CONFERENCE RECORD	**2-6 (t-9th)**
OFFENSIVE STARTERS RETURNING	**8**
DEFENSIVE STARTERS RETURNING	**8**
NICKNAME	**Hoosiers**
COLORS	**Red, White & Black**
HOME FIELD	**Memorial Stadium (52,354)**
HEAD COACH	**Cam Cameron (Indiana '83)**
RECORD AT SCHOOL	**13-31 (4 years)**
CAREER RECORD	**13-31 (4 years)**
ASSISTANTS	
	James Bell (Central Arkansas '82)
	Defensive Coordinator/Defensive Backs
	Ron Burton (North Carolina '92)
	Linebackers
	Gerald Carr (Southern Illinois '82)
	Quarterbacks
	Marty Fine (Western New Mexico '83)
	Tight Ends
	Dick Flynn (Michigan State '65)
	Defensive Ends
	Hal Hunter (Northwestern '82)
	Offensive Coordinator/Offensive Line
	Anthony Thompson (Indiana '90)
	Assistant Head Coach/Running Backs
	T.J. Weist (Alabama '88)
	Wide Receivers/Recruiting Coordinator
	Diron Reynolds (Wake Forest '93)
	Defensive Tackles
TEAM WINS (last 5 yrs.)	**3-2-4-4-3**
FINAL RANK (last 5 yrs.)	**35-57-51-44-62**
2000 FINISH	**Lost to Purdue in regular-season finale.**

COACH AND PROGRAM

In 1997, Cam Cameron returned to his alma mater promising to infuse some excitement into Indiana football. During his four-year tenure, the Hoosiers have indeed become more entertaining, but they have not been successful.

Cameron's record at IU is worse than his predecessor's in a similar time span. Bill Mallory won 18 games and reached a bowl game by his third season.

Cameron was hand picked to replace Mallory, who was fired. He may suffer a similar fate if he doesn't turn IU around. IU—with the football program in mind—has hired a new athletic director in Michael McNeely. McNeely, a former San Diego Chargers executive, probably will be given carte blanche when it comes to fixing a stagnant program with declining attendance.

The pressure is definitely on Cameron, who realizes patience might be wearing thin.

"There's an urgency," he said. "We're four plays away [last year] from what everybody wants us to be—a team that's going to a bowl game. And we should have gone to a bowl game. We should have won those games, but we didn't. But it's not like we're very far away. I like our approach. Every thing is in place. If we were just struggling in every area and weren't competitive, I'd be disappointed. We're not far away. It doesn't matter how it's perceived.

"That's the truth of it all."

Some statistics support Cameron's argument. In his first year, the Hoosiers scored 120 points. Last year they rolled up 337. The 30.6 points per game average was the second-highest in school history. In 1997, IU lost by more than 30 points six times. That happened only once last season.

The Hoosiers can score points. They are (usually) competitive. So then why have they been unable to turn the corner? This program has habitually been saddled with a defense that drags it down like an anchor. IU blew leads of 21-3 against North Carolina State, 20-7 at Kentucky and was tied against Penn State and Illinois before crumbling.

Name a category and the IU defense ranked either at the bottom or near the bottom in the Big Ten. The Hoosiers gave up more yards (457.3 per game), more points (38.8), and more completions (21.8) for a higher percentage (64.7) than any other school in the 11-team league. And they gave up the second most touchdowns (49). This program will continue to go nowhere until it puts a decent defense on the field.

The man in charge of this arduous task is James Bell, hired last year to fix a habitually poor unit. His credentials as an assistant at Wake Forest were impressive, but Bell could not improve IU's defense. In fact, the unit regressed in many categories. In 1999, IU surrendered 430.1 yards per game, 35.1 points, 17.1 completions, and allowed the opposing quarterback to complete 60 percent of his passes. The Hoosiers allowed 42 touchdowns.

Cameron expects improvement, but IU fans have been hearing that for years.

"We have got to get better on defense," he said.

The pressure mounting on Cameron cannot be described as unfair. He was hired the same year as Purdue's Joe Tiller, Illinois' Ron Turner, and Minnesota's Glen Mason. All three delivered winning records and bowl trips in their first three years. Cameron is still playing catch up. To make matters worse, he is winless against IU's biggest rivals: Purdue (0-4) and Kentucky (0-4).

There was speculation toward the end of last season that Cameron might return to the National Football League, where he was a successful assistant. But after his team was blasted at Purdue, 41-13, in the season finale, he denied that he would opt out of his seven-year deal.

If he doesn't turn things around this year, the school administration might make that decision easy for him.

2001 SCHEDULE

Sept.	6	@North Carolina State
	15	Kentucky
	22	Utah
	29	Ohio State
Oct.	6	@Wisconsin
	13	Illinois
	20	@Iowa
Nov.	3	Northwestern
	10	@Michigan State
	17	@Penn State
	24	Purdue

QUARTERBACKS

This time they appear to be serious. Check out senior **Antwaan Randle El**'s uniform during practice if you have any doubts. He no longer dons a green jersey, the uniform reserved for Hoosier quarterbacks participating in drills.

If everything works according to plan, Randle El will play wide receiver this fall after starting 33 games at quarterback for the Hoosiers. Ever since his freshman year there has been speculation surrounding the diminutive Randle El. Wouldn't the 5-foot-10, 190-pounder be better suited somewhere other than behind the center? Randle El re-wrote the school's record books with his feet as well as his arm, but the team hasn't prospered.

The Hoosiers are 11-22 in the Randle El era. That's only a four-game improvement in the program's record in the 33 games before his arrival.

Cameron has always maintained that he would put the best 11 players on offense. For the last two seasons, back-up quarterback **Tommy Jones** (6-3, 241), a junior, was not included in that group. But now the coaching staff apparently thinks Jones is ready and Randle El is best equipped to help IU in another role.

"We've told Tommy that he has got to take this opportunity and make the most of it," Cameron said. "If he can do that, that's the direction we're going to go for sure. Last year it was kind of an experiment. This is something we would like to do."

This is a bit of a gamble. Jones is a third-year junior, but in many ways he's almost like a redshirt freshman. Because of Randle El's durability, Jones has rarely played. Jones has appeared in either mop-up or spot duty in 10 games. For his career, Jones has thrown 25 passes, completing 10 for 134 yards with two interceptions. He is still awaiting his first touchdown pass.

If Jones is chosen as the opening day starter at North Carolina State, the only video footage the Wolfpack will have probably will last about as long as a television commercial. Jones' biggest career highlight was going 16-of-28 for 301 yards and two scores in the 2000 Red-White game.

But when you consider that every opposing quarterback looked like a Heisman Trophy candidate against IU, perhaps that wasn't all that impressive. While Jones can't wait for the fall, he knows he is not assured of supplanting Randle El. He's heard this kind of talk before.

"I'm going to do everything I can right now to put myself in that position," Jones said. "But it's early right now. I'm not even worried about that. It's going to be a challenge. But when your time comes, you have to be ready. I've been here three years counting my red-shirt year. I'm [eager] every year and I ask Twaan what it's like out there."

Jones and Randle El have played pitch-and-catch throughout winter conditioning, sometimes during seven-on-seven drills, sometimes on their own. Randle El is embracing his new role because this is the best way for him to have a professional career. He still figures to see some action at quarterback in special situations for IU. The team, however, will move from an option game to more of a traditional offense.

Randle El thinks he can be "a great receiver." This despite the fact he has caught just three career receptions for 60 yards, including a 51-yard score on a catch-and-run as a freshman. He acknowledges he has a ways to go and doesn't think he'll miss being a quarterback too much. At quarterback, he was pretty good. He rushed for a career-high 1,270 yards and 13 yards and passed for 1,783 and 10 touchdowns. But he also threw a career-high 14 interceptions.

"I don't think it will be strange because I'm doing it now," he said. "On opening day, I'll get some [jitters]. But other than that I think I'll be all right. I'm working at it every day and I'll be working at it all summer."

RUNNING BACKS

When senior **Levron Williams** signed a letter-of-intent with Indiana, it was hailed as one of the more important gets in school history. Williams was a stud, a homegrown runner from Evansville who could have gone anywhere. Instead he became a Hoosier and the coaching staff quietly rejoiced. Williams has had a very good career. Is this the season he final breaks out with a monster year?

Williams (6-4, 222) is a speedy tailback who

operates best in space. The option game was a perfect fit for him because he could catch the ball off the pitch from Randle El and turn the corner with plenty of room. He rushed 116 times for 821 yards with 10 scores. For his career, he has averaged 7.1 yards a carry. Now that IU is going to a more traditional offense, it will be interesting to see how effective Williams will be. He has not been a great runner between the tackles. Most of his big runs have come off the option.

The coaching staff's other challenge is to get Williams involved in the passing game. Two years ago, he caught 33 passes for 360 yards and three scores. But in 2000, he had only 20 receptions for 116 yards and no scores. Williams is a very skilled receiver with good hands and concentration. He actually played wide receiver as a sophomore and can easily line up in that position in a pinch.

"We wanted to find out what kind of runner he could be," Cameron said.

"If he hadn't gotten hurt in the latter part of the season he would have rushed for over 1,000 yards. But we have to even out what we've done the last two years. We have to ask him to run the ball and at the same time use him as a receiver."

Brian Lewis (5-7, 197) is a capable backup who saw action in all 11 games, starting four. As a redshirt freshman, he carried 67 times for 373 yards and three scores. In the second game of the season, Lewis broke out a 43-yarder against Kentucky. Lewis, however, isn't the receiving threat that Williams is. Cameron does have a lot of confidence in Lewis and usually won't hesitate to put him in.

Sophomore **Rashon Myles** (6-1, 218) should also compete for playing time. In 2000, the freshman displayed power and persistence as a runner. He might be the best inside rusher on the team. In the tail end of a 42-6 victory over Cincinnati, Myles rushed 11 times for 61 yards. For the season, he finished with 91 yards on 17 carries.

The IU starting fullback job will finally belong to junior **Jeremi Johnson**. After sharing time with De'Wayne Hogan, Johnson (6-2, 277) should be primed for a breakout season. He is a hard runner who is very effective in short yardage situations. He gained 103 yards on 20 carries and scored a pair of touchdowns last year. He also isn't a bad receiver—he made 11 catches for 83 yards a year ago. The team is even considering playing Johnson at tailback in certain packages.

"Jeremi Johnson has to have a great [season]," Cameron said. "Now that he doesn't have De'Wayne Hogan to push him."

Johnson's weight is a concern. He initially came to the program at 298. He hasn't ballooned back, but he hasn't always been in shape. If he keeps his weight down, there's no reason for him not to be effective.

WIDE RECEIVERS/ TIGHT ENDS

The departure of IU's top three wideouts leaves the Hoosiers in a possible bind. Jerry Dorsey, Versie Gaddis and Derin Graham combined for 73 catches for 1,266 yards. Dorsey and Gaddis, who finished their careers with more than 1,000 receiving yards, were great deep threats that could stretch a defense, and Graham was a competent third-down receiver.

"We are concerned from a standpoint of experience but we put Antwaan out there," Cameron said. "At receiver, I think we have tremendous talent with senior **Henry Frazier**, sophomore **L.J. Parker**, junior **Glenn Johnson**, freshman **Travis Haney**, freshman **David Lewis** and obviously Antwaan."

The thinness of the position is one major reason Randle El will be lining up at wide receiver. Randle El is embracing his new role because this is the best way for him to have a professional career.

Randle El is an excellent runner after the catch, showing tremendous burst. For this reason, the Hoosiers have put in a number of bubble screen plays in which Jones can just dump the pass off and let Randle El create. Randle El has the ability to get deep and can make big plays. But he has not had to go against the better Big Ten cornerbacks that undoubtedly will be physical with him.

One player that can make things easier on Randle El is Frazier, who came to IU as a highly touted junior college player. He was offered a scholarship at Nebraska before deciding to come to Bloomington. At Chabot (Calif.) Junior College, Frazier (6-1, 171) caught 37 passes for 544 yards and six touchdowns. But as a junior at IU, Frazier had only four receptions for 41 yards. Still, Cameron expects big things from him.

"Henry Frazier is as talented, if not more talented than [Dorsey and Gaddis]," he said. "It's just a matter of him having the kind of year he is capable of having."

Parker and Johnson have seen limited action at wideout. At 6-1 and 210 pounds, Parker possesses good size and he and Johnson (5-11, 186) run their patterns very well. Redshirt freshman Haney (6-4, 206) was a first-team all-state selection in Florida in 1999.

Redshirt freshman Lewis (6-1, 174), brother of Purdue basketball player Maynard, is an outstanding talent. Before he's done, he could be among the best wide receivers the school has produced.

"We don't have the experience, we're going to have to bring them along slowly," Cameron said. "But [wide receiver] is one of the easier positions for a guy to come in and play. It's just a matter of how mentally tough they are. They have to believe in themselves and have to believe in what they're doing."

IU has high hopes for freshman tight end **Aaron Halterman**, which is saying a lot. Not only has Halterman (6-5, 258) yet to catch a pass in collegiate play, he has barely played. In the 2000 season opener, Halterman made his debut as a true freshman only to suffer a stress fracture in his lower leg. He received a medical redshirt and now Cameron and the coaching staff are eager to see what he can do.

Halterman has already impressed enough to play with the first-string offense. In one spring scrimmage he caught four passes for 55 yards. To put that in perspective, IU tight ends combined for 12 catches for 124 yards during the entire 2000 season. Simply put, Halterman gives IU an option it hasn't really had in its offense.

"He can run and he can catch the football," Cameron said. "He just needs to prove he can do it consistently. The thing I really like about him is that he is a tough, hard-nosed football player that loves contact. He loves to play the game. The early indications are that this guy wants to be a great player."

Halterman isn't the only quality tight end in the IU fold. He might be asked to be part of a rotation that will include junior **Kris Dielman** (6-4, 293) and junior **Stephen Anthony** (6-3, 267). With Brandt being moved from tight end to right tackle, this is still a pretty green group. Anthony is a converted defensive end. Dielman is the more experienced, having played all eleven games. He had seven catches for 46 yards and two touchdowns.

"Our tight ends are guys that I'm excited to see," Cameron said. "I like all three of them. Who's going to end up starting? I'd like to think all three guys are going to come back thinking they are going to start. We should be pretty solid at tight end."

OFFENSIVE LINE

There's a feeling that this could be the best unit Cameron has ever had. The Hoosiers finally have the type of line that will not only boast talent but has enough depth to compete when a starter gets knocked out with an injury.

First-year offensive line coach Hal Hunter started the process a year ago by revamping the line. Junior **A.C. Myler**, a defensive tackle, moved to left tackle, senior **Craig Osika** switched from tight end to center and junior guard **Enoch DeMar** moved to tackle.

There was considerable skepticism, but the unit held up fairly well. The IU offense rolled to 439.5 yards a game and gave up just nine quarterback sacks. The Hoosiers led the Big Ten in rushing (266.4 yards a game) with 34 rushing touchdowns and finished second nationally in yards per carry (5.8).

A big reason, however, for the line's statistical success was the brilliance of Randle El. The group won't have that luxury with the considerably less mobile Jones.

"We've probably gotten spoiled the last few years," Cameron said. "A guy will miss a block and then what is normally a 10-yard sack, Antwaan will go run for 30 yards. So when you miss an assignment now, you won't have a guy back there that's going to bail you out every time."

Cameron has never been afraid to shuffle players around to fill a need.

He moved Williams from tailback to wide receiver back to tailback and Williams was successful in both roles. He switched Hogan from tailback to fullback and he's become one of team's better blockers. Cameron had similar success with Osika. Early on, it didn't look too promising. By Randle El's count, the first 13 or so snaps in 2000 spring practice were an adventure. Osika called Randle El's estimate kind.

Osika (6-4, 293) played well enough that the program is touting him for All-Big Ten honors. Cameron hopes another switch will pay off. Junior **Bobby Brandt** (6-8, 304) is moving from tight end to right tackle. DeMar (6-4, 313), possibly the most talented lineman, might be moved back inside to right guard. Myler (6-4, 334) is a powerful road-grader at left tackle. He will have to be a better blocker for Jones' sake.

Sophomore **Anthony Oakley** (6-3, 290) will return at left guard. He is possibly the team's strongest player. IU should have quality depth with junior guard **Jarmarkus Gorman** (6-4, 317), who can start in a pinch, and sophomore **Colin Christopher** (6-2, 281). Junior **Brett Taylor** (6-8, 304) is also much improved.

2000 STATISTICS

Rushing offense	266.4	7
Passing offense	172.7	90
Total offense	439.1	15
Scoring offense	30.6	34
Net Punting	26.2	114
Punt returns	8.3	80
Kickoff returns	19.6	59
Rushing defense	186.4	91
Passing efficiency defense	152.2	109
Total defense	457.3	112
Scoring defense	38.8	112
Turnover margin	-16	111

Last column is ranking among Division I-A teams.

KICKERS

The solid Andy Payne is gone. Payne was arguably the team's most dependable special teams player. He converted 9-of-12 field-goal kicks last season and 43-of-58 for his career. Now the Hoosiers need to find someone just like him.

Sophomore **Adam Braucher** is the early favorite. Braucher (5-7, 195) has a stronger leg than Payne but lacks experience. Payne attempted only five 50-yard kicks in his career. Braucher, who handled kick-off duties last year, might be asked to attempt a few more from long distance.

Signee **Bryan Robertson** (5-9, 180) was a first-team All-America selection. He's a hometown boy from nearby Seymour, Ind., and he has a world of talent. Robertson will be given a chance to win the job but might not factor into the equation until the following season.

Freshman **Brett Gaudin** (6-0, 186), a walk-on, could also figure into the mix.

DEFENSIVE LINE

The Hoosiers will return three starting linemen, including both starting ends. This unit needs to generate more of a pass rush. IU had only 18 sacks—down five from 1999. Last season the defensive line had 11. The year before that, starting ends Adewale Ogunleye and senior **Kemp Rasmussen** combined 15 for by themselves.

"We have to find guys up front who can get to the quarterback," Cameron said. "These days, if you can't get to the quarterback, that's the difference because these teams will spread you out. You have to be able to get to the quarterback."

Rasmussen (6-3, 250) is being moved to tackle. The fifth-year senior seemed to be on his way to promising career after collecting seven sacks as a sophomore. But last fall his production dropped off. He had 30 tackles, including nine for a loss and three sacks. He also broke up seven passes. Rasmussen is active and quick but a bit small for an interior lineman.

But Cameron doesn't think size will be that much of an issue.

"In college you can do some things," he said. "Is he going to line up over the center and guard and pound away? No. But with his athletic frame, I think he can make some plays."

Sophomore **Derek Barnett** has been groomed to be the successor to Ogunleye, IU's all-time sacks leader. In his first season of major action, Barnett (6-3, 246) started all 11 games and had 32 tackles and three sacks. He is probably the team's fastest defensive lineman. Barnett must show greater stamina. He had only one sack in the Big Ten season.

Senior **Dominique Smith** (6-3, 293) is the third returning starter. The former junior college player started 10 games and recorded 25 tackles and three sacks. Smith has the talent to be an above-average player.

Competing for the other defensive end position will be junior **Sean Nelson** (6-3, 261) and sophomore **Steve Williams** (6-3, 242). Nelson, a junior, missed the entire 2000 season with a shoulder injury. Williams played 10 games at defensive tackle as a freshman.

The Hoosiers need to be more competitive in this area. Nothing makes an entire defense more effective than a strong defensive line. A strong pass-rush is critical, especially given the problems Indiana has had in the secondary.

"The defensive line has probably been the most pleasant surprise of the spring," Cameron said.

LINEBACKERS

This is another area in need of improvement. The IU linebackers were inconsistent and seemed to struggle the most in adjusting to the new defensive scheme that called for multiple looks.

The most dependable of the trio is second-team All-Big Ten selection **Justin Smith** (6-0, 213). Smith, a Butkus award nominee, is undersized but quick to the ball and quarterback.

The coaching staff turned Smith, a senior, loose on quarterbacks last season. As a result he picked up a career-best six sacks. He earned league player-of-the-week honors when he had four sacks in a victory over Iowa. Smith entered last year with two for his career and none in 1999. He was the second-leading tackler with 74 stops, including 14 for a loss. He also was credited with four passes broken up and two forced fumbles. One of those forced fumbles helped seal a win over Minnesota. How much more can IU ask from Smith?

"I think a lot," Cameron said. "Justin has not been healthy for an entire season yet. If he can stay healthy I think he can be one of the best, if not the best linebacker in the league. He has a knack for [blitzing]. We'll pick and chose. Probably if anything we did a little too much at the latter point of the season. People [adjusted] after a while."

The other outside linebacker will be senior **Devin Schaffer** (6-2, 242). Shaffer moved from middle linebacker before the 2000 season. He started all 11 games at his new position. He finished fourth on the team with 47 tackles, including nine for a loss, and a sack. The fifth-year senior had trouble occasionally when he was caught out of position in pass coverage.

Middle linebacker is the biggest question mark. The most likely candidate appears to be sophomore **Brandonn Baker** (6-1, 240). He started three games as a freshman last year—all in the Big Ten. Baker is a very good athlete who runs well. He was hampered by a knee injury last season.

"We know we have Justin Smith and Devin Schaffer," Cameron said. "We don't know who is going to be our middle linebacker. Whoever it is will have to be smart and tough. We're going to have to wait and see. It's going to come down to who works the hardest this summer."

DEFENSIVE BACKS

This is easily the most glaring weakness on the team. A year ago, opposing quarterbacks torched the Hoosiers for 240-for-371 passing (64 percent), good for 2,980 yards and 25 touchdown passes. Indiana made just four interceptions. The pass defense was so bad that North Carolina State freshman quarterback Philip Rivers passed for 401 yards and five scores to rally the Wolfpack from a 38-26 deficit for 41-38 victory.

Indiana's secondary was so inept that Wisconsin lost its starting quarterback to injury and backup Jim Sorgi came off the bench to go 16-of-21 for 207 yards and three scores in the Badgers' 43-22 triumph.

For opposing offenses, it was no mystery. When in doubt, pass, because the Hoosiers couldn't cover. Cameron said his team's secondary woes are more mental than physical.

"It's about confidence, period," he said. "It's getting through to the guys and them having confidence in what they're doing. The secondary is the last line of defense. If you're back there playing in fear, you're going to have a tough time. You have to believe in what you see. Read and react. And you to have the courage to make some plays. I think we'll have a different mental attitude."

Senior cornerback **Sharrod Wallace** (5-8, 183) is the steadiest backfield performer. Last season, he had 49 tackles with two interceptions, broke up nine passes and had a fumble recovery. This will be Wallace's third year as a starter and he will be looked upon to have a big year. He has to because the other cornerback position is very much unsettled.

Senior **Marcus Floyd** (5-9, 184), junior **A.C. Carter** (5-7, 188) and sophomore **Duane Stone** (5-9, 177) all tried, with lukewarm results at best. Floyd and Carter are both converted tailbacks.

Floyd and Stone saw the most action. Floyd started the final four games, finishing the year with 40 tackles. Stone started six games before being benched in favor of Floyd. He had 44 tackles.

Sophomore **Michael Hanley** (5-11, 172) might be the solution. Hanley missed the 2000 season because of academics. The sophomore has ideal size and has the kind of coverage skills that this unit is in dire need of.

"Sharrod and Michael Hanley did some good things this spring," Cameron said.

At strong safety, junior **Ron Bethel** (6-3, 215) returns. Bethel isn't just the tallest and bulkiest defensive back on the team; he's also one of the tallest in the league. He was tied for fifth on the team in tackles with 44 and had a sack.

The team also should get a boost from junior college defensive back **Antonio Watson** (6-1, 198), a junior.

PUNTERS

Last season IU tried punting by committee. Sophomore **Ryan Hamre**, Payne and even Randle El all tried. Hamre (6-2, 215) probably will take over full-time duties. He punted 16 times a year ago for a 37.4 average. That was a big drop off from the punting the team had in 1999 with All-Big Ten pick Drew Hagan.

Of course, perhaps Hamre will feel better if he knows he won't be rushed. The Hoosiers had three punts blocked last season.

SPECIAL TEAMS

With the exception of the field-goal unit, IU's special teams took a step back last year. Opponents returned two punts and kickoffs for touchdowns. In contrast, the Hoosiers did not have any special team returns for scores. The team will be in a further bind this year without Derin Graham, who in his career had a pair of kickoff returns for scores.

The punt coverage team did have a noteworthy achievement. Johnny Anderson blocked a punt against Cincinnati, the program's first since 1996.

This season the punt return team should get a boost from Randle El, whose speed will be a real asset. Randle El should be motivated to do well. NFL scouts want to see how he does in this department. He appears to have the tools to be a good one.

RECRUITING CLASS

Cameron has continued to make good on upgrading IU's recruiting. While IU hasn't landed that one knockout class, it has put together a solid string.

Twenty-two players have signed. The class, which features players from nine different states and Canada, is highlighted by *SuperPrep*'s first- and third-rated junior college defensive backs in the country in **Antonio Watson** (6-1, 198) and **Willie Northern** (6-1, 195). The two highly regarded defensive backs enrolled in school in time to participate in spring drills. Watson played at Hinds (Miss.) Community College and Nothern at Community College of San Francisco.

The emphasis in recruiting has been on

defense. Cornerback **Damien Jones** (5-10, 185), from Houston (Texas) Sterling High, might be the most talented of all the recruits. Cameron managed to pry Jones away from the powerhouses like Kansas State, Arizona, Purdue and national champion Oklahoma. Jones probably will compete for the starting cornerback position soon.

Some other key defensive backs are Indianapolis Cathedral's **Buster Larkins** (5-11, 180), **Will Lumpkin** (5-11, 192) of Ohio and **Leonard Bryant** (5-10, 180) of Immokalee, Fla. Bryant hails from the same high school that produced Indianapolis Colts All-Pro tailback Edgerrin James.

On the offensive end, one notable recruit is Cincinnati fullback **Kyle Koester**. The 6-1, 235-pounder rushed for more than 1,500 yards in his junior and senior seasons. He also averaged more than six yards per carry. Widely regarded as one of the finest fullback prospects in the Midwest, this Cincinnati Elder product was the *Cincinnati Post's* Division I Player of the Year as he finished his career with more than 4,300 career rushing yards. As a senior in 2000, Koester rushed for 1,474 yards and 17 touchdowns. He also caught 25 passes for 271 yards.

Robertson, considered the top kicker in the Midwest, owns state records for most career field goals (34), most in a single season (13), and longest field goal—a 61-yarder he kicked as a junior. After converting 13-of-23 attempts in 1999, Robertson struggled this year by making only 7-of-21 tries.

Recruiting analyst Tom Lemming rated this class in the top second half of the 11-team Big Ten.

"I think they have done O.K.," he said. "The whole Big Ten has done pretty good. Indiana went after some athletic guys and it looks like they came up with some this year."

BLUE RIBBON ANALYSIS

OFFENSE	B
SPECIAL TEAMS	D
DEFENSE	D
INTANGIBLES	C-

The chances of IU having a breakthrough season appear to be slim. While the Hoosiers have proven they can be competitive, they have yet to show they are ready to take the next step to bowl eligibility. Cameron is taking a gamble by putting Jones in charge of the offense. At least Randle El had the ability to create offense out of a broken play. Jones doesn't appear to have those physical or mental instincts.

The offense has to score points because the defense is going to give up a ton. Jones is also going to be hampered by the lack of veteran receivers. With the Hoosiers going to a more conventional offense, tailback Williams becomes a very, very important player. They need to play keep away because of the defensive problems. The Hoosiers also have to cut down on turnovers. They had 30 last season—too many for a poor defense to overcome.

Can the defense get better? Defensive coordinator James Bell has a good track record and improvement doesn't seem to be out of the question. The talent base on defense is getting better. But it needs an impact player to emerge, especially in the front seven. If the Hoosiers had merely an average defense, they would have been to two bowl games by now.

The key might be getting off to a good pre-conference start. IU opens up at North Carolina State and plays Kentucky and Utah at home. A three-game sweep won't be easy, but it is possible. But during the Cameron era, the program has never opened up 3-0. The Big Ten season is, as usual, a bear. Ohio State, Illinois, Northwestern and Purdue come to Memorial Stadium. All but Illinois went to a bowl game last year and the Illini are two seasons removed from a bowl victory. Winning league road games figures to be even tougher. The Hoosiers were outscored, 192-81, in such games last year. In Cameron's tenure, they have won only one Big Ten road game.

This is Cameron's make-or-break year. He's fighting long odds.

(M.G.)

2000 RESULTS

North Carolina State	L	38-41	0-1
Kentucky	L	34-41	0-2
Cincinnati	W	42-6	1-2
Iowa	W	45-33	2-2
Northwestern	L	33-52	2-3
Michigan	L	0-58	2-4
Minnesota	W	51-43	3-4
Penn State	L	24-27	3-5
Illinois	L	35-42	3-6
Wisconsin	L	22-43	3-7
Purdue	L	13-41	3-8

Iowa

LOCATION Iowa City, IA
CONFERENCE Big Ten
LAST SEASON 3-9 (.250)
CONFERENCE RECORD 3-5 (8th)
OFFENSIVE STARTERS RETURNING 8
DEFENSIVE STARTERS RETURNING 8
NICKNAME Hawkeyes
COLORS Old Gold & Black
HOME FIELD Kinnick Stadium (70,397)
HEAD COACH Kirk Ferentz (Connecticut '78)
RECORD AT SCHOOL 4-19 (2 years)
CAREER RECORD 26-40 (5 years)
ASSISTANTS
Ron Aiken (North Carolina A&T '77) Defensive Line
Bret Bielema (Iowa '92) Linebackers
Lester Erb (Bucknell '92) Receivers/Special Teams
Carl Jackson (Prairie View A&M '63) Running Backs
Reese Morgan (Wartburg '73) Recruiting Coordinator/Tight Ends
Ken O'Keefe (John Carroll '75) Offensive Coordinator/Quarterbacks
Norm Parker (Eastern Michigan '65) Defensive Coordinator/Outside Linebackers
Phil Parker (Michigan State '86) Defensive Backs
Joe Philbin (Washington & Jefferson '84) Offensive Line
TEAM WINS (last 5 yrs.) 9-7-3-1-3
FINAL RANK (last 5 yrs.) 10-20-58-74-68
2000 FINISH Lost to Minnesota in regular-season finale.

COACH AND PROGRAM

It's not unusual for a young head coach to struggle in the shadow of a legendary predecessor. But Iowa's Kirk Ferentz has to deal with a different problem. He operates in the shadow of a legend who never even coached at Iowa.

Ferentz took the reins of the Iowa program from the hands of Hayden Fry in 1999. In his 20 seasons in Iowa City, Fry led the Hawkeyes to 14 bowl games, won three Big Ten titles and helped Iowa crack the season-ending AP Top 10 twice, its first such honors since 1961. His 143-89-6 record is the best ever at Iowa and will be tough for Ferentz or any coach to top.

But ask any Iowa booster and you'll discover that Ferentz was not the Hawkeyes' first choice to succeed Fry. In the fall of 1998, Florida defensive coordinator Bob Stoops was the hot coaching candidate throughout the nation, and his status as a former Hawkeye star and former Fry assistant led many to believe he was holding out for the Iowa job.

But after Fry retired, Iowa officials couldn't come to terms with Stoops, and on Dec. 1, 1998, he was hired as the head coach at the University of Oklahoma. One day later, Ferentz was introduced as the new head coach at Iowa. And the rest, as they say, is history. As Stoops led the Sooners to 13 straight victories and the national championship last season, Hawkeye fans could be heard to mutter, "That's supposed to be our coach!" on a weekly basis.

Meanwhile, to say that Ferentz has struggled in his first two years would be putting it mildly. A 1-10 debut was followed by a 3-9 mark last year, and although the Hawkeyes showed some signs of life, there's clearly much work to be done.

Aside from Stoops and his success at Oklahoma, there are a couple other factors that played into the grumbling at Kinnick Stadium the last two autumns. One is the widely held belief that ol' Hayden left the cupboard bare when he packed up his cowboy hat and sunglasses and headed off into the sunset. In his last seven seasons, Fry's Hawkeyes were above .500 in the Big Ten only once, and his 3-8 swan song in 1998 ended with a five-game losing streak. That left a sour taste in the mouths of the Hawkeye faithful, who grew critical of Fry's recruiting efforts toward the end of his career.

Even more damning was Ferentz's head coaching résumé, or lack of same, before taking over at Iowa. His only experience as the top man at a program was a three-year stint at Maine in the early '90s. The Black Bears were 12-21 under Ferentz, who then jumped to the NFL's Cleveland Browns. His last position before taking over at Iowa was as the assistant head coach and offensive line coach of the Baltimore Ravens in 1998.

So in the minds of many Hawkeyes followers, the cards were already stacked against Ferentz when he took over—because of the state of the program when Fry left, because he wasn't Stoops, and because he wasn't a proven winner anywhere else.

Fry did no favors for Ferentz when he created the schedule. Playing the fourth-toughest schedule in the country, the Hawkeyes went 1-10 in the first year of the Ferentz Era, and last year's 3-9 team faced eight bowl teams scattered across the NCAA's sixth-toughest schedule.

But to say that 2000 was a complete failure for Iowa would be viewing the glass as half-empty. After a 1-8 start (and a 2-18 career start for Ferentz), the team rebounded to win two of its last three, including a win at free-falling Penn State and an upset of a Northwestern team that would have been Rose Bowl-bound had it beaten the Hawkeyes.

Iowa was also highly competitive in its final two losses. Wisconsin's potent offense struggled to a 13-7 victory in Iowa City, and in the season finale the Hawks coughed up a 12-point fourth-quarter lead in a loss at Minnesota. But after that final stretch the light was clearly visible at the end of the tunnel for the Hawkeyes.

This year's challenges include settling on a quarterback and an offensive line combo that can maximize the potential of a couple of exciting offensive threats, shoring up the conference's second-worst pass defense and finding a way to get a few breaks that didn't bounce Iowa's way in close losses last year.

"We have to realize that a lot of good things are taking place," Ferentz told *The Daily Iowan*. "But we are nowhere near where we want to be, and we just have to stay after it in a workman-like fashion. I'm real confident if we do that and stay healthy, we'll take our chances with the 2001 season."

If the Hawkeyes can achieve those goals, look for fans to stop whispering the names of Fry and Stoops around Iowa City this fall.

2000 STATISTICS

Rushing offense	90.8	105
Passing offense	215.0	59
Total offense	305.8	101
Scoring offense	16.9	98
Net Punting	39.0	8
Punt returns	9.0	66
Kickoff returns	23.4	7
Rushing defense	194.2	95
Passing efficiency defense	135.4	100
Total defense	440.9	106
Scoring defense	27.5	78
Turnover margin	-3	73

Last column is ranking among Division I-A teams.

QUARTERBACKS

The highest-profile position on the team is the one giving Ferentz the most headaches this year. Not because he doesn't have options, but because he has too many.

Still, it's a good problem to have, and you won't catch Ferentz complaining about it.

"There will come a time when we have to settle on one candidate, but that time isn't now," Ferentz told *The Daily Iowan* during spring practice. "Right now it's just too close to call."

The incumbent appears to be senior **Kyle McCann** (6-5, 214), who started the final four games last year. That happens to coincide with the Hawkeye's four-game season-saving resurgence against Wisconsin, Penn State, Northwestern and Minnesota, so you'd have to call that a big plus in McCann's favor.

In four-and-a-half games last season, McCann connected on 79-of-136 passes (58 percent) for 862 yards and five touchdowns with only four interceptions. That kind of efficiency could help lead the Hawkeyes back to respectability this season if he can keep it up for 11 games instead of just four.

His main competition for the starting job is sophomore **Jon Beutjer** (6-5, 200), who also started four games last season. He took over from the now-departed Scott Mullen in the fifth game, at Indiana, and led the Hawkeyes to a 21-16 upset over Michigan State the next week. But two weeks later, Beutjer went down with an injury against Ohio State, opening the door for McCann to show his stuff.

For the season, Beutjer's numbers were slightly better than McCann's—77-for-125 (62 percent) for 841 yards with six touchdowns and three interceptions. Which gives you a sense of why Ferentz and his staff are still undecided about their starting quarterback.

"It should be fun and competitive around here this summer," Beutjer told the *Des Moines Register*. "Everyone's going to be staying around campus and working out on a daily basis. I'm going to live in the film room, because I need to learn to recognize defenses. I need to put on about 10 pounds, too."

A third name has joined the mix since the last time the Hawkeyes laced up their cleats. Junior **Brad Banks** (6-1, 180) transferred from Hinds (Miss.) Community College, and he opened some eyes in spring practice.

Unlike McCann and Beutjer, who will stay at home in the pocket, Banks gives defenses fits with his scrambling ability.

Last year at Hinds he passed for more than 2,000 yards, ran for more than 500 yards, and scored 13 rushing touchdowns. While Ferentz is looking for either McCann or Beutjer to win the job, Banks is clearly in the mix. His mid-year transfer only helped his cause.

Banks started his college career at Central Florida, but left there after his redshirt freshman season. He was a receiver at Hinds in 1999 before being moved to quarterback in 2000.

"The fact that he could be here right now and jump in made that attractive to us," Ferentz told the *Register*. "First and foremost, we were impressed with his throwing. We want a quarterback who is a thrower. We're not going to veer too far from that."

Providing depth will be junior **Nick Whisler** (6-3, 205) and sophomore **David Raih** (6-5, 190)

RUNNNING BACKS

If there's one spot where there will be no competition, it will be at starting tailback. Senior **Ladell Betts** (5-11, 215) piled up 1,090 yards and a 4.7 yards per carry average last season, putting him head and shoulders above the competition. He earned honorable-mention All-Big Ten status as a junior and has a shot at becoming the Hawkeyes' all-time leading rusher this year. He's currently third on the career list and needs 1,530 to pass Sedrick Shaw for that honor.

Betts' caddy will be junior **Siaka Massaquoi** (5-11, 200), who had a strong spring practice and jumped ahead of sophomores **Aaron Greving** (5-11, 207) and **Fred Russell** (5-8, 177) in the battle for the backup role. Greving and Russell were key special-teamers last year but didn't carry the ball out of the backfield all season. Greving, who sat out the spring game when he tweaked a knee in practice, is a banger while Russell is more of an elusive back who could make some noise as a pass receiver as well. Both players could return kicks for the Hawkeyes this season.

The star-in-the-making in the Hawkeye backfield could be redshirt freshman **Jermelle Lewis** (5-11, 208), who rushed for 1,623 yards and 25 touchdowns as a prep senior at Bloomfield (Conn.) High School. He was the prize of the 2000 Iowa recruiting class, but he'll have to bide his time again unless injuries strike the running backs. Still, he's one to keep an eye on for the future.

At fullback, the Hawkeyes have only one player with college experience—senior **Jeremy Allen** (6-1, 240), who started six games last season and carried the ball 34 times for 135 yards. He has a lock on the starting job this year, with senior **Robbie Crockett** (6-0, 207) moving up from tailback to fill the backup role. Also pushing for playing time will be junior **Scott Rathke** (6-0, 235), sophomore **Edgar Cervantes** (6-3, 240)—a converted linebacker—and redshirt freshman Aaron Mickens (5-10, 235), who could also wind up on the defensive line.

"We have a pretty good idea what Ladell can do and we have a pretty good idea what Robbie can do as well," Ferentz told the *Register*. "The guys underneath those two are the ones we're really interested to see sift themselves out. We've got to get a better feel for what that group can do."

No matter who carries the ball for Iowa, Ferentz has made it clear that he wants to do a better job of establishing the run this year. The Hawkeyes ranked last in the conference in rushing offense last year, and that was a big factor in exposing the Iowa defense. This year, ball control and time of possession will be important statistics for the Hawkeyes, whose fifth-ranked passing game would benefit from an improved rushing attack.

WIDE RECEIVERS/TIGHT ENDS

The biggest hole the Hawkeyes have to fill is the vacant spot left by the departure of wide receiver Kevin Kasper. The career leader in pass receptions at Iowa hauled in a school-record and Big Ten-high 82 catches last year for 1,010 yards, second-best in Iowa history, and was a second team All-Big Ten honoree. His seven touchdowns were also a team high. They will also have to replace No. 3 receiver Ryan Barton and his 18 grabs.

Fortunately for Ferentz, he's got another deep threat in senior **Kahlil Hill** (6-3, 195) who is a threat to make a game-breaking play any time he steps on the field. Hill was an honorable-mention All-Big Ten selection and his 58 catches for 619 yards and five touchdowns were second to Kasper in all three categories.

Hill's main running mate has yet to be chosen, but the leader appears to be senior **Chris Oliver** (6-2, 210), the only returning wideout with college experience. Last season he caught 10 balls for 206 yards and two touchdowns.

The other main target for the Iowa quarterbacks should be senior **Tim Dodge** (5-10, 180), who makes the switch from cornerback to wide receiver this year after moving from receiver to defensive back the year before. He started eight games at the corner last year but is filling a bigger need for the Hawkeyes on offense this season.

"We moved him to cornerback because we needed his speed back there, and because we had pretty good depth at wide receiver," Ferentz told the *Register*. "We moved him back because we lost two receivers."

Others in the mix are sophomores **Mo Brown** (6-2, 210) and **Ramon Ochoa** (5-10, 189).

Junior college transfer **C.J. Jones** (5-11, 180), who had 42 catches for 927 yards at Garden City (Kansas) Community College last season, is a potential major contributor. Jones was chosen to the NJCAA All-America team in 2000 after making the team as a return specialist in 1999.

The tight end position is wide open, because both of last year's starters are gone. Kyle Trippeer, who caught 19 passes for 188 yards, has graduated, and **Robert Gallery** was moved to tackle midway through the season.

The early leader appears to be sophomore **Erik Jensen** (6-3, 259), who earned a letter last year when he caught two passes for 37 yards. He'll be pushed by redshirt freshman **Tony Jackson** (6-3, 235) and junior **Dallas Clark** (6-4, 240). Clark played linebacker his first three years at Iowa, but he had a great spring practice at his new position and impressed coaches with his soft hands.

"Dallas Clark has been a pleasant surprise," Ferentz told the *Cedar Rapids Gazette*. "We knew he could give us something in the passing game we haven't had for a while."

Two incoming freshmen have a shot at some playing time immediately if they are not redshirted—**C.J. Barkema** (6-8, 235) of Muscatine, Iowa, and **Ben Gates** (6-6, 235) of Toledo, Iowa.

OFFENSIVE LINE

This is an area of expertise for Ferentz, who was the offensive line coach for the Baltimore Ravens before coming to Iowa. He says that barring injury, the Hawkeyes will have the best line since he arrived on campus.

That's good, because last year's line allowed a Big Ten-high 57 sacks. That number is partly inflated by the stationary nature of the quarterbacks on the roster—thanks to the fleet feet of Antwaan Randle El, Indiana allowed only nine sacks all year—but even so, the Hawkeye offense cannot afford to be knocked backward five times a game.

The only hole to fill is at center, where the graduated A.J. Blazek started all 12 games and was the offensive captain last season. Junior **Bruce Nelson** (6-4, 290), who started 11 games at left guard last year, appears poised to make the switch to center this season. He will be backed up by junior **Pete Traynor** (6-3, 290).

The starting guards should be junior **Eric Steinbach** (6-7, 284) and sophomore **Sam Aiello** (6-5, 310). Steinbach was slated to start at center last season but missed most of the season with an injury; he was shifted to guard when he returned and started the final game of the season. Aiello had five starts last season, four coming at tackle. Pushing them will be junior **Andy Lightfoot** (6-6, 284) and sophomore **Eric Rothwell** (6-3, 300).

A pair of 300 pounders will bookend the line at tackle. On the right side should be Gallery (6-7, 300), the converted tight end who started the final six games last year. Over on the left, look for senior **Alonzo Cunningham** (6-4, 305), who started eight games last season. Waiting in the wings will be senior David Porter (6-7, 305) and sophomore **Kory Borchers** (6-6, 290).

The line will also benefit from the return of senior **Ben Sobieski** (6-5, 305). He started all 11 games at tackle as a sophomore two years ago, but he's missed the last two years because of an injury. If he can stay healthy, Ferentz might be right—this could be a solid line and a reason for hope, not dismay, in Iowa City.

2001 SCHEDULE

Sept.	1	Kent State
	8	Miami (Ohio)
	15	@Iowa State
	29	Penn State
Oct.	6	@Purdue
	13	@Michigan State
	20	Indiana
	27	Michigan
Nov.	3	@Wisconsin
	10	@Northwestern
	17	Minnesota

KICKERS

No need to worry here for the Hawkeyes. Sophomore **Nate Kaeding** (6-0, 165) returns after a solid freshman year. He hit 14-of-22 field goal attempts and all 20 of his PATs, and was voted third-team freshman All-America by *The Sporting News*. His four field goals—three of them from 46 yards or beyond—were the key in Iowa's victory at Penn State, and he led all Iowa scorers with 62 points. His season long was a 49-yarder at Penn State, and he connected on his final seven attempts, five of them from 40-plus yards.

Backing up Kaeding will be redshirt freshman **Ryan Clark** (6-4, 210).

DEFENSIVE LINE

The defensive line made big steps last season but it must continue to improve if the Hawkeyes hope to make up ground in the Big Ten. Iowa finished ninth in rushing defense, allowing 194.3 yards per game on the ground, and sacked the quarterback only 24 times in 12 games. The Hawkeyes lose starting defensive end Anthony Herren, who had 64 tackles and three sacks last year and was an honorable-mention All-Big Ten pick.

But the bulk of the line will have plenty of experience. The leader will be senior **Aaron Kampman** (6-4, 282), a legitimate All-America candidate after moving from linebacker to end last year. He finished third on the team with 94 tackles and had three sacks. The other end will be junior **Colin Cole** (6-2, 300), who doesn't have much starting experience but saw plenty of action off the bench last season.

Pushing for playing time at defensive end will be sophomore **Howard Hodges** (6-2, 235), senior **Joe Uselman** (6-3, 255) and senior **Cody O'Hare** (6-4, 270). If Cole isn't up to the task of replacing Herren, one of these three could step up to fill the void.

The tackles should be a pair of seniors, **Jerry Mongtomery** (6-3, 300), who started all 12 games last season, and **Derrick Pickens** (6-2, 284), who racked up 11 starts in 2000. Montgomery led the Hawkeyes with 11 tackles for loss, one more than Pickens, who had a team-high seven sacks.

Sophomore **Jared Clauss** (6-5, 287) could also be a factor on the line this year—he will get a look inside, as will junior **Scott Webb** (6-2, 295). Another player to watch is sophomore **Jonathan Babineaux** (6-2, 255), who joins the defense after time spent at fullback as a freshman last year.

LINEBACKERS

Leading tackler LeVar Woods and backup Derrick Davison have moved on, but the linebackers should still be a strength of the defense this season. If senior **Mike Dolezal** (6-3, 240) can stay healthy, he will anchor the middle of the field for the Hawkeyes. He missed five games in the second half of the season last year but still managed to finish fourth on the team in tackles with 72. He will team with senior **Roger Meyer** (6-3, 244), who filled in to the tune of 95 tackles last season, second on the team.

Sophomore **Grant Steen** (6-3, 238) should get the nod at one outside spot, while junior **Fred Barr** (6-2, 238) looks strong at the other. Steen saw action in all 12 games last year as a freshman backing up Woods. Barr replaced Davison midway through the season and racked up 72 tackles.

Look for sophomore **George Lewis** (6-2, 230) to back up Steen on the strong side, and sophomore **Kevin Worthy** (6-2, 235) to spell Barr on the weak side. Freshman **Charlie Bodiford** (6-2, 235) and junior **Tony Burrier** (6-4, 212) will add depth to a linebacking corps that could be a pleasant surprise for Iowa this fall.

DEFENSIVE BACKS

The much-maligned Hawkeye secondary gave up 21 touchdowns and almost 247 passing yards per game last season, second-worst in the Big Ten, but experience and a couple of new faces should help improve those numbers this year. The biggest loss will be free safety Ryan Hansen, who started all 12 games last year and totaled 72 tackles, three interceptions and 10 passes defensed. Dodge, who started the first eight games at corner, was moved to wide receiver in the off-season, creating another opening.

Sophomore **Chris Smith** (5-11, 195) will get the first shot at replacing Hansen at free safety. He started two games last year at strong safety, but sophomore **Bob Sanders** (5-8, 194) finished the season there and should throw his weight around from that position again this fall.

Junior **Derek Pagel** (6-1, 203) will push Sanders at strong safety, and junior **D.J. Johnson** (5-10, 192) is in the mix at free safety.

Another candidate for both positions is junior college transfer **Jermire Roberts** (6-2, 210), who had a an excellent 2000 season at Trinity Valley Community College in Port Arthur, Texas. Roberts set school and conference records with 11 interceptions and made 130 tackles as a sophomore. He earned second-team NCJAA All-America honors.

Sophomore **Benny Sapp** (5-10, 181) returns at one corner, and senior **Matt Stockdale** (5-10, 188) has the edge at the other corner. Sapp started the final eight games last season as a freshman, and although he struggled at times, he's got enough speed and athletic ability to expect improvement. Stockdale started the final three games last season and needs to make plays to keep his job this fall.

Waiting in the wings are redshirt freshman **Aramis Haralson** (6-3, 197), senior **Mikkel Brown** (5-10, 195), junior **Marqueas McLaurin** (5-8, 175) and senior **Shane Hall** (5-11, 201).

PUNTERS

The Hawkeyes lost four-year starter Jason Baker, whose 42.5-yard average last year was third in the Big Ten and 17th in the NCAA. He tops the Iowa career lists and is second all-time in the conference in punts (272) and yardage (11,304).

Baker has been working in the off-season with red-shirt freshman **David Bradley** (6-2, 205), who averaged 42.1 yards on 10 kicks in the spring game. Bradley, who was recruited to Iowa as a quarterback, will compete with Keading for the punting job.

"Those are going to be some pretty tough shoes to fill," Bradley told the *Cedar Rapids Gazette*. "Nate [Kaeding] and I worked out all winter, but the coaches came to us at the start of spring with an idea of me punting and Nate concentrating on being the kicker."

SPECIAL TEAMS

Hill is an electrifying kick returner who won first-team all-Big Ten honors from *The Sporting News* last year. He averaged 9.6 yards per punt return, fifth in the conference, and was second in the Big Ten with a 27.2-yard average on kickoff returns.

Dodge will team with Hill on the kickoff return team. Last year he brought back 12 kicks for a 24.8-yard average. Oliver is the backup punt returner—he averaged 6.6 yards per return in limited duty last fall.

Junior college transfer C.J. Jones could well get a serious shot as a punter return. Last season in junior college he returned two punts for touchdowns. In 1999, he made the NJCAA All-America team as a return specialist.

RECRUITING CLASS

The Hawkeyes' recruiting class ranked somewhere in the middle of the Big Ten. Junior college transfers like Banks, Jones and Roberts could supply some immediate help, but a few of the true freshman will get a shot at playing this fall.

The highlights of the class are linebacker **Matt Roth** (6-4, 245) of Villa Park, Ill., a relentless ballhawk with an NFL future; offensive lineman **Blake Larsen** (6-7, 304) of Atlantic, Iowa, the state's top recruit who has been compared to Mike Munoz; and center **Ben Cronin** (6-5, 270) of Ames, Iowa, another highly regarded in-state prospect stolen from rival Iowa State's backyard.

Roth was chosen to the ESPN and Reebok All-America teams after his senior season. In his final two years at Villa Park, Roth made 271 tackles, 52 tackles for loss and 15 sacks.

Larsen was a consensus All-America pick, having been chosen to the *Parade*, *USA Today*, ESPN and Reebok teams. Some experts considered Larsen the premier offensive lineman in the class of 2001.

Cronin was rated a four-star recruit by analyst Tom Lemming, and he was also a two-time first-team all-state seletion.

BLUE RIBBON ANALYSIS

OFFENSE	B
SPECIAL TEAMS	B-
DEFENSE	C+
INTANGIBLES	C

If all goes according to plan, this could be the year Hawkeye fans identify in a few years as the turning point for Ferentz and the football program. You can't overlook the way the Hawkeyes finished last season, with two wins and two gut-wrenching defeats in their final four games. After looking more or less overmatched in the first eight games, that kind of in-season improvement is the sign of a team on the rise.

This year fans can expect the Hawkeyes to at least be competitive, and with a few breaks that they didn't get last season, a bowl berth is not out of the question. Even if they don't completely reverse their fortunes, Ferentz should be able to rely on a solid offense and an improved defense as a reason for hope for the future.

"We're a better football team—there's no question about that," Ferentz told *The Daily Iowan* during spring practice. "How much better? That remains to be seen. Hopefully the improvement we had at the end of last season will show up for the entire season next year.

"I'm excited about the direction things are going. The way we are going to get to where we want to be is to be committed and keep preparing on a consistent basis. What enabled us to play well in the last four games last year is that we stayed the course. We stayed mentally tough and kept focused and that will also determine our fate this year."

(P.D.)

2000 RESULTS

Kansas State	L	7-27	0-1
Western Michigan	L	21-27	0-2
Iowa State	L	14-24	0-3
Nebraska	L	13-42	0-4
Indiana	L	33-45	0-5
Michigan State	W	21-16	1-5
Illinois	L	0-31	1-6
Ohio State	L	10-38	1-7
Wisconsin	L	7-13	1-8
Penn State	W	26-23	2-8
Northwestern	W	27-17	3-8
Minnesota	L	24-27	3-9

Michigan

LOCATION	**Ann Arbor, MI**
CONFERENCE	**Big Ten**
LAST SEASON	**9-3 (.750)**
CONFERENCE RECORD	**6-2 (t-1st)**
OFFENSIVE STARTERS RETURNING	**4**
DEFENSIVE STARTERS RETURNING	**8**

NICKNAME	**Wolverines**
COLORS	**Maize & Blue**
HOME FIELD	**Michigan Stadium (107,501)**
HEAD COACH	**Lloyd Carr (N. Michigan '68)**
RECORD AT SCHOOL	**58-16 (6 years)**
CAREER RECORD	**58-16 (6 years)**
ASSISTANTS	**Teryl Austin (Pittsburgh '88)** **Defensive Secondary** **Erik Campbell (Michigan '88)** **Wide Receivers** **Jim Herrmann (Michigan '82)** **Defensive Coordinator/Linebackers** **Brady Hoke (Ball State '81)** **Defensive Line** **Fred Jackson (Michigan '75)** **Assistant Head Coach/Running Backs** **Terry Malone (Arizona '84)** **Offensive Line** **Andy Moeller (Michigan '87)** **Offensive Tackles/Tight Ends** **Bobby Morrison (Findlay '67)** **Recruiting Coordinator/Special Teams** **Stan Parrish (Heidelberg '68)** **Offensive Coordinator/Quarterbacks**
TEAM WINS (last 5 yrs.)	**8-12-10-10-9**
FINAL RANK (last 5 yrs.)	**16-2-10-6-12**
2000 FINISH	**Beat Auburn in Citrus Bowl.**

COACH AND PROGRAM

Lloyd Carr is so matter-of-fact at times that you would think he was working at a library. Say what you want. He gets results and has been the Big Ten's most successful coach over the last four years. Last season, Carr became the first Wolverine coach to win four straight bowl games by beating Auburn, 31-28, in the Citrus Bowl.

The sixth-year coach has led Michigan to a bowl game every season since he took over for Gary Moeller. The school didn't know what it had when Carr was promoted from assistant head coach before the start of the 1995 season. A guy who hadn't been a head coach since he was in charge of John Glenn High School in 1975 is en route to becoming one of the best coaches in school history. And Michigan has had some good ones: Fielding Yost, Fritz Crisler, and Bo Schembechler, among others.

Carr has claimed the Big Ten championship in three of the last four years (1997, '98, '00). His 58-16 overall record is the seventh-best start ever by a Division I-A coach. But by far, the most impressive Carr statistic is this: he is 11-1 against Top 10 teams.

Last season, Carr's team earned a share of the league title with a 38-26 victory at Ohio State. The Wolverines lost three games by a total of seven points. In the loss at UCLA, Michigan missed a pair of potential game-tying field-goal attempts. At Purdue, the team blew a 28-10 halftime lead and was beaten by a late field goal in a 32-31 setback. Michigan's final loss—54-51 to Northwestern—came on a touchdown pass with 20 seconds left.

Michigan might have had the most talented offensive personnel in the league. It had three starters drafted in the NFL's first round, two in the second. And arguably the most skilled athlete, quarterback Drew Henson, might have been the top overall pick in the 2002 draft if he hadn't decided to play pro baseball instead.

The Henson-Anthony Thomas-David Terrell trio might have been the best quarterback-tailback-wide receiver combination in the league. Henson ranked first in pass efficiency rating, Thomas was third in rushing yards per game, and Terrell was first in receiving yards and touchdown catches. The threesome helped Michigan average 33.7 points a game—second in the Big Ten.

But the offensive talent couldn't make up for a leaky defense. Michigan ranked second in the league in points allowed, but that was misleading. Take away consecutive shutouts against lowly Indiana and Michigan State and that number balloons up to 25.4 points per game.

And including the Indiana and Michigan State games, Michigan still allowed an astonishing 369.2 yards a game. How bad was that? It was the worst performance by a Michigan defense in the history of the school, breaking the mark of 366.8 set in 1982.

In the Purdue loss, the Wolverines surrendered a school-record 530 yards. That mark was later eclipsed when Northwestern mauled its way to 654 yards.

Despite the offensive losses and the defensive struggles, Carr sounded optimistic in the spring about the future. With his track record, who could blame him?

"I think we have made a lot of progress as a team," he said. "I think the strength of the team has increased. We made some strides at developing team speed. I like the attitudes so far. I think the question that is always present is leadership. What type of leaders will this team have?

"One of my goals is to always have developed practices and teaching progressions that will enable every player to improve as much as he can. My thinking has always been that if you come out of spring football and every individual has improved, then you will be a better a football team."

2000 STATISTICS

Rushing offense	220.2	14
Passing offense	225.3	45
Total offense	445.5	12
Scoring offense	33.9	19
Net Punting	36.1	32
Punt returns	10.9	36
Kickoff returns	17.1	100
Rushing defense	152.1	59
Passing efficiency defense	115.7	48
Total defense	381.2	72
Scoring defense	18.3	19
Turnover margin	+11	11

Last column is ranking among Division I-A teams.

QUARTERBACKS

Henson left Michigan to pursue a baseball career with the New York Yankees. Henson, who would have been a leading Heisman Trophy candidate had he remained with the Wolverines, signed a $17 million, six-year contract. He probably would have been in position to make millions in the NFL, but he couldn't resist the lure of the storied Yankees.

Henson was an outstanding pro football prospect with talent and size. Last season, he was limited to nine games because of injury. But when he came back, he came back with a vengeance. Henson completed 61.6 percent of his passes for 2,146 yards and 18 touchdowns to just four interceptions.

Where does this leave the Wolverines?

With **John Navarre** (6-6, 242), probably. Navarre, a sophomore, is the favorite to start the season. That's not exactly new territory for him. He started Michigan's first four games as a redshirt freshman when Henson was out with a broken bone in his foot. In his debut, Navarre was 15-of-19 for 265 yards and a school-record tying four touchdown passes against Bowling Green. He was selected the Big Ten's Offensive Player of the Week for his performance against the Falcons. The following week, Navarre was 10-of-15 for 129 yards and three touchdowns in a win over Rice.

Navarre did come down to earth. In the loss to UCLA, he went 8-of-28 for 111 yards. For the season, he finished 40- of-77 for 583 yards and eight touchdowns. He was intercepted only one time. Navarre (147.2) played so well that he ranked second only to Henson (152.7) in pass efficiency.

At 6-6, Navarre is an inch taller than Henson. Whether he can be as good remains to be seen. He won't have the benefit of a veteran offensive line, a star tailback to hand off to, and a star wide receiver to throw to.

Navarre did not take a direct path to Michigan. The native of Cudahy, Wisc. said he felt some "arm-twisting" from locals to stay closer to home. He didn't want to go to Wisconsin, so he gave a commitment to Northwestern. That stuck only as long as coach Gary Barnett, who left Northwestern for Colorado. With Barnett leaving, Navarre rethought his commitment and decided to go to Michigan.

Navarre has drawn comparisons to former Michigan quarterback Elvis Grbac, now with the Kansas City Chiefs, although Navarre is bigger.

"He's got a great arm," Carr said. "There aren't any throws he can't make. He's tough. He's got a great release, and he can get the ball out there. The most important thing is John Navarre has confidence. I don't have any question he'll do a good job."

Another interesting quarterback candidate is **Spencer Brinton**, who in late April completed a two-year Mormon mission in Durban, a city on the East Coast of South Africa. Brinton, a transfer from San Diego State, could be in the middle of the Wolverines' quarterback situation.

The 6-foot-5, 220-pounder was ranked the No. 3 high school quarterback in the Pac-10 region coming out of Temecula Valley High (Hemet, Calif.). He was among four quarterbacks recruited by Ohio State. But Brinton hasn't played since 1998.

Carr had never met Brinton and the player hadn't visited the Michigan campus when his recruitment began. But Carr found out all he needed to know by watching game film.

"As we watched the film of Spencer's freshman year at San Diego State, I thought for a true freshman he was very, very impressive," Carr said.

Brinton came on in relief of injured San Diego State starter Kevin McKechnie in the sixth game of the 1997 season and started the last five games, leading the Aztecs to a 4-2 record. The left-hander completed 72-of-162 passes for 1,097 yards and six touchdowns as a freshman. He was intercepted 10 times.

The next season, Brinton suffered sprained ligaments in his left hand during the second game and sat out the rest of the year. During his time away from the game, he decided to take his mission. Brinton didn't leave football behind when he went to South Africa. He managed to take a football with him.

"I'm not going to be totally out of sync," he told the *Detroit News*. "But timing-wise, I'm obviously going to be out of shape."

Brinton, who enrolled in summer classes in May, will make up for lost time.

"I'm going to come in and do the best job I can," Brinton told the *News*. "And we'll see what happens from there. Obviously, John Navarre is the No. 1 guy now. [But] I'm not going to take a back seat and just relax."

Brinton, who turned 23 in late July, is a junior but has sophomore eligibility.

Sophomore **Jermaine Gonzales** (6-2, 201) is penciled in as Navarre's backup, and sophomore **Andy Mignery** (6-3, 230) is third-string.

RUNNING BACKS

The A-Train is gone. Thomas, the school's all-time rushing leader, is now playing for a paycheck in the NFL. It will be tough to replace Thomas' production. He rushed a school-record 319 times to gain 1,773 yards and 18 touchdowns. The rushing yardage was the third-highest single-season mark in school history and the touchdowns were the second-best mark.

Sophomore **Chris Perry** (6-1, 228) is the heir apparent. Perry is faster than Thomas. Will he be as good? Possibly. Perry was Michigan's second-leading rusher last season as a freshman. He had 77 carries for 417 yards and five touchdowns. His 5.4 yards per carry average was equal to Thomas, so there's reason to believe he will be up to the task.

Perry even has a 100-yard game to his credit. In his debut, he rushed for 103 yards on 10 carries, including a 42-yard scoring run against Bowling Green. He joined senior teammate **Walter Cross** as only two players in school history to rush for 100 yards in their debuts.

Cross (5-11, 209) has an edge on experience. The three-year letterman has played in 32 career games. But he has been relegated to back-up duty behind Thomas. For his career, Cross has rushed 92 times for 363 yards and two touchdowns. He is best known for being the first Michigan back to rush for 100 yards (10 carries, 104 yards against Syracuse in 1998) as a freshman. Last season was his best as he gained 151 yards on 27 attempts.

Cross is mainly used on special teams for kick-off returns, and it seems unlikely that he will beat out Perry.

Sophomore **Ryan Beard** (5-9, 209) appeared in eight games, rushing for 81 yards on 16 carries with no touchdowns.

One player to watch could be freshman **Kelly Baraka** (6-0, 180). He was a *USA Today* and *Parade* All-American after rushing for 1,624 yards and 26 touchdowns at Portage (Mich.) Northern High School despite missing two games.

Junior fullback **B.J. Askew** (6-3, 224) is one of four returning starters on offense. He has played in all 24 possible games and started six games last year. He rushed 34 times for 110 yards and caught 21 passes for 261 during his career. Last season, he was particularly effective as a receiver with career highs of 18 receptions for 257 yards and three scores. Askew might not get more than the 11 carries for 40 yards that he did last year, but he might see increased duty as a pass-catcher.

WIDE RECEIVERS/TIGHT ENDS

Terrell, a first round NFL draft pick of the Chicago Bears, is another player Michigan is going to miss a lot. He might have been the been the most talented wide receiver to ever play for the Wolverines. Considering this program produced guys like Anthony Carter, Derrick Alexander, and Desmond Howard, that's saying a lot. Terrell's final season was brilliant. The junior led the Big Ten in receiving yards (1,130) and touchdown catches (14).

You don't replace a David Terrell. But senior **Marquise Walker** (6-3, 212) will try his best to be the go-to receiver. Walker, playing in Terrell's shadow a year ago, had 49 catches for 699 yards and four touchdowns. He has quietly moved his way up the school record books. Walker needs 10 receptions to become only the 11th player in school history with 100. He is already 14th on the all-time list. His 1,126 receiving yards is 267 shy of 15th place.

Walker started out in a big way last season. After never having more than 75 yards receiving, he had three 100-yard games. His best effort came against Northwestern as he had nine receptions for 134 yards. He also starred in the Citrus Bowl with four catches for 100 yards.

Ron Bellamy (6-0, 193) will be in position to do more. The junior probably will start opposite of Walker. He appeared in all 12 games, even starting six, but had just seven catches for 106 yards and two touchdowns. Bellamy, who has very good speed, was used primarily as a punt returner. Bellamy has talent to become a top-notch receiver. He was rated as the fourth-best wide receiver in the nation by *SuperPrep*.

Sophomores **Calvin Bell** (6-1, 190) and **Tyrece Butler** (6-3, 204), who missed 2000 with a knee injury, will round out the receiver corps. Bell was one of six freshmen to play last season, seeing action in all 12 games. He finished with six catches for 101 yards. Butler had season-ending knee surgery during fall camp and was redshirted. He earned a varsity letter in 1999 after playing in six games as a freshman. He has yet to catch a pass.

At tight end, **Bill Seymour** (6-3, 252) is a returning starter. The fifth-year senior set career best marks with eight catches for 95 yards and two touchdowns. He caught his first career touchdown pass against Indiana on an 11-yard reception from Henson.

Senior **Shawn Thompson** (6-4, 254) started the season-opener against Bowling Green but was lost for the season with a knee injury. In 1999, Thompson had 14 receptions for 162 yards and two touchdowns. If the fifth-year senior is completely healthy, it will be tough to keep him out of the lineup.

OFFENSIVE LINE

Michigan has a major rebuilding project on its hands. Four starters are gone; Steve Hutchinson (guard), Jeff Backus (tackle), David Brandt (center) and Maurice Williams (tackle). This cripples what was one of the best offensive lines, if not the best, in the Big Ten. Two starters were first-round draft choices—Hutchinson by Seattle and Backus by Detroit—and a third was a second-round selection (Williams was chosen by Jacksonville).

"You don't replace those guys overnight because they took so much experience with them," Carr said. "That will probably be the major position area that we need to address."

The sole returning starter is senior **Jonathan Goodwin** (6-4, 294). Goodwin missed spring practice with a minor shoulder injury but is expected to play either guard or center. However, he started at right guard during the final nine games of the season and could wind up back there. Goodwin is versatile, having played four different offensive line positions at some point during the 2000 season.

Sophomores **Tony Pape** (6-6, 299) and **Demetrius Solomon** (6-6, 280) are projected to start at the tackles. Pape played primarily on special teams as a redshirt freshman. He made his debut at right tackle against Rice. Solomon played in three games as a redshirt freshman. He made his debut at left tackle against Rice.

"Tony Pape is a tackle in the same mold as Backus—very talented, big, strong, tough and smart," Carr said. "I expect him to be a very good football player. Demetrius Solomon took every snap this spring, as did Tony as a backup tackle."

If **Ben Mast** (6-4, 298) is ready, he will be the starting center. The fifth-year senior can play any position on the line. He started at right guard against Bowling Green. He played in five games, starting three. If he isn't ready to play center, he will switch to guard and Goodwin will play center.

"We will start out with Ben Mast, to see if he is a guy who can play center," Carr said. "He played some last fall. He will get a good look."

Joe Denay (6-7, 298) will be the other guard. The junior has five career games of experience.

Michigan's offensive line was a big reason the Wolverines were one of only three teams to average more than 200 rushing yards and 200 passing yards per game last season. It also allowed only 18 sacks. Can this line be remotely as good as its predecessor?

"Goodwin had an outstanding season last year," Carr said. "Ben Mast has been around. I think you build around guys who have experience and have been around the program for a while. I think we have some very talented young guys, some guys that have been around that have not had opportunities to play."

2001 SCHEDULE

Sept.	1	Miami (Ohio)
	8	@Washington
	15	Western Michigan
	22	Illinois
Oct.	6	@Penn State
	13	Purdue
	27	@Iowa
Nov.	3	@Michigan State
	10	Minnesota
	17	@Wisconsin
	24	Ohio State

KICKERS

Hayden Epstein (6-2, 205) pulls double duty as a place-kicker as well as a punter. The senior should be a Lou Groza candidate as a kicker. He finished third on the team in scoring with a career-best 50 points. Epstein converted 8-of-14 field goals and 26-of-28 PATs.

For his career, he has made 13-of-22 field goals, including a career-long 56-yarder into the wind against Michigan State in 1999.

"I looked for Hayden Epstein next fall to be a great kicker," Carr said. "I think he did a tremendous job last fall down the stretch. I think he proved his toughness from the standpoint that he struggled early and he continued to work and compete. He didn't let his lack of success early wreck him mentally. That is a sign of a mentally tough guy, so I have tremendous confidence in him."

DEFENSIVE LINE

This was not a great unit. Injuries were partly to blame. Defensive lineman **Jake Frysinger** missed the rest of last season after hurting his foot in the first game. Nose tackle Eric Wilson sat out four games with injuries. Wilson has graduated but Frysinger (6-4, 277), a senior, is back. Frysinger is a four-year letterman who has played in 34 games with two starts (2000 Orange Bowl and 2000 season-opener against Bowling Green).

Frysinger has 44 career tackles and four sacks. His best season came in 1998 when he had 30 tackles and three sacks. The coaching staff was counting on big things from him last year until he hurt his right foot against Bowling Green.

"In the long run, having a fifth year is going to be an advantage to him and the team," Carr said. "If you remember, he came here as a standout linebacker and a good basketball player in high school. He is athletic and strong, and he is really excited about the opportunity to come back. In the beginning, I think that is something he didn't want to do, but now I think he looks at it as a real blessing."

Dan Rumishek (6-3, 277) slid over from tackle to end to fill in for Frysinger last year. Rumishek came on as the season progressed. He was the winner of the Dick Katcher Award as Michigan's top defensive lineman. The junior started 10 games last year. He finished with 24 tackles and also had a sack, an interception and a fumble recovery. His first career interception came in the regular-season finale against Ohio State.

"Danny Rumishek a year ago proved to be a very good football player," Carr said. "He's tough and durable."

Grant Bowman (6-1, 281) and **Shawn Lazarus** (6-3, 278) could wind up being the tackles. Bowman, a nose tackle, started five games as a redshirt freshman. He had 10 tackles, four for a loss, and broke up a pass. Lazarus was a starter for the final five games of the season. As a sophomore, he had four tackles a sack and recovered two fumbles.

Sophomore **Alain Kashama** (6-4, 236) will also push for playing time along the defensive line. He played as a freshman, amassing 14 tackles and a sack.

"I look for our defensive line to be a tremendously improved part of our football team," Carr said. "I think we've got the makings [of a good line], in terms of not only individual improvement. But I think our depth is going to be much better."

LINEBACKERS

The Wolverines could boast the best linebackers in the Big Ten. You would be hard-pressed to find a better threesome than senior **Eric Brackins** (6-2, 235), senior **Larry Foote** (6-1, 228) and junior **Victor Hobson** (6-1, 242). They do as good a job as any linebacking crew when it comes to plugging up the middle. They combined for 31 tackles for losses last season.

Brackins is an All-America type of inside linebacker. The fifth-year senior needs just five tackles to reach 100 for his career. He started in six games last season and finished fifth on the team with 57 tackles. He also added nine for losses and had a pair of sacks. Brackins set a career high with 14 tackles against Auburn in the Citrus Bowl.

"Brackins is 235 pounds and runs about the same as when he got here," Carr said. "He's one of those guys that this program has helped to develop. He is one of those guys in the same line as Dhani Jones and Ian Gold. He's not particularly big, but he's a guy that can run and he's tough."

Foote is another All-America candidate. The inside linebacker is the only returning All-Big Ten performer on the squad. The senior is the team's active leader in tackles (130), tackles for a loss (18 for 60 yards), sacks (five for 39 yards) and starts (16). He has played in 36 of a possible 37 games in his career.

Foote, who was second on the team with 84 tackles last year, averaged 10.6 stops in his last five games. He also had a sack, a fumble recovery and intercepted two passes. He tied his career-high with 14 tackles against Northwestern. As good as he was, Carr expects better.

"He has increased his speed, so this defense is going to be improved," Carr said.

Hobson is the team's top returning sack and tackles-for-loss leader. The junior had four sacks and 12 tackles for a loss. For his career, he has four sacks and 17 tackles for a loss. Hobson was the Roger Zatkoff Award winner as Michigan's top linebacker. He set a career best with 58 tackles. He was an honorable mention All-Big Ten player.

Backup linebacker **Carl Diggs** (6-1, 245) will be tough to keep out of the lineup. The redshirt freshman played in every game and had a pair of starts. Diggs had 30 tackles. One of those came against Ohio State.

"He did an excellent job," Carr said.

DEFENSIVE BACKS

This unit was a major problem. Michigan gave up 2,914 passing yards—the highest mark since it surrendered 3,052 in 1982. The Wolverines had the third-worst pass defense in the Big Ten in terms of yards given up. Opponents gorged themselves for 242.8 yards a game. The opponents' 58.5 percent completion percentage was also the third worst in the conference.

The healthy return of junior free safety **June Cato** (6-1, 213) should help. Cato missed the 2000 season after off-season knee surgery. In 1999, he played all 12 games and finished with 27 tackles and a sack.

"Cato will be able to do some things," Carr said. "He is running extremely well. He made an excellent recovery and is working hard. His strength is very good and he is probably a few pounds too heavy right now. The mentality of most players is to get as big as they can. There is always a point where you don't want to sacrifice speed and quickness for size. He needs to lose a few pounds, but the one thing June brings is enthusiasm, intensity and love for playing. He is one of those guys that unifies the defense. It will be good to have him back."

Julius Curry (6-0, 191) returns at strong safety. The junior is probably the best of the defensive backs. The two-year letterman has played in 21 games, starting 12. He started all but one game last season. Curry finished third on the team with a career-best 59 tackles. He made 50 of those during Big Ten play. Curry tied for second in the league with three forced fumbles. His lone interception came against Auburn in the Citrus Bowl.

Veteran senior cornerback **Todd Howard** (5-10, 183) led the team with six interceptions. He need just three passes broken up to surpass 1997 Heisman Trophy winner Charles Woodson's record of 30 in a career. Howard has recorded back-to-back double-digit pass breakup seasons (14 in 1999 and 13 in 2000). He has played in 26 of a possible 37 career games.

Sophomore **Jeremy LeSuer** (6-0, 191) and freshman **Markus Curry** (6-0, 180) will battle for the other corner spot. LeSuer, who missed most of the 1999 season with a knee injury, played in every game, starting two. He had 32 tackles and a sack. Curry is the brother of Julius.

"He is just like his brother from the standpoint that he is not intimidated," Carr said. "I would look for him to be a factor."

PUNTERS

Espstein punted 55 times for a 40.4 average last season. He had a career-best 19 punts downed inside the opponent's 20-yard line. For his career, Epstein has 96 kicks for an average of 40.3 yards. He enters the season as a Ray Guy Award candidate. Epstein was particularly effective in the Citrus Bowl when he punted four times for 43.5 yards.

SPECIAL TEAMS

Michigan needs to upgrade its kickoff return team. The Wolverines ranked last in the league in that category, averaging only 17.1 yards a return. They failed to score a touchdown on a return. Cross handled that duty last season. He had 14 returns for an 18.6-yard average. Cross ranks eighth in career return kickoff return average (22.1), is tied for 10th in career returns (26) and

12th in career yards (575).

The Wolverines were better at punt returns. The team was fourth in the Big Ten, averaging 10.4 yards a return with one score.

Bellamy will return punts. Last season he had 27 returns for 297 yards. Walker had one punt return for a 41-yard touchdown.

Epsein has 86 kickoffs for touchbacks in his career.

RECRUITING CLASS

Michigan bounced back from an average class last year to field possibly one of the best in the nation. Analyst Tom Lemming ranked the Wolverines second in the nation. The prize might be tailback **David Underwood** (6-0, 220) from Madisonville (Texas) High School. He has good size and excellent speed. Underwood rushed for 1,548 yards and 34 touchdowns as a senior. He gained 1,231 rushing yards and 11 scores as a junior. He also ran the 100-meter dash for the school track team.

Another quality tailback is Baraka. He gained 1,624 rushing yards and scored 26 touchdowns despite missing two games. Baraka also added seven receptions for 115 yards. He set a school record with 309 rushing yards and once scored six touchdowns in a game on just 13 carries. He was also the state champion in the 100- and 200-meter dashes.

The Wolverines also bulked on defensive backs with Markus Curry, **Braylon Edwards** (6-3, 192), **Malin Jackson** (6-1 180), **Ernest Shazor** (6-4, 210) and **Jacob Stewart** (5-11, 198). Curry, brother of Michigan safety Julius Curry, could break into the starting lineup.

Edwards, from Bishop Gallagher High in Detroit, Mich., is intriguing. He played only one year but had 73 tackles, seven sacks and five interceptions. Jackson was a *USA Today* All-American. He had 84 tackles, five interceptions and broke up 11 passes as a senior. He also has 4.4 speed.

Shazor, from King High School in Detroit, Mich., could be the best of the bunch. The *Parade* All-American had 97 tackles, eight interceptions and blocked two punts as a senior. He played free safety and cornerback.

Linebacker **Joey Sarantos** (6-3, 215) bears watching. He is going to walk on at Michigan after turning down scholarship offers from other schools. He had 100 tackles, including 15 for a loss, and five sacks as a senior at Portage Northern High in Portage, Mich.

Jackson played at Sharon (Pa.) High and Stewart played at Ypsilanti (Mich.) High School.

BLUE RIBBON ANALYSIS

OFFENSE	B-
SPECIAL TEAMS	B
DEFENSE	B-
INTANGIBLES	A-

If Henson had stuck with football, Michigan would have been considered a national championship contender. Without him, the Wolverines are going to scramble to have an offense as good as the one it had last season. The Big Ten title is not out of reach, but it will be hard to put up enough points, especially with a suspect defense.

Navarre's statistics were good, but most of his numbers came against weaker competition. He is going to have to prove he can be a consistent quarterback. Navarre struggled in particular on the road. He completed just 1-of-10 passes and threw his only interception of the season in the second half of a 23-20 loss at UCLA. He struggled in the first half at Illinois before being replaced by Henson.

Navarre is drop-back quarterback with good vision and arm strength. While he's not particularly mobile, he can make plays. But he'll be a sitting duck if the revamped offensive line cannot protect him. The coaching staff isn't expecting him to be Henson, but to at least be productive.

The biggest key of the season will be the defense. Before last season, Carr said he was worried about his defense and he turned out to be right. Conversely, he is now expressing optimism. With its star linebacker and a better effort from the defensive front, the Wolverines could make a quantum leap.

"I think we're going to have an extremely good defense," Carr said. "I think up front we're much bigger, much more experienced, much stronger. Our linebackers are good and our secondary is much improved. We have a much more physical defense."

Michigan has never won fewer than five league games under Carr and is 27-5 in Big Ten play since 1997. Expect more of the same success.

(M.G.)

2000 RESULTS

Bowling Green	W	42-7	1-0
Rice	W	38-7	2-0
UCLA	L	20-23	2-1
Illinois	W	35-31	3-1
Wisconsin	W	13-10	4-1
Purdue	L	31-32	4-2
Indiana	W	58-0	5-2
Michigan State	W	14-0	6-2
Northwestern	L	51-54	6-3
Penn State	W	33-11	7-3
Ohio State	W	38-26	8-3
Auburn	W	31-28	9-3

Michigan State

LOCATION	**East Lansing, MI**
CONFERENCE	**Big Ten**
LAST SEASON	**5-6 (.455)**
CONFERENCE RECORD	**2-6 (t-9th)**
OFFENSIVE STARTERS RETURNING	**6**
DEFENSIVE STARTERS RETURNING	**6**
NICKNAME	**Spartans**
COLORS	**Green & White**
HOME FIELD	**Spartan Stadium (72,027)**
HEAD COACH	**Bobby Williams (Purdue '82)**
RECORD AT SCHOOL	**6-6 (1 year)**
CAREER RECORD	**6-6 (1 year)**
ASSISTANTS	**Bill Miller (Texas-Arlington '78)** **Defensive Coordinator** **Morris Watts (Tulsa '61)** **Offensive Coordinator/Quarterbacks** **Brad Lawing (Lenoir-Rhyne '79)** **Defensive Line/Recruiting Coordinator** **Reggie Mitchell (Central Michigan '81)** **Running Backs** **Pat Perles (Michigan State '87)** **Tight Ends** **Jeff Stoutland (Southern Conn. State '84)** **Offensive Line** **Don Treadwell (Miami-Ohio '82)** **Wide Receivers** **Sal Sunseri (Pittsburgh '82)** **Linebackers/Special Teams** **Troy Douglas (Appalachian State '88)** **Defensive Backs**
TEAM WINS (last 5 yrs.)	**6-7-6-10-5**
FINAL RANK (last 5 yrs.)	**38-27-38-5-55**
2000 FINISH	**Lost to Penn State in regular-season finale.**

COACH AND PROGRAM

In his year and change as the head coach at Michigan State, Bobby Williams' life has pretty much followed the script of most episodes of VH-1's *Behind the Music*.

If you have cable TV, you know the drill: 1.) Man is on top of the world (Williams after getting the Michigan State job). 2.) His star rises even higher (Williams wins his first-ever college game over Steve Spurrier and the Florida Gators in the Citrus Bowl and the Spartans end up No. 5 in the final polls. Williams then lands lots of top-shelf recruits. 3.) Williams is a still a big hit the following September as the Spartans won the first three games, including a win over Notre Dame.

But as anyone who watches VH-1 can tell you, step 4 is a killer. That's when everything comes crashing down. Suddenly, in fact. And that's what happened to Williams in the last two months of the 2000 football season.

Michigan State suffered from inconsistent quarterback play as freshman **Jeff Smoker** was forced to play sooner than expected when projected starter **Ryan Van Dyke** got hurt. The Spartans also couldn't generate a consistent pass rush (a Big Ten-low 17 sacks) and didn't have big-play wideouts. The final result was a 5-6 season, quite a comedown from the 10-2 mark in 1999.

But like the bands profiled on *Behind the Music*, Williams is hoping for a revival rather than being deemed a one-hit wonder. In 2001, the Spartans will use a version of the spread offense, often employing a three-wide receiver set, all of which should take the heat off his battering ram of a tailback, junior All-America candidate **T.J. Duckett**.

If the spread offense—today's cure-all which has worked wonders at such schools as Oklahoma, Northwestern, Purdue, Clemson and others—clicks in East Lansing and MSU can improve its pass rush and special teams play, Williams and Co. could get themselves a bowl berth at season's end. Probably not a BCS bowl berth, but a trip to a bowl nonetheless.

"When you look at last year's personnel, we were limited from an offensive standpoint," Williams said. "I don't think we had the big-play threat that we had in our passing game in 1999. It seems like we have a chance to have that deep threat this year with our receiving corps. Defensively, we didn't have the pass rush and sack production that we had in 1999. It seems that is an area where we will be a little better.

"And on special teams, we really wanted to improve because I felt we had outstanding special teams in 1999. We were winning games with our special teams and putting ourselves in position to win games. That's something where I think we will make real improvement. Those are three areas where I think we will be a much-improved team."

2001 SCHEDULE

Sept.	8	Central Michigan
	15	Missouri
	22	@Notre Dame
	29	@Northwestern
Oct.	13	Iowa
	20	@Minnesota
	27	@Wisconsin
Nov.	3	Michigan
	10	Indiana
	17	@Purdue
	24	Penn State

QUARTERBACKS

The duel for the starting quarterback job between sophomore Smoker (6-3, 203) and senior Van Dyke (6-5, 220) will continue in August. The race was too close to call during spring ball.

"Today's not game day," Williams said of a possible quarterback controversy. "On Sept. 8 [opening day against Central Michigan], that's when it becomes an issue. I'm very confident this quarterback situation will be straightened out before we play."

Before the 2000 season, Van Dyke was anxious to take over the team. But he injured his right thumb in the first quarter of the season opener against Marshall last season. The former Marshall High School star started five games in MSU's disappointing 5-6 season, 2-6 in the Big Ten, and his thumb never fully healed. Even now, Van Dyke said his throwing hand isn't completely healthy because of calluses built up on his bone.

Still, he was sharp this spring and gained ground on Smoker, who played admirably last season for a guy who was supposed to redshirt. Smoker learned the offense on the fly and led the Spartans to a 3-0 start (with wins over Marshall, Missouri and Notre Dame). Smoker appeared in 9-of-11 games, completing 103-of-197 passes (52.3 percent) for 1,365 yards, six touchdowns and seven interceptions. Van Dyke completed 70- of-122 throws (57.4 percent) for 796 yards, four touchdowns and nine interceptions.

"Jeff did not fall off," Williams said. "I think Ryan raised his game. The fact we said we're going to open this race up really brought out the best in everybody. Ryan went into [last] season as the starting quarterback and really was sharp. But when he injured his hand, he never really got back [to the same level]. Now he's where he was going into the season [and] a lot more mature.

"If we get down to game week and it's still there [no clear starter], we're going to have to play both of them and then see how they play in a game situation. If today was Sept. 8, Jeff would start the game, but then at some point in time, Ryan would come in."

The No. 3 man on the depth chart is redshirt freshman **Damon Dowdell** (6-1, 211). Dowdell pleaded no contest to misdemeanor assault and battery last August for his alleged involvement in sexual assault incident with a 13-year-old girl (along with former high school teammate Eric Knott, a prep All-America tight end who hopes to attend MSU, too). Dowdell joined the Spartans last September, although he was redshirted last season.

RUNNING BACKS

The Spartans are just fine in this department with the return of junior Duckett (6-2, 252), a legitimate Heisman Trophy candidate if the new offensive line comes together. Duckett is a bigger, faster version of Ron Dayne and running out of a one-back, spread attack, he will cause headaches for opposing defensive coordinators and would-be tacklers alike.

Duckett is a load. As a freshman, "Diesel" Duckett rushed 118 times for 606 yards (5.1 yards per carry) and 10 touchdowns for the 10-2 Spartans. As it turned out, that was a glimpse of what he could do. Despite running behind a beat-up offensive line with an unproven quarterback and no game-breaking wideouts, Duckett tallied 1,353 yards on the ground and seven rushing touchdowns on a whopping 240 carries.

"He's a great tailback," Ohio State linebacker Joe Cooper said. "He's one of those backs that you can't allow to come to you; you can't sit and wait on him. If you do, he'll run you over and keep on heading down the field."

With better wide receivers and an offense designed to spread the field and give him more running lanes a la Northwestern's Damien Anderson, Duckett should gain between 1,500 and 2,000 yards rushing, if he stays healthy. He was slowed by groin and shoulder injuries late in the 2000 season and missed the end of spring ball after undergoing minor shoulder surgery, but he'll be fine by August. Plus, he won't have to face as many eight- and nine-man fronts, if MSU's passing game improves as expected.

"T.J. should reap the benefits of a much better offense," Williams said. "He had a very good season last year, but he's still improving."

That is a scary thought, because Duckett is already 12th on Michigan State's all-time rushing charts with 1,959 career yards. He could rise as high as No. 3 or No. 4 all-time with a productive junior season, surpassing current No. 3 man Blake Ezor (3,749 yards from 1986-89) and No. 4 Sedrick Irvin (3,504 yards from 1996-98).

While Duckett will once again be a workhorse, Williams has other options in senior **Little John Flowers** (6-0, 227) and sophomore **Tyrell Dortch** (5-10, 194). Flowers, like Duckett, is from Kalamazoo. He too is a tough between-the-tackles runner. Last season, Flowers carried the ball 54 times for 281 yards and two scores.

Flowers and Dortch (36 carries, 210 yards) both average more than five yards per pop after opposing defenses tire from trying to tackle Duckett (which is like trying to tackle a Coke machine over and over again). Dortch, in particular, figures to get a lot more work in 2001, because his 4.4 speed will allow him to break off long runs in MSU's spread offense.

Opening holes once again is junior **Dawan Moss** (5-10, 260), a tough-as-nails run blocker who could probably clothes shop with Duckett. He doesn't get many carries (31 for 81 yards and three touchdowns in 2000), but he's one of the best blocking backs in the nation.

If Moss needs a breather, then sophomore **Bradshaw Littlejohn** (6-1, 248) enters the fray. He's cut from the same cloth as Moss in that he'll rarely get to tote the ball himself. But Littlejohn, a converted linebacker, figures to take great pleasure in knocking an opposing linebacker on his backside.

WIDE RECEIVERS/TIGHT ENDS

This position was an area of weakness in 2000 after the departures of superb split end Plaxico Burress and steady flanker Gari Scott to the play-for-pay ranks. But Williams believes his 2001 collection of wide receivers—sophomore **Charles Rogers** (6-4, 207), junior college transfer **B.J. Lovett** (6-4, 200), returning sophomore **Marcus Waters** (6-4, 233) and returning senior **Herb Haygood** (6-0, 191)—will give his team a more balanced attack.

"I think probably the biggest difference in our offense this year is we've got some wideouts who can make some plays down the field," Williams said. "We should have the ability to make some plays with the receivers we have."

Rogers was one of the nation's top recruits coming out of high school in 2000, but he had to sit out last year because he was academically ineligible. Rogers is often compared to former MSU star Plaxico Burress, thanks to his size and sub-4.4 speed.

Lovett is another prize newcomer. He caught 29 balls at SUNY-Morrisville last year. Combine those two with senior co-captain Haygood, who caught a MSU-best 35 passes for 539 yards and two scores last fall, and one of the nation's most gifted tight ends in senior **Chris Baker** (6-3, 260) and no wonder folks in East Lansing are excited.

Haygood has 58 career catches for 832 yards (a 14.3-yards-per-catch average) and three scores. Haygood already ranks among MSU's all-time leaders (fourth) in kickoff returns with 1,138 career yards (21.9 average). Baker hauled in 33 passes for 461 yards (14.0 average) and two touchdowns last season. He flirted with the idea of turning pro before deciding to come back to school.

"Chris Baker has always been a productive tight end for us and he's an important player in our offense, so I'm glad we got him back for another year,' said Williams. "Chris has had a very good spring and this is a big year for him in terms of improving his stock as a pro prospect. He's an important part of our offensive playbook."

"This year, we've got more depth at wide receivers where we can have that deep ball threat," Rogers said. "You've got guys like Marcus Waters, myself and B.J. Lovett [where] I feel we can concentrate and contribute."

Rogers said with Duckett, Baker, and two solid quarterbacks, the Spartans' offense this year could draw comparisons to a particular powerhouse offense in the NFL.

"I feel we can have that St. Louis [Rams] type offense where we have three wide receiver sets," Rogers said.

Actually, Williams would settle for a reasonable facsimile of Northwestern's 2000 offense. He's implementing the spread attack. He has the tall, speedy wideouts needed to run the spread, as well as the lethal runner in Duckett and speedy tight end in Baker.

OFFENSIVE LINE

After losing as many seniors as one would find at a church bingo night, this a major area of concern on the offensive side of the ball for MSU, along with the quarterback spot. The Spartans lose four starters to graduation (tackles Siitupe Peko and Matt Bonito and guards Shaun Mason and Dave Sucura) from last year's injury-plagued unit that surrendered a whopping 43 sacks.

Peko, a 6-4, 300-pound tackle, battled a sprained right knee in 2000, but still showed enough that he was sixth round draft pick (217th overall) of the New York Jets.

The 6-5, 302-pound Mason was expected to be an NFL draft pick last spring, but a cancerous tumor was found in his right shoulder last January. Doctors had thought the growth in Mason's shoulder was a cyst until they operated Jan. 30. The cancer, plasmacytoma, is extremely rare in someone his age. It had not spread, but there are no guarantees about whether it will return. So, Mason's football career is likely over.

This nearly all-new unit will be athletic, but young. Hence the concern. The Spartans were 10th in the Big Ten in scoring (17.9 points per game) and that was with a veteran offensive line.

The new offensive line figures to be led by sophomore center **Brian Ottney** (6-6, 306), who looks like a star in the making. Thrown into the starting center position after two games last season while still recovering from a torn ligament in his left leg, Ottney said contributing on the field in 2000 was a challenge because of his limited athleticism.

"I was playing with one leg, but have really worked hard to get back to 100 percent now," said Ottney, who missed all of last year's preseason camp and much of September. "I'm doing things now that I couldn't have dreamed of doing last fall. Our whole offensive line now has a year's worth of experience and it should prove to be valuable this year."

Now healthy for the first time in his college career, Ottney is expected to be a team leader in what will be an extremely young offensive line.

Duckett, for one, has noticed an increased amount of focus in Ottney on the field.

"Brian is a lot more confident now, he's making more plays and has really found a way to make big plays," Duckett said. "The whole line looks a lot more confident. If you look at the offensive unit now, it looks like we have been together for a couple of years, things are that much better as far as communication and execution."

Joining in Michigan State's re-tooled forward wall will be redshirt freshman right guard **William Whitticker** (6-6, 303) and junior **Paul Harker** (6-3, 298), a part-time starter in 2000, at the left guard spot. Sophomore **Steve Stewart** (6-5, 310) and junior **Ulish Booker** (6-7, 291) are penciled in as the starting tackles.

If injuries occur, the backups who will get the first call include sophomore left tackle **Joe Tate** (6-5, 275), sophomore left guard **Joe Patrick** (6-5, 304), sophomore center **DeMarco Monroe** (6-4, 300), sophomore **Joe Brooks** (6-3, 285) and redshirt freshman right tackle **Sean Poole** (6-6, 290).

Aside from problem No. 1 (the Spartans have no senior starters up front), this group must learn a new offensive system. Plus, there are questions about depth. Things were so bad in the spring that MSU often didn't have enough linemen for practice.

That is why Williams will need some of his new recruits to ready. None of them will start, but a couple should appear on the depth chart, most probably the ballyhooed German import Heyer and giant lineman **Alphonso "Biggie" Townsend** (6-6, 310), who will get looks on both sides of the ball in August.

Townsend, a year removed from the 2000 *SuperPrep* All-America team, signed with Ohio State out of Lima (Ohio) High School, spent a year at Fork Union (Va.) Military Academy (the same prep school that produced former MSU star wideout Plaxico Burress), and is now one of the Spartans' top newcomers.

"I think depth is real critical because when you look at our depth, we only have a few guys with game experience and most of those guys are on the first team," Williams said. "When you look at the second unit, those guys don't have much game experience. From a talent standpoint, I think we will have 10 solid offensive linemen and then we have to look at the guys that are coming in this fall.

"Hopefully, a few of them will fit in and make the travel squad to give us some more depth there. We don't have a whole lot of experience up front so that will be a concern to get some guys experience early."

2000 STATISTICS

Rushing offense	170.4	31
Passing offense	196.5	72
Total offense	366.8	61
Scoring offense	17.9	97
Net Punting	37.3	22
Punt returns	7.7	90
Kickoff returns	21.5	26
Rushing defense	154.2	61
Passing efficiency defense	104.5	26
Total defense	318.3	23
Scoring defense	21.2	41
Turnover margin	-8	90

Last column is ranking among Division I-A teams.

KICKERS

Former All-Big Ten kicker Paul Edinger proved quite tough for the Spartans to replace last fall. A sixth-round draft pick of the Chicago Bears in the spring of 2000, Edinger made all 21 of extra points and 21-of-27 field goals last year for the Bears (77.8 percent), including makes on both of his attempts from 50-plus yards.

Edinger's replacement, senior **David Schaefer** (5-10, 197), wasn't nearly as reliable. Schaefer was 11-of- 17 on field-goal attempts and missed three of his 21 extra-point tries. In a 21-16 upset loss at Iowa, Schaefer had an extra point and a field goal blocked. He seems much more comfortable kicking on artificial turf than on natural grass.

Schaefer looked better in the spring, but Williams remains unsure about him. As a result, come August MSU will have a kick line long enough to rival the ones in *The Producers*.

Senior **Michael Servis** (6-1, 198) is also back. Servis was recruited out of St. Petersburg (Fla.) Junior College to replace Edinger, but he was unable to beat out Schaefer last fall. Servis had a very good spring and will battle Scahefer, along with a pair of incoming freshmen—**David Raymer** (6-3, 200) and **J.J. Danhof**.

Raymer was a star kicker and soccer player at Oxford (Mich.) High School, while Danhof was a two-time Class B all-state kicker at Haslett (Mich.) High School. A walk-on, Danhof connected on 21-of-30 career field goals and his average kick-off last year landed at the opponents' three-yard line.

DEFENSIVE LINE

This fall, getting pressure on opposing quarterbacks is one of the top things on Williams' to-do list. The reason? The Spartans were last in the Big Ten with 17 sacks a year ago. The Spartans should improve significantly on that number, led by seniors **Josh Shaw** (6-3, 280) and **Nick Myers** (6-2, 263).

Shaw, a Fort Lauderdale native, first made headlines in East Lansing back in 1998 for his involvement with three other athletes (the most famous being former MSU point guard Mateen Cleaves) in an off-campus fight. Since then, Shaw has been a model citizen and a productive football player.

With Jace Snyder (49 tackles in 2000) lost to graduation, Shaw will be asked to provide an inside push. He should be up to the job after recording 61 tackles in 1999 and 68 last fall. Shaw will be joined by sophomore **Kyle Rasmussen** (6-4, 265) in a smallish set of starting defensive tackles.

Because of their lack of girth (by Big Ten standards), both Shaw and Rasmussen will need an occasional rest. That's where a pair of burly redshirt freshmen, **Dwight Whitfield** (6-2, 300) from St. Louis and Lonnie Simmons (6-2, 287) from Columbus, Ohio, will come in handy.

Williams will play a number of ends too, in order to keep fresh legs in the game at all times. The projected starters are Myers, a two-year starter who registered two sacks last season, and sophomore **Greg Taplin** (6-5, 269). Myers (41 tackles in 2000) was suspended in the spring for violating team rules, but he is expected back in the fall.

Taplin (21 tackles as true freshman) looks like he'll be a future stalwart. In his first career start, Taplin registered eight tackles and a sack versus Northwestern. Converted tight end **Ivory McCoy** (6-4, 232) will also put some heat on the quarterback from his strong-side linebacker spot.

Backing up Myers and Taplin at the defensive end spots will be redshirt freshman **Clifford Dukes** (6-3, 239), a converted linebacker, and sophomore **Samalj Gordon** (6-0, 265), along with a slew of newcomers.

Williams signed lots of defensive line help, including **Van Brown** (6-5, 250) from Pasadena (Calif.) City College. Brown, the younger brother of NFL player Chad Brown, had 44 tackles and six sacks last year at Pasadena City. He has three years of eligibility remaining.

Linebacker **Michael Bazemore** (6-4, 228) from Philadelphia's West Catholic High and mammoth **Matthias Askew** (6-7, 290) from the same high school (Dillard in Fort Lauderdale, Fla.) as current MSU defensive tackle Josh Shaw, could also play sooner rather than later.

LINEBACKERS

T.J. Turner is gone after being one of the last players picked in last April's NFL draft (239th overall by the New England Patriots in a 246-player draft). He will be missed, as will Drew Young, a starting linebacker last season who left the team for medical reasons. Young (57 tackles in 2000) was at risk for a catastrophic neck injury because of a narrowing of the nerve canals in his vertebrae. He will remain in school on scholarship.

Despite the personnel losses, Williams and his staff are smiling because senior middle linebacker **Josh Thornhill** (6-2, 234) will be one of the nation's best at his position this fall. A first-team All-Big Ten selection last year, Thornhill was listed among 52 preseason candidates for the 2001 Lombardi Award, presented annually to the outstanding college lineman of the year by the Rotary Club of Houston.

Thornhill led the Spartans in tackles with 114 in 2000, including 68 solos and 46 assists. The middle linebacker anchored a defensive unit that led the Big Ten in total defense, allowing 318.3 yards per game. He reached double figures in tackles seven times last season and ranked third in the Big Ten in tackles, averaging 10.4 per game. The Lansing, Mich., native earned Spartan Defensive Player of the Week honors twice in 2000, recording 14 stops against Purdue and a season-high 15 tackles against Northwestern. Thornhill also earned second-team Academic All-America honors last season.

"Josh Thornhill possesses everything you want in a linebacker," Spartan defensive coordinator Bill Miller said. "Josh plays with tremendous toughness and has the explosiveness to make big plays. He's a dream to coach because he gives that extra effort on every down. He studies a ton of film and he's one of the best practice players that I've ever been around. Josh has been a model of consistency throughout his career and he plays at that level because he prepares the same way each and every week."

Thornhill enters his fourth season as a starter, including 28-straight starting assignments, with 267 career tackles. He has 14 career double-figure tackle games.

Splitting time at weak-side linebacker will be sophomore **Mark Goebel** (6-2, 217) and redshirt freshman **James Cooper** (6-3, 211). Both are smallish, but possess great foot speed that will enable them to pursue ball carriers quite effectively.

McCoy was moved from tight end to rush linebacker as an experiment to help improve MSU's pass rush. The early results were encouraging and Williams believes that McCoy, who has 13 career starts at tight end, will be an excellent situational pass rusher, a la Julian Peterson in 1999.

Peterson was the 16th overall pick by the San

Francisco 49ers in the spring of 2000 after recording 15 sacks and 30 tackles for loss as a senior. The position never had the same type of zip last season. Perhaps McCoy can remedy that problem.

Backing up McCoy at the strong-side linebacker slot will be sophomore **Dominick Brown** (6-3, 247), an outstanding homegrown physical specimen from Lansing. Redshirt freshman **Jason Bradley** (6-0, 248) is the heir apparent to Thornhill in the middle.

DEFENSIVE BACKS

MSU defensive coordinator Bill Miller has two gaping holes to fill here with stud corner Renaldo Hill and free safety Richard Newsome both gone. With pass-happy offenses coming into vogue in the Big Ten, Hill, a seventh-round draft pick of the Arizona Cardinals, is the much bigger loss.

A first-team All-Big Ten performer in 2000, Hill started 35 games at MSU. He had 182 tackles, nine interceptions and 36 deflections. Newsome was no slouch either. He was third on the Spartans in tackles a year ago with 96 stops.

Returning senior **Cedric Henry** (5-1, 180)) who had five interceptions and a team-best 22 pass deflections in 2000, will be joined by fellow senior **DeMario Suggs** (5-11, 190) as the Spartans' starting corners. Suggs had 42 tackles in 2000.

Like Henry, junior strong safety **Thomas Wright** (6-1, 195) is a proven commodity. He recorded 107 tackles (second on the team) and a pair of interceptions in 2000.

Senior **Lorenzo Guess** (6-1, 190), who has helped out Tom Izzo's powerful hoops squad on occasion, is battling with fellow senior **Duron Bryan** (6-0, 205) for Newsome's vacant free safety spot.

"Duron Bryan and Lorenzlo Guess have a good competition going there at free safety," Williams said in the spring.

The loser of the Bryan-Guess battle will provide depth at safety, while junior **Broderick Nelson** (6-0, 170) should be the team's nickel back. He was light years better in spring ball.

Additional depth at cornerback will be provided by sophomore **Jeremiah McLaurin** (5-11, 180), a former teammate of Charlie Rogers at Saginaw (Mich.) High.

PUNTERS

As it turns out, punters aren't immune to the "sophomore jinx." Junior **Craig Jarrett** (6-2, 212) followed a sensational freshman year (43.5 punting average) in 2000 with a somewhat disappointing sophomore season. He still managed 40.8 yards per boot (sixth best in the Big Ten), but was inconsistent.

Jarrett had punts of five yards, 23 yards and 27 yards in an upset loss at Iowa in the fifth game of the 2000 season. In the spring, Jarrett appeared to have regained his 1999 form, which brought smiles to the faces of MSU's coaching staff. They need Jarrett to boom the ball when called upon, if the Spartans are to win the all-important field position battle week in and week out.

If Jarrett struggles, then freshman **Dave Raymer** (6-3, 200) might warrant a look. A member of the *Detroit Press*' 2000 Dream Team, Raymer averaged 44.7 yards on his 30 punts last fall at Oxford (Mich.) High School.

SPECIAL TEAMS

This area needs improvement in 2001. After losing top-notch kicker Paul Edinger to the Chicago Bears, his understudy David Schaefer wasn't nearly as effective a weapon as his predecessor. Schaefer was 11-of-17 on field-goal attempts and missed three of his 21 extra point tries in 2000.

He kicked the ball better this spring, but Williams will have open auditions late this summer with Servis, Raymer and Danhof all getting a crack at the No. 1 job.

Jarrett has one of the strongest legs of any Big Ten punter, but he needs better consistency in 2001. After a brilliant freshman season during which he averaged 43.5 yards per punt, Jarrett averaged just 40.8 yards as a sophomore. He'll need to regain his old form.

The return game should get a lift with gifted split end Rogers returning punts and JUCO transfer Lovett, a former high school track star, helping out in the kickoff return game.

RECRUITING CLASS

Williams and his staff landed a Top 35 recruiting class. It was bolstered by the late signing of defensive lineman **Kevin Vickerson** (6-5, 270) and the addition of Alphonso Townsend, a Detroit Martin Luther King High School star who was listed as the No. 42 overall prospect in the Midwest *SuperPrep*. There is still some question whether he will qualify academically. There is no question about his skills. Vickerson had 97 tackles and 17 sacks last year.

Townsend, a year removed from the 2000 *SuperPrep* All-America team, originally signed with Ohio State in the spring of 2000. But he was an academic non-qualifier and had to attend Fork Union (Va.) Military Academy last year. He had 16 tackles for loss, including nine sacks for Fork Union.

Most assumed he was headed for Ohio State. When OSU coach John Cooper was fired, Townsend considered and eventually chose Michigan State. He can play either offense or defensive line, but he will be tried first at right guard.

The reason? Williams signed lots of defensive line help, including Brown from Pasadena (Calif.) City College. Brown, the kid brother of NFL player Chad Brown, had 44 tackles and six sacks last year at Pasadena City. He has three years of eligibility remaining. Linebacker Bazemore from Philadelphia's West Catholic High was in on 158 tackles (89 solo, 69 assists) and had eight sacks as a senior. And jumbo-sized Askew had 125 tackles and a whopping 21 sacks as a prep senior.

Offensively, Heyer, a 21-year-old offensive lineman from Germany, and JUCO receiver Lovett are both expected to make an impact. Lovett caught a total of 79 balls for 1,233 yards in two years at SUNY-Morrisville.

Freshman **Robert Strickland** (6-4 205) could also contribute. Strickland was rated the No. 3 player in Michigan by the *Detroit News*. He snared 31 balls for 330 yards and six touchdowns as a senior at Detroit's Derby High.

BLUE RIBBON ANALYSIS

OFFENSE	B-
SPECIAL TEAMS	C+
DEFENSE	B
INTANGIBLES	C+

Despite the lack of a deep threat, an unsettled quarterback situation, a non-existent pass rush and spotty special teams play, the Spartans would have gone bowling if they could have beaten Penn State in the 2000 season finale. Instead, they were hammered, 42-23, to close out a 5-6 season.

So which team is the real Michigan State—the one that won a school-record 10 games in 1999 or the team that won half as many in 2000? The answer in 2000 is probably somewhere in between. With the addition of many new wideouts (including a supposed Plaxico Burress-clone in sophomore Rogers), Williams will install a spread offense, a la Northwestern last year.

The offensive line is young, but if Williams can get any kind of quarterback play, then MSU's offense should be much improved. The reason? Duckett (1,353 rushing yards in 2000) is a legitimate Heisman candidate at tailback. Haygood and new faces Lovett and Rogers should combine to form a potent group of receivers and senior tight end Baker is one of the nation's best at his position.

In fact, if the quarterback play improves and both lines hold up, then Michigan State could win eight or nine games and make a trip to a big-time bowl. If the results are just OK, then six or seven wins are still possible in the wide-open Big Ten. Either way, it's a second-tier bowl for the Spartans in a powerful league where as many as three-quarters of the teams could go bowling.

(B.D.)

2000 RESULTS

Marshall	W	34-24	1-0
Missouri	W	13-10	2-0
Notre Dame	W	27-21	3-0
Northwestern	L	17-37	3-1
Iowa	L	16-21	3-2
Wisconsin	L	10-17	3-3
Michigan	L	0-14	3-4
Illinois	W	14-0	4-4
Ohio State	L	13-27	4-5
Purdue	W	30-10	5-5
Penn State	L	23-42	5-6

Minnesota

LOCATION	**Minneapolis, MN**
CONFERENCE	**Big Ten**
LAST SEASON	**6-6 (.500)**
CONFERENCE RECORD	**4-4 (t-5th)**
OFFENSIVE STARTERS RETURNING	**9**
DEFENSIVE STARTERS RETURNING	**3**
NICKNAME	**Golden Gophers**
COLORS	**Maroon & Gold**
HOME FIELD	**Metrodome (63,669)**
HEAD COACH	**Glen Mason (Ohio State '72)**
RECORD AT SCHOOL	**22-25 (4 years)**
CAREER RECORD	**81-89 (14 years)**
ASSISTANTS	**Moe Ankney (Bowling Green '64)** **Defensive Coordinator** **Mitch Browning (Capital University '79)** **Co-Offensive Coodinator** **Tony Peterson (Marshall '88)** **Co-Offensive Coordinator** **Vic Adamle (Eastern Michigan '83)** **Running Backs** **Greg Hudson (Notre Dame '90)** **Linebackers/Recruiting Coordinator** **Gordon Shaw (Cal Poly-San Luis Obispo '78)** **Guards/Centers** **Tom Sims (Pittsburgh '89)** **Defensive Line** **David Turner (Davidson '85)** **Defensive Ends** **Richard Wilson (Arkansas '81)** **Wide Receivers**
TEAM WINS (last 5 yrs.)	**4-3-5-8-6**
FINAL RANK (last 5 yrs.)	**42-49-49-18-58**
2000 FINISH	**Lost to North Carolina State in Micron PC.com Bowl.**

COACH AND PROGRAM

The opportunity of a lifetime opened up for Minnesota coach Glen Mason when his alma mater Ohio State was in need of a coach. Mason, a former Buckeye player and assistant coach, thought he had a very good shot at the job.

After all, he had just completed a season where he led Minnesota to its second straight bowl game. It was only the third time in school history the Golden Gophers accomplished such a feat.

After his interview at Ohio State, Mason told reporters that his visit went well. Well, imagine Mason's dismay when Ohio State picked Jim Tressel, a coach at Division I-AA Youngstown State, to be the Buckeye's 22nd head coach. Reports described Mason as "devastated" when told that Tressel would be the new coach. Mason had a strong Division I-A resume. He is only the third man ever to earn coach-of-the-year honors in three different Division I-A conferences—Mid-American (Kent), Big Eight (Kansas) and Big Ten.

Mason had the backers in Columbus. What he was missing was apparently the support of Andy Geiger, Ohio State's athletic director. Geiger is a hands-on kind of guy. It can be presumed that he wanted a coach over whom he can exercise considerable control.

When Mason finally met with the media, he was contrite, apologizing for avoiding local media and failing to return phone calls during Ohio State's 16-day search. He was passionate in expressing his desire to become Ohio State's coach. He said he hoped Tressel and the Buckeyes go 10-1 every year, losing only to Minnesota.

"It was a win-win situation for me," he said. "On the one hand, there was the opportunity for me to coach at the school that provided me with my beginning and gave me the tools that allowed me to get to where I am today.

"On the other hand, I remain at Minnesota with some of the most compassionate, understanding people I know; and a football team that will continue to improve."

But is the commitment really there? Mason's flirtation and subsequent disappointment did not sit well with some in Minnesota. This was hardly anything new. Mason interviewed for jobs at Michigan State and LSU after last season.

"I can tell you something: This guy is done interviewing for jobs," Mason said. "Regardless of what I say, and I really believe this, people are going to say, 'Oh, sure.' ... I guess I'll let my actions speak for themselves, and let time be the judge."

For the time being, the surest way for Mason to win over disgruntled Gopher fans is to keep the program upright. Before Mason's arrival in 1997, Minnesota won 14 games. But since he came aboard, the team has surpassed that figure by eight. When the Gophers leapfrogged from 5-6 to 8-4 in 1999, it marked the first time since 1990 that they had a winning record.

In 2000, Minnesota stumbled a bit, but it was still a successful season. It ran out to a 5-2 start by beating Illinois, Penn State, and Ohio State in consecutive weeks. The Gophers' 29-17 victory over the sixth-ranked Buckeyes broke a 51-year losing streak in Columbus. But a stunning 51-43 defeat at Indiana started a three-game losing streak. Minnesota had to rally for 27-24 triumph in the regular-season finale to become bowl eligible.

Can Minnesota make it to three straight bowl games? It has the offense to hang with any Big Ten team. But with so many defensive players gone, the offense is going to have to carry the load. And what about any remaining bad feeling about Mason's flirtation with Ohio State?

"I hope I have not burned any bridges," he said. "That was not my intent. I love my job. I really am happy at Minnesota. I like the people here, I like the area and I like my players. I like the people I work with. I have a terrific staff and I am still very excited about the direction this program is headed."

2001 SCHEDULE

Aug.	31	@Toledo
Sept.	8	Louisiana-Lafayette
	15	Baylor
	29	Purdue
Oct.	6	@Illinois
	13	@Northwestern
	20	Michigan State
Nov.	3	Ohio State
	10	@Michigan
	17	@Iowa
	24	Wisconsin

QUARTERBACKS

Who's the man? Right now it appear to be **Travis Cole** (6-3, 205). The senior started the final eight games of the season. Cole is a traditional drop-back passer with a solid arm. He established himself as the starter over sophomore **Asad Abul-Khaliq** when he led the Gophers to consecutive victories over Illinois, Penn State and Ohio State. In his starting debut, the junior college transfer was 8-of-13 for 170 yards and rushed for 82 yards and a pair of touchdowns.

Cole capped his strong season by leading his team from a 24-12 deficit against Iowa with 12 minutes left to play. He engineered an 82-yard drive, culminating with a 15-yard touchdown pass and completed an 81-yard scoring pass. His third touchdown pass of the day put the Gophers ahead for good.

For the season, Cole was 147-of-252 for 1982 yards with 11 touchdowns and seven interceptions. He also has some mobility, with five scores. He ranked 16th in the nation in passing efficiency (137.6) at the end of the regular season.

"Travis probably excelled a little bit over Asad as far as being more poised and mature," Minnesota offensive coordinator Tony Petersen said. "Travis' confidence in his ability is his big asset. Travis started and did a good job, but we were still able to get Asad in there to get some reps.'"

Abul-Khaliq (6-0, 201) came to Minnesota with impressive credentials. At Fork Union (Va.) Military Academy, he completed 62 percent of his passes in '98 and had 18 touchdowns to just three interceptions. He broke Vinny Testaverde's school record for touchdown-to-interception ratio.

Abul-Khaliq started the first four games of the season as a red-shirt freshman. He threw three touchdown passes in his debut against Louisiana-Monroe before leaving the game with a concussion in the first half. Abul-Khaliq played decently in the first three games, with seven touchdown passes to two interceptions in the non-conference season. But at Purdue, he hit the skids while completing just 5-of-12 for 34 yards in a 38-24 loss. He was replaced by Cole and lost his starting job.

Abul-Khaliq played in 10 games, passing for 676 yards and five touchdowns. He was intercepted four times. Abul-Khaliq is a better runner than Cole; he gained 200 yards on 42 carries with four scores a year ago. Publicly they will both compete for the starter's job. Realistically given Cole's season, it will be difficult for the young passer to beat him out. But expect Minnesota to sprinkle in Abul-Khaliq for a few meaningful snaps at quarterback.

"We return two quarterbacks with Big Ten experience," Mason said. "They both bring different tools to the table and have proven that they can be successful at this level. As was the case last year, I expect both quarterbacks to contribute."

Benji Kamrath (6-3, 198) is penciled in as the No. 3 quarterback. He appeared in two games as a redshirt freshman and was 2-of-3 for 19 yards. At Mayville High School, Kamrath was the Wisconsin Player of the Year when he threw for 18 touchdowns against just four interceptions.

RUNNING BACKS

Junior **Tellis Redmon** (6-0, 192) did an outstanding job filling in for All-Big Ten tailback Thomas Hamner. As a sophomore, he rushed for 1,368 yards—the fourth-highest total in school history and added eight scores. He also added 327 receiving yards on 32 receptions and two touchdowns. Redmon finished with 2,024 all-purpose yards, the second-highest total in school history.

"Tellis had a very good year for us and improved as the season went along," Mason said. "He is a hard worker and should improve like he did in 2000."

Redmon wrapped up the season in fine fashion. He rushed 42 times for 246 yards and two touchdowns in the Micronpc.com Bowl. That was the fifth-best rushing day in school history. His seven 100-yard games tied Darrell Thompson's record.

"I wasn't surprised [by Redmon]," Petersen said. "I think we have a good system and we execute it well. If the running back does what he is supposed to do and runs the holes the way he's supposed to run it, he'll [be successful]. Our offensive did a good job and Tellis took advantage of it."

All the publicity wasn't good, however. Redmon earned the nickname "TV Tellis." He was arrested in October on charges of driving with a revoked license when officers allegedly saw a television playing inside his 1999 Honda Accord. Earlier that day, Redmon rushed for 150 yards to lead the Gophers to a 25-16 victory over Penn State. Charges were later dismissed.

Redmon could lose some of his 293 rushing attempts. The coaching staff is welcoming the return of sophomore **Thomas Tapeh** (6-1, 231). Tapeh played in seven games last year before suffering a season-ending foot injury. When he did play, Tapeh was effective, rushing 81 times for 344 yards and two scores. He gained 183 yards against Baylor.

Terry Jackson (5-11, 185), a redshirt freshman, will also compete for time. Jackson rushed for 1,774 yards and 21 touchdowns as a senior when he helped Saginaw High School to its first-ever state championship.

"At running back, we are looking pretty deep," Mason said. "Tellis Redmon improved throughout the season last year and we look forward to him. Terry Jackson was an impressive freshman. Thomas Tapeh is still waiting and we hope to use him."

With Minnesota using a three-receiver, one-back offense, freshmen fullbacks **Larry Pinson** (6-1, 220) and **Jason Beckum** (6-0, 186) are strictly short-yardage runners.

WIDE RECEIVERS/TIGHT ENDS

Minnesota has, hands down, the best wide receiver in the Big Ten and perhaps the best in college football. **Ron Johnson** (6-3, 216) is a terrific player who should finish his career owning every major school receiving record. He has the size and breakaway speed to beat any cornerback in the country. The senior is already Minnesota's all-time leader in receiving touchdowns and is just 29 catches and 496 yards away from breaking the career records in those categories.

Peterson, who coached Randy Moss at Marshall—where he was the offensive coordinator—had high praise for Johnson.

"Ron has a lot of ability," he said. "He's a big-time play-maker and when you need a big play, he makes it. When the game's on the line, that's the guy you want to be throwing the ball to. Somehow Ron is going to come down with it."

Johnson, who has gotten better every season, had 61 catches for a school-record 1,125 yards and 11 scores a year ago. After having just two 100-yard games in his first two seasons, Johnson had five last year. He has caught a pass in all 35 games of his career. Johnson, the team co-MVP in 2000 with center Ben Hamilion, is the only Golden Gopher to catch at least one pass in each game of the 1998, '99 and '00 seasons. His 61 receptions were one shy of the school record set by Tutu Atwell in 1996, and he stands in second place on the school's career receptions list with 142. Last season Johnson moved into third place on the Golden Gopher all-time list for receiving yards (2,144).

Johnson had one of the best stretches in recent memory when over a three-game span he absolutely dominated. Against Penn State, Ohio State and Indiana, he had a combined 19 catches for 454 yards and four touchdowns. He capped the run with a career-high 177 yards at Indiana, including an electrifying 82-yard catch-and-run.

In short, Johnson is destined to be a top 10 NFL draft choice. He could have left school early but decided to stay.

"Johnson has shown that be can make the best plays against the best talent in the country and we are very pleased that he passed up the draft to stay with us another year," Mason said. "I really don't think there is a harder working player in our program than Johnson."

Jermaine Mays (6-0, 191) is a complementary receiver with good play-making ability. The senior had 21 receptions for 321 yards. He had a career-best six catches for 119 yards and a touchdown against Iowa. His 81-yard game-winning score to beat the Hawkeyes was his lone touchdown on the season.

Antoine Henderson (5-8, 162) is another senior with good speed. A converted tailback, he missed virtually all of last year after injuring his knee in the season opener. For his career, Henderson has 25 catches for 326 yards and three scores. Senior **Elvin Jones** (6-3, 214), junior **Antoine Burns** (6-1, 192), sophomore **Tony Patterson** (6-3, 200) and sophomore **Keith Matthews** (6-2, 195) will all factor in. Jones had the most production with 17 catches for 217 yards and a touchdown.

"We expect them to make all the plays that they are supposed to make," Petersen said. "They might make some of the big-time catches that Ron does but you never know. I don't think we win the Iowa game unless Mays makes that 81-yard touchdown catch in the fourth quarter."

Former wide receiver **Jack Brewer** (6-1, 189), who had 22 catches for 286 yards, was switched to free safety.

The tight end wasn't a huge factor in the passing game. Most of Minnesota's sets require only one. But sophomore **Ben Utecht** (6-6, 244), a converted wide receiver, has ability. He had eight receptions for 128 yards and two touchdowns.

OFFENSIVE LINE

The offensive line will have to replace a pair of stalwarts. Center Ben Hamilton and tackle Adam Haayer were anchors that helped Minnesota churn out 429.1 yards per game. The NFL drafted both—Hamilton was a fourth-round pick of the Denver Broncos and Haayer, a sixth-round selection by Tennessee.

"We're not going to change anything," Petersen said. "We're still going to do what we do. We might not be able to do as much with a center that Ben was able to do. He'd pull a lot. He could do some things that not too many people can do. It might limit some of the things we do up front. But it won't change what we do."

Minnesota will make one change. Left guard **Derek Burns** (6-5, 277) will move to center. Burns is an aggressive, physical blocker. He started every game and has a streak of 18 straight dating to last season. Burns, who saw action in 897 plays, helped Minnesota average 196.9 rushing yards.

Dan Gitlewski (6-6, 296) will step into the left guard spot. He showed signs of promise as a redshirt freshman last season.

Jake Kuppe (6-7, 338) is being shuffled to left tackle to replace Haayer after playing on the right side. Kuppe will have to assume more pass-protection duty now with the switch. The junior has the skills to be an All-Big Ten performer.

Ryan Roth (6-3, 302) returns at right guard. He started all but one game and played in all. Ryan has been instrumental in the steady improvement of Minnesota's offensive line in the past three years.

Arthur Smith (6-8, 344) will move in at right tackle. He saw action as a freshman last year. Senior **Akeem Akinwale** (6-3, 274) will also figure in, probably at center.

"We feel pretty good about the first five," Petersen said. "We just have to get some depth there. You've got to have depth in the offensive line. Guys are going to end up playing."

2000 STATISTICS

Rushing offense	187.5	27
Passing offense	234.9	36
Total offense	422.5	26
Scoring offense	31.4	29
Net Punting	40.9	2
Punt returns	13.3	16
Kickoff returns	18.7	77
Rushing defense	171.3	77
Passing efficiency defense	115.5	47
Total defense	364.6	57
Scoring defense	25.5	60
Turnover margin	+2	54

Last column is ranking among Division I-A teams.

KICKERS

Mason didn't pull any punches when asked about star kicker **Dan Nystrom** (5-11, 205).

"Not to criticize, but Dan had an awful year last year," he said.

Nystrom was a second-team All-Big Ten selection. He set a conference record for field goals (25) and was a point shy (109) for the league mark in kick scoring. However, he was probably the most inconsistent kicker in the Big Ten. Nystrom was 25-of-37 on field goals. That's a substantial drop-off from his stellar freshman season when he was 17-of-21.

Nystrom didn't just miss long kicks. He missed several he was capable of making. He was 20-of-28 from within 39 yards in 2000. As a freshman he was 13-of -15 from that distance.

"Our kicker had an atypical year in his consistency," Mason said. "We are looking for him to regain his form as one of the top kickers in the nation."

Assuming Minnesota's offense is more productive, Nystrom probably won't attempt as many kicks as last year. He needs 16 to pass Chip Lohmiller on the school's all-time list. He remains consistent on extra points, having converted 75-of-79 in his career.

DEFENSIVE LINE

The defensive line, as well as most of the defense, is basically revamped. The biggest loss is Karon Riley, the Big Ten sacks leader last year with 12. Chicago drafted him in the fourth round. With Riley, John Schlecht, and Matt Anderle gone, the Gophers are going to have to find replacements.

"We lost a lot of people," Mason said. "We have a great deal of new faces, including the coaching staff. We've got some depth concerns up front where we lost a lot of guys. The only player we really have returning is defensive tackle **Dan Kwapinski**, who ended up being an alternate last year. We have **Gregg White** returning at defensive end, and we look forward to him having an outstanding year."

The sole returnee is White (6-2, 259) at end. He was a top-notch bookend to Riley as he collected 69 tackles, 50 solo and had six sacks. The senior had a tackle for a loss in 10 of 12 games. He also blocked five passes. White's best game might have been when he had 13 tackles and a sack against Ohio.

Steve Watson (6-3, 218) figures to play at left end as a redshirt freshman. Watson was one of the top defensive end prospects in the Midwest according to *SuperPrep.* He logged 115 tackles, 12 sacks, and forced six fumbles as a senior high school player in Defiance, Mo. Watson led Francis Howell to a 29-6 record over three seasons.

At defensive tackle is sophomore Kwapinski (6-5, 278), who played in nine games with one start. He had five tackles and a sack as a redshirt freshman. He has a solid background. Kwapinski was the 1998 North Dakota Gatorade Player of the Year. He had 160 tackles and seven sacks.

The other defensive tackle could be **Brandon Harston** (6-3, 290) as Minnesota continues the youth movement. The redshirt freshman was voted to the *SuperPrep* All-Southwest team. Harston had 120 career tackles, 15 sacks and 15 forced fumbles. He might be a little rusty. Harston hasn't played a full season since 1998. In 1999, he played just four games as a senior because of a high ankle sprain.

The young players on the line will have to produce because there isn't much veteran depth. Senior **Zach Vevea** (6-4, 263) and junior **Dave Sykora** (6-6, 288) don't have a lot of experience. There is evidence to believe that Minnesota's youngsters will thrive. With improved team speed, perhaps the Gophers can improve upon a defense that allowed 26.5 points. That was the most points allowed by a Big Ten team that went to a bowl game.

LINEBACKERS

Minnesota will have some new faces at linebacker also.

"All of our linebackers are new, but we think we have some young depth that we have confidence will play pretty well," Mason said.

The most experienced player is **Astein Osei** (6-2, 238). The senior will man the outside after he got hurt in the third game last season and missed the rest the year. In limited duty he had three tackles. In 1999, Osei started in five of the last six games and played in all 12 games as Minnesota reached the Sun Bowl. Osei finished the year with 49 tackles and one sack.

The middle linebacker spot is a question mark. Redshirt freshman **Darrell Reid** (6-3, 246) and sophomore **Phil Archer** (6-2, 228) will compete for the position. Reid has a huge upside. As a high school player in Farmingdale, N.J., he was ranked the second-best linebacker in the Northeast by *SuperPrep.* Reid had 99 tackles, blocked five kicks, broke up five passes and forced three fumbles as a senior. He played six games with a cast on his arm.

Archer played in 10 games but saw limited action as a redshirt freshman. He was a two-time all-state selection out of St. Paul who had 121 tackles, 19 tackles for a loss and two interceptions.

Senior **Jimmy Henry** (6-0, 189), a converted strong safety, is expected to contribute at outside linebacker. He played in all but one game last year, finishing with 28 tackles and a sack. Henry is one of the faster linebackers on the team.

DEFENSIVE BACKS

Cornerback Willie Middlebrooks and free safety Delvin Jones left early to the NFL. Even with those losses, the unit could be better. **Mike Lehan** (6-0, 187) is the sole returnee in the secondary. The junior cornerback has been clocked at 4.39 in the 40. He started 10 of the 12 games. Lehan participated in 762 plays—the third most among defensive backs.

Lehan led the team with eight pass breakups. He had 43 tackles, including his first tackle for a loss against Wisconsin. He had a career-high nine tackles against Indiana. Lehan recorded a tackle in every game but the Iowa game. He has one career interception.

Redshirt freshman **Justin Fraley** (6-1, 198) could be the other cornerback. He was a two-time all-state selection out of Cleveland. Fraley intercepted 34 passes and forced 28 fumbles during his career at Benedictine High School. He had an interception to seal a state championship victory as a freshman.

Senior Jack Brewer lettered as a free safety and wide receiver in 1999 and played primarily wide receiver last season. Late in the year he returned to defense and heads into 2001 as the top free safety. He possesses excellent speed and toughness and brings experience to the group. Brewer had 14 tackles in 11 games. As a sophomore in '98, Brewer had 35 tackles. He also tied for the team lead with two interceptions. Brewer is a cousin of fellow Golden Gopher Tellis Redmon.

Sophomore **Eli Ward** (6-0, 195) will probably line up at strong safety. He had 16 tackles in 11 games last year. He has good size and speed. Ward will be expected to contribute more.

"We have guys that we are high on; there's youth there, but there's talent and I think it's just a matter of time that we feel really good about it," Mason said. "If you ask me what area do we feel best about on defense, it's our back end; I think we have good talent there."

PUNTERS

Preston Gruening (5-10, 204) was an All-America selection by *The Football News.* The junior led the nation with a 45.2 punting average. He led the nation in average yards per punt from week one of the 2000 season until the final week. Gruening dropped 17 punts inside the 20-yard line, 13 of which were downed. Two of those punts were downed inside the 10.

Seventeen of his 46 punts went for 50 yards or more. Opponents averaged only 7.2 yards a return.

Gruening was chosen to preseason All-America teams by *Blue Ribbon* and *Playboy.*

SPECIAL TEAMS

Minnesota had the best punt return team in the Big Ten. The Gophers averaged 13.1 a return and scored a touchdown. Redmon was the second-leading return man and had an 83-yard touchdown return, but he might not have to do the job this season.

Antoine Burns (6-1, 195), a junior transfer, had three punt returns for scores at Rochester (Minn.) Community College.

Kick returning duties will fall to Henderson, who returns after injuring his knee in the first game of the year on a punt return. The senior has 25 career returns for 566 and no touchdowns. He did, however, bring one back 83 yards against Indiana in 1998. Mays also will factor in. He had 21 returns for 497 yards and a touchdown. Mays had a 100-yard return for a score against Indiana.

RECRUITING CLASS

Minnesota signed 22 players, many of them with specific needs in mind.

"One of our main goals in the recruiting process was to add speed and athleticism to the roster and I think we've done a good job with that," Mason said. "We signed 12 players on defense and 10 on offense, enabling us to fill some needs on both sides of the ball. We are very excited about the players that have committed to our program and look forward to seeing them in a Minnesota uniform."

The best player might be **Damian Haye** (6-2, 245) out of Hialeah-American in Miami. He was an Associated Press all-state selection who has tremendous quickness and athleticism. He was considered the top player on one of Dade County's top defenses. Haye tallied 45 tackles, 15 for loss with nine sacks last season. He's a hard hitter who forced seven fumbles and recovered six.

Jarod Posthumus (6-4, 215) is the sole quarterback in the class. He threw for 5,844 yards in his prep career at Becker High in St. Cloud and was a *PrepStar* All-Midwest Team selection and one of the top 10 quarterback prospects in the Midwest. Posthumus threw for more than 3,400 yards and 30 touchdowns the last two seasons and completed 60 percent of his passes. He also played safety, amassing 79 tackles with four pass breakups and four interceptions. Posthumus led his team to a 30-13 record in four years as a starter.

From the junior college ranks, **Dee Saunders** (5-10, 170) was rated the second-best corner in the country by *Blue Chip Illustrated.* Saunders signed with Miami out of high school. He tallied 36 tackles, 29 of them solo with 11 pass breakups and three interceptions at SUNY-Morrisville. Saunders was a *SuperPrep* and *PrepStar* All-Southeast selection at Glades Central High School (Belle Grades, Fla.), where he was all-state, all-area and all-conference selection.

His team was ranked No. 1 in Class 4A, posting a 14-1 record, losing in the state title game. Saunders returned 29 punts for an average of 16.5 yards and took two of them for touchdowns.

BLUE RIBBON ANALYSIS

OFFENSE	A-
SPECIAL TEAMS	B+
DEFENSE	C-
INTANGIBLES	C

Minnesota has a chance to do something that no previous Gopher team has done before—play in a bowl game for the third straight year. Minnesota is one of just four Big Ten teams to earn bowl bids the last two years.

Offensively, the Gophers have enough personnel to compete with anybody. They have solid depth at quarterback, a quality running back and game-breaking receivers. If the offensive line holds up, the Gophers should be among the highest-scoring teams in the league. But they can't settle for field goals like they did last season.

"We have to go back and establish the run," Mason said. "With the wide receivers we have returning, there's a natural tendency to spread them out and throw the ball all over the lot, which is fine as long as you also have the ability to run the ball. We're going to expand our offense and work very hard on red zone and goal-line; last year the number of times we got in scoring situations and didn't come away with points really hurt us."

Redmon is a quality back, but the guy who makes the offense go is Johnson. Minnesota needs to make sure it gets the most out of its star wideout. Johnson should surpass last year's outstanding production, at least in number of catches. The team might also involve him more with reverses or end-around plays.

"Ron is one of our most consistent performers and our big-play, go-to receiver," Mason said. "We feel that he is as good as any receiver in the Big Ten and will be one of the keys to out offense."

The defense will be new, but that isn't bad. Minnesota needs to get more stops because it gave up way too many points (26.5 points per game). The Gophers have enough talent on offense and special teams to ease the burden on defense.

They should reach a bowl despite not finishing in the upper echelon in the league.

(M.G.)

2000 RESULTS

Louisiana-Monroe	W	47-10	1-0
Ohio	L	17-23	1-1
Baylor	W	34-9	2-1
Purdue	L	24-38	2-2
Illinois	W	44-10	3-2
Penn State	W	25-16	4-2
Ohio State	W	29-17	5-2
Indiana	L	43-51	5-3
Northwestern	L	35-41	5-4
Wisconsin	L	20-41	5-5
Iowa	W	27-24	6-5
NC St. (Micron PC.com)	L	30-38	6-6

Northwestern

LOCATION	**Evanston, IL**
CONFERENCE	**Big Ten**
LAST SEASON	**8-4 (.667)**
CONFERENCE RECORD	**6-2 (t-1st)**
OFFENSIVE STARTERS RETURNING	**10**
DEFENSIVE STARTERS RETURNING	**6**
NICKNAME	**Wildcats**
COLORS	**Purple & White**
HOME FIELD	**Ryan Field (49,256)**
HEAD COACH	**Randy Walker (Miami-Ohio '76)**
RECORD AT SCHOOL	**11-12 (2 years)**
CAREER RECORD	**70-45-5 (11 years)**
ASSISTANTS	**Kevin Wilson (N. Carolina '84)**

Offensive Coordinator/Quarterbacks/ Assistant Head Coach
Jerry Brown (Northwestern '72)
Defensive Coordinator
Brad Bolinger (Franklin '94)
Defensive Backs
Mike Dunbar (Washington '72)
Tight Ends/H-Backs/Special Teams
Howard Feggins (North Carolina '87)
Wide Receivers
Jeff Genyk (Bowling Green '82)
Running Backs
Jack Glowik (Miami-Ohio '78)
Defensive Line
James Patton (Miami-Ohio '93)
Offensive Line
Jay Peterson (Miami-Ohio '85)
Linebackers
TEAM WINS (last 5 yrs.) 9-5-3-3-8
FINAL RANK (last 5 yrs.) 15-17-62-68-27
2000 FINISHLost to Nebraska in Alamo Bowl.

COACH AND PROGRAM

If there has been a more schizophrenic program in the NCAA than Northwestern the past 20 years, we don't know which one it would be. The Wildcats were one of the worst teams in the 1980s, winning a grand total of 18 games in the decade. They started the '90s with a five-year run that featured just 13 more victories. Football success, it appeared, just wasn't meant to be in Evanston.

Naturally, the next two years the Wildcats won back-to-back Big Ten championships under head coach Gary Barnett. But as quickly as they surged, the Wildcats slid back to the bottom tier of the conference as Barnett's magic began to wear off. After a 3-9 season in 1998, Barnett high-tailed it out of Evanston for the mountains of Colorado, and Northwestern turned the program over to Randy Walker.

Who?

Yes, Randy Walker probably still leads the Big Ten in the "Who's he?" factor, though that should change this year. After all, he was the 2000 Big Ten Coach of the Year and was voted Region 3 Coach of the Year by his peers in the American Football Coaches Association.

Sure, Walker is a rather nondescript fellow. He doesn't fire off one-liners with the ease of a standup comic at his post-game press conferences. You won't see clips of him raving on the sideline, grabbing his players by the facemask or hugging them after big plays. He defines "low profile," at least until you look at his record.

This will be the year the country's football fans get to know Randy Walker, because his Wildcats are the preseason favorites to win the Big Ten. And one reason that they're so highly regarded is that Walker has crafted an offense that maximizes the unique skills of two of the country's most exciting offensive players, running back **Damien Anderson** and quarterback **Zak Kustok**.

Walker, 46, has always specialized in offense. He was a fullback on three 10-plus win teams at Miami (Ohio) in the mid-70s, then spent 10 years at North Carolina, where he coached the running backs and quarterbacks and eventually served three seasons as offensive coordinator.

After a two-year stint coaching the running backs at Northwestern, Walker took over the program at his alma mater and became the winningest head coach in school history, with a 59-35-5 record. That's a decent feather in the cap, especially considering Miami's reputation as the "Cradle of Coaches"—the school has spawned such coaching giants as Red Blaik, Paul Brown, Sid Gillman, Weeb Ewbank, Woody Hayes, Ara Parseghian and Bo Schembechler.

Someday Randy Walker's name could be featured prominently among that list, at least if his early success at Northwestern is any indication. The 'Cats wound up 3-8 in Walker's first year, but after installing a wide-open spread offense, last year's team shocked the nation, going 6-2 in Big Ten play and winning a share of the conference title.

After a 2-1 non-conference season, the Wildcats traveled to Madison and upended Wisconsin, 47-44, in double overtime. And that was just the start of a series of wild games for the Wildcats that usually found them on the winning end. They put 52 on the board at Indiana, roared back from 21 down in the second half to beat Minnesota, 41-35, on the final play of the game, and toppled Michigan, 54-51, on another miracle finish. That time, Northwestern recovered a fumble in the final minute and scoring a game-winning touchdown in the final 20 seconds.

The 'Cats controlled their own destiny with two games to play, but their Rose Bowl dreams fizzled when they fell flat at Iowa and lost by 10 to the Hawkeyes. After a 61-23 drubbing of Illinois, the lack of a consistent defense caught up with Northwestern in the Alamo Bowl, where Nebraska ran wild in a 66-17 blowout in San Antonio.

This year's priorities obviously center on finding a better way to stop the opposition, because the Wildcats seem to have this whole offense thing figured out.

"We have to become a better defense," Walker said. "We were near the bottom in many defensive categories last season in the Big Ten. We feel we have better personnel and a better plan than that indicates.

"We need 11 guys playing together with great effort, flying around to the football, and we think that is possible. We have some quality players returning on that side of the ball anchored by a very deep linebacker corps. We think some of the young guys up front are of high quality and we think the same is true of the back half."

But don't think Walker's going to rest on his laurels and expect the offense to throw 36.8 points a game on the scoreboard again.

"There are some things on offense that right now we don't do very well. Despite leading the Big Ten in total offense and scoring," he said. "We think we can be more of a complete and balanced offense. And that's the direction that we want to take."

The possibility that the offense could be even better this year is enough to cause more than a few sleepless nights for defensive coordinators around the Big Ten. Add in a better defense and the Wildcats—ranked in the mid-teens in most national preseason polls—could take that next step for Walker this fall, to an outright Big Ten title and a BCS bowl.

And then we'll all know the answer to the question, "Who's he?"

2001 SCHEDULE

Sept.	7	@UNLV
	15	Navy
	22	@Duke
	29	Michigan State
Oct.	6	@Ohio State
	13	Minnesota
	20	Penn State
	27	@Purdue
Nov.	3	@Indiana
	10	Iowa
	22	@Illinois

QUARTERBACKS

If Walker was a relative unknown in big-time college football circles, then Kustok (6-1, 200) wasn't even a blip on the radar screen. Heading into his junior season, his sole collegiate experience consisted of seven starts as a sophomore in Walker's ho-hum debut season.

But last year Kustok thrust himself into conversations that included names like Brees, Weinke and Henson. He started all 12 games and helped the Wildcats win in a variety of ways. His 2,389 yards passing were second in the conference. His 19 touchdown passes were a school record, as is his streak of consecutive games with a touchdown pass—13 and counting. His 505 yards rushing set a school record, and his nine rushing touchdowns tied a mark held by Otto Graham. And perhaps most impressively, he finished the season on a streak of 189 straight passes without an interception—yes, another school record.

Kustok is cool under fire, which is crucial when you're running an offense that to the untrained eye resembles an elementary school playground at recess. He ran the no-huddle, multiple set offense with dazzling efficiency, taking play-calling signals from the sideline, relaying them to his teammates, and then executing with deadly precision.

"He managed our offense very well, and it's a difficult offense to manage," Walker said. "He made great decisions, protected the football and just did a marvelous job of handling and manipulating our no-huddle offense. He's a versatile kid who throws the ball as well as he runs it, and that gives the defense a lot of problems."

Kustok earned honorable mention All-Big Ten and All-America status as a junior, and if he lives up to the lofty expectations he's established, he could find himself in New York in December as a Heisman Trophy finalist.

Walker is making no predictions about the Heisman, but he thinks Kustok is the best the Big Ten has to offer.

"... I think he's the best quarterback in the Big Ten," Walker said. "I know there are a lot of good quarterbacks, but I wouldn't trade him for anyone."

Kustok's top backup will be sophomore **Matt Danielson** (6-0, 222), who saw spot duty as a freshman in garbage time. He will be pushed by redshirt freshman **Tony Stauss** (6-1, 202), who had a strong spring practice. His experience running the spread offense in high school could give him a leg up on Danielson in the long run.

"I'm excited about our young quarterbacks," Walker said. "I think we are a lot better off today than we were a year ago. Now we believe we have an exceptional No. 1 quarterback and the young guys are stepping up."

RUNNING BACKS

Another player who made a name for himself nationally with his play last year is senior running back Anderson (5-11, 204). He set or tied 23 school records en route to piling up these eye-popping statistics: 2,063 yards rushing, 6.6. yards per carry and 23 touchdowns. He rattled off 219 yards at Michigan State, 230 at Minnesota, 240 against Nebraska in the Alamo Bowl, 268 against Michigan and 292 against Indiana. Toss in four more games over 100 and all those touchdowns, and you can see why he received a slew of All-America honors and finished fifth in Heisman voting.

He will have the school's career rushing record wrapped up by halftime of the season-opener (he needs 65 yards) and will graduate in June 2002 with a degree in communications. By then, one NFL team will feel very lucky to have landed this multi-talented back, who could have been a first-round pick this spring if he hadn't decided to return for his senior year.

What's left for Anderson to accomplish? Besides the school rushing record and the degree, that is? Well, that stiff-arming hunk of metal would look great on any mantel, and then there's the national championship to consider. After all, if Oklahoma could do it, why not Northwestern?

"We know Damien Anderson is a great player and an All-American on just about everyone's list," Walker said. "Certainly he's a legitimate candidate who will be considered strongly for the Heisman Trophy. Two thousand yards rushing is no small feat. He had a great season in 2000, and we expect him to have another great season."

When Anderson needs a breather or gets pulled in a blowout, the Wildcats will turn to junior **Kevin Lawrence** (5-11, 200) and sophomore **Torri Stuckey** (5-11, 197). Lawrence averaged 5.0 yards a carry and totaled 374 yards and three touchdowns last year, while Stuckey chipped in 105 and a score.

Redshirt freshman **Noah Herron** (5-11, 219) provides depth at running back.

"Our goal is to develop some guys to give [Anderson] quality backup," Walker said during the spring. "Kevin Lawrence had a great season in 2000 and we expect him to continue to grow. We [also] have Torri Stuckey, who got his feet wet last season, and Noah Herron. We have some young guys who we want to see more of to see who can really be a quality player for us in the future."

Don't look for much action from the fullbacks in the spread offense, but when the 'Cats do use one, it should be junior **Vincent Cartaya** (6-3, 233) or sophomore **Gilles Lezi** (6-0, 229). Redshirt freshman **Rob Shirley** (6-0, 230) is also in the mix. If Walker truly wants to make this offense more diverse and versatile, the fullback position could play a bigger role than last year.

WIDE RECEIVERS/TIGHT ENDS

The only offensive starter not returning is wide receiver Teddy Johnson, who led the team with seven touchdowns. But the team's leading receiver was senior **Sam Simmons** (5-10, 201), who hauled in 38 passes and five touchdowns, including back-to-back game-winners against Minnesota and Michigan. When Kustok isn't sticking the ball into Anderson's bread basket, he'll be looking downfield for Simmons to get open.

"When he's in the lineup and playing effectively, we're hard to beat," Walker said. "He adds the other dimension. He's a big-play player at wide receiver and couples with Damien to give us a very good 1-2 threat. If he's healthy all 11 weeks, and shows up to play all 11 times, we're going to have a great chance at winning."

Kustok's secondary target will be junior **Jon Schweighardt** (5-11, 189), who was second on the team with 35 catches last year.

When four receivers are on the field, look for sophomores **Roger Jordan** (6-3, 202) and **Kunle Patrick** (6-0, 204), who teamed for 60 catches last season. Talented sophomore **Jovan Witherspoon** (6-3, 203), a transfer from Notre Dame who sat out last season, should find some playing time as well, if he heals from a broken foot suffered in spring practice.

Junior **Louis Ayeni** (5-11, 198) and sophomore **Jason Wright** (5-10) are also in the mix at wide receiver.

The tight end isn't used much in this offense, but the Wildcats do welcome back junior **David Farman** (6-5, 253), who started all 12 games and caught six passes last season. He will be backed up by sophomore **Eric Worley** (6-4, 247).

OFFENSIVE LINE

Any team that rushes for 3,062 yards must be doing something right up front—like putting together an experienced, athletic line capable of clearing holes for a thoroughbred like Anderson. Continuity is vital for an elite offensive line, and the Wildcats have it. They were fortunate in the injury department last year; all five starters remained healthy and started 12 games last season, and the same five will return this year, so look for more of the same up front.

Junior **Austin King** (6-4, 281) is probably the best in the conference with Ben Hamilton and Casey Rabach now playing on Sundays. He and junior guard **Jeff Roehl** (6-4, 299) are candidates for postseason honors. King has started 21 straight games, dating back to 1999 when he played as a freshman. Roehl was voted *Football News* honorable mention All-America last season.

They will be joined by three seniors—tackles **Mike Souza** (6-6, 294) and **Leon Brockmeier** (6-7, 302), and guard **Lance Clelland** (6-6, 317)—to form the best line in the Big Ten.

"It's the strength of our football team," Walker said. "It always starts up front. Damien doesn't gain all of those yards and we don't throw the ball effectively if we don't play well up front."

Walker expects some of the younger linemen to push for playing time this season as well. He singled out sophomores **Carl Matejka** (6-4, 295) at center and **Derek Martinez** (6-5, 292) as future stars and noted the improvement of freshman tackle **Ikechuku Ndukwe** (6-6, 333) and freshman guard **Matt Ulrich** (6-2, 292). Senior **Adam Fay** (6-4, 313) adds experience off the bench for the offensive line.

2000 STATISTICS

Rushing offense	257.3	8
Passing offense	218.4	52
Total offense	475.6	3
Scoring offense	38.5	8
Net Punting	36.6	25
Punt returns	10.1	45
Kickoff returns	19.6	60
Rushing defense	180.1	82
Passing efficiency defense	124.4	80
Total defense	408.1	89
Scoring defense	30.4	85
Turnover margin	+12	8

Last column is ranking among Division I-A teams.

KICKERS

The 'Cats are looking for a replacement for Tim Long, who connected on 13-of-17 field-goal attempts last season, including a 6-for-8 performance from beyond 40 yards. His season long was a 46-yarder at the gun that sent the Wisconsin game into overtime. He also went 3-for-3 in the win over Michigan State and 4-for-4 in the nail-biter against Michigan. That kind of clutch performance will be hard to replace this fall.

Junior **David Wasielewski** (5-10, 229) and sophomore **Brian Huffman** (6-1, 202) will battle it out for this position. Wasielewski is a transfer from Florida and should get first crack at the job, but at this point it's still wide open.

DEFENSIVE LINE

For all the impressive numbers posted by the Northwestern offense, the picture isn't so pretty on the other side of the ball. The Wildcats were near the bottom of the Big Ten in a number of significant categories—10th in scoring defense, 10th in rushing defense, ninth in total defense, ninth in passing defense efficiency and 10th in opponent first downs.

The rushing defense, in particular, yielded some shocking totals last season—243 yards to TCU's Ladainian Tomlinson, 293 yards to Wisconsin's Michael Bennett, 199 yards to Michigan's Anthony Thomas, and 240 yards to Nebraska's Dan Alexander.

Of course, an optimist could look at those numbers and say that at least Walker and his staff know where to focus their efforts this fall. The 'Cats lost five starters on defense, including defensive end Dwayne Missouri, defensive tackle Javiar Collins and end/linebacker Conrad Emmerich, who were 1-2-3 in sacks last season. But again, the positive view would be that the defense was lousy with those five starters, so how much worse could the new guys do?

Senior **Salem Simon** (6-4, 270) and junior **Pete Chapman** (6-4, 294) will anchor the line at the tackle position. The ends will likely be senior **Pete Konopka** (6-4, 242) and junior **Onaje Grimes** (6-3, 247).

There are plenty of candidates to push for playing time along the line, which is the team's biggest weakness entering the season. Among them are sophomores **Ray Bogenrief** (6-3, 260), **Matt Anderson** (6-3, 281), **George Woods** (6-1, 275) and **Ben Kennedy** (6-6, 265), with red-shirt freshman **Colby Clark** (6-2, 272) also in the mix.

"I've been impressed with Pete Chapman and the work ethic that he brings, as well as Salem Simon," Walker said. "Those two guys inside will anchor us. Outside, we took our most significant hit. We're looking at some guys. We even took a guy from the offensive line, Ben Kennedy, over to the defensive side of the ball just to see if he could get into the mix. He's probably our fastest, most explosive big man."

One possible fix for the line that the coaches have tinkered with is a 3-4 formation, which would get more of the team's best athletes—the linebackers—on the field.

LINEBACKERS

The defense's strongest unit is loaded with experience and talent, and might be the Big Ten's best. Senior **Billy Silva** (6-3, 248) was second in the Big Ten last year with 124 tackles, while senior **Napoleon Harris** (6-3, 243) was third with 117. Both players received various All-Big Ten honors last season, and both are legitimate All-America candidates this season.

Silva will once again anchor the middle, while Harris will line up outside or possibly at defensive end in the 3-4. Harris is an athlete who can rush the passer, stuff the run and cover a receiver, while Silva is the prototype middle linebacker. They each had six double-digit tackle games last year, and the defense will once again lean heavily on both.

"[Linebacking is] the strength of our defense," Walker said. "It's the most experienced position on the defensive side of the ball. All of our returns have been starters for a couple of years. We feel like we have four quality and proven performers. They are guys who can certainly be the anchor of your defense."

Senior **Kevin Bentley** (6-1, 233) will be the other starter outside, and look for junior **Pat Durr**

(6-1, 228) to get plenty of action as well, especially if the 3-4 is a hit.

Sophomores **Ryan Peterson** (6-2, 211) will spell Silva, and sophomore **Syga Thomas** (6-0, 208) will fill in outside.

DEFENSIVE BACKS

Gone are cornerback Harold Blackmon and free safety Rashad Morton, as well as reserve Shegun Cummings-John, so a secondary that already faced its share of adversity now has to retool as well.

Junior **Raheem Covington** (5-9, 182) looks like the new leader of the defensive backfield. Starting all 12 games at right corner last year, Covington made 81 tackles, broke up four passes and had one interception. Coaches think he has the skills to be a star for the Wildcats this year.

Junior **Chasda Martin** (5-11, 194) and sophomore **Brandon Evans** (5-11, 182) will battle on the left side for the opportunity to replace Blackmon. Each of them got some seasoning last year, but if the secondary is to hold together this year, one of them will have to step up and prove he's worthy of the playing time.

Senior **Rashidi Wheeler** (6-0, 212) mans the strong safety spot, where he started all 12 games last year and finished third on the team with 88 tackles. Senior **Marvin Brown** (5-11, 200) will back him up.

Junior **Sean Wieber** (6-1, 207) started four games in place of Morton last fall, and he will battle sophomore **Mark Roush** (6-0, 184) for the full-time starting position this year.

One wild card to keep an eye on is redshirt freshman **Marvin Ward** (5-11, 196), who opened some eyes in spring practice and could be a factor this fall.

"We have some young players who have not played and not received a lot of opportunity," Walker said of his secondary. "How big a contribution they can make is what we have to find out. We know Raheem is a quality corner, but who else is going to step up?"

PUNTERS

Senior **J.J. Standring** (6-1, 212) is the incumbent after a season in which he averaged 40.9 yards on 74 punts. He dropped 17 kicks inside the 20 and had only seven touchbacks, crucial numbers in the all-important battle for field position.

Standring is an excellent athlete and also pitches for the Northwestern baseball team. However, that posed a bit of a conflict in spring practice, which didn't exactly please Walker, who's a stickler for commitment to the program.

Standring will have to fight off a challenge from Wasielewski, the Florida transfer who also will challenge for the place kicking duties. Walker said this spring that Wasielewski will be given every opportunity to win both jobs.

SPECIAL TEAMS

The biggest change this year will be on the sideline, where Mike Dunbar moves into the special teams coordinator role. He is fortunate to have a veteran kick returner like Simmons in the fold. Last year Simmons brought back 13 punts for a 13.2-yard average. He shared the kickoff return duties with Johnson last year, and averaged 22.0 yards in nine returns. However, Walker is concerned about wearing out his top receiver with special teams work, and is looking for other players to spell him from time to time.

"Obviously Sam is a special player back there, but the issue with Sam is will he be able to go 11 games," Walker said. "I don't know the answer to that. If I had my way, Sam would return every kick. But I'm not sure that's in the best interest of our football team. Right now I don't have an answer other than Sam Simmons is a guy we can count on.

"Along with Sam we're going to take a look at guys like Louis Ayeni or Torri Stuckey. Ayeni has done it in the past. We have some young players that we're taking a look at."

The Wildcats lost long snapper Jack Harnedy to graduation. Candidates to replace him include redshirt freshman **Joel Layfield** (6-1, 196) and redshirt freshman **Mike Griffin** (6-3, 224), a backup quarterback who recently took up long-snapping.

Standring has served as the holder in the past, and should be available to fill that role again this fall, although Walker said Stauss and Patrick could also take over.

RECRUITING CLASS

Walker isn't shy about admitting his team's defensive deficiencies, and that's why 13 defensive players will be joining the squad in Evanston this fall.

"We brought in a couple of defensive tackles that can compete there," Walker said. "If a guy can move his hips and cover and pick up the defensive path, he can go back and play the secondary. We are going to give some defensive guys a close look. And those guys are going to have a great chance to come in and contribute."

Contending for spots on the line will be **Greg Lutzen** (6-5, 250), an all-state selection from Pewaukee, Wisc.; **David Thompson** (6-3, 245) of Rockledge, Fla.; **Luis Castillo** (6-4, 265), an all-stater from Garfield, N.J.; and **Tom Derricks** (6-1, 295), a competitor from Dallas with a non-stop motor.

On offense, tight end **Trai Essex** (6-4, 240) of Ft. Wayne, Ind., was one of the top two recruits in his state; **Ashton Aikens** (6-2, 190) is a highly regarded running back out of Detroit Country Day; and quarterback **Brett Basanez** (6-2, 175) of Arlington Heights, Ill., was his state's player of the year as a senior with 3,200 yards and 41 touchdowns through the air.

In addition to the defense, a newcomer might find some work on offense.

"I think there is a possibility that an offensive skill player can contribute," Walker said. "There might be an opportunity at wide receiver or running back."

BLUE RIBBON ANALYSIS

OFFENSE	A
SPECIAL TEAMS	B-
DEFENSE	C-
INTANGIBLES	A-

The pieces seem to be in place for Northwestern to continue its return to prominence in the Big Ten. The offense is peerless in the conference, the defense should be improved, and in Walker they have one of the best unknown coaches in the game. Well, unknown for now, at least.

No team in the Big Ten can boast a quarterback-running back-wide receiver trio like Kustok, Anderson and Simmons. Put them behind a line that's working together for its second straight season as starters, and they should be even more potent than last season.

The schedule has a few potential landmines to keep an eye on. The season opener is no picnic, a trip to the desert to take on a UNLV team that won the Las Vegas Bowl last season. The Rebels will already have one game behind them by the time the untested Wildcats head west for the Sept. 7 opener.

While Northwestern drops Wisconsin and Michigan from its Big Ten schedule, it adds Penn State and Ohio State. The Oct. 6 trip to Columbus could prove to be dicey for this crop of players, which has never won at OSU. And the season finale at cross-state rival Illinois could be trouble—a Thanksgiving Day matchup against a team the 'Cats humiliated, 61-23, last year.

However, if Northwestern can avoid those pitfalls, don't be surprised to be sharing your thoughts on Randy Walker and how his spread offense will look on New Year's day when you visit your water cooler next December.

(P.D.)

2000 RESULTS

Northern Illinois	W	35-17	1-0
Duke	W	38-5	2-0
Texas Christian	L	14-41	2-1
Wisconsin	W	47-44	3-1
Michigan State	W	37-17	4-1
Indiana	W	52-33	5-1
Purdue	L	28-41	5-2
Minnesota	W	41-35	6-2
Michigan	W	54-51	7-2
Iowa	L	17-27	7-3
Illinois	W	61-23	8-3
Nebraska (Alamo Bowl)	L	17-66	8-4

Ohio State

LOCATION	**Columbus, OH**
CONFERENCE	**Big Ten**
LAST SEASON	**8-4 (.667)**
CONFERENCE RECORD	**5-3 (4th)**
OFFENSIVE STARTERS RETURNING	**5**
DEFENSIVE STARTERS RETURNING	**6**
NICKNAME	**Buckeyes**
COLORS	**Scarlet & Gray**
HOME FIELD	**Ohio Stadium (98,000)**
HEAD COACH	**JimTressel (Baldwin-Wallace '75)**
RECORD AT SCHOOL	**First Year**
CAREER RECORD	**135-57-2 (15 years)**
ASSISTANTS	
	Mark Dantonio (South Carolina '79) **Defensive Coordinator**
	Jim Bollman (Ohio '77) **Offensive Coordinator/Offensive Line**
	Mark Snyder (Marshall '87) **Linebackers**
	Joe Daniels (Slippery Rock '64) **Wide Receivers**
	Tim Spencer (Ohio State '93) **Running Backs**
	Ken Conatser (Cincinnati '62) **Special Teams**
	Jim Heacock (Muskingum '70) **Defensive Line**
	Mel Tucker (Wisconsin '95) **Secondary**
	Bill Conley (Ohio State '72) **Tight Ends/Recruiting Coordinator**
TEAM WINS (last 5 yrs.)	**11-10-11-6-8**
FINAL RANK (last 5 yrs.)	**3-7-3-30-23**
2000 FINISH	**Lost to South Carolina in Outback Bowl.**

COACH AND PROGRAM

Ohio State coach John Cooper was given the heave-ho after losing to Michigan in the 2000 regular season finale (yet again) and then to South

Carolina in the Outback Bowl. The bowl loss was particularly tough to swallow because the Buckeyes were done in by Ryan Brewer, a Troy, Ohio native Cooper didn't recruit. Brewer, who rushed for 7,656 yards in high school, accumulated 219 total yards and three touchdowns to earn MVP honors in the Outback Bowl.

After pink slipping Cooper, Ohio State flirted with many of the hottest names in the college coaching ranks. Pittsburgh's Walt Harris, Minnesota's Glen Mason, Stanford's Tyrone Willingham, Oregon's Mike Bellotti, Oakland Raiders head coach Jon Gruden, Ohio State assistant Fred Pagac and former Buckeye star Chris Spielman were among the names floated as possible successors. Fifteen days after canning Cooper, the school surprised many when it picked Youngstown State's Jim Tressel.

Cooper was fired on Jan. 2 after Ohio State lost, 24-7, to South Carolina in the Outback Bowl. He was 111-43-4, shared three Big Ten titles and played in bowls in 11 of his 13 seasons.

But he was 3-8 in those bowl games and was just 2-10-1 against Ohio State's chief rival, Michigan, a game Ohio State fans refer to as "The Game."

After Cooper's firing, Ohio State athletic director Andy Geiger also cited poor academic performance, on-the-field taunting and off-the-field brushes with the law by the Buckeyes players as reasons for the need for a change.

Tressel's Youngstown State teams won national titles in 1991, 1993, 1994 and 1997—the most for a head coach in I-AA history—and had 12 winning seasons. Tressel took over the Penguins program in 1986. After suffering through a 2-9 season, he guided the Penguins to their first I-AA playoff appearance with an 8-4 mark the next season and won their first Ohio Valley Conference title.

Tressel is the son of Dr. Lee Tressel, who compiled a 155-52-6 record as head football coach at Baldwin-Wallace College. He lettered four years as a quarterback for his father. The Berea, Ohio native served as an assistant coach at Akron, Miami (Ohio) and Syracuse before handling quarterbacks and receivers for three years at Ohio State. After taking over at Youngstown State, he kept an eye on Ohio State but didn't waste time dreaming about following in Woody Hayes' footsteps.

"I've learned some good things growing up in this profession," Tressel said. "Woody said in his book that one cardinal rule is you never apply for a job that is not open. The Ohio State job has not been open for 13 years, and I've been awfully busy trying to get things done."

Is Tressel the right man for job? Sure, he's been one of the nation's most successful Division I-AA coaches, winning four national titles in his 15 years at Youngstown State. But it's a world of difference between Youngstown State and Ohio State, so we'll have to wait and see how he does.

"The biggest difference is in the operation," Tressel said. "At Youngstown State, you're the head coach, the director of football operation and the athletics director. You can't have that here.

"Otherwise, it has been the same. We're still only allowed to put 11 players on the field. The time investment also has been the same. These are young people who want to be part of something special. I know these guys are interested in doing something special in 2001."

With 11 starters back (five on offense, six on defense) and non-league games against Akron and San Diego State to start the season, Tressel should get out of the blocks at 2-0. That will keep critics off his back until mid-September, at which time all bets are off. Tressel inherits a team with a brutal schedule. Ohio State plays at UCLA, Indiana, Penn State, Minnesota and Michigan this fall.

Some good news for the new sideline boss is that lefty quarterback **Steve Bellisari**, who has started the last two years, returns under center. Bellisari was inconsistent last year, but at least he's been through the Big Ten wars. But he'll have to find new guys to play catch with as wideouts Ken-Yon Rambo and Reggie Germany are both gone. However, the ground game should be just fine, led by a beefy offensive line and a bruising tailback in senior **Jonathan Wells**.

On defense, **Joe Cooper**'s return can be seen as an unexpected win for Tressel, who now inherits a defense that has six returning starters, including all three linebackers. Cooper is a legit Butkus Award and All-America candidate. His return helps solidify the middle of a defense which lost two players to substantial NFL riches when early entrants Nate Clements and Ryan Pickett went in the first round of the 2001 draft. Clements and Pickett were the fifth OSU pair to be first-round picks within the last seven drafts—showing just how much talent Cooper was able to attract to Columbus.

But Tressel has already answered one of the biggest questions facing him: Can he recruit? Despite Cooper's firing, Ohio State salvaged its recruiting season by landing commitments from four prep All-Americans—running backs **Maurice Hall** (5-10, 180) from Columbus, Ohio and **Lydell Ross** (6-0, 205) from Tampa, Fla.; wide receiver **Angelo Chattams** (5-11, 185) from Dayton, Ohio; and safety **Dustin Fox** (6-0, 185) from North Canton, Ohio.

Tressel also experienced some key losses this off-season. First, running back Drushaun Humphrey—a high school senior from Toledo who had committed early to Tressel and the Buckeyes and whom many folks compared favorably to former OSU great Eddie George—died of a heart attack on May 1. Then, one of the nation's most widely respected strength and conditioning coaches, Dave Kennedy, resigned on May 9. Many of OSU's recent first-round draft picks credit Kennedy's weight training regime with helping improve their draft position.

But, then roughly 100 days before the opening kickoff, Tressel picked up a huge "W" when Massillon (Ohio) Washington High School quarterback **Justin Zwick** announced he will play college football at Ohio State in 2002. The 6-5, 205-pound Zwick, who chose Ohio State over Michigan, Miami (Fla.), Tennessee and Texas, is considered the most high-profile quarterback to commit to the Buckeyes in a long time.

"Ohio State has landed some very good quarterbacks since then; for instance, Bobby Hoying," said Bill Kurelic, publisher of *Ohio Football Recruiting News*. "But they really haven't landed a quarterback of Zwick's caliber since Art Schlichter."

While proximity was a big factor in Zwick's commitment, the hiring of Tressel from Youngstown State in January to replace John Cooper should not be discounted.

"It was a big thing because I know what coach Tressel is like, what he's about with his program," Zwick said. "I know what he likes to do and how he studies and cares about the players."

He knows because his brother Jared, five years older than Justin, played quarterback for Tressel at YSU. Jared Zwick is in dental school at Ohio State, where he has met with Tressel several times in recent months.

With one full high school season remaining, Zwick already has thrown for more than 7,000 yards. His first two seasons were at nearby Orrville, which he led to a state championship as a freshman. He transferred to larger Massillon last year and rang up 2,460 yards passing and 24 touchdown, increasing his career touchdown pass total to 70. Couple all of that with a nearly 4.0 grade-point average, and the package borders on perfection.

His commitment was a huge coup for Tressel, who in his first six months on the job, appears to be more popular than the man he replaced. Cooper produced first-round draft picks at Bobby Bowden-speed, but couldn't produce wins over Michigan or in bowls.

If Tressel can find a way to beat the hated interlopers to the North and win bowls with regularity, he'll enjoy a long reign as the Buckeyes coach. But if he can't beat Michigan on a regular basis, he'll get a pink slip—just like Cooper.

2001 SCHEDULE

Sept.	8	Akron
	15	San Diego State
	22	@UCLA
	29	@Indiana
Oct.	6	Northwestern
	13	Wisconsin
	27	@Penn State
Nov.	3	@Minnesota
	10	Purdue
	17	Illinois
	24	@Michigan

QUARTERBACKS

Tressel isn't taking over a down-and-out program, just one with a down-and-out veteran quarterback in senior Bellisari (6-3, 220). At times, Bellisari brings to mind a much more famous Steve (former NFL great Steve Young), with his mobility, strong left arm and the No. 8 he wears. But unlike the recently retired Young, Bellisari's aim isn't always true.

Bellisari needs to be more productive in 2001, if the Buckeyes are to challenge for the Big Ten crown. Bellsari threw for 2,319 yards last season, but completed only 52.6 percent of his tosses and had just 13 touchdown passes. And he wasn't as dangerous as expected as a runner, accounting for only 179 yards on the ground in 2000.

Still, there's no disputing that Bellisari has skills. He has the ability to hurt opposing defenses with his arm and his legs, if he's feeling 100 percent confident. It will be up to Tressel (who coaches the quarterbacks) to instill that much-needed confidence in Bellisari, so that he can win big games and be a much more consistent performer.

While the Bellisari bashers are plentiful in Columbus and throughout the state, figure on him being the opening day starter. The reason? Most coaches choose experience over youth. And Bellisari is a veteran of 22 starts and stands sixth on the school's all-time total offense list with 4,470 yards.

Still, Tressel is an advocate of developing a backup who can play—which means that sophomore **Scott McMullen** (6-3, 195) could get some snaps in the first two games to ensure that he's ready in the event of an injury.

McMullen's nickname is "The Gunslinger." The moniker seems apt because he possesses the biggest gun of OSU's four quarterbacks. But McMullen isn't seasoned and doesn't figure to be handed the keys to Tressel's offense until 2002—unless Bellisari is completely ineffective or gets hurt.

The fact that McMullen has worked his way into the mix is a tribute to him. When he was recruited out of Granville High School in 1999, most OSU backers thought that this small-town phenom was destined to be a career backup with the Buckeyes.

While McMullen is the No. 2 man right now, his spot is anything but sewn up. That's because sophomore **Craig Kenzel** (6-4, 215) was impressive in the spring game. But redshirt freshman **Rick McFadden**, a 6-7, 210-pound lefty, made more progress in the last two weeks of spring ball than the other three and appeared to be coming up on the outside.

Bellisari did enough in the spring to maintain his position at the top. But this spring revealed the other three aren't slouches, and the battle to be Bellisari's understudy should be quite interesting indeed.

RUNNING BACKS

Wells (6-2, 230), a senior, appears to have learned his lesson. Wells was suspended last year for the last half of Ohio State's spring drills and the spring game and watched Derek Combs go right past him on the depth chart. Combs remained ahead of him through the season.

Wells is expected to step in for Combs, a seventh-round draft pick of the Oakland Raiders, at tailback. He ran for 598 yards and a team-best six touchdowns last year in a backup role. He hopes to make this, his final season, a year to remember.

Sophomore **Sammy Maldonado** (6-0, 230) is the only other scholarship tailback on the roster. He showed flashes of promise last year in practice, but needs to be more consistent in order to garner more playing time.

Still, the hard-running Wells rushed for 598 yards and six scores. With Combs gone, Wells is the No. 1 tailback at Ohio State, carrying on quite a tradition. In the last 30 years, the list of Buckeye tailbacks has included Heisman Trophy winners Archie Griffin (twice) and Eddie George as well as 1984 Heisman runner-up Keith Byars, Raymont Harris, Robert Smith, Tim Spencer and Pepe Pearson.

"It's a huge responsibility; it's a huge honor," Wells told reporters in the spring. "They are big shoes to fill. We can go on and on about the tailbacks who have been through this building, been through this program. It's a big responsibility, but I'm up for the challenge."

Wells came on strong at the end of last season and with his size and speed (sub 4.5 in the 40, he should be able to handle the job full time. Wells led the comeback victory at Illinois that put the Buckeyes in position to play for a share of the Big Ten title the next week against Michigan. He started in the Outback Bowl loss to South Carolina, but after a productive first series was pretty much the forgotten man the rest of the day.

The bowl game disappointment has given Wells a fire in his belly. If that burns all season long and he can do a better job of reading blocks, Wells will be one of the Big Ten's top runners.

And with the super sophomore Maldonado closing fast at the end of spring and the arrival of the talented trio of Hall (5-10, 180), Ross (6-0, 205) and **JaJa Riley** (6-2, 188) in the fall, running the ball will not become an afterthought in the land once known for its "Three Yards and a Cloud of Dust" offense.

Wells will be the primary ball carrier, but Maldonado will get to tote the ball, too. A former Parade All-American from Harrison, N.Y., Maldonado gained 7,581 yards and scored 99 touchdowns in high school. He was one of the crown jewels in the high school class of 2000, as evidenced by the fact that he was the top-rated eastern player by *SuperPrep* that year.

Another running threat is bullish senior fullback **Jamar Martin**, whom the coaches praise every chance they get. Tressel's aim is to install Martin as a running and pass-catching threat from the single-back set along with maintaining his blocking expertise in the I. Martin, a 6-0, 245-pounder and the prototypical Ohio State fullback, is a bruising blocker and powerful runner.

WIDE RECEIVERS/TIGHT ENDS

Gone are OSU's top four receivers from last year: Ken-Yon Rambo, Reggie Germany, Chad Cacchio and Vaness Profit. Rambo is the biggest loss of the foursome, although he was a lightning rod of criticism from both the media and some of his OSU teammates after the team went 6-6 in 1999 and faded down the stretch a year ago.

Despite battling a sprained left knee, Rambo caught a team-high 53 balls in 2000, but his yards per catch (20.5 in 1999, 15.0 in 2000) and his touchdown catch numbers (six in 1999, two in 2000) both plummeted last fall. As a result, so did his draft position. Rambo was talked about as a late-second or third round pick before last spring's draft. Instead, Rambo was the 32nd receiver—and 229th overall player—taken as teams were scared off by his knee woes and cocky attitude.

Like Rambo, Germany (22 receptions in 2000) ended up being a seventh-round NFL draft pick, going to Buffalo with the 17th pick in that round.

In spite of the personnel losses, there are still plenty of pass catchers on campus. Rangy sophomore **Drew Carter** (6-4, 187) has established himself as a sure starter, while junior college transfer **Chris Vance** (6-2, 185), diminutive sophomore speedster **Ricky Bryant** (6-0, 175), redshirt freshman **John Hollins** (6-2, 185) and cornerback-turned-wideout **Bam Childress** (5-10, 175) seem locked in a duel for the other starting spot. All will play in the fall.

Childress, a redshirt freshman who started the spring playing cornerback, showed everyone he needs to touch the ball four or five times a game just for the heck of it. In Peter Warrick fashion, he possesses escapability. Keep an eye on Vance too. A highly regarded transfer from Fort Scott Community College, Vance, a junior, enrolled for the winter quarter and was able to practice in the spring. He will contribute this fall after catching 37 balls for 598 yards and 10 scores at Fort Scott (Kansas) Community College in 2000.

As for tight end, returning starter **Darnell Sanders** (6-6, 265), a junior, and **Ben Hartsock** (6-3, 255), a sophomore, left the spring in a deadlock for the starting job. Both are willing to block hard, both have the ability to stand up and run routes downfield, and both can catch the ball. Opposing defensive coordinators, beware: New OSU offensive coordinator Jim Bollman, who spent the last two years coaching tight ends for the Chicago Bears, loves using the tight end as a weapon.

Sanders was the Buckeyes' second leading receiver last year with 23 catches for 270 yards and a team-leading five touchdowns. He is an eventual NFL talent who is going to get better and better. Hartsock is a fine player in his own right. As a result, the tight end position is literally in good hands.

OFFENSIVE LINE

The starting unit of senior left tackle **Tyson Walter**, sophomore left guard **Alex Stepanovich**, senior center **LeCharles Bentley**, sophomore right guard **Shane Olivea** and sophomore right tackle **Adrien Clarke** could be better than average, which beats the heck out of the last two years.

It's Walter's return—from a one-year hiatus to fight a mysterious infection in his hip—that gives this line a chance to be special. Having started the three previous seasons, Walter (6-5, 300) stepped back in at left tackle and proved to be the most technically sound and aggressive member of the bunch in spring ball.

The 6-3, 325-pound Clarke, who started nine games last year as a redshirt freshman and was selected to *The Sporting News* Freshman All-America team, joins Walter to give the Buckeyes a pair of outstanding tackles. Both are natural left tackles, so Clarke was moved to the right side this spring. Clarke has "future pro" written all over him, if he can stay healthy the next couple years.

Bentley, the team's lineman of the year the last two seasons, had to miss most of the spring after suffering a dislocated kneecap but returned in time to play in the spring game. But Bentley is the least of Tressel's worries. The dependable Bentley (6-2, 290) has developed into one of the best centers in college football and should be in the hunt for All-America honors this year. He is already being mentioned as a possible Outland Trophy candidate.

The picture at guard is a bit more clouded. Stepanovich (6-5, 275) revealed versatility by subbing for Bentley at times at center. But Stepanovich displayed his true strength at guard, where he could pull and show his speed and glee while leading a back on a counter rip.

The real comer was Olivea (6-5, 315), who played in five games as a freshman in 2000. Regarded as one of the top line prospects in the nation two years ago, he finished strong in the spring. He jumped to the top of the chart at right guard.

Sophomore **Ivan Douglas** (6-6, 295), senior **Jim Massey** (6-5, 290), junior **Scott Kunhein** (6-4, 285) and sophomore **Bryce Bishop** (6-3, 315) are all solid reserves. Bishop, one of the most sought-after players in the country out of Miami in 1998, did not play in 1999 and was red-shirted last year. His return to form would prove to be a gigantic plus for OSU.

2000 STATISTICS

Rushing offense	161.9	41
Passing offense	208.4	64
Total offense	370.3	58
Scoring offense	29.5	40
Net Punting	36.3	28
Punt returns	12.6	21
Kickoff returns	24.6	4
Rushing defense	91.6	11
Passing efficiency defense	110.3	39
Total defense	319.4	25
Scoring defense	18.0	14
Turnover margin	+10	15

Last column is ranking among Division I-A teams.

KICKERS

Just as he did during his successful tenure at Youngstown State, Tressel will place a great deal of emphasis on special teams play at Ohio State. To that end, he has hired long-time assistant Ken Conatser as the Buckeyes' special teams coordinator.

One of Conatser's primary responsibilities this spring will be the development of redshirt freshman **Josh Huston** (6-2, 190) as the Buckeyes' place-kicker. Huston is the heir apparent to four-year starter Dan Stultz, who closed out his career as OSU's second all-time leading scorer (342) and career leader in field goals made (59). A first-team All-Big Ten kicker in 2000, Stultz was the only player in OSU history to score 90 or more points in three different seasons. Huston was a bit inconsistent in spring ball.

DEFENSIVE LINE

The graduation of defensive ends Brent Johnson and Rodney Bailey and the unexpected departure of tackle Ryan Pickett for the NFL means nose guard **Mike Collins** is the lone holdover on the defensive line. But the 6-3, 290-pound senior is a good one, good enough to be in the hunt for postseason honors in the fall. Despite being constantly double-teamed, Collins finished the 2000 season with 46 tackles, tops among OSU's defensive linemen. Sophomore **Fred Sturrup** (6-3, 295) will serve as his backup.

The return of Collins is a positive, but this is a major area of concern for the OSU coaching staff. Many draftniks questioned Pickett's decision to leave early and join what was already a defensive tackle-loaded 2001 NFL draft, but Pickett got the last laugh when he was picked 29th overall by the St. Louis Rams.

Pickett wasn't the only OSU defensive lineman lost to the NFL draft. End Rodney Bailey was a sixth-round selection of the Pittsburgh Steelers.

So who will fill the vacancies in the trenches for the Buckeyes? Either **Tim Anderson** or **David Thompson** is expected to occupy the slot held down by Pickett the last three years. Bet on the 6-3, 295-pound sophomore Anderson, who played behind Collins last season. Thompson is a 6-5, 280-pound junior who has seen only limited action to date.

A former state wrestling champ, Anderson (two sacks in 2000) possesses a never-say-die motor and excellent balance and strength, but he must learn to stay lower and use his hands better this fall. If he does that, he'll be solid in the middle.

Junior **Kenny Peterson** (6-4, 265) and sophomore **Will Smith** (6-3, 235) give the Buckeyes a pair of quality defensive ends. They combined for 12 tackles for loss and six sacks last year in a reserve role. Smith is blessed with outstanding speed and quickness and should be one of the top pass rushers in the Big Ten.

Sophomore **Darrion Scott** (6-3, 245) and senior **Tim Cheatwood** (6-4, 250) also will figure in the rotation. Scott is highly regarded. Cheatwood, who moves back to defense after a year at tight end, has excellent speed and should be right at home at rush end.

LINEBACKERS

Linebacker is an area of strength for the Buckeyes. All three starters—seniors Cooper (6-0, 225) and **Courtland Bullard** (6-3, 227) on the outside and junior **Matt Wilhelm** (6-4, 245) in the middle—return. So do the backups: sophomore **Robert Reynolds** (6-4, 225), sophomore **Fred Pagac, Jr.** (6-1, 225), sophomore **Marco Cooper** (6-2, 235) and redshirt freshman **Thomas Matthews** (6-1, 205).

The fiery Cooper, one of 20 returning lettermen on the defense, was the Buckeyes' second-leading tackler last year with 80 total stops and was voted by his teammates as the co-most inspirational player. He also was a consensus All-Big Ten pick and a third-team Associated Press All-American. A Butkus Award candidate, Cooper has a penchant for playing well in big games.

Wilhelm was moved inside at the start of the season and responded by leading the team in tackles for loss with 15. Wilhelm finished the year with an impressive 66 tackles (third best on the team) and also had three sacks. He was voted Big Ten Defensive Player of the Week after a 12-tackle performance at Illinois. Wilhelm has the size to plug the hole and the lateral speed to collar the ball carrier. He seemed to show improvement each week and was selected to a second-team berth on the coaches' All-Big Ten team. He's a star in the making.

Bullard, who will be in his third year as a starter, is a solid all-around player with stunning speed. Bullard finished with a career-best 46 tackles in 2000 and also registered 11 tackles for loss, six sacks (third-best on the team) and had his first career interception against South Carolina in the Outback Bowl. A ball hawk, Bullard also forced fumbles at Wisconsin and against Minnesota and recovered a fumble at Iowa in 2000.

Reynolds, Kentucky's Prep Player of the Year in 1999, played in all 12 games last year as a freshman and has a chance to be very good. Pagac, the son of OSU's former assistant head coach Fred Pagac (who took a job with the Oakland Raiders this off-season after Cooper's ouster), hopes to battle back from a series of injuries that have haunted him the last two years. Matthews and Cooper, a Parade and USA Today All-American from Michigan, were redshirted last year.

DEFENSIVE BACKS

Nate Clements' decision to leave school a year early turned out to be a wise one. He's now an instant millionaire. Clements was the 21st overall pick in last spring's draft by Buffalo, where he will re-team with former Buckeye teammate Antoine Winfield. Clements kept alive the recent conveyor belt of first-round cornerbacks taken from Ohio State, going back to Shawn Springs in the 1997 draft and continuing with Winfield in 1999 and with Ahmed Plummer in 2000.

Clements' defection hurts, but NFL scouts figure to be sniffing around OSU's campus again this fall and winter to check out junior All-America candidate **Mike Doss**. The hard-hitting Doss (5-11, 197) led the Buckeyes in tackles last year with 90, including 16 in the season finale against Michigan. He also had 13 tackles for loss, three interceptions and three fumble recoveries, returning two of the latter for touchdowns. Doss won first-team All-Big Ten honors last year as a sophomore and was chosen to *The Sporting News* All-America team. He will be a serious Thorpe Award candidate this year.

Free safety **Donnie Nickey** returns for his third year as a starter. The 6-3, 205-pound junior was in on 64 tackles last year and has been a solid player throughout his career. One of the Buckeyes' most experienced defenders with 24 games and 22 starts behind him, Nickey started at strong safety as a redshirt freshman in 1999, but moved to free safety last year.

He's an intelligent player who makes the defensive calls in the secondary and had a season-high nine tackles three times (Wisconsin, Minnesota and Michigan State) in 2000. Suffice to say OSU will have one of the nation's best sets of safeties in 2001.

Junior **Derek Ross** (6-1, 197) and sophomore **Richard McNutt** (5-10, 178) appear to have the inside track at the two corner spots. Ross was the Buckeyes' nickel back last season and had his best year with 37 tackles and two interceptions. Ross is a superb athlete, but he must take care of business in the classroom to Tressel's satisfaction to get the starting job.

McNutt backed up Clements last year and is regarded as a good cover corner. He will battle with converted wide receiver **Maurice Lee** (5-9, 170), a sophomore, for the starting nod.

Additionally, sophomore **Will Allen** (6-2, 175), sophomore **B.J. Barre** (6-1, 185), redshirt freshman **Bobby Britton** (5-11, 175), sophomore **Curtis Crosby** (5-11, 195) and redshirt freshman **Harlen Jacobs** (6-2, 175) are waiting in the wings for the opportunity to show what they can do. All are young players who came to OSU with bulging high school scrapbooks. Any of them could challenge for playing time this fall.

PUNTERS

Sophomore **B.J. Sander** (6-3, 210) returns to handle the punting chores. He averaged 41.9 yards per kick last season. Tressel, who stresses special teams play, is happy to have one of the Big Ten's best punters on his team. Tressel wants Sander to get his punts off more quickly though. He thinks that Sander takes too many steps before booting the ball and as a result, Tressel frets about getting punts blocked.

If Sander doesn't speed up his act, then Tressel might give walk-on **Andy Groom** (6-1, 180) a look-see in August.

SPECIAL TEAMS

Make no mistake, Tressel places a huge emphasis on special teams.

"Special teams win championships," Tressel said. "It is an area that will be a difference maker."

The Buckeyes should have the personnel to be solid here.

As one might expect. Ohio State's roster is loaded with speedballs who can return punts and kicks. Childress, the fifth Ohio Mr. Football to attend OSU (the others being Robert Smith, Bobby Hoying, Andy Katzenmoyer and Derek Combs), is one suspect. He has sprinter speed and knack for making guys miss. Lee, a former wide receiver, is another distinct possibility.

RECRUITING CLASS

Despite Tressel's late hiring, Ohio State somehow put together a class that *Midwest Football Recruiting News* publisher Bill Kurelic said was the third best in the Big Ten behind Michigan and Penn State. Among the 17 signees were four prep All-Americans—Hall, Ross, Chattams and Fox.

The Buckeyes welcome two of the nation's top running backs, Hall and Ross, into the fold. Add running back Riley of San Diego and Ohio State has one of its more impressive recruiting hauls ever at one position.

"I think that speaks to the tradition of being a running back at Ohio State," Tressel said. "When they walk in and see those Heisman Trophies ... and see those big pictures up on the wall, and I think the other thing it speaks to is those are two top-notch students who recognize a good school and they know that's important to us. And it's important to them, or they wouldn't be getting 4.0s or 3.5s [grade-point averages]—you don't do that by accident.

"And I have to point out that [running backs coach] Tim Spencer is a factor. He's a quality guy. They can make an immediate bond with him as they sit and speak with him. You put all those things together and I'm not surprised that we've got three good ones."

Riley committed in December and never wavered. Hall and Ross waited until the final day, fighting off offers from Florida State (Hall) and Florida and Notre Dame (Ross). Ross rushed for 2,676 yards and 28 touchdowns for Gaither (Fla.) High last fall. In picking up Hall, Ross, Fox and Dayton Ohio's Chaminade-Julienne High School receiver Angelo Chattams in the last three days, "the finish was extremely impressive, spectacular," Kurelic said.

The only blemishes were signing only one defensive back (Fox) and losing offensive lineman Alphonso Townsend of Fork Union (Va.)

Military Academy. Townsend, of Lima, Ohio, had been a member of the OSU class of 2000 before opting to go to Fork Union to improve his academics. He had committed again to the Buckeyes, then opted to sign with Michigan State after Cooper's ouster.

BLUE RIBBON ANALYSIS

OFFENSE	B
SPECIAL TEAMS	C+
DEFENSE	B-
INTANGIBLES	B

Geiger rolled the dice in choosing former Youngstown State coach Jim Tressel. And he knows it.

Geiger hired a man who has proven that he can beat the Hofstras and Delawares of the Division I-AA world, but a guy who has never coached a game of Division I-A football. Hiring Tressel over Minnesota coach Glen Mason sets up an interesting matchup between the two when Ohio State plays at Minnesota on Nov. 3. Both men were assistants under Earle Bruce at Ohio State from 1983-85, after which Tressel left to become the head coach at Youngstown State and Mason was hired as the head man at Kent State.

Both men have outstanding football minds. Tressel has been the Bear Bryant of the I-AA ranks for the last 15 years, winning four national titles and 70 percent of his games. Mason has resurrected the programs at Kent State, Kansas and now Minnesota (which whipped Ohio State last year).

Did OSU make the right choice? We'll see. Xs and Os won't be Tressel's problem, but recruiting on a national scale might be. Because the school is in a populous, football-crazy state, the Buckeyes have a great recruiting advantage. But Tressel will have to be able to go outside the state to get speed merchants, like Cooper and his staff were able to do.

This year, Tressel faces a rugged schedule, but has the talent to push for third or fourth in the Big Ten, behind Northwestern and Michigan. We'll call it a middle-of-the-pack finish, which still means a bowl berth.

(B.D.)

2000 RESULTS

Fresno State	W	43-10	1-0
Arizona	W	27-17	2-0
Miami (Ohio)	W	27-16	3-0
Penn State	W	45-6	4-0
Wisconsin	W	23-7	5-0
Minnesota	L	17-29	5-1
Iowa	W	38-10	6-1
Purdue	L	27-31	6-2
Michigan State	W	27-13	6-3
Illinois	W	24-21	7-3
Michigan	L	26-38	7-4
South Carolina (Outback)	L	7-24	7-5

Penn State

LOCATION	**University Park, PA**
CONFERENCE	**Big Ten**
LAST SEASON	**5-7 (.417)**
CONFERENCE RECORD	**4-4 (t-5th)**
OFFENSIVE STARTERS RETURNING	**4**
DEFENSIVE STARTERS RETURNING	**6**
NICKNAME	**Nittany Lions**
COLORS	**Blue & White**
HOME FIELD	**Beaver Stadium (103,500)**
HEAD COACH	**Joe Paterno (Brown '50)**
RECORD AT SCHOOL	**322-90-3 (35 years)**
CAREER RECORD	**322-90-3 (35 years)**
ASSISTANTS	**Tom Bradley (Penn State '79)** **Defensive Coordinator** **Fran Ganter (Penn State '79)** **Offensive Coordinator** **Ron Vanderlinden (Albion '78)** **Linebackers** **Kenny Carter (The Citadel '90)** **Wide Receivers** **Bill Kenney (Norwich '82)** **Tight Ends** **Dick Anderson (Penn State '63)** **Offensive Line** **Larry Johnson (Elizabeth City State '73)** **Defensive Line** **Jay Paterno (Penn State '90)** **Quarterbacks**
TEAM WINS (last 5 yrs.)	**11-9-9-10-5**
FINAL RANK (last 5 yrs.)	**7-13-11-8-44**
2000 FINISH	**Beat Michigan State in regular-season finale.**

COACH AND PROGRAM

The 2000 season was largely a disappointment for the Nittany Lions, whose 5-7 finish left them in the unaccustomed role of being home for the holidays.

That sub-.500 record was hard for anyone who knows about college football to believe. And it was especially hard for folks in the Keystone State to swallow, whether they were from Altoona or Allentown. The reason? Penn State football has a tradition of winning. Over the last 50 years, the Nittany Lions have won 75.2 percent of their games, tops in Division I-A football over that stretch. The one constant in those 50 years of success is the man in the Coke-bottle classes and flood pants, legendary 74-year-old coach Joe Paterno.

During his 35 years as Penn State's top man, Paterno has a gaudy 322-90-3 record. But, in his last 16 games, Paterno is just 6-10. Unfortunately, Joe Geritol's losing ways continued this off-season.

First, PSU's recruiting coordinator Al Golden left Happy Valley in the middle of recruiting season to run Al Groh's defense at the University of Virginia. Then, two players who had given commitments to the Nittany Lions—Aliquippa (Pa.) all-state defensive back Bernard "Josh" Lay and Kiski Prep running back Elley Moore—backed out.

But the most crushing blow came just before signing day when the nation's top-rated high school senior running back, Kevin Jones of Cardinal O'Hara (Pa.), announced early that he would attend Virginia Tech (where he's been offered Michael Vick's old No. 7) rather than the play for the Nittany Lions.

The 6-1, 208-pound Jones was the leading rusher in Philadelphia Catholic League history (5,728 yards) and was the No. 1 priority on PSU's recruiting board. After the loss of Jones, Paterno had to endure one more loss, when key recruiter Kenny Jackson left the nest to be the receivers coach of the Pittsburgh Steelers.

Jackson had been a secret weapon against Big Ten schools who recruited negatively against Paterno, citing his age and the fact that there aren't many recreational outlets for African-American kids in the middle-of-nowhere State College, Pa. Jackson could look recruits in the eye and say that African-Americans could thrive and survive at Penn State, because he had done it himself.

So, for the first time in several years, Paterno went outside the system to bring in secondary coach Brian Norwood (from Texas Tech), wide receivers coach Kenny Carter (Pittsburgh) and linebacker coach Ron Vanderlinden (Maryland). The trio replaces Golden (to Virginia), Jackson (Pittsburgh Steelers) and Bob White (Penn State administration).

"I think it's been invigorating," Paterno said of the coaching changes. "It's been interesting. There's a lot of ways to skin a cat. I think that they've brought some ideas. I think it's been good. It's been interesting for me because I've sat back and learned some things."

Paterno said bringing in coaches with no Penn State background wasn't by design. He targeted a couple former players, but they had never coached the positions he needed to fill. Vanderlinden, fired as Maryland's head coach after last season, was the only one of the three Paterno had any prior knowledge about. Paterno had coached against Vanderlinden when he was a defensive coordinator at Northwestern. Carter and Norwood were "highly recommended" minority coaches who fit Paterno's needs.

"I wanted to hire two minority coaches," Paterno said. "I feel that when your squad has as many minority kids as we have, particularly African-American kids, you should have some people there to represent their culture and their background and those things."

While the hiring of Carter and Norwood should help Paterno on the recruiting trail with African-American players (including those who might have been scared off by a student protest before the 2001 Blue-White spring game to point our the racism problem on PSU's main campus), the other question lingers: Is the end of the line near for JoePa? Now, entering his 36th year at Penn State, Paterno is getting up in years—a fact that is used against him on the recruiting trail. Many are suggesting that he'll coach another year or two before handing over the keys to long-time assistant Fran Ganter.

But that's in the future. Paterno will begin this season with 322 career wins, one behind Bear Bryant's all-time D-I wins record. But Florida State's Bobby Bowden (315 wins) is just seven wins behind Paterno in the Bear hunt. Getting to the top spot won't be a formality—Penn State opens with national title contender Miami at newly renovated Beaver Stadium (the House that Paterno built now seats 103,500), then plays at Virginia before a steady diet of Big Ten foes and a Nov. 3 homecoming game against Southern Miss. The Nits must tackle this tough schedule with only 10 returning starters (four on offense, six on defense).

Paterno will be breaking in a new quarterback and must re-tool the offensive line and secondary. However, his defensive line should be one of the best in college football and he has a nice stable of running backs. So the pieces are in place for Paterno to play the defense-first, special teams-second, offense-third approach that has served him so well over the years.

Can it work again? Or will the losses continue to mount for a guy who will become college football's all-time winner sometime this fall?

We'll see.

2001 SCHEDULE

Sept.	1	Miami
	13	@Virginia
	22	Wisconsin
	29	@Iowa
Oct.	6	Michigan
	20	@Northwestern
	27	Ohio State
Nov.	3	Southern Miss
	10	@Illinois

17 Indiana
24 @Michigan State

QUARTERBACKS

Redshirt junior **Matt Senneca** (6-3, 226) isn't blessed with the strongest arm in the nation and doesn't have the foot speed or elusiveness of his predecessor, Rashard Casey. He's also rather inexperienced. But Senneca, scheduled to succeed Casey as quarterback this fall, is far and away the best option Penn State has.

"The best part of my game is my leadership qualities," Senneca said. "When I'm in the huddle, it's my huddle, and no one is going to do anything about that. The other thing is, I'll stand in there and try and get the ball downfield. Those are the two things I do best."

So, don't expect Senneca to improvise like Casey. And don't expect the shotgun formation too much either. Senneca is someone in whom Paterno believes he can entrust his offense. Senneca has been in the system for four years, learning at the knees of Kevin Thompson and Casey. He's been the loyal soldier, taking his playing time in bits and pieces, watching Casey's eligibility clock wind down. He might be the prototypical Penn State quarterback.

"I think I'm the more traditional quote-unquote Penn State quarterback," Senneca said. "Coach Paterno always says don't move around in the pocket if you don't have to. If it's his choice, he wants you to stay in the pocket and throw the ball."

Senneca appeared in every game in 2000, completing 20-of-46 passes for 200 yards, one touchdown and one interception. Nonetheless, becoming the starting quarterback presents another step in the learning process for Senneca.

"There's a lot more responsibility," Senneca said. "Everyone has their eyes on you on and off the team. You're the guy everyone looks up to when it's crunch time in the big game. They're counting on you. So yeah, there's a lot more responsibility, and I'm ready for that."

Two things are certain at this position, though. First, at least this year there shouldn't be a quarterback controversy at Penn State. And second, Senneca must stay healthy or the Nittany Lions are doomed, because both of his backups are as raw as sushi.

So while Senneca is a clear No. 1, can unproven redshirt freshman **Zack Mills** handle being No. 2? Back in the fall of 2000, a pair of freshmen (Zac Wasserman and Zack Mills) arrived at State College with impressive high school resumes. Wasserman was part of the deep California quarterback crop in the high school class of 2000, a group which includes Tennessee star quarterback Casey Clausen, Florida State quarterback Chris Rix and current USC backup Matt Cassel. The left-handed Mills came from Ijamsville, Md. Both were redshirted last year before being unveiled this spring. Mills was much more impressive than Wasserman in the annual Blue-White spring game.

By early May, Wasserman could read the writing on the wall and asked Paterno for a release from his scholarship. According to published reports, Wasserman was looking to transfer somewhere closer to his family's Tarzana, Calif. home. The reason? Zac's mother Candace recently was diagnosed with cancer.

Wasserman's decision to leave after the completion of the spring 2001 semester leaves Paterno a little thin at the quarterback spot. When the season begins this fall, Penn State will only have three quarterbacks on scholarship: Senneca, Mills and incoming freshman **Michael Robinson** (6-3, 210).

This summer, Paterno and his staff will be forced to work double-time to get Robinson up to speed at quarterback. A Richmond, Va. product whom Virginia Tech coach Frank Beamer coveted as a possible heir to Michael Vick, Robinson chose Penn State instead. Like Vick, Robinson is a 21st century quarterback, a guy capable of causing fits for defenders both with his arm and his feet. Still, given how uncomfortable Paterno seemed with the scrambling ways of Casey, the smart money was on Robinson playing strong safety at Penn State. But with Wasserman gone and Chris Ganter, the son of PSU assistant head coach Fran Ganter, not in school until January of 2002, Paterno has no choice but to play Robinson at quarterback—at least for his first year.

RUNNING BACKS

Blue-collar fullback Mike Cerimele is gone, signing as a free agent with the Redskins hours after the 2001 NFL draft ended. A three-year starter at fullback, Cerimele was used primarily as a blocking back in 2000. He rushed for 47 yards on 22 carries and had nine catches for 61 yards.

Even with the tough-as-nails lead blocker Cerimele no longer on campus and with all-everything Pennsylvania prep star Kevin Jones choosing Virginia Tech over Penn State, Paterno has a nice stable of runners in 2001. In fact, next to the defensive line, the deepest position on the team next fall might be running back. The question is whether top returning rusher **Eric McCoo** (5-10, 209) will be part of that mix.

McCoo, a senior who rushed for 692 yards last season in Paterno's tailback-by-committee offense, sat out most of the spring to concentrate on his academics. Paterno did not rule out the possibility that McCoo will redshirt next season, depending on his academic situation. But if he can win his personal battle with the books, McCoo, owner of 2,253 career rushing yards at Penn State (10th best on PSU's all-time rushing list), would give the Nittany Lions another much-needed playmaker on offense.

If McCoo is unable to get his academic house in order, then junior **Larry Johnson** (6-2, 214) and senior **Omar Easy** (6-1, 245) will get the majority of the carries. During spring practice, Johnson was a changed man, letting his actions and not his mouth do the talking for him. Johnson, who criticized the coaching staff's predictable offensive calls and the quality of the Lions' offensive line play after a 24-6 loss to Toledo last season, emerged as a force this spring.

Johnson, the new No. 1 tailback, completed his strong spring with 56 yards on 13 carries and a touchdown in the annual spring scrimmage. Johnson, second to McCoo in rushing with 529 yards last season, added 10 pounds of muscle during the off-season and should be a much more determined runner.

"I added weight and really didn't lose any of my speed," said Johnson, who runs a 4.45 40-yard dash. "I'm more patient now. I know where I'm running the ball."

Like Johnson, Easy (463 yards in 2000) looked like a more confident performer this spring. A former Jamaican soccer star, Easy has a huge upside. He's got a well-chiseled NFL body (6-1, 245), but has only been playing organized football since his junior year at Everett (Mass.) High School. Now, Easy just needs to do it on fall Saturdays for the Nittany Lions to improve their anemic ground game (10th in the Big Ten in 2000).

"Johnson and Easy had good springs," Paterno said. "They run hard. They've done things very well. They're blocking well. They're catching the ball well. Both of those kids are very good. So is **Ricky Upton** (6-0, 238); he's had the best spring since he's been here. Overall, the running back situation should be very, very good."

If the veteran McCoo doesn't play, Upton, a sophomore, appears poised to get some carries in 2001. Upton has more home run hitting ability than either McCoo or Easy, but isn't as polished a between-the-tackles runner as those two. But, Upton flashed his skills in mop-up duty last fall (11 carries, 66 yards, one touchdown) and again in the spring game (41 yards). Upton must stay out of trouble, though. He was arrested for disorderly conduct March 24 after Penn State's loss the day before to Temple in the NCAA men's basketball regional semifinals.

At fullback, three different players—**R.J. Luke**, **Paul Jefferson** and **Mick Blosser**—will replace Cerimele. The senior Blosser (6-0, 237), a former walk-on, and the jumbo-sized Jefferson (6-1, 267), both saw limited duty as backups to Cerimele in 2000. Blosser had three carries for 16 yards, while Jefferson, a sophomore, got 13 carries for 28 yards and one touchdown last fall. The junior Luke (6-3, 236) is back after redshirting last season to rehab a knee injury. All three guys in the fullback rotation bring something slightly different to the table.

"Right now, if we had to play tomorrow, Blosser would probably start," Paterno said. "Jefferson is a strong kid, Luke is a great receiver and Blosser is probably the best, all-around. He's the most consistent although he's not the athlete the others are. But they are all solid fullbacks."

WIDE RECEIVERS/TIGHT ENDS

Penn State will have to replace highly productive tight end Tony Stewart, an Allentown native who was drafted by the Philadelphia Eagles, the team he cheered for as a kid. The 147th overall pick in last April's NFL draft, the 6-5, 260-pound Stewart caught 38 balls for 451 yards and two scores in 2000 and earned second-team All-Big Ten honors.

Suffice to say Stewart will be missed. Also gone is Kenny Watson, a free agent signee of the Washington Redskins. Shifted between wideout, tailback, punt returner and kick returner, Watson never really established himself at any position during his five injury-riddled years at Penn State.

At tight end, the primary guy will be **John Gilmore** (6-4, 265), who will be out to prove that he's a tight end who can catch as well as block. The senior from Reading shared the starting role with Stewart last season. Gilmore caught three balls for 37 yards and a touchdown in the spring game.

"I feel I catch the ball as well as any tight end in the nation," Gilmore said this spring. "I'm proud of my blocking, but I want to get rid of that blocking label. I want to be known as an all-purpose tight end."

As good as he is, Gilmore is probably just keeping the tight end spot warm this season for superb sophomore **Sean McHugh** (6-5, 257), who caught two balls as a freshman in 2000, or highly touted freshman **Andrew Richardson** (6-5, 245), from the same Pittsburgh high school as recent PSU great LaVar Arrington.

Gilmore and his fellow receivers must avoid the drops that plagued the team last year. This spring, if a receiver dropped a pass, they had to sprint back to the huddle and do pushups before the next play was called. That tactic, and others that new receivers coach Kenny Carter brought with him from Pitt, seemed to work wonders on junior **Bryant Johnson** (6-2, 203), who made five catches for 103 yards and one score in the Blue-White game. Widely criticized for dropping passes last season, Johnson looks poised to become the finest PSU receiver since Bobby Engram the next two years. Johnson (four catches, 85 yards in 2000) is blessed with NFL size and speed.

Johnson's maturation resulted in him earning Penn State's Red Worrell Award, given each year to the offensive player who displays the most improvement, exemplary conduct and attitude during spring drills.

Incumbent starter **Eddie Drummond** (5-9, 192) did not practice this spring because of academic problems. If he does the work in the classroom, Drummond, a senior, should be the starting split end. He caught 35 passes for 652 yards and five touchdowns in 1999 and seemed to be poised for an All-Big Ten season in 2000.

Instead, like many aspects of Penn State's 2000 football season, Drummond's problems began from the get-go—he sprained his right knee on the first play of the opening game against USC and didn't play the next two games. He returned for the Pittsburgh game unsure of the status of the injury, but proceeded to grab a career-high eight catches for 54 yards, the most receptions for a Penn State receiver since Joe Jurevicius made eight against Michigan State in 1996.

Still, the knee injury nagged him the entire season and Drummond never became the offensive game breaker many coaches and fans hoped he would. One of the squad's most athletically gifted athletes (4.35 in the 40 speed), Drummond is once again healthy and hungry to increase his output after catching just 29 balls for 365 yards and no touchdowns last year.

If Drummond is unable to go, then Paterno might employ a Johnson & Johnson approach at receiver. That's because sophomore **Tony Johnson**, the son of PSU assistant coach Larry Johnson and the kid brother of Penn State tailback Larry Johnson, made huge strides this off-season. Tony Johnson (5-11, 198) caught 14 balls for 204 yards (14.6 average) and one touchdown last season, but was much more self-assured this spring and will push Drummond for the No. 1 split end spot.

"They're older," Paterno said of the receivers. "Tony Johnson was a legitimate freshman last year, and it was a new position for him. He was a high school running back. Bryant Johnson had to grow up a little bit. He goofed around a little bit academically. He and I had a problem last season and that problem probably affected the way he played. He's more mature. He has more confidence in himself. Those two guys will do a great job."

Besides the two Johnsons (no relation) and Drummond, Paterno might have another viable option in senior **Rod Perry**, a USC transfer who caught two balls for the Nittany Lions last season. The 5-10, 185-pound Perry can also make an impact as a punt returner (14 returns for 65 yards in 2000). How good an athlete is Perry? He also plays centerfield for the Penn State baseball team. But word around State College is that Perry might quit football to concentrate full-time on baseball.

He isn't a threat to displace Maurice Greene on the U.S. 4 x 100 relay team, but sophomore wideout **Matt Kranchick** (6-6, 224) is a tall, possession receiver who can help the Nits in three wide receiver sets. He reminds some of a Wal-Mart version of former PSU star Joe Jurevicius. This spring, Kranchick showed that in addition to possessing a Jurevicius-like build that he has also had the ability to throw a solid block and get some vital yards after the catch.

The emergence of the two Johnsons and Kranchick as well as the heavy graduation in the secondary have allowed Paterno to move senior **Sam Crenshaw** (6-2, 215), who missed most of last season with a shoulder injury, from wide receiver to safety.

OFFENSIVE LINE

This was a trouble spot last year. Paterno and his staff will spend lots of time and effort tinkering with the line between now and the time Miami visits Happy Valley on Sept. 1. Injuries and inconsistency hurt this unit that struggled in 2000. Penn State ranked tenth in the Big Ten in rushing offense and surrendered 34 sacks, which looks even worse considering an athlete as gifted as Rashard Casey was playing quarterback. From that unit, both starting tackles Kareem McKenzie and Imani Bell must be replaced. Of the duo, McKenzie, a third round draft choice of the New York Jets, is the much bigger loss.

A three-year starter, the 6-7, 314-pound McKenzie was selected second team All-Big Ten in 2000, becoming just the fifth Nittany Lion to earn All-Big Ten honors three times. McKenzie also played in the Senior Bowl.

With three big holes on the offensive line left by the graduation of McKenzie, Bell and guard Jordan Caruso, senior **Gus Felder**, one of Penn State's biggest players (6-5, 317), is one guy who can step in and fill those oversized shoes. Felder will be asked to be a leader on this season's offensive line and after starting the last five games of the 2000 season, he has the experience to respond to the challenge. Felder, who played his prep ball at the same powerful Berwick (Pa.) High School where Ron Powlus was a schoolboy legend, will move from guard to left tackle.

Fifth-year senior **Joe Hartings** will man the left guard spot, making that the much stronger of the two sides of Penn State's line. Hartings made a comeback to the Lions' program last season after enduring an off year because of back surgery in 1999. Because of hard work, dedication and perseverance, Hartings' comeback was a success. He started six games at left guard. He proved to be an effective blocker and honed his leadership skills, which will prove handy this season with several fresh faces on the line. Hartings hits the books as hard as the blocking sleds as he holds a 3.40 grade-point average.

Junior **Matt Schmitt** (6-4, 290) has moved from center to tackle and figures to hold down a starting job there. Junior **Tyler Lenda** converted to guard last season and actually earned two starts at left guard after coming to Penn State as a tight end. He'll be an opening day starter at right guard. One reason for concern is that Hartings (6-4, 265) and Lenda (6-3, 278) lack the gigantic size of the typical Big 10 lineman.

If Lenda can't hold down the job, then fifth-year senior **Greg Ransom** could start at guard. The 6-2, 300-pound Ransom was redshirted last year by Paterno, who cited Ransom's struggles in the classroom as the reason he was held out. Ransom was slowed by a foot sprain in spring ball, but he has seven career starts.

Sophomore right tackle **Chris McKelvy** along with redshirt freshmen **Nick Marmo** (6-5, 287), a left tackle, and **Scott Davis** (6-2, 282), a guard, should provide quality depth up and down the line. McKelvy in particular bears watching. The 6-4, 300-pound McKelvy was viewed as one of the nation's Grade-A offensive linemen when he was at North Penn High in suburban Philadelphia.

2000 STATISTICS

Rushing offense	142.2	62
Passing offense	183.4	84
Total offense	325.7	86
Scoring offense	22.0	80
Net Punting	34.4	61
Punt returns	4.5	112
Kickoff returns	21.3	31
Rushing defense	155.6	63
Passing efficiency defense	117.2	51
Total defense	363.8	56
Scoring defense	24.4	53
Turnover margin	+4	43

Last column is ranking among Division I-A teams..

KICKERS

Accurate kicker Ryan Primanti is gone, so sophomore **David Kimball** (6-2, 188) will take over. He's a big-time prospect from State College (Pa.) High. Kimball made a 54-yard field goal in high school and was rated the No. 1 place-kicker in the high school class of 2000 by *SuperPrep*.

Kimball was slowed this spring by a sore knee, but should be ready by the opener against Miami.

DEFENSIVE LINE

With nine new starters, Penn State finished in the middle of the Big Ten rankings in almost every defensive statistical category last season. But the defensive line is the one area where PSU defensive coordinator Tom Bradley is comfortable. Quite comfortable, in fact. Three starters return, as well as experienced reserve **Michael Haynes** (6-3, 263) to take Justin Kurpeikis' place at left defensive end.

"I'm pretty confident with the guys we have up front. It's the same core of guys, except for Justin," said Bradley. "We have a lot of experience up front. Haynes will have to assume that role of playmaker now that Justin is gone."

Kurpeikis will be missed, though. A two-year starter as an undersized defensive end for the Lions, Kurpeikis led the Lions in tackles for loss (18 for 70 yards), tied for the team lead in sacks (six) and finished second in tackles last season with 76. What he lacked in size, Kurpeikis (18 career sacks) made up for with his non-stop motor.

The leadership mantle will be passed to mammoth and gifted junior defensive tackle **Jimmy Kennedy** (6-5, 320). Kennedy, who had to slim down from 420 pounds when he arrived at Penn State in 1998, racked up six sacks and 42 tackles last season, including nine tackles for losses. While he believes he improved last fall, Kennedy wants to be more of a force this season—his third as the Lions' starting defensive tackle.

"I've got to become more of a dominant player overall," Kennedy said. "I have to assume that role that Justin (Kurpeikis) had. Just dominate a game."

His unbelievable nimbleness for a man his size could result in Kennedy being a first-round NFL draft pick. He'll have lots of experienced hands to work alongside. Starting tackle **Anthony Adams** (6-0, 292), a tough-to-block junior, is back. So are defensive ends **Bob Jones** (6-5, 256) and the aforementioned Haynes, who split time starting opposite Kurpeikis last season. Said Adams: "We're really going to get after the quarterback this year."

Adams is an interesting case study. He's the team comedian, doing everything in his power to keep the team loose. But, he's also one of the team leaders, because his teammates respect Adams' never-say-die attitude which was borne on the drug-infested streets of East Detroit. Adams is always in attack mode, even though he is often double-teamed. It's possible that Adams and Kennedy could blossom into the best tandem of PSU defensive tackles since Bruce Clark and Matt Millen way back in 1978.

Last season, Jones, a senior, stepped in at left

defensive end to fill the hole left by the departure of top NFL pick Courtney Brown and did a formidable job. He notched 30 tackles, 22 of those solo, and tied James Boyd for the team lead with two fumble recoveries. Jones then trained this winter in his own way, by participating in another sport. He was the captain of the wrestling squad and was chosen an honorable mention All-American.

The son of retired military parents, Haynes, a junior, grew up in a structured atmosphere where academics and adaptability were stressed. He played fullback during his redshirt season, but before the 1999 season was shifted to defensive end, where he has emerged as a starter. He has the quickness (4.75 in the 40) to be an outstanding off-the-edge pass rusher, especially with Kennedy and Adams occupying multiple blockers inside.

Adams will be backed up by junior tackle **Tim Falls** (6-3, 270), who was slowed by a minor knee sprain in spring ball, and redshirt freshman **Jason Robinson** (6-3, 263).

When Kennedy needs a blow, either redshirt junior **Tyler Valoczki** (6-4, 281) or redshirt freshman **Erik Noll** will enter the game. Noll entered Penn State with a thick high school scrapbook. Noll (6-5, 290) was Maryland's Gatorade Player of the Year at Watkins Mill High School in Gaithersburg.

Behind Jones at left end will be sophomore **Sam Ruhe** (6-5, 250), who intercepted a pass in the spring game. Ruhe was a former Ohio Division II Defensive Player of the Year in high school.

Ruhe is just one of many young linemen worth tracking. That's because a pair of redshirt freshmen **John Bronson** (6-3, 261), the biggest single surprise in PSU's spring camp, and **Jeremiah Davis** (6-4, 251) will back up Haynes at right end.

The wild card in the defensive front is junior **T.J. Gohlston** (6-3, 280), who could see significant time at end and tackle, if he can keep his grades in order. Add in this year's newest defensive line gem, true freshmen **Charles Rush** (6-3, 280) from Erie (Pa.) Cathedral Prep, in August and the Nittany Lions have an embarrassment of riches here. Rush, a Parade All-American, was the Pennsylvania Big School Player of the Year and chose Penn State over Michigan, Notre Dame, Miami and UCLA.

LINEBACKERS

One year after "Linebacker U" fielded one of its best threesomes in the school's storied history in LaVar Arrington (the No.2 overall pick in the 2000 NFL draft), Brandon Short (a Butkus Award finalist) and the rock-steady Mac Morrison, the Nits were a little soft in the middle last season. That was particularly true against the run.

"We didn't get the play out of our linebackers we wanted to last season," PSU defensive coordinator Tom Bradley said. "We're trying to get them to play better in a lot of different areas. We're looking for our linebackers to make more plays, to come up with bigger plays. We need them to control the line of scrimmage better than they did last season."

From last year's group, outside backers Eric Sturdifen and Aaron Gatten are gone. That's no big deal, though Gatten came on down the stretch last year. Senior **Shamar Finney** (6-2, 237) will be the anchor in the middle. Finney, Penn State's undisputed king of colorful gameday suits, was the only Lions linebacker to start every game last season. He also made his presence felt throughout the rest of the year, starting all 12 games—the first six at outside linebacker and the final six on the inside—and leading the team in interceptions with three. Those interceptions included a 49-yard return against Illinois for Finney's first collegiate score, and his 55 tackles placed him fourth on the team in 2000.

With senior **Ron Graham**'s status in limbo (academic woes) and redshirt freshman **Tim Johnson** (6-3, 226) limited by nagging injuries this past spring, Finney emerged as the leader of the defense. He knows that he'll be asked to continue to lead and he relishes the opportunity.

"Oh definitely, I'm willing to take that role," said Finney, who expects to play inside linebacker again. "Basically, they wouldn't even have to ask me. I know that's my role this year."

A former *Parade* and *USA Today* high school All-American, Finney said this spring that he's as healthy as he's been since he came to Penn State. He didn't miss a practice this spring, a valued experience for a player slowed by a chronic hamstring pull the last three years.

"If he wants to be a dominating linebacker, he has to stay healthy," Paterno said this spring. "He certainly could be one of the better athletes we have and is the kind of kid you want to play. He's gonna be a good leader. He's just got to stay healthy."

Further muddling the linebacking situation this spring was the fact that the 6-2, 255-pound Graham did not practice because Paterno ordered him to concentrate on his studies. If Toles can't go and Graham doesn't make the grade, then Bradley is prepared to throw sophomores **Gino Capone** (6-1, 236) and **Derek Wake** (6-3, 233) into the fray. Of the two, Wake has the God-given ability to be an All-American linebacker before he's through at State College.

Bet on Graham making the grade after getting a loud and clear message from Paterno. But the books aren't the only battle facing Graham (29 tackles, two interceptions in 2000), who must keep his weight under 250 pounds to be an effective player. During his career, Graham has often ballooned up to 265 pounds.

Sam Ruhe (see defensive line section) could also figure in the mix as a tall, pass-rushing outside linebacker.

DEFENSIVE BACKS

Along with quarterback and offensive line, the secondary is a huge area of concern for the Nittany Lions, because cornerback Bhawoh Jue, free safety James Boyd and cornerback Titcus Pettigrew are gone. In addition, senior safety **Shawn Mayer** (6-0, 205), whose left anterior cruciate ligament was torn last summer, took part in only non-contact drills in the spring because his knee had been slow to heal. Fifth-year senior **Sam Crenshaw**, who played receiver during his first four seasons, has been moved to safety. And sophomores **Horace Dodd** (6-1, 213) and **Deryck Toles** (6-0, 208), who both played outside linebacker last season, have been moved to safety.

The loss of Jue, an honorable-mention All-Big Ten pick in 2000, on the corner is a huge one. A two-year starter, Jue was tied for the team lead with three interceptions. The former Chantilly (Va.) High standout made 43 tackles (33 solo) and lead the team with 13 pass breakups. The 71st overall selection in April's NFL draft, Jue joins former Nittany Lion guard Marco Rivera with the Packers.

A late third-round pick of the Jacksonville Jaguars, Boyd won't be an easy man to replace either. A semifinalist for the Jim Thorpe Award, presented to the nation's top defensive back, Boyd was selected a third team All-American by *The Sporting News* and first team All-Big Ten by the league coaches last year. A co-captain, Boyd recorded the most tackles ever by a Penn State defensive back with a team-high 109 last season.

With Jue gone, senior left corner **Bruce Branch** (5-11, 190) and junior right cornerback **Bryan Scott** (6-2, 215) have secured the starting jobs, but there is little depth behind them. Scott looks like he has the tools to be a future, although he was slowed by a sprained knee this spring. The question is: Are Branch and especially Scott fast enough to play lots of man-to-man coverage? The Lions also are thin at cornerback because of injuries to freshmen Adam Taliaferro and Gerald Smith.

Taliaferro's career ended Sept. 23 when his spinal cord was injured against Ohio State. Miraculously, Taliaferro is able to walk and has returned to classes at State College, but his career is over. Smith was forced to move from cornerback to wide receiver because of a neck injury sustained in the Louisiana Tech game last season. This year, Smith returns to corner and will fight aggressive sophomore **Eric Dare** (5-9, 185) and some of the incoming freshmen to be the team's third man in PSU's nickel defense packages.

The favorites to win the battles for the starting safety spots in what should be a super-sized Penn State secondary are Dodd and Toles. Both are fearless hitters, but there are health questions surrounding Toles, who started five games last season on the outside. Toles sat out this spring because of a rare enzyme disorder that limits the amount of time he can spend on the field. He was able to play only about 30-40 plays per game last season because of the condition, an incurable ailment that limits his body's ability to metabolize fat and forces it to use his muscles for energy instead of sugar.

Sophomore **Yaacov Yisrael** (5-11, 198) could be a factor at the hero spot, too. Mayer, whose left ACL was torn last summer, was treated with kid gloves all spring. He has the experience, the question is: Does Mayer have the wheels to keep up with Big Ten wideouts? If his knee is not 100 percent sound, then Crenshaw and redshirt freshman **Jimi Mitchell** (6-2, 215) will zoom past him on the depth chart.

Because the secondary is the team's primary need area, some faces who could play sooner rather than later are speedy freshman **Allen Zemaitis** (6-2, 198), a 4.36-40 sprinter out of Spencerport Central (N.Y.) High School, and **Terrance Phillips** (6-1, 185), who was part of a Sharon (Pa.) High defense that handed out seven shutouts and allowed only 105 points in 14 games. An all-stater, Phillips was recruited by Michigan, Notre Dame, and Kentucky, but opted to sign with the Lions.

PUNTERS

Junior **David Royer** (38.9 yards per punt in 2000) solidified his grip on the No. 1 punting job with his solid work this spring. In the annual Blue-White spring game, Royer (6-3, 210) averaged 41.4 yards in his seven punts and dropped two inside the 20.

SPECIAL TEAMS

Penn State's kickoff returns should be in good shape with Larry Johnson (24.7). Either wideout Rod Perry, if he doesn't quit football to concentrate on baseball, and cornerback Bruce Branch, who ran back two punts for touchdowns in 1999, will return punts.

RECRUITING CLASS

The shot heard around the Keystone State

occurred last Jan. 25 at a press conference at Cardinal O'Hara High School in suburban Philadelphia. On that date, Kevin Jones, the most highly recruited running back in the nation who has been compared to a young Herschel Walker and Bo Jackson, entered the room with a black Reebok gym bag. Once he sat down at the podium with his mom, dad and two grandfathers, Jones (a self-professed "huge" wrestling fan) started the show, saying: "I've been going back and forth between Penn State and Virginia Tech, my two schools."

He then sighed deeply, for effect, of course—which drew a reassuring pat on the back from his father Tom. "It's been so much pressure, but right now my decision is ..."

Jones then reached into his black bag and tossed a Penn State jersey on to the table in front of him and said: "Not Penn State."

The reaction from the stunned pro-Penn State crowd ranged from "ooooo" to "ah, maaaann" as Jones told the assembled students, media and faculty that his choice was Virginia Tech. He then peeled off his blue sweater to reveal a Michael Vick No. 7 Tech jersey—a jersey that Hokies coach Frank Beamer said that the prize running back can wear, if wants.

While most of the post-signing date focus was on Jones' decision to go elsewhere, Paterno and Co. still enjoyed a stellar recruiting class. It's not as sexy as adding a franchise tailback, but PSU landed plenty of Grade-A beef to both lines, led by prep All-Americans **Charles Rush** (603, 280) and **Tyler Reed** (6-6, 305). The 2000 Pennsylvania Big School Player of the Year, Rush chose the Nittany Lions over Michigan, Notre Dame, Miami and UCLA. Rush was rated the 95th-best player in the country by Tom Lemming. He had 18 tackles in Erie Cathedral Prep's PIAA Class AAAA state title game win over Central Bucks West. He'll be a force at defensive tackle before he's through at Penn State.

One of the best offensive tackles in the high school Class of 2001, Reed was a great get for the Nittany Lions. Coming out of Pittsburgh's Thomas Jefferson High, Reed had 35 D-IA scholarship offers (including from Pitt, Michigan, Michigan State and Tennessee), but chose Penn State. The 305-pounder is blessed with 5.1 speed in the 40 and 78-inch wing span. No wonder he was rated the nation's No. 55 prospect by Lemming.

What wasn't written about was that Paterno exacted a measure of revenge on Beamer for the Jones' signing by landing 6-3, 210-pound quarterback/safety Robinson from Varina High School in Richmond. Beamer viewed Robinson as a possible heir apparent to new Atalnta Falcon Vick, but Robinson took his 4.4 speed to Happy Valley instead. A four-year starter at quarterback, he threw for 820 yards and rushed for another 800 last season. He'll be the No. 3 quarterback as a freshman at Penn State, behind junior Senneca and Mills.

BLUE RIBBON ANALYSIS

OFFENSE	C+
SPECIAL TEAMS	C
DEFENSE	B
INTANGIBLES	B+

In a league with many mystery guests (i.e. Purdue without Drew Brees, Michigan without Drew Henson, Anthony Thomas, David Terrell and most of its 2000 offensive line), Penn State has a chance to rebound from its worst season in 50 years.

But it won't be easy. The non-league schedule is rugged, especially for a team breaking in a new quarterback and re-tooling its linebacking corps and secondary. There will be lots of pressure on new quarterback Matt Senneca, a junior built like Kerry Collins but who lacks experience. If he's steady and the Lions' re-tooled secondary holds up against the Ken Dorseys, Zak Kustoks and Kurt Kittners they'll face, then Penn State might be able to finish a game or two over .500.

If not, it could be another sub-.500 season for Paterno, who will become Division I-A's all-time winner some time this autumn.

(B.D.)

2000 RESULTS

USC (Kickoff Classic)	L	5-29	0-1
Toledo	L	6-24	0-2
Louisiana Tech	W	67-7	1-2
Pittsburgh	L	0-12	1-3
@Ohio State	L	6-45	1-4
Purdue	W	22-20	2-4
@Minnesota	L	16-25	2-5
Illinois	W	39-25	3-5
Indiana	W	27-24	4-5
Iowa	L	23-26	4-6
Michigan	L	11-33	4-7
Michigan State	W	42-23	5-7

Purdue

LOCATION	**West Lafayette, IN**
CONFERENCE	**Big Ten**
LAST SEASON	**8-4 (.666)**
CONFERENCE RECORD	**6-2 (t-1st)**
OFFENSIVE STARTERS RETURNING	**5**
DEFENSIVE STARTERS RETURNING	**10**
NICKNAME	**Boilermakers**
COLORS	**Old Gold & Black**
HOME FIELD	**Ross-Ade Stadium (67,332)**
HEAD COACH	**Joe Tiller (Montana State '65)**
RECORD AT SCHOOL	**33-16 (4 years)**
CAREER RECORD	**72-46-1 (10 years)**
ASSISTANTS	**Scott Downing (Sterling '79)** Assistant Head Coach/Running Backs/Special Teams
	Brock Spack (Purdue '84) Defensive Coordinator/Linebackers
	Jim Chaney (Central Missouri State '84) Offensive Coordinator/Offensive Line/Recruiting
	Blaine Bennett (Washington State '87) Quarterbacks
	Gary Emanuel (Plymouth State '82) Defensive Ends
	Ted Gilmore (Wyoming '91) Receivers
	Ken Greene (Washington State '78) Defensive Backs
	Mark Hagen (Indiana '91) Defensive Tackles
	Danny Hope (Eastern Kentucky '81) Offensive Line
TEAM WINS (last 5 yrs.)	**3-9-9-7-8**
FINAL RANK (last 5 yrs.)	**41-23-22-20-20**
2000 FINISH	**Lost to Washington in Rose Bowl.**

COACH AND PROGRAM

Is Joe Tiller the best coach in Big Ten? You can make that argument. He has put together a four-year run surpassed only by Michigan's Lloyd Carr. But in some respects what Tiller has done is more impressive.

When Carr took over the Wolverines in 1995, he inherited an 8-4 team that won the Holiday Bowl. By contrast, when Tiller came aboard in 1997, the Boilermakers were coming off a 3-8 season. Tiller is Captain Turnaround. He got Purdue to 9-3 record and an Alamo Bowl victory that year.

"We were not going to wait four years to figure this out," Tiller said. "If I would have waited four more years, I wouldn't have any hair left. We're here to win a championship. We've won in the past and we will win again in the future."

In 2000, Purdue reached the apex by tying for the Big Ten championship, the program's first league title since 1967. It reached the Rose Bowl for the first time since the end of the 1966 season. Tiller has put the Boilermakers in elite company. Purdue, Michigan, and Wisconsin are the only league teams to go to a bowl every year since the 1997 season.

The coach who other coaches in the Big Ten regard as a bit of mad scientist believes in his system. Tiller has created a monster. When all else fails, the pass is the first, second and third option. Purdue has—by far—thrown for more yards and more touchdowns than any team in the conference in the Tiller era. It's not a gimmick. The proof is in the success.

A year ago, the Boilermakers won their eighth Big Ten title, finishing in a three-way tie with Michigan and Northwestern. They earned the Rose Bowl trip by virtue of victories over the Wolverines and the Wildcats. Purdue was fueled by an offense that finished fourth in the nation (471.2 yards per game) and a passing attack that ranked sixth (312.5).

Can Purdue keep its string of success alive? Given Tiller's track record that seems very likely. Quarterback Drew Brees, the most prolific passer in Big Ten history, is gone. But Tiller won before Brees became a starter, so he probably will be able to win without him. The offensive system allows for a quarterback to be productive and the defense returns all but one starter.

"We're going to be new at quarterback and we're going to be new at some positions offensively that will involve a lot of learning," Tiller said. "The question to us is how is an inexperienced offense going to fare? I hope we have enough success that we don't get discouraged."

Purdue has not finished lower than 16th in the nation in offense in the Tiller era. Nor has it won fewer than seven games. Despite the loss of Brees, the program did keep its most important component. There had been routine speculation that another program might give Tiller an offer he couldn't refuse. Athletic director Morgan Burke, who hired Tiller in November 1996, said he has not been contacted by any athletic directors seeking permission to talk to Tiller. If Burke has his way, that will continue to be the case.

"We annually review the earnings opportunities for the football staff to ensure that their compensation is market-competitive and that their performance is rewarded," Burke said.

Successive contract extensions negotiated in past years by Burke and Tiller guarantee that Tiller will remain the Purdue head coach until at least December 2007.

"The market for high-achieving head coaches is more active than it has ever been," Burke said. "We are committed to Joe Tiller for the long term and I'm happy to say, he shares that commitment."

2001 SCHEDULE

Sept.	2	@Cincinnati
	15	Notre Dame
	22	Akron
	29	@Minnesota
Oct.	6	Iowa
	13	@Michigan
	27	Northwestern

Nov. 3 Illinois
10 @Ohio State
17 Michigan State
24 @Indiana

QUARTERBACKS

So how do you replace Drew Brees, who was picked in the second round of the NFL draft by the San Diego Chargers? Not too long ago, college pundits were wondering how Tiller was going to replace Billy Dicken, who quarterbacked the Boilermakers to an Alamo Bowl victory in Tiller's first season as he threw for 3,136 yards and 21 touchdowns as a senior. Dicken was a 1997 first-team All-Big Ten pick a year after throwing for just one touchdown.

Dicken's rise would indicate the Tiller system is quarterback friendly. Brees just took it to another plateau. Brees came out of nowhere to rewrite the Big Ten passing records in just three full years of action. He went from a guy who didn't have a touchdown pass as a freshman to a Big Ten record 39 as a sophomore. Brees finished with 90 touchdown passes—a record that might not be broken. Unless it's broken by another Purdue passer.

No one is predicting such lofty achievements for **Brandon Hance** (6-1, 190). But for now, he is the heir apparent to Brees. The redshirt freshman barely played last year. He appeared in only two games, going 5-for-9 for 40 yards and a touchdown. Hance also rushed for 37 yards on seven carries.

Hance has a solid prep background. The Californian was list as the ninth-best quarterback by *Prep Football Report*. In his senior year at Taft High School in Woodland Hills, he passed for 2,400 yards and 19 touchdowns and rushed for more than 500 yards and 19 scores.

But is he ready for the big time? So far the results have been promising. In the spring game, Hance went 27-of-47 for 310 yards with five touchdowns and two interceptions. He completed 11 of his last 19 attempts and was 6-of-6 for 99 yards in the red zone. Tiller said Hance is the likely starter. But he also noted that things change.

"He is [the starting quarterback today]," Tiller said in the spring. "And I emphasize today because who knows what's going to happen into the future. Particularly when we open fall camp. Go back to '97 when we came out of spring football with John Reeves as our starting quarterback. But we opened the '97 campaign with Billy Dicken at quarterback and he never surrendered the position.

"But we quite frankly hope that Brandon really develops and continues to be the starter and there never is a question."

If Hance falters, Tiller might have to turn to a freshman. **Kyle Orton** (6-3, 205) was a *USA Today* Super 25 selection and was rated the nation's second-best high school quarterback by *SuperPrep*. Orton passed for 3,176 yards and 24 touchdowns during his career at Southeast Polk High School in Altoona, Iowa. His physical talents will give him a shot to play.

Tiller acknowledged that he was leery of turning to a freshman, but in the same breath admitted that more high school passers are coming in ready.

Michigan State played Jeff Smoker and North Carolina State turned to Philip Rivers last year.

"He's certainly talented. I don't know if he's talented enough," Tiller said. "I've never been around a freshman quarterback that was capable of starting his first fall on campus. But I also recognize that last fall there were more true freshmen that played than at any time in the history of college football. There are players that are doing it and perhaps Kyle Orton is that kind of player."

Ben Smith (6-3, 210) will compete for the backup job. Smith, converted to a strong safety two years ago, will return to quarterback. But the senior hasn't played quarterback since 1996. As a senior in Nebraska, he passed for 1,800 yards and 22 touchdowns.

RUNNING BACKS

Tailbacks can often be lost in the shuffle in Tiller's pass-happy offense. No running back caught more than 11 passes and Brees was the team's second-leading rusher. This season, the Boilermakers might have to lean more on the running game with an inexperienced passer running the offense.

Whoever lines up at center will have the benefit of handing off to **Montrell Lowe** (5-8, 192). The junior is a nice fit to Tiller's offense. He rushed for 998 yards on 226 carries last year. That was the most yards gained by a tailback in the Tiller era. Lowe closed out the regular season with a bang, amassing a career-high 208 yards in a victory over Indiana that put Purdue in the Rose Bowl. He already ranks 10th on the school's all-time rushing list with 1,839 yards.

Lowe is a shifty runner but does not have overwhelming speed. He averaged only 4.4 yards a carry. As a freshman, he averaged 4.9 yards. With a veteran offensive line, Lowe might be hard-pressed to improve his numbers across the board.

Sedrick Brown (6-1, 246) is bigger, a little more versatile and was effective in spot duty. Brown appeared in all 12 games, including two starts. He finished third on the team with 260 rushing yards on 44 carries. He also led all tailbacks in receptions with 11. Brown could figure a little more in the offense.

Brown, a junior, was the leading ground gainer in the spring game with 111 yards on 12 carries, including a 70-yard touchdown run.

"With Montrell and Sedrick we have two experienced backs," Tiller said. "We think with the guys we're going to add there is going to be a real injection of speed on the roster."

Freshman **Joe Harris** (5-11, 200) is a player everyone is eager to see. Harris sat out last season and missed spring practice because of academics. Harris, a native of Tomball, Texas, rushed for 1,150 yards with 10 touchdowns as a senior. *SuperPrep* rated him the 19th best back in the nation. Harris has outstanding speed. He finished second in the state in the 200 meters with a time of 21.07—the 11th fastest time in the nation.

Another youngster to watch is **Reggie Benton** (6-1, 210). The freshman rushed 227 times for 1,995 yards with 29 touchdowns at Michigan's Grand Blanc High School. He also returned for kickoffs for 205 yards and a score. For his career, Benton amassed 70 touchdowns and 6,504 yards.

WIDE RECEIVERS/TIGHT ENDS

Being a wide receiver in Tiller's spread offense is like being a kid in a candy store. Purdue is one of the few teams in the league that routinely lines up in a spread formation with three receivers and one back. And so far the system has worked. So most expect that Purdue will be able to compensate for the loss of leading receiver Vinny Sutherland. The senior had a career year last season with 72 catches for 1,014 yards and a school-record 13 scores.

Boilermaker receivers must be able to run after the catch because a lot of the routes are short- to intermediate ones. Returnees **John Standeford**, **Seth Morales**, and **A.T. Simpson** all will have opportunities to showcase their skills. Standeford (6-4, 187), a sophomore, appears to have a huge upside. As a freshman, he played every game and led all freshmen nationally with 67 catches for 744 yards. He also had six touchdowns. Standeford's impact was all over the Purdue record books. He set a school record for catches by a freshman, breaking Sutherland's mark of 34 in 1997. And his receptions tied for sixth most in school history. He should be the go-to guy for next season.

Morales (5-10, 170) should also figure in the mix. The Butler transfer finished fourth on the team with 35 receptions for 556 yards. His touchdowns were both from long-distance. He had a 78-yard score against Wisconsin and a 64-yarder against Ohio State. The junior had his best game against Ohio State, finishing with seven catches for 115 yards.

Simpson (6-4, 232) is a big target. Last season he set career bests with 25 catches for 275 yards and two scores. The senior has not displayed great playmaking ability. For his career, he has averaged 9.9 yards a catch and his longest reception is 35 yards.

"It's another one of the positions where we're anxious to see what the new guys will bring," Tiller said. "We like our talent level."

Taylor Stubblefield (6-1, 166) has the kind of speed that turns heads. The redshirt freshman will compete for time along with sophomore **Andre Henderson** (6-3, 197), who had seven catches for 63 yards last year.

As a high schooler in Yakima, Wash., Stubblefield's best season came as a sophomore when he had 51 catches for 900 yards.

"A lot of folks are talking about him," Tiller said. "I guessed we goofed up and made a comment to the fact that we like his speed and think he could be a good player. He hasn't caught a ball for us yet and he seems to be getting a lot of media attention. That's fine. We do think Taylor has the explosiveness and the quickness to be an effective player in this system. We're anxious to see exactly how good this guy is going to be."

At tight end, Purdue is pretty well stocked. **Tim Stratton** (6-4, 258) should be an All-Big Ten player for the third straight year. Last season, the senior won the inaugural John Mackey Award, which honors the nation's best tight end.

Stratton was third on the team with 58 receptions and 609 receiving yards. He was seventh in the Big Ten in receptions. Stratton has been a consistent target and may pick up even more receptions because he is the most experienced pass-catcher. He has caught a pass in 31 straight games and in all but one during his 37-game career.

Chris Randolph (6-4, 249) is another fifth-year senior who will give the Boilermakers some depth. He caught only one pass for 12 yards last year and has three receptions for his career. Still, the coaching staff is confident in his abilities. He isn't the receiver Stratton is, but does provide blocking.

Junior **Pete Lougheed** (6-5, 279) is moving from tight end to offensive tackle. He is the biggest and most physical of the tight ends, but will play primarily on the offensive line. Don't be surprised to see him at tight end, though occasionally. He has four career receptions for 56 yards and a touchdown.

"Tight end is one of the positions where we are three deep," Tiller said. "But we're not going to play with three tight ends."

OFFENSIVE LINE

Brees deservedly received a lot of credit for the Rose Bowl run. The unsung heroes, however, might have been the four senior offensive linemen who helped to protect him. The Boilermakers now must cope without Ian Allen, Brandon Gorin, Matt Light, and Chukky Okobi. Only left guard **Gene Mruczkowski** (6-2, 310) returns for a completely revamped unit.

Mruczkowski won't be playing the same position. The junior will play center—and for good reason, Tiller says. Mruczkowski was a two-year starter on an offensive line that allowed only 25 sacks the last two seasons. Tiller said the move isn't all that radical.

"It's very similar to what we did this past fall with Chukky Okobi making the move from guard to center," he said. "Gene has worked at center for us and was really our backup center in an emergency case last year. Our center calls a lot of our blocking schemes for us, and it's always good to have an experienced player at center. That's what prompted the move."

Another position change will take place as Lougheed makes the transition from tight end to left tackle. The junior played all 12 games at tight last season and started three. Tiller said it's important to have a physical, veteran presence at tackle.

"Most people probably didn't recognize him as a tight end because he was there in a blocking role," Tiller said. "But we feel like he's a big, physical smart guy. We think this move is to Pete's benefit and the team's benefit. It gives us an experienced player at that position."

Kelly Kitchel (6-6, 306) will probably handle left guard. The junior appeared in 11 games as a reserve and a special teams player. He has limited experience with 15 games under his belt and none as a starter.

At right guard, junior **Rob Turner** (6-4, 304) is slated to start. Turner played in every game and had three starts. He contributed to a line that allowed only 10 sacks in 528 pass attempts. He has played in every Purdue game since his redshirt freshman year.

Right tackle **Kelly Butler** (6-8, 297) has talent but is also inexperienced. The redshirt freshman was rated the 24th-best offensive lineman by *Prep Football Report* as a star at Union High School in Grand Rapids, Mich.

2000 STATISTICS

Rushing offense	158.6	46
Passing offense	312.5	8
Total offense	471.2	4
Scoring offense	32.5	23
Net Punting	31.7	93
Punt returns	9.1	65
Kickoff returns	20.7	33
Rushing defense	139.1	47
Passing efficiency defense	123.8	79
Total defense	340.5	38
Scoring defense	21.1	40
Turnover margin	+0	60

Last column is ranking among Division I-A teams.

KICKERS

Travis Dorsch (6-6, 211) is a large and in-charge kicker. He is Purdue's career leader with 46 field goals and 56 consecutive PATs (Oct. 31, 1998-Jan. 1, 2000) and 269 points. He ranks third with a .657 field-goal percentage (46-of-70). Dorsch was an honorable mention All-Big Ten player.

The senior made 12-of-17 kicks and converted 25-of-27 PATs. His 70.6 field-goal percentage ranked fifth in the Big Ten and was fifth best on the school season list.

Dorsch doesn't have great range—his career long was 47 yards. But he has been a consistent performer. After a so-so 1999 when he made just 18-of-31.

He made a game-winning 33-yarder with four seconds left against Michigan after missing a potential 32-yarder with 2:11 left.

DEFENSIVE LINE

Akinola James Ayodele's first name is African for "a warrior who has gone through many wars and has never been defeated."

Ayodele (6-3, 253), a senior, is indeed a warrior and the best player on a Purdue defense that should be among the best in league. In just two seasons the former junior college player is already third on Purdue's all-time sacks list with 20. With a good season, the senior could finish second in school history.

Ayodele was a second-team All-Big Ten selection in 2000 after getting nine sacks and 15 tackles for a loss. He started all 12 games, the first five at linebacker and the final seven at right defensive end. He led the team and tied for sixth in the league in tackles for a loss. He was also second on the team with a pair of interceptions. Ayodele had perhaps his best game against Wisconsin when he had career highs of nine tackles for loss, three sacks and recovered a fumble.

Ayodele is a bit small but is very quick and has a nose for the football. A year ago, he finished fourth on the team with 66 tackles. That was in line with his production from 1999 when he had 64 tackles. Because all four defensive linemen return, there is every reason to believe he will at least equal his 11 sacks from 1999.

"Around here, you always hear about the offense, but this year we have a chance to go into the season as the guys who are going to carry the team," Ayodele said. "I don't think we know yet the full potential of this defense. I think we can still take it up to another level. As a group, I definitely think it's by far the best defense since I've been here. I don't see any weaknesses."

Tackle **Matt Mitrione** (6-3, 281) is another senior who should shine this season. He was also a second-team All-Big Ten selection after amassing 47 tackles, including 13 for a loss. He also blocked a 33-yard field-goal attempt against Central Michigan. Mitrione saved his best for last, making a career-high seven tackles in the regular-season finale against Indiana.

Mitrione has an interesting background. He once placed second in a Tough Man competition. His nickname is "Meathead."

Shaun Phillips (6-3, 252) is a promising young player. The sophomore was an honorable mention All-Big Ten selection after collecting seven sacks as a redshirt freshman. He started every game with the first five at right end and the last seven at left end after the move of Ayodele from linebacker. His sacks placed him 16th on the career list and represented the 10th-best effort all-time by a Purdue pass-rusher.

Sophomore **Craig Terrill** (6-3, 289) was third on the team with six sacks and had 23 tackles. His biggest play came when he blocked a 58-yard kick by Wisconsin that was returned for a game-winning score in overtime.

LINEBACKERS

In keeping with the rest of the defense, Purdue's linebackers emphasize speed rather than size. All three starters are back. Sophomore outside linebacker **Landon Johnson** (6-2, 212) is small, but has a big upside. As a redshirt freshman, he started 10 games and finished second on the team with 71 tackles. The only time he missed a game was when he sat out the Michigan game with an ankle sprain. Johnson tied for the team lead along with Ayodele with a pair of fumble recoveries. One of those helped seal a victory over Ohio State.

Johnson's best game came against Central Michigan when he had 10 tackles, including two for a loss and one sack. He set a career high with 11 stops against Indiana, including a pair of pass break-ups. He also had nine tackles in the Rose Bowl loss to Washington. Johnson could add some pounds without sacrificing speed and should contend for All-Big Ten honors.

The other outside linebacker will be sophomore **Gilbert Gardner** (6-2, 220). A freshman All-American pick by Rivals.com, he appeared in all 12 games and started 11 after being moved from wide receiver to linebacker in training camp. Gardner had 47 tackles, including four for a loss and a sack. He tied for the team lead with two forced fumbles. Gardner had a season-high six tackles and forced a fumble against Central Michigan. He had five solo tackles in the Rose Bowl.

Tiller moved Gardner to defense with the future in mind. Purdue needed more speed on the other side of the ball and Gardner uses his quickness to track down ball carriers in a hurry. Gardner was a standout wide receiver at Angleton High School in Texas with 35 receptions for 453 yards as a senior.

At middle linebacker is junior **Joe Odom** (6-2, 243). Odom, who missed the team's first three games with a back injury, was a key part of the Boiler's success on defense. After registering two tackles and a sack in limited action during Purdue's 38-24 win over Minnesota, Odom started at middle linebacker in place of Gardner and excelled immediately. He had an interception against Penn State that set up a touchdown and also made five tackles in that game. He finished the season with 53 tackles and two sacks.

DEFENSIVE BACKS

Purdue's pass defense took a step forward in 2000. It allowed 363 less yards and one fewer touchdown than the season before. Opponents completed a higher percentage (61.0 percent as compared to 55.8) but generally speaking the cornerback play was pretty solid. Cornerback Chris Clopton is the sole starter lost on defense. The feeling is that the cornerback play should be as good or better as last year.

Cornerback **Ashante Woodyard** (6-2, 201) made an immediate impact as a junior college player. The senior started every game and was second on the team with seven pass breakups and tied for fourth on the team with 65 tackles.

Woodyard collected a career-high 10 tackles in the victory over Northwestern. Woodyard's shining moment was his recovery of a blocked field goal at Wisconsin. He was selected Co-Big Ten Special Teams Player of the Week for his effort. Woodyard finished up in style, tying a career-high with 10 tackles and a recovered fumble against Washington.

The frontrunner to replace Clopton is redshirt freshman **Antwaun Rogers** (6-2, 166). He was ranked the 16th best defensive back by *Prep Football Report*. As a senior at Middletown, Ohio, he had 30 tackles and one interception and blocked six kicks.

"The redshirt year really benefited him," Tiller said. "He was able to get a little stronger and adjust to the college game. We're not so sure that he isn't our best cover corner right now. Maybe even better than Woodyard on the other side. He's a good young prospect."

Also competing for playing time are sophomores **Jacques Reeves** (6-1, 180) and **Deaunte Ferrell** (5-11, 190), who both played as freshmen.

Reeves played in all but one game and had 11 tackles. Ferrell appeared in every game and had five tackles and broke up two passes.

Strong safety **Ralph Turner** (6-2, 210), a junior, had a promising sophomore season. The converted quarterback started every game and finished fourth on the team with 65 tackles, including 10 for a loss. He also had four sacks, five pass breakups and one interception. He had eight tackles in consecutive games against Northwestern and Wisconsin. Turner should be primed for a great season.

Sophomore free safety **Stuart Schweigert** (6-3, 202) was the freshman defensive player of the year by Rivals.com. He also earned Big Ten Freshman of the Year honors, becoming just the fourth Purdue player to receive that honor, along with quarterback Brian Fox (1988), quarterback Eric Hunter (1989), and running back Corey Rogers (1991). Schweigert appeared in every game, starting the final nine. He led the team in tackles with 85 and had 10 pass breakups and five interceptions. He was the first freshman to pace Purdue in tackles since 1976 when Kevin Motts had 121. The five interceptions were the most ever by a freshman.

PUNTERS

Scott Kurz (6-1, 195) began the season as the team's pooch punter before taking over full-time duties against Michigan. The senior averaged 36.4 yards per kick—which didn't place him among the league leaders. He did, however, land 15-of-30 attempts inside the opponent's 20-yard line. Kurz's season-long punt was a 54-yarder at Wisconsin. His best punting day was at Michigan State, when he averaged 42.2 yards on five kicks.

SPECIAL TEAMS

Purdue must find a way to replace Sutherland, who not only returned kicks but punts as well. Sutherland did not have a return for a score but he fulfilled both duties capably. Sutherland was seventh in the league in kickoff returns (24.3) and fifth in punt returns (9.9).

Still, there is room for improvement—the Boilermakers did not have a kickoff or punt return for a score last season.

The kickoff return duties will be given to Ferrell and Schweigert. Ferrell has the most experience on special teams. He returned four kickoffs for a 10.2 average. Punt returning should be given to Stubblefield. He is one of Purdue's fastest players.

Purdue also blocked a pair of field goals and didn't have one blocked.

RECRUITING CLASS

Purdue signed 22 last February, including 11 offensive players and nine defensive players, plus two players listed as athletes. There are six linebackers, three offensive linemen, two quarterbacks, two wide receivers, two tight ends, two running backs, one defensive lineman, one defensive end and one defensive back in the class.

"We certainly feel that this class could be the best one we have signed at Purdue," Tiller said. "That's a strong statement based on the success of last year's class. Each year we have been here, we have made progress in attracting the best student-athletes to Purdue. I'm excited and anxious to get them here and watch them compete.

"The strength of the class is the linebackers, which already is a strong position on our team. In addition to the balance you look for in every class, we went hard after linemen and tight ends. I really like the running backs. Overall, the athleticism and speed of the class is good."

The Boilermakers' recruiting fortunes got a boost from reaching their first Rose Bowl in 34 years.

"The Rose Bowl certainly helped us with a guy like **Kevin Noel**," Tiller said. "That might be huge. He's a guy that has star billing coming in, which leads you to believe that he can play right away and be a big-time receiver for us."

Noel, a 6-3, 185-pounder from Naperville, Ill., is the most highly touted receiver to sign with Purdue since Tiller became coach.

Tiller said perhaps two running backs and one of the two quarterbacks also could play immediately as freshmen.

One prime running back candidate is **Reggie Benton**, who originally committed to Michigan's class of 2000. The 6-1, 210-pound Benton, from Grand Blanc, Mich., learned he needed to take two more classes to graduate, so he had to sit out last season.

"Benton is a physical running back who has outstanding speed," Tiller said. "I'd be surprised as well as disappointed if he doesn't play for us [this] year."

The two quarterbacks are Kyle Orton from Altoona, Iowa, and **Mike Rhinehart** (6-5, 235), from Fort Wayne (Ind.) Homestead High School.

In December, the Boilermakers signed defensive end **Jarod Ramirez**, a junior college transfer from Fresno (Calif.) City College. He enrolled in January and took part in spring practice. The 6-4, 255-pound Ramirez played for former Purdue assistant coach Tony Caviglia, now the head coach at Fresno City College.

BLUE RIBBON ANALYSIS

OFFENSE	B-
SPECIAL TEAMS	B-
DEFENSE	D
INTANGIBLES	C-

This could a team unlike any previously seen under Tiller. The defense is loaded with good young players and the offense is a major question mark with Brees and most of the offensive line gone. Tiller's system has been productive before without Brees, but this will be his greatest challenge.

The Boilermakers do have good depth at tailback with Lowe and Brown. The running game might have to carry the load while Hance gets up to speed. Hance took 75- to 80 percent of the snaps in spring to get ready. That approach worked for his predecessor. Brees took almost all of the spring snaps en route to becoming the Big Ten's all-time passing leader. This was actually Hance's second spring practice. He graduated early from high school and participated in the 2000 session.

Hance's best friends will be the tailbacks and defense. The speedy Lowe and powerful Brown give him a pair of capable runners and the defense has almost everyone back. Would Tiller turn down his high-octane offense a notch? Or at least change the strategy that has led the Boilermakers to four straight bowl trips?

"That's a good question," he said. "I don't know. I would suggest that our defense would have to carry us early until our offense could catch up. I made that statement in the past about our offense carrying us early until the defense catches up, and just the opposite happened.

"A year ago we came out strong early [on defense] and it took a little bit of time for our offense to get the cobwebs out. But certainly on the surface it would appear that the strongest part of football team is our defense."

The belief here is that Purdue will field one of its best defenses in years and the offense will manage enough points to win. Tiller's track record on offense is too good not to expect a productive season from Hance. The Boilermakers will finish in the top half of the Big Ten and will make it to another bowl.

(M.G.)

2000 RESULTS

Central Michigan	W	48-0	1-0
Kent State	W	45-10	2-0
Notre Dame	L	21-23	2-1
Minnesota	W	38-24	3-1
Penn State	L	20-22	3-2
Michigan	W	32-31	4-2
Northwestern	W	41-28	5-2
Wisconsin	W	30-24	6-2
Ohio State	W	31-27	7-2
Michigan State	L	10-30	7-3
Indiana	W	41-13	8-3
Washington (Rose Bowl)	L	24-34	8-4

Wisconsin

LOCATION	**Madison, WI**
CONFERENCE	**Big Ten**
LAST SEASON	**9-4 (.692)**
CONFERENCE RECORD	**4-4 (5th)**
OFFENSIVE STARTERS RETURNING	**5**
DEFENSIVE STARTERS RETURNING	**5**
NICKNAME	**Badgers**
COLORS	**Cardinal & White**
HOME FIELD	**Camp Randall Stadium (76,129)**
HEAD COACH	**Barry Alvarez (Nebraska '69)**
RECORD AT SCHOOL	**79-48-4 (11 years)**
CAREER RECORD	**79-48-4 (11 years)**
ASSISTANTS	
	Todd Bradford (Southern Utah '86) Secondary
	Kevin Cosgrove (Wisconsin-Oshkosh '79) Defensive Coordinator/Linebackers
	Tim Davis (Utah '82) Tight Ends
	Jeff Horton (Nevada '81) Quarterbacks
	Jim Hueber (South Dakota '71) Running Game Coordinator
	Henry Mason (Central Missouri State '79) Wide Receivers
	John Palermo (Florida State '74) Defensive Line
	Brian White (Harvard '86) Offensive Coordinator/Running Backs
	Darrell Wilson (Connecticut '81) Offensive Line/Special Teams
TEAM WINS (last 5 yrs.)	**8-8-11-10-9**
FINAL RANK (last 5 yrs.)	**28-30-5-7-26**
2000 FINISH	**Beat UCLA in Sun Bowl.**

COACH AND PROGRAM

After the Shoe Box scandal of 2000, the only way the 2001 season could start any worse for coach Barry Alvarez and his Wisconsin Badgers would be if the team mascot contracts rabies.

Last year, the defending Rose Bowl-champion Badgers were a consensus preseason top 10 pick—they even reached the lofty status of No. 1 in some polls—and were poised to dominate the Big Ten and earn a BCS bowl berth. But on the eve of their season opener against Western Michigan, Madison media outlets began buzzing about NCAA violations within the football program.

Badger athletic officials called a press conference just hours before kickoff and announced a series of suspensions that would sideline numerous starters and top reserves from one to three games. Players had admitted receiving illegal discounts on shoes and clothing at the Shoe Box, a local sporting goods store owned and operated by a longtime Badger booster. And because the NCAA doesn't look kindly on benefits given to athletes that aren't available to the general public, the Wisconsin athletic department found itself face-to-face with its biggest scandal in years.

In the wake of the press conference, the undermanned Badgers looked shell-shocked as they struggled to an unimpressive victory against pesky Western Michigan. Amazingly, they stuck together through the rest of their non-conference games, including an overtime victory against soon-to-be-mighty Oregon, and appeared to have weathered the storm as the remainder of the suspensions were served.

But the lack of continuity in practice and on game day finally manifested itself in the Big Ten opener, as Wisconsin's dreams of an undefeated season came to a crashing halt with a double-overtime home loss to Northwestern. The Badgers went on to lose three of the next four and at 1-4 in the conference were in danger of becoming road kill on the Big Ten highway.

But the season turned in a 13-7 victory over a feisty Iowa squad, and then the Badger offense really hit its stride, posting almost 40 points per game in the final three games. Their fifth-place conference record earned the Badgers a slot in the Sun Bowl, where they pulled out a one-point victory over UCLA to put a bright red bow on an otherwise unsatisfying season.

Once the 2000 Badgers got rolling, the amazing talent on display proved that their preseason hype was indeed deserved. But much of that talent must be replaced if this year's team hopes to reach the lofty expectations that now accompany Wisconsin football.

The offense lost five starters, including leading rusher Michael Bennett, top receiver Chris Chambers and a trio from the offensive line—Casey Rabach, Bill Ferrario and Dave Costa—who started 139 games combined in their careers.

On the other side of the ball, Alvarez and his staff are searching for a replacement for All-America cornerback Jamar Fletcher, the Big Ten Defensive Player of the Year and Jim Thorpe Award winner. And the kicking game is in disarray with the departure of Ray Guy Award winner Kevin Stemke at punter and the steady Vitaly Pisetsky at kicker.

Alvarez himself was the focal point of some off-season speculation. It seems that whenever a high-profile program has an opening at head coach, Alvarez's name is at the top of the list of potential candidates. Whether it's Notre Dame, UCLA or the Green Bay Packers, Alvarez has found himself denying his interest in leaving Madison.

This off-season, however, one rumor just wouldn't go away—Alvarez replacing Butch Davis at the University of Miami. This time it appeared that Alvarez was actually weighing the possibility of taking over the Hurricane reins, and the specter of further NCAA sanctions against the Wisconsin program gave this story some serious legs. Alvarez finally withdrew from the Miami discussions and reaffirmed his commitment to finish his career at Wisconsin, but not before his reputation took a bit of a hit in dairy country.

The grumbling of the Badger Nation represents the first chink in the armor of a coach who took over a moribund program and turned it into a consistent winner. Under Alvarez's guidance, the Badgers have won more games (30) than any Big Ten team the last three years, including back-to-back league titles in 1998 and '99, the first time in 100 years that Wisconsin could claim that feat. The Badgers have been to a bowl in seven of the last eight seasons—and won the Rose Bowl three times in that span—and Alvarez's 79 career victories are the most of any coach in Wisconsin history.

With only 10 starters returning—the fewest of his career—this will be Alvarez's toughest challenge since he took over the program in 1990. Will the new faces on the field be up to the task of building on the success of this now elite program? Or will 2001 go down as a rebuilding year for the boys in Madison?

2001 SCHEDULE

Aug.	25	Virginia (Eddie Robinson Classic)
Sept.	1	@Oregon
	8	Fresno State
	15	Western Kentucky
	22	@Penn State
Oct.	6	Indiana
	13	@Ohio State
	20	@Illinois
	27	Michigan State
Nov.	3	Iowa
	17	Michigan
	24	@Minnesota

QUARTERBACKS

This should be a position of strength. Most programs would be happy with one quarterback who has experience in leading the squad to victory. Wisconsin has two.

Alvarez has made it clear in the off-season that there will be no controversy—his starter will be junior **Brooks Bollinger** (6-2, 204). His 17-3 record as a starter over the last two years makes it clear why he will get the nod over sophomore **Jim Sorgi** (6-5, 178), who led the team to comeback wins at Michigan State and Indiana after Bollinger left with injuries.

Alvarez knows that with a young team, he needs to be able to rely on his seasoned quarterbacks to carry it.

"If your quarterback isn't effective, then you struggle," he said. "If there's one place you want experience, it's under center. We're blessed to have two guys at the position that are proven winners."

Both quarterbacks looked sharp in the spring game, where Bollinger—the Big Ten Freshman of the Year in 1999—solidified his hold on the top spot despite an efficient (13-for-15, 198 yards) performance by Sorgi. Bollinger is a threat on the ground; his 913 rushing yards in two years already ranks him second all-time among Wisconsin quarterbacks. He's also rushed for six touchdowns in each of his first two seasons and had 10 runs of at least 20 yards last year.

The Badgers did finish last in the conference in passing offense last season, but that should change this year because of a change in philosophy, in addition to Bollinger's added experience. In their Sun Bowl preparations last year, the coaches began tinkering with a spread offense, which was used effectively in spring practice as well. Although he doesn't want to tip his hand too much, Alvarez said, "The players liked it [during bowl preparations], and it adds a bit to our offense. We'll continue to experiment with it."

When he did pass, Bollinger connected on 52.6 percent of his 209 attempts, a six percent drop-off from his freshman year, when his main duty was to hand the ball to Ron Dayne and celebrate the Heisman Trophy winner's touchdowns. He'll have to get that completion percentage back up in the 60-62 range if the spread offense is to be effective this fall.

If Bollinger struggles or suffers another injury—ankle sprains and a concussion dogged him in 2000—Alvarez will have no qualms about putting Sorgi behind center. His quarterback rating was an eye-popping 164.4 in spot duty last year, and his lanky frame and strong arm would be a perfect fit for a wide-open passing attack. You won't see him ramble downfield like Bollinger, but he gave a glimpse of his promise last year when he outperformed Drew Brees (21-of-29, 243 yards, two touchdowns) in a loss to Purdue. There should be little if any drop-off if Sorgi is called into extensive duty this year.

"It's a great feeling to know that we have two guys capable of leading us to victory at the quarterback position," Alvarez said.

Depth will be provided by sophomore **Scott Wille** (6-3, 205) and redshirt freshman **Matt Schabert** (6-2, 193).

RUNNING BACKS

With Dayne and Bennett (Minnesota Vikings) going in the first round in the NFL draft in back-to-back years, Wisconsin is compiling something of a reputation as a mini-Tailback U. But this year's backfield will at least start the season as a three-headed monster because sophomore heir-apparent **Broderick Williams** (6-0, 207) blew out his knee in spring practice and will miss the season.

"Contrary to a lot of the experts who predicted that we wouldn't have any running backs next year, we have three quality kids," offensive coordinator Brian White told the **Milwaukee Journal-Sentinel**. A trio of redshirt freshman will be called on to replace the 1,681 yards and 11 touchdowns Bennett contributed last season.

The biggest of the backs is **Tyron Griffin** (6-0, 231), who might be able the team's secret weapon if it indeed uses the spread offense more frequently. If opponents try to counter the spread by playing only six men in the box, he could exploit the gaps in the line by banging his Dayne-like frame through for chunks of yardage. He'll also probably be the third-and-short back for Wisconsin this year. His bulk and straight-forward style will be a nice counter to Bollinger's downfield free-lancing.

The other two backs sharing time will be **Jerome Pettus** (5-9, 176) and **Anthony Davis** (5-8, 185). Both are cut from the scatback mold—speedy, elusive runners who can stretch the defenses coming out of the backfield as receivers. All three backs had strong spring practices and all three had big days in the spring game—Griffin with 15 carries for 100 yards and a touchdown, Pettus with 98 yards and two scores, and Davis with 69 yards and a pair of touchdowns in just six carries.

Before Williams' injury, Alvarez said of the tailback battle, "I would say it's a position by committee. We have four players with unique styles competing for the job. I think there will be a place for all of them unless one separates himself from the pack."

Now down to a three-man battle, the competition seems as wide open as ever and will be something Badger fans should monitor throughout the season.

Clearing the way for the tailbacks—and perhaps getting a few carries in a one-back set—will be senior fullback **Chad Kuhns** (6-1, 230). He's known as a bruising blocker who can catch a pass—his 5-yard touchdown reception gave Wisconsin a short-lived fourth-quarter lead at Michigan last season. He carried the ball only 16 times for 53 yards because his primary role was to block for Bennett, but that could evolve a bit this season, especially if the young tailbacks struggle.

Kuhns' backups will be a couple of juniors—kid brother **Russ Kuhns** (6-0, 232) and **Erik Bickerstaff** (6-0, 219).

WIDE RECEIVERS/TIGHT ENDS

With Chambers (Miami Dolphins, second round) now going deep in the NFL, the Badgers are going to have to find some more targets if the wide-open offense is going to be successful. The star of the show should be junior flanker **Lee Evans** (5-11, 190), whose 33 catches and 634 yards were second on the team last year.

Evans was Bollinger's primary target when Chambers missed the first four games with an injury, and he hauled in a 45-yard bomb from Sorgi in the final minute to beat Michigan State. His 19.2 yards per catch average was the fourth-best season total in school history, and he'll be the main home-run threat again this year.

Senior **Nick Davis** (5-10, 183) is better known as a dynamic kick returner, but he'll be asked to make his mark as a split end this year. Davis has had a difficult time staying out of trouble off the field as of late, but if he can right himself, he could be an important part of the Badger offense.

Davis is a shifty runner with speed to burn, so if the Badgers run a four-wideout set, look for them to try to get him the ball on some receiver screens or quick-hitters that will give him room to work. His 21 receptions were a career high last year, even though he missed four games to suspension and injury.

Depth will be an issue at this spot, as the remaining receivers on the roster caught a total of eight passes last season. Junior **David Braun** (5-11, 188) and sophomore **Byron Brown** (6-0, 184) will get the first crack at playing time among the backups. Brown surprised many in spring camp with his quick adjustment to the position after a switch from quarterback.

Senior **Conroy Whyte** (5-7, 165) and junior **Stephon Watson** (6-3, 190) could be part of the mix if the spread offense really catches on. Watson is in his first full season as a flanker after being shifted from safety. Four freshmen will add depth when they arrive on campus in the fall.

Only one tight end on the roster has played a down in the Big Ten—senior **Mark Anelli** (6-5, 255), who was the No. 2 man last season when he caught 10 passes for 78 yards. He will be the starter this year, but will be pushed by a pair of redshirt freshmen, **Mark Bell** (6-4, 244) and **Tony Paciotti** (6-4, 245).

OFFENSIVE LINE

The Wisconsin offensive line has produced a 1,000-yard rusher in the last eight seasons, a Big Ten record. They will be hard-pressed to keep that streak alive this year, and not only because it's unlikely that one back will get enough carries to reach 1,000 yards.

While bigger names were lost at other positions, the offensive line was the unit that suffered the most defections. Rabach was a consensus first-team All-Big Ten and second-team All-American who played center and guard. He was taken in the third round of the NFL draft by the Super Bowl champion Baltimore Ravens.

Ferrario was a consensus second-team All-Big Ten guard who was drafted by the Green Bay Packers in the fourth round. And Costa was a four-year starter. That's a lot of beef to replace.

This year the line will be anchored by its only returning starters, cousins **Al Johnson** (6-4, 280), a junior center, and **Ben Johnson** (6-7, 319), a junior slated for left tackle. The coaching staff was excited about Al Johnson's play in spring practice, while Ben Johnson is touted as a potential Outland Trophy candidate who is an outstanding run blocker.

At least five players will compete for the final three spots on the line. Junior **Jason Jowers** (6-6, 310) is the main man at right tackle, and redshirt freshman **Dan Buenning** (6-4, 299) should take over the left guard spot.

The starting right guard will probably be either redshirt freshman **Kalvin Barrett** (6-2, 316) or fellow first-year man **Jonathan Clinkscale** (6-3, 302). But keep an eye on redshirt freshman **Mike Lorenz** (6-5, 296) to push for playing time.

The Badgers' rushing offense has been ranked in the top 25 in the NCAA in each of the last four seasons. This year's offensive line might be asked to do a bit more pass protecting, but you can bet that if this crew proves its mettle as run blockers, the Wisconsin ground game will ride high again.

2000 STATISTICS

Rushing offense	192.5	25
Passing offense	160.9	95
Total offense	353.5	69
Scoring offense	24.8	63
Net Punting	43.5	1
Punt returns	9.6	53
Kickoff returns	18.8	75
Rushing defense	163.8	72
Passing efficiency defense	108.2	31
Total defense	390.7	78
Scoring defense	20.6	33
Turnover margin	+8	25

Last column is ranking among Division I-A teams.

KICKERS

Last year the steady Pisetsky converted 28-of-29 PATs and 13-of-22 field goals in his second year as the starting kicker. Replacing him will be a challenge because there is no experience on the bench.

Entering spring practice, Alvarez addressed his worries about the kicking and punting game.

"It's a concern because I haven't had to worry about it for several years," Alvarez said. "We've got some candidates, and we'll certainly encourage competition. Whoever is in there will be brand new, but we'll work hard on it during camp."

After the spring game, nothing much had changed—no one had claimed the position. The kicking job will come down to sophomore **Mark Neuser** (5-9, 164), a walk-on who has limited range, and freshman **Adam Espinoza** (5-10, 166), who was strong but erratic in the spring.

The Badgers did not recruit a prep kicker last year, so it will be up to Neuser and Espinoza to improve if Alvarez is to have a reliable kicker for the next couple of years.

DEFENSIVE LINE

Any discussion of the Badger defensive line must begin with **Wendell Bryant** (6-4, 293). The senior shared the Big Ten Defensive Lineman-of-the-Year honors with Minnesota's Karon Riley last year and was a semifinalist for the Lombardi Award. He regularly shook off two- and three blockers and came up with a team-high six sacks. He added 11 more tackles for losses.

"There aren't many defensive linemen in the nation that cause as many headaches for the opponent as Wendell Bryant," Alvarez said. "He gets special treatment every play, and that's a tribute to his abilities."

Bryant will need another big year if the line is to bounce back from a disappointing year. The Badgers finished seventh in the conference in total defense, but they surrendered nearly 100 yards and a touchdown more per game than in 1999. And the defensive line has lost starters John Favret, Ross Kolodziej and Eric Mahlik. Kolodziej was a seventh-round pick of the New York Giants.

Starting at the "junk" tackle will be fellow senior **Jake Sprague** (6-4, 283), who missed spring practice with a shoulder injury. If he can't go in the fall, senior **Chuck Smith** (6-6, 267) or freshman **Jason Jefferson** (6-3, 292) could fill in.

The rush end will be sophomore **Darius Jones** (6-3, 268), who began his career as a linebacker but came on strong after his move to the line. He's got the size and speed to be a star. Senior **Delante McGrew** (6-4, 215) will spell him.

The coaches will likely use a pair of undersized nose guards, senior Ben Herbert (6-4, 238) and redshirt freshman **Traison Lewis** (6-2, 235), both converted rush ends who were moved inside to get more speed into the lineup. Sophomore **Nick Cochart** (6-1, 259) could push for playing time.

LINEBACKERS

Senior **Nick Griesen** (6-2, 234) led the Big Ten with 146 tackles last year and he will spearhead the charge at inside linebacker. Griesen was chosen first-team All-Big Ten by the media, led the team with 14 tackles for loss and tied with Bryant for the sack lead with six. His backups include junior **P.J. Cannon** (6-1, 237) and senior **Mark Downing** (6-2, 233).

The other inside spot will go to senior **Bryson Thompson** (6-1, 212), who looked good in the spring after an inconsistent and injury-plagued three years. He will be backed up by redshirt freshman **Howard Boye-Doe** (6-2, 225), a converted running back.

Sophomore **Jeff Mack** (6-0, 237) returns for his second year as a starter, moving from inside to outside, and his 55 tackles last season were the most for a freshman linebacker under Alvarez.

The wild card in this bunch is redshirt freshman **Kareem Timbers** (6-3, 207), who moves up from safety and has blown people away with his speed. With some size and experience, he could be a star.

Providing depth will be redshirt freshmen **Jerron Smith** (6-1, 229) and **Ryan Keepman** (6-4, 214) and sophomore **Jason Clemens** (6-1, 220).

DEFENSIVE BACKS

The secondary took a huge hit with the departure of Fletcher, the nation's fourth-leading interceptor with seven, and steady-tackling safety Jason Doering. Fletcher was chosen in the first round of the NFL draft by the Miami Dolphins and Doering went in the sixth round to the Indianapolis Colts

That's a lot of talent to lose, but senior **Mike Echols** (5-10, 171) is back at corner and is a preseason All-Big Ten pick. His 75 tackles ranked fourth on the team last year and he earned second-team conference honors. Echols intercepted five passes last year, returning one for a touchdown, and set a school record with a conference-leading 25 passes broken up.

"Echols' abilities have been somewhat overshadowed because of Fletcher's play," Alvarez said. "We need Echols to take over a leadership role in the back end, and he's ready for that assignment."

The rest of the secondary is unsettled. Senior **Joey Boese** (5-11, 170) was set to play free safety but appears headed for the other corner spot ahead of **B.J. Tucker** (5-11, 171), who struggled there last year as a sophomore and again this spring.

Last year's nickel back, sophomore **Michael Broussard** (5-10, 185), could fill the strong safety role, while senior **Carlease Clark** (5-11, 192) was tabbed to take over at free safety. But academic problems have put Clark's eligibility in question.

If Clark isn't eligible, sophomore **Ryan Aiello** (6-1, 204) could step in a free safety. Other candidates for the defensive backfield include junior **Ryan Simmons** (5-11, 185) and redshirt freshmen **Chris Holznecht** (5-9, 159) and **Chris Catalano** (6-1, 213).

PUNTERS

It's never easy to replace the Ray Guy Award winner. Stemke's booming leg and directional punting ability kept opposing offenses from getting decent field position—in fact, his 42.5 yard net average was a Big Ten record.

Sophomore **Kirk Munden** (5-9, 172) is the leading candidate to replace Stemke, but he didn't secure the job with his performance in the spring. His backup, freshman **Chris Koth** (5-9, 170), was not impressive in the spring game.

SPECIAL TEAMS

The Badgers boast one of the leading kick returners in the game in Davis. On punt returns, he averaged 15.3 yards per return as a freshman and 12.6 yards as a sophomore. Last year opponents finally got smart and started kicking away from him, and he had career lows in returns (15) and average (5.5 yards). Still, his five career kick return touchdowns strongly suggest he's a threat every time he touches the ball.

Davis has a good chance this year to become the first Badger ever to amass 1,000 career yards in three categories—receiving, punt returns and kickoff returns. His 23.7 yard career average on kickoff returns is third in Wisconsin history, and to keep opposing teams honest, look for Evans to join him on the goal line on kickoffs.

RECRUITING CLASS

The Badgers' class was generally ranked among the top three in the Big Ten, along with Michigan and Ohio State.

The key recruits for Wisconsin were defensive lineman **Anttaj Hawthorne** (6-3, 310) from Hamden, Conn.; defensive back **Brett Bell** (6-0, 190) of Wheaton, Ill.; and quarterback **Owen Daniels** (6-3, 215) of Naperville, Ill.

Hawthorne, who played for Hamden High School, was rated by recruiting analyst Tom Lemming as the ninth-best prospect in the country and the second-best defensive player. He piled up 102 tackles and 17 sacks a year ago and also forced seven fumbles.

Bell played just two games because of a knee injury, but he was generally considered the top prospect in Illinois. Bell, who played for Warrensville South High School, was Lemming's ninth-ranked defensive player.

Daniels, who played for Central High School, also suffered a knee injury that limited him to two games a year ago. He completed 30-of-35 passes for 562 yards and seven touchdowns in his limited action. The year before, he threw for 1,750 yards and 17 touchdowns and was intercepted just once.

BLUE RIBBON ANALYSIS

OFFENSE	C+
SPECIAL TEAMS	C-
DEFENSE	B-
INTANGIBLES	B

The Badgers catch a scheduling break by missing Northwestern and Purdue this year and getting the two Michigan schools at home. They will have their hands full with non-conference foes Virginia and Oregon—the Ducks will have revenge on their minds as the Badgers head to Eugene—and back-to-back games at Ohio State and Illinois in October could prove troublesome.

(P.D.)

2000 RESULTS

Western Michigan	W	19-7	1-0
Oregon	W	27-23	2-0
Cincinnati	W	28-25	3-0
Northwestern	L	44-47	3-1
Michigan	L	10-13	3-2
Ohio State	L	7-23	3-3
Michigan State	W	17-10	4-3
Purdue	L	24-30	4-4
Iowa	W	13-7	5-4
Minnesota	W	41-20	6-4
Indiana	W	43-22	7-4
Hawaii	W	34-18	8-4
UCLA (Sun Bowl)	W	21-20	9-4

Baylor

LOCATION	**Waco, TX**
CONFERENCE	**Big 12 (South)**
LAST SEASON	**2-9 (.182)**
CONFERENCE RECORD	**0-8 (6th)**
OFFENSIVE STARTERS RETURNING	**9**
DEFENSIVE STARTERS RETURNING	**7**
NICKNAME	**Bears**
COLORS	**Green & Gold**
HOME FIELD	**Floyd Casey Stadium (50,000)**
HEAD COACH	**Kevin Steele (Tennessee '81)**
RECORD AT SCHOOL	**3-19 (2 years)**
CAREER RECORD	**3-10 (2 years)**
ASSISTANTS	**Scott Smith (Baylor '82)** **Tight Ends/Special Teams** **Brick Haley (Alabama A&M '89)** **Defensive Coordinator/Linebackers** **Greg Meyer (North Colorado '74)** **Offensive Coordinator/Quarterbacks** **Doug Fertsch (Baylor '77)** **Offensive Line** **Paul Jette (Texas '77)** **Defensive Backs** **Tommie Frazier (Nebraska '96)** **Running Backs** **Lonnie Hansen (Ottawa University '76)** **Defensive Tackles** **Robert James (Snyder '57)** **Defensive Ends** **Dale Steele (South Carolina '76)** **Wide Receivers/Recruiting Coordinator**
TEAM WINS (last 5 yrs.)	**4-2-2-1-2**
FINAL RANK (last 5 yrs.)	**74-71-59-92-98**
2000 FINISH	**Lost to Oklahoma State in regular-season finale.**

COACH AND PROGRAM

The subject was fan support. Baylor second-year coach Kevin Steele offered this opinion:

"From a coaches perspective, 95 percent of the fans already give us more than enough support. The other five percent, who make a lot of noise, would be disappointed if they knew they really go unheard."

That comment was made at the end of an online chat with Baylor fans. Most of the two dozen or so questions were innocuous, dealing with depth charts and recruiting. But one of the contributors wasn't afraid to vent.

"I go to school here and love football. But there wasn't very much to look forward to this past year," said someone with the electronic handle of WantToBeABearFan. "Every game we were down by 20 at halftime and most of the time we had a big zero points at half time. It was horrible to watch and embarrassing to see more visiting fans than home fans...

"*Sports Illustrated* thinks we should be kicked out of the Big 12. Please tell me we will win one game in the Big 12 next year, or even score a touchdown in more than three games. Hopefully this will happen before I graduate. I want to cheer for you guys. But you have to give me something to cheer about ... You guys suck. Is there any hope next year?"

Steele's response, was, well, steely: "I understand your frustration, and I'm sorry that you choose to vent it in such [an] aggressively negative manner. Yes, we will win in the Big 12, and yes, we will score touchdowns. ... This is a tough, intense, difficult process. It takes time."

In November, Steele's contract was extended. For now, his job appears safe, but it's obvious that Baylor fans—if not particularly the school's administrators—are growing impatient and frustrated from the last five seasons that have produced a total of 11 victories.

"Kevin Steele is a great coach and a man of impeccable character," Baylor president Robert B. Sloan said last November after the contract extension was announced. "We are fortunate to have him leading our football student-athletes. Because of the quality Kevin represents, we want to ensure he has the necessary time and resources needed to build our football program the right way."

Steele, though, is fighting tanks with spit wads. Baylor's athletic department budget of $18.5 million a year is last in the Big 12. By comparison, Texas' budget is $42.2 million while Nebraska's is $41.2 million.

Still, Baylor tries to do its best. Over the last decade, it has improved the athletic department facilities at functional Floyd Casey Stadium. And in the last year, Baylor more than doubled the size of its weight and training rooms. Also, the Bears will dress in a new 8,000-square foot locker room featuring the same lockers NFL players use.

"It's a reward for our players," Steele said. "It's a recruiting tool no question. You'd be surprised what impresses an 18-year old kid."

What impresses fans are victories. And while the Bears doubled their win total last season (from one to two), the progress was minimal. True enough, there were no pratfall losses like the second game of the Steele Era when an ill-advised running play led to a fumble that gave UNLV an eye-rubbing victory in Waco.

But the offense imploded in October. During a three-week stretch, the Bears lost to Texas Tech, 28-0, to Texas A&M, 24-0, and to Nebraska, 56-0. The Bears had 568 yards of total offense in those three games. Statistically, the Bears finished last in the Big 12 in scoring offense, scoring defense, turnover margin, total offense, total defense and first downs.

Much of the offensive impotence can be traced to the season-ending injury suffered by quarterback Greg Cicero in the second game. And, Steele is hoping to continue to integrate a spread offense like the one favored by Clemson. But one of the major problems facing Steele is getting his players to believe they can win again. In particular, the Bears have lost 21 consecutive Big 12 games. Overall in Big 12 play they are 3-37.

"Winning is the biggest confidence builder,"

BIG 12

BLUE RIBBON FORECAST

North Division
1. Nebraska
2. Kansas State
3. Colorado
4. Iowa State
5. Kansas
6. Missouri

South Division
1. Oklahoma
2. Texas
3. Texas Tech
4. Texas A&M
5. Oklahoma State
6. Baylor

ALL-CONFERENCE TEAM

OFFENSE
POS. PLAYER SCHOOL HT. WT. CL.

WR Roy Williams, Texas, 6-5, 210, So.
WR Aaron Lockett, Kansas State, 5-7, 160, Sr.
OL Seth McKinney, Texas A&M, 6-3, 295, Sr.
OL Andre Gurode, Colorado, 6-4, 305, Sr.
C Toniu Fonoti, Nebraska, 6-4, 340, Jr.
OL Frank Romero, Oklahoma, 6-4, 286, Sr.
OL Mike Hayes, Missouri, 6-3, 308, Sr.
QB Eric Crouch, Nebraska, 6-1, 200, Sr.
RB Ennis Haywood, Iowa State, 5-11, 218, Sr.
RB Quentin Griffin, Oklahoma, 5-6, 187, Jr.
TE Tracey Wistrom, Nebraska, 6-5, 240, Sr.

DEFENSE
POS. PLAYER SCHOOL HT. WT. CL.

DL Chad Kelsay, Nebraska, 6-5, 270, Jr.
DL Nate Dwyer, Kansas, 6-3, 300, Sr.
DL Ty Warren, Texas A&M, 6-4, 297, Jr.
DL Cory Redding, Texas, 6-5, 260, Jr.
LB Rocky Calmus, Oklahoma, 6-3, 234, Sr.
LB Ben Leber, Kansas State, 6-4, 250, Sr.
LB Jashon Sykes, Colorado, 6-3, 230, Sr.
DB Kevin Curtis, Texas Tech, 6-3, 209, Sr.
DB Roy Williams, Oklahoma, 6-0, 221, Jr.
DB Quentin Jammer, Texas, 6-1, 198, Sr.
DB Derrick Strait, Oklahoma, 5-11, 194, So.

SPECIALISTS
POS. PLAYER SCHOOL HT. WT. CL.

PK Tim Duncan, Oklahoma, 6-2, 198, Sr.
P Jeff Ferguson, Oklahoma, 5-10, 190, Sr.
RS Aaron Lockett, Kansas State, 5-7, 160, Sr

OFFENSIVE PLAYER OF THE YEAR
Eric Crouch, QB, Nebraska

DEFENSIVE PLAYER OF THE YEAR
Roy Williams, DB, Oklahoma

NEWCOMER OF THE YEAR
Cedric Benson, RB, Texas

BIG 12 NOTEBOOK
After five seasons, the Big 12 Conference is down to just three coaches who have been with their teams since the league made its debut in 1996—Iowa State's Dan McCarney, Kansas State's Bill Snyder and Texas A&M's R.C. Slocum. Oklahoma State (Les Miles) and Missouri (Gary Pinkel) will have new coaches this season. In the Big 12's brief history, there have been eight first-year coaches (Oklahoma has had two). Those coaches have combined for a 48-47 record in their rookie seasons. Five first-year coaches have had winning seasons—Colorado's Gary Barnett (7-5 in 1999), Nebraska's Frank Solich (9-4 in 1998), Oklahoma's Bob Stoops (7-5 in 1999), Texas' Mack Brown (9-3 in 1998) and Texas Tech's Mike Leach (7-6 in 2000). ... The Big 12 championship game will be played at Texas Stadium in Irving, home of the Dallas Cowboys. In the first five years of the Big 12 title game, there has been an interesting trend. Each year when the event has been in a "North" city, a South Division team has won, and vice versa. Texas won in 1996 in St. Louis, Nebraska won in 1997 in San Antonio, Texas A&M won in 1998 in St. Louis, Nebraska won in 1999 in San Antonio and Oklahoma won in 2000 in Kansas City. ... Oklahoma overcame the championship stumbling block that had tripped up Nebraska in 1996 and Kansas State in 1998. Losses in the Big 12 title game cost the Huskers and the Wildcats shots at the national title. The Sooners prevailed over Kansas State, 27-24, in their penultimate step to the national title. However, that doesn't mean that OU administrators are happy with the championship game format. They moved behind the scenes to put together a sub-committee to study the feasibility and need for the title game. However, with television contracts in place through 2006, it's unlikely that the championship game will be discontinued. The Big 12 title game earns the conference more than $8 million in television, corporate sponsorship and ticket revenue. Big 12 schools share equally in the championship game revenue; that works out to nearly $700,000 for each school. ... Oklahoma had just two players—quarterback Josh Heupel and linebacker Torrance Marshall—selected in the NFL draft. That's the fewest number of players drafted from a No. 1 team since 1993, the year the NFL shortened the draft to seven rounds.

Steele said. "It's no different than any other human being in any other field or endeavor. It takes constant attention and care, and in many ways, to rebuild one's confidence. Sometimes the progress early is slow and then explodes."

Playing in the Big 12 Conference, though, sometimes turns explosions into fizzles. True enough, Iowa State had a breakthrough season in 2000, winning nine games and the first bowl game in school history. But for a school like Baylor, climbing the ladder in the Big 12 South is a tedious process. This season, Baylor knows it will face the defending national champion (Oklahoma) plus a school that has its sites set on a national title (Texas).

"We are on track because there are so many positive things happening within this program," Steele said. "We're not where we need to be depth-wise, but we're becoming a more broad-based talented football team. We now have a sense of competition at almost every position.

"The toughest part of the rebuilding process is behind us."

That's a statement of incredible confidence. Steele and his team will try to prove that statement to be correct over the next few seasons.

2001 SCHEDULE

Sept.	8	Arkansas State
	15	@Minnesota
	22	New Mexico
	29	@Iowa State
Oct.	6	@Texas A&M
	13	Nebraska
	20	@Oklahoma
	27	Texas Tech
Nov.	3	Texas
	10	@Missouri
	17	Oklahoma State

QUARTERBACKS

The plan was simple: bring in a junior-college quarterback, someone with experience to lead the offense. Baylor's choice was **Greg Cicero**, a Californian who started his career at Texas, then transferred to Palomar College in San Marcos, Calif.

In his first game as Baylor's quarterback, he directed the Bears to a 20-7 victory over North Texas, completing 17-of-28 passes for 213 yards. He ran an offense that had just two penalties, an eye-catching statistic for a season opener.

Then, in the first quarter of game two against Minnesota, Cicero broke his collarbone. Baylor would try four other quarterbacks, but none were able to run the offense like Cicero.

"We recruited Cicero out of junior college because we knew we had no experience at quarterback." Steele said. "That means all those we started last year, they were all freshmen or redshirt freshmen. That's a tough thing to do in the Big 12."

A 6-4, 213-pound junior, Cicero has recovered from his injury. He participated in spring drills, during which he tried to master the Bears' spread offense. Baylor hopes to copy the success achieved at Tulane and Clemson with the spread attack. The Bears' coaching staff spent a week at Clemson and also talked with new West Virginia coach Rich Rodriguez to learn the best ways to implement the new offense.

"We've had the intent from the very beginning of spreading things out gradually; it's never seemed to work as we first intended," Steele said.

There is concern that Cicero doesn't have the speed or mobility to run the spread attack. Steele says that while Clemson has a running threat in quarterback Woodrow Dantzler, Tulane was successful with Shaun King, a quarterback who rarely ran.

"Cicero does have straight line speed, but he is no Dantzler," Steele said. "In the off-season, we've watched repeatedly the offense of different schools running different versions of it. One of our coaches who thought Shawn was a runner was shocked how rarely he did in fact carry the football."

One thing is certain. If Cicero is healthy, Baylor's offense should improve considerably compared to last season. And if Cicero goes down, at least Steele knows he's got a number of quarterbacks who were force-fed experience last season.

Sophomores **Josh Zachry** (6-3, 183), **Kerry Dixon** (6-1, 190) and **Guy Tomcheck** (6-4, 227) all took turns trying to salvage the offense last season. Zachry has the edge as the backup, but the competition during preseason workouts should be intense.

Last season, Tomcheck saw the most action. He played in eight games, completing 53-of-144 passes for 602 yards and six touchdowns. Zachry played in three games, completing 34-of-66 passes for 428 yards and four touchdowns.

Dixon played in seven games, completing 20-of-65 attempts for 203 yards and no touchdowns. He threw nine of the team's 20 interceptions (as a team, Baylor had just 10 touchdown passes.)

Redshirt freshman **Aaron Karas** (6-2, 195) had a solid spring and finished No. 3 on the depth chart.

RUNNING BACKS

Baylor was last in Division I-A in total offense last season. A big reason for the inability to move the ball was the fact that the Bears averaged just 2.2 yards per rushing attempt (but at least the Bears weren't last nationally in rushing—they were 110th out of 114 teams). For the season, Baylor averaged just 72.9 yards a game and scored just five rushing touchdowns.

Unfortunately for Baylor, one of the key losses from last year's offensive unit is running back Darrell Bush. A plugger, Bush led the Bears with 517 yards. Bush closed out his career as the fourth-leading career rusher in Baylor history with 2,249 yards on 503 attempts.

The two main ball carriers for 2001 probably will be junior **Chedrick Ricks** (5-8, 200) and sophomore **Jonathan Golden** (6-0, 208). Both are tailbacks who played last year as Bush's backups.

Ricks played in all 11 games, primarily in third-down situations. He gained 122 yards on 38 carries and caught four passes for 46 yards. Golden played in 10 games during his freshman season, gaining 90 yards on 35 carries.

Senior **Melvin Barnett** (6-0, 243) is the probable starter at fullback. He played in all 11 games last season, starting five. He finished with 79 yards on 29 carries and tied for the team lead with two rushing touchdowns.

Also in the mix at fullback is redshirt freshman **Jonathan Evans** (6-1, 250). He was moved from tailback to fullback during spring practice.

"He has fluidity there," Steele said. "He's one of those guys who can slither through all that trash and find his block. There's not a lot of guys who are real good at that."

The running game could get a boost from the return of senior **Derek Lagway** (6-1, 265). Projected to be one of the team's top running backs last season, he had to sit out the season as a medical redshirt after his motorcycle was hit by a car last June. He suffered a broken kneecap and had to undergo surgery.

In 1999, Lagway was the team's second-leading rusher, gaining 226 yards on 51 carries. Lagway has the ability to play both fullback and tailback. However, the year away from football will be difficult to overcome. After spring practice, he was not listed on the two-deep charts at either position.

WIDE RECEIVERS/TIGHT ENDS

There is potential at this position, but with Baylor going to a spread offense, there's got to be more bodies so that when the Bears go to four receiver looks, they've got legitimate targets on the field.

Junior **Reggie Newhouse** (6-1, 197), the son of former Dallas Cowboys fullback Robert Newhouse, was Baylor's top receiver last season. He became the first Baylor receiver in 17 years to catch at least 40 passes in a season. He averaged 15.7 yards on 40 catches and four touchdowns.

Redshirt freshman **John Martin** (5-11, 182) is listed as the starter at flanker.

Sophomore **Robeert Quiroga** (6-2, 185) was limited in his spring practices because he competes on the Baylor track team. He showed flashes of potential as a freshman last season, catching 17 passes for 199 yards and three touchdowns. His ability to stretch the field provides a nice complement to Newsome's steady play.

Juniors **Lanny O'Steen** (5-11, 187) and **Bobby Darnell** (5-11, 188), along with redshirt freshman **Marques Roberts** (6-1, 218), should also see playing time.

Last season, O'Steen was second on the team with 21 receptions for 279 yards and one touchdown. Darnell played in six games last year, making one catch for 11 yards. In two seasons, Darnell has five receptions for 54 yards.

Junior **Ray Harrington** (6-3, 195), from Southwestern (Calif.) Junior College in San Diego, could also see playing time at wide receiver. He originally signed with Hawaii out of high school.

The Bears have solid depth at tight end. Seniors **Andrew Obriotti** (6-3, 238) and **Anthony Dozier** (6-5, 251), along with sophomore **Shane Williams** (6-3, 240), all caught Steele's attention.

"They all had a good spring," he said. "All three are talented tight ends and very similar. Dozer and Obriotti are seniors, and Williams is a redshirt sophomore with a bright future."

Obriotti is the most experienced of the trio, with 24 career starts. He started 10-of-11 games in 2000, finishing with 10 catches for 96 yards. Williams played in all 11 games last season as a backup and did not have a reception.

Dozier, who sat out the 1999 season after transferring from Louisiana-Lafayette, started three games and played in all 11 last season. He had five catches for 58 yards.

Redshirt freshman Luke Groth (6-5, 254) provides more depth at tight end.

OFFENSIVE LINE

With his background of coaching at Nebraska, Steele realizes that offensive line is one of a team's most important positions. Baylor is still struggling to not only improve its talent level but its depth on the offensive line.

All five starters return from last year's line, but as the ineffective running game statistics indicate, Baylor needs to pull a Spike Lee—Mo' Better players.

Steele went the quick-fix route, signing three junior-college offensive linemen.

"We recruited the JUCO talent based on the premise that we felt they could compete for starting positions," Steele said. "We want the JUCO guys to either start or make others around them better through competition."

Matt Bickel (6-5, 340) from Grossmont (Calif.) Community College, **Antoine Murphy** (6-4, 325) from William Rainey Harper (Ill.) Junior College and **Charles Bungert** (6-8, 350) from Moorpark (Calif.) Junior College all should see extensive playing time.

Of the returning starters, seniors **Joe Jackson**, a 6-3, 277-pound center, and left tackle **Jon Erickson** (6-5, 299) are expected to keep their starting jobs.

Sophomore **Cedric Fields** (6-2, 295) made a lot of improvement during spring drills as Jackson's backup at center.

Three redshirt freshmen also made strides during the spring—**Brad Schlueter** (6-5, 283), listed as the third-team center; **Ryan McDaniel** (6-5, 288), listed second-team at left tackle; and **Chris Sipes** (6-4, 306), the backup at right tackle.

Junior **Ethan Kelley** (6-2, 231) started 10-of-11 games at left guard. Sophomore **Derek Long** (6-6, 296) started four of the last five games at right guard as a redshirt freshman. Senior **Greg Jerman** (6-5, 292) started 10-of-11 games at right tackle. As a sophomore, he started all 11 games at left tackle.

With the junior-college additions and with depth at certain positions, preseason practice could see a number of linemen switching positions in order to balance the depth chart and get the Bears' best linemen on the field.

2000 STATISTICS

Rushing offense	72.9	110
Passing offense	148.9	106
Total offense	221.8	114
Scoring offense	12.6	111
Net Punting	30.9	101
Punt returns	9.7	53
Kickoff returns	19.0	76
Rushing defense	209.0	102
Passing efficiency defense	129.5	92
Total defense	441.4	109
Scoring defense	36.1	107
Turnover margin	-9	97

Last column is ranking among Division I-A teams.

KICKERS

In an offense that struggled to score points, inconsistency in the kicking game is a mortal sin. Unfortunately for the Bears, they don't have one kicker they can rely on.

"We worked extensively on the kicking game this spring," Steele said. "We've got to get more consistency from them. They are very talented and have good legs, but we need more consistency to really see improvement."

Senior **Adam Stiles** (6-5, 236) handles both the long-range kicking and punting duties. He started the season handling all the kicking chores, but missed 2-of-4 tries in the season opener. For the season, he was 3-of-6 on field-goal tries. He also handles kickoffs.

Junior **Danile Andino** (6-0, 230) is listed as Stiles' backup. The former walk-on made 12-of-13 extra-point attempts and was 2-of-3 on field goals.

Redshirt freshman **Kenny Webb** (5-7, 155) also is competing for the kicking job.

DEFENSIVE LINE

Steele believes he has more talent and depth on defense and he's particularly pleased with how his defensive line is developing.

"The defensive line is actually the most improved segment of our team coming out of the spring," he said. "We have some junior college players who will help, so our depth is much improved, but more importantly, we're older, more experienced."

Two junior college recruits and a prep school signee should shore up the defensive line—junior **A.C. Collier** (6-3, 235) from Tyler (Texas) Junior College; freshman **Jason Geter** (6-5, 306) from Georgia Military; and junior **Shaun Jackson** (6-3, 238) from Grossmont (Calif.) Community College.

Collier led his league in quarterback sacks with 12 despite missing a pair of games. He was a second-team NJCAA All-American who made 68 tackles as a sophomore. The mammoth Geter, a North Carolina native, played in the 1998 Shrine Bowl All-Star game, which features North Carolina high school all-stars against those from South Carolina. Jackson originally signed with Hawaii and started for the Warriors in their 1999 Oahu Bowl win over Oregon State.

Junior **Kevin Stevenson** (6-2, 274) is starting to develop into a force at defensive tackle. Last season, he started 10- of-11 games, finishing with

67 tackles, four tackles for loss and one quarterback sack. Stevenson teams with nose tackle **Travis Hicks**, a 6-3, 303-pound junior, as the starters in the middle of the defensive line. Hicks totaled 38 tackles during the 2000 season, starting 2-of-11 games.

Senior **Demetrio Phillips** (6-4, 285) and sophomore **Eric Sims** (6-5, 281) provide depth at both tackle spots. Junior **Ethan Kelley** (6-2, 321) was impressive during spring practice after being moved from the offensive line.

Junior **Charles Mann** (6-4, 252) and sophomore **Aaron Lard** (6-1, 266) give the Bears a solid pair of defensive ends. Mann started nine times last season, totaling 35 tackles with eight quarterback hurries. Lard started 10 games, finishing with 50 tackles, four tackles for loss and two quarterback sacks.

Sophomore **Joe Simmons** (6-4, 232), along with redshirt freshmen **Khari Long** (6-5, 240), **Billy Crawford** (6-2, 229), **David Wren** (6-3, 250) and **Luke Groth** (6-5, 254), should all see action as backups. Groth had an impressive spring after being moved from tight end.

LINEBACKERS

This is a talented and young area. Of the top six projected players in the spring, there were three sophomores and two were redshirt freshmen. The other was a junior.

Sophomore **John Garrett** (6-1, 235), a 2000 signing day coup, had an impressive season as a freshman. He played in all 11 games, starting five. He had 54 tackles, including six tackles for losses.

Garrett was moved to the middle linebacker spot in the spring and should bring his enthusiastic hustling style to the middle of the Baylor defense.

Garrett probably will be flanked by sophomores **Stephen Sepulveda** (6-2, 218) and **Anthony Simmons** (5-11, 201).

Junior **Kevin Chaisson** (6-1, 243), along with redshirt freshmen **Mike Tolbert** (6-0, 238) and **Jack Wallace** (6-3, 205), are projected as backups.

Freshman **Greg Wade** (6-3, 230) was signed out of Georgia Military College. He originally signed with Duke. Wade could compete for one of the outside linebacking spots or provide depth.

DEFENSIVE BACKS

Through the last two seasons of 3-19 football, one thing that Baylor fans could count on was the stellar play of defensive back Gary Baxter. Last season as a senior he led the team with 95 tackles and added 11 pass deflections and two forced fumbles. And, he was the only Bear selected in the NFL draft, going to the Super Bowl champion Baltimore Ravens in the second round.

"Obviously the loss of a player as talented as Baxter is tough, but it's part of the college game," Steele said. "We have some very good young corners who have played well for us."

Sophomores **Eric Giddens** (5-11, 189) and **Bobby Hart** (5-11, 183) are projected as the starters at the corners. Giddens played in 10 games last season as a redshirt freshman, with four starts. He finished with 36 tackles and two interceptions. Hart played in all 11 games as a freshman, with two starts. He totaled 22 tackles.

Junior **Randy Davis** (5-9, 173), sophomores **Matt Johnson** (5-8, 182) and **Danielle McLean** (5-11, 178) and redshirt freshman **Marcus Stenix** (6-0, 185) figure to be cornerback reserves. Davis and McClean were moved to the corner from free safety during spring practice.

There is experience and talent at both safety spots. Seniors **Samir Al-Amin** (6-1, 219) at free and **Kyle Staudt** (6-3, 212) at strong will have plenty of opportunity to provide leadership for the Bears' young defensive backs.

Al-Amin, who moves from strong to free safety, has started 17 games during his career. Last season, he finished with 68 tackles and also had seven pass breakups and two interceptions. Staudt's development has allowed Baylor to shift Al-Amin. Last season, Staudt started in 3-of-11 games, finishing with 33 tackles.

Sophomores **Derrick Cash** (5-11, 206) and **Matt Amendola** (5-11, 194) figure to be the backups at the safety spots. Cash was moved to the secondary after spending time at linebacker.

Paul Jette is the new secondary coach and is the only coaching change for the Baylor staff. He comes to Baylor after seven years at East Carolina as the defensive coordinator and secondary coach. The Bears figure to play press coverage, but they didn't show much of that during the spring game.

PUNTERS

If Stiles is allowed to concentrate only on punting, he could have a solid season. Last season, he finished fourth in the Big 12 with a 40.1 average. He certainly got plenty of practice; his 81 punts easily ranked as the most attempts by a Big 12 punter. Stiles had 12 of his punts downed inside the 20.

Senior **Ryan Chapdelaine** (6-1, 205) is available if anything happens to Stiles. In 2000, Chapdelaine saw his only action against Oklahoma State, punting twice for an average of 39 yards with a long kick of 45 yards.

SPECIAL TEAMS

"We've got 13 seniors and 14 juniors and the rest are freshmen and sophomores," Steele said. "As far as the coverage teams, we will have to stay healthy and avoid using too many young people on coverage teams."

The dilemma for coaches in positions like Steele's is this: play your veterans on special teams with the additional risk of injury and certain fatigue or gamble that younger, inexperienced players won't make special teams blunders that can change the course of a game.

Last season, the kickoff and punt coverage teams didn't do their jobs. On 19 kickoffs, Baylor allowed an average return of 21.3 yards. And opponents averaged 12.3 yards and scored three touchdowns on 54 punt returns.

Baylor must replace its top two kickoff returners in Martin Dorsett and Elijah Burkins. Davis and Ricks have experience returning kickoffs. Hard, who returned 18 punts for an 8.4-yard average, is expected to continue in that role.

RECRUITING CLASS

Signing day 2000 was a celebration in Waco when linebacker Garrett of Mart, Texas, signed with the Bears. Steele saw that as an indication Baylor was making progress in keeping Central Texas players close to home.

Signing day 2001 brought disappointment when Quan Cosby of Mart opted to sign with Texas instead of Baylor. That strikeout, plus the fact that the Bears' '01 class wasn't filled with blue-chip names, had Steele trying to put a positive spin on Signing Day.

"The signing day rankings are strong evidence that very rarely do the most prominent names and the highest ranked signing classes pan out," he said. "We recruit the big names and we 'kick the weeds' [looking for players].

"Players are found everywhere; Jerry Rice was found by the 49ers at Mississippi Valley. It's no different from high school to college."

In addition to the junior college signees who will be counted on to make an immediate impact, Baylor needs some of its freshmen to step in and add depth at wide receiver and linebacker.

Linebackers **Justin Crooks** (6-1, 217) of Round Rock McNeil High School and **Jamaal Harper** (6-2, 220) of Dallas Bryan Adams High School should get long looks during preseason practices. Also, wide receiver **J Fields** (6-3, 190) of Caprock High School is the only freshman wide receiver on the roster.

BLUE RIBBON ANALYSIS

OFFENSE	C-
SPECIAL TEAMS	C
DEFENSE	C+
INTANGIBLES	D+

Steele is pushing a large rock up a steep hill. Ending the Big 12 losing streak could help elevate the program, but even that won't be easy. Of the Bears' eight conference foes, the first six—Iowa State, Texas Tech, Texas A&M, Nebraska, Texas and Oklahoma—all appeared in bowl games last season.

The rest of the schedule offers no respite. After opening at home against Arkansas State, Baylor plays at Minnesota, a team that whipped the Bears, 34-9, in Waco. That game could help define the season. If Baylor could win on the road against a Big Ten Conference team, it could provide a huge boost of confidence. However, a loss to the Gophers—particularly if it's a blowout—could set the stage for another one- or two-win season.

When he took the job two years ago, Steele said the Bears had the talent needed to win in the Big 12. He admits now that he was trying to whistle his way past a graveyard.

"In assessing this situation at the time, I felt like Colin Powell said of war: If you tell everything, the people back home will know it [fans], the enemy will know it [opponents], and worst of all, the troops [your team] will know it," Steele said. "I made the assessment that we needed hope no matter how difficult the task. I would do it the same way again, in terms of assessment. We are much improved across the board, but ultimately it has to show up on the field. Win."

Like many programs trying to swim up from the deep end of the pool, Baylor is working with a small margin of error. The Bears need to keep their front line players healthy. They need young players to develop quickly. They need Cicero to give the offense direction. They need Newhouse and others to make big plays. And they need to steal a few victories (games with Minnesota, Texas Tech, Missouri and Oklahoma State are the most eligible for pilfering).

That's a lot to ask.

"Look, the bottom line is that Baylor needs a good dose of winning for a couple of years," Steele said. "That would solve a lot of problems. We need to win some football games.

"I know it's tough. I know it's frustrating. We're going to get this thing turned. We're going to win. If I don't get it turned, they're going to fire me."

(W.B.)

2000 RESULTS

North Texas	W	20-7	1-0
Minnesota	L	9-34	1-1
South Florida	W	28-13	2-1
Iowa State	L	17-31	2-2
Texas Tech	L	0-28	2-3

Texas A&M	L	0-24	2-4
Nebraska	L	0-59	2-5
Texas	L	14-48	2-6
Oklahoma	L	7-56	2-7
Missouri	L	22-47	2-8
Oklahoma State	L	22-50	2-9

Colorado

LOCATION Boulder, CO
CONFERENCE Big 12 (North)
LAST SEASON 3-8 (.273)
CONFERENCE RECORD 3-5 (4th)
OFFENSIVE STARTERS RETURNING 10
DEFENSIVE STARTERS RETURNING 8
NICKNAME Buffaloes
COLORS Black, Gold & Silver
HOME FIELD Folsom Field (51,650)
HEAD COACH Gary Barnett (Missouri '69)
RECORD AT SCHOOL 10-13 (2 years)
CAREER RECORD 53-69-2 (10 years)
ASSISTANTS Brian Cabral (Colorado '78)
Assistant Head Coach/Inside Linebackers
Shawn Watson (Southern Illinois '82)
Offensive Coordinator/Quarterbacks
Vince Okruch (Culver-Stockton '77)
Co-Defensive Coordinator/OS Linebackers
Tom McMahon (Montana '71)
Co-Defensive Coordinator/Secondary
Chris Wilson (Oklahoma '92)
Defensive Line
Steve Marshall (Louisville '79)
Offensive Line
John Wristen (Southern Colorado '84)
Tight Ends
Eric Bieniemy (Colorado '01)
Running Backs
Jon Embree (Colorado '87)
Receivers
TEAM WINS (last 5 yrs.) 10-5-8-7-3
FINAL RANK (last 5 yrs.) 6-34-28-14-56
2000 FINISH Lost to Nebraska in regular-season finale.

COACH AND PROGRAM

Watching Colorado approach last season was like standing on an overpass with a full view of train tracks. Approaching from one side was a team full of youthful optimism. From the other side was a schedule so ridiculous that coach Gary Barnett was griping about it the previous spring.

Another time in Colorado history and the Buffs would have increased their speed and blown through the obstacles. Since Bill McCartney turned the program around in the mid-1980s, Colorado never backed away from a challenge. The Buffs were September television favorites, taking on all comers.

Who can forget Kordell Stewart's Hail Mary touchdown bomb at Michigan, the near brawl that broke out in the home loss to Miami, the final-second field goal to beat Texas, victories over Washington and Wisconsin? Colorado became a program forged of steel because of who it played, and the Buffs, who started the 1990 season with an 0-1-1 record, would never have rallied to win a share of the national championship that season had it not built credentials against worthy opponents.

Those teams were fortified with All-America talent. The 2000 Buffaloes were not. On came the schedule—Colorado State, Southern Cal, Washington, Kansas State, Texas A&M and Texas. It didn't take a pessimist to forecast an 0-6 start, especially with the Buffs breaking in a new starting quarterback.

The opener was the critical game. In 1999, upstart Colorado State embarrassed the Buffs, 41-14, in Gary Barnett's debut. The debacle ended with police firing tear gas into Mile High Stadium to end fan battles. Revenge was with Colorado this time but not fortune as the pesky Rams did it again, although not as comfortably, 28-24.

From there, a pair of three-point losses put the season in a tailspin. The only good thing to come out of the fourth loss, by 23 at home to Kansas State, was the emergence of freshman quarterback **Craig Ochs**, who entered in the second quarter and didn't leave for the rest of the season.

Colorado somehow found a way to win at Texas A&M, but gave it back two weeks later with a loss at Kansas.

By Oct. 21 and with four games remaining, the bowl-regular Buffs were mathematically eliminated from the postseason. The program was headed for a season it hadn't lived in nearly two decades.

But Colorado was not a bad team. Running back **Cortlen Johnson**, linebacker **Jashon Sykes**, tight end **Daniel Graham** and center **Anthony Gurode** were all-conference caliber. Also, the Buffs had one of the nation's top recruits in running back **Marcus Houston**.

The team couldn't handle the schedule. Shouldn't have had to, really. Turns out, the Buffs played Washington as well as anybody. In the regular-season finale at Nebraska, Colorado went ahead with 47 seconds to play only to have the Huskers drive for a game-winning field goal that just beat the clock. Colorado had the talent to play with anybody. But not the experience, or, after a few weeks, the confidence. That's what the off-season was all about for Colorado—regaining confidence.

"There's no doubt we were shaken, but I think everybody came away more disgusted than anything else," Barnett said. "Spring practice has always been important but it was more so for us this year because we wanted our kids to feel confident about every phase of the game."

They would have had they not all been injured. For reasons the coaches and medical staff are still trying to determine, Colorado had the most injury-plagued off-season in memory. Barnett counted 23 who missed spring workouts, including eight who needed shoulder surgery.

"That seems way out of proportion to me," said Barnett, who ordered a full review of the team's practice drills, strength and conditioning work, equipment and medical procedures. He is also digging to find out how Colorado worked out before he arrived in 1999. Barnett also guessed that some players arrived on campus with shoulder injuries that weren't properly treated in high school.

Barnett had already moved ahead with another form of surgery, to his schedule. Washington and Southern Cal have been replaced by Washington State and San Jose State. The date against Colorado State in Denver remains. That's a cash cow game for both schools.

Barnett felt good enough about his team to take on an additional game, at home against Fresno State on Aug. 25. If Colorado can't find some confidence by October this year, then Barnett needs to be evaluating more than sore shoulders.

2001 SCHEDULE

Aug.	26	Fresno State
Sept.	1	Colorado State
	8	San Jose State
	15	@Washington State
	22	Kansas
Oct.	6	@Kansas State
	13	Texas A&M
	20	@Texas
	27	@Oklahoma State
Nov.	3	Missouri
	10	@Iowa State
	23	Nebraska

QUARTERBACKS

During last year's fall camp, Barnett said it was possible that Ochs (6-2, 210), who had been on campus for all of a few weeks, was the best quarterback in the program.

How prophetic that statement proved.

But at the time it seemed like a statement Barnett made to light a fire under his two top candidates, **Bobby Pesavento** (6-5, 230) and Zac Colvin. They were battling to replace Mike Moschetti, a two-year starter after arriving from junior college.

Pesavento had the better spring practice, Colvin the better spring game. The battle would continue into the early weeks of the season. Each started a September game. Neither could get the job done. Especially disappointing was the way the offense bogged down late in 17-14 losses to Washington and Southern Cal.

The fourth week and Kansas State approached. Colorado stood 0-3. Ochs was starting to take more snaps in practice but Pesavento would start against the Wildcats. K-State jumped to a 13-0 lead. The Buffs tacked on a pair of field goals, but after one possession of the second quarter, the margin was 20-6.

Enter Ochs, the hometown hero, a product of Boulder High. Immediately the offense and entire team was energized. He directed a touchdown drive on his first possession, capping it with his own scoring run.

Colorado had its starter. The next week, in his first-ever start, Ochs directed the Buffs to an improbable win at Texas A&M, ending the Aggies' 22-game home winning streak. Ochs kept his poise before more than 75,000 hostile fans, scoring a touchdown on an 18-yard run, passing 52 yards for another and delivering several key third-down plays.

"For a freshman, he's just incredibly poised," Barnett said after that game. "To come in here and win in these conditions, in front of a hostile crowd, speaks volumes for the kind of player he can be."

Ochs went on to set school freshmen records for passing yards (1,778) and total offense (1,884), and he became the first player in school history to throw for a touchdown, rush for a touchdown and catch a touchdown pass in the same game in the Buffs' 37-21 victory over Oklahoma State. He threw seven touchdown passes and was intercepted seven times.

Maybe Ochs' most impressive performance came in the season finale against Nebraska. After a lousy start, Ochs rallied to complete 21 of his last 30 passes for 235 yards and a touchdown. He also rifled a conversion pass with 47 seconds to play that gave Colorado a lead.

"We're looking to go to the next level in the passing game," Barnett said. "We want Craig to have greater control."

Ochs didn't get that chance in the spring. He was one of several who sat out because of injury.

Pesavento, a senior, remains as the top reserve, but Colvin has transferred. A year ago, Pesavento completed 43-of-72 passes for 536 yards and three touchdowns. His completion ratio was 59 percent, and he wasn't intercepted.

There's another name in the quarterback mix, **Robert Hodge** (5-11, 180), who enrolled in

January from El Camino (Calif.) Junior College and was one of the nation's best last season. The only other player who got snaps at the position in the spring was walk-on freshman Adam Drill (6-4, 210).

RUNNING BACKS

Not since the days of Rashaan Salaam has Colorado potentially looked this good at running back.

Last year, the Buffs essentially got a full season out of senior Johnson (5-9, 195), Houston (6-2, 205) and sophomore **Bobby Purify** (6-0, 195), who combined to rush for 1,131 yards in 16 games.

All three battled injuries throughout the season. Johnson hurt a toe, ankle and knee. Houston suffered a hip flexor tear in the third game and his promising rookie season came to an end. Purify broke a bone in his foot on the first day of fall camp and didn't play until the seventh game.

The problems didn't stop after the season. Johnson was suspended indefinitely by Barnett during spring workouts for academic problems.

"Indefinite means indefinite," Barnett said at the end of spring.

Johnson was not listed on the team's post-spring roster. If he makes it back, Johnson gives the Buffs a potential all-conference running back. A year ago, he was on the Doak Walker preseason watch list before the injuries slowed him down. Johnson wound up with 622 yards in eight games, including a 155-yard performance against Nebraska. His biggest day as a Buff came in a bowl-game victory over Boston College after the 1999 season, when he rushed for 201 yards and a pair of touchdowns.

Houston was, in the opinion of some recruiting analysts, the nation's top running back out of Denver's Thomas Jefferson High two years ago. Then came the injury. Houston received a medical redshirt and has four years remaining.

Houston gave a tantalizing glimpse of things to come in his debut game, rushing for 100 yards on 18 carries in the season opener against Colorado State. He followed that with an even more impressive effort, carrying 25 times for 150 yards against Southern Cal. He tacked on 82 yards on 23 carries against Washington before his season ended.

Houston ran 66 times for 332 yards and a touchdown in his abbreviated rookie year. That's a 110.7 yards-per-game average. He also caught three passes for 33 yards.

Houston is more than just a special player. He's also a special person. In high school, Houston was disturbed by the number of freshmen in his school district who were ineligible for sports because of poor grades and behavior.

His solution was to develop an educational program called "Just Say Know" that helped show middle school students what it takes to achieve academic, social and athletic success in high school."

Houston has taken his message across the country, and has traveled all the way to Amsterdam to speak on human rights.

At fullback, senior **Scott Nemeth** (6-2, 235) is a returning starter. Fullbacks don't get many attempts in Barnett's offense. Nemeth had nine attempts for 44 yards and a touchdown last season. He was pushed in the spring by junior **Brandom Drumm** (6-2, 230), who has tailback like moves and could see some action there.

WIDE RECEIVERS/TIGHT ENDS

The Big 12's top receiving tight end wears a Colorado uniform. Graham (6-3, 245), a senior, is one of the nation's best. He led league tight ends with 33 receptions and 443 yards. The coaching staff keeps up with domination blocks, where a player controls his opponent by either knocking him on his back or taking him five yards downfield. Graham recorded an unusually high number, 93, last season.

Graham figures to be more of a target in 2001. His speed and soft hands make him Shannon Sharpe-like. Graham was voted the team's outstanding offensive player in the spring. He'll be spelled by sophomore **Quinn Sypniewski** (6-6, 255), who started twice last year when the Buffs opened in a two-tight end set.

Senior **John Minardi** (6-2, 200) once again figures to be Ochs' go-to wide receiver. He caught 48 passes for 592 yards, two touchdowns and 27 first downs and was much better in the second half of the season than the first.

Seniors **Roman Hollowell** (5-6, 160) and **Cedric Cormier** (5-11, 185) are also front-liners. Hollowell caught a pass in every game last season and finished with 26 for 248 yards.

Cormier is looking to regain the form he flashed as a freshman before tearing his ACL in the fifth week. He had caught seven passes for 131 yards, returned a punt 82 yards for a touchdown and three kickoffs for a 29-yard average before the injury. Cormier was Colorado's special teams' player of the game twice in four games.

Behind Minardi are sophomores **Derek McCoy** (6-3, 210), John Donahoe (6-0, 185) and **Marcus Moore** (5-11, 185), a former tailback. Backing up Hollowell and Cormier are junior **Jason Burianek** (6-0, 170) and sophomore **Corey Alexander** (5-10, 165).

OFFENSIVE LINE

A weakness when last season started, the Buffs' line got better throughout the year and an All-America candidate emerged in Gurode (6-4, 320), a senior so massive he held down two offensive line positions—center and left guard.

Injuries forced Gurode to shift from center, where he started the first six games, to right guard, where he finished the season. That's where he'll line up this year.

Gurode made the coaches' all-conference team and was a standout in the final game against Nebraska in which he recorded 15 domination blocks. Gurode rarely came off the field. He played 771 snaps, four away from a school record, and led the Buffs in all the offensive line blocking categories that coaches glean from game film.

In a rarity for a lineman, Gurode was voted the team's offensive MVP last season, and he easily captured the team's top offensive lineman award for the spring. His starting string of 24 games is a team best.

Gurode will team up in the right side with senior **Victor Rogers** (6-7, 320), the walking human surgery. At one point over a 15-month span, Rogers had seven operations. He missed the spring but is expected to be at full strength for fall camp.

Junior college transfer **Wayne Lucier** (6-4, 300) and senior **Neal Hannifan** (6-3, 290) are battling for the center spot. On the left side, junior tackle **Justin Bates** (6-4, 295) and sophomore guard **Marwan Hage** (6-3, 295) are each coming off shoulder surgery. They shared the guard position last season. Bates is making the switch.

2000 STATISTICS

Rushing offense	122.0	82
Passing offense	240.0	32
Total offense	362.0	66
Scoring offense	22.9	77
Net Punting	35.0	47
Punt returns	17.8	2
Kickoff returns	20.5	33
Rushing defense	175.1	78
Passing efficiency defense	134.4	98
Total defense	422.1	99
Scoring defense	25.8	63
Turnover margin	+5	35

Last column is ranking among Division I-A teams.

KICKERS

Once again, injuries slowed development of a position in the spring. Coaches had hoped senior **Jeremy Flores** (5-10, 185) would emerge as the clear frontrunner at place-kicker but an ankle sprain limited his action.

Still, Flores is the guy. He came to Colorado as a kicker-punter out of junior college last season, but handled only the punt duties as junior **Mark Mariscal** (6-2, 195) struggled as the kicker, missing 11 of 18 field-goal tries.

Mariscal has been moved to punter, Flores continues to be the front-runner at kicker, but he'll get pushed by senior **Derek Moore** (5-9, 180), junior **Pat Broughtman** (5-11, 185) and freshman **J.T. Eberly** (6-1, 175).

One kicker you won't see is Katie Hnida, who became the first woman on Colorado roster and first in Big 12 history last season. She dressed for a regular-season and bowl game in 1999 but left the team before last season.

DEFENSIVE LINE

The line didn't hurt Colorado last year like other areas of the defense, but it didn't distinguish itself and this unit has more rebuilding to do than the others.

The Buffs finished ninth in the league in rushing defense, surrendering 175 yards per game. Three starters are gone, and the only returning player is senior tackle **Justin Bannan** (6-3, 295), probably the best of the bunch, having been a second-team all-league pick in 1999 and third-team last year.

Despite being double-teamed, Bannan managed 39 tackles, 30 solo, with five for losses and two forced fumbles.

The battle for most of the other starting spots continues in the fall because of spring injuries. Sophomore **Marcus Harris** (6-2, 220) and junior **Tyler Brayton** (6-6, 265) are competing at end and Barnett may decide to start both of them. Also looking for time at end is sophomore **Matt McChesney** (6-5, 280) and freshman **Sam Wilder** (6-5, 265).

The most interesting candidate at end is senior **Ernest Renfroe** (6-6, 250), a bruising forward on the basketball team who is finishing up school this year.

The other starting tackle will come from a pool of junior **Sam Taulealea** (6-0, 320), redshirt freshman **Brandon Dabdoub** (6-1, 295) and sophomore **Pete Friedrich** (6-3, 290). Friedrich missed all of last year with a hamstring injury.

Junior **DeAndre Fluellen** (6-1, 300) is a newcomer who could vault into the starting lineup at tackle.

LINEBACKERS

This is the strongest of the defensive positions but also the most puzzling. There's no way a player like senior inside linebacker Sykes (6-3, 230) should have let Colorado slip to the Big 12's second worst defense (422.1 yards allowed) last season.

Sykes' unexpected poor performance last year

not only cost the Buffaloes, it cost Sykes a chance of an early exit to NFL riches. He was the Big 12's most highly touted defensive player heading into last season, every publication's first-team All-American after coming off a sophomore year in which he was the team's most valuable player.

And, by the way, he was *Blue Ribbon*'s preseason defensive player of the year in the Big 12. He wound up honorable mention All-Big 12.

"I've got something to prove this year," Sykes said.

Not that his year was a total loss. He was second on the team in tackles with 107, 74 unassisted. He had six tackles for loss and four quarterback sacks, and even contributed a fumble recovery (returning it 50 yards) and an interception.

Once again, Sykes will try and become the third Colorado player to win the Butkus Award. He'd join some elite company in Alfred Williams (1989) and Matt Russell (1996) .

The other starting inside linebacker, senior **Andy Peeke** (6-0, 200), isn't flashy, but he's effective. He was fourth on the team with 72 tackles.

Backing up the inside linebackers are junior **Aaron Killion** (6-3, 235), sophomore **Sean Tufts** (6-4, 225 pounds) and junior **Joey Johnson** (6-3, 220).

DEFENSIVE BACKS

This was the problem, a big problem.

"We gave up too many big plays, particularly at the corner," Barnett said. "We've got to get some confidence in the secondary."

It's hard to instill confidence after last season's handiwork. Colorado finished dead last in the Big 12 in pass defense. Opponents threw for 2,717 yards and 17 touchdowns. The Buffs gave up 23 first downs per game.

A major issue was big plays, a condition that reared its ugly head in the season-opening loss to Colorado State. The Rams scored four touchdowns on long plays in a 28-24 victory.

There is some talent. Senior strong safety **Michael Lewis** (6-1, 210) is a three-year letter winner and was voted the team's defensive MVP last season. He led the Buffs in interceptions (three), tackles (117), deflections (six) and forced fumbles (four). He won the Hale Irwin Award as the top defensive back in spring practice.

Senior **Robbie Robinson** (5-11, 200) will be the starting free safety, and sophomore **Phil Jackson** (6-1, 180) has a stranglehold on one of the cornerback spots. Both were starters last season.

Senior **Roderick Sneed** (6-0, 180) should get the nod over junior **Donald Strickland** (5-10, 180) at the other corner. They shared the position last season, but Strickland was sidelined in the spring with shoulder surgery.

A junior college transfer who could make a difference is **Omar Stewart** (5-11, 190). He'll get a look at left corner.

PUNTERS

Mariscal and Jeremy are switching identities. Mariscal made only 39 percent of his field goals last year and is now the Buffs' punter. Flores averaged 35.2 yards per punt, not good enough for a program that has produced some tremendous punters. So Flores was switched to place kicking duties this year.

SPECIAL TEAMS

Colorado ranked second nationally in punt returns last year, averaging nearly 18 yards per return. Hollowell averaged 15 yards, including a 66-yard touchdown against Kansas. He would have finished among the national leaders but didn't have enough attempts to qualify.

Minardi averaged 24.3 yards per return.

The Buffs weren't as good on kickoff returns, averaging about 21 per attempt with Hollowell and senior wide receiver **Matt Brunson** (5-11, 175) handling the duties.

The return achievements were overshadowed by poor kick coverage. Kickoffs and punts tended to be short and low. The Buffs gave up six kickoffs and punts longer than 30 yards.

RECRUITING CLASS

Barnett didn't sign a big class, 17 in all. Colorado went heavy for line help, signing three offensive linemen and five defensive linemen among the 13 high school signees.

"You've got to have a big-picture overview to understand this class," Barnett said. "Lots of times those kinds of recruits don't attract a lot of attention nationally. This class for us, down the road, fills the needs we have in our program."

Two linemen figure to play right away. **DeAndre Fluellen**, a 6-1, 300-pound defensive lineman, and freshman **McKenzie Tilmon**, a 6-3, 285-pounder from Irving, Texas, might get plugged into the two-deep.

Fluellen played one year at Northeastern Oklahoma A&M. He sat out his freshman season while recovering from a broke fibula suffered in his final high school game. He has three years remaining.

Tilmon is an interesting character. He's an accomplished drag racer and belongs to a racing club that participates in an annual event called "Texas Drag Wars."

Barnett is especially high on offensive lineman **Drew Shader**, a 6-3, 285-pound home grown product from Mullen High in Boulder.

"I can't remember a better offensive lineman coming out of high school," Barnett said. "Everyone who sees him is awestruck."

Barnett is doing a better job recruiting Colorado than his predecessor, Rick Neuheisel. In four years, Neuheisel signed 13 Colorado players. In three recruiting classes, Barnett has signed 20.

BLUE RIBBON ANALYSIS

OFFENSE	B
SPECIAL TEAMS	C+
DEFENSE	C+
INTANGIBLES	C+

Colorado is sneaking into some preseason polls, and lately that hasn't been a good thing. Who can forget a national magazine making the Buffs their preseason No. 1 team in 1997? Colorado lasted a few weeks in the top 10, dropped out and haven't been back since.

This probably isn't the year for a return. There's plenty to like about Colorado. Not many other programs will start 18 seniors.

Ochs may be a terrific quarterback. Houston should be the program's next great running back. They never appeared on the field together last year.

Graham and Gurode rank among the best at their positions in the Big 12. On defense, Sykes has been and could be one of the nation's best. This season will be a test of his character.

The schedule is easier than last year, although Barnett gambled by adding Fresno State as a 12th game in the inaugural Jim Thorpe Classic. At least Washington is gone, replaced by Washington State.

The "Return to Dominance" theme introduced by Barnett when he took over in 1999 continues. But Colorado needs to return to respectability first. That happens with an upper-division finish in the Big 12 North and a bowl game. It's too much to ask to finish first, but this team could win seven or eight and climb back into the final polls.

(B.K.)

2000 RESULTS

Colorado State	L	24-28	0-1
USC	L	14-17	0-2
Washington	L	14-17	0-3
Kansas State	L	21-44	0-4
Texas A&M	W	26-19	1-4
Texas	L	14-28	1-5
Kansas	L	15-23	1-6
Oklahoma State	W	37-21	2-6
Missouri	W	28-18	3-6
Iowa State	L	27-35	3-7
Nebraska	L	32-34	3-8

Iowa State

LOCATION	**Ames, IA**
CONFERENCE	**Big 12 (North)**
LAST SEASON	**9-3**
CONFERENCE RECORD	**5-3 (2nd)**
OFFENSIVE STARTERS RETURNING	**6**
DEFENSIVE STARTERS RETURNING	**4**
NICKNAME	**Cyclones**
COLORS	**Cardinal & Gold**
HOME FIELD	**Jack Trice Stadium (43,000)**
HEAD COACH	**Dan McCarney (Iowa '75)**
RECORD AT SCHOOL	**22-45 (6 years)**
CAREER RECORD	**22-45 (6 years)**
ASSISTANTS	**Bob Elliott (Iowa '75)**

Assoc. Head Coach/Secondary/Spec. Teams
Nick Quartaro (Iowa '77)
Assistant Head Coach/Receivers
John Skladany (Central Connecticut St. '72)
Defensive Coordinator/Linebackers
Steve Laney (Iowa State '74)
Offensive Coordinator/Offensive Line
DeMontie Cross (Missouri '97)
Outside Linebackers
Mike Woodley (Northern Iowa '74)
Tight Ends
Steve Brickey (Missouri '76)
Quarterbacks
Mike Nelson (Dayton '69)
Defensive Line
Mike Grant (Nebraska '93)
Running Backs

TEAM WINS (last 5 yrs.)	**2-1-3-4-9**
FINAL RANK (last 5 yrs.)	**59-72-66-75-30**
2000 FINISH	**Beat Pittsburgh in Insight.com Bowl.**

COACH AND PROGRAM

Iowa State's media guide, like every other in Division I-A football, includes a section on tradition. There are plenty of interesting stories, photographs, a page devoted to the 1915 team that won the state championship, two pages on the "Dirty Thirty" of 1959, a wonderful tribute to stadium namesake Jack Trice, pioneer football player in the 1920s who died after a vicious tackle.

All good stuff. What you don't find in the tradition section is a lot of winning. That's not an Iowa State football tradition. The Cyclones have one of the worst programs in Division I-A. It's down there with Indiana and Wake Forest among the all-time losers. In the 1990s, only Texas-El Paso, Temple and Kent State had a worse losing percentage than the Cyclones' .259 (27-80-3).

It was this bad in Ames: Coach Dan McCarney, hired from Barry Alverez's wildly successful turnaround program at Wisconsin in 1995, entered last year with a five-year 13-42 record and he wasn't in hot water. Oh, a few folks weren't happy with the progress, but this was Iowa State, where beating Iowa is the top priority and anything else is gravy.

McCarney had helped himself immensely by ending the program's 15-game losing streak to the Hawkeyes in 1998 and tacking on another victory in 1999. While the team continued to struggle in league play, knocking off Iowa smoothed things over with the fans.

But a funny thing happened after the 1999 triumph over the Hawks. The Cyclones followed it up with a 24-0 victory at UNLV, and suddenly Iowa State was 3-0 and getting votes in the polls. Then the breaks started going the other way. Iowa State blew a big halftime lead and lost to Kansas State. It suffered heart-breaking losses to Texas and Colorado. The demoralized Cyclones finished without a bowl bid. But McCarney knew he was on to something. For the first time in his tenure at Ames, the Cyclones didn't get pushed around by the big boys. Texas needed a final-play field goal to win.

Iowa State was getting 15 starters, including its best offensive and defensive players—quarterback Sage Rosenfels and defensive end Reggie Hayward—back.

Selling Iowa State as a potential bowl team entering 2000 took some doing. After all, it shared with Rutgers the nation's longest postseason drought among teams in Bowl Championship Series conferences—23 years. And the early schedule, as it had the previous year, probably wouldn't be an indicator. It was pretty much the same cast, although the third straight triumph over Iowa had 'em dancing in Ames.

The big difference came in the next few weeks. A hearty thumping at Baylor was followed by an expected home loss to Nebraska. But Iowa State trailed by only one to the nation's top-ranked team in the fourth quarter.

The next week, Iowa State pulled out a victory at Oklahoma State. One more triumph and fans could start making holiday travel plans. It would have been great to do it at home against Texas A&M, but Iowa State played its worst game of the season and the fears of those who had waited so long to celebrate began to surface. The Cyclones weren't going to retreat, were they?

Indeed they would not. The next week Missouri arrived and Iowa State roared to a resounding 39-20 victory. In the final two weeks, the Cyclones would pull out triumphs at Colorado and against Kansas to not only solidify its postseason standing but actually force some bowls higher in the Big 12 pecking order, like the Holiday, to take a hard look at the upstart.

It couldn't have worked out better for the program when it was lined up against Pittsburgh in the Insight.com Bowl. More than 20,000 of the bowl-starved faithful made the trek and were rewarded with a 37-29 victory that meant so much more than the program's first bowl triumph. Consider:

- The nine victories matched a school record and were the most by the program since 1906.
- The 5-1 record away from Ames was a school record. Iowa State was 6-43-1 on the road in the 1990s.
- The Cyclones are 14-10 over their last 24 games, the best record over such a stretch since 1976-1977.

Iowa State had arrived. A football season had started in late July and progressed through the holidays and the Cyclones got to play the entire time.

After years of preaching patience and progress, McCarney got it done. And he was rewarded handsomely with a new $600,000 a year deal that raised a few eyebrows after the school was forced to drop its baseball and men's swimming programs.

Season ticket sales are up, and Iowa State might even fill the place for an opponent besides Iowa this season. A winning spirit permeates the football program. Players walk around campus in their bowl jackets, talk confidently of building on what's been accomplished.

"There's an air of confidence that comes from going 9-3 and winning a bowl game," McCarney said. "What we're not going to lose is our work ethic."

The losses are steep with Rosenfels and Hayward gone. The top returning player is running back **Ennis Haywood**, who led the Big 12 with 1,237 yards last season. Plenty of shoring up on defense will be necessary with seven departed starters.

This isn't one of those deals where folks are thinking the Cyclones will be better this year than last. But the program clearly is better off in so many areas heading into a new season than at any other time. Recruiting went better, fans are interested and no opponent is looking at Iowa State as an easy mark.

2001 SCHEDULE

Sept.	8	Northern Iowa
	15	Iowa
	22	@Ohio
	29	Baylor
Oct.	6	@Nebraska
	13	@Missouri
	20	Oklahoma State
	27	@Texas A&M
Nov.	3	Kansas State
	10	Colorado
	17	@Kansas

QUARTERBACKS

Maybe the Cyclones won't be hurting at this position as much as initially thought. Sage Rosenfels was one of the best ever in Ames. Last season, he completed 52 percent for 2,298 yards and eight touchdowns in a nearly perfectly balanced offense. He rushed for 10 touchdowns and 381 yards.

Rosenfels didn't make any headway for postseason honors because of Oklahoma's Josh Heupel, but he was his team's most valuable offensive player.

McCarney isn't looking for drastic changes at the position, but in junior **Seneca Wallace** (6-1, 185), he has a better runner with a strong arm.

Wallace is originally from Sacramento and played last season at Sac City Junior College, where he passed for 3,675 yards with 22 touchdowns. He also rushed for 550 yards on 49 tries and nine touchdowns. His two junior college teams finished 9-2.

It was difficult to keep the lid on the enthusiasm after spring practice, when Wallace strong-armed the starting position away from redshirt freshman **Cris Love** (6-5, 210). Wallace also should stay ahead of another California junior college transfer, junior **Dustin Ochs** (6-3, 220), who passed for 2,308 yards and 15 touchdowns at San Bernadino Valley Community College last season. Ochs didn't arrive until the fall.

Wallace got the jump on everybody in a spring game that included eight rushes for 72 yards and 7-of-11 passing for 124 yards and a touchdown.

"You saw the potential there," McCarney said after the spring game. "I think you saw his abilities. You saw he has a strong arm and good accuracy. He's got real good feet. He's got speed. He's got a lot of room for improvement and he still hasn't done it against a No. 1 Big 12 defense that's coming after him. But I'm really, really proud of him and Cris Love both. By kickoff Sept. 8, we're going to have a nice group of quarterbacks."

McCarney and his staff think they uncovered a sleeper when they lured Wallace to Ames.

"Seneca's exactly what we're looking for in our offense," McCarney said. "I think when it's all said and done people will be shocked at how few schools recruited him."

Iowa State coaches were comparing Wallace to a pair of former league quarterbacks Tommie Frazier of Nebraska and Michael Bishop of Kansas State. Both were Heisman Trophy runners-up.

"[Wallace] wants to do what we're asking him in the offense and throw the ball and deliver it on time and do it accurately and as a last resort pull it down and run," McCarney said. "But when he does, he's dangerous.

"He's real explosive. He gets to the edge of the defense real fast. But as we all know, we're taking a guy that's going to be drafted pretty high in the NFL draft today [Rosenfels was taken in the fourth round by the Washington Redskins] versus a guy that hasn't taken a snap in Division I football, so that's the trade off right now. He really lacks in experience, but I think there's really a lot of ability there and I'm just really proud of the way he's handled things."

It will be difficult for Seneca to live up to the hype. Frazier and Bishop were surrounded with top-ranked talent.

"All I want to do is bring a dimension to the offense that schools don't usually see," Wallace said. "I can run, and I can throw it pretty well."

RUNNING BACKS

As bad as Iowa State football has been, there's no arguing its recent history of talent at running back. Troy Davis became the first player in college history to post consecutive 2,000-yard seasons. His brother, Darren, posted three 1,000-yard seasons.

Last season, Haywood (5-11, 218) joined the circle. He led the Big 12 with 1,273 yards in only 10 regular-season games. He ran for more than 190 yards three times and also caught 25 passes for 211 yards. Haywood's goals for his senior season are to improve those numbers and become more of a big-play back.

"I've been around a lot of backs that have gotten 60- or 70-yard runs and a lot of it is knowing how you use your downfield blocking," running backs coach Mike Grant said. "We really want to focus on that, keep improving his change of direction, speed, change of speed through the hole."

Grant has had Haywood study tapes of Marshall Faulk and Jamal Lewis—and of himself.

"I've watched film when I've been one-on-one with a guy and he's brought me down," Haywood said. "I want to eliminate that. When I get to the open field I want to score."

Running back is Iowa State's deepest position. Besides Haywood, three sophomore lettermen return—**Michael Wagner** (5-7, 187), **Hiawatha Rutland** (6-0, 206) and **JaMaine Billups** (5-10, 198).

Of the reserves, Wagner has the most experience. Haywood missed the Oklahoma State game. Wagner stepped in and rushed for a school freshman record 170 yards and two touchdowns. He also caught a scoring pass. In the regular-season finale, Wagner rushed for 102 yards against Kansas.

Rutland averaged 7.1 yards per carry. And all Billups did was win the bowl game with an electrifying 72-yard punt return for a fourth-quarter touchdown.

"I've never felt better about a position going into the spring," McCarney said.

And he shouldn't. The only question will be how many attempts will Wallace take away from his talent stable?

WIDE RECEIVERS/TIGHT ENDS

Gone are starters Chris Anthony and J.J. Moses, two of the best pass catchers in the program's history. But the Cyclones aren't scrounging for replacements.

Unless somebody else steps up, senior **Craig Campbell** (5-11, 185) will be the go-to receiver. He caught 20 balls for 353 yards and showed his big-game ability with three receptions for 119 yards and a touchdown against Nebraska and five catches for 62 yards in the bowl game.

Sophomore **Lane Danielsen** (6-0, 195), a former walk-on, averaged 30.5 yards on five receptions and turned in one of the biggest plays of the season, a 33-yard touchdown catch with 18 seconds to play for the winning touchdown at Oklahoma State.

Another part-timer who came up big when given the opportunity was sophomore flanker **Jamaul Montgomery** (6-0, 196). Against Pittsburgh, when Moses sat out the second half with a concussion, Montgomery caught three passes for 57 yards, equaling his regular-season output.

Also part of the equation is junior **Larry Anglin** (5-7, 184), a junior college transfer who missed all of last season with an ankle injury.

Tight end is set. Senior **Mike Banks** (6-4, 248) is one of the league's best. His soft hands allowed him to grab 27 passes for 273 yards. And he's one of the team's top blockers.

OFFENSIVE LINE

Even in the lean years, Iowa State has always put together a respectable offensive line. At least that's how things turn out. The Cyclones usually go into the season with plenty of question marks, but somehow things work out.

We know this is true because Iowa State has produced a 1,000-yard rusher in each of the last six seasons, and the team has allowed a mere 29 sacks in the last three seasons.

There are a few questions this time because three seniors from a year ago have departed. The most significant loss is center Ben Bruns. This season, the Cyclones will build around senior right guard **Lorenzo White** (6-5, 344), junior center **Zach Butler** (6-4, 290) and senior left tackle **Marcel Howard** (6-6, 321), who is bidding for his fourth letter.

White didn't arrive on campus until last year's fall camp was under way and he checked in weighing more than 360. The idea was to redshirt him, but McCarney was so impressed that he inserted White in the starting lineup for the opening game and the big man answered the call for all 12 games.

The leaders for other starting spots are sophomore left guard **Bob Montgomery** (6-3, 302) and right tackle **Corey Hannen** (6-5, 307), who started last year's opener. Hannan is a three-year letter winner.

One advantage is experienced backups. Tackle **Jared Bucksa** (6-3, 273) and guard **Brian Donahue** (6-5, 275) are seniors and letter winners.

2000 STATISTICS

Rushing offense	209.0	17
Passing offense	215.5	54
Total offense	424.5	21
Scoring offense	27.8	48
Net Punting	32.6	85
Punt returns	10.2	47
Kickoff returns	17.0	103
Rushing defense	196.3	95
Passing efficiency defense	116.7	50
Total defense	406.1	88
Scoring defense	26.6	70
Turnover margin	+5	35

Last column is ranking among Division I-A teams.

KICKERS

The Cyclones got lucky with punter Carl Gomez, who has graduated. He took over the place kicking duties in the second half of last season and converted 7-of-8 field goals. He did this while building on a fine punting season in which he averaged 39.9 yards.

Gomez was a hero in an eight-point triumph at Colorado, where he kicked field goals of 43, 27 and 46 yards in the snow.

Iowa State clearly will miss Rosenfels and Hayward and other starters. But replacing a kicker/punter as dependable as Gomez might be the most difficult task facing the coaching staff.

The place kicking replacement will be **Tony Yelk** (6-0, 201), a redshirt freshman who was Wisconsin's top high school kicker two years ago. Yelk was an all-conference kicker, punter and quarterback at Poynette High in Arlington, Wisc., where 71 percent of his kickoffs went for touchbacks.

Iowa State signed freshman **Troy Blankenship** (6-2, 190) to give Yelk competition. Blankenship was a second-team all-state punter for Kennedy High in Cedar Rapids, Iowa last fall.

DEFENSIVE LINE

Probably more than any unit over the years, defensive line has made the greatest strides at Iowa State. For the last two decades or so, opposing running backs licked their chops when the Cyclones appeared on the schedule.

Sure, the Davis brothers and Ennis Haywood were having big days. But often opposing backs would have even bigger days, like the time Texas' Ricky Williams rushed for 350 yards on the Cyclones. Nebraska regularly pushed two backs over the century mark against Iowa State.

And hey, it wasn't like the Cyclones built a wall along the defensive line in 2000. Foes still managed to average 196 rushing yards. But it was nothing like the days of yore. That Iowa State could actually promote a defensive lineman for all-conference—Reggie Hayward—said plenty about the program's progress.

The improvement must continue for Iowa State to remain competitive, but if that's going to happen this year, it will be done with many new faces.

Besides Hayward—who was taken by the Denver Broncos in the third round of the NFL draft—the Cyclones lose tackle James Reed—a seventh-round pick by the New York Jets—and nose guard Ryan Harklau. Each were four-year letter winners and Reed got some all-conference consideration. Also gone is another four-year letter winner, reserve Nigel Tharpe.

"When you lose four guys who will probably make it to NFL camps there's going to be a drop off at the position," McCarney said.

Rebuilding begins around the lone returning starter, senior end **Kevin DeRonde** (6-5, 257). He had a breakout season in 2000, recording 60 tackles and seven behind the line. DeRonde is a Pella, Iowa native who was one of the state's top prospects in high school. The former prep sprinter has more speed than most at his position.

Redshirt freshman **Brett Kellogg** (6-2, 248), another former high school track standout, is the leader at the other end. He was the Cyclones' defensive scout team player of the year last season. Kellogg will be pushed by junior **Beau Coleman** (6-1, 235), who recorded 23 sacks in two years at Southwestern (Calif.) Junior College.

Everybody is pulling for sophomore defensive tackle **Jordan Carstens** (6-5, 291). He arrived on campus two years ago as a 228-pound walk-on from Bagley, Iowa (population 303) and was considered the last man on the 105-man roster. Carstens practically lived in the weight room during his first year, worked hard enough on the practice field to be selected the scout team's top defensive player and entered last season weighing 275 pounds. He started behind Reed and finished with 48 tackles, 26 unassisted, and a sack.

Ready to step up at nose guard is senior **Willie Judd** (6-3, 282), who arrived from junior college last season and appeared in 10 games as Harklau's backup. Judd recorded 25 sacks in two years at Butte (Calif.) Junior College.

Redshirt freshman **Cal Stubbe** (6-4, 275) also will get a look at the position.

It's a good year for reserves to make their case. Guys like redshirt freshman end **Tim DeBrink** (6-3, 258) and redshirt freshmen tackles **Andy Leders** (6-3, 250) and **Paul Jarrett** (6-4, 260) will get opportunities.

LINEBACKERS

The Cyclones can feel pretty good about their linebackers. Three with starting experience are back and there's enough in reserve to keep the unit strong.

Junior middle linebacker **Chris Whitaker** (6-0, 227) came up big toward the end of the season after struggling with an ankle injury early. He recorded 14 of his 39 tackles against Colorado and Kansas.

Junior **Matt Word** (6-0, 230) played in the middle most of last year but was shifted to the weak side, where he'll knock heads with senior **Justin Eilers** (6-2, 230) for playing time.

Word finished fourth on the team in tackles with 63 and was the team's top tackler in the bowl game with 10. Eilers, in his first year after transferring from junior college, recorded 21 tackles in the final four games.

On the outside, sophomore **Tyson Smith** (6-2, 230) saw enough action last year as a reserve to win a letter and now will be the starter. He was Iowa's top high school prospect two years ago out of West Des Moines, and big things are expected.

Junior **Jeremy Loyd** (6-2, 220), a transfer from Tyler, (Texas) Junior College, will back up Smith. Loyd recorded 12 sacks and two interceptions last season.

Behind Whitaker will be redshirt freshman **Brent Nash** (5-11, 240) and sophomore **Derek Walters** (6-0, 224).

DEFENSIVE BACKS

The Cyclones have made great strides in recent years in the secondary. And it's a measure of progress that despite the loss of three starters, Iowa State shouldn't drop off much from last season.

Strong safety **Adam Runk** (6-2, 183) is a three-year letter winner who will move into the starting role as a senior. Runk came up with 10 tackles against Missouri and Kansas State and five against Pittsburgh in the bowl game. He's bidding to become a four-time first-team all-academic Big 12 selection.

Sophomore free safety **Marc Timmons** (5-9, 168) started one game last season and made the most of the opportunity. Against Missouri, Timmons became the first Iowa State player in eight years to intercept two passes in one game. He returned one 78 yards for a touchdown, the sixth-longest pick return in school history.

Timmons finished the season with three interceptions, 58 tackles, 39 solo and a fumble recovery. Big things are expected from him this season.

Cornerback is the land of opportunity. Sophomores **Johnny Smith III** (5-11, 170), **Harold Clewis** (5-10, 183), **Bryan Ollie** (5-8, 180) and **DeAndre Phillips** (5-9, 195) played enough to earn letters last season.

A key to the position is the health of junior **Atif Austin** (5-9, 180). He started 10 games last season but missed the spring after undergoing shoulder surgery. Austin came up with one of the biggest plays of 2000, a late interception at Oklahoma State to preserve the victory. The Cyclones get a big boost if Austin is 100 percent for the fall.

PUNTERS

The issue will be settled in the fall between newcomer **Troy Blankenship** (6-2, 190) and sophomore **Casey Baldwin** (6-2, 210), who appeared in every game last season as a holder for extra points and field goals.

Baldwin averaged 35.6 yards on 50 punts as a senior at Perry (Iowa) High. Blankenship averaged 42.2 yards on 45 punts with a long of 68 yards for Kennedy High in Cedar Rapids last fall.

SPECIAL TEAMS

A pair of sophomores, JaMaine Billups and Michael Wagner, figure to handle all the return action. Wagner was the only player besides Moses to return more than one punt last season. Wagner's two returns went for four yards.

Billups returned only eight kickoffs for a 14.8-yard average in the regular season, but his 72-yard punt return for a touchdown against Pittsburgh was the biggest play in the bowl game. He also returned three kickoffs for 17 yards in that game.

The Cyclones seek to improve their kickoff coverage. They ranked 10th in the Big 12, allowing an average 21-yard return. But one number that made McCarney and his staff happy was seven blocked kicks. Nobody in the Big 12 had more.

RECRUITING CLASS

The class played to the usual reviews. It ranked behind at least three others in the Big 12 North (Nebraska, Kansas State and Colorado), and nearly everybody in the South. Funny how this works.

The recruiting class rankings are always a few years behind the team's improved ranking. Just ask Kansas State. It took years for the Wildcats' class to be rated near a level with those at Texas, Oklahoma, Texas A&M and Nebraska—teams Kansas State was beating.

The Cyclones hit the junior college ranks hard, especially in California, where they signed quarterbacks Wallace and Ochs and defensive linemen **Kevin Hines** (6-1, 282) and Beau Coleman. The linemen will get plenty of playing time, and so will another Golden State transfer, wide receiver **David Banks-Bursey** (5-11, 175), who caught 38 passes for 625 yards at West Los Angeles College.

The Iowa State recruiting class breakdown by state reflects a condition that is somewhat sad but based in cold reality. The Cyclones understand there aren't enough players in the Midwest to stock a team. They signed 10 from Texas schools, five from California and two from Florida. Only three came from Iowa.

BLUE RIBBON ANALYSIS

OFFENSE	C
SPECIAL TEAMS	B
DEFENSE	C
INTANGIBLES	C+

The program got everything it deserved last season, a winning Big 12 record, eight regular-season victories and a bowl triumph.

More than two decades of frustration were released in one season. Now comes the hard part. Sustaining success, which is difficult at the lower-budget Big 12 schools. Kansas went 10-2 in 1995 and hasn't had a winning season since. Missouri went to bowl games after the 1997 and 1998 seasons. It hasn't posted a winning season since.

Only Kansas State has maintained its winning pace, and that's what Iowa State is shooting for. Another winning record isn't out of the question if Wallace delivers. But it's asking a lot of a first-year quarterback to carry a team.

Haywood must stay healthy for Iowa State to succeed. There can be no major malfunctions in the defense. The defensive line must find an identity and it would help the Cyclones to find a go-to wide receiver.

Can Iowa State build on last year's success?

"We have to continue to make major improvement between now and September defensively, physically, athletically, getting everybody ready to play," McCarney said after the spring game. "I think it's hard to compare [the 2000 and 2001 teams]. I know this much right now—you see the success of last year carrying through this football team.

"These kids know how to win, they've got a great attitude, they know how to practice. There's no doubt about that. I think you'll see as many play makers on our offense as you saw last year. Hopefully by kickoff there'll be more. Defensively we're not as good right now as we were last year, but we just lost nine starters and a lot of seniors, so I'm not saying we can't be by fall."

The schedule is favorable. Iowa State should jump out of the box 4-0. After a trip to Nebraska come swing games against teams with a revenge motive, Missouri and Oklahoma State. If Iowa State can win those, the Cyclones can be back in the bowling lane and not be remembered as a one-year wonder.

(B.K.)

2000 RESULTS

Ohio	W	25-15	1-0
UNLV	W	37-22	2-0
Iowa	W	24-14	3-0
Baylor	W	31-17	4-0
Nebraska	L	27-49	4-1
Oklahoma State	W	33-26	5-1
Texas A&M	L	7-30	5-2
Missouri	W	39-20	6-2
Kansas State	L	10-56	6-3
Colorado	W	35-27	7-3
Kansas	W	38-17	8-3
Pitt (Insight.com Bowl)	W	37-29	9-3

Kansas

LOCATION	Lawrence, KS
CONFERENCE	Big 12 (North)
LAST SEASON	4-7 (.364)
CONFERENCE RECORD	2-6 (5th)
OFFENSIVE STARTERS RETURNING	6
DEFENSIVE STARTERS RETURNING	7
NICKNAME	Jayhawks
COLORS	Crimson & Blue
HOME FIELD	Memorial Stadium (50,250)
HEAD COACH	Terry Allen (Northern Iowa '79)
RECORD AT SCHOOL	18-27 (4 years)
CAREER RECORD	93-53 (12 years)
ASSISTANTS	Tom Hayes (Iowa '71) (Assistant Head Coach/Defensive Coordinator/Secondary); Tim Burke (Luther '77) Defensive Ends; Mark Farley (Northern Iowa '86) Linebackers; Travis Jones (Georgia '94) Defensive Line; Bill Salmon (Northern Iowa '76) Running Backs; Clarence James (Langston '73) Wide Recievers; Jay Johnson (Northern Iowa '92) Quarterbacks; Sam Pittman (Pittsburg State '83) Offensive Line; Clint Bowen (Kansas '93) Tight Ends
TEAM WINS (last 5 yrs.)	4-5-4-5-4
FINAL RANK (last 5 yrs.)	61-66-71-72-60
2000 FINISH	Lost to Iowa State in regular-season finale.

COACH AND PROGRAM

In his first season at Kansas, Terry Allen got to the final quarter of the final game with a chance at a winning record and bowl game. The Jayhawks led Texas. Hang on and Kansas finishes 6-5 and sneaks into a bowl game.

And a bowl game in Allen's first season could have been huge. The bad feelings left from the Glen Mason departure would have been forgotten. The program would have gotten some momentum and Allen could have renegotiated his contract.

Of course, it didn't happen and Allen's program has never had any momentum, which is why he finds himself on the hot seat. Allen has to get it done this year, win at least six games, or there probably will not be a sixth year.

That was the sense after last season's crushing 4-7 record. In sharp contrast to Allen's first year, last season ended in the first quarter of the first game. The Jayhawks visited SMU in a game they had to win. What happens? Special teams break down with four bad punt snaps and the Mustangs go up 24-0 by the end of the first quarter.

Kansas fans, unaccustomed to football success, are choosy. They wait until some progress is made before committing their hearts to the team. Last season, they truly wanted to believe. And there were reasons to feel upbeat about the Jayhawks.

The Jayhawks returned 17 starters from a team that won three of its final five games in 1999. Quarterback Dylen Smith was an exciting athlete. Running back David Winbush could deliver big games, fullback Moran Norris was considered an NFL prospect, free safety Carl Nesmith promised success and showed up at an early press conference asking reporters to call him "the butcher."

It all went up in smoke in the opener, a game in which Nesmith got himself suspended. Kansas fans immediately turned their backs. The shame is, the Jayhawks played their best ball of the season over the next six weeks, nearly climbing back into bowl contention.

After a pair of expected non-league victories, Kansas played Oklahoma tough before falling in Norman. The usual slaughter by Kansas State followed. Then the Jayhawks hit a mid-season hot streak. They won at Missouri and beat Colorado at home. Suddenly, Kansas stood 2-2 in the Big 12 and 4-3 overall. A home victory over Texas Tech the next week could change the entire posture of the season.

The fans weren't excited. Only 26,000, the smallest crowd of the season, showed up to watch a Kansas rally fall short when a final pass fell incomplete, seating a six-point loss. Kansas was done. No winning season, no bowl. Plenty of disappointment, and now pressure on Allen as well.

"It was as difficult a year as I've ever been involved with," Allen said.

The Jayhawks were left to play what-if throughout the off-season. The biggest came in the first week. Allen knew he made a bad choice with the long snapper at SMU, and not making an early change compounded the problem.

"There's no reason for Kansas to lose to SMU," Allen said. "If we win that game, we're 5-5 going into our last game, and if we're playing for something I think the outcome (a 38-17 loss to Iowa State) is different."

And maybe several assistant coaches keep their jobs. Allen knew he had to make a statement and more than half the staff was turned over. The most significant change was the hiring of Tom Hayes as assistant head coach and defensive coordinator. Hayes came to Kansas in February from the Washington Redskins, where he spent the previous five seasons as the secondary coach. Among his pupils there was Champ Bailey, who won NFL Rookie of the Year in 1999. Hayes got caught up in the Redskins' house cleaning after the 1999 season and he didn't coach last season.

"Only two people in the entire organization were left, the trainer and receptionist," Hayes said. "We had won 10 games and won the division in 1999, and we all got fired. Then the big team they spent all that money on went 8-8."

During spring practice, Hayes as much as any player was the focus. Players talked about how impressed they were just walking into his office.

"Everything is so neat and stacked so nicely," nose tackle Nate Dwyer said. "He opens the refrigerator and all the water bottles are lined up perfectly, right in a row."

Said Allen, "He's not a guy to leave any stone unturned. He's into structure, let's just say that."

Hayes needs to be into improving a unit that gave up 400 yards per game a year ago. In its final three games, the Jayhawks gave up 145 points.

Hayes and the other new assistants signed two-year contracts, so they're guaranteed if this is Allen's final year. Not making it any easier for Allen is the athletic director's job, which was open at the time this publication went to press.

The man who hired Allen, Bob Frederick, resigned in the spring. Allen's fate might not have been any different this season under Frederick if Kansas produces a losing record. But now there seems to be little doubt that Allen must impress a new regime to keep his Lawrence address.

2001 SCHEDULE

Sept.	1	Southwest Missouri
	8	UCLA
	15	Wyoming
	22	@Colorado
Oct.	6	@Texas Tech
	13	Oklahoma
	20	Missouri
	27	@Kansas State
Nov.	3	Nebraska
	10	@Texas
	17	Iowa State

QUARTERBACKS

It's doesn't bode well for Allen that he's entering the most important season of his coaching career without a proven quarterback.

Spring practice did not produce a winner between sophomore **Zach Dyer** (6-3, 200) and redshirt freshman **Mario Kinsey** (6-1, 195), with redshirt freshman **Kevin Long** (6-5, 210) lurking in the background.

Dyer was last year's No. 2 and had a few nice moments. In six games, he completed 6-of-12 passes for 60 yards. His best game came against Nebraska when he directed a 12-play, 80-yard scoring drive in which he passed for 40 yards and rushed for seven.

"That let me know that I belonged," Dyer said.

Dyer is a local product from nearby Olathe, Kansas. He's a strong player with such a tough-minded approach that coaches toyed with the idea of moving him to safety last season just to get some attitude on the field. He's one of the team's most dedicated weight lifters and his powerful upper body strength rivals most linebackers.

"He's our most athletic quarterback," Allen said. "If you look at all the numbers and activities we do, he jumps off the page at you with his 40-yard dash time, his change-of-direction and his vertical jump."

Just because of the experience factor, Dyer heads into fall camp slightly ahead of Kinsey, but not because he won a decisive victory in spring ball. Dyer went 6-of-11 for 76 yards and an interception in the spring game. Kinsey went 6-of-12 for 106 yards, including a touchdown.

Kinsey came to Kansas as a football-basketball package. He redshirted last season but was so impressive in fall camp that Allen nearly kept him away from hoops. Allen resisted the temptation and Kinsey joined the basketball team in mid-October. He played in 16 games for Roy Williams, and left that team early to try and win the quarterback slot in the spring.

Kinsey isn't as fast as Dyer, but he's more elusive. He also has a stronger arm. Now Allen wants to see a better attitude. He wants his quarterback candidate to be more of a leader. Kinsey said basketball helped him grow up because he was no longer the star attraction, merely a role player.

"Mario is the type of quarterback you're seeing more and more in the NFL," Allen said. "He's as much a threat to run the ball as he is to throw it. He can really make you miss."

Both will get snaps with the first team in fall camp and they might split time in the opener against Division I-AA Southwest Missouri State, but Allen certainly wants the issue settled by the second game against UCLA.

"Mario is more flamboyant," senior wide receiver **Harrison Hill** said. "He's got the best arm of anyone out there. He's outspoken, and, to a degree, you want that in your quarterback. Zach is a little more quiet. But everyone respects him because he busts his butt out there. He's a real competitor. I think either one can be a leader."

Long is the third party candidate. He was one of the most heralded recruits when he signed out of Iowa City, Iowa two years ago, but he didn't make much of an impression until the final few weeks of practice last fall.

"I was homesick and was doubting my decision on whether I should have come here or not," Long told the *Kansas City Star*. "But I think a lot of freshmen go through that. Now, I'm glad to be where I am."

Junior **Jonas Weatherbie** (6-2, 205) also will get some reps at quarterback.

RUNNING BACKS

At least sophomore **Reggie Duncan** (5-9, 215) is familiar with the role. At Ellison High in Killeen, Texas, Duncan followed Winbush, who went off to Kansas. Four years later, it's the same deal. Winbush leaves Kansas sixth on the career rushing list, and Duncan is poised to step in.

Duncan is the top returning rusher, gaining 207 yards and two touchdowns in nine games as a reserve. He got nearly half those yards (96) against Nebraska. His season long run of 38 yards set up the Jayhawks' winning touchdown against Colorado.

Duncan is powerfully built and is as much a threat to bulldoze for yards inside as he is to turn the corner. Allen is so high on Duncan that he pulled him out of the spring game to avoid an injury. Duncan had rushed for 53 yards on nine carries and scored a touchdown.

"If he can stay healthy, he's our guy," Allen said. "He could run it 25 times a game."

Behind Duncan on the depth chart is sophomore **Daniel Coke** (6-1, 205), who picked up 54 yards on 10 carries in six games. **Mitchell Scott** (6-3, 235), a junior, and redshirt freshman **Austine Nwabuisi** (6-1, 230) will be taking their first snaps as fullbacks this season. The position was a let down for the Jayhawks, who were looking for big things from Norris. But injuries limited Norris to 313 yards and only two touchdowns in seven games.

Kansas has never been the kind of running team under Allen it was under Mason, when 1,000-yard rushers were the norm. But that could change this year with Duncan.

WIDE RECEIVERS/TIGHT ENDS

This is the deepest and most talented position on the team.

Kansas returns eight wide receivers who have earned 14 letters among them. The most productive over the years is Hill (5-11, 190), who will serve as a co-captain this season.

Hill probably will become the program's career leader in receptions. He has caught 106 passes and needs 28 to hold the mark. Last season, he ranked fifth in the Big 12 with 47 receptions and had a career best day against Oklahoma with eight catches for 144 yards. Hill was selected honorable mention All-Big 12.

Senior **Trumaine Fulton** (5-10, 190) will start at flanker. He is fourth in career touchdown receptions with 11 and 12th in yards (1,168). Fulton has had at least one catch in 25 of his 35 games at Kansas. He's one of the team's top athletes who recorded a team best 32-inch vertical leap in off-season testing.

Fulton shares time with junior **Byron Gasaway** (6-4, 180), who was converted to receiver from quarterback. Gasaway suffered a broken jaw two years ago in a weight room accident that cost him the 1999 season, and he wasn't as productive in 2000 (six catches, no touchdowns) as he was in 1998 (12 catches, two scores).

Senior **Roger Ross** (5-7, 175) made a big splash in his Kansas debut last season, catching 29 passes for a 16.6-yard average and team best four touchdowns. Ross' 77-yard touchdown reception against Oklahoma was the longest pass play against the Sooners last season.

Sophomore **Derick Mills** (5-7, 155) and junior **Marcellus Jones** (5-1, 200) back up Ross. Junior **Derek Vann** (6-1, 185) will get reps at flanker. The most productive reserve again figures to be sophomore **J.T. Thompson** (5-10, 190), who caught eight passes for a 16.2-yard average last season.

Kansas doesn't usually start a tight end, opting for a third receiver. But Junior **David Hurst** (6-3, 245) has a chance to be a good one. He has caught 13 passes and a touchdown over the past two seasons.

Sophomore **Adrian Jones** (6-5, 255) and redshirt freshman **Jason Farley** (6-3, 235) will back up.

The depth at the receiver spots reflects Allen's pass-happy philosophy that was wildly success at Northern Iowa. It has never gotten a chance to succeed at Kansas because he has never had the quarterback who could make it happen. If Dyer or Kinsey emerges this season, the Jayhawks could have one of the league's top passing attacks.

OFFENSIVE LINE

This was the recruiting emphasis and Kansas went hard into the junior college ranks to fill holes.

"We wanted big, physical players and we wanted guys that could get into school at midsemester," Allen said.

Four of the nine junior college signees were offensive linemen—**Brock Teddleton** (6-6, 330) from Coffeyville (Kansas) Community College, **Jawad Pearson** (6-5, 300) from Chaffey (Calif.) Community College, **Danny Lewis** (6-5, 290) from Phoenix (Ariz.) Community College and **John Harvey** (6-6, 305) from Mesa (Ariz.) Junior College.

Harvey is the most heralded of the group. A first-team All-Arizona selection and All-Western States Football League choice last year, Harvey was considered one of the top offensive linemen in junior college last season.

Teddleton sat out the 2000 season as a medical redshirt and will have three years of eligibility remaining. He was the No. 4-rated offensive lineman in the Kansas junior college ranks last season. The long-armed Pearson excels at pass blocking. He was a two-year starter at Chaffey, during which time his team was 17-4.

The newcomers were immediately plugged into the depth chart.

Kansas has three returning starters in right tackle **Justin Hartwig** (6-4, 295), junior center **Nick Smith** (6-4, 280) and left guard **Bob Smith** (6-4, 290).

Hartwig has started 23 straight games and is the Jayhawks' top honors candidate. He was the team's second-highest graded offensive linemen last season.

Junior **Justin Sands** (6-7, 295) moved from the defensive line to offense last season and looks to hold off junior college talent to start at left tackle.

Kyle Grady (6-5, 305) was projected as a starting left guard last season before being sidelined with a season ending knee injury. He's battling Smith for the start.

At right guard, senior **Jason Stevenson** (6-2, 285) is competing against junior **Tony Damiani** (6-4, 290) and Middleton for the start.

What Allen has created on his offensive line is competition. It has been a weak area for most of his previous four seasons. That shouldn't be the case this year.

2000 STATISTICS

Rushing offense	157.4	46
Passing offense	183.9	82
Total offense	341.3	77
Scoring offense	23.7	70
Net Punting	29.9	105
Punt returns	8.7	71
Kickoff returns	17.6	100
Rushing defense	198.0	98
Passing efficiency defense	126.4	85
Total defense	400.6	80
Scoring defense	32.6	95
Turnover margin	-7	93

Last column is ranking among Division I-A teams.

KICKERS

Joe Garcia, who handled all the place kicking chores for the last four seasons, is gone, and there is no player on the team who has kicked in a game.

As he did four years ago, Allen signed a high school kicker to come in and take over. This time it's **Johnny Beck** (6-1, 200), a local product from Kansas City, Kansas who was considered one of the top kickers in the Midwest.

Beck made 10-of-12 field goals from beyond 50 yards in his career at Piper High. He set a school record for longest field goal (54 yards), most field goals in a career (28), most in a game (three) and season (12).

Three other kickers on the roster will try to prevent the freshman from taking over. They are sophomore **Case Collard** (6-0, 190), senior **Brian Tracy** (5-9, 165) and sophomore Phil Garlin (5-9, 205).

DEFENSIVE LINE

Nearly everybody's back, and that's good news for new defensive coordinator Tom Hayes and defensive line coach Travis Jones.

The Jayhawks haven't produced many quality defensive linemen since the days of Dana Stubblefield, Gilbert Brown and Chris Maumalanga. But the Jayhawks are high on this group.

It is led by senior nose tackle **Nate Dwyer** (6-3, 300), a co-captain who was selected second team All-Big 12 last season. Dwyer led Kansas with 14 tackles for loss, the second most ever by a Kansas down lineman. He is surprisingly athletic and even has two career interceptions on his resume.

Also plugging the middle at tackle is senior **Ervin Holloman** (6-3, 290), who moves from end this season. Holloman finished with 21 total tackles and recovered a fumble in his first year at Division I-A. He was a terror at Garden City (Kansas) Community College two years ago, earning junior college All-America honors.

Making a huge impact at end in the spring was junior college transfer **Charlie Dennis** (6-5, 230). He vaulted to the top of the depth chart.

"He's so athletic, and plays as hard as anybody on defense," Allen said.

Dennis recorded 26 sacks in two years at Butler (Kansas) Community College. He was rated as the No. 2 defensive lineman in the Kansas junior college ranks last season.

A pair of redshirt freshmen—**Travis Watkins** (6-4, 270) and **Clarence Laws** (6-4, 260)—are likely to produce a starter at left end.

The Jayhawks are deep in the middle with senior **Marquis Hayes** (6-4, 265), sophomore **Tony Strickland** (6-6, 265) and senior **Ryan Atkinson** (6-2, 290) all returning letter winners.

LINEBACKERS

Fifth-year senior **Marcus Rogers** (6-1, 235) has been with Allen since the beginning and looks to come up big in his final year. He's a co-captain and one of the team's top defensive honors candidates.

Rogers, a middle linebacker, is the top returning tackler. He had 91 last season. Only Nesmith had more. His best game came against Nebraska, when he turned in 10 solo tackles. He was voted the league's top defensive player of the week for his 11-tackle performance against Colorado.

Senior **Algie Atkinson** (6-5, 240) will start for a third straight year on the strong side. His seven sacks tied Dwyer for the team lead.

Allen signed **Greg Cole** (6-3, 235) from Hutchinson (Kansas) Community College, to push Atkinson. Cole was rated the top junior college linebacker in Kansas last season, his first year at the position after playing tight end as a freshman.

A year ago, Cole was credited with 91 total tackles, including 14 for loss and eight quarterback sacks. As a freshman tight end, he caught 14 passes, three of which went for touchdowns. A track star at Miami's Killian High School, Cole won the 200 meters in district competition. He should have the speed to run down ball carriers.

Sophomore **Glenn Robinson** (6-3, 230) excelled on special teams last season and will get first crack at weak-side linebacker.

Again, a junior college transfer from Hutchinson will push for the start. **Leo Etienne** (6-0, 215) lined up beside Cole and was chosen first-team All-Jayhawk Junior Conference last season. Etienne had a team-best 118 tackles and nine sacks and was also chosen an All-American by J.C. Gridwire. Like Cole a great athlete, Etienne was drafted by the Tampa Bay Devil Rays as an outfielder after his senior year in high school at Auburndale, Fla.

DEFENSIVE BACKS

The Jayhawks' pass defense was stronger than the rush defense, and the starting cornerbacks are back.

Senior **Andrew Davison** (5-11, 185) owns a team-best streak of 27 starts. He has been one of the Jayhawks' more consistent defensive players over the last three seasons. The highlight of his season was a 40-yard interception return for a touchdown against Texas.

Not long after arriving at Kansas, Davison switched his uniform number from No. 2 to No. 24 to honor his favorite player, Charles Woodson.

Quincy Roe (5-9, 185) enters his senior season with 19 straight starts. He shared the team lead in interceptions last season with three and led Kansas in pass deflections with 14. He's the hard hitter of the defense.

Kansas is finding it difficult to keep sophomore **Carl Ivey** (5-11, 180) out of the lineup. After spring, he was listed as a co-starter with Roe. Ivey started two games last season.

The safety positions are unsettled. Senior **Jamarei Bryant** (5-11, 190) will get the first look at free safety, and junior **Jake Letourneau** (6-2, 195) at strong safety. Neither played much last season. Bryant got in 10 games and was credited with four tackles. Letourneau played in nine games and had 11 stops.

At free safety, redshirt freshman **Leo Bookman** (6-1, 205) and senior **Brandon Wier** (6-2, 200) should see more playing time, and so should redshirt freshman **Santana Lane** (6-0, 180) at strong safety.

PUNTERS

Joey Pelfanio had been a steady kicker for the last two seasons. His departure leaves redshirt freshman **Chris Tyrrell** (5-11, 220) as the only scholarship punter on the roster.

Tyrrell averaged 41.8 yards as a punter and kicked nine field goals in his senior season at Liberty (Mo.) High School.

Kansas signed a junior college punter, **Curtis Ansel** (6-1, 185) from Garden City (Kansas) Community College. Ansel helped Garden City to the junior college national championship game and had punts of 58 and 52 yards in the title game. He averaged 39.2 yards per punt last season.

Ansel, who also handled kickoffs in junior college, has three seasons of eligibility remaining after redshirting his first season at Garden City.

SPECIAL TEAMS

One of the big losses is long snapper Marc Owens, who proved to be a steady hand. Allen said his biggest regret of last season was not playing Owens from the opening game.

The return game appears to be in good shape. The Jayhawks dip into their well of wide receivers and go with Ross and Hill as punt returners. Ross averaged 7.1 yards and scored a 62-yard touchdown against Missouri.

Ross and Mills are the top kick return men. Mills averaged 18.7 yards and Ross 13.3.

RECRUITING CLASS

The nine-member junior college recruiting class reflects Allen's desire to win immediately. The offensive line group is probably the best in the nation, and the linebacking teammates from Hutchinson, Cole and Etienne, will provide immediate dividends.

Remuise Johnson (5-8, 175), a cornerback from Garden City, is another junior college transfer who could see plenty of early action. He's an athletic cover corner who intercepted nine passes in his two seasons at Garden City. As a sophomore, Johnson had 29 tackles, three tackles for loss, one sack, three interceptions and 12 pass break-ups. He had six interceptions and seven pass deflections as a freshman.

Among the freshmen, running back **Marshell Chiles** (5-10, 205) from El Reno, Okla., is probably the best. Chiles rushed for 2,008 yards and 44 touchdowns last season and was listed as the 12th-best running back in the Midwest by one recruiting analyst.

The freshman who could be given an opportunity to make a big splash early is Beck, the kicker.

There was another reason for heavy emphasis on junior college talent. Allen's job security probably cost the Jayhawks freshmen recruits. Junior college players aren't as concerned about long-term prospects.

"The most negative thing that's always thrown out there after a disappointing season is job security," Allen said. "You can't overcome that until you have some success."

BLUE RIBBON ANALYSIS

OFFENSE	C
SPECIAL TEAMS	C
DEFENSE	C+
INTANGIBLES	C

A few changes should help the Jayhawks. The coaching staff turnover has brought fresh faces and new ideas. And these guys are coaching for their jobs. They know Allen is on thin ice.

Also, opening with Division I-AA Southwest Missouri State is smarter than last season, when the Jayhawks wrecked their season at SMU. Kansas should have some good feeling from the opener.

They're going to need them because the make-or-break game comes the next week when UCLA visits. Kansas can't count on finding four Big 12 victories.

What needs to happen is a sweep of non-league games and three league triumphs to reach a winning record, bowl game and happiness.

UCLA is pivotal. Kansas is hoping for a big crowd, plenty of exposure and the victory that could change the fortunes of the Allen regime. The program needs to settle on a quarterback, fill holes in the secondary and on the offensive line and find a way to win games it hasn't won in the past.

Allen no longer has the luxury of time. It needs to happen this season or there probably won't be a next.

(B.K.)

2000 RESULTS

SMU	L	17-31	0-1
UAB	W	23-20	1-1
Southern Illinois	W	42-0	2-1
Oklahoma	L	16-34	2-2
Kansas State	L	13-52	2-3
Missouri	W	38-17	3-3
Colorado	W	23-15	4-3
Texas Tech	L	39-45	4-4
Nebraska	L	17-56	4-5
Texas	L	16-51	4-6
Iowa State	L	17-38	4-7

Kansas State

LOCATION	**Manhattan, KS**
CONFERENCE	**Big 12 (North)**
LAST SEASON	**11-3 (.846)**
CONFERENCE RECORD	**6-2 (1st)**
OFFENSIVE STARTERS RETURNING	**6**
DEFENSIVE STARTERS RETURNING	**3**
NICKNAME	**Wildcats**
COLORS	**Purple & White**
HOME FIELD	**KSU Stadium (50,000)**
HEAD COACH	**Bill Snyder (William Jewell '62)**
RECORD AT SCHOOL	**99-43-1 (12 years)**
CAREER RECORD	**99-43-1 (12 years)**

ASSISTANTS

Phil Bennett (Texas A&M '78)
Defensive Coordinator/Defensive Backs
Ron Hudson (California '69)
Offensive Coordinator/Quarterbacks
Bob Fello (Kent '74)
Defensive Ends
Mo Lattimore (Kansas State '76)
Defensive Tackles
Jim Gush (Bucknell '81)
Linebackers
Paul Dunn (Pittsburgh '83)
Offensive Line/Running Game Coordinator
Greg Peterson (Nebraska Wesleyan '84)
Receivers/Passing Game Coordinator
Michael Smith (Kansas State '95)
Running Backs
Matt Miller (Kansas State '96)
Tight Ends

TEAM WINS (last 5 yrs.)	**9-11-11-11-11**
FINAL RANK (last 5 yrs.)	**23-10-6-4-8**
2000 FINISH	**Beat Tennessee in Cotton Bowl.**

COACH AND PROGRAM

Kansas State may be the ultimate, "Well, yes, but ... " program:

• The Wildcats won 11 games for the fourth straight season in 2000. Well, yes, but, they played their usual gosh awful non-league schedule. Beating Ball State, 76-0, helped the program how?

• K-State won the North Division title for the second time in three years and shares the top overall record in five years of league play with mighty Nebraska. Well, yes, but, K-State lost the conference championship game for the second time in three years. It has never been a Big 12 champion.

• The 'Cats won the Cotton Bowl. Well, yes, but they should have. K-State entered the game ranked ninth, Tennessee 21st.

It's an interesting time to be a Kansas State fan. Are you thrilled about the sustained success of eight straight bowl appearances, your team's place in the Big 12 elite, taking chief rival Kansas for granted? Or are you disappointed that in two of the last three years the program has reached the brink of ultimate success only to fall short?

In 1998, Kansas State merely needed to hold on to a 15-point fourth quarter lead against Texas A&M in the Big 12 championship game to play for the whole enchilada. The Aggies won. Last year, K-State was ranked second when Oklahoma visited in the seventh week. But the Sooners jumped ahead early and never looked back.

The result both times was a final Top-10 ranking, but less than satisfying finish. Last season, after the Wildcats had lost to Oklahoma and Texas A&M in a three-week period, Kansas State followers seemed to take a hard look at themselves. The team stood 7-2 but they were gloomy over the lost opportunity of a national title.

But here's where coach Bill Snyder started pushing the right buttons. Yes, the goal of a national title was gone. But Kansas State could still win the division and have a shot at the league championship and BCS bowl. Fans may have been down, but Snyder didn't let that happen to the team.

The next weekend, K-State pounded bowl-bound Iowa State, 56-10. Nebraska was next. The Cornhuskers' national title hopes were alive, but on a snowy evening in Manhattan, the Wildcats made their stand, winning by 29-28. A season was salvaged.

Losing to Oklahoma in the Big 12 title game was no crime. Beating Tennessee felt as good as any of Snyder's five bowl victories. The Vols may have not have held the ranking, but the 1998 national champions had the reputation. K-State doesn't play many quality non-league teams. When it does, it cannot afford to leave a bad impression.

Where does this leave Kansas State this season? In a good place.

Expectations are lower. Playmakers in quarterback Jonathan Beasley and wide receiver Quincy Morgan along with eight defensive starters and an All-America kicker are gone. The Wildcats will be forecast no higher than second, which is where they started last season.

But this is a good team. Running back **Josh Scobey** and fullback **Rock Cartwright** should give the Wildcats their best rushing attack under Snyder. Defensive players like linebackers **Terry Pierce** and **Josh Buhl** and end **Melvin Williams** are candidates to step into stardom.

The quarterback competition between **Ell Roberson III** and **Marc Dunn** wasn't settled after spring practice, but Snyder said the vibes he got from his team in the spring were as good as any he's encountered in coaching.

"There is a sense that this team is coming together," Snyder said.

The schedule doesn't break favorably for the Cats. The opener at Southern Cal will be the program's most difficult non-league test in years. The Trojans aren't the perennial power of the past, but this was a quick starting team last season.

The Wildcats turned down a chance to open the season against Southern Mississippi in Manhattan, which was probably a wise move. Beating the Trojans should be the focus.

Kansas State opens Big 12 play at Oklahoma and its other league road games are against bowl teams: Texas Tech, Iowa State and Nebraska, all with a revenge motive.

A ninth straight bowl game should happen and a Bowl Championship Series game would be well deserved if Kansas State can go 9-2 against this schedule. It might be difficult to reach 11 victories this year, but that's a tough task every season, even with three easy wins in September.

2001 SCHEDULE

Sept.	8	USC
	15	Louisiana Tech
	22	New Mexico State
	29	@Oklahoma
Oct.	6	Colorado
	13	@Texas Tech
	20	Texas A&M
	27	Kansas
Nov.	3	@Iowa State
	10	@Nebraska
	17	Missouri

QUARTERBACKS

Before we get to this year's situation, last year's guy deserves a final salute. Jonathan Beasley was treated as poorly by the fans and media as any K-State quarterback under Bill Snyder. He didn't run as well as Heisman runner-up Michael Bishop, didn't throw as well as some of Snyder's earlier quarterbacks. He didn't have what it takes to get the Wildcats to a conference championship and in the national title picture.

Well, it's true the Wildcats didn't win a Big 12 title or play in a Bowl Championship Series bowl with Beasley. But you know what? The only quarterback in Kansas State history who can make either of those claims is Bishop, who guided the team to the Fiesta Bowl as a junior, not as a conference champion but as an at-large selection.

All Beasley did in his two years as a starter was lead K-State to consecutive bowl victories. No other quarterback under Snyder can make that claim. Beasley set eight school records in his senior season.

In the final analysis, the quarterback position isn't why the Wildcats didn't win a conference or national title the last two seasons. In fact, Beasley helped make Kansas State as good as it was.

Onward. Beasley's replacement is either sophomore Roberson III (6-1, 190) or junior Dunn (6-4, 205), and their styles couldn't stand in greater contrast.

Roberson is speed and quickness. He is the guy who ran 73 yards for a touchdown the first time he touched the ball in the spring game two years ago. His athletic ability is mindful of Bishop, but accuracy is a problem.

Last season, Roberson completed 10-of-23 (43.5 percent) for 119 yards, two touchdowns and two interceptions.

That didn't stop Kansas State fans from chanting "E3" last September, while Snyder was trying to build confidence in Beasley. Roberson played in six games, all in mop-up situations. At the same time, Snyder was trying to bring Roberson along slowly, and he thinks that long touchdown run two springs ago may have done everybody a disservice.

"In retrospect, I cringed when it happened," Snyder said. "We start the first ball game the next season and everybody thinks I'm an idiot because Ell Roberson is not on the field. Here's a young guy who comes out of high school, where he had tremendous success, and bang, all of a sudden he makes it look so easy.

"Now, that's not entirely a bad thing because it made him feel a little more at ease. But it gave him the impression that, 'Hey, all I need to do to is step out here and all those things will happen.' "

They don't, and Roberson has needed every bit of his two-plus years as an understudy to pick up the offense. But if Roberson, the Houston area high school player of the year in 1999, was the obvious successor to Beasley, why did the Wildcats sign Dunn, one of the top passing quarterbacks in junior college last season?

Competition is healthy for everybody, but the Wildcats essentially have two starters. Dunn was last year's National Junior College Athletic Association Offensive Player of the Year at Ricks College in Idaho. He threw for an NJCAA-record 4,351 yards, 42 touchdowns and 17 interceptions in 11 games, completing 60.4 percent. He passed for 605 yards in one game.

A year ago, Dunn broke eight school records: passes completed in a game (34), most yards passing in a game (605), most touchdowns in a game (8), most passing yards in a season (4,351), most yards total offense in a season (4,237), most touchdown passes in a season (42), most passes attempted in a season (464) and most passes completed in a season (281).

Dunn is a Mormon who finished high school in 1995, redshirted in 1996, went on a two-year mission to Chile in 1997 and 1998 and played at Ricks for two seasons. So at 23 he brings some maturity to the mix. Dunn's father, Richard, played at Brigham Young.

Dunn looks like the kind of drop-back passer Kansas State hasn't seen since Brian Kavanagh in 1996. But Dunn also ran the option in high school, and the question remains whether Snyder will use Dunn the way he expects to use Roberson.

"Marc is a better athlete than people might have projected when they see he's 6-4," Snyder said. "You don't expect a guy that size running around and doing athletic things. We'll move our offense in a direction where we think both of them can fit."

Third on the depth chart is senior **Jeremy Milne** (6-0, 210), who has seen mop-up action in each of his previous three seasons. Last year, Milne got in two games but didn't attempt a pass.

RUNNING BACKS

Kansas State has rarely been one of those programs where you lick your chops at the running game prospects. Not that's it has been ineffective. Kansas State typically has operated by committee and the big-play men have been the quarterbacks and wide receivers. This year, the Cats are running.

Starters Scobey (6-0, 205) and the appropriately named Cartwright (5-8, 242) return. Scobey had a breakout season in 2000 and earned third team all-conference after leading the Wildcats with 718 rushing yards. He set a school record for rushing touchdowns by a running back with 16 (Beasley, the quarterback, had 17.) None of those totals include the 147 yards and two touchdowns against Tennessee in the Cotton Bowl.

Scobey is a senior from Oklahoma City who signed with Wildcats out of high school but attended Northeastern Oklahoma A&M for two years. He didn't start until the sixth game and got only six starts for the season, but proved to be one of the team's top offensive weapons. He is clearly the team's top back and could take aim at the school rushing record of 1,173 yards set by Isaac Jackson in 1973.

Cartwright, a senior, joined Scobey in forming the starting backfield of the season's second half. Cartwright was a reserve behind Johnno Lazetic through six games, then got his first start against Texas Tech. His 6-yard rushing average was the team's best and his 278 yards ranked fourth. Cartwright is a punishing back as his frame suggests. Like Scobey, he transferred in from junior college last season. Look for Cartwright to be featured in some one-back sets.

Sophomore **Danny Morris** (5-11, 200) was a special teams regular last season who will back up Scobey. Morris picked up 64 yards on 17 carries in three games last season. Also in reserve is sophomore **Rashad Washington** (6-3, 200), who saw action on the Kansas State basketball team last season.

Reserve fullback **Nick Hohiesel** (6-1, 225), a junior, is one of those overachievers who earns his stripes through his devotion to duty. It comes as no surprise that Hohiesel makes the most of every day. He had an ideal mentor in his father, John, a former Wichita State football player who survived the plane crash that killed 14 teammates.

WIDE RECEIVERS/TIGHT ENDS

Catching his brother is a tall task, but all that means is that senior wide receiver **Aaron Lockett** (5-7, 165) is planning on a big season.

Lockett owns 113 receptions for 2,043 yards and 11 touchdowns in his career. Kevin Lockett caught 213 passes for 3,032 yards and 26 touchdowns from 1993-96. Out of the question? Not for Lockett, who has succeeded in all of his sports endeavors.

In 1998, Lockett was a freshman All-American with 44 receptions and six touchdowns. His 928 yards that season were the second best in school history at the time.

In 1999, Lockett made second team All-Big 12, and last year he went to first team all-conference and second-team All-American, not as a wide receiver, but as a kick returner.

In his first season returning punts, Lockett averaged a nation's best 22.8 yards per return and scored three touchdowns, including one against Oklahoma in the Big 12 championship game. He was subbing for David Allen, the reigning All-America return man who had injured an ankle in the season opener.

Even as Allen's health improved, he couldn't dislodge Lockett from the position. Lockett wound up leading the team in all-purpose yards (rushing, receiving and return) with 1,459. He averaged 18.5 yards on the 79 times he touched the ball last season.

When he's not in the end zone, Lockett is on the track or cutting tracks. He is a member of the indoor team and holds the school record for the 60 at 6.69 seconds. Lockett also is an accomplished hip hop performer who has produced a CD called *Strange State of OK.* On stage, he goes by "Strange."

With the departure of leading receiver Quincy Morgan, Lockett is by far the Wildcats' most potent weapon on the outside. If he doesn't catch his brother on the career lists, Lockett should finish his life as a Wildcat no worse than two or three on the charts.

Where else will Kansas State go to find receptions? The only other returning players who caught a pass last season are seniors **Brandon Clark** (6-3, 220), set to start at the other wide receiver position, and **Ricky Lloyd** (5-10, 160). Senior **Chris Devore** (6-2, 200) and sophomore **Derrick Evans** (5-11, 175) each saw action in three games last season.

Clark has size and speed (4.4 in the 40) and has shown glimpses of excellence in the past. He is listed as a senior, but because of several foot injuries that have kept him off the field, he has been granted a sixth year of eligibility this season.

Another backup wide receiver is senior **Drew Thalmann** (6-2, 190), also a special teams standout.

Senior tight end **Nick Warren** (6-7, 255) turned down scholarship offers from elsewhere to walk on at K-State. He will get his first crack as a regular after backing up Shad Meier most of last year. Warren started twice when Meier went down and had his best game at Texas A&M, when he caught three passes for 50 yards.

OFFENSIVE LINE

Senior guards **Andy Eby** (6-3, 280) and **John Robertson** (6-4, 291) have been teammates ever since high school in Olathe, Kansas, and they're bidding to become teammates on the all-conference team this season.

Eby broke into the starting lineup as a sophomore but finished the season coming off the bench. Last season, Eby was a starter for good and helped the Wildcats rack up some impressive figures. The offensive line allowed a mere nine sacks and helped the running game cross the goal line 42 times, matching a school record.

Robertson will start for a third season and owns a 24-game starting streak. He comes from hearty stock. Robertson's father, John, played at Illinois and for the Houston Oilers.

Senior **Thomas Barnett** (6-5, 290) has started 20 straight games at right tackle, but Snyder has said that streak may be in jeopardy. Working with the starters in the spring at center is sophomore **Nick Leckey** (6-4, 285), who was one of two first-year freshmen to see playing time last season. Leckey played in nine games, starting twice at left guard when Eby went out with an injury.

It is a three-man battle for the left tackle spot among seniors **Matt Martin** (6-5, 270), **Oshin Honarchian** (6-5, 290) and junior **Steve Washington** (6-4, 315). Martin appeared in nine games last season and Honarchian played in five. Washington is listed as the backup center, but can play all the line positions.

Filling in are sophomore **Ben Rettele** (6-7, 282), junior **Jarvis Miller** (6-3, 280) and redshirt freshman **Chris Boggas** (6-5, 315)

2000 STATISTICS

Rushing offense	198.1	22
Passing offense	211.9	58
Total offense	410.0	33
Scoring offense	39.5	6
Net Punting	34.2	67
Punt returns	17.3	4
Kickoff returns	18.6	82
Rushing defense	98.2	14
Passing efficiency defense	94.9	6
Total defense	270.5	4
Scoring defense	18.5	17
Turnover margin	+6	34

Last column is ranking among Division I-A teams.

KICKERS

A position of excellence gets tested this season.

For the past four years, Kansas State has had the all-conference place-kicker—Martin Gramatica in 1997 and 1998 and Jamie Rheem the last two seasons.

Now the spotlight falls on sophomore **Jared Brite** (6-2, 185), who was 5-for-5 on extra-points kicks last season.

Brite also is a punter who had four attempts last season for a 36.8-yard average. Two of his kicks were downed inside the 20. Brite's future may be on the baseball diamond. He pitches for the Wildcats and his fastball's been clocked at 95 mph.

Regular punter **Travis Brown** (6-4, 215), a junior, can also kick. He stepped in for an injured Rheem two seasons ago and made one of two field goals.

DEFENSIVE LINE

This is the area of great unknown for the Wildcats. Gone are ends Monty Beisel and Chris Johnson, who combined for more than 21 sacks last season. Also departed is All-America tackle Mario Fatahehi and tackle DeVane Robinson.

The entire line must be rebuilt, and Snyder and his staff will fill some holes with junior college transfers. The most experienced returning player is junior end Williams (6-3, 250), who had 4 1/2 sacks last season.

Williams is one of the team's better athletes. At Mehlville High in St. Louis, he was a basketball standout. But he followed the path of older brother Turelle, a former K-State linebacker.

In the spring, the other end slot was up for grabs between sophomore **Thomas Houchin** (6-3, 235) and redshirt freshman **Alax Carrier** (6-4, 230). Houchin played in one game last season. Carrier will see his first action this season.

On the inside, senior **Jerry Togiai** (6-4, 291) is ready to earn the starting tackle slot. Togiai started twice and had his best game against Oklahoma in the Big 12 championship game when he recorded six tackles, including a 10-yard sack of Josh Heupel.

Senior **Eric Everley** (6-6, 332) will start fall workouts as the starting nose tackle, beating out junior **Corey Hoffman** (6-5, 275). But help is arriving across the line in the fall.

Junior **Henry Bryant** (6-1, 255) was a first-team junior college All-America end from Garden City (Kansas) Community College. He finished with103 tackles and nine sacks. His 18 tackles behind the line of scrimmage ranked fourth in the Jayhawk League.

Ahead of Bryant in that category was junior **Allen "Tank" Reese** (5-11, 280), a second-team all-conference selection from Hutchinson (Kansas) Community College. Reese also punted for Hutch last season.

Also providing immediate help will be junior tackle **Corey White** (6-3, 285), a first-team All-Southwest Junior College Conference pick from Navarro (Texas) Junior College. White had 65 tackles and four sacks.

LINEBACKERS

K-State's linebackers are the strength of the defense. The unit will be among the best in the Big 12.

Senior **Ben Leber** (6-4, 250) will start for a third straight season and look to continue his climb up the honors ladder. From honorable mention All-Big 12 two years ago to second-team last season, Leber will be the center of attention for the K-State defense, and he is up to the challenge.

He will be the team's captain player representative for the second straight year.

Senior **Warren Lott** (6-3, 235) started four games last season, his first full year of action since 1997 when he played at Georgia Military College. Lott originally signed with Clemson and was so highly regarded that he was voted the ACC's Preseason Defensive Newcomer of the Year.

But Lott had a change of heart and landed in Manhattan. He is battling sophomore Buhl (6-0, 200) for the starting weak-side job, and Buhl had a terrific spring, which he capped with a seven-tackle performance in the spring game. There was some concern about Buhl's small stature, but he put those questions to rest with his performance.

Also in the mix there is **Bryan Hickman** (6-3, 220), a teammate of Buhl's at Mesquite North High in Mesquite, Texas. Hickman played in two games last season.

Ready to build on his solid freshman season is sophomore middle linebacker Pierce (6-3, 245). He is already being compared to great Kansas State linebackers of recent vintage like Mark Simoneau and Jeff Kelly.

A year ago, Pierce was voted the Big 12's Defensive Newcomer of the Year and was selected second-team freshman All-America. During the spring he was chosen one of five team captains and he's the only one who isn't a senior. But it is what he does on the field that is impressive.

"We've got a sophomore middle linebacker who made 11 tackles in our spring game," defensive coordinator Phil Bennett said. "That's impressive."

Junior **Andy Klocke** (6-2, 220) bids for his third letter as a reserve.

DEFENSIVE BACKS

Kansas State has established a standard in the secondary. It never seems to matter how great the losses. The Wildcats find great defensive backs to plug in.

This season K-State gets put to the test again. The lone returning starter is senior **Jon McGraw** (6-3, 200), who could move from free safety to strong safety. McGraw was the team's second-leading tackler with 81 and fifth on the team in tackles for loss with 10. He is bidding to become a four-time first-team academic All-Big 12.

If McGraw moves over, senior **Derrick Yates** (6-2, 185) could move up. Yates was voted Big 12 Defensive Newcomer of the Year last season after transferring from Coffeyville (Kansas) Community Colleges. Yates had 29 tackles and broke up six passes. He came on strong at the end of the season, recording 12 tackles in the regular-season finale against Missouri.

Also vying for time at strong safety are junior **Milton Proctor** (6-0, 200) and sophomore **Alan Walker** (6-2, 175). Proctor started four games last season in place of injured Jarrod Cooper and has intercepted a pass in each of his three seasons. Walker (6-2, 175) played in three games.

Junior **Terence Newman** (5-11, 170) looks to apply his track speed to cornerback. Newman owns the school record for the indoor 60 and 200 as well as the outdoor 100 (10.26). He played in all 14 games last season and started against Louisiana Tech.

Newman's best moments came in the Cotton Bowl. He filled in for injured Jerametrius Butler and threw a blanket over Tennessee's Cedrick Wilson.

"What happened in that game was a big confidence boost," Newman said.

Newman will battle with junior **James Dunnigan** (5-7, 180), who began his career at Purdue, where he started 8-of-12 games in 1999. Dunnigan was injured at Garden City (Kansas) Community College most of last season.

Senior **DeRon Tyler** (5-8, 170) or **DeMarcus Faggins** (5-11, 175) are battling for the other corner. Tyler started five games when the Wildcats opened in nickel or dime packages. He has a pair of interceptions in his career. Faggins also started when the Wildcats opened in pass defense. His lone interception last season came in the Cotton Bowl.

PUNTERS

Brown averaged 38.5 yards on 51 punts last season. Only 24 of his punts were returned and that was for a paltry 4.7-yard average.

At the Cotton Bowl, three of Brown's four punts were downed inside the Tennessee 20. He is starting his second year as the regular punter and also can kick in a pinch. In 1999, Brown converted a 36-yard field goal.

Brite, also a pitcher on the Wildcats' baseball team, was one of two freshmen to play last season and will handle the place kicking chores. But Brite also punts and kicked twice against Oklahoma in the Big 12 title game.

Rick Gerla (6-1, 210), a junior, will also battle for the job. He finished second among junior college punters with a 43-yard average for Blinn (Texas) Junior College.

Senior **Mike Ronsick** (6-2, 190) split time with Brown in 1999 and averaged 37.1 yards. He is the Wildcats' holder on place kicks.

SPECIAL TEAMS

Kansas State has the nation's top return man in Lockett, who led Division I-A in punt returns. He also is the team's top kick returner with a 22.3-yard average on 14 returns.

The Wildcats also cover kicks as well as any team this side of Virginia Tech. Opponents averaged a mere 4.7 yards per punt return with none going longer than 12 yards. Foes averaged 15.8 yards on kick returns and that included a 93-yarder that set up a touchdown for Oklahoma.

Kansas State will miss Brice Libel and Chris Claybon, who were excellent blockers and made the coverage teams special. But once again, the Wildcats should boast some of the best special teams in the nation.

RECRUITING CLASS

Kansas State may have signed the nation's best junior college class, which means fans are going to see plenty of new faces immediately.

The most heralded of the group is quarterback Dunn. But he might not start. Others should. Help arrived on the defensive line in Reese, White and Bryant.

The Wildcats looked to soften the blow of losing Morgan by signing junior **Lawrence "Taco" Wallace** (6-1, 190) from Mount San Jacinto (Calif.) College. Wallace caught 49 passes for 1,072 yards and was voted honorable mention All-America.

Dralinn Burks (6-4, 305), a two-year starting offensive tackle at Trinity Valley (Texas) Community College, and punter Gerla also will battle for starts.

The most heralded freshman might be running back **Darren Sproles** (5-7, 170), who continues an Olathe, Kansas, pipeline to Kansas State. Sproles swept all the state and area player-of-the-year awards, rushing for 2,485 yards and 49 touchdowns in leading North High to its fourth large-class state championship in five years.

The Wildcats want to continue the recent place kicking success by signing the younger brother of departed Jamie Rheem, Joe. He was the only kicker chosen to the *Parade* All-America team. **Joe Rheem** (6-2, 210) made 11-of-13 field goals, including a 53-yarder, last season.

Ayo Saba (6-0, 260) of Erial, N.J., was considered one of the best high school fullbacks in the nation. He rushed for 1,225 yards and 15 touchdowns and got seven starts at halfback. Saba chose the Wildcats over Nebraska, Wisconsin, Miami and Iowa.

BLUE RIBBON ANALYSIS

OFFENSE	B+
SPECIAL TEAMS	A
DEFENSE	B
INTANGIBLES	B

So much of what to think about Kansas State rides with the success of the quarterback. Snyder has entered seasons without a definitive No. 1 in the past and it has never affected a team the way it did at Texas last season.

Still, you just don't know what you're getting with Roberson or Dunn. Roberson has had two years to grasp the system, and you figure the experience will give him an early edge. But don't be shocked if Dunn splits time.

Snyder and Kansas State were overwhelmed by the excellence displayed by Oklahoma's Josh Heupel in Manhattan last season. Heupel, in his second year after transferring from junior college, passed for 375 yards on 29-of-37 completions. Dunn can be that kind of passer.

Kansas State isn't alone in the Big 12 as far as not choosing a starter entering fall. Oklahoma, Kansas, Missouri are also uncertain. But the programs on solid ground also find a way to work through the issue, and Kansas State will do that.

The schedule is more difficult, the personnel losses, especially on defense, are heavy. But it is hard to see Kansas State finishing any worse than 8-3. The Cats will start the season behind Oklahoma, Texas and Nebraska in the polls. The good news for Kansas State is it will have a chance to do something about the Sooners and Cornhuskers, who appear on the regular-season schedule.

(B.K.)

2000 RESULTS

Iowa (E.Robinson Classic)	W	27-7	1-0
Louisiana Tech	W	54-10	2-0
Ball State	W	76-0	3-0
North Texas	W	55-10	4-0
Colorado	W	44-21	5-0
Kansas	W	52-13	6-0
Oklahoma	L	31-41	6-1
Texas Tech	W	28-23	7-1
Texas A&M	L	10-26	7-2
Iowa State	W	56-10	8-2
Nebraska	W	29-28	9-2
Missouri	W	28-24	10-2
Oklahoma (Big 12 Champ.)	L	24-27	10-3
Tennessee (Cotton Bowl)	W	35-21	11-3

Missouri

LOCATION	**Columbia, MO**
CONFERENCE	**Big 12 (North)**
LAST SEASON	**3-8 (.273)**
CONFERENCE RECORD	**2-6 (6th)**
OFFENSIVE STARTERS RETURNING	**8**
DEFENSIVE STARTERS RETURNING	**6**
NICKNAME	**Tigers**
COLORS	**Black & Old Gold**
HOME FIELD	**Faurot Field (69,349)**
HEAD COACH	**Gary Pinkel (Kent '75)**
RECORD AT SCHOOL	**First Year**
CAREER RECORD	**73-37-3 (10 years)**

ASSISTANTS

Dave Christensen (Washington '83)
Assistant Head Coach/Offensive Coordinator/Offensive Line
Brian Jones (Connecticut '81)
Running Backs
Andy Hill (Missouri '85)
Wide Receivers
Bruce Walker (Central Washington '83)
Tight Ends
David Yost (Kent '92)
Quarterbacks
Matt Eberflus (Toledo '93)
Defensive Coordinator/Secondary
Cornell Ford (Toledo '91)
Safeties
Craig Kuligowski (Toledo '91)
Defensive Line
Dave Steckel (Kutztown '82)
Linebackers

TEAM WINS (last 5 yrs.)	**5-7-8-4-3**
FINAL RANK (last 5 yrs.)	**57-36-20-73-73**
2000 FINISH	**Lost to Kansas State in regular-season finale.**

COACH AND PROGRAM

With every loss the groaning grew louder. Larry Smith, who had led Missouri out of the darkness with consecutive bowl appearance to end a 13-year streak of losing seasons, was now headed for a second straight awful season.

The problems started early with an embarrassing 62-9 loss to Clemson. Then came an incident in the Michigan State game the next week. Smith decided to punt late in the game. The Tigers never got the ball back and lost by a field goal.

As the losses mounted, Smith's fate became inevitable. But in these days of rampant media speculation and college football's recent trend of axing coaches with games remaining, it became excruciating to watch the Tigers in the final weeks of the season.

No interview with Smith was complete without a comment on his future. Athletic director Mike Alden was quoted nearly every day about the situation. Media types were beginning to interview potential replacement candidates with weeks left in the season. TCU's Dennis Franchione became a popular target.

Meanwhile, the players and coaching staff had to find a way to block it all out. To their credit, they did just that. Missouri pounded Baylor in the 10th week, and the Tigers took Kansas State to the brink before falling, 28-24. Smith got the news the next day.

Enter Gary Pinkel, a consistent winner at Toledo who opened everybody's eyes with a dominating 24-6 victory at Penn State earlier in the season. The Rockets probably were the best—certainly they were the most deserving team—not to play in a bowl game last season.

Pinkel's charge is simple: get Missouri back to regular bowl status and go from there. He's making no predictions about the Tigers' success, offers no timetable. That's not his style.

"We don't talk about the past, and I never talk about 'We're going to win this, we're going to get this done or get that done," Pinkel said. "I focus on the next game. I focus on the things necessary so that we can be the best we can be at that moment. I know that sounds boring. But I've done that every year I've been in coaching.

"I have a one-day plan. That's all."

Pinkel studied at the Don James school of football philosophy. He played tight end for James at Kent State and coached under him at Washington. He immediately bought into James, who had become Kent State's coach in the aftermath of the National Guard shootings of May, 1970 in which four students were killed during Vietnam protests. Pinkel entered school that fall.

"It was a pretty ugly time there," Pinkel said. "Don James came in and within two years we won a [Mid-American] championship and played in the Tangerine Bowl. I was thinking about going into teaching or business. I wasn't sure what I really wanted to do. But when I saw him and what he did at the worst time that you could ever recruit at that school, that inspired me."

Missouri seemed inspired with Pinkel's hiring. He was warmly received in Columbia and was overwhelmed with a standing ovation at his introductory press conference. Fans like what they hear, the switch to a one-back offense that will typically employ three wide receivers, a 4-4 defense, and improved special teams.

That last one is important. Special teams were a consistent weakness under Smith. It not only cost the Tigers games during the losing seasons, but better bowls in the winning ones. Pinkel, with his attention to detail, won't let that happen.

"I believe in our system," Pinkel said. "I watched Don James make decisions every day for 12 years and I made many of the same decisions he made. Sometimes I agreed and sometimes I disagreed. But I learned a lot from him, and he's one of the most successful coaches ever in Division I."

One decision Pinkel couldn't change was that of defensive end Justin Smith, the All-America tackle who skipped his senior season to enter the NFL draft. Smith, who holds Missouri's all-time record for sacks, was chosen by the Cincinnati Bengals with the fourth pick in the first round. Smith and Russ Washington, the fourth overall choice in the 1968 draft, are the highest-ever picks out of Missouri. Smith's departure leaves a gaping hole of talent and leadership.

A winning season is too much to expect in Pinkel's first season, but steady improvement is not. That's his goal.

"The foundation of this program will never change," Pinkel said. "We will consistently try to make every area better while maintaining a basic philosophy of how to win. All the details in the program are geared toward increasing our chances of winning.

"... We want our players to be winners. That means changing attitudes and habits and we do that in everything we do, from meetings, to the weight room, to our 6 a.m. morning workouts."

2001 SCHEDULE

Sept.	1	Bowling Green
	8	Southwest Texas
	15	@Michigan State
	29	Nebraska
Oct.	6	@Oklahoma State
	13	Iowa State
	20	@Kansas
	27	Texas
Nov.	3	@Colorado
	10	Baylor
	17	@Kansas State

QUARTERBACKS

It looks like junior **Kirk Farmer** (6-5, 210) will be the man here, but don't write it in ink just yet.

The Missouri depth chart lists Farmer over junior **Darius Outlaw** (6-4, 192), but Pinkel wasn't ready to make a pronouncement during spring ball, so the competition continues into the fall.

Farmer, though, has other ideas.

"I just think, 'This is my job, I'm going to do this," he said. "I'm a veteran, getting older and older, and I've had a couple of injuries, but I'm ready to go."

Those injuries have knocked Farmer's career off track. Two years ago he was splitting time with **Jim Dougherty** (6-4, 195), a senior, when he broke his leg against Iowa State. Farmer had made his first career start the previous week against Colorado.

Last season, the injury was even more devastating. The Tigers were hanging with Nebraska in Lincoln, roughing up the Cornhuskers' defense.

Through 2 1/2 quarters, Farmer had rushed for 83 yards, passed for a career-best 214 and even caught a 35-yard pass. But on the end of a 48-yard scramble, Farmer was tackled and his shoulder was buried into the turf. He had broken his collarbone and would miss the next seven games.

Farmer wound up with three touchdown passes, three interceptions and 669 yards in the abbreviated season. Outlaw started the rest of the way and completed 105-of-225 passes for 1,391 yards. He had nine touchdown passes and 16 interceptions. He also rushed for 259 yards and five touchdowns. Outlaw also is competing as if the job is open.

"There's a job out there that needs to be won," Outlaw said. "[Farmer] won it last year, and I'm getting a fair opportunity to win it this year. If I win it, I win it. If I don't, then I've got to be what I can be, a reliable backup."

Farmer is a better thrower, Outlaw a better runner. Farmer's been in the program for three full years. Outlaw for two. Outlaw, a Georgia native, came to Missouri after attending the Tigers' football camps in 1997 and '98. For what Pinkel wants to run, Farmer seems the better choice. But he's not willing to hand Farmer the keys to the offense just yet.

"They're competing," Pinkel said. "Just like every other position."

Dougherty is back for his senior year. He started 10 games as a sophomore and hasn't started since. He didn't get a chance to compete in the spring after undergoing elbow surgery.

Redshirt freshman **Brock Harvey** (6-2, 194) was moved to quarterback when Farmer went down last year. He was recruited as a cornerback and was also a punter in high school, but quarterback is where he will play this season.

RUNNING BACKS

The Z-backfield returns. Senior **Zain Gilmore** (6-1, 215) and sophomore **Zack Abron** (5-10, 228) are knocking heads for the starting tailback slot. Gilmore led the Tigers in rushing last season with 632 yards. He averaged 4.5 yards per carry and scored seven touchdowns. Abron gained 502 yards, owned a 3.8-yard average and found the end zone five times.

The big difference between the backs this year is their weight. Pinkel wanted them leaner. Gilmore dropped 17 pounds between the end of the season and beginning of spring workouts. Abron dropped about 10 pounds.

"They're both quicker," Pinkel said. "And they're faster."

Gilmore has led Missouri in rushing for two years, and he's only started nine games in that period. He came to Missouri to follow All-America running back Devin West and is looking for an all-conference season as a senior.

Abron excited the Tigers last season after emerging from spring practice as a force. He actually entered last season as the No. 1 back.

Another possibility at running back is junior **T.J. Leon** (6-0, 225), who moves from fullback in the new offense. Leon was battling for the starting fullback role a year ago when he broke a leg early in two-a-day workouts. But he logged an impressive spring and was timed at 4.4 in the 40-yard dash.

Leon comes from an athletic family. His father was a four-year letterman in wrestling at St. Francis, Pa., and his sister, Monica, was a track athlete at Oklahoma.

Toledo ranked among the nation's top 10 rushing teams in Pinkel's final two seasons, but in the two previous years the passing game was the team's strength.

The Tigers under Smith went from primarily an option team under Corby Jones and West to a passing attack under Farmer. These Tigers appear to have elements of both phases, which should make them more balanced than in recent seasons.

WIDE RECEIVERS/TIGHT ENDS

Missouri entered last year feeling great about its fleet of pass catchers. Guys like Travis Garvin, John Dausman, **Brandon Barnes** and **Justin Gage**. Injuries took all of them away except Gage. Garvin and Dausman have moved on, and now it's up to Gage and Barnes to pick up the pieces.

Gage (6-5, 200), a junior, could be on the cusp of stardom. The injury-depleted ranks gave him an opportunity to show his stuff last year and Gage didn't disappoint. He caught 44 passes for 709 yards and four touchdowns, a year after he had been switched from quarterback.

He's also the most successful football-basketball talent in the Big 12, getting quality minutes off the bench for Quin Snyder's team. But Gage's future is football. He's got the body, strength and speed to be a premier wide receiver. When his career is over, Gage might be one of the best athletes ever produced by the university.

Barnes (6-4, 214), a sophomore, is ready to put in a complete season. He suffered a broken leg on special teams in the second week against Clemson. The injury situation forced sophomores **Tay Jackson** (5-10, 178) and **Marcus James** (5-8, 169) into duty as freshmen. They could have used redshirt seasons but now must develop ahead of schedule.

Sophomore **Shirdonya Mitchell** (6-0, 175) came to campus two years ago heralded as one of the top high school wide receivers in Texas. But he sat out last year as a partial qualifier. He will get a chance to establish himself as a top threat, as will sophomore **Brandon Severino** (6-3, 198), a sure-handed pass catcher.

Without a fullback in the new offense, the tight end is an emphasis. Pinkel calls the position the R-back. They can line up in the backfield and are used as primary pass catchers.

Missouri has a good one returning in senior **Dwayne Blakley** (6-4, 256). He has caught 45 passes in his career and was third on the team last season with 18 receptions for 211 yards.

Sophomore **J.D. McCoy** (6-3, 250) was one of three freshmen to play last season, and Pinkel has moved two players into the position, former fullback **Joe Chirumbolo** (6-2, 234) and former wide receiver **Darren Baldwin** (6-4, 216).

OFFENSIVE LINE

Three returning starters and a pair of returning part-time starters give the offensive line a chance to be a team strength. Now, it a matter of picking up the new sets.

The best of the group is senior right guard **Mike Hayes** (6-3, 308), a returning third-team All-Big 12 selection. He was the unit's vocal leader a year ago and helped the Tigers finish in the top half among league rushing leaders at 154 yards per game.

Also on the right side is senior tackle **Justin Bland** (6-6, 344), who will be a third-year starter. He's the biggest of the linemen, although Pinkel believes bigger isn't necessarily better among linemen. He wants Bland and others trimmed down.

Sophomore **A.J. Ricker** (6-5, 287) started all 11 games at center last season. Tigers coaches think Ricker should be in line for honors this season.

The left side projected starters, senior tackle **Aaron Crittendon** (6-5, 342) and senior guard **Adrian Cole** (6-4, 339) have started in the past. Crittendon has missed time with injuries each of the last two years but came on strong at the end of last season. Cole has been looking for consistency while moving in and out of the starting lineup for the last two years.

Sophomore guard **Rob Droege** (6-6, 290), redshirt freshmen guard **Joe Giannio** (6-4, 285) and tackle **Tony Clinker** (6-2, 272) are returning letter winners.

"I expect some great competition out of this group," Pinkel said. "It is going to be interesting how it all sorts out."

2000 STATISTICS

Rushing offense	154.2	49
Passing offense	196.8	72
Total offense	351.0	71
Scoring offense	23.2	74
Net Punting	30.6	103
Punt returns	7.8	87
Kickoff returns	17.7	97
Rushing defense	159.0	68
Passing efficiency defense	121.4	65
Total defense	366.9	60
Scoring defense	31.6	88
Turnover margin	-5	82

Last column is ranking among Division I-A teams.

KICKERS

Place kicking is the one special teams unit that Pinkel inherited in reasonably good shape.

Senior **Brad Hammerich** (6-3, 191) was rolling along well, having made 7-of-9 field goals and all of his extra points, until he went down with a broken collarbone making a kickoff coverage tackle against Texas in the seventh week.

The Tigers had to the pull the redshirt off sophomore walk-on **Justin Scott** (6-0, 171), who will provide Hammerich with competition this season.

Missouri went with senior **Mike Caldrone** (5-2, 147) in the fourth quarter of the Baylor game and against Kansas State in the season finale and he made his only field goal and all five extra points.

DEFENSIVE LINE

Missouri switches from a 4-3 to a 4-4, but the biggest adjustment will be life without Smith, who became the school's career sack leader in only three seasons.

The candidates to replace Smith are a pair of junior college transfers who enrolled last season, juniors **Antwaun Bynum** (6-0, 240) and **Keith Wright** (6-4, 256). Bynum played three games at linebacker last season, a year after he was voted junior college All-America at Hutchinson (Kan.) Community College.

Wright also was a junior college All-American in 1999 at Sacramento City (Calif.) Junior College. He was redshirted last season after choosing the Tigers over Arizona, Miami, Florida and Illinois.

Other defensive end candidates come from a pool of junior **Josh O'Neal** (6-1, 235), redshirt freshmen **Nick Tarpoff** (6-3, 245) and **Terrell Mills** (6-4, 255) and **Dan Davis** (6-2, 246), a sophomore who was converted from running back. Mills was a linebacker last season.

The sleeper on defense is junior nose tackle **Cedric Harden** (6-3, 311), who had his best games against Nebraska, Kansas State and Oklahoma. He steps in for Pat Mingucci, who earned honorable mention all-league honors.

Senior **Michael Gavins** (6-6, 292) shared the tackle position with Danny McCamey last year and has the chance to win it outright this season. His height makes Gavins a top-notch pass deflector and his interception at Oklahoma State last season preserved a victory.

Senior **Chris Ryan** (6-3, 291) and sophomore **Howard Brown** (6-3, 283) are the top reserves at nose tackle.

LINEBACKERS

Linebacker is another position where injuries became a major factor.

Senior **Jamonte Robinson** (6-2, 209) was on the Butkus Award watch list last fall, but a nagging ankle injury kept him from reaching his full potential. He finished fourth on the team in tackles with 79 and had four sacks.

Junior **Sean Doyle** (6-0, 227) battled ankle and hamstring injuries all last season but missed only one game. He came up with 80 tackles and six sacks. He was second on the team in tackles for loss with 15. How tough is Doyle? He sat out the Oklahoma State game and appeared doubtful for the next game, against Kansas. Doyle not only played against the Jayhawks, he recorded 17 tackles.

Getting more playing time than scheduled because of the injuries were seniors **David Monroe** (6-0, 229) and **Duke Revard** (6-3, 225). They combined for 81 stops and seven tackles for loss. Revard also had three sacks and recovered a fumble for a touchdown.

In the Tigers' new 4-4 alignment, Robinson, Doyle, Monroe and Revard are inside linebackers. Pinkel calls the outside players outside safeties. At the top of the depth chart are junior **Gary Anthony** (6-0, 209) and **Marcus Caldwell** (6-0, 207), a former walk-on who started five games, made 27 tackles and had two interceptions last season.

The big move at the position involves former junior college All-America running back **Taurus Ferguson** (5-11, 202). Ferguson wasn't happy with the switch, and Pinkel understood.

"He didn't feel real good about it," Pinkel said. "He sees himself as a running back, but when we evaluated him during the off-season we saw he had a chance to a great player at [outside safety]."

DEFENSIVE BACKS

This area could be big trouble for the Tigers, who return only one scholarship cornerback from last year—junior **Cedric Duncan** (5-10, 177).

Duncan had four interceptions last season and broke up seven other passes. He starts at one corner in the new alignment that uses only three defensive backs—two corners and a free safety.

The Tigers will return junior **Terrence Curry** (5-11, 175) to cornerback, his original position, after shifting him to wide receiver last year. Curry went over when injuries piled up on offense, but now he's needed in the secondary, where he started two games as a freshman in 1999.

Also in the mix immediately is junior college transfer **R.J. Jones** (6-1, 151).

Free safety belongs to senior **Clarence Jones** (6-1, 199), a three-year letter winner who was second on the team in tackles with 87 and intercepted three passes. He'll be backed up by redshirt freshman **Kevin Johnson** (6-3, 204).

The new Missouri defense, headed by coordinator Matt Erberflus, should take some comfort in last year's statistics at Toledo. The Rockets led the nation in turnover ratio for the second time in six years.

"Our teams were in the top ten in turnover ratio for the last seven or eight years," Pinkel said. "Turnovers are a big deal with me. That's a way you help yourself win games."

PUNTERS

Senior **Jared Gilpin** (5-10, 175) is back but he didn't kick in the spring after off-season surgery to his neck. Gilpen averaged 39.8 yards per kick with a long of 55 yards. He put 22 punts inside the opponents' 20, compared to 10 the previous year.

The punting was acceptable. The punt coverage was not. Missouri gave up three returns for touchdowns last season and opponents averaged a whopping 15.4 yards per return.

SPECIAL TEAMS

They've been mostly a disaster for the last few years, and it's usually a different unit every year. In 1998, the Tigers couldn't buy a field goal.

Last season, the punt coverage was terrible. Pinkel isn't the kind of coach who will let special teams slide. Toledo has been solid in all phases of the kicking game. You'll see top-line players on coverage teams.

James handled many of the return chores last season. He averaged 5.9 yards on nine punt returns and 20 yards on nine kick returns.

RECRUITING CLASS

It never fails. When a new Missouri coach is introduced, the topic inevitably turns to recruiting Missouri players. So many good ones get away.

The Tigers do well in the central and southern parts of the state, but for every recruit out of the St. Louis and Kansas City areas that signs with the Tigers, another gets away.

That prospect faced Pinkel, who had only a few weeks to put together his first class. By all accounts, the Tigers did well in Missouri, and especially St. Louis by signing eight area players.

"I think we did OK in the state of Missouri and St. Louis," Pinkel said. "We made some strides. For the most part, we certainly improved in that area. I think based on what happened in the past and all the horror stories I heard I was surprised [at the success]. But the key is to do it year after year."

Probably the best recruit from the St. Louis area is running back **Damien Nash** (5-11, 195), who's from East St. Louis, Ill. Nash signed with the Tigers instead of Nebraska.

"Damien's a great prospect," Pinkel said. "He's got great balance, quickness, explosiveness and can change direction."

Nash was rated among the nation's top 15- to 30 running backs, depending on which recruiting guru you believe. A year ago, he rushed for 1,444 yards and 28 touchdowns despite missing the first game of the season. Nash also caught four passes for 87 yards and completed three passes for 97 yards and a touchdown.

Other St. Louis-area players signed were athlete **Arnold Britt** (6-2, 180) from Vashon High School, wide receiver/defensive back **Chris Crosby** (6-3, 185) of CBC, running back/defensive back **Orlando Gooden** of East St. Louis Cahokia High School, running back/defensive back **A.J. Kincade** (5-11, 185) of Hazelwood Central, running back/cornerback **Derrick Ming** (6-0, 230) of Webster Groves High School, running back/defensive back **Tyrone Robertson** (5-10, 185) of Pattonville and running back/defensive back **Quincy Wade** (5-9, 178) of Lindbergh High School.

Among the more decorated of the St. Louis-area recruits is Robertson, who was chosen the city's offensive player of the year by the *St. Louis Post-Dispatch* and was generally considered the top running back in the state. Last year, he piled up 2,766 all-purpose yards and scored 28 touchdowns. Robertson rushed for 1,569 yards and caught passes for 451 more.

Missouri signed six running backs, and in a major emphasis, signed 14 who could play in the secondary.

"We were looking for speed," Pinkel said. "What we tried to do with this recruiting class is improve our overall team speed."

Perhaps the best of the defensive backs is **Thompson Omboga** (6-1, 168), who also played wide receiver at Grand Prairie, Texas.

Omboga was ranked as the 27th-best wide receiver in the nation by Rivals.com and was ranked as the fifth-best receiver in the Midlands (Texas, Colorado, Missouri and Oklahoma) by *PrepStar.* He was a first team all-state selection last year after catching 50 passes for 1,027 yards and nine touchdowns.

BLUE RIBBON ANALYSIS

OFFENSE	C
SPECIAL TEAMS	D
DEFENSE	C
INTANGIBLES	B

If nothing else, Missouri will be a better-organized team this season. Players seemed to have bailed out on Larry Smith in 2000, a true shame because the veteran Smith deserved better.

Pinkel brings the excitement of a new regime and the promise of improved play. The best thing that could happen to the Tigers this season is to win the non-league home games (Bowling Green, Southwest Texas State), defeat the Big 12 teams it beat last year (Oklahoma State and Baylor) and find a way to defeat Kansas.

If that happens, the Tigers will find themselves one victory away from a bowl game in Pinkel's first year and Missouri athletic director Mike Alden will know he found the right man.

(B.K.)

2000 RESULTS

Western Illinois	W	50-20	1-0
Clemson	L	9-62	1-1
Michigan State	L	10-13	1-2
Nebraska	L	24-42	1-3
Oklahoma State	W	24-10	2-3
Kansas	L	17-38	2-4
Texas	L	12-46	2-5
Iowa State	L	20-39	2-6
Colorado	L	18-28	2-7
Baylor	W	47-22	3-7
Kansas State	L	28-24	4-7

Nebraska

LOCATION	**Lincoln, NE**
CONFERENCE	**Big 12 (North)**
LAST SEASON	**10-2 (.833)**
CONFERENCE RECORD	**6-2 (2nd)**
OFFENSIVE STARTERS RETURNING	**4**
DEFENSIVE STARTERS RETURNING	**9**
NICKNAME	**Cornhuskers**
COLORS	**Scarlet & Cream**
HOME FIELD	**Memorial Stadium (74,031)**
HEAD COACH	**Frank Solich (Nebraska '66)**
RECORD AT SCHOOL	**31-7 (3 years)**
CAREER RECORD	**31-7 (3 years)**
ASSISTANTS	
	Craig Bohl (Nebraska '81) Defensive Coordinator/Linebackers
	Nelson Barnes (North Texas '82) Rush Ends
	Ron Brown (Brown '79) Receivers
	George Darlington (Rutgers '61) Secondary
	Turner Gill (North Texas '90) Quarterbacks
	Dave Gillespie (Nebraska '77) Running Backs
	Jeff Jamrog (Nebraska '87) Defensive Line
	Milt Tenopir (Sterling College '62) Offensive Line
	Dan Young (Kearney State '62) Offensive Line/Kickers
TEAM WINS (last 5 yrs.)	**11-13-9-12-10**
FINAL RANK (last 5 yrs.)	**5-1-18-2-6**
2000 FINISH	**Beat Northwestern in Alamo Bowl.**

COACH AND PROGRAM

As he stood in the back of the interview room, waiting for his turn at the podium, Nebraska coach Frank Solich was trying to get water out of his ear, an unwanted byproduct from a post-game ice-bucket shower. Somehow it seemed appropriate that the most enjoyable moment of Nebraska's 2000 season—the celebration of a 66-17 thrashing of Northwestern in the Alamo Bowl—could not be unconditionally enjoyed.

That's how it goes at Nebraska, where a 10-2 season, a Top-10 finish and a resounding bowl triumph buys the Cornhuskers a momentary smile and an earache. This after the program spent most of the season ranked No. 1.

Looking back on it, the voters had it wrong.

"I thought going into the year that we were an inexperienced football team," Solich said. "When you have that, all bets are off. I think we did a lot right this year."

Solich has done plenty right in three seasons. He owns 31 career victories, three more than Tom Osborne and Bob Devaney had at the same juncture. He's won a conference championship and a bowl game. Osborne also had one league title in his first three years, and two in his first six.

On a national scale, only three coaches in major college football history have won more games in their first three seasons—Walter Camp at Yale, George Woodruff at Penn and Oklahoma's Barry Switzer.

"I feel very good about things in a lot of ways," Solich said. "Thirty wins in three years ... wins aren't automatic."

But overall Nebraska couldn't help but be disappointed in the season. The Huskers had expected to play in the Orange Bowl for the national championship. Instead, they played in the Alamo Bowl against the team picked to finish last in the Big Ten.

"To say we were disappointed in the year is correct," quarterbacks coach Turner Gill said. "We had hoped to be in Miami, and thought we were good enough to be there."

Nebraska knew otherwise at mid-season. After running through its first seven games with only one major scare, the Huskers' poor special teams kept Notre Dame alive through regulation before Nebraska prevailed in overtime.

Otherwise, there had been nothing but pummelings.

Then came Oklahoma. Top-ranked Nebraska played the third-ranked Sooners in the first significant meeting between the programs in more than a decade. Oklahoma was coming off a big victory at Kansas State but nobody was sure if that meant the Sooners were underrated or the Wildcats overrated.

Sixty minutes of Oklahoma dominance over Nebraska told the story. Actually, it was more like 45 minutes. The Huskers scored two touchdowns to open the game before Oklahoma stormed back to win, 31-14.

Nebraska's payback opportunity was contingent on defeating Kansas State at Manhattan. But in a snowstorm, the Wildcats prevailed, and for only the second time in five years the Cornhuskers would not play for the Big 12 championship. The depression nearly cost the program an embarrassing loss the next week. It took a field-length drive in the final minute for a game-winning field goal against a Colorado team that finished 3-8.

Because of the changing landscape of college football, a world in which an Oregon State can pop up out of nowhere to win a BCS bowl, perhaps it's unrealistic to expect annual double-digit victory seasons at Nebraska. After all, the Huskers don't play in Florida State's ACC, where the Seminoles are rarely challenged.

Nebraska plays in the Big 12, with Oklahoma, K-State, Texas and Texas A&M. Every league school except Kansas has played in a bowl game in the last five years. In that regard Solich coaches in a different era than Osborne and Devaney, who could build their seasons for one or two key games.

The fans are slow to understand this. Solich came under some fire last season. A usually enthusiastic breakfast meeting with boosters toward the end of the season was less than enthusiastic. Maybe Solich isn't head-coach material, fans wondered.

The coach knows it's all part of the game.

"You're always going to get criticized," Solich said. "What I have had a hard time seeing is a lot of the things that don't go well always get reflected upon.

"For me, it hit home on the day we played at Kansas State. The paper in Manhattan came out and talked about Bill Snyder's record being 1-18 against Top 10 teams. All the good things he's done for that program, and that's the headline.

"You get criticized so much anymore, in the media, on the Internet, that you sometimes get the feeling everybody's against you. When it's really the opposite. What I've learned as a head coach is that I have to keep moving forward in this profession in the manner that I have up to this point. This is where I want to coach. I want to keep this going. Whether that's enjoyable or not, I don't know."

2001 SCHEDULE

Aug.	25	Texas Christian (Pigskin Classic)
Sept.	1	Troy State
	8	Notre Dame

	15	Rice
	29	@Missouri
Oct.	6	Iowa State
	13	@Baylor
	20	Texas Tech
	27	Oklahoma
Nov.	3	@Kansas
	10	Kansas State
	23	@Colorado

QUARTERBACKS

A second shoulder surgery in as many years kept senior **Eric Crouch** (6-1, 200) out of spring practice. He's expected to be at 100 percent when the season begins, but it's natural to wonder just how much punishment Crouch can take.

Make no mistake, Crouch is one tough customer. He's a running back with a quarterback's number. A case could be made that he's been the team's top runner in each of his three years. He's one of the team's fastest players.

Crouch runs the 40 in 4.47, and has flashed better moves that any of his running backs. He even ran with the track team this winter, though he didn't compete in any meets.

Crouch is starting to pile up some pretty impressive career numbers: 2,319 rushing yards, 41 touchdowns, a 4.9-yard average. Take out the yards lost by sacks and Crouch is over 1,000 in each of the last two years.

Crouch is already the program's top rushing quarterback, and should pass Tommie Frazier for the school's career total offense record in the first half of the season opener. With the ball in his hands so often, Crouch is going to get banged up.

The problem is, Nebraska needs him to throw the ball to make the offense work, which it didn't at clutch times last season. The Cornhuskers couldn't engineer a final drive at Kansas State, and after scoring two touchdowns on the opening possessions at Oklahoma, didn't cross the goal line.

Simply put, Crouch needs to be a better passer, which may mean fewer keeps on the option.

"We have to throw the ball more consistently," Solich said. "We didn't always throw it well enough to win games."

Crouch completed 75-of-156 (48.1 percent) with 11 touchdowns and seven interceptions. The percentage was down from the previous season. Nebraska doesn't appear to have the talent at I-back to be a third down-only passing team. The offense needs to open, and Crouch has shown the ability to be an effective thrower.

Suffice to say he wasn't pleased with having to sit out spring practice for the second straight year, but Crouch made the best of his situation.

"It's been tough and it's kind of plagued me throughout my career, kind of taking it off a little bit," Crouch said. "It's nothing that I like to do, of course, it's something that helps me prepare to become a better player. ... There are different avenues that I have to take to get on track. One of them begins in the weight room—extra things as far as rehab, as far as my shoulder goes, kind of help me mentally through it and help me physically also."

Backup **Jammal Lord** (6-2, 215) got plenty of snaps with the starters during spring practice, which will serve him well. Lord, a sophomore, is in the Husker quarterback mold—a terrific runner with a strong arm who needs plenty of target practice. Lord is next year's starter.

"Right now I feel confident that if we have to go to [Lord] in a game situation, he can move our offense and do the things we want our quarterbacks to do," Gill said during spring practice. "He's put himself in the position where he can succeed if he's called upon."

Solich seconded that opinion.

"Jammal has had an excellent spring," Solich said in April. "He has really improved his passing and has shown excellent leadership. I feel very comfortable with Jammal at quarterback."

Lord's impressive spring was his second straight. In 2000, Crouch was also held out of spring practice, and Lord looked good in his stead. But Lord suffered a partial tear of this left posterior cruciate ligament in the third week of spring and missed the Red-White game.

This spring, Lord played without a knee brace, but he wore a green jersey, meaning he was protected from would-be tacklers. Neither Solich nor Gill wanted to take a chance of anyone tagging Lord and knocking him out of action for an extended period. Given the beating Crouch takes, Lord could well be needed.

Junior **Joe Christman** (5-11, 190), is the emergency quarterback and holder for place kicks.

The Huskers are going to miss Bobby Newcombe, whose star-crossed career ended in the Alamo Bowl. Newcombe was hailed as the next Frazier, but a torn knee ligament in his first game as a starter in 1998—one of those added-to-the-schedule games in August, effectively ended his season and career as quarterback. Crouch took over later in the season and was not dislodged.

Newcombe played wingback in his final two seasons, but there was a certain comfort knowing that if Crouch suffered a season-ending injury, a player with Newcombe's experience could step in.

As something of a going-away gift to Newcombe, Solich called his number in the second half of the Alamo Bowl. Newcombe took a lateral and fired a long touchdown pass. The game was already out of reach for Northwestern and the Wildcats howled, but Nebraska wanted to give its former quarterback of the future one final feeling of glory.

RUNNING BACKS

Let's start with 1983, with one of the great offensive teams in college football history. Nebraska averaged a nation's best 401 yards rushing that season, Solich's first as a Cornhuskers assistant.

Nine more times in the next 17 years, Nebraska would lead the nation in rushing, including last year's 349.9-yard average. When others talk about beefing up the running game, Nebraska is always the standard, the reference point.

And yet, the running game can take some of the responsibility of Nebraska falling short of its national championship goals over the previous two seasons. In 1999, a fumble epidemic spread through the season and contributed to the team's only loss, at Texas.

Fumbling wasn't a problem last year. But Nebraska didn't have the benefit of a classic I-back, a player with all the power and speed that are basic requirements of the position along with a shiftiness that separates the great ones.

Maybe the last back to fit that mold was Ahman Green, who finished in 1997. Dan Alexander was powerful. Correll Buckhalter could be acrobatic at times. Both were effective, as Alexander rushed for 1,154 yards and Buckhaler 750. Neither was a classic I-back. Maybe DeAngelo Evans would have been, but the highly regarded running back left the program early in the 2000 season and never played at Nebraska at full strength.

Where does this leave the Huskers? Largely unproven, which is a strange place for Nebraska. All eyes are on junior **Dahrran Diedrick** (6-0, 225), the best darn Canadian running back ever to wear the Scarlet and Cream. Diedrick hails from Scarborough, Ontario. He's rushed for 515 yards and five touchdowns in two seasons, getting his most significant playing time as a sophomore when the guys ahead of him on the depth chart were suffering fumble-itis.

Diedrick's biggest contribution last year was a 12-yard kickoff return of a Colorado pooch kick with 47 seconds remaining to set up a short drive and game-winning field goal. Much more will be expected this year.

"When he's gotten a chance throughout his career, Dahrran has been excellent," Solich said.

That may be stretching things a little. But Diedrick appears to possess some of the qualities that have been missing from running backs in recent years. He goes east to west better than Alexander and has more breakaway speed than Buckhalter.

"He's proven himself to be a guy you can win with," running backs coach Dave Gillespie said.

Solich agreed.

"I think he's got excellent feet, excellent running instincts," Solich said. "Those were obvious to many people over the last two seasons. We expect that he'll be an excellent player for us as an I-back."

After Dietrick comes a guy with the best name in college football, **Thunder Collins**. He arrived from Los Angeles as a junior college All-America and much was expected. But Collins, a junior, never made an impact. He couldn't play in the spring while cleaning up an academic issue, and an injury in preseason camp limited his effectiveness.

Collins (6-2, 190) played in only three games. He gained 77 yards and had a 17-yard run against Kansas. He was the fourth running back last season, and he's battling for the No. 2 spot this year with sophomores **DeAntae Grixby** (5-8, 205) and **Robin Miller** (5-11, 225).

Miller came to Nebraska as an I-back in 1999, was moved to fullback last spring, and is back at I-back. Nebraska feels good enough about the fullback slot to make the move. Sophomore **Judd Davies** (6-0, 240) sat out spring with a back injury and there's some concern that the damage could be long-lasting. But if Davies is healthy he figures to join the long line of excellence at the position.

Davies rushed 18 times for 183 yards, a healthy 10.2 yards per carry last year. He had the team's second longest run of the season, a 57-yarder against Baylor. Miller and junior **Paul Kastl** (5-10, 230) will fight for backup time.

WIDE RECEIVERS/TIGHT ENDS

In a conference full of terrific tight ends, Nebraska may have the best in senior **Tracey Wistrom** (6-5, 240). Entering last year, Wistrom said he didn't think he'd have a shot at professional football. But the pros are going to love a guy with his size, blocking toughness and hands soft enough to haul in 37 passes for a 22.4-yard average and eight touchdowns in a career.

Wistrom picked Nebraska over Northwestern. Few others were recruiting him with anything like the fervor of his brother Grant, and it was Grant who helped him get a strong look in Lincoln.

Wistrom's pass catching numbers were a little down last year (16.5 yards per catch verses 26.8 in 1999), but that had something to do with Crouch's injured shoulder and the idea that Wistrom is no longer a secret.

When he comes off the line and isn't drilling somebody, more often than not Winstrom is Nebraska's primary target. He's hard to stop even when the opponent knows it's coming. On a third-

and-9 from the 24, Crouch fired a 9-yard bullet to Wistrom, who was surrounded by Notre Dame defenders, to keep the game-winning overtime drive alive.

Expect Crouch to find back up tight ends **Aaron Golliday** (6-4, 285) and **Jon Bowling** (6-3, 245), both juniors, more often. They combined for five receptions, but are sure-handed pass catchers. Golliday caught a touchdown pass in the Fiesta Bowl two years ago.

Nebraska must develop options at split end. Gone are the sure hands of Matt Davison, the program's No. 2 career pass catcher, and the speed of Bobby Newcombe. The cupboard is so bare that the Huskers have toyed with kicker **Josh Brown** taking snaps as a wideout. The depth chart lists junior **Wilson Thomas** (6-5, 205) at split end. Nobody else is listed.

Thomas caught one pass for eight yards last season and by default will be the No. 1 end heading into the fall. He played in eight games and got as much time on the Huskers basketball team, where he averaged 1.8 points and 1.7 rebounds when he joined after the bowl game.

After spring workouts, Nebraska still did not know about the status of wingback John Gibson, who was petitioning the NCAA for a sixth year of eligibility. Gibson caught eight passes for 41 yards and a touchdown last season and would be the starter.

Junior **Troy Hassebroek** (6-4, 220), who played in all 11 games but didn't catch a pass, entered spring as the No. 1 wingback.

OFFENSIVE LINE

A few days after its biggest victory, Nebraska suffered its biggest loss.

Junior center Dominic Raiola cast his lot with the NFL after the bowl game. This one hurt. Raiola was the heart and soul of the program's best line over the previous three years. Nebraska can get away without an all-conference running back when the line is good and that was the case last season.

Raiola, a finalist for the Outland and Lombardi Trophies, was a two-time first-team All-Big 12 selection and consensus All-American, the first from the Nebraska line since Aaron Taylor in 1997. Raiola was chosen by the Detroit Lions in the second round of the NFL draft.

The Huskers must also find replacements for Russ Hochstein, a three-year starter and all-conference guard, and Jason Schwab, who went from a walk-on to two-year starter at tackle.

Senior **Jon Rutherford** (6-3, 300), the top offensive line reserve last season, is ticketed to replace Raiola. Rutherford played every line position and although he missed three games he finished sixth on the team in pancake blocks. Rutherford missed the spring after knee surgery.

"Jon's the key if he comes back as healthy as we think he will," offensive line coach Milt Tenopir said.

Junior **John Garrison** (6-4, 285) and **Matt Shook** (6-2, 300) will battle for the backup role. Garrison has been excellent in his career as deep snapper.

Right tackle **Chris Loos** (6-3, 310) will step into Schwab's spot. Loos, a sophomore, played in all 11 regular season games mostly as the tackle on the field goal and extra point teams. He sat out the spring mending a torn knee ligament.

Right guard is the big question mark. Junior **Wes Cody** (6-2, 295) and sophomore **Jon Dawson** (6-2, 295) are the top candidates with Cody leading heading into fall. Cody was on the travel squad last season and played in six games.

Those are the unknowns.

Junior guard **Toniu Fonoti** (6-4, 340) and senior tackle **Dave Volk** (6-5, 300) give Nebraska a definite direction this season—left. Both returning starters and Outland candidates are on the left side.

Fonoti (Toe-NEE-you Foe-no-tea) came on strong last year and picked up some all-conference consideration after shattering the program's record for pancake blocks with 155. Raiola had set the record of 140 the previous season. And Fonoti's total did not include the school-record 21 pancake blocks against Northwestern, a game in which Fonoti played with a cast to protect a broken right hand.

A three-year starter, Volk is Nebraska's most experienced lineman. He moved from right to left tackle last year and earned honorable mention all-league honors. Volk was at his best in the season finale against Colorado, when he recorded 12 pancake blocks.

Plenty of left turns in store for Crouch and company this season? Not necessarily, said Tenopir.

"We would have loved to plug Dominic in at center this year, but one of the fun challenges is to see who's going to step up," he said.

2000 STATISTICS

Rushing offense	349.3	1
Passing offense	110.6	111
Total offense	459.9	6
Scoring offense	41.5	4
Net Punting	34.5	59
Punt returns	11.0	36
Kickoff returns	16.7	105
Rushing defense	113.5	27
Passing efficiency defense	95.8	7
Total defense	321.8	26
Scoring defense	19.4	26
Turnover margin	+2	51

Last column is ranking among Division I-A teams.

KICKERS

As 100 teammates swarmed Brown (6-2, 190), whose 29-yarder with no time remaining beat Colorado, press box wags were trying to determine the last time Nebraska won a game on a final-play field goal.

It had never happened, at least since such information was first recorded in 1960. (It could have happened in the Orange Bowl after the 1993 season, but Byron Bennett's 45-yarder was wide left, giving Florida State a victory and sealing Bobby Bowden's first national title).

Brown, a junior, is as solid as they come. He missed a point after early in the 1999 season and hasn't missed one since, entering the season with a streak of 108 (including bowl games). He's made 19-of-30 field goal tries, including 14 of his last 20.

Brown also punted once last year and in the spring ran plays at wingback for the second straight year.

DEFENSIVE LINE

Juniors **Chris Kelsay** (6-5, 270) and **Demoine Adams** (6-2, 235) shared the left rush end position last year. Kelsay will keep the job and Adams will move to the right side.

Kelsay is the younger brother of former all-conference end Chad Kelsay, who played the same position from 1995-98. Chris even took his brother's No. 57 uniform. Chris Kelsay started seven games last year and got one sack. The production should increase this season.

Adams earned a starting spot at the beginning of last season before giving way to Kelsay. Adams is the team's quickest end but his linebacker-like size gave him problems getting penetration. But coaches are high on Adams, and will give him another chance to prove himself as a starter this fall.

Sophomore **Benard Thomas** (6-4, 250) played in a few games as a freshman in passing situations and has a bright future at end. Senior **J.P. Wichmann** (6-4 230) is a workhorse lineman who will get snaps at end along with junior **Justin Smith** (6-4, 260).

Nebraska is solid in the middle with senior nose tackle **Jason Lohr** (6-2, 275) and senior tackle **Jeremy Slechta** (6-6, 285). Lohr and Slechta were two of three freshmen who played in 1998.

Lohr finished sixth with 46 tackles and was at his best in the big games. He logged six stops against Notre Dame, eight against Oklahoma and a team-best 11 against Colorado.

Slechta backed up Loran Kaiser at tackle and started four games when Kaiser was injured. Now, if Slechta can keep from getting hurt, not on the football field but in the garage. He suffered a hand injury in January while helping a friend work on a car.

Reserve nose tackle **Jon Clanton** (6-2, 285) had one of the best speed testing days in school history last spring and needs for that to translate on the field. Backup tackle **Patrick Kabongo** (6-6, 290) has shed nearly 40 pounds since arriving two years ago from Montreal.

The line needs to find an identity. Kyle Vanden Bosch provided it last year.

"We're looking for the kind of play that we got from Kyle, especially at the end of last year," defensive coordinator Craig Bohl said. "We need some guys to step up."

LINEBACKERS

Much depends on the status of weak-side starter **Randy Stella** (6-0, 210), who was suspended from the team before spring workouts and not reinstated during the spring semester. Solich said Stella, a senior, violated unspecified team rules, and did not speculate on Stella's chances of returning in the fall.

Stella was the Huskers' second leading tackler last year with 58 solo stops and tied end Kyle Vanden Bosch for the team lead in sacks with 5 1/2.

Senior **Mark Vederal** (6-1, 210) took over the starting spot in the spring and could wind up being a starter for the first time this fall. Vederal, a coverage team specialist, was Nebraska's top defensive reserve last year, making 23 tackles.

The strong side is in good shape with junior **Scott Shanle** (6-2, 235), a returning starter who had his best outing against Kansas State with 11 tackles.

The hole is in the middle, where Carlos Polk was one of the nation's best the last couple of years. Beyond his skills, Polk was the unit's vocal leader. That has to come from a different position this year. It's too much to expect of senior **Jamie Burrow** (6-1, 245), who will probably start in the middle.

Burrow has played in every game over the last three seasons. Burrow was born in Ames, Iowa, because his father, Jimmy, was an Iowa State assistant at the time. But he's a fifth-generation Husker—dad lettered in the mid-1970s.

Sophomore **T.J. Hollowell** (6-0, 220) played as freshman last season and will continue to back up Shanle. Junior **Tony Tata** (6-1, 245), one of three in the two-deep from Hawaii, battles Burrow, and senior **Jon Penny** (6-1, 220) and sophomore **Blanchard Johnson** (5-11, 205) could get more time than expected if Stella doesn't return.

DEFENSIVE BACKS

The top three corners and starting strong safety are back, which should make the secondary the strongest unit.

Left corner **Keyuo Craver** (5-10, 190), a senior, has started the last 23 games and is on the Jim Thorpe watch list. He's one of the team's top athletes with four career interceptions. He's also blocked four kicks and he spent the 1999 season as a punt returner.

Craver might be the guy Nebraska turns to for its leadership. He already ranks second in career pass breakups with 28 and needs 22 more to catch Ralph Brown.

But chasing Craver in that category is senior **Erwin Swiney** (6-0, 185) at right corner. Swiney owns 27 career breakups. He's the team's most experienced player with 33 career starts. Swiney is the only player on the roster who started for the 1997 national championship team.

Swiney sat out the 1999 season as a medical redshirt. Last season, he split time with junior **DeJuan Groce** (5-10, 190) and that should be the case this season. Groce also plays left corner in the nickel package when Craver goes to the nickel spot.

Groce was terrific last year with a team-record 17 pass breakups, including five against Iowa State.

The other returning starter is senior free safety **Dion Booker** (6-1, 205), who had a big game in the Alamo Bowl with eight tackles. After seven games, Booker gave up his starting spot to Troy Watchorn, who led Nebraska with five interceptions last season. Now that Watchorn is gone, Booker's top challenger for the position is sophomore **Willie Amos** (6-0, 185), who played as a freshman last season and set conditioning test records for defensive backs in the spring.

Junior **Aaron Terpening** (5-11, 190) and senior **Wes Woodard** (5-8, 185) are the only players who have taken a snap at rover, or strong safety. Terpening gets the first look at the spot, but rover is as wide open as any position on defense.

PUNTERS

Sophomore **Kyle Larson** (6-0, 205) is the favorite to replace Dan Hadenfeldt, who had been granted a sixth year of eligibility last season.

Larson hasn't punted in a game since high school in Funk, Neb. Hadenfeldt finished eighth in the nation with 43.8-yard average and finished his career at 44.4 yards, shattering the school record.

SPECIAL TEAMS

The Cornhuskers were alarmingly bad in one game. Poor kick coverage nearly cost them the victory at Notre Dame, where Julius Jones returned a kickoff 100 yards and Joey Getherall a punt 83 yards for touchdowns.

Nebraska came back and won in overtime, and then Solich rattled the cages of the coverage teams and things got a little better.

The Huskers still wound up next to last in the Big 12, allowing nearly 22 yards per kick return (while averaging only 16.7 yards on returns). They also surrendered 12.6 yards per punt return.

Nebraska was above average kicking the ball, making all its extra points, big field goals and getting maximum effort from its punt team.

Groce, who returned two punts last year, will get the call this season, along with Craver and Cornelson. The Huskers haven't settled on kickoff return man.

RECRUITING CLASS

The class slipped into a few analysts' Top 10 lists without a player who would be considered one of the top three in the nation at his position. That's typical for the Cornhuskers, whose seniors in the national championship years of 1994, '95 and '97 weren't part of any top-ranked recruiting class.

One thing about the Huskers—they like the guys who attend their camps. Nine of the 18 in this class were football campers in Lincoln.

"If you can see them first hand as you coach them, without question you're going to have a better feel for a young man," Solich said. "One good thing about our camp is that it fills up. We have people come in from around the country and we get to look at players from all over."

Like Chattanooga, Tenn., hometown of the first set of twins to ever sign with Nebraska—the Bullocks. **Daniel Bullocks** (6-2, 200) will get a first look at free safety, although he played quarterback and returned kicks on his way to a Mr. Tennessee senior season for Hixson High School. **Josh Bullocks** (6-2, 200) is a rover. Last season, he took handoffs from his brother and rushed for eight touchdowns.

The top defensive back in the class is **Antown Guidry** (6-1, 185) of Campbell, Calif., who also starred as a running back in high school.

Defense was the trend for Nebraska with 11 of the 18 signees on that side of the ball. And Solich was influenced by some recent football champions.

"We went heavy on defensive players, no question about it," Solich said. "If you looked at the Super Bowl, if you looked at the Big 12 championship game, if you looked at the national championship game, you saw great defense played."

Cory Ross (5-7, 190) of Denver may be the top player in the class. He was an outstanding running back but also was ranked as the nation's 12th best corner by one service. Another top pick is defensive tackle **Le Kevin Smith** (6-3, 295), the player of the year in Georgia.

Help is needed immediately at wide receiver, and **Clifford Brye** (5-10, 175) is the only junior college transfer in the class. Brye had 20 receptions for 344 yards and five touchdowns last season at Hutchinson (Kansas) Community College. He originally enrolled at Wyoming and played running back for the Cowboys as a freshman, leading the team with 451 yards (5.9 yards per carry). He grew up in Lincoln.

"He's an excellent example of the athleticism we have in this class," Solich said. "He could play on either side of the ball [also cornerback]. We'll line him up at wide receiver and he'll be a guy who can get deep on people as well as catch the short one and make people miss."

BLUE RIBBON ANALYSIS

OFFENSE	A
SPECIAL TEAMS	B
DEFENSE	B
INTANGIBLES	A

Quick. Name the last senior starting quarterback who did not win a national championship at Nebraska.

The most recent, Scott Frost, got his team a share of the 1997 title. Before that, Tommie Frazier and Brook Berringer were seniors in 1995, winning a second straight championship.

You have to go back a whole decade to Keithen McCant in 1991 to find a senior QB who got shut out of the championship. That's how it works in Nebraska. A quarterback is identified and groomed. But the time he's a senior, pieces are in place for a national title.

This is a senior quarterback season at Nebraska and Crouch may statistically become the greatest at his position in Husker history. But are the pieces in place around him for a championship?

The schedule is. The three toughest opponents—Notre Dame, Kansas State and Oklahoma—are in Lincoln. Nebraska has a revenge motive against the Wildcats and Sooners. The only road game that could be trouble is the season finale at Colorado. The Buffs have played Nebraska to the final series in each of the last four years. They'd love nothing better than to dash the Huskers' title hopes this year.

There are more question marks entering this year than before the championship seasons. Then, Nebraska went into battle with an established I-back (although Lawrence Phillips got suspended for most of the 1995 season). There weren't as many questions at receiver, the defensive line or middle linebacker.

But as long as Crouch remains healthy, Nebraska will be a Top 10 team throughout the season. The Huskers should start high enough in the polls to be in title contention. When Oklahoma visits on Oct. 27, Nebraska could very well be 8-0. Then things get difficult with Kansas State and Colorado coming in the final two games. Nebraska is likely to face the Sooners or Texas in the Big 12 championship game in Dallas, but a Texas destination hasn't bothered the Huskers in the past. Both of their Big 12 championship game victories have come in San Antonio over Texas schools.

The Rose Bowl is possible. But Nebraska will have to win a game or two as an underdog somewhere along the way.

(B.K.)

2000 RESULTS

San Jose State	W	49-13	1-0
Notre Dame	W	27-24	2-0
Iowa	W	42-13	3-0
Missouri	W	42-24	4-0
Iowa State	W	49-27	5-0
Texas Tech	W	56-3	6-0
Baylor	W	59-0	7-0
Oklahoma	L	14-31	7-1
Kansas	W	56-17	8-1
Kansas State	L	28-29	8-2
Colorado	W	34-32	9-2
Northwestern (Alamo Bowl)	W	66-17	10-2

Oklahoma

LOCATION	**Norman, OK**
CONFERENCE	**Big 12 (South)**
LAST SEASON	**13-0 (1.000)**
CONFERENCE RECORD	**8-0 (1st)**
OFFENSIVE STARTERS RETURNING	**8**
DEFENSIVE STARTERS RETURNING	**8**
NICKNAME	**Sooners**
COLORS	**Crimson & Cream**
HOME FIELD	**Memorial Stadium (75,004)**
HEAD COACH	**Bob Stoops (Iowa '83)**
RECORD AT SCHOOL	**20-5 (2 years)**
CAREER RECORD	**20-5 (2 years)**
ASSISTANTS	**Mike Stoops (Iowa '84)** **Co-Defensive Coordinator** **Mark Mangino (Youngstown State '87)** **Offensive Coordinator/Offensive Line** **Brent Venables (Kansas State '92)** **Co-Defensive Coordinator/Linebackers**

Jonathan Hayes (Iowa '84)
Tight Ends/Special Teams
Cale Gundy (Oklahoma '94)
Running Backs
Steve Spurrier, Jr. (Duke '94)
Wide Receivers
Jackie Shipp (Langston University '92)
Defensive Line
Bobby Jack Wright (SW Texas State '73)
Defensive Ends/Recruiting Coordinator
Chuck Long (Iowa '85)
Quarterbacks/Passing Game Coordinator

TEAM WINS (last 5 yrs.) 3-4-5-7-13
FINAL RANK (last 5 yrs.) 63-62-53-34-1
2000 FINISH Beat Florida St. in Orange Bowl.

COACH AND PROGRAM

Yes, this is the way it's *supposed* to work: Hire an athletic director to fire the unsuccessful coach. The AD then will hire the right man for the job, who will resurrect the past glories of a proud program that has wandered in the wilderness for a decade.

And, no, it rarely happens like it did at Oklahoma. The school hires Joe Castiglione to run its athletic department in April of 1998 and his first major move is to fire John Blake, who in three seasons has a 12-22 record, extending the school's streak of non-winning seasons to five. To replace Blake, Castiglione appoints himself as a one-man search committee. His ability to strike fast allows him to hire Bob Stoops away from Florida before Iowa's search committee can firm its offer to Stoops, an Iowa graduate. It takes Stoops two years and 25 games to win the school's seventh national championship.

Fairy tales do come true, and one happened at OU. What Stoops, his staff and his players accomplished in 2000 was truly remarkable. Not only did the Sooners record the first 13-0 season in school history, they did it with a group of players who were still scarred from being involved in a program that spent the 1990s regressing into a modern-day version of the Keystone Cops.

"We were a pretty fractured group before coach Stoops came in," defensive tackle Ryan Fisher said after Oklahoma's 13-2 victory over Florida State in the Orange Bowl. "He was just so positive. He made us believe in ourselves again."

Barry Switzer's dismissal begat Gary Gibbs, whose failing was that he wasn't Barry Switzer. After six years and a 44-23-2 record, Gibbs was fired.

The bombastic Howard Schnellenberger was hired away from Louisville (which, in basketball terms, is like Duke hiring its next basketball coach from Southern Mississippi) Schnelly boasted that people would be making movies of OU during his era, but his one-season 5-5-1 tenure wasn't worth a highlights video.

To replace Schnellenberger, Oklahoma hired Blake—at the urging of Switzer—off the Dallas Cowboys' staff. Blake had no head coaching or coordinator experience. That became painfully obvious during Blake's three seasons in Norman. Brain-dead penalties, offensive schizophrenia and the challenge of kicking extra points became the signatures of the Blake regime.

Stoops, who had distinguished himself as defensive coordinator in stops at Kansas State and Florida, turned the Sooners into winners. OU went 7-5 in Stoops' first season. The players gained the confidence that they could again be winners.

"We never had a timetable," Stoops said in a way to explain the inexplicable. "We just wanted to work each week. I said this—we didn't come in [here] the first month and first week and start talking about what we were going to win. We talked about initially let's learn how to go through a winter workout like we're supposed to. Let's train in a way that athletes train to give us a chance to win.

"And then we get into spring ball and we talked about learning how to play football on the field the correct way and a winning way. Then summer, same thing; let's learn how to get ourselves in condition to compete for a championship, so it is just an evolving process, just working week-to-week, month-to-month to improve."

Stoops and his staff made all the right moves. For instance:

• In the first season, the OU coaches correctly assessed the roster's talent level and decided that several players were out of position. They moved J.T. Thatcher to safety, where he had an All-American senior season. They moved Frank Romero, one of four captains on the 2001 team, from defensive line to offensive tackle. He was instrumental in the Sooners' stifling blocking on Florida State's pass rushers in the national championship game.

• When Mike Leach, who was offensive coordinator in 1999, left to become Texas Tech's head coach, Stoops promoted from within, moving Mark Mangino to offensive coordinator. Mangino, who also coaches the offensive line, increased the team's emphasis on running the ball. As a result, the 2000 Sooners averaged 134 yards a game rushing and had 33 rushing touchdowns.

In 1999, those numbers were 105 yards per game and 18 rushing touchdowns.

• They approached a killer October schedule, including games with Texas, at Kansas State and at home with Nebraska, with a quiet confidence. The Sooners responded with three victories that vaulted them to the top of the polls heading into November.

• Against the Seminoles, defensive coordinators Mike Stoops and Brent Venables devised a kaleidoscope defense that befuddled Heisman Trophy winning quarterback Chris Weinke and accomplished the unthinkable, an offensive shutout of a team that was averaging 42 points and 549 total yards a game.

The undefeated season, the national championship, was accomplished with a team that was relatively inexperienced. Eight starters return on offense and defense, plus the punter and kicker are back. The Sooners spent nearly an hour on the field celebrating the national championship game, but for Stoops and his staff, the accomplishment was quickly filed away in the "Old News" category.

"In the short period of time after the game, that was all I needed," Stoops said. "I don't sit there and relish it, keep thinking about it. Because we want more. It's good, it's special, it's exceptional to win one. I don't take it for granted. I don't make too much of it, either. Because it's over.

"Coaches and players have a much easier time putting it behind them. The fans and the general public are supposed to relish it. We experienced it. That's what's special, the quest for it. It's kind of anti-climactic. For us, it's over that night. There's nothing to compare to the two hours before the game, the game itself and the hour or so after it."

With the nucleus of a championship team returning, it wasn't long after winning his first national title that Stoops was asked about going for his second. The Sooners, who open their season Aug. 25 against North Carolina, face the challenge of going 14-0 to win consecutive titles.

"That would be about the only place you can go from here," Stoops said. "But doing it again would be pretty special, too. And Oklahoma has done that before."

2001 SCHEDULE

Aug.	25	North Carolina
Sept.	1	@Air Force
	8	North Texas
	15	Tulsa
	29	Kansas State
Oct.	6	@Texas (Dallas)
	13	@Kansas
	20	Baylor
	27	@Nebraska
Nov.	10	Texas A&M
	17	@Texas Tech
	24	Oklahoma State

QUARTERBACKS

Josh Heupel's departure creates a void at quarterback, but an even bigger void in Oklahoma's leadership. Heupel never threw with Elway-type velocity—and his passes were even softer over the last half of the 2000 season thanks to a well-disguised elbow injury. But whenever Oklahoma needed a big offensive play—a key pass, a scramble, even an option pitch—Heupel did it.

In OU's three Hunt for Red October games (victories over Texas, Kansas State and Nebraska), Heupel was marvelous. He completed 66-of-98 passes for 949 yards and four touchdowns as the Sooners established themselves as a national championship favorite.

And, in Oklahoma's toughest test, Heupel proved himself again. Before the largest crowd in Kyle Field history (87,188), the Sooners turned back Texas A&M's upset bid. Trailing, 31-21, Heupel directed a 15-play, 77-yard drive that pulled the Sooners within three points and set the stage for Torrance Marshall's game-winning interception return for a touchdown.

For the season, Heupel completed 64 percent of his passes for 3,392 yards and 20 touchdowns. He was runner-up to Weinke in the Heisman Trophy balloting.

Spring drills didn't produce a clear No. 1 quarterback. Junior **Nate Hybl** (6-3, 215), who started his career at Georgia before transferring, and sophomore **Jason White** (6-2, 220) battled to a draw in the spring.

In the annual Red-White scrimmage to end spring drills, Hybl was 23-of-31 for 180 yards and threw a touchdown and two interceptions. White was 19-of-28 for 155 yards and threw a touchdown and an interception.

"Spring was great at the quarterback position," Stoops said. "I really believe we have two players that we can compete for a championship with. I believe they're both excellent players. We'll figure it out as the season goes. It would only be a problem if neither one of them was ready, then we'd have a major problem."

Redshirt freshman **Hunter Wall** (6-4, 220) practiced with the scout team in the spring.

"All three of them have very powerful arms, but that's not all of our offense," quarterbacks coach Chuck Long said of Hybl, White and Wall. "It helps, but you have to have great intelligence and a good feel for our passing game, which is a short-intermediate game, so it requires great accuracy and timing, which Josh really had. But they are all very capable of becoming a Josh Heupel in time."

"They both do a lot of very positive things and they're similar in a lot of ways," Stoops said. "The players have confidence in both of them. They have leadership ability, they both have excellent character and work ethic. It's a positive situation. They help each other and work together really well.

"We can win a lot of games and compete for a championship with either one of them."

Stoops says the only difference he can tell between Hybl and White is that "Nate's a scratch golfer, and Jason isn't. Outside of that, they're pretty similar in a lot of ways."

Hybl was a member of Georgia's national championship golf team, giving him two national title rings in two sports at two schools. The difference that matters—who starts—will be determined by preseason practices. Stoops won't pick a starter until the week of the season opener against North Carolina and he has not ruled out the possibility of rotating quarterbacks.

Last season, Hybl played in five games, completing 9-of-16 passes for 144 yards with two touchdowns and two interceptions. He spent the 1999 season sitting out under NCAA transfer rules and played for the Sooners' scout team.

White spent most of his time working with the scout team last season. He played in the Nebraska and Baylor games, but didn't attempt a pass in either. As a freshman in 1999, he played in two games, completing 1-of-2 passes for nine yards. He suffered a back injury and was able to gain an extra year after a redshirt season.

If Hybl and White sputter—during the season or especially during a game—Mangino has come up with a wrinkle that will force opposing defenses to prepare for something different.

During the spring game, the Sooners used junior wide receiver **Antwone Savage** for a few series at quarterback. Savage took four snaps, running the ball four times for 13 yards.

"It's a good little package to have," Stoops said. "Antone is an option quarterback from high school. We couldn't resist. We've got about eight, nine plays we can run with him in there. Quarterback draws, option game ... and if they don't cover somebody, he can throw the ball. To throw that in for a few series, here and there, it creates some problems.

"Coaches always want more depth. We're better off than we were two years ago [at quarterback], no question. It's making use of what you have."

Savage, who figures to be one of the Sooners' top receivers this season, doesn't figure to spend much time under center.

"It was fun, but those guys are safe," said Savage, who caught five passes for 18 yards in the spring game.

RUNNING BACKS

In 1999, with Mad Professor Mike Leach calling the plays as offensive coordinator, Oklahoma's running game was an afterthought. The Sooners set all sorts of passing game records, but the ground game was, well, grounded.

When Mark Mangino succeeded Leach after Leach left for Texas Tech, the offense became more balanced. Last season, the Sooners scored their most rushing touchdowns (33) since 1988.

The two main producers were junior **Quintin Griffin** (5-6, 187) and sophomore **Renaldo Works** (5-11, 208). Griffin, whose 10-yard run on a draw play in the fourth quarter clinched Oklahoma's Orange Bowl victory, carried 189 times for 783 yards and 16 touchdowns. Works carried 432 yards for 377 yards and five touchdowns. As the two main ball carriers, they combined to give OU a consistent running attack.

In the spring, however, Griffin and Works were limited by injuries. Both are expected to be healthy when preseason workouts begin.

"Renaldo and Quintin were impressive in the time they got to practice," Stoops said. "They both continue to improve and we feel good about both of those guys."

While Griffin and Works were effective, neither were the types of back who could be counted on to carry an offense that was sputtering in other areas.

With the quarterback situation unsettled, a consistent ground game will be even more important. The injuries to Griffin and Works allowed more time for redshirt freshman **Jerad Estus** (6-1, 177), who took advantage of the extra snaps to display his abilities.

"He was impressive [in spring practice]," Stoops said. "He's got incredible speed but he plays in a physical way. For a guy who doesn't appear to have a physical stature to him, he plays hard and physical all the time."

Sophomore **Jamar Mozee** (5-10, 216) and redshirt freshman **Brian Odom** (5-10, 205) also could be factors at running back. During spring practice, junior **Jay Hunt** (5-11, 200) was working with the first and second team at tailback before suffering a knee injury late in spring drills.

The departure of fullback Seth Littrell means the Sooners must replace one of their unsung heroes. Littrell produced 179 yards of total offense (22 carries, 10 pass receptions) but his blocking and leadership never showed up on the stat sheet.

There are no fullbacks listed on the Sooners' spring roster. Works could wind up there in some formations, but the person who'll be the full-time starter will be the player who does the best job as lead blocker on running plays and picking up blitzes to protect the quarterback.

WIDE RECEIVERS/TIGHT ENDS

When Stoops arrived two years ago and decided to bring OU's offense into the 21st century, that meant an emphasis on throwing the ball. One problem: The Sooners didn't really have anyone who could catch it.

Oklahoma's Mr. Fix It turned out to be receivers coach Steve Spurrier, Jr. He was allowed to scavenge the roster in an effort to find athletes who could be converted or returned to wide receiver positions.

The result was a 2000 group of pass catchers who combined for 184 catches, 2,482 yards and 17 touchdowns. All of the Sooners' top wide receivers return from last season. And, combined with a group of quality newcomers, Oklahoma should have plenty of depth.

"The more competition at the receiver spot, the better," said Mangino, who jokes that he'd like to play six wideouts and three offensive linemen. "We've got some young kids who are really talented."

Five juniors return to provide a variety of targets—speedy deep threats, physical slant runners and combinations of those talents.

Antwone Savage (6-0, 190) had 48 receptions for 598 yards and three touchdowns last season. Savage is also a dangerous threat on reverses. On 13 attempts, he gained 160 yards, an average of 13.3 per carry.

Curtis Fagan (6-0, 175) had 40 catches for 567 yards and seven touchdowns, including a key touchdown reception against Nebraska. **Andre Woolfolk** (6-1, 175) had 39 catches for 573 yards and five touchdowns. **Josh Norman** (6-2, 233) had 31 receptions for 469 yards and one touchdown. **Damian Mackey** (5-11, 185) had 26 receptions for 275 yards and one touchdown.

The Sooners' receivers are an example of the whole being greater than the sum of the parts. Their numbers indicate that any are capable of making a big play. In OU's four wide receiver sets, it's very difficult for a defense to find one receiver to concentrate on. And if one Sooner is double-teamed that means another threat should be uncovered.

Redshirt freshmen **Mark Clayton** (5-11, 170), **Ataleo Ford** (6-1, 178), **Will Peoples** (6-1, 190) and **Jarvis Smith** (5-9, 170) give the Sooners depth and talent for the future. Clayton had a solid spring practice.

Also, junior **Quentin Morgan** (6-0, 185) should be in the mix. He sat out last season after transferring from Washington.

The tight end position provides yet another threat. Junior **Trent Smith** (6-5, 229) came on strong over the last half of the 2000 season. He finished with 29 receptions for 310 yards and three touchdowns. He had a career-best eight catches in the Big 12 championship game victory over Kansas State.

And Smith theorizes that OU's tight ends will be an even greater part of the passing game this season with either Hybl or White at quarterback. Both are right-handed. Heupel was left-handed. Usually, the tight end lined up on the right side of the formation, which meant that Heupel looked in that direction only as a last resort. Smith figures that the tight end spot will move up the progression chart with right-handers at quarterback.

OFFENSIVE LINE

Mangino has proven that he can successfully build lines that get the job done. Last season, the Sooners allowed 17 sacks on 450 pass attempts (one sack for every 26 passes). And while the running game didn't approach yard-gobbling Wishbone levels, OU did average 3.9 yards per attempt with 33 rushing touchdowns.

However, the pressure to perform should increase this season. Whoever is at quarterback, he'll be inexperienced. That means the sack totals could increase now that the savvy Heupel has departed. And, with a rookie quarterback, the Sooners' offense will probably rely more on balancing the attack with a productive running game.

There is work to be done on the offensive line. Center Bubba Burcham and right tackle Scott Kempenich were the senior anchors and leaders of last year's unit.

The returning starters on the line are led by senior **Frank Romero** (6-4, 286), a former defensive lineman. Romero's shift to the offensive side has paid great dividends. This season, he's an All-America candidate. He realizes his success and his unit's success will depend on how the line comes together.

"We've got a ways to go on the offensive line and it just takes time," Romero said. "We've got some new players at key positions and it will just take some time to get the chemistry down."

Senior **Howard Duncan** (6-3, 299), who started at guard last season, and junior **Mike Skinner** (6-4, 305), who started every game at right guard, also return.

Duncan is one of several candidates to replace Burcham at center. Others being considered to start in the middle are sophomore Josh Tucker (6-3, 250), junior **Josh Smith** (6-1, 281), redshirt freshman **Cliff Takawana** (6-3, 300) and sophomore **Adam Panter** (6-1, 251).

If Duncan winds up starting at center, Mangino will have to find another starting guard. And he also must find a replacement for Kempenich. The candidates there are **Clint Werth** (6-6, 275), a junior-college transfer from Garden City (Kan.) Community College, redshirt freshman **Wes Sims** (6-5, 300) and freshman **Jerod Fields** (6-7, 280). He signed with Oklahoma a year ago, but didn't qualify academically. Werth and Fields each got a head start by participating in spring practice.

Mangino knows that last season the Sooners were fortunate to not have any serious injuries.

"I'd like to have a competitive situation at all five positions," Mangino said. "We need to develop a two-deep. We didn't have one last year. I want to give those kids credit. They fought all the way through the fourth quarter of all those games, but boy, we sure would have liked to rest them. Hopefully this year, we can.

"We didn't have much continuity in the offensive line [during spring practice]. We need some leadership on the offensive line. We need Frank Romero and Howard Duncan, those kinds of guys, to step up and display leadership. I think that will occur and we need that to occur to have a good offensive unit."

2000 STATISTICS

Rushing offense	161.5	42
Passing offense	294.7	13
Total offense	429.2	18
Scoring offense	39.0	7
Net Punting	36.5	23
Punt returns	15.4	9
Kickoff returns	20.6	31
Rushing defense	108.2	23
Passing efficiency defense	89.1	2
Total defense	278.9	8
Scoring defense	16.0	7
Turnover margin	+6	30

Last column is ranking among Division I-A teams.

KICKERS

Lost in the glare of a national championship is the fact that, under Stoops, Oklahoma's kicking game has gone from putrid to nearly perfect. Before Stoops, OU struggled to complete the snap from center, had trouble getting the right number of people on the field and every extra-point was an adventure.

Senior **Tim Duncan** (6-2, 198) returns and could wind up in the running for the Lou Groza kicking award. Last season, he made all but one of his 60 extra-point tries and 13-of-21 field-goal attempts. But he was particularly effective when the pressure was on. His leg provided the only points OU would need against Florida State in the Orange Bowl as he connected on kicks of 27 and 42 yards to give the Sooners a 6-0 lead going into the fourth quarter.

In Big 12 Conference play, Duncan made 10-of-12 attempts. In the Big 12 title game, his career-best 46-yarder gave the Sooners a championship-clinching 10-point lead. Senior **Ben Panter** (5-10, 215), whose younger brother, sophomore **Adam Panter** (6-1, 251) is in the mix on the offensive line, has been the Sooners' deep snapper for 37 consecutive games.

DEFENSIVE LINE

Starters Corey Callens, Ramon Richardson and Ryan Fisher (an All-Big 12 selection) must be replaced. Those three combined for 103 tackles, 19 tackles for loss, nine sacks and 32 quarterback hurries. Also gone is top reserve Darryl Bright.

Six players who saw extensive playing time return and the OU coaches think that the defensive line could become a strength for this season.

The returnees are led by sophomore **Kory Klein**, a second-team freshman All-American last season. Klein (6-2, 270) played in 13 games and recorded 30 tackles, five tackles for losses and three sacks.

Other defensive linemen who saw playing time last season are senior **Bary Holleyman** (6-4, 284), sophomore **Dan Cody** (6-4, 230), senior **Marcus Chretian** (6-3, 241) and junior Chike Ozumba (6-3, 278). The six who played last year combined for 114 tackles, six sacks, 16 tackles for loss and 12 pass deflections.

The unit is also getting a boost from sophomore **Jimmy Wilkerson**'s move from linebacker to the defensive line.

"Jimmy Wilkerson will be a guy we've been moving around," co-defensive coordinator Mike Stoops said during spring practice. "We need to find a home for him. Because we're not where we're at depth-wise, we're moving him back and forth from tackle to end. He's too good a player not to have on the field. He's going to be on the field for 70 snaps a game."

The 6-4, 230-pound Wilkerson's ability excites Bob Stoops, who envisions using him on the edge.

"It just makes sense to use him as a defensive end in passing situations, long yardage situations," Stoops said. "He just has a knack for it. In just a very little time of working at it, he knows how to stay low, jumping the ball, turning the corner on the linemen and making plays. You need to utilize that."

Juan Prishker (6-2, 272) a junior college All-American at Blinn (Texas) Junior College, figures to see significant action on the defensive line. Also, redshirt freshman **Jamal Brown** (6-6, 310) is expected to live up to his high school All America reputation.

In the Sooners' defensive scheme, the defensive linemen are there to peel off blockers to free linebackers and safeties to come up and make the play. Any sacks or tackles for loss made by a defensive lineman is a bonus. If the Sooners start getting above-average numbers from their defensive linemen, this defense could rival some of the best in school history.

LINEBACKERS

Perhaps no one player better illustrated Oklahoma's championship season than linebacker Torrance Marshall. Like the Sooners' program, Marshall was in trouble at one point during his college career. Poor academics kept him from attending Miami, his hometown choice of college. After knocking around at junior colleges, Marshall landed at OU because an old friend called Mark Mangino and said he knew of a player who might help Oklahoma.

Marshall spent his first season adapting to OU's defensive scheme and to playing Division I-A ball. Last season, he became a dominant player. His interception and return for a touchdown gave the Sooners a come-from-behind victory at Texas A&M and he was the MVP of the Orange Bowl.

Replacing Marshall will be difficult, but the Sooners' second-best linebacker last season will simply become their best linebacker this season.

Senior **Rocky Calmus** (6-3, 234), a consensus All-American and a finalist for the Butkus Award, figures to be one of the nation's top defenders in 2001. Last season, Calmus led OU with 125 tackles. He had 17 tackles for loss, four sacks, three forced fumbles and an interception.

There is little question about Calmus' grit and courage. In 1999, he played most of the game against Oklahoma State with a broken bone in his leg. He played almost the entire 2000 season with a broken right thumb. And during his entire career, he's played despite a broken right wrist.

"I broke it freshman year," Calmus said. "It never really healed, then I broke it again. I had surgery two days after the [Orange Bowl]. They did a bone graft and took a piece of my hip. So this is my first [season] without a broken wrist. I have great range of motion and can grab a little bit better."

Calmus is the only returning starter among OU's trio of linebackers (Roger Steffen, who was a steady player last season, also must be replaced). However, the Sooners believe they have a solid corps of talented linebackers whose only shortcoming is experience.

Sophomore **Teddy Lehman** (6-1, 232) had an impressive spring and figures to be one of the starters alongside Calmus. Lehman probably will start at middle linebacker. The other outside linebacker should be senior **Brandon Moore** (6-1, 232) who missed last season with a knee injury.

Sophomore **Scott Secrest** (6-0, 225), junior **Brandon Pryor** (5-11, 229), sophomore **Brian Jimerson** (6-2, 228), and sophomore **Derrick Hurst** (6-1, 227) provide depth and should all figure into the two-deep.

DEFENSIVE BACKS

This unit received a major set back with the loss of junior cornerback Michael Thompson. He was seriously injured in a one-car accident in Norman in early May. His injuries were so severe that not only is Thompson expected to miss this season, his future playing status is in doubt.

"The biggest concern with all of us is just getting him healthy and getting him to walk out of that hospital," Stoops said. "There's just so much to the kid. Football is just a small part of who he is. He's a better person than he is a player. That says it all."

As a sophomore, Thompson started every game. He had 54 tackles, an interception and broke up 13 passes.

"He always had the hardest job of anybody in the secondary," co-defensive coordinator Mike Stoops said. "He's the guy we put out there on everybody's top receiver."

Last season, Thompson and **Derrick Strait** provided OU with exemplary coverage. Both were able to lock down their man in one-on-one coverage, which allowed the rest of the defense to worry about stacking the line of scrimmage and attacking the quarterback.

Strait, a 5-11, 191-pound sophomore, finished 2000 with 62 tackles, two interceptions and 14 pass breakups. He has the potential to become a great coverage corner.

Redshirt freshman **Antonio Perkins** (6-0, 198) had a solid spring. He was just a notch below Strait and Thompson. If he can continue to play like that, he should be able to step in for Thompson and team with Strait to give the Sooners more outstanding play on the edges of their defense.

There's a basketball coach at Kansas and a hot shot wide receiver at Texas by the same name, but Oklahoma's **Roy Williams** is at the top of the "Same Name List." A 6-0, 221-pound junior, Williams is a dominating player who is a versatile, teeth-rattling tackler.

"Roy has been the best player on the field the last two years for us. Roy will have to be a big-play guy for us," Mike Stoops said. "He can play linebacker, safety and corner. He's got cover skills and his tackling is really special. He's a great player. His presence is felt on the field. You can't not know where he's at because he can single-handedly destroy some plays."

Said Bob Stoops, "Roy Williams at times just dominates our offense. He's just an amazing player. He's the best safety I've ever been around."

Last year, Williams teamed with J.T. Thatcher, who had an All-America season and led the Sooners with eight interceptions. The Sooners must also replace Ontei Jones, who was valuable as an extra defensive back.

Sophomore **Brandon Everage** (5-11, 192), who played in 12 games last season, is tabbed to replace Thatcher at safety.

Others in the mix in the secondary include sophomore **Matt McCoy** (5-11, 195), sophomore **Matt Mayhew** (5-11, 195), redshirt freshmen **Darren Stephens** (6-3, 185) and **Brandon Shelby** (5-10, 185), junior **Terrance Sims** (6-1, 185), a transfer from Hutchinson (Kansas) Community College, junior **Moses Washington** (6-0, 180) and redshirt freshman **Antonio Perkins** (6-0, 178).

Washington and Perkins are projects; Washington is a former track standout while Perkins has been moved from wide receiver.

PUNTERS

In a league where kickers and punters are usually top notch, being selected all-conference is a significant accomplishment. Senior **Jeff Ferguson** (5-10, 190) was voted the Big 12's outstanding punter. He averaged 43.9 yards per punt to lead the league, which placed him sixth nationally. That average was the fourth-best single-season effort in school history.

While Ferguson has a big leg, his hang time is outstanding. Of his 48 punts, 14 were downed inside the 20. Ferguson was particularly effective in the Orange Bowl. He pinned Florida State deep in its own territory with three punts downed inside the five-yard line.

SPECIAL TEAMS

What was a joke during the Blake era has become a strength under Stoops. Last season, the Sooners had significant edges in kickoff return and punt return averages compared to their opponents. Oklahoma's talented roster was used properly, with speedy wide receivers and defensive backs helping to swarm on punt and kick return units.

The biggest challenge will be replacing Thatcher, who was OU's top return man. Thatcher averaged 15.8 yards on punt returns and scored two touchdowns and he also averaged 20.2 yards on kickoff returns. Receivers Fagan, Savage, Norman and Mackey are all candidates to return punts and kickoffs.

RECRUITING CLASS

OU's seventh national championship plus the hard work of Stoops and his personable staff helped produce what was rated by some analysts as the nation's best recruiting class. Other analysts ranked the Sooners' class just behind Florida State.

"We're really excited about this recruiting class," Stoops said. "It's the best class we've had even though the players we've had the first two years have been a big impact in this program, and a big reason why we won the Big 12 championship and the national championship last year.

"I love the balance we've got between big players, speed players, athletic players, middle-of-the-road, linebacker, tight end types, While everyone is excited about this class, I believe that a true measure of a recruiting class should come three years down the road, not on the day that the class is announced."

During Switzer's years in Norman, Oklahoma wasn't neighborly when it came to crossing the Red River and raiding Texas for some of its top high school players. **Tommie Harris** (6-3, 285), one of the nation's top defensive line recruits, is from Kileen, Texas. And one of the nation's top running backs, **Danta Hickson** (5-10, 180), is from McKinney, Texas.

"Our success in Texas, as well as across the country, has been helped by the success we had last year,'" Stoops said.

One of the other top players in OU's class is linebacker **Gabe Toomey** (6-3, 215), who is from Valley, Iowa.

"We had a great need this year at linebacker," Stoops said. "Each one of the linebackers we signed are outstanding athletes, most of them two-sport athletes in high school.

"We also had a need for defensive linemen, and once again, the players we have signed are strong athletes who excel in two-sports. We signed five secondary guys who are very much the same. They all have great range, size and speed. We recognized the need for depth in this area, and the five guys here are capable of competing for playing time immediately."

BLUE RIBBON ANALYSIS

OFFENSE	B+
SPECIAL TEAMS	A-
DEFENSE	A-
INTANGIBLES	B+

A year ago everyone looked at Oklahoma's killer October schedule—Texas, Kansas State and Nebraska—and figured, "Well, two out of three would be pretty good, but three for three? Nope, no way, no how."

The Sooners swept their three games that month, survived scares against Texas A&M and Oklahoma State, gutted out a Big 12 championship game victory over Kansas State and then throttled Florida State for the national championship.

And the talk around Norman right now is the 2001 Sooners might be better.

"We were such a young team last year. We had 23 freshmen and sophomores in the two-deep going into the championship game," Stoops told *USA Today*. "Now those guys have a year more of experience, a lot of experience in big games, plus more maturity, increased strength and increased speed. We're a little deeper than we were a year ago. Whether that results in more wins or not depends on how hard we work, our chemistry and toughness."

Yes, the Sooners might be as good or better than last year ... and they might wind up with a Holiday Bowl trip to show for it. To win another national championship, the Sooners can do no worse than 13-1. With a preseason game against North Carolina on Aug. 25, OU could play 14 games if it wins the Big 12 South and plays in the league title game in Texas Stadium on Dec. 1.

That's a long season, with little margin for error. After opening against the Tar Heels, Oklahoma plays at Air Force, gets North Texas at home and is at Tulsa.

The Sooners open Big 12 play at home against Kansas State on Sept. 29. The next Saturday, Oklahoma faces Texas in the annual Red River Shootout in Dallas. Games with Kansas and Baylor precede a trip to Nebraska on Oct. 27. After a week off, OU plays host to Texas A&M.

Certainly, there are a lot of land mines. And, as defending national champions, the Sooners add a bull's eye to their regular uniform jerseys.

"We're not worried about repeating," Stoops said. "All our focus is on is trying to go out and earning it, fighting for it again. We don't have any more claim to it than anyone else. That's our attitude."

(W.B)

2000 RESULTS

UTEP	W	55-14	1-0
Arkansas State	W	45-7	2-0
Rice	W	42-14	3-0
Kansas	W	34-16	4-0
Texas	W	63-14	5-0
Kansas State	W	41-31	6-0
Nebraska	W	31-14	7-0
Baylor	W	56-7	8-0
Texas A&M	W	35-31	9-0
Texas Tech	W	27-13	10-0
Oklahoma State	W	12-7	11-0
Kansas State (Big 12)	W	27-24	12-0
Florida St. (Orange Bowl)	W	13-2	13-0

Oklahoma State

LOCATION	**Stillwater, OK**
CONFERENCE	**Big 12 (South)**
LAST SEASON	**3-8 (.273)**
CONFERENCE RECORD	**1-7 (5th)**
OFFENSIVE STARTERS RETURNING	**8**
DEFENSIVE STARTERS RETURNING	**7**
NICKNAME	**Cowboys**
COLORS	**Orange & Black**
HOME FIELD	**Lewis Field (48,000)**
HEAD COACH	**Les Miles (Michigan '76)**
RECORD AT SCHOOL	**First Year**
CAREER RECORD	**First Year**
ASSISTANTS	
	Mike Gundy (Oklahoma State '89) **Offensive Coordinator**
	Bill Clay (Arkansas '63) **Defensive Coordinator/Linebackers**
	Darrell Wyatt (Kansas State '89) **Passing Coordinator/Wide Receivers**
	Chuck Moller (Minnesota-Morris '83) **Offensive Line**
	Calvin Miller (Oklahoma State '76) **Defensive Line**
	Doug Mallory (Michigan '88) **Secondary**
	Tommy Robinson (Troy State '85) **Running Backs**
	Josh Henson (Oklahoma State '97) **Tight Ends**
	Joe DeForrest (Southwestern Louisiana '87) **Special Teams**
TEAM WINS (last 5 yrs.)	**5-8-5-5-3**
FINAL RANK (last 5 yrs.)	**69-44-43-47-67**
2000 FINISH	**Lost to Oklahoma in regular-season finale.**

COACH AND PROGRAM

Oklahoma State athletic director Terry Don Phillips had his man. After dismissing Bob Simmons following six seasons that produced just a single winning record, Phillips looked West and found Boise State coach Dirk Koetter to become the Cowboys' 21st coach.

There was just one problem. Koetter never arrived in Stillwater. He changed his state of mind, backing out of the verbal deal with Oklahoma State to accept the job at Arizona State.

Phillips then tried to make the best of a bad situation by offering the job to Dallas Cowboys tight end coach Les Miles, who was an Oklahoma State assistant from 1995-97. Miles said yes and didn't change his mind.

Cowboys fans can only hope that Phillips' second choice turns out to be the right one.

"He's got fire in his breeches," Phillips said. "He's very competitive. I feel very good."

Said Miles, "I don't care how they got the best

guy. But I definitely think they got the best guy."

Miles was offensive coordinator during Oklahoma State's last winning season (8-4 in 1997). He inherits a program that has had one winning season (8-4 in 1997) since 1988. Stillwater is not a college football backwater, but it's not South Bend, either. Oklahoma State's $18.8 million athletic budget ranks 10th in the Big 12 Conference.

Miles understands the economics and he gave his boss a budget break. When Phillips offered Miles an annual salary of $700,000, Miles turned it down. And took less. He asked Phillips to take $300,000 of the money he had been offered and give it to his assistant coaches.

"We aren't in a hurry to raise a salary for me," Miles said. "We are in a hurry to have success on the gridiron here. I've been places where the head coach did not make more money than other people in the conference and was the league's finest coach. I really don't see this as that unusual. It caught some notoriety, which is a kind thing. I think this is a way that athletics is headed."

With the extra money, Oklahoma State was able to hire the staff Miles wanted. The Cowboys' assistant coaches' salaries will total $1.078 million.

Assistant head coach/offensive coordinator Mike Gundy, the school's all-time leading passer, will earn $250,000. Gundy was one of the finalists for the head-coaching job.

"You can't hire a staff of quality guys and not pay them," Miles said. "I've been lucky to hire a group of guys from quality programs who are into it. The thing you're going to want to do is maintain consistency with your coaches. Not that we're going to keep 100 percent of our coaches intact while I'm here.

"But their comparison will now be slanted many times in our favor. If they enjoy a great college town, the people of Oklahoma, living and raising a family in Stillwater, it will be hard for that assistant coach to leave."

Now, if Miles can just find a way to defer enough salary to refurbish Lewis Field. With Gallagher-Iba Arena's stunning facelift completed, attention now turns to Oklahoma State's football venue. With a capacity of 50,614, Lewis Field can best be described as a rusting erector set. It's clearly the worst football facility in the Big 12.

"It's a very uncomfortable stadium for our fans," Phillips admits. "I've got to make that stadium a fan-friendly, attractive facility that we can recruit to and our people feel good about."

Miles is confident that Phillips and the administration will find the money (an estimated $100 million) to renovate his team's home.

During Miles' three-year stint as an Oklahoma State assistant, the Cowboys were equal—if not a half step ahead—of Oklahoma. Now that Miles returns as the team's head coach, Oklahoma State looks down I-35 at the national champion.

"We're competing against all the programs in the country, not just against Oklahoma," Miles said. "I was really proud of the job they did, how that staff took a program that was not on top and turned it around. We'd like to have the same transformation at Oklahoma State. There's room for two good football programs in the state of Oklahoma.

"Yes, it is our state, they are the team right down the street, but we're going to compete against all the programs and do the best we can to promote Oklahoma State and just not worry about those very capable Sooners just down the road."

2001 SCHEDULE

Sept.	1	@Southern Mississippi
	8	Louisiana Tech
	15	Northern Arizona
	22	@Texas A&M
Oct.	6	Missouri
	13	Texas
	20	@Iowa State
	27	Colorado
Nov.	10	Texas Tech
	17	@Baylor
	24	@Oklahoma

QUARTERBACKS

During Miles' previous stint in Stillwater, Tony Lindsay was a redshirt freshman quarterback who led the '97 Cowboys to an 8-4 record and a spot in the Alamo Bowl.

Over the next three seasons, however, Lindsay was never able to regain his form. Injuries had a lot to do with that. Lindsay's final season with Oklahoma State was ruined when he tried to make a tackle after throwing an interception in a preseason scrimmage. Lindsay injured his shoulder and, after struggling through the first five games, had to undergo season-ending shoulder surgery.

Simmons and his staff had little choice but to turn to redshirt freshman **Aso Pogi**, which ironically should help Miles and his staff this season. If nothing else, the Cowboys know they have a talented player at quarterback.

Should Pogi, a 6-3, 225-pound sophomore, continue to post numbers like he did as a rookie, opposing defenses could have as much trouble with the OSU offense as people have spelling Pogi's first name (it's Asoteletangafamosili). Pogi set a school single-season record for passing yards by a freshman. Playing in 10 games, Pogi completed 139-of-247 passes for 1,550 yards. However, he had just six touchdown passes to counter 11 interceptions.

"What we're most excited about is that he wants to work hard and improve himself," Miles said of Pogi. "He could be a long-term leader for us.

"He's got effective mobility, good quickness and he's got the ability to get the ball to the receivers he's supposed to. Aso will be a very competitive Big 12 quarterback."

One of the strengths of the multi-dimensional I-formation offense that Miles plans to run is a corps of talented wide receivers. Pogi believes that he's got enough targets to make for a potent passing game.

"We've got a lot of talent," Pogi said. "And I think coach Miles knows the type of weapons we have on the outside, and he knows we need to use them. They need to have the football. That's always a great thing for me, because that means I get to wing it more."

One of the biggest weaknesses on the roster is a lack of depth behind Pogi. Miles, his staff and Cowboys fans held their breath during a spring scrimmage when Pogi made a diving tackle after throwing an interception.

"If there was a guy who got the most snaps this spring, it was Aso," Miles said. "He had a new offense to learn. As long as Aso is our quarterback, it's an advantage to take most of the snaps. If something happens, that becomes a disadvantage."

Redshirt freshman **Andre McGill** (6-0, 180), a former safety, came out of spring practice listed as the No. 2 quarterback. All the other quarterbacks on the roster are walk-ons—juniors **Curtis Cornell** (6-3, 200) and **Michael Cox** (5-11, 170), sophomore **Tom Campos** (5-11, 175) and redshirt freshman **Jake Hammond** (6-2, 195). None of Oklahoma State's backup quarterbacks have played in a Division I-A game.

Junior **Chris Massey** (6-0, 205) was working at quarterback before being moved to safety during spring practice.

"We have a strong backup plan," Miles said. "But I don't know ... we have a number of guys who competed there in the spring, and they could come in and finish a game for us. If something happened that we felt we needed a long-term answer for, Chris Massey may in fact have to play a little bit more quarterback than we want."

Freshman **Josh Fields** (6-2, 210), a blue-chip recruit from Stillwater High School, could wind up being Pogi's backup. Oklahoma State's coaches were concerned that Fields, a shortstop who will play for the school's baseball team, would be selected in the June major-league draft. Fields, however, was not selected.

"We knew that if Josh was drafted high and he got a lot of money, he would have to take it," said Mike Gundy, Oklahoma State's offensive coordinator. "But I also wanted him, and we're breathing a little easier [now]."

RUNNING BACKS

Oklahoma State, if nothing else, has been strong when it comes to productive tailbacks. However, under Simmons, the Cowboys often struggled to pound the ball on the ground.

Last season, Reggie White was steady, gaining 1,049 yards and averaging 5.0 yards per carry. White, though, decided to pass up his senior season and declare himself available for the NFL draft.

That meant that spring drills provided a chance for someone to fill the void. Sophomore **Tatum Bell** (5-11, 190) indicated that he has the potential to restore some of the school's reputation for producing exciting running backs.

As a freshman last season, he was the team's second-leading rusher, gaining 251 yards and averaging 5.1 yards per carry. In the season-ending near-upset of top-ranked Oklahoma, Bell scored his only touchdown on a 60-yard scamper.

"Tatum Bell is not only fast but he really pounds it in there," Miles said. "He's a lot tougher runner than I would have thought, but I had never seen him play. I'm excited about his potential at running back. He's going to be a good Big 12 tailback."

Bell is ready for the workload that usually comes with being Oklahoma State's starting tailback.

"I'm very comfortable," Bell said during the spring. "I feel like I can do it—25, 30 carries a game. And it doesn't have to be 20 carries, as long as we win the game."

Bell's backup will be redshirt freshman **D.D. Cox** (5-10, 200). Sophomore **Richard Schwarz** (5-11, 190) is also in the mix at tailback.

Miles is also confident that the fullback position will be productive in providing blocking, yards and receptions. Junior **Mike Denard** (5-11, 240) and sophomore **Tim Burrough** (5-11, 190) are the top two players at that position.

WIDE RECEIVERS/TIGHT ENDS

One of the strengths of the 1997 Cowboys was wide receiver. As offensive coordinator, Miles could choose from Terence Richardson, Sean Love, Willie Grissom and sometimes-defensive back R.W. McQuarters as his targets in the passing game. Any of those players were capable of a game-breaking play. Miles believes the 2001 Cowboys are stronger.

"There's no question, we're better off at wide receiver," he said. "Not even close. I feel like we have some real weapons at wide receiver."

Miles wants his versatile offense to hit the defense from any and all directions. The receivers will be a major part of that.

Juniors **Terrance Davis-Bryant** (5-9, 185), whose nickname is T.D., and **Gabe Lindsay** (5-8, 180), Tony's little brother, are the most experienced receivers.

Redshirt freshman **Rashaun Woods** (6-2, 185), sophomore **Willie Young** (6-1, 210) and junior **John Lewis** (5-11, 185) provide talent and depth. Woods was perhaps the standout of the spring. Young had two touchdowns in last season's first game while Lewis originally signed with Oklahoma State but attended junior college before winding up back in Stillwater. Lewis, who has 4.5 speed, was a first-team All-Mississippi Junior College Conference selection.

"Rashuan Woods had a great play in every scrimmage we had during the spring," Miles said.

Oklahoma State must replace its top three tight ends from last season. Marcellus Rivers, Khary Jackson and Bryan Blackwood accounted for 41receptions last season.

Senior **Tarrick McGuire** (6-3, 225) has potential to be a key cog in the passing offense. Redshirt freshman **Mark Milosevich** (6-5, 240) could also see plenty of playing time.

Redshirt freshmen **Derrius Whitehead** (6-2, 270) and **Kyle Williams** (6-4, 260) plus junior **Willis Holdeman** (6-2, 220) provide plenty of depth.

"I think wide receiver is the deepest position that we've got," Miles said. "I like the speed and experience we've got at that position. And with Pogi at quarterback, I like the fact that we've got a bunch of guys for him to throw to. We've got guys who can catch and run with it. I think we've got guys who can make us a viable threat through the air."

OFFENSIVE LINE

There is a lot to like in this unit. Three of five starters return, plus there is depth and talent in good supply.

Junior tackle **Kyle Eaton** (6-8, 305), senior guard **Jeff Machado** (6-3, 300) and senior center **Jon Vandrell** (6-0, 285) started last year, so the Cowboys are solid from center to the left.

Senior **Bryan Phillips** (6-4, 335), who started 10-of-11 games last season at right guard, is listed as the starter at that position. Junior **Jason Russell** (6-5, 310) started three games last season and he is the projected starter at left tackle.

Senior **D.J. Grissom** (6-3, 345), sophomore **John Hayhurst** (6-3, 295), junior **Dustin Vanderhoof** (6-3, 300), senior **Jason Johnson** (6-2, 305), redshirt freshman **Sam Mayes** (6-5, 325), sophomore **Doug Koenig** (6-4, 275), senior **Jason Rannebarger** (6-5, 340), sophomore **Bob Hafler** (6-2, 295) and sophomore **Derek Lafargue** (6-4, 255) are all in the mix to see backup duty on the line.

"We've got a number of offensive linemen who can fit the bill. I don't feel like we've got the depth that we'd like," Miles said. "We've got six, seven or eight linemen who will be pretty good."

2000 STATISTICS

Rushing offense	161.5	42
Passing offense	198.5	70
Total offense	360.0	67
Scoring offense	18.4	95
Net Punting	34.0	73
Punt returns	9.0	69
Kickoff returns	18.0	92
Rushing defense	126.8	34
Passing efficiency defense	125.9	84
Total defense	379.8	68
Scoring defense	27.5	77
Turnover margin	-4	80

Last column is ranking among Division I-A teams.

KICKERS

Seth Condley, who had a so-so 2000 season, must be replaced. Condley made 12-of-20 field-goal attempts and had two kicks blocked. Condley also missed 2-of-21 extra points. He and Russ Schwettman were the only experienced kickers. Schwettman missed his only field-goal try and was 1-of-1 on extra points.

Sophomore **Luke Phillips** (6-0, 160) is listed as the No. 1 kicker after spring practice. Junior **Chris Calcagni** (5-10, 180) provides kicking competition.

Miles expects freshman **Cole Farden** (5-11, 180), one of the Cowboys' top recruits, to compete for the kicking job.

"He's got a real strong leg, can kick it off and punt it, kick field goals and extra points," Miles said of Farden. "He's going to develop and compete for a starting job. We feel we came out of the spring with a kicker in Luke Phillips."

DEFENSIVE LINE

This is a unit in transition. Four players—Juqua Thomas, Zac Akin, Sean Barry and Zac Warner—who started last year at various times, must be replaced. Thomas was a big-time playmaker. He made 21 tackles for loss and had 10 sacks last season.

Junior **Kevin Williams** (6-5, 275) should be the cornerstone of the rebuilding process. He played defensive tackle and end last season, totaling 35 tackles and 11 tackles for loss. He will probably play at defensive tackle this season.

The other projected starters on the defensive line are junior **Jake Riffe** (6-3, 235), sophomore **LaWaylon Brown** (6-5, 290) and sophomore **Greg Richmond** (6-2, 230). Riffe and Richmond are ends while Brown should team with Williams in the middle of the Cowboys' new 4-2-5 scheme.

The defensive line reserves are junior end **Kyle Beck** (6-2, 240), senior tackle **Chris Tyler** (6-2, 290), redshirt freshman tackle **Clay Coe** (6-1, 260) and sophomore end **Thomas Glapion** (6-6, 250).

LINEBACKERS

The strongest unit on the defense, ironically, needs the fewest players in the new 4-2-5 alignment. The top linebacker is senior **Dwayne Levels** (6-2, 250), a blue-collar, hard-working linebacker. Last season, he led the Cowboys in tackles with 95, had three pass deflections, three quarterback hurries and nine tackles for loss.

Junior **Terrence Robinson** (6-0, 215) is projected to start alongside Levels.

"The mentality is still the same—attack," Levels said of Oklahoma State's new defensive scheme. "I'm all for that. I don't like sitting and waiting. With the way the conference is going to more pass-oriented offenses, the extra defensive back is really going to help us out. We're still strong enough on the run yet strong enough on the pass. It's more of a balanced attack now."

Sophomore **Fath'** (pronounced Fa-da) **Carter** (6-2, 210) and senior **Ron Able** (6-0, 240) saw plenty of playing time last season and provide solid backups to the starters.

DEFENSIVE BACKS

Last season, Oklahoma State's blitz-oriented defense got singed. When Alvin Porter, the team's best one-on-one defender, was declared academically ineligible just before the season opener, a young secondary was headed toward a long season. The Cowboys allowed 253 yards per game through the air, a school record.

Miles and defensive coordinator Bill Clay believe that the 4-2-5 defensive scheme will help stop the pass while not sacrificing the ability to stop the run.

"A year ago, there was more man coverage, with their corners out there on an island," Miles said. "Going to this scheme, we've got the ability to help those corners. Having five defensive backs on the field, it adds some speed to the scheme. Being able to change coverage, it gives an edge to those corners who need some advantage."

All of last year's starters return—senior cornerback **Michael Cooper** (5-9, 195), junior cornerback **Ricklan Holmes** (5-11, 195), junior safety **Chris Massey** (6-0, 205) and sophomore safety Elbert Craig (6-2, 195), who was second on the team in tackles and whose three interceptions led the team.

Senior **Roger Bombach** (5-11, 190) is projected to be the third safety in the starting lineup.

"This defense is interesting," Miles said. "We're going to have an opportunity to have an extra guy to defend the running game and the passing game. The offense is going to have to look us over and figure where that guy is. They're going to be guessing. We feel like the scheme will be a benefit.

"When you face teams that are good at throwing the football, you'd better be able to adjust your coverage with something that is not difficult for your players to grasp. That's what we were looking for when we went to that scheme."

The secondary reserves are sophomore **Chris Cole** (5-9, 180), senior **Marcus Jones** (5-8, 195), junior **Paul Jones** (6-1, 200), senior **Robbie Gillem** (5-11, 210).

Junior **Kobina Amoo** (5-10, 180), a transfer from Northeastern (Oklahoma) A&M Junior College, is expected to have an impact as a cornerback. Amoo, who has 4.4 speed, originally signed with Oklahoma State two years ago. He was a two-year starter at NEO. A year ago he made 27 tackles—19 unassisted—and intercepted three passes.

PUNTERS

Junior **Scott Elder** (6-1, 190) had a solid 2000 season. He was busy, punting 56 times for a 37.6-yard average. He had one punt blocked. Of his 56 punts, 20 were downed inside the 20 and 11 were fair caught.

If Elder falters, sophomore **Sky Rylant** (6-0, 195) is available. Also, freshman **Ryan Wimberly** (6-0, 190) from Houston (Mo.) High School, is regarded by Miles as the team's "most heralded signee." Miles was chosen a first-team All-American punter by *USA Today.* A versatile athlete, Wimberly rushed for close to 1,000 yards as a running back, played safety and returned kicks for Houston High. He averaged 49.2 yards per punt as a senior and 48.5 yards a punt as a junior.

SPECIAL TEAMS

An overall lack of depth could mean that too many players will be seeing action as starters and on special teams. Miles won't be able to do much about that until he fills out the roster with more players over the next few years.

Lindsay (a receiver) and Massey (a safety) are listed as the team's top punt returners. Lindsay handled that job last season, returning 25 punts for a 9.2-yard average with one touchdown.

Jones (a defensive back) and Davis-Bryant (a receiver) are the top kickoff returners. Davis-Bryant averaged 24.2 yards on six kickoff returns last season.

Juniors **Jed Newkirk** (6-4, 305) and **Scott Smith** (5-8, 200) are the team's top deep snappers while punter Elder holds on place-kicks.

RECRUITING CLASS

Programs like Oklahoma State can't afford recruiting mistakes. To that end, Miles and his staff concentrated on recruiting "utility" players.

"We wanted to recruit people who can play more than one position," Miles said. "Both of the tailbacks we recruited can play corner and or wide receiver if they don't wind up at tailback."

Errick McCown (5-11, 170) of Arlington, Texas and **Greg Jones** (5-10, 185) of Carrollton (Texas) Newman Smith High School are the running backs that Miles referred to. Jones played quarterback, wide receiver, running back and cornerback as a senior.

One of the Cowboys' top signees was **Billy Bajema** (6-5, 240), a tight end/defensive end from Oklahoma City Westmoore High School.

"He's a perfect example of that," Miles said of the versatility philosophy. "He can play tight end or defensive end. He's big and can run. We had that kind of athlete all through this class.

"That is a philosophy that we will continue to follow. The quarterbacks who can only play quarterback will be few and far between. Those quarterbacks who can play linebacker and quarterback, that helps us. We've got a quarterback who's athletic who improves your offense. If he doesn't play at quarterback, he's at a position where he can use his athletic ability.

"If a player is good enough to play defensive line, he can play offensive line."

Miles thinks that kicker Farden and punter Wimberly will fill those roles for the Cowboys for the next three or four years.

"We feel with this recruiting class, we really shored up our kicking game," Miles said.

BLUE RIBBON ANALYSIS

OFFENSE	B
SPECIAL TEAMS	C+
DEFENSE	B-
INTANGIBLES	B+

Thus far, Miles has been popular among Oklahoma State fans with his positive, meet-and-greet Cowboys caravans. The honeymoon period is still in effect.

There is talent on the roster. Bob Simmons was no buffoon as a recruiter. Oklahoma State, after all, played national champion Oklahoma within a few minutes of its undefeated season before losing, 12-7.

The challenge for Miles will be convincing the Cowboys that they can compete with Big 12 South Division powerhouses like Oklahoma and Texas.

The schedule is formidable. The Cowboys open at Southern Mississippi, then have two must-win home games against Louisiana Tech and I-AA Northern Arizona. That's the non-conference schedule. Oklahoma State faces Texas A&M, Iowa State, Baylor and Oklahoma on the road, with Missouri, Texas, Colorado and Texas Tech coming to Stillwater. If the Cowboys can defeat Iowa State, Baylor and Missouri, Miles' first season could be a roaring success.

"There is some talent here," Miles said. "We've got to keep working at it. If we do that, we'll have an opportunity to get after some of the folks we are going to play.

"I promise you, we will win here. This team is loaded with good people and I just have a real strong feeling that good people work their butt off to get better."

(W.B.)

2000 RESULTS

Tulsa	W	36-26	1-0
Southwest Texas	W	23-0	2-0
Southern Miss	L	6-28	2-1
Texas	L	7-42	2-2
Missouri	L	10-24	2-3
Iowa State	L	26-33	2-4
Colorado	L	21-37	2-5
Texas A&M	L	16-21	2-6
Texas Tech	L	0-58	2-7
Baylor	W	50-22	3-7
Oklahoma	L	7-12	3-8

Texas

LOCATION **Austin, TX**
CONFERENCE **Big 12 (South)**
LAST SEASON **9-3 (.750)**
CONFERENCE RECORD **7-1 (2nd)**
OFFENSIVE STARTERS RETURNING **9**
DEFENSIVE STARTERS RETURNING **8**
NICKNAME **Longhorns**
COLORS **White & Burnt Orange**
HOME FIELD **Darrel K. Royal/Memorial Stadium (80,082)**
HEAD COACH **Mack Brown (Florida State '74)**
RECORD AT SCHOOL **27-11 (3 years)**
CAREER RECORD **113-85-1 (17 years)**
ASSISTANTS **Greg Davis (McNeese State '73)**
Offensive Coordinator/Quarterbacks
Carl Reese (Missouri '66)
Defensive Coordinator/Linebackers
Everett Withers (Appalachian State '87)
Defensive Backs
Mike Tolleson (Delta State '70)
Defensive Tackles/Special Teams
Tim Nunez (Lamar '70)
Offensive Line
Hardee McCrary (Austin College '73)
Defensive Ends
Bruce Chambers (North Texas '82)
Running Backs
Tim Brewster (Illinois '83)
Tight Ends
Darryl Drake (Western Kentucky '80)
Wide Receivers
TEAM WINS (last 5 yrs.) **8-4-9-9-9**
FINAL RANK (last 5 yrs.) **19-63-14-29-11**
2000 FINISH **Lost to Oregon in Holiday Bowl.**

COACH AND PROGRAM

In three years under Mack Brown, Texas has been consistent. The Longhorns have won nine games each season. After nearly two decades of maddeningly inconsistent year-to-year performances, the Horns have stabilized.

The last time UT had this good a three-year run was 1981-83 under Fred Akers (30 victories). Add that winning to stellar recruiting classes and it's no surprise that Texas is tabbed as one of several teams with a legitimate shot at winning the national championship. And the pressure is on Brown to make sure that the Horns don't stumble out of that race early, as they have in the last two seasons.

"The program is growing at the pace we'd hoped it would," Brown said. "Each year we have developed more depth and experience from top to bottom. The key to our continued success is developing more depth.

"We want to win our conference championship and hope that puts us in a position to win the national championship. That's going to be our goal every year. We put pressure on ourselves to win every game, every year, and we will continue to strive for that."

For some Orangebloods, striving won't be as important as arriving. Oklahoma proved that a sudden turnaround is possible, that national champions do grow in the Big 12 Conference. The pressure is clearly on Brown to deliver a national championship—or at the very least, a contending team—this season.

Since arriving in Austin from North Carolina before the 1998 season, Brown has done a masterful job of restoring Texas' football pride. The program embodies class, from the secretaries to the weight room to the football offices to expanded Darrell K. Royal/Memorial Stadium. The Horns are no longer jokes.

In his first year, Brown was masterful in handling Ricky Williams' Heisman Trophy season. Last season, however, a quarterback controversy blew up in Brown's face. **Major Applewhite** and **Chris Simms** spent most of the year battling for the starting job. No matter what Brown said or did, the Applewhite/Simms, Simms/Applewhite competition appeared to be a season-long distraction.

While having a Heisman-winning running back and a quarterback quandary is nice, Brown has restored tradition on the defensive side of the ball. Under coordinator Carl Reese, the Horns have steadily improved. In the seven seasons before Brown and Reese arrived in Austin, Texas had finished no higher than 55th in total defense. In 1999, Texas was seventh and last year it was sixth in total defense.

"We have better speed at all positions than at any time since I've been here," Reese said after the spring drills saw some position switches to get more speed on the line, at linebacker and in the secondary. "Speed is the answer, and we have more of it than we've had."

The schedule is certainly conducive to a national championship run. The non-conference foes—New Mexico State and North Carolina at home, Houston on the road—pose no great threats. Texas opens conference play with a home game against Texas Tech on Sept. 29. All eyes will be on Dallas on Oct. 6 when the Horns face the defending national champions. That game could match a pair of top five teams. The loser goes to the back of the contenders' line.

After the annual Red River Shootout, Texas plays at Oklahoma State, is at home against Colorado, then travels to Missouri and Baylor. The regular season ends with a home game against Kansas and a road game at rival Texas A&M on Nov. 23.

All things considered, that's a schedule that adds to the championship heat in Austin. The two big games are against Oklahoma and A&M. If the Horns win those two games, they'll be expected to win the other nine regular-season games, too. A loss to a North Carolina, a Texas Tech or a Colorado will be unacceptable.

In some media outposts, before last season Texas was selected as a long shot national championship contender. But in the second game of the season, the Horns lost a shocker at Stanford, 27-24. The national title hopes and dreams were officially squashed three weeks later when Oklahoma made its national championship with an eye-opening 63-14 whacking of the Horns in the Cotton Bowl on Oct. 7.

"As our program continues to evolve, it's extremely important for us not to allow preseason expectations to get into our head, like I'm afraid it did some last year," Brown said. "Certainly we want to be a well-respected program and with that comes continued high expectations.

"But, ultimately preseason expectations don't matter. It's our performance week in and week out that will be judged at the end of the year. Our players need to understand that."

2001 SCHEDULE

Sept.	1	New Mexico State
	8	North Carolina
	15	@Houston
	29	Texas Tech
Oct.	6	Oklahoma at Cotton Bowl
	13	@Oklahoma State
	20	Colorado
	27	@Missouri
Nov.	3	@Baylor
	10	Kansas
	23	@Texas A&M

QUARTERBACKS

This is now Simms' team. The 6-5, 222-pound junior won the starting job during spring practice. That means that Applewhite, a 6-1, 207-pound senior, will play only in blowouts or if Simms is injured. Considering that Applewhite is the school's leader in career passing yards and touchdown passes, the two quarterbacks provide Texas with uncommon depth at the position.

"Very few teams have two quarterbacks who have started and been successful," Brown said. "We are fortunate and excited to have that situation."

The starting/backup situation is a complete reversal from last season. Applewhite, who in the 1999 Cotton Bowl suffered a knee injury that required surgery, came back to claim the starting spot heading into last season. However, Brown tried to keep Simms happy by using him in certain situations. The two-quarterback system worked for Brown at North Carolina. He did not have similar results last season with the Longhorns.

"I thought that there was too much emphasis put on the quarterback situation and not enough on our team last year," Brown said. "We will handle that differently this year. I'm sure at times we will need to play both. We have two guys who can step in and play, but will have a determined starter."

Brown announced in the spring that Simms would enter preseason drills as No. 1. The decision was a no-brainer. Simms needed a vote of confidence. And Applewhite was limited during the spring while he recovered from a sprained right knee (his left knee was the problem a year ago) suffered near the end of last season.

"The only thing that's important to us," Brown said, "is the guy who can help us win."

For most of his three seasons, Applewhite has been that guy. He's small in stature, his passes lack zip, his mobility is average. But all he's done is be the guiding force in three nine-win seasons. Last season, before he suffered his knee injury against Texas Tech, Applewhite completed 152-of-279 passes for 2,164 yards. He had 18 touchdown passes and seven interceptions.

Applewhite's injury opened the door for Simms. Before replacing Applewhite, Simms had shown flashes of brilliance in spot duty. But he had also shown a troubling tendency to throw the wrong pass at the wrong time—the anti-Applewhite.

In his first start, Simms rallied Texas from a 14-0 deficit at Kansas—the second touchdown an interception returned for a touchdown. He also led the Longhorns back from a 14-0 deficit against Oregon in the Holiday Bowl. However, he threw four interceptions against the Ducks, the last killing any chance of a victory.

Last season, Simms played in 10 games. He completed 67-of-117 passes for 1,064 yards and eight touchdowns. But he also had seven interceptions, and in his career has thrown one interception for every 15 attempts.

"We are obviously very solid at quarterback," offensive coordinator Greg Davis said. "Both of those guys have proven themselves and are among the best in the nation at their position."

Junior **Beau Trahan** (5-11, 200) moved up to No. 2 as Simms' backup after Applewhite was injured. However, Trahan saw plenty of action on special teams, distinguishing himself to the point that he was the team's co-most valuable special teams player. He appeared in one game at quarterback last season, completing one pass for one yard.

Freshman **Chance Mock** (6-2, 205) is the designated quarterback of the future. He spent last season as a redshirt and will try to battle his way up the depth chart in preseason drills.

RUNNING BACKS

Hodges Mitchell might have gotten more out of less than any back in UT history. The 5-7, 185-pound Mitchell was a perfect fit in Texas' pass-oriented offense under Brown. He finished his career sixth on the all-time rushing list (2,664 yards) and wound up fourth in all-purpose yardage (4,945 yards).

Mitchell was an effective receiver who got a lot of his yardage on well-timed draw plays that allowed him to pick his openings. With his small stature, Mitchell wasn't going to blast his way through opposing lines.

But now Mitchell has departed with the memories of a wonderful three-year career. Davis will be hard-pressed to find a replacement.

"A year ago, we were trying to determine who our fullback would be," Davis said. "Now, we need to find out who the tailback is—or who the tailbacks are."

Yes, there's a crowded depth chart. A tailback by committee could be in the works.

Juniors **Victor Ike** (5-11, 195) and **Kenny Hayter** (5-11, 215) are battling for the starting spot. Ike, 13th nationally in kickoff returns last season (24.8 yards per return), had 156 yards and four touchdowns on 36 attempts in 2000. During his career, he's averaged 9.2 yards every time he's touched the ball. Hayter, who a year ago gained 122 yards against Oklahoma State, was the Horns' second-leading rusher with 220 yards on 60 attempts.

Sophomore **Ivan Williams** (6-1, 235) and redshirt freshman **Sneezy** (his real first name is Arturo) **Beltran** (5-10, 205) also figure to see some playing time.

UT fans no doubt will be clamoring for **Cedric Benson** (6-foot, 200) to be chosen the team's starting tailback. Benson, from Midland Lee High School, is the school's most ballyhooed running back recruit since Earl Campbell. In high school, Benson gained 8,423 yards—the fourth most in state history and the most for a Class 5A (the biggest schools) running back.

Benson had something to ponder in early June when the Los Angeles Dodgers chose him in the 13th round of the Major League Baseball draft.

Junior **Matt Trissel** (6-0, 235) filled the void at fullback last season. Used exclusively as a blocker—he didn't carry the ball once—Trissel caught five passes for 43 yards and a touchdown.

Junior **Chad Stevens** (6-4, 245) and sophomore **Brett Robin** (5-11, 19) provide depth. Stevens started the last three games of the 2000 season at tight end while Robin also has the speed and quickness to play tailback. Redshirt freshman **Will Matthews** (6-3, 235) could also be a factor at fullback.

WIDE RECEIVERS/TIGHT ENDS

The foundation of last year's recruiting class was a high-profile group of wide receivers. And, yes, these kids are all right. After "making do" at wide receiver during his first two seasons, Brown now has a group of game-breaking pass catchers who should keep the Longhorns' offense potent.

Last season, sophomores **Roy Williams** (6-5, 210) and **B.J. Johnson** (6-1, 190) had impressive rookie seasons.

"Roy and B.J. had phenomenal freshman years, especially when you consider all they had to learn in a short period of time," Davis said. "And that's just the tip of the iceberg. They will get so much better."

Johnson set a school freshman record with his team-high 41 receptions. Those catches produced 698 yards and three touchdowns. Williams had 40 receptions and his 809 yards was a freshman record. He also had eight touchdown receptions.

Williams and Johnson are five of the six wide receivers returning who caught passes last season. Texas returns 85 percent of the yardage produced by wide receivers in 2000.

While Williams and Johnson set most of the records, sophomore **Sloan Thomas** (6-2, 195) proved that he might be the big-play threat of last year's rookie crop. He played in just eight games, catching nine passes for 208 yards (23.1 yards per catch). And three of his receptions went for touchdowns.

Senior **Montrell Flowers** (5-9, 182) caught 22 passes for 343 yards and two touchdowns; he might be the team's fastest wideout. Junior **Kyle Shanahan** (6-3, 170), the son of the Denver Broncos' coach, sat out last season after transferring from Duke. He's known for his route running and sticky fingers.

Redshirt freshman **Tony Jeffery** (6-2, 180), who was a top-notch high school quarterback, spent last season learning to play receiver.

"This is a great group of young receivers coming back," Davis said. "I think we will have great competition at that position."

The biggest problem that Williams, Johnson and some of the other Texas receivers had was a tendency to drop passes. Particularly in the Holiday Bowl loss against Oregon, it seemed that the Longhorns' receivers would drop a pass for each big play they would make. Reaching a consistent level of performance will be crucial this season, particularly if quarterback Simms is to play with confidence.

Tight end was a disaster last season. Sophomore **Bo Scaife** (6-3, 240) was being counted on to have a 40-catch season, but he suffered a season-ending knee injury in the team's first practice last August. Scaife, who has had a history of knee injuries, could be a valuable weapon if he could stay healthy. He has speed to stretch the field and is an excellent receiver.

Sophomore **Brock Edwards** (6-5, 265) started nine games as a freshman last season, taking over when senior **Mike Jones** was injured. Edwards had eight receptions for 107 yards before missing the final two regular-season games with a knee injury.

Jones (6-4, 260) went out in last season's seventh game. Before being hurt, he had 17 receptions for 199 yards. If he returns to form, he'll provide a combination of blocking and receiving ability.

Sophomore **Artie Ellis** (6-4, 205) had eight catches for 77 yards and three touchdowns last season—as a flanker. Because of the talent glut at wide receiver and in order to add some punch at tight end, Ellis moved to that position during spring drills.

OFFENSIVE LINE

Four of five starters return here, but there's a hole to plug. A BIG hole. The missing starter from last year's unit is left tackle Leonard Davis. The consensus first-team All-American and Outland Trophy finalist was blot-out-the-sun big—6-6 and 365 pounds.

Junior **Robbie Doane** (6-6, 305) won the left tackle spot during spring drills and Davis isn't worried that the unit will suffer greatly from Davis' departure.

"Obviously, we have to fill the void Leonard leaves at left tackle," Davis said. "But offensive line is a very solid position where we are developing more depth."

Three seniors with playing experience should anchor the line. **Matt Anderson** (6-4, 300) is a two-year starter at center. **Mike Williams** (6-6, 339) and **Antwan Kirk-Hughes** (6-3, 310) were both honorable mention Big 12 performers last season. Anderson was voted the team's most consistent offensive player last season. Williams started all 12 games and allowed just one sack. Kirk-Hughes missed spring practice after undergoing shoulder surgery. That injury limited him last season.

Junior **Derrick Dockery** (6-6, 330) started nine games last season at guard. Sophomore **Tillman Holloway** (6-3, 297), who began his career as a defensive tackle, started seven games at guard last season as a redshirt freshman. Holloway suffered a knee injury during spring practice, but is expected to be ready for preseason drills.

Alfio Randall (6-6, 300), a transfer from Blinn Junior College in Brenham, Texas, should push Doane at left tackle and his arrival increases the experience and depth. Redshirt freshman **Lionel Garr** (6-7, 335) should also provide some depth at tackle.

2000 STATISTICS

Rushing offense	145.5	60
Passing offense	293.2	14
Total offense	438.6	14
Scoring offense	38.6	8
Net Punting	35.4	58
Punt returns	11.6	32
Kickoff returns	22.9	10
Rushing defense	93.4	11
Passing efficiency defense	88.3	1
Total defense	277.6	7
Scoring defense	17.9	11
Turnover margin	+8	19

Last column is ranking among Division I-A teams.

KICKERS

In three seasons in Austin, Brown has tackled problems faced by every coach—pleasing alums, improving facilities, recruiting, plugging personnel holes.

One thing the Texas coach hasn't had to worry about has been his team's kicker. For four seasons, Kris Stockton was a steady, reliable scorer. In his career, he made 58-of-77 field goals and that 75.3 percent success rate is the best in school history—an impressive feat when you consider the long line of kickers the school has produced.

Last season, Stockton was a semifinalist for the Lou Groza Award. He was second nationally in field goals (two per game) and was 10th nationally in scoring (9.7 points per game). His 58 career field goals are second in school history and his 22 field goals last season were a Texas single-season record.

"The loss of Kris Stockton is one that will really hurt us," Brown said. "Kris was an outstanding player for us in all phases for the past three years and he's someone we are going to have a hard time replacing."

Redshirt freshman **Matt McFadden** (5-11, 180) is the heir apparent. A product of Coppell High School (a Dallas suburb school), McFadden was a first-team all state (Class 4-A) kicker who displayed excellent range and consistency.

DEFENSIVE LINE

For the last two years, Texas' defense against the run has been excellent. Last year, the Horns were 12th nationally in stuffing opposing ball carriers.

The two biggest reasons for that success were defensive tackles Casey Hampton and Shaun Rogers. Hampton was a two-time first-team All-America selection. Rogers was slowed last season by an ankle injury. They formed one of the nation's best tackle duos and gave Reese the kind of middle-of-the-line defense that coordinators crave.

"Our biggest loss obviously is the tackle position," Reese said. "We lost two veteran guys. One of the things Casey could do so well was his ability to make plays."

While Rogers' ankle injury prevented Reese from getting all he had hoped for out of the dynamic duo, it was a blessing in disguise. With Rogers' playing time limited, other players were forced to get more experience.

"(Rogers' injury) hurt us in the short run but hopefully will pay dividends for us now," Reese said.

Sophomore **Marcus Tubbs** (6-4, 280) is expected to fill one of the tackle spots. Last season as a redshirt freshman, he had 5.5 sacks, 10 tackles for loss, 37 tackles and seven quarterback pressures.

Redshirt freshman **Stevie Lee** (6-4, 300) is expected to join Tubbs as the other starting tackle. But he's been hobbled by a foot injury sustained last season. He played in the first two games before being sidelined and being granted a medical redshirt. Lee, regarded as the best run stopper on the defensive line, had foot surgery that forced him to miss spring practice. He's expected to be ready for preseason practice.

Junior **Miguel McKay** (6-1, 275) and sophomores **Adam Doiron** (6-4, 260) and **Ryan Haywood** (6-5, 260) are expected to be in the tackle rotation as reserves. And in the spring, Texas moved senior **Maurice Gordon** (6-1, 246) from defensive end to tackle to utilize his speed there. Gordon could be a factor on passing downs when Reese wants to get another pass rusher on the field.

"We have better athletes now than we've had at that position and that will make things interesting," Reese told the *Houston Chronicle*. "We can do more with these guys, especially against the passing teams we have to play, because of their athletic ability."

While the emphasis last season was on Hampton and Rogers at tackle, much of the defensive line focus this season should be on the ends. In junior **Cory Redding** (6-5, 260) and sophomore **Kalen Thornton** (6-3, 270), Texas has two of the best defensive ends in the Big 12.

"For the first time since we've been here, we have two guys who have started and who are the type of athletes we are looking for at the end position," Reese said. "Cory and Kalen are two young guys who are steadily improving. We are looking for big things out of them this year."

Last season, Redding started to blossom. He led the Horns with 6.5 sacks and also had a team-high 22 quarterback pressures. His 17 tackles for loss were second on the team. Thornton had 3.5 sacks and was third on the team with 20 quarterback pressures.

If Redding and Thornton can show continued improvement and keep hounding opposing quarterbacks while they're trying to pass, the Horns' defense could be lethal.

To add depth and increase speed at defensive end, Texas moved junior **O.J. McClintock** (6-2, 235), a backup at weak-side linebacker last season, to defensive end during spring practice. McClintock should be familiar with position switches; he played quarterback and wide receiver in high school.

Senior **Jermain Anderson** (6-3, 332) and junior **Adam McConathy** (6-4, 250) figure to see time as backups at defensive end.

Tragedy struck the Texas program in early March when Cole Pittman, a sophomore defensive tackle, was killed in a one-car accident while he was driving from his home in Shreveport to Austin for the start of spring practice.

Pittman earned letters in each of his first two seasons at Texas. Playing defensive end and tackle, he saw action in 23 games and started three contests for the Longhorns. He had 30 tackles, two sacks, five tackles for loss, five quarterback pressures and caused one fumble during his career.

The team voted to keep Pittman's locker intact for two years (which corresponds to his graduation date) and not allow his number 44 to be worn during that time. The Longhorns will dedicate a game in Pittman's memory.

LINEBACKERS

In the years before the Brown Era, this position was a wasteland. Texas seemed to lack not only linebackers who could run and hit. It didn't have enough linebackers who were even marginally talented. That was then, this is now. The Longhorns are three deep at the middle, strong and weak-side linebacker spots. This position has quickly become one of the team's strengths.

"We are in good shape at linebacker, with nearly all of the starters and backups back from last season," Reese said. "With the athletic ability and competition we have at the linebacker spot, I think we have the potential to be very solid there. I'd like to see our linebackers play tougher, more with a linebacker mentality."

All three starters return for their senior seasons. **D.D. Lewis** (6-1, 245) is back in the middle, **Everick Rawls** (6-1, 235) is the weak-side linebacker and **Tyrone Jones** (6-4, 235) plays the strong side. Lewis is a three-year starter. He tied for the team lead in tackles last season (78), had 4.5 sacks, 15 tackles for loss and 12 quarterback pressures.

"D.D. is what you want in a linebacker," Reese said. "He can run like a deer and when he gets there, he's going to hit you. We need him to fill the role that Casey Hampton provided in being the leader on the defensive side of the ball."

Rawls has started 25 of the last 26 games. Last season, he had 69 tackles and led UT linebackers with seven pass breakups. Jones has the least experience of the starting trio.

With Texas' continued emphasis on speed, the Horns decided to move senior **Lee Jackson** (6-3, 205) from strong safety to linebacker. After a stellar 1999 season, Jackson battled injuries in 2000. If he can make a smooth transition to the outside linebacker/rover position, he'll help UT's defensive flexibility, particularly when it comes to defending the pass.

Redshirt freshmen **Austin Sendlein** (6-3, 240) and **Rashad Thomas** (6-2, 235) should work into the mix on the three-deep roster.

DEFENSIVE BACKS

Texas' defense got a boost when **Quentin Jammer** (6-1, 198) decided to return for his senior season instead of entering the NFL draft. Jammer was listed as the nation's top junior cornerback by draft expert Mel Kiper, Jr.

"Jammer is the first guy who jumps out at you," Reese said. "He is coming off a great season. We challenged him in a lot of games to shut down the other team's best receiver and he did. We hope he will continue to work hard and get better and be a real force in the secondary."

Last season, Jammer had 43 tackles, three interceptions, forced four fumbles and broke up 20 passes. He's a leading candidate for the Thorpe Award that goes to the nation's top defensive back.

Jammer's return means that the Horns have seven of their top eight defensive backs from last season returning in 2001. The only loss is safety Greg Brown, an All-Big 12 performer who started 25 of the last 26 games of his career.

Junior **Roderick Babers** (5-10, 183) will man the cornerback spot opposite Jammer. He's a steady player with 14 career starts.

With Brown's departure and Jackson's move to linebacker, both safety positions are in flux. Sophomore **Dakarai Pearson** (5-10, 180) started the last 10 games of 2000 when Jackson was injured, so he should be able to take over at that position.

"Dakarai is a tremendous athlete who gives us great flexibility in our coverage packages," Reese said.

And, to increase the speed at safety, Texas moved senior **Ahmad Brooks** (5-8, 180) from corner to safety.

Senior **Ervis Hill** (5-9, 185) plus sophomores **Nathan Vasher** (5-11, 170) and **Monti Collier** (5-11, 170) provide depth at cornerback while sophomore **Phillip Geiggar** (5-11, 185) should be a backup at safety after seeing most of his action on special teams last season.

PUNTERS

The loss of Kris Stockton not only means that Texas needs to find someone to score points in the kicking game. The Horns must also find a punter and someone to handle kickoffs. Ryan Long, who shared punting and kickoff duties with Stockton, also graduated. While Stockton took over as the punter last season, he and Long shared kickoff duties. Of their 83 kickoffs, 26 went for touchbacks.

Redshirt freshman **Justin Smith** (6-5, 185) is one of the candidates to handle the punting chores. He figures to be challenged by junior **Brian Bradford** (6-2, 215), who was a junior-college All-American at Trinity Valley (Texas) where he averaged 44.3 yards a punt last season.

Either Smith, Bradford or top place-kicking candidate Matt McFadden figure to handle kickoff duties.

SPECIAL TEAMS

Going into last season, Brown wanted to boost his team's punt and kickoff return units. Both quests were successful. Hodges Mitchell helped Texas improve from 108th nationally in punt returns in 1999 to 32nd nationally last year. And Ike led the Big 12 and was ranked 13th nationally in kickoff returns.

"We need to continue to make big plays in the kick return game," Brown said. "It's critical that your kicking game is explosive. I think with that area gaining more experience each year, we can become more effective."

While Ike returns, Texas must find a replacement for Mitchell on punt returns. Sophomore cornerback Vasher is the likely candidate to fill that job.

Overall, the Longhorns' special teams have benefited from the increased talent brought by recent recruiting successes. The improved depth and ability at all positions has helped Texas' special teams improve.

"We have put a tremendous amount of preparation time into developing our kick coverage units," Brown said. "I think that paid dividends last year."

RECRUITING CLASS

Texas had another stellar recruiting class, but the Longhorns' February euphoria was tempered in early June, thanks to the Major League Baseball draft.

Brown lost Quan Cosby, a 5-11, 190-pound speedster who played quarterback in high school but was projected as a wide receiver in college. Cosby, from Mart High School, was drafted by the Anaheim Angels in the sixth round. Terming the baseball contract too tempting to refuse, Cosby signed a five-year deal.

"I hate to give up football, but the Angels really stepped to the plate," Cosby said. "It was a hard decision because I was looking forward to playing football at Texas. Coach Brown told me that if I don't like baseball, I could always come back and play for him at Texas. But I doubt if that will happen."

UT's top recruit, running back Cedric Benson, was drafted in the 12th round by the Los Angeles Dodgers. Benson is considering playing pro baseball in the summer and college football in the fall. That would follow the path similar to the one taken by Ricky Williams, Texas' Heisman Trophy winning running back.

Benson, considered the best high school running back to come out of Texas since Earl Campbell, was the centerpiece to a Texas recruiting class ranked as the top five in the nation. Benson led Midland Lee to three consecutive state championships.

The only area where the Longhorns fell short was in signing defensive tackles.

"Everything fell nicely into place," recruiting expert Jeremy Crabtree told the *Fort Worth Star-Telegram*. "The pieces of the puzzle are in place for Texas to be competing for national championships over the next four or five years."

The reason Brown has had such highly rated classes is that he and his staff have done a good job of signing most of the top Texas high school players.

The 2001 signees included offensive lineman **Jonathon Scott** (6-7, 285) of Dallas Carter, linebacker **Derrick Johnson** (6-4, 210) of Waco, offensive lineman **William Winston** (6-7, 350) of Houston Madison, defensive back **Rufus Harris** (5-11, 185) of LaPorte and defensive back **Kendal Briles** (6-0, 190) of Lubbock.

"Texas will always be our lifeblood in recruiting," Brown said. "We will always look hard at the guys in state first and if we can't find the perfect fit, then we will go out of state to fill our needs."

BLUE RIBBON ANALYSIS

OFFENSE	A-
SPECIAL TEAMS	B-
DEFENSE	B+
INTANGIBLES	A-

The word "patience" isn't in the vocabulary of most Texas fans. While Brown has returned pride to the program, the memories of the school's last national championship (1970) continue to fade. And, dad gum it, if those @#$&^!!? Sooners can win a national championship, why can't the Longhorns?

This is the season when Brown needs to deliver a team that won't trip over its own shoelaces, a team that will enter November undefeated and on the trail of a national title.

Brown's recruiting crown slipped during February when Oklahoma and Bob Stoops were ranked ahead of UT's class on signing day. That doesn't mean that Brown signed a bunch of Division III-level players. But the gauntlet has definitely been placed in front of Texas by its rivals north of the Red River.

Texas, which for years seemed to be scraping by in the talent department, has enough All-American and all-conference types to compete with the nation's best. If the defense continues to get better and faster, it should be able to match an offense which could be potent if a productive tailback is discovered.

But much of the offense's success will depend on the quarterback. Simms must turn his potential and promise into results on the field. If he does, he should follow in the footsteps of sons of quarterbacks such as Peyton Manning and Brian Griese. And if that happens, figure that Brown's program will break through to the next level—for this season at least—and be in the running for the Rose Bowl and the national championship.

(W.B.)

2000 RESULTS

Louisiana-Lafayette	W	52-10	1-0
Stanford	L	24-27	1-1
Houston	W	48-0	2-1
Oklahoma State	W	42-7	3-1
Oklahoma	L	14-63	3-2
Colorado	W	28-14	4-2
Missouri	W	46-12	5-2
Baylor	W	48-14	6-2
Texas Tech	W	29-17	7-2
Kansas	W	51-16	8-2
Texas A&M	W	43-17	9-2
Oregon (Holiday Bowl)	L	30-35	9-3

Texas A&M

LOCATION College Station, TX
CONFERENCE Big 12 (South)
LAST SEASON 7-5 (.583)
CONFERENCE RECORD 5-3 (3rd)
OFFENSIVE STARTERS RETURNING 6
DEFENSIVE STARTERS RETURNING 5
NICKNAME Aggies
COLORS Maroon & White
HOME FIELD Kyle Field (80,322)
HEAD COACH R.C. Slocum (McNeese St. '67)
RECORD AT SCHOOL 109-37-2 (12 years)
CAREER RECORD 109-37-2 (12 years)
ASSISTANTS Mike Hankwitz (Michigan '70)
Defensive Coordinator/Outside Linebackers
Dino Babers (Hawaii '84)
Offensive Coordinator/Quarterbacks
J.B. Grimes (Northeast Louisiana '70)
Offensive Line
Tam Hollingshead (Sul Ross State '79)
Tight Ends
Ken Rucker (Carson-Newman '76)
Running Backs

Shawn Slocum (Texas A&M '87)
Defensive Backs/Special Teams Coordinator
Allan Weddell (Houston-Victoria '87)
Inside Linebackers
Kevin Sumlin (Purdue '86)
Wide Receivers
Buddy Wyatt (TCU '89)
Defensive Line

TEAM WINS (last 5 yrs.)	**6-9-11-8-7**
FINAL RANK (last 5 yrs.)	**32-22-9-15-25**
2000 FINISH	**Lost to Mississippi State in Independence Bowl.**

COACH AND PROGRAM

Close your eyes and listen to R.C. Slocum talk. Listen to the deep voice, twinged by the Louisiana accent, and you can't help but think, "Yeah, sounds like this guy's a football coach."

And while Slocum's speech patterns make for easy imitation and lead his detractors to declare him an old-school relic, Slocum is far from out of touch. For gosh sakes, he even answers his own e-mail.

And the 57-year-old Slocum is far from out of touch when it comes with knowing what's what. Here is Slocum's take on the revolving door that seems to sweep out about 25 Division I-A coaches each season.

"There does seem to be a little more change these days," he said. "I think it is a sign of the times. Everyone wants a quick fix. We want what we want and we want it now. Young people getting out of college are not as ready to go to work at a low salary and work their way up the ladder. We want fast food, etc. When things don't go as we would like, we want to blame someone."

Slocum is well aware that the days of multi-decade careers (Tom Osborne at Nebraska, Bobby Bowden at Florida State, Joe Paterno at Penn State) are history. Southern Cal gave Paul Hackett three years before he got canned. In the Big 12 Conference, Oklahoma State fired Bob Simmons after six below-average seasons and Baylor coach Kevin Steele is feeling moderate heat after just two seasons in Waco.

And it took Bob Stoops just two seasons at Oklahoma to win a national championship. Fans and administrators, Slocum is saying, seem to think that you can plop the program in the microwave, hit "championship" and DING, pull out the Sears Trophy.

"I realize that there will be those that point to OU and the quick success that coach Stoops has had," Slocum said. "I would argue that the program would have been far better off if they had been more patient with Gary Gibbs. He was a good coach and was charged with 'cleaning' up their program.

"With a new set of rules, Gary's teams were not quite as successful as their fans expected, although they were very competitive as far as I was concerned. I have now faced four different coaches at OU. ... Who knows what would have happened if the program had been stable and Gary remained as coach? I have no doubt their record over the last several years would have been much different."

Slocum said that Baylor had a great coach in Grant Teaff.

"He was respected throughout the country and their program was as well," Slocum said. "Again, there was a group of Baylor fans that grew discontented and thought they should be much better. Eventually Grant grew tired of not being appreciated and resigned. The malcontents got their wish, but the reality is they would love to have the program they once had under Grant. They have now discovered that he was actually doing a great job."

Slocum has been coaching the Aggies for 12 seasons and he has a glittering 109-37-2 record during that time. But the drum beat in College Station has started. Last year's middling 7-5 season included too many negatives:

• The Aggies finished out of the final Associated Press Top 25 poll for just the second time in Slocum's dozen years as the coach.

• The Aggies closed out the season by losing their last three games, including a galling 43-41 Independence Bowl overtime loss to Mississippi State and former A&M coach Jacki Sherrill. The last time A&M closed the season with three consecutive losses was 1970.

• The Independence Bowl loss was A&M's fourth consecutive loss in a bowl game. Under Slocum, the Aggies are 2-8 in bowl games.

• Despite an expanded Kyle Field (80,650), A&M lost two home games (to Colorado and to Oklahoma) for the first time since 1985.

"I was very disappointed with the season," Slocum said. "Going 7-5 is certainly not up to the standard that I expect for Texas A&M. It was very close to being much better but it was not. We an unusual number of injuries that impacted our team. Few teams have enough depth to sustain the number of injuries we had this past season. Oklahoma was a great example of how important it is to stay healthy. They did not lose a starter on either side of the ball."

Oklahoma is also a great example for Slocum's detractors. The Sooners reclaimed their seat at the championship table in just two seasons under a young, firebrand coach. The Aggies won their only national championship in 1939, they haven't been ranked No. 1 since the 1957 season and they haven't gone through a regular season undefeated since 1992.

"Yes, I do feel pressure but maybe not the kind that you imagine," Slocum said. "I don't feel the pressure of job security. I am a good football coach and I will be able to coach for as long as I want somewhere. I have had many opportunities to leave A&M but have felt that there is still work to be done here. I am proud of the progress that has been made but there is still a lot to be accomplished."

Slocum says that one of his team's annual goals is the national championship. But to win it all, the Aggies must first win the Big 12 South Division title (they've done that twice), the Big 12 championship (once). But with Oklahoma and Texas both top five teams this season, the Aggies don't look to be anything more than a dark horse choice.

"We're not a team that's going to dazzle anybody with our talent level," Slocum said. "But I do think there's enough talent there if we can keep guys healthy and everybody will be in great shape coming back in August. If we get everybody hitting on the same cylinder and have a little luck in keeping guys healthy, then we can have a pretty good team. Anything short of that, and we're not going to be a real good team."

Not exactly the kind of comments that will inspire the faithful. Slocum, though, is being honest. His team lost three of its top playmakers—linebacker Jason Glenn ran out of eligibility while wide receiver Robert Ferguson and fullback Ja'Mar Toombs both left school early to make themselves eligible for the NFL draft. If Ferguson and Toombs were still in school, the Aggies' offense probably would be ranked on a level with the Oklahoma and Texas attacks.

Slocum also had to spend the off-season reworking his coaching staff. For the third time in the last four years, A&M has three new assistant coaches. Pete Hoener (Arizona Cardinals), Steve Kragthorpe (Buffalo Bills) and Larry Kirksey (Detroit Lions) all left for NFL assistants jobs. Dino Babers is the new offensive coordinator (replacing Kragthorpe), Kevin Sumlin takes over for Kirksey as wide receivers coach and Ken Rucker replaces Hoener as running backs coach.

Slocum, though, believes that the defections and changes are just part of college football in the 21st century. And he prefers to look at his program as half full instead of half empty. The positives far outweigh the negatives.

"There were three times in the '90s when we finished in the top 10. We need to get back to that level of play and have some luck," Slocum said. "One year, we won 12 straight games. With a little luck we could have played for [the national championship] that year.

"We will eventually get the stars in the right alignment and get our [national championship]. It would be a tragedy to be chronically unhappy as a fan until that time comes, and I don't think that would be fair to our players either."

2001 SCHEDULE

Sept.	1	McNeese State
	6	@Wyoming
	22	Oklahoma State
	29	Notre Dame
Oct.	6	Baylor
	13	@Colorado
	20	@Kansas State
	27	Iowa State
Nov.	3	@Texas Tech
	10	@Oklahoma
	23	Texas

QUARTERBACKS

One of the major complaints from fans during the Slocum Era has been this: The only way his quarterbacks could move the offense was with option pitches or handoffs. The passing game was always a work in progress. It took a former minor-league baseball player to finally get the Aggie moving through the air.

Junior **Mark Farris** (6-2, 206) spent five seasons in the Pittsburgh Pirates' farm system before giving up his baseball dream and joining the Aggies in 1999. Last August, the 25-year-old won the A&M quarterback job during preseason workouts. Farris showed that Slocum made the right choice by setting a single-season school record for passing yards (2,551) and total offense.

Farris completed 208-of-347 passes for 10 touchdowns and nine interceptions. One of those interceptions, though, was critical. His fourth-quarter pass against top-ranked Oklahoma was picked off by Torrance Marshall and returned for the game-winning touchdown, preventing the Aggies from springing the season's biggest upset.

"My emphasis is on getting better," said Farris, who signed with A&M in 1994 before trying baseball. "If you stay the same, you're going to get passed. And to be honest, I think I could have played a lot better last year.

"While I'm 26, it was my first year as a starting quarterback in college football. Hopefully, I can build on last year, maybe throw for 3,000 yards this year and win more games. That's my objective."

Farris was impressive during spring drills.

"Mark Farris really improved this spring," Slocum said. "Last year at this time he had not played but a few plays. I expect bigger things out of him this year. He can be a real good quarterback for us this year. He needs to continue to study football and become better from a knowledge standpoint."

Junior **Vance Smith** (6-4, 226) will be Farris' backup. Last season, he saw mop-up duty in three games, completing 1-of-3 passes. For his career, Smith has completed 6-of-17 passes for 97 yards and one touchdown.

RUNNING BACKS

Ja'Mar Toombs was asked to shift to fullback last season. He gave the Aggies a powerful runner at that position, gaining 355 yards and scoring a team-high 14 touchdowns. But his decision to pass up his senior season for the NFL draft left A&M without a power runner in the backfield. Slocum is particularly concerned about his team's ability to shove the ball into the end zone from close range.

"That's [scoring in the red zone] something that is a point of emphasis," Slocum said. "Last year we had some problems getting it in. That's something that we need to work on and that is something we are going to work on this spring."

Former walk-on **Stacy Jones**, a 5-11, 229-pound junior, was the only other fullback with significant experience, so the coaching staff decided to shift some of the team's tailbacks to fullback. Junior **Joe Weber** (6-0, 233), who gained 444 yards and averaged 4.4 yards a carry last year as a tailback, will probably be the starter at fullback.

"Joe made the move this spring and can develop into a good fullback," Slocum said. "He needs to continue to work on his blocking. He has good hands and good running skills."

Sophomore **Richard Whitaker** (5-10, 197), the team's leading rusher last season with 455 yards (5.4 yards per carry and six touchdowns) will get the bulk of the carries at tailback. Redshirt freshman **Keith Joseph** (6-2, 221), whose running style has been likened to Eric Dickerson, provides a bigger option at tailback. Slocum said that Joseph had a good spring and "demonstrated that he will help the team."

Last season, Joseph was impressive playing for the scout team.

A&M averaged 146 yards per game and 3.8 yards per carry. Not bad, but not that good. In fact, for the last two seasons, the Aggies haven't been a dominant running team.

"We've got to be able to run the football better than we did last year," Slocum said. "We're making a big emphasis on that."

WIDE RECEIVERS/TIGHT ENDS

Robert Ferguson made a significant impact as a junior college transfer. He led the Big 12 in receiving, with 58 catches for 885 yards and six touchdowns. However, after just one season as a Division I-A receiver, Ferguson decided to skip his senior season for the NFL draft. He was taken in the second round by the Green Bay Packers.

The Aggies also lost their third-leading receiver as Chris Taylor ran out of eligibility. He too was drafted, by the Pittsburgh Steelers in the seventh round.

The Aggies have four experienced receivers—seniors **Bethel Johnson** (5-11, 188) and **Mickey Jones** (5-9, 178) plus juniors **Dwain Goynes** (5-10, 179) and **Greg Porter** (6-4, 228).

Johnson was the team's second-leading receiver, with 42 catches for 440 yards. However, the Aggies are still waiting for the talented Johnson to have a breakout season.

"We've got to have some guys step up there," Slocum said. "Bethel is showing some signs of maturing. Hopefully he'll step up as a senior."

Goynes, who averaged 25.7 yards on his six receptions last season, had a solid spring. If he continues to develop, he should provide a legitimate deep threat.

"Dwain's a guy that is very fast," Slocum said. "He's probably the fastest guy on our football team. He's someone we're going to try to get the ball to. He showed some signs of making some plays, he's a tough guy and I am really pleased with the way he is developing as a player.

"With the loss of Robert Ferguson, we need a receiver with big-play potential. Dwain's speed makes him a dangerous player. He's been catching the ball much better. He's maturing as a player. We have plans of finding ways to get the ball into his hands."

In A&M's offense, the tight end position is not much more than a glorified offensive lineman. Last season, incumbent tight ends **Michael de la Torre**, a 6-5, 244-pound junior, and **Lonnie Madoison**, a 6-3, 236-pound senior, combined for four catches that totaled 37 yards.

OFFENSIVE LINE

The Aggies return three starters from a unit that was surprisingly solid last season. While A&M struggled to consistently run the ball, the offensive line did a good job protecting Farris. He was sacked just 10 times out of 347 pass attempts.

The only senior lost from last year's unit was guard Chris Valletta. However, the offensive line lost a projected starter when senior Tango McCauley (6-3, 288) was dismissed from the team during the spring.

"He had a serious violation of team rules and I could not allow him to remain on the squad," Slocum said. "I am really sorry for the young man's sake and it is certainly a loss to our team. We are thin at the tackle position and he was one of our most experienced linemen."

The anchor of the line is senior **Seth McKinney** (6-3, 290). He's a steady blocker and leader who has All-America potential.

Junior **Taylor Whitley** (6-4, 305) is a returning starter at right guard while junior **Michael Mahan** (6-6, 299) is the starter at left tackle. Mahan had decided to give up football after last season because of heart irregularity but returned in spring practice to earn a starting job.

Sophomore **Andre Brooks** (6-4, 298) is projected to start at right tackle while junior **Billy Yates** (6-1, 292) is listed as first team at left guard.

Sophomores **Alan Reuber** (6-6, 289), **Britt Lively** (6-5, 311) and **John Kirk** (6-4, 282) plus redshirt freshmen **Kasey Cheshier** (6-4, 279) and **Geoff Hangarter** (6-5, 287) are the reserves.

2000 STATISTICS

Rushing offense	146.4	59
Passing offense	235.3	35
Total offense	381.6	49
Scoring offense	27.9	46
Net Punting	34.2	69
Punt returns	11.7	31
Kickoff returns	20.1	48
Rushing defense	106.3	22
Passing efficiency defense	109.3	36
Total defense	321.6	25
Scoring defense	17.8	10
Turnover margin	+6	28

Last column is ranking among Division I-A teams.

KICKERS

Terrence Kitchens will be difficult to replace. After an inconsistent junior season during which he missed eight field goals, he came back as a senior to make 15-of-18 field goal tries. His 83.3 percent success rate was a school single-season record.

Slocum is confident that redshirt freshman **Chris Sims** (6-0, 183) will step forward as the team's kicker. Also in the picture is sophomore **Cody Scates** (6-0, 180), who handled the team's punting last season and will fill that role again this season.

DEFENSIVE LINE

There is one returning starter up front in the Aggies' 3-4 defensive scheme. Nose tackle Ron Evans and right defensive end Ronald Flemons must be replaced, but actually there will be three new starters on the line. Evans and Flemons were both drafted—Evans by the Buffalo Bills in the third round and Flemons by the Atlanta Falcons in the seventh.

Junior **Ty Warren** (6-4, 300) started the last eight games of last season at defensive end. He tied for the team lead in tackles for loss with 16. However, Warren has been moved from the edge to the middle, where he's projected to be the starter at nose tackle. His size and quickness should make him a terror for opposing centers and guards.

Redshirt freshman **Marcus Jasmin** (6-4, 323) is projected as Warren's backup. Senior **Evan Perroni** (6-5, 265), who was Warren's backup last season, is slated to start at left defensive end. Sophomore **Linnis Smith** (6-4, 250) will start at right defensive end.

There is a troubling lack of depth on the defensive front. Smith was slated to spend last season as a redshirt, but injuries forced him to start playing toward the end of the season. And, there are only five scholarship defensive linemen on the roster.

Senior **Rocky Bernard** (6-3, 294) is this unit's most experienced player. He is listed as the backup at both end positions. Bernard sat out the 2000 season as a redshirt after suffering a knee injury during preseason practice. He was limited in his work during spring drills.

"He is actually behind where I hoped he would be at this time," Slocum said. "He had a major injury and it has not responded as well as we would have liked. He needs to have a great summer of rehab. He can be a big help to us. This time last year, I thought he was perhaps our best defensive player."

LINEBACKERS

Next to Penn State, Texas A&M is a school synonymous with producing quality linebackers. This season, the Aggies will have to crank up the production line in order to replace three of the four starters from last year's unit—Roylin Bradley, Jason Glenn and Cornelius Anthony. Glenn was chosen by the Detroit Lions in the sixth round of the NFL draft.

"Linebacker is a big position for us in terms of transition, both inside and outside," Slocum said.

The lone returning starter is junior **Brian Gamble** (6-2, 227). He is a blue-collar player, a son of coach who studies the game and loves to play. Last season he led the team in tackles and was second in sacks. Gamble's heart and desire outweigh his overall ability, so in some ways he resembles Dat Nguyen.

Glenn, who suffered a season-ending knee injury in the Aggies' loss to Oklahoma, was the linebacking unit's playmaker; he led the team with 16 tackles for loss and also had five sacks. Finding someone to replace Glenn's dynamic effort will be difficult.

Gamble mans one of the inside linebacking positions. The other inside linebacker will be either sophomore **Jared Morris** (6-3, 240) or senior **Harold Robertson** (6-3, 217). Morris, though, lacks foot speed while Robertson has lots of ability but has been slowed by injuries. Also in the picture at the inside spots are senior **Amon Simon** (6-1, 224) and redshirt freshman **LeBrandon Shepard** (6-1, 235). Coaches are high on Shepard because he plays with a lot of attitude.

Senior **Christian Rodriguez** (6-2, 235) and sophomore **Jarrod Penright** (6-3, 232) are expected to start at the outside linebacker posts. Rodriguez goes by "C-Rod" because he's a distant relative of Texas Rangers' shortstop Alex Rodriguez. A&M coaches hope that "C-Rod" finally starts playing with some confidence during his senior year.

The reserves on the outside are sophomore **Everett Smith** (6-2, 215) and junior **Jesse Hunnicutt** (6-3, 237). Hunnicutt, a converted running back, could give Rodriguez a run for the starting spot during preseason drills.

DEFENSIVE BACKS

Despite fielding a group of unproven defensive backs, the Aggies survived last season. A&M finished sixth in the Big 12 and 35th nationally in pass defense. The Aggies allowed 13 touchdown passes and picked off 18 passes.

The only starter who must be replaced is free safety Michael Jameson, who finished the season strong and was later chosen in the sixth round of the NFL draft by the Cleveland Browns. He will be replaced by senior **Jay Brooks** (5-9, 190), who as a reserve cornerback made his presence felt by making big plays.

"We've got a lot of guys who are capable of being playmakers," Brooks said. "The key is for them to gain the confidence and to take the attitude that they are definitely going to get the job done."

The returning starters at cornerback are sophomore **Sean Weston** (5-9, 163) and junior **Sammy Davis** (6-0, 180). Weston tied for the team lead in pass breakups with 15 while Davis is regarded as the Aggies' top defender; most of the time opposing quarterbacks threw to the other side of the field.

The cornerback reserves are sophomores—**Adam Black** (5-10, 173) and **Jonte Buhl** (5-9, 163). Junior **Terrence Keil** (5-11, 196) is the returning starter at strong safety.

Last season, he had four interceptions and 57 tackles, and was second on the team in both categories. The backups at safety are senior **Wes Bautovich** (6-2, 210) at strong and sophomore **Dawon Gentry** (5-11, 189) at free.

PUNTERS

Scates became the fourth freshman in A&M history to average more than 40 yards a punt. As a freshman, he had little difficulty in replacing departed All-American Shane Lechler, the best punter in NCAA history.

Scates, who also handled kickoffs, averaged 40.2 yards on 52 punts. He had one punt blocked. More than half of his punts resulted in fair catches (11) or were downed inside the 20-yard line (17).

SPECIAL TEAMS

"The biggest area of concern is at the punt returner and kick returner areas," Slocum said.

Wide receiver Taylor was steady but unspectacular handling punt returns (7.4-yard average, no touchdowns). His likely replacement will be senior wide receivers Jones or Johnson.

The Aggies' top kickoff returners are back. Tailback Whitaker averaged 21.7 yards per return while speedy wideout Goynes averaged 22.2. The problem with using those two to return kicks is that both will be counted on to be key producers in the running and passing games.

A&M has two experienced deep snappers in junior **Chance Pearce** (6-2, 223) and sophomore **Don Muhlbach** (6-4, 255). Senior defensive back Bautovich is back to hold for extra points and field goals.

RECRUITING CLASS

Slocum and A&M are battling the perception that they've come a third wheel in the Big 12's South Division. Texas has been in the top five with its last three classes and Oklahoma had a top five recruiting class this season, sparked by the Sooners' national championship.

"Sure, Oklahoma had a good year," Slocum said. "Texas did, too. But if you're at any one of the schools in this league, you'll get some players. Maybe we were accustomed for awhile to one or two schools getting all the guys. The Big 12 has made it a lot more competitive. Fans haven't adjusted to it."

Slocum expects three areas where freshmen can have an impact in 2001: wide receiver, the secondary and offensive line.

"We have some guys in this class of offensive linemen who, because of their size and ability, could step up and lend some depth to the line," Slocum said.

Two teammates from Jacksonville (Texas) High School are at the top of the signees list—**Jami Hightower** (6-5 305) and **Quentin Holman** (6-2, 310). **Cole Smith** (6-4, 280)—the younger brother of Aggies' backup quarterback Vance—and **Dominique Steamer** (6-5, 300) are the other offensive linemen who could wind up playing this season.

The top first-year defensive backs are **Jaxson Appel** (5-11, 195), **Byron Jones** (5-10, 180), **Ronald Jones** (5-11, 175) and **Jarvis Mays** (6-3, 185). Freshmen wide receivers who could see action are **Terrence Murphy** (6-1, 190), **John Roberson** (5-10, 175), **Bryant Singleton** (6-0, 175), **Terrence Thomas** (5-11, 185) and **Jesse Woods** (6-4, 185).

The most decorated of the new receivers was probably Roberson, a prep All-American pick by *USA Today* and *PrepStar*. He caught 64 passes for 15 touchdowns last season at Bay City (Texas) High School, where he was a first-team Class 4-A All-State selection.

"John is the type of player who makes things happen when he touches the football," Slocum said. "He can take a short pass and turn it into something big. He averaged over 23 yards per catch and is a difference maker."

Singleton didn't have near the numbers while playing for Ball High School in Galveston, Texas (21 catches for 419 yards and six touchdowns) but Slocum likes his potential.

"Bryant is another big-play receiver," Slocum said. "He played in a wishbone offense and didn't post the numbers of some of the other prospects, but we think he is a player."

On signing day, A&M coaches were pleased to get a signed scholarship back from **Derek Farmer**, a 6-0, 190-pounder from Tyler (Texas) Lee High School. Farmer was the only running back the Aggies signed. Farmer had considered signing with Alabama before changing his mind.

Farmer was a prep All-American as chosen by *PrepStar*, and he earned second-team Class 5A all-state honors as a senior after rushing for 1,800 yards and 21 touchdowns. He produced 1,934 yards and 18 scores as a junior.

"Derek is an excellent running back," Slocum said. "Every time you see him run, he gets positive yards. He can get the tough inside yards and yet has the speed to break some big gainers."

BLUE RIBBON ANALYSIS

OFFENSE	B+
SPECIAL TEAMS	B
DEFENSE	B
INTANGIBLES	C+

Texas A&M optimists point out that Oklahoma went 7-5 and suffered a two-point loss in the Independence Bowl before going 13-0 and winning the 2000 national championship. The Aggies, remember, went 7-5 last year with the final game a two-point loss in Shreveport.

"College football is a crazy game," Aggies junior linebacker Gamble said. "Anything can happen. We have to start preparing that way, preparing for anything that happens down the road. If luck comes our way, then we could be that next team to win the national championship."

Ah, youth.

True enough, the Aggies have the makings of a solid offense if they can find some receivers to make plays. However, the defense has several question marks in the front seven. The lack of depth on the defensive line is a major concern.

The schedule does A&M few favors. After a gimme home opener against McNeese State, the Aggies travel to Wyoming for a dicey Thursday night game. On Sept. 29, Notre Dame visits College Station. The Big 12 road games are all troublesome—Colorado, Kansas State, Texas Tech (always a problem for the Aggies) and Oklahoma. Winning all four of those games would appear to be impossible.

After consecutive 5-3 Big 12 records and seasons that ended with bowl losses, the Aggies find themselves on a slippery slope. If they don't get a grip, the whispers about the need to change coaches will increase in volume.

(W.B.)

2000 RESULTS

Notre Dame	L	10-24	0-1
Wyoming	W	51-3	1-1
UTEP	W	45-17	2-1
Texas Tech	W	33-15	3-1
Colorado	L	19-26	3-2
Baylor	W	24-0	4-2
Iowa State	W	30-7	5-2
Kansas State	W	26-10	6-2
Oklahoma State	W	21-16	7-2
Oklahoma	L	31-35	7-3
Texas	L	17-43	7-4
Mississippi St. (Ind. Bowl)	L	41-43	7-5

Texas Tech

LOCATION	**Lubbock, TX**
CONFERENCE	**Big 12 (South)**
LAST SEASON	**7-6 (.538)**
CONFERENCE RECORD	**3-5 (4th)**
OFFENSIVE STARTERS RETURNING	**8**
DEFENSIVE STARTERS RETURNING	**4**
NICKNAME	**Red Raiders**
COLORS	**Scarlet & Black**
HOME FIELD	**Jones Stadium (50,500)**
HEAD COACH	**Mike Leach (BYU '83)**
RECORD AT SCHOOL	**7-6 (1 year)**
CAREER RECORD	**7-6 (1 year)**
ASSISTANTS	

Greg McMackin (Southern Oregon '69)
Defensive Coordinator
Manny Matsakis (Capital University '84)
Assistant Head Coach/Special teams

Art Briles (Houston '77)
Running Backs
Sonny Dykes (Texas Tech '93)
Wide Receivers
Dana Holgorsen (Iowa Wesleyan '93)
Inside Receivers
Ron Harris (Cal Lutheran '80)
Defensive Line
Robert Anae (BYU '85)
Offensive Line
Ruffin McNeill (East Carolina '80)
Linebackers
Dave Brown (Michigan '76)
Secondary

TEAM WINS (last 5 yrs.) **7-6-7-6-7**
FINAL RANK (last 5 yrs.) **30-52-42-37-50**
2000 FINISH **Lost to E.Carolina in Gallery Bowl.**

COACH AND PROGRAM

Mike Leach and his Texas Tech football program are battling perception and reality. The perception is that, in the Lone Star state, the Red Raiders' program is a distant third behind Texas and Texas A&M.

The reality is that in the Big 12 Conference's South Division, Texas Tech gets to line up against the defending national champions when Oklahoma comes to Lubbock on Nov. 17.

"I believe the Big 12 is the best football conference in America," Leach said. "There are no easy games on the league schedule. Every week is a battle."

All that Texas Tech can do is spend money to try to make its athletic department competitive. Tech's budget of $19.9 million ranks eighth in the Big 12 (Texas is first with $42.2 million, Oklahoma is third at $27.4 million and Texas A&M is fifth at $26 million). But in hiring Leach and his staff, Tech athletic director Gerald Myers spared no expense. And Tech's recruiting budget is $200,000, more than triple the $63,000 that was budgeted for recruiting in Spike Dykes' final season.

Tech even showed it was serious about men's basketball when it got the college hoops world to take notice by hiring Bob Knight. Lubbock figures to be on the itinerary of more than a few national writers. What Leach and the Red Raiders must hope is that they'll play well enough to piggyback on some of that media attention.

"I'd just say to all the fans who are itching for basketball to start that they're going to have a fun fall, too," junior quarterback **Kliff Kingsbury** said. "We're going to put on a good show for them. We're capable of generating plenty of excitement on the football field, too."

Leach's first season didn't generate quite the excitement that Myers and the school leaders hoped. Sure, Tech finished with a 7-5 regular-season record that earned a bid to the inaugural galleryfurniture.com Bowl (which wound up as a 40-34 loss to East Carolina of Conference USA).

Known as a Mad Professor of the passing game, Leach wasn't able to get the Red Raiders moving the ball like he had done in offensive coordinator stops at Kentucky and Oklahoma. Tech averaged 296 yards passing per game and averaged 25.3 points per game. But the 2001 season was disjointed because of a poor running game and inconsistencies on the offensive line. Plus, Kingsbury struggled to master Leach's complicated playbook.

Tech's defense was the team's strength last season. In seven victories, the Red Raiders had three shutouts and allowed a total of 26 points in three of the other four victories (the only Tech victory in a shootout was a 45-39 decision over Kansas). However, in the team's six losses, Tech allowed 33, 56, 28, 29, 28 and 40 points.

"The first two years I was here, we lost games we shouldn't have," said senior strong safety **Kevin Curtis**, an All-America candidate. "Last year, we beat the teams we were supposed to, but we didn't beat any of the better teams. This year we have to do it and put it all together. This up and down stuff won't cut."

True enough. But the defense must replace seven starters. In an effort to counter those personnel losses, defensive coordinator Greg McMackin did some tinkering in the spring. In addition to the team's 4-3 base defensive package, McMakin plans on playing a "45" scheme, a 4-2-5 that will get three safeties on the field in passing situations.

With a year's experience as a starter, Kingsbury should make progress in Leach's offense. He's got a talented group of receivers. The key will be improving the running game.

"I think we need to polish up the running game," Leach said. "The thing we were up against last year was we didn't have a consistent group of offensive linemen."

2001 SCHEDULE

Sept.	8	New Mexico
	15	@UTEP
	22	North Texas (Texas Stadium)
	29	@Texas
Oct.	6	Kansas
	13	Kansas State
	20	@Nebraska
	27	@Baylor
Nov.	3	Texas A&M
	10	@Oklahoma State
	17	Oklahoma

QUARTERBACKS

You won't find this weight-loss program being sold during a 30-minute infomercial and you won't see it any health magazines. But Kingsbury can tell you all about the Big 12 Diet.

Last season, his first as a starter, Kingsbury not only attempted 585 passes in Leach's fling-and-wing offense, he was sacked 30 times. All of that action during a 13-game season caused him to lose more than 12 pounds. By season's end, he was down to 188 pounds on his 6-4 frame.

"Yeah, I'd like to see him get a little heavier, but with some of it, nature's just got to take its course," Leach said. "He did seem a little thin at the end of last year."

This season, Kingsbury hopes to open the season weighing closer to 220 pounds. Sure, he's hitting the weight room. But he's also trying to eat like an offensive lineman. During the off-season he ate a peanut butter and jelly sandwich between meals and tried to eat four meals a day.

"I can use all the good weight I can get," Kingsbury said. "One of these days in the future, I may not have any trouble putting on the pounds, but right now, it has been hard to keep the weight on."

As long as the pounds don't slow him down, Kingsbury should benefit from his continued exposure to Leach's system. Last season, Kingsbury completed 61.9 percent of his passes for 3,418 yards, 21 touchdowns and 17 interceptions. Kingsbury led the Big 12 in passing yardage and touchdown passes and was second to Oklahoma's Josh Heupel in completion percentage. He was also second to Heupel and 10th in the nation in total offense, averaging 286.4 yards per game.

At times, the offense looked as explosive as Leach envisioned; at other times, it struggled as Kingsbury tried to sort out the multiple receiver sets while dodging opposing pass rushers. All those interceptions hurt his passing efficiency rating; Kingsbury was just seventh in the Big 12 in that stat (117.0).

"The off-season was a much-needed rest," said Kingsbury, who completed 30.1 passes per game last year, tops in the nation. "I was kind of beat up, but I feel good now. There was a lot of healing and a lot of gaining weight back that I lost at the end of the season. Now I'm just trying to get stronger and better mentally."

Kingsbury's backup is sophomore **B.J. Symons** (6-2, 204). He appeared in five games last season, completing just 8-of-25 passes for 56 yards.

Should the offense falter behind Kingsbury's leadership, Tech fans will probably start clamoring to see redshirt freshman **Jason Winn** (6-2, 185). The Granada Hills, Calif. product was one of Tech's top signees last season.

Redshirt freshman **Sonny Cumbie** (6-4, 202) also showed some positive signs during spring drills.

RUNNING BACKS

Raise your hand if you think Ricky Williams has been around longer than Dick Clark. It's particularly puzzling to fans around the country who confuse Tech's **Ricky Williams** with Texas' Heisman Trophy winning running back whose final season was 1998.

A 5-9, 203-pound senior, Williams could have bolted after a so-so 2000 season. After a 1999 season that was a wash because of a knee injury, Williams was granted an extra year of eligibility. Reasoning that he needed another season to strengthen his knee and prove that he's healthy before heading to the NFL, Williams decided to spend a final season in Lubbock.

Last season, Williams gained 421 yards on 127 carries with 52 carries for 228 yards. However, he did not have the old explosiveness that made him a 1,000-yard rusher as a sophomore in 1998.

In the spring, a healthy and heavier (an extra 10 pounds) Williams had 25 carries for 143 yards in three scrimmages. The old Ricky Williams appears to be back.

"He's in better shape, and he's healthier," Leach said. "You can tell he's quicker than he was."

"The past spring was really the first time I've seen him look like the old Ricky Williams," Kingsbury said. "It's awesome to have him back at full strength. Probably the biggest thing he brings to this team is his leadership and his passion for the game. Having him back will really make a huge difference."

Shaud Williams decided to leave the program and in late May he announced plans to transfer to Alabama. Williams was the Big 12 Offensive Freshman of the Year in 1999 when he gained 658 yards on 112 carries during Spike Dykes' last season. Williams wasn't happy with his role in Leach's pass-oriented attack and he decided to transfer. After sitting out a season, he'll have two years of eligibility remaining.

Williams' transfer options were limited by some stern restrictions imposed by Leach. Williams couldn't transfer to another Big 12 school, a school within the states of Texas and New Mexico and a school appearing on the Tech schedule the next two seasons.

"We wish Shaud the best," Leach said after Williams announced he was leaving. "I'll do anything I can to help him, but we have a team policy with regard to releases. We're not running a free-agent camp."

In Leach's four-wide receiver offense, there's not a lot of room for running backs. Tech has just six players on its roster, including Ricky Williams, listed as running backs.

Sophomore **Foy Munlin** (6-0, 210) had 13 carries for 55 yards last season, while sophomore **Wes Welker** (5-9, 185), who is listed as a starting wide receiver, had six carries for 72 yards. He's a player who can use his quickness and speed as a receiver, running back and return man.

Sophomores **Kenny Hogan** (5-11, 220) and **Clay Stephens** (5-11, 205) plus redshirt freshman **Trevor McKenzie** (5-8, 175) are also in the backfield mix.

Stephens is the only player on the roster listed as a fullback.

WIDE RECEIVERS/TIGHT ENDS

Last season, Texas A&M had the Big 12's leading receiver in Robert Ferguson, who was in his first season at the Division I-A level after spending two seasons playing junior college ball.

Texas Tech thinks it has this season's version of Ferguson—a receiver capable of leading the league in receptions—in junior **Anton Paige** (6-5, 205). Paige was able to join Texas Tech for spring practice and took over as the starter at flanker.

"He really has been impressive," Kingsbury said. "He's about 6-foot-6, and for the way he moves, it's just amazing. He's going to be a big asset, and he's a great guy who really fits in well with the team. He also has great hands and will be a fun guy to throw it to."

Paige started his career at Kansas, where he redshirted in 1998 and played sparingly (four catches for 49 yards) in 1999. Last season, he played at Northwest Mississippi Community College, where he caught 64 passes for 1,237 yards and 16 touchdowns to earn honorable mention NJCAA All-American honors. Recruiting guru Max Emfinger ranked him the ninth-best junior college prospect in the country.

Paige's arrival should ease the departure of Tim Baker and Derek Dorris, who combined for 125 catches and 16 touchdowns last season.

Leach said that **Wes Welker** (5-9, 185) was "one of the best true freshmen in the country" last season. He's listed as the starting inside wide receiver. Last season, he had 26 catches for 334 yards.

Senior **Darrell Jones** (6-3, 195) is the starter at split end. Last season, he had 27 catches for 361 yards. Sophomore **Mickey Peters** (6-3, 194), who moved from quarterback before last season, is listed as the tight end.

Seniors **Cole Roberts** (6-6, 245) and **King Scovell** (5-11, 184), sophomore **Carlos Francis** (5-9, 188) and redshirt freshman **Nehemiah Glover** (5-8, 165) are the receiver reserves.

Sophomore **Chris Garner** (6-3, 233), a former defensive lineman, was impressive during spring drills after being moved to tight end. A walk-on, his main role will be as a blocker when Tech goes to double tight-end formations.

OFFENSIVE LINE

For an offensive line that struggled most of last year, the fact that three starters—junior tackle **Paul Erickson** (6-5, 284), sophomore center **Toby Cecil** (6-4, 262) and junior guard **Rex Richards** (6-4, 299)—missed spring practice as they recovered from off-season surgeries is not the kind of news to make an offensive line coach feel good.

But Robert Anae decided to look at the glass as half full. The absence of three starters meant that Anae was able to look other players, which he believes will improve the offensive line depth.

Last year, Tech used eight different starting combinations on the offensive line, allowed 30 quarterback sacks and could run block well enough to average only 2.6 yards per attempt. The instability was caused by injuries. Only Erickson, Cecil and Richards were able to start 10 games last season. On top of that, the Red Raiders' offensive linemen spent much of the season trying to master new blocking schemes.

"I can't say enough about the progress we've made," Anae said. "I say that if only because our guys made every practice and every drill with no new injuries. I'm also not having to put out five spot fires this year on most plays. Now it's like one fire every other play. Now we just have more [practice] to go."

In addition to the three starters, sophomore tackle **Casey Keck** (6-3, 247) and senior guard **Matt Heider** (6-5, 305) are back.

Senior **Lance Williams** (6-2, 302) is battling Richards for the right guard spot. Junior **Jason May** (6-4, 295) also got plenty of action during the spring while filling in for Erickson. Two redshirt freshmen—**Dylan Gandy** (6-4, 260) and **Daniel Loper** (6-7, 280)—are expected to see action as backups at center and tackle, respectively.

"We're definitely coming together as a group," Heider said. "We term last year as a starting point, which is what it was. Last year, we had to focus on a lot of assignment stuff. Now, it's second nature to us so we're able to focus more on technique than assignment."

2000 STATISTICS

Rushing offense	66.4	113
Passing offense	296.2	11
Total offense	362.6	65
Scoring offense	25.2	61
Net Punting	34.8	50
Punt returns	10.7	39
Kickoff returns	17.9	95
Rushing defense	156.6	67
Passing efficiency defense	97.8	10
Total defense	320.7	24
Scoring defense	19.8	30
Turnover margin	+6	30

Last column is ranking among Division I-A teams.

KICKERS

Replacing the steady Chris Birkholz is a top priority. Last season, Birkholz made 12-of-19 field goals and missed just 1-of-36 extra point attempts.

The top two candidates for the kicking job are junior **Clinton Greathouse** (5-11, 201) and sophomore **Wich Brenner** (6-2, 225). Greathouse handled most of the punting last year and is first in line to handle those duties again this year. Brenner has a strong leg and handled most of the kickoffs last season, but he was hampered by a hip injury during spring practice.

Freshman **Ryan Bishop** (5-8, 190) is a straight-on kicker. He's accurate, but there's concern about his ability to kick from long distance.

During one of the spring games, Tech conducted kicker auditions, with six candidates trying extra points and field goals. The top survivor was **Brandon Stroud** (6-2, 194), a sophomore transfer from Tyler (Texas) Junior College. He made a 48-yard field goal and an extra-point attempt.

DEFENSIVE LINE

Half of last year's unit must be replaced. Starting tackle Kris Kocurek and defensive end Devin Lemons were steady producers up front.

Junior tackle **Robert Wyatt** (6-1, 305) could step up to become an all-conference caliber player. However, he missed spring practice to recover from a knee injury.

Junior defensive end **Aaron Hunt** (6-3, 239) is an undersized defensive end, but he's an effective pass rusher. Junior **Josh Ratliff** (6-3, 240) is expected to be Hunt's opposite number at defensive end.

The talent and depth of the defensive line should be improved by the return of sophomore **Lamont Anderson** (6-1, 283). He suffered a broken leg last September. Anderson is an effective run stopper.

"Based on what we knew two weeks ago at start of spring, yes, it's a surprise to have him back," Tech defensive line coach Ron Harris said. "Anything we can get out of him from here on out is just a plus. Now we just have to guard against being too greedy and wanting to get him back all the way. We still need to control his reps."

Junior Zeno McCoy, who was a solid backup last season and who was projected to be a starter this season, quit the team during spring practice.

The backups at tackle should be juniors **Josh Page** (6-2, 277), sophomore **Jeremy Milam** (6-2, 272), redshirt freshman **John Sellers** (6-4, 245), a walk-on, and sophomore **Beau Radney** (6-3, 304), a converted offensive lineman.

Junior **Rodney McKinney** (6-2, 285), a transfer from Mississippi Delta Community College, should add depth in the middle. Tech swiped McKinney from Southeastern Conference country. McKinney—originally from Tuscaloosa, Ala.—was recruited by Auburn in high school and by Alabama, Auburn and Mississippi State a year ago. He was a first-team Mississippi junior college all-state pick last season, when he made five sacks.

LINEBACKERS

Junior **Laurence Flugence** (6-1, 240) had an outstanding season. His 156 tackles led the Big 12 in tackles. As evidenced by his statistics, he is a sure tackler who usually gets his man.

The main concerns are replacing the players who flanked Flugence—John Norman and Dorian Pitts. Junior **Rusty Bucy** (6-1, 226) and senior **Jonathan Hawkins** (5-11, 224) are listed as the starters who will replace those two.

Hawkins was sidelined after two games with a broken ankle and Bucy has been battling hamstring problems.

The linebacking unit got a boost during the spring when redshirt freshman **Mike Smith** (6-2, 195) returned after suffering a broken left wrist last November. Sophomores **Toby Shain** (5-11, 241) and **Jason Wesley** (5-11, 201) are the backups.

DEFENSIVE BACKS

Senior **Kevin Curtis** (6-2, 209) was second on the team in tackles last season with 121. He considered declaring himself eligible for the NFL draft, but his decision to return for this season solidified a young secondary. Curtis plays strong safety with a nose for the ball.

The rest of the secondary candidates have more experience on special teams than they do covering opposing receivers.

Seniors **C.J. Johnson** (5-10, 190) and **Ronald Ross** (5-11, 193) should start at the corners. Ross moved up to the starting spot during the spring when sophomore Eric Cooper (5-11, 198) sat out spring drills to concentrate on academics, as did senior safety **Anthony Terrell** (5-11, 174).

Tech's cornerback depth was depleted in June when Cooper was ruled academically ineligible. Cooper played in nine games last season and Tech coaches hoped he would be the starter. **Ricky Sailor** (5-11, 190), a junior transfer from

Butte (Calif.) Community College, also could wind up as a starter at one of the corner spots.

Sophomore **B.J. Johnson** (6-1, 192), who spent most of last season playing corner, is back at free safety, a position at which he is much more comfortable. Johnson is aggressive at flying to the ball, so he should make a fine complement to Curtis.

Senior **Paul McClendon** (5-10, 178) should be the main backup at free safety while sophomore **Ryan Aycock** (6-0, 187) will be Curtis' backup.

McClendon should get the call when Tech goes to its "45" defense, which will use three safeties when the opposition is facing long-yardage situations.

PUNTERS

Greathouse took over for Eric Rosiles as Tech's punter. Greathouse punted 36 times, averaging 39.5 yards per punt. Eight of his punts were downed inside the 20.

The punting job is Greathouse's to lose. He's also in the running to become the team's field goal kicker.

SPECIAL TEAMS

Welker and Francis, both sophomore wide receivers, should handle the return duties.

Welker averaged 12.6 yards on 28 punt returns and had two punt returns for touchdowns. Welker also led the Raiders in kickoff returns, taking back 17 kicks for an 18-yard average. Francis averaged 21.2 yards on eight kickoff returns.

Tech's coverage units were no better than average.

Tech must replace steady long snapper Robert Monroe. Junior **Eric Bartee** (6-2, 220) had a solid spring in that role and should open the season in that role.

Bartee added about 20 pounds so that he could stand up to the pounding.

RECRUITING CLASS

Leach and his staff appear intent on spending all of their department's recruiting budget. In the final days leading up to signing day, Leach visited Los Angeles, Sacramento, Oroville, and Salinas, all in California, plus Tallahassee, Fla., Memphis, Tenn., Moorhead, Miss., Atlanta and Houston.

"We wanted to go coast-to-coast and recruit from everywhere," Leach said. "The trips all run together. But all of our coaches on the road worked tirelessly for this. I'd put our time and our flight plans and our effort on the road against anybody in the country."

Tech's class of 24 newcomers includes seven junior college transfers plus nine out-of-state players. One of the signees, if nothing else, figures to make a number of all-name teams—running back **Loliki Bongo-Wanga** (6-0, 200) of Hartnell (Calif.) Community College. Bongo-Wanga has some game to go along with his name. He was the California Junior College Player of the Year last season after rushing for 1,264 yards and 16 touchdowns.

Tech signed five defensive linemen and six defensive backs.

"This year, we really went after defensive linemen and defensive backs," defensive coordinator Greg McMackin said. "For whatever reason, we had a hole in our depth there, and we had to get the numbers back right."

Two Texas high school products are expected to make contributions this season. **Armon Dorrough** (6-2, 175) from Lancaster could see playing time at wide receiver while **Fred Thrweatt** (6-3, 300) from Midland Lee is a Warren Sapp lookalike and play-alike who could wind up playing in the rotation on the defensive line.

Another junior college recruit who could pay quick dividends is Ratliff, from Butte (Calif.) Community College. Like Paige, he was able to join the program for spring drills. A year ago, Ratliff was a first-team NJCAA All-American.

"He is tall, rangy and has great feet with the potential to put on weight," Leach said.

BLUE RIBBON ANALYSIS

OFFENSE	B+
SPECIAL TEAMS	B
DEFENSE	B
INTANGIBLES	B-

With another year to absorb the offensive system, Tech should be more explosive offensively—especially if Ricky Williams returns to the form he showed as a sophomore in 1998. However, there are lingering doubts about Kingsbury's ability to make the kinds of reads and throws necessary to make Leach's offense work.

Last season, all seven of Tech's victories came against teams that failed to play in bowl games, while all six of its losses came to bowl teams.

This season, the Red Raiders should be 2-1—at worst—after a non-conference schedule of New Mexico, UTEP and North Texas. Tech opens Big 12 Conference play at Texas on Sept. 29 and also has a road game at Nebraska on Oct. 20. Kansas State, Texas A&M and Oklahoma all visit Lubbock, which at times during the past has become a Voodoo Palace for visiting teams.

It will be a major disappointment if Tech doesn't find a way to win six games and qualify for another bowl trip. Progress, though, would be moving up the Big 12's bowl list by winning seven or eight games. If the defensive holes can be plugged and the defense plays like it did last year, then Tech might be able to pull an upset or two and move up in the world.

(W.B.)

2000 RESULTS

New Mexico	W	24-3	1-0
Utah State	W	38-16	2-0
North Texas	W	13-7	3-0
Louisiana-Lafayette	W	26-0	4-0
Texas A&M	L	15-33	4-1
Baylor	W	28-0	5-1
Nebraska	L	3-56	5-2
Kansas State	L	23-28	5-3
Kansas	W	45-39	6-3
Texas	L	17-29	6-4
Oklahoma State	W	58-0	7-4
Oklahoma	L	13-27	7-5
E. Carolina (Gallery Bowl)	L	27-40	7-6

Army

LOCATION	**West Point, NY**
CONFERENCE	**Conference USA**
LAST SEASON	**1-10 (.090)**
CONFERENCE RECORD	**1-6 (9th)**
OFFENSIVE STARTERS RETURNING	**8**
DEFENSIVE STARTERS RETURNING	**5**
NICKNAME	**Cadets, Black Knights**
COLORS	**Black, Gold & Gray**
HOME FIELD	**Mitchie Stadium (39,929)**
HEAD COACH	**Todd Berry (Tulsa '82)**
RECORD AT SCHOOL	**1-10 (1 year)**
CAREER RECORD	**25-34 (5 years)**
ASSISTANTS	**John Bond (Arkansas '85)** Offensive Coordinator/Quarterbacks
	Dennis Therrell (Tennessee Tech '78) Defensive Coordinator/Snipers
	Harold Etheridge (Western New Mexico '81) Offensive Line
	Chip Garber (Maryland '78) Inside Linebackers
	John Mumford (Pittsburg State '79) Defensive Line
	Travis Niekamp (Illinois State '97) Tight Ends
	Jody Sears (Washington State '91) Cornerbacks
	Junior Smith (East Carolina '97) Running Backs
	Tucker Waugh (DePauw '93) Wide Receivers
	Derrick Jackson (Duke '93) Defensive Ends
	Tom Jordan (Southeast Missouri State '92) Offensive Line
TEAM WINS (last 5 yrs.)	**10-4-3-3-1**
FINAL RANK (last 5 yrs.)	**29-88-77-82-99**
2000 FINISH	**Lost to Navy in regular-season finale.**

COACH AND PROGRAM

Todd Berry was under no illusion that his first season at Army would be easy. He knew he had new offensive and defensive systems to install, and, more important, a new mentality for a group of players that had not experienced success on the college level.

Record-wise, Berry's 1-10 debut was Army's worst showing since 1973's 0-10 showing. Had it not been for a 21-17 victory over Tulane on Oct. 21, the Cadets would have again gone winless. And speaking of winless, previously winless Navy enjoyed its only celebration of the season at Army's expense, 30-28, in the season finale in Baltimore.

The real story on Berry's second season at West Point will not be written until the 11 Saturdays to come this fall, but the 40-year-old Oklahoma native feels good about the groundwork that has been laid in his first season and second spring practice.

"So much of that first year is about truly understanding the young people you are dealing with," said Berry, who came to Army after leading Illinois State to a school-record 11 wins in 1999. "The thing that is exciting about the second year is that you are very knowledgeable of the people in your program. As a coach, you know how to motivate your young men and you understand their strengths and weaknesses."

And for Berry, the understanding of what life at Army means has also been enriched. He made his second off-season tour of several bases, the point being driven home what a unique scenario West Point offers.

Think Steve Spurrier ever jumped out of a plane at 11,000 feet with a bunch of Florida boosters? Berry did last spring, making a tandem-jump with the 82nd Airborne at Ft. Bragg, N.C. He also spent time observing the inner-workings of the Pentagon.

"I have been at nine different institutions," Berry said, "and everyone takes pride in their school and the teams they played on. But West Point is different. It's incredible learning that so many players attribute their success to being an Army football player."

Here lately, Army players have been forced to build character in defeat. The Cadets haven't been a juggernaut on the field since Jim Young produced six winning seasons in a seven-year span (1984-90), a run that included two bowl victories. Bob Sutton followed, but managed only two winnings seasons out of nine before getting the boot.

Berry, a history buff who possesses a deep appreciation of the military institutions, has a burning desire to get Army back on track. He sees his second season as a step in that direction. Comparing his second spring practice to his first was like night and day, things were so much more evolved.

"Last year was about installing schemes," he said. "This year is about creating competition. Competition is a great motivator.

"We have the potential to put a much more athletic team on the field this season. I'm very excited our players recognize we have so much room left for growth. They realize they haven't come close to reaching their potential."

After having observed his talent pool for a season, Berry and his staff made several personnel switches for year two. A couple of running backs, **Brian Todd** and **Alton McCallum**, were moved to outside linebacker and tight end, respectively. Guard **Dustin Plumadore** has shifted from starting guard to center. Free safety **Ben Woodruff** has become an outside linebacker and starting corner **Ben Dial** is the new free safety. **Ryan Kent**, a quarterback buried in the depth chart, is also an outside linebacker.

Switching from the wishbone to a pass-oriented offense was, predictably, a tough transition. Rotating three quarterbacks didn't make it any easier.

Army ranked seventh of nine teams in Conference USA in total offense and was better running than throwing. Berry describes his offense as a "throwing man's wishbone." Instead of pitching the ball to get it on the corner, the quarterback throws a quick-hitting pass that accomplishes the same goal.

The departure of senior quarterback Joe Gerena leaves a two-man competition between **Chad Jenkins** and **Curtis Zervic** instead of last year's three-man circus. Michael Wallace, who led Conference USA in rushing last year, is gone from the one-back running game.

But the bigger concerns are on the other side of the line of scrimmage. The Cadets ranked 101st out of 114 Division I-A teams in scoring defense (33.8 points per game), 101st in pass-efficiency defense, 106th in total defense (439.7 yards per game) and 109th in rushing defense (216 yards per game).

Obviously, the offense's chance of success is undermined when the opponents are averaging 5.8 yards every time they snap the ball. Injuries took a heavy toll, particularly in the defensive front four last year. There was a shortage of the quickness necessary to pressure receivers in man-to-man coverage, forcing the Cadets to play soft.

Berry and his staff can't control the injury factor, but they have made moves to get a quicker unit on the field defensively. They also think depth is better.

The schedule is very similar to last season, with two changes. Non-conference foe New Mexico State is replaced by Buffalo and Conference USA champ Louisville goes off, replaced by a first-ever meeting with new league member Texas Christian.

CONFERENCE USA

BLUE RIBBON FORECAST

1. East Carolina
2. Southern Mississippi
3. Louisville
4. UAB
5. TCU
6. Memphis
7. Tulane
8. Cincinnati
9. Houston
10. Army

ALL-CONFERENCE TEAM

OFFENSE

POS. PLAYER SCHOOL HT. WT. CL.

WR Deion Branch, Louisville, 5-10, 195, Sr.
WR Brian Robinson, Houston, 6-4, 204, Jr.
OL Paul Henderson, Army, 6-3, 294, Sr.
OL Victor Payne, TCU, 6-1, 305, Sr.
C Dustin Plumadore, Army, 6-1, 305, Sr.
OL Aaron Walker, East Carolina, 6-3, 310, Sr.
OL Jeremy Bridges, Southern Miss, 6-4, 300, Sr.
QB Dave Raggone, Louisville, 6-4, 240, Jr.
RB Jegil Dugger, UAB, 5-11, 212, Sr.
RB Leonard Henry, East Carolina, 6-1, 200, Sr.
TE Ronnie Ghent, Louisville, 6-2, 230, Jr.

DEFENSE

POS. PLAYER SCHOOL HT. WT. CL.

DL Andre Arnold, Memphis, 6-4, 234, Sr.
DL Michael Josiah, Louisville, 6-4, 235, Jr.
DL Marion Bush, UAB, 6-3, 280, Sr.
DL Pernell Griffin, East Carolina, 6-3, 240, Sr.
LB Chad Bayer, TCU, 5-11, 231, Sr.
LB Brian Zickefoose, Army, 5-10, 210, Sr.
LB Rod Davis, Southern Miss, 6-3, 238, So.
DB Jason Brown, Memphis, 5-10, 187, So.
DB Lynaris Elpheage, Tulane, 5-9, 168, So.
DB Chad Williams, Southern Miss, 5-10, 201, Sr.
DB Anthony Floyd, Louisville, 5-10, 195, Jr.

SPECIALISTS

POS. PLAYER SCHOOL HT. WT. CL.

PK Jonathan Ruffin, Cincinnati, 5-10, 185, Jr.
P Casey Roussel, Tulane, 6-1, 223, Sr.
RS LaTarence Dunbar, TCU, 5-11, 187, Jr.

OFFENSIVE PLAYER OF THE YEAR

Dave Ragone, QB, Louisville

DEFENSIVE PLAYER OF THE YEAR

Pernell Griffin, LB, East Carolina

NEWCOMER OF THE YEAR

Derrick Ducksworth, LB, Southern Mississippi

C-USA NOTEBOOK

Two head coaches make their C-USA debuts this year, but neither is a stranger to his program. Memphis coach Tommy West, the former Clemson head coach, was the Tigers' defensive coordinator under Rip Scherer. TCU coach Gary Patterson was the defensive coordinator under Dennis Franchione the previous three seasons. Patterson, however, won't be making his debut with the Horned Frogs; he coached them in the GMAC Mobile Alabama Bowl against Southern Miss last December. ... C-USA had six bowl-eligible teams last season, starting with regular-season champion Louisville. The others were Southern Miss, East Carolina, Cincinnati, UAB, and Tulane. All had at least six victories. Before last year, C-USA had not had more than four bowl-eligible teams in a season. ... C-USA has four bowl tie-ins this season. The conference champion will play in the AXA Liberty Bowl in Memphis, Tenn. The league will also send teams to the GMAC Mobile Alabama Bowl, the galleryfurniture.com Bowl, and the Motor City Bowl. Last season, Colorado State beat Louisville in the Liberty Bowl, 22-17; Southern Miss beat TCU in the Mobile Alabama Bowl, 28-21; East Carolina beat Texas Tech in the inaugural galleryfurniture.com Bowl, 40-27; and Marshall beat Cincinnati in the Motor City Bowl, 25-14. ... Louisville will play the first college football game of the season on Aug. 23 when it plays New Mexico State in the John Thompson Foundation Challenge Football Classic at Papa John's Cardinal Stadium in Louisville, Ky. ... TCU plays at Nebraska on Aug. 25 in the Pigskin Classic. ... Cincinnati's Jonathan Ruffin won the 2000 Lou Groza Award as the nation's top place-kicker. Ruffin led the nation with 26 field goals, setting a C-USA regular-season record. ... Louisville's Anthony Floyd led the nation in interceptions with 10, also a C-USA record. Louisville led the nation in total interceptions with 27. ... Memphis led the nation in rushing defense, allowing only 72.7 yards per game.

2001 SCHEDULE

Sept.	8	Cincinnati
	15	Buffalo
	22	@UAB
	29	@Boston College
Oct.	6	Houston
	13	East Carolina
	20	@TCU
	27	Tulane
Nov.	3	@Air Force
	10	@Memphis
	17	Navy (Philadelphia)

QUARTERBACKS

Last year, the Cadets labored with a three-man quarterback derby. The graduation of Joe Gerena leaves Berry with a two-man duel between seniors Jenkins (5-11, 175) and Zervic (6-4, 195). Both saw roughly equal duty last year, although Jenkins had five starts to only one for Zervic. Gerena had five starts, including Army's only win (against Tulane), and played in eight games.

Jenkins and Zervic are very different quarterbacks, but Berry believes both can be effective in the system. Jenkins, who is from Ohio, won the opening-game nod last year but drifted in and out of the lineup, partly because of an ankle injury and partly because he completed only 46 percent of his passes. That didn't help an already difficult transition from the wishbone to a passing game.

Jenkins was 58-of-125 with seven interceptions and only two touchdowns. Zervic, known as the "Gunslinger," was 65-of-104, completing 62.5 percent of his passes, with six interceptions and four scores. His pass-efficiency rating of 113.49 dwarfed Jenkins' 76.77.

The spring competition was inconclusive, with Jenkins perhaps the leader.

"I was disappointed early in the spring," Berry said, "because our quarterbacks were trying to be somebody they could not be. Chad was trying to be a drop-back thrower, and that's not what he is. Curtis was trying to be a scrambler and get out of the pocket. Curtis was trying to do what Chad can do and Chad was trying to be like Curtis.

"Once Chad got the message [to play to his

own strengths] all of a sudden his completion percentage improved dramatically and he started to move around in the pocket. That's where he's really dangerous. Curtis had so much faith in his arm that he was forcing the football. Once he started to have a little more patience and we forced him to throw to the outlets, he was much more consistent. If I had to give an edge to somebody right now, I'd give it to Chad."

Zervic, who came to the Academy from Buffalo Grove, Ill., should show more comfort this fall. In 2000, he was moving up to the varsity after two years with the jayvee squad. He completed better than 50 percent of his attempts in four of his five appearances, while Jenkins did so in only one of his five.

The third quarterback in the spring was senior **Jon Hall** (5-11, 192).

RUNNING BACKS

Michael Wallace, gone after leading the Cadets in rushing the last two seasons, leaves an opening in the one-back offense up for grabs. Wallace put together a terrific season last fall, averaging 115 yards per game (6.0 per carry) to account for 75 percent of Army's rushing yardage.

Because McCallum, the second-leading rusher (231 yards) has been moved to tight end, junior **Josh Holden** (6-0, 208) is the heir apparent. However, the fact that Holden, who netted 127 yards last fall, spent the spring playing center field for the Army baseball squad leaves the job very much open when fall camp begins.

Sophomores **Marcellus Chapman**, **D.J. Stancil** and veteran **Demetrius Ball** took advantage of Holden's absence to state their case in the spring. Chapman (5-8, 183), from Houston, put together several good scrimmages and popped a couple of 50-plus-yard runs in the spring. Stancil (5-8, 192) has decent hands and some shiftiness and would be a nice receiving option who might turn a short hitch into a long gainer. Ball (5-10, 205), a senior, finally got Berry's attention in the spring when he started running north-south.

Once Holden returns full-time to football, he will try to cash in on his experience, though limited, and athleticism. His busiest day last fall was 56 yards on 13 attempts against UAB.

Also looking for playing time is **C.J. Young** (5-8, 196), a sophomore out of Detroit.

Even though Wallace's production was valuable last year, Berry thinks this year's candidates are more suited to the one-back offense he brought with him when he took the job.

"The running backs we have now, I think, are more our style of running backs," Berry said. "While we're certainly going to miss Mike I don't think we will see a lot of dropoff there.

"We have guys that can be effective in our style of play. Marcellus Chapman had a great spring. He showed speed, good quickness and he's durable. Demetrius Ball started playing within his capabilities. He is a power back. In the past, he tried to be flashy and show some wiggle. He became a much more productive runner when he started playing within himself."

WIDE RECEIVERS/TIGHT ENDS

Making the transition from a wishbone to an open passing game last year gave Army's new staff some understandable willies. Would, for example, Army's receivers be able to step up from a supporting role to the center ring?

In senior **Omari Thompson**'s case, the answer was a resounding yes. Thompson (5-7, 160) multiplied his 1999 receptions (eight) by five to come up with 40 in 2000.

Thompson, a speedster from Miami, was busier as a halfback in '99, getting 37 carries. He became Army's go-to target in the new offense and will be so again this fall.

Calvin Smith (5-10, 165), who had three starts last year and caught 12 passes, is a threat to make the top rotation this fall. Like Thompson, Smith, a senior, runs on Army's track team and has some big-play ability.

Experience will be a strong suit in the receiving corps, as 13-of-15 players who caught passes last year are back. Recruiting quality receivers to a wishbone offense was a difficult proposition, which is why several of the Cadets' top targets, such as Thompson and Smith, are converted backs. Over time, Berry's system should allow Army to attract a higher grade of receivers out of high school.

Last year's group accounted for only seven touchdown catches and Thompson didn't have a single one among his 40 catches. Of course, the point of origination of a touchdown pass was as big a factor as the receivers.

The departure of senior Bryan Bowdish (17 catches) leaves a vacancy in the starting rotation. The best bet to join Thompson and Smith in the three-receiver set is **Anthony Miller** (5-8, 176), a sophomore who had 11 catches for 141 yards last year. Miller was playing well at the end of last season.

"I like this group as a whole," Berry said. "Overall, the group of receivers has some maturity within the scheme. I know these players will catch the ball and block.

"Omari had a very productive season for us. We need to find ways to get him the ball because he can make things happen. Calvin Smith grew more comfortable throughout the season and developed into someone who can go the distance. We hope to utilize his speed more often this season."

Senior **Brian Bruenton** (6-2, 215) started six games last year and came on strong at the end. He wound up with 13 catches. Junior **Aris Comeaux** (5-10, 178), who started one game in 2000, is likely to improve on last year's 12 receptions. Like Thompson and Smith, Comeaux is a track man.

The low men on the depth chart are junior **Chris Pestel** (5-11, 177), sophomore **Clint Woody** (6-5, 200) and sophomore **Jonathan Woollam** (6-2, 211). Pestel, from Lombard, Ill., had a busy spring while several of his teammates were running track and made up some ground.

The Cadets are blessed with an excellent receiving option at tight end in senior **Clint Dodson** (6-4, 235). Dodson, a Pennsylvanian, can get physical and block when required, but is more effective as a target. He caught 37 balls last year for 383 yards. Only Thompson had more catches and nobody could equal Dodson's two touchdown receptions.

"Clint is the perfect tight end for our system," Berry said. "He blocks well and he is a go-to guy in our offense, especially on third down."

Dodson missed spring to recover from knee surgery, but is expected to be full speed in the fall.

Senior **Tyler Sheble** (6-2, 217) can figure on playing time when Army uses two tight ends. McCallum (6-0, 259), a senior, has spent his career at running back but was moved to tight end in the spring.

OFFENSIVE LINE

Unlike the rest of the offensive unit, the line has some major rebuilding after losing three two-year starters. Gone are center Jim Calhoun, guard Josh Gonzalez and tackle Mike Larkin.

A good place to start is left tackle **Paul Henderson** (6-3, 285), a senior who earned second-team all-conference honors last fall. Henderson, from Mobile, Ala., entered the season projected as a backup but emerged as one of the league's better surprises among linemen.

The other returning starter is Plumadore (6-1, 305). Plumadore is likely to return to center, where he started his career, after starting two years at right guard. A senior, he has 22 consecutive starts and earned second-team all-conference in 1999.

Henderson and Plumadore should feel more comfortable in their new offense with a year's experience behind them. Last fall was an adjustment from a run-blocking system to a pass-blocking system. The line allowed 21 sacks, which probably wasn't bad under the circumstances.

Three new starters must be blended in. Senior **Nolan Gordon** (6-2, 278) probably would have been one of them. Gordon was the early favorite to succeed Calhoun at center, but a knee injury ended his spring practice early, necessitating the move of Plumadore from guard to center.

If Plumadore sticks at center, juniors **Aaron Burger** (6-3, 298) and **Alex Moore** (6-2, 279) are possibilities to win the starting nod at the two guard positions. Burger got ample reserve duty last fall, while Moore has little experience.

Another pair of juniors, **Mike Hastings** (6-2, 270) and **Steve Schmidt** (6-2, 267) will provide depth.

Replacing Larkin at right tackle will be either senior **Jared Churchill** (6-1, 288) or junior **Craig Cunningham** (6-4, 296). Senior **Mark Riegel** (6-2, 280) is also a consideration and his ability to play guard or tackle is an asset.

Probably at least one youngster will merit getting in the rotation. It could be sophomore **Peter Stewart** (6-1, 250), sophomore **Josh Davis** (6-0, 310), sophomore **Adam Wojcik** (6-3, 245) or sophomore **Mark Conliffe** (6-3, 270).

2000 STATISTICS

Rushing offense	143.2	61
Passing offense	176.0	87
Total offense	319.2	91
Scoring offense	20.4	88
Net Punting	31.4	96
Punt returns	17.1	5
Kickoff returns	19.7	56
Rushing defense	216.3	109
Passing efficiency defense	135.9	101
Total defense	439.7	106
Scoring defense	33.8	101
Turnover margin	-6	87

Last column is ranking among Division I-A teams.

KICKERS

With Brendan Mullen's departure, the kicking job is wide open, which isn't a bad thing because Mullen was only 5-of-11 on field goals last fall. Punter **Dan MacElroy** (6-0, 190), a senior, could become a double-duty man if someone else doesn't step up and win the job in two-a-days.

Candidates are sophomores **Zachary Kaye** (5-7, 171) and **Anthony Zurisko** (5-10, 190), plus junior **Paul Stelzer** (6-4, 186). Kaye made a 22-yard field goal in the spring game, but also missed from 21 yards.

Berry could also rush a freshman into duty. The incoming class includes a couple of kickers.

Veteran long snapper **Reid Finn** (6-2, 225), a senior, is back.

DEFENSIVE LINE

There is room for improvement everywhere on a unit that ranked 106th of 114 teams in Division I-A in total defense and 109th in rushing defense.

The Black Knights got off on the wrong foot last year when early injuries rearranged the depth chart on the defensive front. Therefore, a key to improvement this year is obviously staying healthier.

"We felt like we lost half our defense last year," defensive coordinator Dennis Therrell said. "We'd get the dike plugged over here and then we'd lose somebody somewhere else."

Berry feels more confidence in his two tackle positions than the ends. One reason is losing end Zac Hurst, the school's career sack leader. **Brandon Perdue** (6-2, 225), a senior out of Georgia, stepped into an unexpected starting role last year when Ron Sporer was injured. Perdue is back, older and wiser, and should hold onto his job.

The other end spot is likely to go to **David McCracken** (6-3, 236), a senior who hopes he can get through a year without the injuries that have held him back in the past. The former inside linebacker should start as long as he stays healthy.

Depth will come from **Odene Brathwaite** (6-3, 240), a sophomore who earned a spot on the C-USA All-Rookie team as a freshman. Brathwaite played seven games last year as a reserve and showed flashes that could indicate a breakout year this fall. Sophomore **Jesse Hall** (6-1, 222) also provides depth.

"Defensive end is a position where we need some of our younger players to step forward and contribute," Berry said. "We have talent. We just need to improve our overall depth."

Inside at tackle, junior **Clarence Holmes** (6-2, 261) and junior **Paddy Heiliger** (6-4, 270) are charged with the assignment of getting tougher against the run. Holmes was among the injury casualties during the 2000 season. He and Heiliger can get the job done if they can stay off the injury list, Therrell said.

"Last year we'd be where we were supposed to be," he said. "We were just getting knocked back off the ball because we weren't big enough."

Depth comes from juniors **Doug Larsen** (6-1, 255) and **Seth Langston** (6-4, 260).

"I feel very good about our tackle spot," Berry said. "The players at that position have experience and athleticism. I think we'll be solid inside in terms of talent and depth."

LINEBACKERS

Therrell believes this should be an improved position in 2001. The Cadets play two inside backers with two outside backers, known as "snipers," to give the defense an eight-man front.

Senior outside linebacker **Brian Zickefoose** (5-10, 210) flourished in the new system last year, recording 128 tackles, second best in Conference USA. The West Virginia product also intercepted three passes and notched three sacks.

"He's a playmaker," Therrell said. "He's probably our best football player on the defense."

"Brian is really primed for a fine senior year," Berry said. He put on about 20 pounds and brings a strong force off the edge. He has developed into the spiritual leader of the defense."

Woodruff (6-2, 197), a senior, makes the move from free safety to outside linebacker and should earn a starting job. The all-around athlete began his career at quarterback before moving to the secondary. Woodruff is tough enough to play the run and can play bump-and-run adequately when the Cadets line up against three-wide sets.

"He's better close to the line of scrimmage," Therrell said.

Therrell considers senior **Ben Edgar** (6-0, 190) a third starter at outside linebacker. Edgar returns from knee surgery and is like a nickel back. He will see a lot of snaps.

Sophomore **Jay Thomas** (6-1, 197) should see some action outside, along with two players who showed promise in the spring after moving over from offense. Junior Brian Todd (5-11, 192) is a former running back and Kent (5-11, 189) was a quarterback.

At inside linebacker, there are at least four Cadets capable of playing. Junior **Mike Lennox** (6-2, 233) and junior **Jason Frazier** (5-11, 227) are the likely starters. Lennox had a consistent sophomore year and made three starts. He picked off two interceptions against Tulane in his first career start. Frazier's 88 tackles were third best on the team last fall.

Junior **Warren Stewart** (6-1, 220) and senior **B.J. Wiley** (5-11, 224) will also see playing time.

"I thought we received a very inconsistent performance from our inside linebackers last year," Berry said. "We ask a lot of our inside linebackers and they must continue to gain comfort within our scheme."

DEFENSIVE BACKS

The defensive backfield will have a different look this year, with Dial (6-0, 183), senior, moving from corner to free safety. The three-deep scheme calls for two corners and one safety. Two starters, free safety Derik McNally and corner Andrew Burke, are gone from last year, and the third starter, Dial, is trying a new position.

Dial's move to free safety to replace McNally looked promising in the spring. Dial had only one interception last year but his move will improve the overall quickness of the secondary.

The key to taking Dial off a corner was the development of junior **Emiko Terry** (5-10, 164) and junior **Mario Smith** (5-8, 170), both of whom played mostly on special teams as sophomores. Getting senior **Brandon Dickens** (5-5, 165) back from a knee injury will improve depth. **Thomas Roberts** (5-9, 180) is a freshman who had an encouraging spring. Junior **Mike Sehzue** (5-10, 175) also got in some good spring work.

Between Terry, Smith and Dickens, Army hopes to come up with two capable starters at corner and a solid reserve.

"We didn't go up and play a lot of bump-and-run last year," Therrell said. "We played a little more of a bend-but-don't-break style. This year we hope we can play more bump-and-run."

PUNTERS

MacElroy (5-11, 191) returns after averaging 38.2 yards last year. MacElroy struggled with consistency in his first year as Army's punter and hopes to be steadier as a senior. He hit a season-long 59-yarder against Boston College.

SPECIAL TEAMS

In Thompson, Army has one of the best punt-return weapons in the nation. Thompson averaged a whopping 17.6 yards last year on 12 returns. He became the first Cadet since Heisman Trophy winner Glenn Davis in 1944 to return two punts for touchdowns. One was 72 yards against Memphis, the other 86 yards against Air Force. Thompson averaged 19.4 yards on kickoff returns, with a long of 51 yards.

The Cadets weren't so successful in coverage.

"Coverage comes down to speed," Berry said, "and that's an area where some of our incoming freshmen will be able to help. But we need to do a better job kicking the football."

RECRUITING CLASS

Berry's first full recruiting class brings in 30 high school prospects, plus 12 who have matured for a year at the U.S. Military Academy Prep School. The breakdown is 23 offensive players, 17 on defense and two kickers. There are 17 all-state selections in the group that includes 10 offensive linemen and seven defensive linemen.

Among the quarterbacks are **Christian Montagliani** (6-4, 220) of Morgantown, W.Va., and **Reggie Nevels** (6-0, 184), who accounted for 32 touchdowns rushing and throwing last year at Marion, Ind.

Heading the running backs are **La'Berrick Williams** (5-11, 185), who averaged 6.8 yards per carry last year in Huntsville, Ala., and **Dwight Blackledge** (5-10, 186), of Ventura, Calif., who was the Ventura County Most Valuable Player. Another Californian, **Lamar Mason** (5-7, 165), was player of the year in Anaheim.

Ardell Daniels (5-9, 188) of North Port, Fla., hopes to work into the receiver rotation before too long. **Joseph Nelson** (6-3, 215) is a tight end out of Barnsdall, Okla.

Among the all-staters joining the offensive line is **Seth Neiman** (6-5, 280) out of Calvin, N.D.

One of the more heralded defensive signees is end **Kennan Beasley** (6-3, 230) of Pomona, Calif. Others who could help up front are **Brandon Holley** (6-2, 275) of Charleston, Ark., **Trey Landry** (6-3, 260) of Lafayette, La., and **William Pyant** (6-5, 220) of Farmington, Mich.

"I'm very pleased with the number of linemen that we brought in with this class," Berry said. "In your first full recruiting year, it's very important to bring in a strong group of linemen because it takes a little longer for those players to develop. Those players will pay big dividends in the future."

One of the outside linebackers who chose Army is **Mikel Resnick** (5-11, 198) of Oak Ridge, Tenn., the son of a retired Navy man. Resnick led his team in tackles despite missing five games. **Britt Cleveland** (6-0, 205) of Mokema, Ill., and **John Perkowski** (5-10, 190) of Hinsdale, Ill., also have good futures at linebacker.

Derek Jacobs (5-10, 186) won all-state kicking honors at Florence, Miss.

"I think we fulfilled our needs," Berry said. "This year, in relation to the year before, we had the time to really comb the country for good players and good people. I think we hit on both of those things."

BLUE RIBBON ANALYSIS

OFFENSE	C
SPECIAL TEAMS	C
DEFENSE	D
INTANGIBLES	C

Berry and the Army players are more comfortable with each other in their second season. That should be a positive to balance against the negative intangible of the lack of a winning mentality. None of the Cadets have experienced a winning record on the college level. Getting off to a good start with wins over Cincinnati and Buffalo at Michie Stadium would do wonders for Army's confidence.

The quarterback situation bears a degree of uncertainty. Jenkins, who finished the spring ahead of Zervic, hasn't proved to be the accurate passer that Zervic is. If Jenkins doesn't considerably improve his 46 percent completion ratio, it will be a hindrance to an offense built around the short passing game.

How much improvement the defense can make could tell the story on how far the Cadets can step up record-wise. In short, things couldn't get much worse than last year. The plan is to play more aggressively, especially in passing situations. If it pans out, the Cadets should produce more than the 18 turnovers they forced last year.

In Thompson, Army has an exciting double threat it must utilize to the max. Thompson should be the featured target in an offensive system designed to create one-on-one matchups that can result in occasional big plays. He is also one of the most explosive punt-return men in the nation. Now, it's up to Army's defense to force some punts.

(M.S.)

2000 RESULTS

Cincinnati	L	17-23	0-1
Boston College	L	17-55	0-2
Houston	L	30-31	0-3
Memphis	L	16-26	0-4
New Mexico State	L	23-42	0-5
East Carolina	L	21-42	0-6
Tulane	W	21-17	1-6
Air Force	L	27-41	1-7
Louisville	L	17-38	1-8
UAB	L	7-27	1-9
Navy	L	28-30	1-10

Cincinnati

LOCATION	**Cincinnati, OH**
CONFERENCE	**Conference USA**
LAST SEASON	**7-5 (.583)**
CONFERENCE RECORD	**5-2 (2nd)**
OFFENSIVE STARTERS RETURNING	**5**
DEFENSIVE STARTERS RETURNING	**5**
NICKNAME	**Bearcats**
COLORS	**Red & Black**
HOME FIELD	**Nippert Stadium (35,000)**
HEAD COACH	**Rick Minter (Henderson St. '78)**
RECORD AT SCHOOL	**34-44-1 (7 years)**
CAREER RECORD	**34-44-1 (7 years)**
ASSISTANTS	
	Dave Baldwin (Cal State-Northridge '78) Offensive Coordinator
	A.J. Christoff (Idaho '71) Defensive Coordinator
	Tyrone Dixon (Indiana, Pa. '86) Receivers
	O'Neill Gilbert (Texas A&M '89) Defensive Line
	Jeff Filkovski (Alleghney '91) Quarterbacks
	Andy Hendel (North Carolina State '84) Linebackers
	Amos Jones (Alabama '80) Running Backs
	Charles McMillian (Utah State '95) Secondary
	Stacy Searels (Auburn '90) Offensive Line
TEAM WINS (last 5 yrs.)	**6-8-2-3-7**
FINAL RANK (last 5 yrs.)	**62-58-94-77-66**
2000 FINISH	**Lost to Marshall in Motor City Bowl.**

COACH AND PROGRAM

Cincinnati could dwell on its 25-14 loss to Marshall in the 2000 Motor City Bowl. Instead, the Bearcats would rather remember ending the regular season with four straight victories en route to a berth in a postseason bowl.

After losing to Louisville last year, Cincinnati earned victories over Miami (Ohio), UAB, Memphis and Southern Mississippi.

"We benefited from playing in the Motor City Bowl because it gave us an additional month of practice where we were able to work closely with our young players," Cincinnati coach Rick Minter said before spring practice. "Since then, we have worked hard in the weight room and in conditioning and it will be good to get everybody out and into a practice situation."

Despite a 7-5 record and a second-place finish at 5-2 in Conference USA, Minter's coaching staff underwent a major facelift in the off-season.

Minter first hired Dave Baldwin as the Bearcats' offensive coordinator. Baldwin had served as head coach the last four seasons at San Jose State, which he guided to a 7-5 record in 2000, the school's best since 1992. The Spartans upset Stanford and then-No. 9 ranked TCU, but fell short of a bowl bid by losing to Fresno State in its final regular-season game. Still, Baldwin was offered a contract extension, but he turned it down.

San Jose State, which featured Doak Walker Award semifinalist Deonce Whitaker, ended the season ranked 26th nationally in total offense and 30th in scoring offense.

"I am excited that we have added to our staff a person with the coaching credentials and history of success like Dave Baldwin," Minter said. "He has worked with some of the most innovative offenses in the country and his teams have played quite well against some very talented opponents.

"Dave complements greatly the offensive scheme that we have been using the last couple of seasons. With him running the offense, our philosophy of spreading the field and taking advantage of a balance between the run and pass will not change."

The offense will continue to feature the one-back, multi-formation spread attack the Bearcats have featured the last two seasons.

Minter also hired Stacy Searels, who had been an assistant at Appalachian State the last seven years, as the Bearcats' offensive line coach.

"Stacy has established himself as one of the top young offensive line coaches in the country," Minter said. "He has worked with some of the best offensive teams in Division I-AA the last seven years at Appalachian State, developing some very solid offensive linemen.

"Stacy's coaching strength comes from the knowledge of the offensive line that he gained as an NFL-caliber tackle. He learned from some of the best offensive line coaches as a player and is able to pass along what he has learned."

Searels, 35, was a first-team All-America in 1987 as a senior at Auburn.

After hiring Searels, Minter still had some work to do as he filled out his staff.

Only two weeks before the start of spring practice, Minter hired four defensive coaches—defensive coordinator A.J. Christoff, linebacker coach Andy Hendel, defensive line coach O'Neill Gilbert and secondary coach Charles McMillian.

Christoff, 53, has 28 years of coaching experience at the collegiate level, most recently serving as linebacker coach at Southern Cal. Gilbert, 36, joins the program after three years as linebacker coach for the Tennessee Titans. Hendel, 40, comes to Cincinnati after five years as the defensive coordinator at Western Kentucky. McMillian, 29, has six years assistant coaching experience at Navy and Boise State.

"I believe that we have put together a coaching unit that will be able to continue the development of the defense that we have seen over the last couple of years," Minter said. "The coaches we have added offer a good balance of experience along with playing and coaching experience at both the collegiate the professional levels. I think it is a great staff with real high energy."

The 10 starters and 42 lettermen who return give the Bearcats a good nucleus for a run at another winning season. One offense, two solid running backs return. The strength of the defense will be on the line and in the secondary.

The schedule is a challenging one with the season opener at home against Big Ten champion Purdue on Sunday, Sept. 2. The game will be broadcast by ESPN2.

"The opportunity to showcase Cincinnati football in front of an exclusive national audience is a perfect way to begin the 2001 season," Cincinnati athletic director Bob Goin said.

The Purdue game will be the first game televised as part of an eight-year agreement between Conference USA and ESPN.

"We are real excited about the whole schedule," Minter said. "Opening up with a team like Purdue is going to be great. A Rose Bowl participant comes into our house on national TV. They lost some players and so did we, but it's going to be a challenge. We're looking forward to it."

Minter's coaching record at Cincinnati is 34-44-1, but he is one of only two coaches to take UC to postseason play. He trails only Hall of Fame coach Sid Gillman as the winningest coach in school history.

The 5-2 record last year was the best performance since the Bearcats joined Conference USA.

Cincinnati closed the regular season last year with a 27-24 victory over No. 20 Southern Miss, giving the Bearcats their second win over a ranked opponent in school history. Minter was honored for his success by being voted as the Conference USA Coach of the Year by *The Sporting News*.

2001 SCHEDULE

Sept.	2	Purdue
	8	@Army
	15	Louisiana-Monroe
	22	@Miami (Ohio)
Oct.	6	Tulane
	13	@UAB
	20	@Houston
	27	Louisville
Nov.	3	Connecticut
	10	East Carolina
	24	@Memphis

QUARTERBACKS

The Bearcats must replace three-year starter Deontey Kenner at quarterback from among senior **Adam Hoover** (6-1, 201), junior **John Leonard** (6-2, 195) and sophomore **Luis Gonzalez** (6-2, 185).

Hoover served as Kenner's backup last year. When Kenner was injured at mid-season, Hoover completed 53-of-106 passes for 665 yards and three touchdowns. He was 15-of-25 for 268 yards in the victory over Houston.

Leonard played one season at El Camino College in Torrance, Calif., and one year at Arizona State before joining the Bearcats last fall. He was 29-of-74 for 340 yards as a sophomore at Arizona State. Leonard came off the bench and led the Sun Devils to a victory over UCLA and started against Wake Forest in the Aloha Bowl.

In the spring game, Hoover completed 9-of-21 passes for 132 yards and two touchdowns while Leonard was 9-of-15 for 74 yards and a touchdown. He also ran for a touchdown.

"The guys have been working hard," Minter said. "I don't know if Adam Hoover has improved since the bowl game, but he has been working hard. Leonard is going to be a tremendous challenge.

"Hoover proved in the Houston game that he can play. Leonard is a similar player. These guys aren't as big a presence in the pocket and making reads, but they can do good things."

Gonzalez begins his third season at Cincinnati, but must continue to show improvement in the mental aspect of the game.

The three quarterback candidates will be joined in the fall by four freshmen quarterbacks, all of whom bring impressive credentials.

RUNNING BACKS

Senior **Ray Jackson** (6-1, 216) and junior **DeMarco McCleskey** (5-11, 216) will split playing time in the one-back set.

Jackson earned first-team All-Conference USA honors last year. He finished third in the league in rushing with 808 yards and had four games of more than 100 yards.

Jackson, who scored eight touchdowns, has the size and strength to be a power runner. He also has quickness and the ability to catch the football coming out of the backfield.

In the spring game, Jackson rushed for 129 yards on 16 carries and scored a touchdown.

McCleskey missed the spring game with an ankle injury. He started four games last year and finished with 500 yards rushing and four touchdowns. He begins his junior season ranked No. 17 on Cincinnati's career rushing list with 1,362 yards.

"One of the strengths of the team will be our ability to run the ball effectively and we proved that this afternoon," Minter said after the spring game. "Even without DeMarco McCleskey in the lineup, we showed that we could use the run to put together several long drives."

Also expected to get playing time are seniors **Charles Spencer** (5-9, 206) and **Nathan Wize** (5-6, 193). Spencer joined the Bearcats from Missouri Western, where he rushed for 1,530 yards and 12 touchdowns in two seasons. He gained 130 yards on 48 carries as a reserve at Cincinnati last year. Spencer ran for 91 yards on 15 carries in the spring game.

Wize is often used as a third down back because he is a good blocker and capable of catching the ball out of the backfield. He had 40 yards on nine carries in the spring game.

There is no fullback in the spread formation, but junior **Joe Harrison** (5-11, 250), Wize, Jackson or possibly a tight end can line up there in a short-yardage situation.

Junior running back Lloyd Garden announced that he would forego his final season of eligibility and graduate with a degree in criminal justice.

Garden, a 5-11, 230-pound junior from Akron, Ohio, was a regular for the last three seasons. He played in 34 games with 17 starts, and rushed for 77 yards on 19 carries last season. He played on special teams and was used primarily as a blocking back during his career.

WIDE RECEIVERS/TIGHT ENDS

Only five players who caught a pass in 2000 return, led by juniors **LaDaris Vann** (5-9, 193) and **Tye Keith** (5-8, 181).

Vann was the 1999 Conference USA Freshman of the Year. He has 837 yards receiving on 60 receptions with six touchdowns in his two seasons with the Bearcats. Cincinnati coaches say he has good speed and a great understanding of the game. He had three catches for 30 yards and a touchdown in the spring game.

Keith made three or more catches in seven of the last eight games last year. He finished with 32 catches for 456 yards.

Also expected to contribute are seniors **Robert Drewery** (6-0, 181) and **Tim Walker** (5-11, 190) and junior **Jon Olinger** (6-3, 212). Drewery caught nine passes for 149 yards last year. He has the ability to be a deep threat. Walker broke his leg early in the 1999 season, but has 4.45 speed in the 40 and could be an impact player this season. Olinger has good size, but has seen action only as a reserve. He caught three passes for 53 yards in the spring game.

Several freshmen signees could see playing time, as well as redshirt freshmen **Daven Holly** (5-11, 171) and junior **Reuben Dunbar** (5-9, 184).

The spread formation often eliminates a tight end. The Bearcats will use different players in different situations there, including seniors **J.R. Deatherage** (6-4, 238) and **Joe Hamilton** (6-2, 244) and redshirt freshman **A.J. Lucius** (6-3, 241).

Deatherage caught only two passes for 13 yards last year even though he played in every game. He is a solid blocker. Lucius gained almost 25 pounds during his redshirt season. Hamilton played the last three seasons at defensive tackle.

Also in the mix at tight end is junior college signee **Dennis Hart** (6-3, 217). The junior caught 74 passes for 1,495 yards and 13 touchdowns in two seasons at Compton (Calif.) Community College.

OFFENSIVE LINE

Three veterans return to help form an anticipated starting lineup averaging 6-3 and 292 pounds and with 66 career starts.

Returning to the starting lineup are senior left tackle **Shawn Murphy** (6-4, 286), junior right tackle **Josh Gardner** (6-4, 286) and junior right guard **Kirt Doolin** (6-4, 303).

Cincinnati coaches say Murphy and Gardner are the backbone of the offensive line. Murphy transferred from Michigan while Gardner has been in the starting lineup for all 23 games of his career.

Doolin played tackle his first two seasons at Cincinnati before moving to guard last fall. He started at right guard six games and also served as the primary backup at left guard.

The other 2001 starters will be senior **DeWayne Johnston** (6-1, 306) at left guard and sophomore **Josh Scneyderov** (6-2, 280) at center. Johnston was supposed to see only backup duty each of the last two years, but started 17 games because of injuries. Schneyderov played behind two-time All-Conference USA center Doug Rosfeld the last two years.

The only backup with significant playing time is senior **Ted Forrest** (6-3, 291) at guard. He is returning to the lineup after recovering from a torn ACL.

Serving as backups will be redshirt freshmen **Adam Shorter** (6-6, 297), **Clint Stickdorn** (6-6, 274), **Kyle Takavitz** (6-4, 307) and **Matt Mercer** (6-3, 305).

Another player being counted on for depth is junior tackle **Chris Rehfuss** (6-3, 286). Junior guard Ricardo Robledo, a transfer from Los Angeles Harbor Junior College, would have factored in, but tragically, he was shot and killed during an altercation at a party in California in early June.

"We are very saddened by the death of Ricardo," Minter said. "Ricardo was really looking forward to joining the Bearcat football program and start a new period in his life. It is unfortunate that he will never be able to enjoy what he worked so hard to accomplish."

Robledo was an honorable mention All-America selection by J.C. Gridwire last year.

2000 STATISTICS

Rushing offense	141.0	63
Passing offense	216.5	53
Total offense	357.5	69
Scoring offense	25.0	63
Net Punting	34.7	51
Punt returns	7.8	85
Kickoff returns	20.4	36
Rushing defense	147.0	56
Passing efficiency defense	119.3	60
Total defense	371.8	63
Scoring defense	23.6	51
Turnover margin	+12	6

Last column is ranking among Division I-A teams.

KICKERS

Returning as the Bearcats' place-kicker is junior **Jonathan Ruffin** (5-10, 185), who led the nation in field goals and earned all the national kicking honors, including the pregtigious Lou Groza Award signifying the nation's top kicker.

It's safe to say Ruffin knows a little something about self-improvement. His sensational year came after a freshmen season when he made only 5-of-12 field goals and was twice replaced as the regular place-kicker. In 2000, Ruffin made 26-of-29 field goals, setting school and Conference USA records for field goals made and attempted. He ended the year with the sixth-highest single-season field goal total in NCAA history.

Ruffin became the first player in school history to earn consensus All-America honors. He will take over the responsibility this year for long field goal attempts and kickoffs.

Ruffin capped his sophomore season off with a class act. In the bowl game, he wore No. 76 instead of his usual 16 in honor of Lou Groza, who had died earlier in the year.

DEFENSIVE LINE

The Cincinnati defense keyed the drive to the Motor City Bowl last year by ranking fourth in the nation with 34 takeaways. The Bearcats were the only team in the top 10 nationally in both fumbles recovered (ninth with 15) and interceptions made (eighth with 19), allowing UC to rank sixth among 114 Division I-A teams in turnover martin (plus 12).

Much of the production on defense the last two seasons came from improvement in the defensive line. The Bearcats have to replace the gigantic Mario Monds, taken in the sixth round of the NFL draft by the Washington Redskins, but a pair of 2000 starters are returning in junior ends **Antwan Peek** (6-2, 235) and **Derrick Adams** (6-0, 242) and senior tackle **Kirk Thompson** (6-1, 260).

Peek is playing his fourth position in three years. He had a sensational season in 2000 with a team-leading 13 tackles for loss and 8 1/2 sacks, ending the year one sack short of the school record. He also led the team in fumbles caused (four), quarterback hurries (nine) and quarterback hits (17).

Peek has vowed to improve those numbers this season.

"I watch the NFL and I see a lot of players like Jevon Kearse constantly chasing the ball," he told the *Cincinnati Enquirer*. "And that's where I want to be [the NFL], so I do what I've got to do to get the ball. That's my goal this year, to get the ball."

Adams is a two-year starter who made 37 tackles last year with 2 1/2 sacks and six tackles for loss. Thompson led all UC linemen with 40 tackles, including seven for loss, and three fumble recoveries.

A transfer from El Camino (Calif.) Community College, **Matt Tupuolo** (6-2, 340), will join the team in August. The junior is expected to claim the other starting position, and has been compared to the departed Mario Monds. Tupuolo was a two-time first-team all-conference and all-state selection at El Camino. He sat out the 2000 season after making 66 tackles with 4 1/2 sacks as a sophomore in 1999.

The defensive line will feature outstanding depth with several players seeking playing time, including junior **Darryll Ransom** (6-1, 260), junior **Ben Piening** (6-5, 270), senior **Dan Wortman** (6-2, 276), senior **Dante Elliott** (6-3, 262), junior **DeMarcus Billings** (6-0, 259) and redshirt freshman **Andre Frazier** (6-5, 205).

Ransom is the brother of former Bearcat and current Kansas City Chiefs standout Derrick. He has played in 20 games his first two seasons at Cincinnati. Piening made the Conference USA All-Freshman team in 1998. He redshirted last year to get stronger.

LINEBACKERS

Three starters who combined to make 283 tackles and accounted for 33 of the 36 starts last year are gone.

Being counted on to fill the void are two players who were good backups last year—senior **Lewis Carter** (6-2, 230) and junior **Willis Edwards** (5-11, 227).

Carter is a three-year backup at outside linebacker, but moves to the middle for his final season. He made 28 tackles last year in the first eight games, but was then sidelined for the last three with a dislocated hip. He returned and played in the Motor City Bowl.

Edwards started two games at linebacker last year and is the leading returning tackler with 38. He has been moved to the outside to take advantage of his open-field instincts.

Providing depth at linebacker will be senior **Ken Wynne** (6-1, 225), junior **Mark Masterson** (5-10, 222), and redshirt freshmen **Jermaine Wilson** (6-0, 209), **Akanni Turner** (6-1, 200), **Jamey Murphy** (6-2, 215) and **Jamar Enzor** (6-2, 221).

Junior college standout **Jason Hunt** (6-3, 230) will join the program in August and should challenge for playing time. The junior earned second-team All-America honors last year at Sacramento (Calif.) City College. He led his team in tackles with 102, including 10 tackles for loss and four sacks. He was voted Sacramento's defensive MVP as a sophomore and freshman.

DEFENSIVE BACKS

Five experienced players return in the secondary, but some shifting has been done to fill the void left by the loss of three players who played safety last year.

Senior **LaVar Glover** (5-10, 178) and junior **Ivan Fields** (5-11, 182) return as starters at cornerback. Glover is the quickest of the defensive backs with 4.42 speed in the 40. He started every game last year and made 38 tackles with one interception. Fields led all Bearcat returnees with 43 tackles in 2000. He has 105 career tackles.

The backups at cornerback will be senior **Anthony Thomas** (6-0, 170) and sophomore **Zach Norton** (6-0, 181). Thomas made 28 tackles last year and shared the team lead with three interceptions. Norton played last year as a freshman, capping his season with an interception and two pass breakups in the Motor City Bowl.

Junior **Blue Adams** (5-10, 184), used exclusively at cornerback his first two seasons, will start at strong safety. Adams missed the 1999 season with a knee injury but came back last year and made 28 tackles. He set a UC record with four interceptions in 1998 and was voted to the Conference USA All-Freshman team. He had an interception in the spring game.

"Injuries limited what we were able to do defensively because five or six guys who will be lining up against Purdue next September weren't able to play," Minter said after the spring game. "Still, guys like Antwan Peek, Ben Piening and Blue Adams showed what they were capable of while a bunch of newcomers were able to see extended playing time."

Junior **Frank Lang** (5-10, 187) is listed as the No. 1 free safety, but will get strong competition in the fall from sophomore **Kelton Lindsay** (6-1, 195). Lang backed up DeJuan Gossett the last two years. He made 25 tackles last year, including a career-high eight against UAB.

Lindsay, a transfer from Ohio State, is returning from a knee injury that kept him out of action last year. He was a two-time all-state running back at Lebanon (Ohio) High School who rushed for more than 5,000 yards and 57 touchdowns in three seasons.

PUNTERS

Returning as the Bearcats' punter will be senior **Adam Wulfeck** (6-0, 236), who earned second-team all-conference honors each of his last two years.

Wulfeck, third in UC history with a 41.4 yard career punting average, punted 51 times for a 41.8 average in 2000. That was good for 22nd in the nation. He has placed 47 of his career 150 punts inside the 20.

SPECIAL TEAMS

With Ruffin and Wulfeck, the Bearcats are in excellent shape with the kicking game.

Spencer, Keith and Vann are the leading candidates to return kickoffs with either Keith or Vann likely to return punts.

Spencer took over as the kick returner last year, returning seven for a 26.3 average. Keith brought back four kickoffs for a 15.8 average.

RECRUITING CLASS

Along with junior college signees Robledo, Tupuola, Hart and Hunt, the Bearcats signed 14 high school players.

"I believe that this year's signing class reflects both the success that we have had on the field and the continued exposure that we have had across the country," Minter said. "We were able to address all of our needs in recruiting this year. We had concerns about our depth at wide receiver, quarterback and on both the offensive and defensive lines and were able to add several players at each of those positions.

Minter and his staff used the junior college route to plug some holes.

"We had some positions where we had an immediate need," he said. "Because we lost (tight end) Ashley Hunt and (defensive tackle) Mario Monds, we felt it was important to sign players (tight end Derrick Hart and defensive tackle Matt Tupuola) to give us a little more experience."

On national signing day, Minter and his staff signed three quarterbacks. Minter hinted of something else to come.

"I feel that this is a pretty good overall class and I am happy with what we have been able to achieve," he said. "There are still a couple of players that we are looking at who have not made a decision yet we may add later this month."

He was right. On the day spring practice began, Highlands High School standout **Gino Guidugli** (6-4, 205), the runner-up for Kentucky Mr. Football honors in 2000, signed with the Bearcats. Guidugli, who originally committed to Kentucky but changed his mind after former coach Hal Mumme resigned in the wake of alleged recruiting improprieties, could have signed with several upper-level Division I-A teams, including Notre Dame.

How did Cincinnati land him? Minter put it all in perspective in a conversation with Guidugli.

"You can go to Notre Dame and have a good career," Minter told the *Cincinnati Post* he said to Guidugli. "Or you can come to Cincinnati and have a hamburger named after you."

Guidugli obviously was intrigued about the possibility of seeing his name on a menu. Minter could barely contain his glee after Guidugli signed.

"We certainly think this was a tremendous coup for the program," Minter told the *Cincinnati Post*. "... Here's a marquee player turning down other programs across the country. Hopefully it can be a windfall for the program."

Guidugli, from nearby Ft. Thomas, Ky., threw for 7,397 yards and 90 touchdowns in his two years as a starter. He helped the Bluebirds become the first school in Kentucky Class AAA history to win three straight state championships. He was 27-2 as a starter.

Guidugli completed 260-of-404 passes for 4,367 yards and 51 touchdowns as a senior. His team was ranked No. 13 in the final *USA Today* Super 25 poll.

"We aren't going to put any pressure on Gino by having any unrealistic expectations," Minter said. "He will be given his opportunity for playing time when fall camp starts and if the cream does indeed rise to the top, then we will take advantage of that."

Guidugli is nothing if not confident.

"I'm going to try to step in and win the starting position sometime this year—if not for the first game—and get in there and win some games," he told the *Cincinnati Enquirer*.

Guidugli's 4,367 yards passing in 2000 was the second-highest season total in Kentucky history. He is also ranked third in completions (260), fourth in touchdown passes (51), and fifth in passing per game (291.1).

The Bearcats also signed quarterbacks **Billy Faulkner** (6-5,185) from Harrison County High in Cynthiana, Ky., **Kenwood Lattimore** (6-4, 208) from Winton Woods in Cincinnati and George Murray (6-2, 190) from Rickards High in Tallahassee, Fla.

Bearcat coaches believe some quick help may come at receiver from freshmen **Carl Jones** (5-10, 180), **Justin LaForgia** (6-5, 210) and **Derick Ross** (6-0, 175).

Jones, from Armwood High in Tampa, Fla., rushed 170 times for a school-record 1,441 yards and 19 touchdowns last year. He added 33 receptions for 614 yards and four interceptions.

LaForgia, from Don Bosco High School in Rutherford, N.J., was rated as the 19th best athlete in his state by *SuperPrep*. He caught 53 passes for 692 yards and eight touchdowns in helping his team to an 11-1 record.

Ross, from Marion Harding High School in Marion, Ohio, caught 39 passes for 650 yards and six touchdowns last season.

BLUE RIBBON ANALYSIS

OFFENSE	C
SPECIAL TEAMS	C
DEFENSE	C
INTANGIBLES	A-

It won't take long in 2001 to find out if the Bearcats can continue the success they had in the second half of the 2000 season.

Cincinnati opens the season on Sept. 2 in a

nationally televised Sunday game against Big Ten champion Purdue.

The Bearcats will begin their sixth season in Conference USA on Sept. 8 at Army, marking the third time in the last four years that UC faced the Golden Knights in September. Cincinnati will then play non-conference games against Louisiana-Monroe on Sept. 15 and Miami (Ohio) on Sept. 22.

The six home games on the schedule mark the sixth consecutive year the Bearcats will play more games at home than on the road.

With five starters returning offense and five on defense, Minter has a good nucleus returning. And the kicking game will once again be one of the nation's best.

The offense returns backs Jackson and McCleskey and the strength of the defense will be the line and the secondary. It will be interesting to see how freshman signee Guidugli fits into the quarterback scramble. Another key is how the new defensive coaching staff comes together.

Regardless, look for Minter and the Bearcats to be competitive in Conference USA once again. It shouldn't be too tough for the Bearcats to finish with at least seven victories.

(S.C.)

2000 RESULTS

Army	W	23-17	1-0
Syracuse	W	12-10	2-0
Wisconsin	L	25-28	2-1
Indiana	L	6-42	2-2
Tulane	L	19-24	2-3
Houston	W	48-31	3-3
Louisville	L	24-38	3-4
Miami (Ohio)	W	45-15	4-4
UAB	W	33-21	5-4
Memphis	W	13-10	6-4
Southern Mississippi	W	27-24	7-4
Marshall (Motor City)	L	14-25	7-5

East Carolina

LOCATION	**Greenville, NC**
CONFERENCE	**Conference USA**
LAST SEASON	**8-4 (.666)**
CONFERENCE RECORD	**5-2 (t-2nd)**
OFFENSIVE STARTERS RETURNING	**6**
DEFENSIVE STARTERS RETURNING	**9**
NICKNAME	**Pirates**
COLORS	**Purple & Gold**
HOME FIELD	**Dowdy-Ficklen Stadium (43,000)**
HEAD COACH	**Steve Logan (Tulsa '75)**
RECORD AT SCHOOL	**59-44 (9 years)**
CAREER RECORD	**59-44 (9 years)**
ASSISTANTS	**Doug Martin (Kentucky '85)**
	Offensive Coordinator/Quarterbacks
	Tim Rose (Xavier '63)
	Defensive Coordinator/Inside Linebackers
	Bob Leahy (Emporia State '69)
	Receivers
	Jerry McManus (Wake Forest '78)
	Running Backs
	Tony Oden (Baldwin-Wallace '95)
	Secondary
	Steve Shankweiler (Davidson '74)
	Offensive Line
	Terry Tilghman (East Carolina '95)
	Tight Ends
	Tim Daisher (Western Michigan '78)
	Outside Linebackers
	Donald Yanowsky (Toledo '81)
	Defensive Line
TEAM WINS (last 5 yrs.)	**8-5-6-9-8**
FINAL RANK (last 5 yrs.)	**33-56-80-62-38**
2000 FINISH	**Beat Texas Tech in galleryfurniture.ccom Bowl.**

COACH AND PROGRAM

Steve Logan has a good thing going at East Carolina. Almost every year, his name pops up for an opening at a high-profile school. One of these days, the Pirates' 10th-year coach may leave, but only if he's sure it's the right move to make.

Until then, Logan will keep building one of the most solid programs in Conference USA.

"I was involved in a job last year that people are suddenly talking a million dollars a year," Logan said. "I was involved in one of those jobs. I really don't want to say which one. I don't think that helps them or me. The point I'm trying to make is I've got a good job here, but the economics from time to time may be the issue that make me do something else later in my career."

East Carolina would do well to keep Logan on board. On his way to becoming the winningest coach in school history, Logan has knocked off some pretty good teams along the way.

Perhaps his biggest victory was over Miami in 1999. Last season, East Carolina beat Syracuse and was the only team in Conference USA to beat Louisville and Southern Mississippi. Logan took the Pirates to their second straight bowl game, beating Texas Tech, 40-27, in the first galleryfurniture.com Bowl.

So what's next for the Pirates? More of the same. Win games. Keep the good thing going.

"I told somebody the other day I think winning championships has an allure to it," Logan said. "I think that's what everybody talks about, but I think Bill Walsh once said winning a lot of games over a long period of time really has more meaning than the occasional championship. I really do believe that.

"I think you'll win some championships if you do win a lot of games over a long period of time. You'll be in constant position. To win a championship you've got to be lucky. Before we went into Conference USA, we were in what we called the Liberty Bowl alliance, which became Conference USA, in 1994 and '95, and we won it both years and went to the Liberty Bowl."

Through all his success, however, Logan has not been able to win the Conference USA title in ECU's four years in the league. The Pirates finished in a four-way tie for second in 1999, finished fourth in '98 and third in '97.

Last year, the Pirates came even closer. If not for an Oct. 28 home loss to UAB, they would have tied Louisville for the league title and gone to the Liberty Bowl as league champion because of their 28-25 victory over the Cardinals on Oct. 23.

"Last year we would have been conference champions," Logan said. "We had one football play in the UAB game that cost us the game. In the meantime, we were the only team in the conference to beat Louisville and Southern Miss. If you give us the UAB victory, we would have been conference champs, but we got beat, 16-13, and fell three points short."

It was a disputed call near the goal line that cost the Pirates a chance for the victory over UAB.

"We had a third down and goal at the 4 and we had our [split end] who was tackled at the line of scrimmage and no call [was made]," Logan said. "It resulted in us kicking a field goal rather than having a first and goal at the 2. ... It was just one of those outrageous blown calls where you get a call on Sunday afternoon from the officials saying 'Sorry', but you know, that doesn't help."

With the return of senior quarterback **David Garrard**, the Pirates seem poised to make another run at the conference title. Garrard has continued the tradition of outstanding quarterbacks in the program.

It started with Jeff Blake (1988-91) and continued with Marcus Crandall (1993-96) and Danny Gonzalez (1994-97). Crandall holds school records for passing yardage, completions and touchdown passes, while Garrard set the record for total offense last season.

"We solidified the program under Blake and he started for two and a half years for us and when he left we kind of started over," Logan said. "We got Marc Crandall integrated into the deal and he had three wonderful years. We went 24-11 over that span of time and he left. We had Gonzalez, who really broke all kinds of records his senior year and then he left.

"Danny's still playing in the Canadian League and Mark is still banging around in the NFL and Blake is in New Orleans. We moved into the David Garrard era and David has gone 6-5, 9-3, 8-4 and he's coming back for his senior year."

And that is a big reason the Pirates will be a contender for the C-USA title again this season. Will it be their breakout year, the year they give Logan the elusive league title? Perhaps. In any case, look for Logan's name to surface again in the off-season when some high-profile positions come open.

"There are a few things out there that could happen," Logan said. "But the main thing is I really don't spend very much time at all on that end of things. I'm just consumed with winning the next game, and here again if you win enough next games, then each year maybe you will have an opportunity and I've had opportunities to leave here almost every year.

"But I always weigh that opportunity against what it is that I'm doing and so far this one has been better."

2001 SCHEDULE

Sept.	1	Wake Forest
	8	@Tulane
	15	@Syracuse
	22	William & Mary
Oct.	6	@North Carolina
	13	@Army
	20	Memphis
	30	@TCU
Nov.	10	@Cincinnati
	15	Louisville
	23	Southern Miss

QUARTERBACKS

In three years at East Carolina, Garrard (6-1, 249) has become one of the most feared quarterbacks in Conference USA. Logan has made a habit of putting good quarterbacks on the field in his nine years with the program, and Garrard could be the best of the bunch.

He is big. He is strong. He can run. He can throw long and short.

"He's got the Blake long ball coupled with the Marc Crandall intermediate throw that I thought were two of the best I've ever been around," Logan said. "He's got a lot of everything. He's so big, strong and durable and he runs very, very well. Of course, he's been four years in the system now and knows what it is we're trying to get done."

Last year, Garrard moved into second on East Carolina's career passing yardage list (6,782) and is second in career touchdown passes (47) and completions (502). He may end his career with those school records to go with his record for total offense, which stood at 7,787 yards after the 2000 season.

Two freshmen will back up Garrard: **Desmond**

Robinson (5-10, 200) and **Paul Troth** (6-4, 217). Robinson was redshirted a year ago.

Junior **Richard Alston** (5-11, 210), who played in eight games last year as Garrard's backup, was moved to halfback during spring practice. Last season, Alston completed 5-of-23 passes for 108 yards with one touchdown and one interception.

Troth (6-4, 217), a high school All-American at Vance High School in Davidson, N.C., should help the Pirates continue their run of outstanding quarterbacks. He threw for more than 2,000 yards in each of his last three seasons of high school, and his 6,835 yards are the fifth most for a high school player in North Carolina. He threw for 26 touchdowns as a sophomore and 79 for his career.

How did Logan land the guy? Troth's father, Mike, played for the Pirates in the early 1970s.

At least this season, though, East Carolina won't be pinning any hopes on Robinson or Troth. It's all on Garrard running the pro-set offense.

"Any time you're not having to break in a new quarterback you've got a really solid chance to have a decent year and that's kind of where we are this particular year," Logan said. "I think next year we'll be in a little bit of a re-tool as we re-tool the quarterback position because we're so quarterback oriented here. Everything we do is that guy and it always has been. We've got a good system that's stood the test of time and it's [revolved around] the quarterback. We've got an awfully, awfully good one right now."

Last year, Garrard was third in the conference in passing efficiency, completing 52.6 percent for 2,332 yards with 19 touchdowns and 11 interceptions. He was second on the team in rushing with 596 yards gained and a net of 358 yards. He ran for five touchdowns.

Last year, Garrard and Tulane's Patrick Ramsey shared second-team all-conference honors. Louisville junior Dave Ragone was the first-team quarterback.

RUNNING BACKS

Senior fullback **Leonard Henry** (6-1, 197) is coming off his best season as a Pirate, and it earned him the team's most-improved offensive player award. Henry led the team with 711 rushing yards and was chosen to the all-conference second team.

The three-time letterman averaged 5.3 yards per carry and scored eight touchdowns. In the 62-20 victory over Houston, Henry rushed for a career-high 167 yards and scored three times.

As the season progressed, Henry became the team's workhorse back. He led ECU in rushing in six games and finished sixth in C-USA in rushing.

Henry was also the team's fourth-leading receiver with 18 catches for 137 yards and a touchdown.

"He's a 212-pound banger," Logan said of Henry. "He's just a slam-bang type of back who runs for about 800 yards a year."

Well, not exactly. Last season, Henry more than doubled his rushing yardage from his sophomore year when he ran for 312 yards. He ran for 634 yards in 1998.

Backing up Henry will be junior **Christshawn Gilliam** (5-11, 218), who played in 11 games but had only one carry, for six yards. Gilliam has also played outside linebacker, but was listed at fullback in the spring. That could change.

"He's gone on both sides of the ball. He'll continue to do that," Logan said. "He's a real talented kid."

Logan is grooming two other fullbacks for the future. Sophomore **Art Brown** (5-9, 205) and freshman redshirt **Marvin Townes** (5-11, 195) will look for playing time this fall, then become more of a factor in 2002 when Henry is gone. Brown played in nine games last season and gained 153 yards, averaging 4.5 yards per carry. He scored a touchdown.

Townes was rated as the No. 10 prospect in North Carolina by the *Fayetteville Observer-Times* after rushing for 5,072 yards at Warren County High School.

"Art Brown and Marvin Townes are really, really, really talented kids that will be special to watch one of these days," Logan said.

Logan calls the running back corps "one of the healthiest situations on the team. ... We're really in good shape there."

WIDE RECEIVERS/TIGHT ENDS

Sure, the Pirates lost their top three receivers, Keith Stokes, Marcellus Harris and tight end Rashon Burns, but Logan isn't about to push the panic button. The three players combined for 72 catches, 1,184 receiving yards and 11 touchdowns.

"We lost Marcellus Harris and Keith Stokes. They were two really good players, but we always play eight to 10 wide receivers a year and we've got six of them coming back," Logan said. "**Arnie Powell** will be good and **Aaron Harris** will be good and **Terrance Copper** is a [sophomore] who will be good. **Torey Morris** is an upcoming junior who's made some big plays for us."

Of the six players Logan mentioned, Powell (6-5, 214) and Morris (6-0, 183) are the leading returning receivers. Both had 12 catches last season. Powell, a senior, had 218 receiving yards, averaged 18.2 yards per catch and caught two touchdown passes. Morris, a junior, had 149 yards and caught a touchdown pass.

Copper (5-11, 204) and Harris (6-2, 197) each caught nine passes. Copper, a sophomore, was second on the team in yards per catch, averaging 20.8 yards, and caught one touchdown pass. Harris, a senior, averaged 14.2 yards and caught a touchdown pass.

In the spring's final depth chart, Copper was listed as the starting halfback (a receiver), ahead of sophomore **Marcus White** (6-0, 190) and Alston. Powell was the starting flanker ahead of Harris, and senior **Derrick Collier** (6-1, 196) was the starting split end. Collier caught seven passes for 100 yards and a touchdown last season.

"We'll have somebody step up," Logan said. "In spring ball, we weren't standing around going, 'Oh my God, we can't catch the football.' We've got kids who can make plays."

With the departure of Burns, the Pirates will have a new starting tight end for the first time in two years. Junior **Ben Thomas** (6-2, 246) played mostly special teams last season. He didn't catch a pass.

Senior **Corey Floyd** (6-2, 250) and sophomore **Seth Yates** (6-4, 247) combined for nine catches and 102 yards. Floyd caught four passes for 22 yards and two touchdowns, one against Virginia Tech and the other against Southern Miss. Yates averaged 16 yards on five catches.

Logan will again look to spread Garrard's passes around in 2001. Last season, nine players caught nine or more passes, and six caught 12 or more.

OFFENSIVE LINE

Two starters are gone from the Pirates' offensive line, but Logan isn't fretting over it. Veteran right tackle Samien Jones is gone. Even the departure of center Sherwin Lacewell, a first-team all-conference player, does not have Logan worried.

"We're playing two complete offensive lines," he said. "It's a deal where [losing starters has] become a non-event. ... So yeah, we lost a couple of starters, but are we worried about it? No, because we're almost always going to have somebody that has been in the game in very meaningful situations."

This year's line has some experience, but is still young. Senior left guard **Aaron Walker** (6-1, 303) started all 12 games last season and senior right guard **Chris Nelson** (6-5, 314) started the last five games of the season.

Replacing Lacewell will be sophomore **Doug White** (6-0, 292), who moved into to the starting job for the last two games when Lacewell broke his ankle against West Virginia.

"We finished the last three games with Doug taking every snap and he did a great job," Logan said.

Two sophomores round out the starting line. **Brandon Pope** (6-4, 279) was slotted as the starter at left tackle when spring practice ended and **Brian Rimpf** (6-5, 301) was at right tackle. Rimpf was chosen to the league's all-freshman team last season.

While those are the starters, Logan will again give their backups ample playing time.

"We're in good shape," he said.

2000 STATISTICS

Rushing offense	161.5	42
Passing offense	224.8	46
Total offense	386.3	47
Scoring offense	30.0	37
Net Punting	29.8	106
Punt returns	14.8	15
Kickoff returns	19.9	53
Rushing defense	142.4	51
Passing efficiency defense	115.0	47
Total defense	346.5	41
Scoring defense	20.8	37
Turnover margin	+4	39

Last column is ranking among Division I-A teams.

KICKERS

Junior **Kevin Miller** (6-0, 214) will again handle the place kicking duties, and he's no stranger to the pressures that go with it. As a redshirt freshman, Miller made 11-of-15 field-goal attempts and all 17 of his extra-point tries before pulling a quadriceps muscle during warm-ups.

Last season, Miller made 42-of-43 extra-point kicks and was 10-of-17 on field-goal attempts. He was 6-of-7 from 30 yards or closer.

Miller was also the punter in 2000, but he won't have to worry about it this year. Jared Preston (5-11, 194), a junior college transfer, takes over as the punter.

DEFENSIVE LINE

Gone are two down linemen, tackle Devone Claybrooks and nose guard Mbayo Ahmadu, but Logan's rotation system assured their backups of enough experience.

Two fifth-year seniors, **Ty Hunt** (6-4, 270) and **Chris Howell** (6-2, 295), should anchor the line.

Hunt, a tackle, started six games during the regular season and had 23 tackles, including nine unassisted. Howell, the backup for Ahmadu at nose guard, played in every game last season and finished with 31 tackles, 22 unassisted.

Senior **Bernard Williams** (6-4, 240) is the other starter at tackle.

"We've been playing about 12 defensive linemen a game the last two years," Logan said. "We lost two defensive linemen this year, Claybrooks and Ahmadu, that were fine players, good senior players, but here again, Howell, Hunt and Williams are all three coming back. We consider them starters even though they may or may not have started at various times of the year.

"Those are the top three coming back. We have youngsters behind them."

Sophomore nose guard **Derek Helms** (6-2, 285) should also see considerable playing time. He is Howell's backup. Sophomore **Damane Duckett** (6-6, 280) should be Hunt's backup, while **Ja'Waren Blair** (6-5, 256) will share time with Williams at the other tackle spot.

Logan is counting on at least a couple of junior college players to contribute on the line, among them **Karl Zubeck** (6-2, 262), **Ronald Pou** (6-1, 270), **Lance Neisz** (6-4, 260) and **Eric Fouchee** (6-4, 285).

Zubeck, from Fort Scott (Kansas) Community College, had 72 tackles last year, 35 of them unassisted. He also recovered four fumbles. Pou, from Georgia Military College, had 47 tackles, 21 unassisted, and was the strongest player on his team. Fouchee, from Montgomery (Md.) College, was a preseason junior college All-American.

LINEBACKERS

Same as last season, the Pirate linebackers are the backbone of the team, with two-time all-conference player **Pernell Griffin** leading the way.

Griffin (6-1, 253), a senior, led the team in tackles last season for the second straight season despite playing just eight games because of a knee injury. He made 87 total tackles, including three for loss, recovered three fumbles and forced a fumble. In a victory over Tulane, Griffin made 18 tackles.

As a sophomore, Griffin made a team high 121 tackles, including 19 against Southern Miss and 17 against Miami. He is among East Carolina's career tackle leaders with 307.

Griffin begins his senior season as one of 52 candidates for the 32nd Lombardi Award, given to the nation's top down lineman or linebacker.

Senior **Greg LeFever** (5-10, 242) lines up alongside Griffin at inside linebacker in the 3-4 defense. Last season, LeFever was fourth on the team in tackles (50), with three for loss. He was limited to seven games because of injuries. LeFever recovered two fumbles, intercepted a pass, and had double-digit tackles against Tulane and West Virginia.

"Pernell is one of the really good players in the country and Greg LeFever is another very good player," Logan said. "When those two kids are on the field, we have two really, really quality linebackers. Then we've got some young kids behind them that are really fine players. **Vonta Leach** is a real good linebacker that played a lot when Pernell got hurt last year."

Leach (5-11, 254), a sophomore, ended the spring as LeFever's backup. He was chosen to the All-Conference USA freshman team. **Kevin Ward** (6-1, 228), a senior, is Griffin's backup.

The Pirates' outside linebackers (defensive ends) may be as talented as the guys inside.

Defensive ends **John Williamson** (6-2, 234) and **Antwane Yelverton** (5-11, 202) have chances to earn all-conference honors. Both are juniors.

Yelverton finished second on the team in tackles last year with 76 and had five tackles for loss and three sacks. Williamson, who was fifth in tackles with 48, had a team-high two interceptions. He was second on the team in tackles for loss with six and was second in sacks with 5 1/2.

"Our outside linebackers are like the running back situation," Logan said. "I think our outside linebackers are one of the healthiest spots on the field. John Williamson and Antwane Yelverton are really good outside linebackers and we've got good kids behind them."

Junior **Reggie Hamphill** (6-1, 235) should play behind Williamson and sophomore **Kent Nealy** (5-9, 219) was listed as Yelverton's backup when spring practice ended.

DEFENSIVE BACKS

Junior twin brothers **Antwan** and **Anthony Adams** will be key players in the secondary, although both may not be in the starting lineup. Antwan Adams (5-11, 176) should be the starter at free safety, while Anthony Adams (5-11, 188) will battle junior **Jerome Steward** (5-8, 182) for the starting job at strong safety.

Last season, Antwan Adams had a career-high 67 tackles, including 23 unassisted. He also had five pass deflections. Antwan started all 11 games, then was the starter in the bowl game, and had a career-high 13 tackles against Memphis. He was third on the team in tackles.

Anthony Adams and Steward will likely share time at strong safety. Anthony Adams started 11 of 12 games last season and had 39 tackles with four pass deflections. His numbers were down slightly from his freshman year when he had 56 tackles.

Steward started the first three games last season at cornerback before moving to strong safety. He finished with 43 tackles and deflected six passes.

Sophomores **Travis Heath** (6-2, 186) and **Kevin Jackson** (5-11, 183) will also see ample playing time at free safety behind Antwan Adams.

Starting cornerbacks will be junior **Kelly Hardy** (5-11, 197) and senior **Charlie Robinson** (5-11, 190).

Hardy started all 11 games last season and finished with 43 tackles, 29 unassisted. He scored the Pirates' first and last touchdowns of the regular season, intercepting a pass and returning it 60 yards for a touchdown in the season opener against Duke and picking up a ball fumbled by LeFever and returning it for a touchdown against Southern Miss. LeFever had intercepted a pass, fumbled the football, and Hardy picked it up and ran 34 yards for a touchdown. Hardy led the team in pass deflections with 10.

The Pirates' secondary was young last year, but its experience from 2000 should make it stronger this time around.

"We started two sophomores and two freshmen in the secondary and they did a fine job and they're coming back. They did well," Logan said. "They had a couple of games that they got pushed around a little bit, but by and large they did well."

PUNTERS

Preston will take over the punting duties this season, allowing Miller to focus only on place kicking. Preston (5-11, 200) averaged 42.1 yards on 61 punts last season at Eastern Arizona Junior College and was chosen to the NJCAA All-America second team.

Preston had an 85-yard punt last season. Miller averaged 40.4 yards on 30 punts in 2000.

"(Preston) has a really strong leg but is kind of raw," Logan said. "We've got to work with him a little bit."

Junior Lee Hunt (5-11, 243) will be Preston's backup.

SPECIAL TEAMS

One of the biggest tasks for Logan will be replacing Stokes, a multi-talented player. Stokes was not only the Pirates' leading receiver but also their top punt and kick returner. He averaged 15.4 yards on 27 punt returns, scoring one touchdown, and averaged 21.0 yards on 24 kick returns with a long return of 52 yards.

In the bowl victory over Texas Tech, Stokes returned a punt 71 yards for the Pirates' second touchdown.

"Stokes was a special guy," Logan said. "I don't know that we'll have anybody like that, with the explosiveness that he had, but we'll have somebody back there who has some skills."

Townes, the redshirt freshman fullback, and the sophomore Cooper will be the top two kick returners. Cooper has some experience after returning four kickoffs and averaging 22.8 per return last season. He ran one for 36 yards.

Cooper and Alston, the junior receiver, will be the top two punt returners, respectively.

RECRUITING CLASS

For the most part, Logan's 2001 class of 29 recruits was assembled for the future, not the quick fix.

The two areas Logan will look for his recruits to make an impact this season are on the defensive line and punter.

Zubeck, Pou, Neisz and Fouchee will be in the mix for playing time on the defensive line, and Logan doesn't mind giving them a chance to play. The coach has already penciled Preston in as the punter.

D'Brian Hudgins (6-0, 200) is an outstanding athlete, and Logan will look to find the right role for him. Hudgins, who played at Fork Union (Va.) Military Academy in 2000, rushed for more than 1,000 yards as a senior at Williamston (N.C.) High School in 1999, but he could be moved to the defensive secondary.

The recruiting class included 15 offensive players, 13 defensive players and the punter. There are five defensive linemen, five linebackers, four offensive linemen, three running backs, three wide receivers, three defensive backs, two quarterbacks, a punter, safety and snapper.

More than 50 percent of the class is from North Carolina, but Logan also signed four players from Florida, two from Virginia, two from New Jersey, and one each from Arizona, Georgia, Maryland, Missouri and South Carolina.

Troth, the highly regarded freshman quarterback from North Carolina, enrolled at East Carolina for the spring semester and took part in spring practice. Preston and Zubeck also took part in spring practice.

"There are a lot of young men that I'm excited about," Logan said. "I'm not going to mention any names because I think that's the only fair way for these kids to come in, learn how to tie their shoes, learn how to get knocked down, learn how to get up and do the things that freshmen have to go through."

BLUE RIBBON ANALYSIS

OFFENSE	A-
SPECIAL TEAMS	C
DEFENSE	B+
INTANGIBLES	B+

Logan says the number of starters returning and lost can't be used as a barometer for projecting success or failure, at least not with his team. He has six offensive starters and nine defensive starters coming back, but more importantly he has 54 lettermen returning.

And you can bet they've had plenty of playing time.

"One of the thing we did starting about four

years ago, we made a commitment. We travel with 65 players," Logan said. 'That's a conference rule. At the end of every game, we've played 63. The only people that don't play, that are not guaranteed to play, are the backup long snapper and sometimes the backup quarterback.

"We average 60, 62 players a game. Last year, we routinely played 38 or 39 players on defense, and I don't mean two snaps and out. I'm talking kids are getting 12, 15, 18 snaps. Nobody plays more than 50 snaps in a 70-snap game."

That is one way Logan has built one of the sturdiest programs in C-USA. His team will always have depth.

Led by the return of Garrard, the Pirates should contend for the conference title again this season. Although five starters are gone from the offense, the Pirates have plenty of guys who were backups last year waiting for their chance to start.

The defense should be better than last year's, which ranked fifth in C-USA in total defense. Griffin is an All-America candidate and he has a solid group around him.

If you ask Logan about strengths and weakness, he can't really find any. That's a good sign to him.

"I don't know particularly what the strengths are, other than the quarterback being exceptional," Logan said. "I don't see a lot of places where you go, 'Oh my God, we just can't do this, or we won't be able to do that.' That's the good news in my opinion. That's what I like, whenever I can look and say, 'Well, we'll be OK there, we'll be kind of OK there, we can get by with this.' "

Once again, the Pirates will be better than OK. After coming close to a C-USA title last season, they could give Logan that elusive championship this season.

(D.L.)

2000 RESULTS

Duke	W	38-0	1-0
Virginia Tech	L	28-45	1-1
Tulane	w	37-17	2-1
Syracuse	W	34-17	3-1
Memphis	L	10-17	3-2
Army	W	42-21	4-2
Louisville	W	28-25	5-2
UAB	L	13-16	5-3
Houston	W	62-20	6-3
West Virginia	L	24-42	6-4
Southern Mississippi	W	14-9	7-4
Texas Tech (gallery)	W	40-27	8-4

Houston

LOCATION Houston, TX
CONFERENCE Conference USA
LAST SEASON 3-8 (.273)
CONFERENCE RECORD 2-5 (t-7th)
OFFENSIVE STARTERS RETURNING 8
DEFENSIVE STARTERS RETURNING 6
NICKNAME Cougars
COLORS Scarlet & White
HOME FIELD Robertson Stadium (32,000)
HEAD COACH Dana Dimel (Kansas St. '86)
RECORD AT SCHOOL 3-8 (1 year)
CAREER RECORD 26-20-0 (4 years)
ASSISTANTS Theron Aych (Northern St. '96)
Tight Ends
Clancy Barone (Cal State-Sacramento '86)
Co-Offensive Coordinator/Offensive Line
Dick Bumpas (Arkansas '71)
Assistant Head Coach/Co-Defensive Coordinator/Defensive Line
Frank Hernandez (Kansas State '92)
Cornerbacks
Cornell Jackson (Sterling College '86)
Linebackers
Bradley Peveto (SMU '87)
Co-Defensive Coordinator/Safeties
Travis Pride (Mesa State '92)
Wide Receivers
Dave Warner (Syracuse '82)
Co-Offensive Coordinator/Quarterbacks
Eric Wolford (Kansas State '94)
Special Teams Coordinator/Running Backs
TEAM WINS (last 5 yrs.) 7-3-3-7-3
FINAL RANK (last 5 yrs.) 55-73-83-42-84
2000 FINISH Lost to Louisville in regular-season finale.

COACH AND PROGRAM

Dana Dimel experienced something new last fall as the head football coach at Houston, and he didn't like it.

Before taking over the Houston program last year, Dimel was one of only 10 current Division I-A head coaches to have won at least seven games in every year in his career. In three years at Wyoming, Dimel's teams were 8-5, 8-3 and 7-4.

In his first year trying to rebuild the Cougars' football program, however, Dimel left the sideline only three times as the winning coach. He didn't like it. It was his first season as a head coach with a losing record and the first time his team didn't win the conference championship.

There were impressive victories over Army and Memphis, and Dimel set the stage for future success by redshirting 25 players. The offensive production of 350 yards per game kept Houston fans dreaming of a return to prominence for their once-storied program.

Still, there were those eight losses. Dimel decided before spring practice that changes must be made.

"One of our goals is to run the football program much better than we did last season," he said. "Both the production and efficiency need to increase in order for us to be a more effective offense.

"Also, we need to work on becoming more mentally and physically tough. We are always looking to improve our physical conditioning, and it's good we have an opportunity to work on that right now. Finally, we need to find the best personnel for our special teams. This will be an area of major emphasis during the spring."

Several changes were also made on the Cougars' coaching staff, with Dimel shifting responsibilities and adding three new coaches.

"This is now an excellent football staff," Dimel said. "We lost some good people, but fortunately we had no problem filling those positions with fine football coaches. We also made some changes on our current staff to reflect the strengths of each individual coach and at the same time solidify an already strong coaching staff.

"All these coaches know what the philosophy of Cougar football is, and in the next few months we will work together to get our players ready for a run for the Conference USA championship."

Bradley Dale Peveto, who was the assistant head coach as well as cornerbacks coach last year, was elevated to co-defensive coordinator and will also coach the safeties. Peveto will relinquish both his former roles with Dick Bumpas taking over as assistant head coach. Bumpus, who coaches the Cougars' defensive linemen, will continue to share the defensive coordinator duties.

Dimel also promoted Eric Wofford, who had been tackles/tight ends coach, to special teams coordinator. Wolford will also coach the running backs as Travis Pride shifts from running backs to wide receivers, where he takes over for Ted Gilmore, who joined the staff at Purdue.

Offensive line coach Clancy Barone was promoted to co-offensive coordinator with the departure of Phil Davis, who joined the staff at Arkansas State. Barone will continue to coach the offensive line.

Former graduate assistant Theron Aych received the final promotion. After coaching the kickers and punters and assisting with the offense last year, Aych will now coach the tight ends.

Dimel also hired three new coaches. Dave Warner, who coached at Connecticut, becomes the new quarterbacks coach and will share the offensive coordinator title with Barone. Frank Hernandez becomes cornerbacks coach and Greg Centilli becomes the new offensive graduate assistant. Hernandez comes to Houston from Wyoming, where he spent the last season as the Cowboys' recruiting coordinator and running backs coach.

The Cougars return 43 lettermen, including eight offensive starters and six defensive starters. The offensive group includes 1999 starter at receiver **Orlando Iglesias**, who along with **Brandon Middleton**, returns from a season-ending injury. Iglesias, a senior, and Middleton, a sophomore, will help Houston enter the season with the best receiving corps in Conference USA. Juniors **KeyKowa Belland** and **Brian Robinson** head into the 2001 season as the nation's No. 2 receiving tendem after finishing fourth best in 2000.

Defensively, the Cougars boast one of the top secondary units in C-USA with four of the five starters returning. Senior **Jason Parker** has been a standout at cornerback for three seasons, and he is joined in the secondary by safeties **Hamin** and **Hanik Milligan** and sophomore **Heard Robinson**.

Hamin Milligan is a senior and brother Hanik is a junior, while Robinson is a sophomore.

In order to have a winning season, Dimel must find a successor for four-year starting quarterback Jason McKinley, who finished his career with several records and a nation's best 41-game starting streak.

While recruiting in Texas through the years Dimel always aspired to be the head coach of a school in the state.

"This has been a career goal of mine," he said after accepting the job a year ago. "I know Houston is on the verge of being a great football program once again, and there is no reason why we cannot keep great players in the state and city at home. We will do whatever needs to be accomplished to be a champion again.

"I am really fired up about this opportunity. I look forward to bringing a high-powered and high-scoring offense to the fans of Houston, and in the process pack the stadium for our home games. This is going to be a lot of fun for everyone."

Dimel doesn't want another losing record. He will move into the 2001 season with one goal: win the Conference USA championship.

"We are hoping to make the natural improvement from the first year to the next," Dimel said. "The biggest thing is this football team understanding the system and understanding what we expect of them. Hopefully, this will translate into some victories for this football team in some close games.

"We think having six home games is definitely a much better situation to be in rather than the four games we had last year. We feel that should be a big advantage for us. The first goal is to get us into the postseason play, and if we can get through a very tough month of September at .500 or better, I think we have a realistic shot at reaching this goal."

2001 SCHEDULE

Sept.	1	Rice
	15	@Georgia
	22	Texas
	29	TCU
Oct.	6	@Army
	13	Memphis
	20	Cincinnati
	27	@Southern Mississippi
Nov.	3	@South Florida
	10	@Louisville
	17	UAB

QUARTERBACKS

The leading candidate to take over for McKinley is sophomore **Bubba Teague** (6-2, 190), who saw limited action last year as a backup. Because Teague is more mobile than McKinley, Houston may run more rollouts and options.

Teague sat out spring drills to concentrate on his academics, which gave his backups a chance for more snaps.

Teague will be challenged by junior walk-on **Kelly Robertson** (6-4, 210), who played baseball at Western Kentucky. Senior **Alvin Lee** (5-10, 177) will also be in the battle at quarterback. He has played both wide receiver and defensive back for the Cougars.

A classic drop-back passer, Robertson was impressive during spring drills. Lee will offer the Cougar offense a quick alternative during goal line and short-yardage situations.

"We were very pleasantly surprised at what Kelly Robertson brought to the table," Dimel said. "I thought Kelly did a great job, even better than what we expected him to do. If we had to pick a starter today, it would be a dogfight between [Kelly] and Bubba for that position. I think it is going to make both of them better players.

"Of course, Alvin Lee did some good things in the spring, and he will be used in strategic spots. Plus, we have the three young guys coming in, and they are all going to be given the opportunity to show what they can do."

In the spring game, Robertson, playing for both teams, completed 16-of-27 passes for 186 yards and two interceptions, while Lee was 4-of-10 for 46 yards.

RUNNING BACKS

The Cougars will have a three-player battle at running back between senior **Leif Penn** (5-9, 198) and juniors **Chris Robertson** (6-1, 220) and **Joffrey Reynolds** (5-10, 215).

Penn finished last season as the Cougars' starter. Reynolds was No. 1 before suffering a toe injury.

Robertson may be the sleeper of the group after sitting out 2000 after transferring from Texas. He has the size, speed and strength to be a factor in C-USA.

Last season, Penn finished second on the team in rushing with 346 yards on 92 carries. He scored three touchdowns. Penn also had seven catches for 24 yards and led the team in kickoffs with 26 for 513 yards (19.7 average). Penn ran for a season- and career-high 144 yards and two touchdowns against Tulane. He was second on the team behind Brian Robinson in all-purpose yardage with 80.3 per game,

Reynolds played in 10 games, leading the team in rushing with 534 yards on 136 carries (3.9 average) and with five rushing touchdowns. Reynolds also chipped in 24 receptions for 193 yards—he was 10th in the nation in receptions per game for a running back (2.7). He was chosen the Conference USA Offensive Player of the Week for his career-best performance against Army. Reynolds rushed for 201 yards and three touchdowns in leading the Cougars to victory. His 34 carries in that game were a season high for UH.

"Right there in those three guys, we feel [they] give us three running backs that are as good as anyone in the conference," Dimel said. "Add in **Anthony Evans** [freshman recruit] and this position becomes even better."

Evans (5-10, 205) played at Pearland (Texas) High School where he was chosen the *Houston Chronicle* Player of the Year. He rushed for 6,192 yards and 66 touchdowns in his career, topping 300 yards rushing time times. He also has a 3.46 grade-point average.

The No. 1 fullback is senior **Tommie Baldwin** (5-11, 237), who will be backed up by freshman **Corbin Moziesek** (6-1, 210).

WIDE RECEIVERS/TIGHT ENDS

The wide receiving duo of Robinson (6-4, 220) and Bell (5-10, 185) returns ranked No. 2 in the nation in tandem receiving. Add in the return of All-America candidate Iglesias, a 6-3, 220 senior, sophomore Middleton (5-11, 182) and junior **Jeremy McCardell** (6-0, 225) from injuries, and it's easy to understand why Dimel thinks he has the best receiving corps in Conference USA.

"With Key Bell and Brian Robinson back, with the numbers they put up," Dimel said, "and then with Orlando and Brandon back from injuries, we think we have some pretty good receivers. We feel right now we have eight receivers that I would feel comfortable if any eight of them were in the game. So we have good depth there."

Bell and Robinson combined for 134 catches and 1,612 yards in 2000.

Robinson was a load after coming on for Iglesias after his injury. He wound up with 80 catches and made second-team All-Conference USA. He had several games with double-figure catches. Robinson's 15 catches against Army were the most by a Cougar receiver in eight years. He finished as one of the top receivers in the nation with seven catches per game.

Robinson had 12 catches against Cincinnati, 12 against East Carolina, 11 (and a career-best 154 yards) against Tulane and 10 against LSU. He scored the winning touchdown in a triple-overtime victor over Memphis.

Bell made a career-best 54 catches for 722 yards and two touchdowns and was second on the team in receptions behind Robinson. He averaged almost five catches per game. Bell set a career high with 10 catches for 157 yards against SMU.

Iglesias caught 59 passes for 750 yards and two touchdowns in 1999 while Middleton's career numbers are 11 receptions for 463 yards and three touchdowns. Iglesias missed last season after suffering a severe ankle sprain in the season opener against Rice. He was granted a medical redshirt.

Providing depth will be sophomores **Choni Francis** (5-6, 170) and **Mark Hopkins** (6-4, 200), who played as freshmen in 2000, while junior **Ethan Ross** (5-10, 170) is a junior-college transfer who also can return punts.

Junior **Jonathan Pritchett** (6-4, 255) returns at tight end after missing all of last season with an injury, while his 2000 replacement, junior **Stephen Cucci** (6-4, 240), caught 16 passes for two touchdowns last year. Cucci spent the spring recovering from shoulder surgery and could be a question mark this fall.

Senior **Grover Thompson** (6-5, 275) and sophomore **Kyle Brown** (6-4, 240) will be the backups.

"Jonathan had a great spring," Dimel said. "He is a good mixture of speed, pass catching and run blocking. Grover is a huge tight end and is improving every day, and Kyle Brown moved over from linebacker and was one of the pleasant surprises of the spring."

OFFENSIVE LINE

Houston must replace tackle Josh Lovelady, who was a three-year starter and two-time member of the all-conference team.

The returning starters are seniors **Jabari Beauford** (6-4, 300) and **Darnerius Watson** (6-2, 300) and sophomore **Al James** (6-0, 295).

Beauford is the most experienced of the returning group, while James was voted to the C-USA All-Freshman squad.

Arizona transfer **Chris Redding** (6-4, 355), a junior, will challenge senior **Josh Demarr** (6-6, 301) for Lovelady's old spot, while either sophomore **Rex Hadnot** (6-1, 310) and junior guard **Tyrone Green** (6-2, 295) will start at the other guard slot.

Senior **Patrick Boatner** (6-1, 285) should back up both James at center and Hadnot and Watson at the two guard positions.

"We were very pleased with what our offensive line did for us this spring," Dimel said. "They improved on the toughness and on being physical, and it obviously showed with the effectiveness and the efficiency we ran the football [during the spring game.]"

2000 STATISTICS

Rushing offense	73.7	111
Passing offense	266.6	19
Total offense	340.4	78
Scoring offense	19.2	92
Net Punting	31.4	95
Punt returns	2.7	113
Kickoff returns	20.3	43
Rushing defense	137.4	44
Passing efficiency defense	117.3	54
Total defense	361.5	54
Scoring defense	33.6	100
Turnover margin	-5	82

Last column is ranking among Division I-A teams.

KICKERS

Dimel wasn't pleased with Houston's special teams last year. He wants to solidify the group this year, and must replace Mike Clark, who did the punting and place kicking last season.

Freshman walk-on **Dustin Bell** (6-2, 210) and senior **Jeff Patterson** (6-1, 205) will compete for the place-kicking job. Patterson was the Cougars' top punter through the first half of the 1999 season.

"Our biggest concern last year was just our consistency in field goals and PATs and punt returns," Dimel said. "Those were our Achilles' heals last year. If we get more consistent with these three areas, I feel things will work out for us."

DEFENSIVE LINE

The Cougars return only one defensive lineman for the second straight year. Back is senior **Lee Ingersoll** (6-3, 275), who is being moved from end to tackle this season.

"For us to be a good as we want to be, we have to be better on defense, and that goes without saying," Dimel said. "We feel good about our pass defense, and we want to make sure we are always shoring up our run defense."

Junior college standout **Bryan Hill** (6-1, 285) and redshirt freshman **Kendrick Goss** (6-4, 270) have the inside track at tackle and end, respectively, facing competition from senior **Robin Tremblay** (6-2, 275) and junior-college transfer and former Florida Marlins' farmhand **Quantaa Jackson** (6-2, 250).

The starter at right end should be sophomore **David Midyett** (6-2, 245), who was impressive last year as a freshman. Junior college transfer **Adrian Lee** (6-2, 235) will provide depth behind Midyett.

"We feel our d-line will come together for us and be quick and athletic," Dimel said. "Even though we only have one starter returning, I feel this is a talented group of players, and all should battle right to the end for playing time."

LINEBACKERS

A key for the Cougars will be replacing middle linebacker Wayne Rogers. Dimel believes Rogers' successor will be sophomore **Justin Davis** (6-2, 226), who sat out last season as a partial NCAA qualifier. Davis lacks Division I-A experience, but Dimel believes he exhibits the true instincts of a middle linebacker.

Dimel can also call on senior **Waymond Ervin** (5-11, 220), who was a part-time starter last year at weak-side linebacker.

"At the middle linebacker position Justin Davis had a great spring for us," Dimel said. "He is a big, physical linebacker who can run, and that is what you want your middle linebackers to look like. It is a tough job replacing someone the caliber of Wayne, but if there is young player out there in Wayne's mold, it is Justin."

Senior **Arthur Gissendanner** (6-2, 225) has battled some injuries in his career, but his athleticism at the weak linebacker spot is needed.

Freshmen **Travis Griffith** (6-4, 235) and **Nick Stavinoha** (6-1, 225) will back Gissendanner this season. Griffith is a former tight end who was a hurdles champion in high school, while Stavinoha moonlighted as a backup catcher for the Cougar baseball team during the early parts of spring.

DEFENSIVE BACKS

Four of five starters from 2000 return, led by outstanding senior Parker (5-10, 180). Parker will be starting for the fourth straight year.

A year ago, Parker led UH in passes defensed with 15 and was second on the team in interceptions with three. He picked off a pair of passes against SMU. Parker recorded career highs with six tackles in the Texas and SMU games.

The other starting cornerback should be freshman **Bobby Tillman** (5-10, 195), a converted running back with blazing speed. If he should have difficulty in adapting to defense, expect junior-college transfers **Roland Cola** (5-10, 170) and **Victor Malone** (5-11, 180) to battle to start at the corner opposite of Parker. Malone, who played at East Mississippi Junior College, runs a 4.3 40. Cola played at Dodge City (Kansas) Junior College and led his team with eight interceptions in 2000.

Junior Hanik Milligan (6-3, 200), who led the Cougars with five interceptions and was fifth in tackles with 86, will start at free safety. His older brother, Hamin (6-2, 185), has overcome two devastating knee injuries to become the starter at weak safety.

Add in sophomore Robinson (6-2, 205), and the Cougars have one of the best defensive backfields in C-USA.

Providing depth will be senior **Clint deGroot** (5-10, 200) and juniors **Greg Holte** (5-10, 185) and **Reggie Medlock** (5-10, 180) and junior college transfer **Jesse Sowells** (5-11, 195). A pair of converted running backs, redshirt freshmen **Chad Davis** (5-11, 185) and **Jermain Woodard** (5-11, 200) could see playing time.

"We addressed the corner situation during the off-season with our recruiting and early signees," Dimel said. "Jason Parker is as good a cornerback as anyone in the conference, so if we shore up the corner spot opposite him, I feel we will be tough to throw against.

"Talking about the safeties, Hamin Milligan is 100 percent healthy and he is a much different player when he's healthy. Hanik Milligan is one of the best safeties in the conference. Those two positions are extremely strong for us. Strong safety is our deepest position. Heard Robinson is the starter, but he is being pushed by Jesse Sowells who is being pushed by Jermain Woodard, so the depth is very impressive at this position."

PUNTERS

The heir apparent for Clark's punting chores is sophomore **Jimmy McClary** (6-6, 214), who spent last season on the sideline observing Clark after transferring from Hofstra.

SPECIAL TEAMS

Using 20-plus redshirts and an experienced group of walk-ons, Dimel believes he can turn the special teams into something "special."

The Cougars went through three long snappers last season and were working with a first-time holder, so PATs and field goals were always an adventure. With more experience at the return and cover teams, the Cougars should be able to improve upon kickoff and punt returns, while limiting the opposition to fewer yards on their returns.

Reynolds and Bell will handle the kickoff returns with Francis serving as the punt returner.

RECRUITING CLASS

The quarterback situation will become even more contested in the fall when three newcomers arrive.

Junior college quarterback **Nick Eddy**, who has three years of eligibility, and freshmen **Blade Bassler** and **Barrick Nealy** will all push for playing time.

Eddy (6-4, 205) comes from American River College in Courtland, Calif., where he threw for more than 2,500 yards and 16 touchdowns last season.

Bassler (6-4, 220) played at Rockdale (Texas) High School. He was ranked as the nation's No. 52 quarterback and No. 4 in Texas by Rivals100.com. Nealy (6-4, 205) played at Adamson High School in Classas, where he started three years at quarterback. He threw for 1,667 yards and 13 touchdowns while rushing for 796 yards last year. He finished with almost 4,000 yards and 30 touchdowns in his career.

"I am extremely pleased with the balance of this class," Dimel said. "We are balanced by position and balanced by geography. We have kids from ever part of this city, from the north, south, east and west. We have the city of Houston covered.

"Of course, our main concern was quarterback, and we addressed our needs with three outstanding players."

Houston signed 13 players from the Greater Houston area, including Evans at running back. The class includes 17 players on the defensive side of the ball and 11 on offense, and was rated No. 51 nationwide by Lone Star Recruting. It was rated No. 1 in Conference USA and No. 4 in the state behind Texas, Texas A&M and Texas Tech.

"This [recruiting] process began last February when we first arrived in Houston," Dimel said. "We began cultivating the Texas high school coaches, which opened up the doors at both ends, and we were able to share knowledge.

"During the spring we invited the coaches to be a part of our development, and this process culminated this fall when we were able to sign not only the diamonds in the rough, but also the top quality football players of this state."

The prizes in the class are Bassier, whose father played for the legendary Bill Yeoman at Houston, and safety **Carlos Jones** (5-10, 190), who turned down an abundance of major offers to stay close to home.

Jones, who played at Clear Lake High School in Houston, was listed as one of the top safeties in the nation. Last year, he made 102 tackles, intercepted two passes and blocked a punt. As a running back, Jones averaged 6.42 yards per carry and scored five touchdowns. He finished his career on defense with more than 300 tackles, six interceptions, four forced fumbles, seven sacks and five fumble recoveries.

BLUE RIBBON ANALYSIS

OFFENSE	B-
SPECIAL TEAMS	C-
DEFENSE	C
INTANGIBLES	B+

Not having Teague present for spring drills didn't help solve the problem at quarterback, but Dimel did find out that Robertson could be an adequate starter or backup in the fall. Davis seems to be the answer as to who would replace Rogers at middle linebacker.

For Houston and Dimel to end the season above .500, the special teams must rebound from a disastrous 2000.

The season begins on Sept. 1 when Rice invades "The Quinn" for the season opener. The Cougars then travel to Georgia on Sept. 15 before coming home to play Texas and TCU.

If the Cougars get through the first four games at 3-1 or 2-2, Dimel's streak should start once again. He endured his first losing season in 2000, and he didn't like it one bit.

(S.C.)

2000 RESULTS

Rice	L	27-30	0-1
LSU	L	13-28	0-2
Army	W	31-30	1-2
Texas	L	0-48	1-3
SMU	W	17-15	2-3
Cincinnati	L	31-48	2-4
Memphis	W	33-30	3-4
Southern Mississippi	L	3-6	3-5
Tulane	L	23-41	3-6
East Carolina	L	20-62	3-7
Lousiville	L	13-32	3-8

Louisville

LOCATION	**Louisville, KY**
CONFERENCE	**Conference USA**
LAST SEASON	**9-3 (.750)**
CONFERENCE RECORD	**6-1 (1st)**
OFFENSIVE STARTERS RETURNING	**8**
DEFENSIVE STARTERS RETURNING	**6**
NICKNAME	**Cardinals**
COLORS	**Red & Black**

HOME FIELD Papa John's Cardinal Stadium (42,000)
HEAD COACH John L. Smith (Weber St. '72)
RECORD AT SCHOOL 23-13 (3 years)
CAREER RECORD 92-51 (12 years)
ASSISTANTS Art Valero (Boise State '81)
Assistant Head Coach/Offensive Line
Scott Linehan (Idaho '86)
Offensive Coordinator/Quarterbacks
Chris Smeland (Cal Poly '74)
Defensive Coordinator/Safeties
Mike Cox (Idaho '89)
Linebackers
Greg Burns (Washington State '95)
Cornerbacks
Steve Stripling (Colorado '76)
Defensive Line
Charles Chandler (Central Washington '88)
Running Backs
Jim McElwain (Eastern Washington '83)
Wide Receivers
Greg Nord (Kentucky '78)
Tight Ends
TEAM WINS (last 5 yrs.) 5-1-7-7-9
FINAL RANK (last 5 yrs.) 60-79-75-70-33
2000 FINISH Lost to Colorado State in Liberty Bowl.

COACH AND PROGRAM

John L. Smith is a coach with a plain brown wrapper name, but his credentials and track record are snazzy. In his third year at Louisville, Smith, 52, directed the Cardinals to a 9-3 record, their first Conference USA title and an unprecedented third consecutive bowl game. The Cardinals are playing a very hard-to-ignore second banana on a campus, in a city and a state where basketball will always be king.

While Louisville's football program has launched a surprising number of recognizable names to the NFL—Johnny Unitas, Joe Jacoby, Doug Buffone, Tom Jackson, Lenny Lyles, Mark Clayton, Otis Wilson—basketball has remained in the center ring. That won't be changing now that Rick Pitino has arrived on the scene. True to form, Pitino swept into Louisville during Kentucky Derby week with a high-priced colt running for the roses. One day leading up to the race, Smith showed up at the backside barns and was asked by a media type if he owned any horses. Smith quipped, "I own the pony that leads Pitino's horse to the gate."

While that comment might be construed as a metaphor for the relative status of the two sports in Louisville, Smith's program stands tall on its own merits. His Cardinals boast an exciting offense. They averaged 35.3 points a game in 2000, scoring at least 32 points in the nine wins.

Junior quarterback **Dave Ragone**'s 27 touchdown passes are the leading figure for a returning Division I-A quarterback. Louisville's defense ranked fourth nationally against the run (79.9 yards per game) and 15th in total defense (304 yards per game). Louisville ranked second in the nation in forced turnovers with 38. The Cardinals have also won two straight against arch rival Kentucky and the series is tied at 4-4 since it was renewed in 1993.

Last season's Conference USA title followed back-to-back 7-5 seasons since Smith was hired away from Utah State to clean up the brief but messy Ron Cooper era that ended with a 1-10 debacle in 1997. In bringing in Smith, Louisville made a smart hire on a guy virtually unknown east of the Mississippi River. The Idaho native started his career with a great run at Division I-AA Idaho, then moved up to I-A at Utah State. In 12 years as a head coach, he's posted only one non-winning record (4-7), that coming in his first year at Utah State. Louisville was his first job east of Wyoming, where he was assistant head coach in 1986.

Smith was one of three nominees for the Eddie Robinson Award for the job he did at Louisville last year. In a move to keep Smith on board (Arizona State made a run at him last year) the school rewarded him with a new contract, virtually doubling his package to $800,000 annually for eight years. Not Pitino money, but not bad.

Recruiting was good last year. The Cardinals have made a living getting the occasional Louisville product to stay home and hitting more traditional talent hotbeds hard. The depth chart reflects Louisville's focus on Ohio, Alabama and Florida.

The Cardinals opened the 2000 season on a momentum-boosting note, knocking off Kentucky, 40-34, in overtime. After getting scalped at Florida State, Louisville won seven-of-eight remaining regular season games, the only setback against East Carolina when Ragone suffered a collarbone injury. The C-USA title sent the Cards to the Liberty Bowl, where they lost, 22-17, to Colorado State.

Optimism in 2001 is high. Eight starters are back on offense, including conference offensive player-of-the-year Ragone. Safety **Anthony Floyd**, a Walter Camp All-American, heads up a defense with several key positions to fill but potential to be very good. Smith had the discipline to redshirt every one of his 2000 signees, so an infusion of first-year talent should help fill in the holes.

The biggest challenge for the Cardinals, though, may be getting used to life wearing a bull's eye on their backs.

"The hard part isn't getting to the top. It's staying there," Smith said. "Our players and coaches have to respond to the challenge that everybody in our league is gunning for us. It's our responsibility not to get complacent and continue to work hard."

This year's schedule includes a late addition of New Mexico State on Aug. 23. That gives the Cards a head start on the Sept. 1 date at Kentucky and pushes the start of fall camp back into July. Colorado State comes to Papa John's Cardinal Stadium for an Oct. 4 rematch of the Liberty Bowl. Playing four of the last five games on the road isn't ideal, especially finishing at TCU, Conference USA's newest member.

Louisville's success is reflected in the Cardinals being invited to play four weeknight games—against New Mexico State, Colorado State, Southern Miss and East Carolina—the latter three of which will be for TV.

2001 SCHEDULE

Aug.	23	New Mexico State (John Thompson)
Sept.	1	@Kentucky
	8	Western Carolina
	15	@Illinois
	29	Memphis
Oct.	4	Colorado State
	16	Southern Mississippi
	27	@Cincinnati
Nov.	3	@Tulane
	10	Houston
	17	@East Carolina
	24	@TCU

QUARTERBACKS

This time a year ago as the post-Chris Redman Era began, Ragone (6-4, 240) was trying to overcome his utter lack of experience and beat out senior challenger Mike Watkins. Turned out it was no contest. Ragone all but made Louisville fans forget Redman, passing for 2,621 yards and 27 touchdowns.

The big left-hander from Middleburg Heights, Ohio ranked 14th in the nation in pass efficiency with a 142.2 rating, hit 61 percent (217-of-354) of his attempts and was voted Conference USA Offensive Player of the Year.

He was an immediate success, beating Kentucky in his starting debut and completing 23-of-30 passes for 256 yards and three touchdowns. He flourished in Louisville's one-back, spread offense, but it would be inaccurate to paint the Cardinals as one-dimensional. Ragone passed for more than 300 yards in just two games.

Ragone says he's miles ahead of where he was going into the 2000 season. After all, he redshirted in '98 and attempted only two throws in all of the '99 season.

"He's grown in about every way imaginable," Smith said. "Everything he did well last season, he'll do better this season."

Ragone has added 15 pounds to get up to 240 and wouldn't mind hitting 250. The extra bulk may come in handy; he was Louisville's second-leading rusher last year with 252 yards. He passed for two scores and rushed for two more in an upset of No. 11 Southern Miss.

Quicker, stronger, more confident and a better team leader. All those positive attributes apply to Ragone in 2001. He hopes to improve his deep throws this year, too, using a little more touch. He is smart enough to realize he doesn't need to add any muscle to his head. He is making it a personal mission to stay hungry.

"I've never been in this position," he told the *Louisville Courier-Journal*. "I've always had to knock somebody off or come out and prove myself against another guy to get to play. Coming out this spring ... the last thing I wanted to do was feel secure."

Offensive coordinator and quarterbacks coach Scott Linehan will be alert to make sure Ragone doesn't get complacent.

"What he did last year was fine," Linehan said. "He's got to up his standard to another level. The other thing we've got to do is keep him healthy."

The backup is redshirt freshman **Stefan LeFors** (6-0, 185) out of Baton Rouge, La. LeFors was the scout team quarterback in 2000. An excellent athlete, he had a good spring, completing 9-of-18 passes for 159 yards in the spring game.

Gerry Ahrens (6-1, 180), a Louisville native, would have probably had the backup job, but he got wanderlust. Ahrens, who got only one pass attempt last year as a redshirt freshman, transferred to Arkansas last spring. But Ahrens had a change of heart and returned to Louisville over the summer. Because of the transfer, he won't be eligible until 2002.

RUNNING BACKS

Ragone wasn't the only instant success on the Louisville offense. Senior **Tony Stallings**, who began his career at linebacker, emerged as the leading rusher with 819 yards. That's 818 more than he accumulated in 1999. Much as Ragone filled Redman's shoes at quarterback, Stallings (5-11, 205) blossomed to ease concerns over the departure of Frank Moreau to the NFL.

Stallings, who started eight games at linebacker in 1998, had only one rushing attempt to his credit in '99. He fended off several challengers in preseason and gave the Cardinals a solid running game. Stallings averged 4.5 yards a carry and had three 100-yard games, including a season-high 144 against Kentucky. One of his most impressive outings was a 93-yard effort against a hard-nosed Southern Miss defense.

Stallings proved durable, with two games of 30 or more carries. He also has decent hands, as evidenced by his 21 receptions and three touchdowns last fall.

Junior **Henry Miller**, seldom seen as a sophomore, took advantage of spring practice to get back in the mix. Miller (6-0, 215) had only five carries last fall, but moved up the depth chart in the absence of **Chris Lester** (6-1, 210) and **T.J. Patterson** (6-0, 210).

Lester, a senior who got 52 carries last year, missed spring practice because of academics. Patterson, a sophomore, had 31 carries a year ago, but had ankle problems. Miller, who had back surgery before the 2000 season, made the most of his increased reps and could start the season as Stallings' backup.

The running game will get ample opportunity to contribute this year because Louisville wants to keep defenses honest.

"If you've followed our offense over the past three years," Linehan said, "where we've rushed the ball effectively, we've won those games. When we're really one-sided throwing the ball, our record drops dramatically. We throw it first to set up the run, but we've got to run to win, even though we're a throwing team."

WIDE RECEIVERS/TIGHT ENDS

Arnold Jackson, who broke the Division I-A all-time receiving record with 300 career catches, is gone, but there's no doubt who will be the featured receiver in 2001. Senior **Deion Branch** actually managed to outshine Jackson last year and is back for his senior season. While Jackson was "held" to 63 catches and a career-low 7.4-yard average by frequent double coverages, Branch (5-10, 180) finished with 71 receptions for 1,106 yards, a 14.3-yard-per-catch average.

Like Ragone at quarterback and Stallings at running back, Branch also emerged from obscurity to lead the offense at his position. The junior college transfer from Albany, Ga. was redshirted in 1999 but came out of nowhere to be among the nation's receiving leaders. He caught at least eight passes in five different games and recorded a team-high nine touchdown catches. After five 100-yard games, Branch was selected first-team all-conference and voted Louisville's team MVP.

Senior **Zek Parker** (5-10, 200) will benefit from a restored fifth year. The former partial qualifier got his academics in order and was rewarded with another season of eligibility. Parker had 30 catches last year but was even more valuable as a kickoff return jet. He averaged 28.9 yards, No. 2 in the nation, in kickoff returns. He has three career return touchdowns and seven of 60-plus yards.

Junior **Damien Dorsey** (5-7, 170) came out of spring practice as the No. 3 receiver in an offense that needs at least that many receivers on the field. Dorsey, who was recruited by several SEC schools, had 11 catches last fall. He has only three career touchdown catches, but two of them are in bowl games.

"Dorsey is gonna be the biggest surprise on the team," Linehan said. "He and Branch are the same type players. They're playmakers. Dorsey does things that don't show up in box scores. He gives an unbelievable effort as a blocker, and makes plays away from the ball that kind of separate him from the average guy."

The Cardinals have three redshirt freshmen eager to get in the mix. **J.R. Russell** (6-3, 185), **Antoine Harris** (5-10, 175) and **Tiger Jones** (5-11, 175) are battling to get on the field. Russell is distinctive in that he's 6-3. He had five catches in the spring game. Sophomore **Victor Glenn** (6-0, 170) is also available.

Tight end is in good shape. **Ronnie Ghent** (6-2, 230) made All-Conference USA first-team last year with 27 catches for 392 yards. He was a pleasant surprise after being academically ineligible in 1999. Ghent's statistics indicate he's a good athlete.

Richard Owens (6-4, 265) is the blocking tight end. As such, he made only one catch in 2000. Look for that to change this fall. Owens was more involved in the passing game during the spring. Smith wants to be able to go more often to a two-tight end formation, but both of them need to be receiving options to keep the defense honest.

OFFENSIVE LINE

There's a hole in the middle of the Cardinal line that measures nearly 600 pounds and 52 consecutive starts.

First-team All-C-USA center Jason Padget and second-team All-C-USA guard Joe O'Shaughnessy are both departed and the Cards spent considerable time in spring practice trying to figure out what to do about it.

There is some good news to report. **Rob Eble** returns at tackle and the senior (6-6, 295) from Marietta, Ga., will likely move from the weak side, where he started 10 games, to the strong side slot.

Senior **Aaron Dardzinski** (6-1, 270) enters his third year as a starter at one of the guard slots. Dardzinski isn't mammoth by today's offensive line standards, but he is the unsung hero of the group.

Junior **Ariel Rodriguez** (6-4, 290) and massive senior **Michael Bowers** (6-3, 320) are battling at center. Bowers will move inside to either center or guard after starting nine games at tackle last year.

"Bowers may end up at center or guard," Linehan said. "He's gonna be one of the five guys in there. He's earned that."

Antoine Sims, (6-2, 295), a junior, will be pushed at guard by whoever doesn't win the center position. There's also huge sophomore **Jason Hilliard** (6-6, 330) in the mix.

One of the spring surprises was **Buster Ashley**, a redshirt freshman from Owensboro, Ky., who made a big move on the starting tackle job. Ashley (6-3, 285) was recognized last year as offensive scout team player of the year. He came on strong last spring after **Jonta Woodard**, (6-5, 325) a projected starter, suffered a sprained knee. Now Woodard, a junior, will have to beat Ashley out of the lineup, but he has the tools to do it and could well be a starter by opening day.

2000 STATISTICS

Rushing offense	134.3	69
Passing offense	256.5	26
Total offense	390.8	42
Scoring offense	35.3	15
Net Punting	35.9	37
Punt returns	8.2	80
Kickoff returns	26.1	2
Rushing defense	79.9	4
Passing efficiency defense	104.1	20
Total defense	304.2	15
Scoring defense	23.6	51
Turnover margin	+12	6

Last column is ranking among Division I-A teams.

KICKERS

Sophomores **Wade Tydlacka** (5-11, 220) and **Nathan Smith** (5-8, 160) shared the kicking chores last fall, but redshirt freshman **Brad Shushman** (5-10, 190) from St. Joseph, Mich., might be the man on opening day. Smith likes to keep his kickers on their toes, so to speak, and promotes competition.

Tydlacka started the season last year but lost the job after a groin injury. He was 6-of-9 on field goals. Smith, who replaced him, was 5-of-7. Combined they were a flawless 44-of-44 on extra points.

Shushman will be a threat to take the field-goal job. Tydlacka has a strong leg and could be the kickoff man if nothing else.

DEFENSIVE LINE

New defensive line coach Steve Stripling replaces Nick Holt and finds a good news-bad news proposition in his Louisville debut. The good news is the return of defensive ends **Dewayne White** and **Michael Josiah**, both of whom are established difference-makers. The bad news is the absence of departed tackles Donovan Arp and Derrick Kennedy.

White (6-2, 270), a sophomore, burst onto the scene as a freshman last fall and recorded 12 sacks while playing both tackle and end. The Marbury, Ala., product also had a team-high 22 quarterback hurries and was an all-conference freshman team selection. A former high school running back, White has obviously beefed up but still has good foot speed.

Whether White spends most of his time at end, or helps fill the void at tackle remains to be seen.

On the other side, Josiah (6-4, 235), a junior, returns as the team leader with 13 sacks. Another Alabama product, Josiah managed to record his 13 sacks last year despite missing one game and playing only three snaps of another. Don't ever question Josiah's toughness. He could play without the pads. He earned a spot on Kenya's under-18 rugby national team before returning to the United States for his final two years of high school. He's working on getting stronger.

"Both Dewayne and Michael were young guys who had nice seasons for us," defensive coordinator Chris Smeland said. "They need to continue to improve off last year, and if they do, they have a chance to be pretty special."

The question of who takes over inside wasn't finalized in the spring. Arp, a second-team All-C-USA pick, and Kennedy both leave big shoes to fill in a defense that ranked No. 4 nationally against the run.

The Cardinals will be young at tackle. The leading candidates to start are sophomore **Scott Lopez** (6-3, 270) and redshirt freshman **Bobby Leffew** (6-4, 270). Leffew, a Danville, Ky., product, has put on weight since his high school days at tight end and was impressive on the scout team last fall. Louisville has high expectatons for him and hopes Leffew is ready to be a prime-time player in 2001. Lopez, a sophomore, made only one tackle last fall but came out of spring with an edge over a couple of more experienced guys.

Senior **Koby Clark** (6-5, 270) and junior **Devon Thomas** (6-1, 250) have been through the wars and are likely to play significant snaps even if they don't start. Redshirt freshman **Tyrone Satterfield** (6-2, 315) is another youngster who will probably be in the mix. Another redshirt freshman, **Marcus Jones** (6-2, 230), will be trying to get his foot in the door.

Junior **Keeshan Lowe** (6-1, 290) hopes to make an impact after transferring at the semester break from Copiah-Lincoln Junior College. The big Mississippian suffered a sprained knee that curtailed his spring practice, but he'll be ready to go in two-a-days.

"We would have liked to have gotten a few more reps out of Lowe in the spring," Smeland said. "We don't have the experience we had last year, but we've got a few more numbers."

LINEBACKERS

The burning question is who can take over for Rashad Harris, the All-C-USA second-teamer at middle linebacker? Harris was Louisville's leading tackler with 105 stops and an emotional leader in the huddle. Losing a four-year starter cannot be minimized.

Junior **Michael Brown** returns at the "Bandit" linebacker spot and senior **Jeromy Freitag** is back at the other outside spot.

Smith, who has a successful track record of switching players from one position to another, is hoping to strike pay dirt again with junior **Chad Lee**. Lee (6-2, 245) contributed as a reserve defensive end last fall, but opened spring at middle linebacker.

"Chad is a heck of a football player," Smith told the *Louisville Courier-Journal*. "The question facing us was, how do we get him on the field for 70 plays instead of 30? And at defensive end that probably wasn't going to happen. He's kind of a tweener as a D-line guy, so we've tried him in Rashad Harris' spot to see what he can do."

Early returns were encouraging. Lee is a playmaker. He had 10 tackles-for-loss in the final five games last fall. The key will be getting to the point where Lee plays on instinct instead of having to think too much.

Another possibility in the middle is junior **Jeremy Collins** (6-1, 240), a two-year letterman.

"He's been in the program a couple of years," Smeland said. "He's a smart kid we're gonna have to count on to spell some time at that spot. He's capable of doing that."

Brown (5-11, 210), a two-year starter, is rock solid at the Bandit position. The homegrown prep star at Butler High School had three interceptions and three sacks last year, along with 94 tackles.

Freitag (6-1, 225) was an immediate contributor last fall after transferring from Sacramento City College. He started five games and had three double-figure tackle performances.

Junior **B.J. Steele** (6-1, 215), redshirt freshman **Ryan McDermond** (6-1, 240), sophomore **Rod Day** (6-1, 215) and sophomore **Michael Everett** (5-11, 190) hope to earn their way onto to the field in some capacity. Everett was a special-teams standout who could be in for more playing time as a sophomore. McDermond looked good on the scout team last fall.

DEFENSIVE BACKS

Safety might be the strongest position on the football team with juniors **Anthony Floyd** and **Curry Burns** returning as established stars. On the other hand, cornerback might be the biggest question mark.

Louisville said farewell to last year's starting corners, Rashad Holman, an All-C-USA second-teamer, and Antonio Roundtree. Holman was the team's undisputed top cover man with a school-record 20 passes broken up. He also had six interceptions. Roundtree was a two-year starter.

Josh Minkins (5-10, 175), a sophomore who is the only returning letterman at corner, pretty much nailed down one spot in the spring. **Laroni Gallishaw** (5-11, 200) is a redshirt freshman who just might win the other job.

"We feel good about both those guys," Smeland said. "We've also got some young guys to get in mix. We've got some junior college guys coming in, but you don't know about them until they start doing it for you."

Junior college transfers **Kayjaei Williams** (5-11, 165) and **Chris Johnson** (6-0, 180), both juniors, arrive in fall camp. **Wilbur Benson** (5-8, 165), also a junior, got an early start in the spring, bringing junior college All-America credentials from San Francisco City College. A Hopkinsville, Ky., product, Benson is glad to be back home.

J.T. Haskins (5-10, 170), a high school quarterback in Lexington, is a redshirt freshman who will probably end up in a reserve role at corner.

Floyd (5-10, 195) is an All-America candidate at free safety. In fact, he made the Walter Camp All-America team as a sophomore. Floyd tied for the national lead with 10 interceptions last fall, which also broke Ray Buchanan's school record.

Floyd, who has a brother Antwan at Penn State, was a steal for the Cardinals out of Youngstown, Ohio. He made two starts as a freshman in 1999.

Burns (6-1, 200) plays his role at strong safety beautifully. He notched 104 tackles last fall, recording 10 or more in six games. He endeared himself to Cardinal fans by blocking a potential game-winning field goal by Kentucky at the end of regulation, allowing Louisville to win in overtime.

When the Cards go to their nickel package, **Brian Gaines** (5-8, 200) usually gets the call. The senior from Daytona Beach is one of the team's biggest hitters. Redshirt freshman **Kerry Rhodes** (6-3, 185) had an impressive spring.

PUNTERS

Junior **Chris Sivori** (6-0, 230), a hometown guy from St. Xavier High School, is back for his third year. His 40.1 average last fall was an improvement over his sophomore year. Sivori proved his toughness averaging 39.2 yards on five punts in Siberia-like conditions at the Liberty Bowl. Sivori also helps out as holder on place kicks and was flawless last fall.

Junior long snapper **Chip Mattingly** (6-2, 245) was Sivori's high school teammate at St. Xavier.

SPECIAL TEAMS

Parker was the nation's No. 2 kickoff return man in 2000, averaging a whopping 28.9 yards per attempt. Parker has seven kickoff returns of 60-plus yards in his career. In '99, he took two kickoff returns the distance.

Departed Arnold Jackson was the top punt-return man last fall, so that job is open. Branch, the team's leading receiver, has some experience, getting seven chances last year.

RECRUITING CLASS

Diversity is the key to this recruiting class. The Cardinals signed players from nine different states and added five junior college signees, including three in the secondary.

The secondary is always a crucial area in a league that throws as much as C-USA, but it's more paramount for Louisville, which lost its starting cornerbacks.

Benson enrolled in the spring. Williams and Johnson arrive in fall camp to compete for the vacancies.

Benson, a former Kentucky all-stater, was a first-team All-America selection by *JC Gridwire* as well as an All-California Junior College selection at San Francisco Community College.

Williams was another first-team All-California selection. He blocked six field goals in two years at El Camino Junior College. Johnson was an honorable mention All-American at Blinn (Texas) Junior College, where he had seven interceptions and two blocked field goals in 2000.

Louisville sought more help for the secondary by signing **Jon Gannon** (5-11, 175) of Cleveland, Ohio. Gannon had seven interceptions as a senior at St. Ignasius High School, where he was a second-team all-state pick.

Michale Troupe (5-11, 190) distinguished himself as a defensive back, running back and quarterback at Athens (Ala.) High School. He was a first-team All-Alabama selection as an athlete.

Lionel Gates (6-1, 205) of Jacksonville, Fla. has great credentials as a running back. He rushed for more than 3,000 yards his last two years at Parker High School.

"As you look at him, he's physical enough," Smith said. "It's just a matter of how quickly he adapts mentally."

Greg Tinch (6-3, 220) of Albany, Ga., could compete early for playing time, even though he didn't play football as a senior. Tinch, who also will play basketball at Louisville, caught 50 passes for 1,112 yards as a junior.

Junior college signee **Chris Thigpen** (6-3, 295) could bolster the offensive line. He was an all-state selection at Copiah-Lincoln (Miss.) Junior College after first making a name for himself at Fairfield (S.C.) Central High School, where he was a consensus all-state tight end.

Jason Spitz (6-4, 290) of Jacksonville, Fla. also might help the offensive line right away. He was a second-team all-stater.

Fred Nolan (6-4, 280) is another Florida all-stater. He played offense and defense at Seabreeze High School in Ormond Beach, Fla.

Montavious Stanley (6-3, 250) of Alabany, Ga., was rated as the No. 33 defensive tackle in the country by Rivals.com. He had 112 tackles and 11 sacks as a senior.

The only quarterback signee was **Adam Ellis** (6-1, 205) of Russell Springs, Ky. Ellis, a two-time all-district pick, passed for a school-record 17 touchdowns last year.

"We've made a living of getting out and finding some guy under a rock who isn't heavily recruited but has a big upside," Smith told the *Louisville Courier-Journal*. "But this year, we had a chance to get after some big-time guys. And we wanted to go after those guys while not getting away from what we've done to be successful."

BLUE RIBBON ANALYSIS

OFFENSE	A
SPECIAL TEAMS	B
DEFENSE	B-
INTANGIBLES	B

Smith has done a terrific job in three seasons, producing 23 wins and three consecutive bowl bids. The Cardinals are knocking on the door of the Top 25 as Smith begins his fourth year.

The offense will be exciting, with Ragone set to expand on his banner debut season. He should be a better quarterback in his second season as a starter, but it'll be tough to improve on the big numbers he put up in 2000.

Ragone is the trigger man, but he doesn't have to carry the entire offense on his shoulders. Branch, the top receiver, and Stallings, the top rusher, are also back along with All-Conference USA tight end Ghent.

The only possible hangup is replacing two stalwarts in the offensive line, but that task appears doable.

"Last year," Linehan said, "every skill position we had on offense was a question mark going into the season. We kind of snuck up on some people. There will be no sneaking up on people this year, so we'll have to step it up a notch."

Defensively, there are some serious holes to fill. Defensive tackles Arp and Kennedy, plus middle linebacker Harris, are all gone, meaning Louisville has to rebuild up the middle.

The Cards ranked No. 4 in the nation against the run last year, but will need fresh faces to step up big-time to achieve that kind of statistical superlative this year.

Replacing both starting corners is a risky prospect at any school, and Louisville is no exception.

But this is a defense with some proven playmakers, namely ends White and Josiah, bandit Brown and safeties Burns and Floyd.

If Louisville can once again produce turnovers in bunches, it should help cut opponents' scoring down from last year's 22.4 points a game.

But the schedule is tricky. Louisville could have two impressive scalps on its belt from Kentucky and Illinois by the time it gets into Conference USA play. Both games are on the road, but Louisville has a solid shot in both.

(M.S.)

2000 RESULTS

Kentucky	W	40-34	1-0
Grambling State	W	52-0	2-0
Florida State	L	0-31	2-1
Connecticut	W	41-22	3-1
UAB	W	38-17	4-1
Cincinnati	W	38-24	5-1
East Carolina	L	25-28	5-2
Tulane	W	35-32	6-2
Southern Mississippi	W	49-28	7-2
Army	W	38-17	8-2
Houston	W	32-13	9-2
Colorado State (Liberty)	L	17-22	9-3

Memphis

LOCATION	**Memphis, TN**
CONFERENCE	**Conference USA**
LAST SEASON	**4-7 (.364)**
CONFERENCE RECORD	**2-5 (7th)**
OFFENSIVE STARTERS RETURNING	**8**
DEFENSIVE STARTERS RETURNING	**7**
NICKNAME	**Tigers**
COLORS	**Royal Blue & Gray**
HOME FIELD	**Liberty Bowl Memorial (62,380)**
HEAD COACH	**Tommy West (Tennessee '76)**
RECORD AT SCHOOL	**First Year**
CAREER RECORD	**33-35 (7 Years)**
ASSISTANTS	
	Randy Fichtner (Purdue '85) **Offensive Coordinator**
	Clay Helton ('94) **Running Backs**
	Charlie Coe (Kansas State '73) **Receivers**
	Rick Mallory (Washington '83) **Offensive Line**
	Russ Huesman (UT-Chattanooga '82) **Tight Ends/Recruiting**
	Rick Whitt (Catawba '76) **Defensive Coordinator/Linebackers**
	Tim Walton (Ohio State '94) **Secondary**
	Joe Cullen (Massachusetts '88) **Defensive Line**
	Tim Banks (Central Michigan '94) **Outside Linebackers**
TEAM WINS (last 5 yrs.)	**4-4-2-5-4**
FINAL RANK (last 5 yrs.)	**67-69-84-57-81**
2000 FINISH	**Lost to Tulane in regular-season finale.**

COACH AND PROGRAM

When Clemson ousted Tommy West in favor of Tommy Bowden in 1998, West felt fortunate to be hired by Rip Scherer as the defensive coordinator at Memphis for the 2000 season.

West headed to Memphis not sure whether he would ever be a head coach again and determined to never get as close to a group of players as the ones he left at Clemson.

"I feel so fortunate to have had to sit out only one year, to coach one year here and then get another shot at being a head coach," West said. "The first thing I had to do was decide whether I wanted to be a head coach again. Once I did that, I became real excited about this opportunity.

"I also swore that I would just come to Memphis and coach and not get so attached to the players. But last year I was so close to the defensive players. I can't help it. I love these kids."

Maybe West is lucky to get the chance to be a head coach so quickly after leaving Clemson. Or maybe Memphis is the fortunate one.

"I am delighted to announce that Tommy West has accepted the head coach's position at the University of Memphis," Memphis athletic director R.C. Johnson said on Nov. 30 last year. "We have talked to numerous applicants over the past 10 days, but when you compare their resumes, look at where they have been and what they have accomplished, it became obvious that Tommy West was the right choice for the Tigers.

"I have received ringing endorsements from athletic officials at Clemson, from other coaches, from players and supporters of this university. There were all complimentary of coach West and the program he ran at Clemson and the work he has done for our football team."

As Clemson's head coach from 1993-98, West guided the Tigers to four bowl appearances, 12 road wins and four wins over Associated Press Top 25 teams. The 1998 Peach Bowl was Clemson's third consecutive bowl appearance, an accomplishment that only 16 other programs could claim. The Tigers were ranked No. 12 in the country that year in rushing defense and No. 25 in total defense. The team threw for more than 2,000 yards, marking just the second time that had happened in Clemson history.

West also did a good job off the field. Sixty-one players were chosen to the ACC Academic Honor Roll in his last year years, twice as many as any four-year period in school history.

Those accomplishments speak volumes about the pressure of coaching at Clemson. They weren't nearly enough to allow West to keep his job.

West's accomplishments in his one season as Memphis' defensive coordinator were also stellar. He took over a Memphis defense that had been ranked 23rd in the nation in 1999 in total defense, but had been unable to defend against the run. Memphis finished the 2000 season ranked No. 5 in the nation in total defense and No. 1 in rushing defense. The Tigers limited nine of their 11 opponents to less than 100 yards rushing. No team rushed for more than 125 yards against the Tigers.

"This is a great opportunity at Memphis," West said. "Of course, any time there is a great opportunity that always means there is a great challenge. This is a program that hasn't had a winning record in six years.

"The most important thing for us to do is get all the people in the right places to be able to compete in this league [Conference USA]. We need to have a winning season. I would love to have 12 wins, but the first order of business is a winning season."

Getting the Tigers to a bowl game is another priority.

"We really need to get to a bowl game," West said. "That's our first tier to reach here, to have a winning season and get to a bowl game. That doesn't mean we can't win our conference championship this year, but that's our pecking order."

West retained six coaches off Sherer's staff and chose Rick Whitt as the Tigers' defensive coordinator. Whitt coached with West at Clemson and Division I-AA Tennessee-Chattanooga.

"I have coached with Rick Whitt for a number of years and I could not think of a better person to serve as my defensive coordinator," West said. "He was instrumental in helping us to our national ranking in defense last year and I'm sure he will continue that tradition with this year's squad."

Whitt served as defensive coordinator at Chattanooga from 1993-99 before joining the Memphis staff in 2000 as outside linebackers coach.

West completed his coaching staff by hiring offensive coordinator Randy Fichtner, defensive line coach Joe Cullen and outside linebacker coach Tim Banks. Fichtner served as offensive coordinator at Arkansas State the last four years.

"I don't believe I had ever met Randy before I started interviewing him for our offensive coordinator position," West said. "However, after the first interview I knew that he was a great fit for our staff. His football philosophy and mine are very similar. Everything just seems to click."

With 44 lettermen returning, including eight offensive and seven defensive starters, West and his staff are eager to start the 2001 season.

"I'm really excited about this staff," West said. "It's a blue-collar group, a hard working group. That fits me perfectly. I'm not fancy, just a hard worker."

West believes Memphis can once again be an outstanding defensive unit.

"I don't know if we can put up those numbers again," he said. "Any time you lead the nation in a category, you're outstanding. Can we beat those numbers? I'm not sure.

"The most important thing we want to work on is scoring defense. That will be our goal. We can't give up as much scoring as we did in the second half last year."

Of offense, the Tigers will join most other teams in the county with the spread offense.

"We have a lot of good defensive players and we expect some people to step up on that side of the ball," West said. "Our problems are on offense. We've torn it to the floor and will try to do things to help our personnel. We'll spread it out and run some no-huddle.

"The speed is so great on teams in the Southeast, so the only way you can combat that is to get some of that speed spread out. Everybody is running some kind of pressure defense, so you have to spread it out offensively."

During the Blue-Gray game in the spring, the Tigers unveiled their new spread offense and posted 35 points during the 100-play scrimmage.

West and his new staff will start the 2001 season short-handed, however, as six Memphis players will miss the season opener Sept. 3 at Mississippi State because of academic irregularities.

Two of the players, defensive starters **Andre Arnold** (end) and **Derrick Ballard** (linebacker), also will miss the second game Sept. 8 against Cincinnati. The other players are **Antonio Harden** (No. 4 tailback), **Garfield Garth** (No. 3 defensive tackle), **Henry Washington** (No. 3 field corner) and **Elijah Bell** (No. 3 strong safety).

"If you make a mistake, you have to pay the price," West said.

The university declined to provide specifics on the academic infractions, citing confidentiality requirements.

2001 SCHEDULE

Sept. 1	@Mississippi State

	8	Chattanooga
	22	South Florida
	29	@Louisville
Oct.	6	Southern Mississippi
	13	@Houston
	20	@East Earolina
	27	UAB
Nov.	10	@Tennessee
	17	Army
	24	Cincinnati

QUARTERBACKS

West was very pleased with the performance during the spring of junior quarterback **Travis Anglin** (6-4,197).

"He had an excellent spring," West said. "Not good enough for me to name him the starter, but very good. He's a step ahead of the others."

In the spring game, Anglin completed 9-of-11 passes for 135 yards and two touchdowns. Showing he has made a complete recovery from the ankle injury that caused him to miss most of the 2000 season, Anglin also rushed for 36 yards and a touchdown in leading the offense to more than 480 yards of total offense and earning Blue-Gray MVP honors.

Anglin opened as the starter last year but was injured in the third game. Senior **Neil Suber** (6-3, 246) took over for Anglin but was knocked out of action two weeks later against Southern Miss.

Junior **Scott Scherer** (5-10, 180) then took over and started the final six games of the season. Also in the quarterback picture are redshirt freshman **Danny Wimprine** (6-1, 216), sophomore **Brian Webb** (5-10, 175) and freshman **Matt Adams** (6-1, 200).

"Wimprine had a very good spring," West said. "But all four of them (Anglin, Suber, Scherer and Wimprine) are still in the mix."

In the spring game, Wimprine completed 3-of-7 passes for 30 yards and a touchdown. He was intercepted once.

Anglin has passed for 1,056 yards and six touchdowns in 12 games for the Tigers. His mobility makes him a threat for opposing defenses.

Suber has thrown for 2,363 career yards and ranks ninth on the Memphis all-time passing list.

Scherer is the son of former coach Rip Scherer. He led the Tigers to a victory over East Carolina last year and was voted the *Houston Chronicle* USA Player of the Week. He finished the season with a team-leading 857 yards passing and four touchdowns. He threw two touchdown passes as the Tigers came within seconds of shocking Tennessee.

Wimprine came to Memphis from J. T. Curtis High School in River Ridge, La., where he was an option quarterback. He led Curtis to back-to-back state championships and an overall record of 53-2.

Wimprine missed the 1999 season because of knee surgery and spent last year learning the Memphis system.

Adams is the grandson of former Memphis coach Fred Pancoast. Also an option quarterback in high school, Adams was signed in the fall of 2000 but elected to return home to Pensacola, Fla., to rehabilitate a shoulder injury.

RUNNING BACKS

In the spring game, tailbacks **Aaron Meadows**, **Sugar Sanders** and **Jeremiah Bonds** rushed for 60, 55 and 49 yards, respectively. Sanders averaged 11.0 yards per carry.

Last year Sanders (5-11, 221), a junior, led all Tiger backs with 646 yards rushing. He scored four touchdowns, including a 62-yarder against Army, and had two 100-yard rushing performances. He is the frontrunner for the starting nod at tailback.

Meadows (6-0, 195) has lettered for two seasons. Last season, the senior rushed for 34 yards and was a key member of the Memphis special teams.

Bonds (5-9, 181) demonstrated his vast skills last year when he caught a swing pass in the Army game and ran 31 yards for a touchdown. The key play by the sophomore broke open a close game as Memphis defeated the Cadets.

Veteran letterman **Dernice Wherry** (6-0, 200) has been moved to free safety. The senior rushed for 159 yards and caught 11 passes for 58 yards and a touchdown as a part-time starter at tailback last fall.

Also competing for time at tailback is senior **Antoine Harden** (5-9, 189), who mostly played on special teams last year.

The starting fullback is expected to be junior **Darche Epting** (6-1, 242), who worked at tailback and fullback last year. He finished the year with 174 yards rushing and three touchdowns. Epting had a season-high 17 rushes for 66 yards in the win over Army.

Expected to push Epting for the start at fullback is sophomore **Shaka Hill** (6-3, 240). Hill came to Memphis from Goodpasture High School in Nashville, where he was chosen the mid-state player of the year. A highly recruited player, big things are expected from Hill.

Joining Epting and Hill at fullback will be redshirt freshman **Robert Douglas** (6-3, 215).

WIDE RECEIVERS/TIGHT ENDS

Last year, junior **Ryan Johnson** (5-11, 190) caught 25 passes for 251 yards and two touchdowns. Most of his yardage came in the final four games. The St. Louis native, who is scheduled to start at split end, had 58 yards and a touchdown against Houston, 73 yards against Cincinnati and 53 yards and a score against Tulane. He also was outstanding as the Tigers' punt returner.

Senior **Bunkie Perkins** (5-9, 155) returns to his starting flanker position. He led the Tigers in receiving last year with 33 catches for 314 yards. He had six catches for 85 yards against East Carolina.

Also in the mix at receiver are junior **Tripp Higgins** (6-3, 198) and sophomore **Darren Garcia** (6-1, 190). Higgins caught 16 passes for 178 yards last year. Garcia played quarterback in high school but has been converted to receiver. He also returns kickoffs.

The competition for starting positions will be good at receiver with several other players expected to earn playing time, including junior **Casey Rooney** (6-0, 201), redshirt freshman **Von Webb** (6-0, 180), sophomore Harden (6-2, 179) and redshirt freshman **Tavarious Davis** (6-1, 196).

Gone from last year is tight end Billy Kendall, who set records at Memphis for receptions, yards and touchdowns. Returning are junior **Jeff Cameron** (6-4, 243) and **Wade Smith** (6-4, 250), who will be joined by redshirt freshmen **Jason Johnson** (6-4, 254) and **Eric Peterson** (6-5, 246) and transfer **Joey Moore** (6-3, 248), a junior.

Cameron and Smith were used mostly as blockers last year. Cameron had six catches for 73 yards and Smith caught five passes for 25 yards.

Johnson and Peterson were highly recruited prep stars from St. Louis and Memphis, respectively. Moore is a transfer from Mississippi College.

OFFENSIVE LINE

"We weren't overly strong anywhere on offense last year," West said. "We were not good up front, and that's our focal point right now.

"We hope to go from being below mediocre in the offensive line to possibly good there. We're looking at some changes, such as moving Wade Smith from tight end to tackle."

The Tigers return three starters, but must find replacements for tackle DeCorye Hampton and guard Lou Esposito. Hampton started 22 straight games for the Tigers and Esposito was a three-year starter.

Senior **Artis Hicks** (6-5, 315) and junior **Jimond Pugh** (6-3, 300) started all 11 games last year and are expected to do so again this year at left tackle and center, respectively.

Pugh did not miss a snap during the 2000 season and is expected to anchor the line this year. Hicks is a three-year starter.

Senior **Justin Eargle** (6-2, 292) should start at left guard. He opened last season as the starter, but suffered a torn ACL against Louisiana-Monroe and missed the rest of the season.

The starter at right guard will be junior **Trey Eyre** (6-3, 300), who had four starts last year after Eargle was injured. Listed as No. 1 at right tackle is junior **Joey Gerda** (6-6, 307), who in 2000 had four consecutive starts at mid-season.

Other key figures in the offensive line will be senior **Jason Austin** (6-3, 310), who started one game at guard last year, junior **Baki Celaj** (6-4, 311) and junior **Matt Gehrke** (6-3, 293).

"We must improve in the offensive line," West said.

2000 STATISTICS

Rushing offense	104.9	95
Passing offense	150.8	104
Total offense	255.7	111
Scoring offense	16.0	103
Net Punting	33.8	75
Punt returns	10.5	41
Kickoff returns	13.5	114
Rushing defense	72.7	1
Passing efficiency defense	100.0	13
Total defense	275.3	5
Scoring defense	18.1	14
Turnover margin	-6	87

Last column is ranking among Division I-A teams.

KICKERS

Returning as the place-kicker will be senior **Ryan White** (5-9, 182), a *Playboy* All-American.

White could finish as the best kicker in Memphis history. He has made 41-of-53 career field goals and has never missed an extra-point kick.

Walk-on **Ryan Ivey** (5-11, 175), a sophomore, will be White's backup.

The deep snapper is sophomore **Chris Moore** (6-1, 258).

DEFENSIVE LINE

The Memphis defense finished first in the nation in rushing defense and fifth in total defense last year. Taking over the defense from West this year is Whitt, who will try to keep the Tigers strong on the defensive side of the ball.

The toughest position for Whitt to rebuild will be the defensive line, where Memphis lost nose tackle Marcus Bell, defensive tackle Calvin Lewis, and backup tackle Jarvis Staton. Bell was a fourth-round pick of the Arizona Cardinals in the NFL draft.

Returning as starters will be senior ends **Tony Brown** (6-3, 274) and Arnold (6-4, 238). Brown appeared in all 11 games last year and made 42 tackles, 10 for losses. Arnold, the rush end, had 35 tackles, including 13 quarterback sacks. The 13 sacks were tops in Conference USA and in the top 10 nationally.

Depth at end is expected to come from junior **Stanley Johnson** (6-6, 235) and junior **Ross Estes** (6-3, 235). Help could also come from redshirt freshman **Jeremy Rone** (6-3, 238), sophomore **Cornell Bazile** (6-3, 218) and sophomore **Treveco Lucas** (6-2, 244).

The most experienced player inside is tackle **Eric Taylor** (6-3, 283), a sophomore who had seven tackles, three for losses, last year.

An impact player at tackle for the Tigers could be sophomore **Albert Means** (6-4, 335), the transfer from Alabama. The Memphis native was a *Parade* All-American at Trezevant High School before starting three games for Alabama last year.

Means left Alabama in January amid a recruiting scandal and signed with Memphis. The NCAA will rule on whether Means will be granted immediate eligibility.

"I'm happy to be enrolling in the University of Memphis and just want to get on with my college career," Means said after filling out his application for admission. "I appreciate the interest the media has shown in me but right now I want to put all of this behind me and get on with my life.

"It was hard for me to leave my mother and family last fall to go to Alabama and I'm glad that I got the opportunity to come back here to go to school."

Listed as the starter at nose tackle is junior **Boris Penchion** (6-4, 269), who will be challenged by junior **Doug Whitaker** (6-4, 283) and redshirt freshman **Kenyun Glover** (6-3, 272).

"We've got some good players in the defensive line," West said. "We're waiting to see who steps up."

LINEBACKERS

Gone is four-year letterman Karnal Shakir, who made more than 400 career tackles in is career and is the Conference USA all-time leading tackler.

Listed as the starter at inside or "Mike" linebacker is senior **DeMorrio Shank** (5-10, 240), who broke his right foot and missed the 2000 season. Shank, who received a redshirt year to rehabilitate his injury, moves to the inside to replace Shakir after playing outside in the past.

Returning on the outside are sophomores Ballard (6-2, 205), **Greg Harper** (6-2, 223) and **Coot Terry** (6-0, 222).

Harper and Terry will share playing time at "Sam" linebacker. Harper had 46 tackles last year and Terry added 58. Depth will come from sophomore **Will Hyden** (6-1, 213) who played mostly on special teams last year.

The "Will" starter will be Ballard, who made 62 tackles last year. His backups will be junior **Derrick Harmon** (6-1, 200) and senior **Draper Hall** (6-0, 236).

DEFENSIVE BACKS

Memphis lost two of its four starters in the secondary in cornerback Michael Stone and free safety Idrees Bashir, who left early for the NFL draft and was taken in the second round by the Indianapolis Colts.

Stone led the Tigers with 74 tackles and Bashir was third with 65. He set a school record in the Army game with a 100-yard interception return. Stone was also picked in the second round of the draft, by the Arizona Cardinals.

Back for 2001 are starting senior cornerback **Marcus Smith** (5-10, 186) and sophomore strong safety **Glenn Sumter** (6-2, 198). They are considered among the best in the conference at their respective positions.

Sumter returned to the lineup last year after suffering a knee injury in 1999. He made 58 tackles and intercepted five passes—good enough for 14th nationally. Smith made 22 tackles last year and broke up six passes. He played most of the season on a sprained ankle.

Sumter's backup will be redshirt freshman **Jamie Green** (6-4, 211), who missed the 2000 season with a shoulder injury. Depth behind Smith will be provided by junior **Quincy Stephenson** (5-6, 167) and redshirt freshman Washington (5-9, 166).

The starter at free safety will be sophomore **Jason Brown** (5-10, 187), who started four games last year when Smith was hurt. Brown had 28 tackles last year. He will be backed up by Wherry, who moves over from tailback. Wherry lettered as a sophomore at linebacker, but was moved to offense last year. He has the speed and hitting ability to excel in the secondary.

Trying to replace Stone at the corner will be sophomores **Anthony Harden** (5-10, 172) and **Bo Arnold** (5-10, 185). Harden has more experience, but Arnold may have the edge in athletic ability.

PUNTERS

Punter Ben Graves graduated, so the Tigers are searching for a replacement.

Johnson, a tight end, and Gehrke, an offensive lineman, worked on their punting skills during spring practice.

The punter, however, is expected to be signee **James Gaither** (6-4, 220) from Grayson County High School in Litchfield, Ky. Gaither punted 38 times for a 44.2-yard average last year and also made 7-of-11 field-goal attempts, including a 51-yarder.

Gaither's career totals were 111 punts for a 43.5 average and 13-of-22 field goals made.

SPECIAL TEAMS

The Tigers have the best place-kicker in Conference USA in White, and Gaither brings in outstanding numbers as the punter.

Epting, a running back, and Johnson, a wide receiver, will return kickoffs. Johnson will also be the punt returner. Last season, Johnson returned 37 punts for 389 yards and finished the season ranked No. 34 in the nation.

The holder will be Scherer, a backup quarterback.

RECRUITING CLASS

Not only did West get Means to return home from Alabama, the staff signed nine other Memphis high school players on national signing day. Memphis signed 21 players.

"We are delighted with this year's recruiting class," West said. "We wanted to make a strong statement in the Memphis area, while filling some very specific needs on our football team and I think that we accomplished our goal.

"As we began our recruiting effort, we knew that we needed offensive and defensive linemen and we set our sights on signing linemen. That was a priority."

The Memphis signings include a *Parade* All-American in Means and several of the state's top-rated prospects. The group contains four highly recruited players from Memphis' Melrose High, three from Trezevant High and one each from East, MUS and Covington High Schools. The 10 signees represent the second-largest number of Memphis area players ever signed in one Tiger class.

The Tigers landed defensive linemen **Dierre Carter** (6-3, 245) and **Jacob Ford** (6-4, 215), defensive back **Derron Johnson** (6-4, 215) and running back **Mario Robinson** (6-0, 205) from Melrose. From Trezevant High, Memphis signed Means and outside linebackers **Sheldon Taylor** (6-2, 220) and **Charles Wellington** (6-0, 225). **LaDarius Price** (6-0, 175), an all-state quarterback from East High, signed with Memphis as did MUS defensive back **Scott Vogel** (6-1, 190) and Covington High multi-purpose back **Darron White** (6-0, 190).

West and his staff did not isolate their recruiting efforts to Memphis and the Mid-South. Six players from the state of Georgia will become Tigers in 2001, including junior college running back **Dante Brown** (6-2, 220).

"We really had a good year in the city of Memphis," West said. "And we feel good about getting Dante Brown, who we originally signed at Clemson. I think a lot of the signees will play next year."

Brown, a junior, comes from Middle Georgia College after playing high school ball in Swainsboro, Ga. He helped Middle Georgia to a 10-1 record and a ranking of No. 5 in the 2000 national rankings. Last season, Brown rushed for 900 yards and 14 touchdowns.

"I really enjoy recruiting the Memphis area," said West, who graduated from Tennessee. "There are a lot of Tennessee graduates here and I'm familiar with the area because I recruiting this area while coaching at Ole Miss [as a graduate assistant] and Clemson."

BLUE RIBBON ANALYSIS

OFFENSE	B-
SPECIAL TEAMS	C
DEFENSE	B+
INTANGIBLES	A

West is feeling fortunate these days that he's back on the sideline as a head coach. And Memphis officials have to be feeling lucky to have been able to hire such a veteran coach from the staff left by Sherer.

West is a defensive genius, and Whitt, his defensive coordinator, is his protégé.

The offense is the problem at Memphis, but West may have fixed it by hiring Fichtner as offensive coordinator. The keys for Fichtner will be who steps up at quarterback and whether the offensive line can improve.

It will be interesting to see what an impact Means will have if the NCAA rules that he is eligible. And don't be surprised if Brown doesn't provide a pleasant surprise for Memphis fans at running back.

Memphis opens the season at Mississippi State, then plays host to Tennessee-Chattanooga and South Florida.

"It will be interesting playing Chattanooga because I coached there," West said. "I've paid them enough money [from a buy-out clause in his contract] that they should name the stadium for me."

The Tigers also have home games against Southern Miss, UAB, Army and Cincinnati and road games at Louisville, Houston, East Carolina and Tennessee.

West has two goals for the 2001 season—a winning record and coaching Memphis to a bowl game. Don't be surprised if he and the Tigers are successful on both counts.

(S.C.)

2000 RESULTS

Mississippi State	L	3-17	0-1
Louisiana-Monroe	W	28-0	1-1
Arkansas State	W	19-17	2-1
Army	W	26-16	3-1
Southern Mississippi	L	3-24	3-2
East Carolina	W	17-10	4-2
UAB	L	9-13	4-3
Houston	L	30-33	4-4
Tennessee	L	17-19	4-5
Cincinnati	L	10-13	4-6
Tulane	L	14-37	4-7

Southern Mississippi

LOCATION Hattiesburg, MS
CONFERENCE Conference USA
LAST SEASON 8-4 (.667)
CONFERENCE RECORD 4-3 (4th)
OFFENSIVE STARTERS RETURNING 9
DEFENSIVE STARTERS RETURNING 4
NICKNAME Golden Eagles
COLORS Black & Gold
HOME FIELD M.M. Roberts Stadium (33,000)
HEAD COACH Jeff Bower (USM '75)
RECORD AT SCHOOL 67-41-1 (10 years)
CAREER RECORD 67-41-1 (10 years)
ASSISTANTS
Randy Butler (Southern Miss '79)
Assistant Head Coach/Defensive Line
Shelton Gandy (Southern Miss '88)
Running Backs
Jay Hopson (Ole Miss '92)
Defensive Backs
Chris Klenakis (Carroll College '86)
Offensive Coordinator/Offensive Line
Tyrone Nix (Southern Miss '95)
Defensive Coordinator/Inside Linebackers
Chad O'Shea (Houston '95)
Special Teams/Recruiting Coordinator
Paul Petrino (Carroll College '90)
Quarterbacks
Lytrel Pollard (Southern Miss '98)
Outside Linebackers/Defensive Ends
Mitch Rodrigue (Nicholls State '98)
Tight Ends/Offensive Tackles
TEAM WINS (last 5 yrs.) 8-9-7-9-8
FINAL RANK (last 5 yrs.) 34-18-52-22-31
2000 FINISH Beat Texas Christian in GMAC Mobile Alabama Bowl.

COACH AND PROGRAM

When you're talking Conference USA football, you've got to start with Southern Mississippi, which in the league's five-year history has won two league titles outright (1997, '99) and shared a title ('96). The Golden Eagles finished second in 1998 with a 5-1 record.

Southern Miss has posted four straight seasons with seven or more victories and has gone to four straight bowls, winning three of them.

Jeff Bower, in his 11th season as the Golden Eagles' coach, has developed a program in the heart of SEC country that can compete with its neighbors.

How has Bower done it?

"I think we've really worked hard to recruit some character into our program," Bower said. "I think you win with character over athletic ability, although we've had good talent here too, but we've had a nucleus of good kids. I think we've had good leadership and been able to develop good leadership on this football team.

"When you've got enough athletic ability and you've got good character on your football team and your work ethic is good, I think you're going to be successful."

Last season Southern Miss' run of top-two finishes ended when it finished fourth with a 4-3 record. As injuries took their toll, the Golden Eagles lost three of their last four games.

Bower said he's never had a team so beset by injuries.

"It all happened primarily on one side of the football, on offense," Bower said. "It was just one of those things. If you're in it long enough, it's going to happen to you sooner or later.

"We're not deep enough, I don't know if anybody's deep enough to miss that many people, but we had a chance to get a little healthier after the last regular-season game, between then and the bowl game, and I think that made a difference."

In their regular season finale, a Golden Eagle rally fell short in a 14-9 loss to East Carolina. Quarterback **Jeff Kelly** scored on a 12-yard run with 3:35 left and the defense held, giving Kelly and Co. a chance for the winning drive. They gained two first downs before Kelly's last pass fell incomplete as time ran out.

Southern Miss then regrouped for the GMAC Mobile Alabama Bowl against No. 13 TCU. After falling behind, 21-14, the Golden Eagles scored two touchdowns in the last 7:24 and won, 28-21.

Kelly's 29-yard touchdown pass to **Kenneth Johnson** won the game with eight seconds left.

With the way the regular season ended, the bowl victory was just what the Golden Eagles needed.

"That was real big because our attitude—after you lose three out of the last four, as you can imagine after starting out 6-1—our attitude wasn't real good at the time," Bower said. "We weren't feeling real good about ourselves, so it's a real credit to our players and our coaches to get ready to go play an outstanding team in a bowl game and do what we did in the fourth quarter.

"We didn't give up a first down in the fourth quarter. We had over 200 yards in total offense, we partially blocked a punt that sets up that winning touchdown, and just the way we won the football game, I think it made us all feel better, no doubt about that. I thought we really got ourselves ready to play and played well and developed a good attitude."

Ranked No. 22 at the start of the season, Southern Miss opened with a near upset of then-No. 12 Tennessee, losing 19-16 in Knoxville. Kelly's two touchdown passes in the fourth quarter pulled the Golden Eagles to within three with 55 seconds left, but they ran out of time.

"It was a good start," Bower said. "We played pretty well up there. We had a little bit of a controversial call that really could have given us an opportunity to win the game, but it was a good start."

After the Golden Eagles' first touchdown of the fourth quarter, Kelly threw a conversion pass to **LeRoy Handy**, who was stopped short of the goal line—at least in the judgement of the officials. Southern Miss trailed 19-9.

"We saw the TV copy of [the ESPN] tape and they had a camera right on the goal line that clearly shows the ball going across the goal line," Bower said. "That would have really changed the whole ball game, but it didn't work out that way. With us scoring the way we did the last score of the game, it would have probably put the game into overtime."

After the loss, the Golden Eagles knocked off then-No. 13 Alabama, starting a six-game winning streak.

"We've always played good opponents outside the conference and for our players to bounce back [from the Tennessee game] and win six in a row, that was a good start," Bower said. "I'll take that every year."

2001 SCHEDULE

Sept.	1	Oklahoma State
	15	@Alabama (Birmingham)
	22	@Louisiana-Lafayette
	29	UAB
Oct.	6	@Memphis
	16	@Louisville
	27	Houston
Nov.	3	@Penn State
	17	Tulane
	23	@East Carolina
	30	TCU

QUARTERBACKS

By the start of fall practice, Kelly (6-2, 210), a senior, should be back at full speed after suffering a broken thumb on his throwing hand during the Gold-Black game in the spring.

Kelly, who has started the last two seasons, suffered the injury while making a tackle after throwing an interception. His thumb was in a cast, but was expected to be 100 percent by the start of preseason workouts.

"He's fine," Bower said in late May. "He has the cast off. He's doing good. He's throwing some now."

During the 2000 regular season, Kelly completed 198-of-341 passes (58.1 percent) for 2,381 yards and 15 touchdowns. He was intercepted 10 times. It was his second straight 2,000-yard passing season.

On the school's single-season record list, his 2000 season was second-best for completions and third-best for passing yardage, attempts, touchdown passes and total offense (2,415).

Among C-USA quarterbacks, Kelly was fifth in total offense, fourth in passing efficiency and fourth in passing yards.

"He's a heady player and a tough guy," Bower said. "He's got a good feel for what we're doing and he's a great kid. What he's accomplished academically here is sort of amazing. He graduated in three years, got an MBA in four years, and I think he's going to get another master's this next year."

Kelly's statistics don't include the bowl victory over TCU when he completed 11-of-23 passes for 159 yards and three touchdowns.

Kelly, along with his teammates, showed plenty of poise in the two games against SEC schools at the start of the season. He was 22-of-30 for 232 yards and two touchdowns in the loss to Tennessee in the season opener. He didn't throw an interception against the Vols.

After an open date, Kelly was 14-of-23 for 159 yards with one touchdown and one interception as the Golden Eagles beat Alabama, 21-13.

Kelly has steadily climbed up the Southern Miss career passing list. He is third in passing yardage (4,482) and touchdown passes (36), fourth in total offense (4,473) and completions (357) and sixth in passing attempts (621).

"He's a good leader for us and obviously has a lot of experience and has played very well for us," Bower said.

With the injury to Kelly, his two backups got a chance for more snaps before spring workouts finished.

Sophomore **Zac White** (6-5, 229) played sparingly last season while **Mickey D'Angelo** (6-3, 212) was redshirted as a freshman.

White played in two games last season, completing 1-of-6 passes. In the spring game, White was 7-of-15 for 153 yards and threw a 60-yard touchdown pass to **Dannye Fowler** with 2:21 left that lifted the Black team to a 14-10 victory.

After an outstanding career at Long Beach High School in Gulfport, Miss., D'Angelo spent his freshman season working with the scout team.

"It's good to have the quality quarterbacks we have returning this year," quarterbacks coach Paul Petrino said. "I challenged them [in the spring] to compete against each other every day in practice and work hard at getting better each day. We talked about improving their footwork, their vision and making good decisions. Now that we have a year in this offense, we didn't have to spend the whole time teaching them plays. We were able to work on the little things."

RUNNING BACKS

After two strong seasons, senior running back **Derrick Nix** (6-2, 232) battled through the 2000 season fighting injury and illness. If Nix returns at full strength this season, the Golden Eagles will have three solid backs.

All have different styles. Nix is a hard-nosed power runner. Senior **Dawayne Woods** (5-7, 187) is an elusive, slashing back, while sophomore **Tim Blackwell** (5-11, 190) has very good speed.

Before the bowl game, Blackwell was moved from wide receiver to running back for depth purposes and will remain in the backfield this season.

Nix, sometimes referred to as "Baby Bull," was off to another good season in 2000 when he suffered an ankle sprain in the fourth game against Memphis. Later, Nix had complications from a reaction to antibiotics that caused kidney problems, and that kept him out for most of the remainder of the season, except for a brief appearance against Louisville on Nov. 4.

"He had a high ankle sprain and he finally got over that and developed a kidney disease," Bower said. "They finally had to biopsy the kidney and he was out for [most of] the year. He's still on medication. Right now I don't know his status, although I am optimistic that he's going to be ready to go."

As a result of the problems, Nix played only five games and gained 156 yards on 68 carries and scored two touchdowns. It was quite a decrease from his sophomore season when Nix gained 1,054 yards and was the team's workhorse. He had 42 carries against East Carolina two years ago and had 29 carries against Nebraska.

Nix was an impact player out of Etowah High School in Attalia, Ala., where he was an listed as the No. 6 prospect in the state by *SuperPrep* magazine. Nix, who played linebacker and running back in high school, played his first two games at Southern Miss as a tight end, then moved to running back and rushed for 1,180 yards—the 19th highest total for a freshman in NCAA history.

Woods was the team's leading rusher last year, gaining 631 yards on 146 carries for a 4.3-yard average. Woods scored seven touchdowns.

Kelby Nance, a senior last season, was the team's second-leading rusher with 250 yards and Nix was third.

Woods, who started six of the last seven games, is also a good receiver out of the backfield. He caught 15 passes for 150 yards and three touchdowns. His 10 touchdowns were a team high.

After being hurt in the regular-season finale against East Carolina, Woods returned for the bowl game and had eight carries for 12 yards, while Nance led the team in rushing with 104 yards on 16 carries.

"Dawayne Woods is a real quick guy that makes you miss, and then we've moved Timmy Blackwell from wide receiver to running back and he had a good spring," Bower said. "He was our most improved offensive player."

Blackwell played in 10 games last season, but had only one carry for a loss of eight yards.

WIDE RECEIVERS/TIGHT ENDS

In his one-back, multiple offense, Bower can never have enough good receivers. Although several of his top receivers return, Bower says developing depth is a must for 2001.

"We're pretty thin there," Bower said. "We only had four on scholarship this spring and of course we're in three wides every snap and do some four and five [receiver formations]."

The only departed senior is Shawn Mills, who led the team with 55 catches for 713 yards and five touchdowns.

Handy (6-1, 196), a junior, and the senior Fowler (5-10, 180) return as the starting wideouts and Johnson (5-10, 165), a sophomore, should move into the starting spot at flanker. All three have all-conference potential.

"Our receivers need to step up and make plays," said Bower, who also coaches the wide receivers. "We challenged them in the spring to do the little things well, run good routes in order to get open, use their speed and catch the ball."

Handy was second on the team in catches, but played only eight games. He caught 40 passes for 481 yards—a 12-yard average per catch—and had two touchdown catches.

After suffering a fractured shoulder blade in the Nov. 4 Louisville game, Handy missed the rest of the regular season, but returned for the GMAC Mobile Alabama Bowl, caught five passes for 84 yards and two touchdowns and was chosen as the bowl's most valuable offensive player. His 56-yard touchdown play from Kelly tied the game in the fourth quarter.

Handy had four catches for 51 yards in the Gold-Black game.

Johnson was third on the team in catches with 27 for 311 yards and one touchdown. His winning touchdown catch in the bowl game was a great way to end a freshman season.

Because of his outstanding speed, Johnson gives the Golden Eagles an added dimension at the flanker position.

In the fourth game of the season, Johnson became the team's punt returner. He was chosen to the C-USA All-Freshman team and was an honorable mention freshman All-American by Rivals.com.

Fowler, who graduated in December, 2000, will return for another season and provide leadership. He started 11-of-12 games in 2000 and was fourth on the team in catches with 23 for 282 yards in the regular season. He had one touchdown catch.

Junior **Kwantrell Green** (5-8, 172) should be Fowler's backup at split end with freshman **Rocky Harrison** (6-1, 192) behind Handy at wide receiver. Junior **Greg James** (5-10, 152) will probably be Johnson's backup at flanker.

Several others will give the Golden Eagles depth, including redshirt freshmen **Aaron Blanchard** (6-1, 175) and **Lanny Beach** (5-10, 168).

At tight end, starter **Bobby Garner** (6-2, 230), a junior, returns along with the second- and third-stringers, senior **Orlando Dantzler** (6-3, 268) and sophomore **Terrell Browden** (6-2, 245).

Garner is an excellent receiving tight end, while Dantzler and Browden are used more as blockers.

Garner started all 12 games last season and was the team's fifth-leading receiver with 19 catches for 262 yards and three touchdowns in the regular season. In the bowl game, Garner had three catches for 42 yards.

Dantzler sat out spring practice while catching up on school work, and the Golden Eagles are hoping he will be back by August. He had four catches for 49 yards last season.

Browden played in 11 games as a true freshman last season and was used mostly on double tight end situations and also on special teams. He was in 172 offensive plays and 60 special teams plays.

OFFENSIVE LINE

All but one starter returns, but the lone loss, Billy Clay, is significant. Clay started the first five games at guard, moved to center for the rest of the season, and earned All-C-USA second-team honors.

Despite the loss of Clay, the Golden Eagles' line is solid.

"We're in pretty good shape there," Bower said. "We've got to solidify our center position. We've worked two or three different guys in there just trying to find the best one."

Before the 2000 season, the Golden Eagles lost starting center Zeb Landers to a career-ending injury. He had suffered several concussions and doctors advised him to give up football.

Junior **Torrin Tucker** (6-6, 316) returns as the starter at strong side guard, while senior **Jeremy Bridges** (6-4, 300) will be the weak side tackle. They will anchor the offensive line.

Tucker was a mainstay on the line last season, playing in 848 snaps and playing 70 or more plays in seven games. He consistently graded out as one of the team's top linemen and was perhaps the team's top protection lineman and leader in knockdown blocks.

Senior **Nathan Grace** (6-6, 342) will probably be Tucker's backup. Grace played in nine games last season and was in on 42 plays. He had an exceptional off-season. The Golden Eagle coaches gave Grace an award for his rigorous work in the weight program.

Sophomore **Adam Gardner** (6-6, 265) should also be a factor at the guard position. Gardner was redshirted in 1999 and missed most of last season with a shoulder injury.

Bridges was the team's iron man; he led the team in overall plays with 849 (809 on offense, 40 on special teams). He also graded out as one of the top linemen. Redshirt freshman **Myron Powe** (6-4, 299) will be Bridges' backup.

Redshirt junior **Buck Miciotto** (6-2, 278) was moved from tight end to guard at the start of the 2000 season and quickly earned the starting job. Miciotto, however, isn't a lock to retain the job.

Redshirt freshman **Jeremy Parquet** (6-7, 318) will also battle for the starting job with Miciotto, who sustained a knee injury in the Oct. 28 game at Houston but returned for the regular season finale and the bowl game.

Parquet spent last season working in the weight room, and it paid off. With a very good spring, Parquet made coaches believe he will be a factor in 2001. He has a big frame and moves well.

Junior **Jason Jimenez** (6-7, 292) made a quick climb up the depth chart last season when injuries took their toll at the strong side tackle position.

Redshirt freshman **Bradley Worthington** (6-4, 283) should be Jimenez' backup.

In the most open battle for a starting job on the line, senior **Kendrick Key** (6-4, 273) enters fall practices with the edge at center over sophomore **Isah Winborne** (6-0, 309), but sophomore **Jim**

Hicks (6-3, 280) also expects to be in the hunt.

Key played guard last season, but moved to center in the spring and made the adjustment well. He showed great improvement in the spring. Last season, Key played in 11 games and started four at guard. He had a season-high 84 snaps against UAB and was used in 333 plays. With all that experience, Key was able to make the move to center because he understood the offense.

Hicks, chosen to the C-USA All-Freshman team, moved into the starting center's job when Landers suffered the career-ending injury. Five games into the season, Hicks suffered a knee injury and missed the rest of the season. He had surgery and should be ready for fall practice.

"Because we had so many injuries last season, we were able to get a lot of players quality playing time," offensive line coach Chris Klenakis said. "We have a good starting point to build around. Now we have to solidify the center position, which is very important.

"That position is the cornerstone of your offensive line, so we need to make sure we find the right fit. If we have to move players around to accomplish our goal, then we will. You always want to put the best five players out there."

2000 STATISTICS

Rushing offense	102.6	98
Passing offense	221.2	49
Total offense	323.8	87
Scoring offense	26.0	57
Net Punting	35.1	44
Punt returns	13.1	19
Kickoff returns	20.4	38
Rushing defense	106.0	21
Passing efficiency defense	91.3	4
Total defense	268.5	2
Scoring defense	16.5	8
Turnover margin	+0	59

Last column is ranking among Division I-A teams.

KICKERS

Brent Hanna (6-1, 217) returns for his senior season after working hard on consistency during the off-season.

Last season, Hanna was 12-of-18 on field-goal attempts and made all 32 of his PAT kicks. He was 3-of-4 on attempts from 40-49 yards, and his long field goal was 49 yards.

Hanna's year ended on a bad note when he missed all four of his field-goal attempts in the bowl game.

Junior **Curtis Jones** (5-9, 170) will continue a battle for the job that carried into spring practice.

"Brant Hanna and Curt Jones had a solid competition this spring," special teams coach Chad O'Shea said. "We need to have a better percentage of field goals made this season. We really challenged the kickers to develop and work hard on their consistency."

Bower said Hanna had a good spring. That should give him the lead in the kicker's job.

"He had a bad, bad bowl game but really had a good spring," Bower said. "We put him in a lot of situations. In our last scrimmage, he kicked 51 and 49 [yarders] into the wind. I think he's got his confidence back."

Junior **Don Urquehart** (5-10, 195) has a stronger leg than Hanna and will probably handle kickoffs.

DEFENSIVE LINE

One of the biggest concerns for Bower heading into the 2001 season is the defensive line.

Gone are three of the four starters from last year. In addition to finding starters, Bower wants to develop some depth.

Last year's defensive front featured four of the team's top 10 tacklers and five of the top 15. They had 27 of the team's 35 sacks and almost half of the tackles for loss.

The biggest gap to be filled was left by defensive end Cedric Scott, who earned a third-team All-American selection by *Football News* and the Associated Press and was chosen as C-USA's Co-Defensive Player of the Year. Scott was fourth on the team in tackles with 69 and had team-highs in tackles for loss (19) and sacks (12). He was the first of four Golden Eagles chosen in the NFL draft, going in the fourth round to the New York Giants.

Also gone are starting tackles Daleroy Stewart and John Nix, who combined for 71 tackles. Stewart had eight tackles for loss and four sacks. Both were drafted by the Dallas Cowboys—Stewart in the sixth round and Nix in the seventh.

"There was a lot of talent on the defensive line with last year's senior class," defensive line coach Randy Butler said. "Not only did we lose talent but quality experience. You could do so many things because the starters were good and you didn't have a drop-off when you turned to the next group. However, we were in the same position four years ago when this group was introduced. We have a talented group of players this year ready to step up and fill the holes left by the seniors."

Southern Miss will look to a couple of junior college transfers to fill two spots. Junior **Carlos Crusoe** (6-3, 277) and senior **Rayshun Jones** (6-2, 275) were both redshirted last season after outstanding seasons in junior college. Jones should start at nose tackle and Crusoe at defensive tackle.

Crusoe was a two-year starter at East Mississippi Community College. Jones, also a two-year starter at the same school, was rated as one of the top defensive linemen in the junior college ranks two years ago. He committed to Iowa before signing with Southern Miss.

Sophomore **Skyler Magee** (6-3, 263) will probably be Jones' backup and redshirt freshman **Chad Ruffin** (6-0, 260) will be Crusoe's backup. Magee practiced at linebacker last season and moved to the defensive line in the spring.

Redshirt freshman Antonio Jones (6-4, 252) and junior **Travis Dorsey** (6-3, 255) may also work their way into the rotation.

Senior **Marchene Hatchett** (6-2, 239), who was Scott's backup last season, should step into the starting job at end this year. Hatchett played sparingly in five games last season. Sophomore **Brian Evans** (6-5, 235) will be Hatchett's backup after spending most of the 2000 season playing special teams.

Terrell Paul (6-3, 226), who was on the C-USA All-Freshman team last year, returns as the starter at bandit end. He moved into the starting job before the Alabama game and retained it the rest of the season. He finished with 11 tackles, two for losses, and one sack.

Redshirt freshman **LeVon Pears** (6-0, 250) will be Paul's backup and junior **Bon Suarez** (5-11, 209) should also see playing time. Suarez missed last season because of numerous injuries.

"We've lost a lot of real good players on defense," Bower said. "... I think we've got some guys who are talented enough to be good players but they haven't played. They're inexperienced but we've got to step up at that position."

LINEBACKERS

While the front is short on experience and depth, this position is sound.

Three-year letterman **Roy Magee** leads the linebackers. Magee (6-2, 214), a senior, will start at weak side linebacker. Last season, Magee was seventh on the team in tackles with 63 in 10 games. He had 14 tackles for loss, five sacks and two fumble recoveries.

Magee missed the last two games of the regular season because of an ankle sprain. He was moved from the strong-side linebacker spot to the weak side to take advantage of his speed. Against Tulane, Magee returned a fumble 38 yards for touchdown, and he had a 55-yard fumble return against Louisville.

Junior **Chris Langston** (6-2, 212) should play behind Magee. Langston played in all 11 games last season, starting three, and had 14 solo tackles and 14 assists. He played a season-high 62 snaps against Cincinnati and had six tackles, also a season-high.

Redshirt freshman **Michael Boley** (6-3, 207) may also work his way into some playing time at weak-side linebacker.

Returning at middle linebacker is sophomore **Rod Davis** (6-3, 238), who was chosen to The *Sporting News* and *Football News* Freshman All-America teams. He was also on *Sports Illustrated*'s All-Bowl team after making 14 unassisted tackles against TCU in the GMAC Mobile Alabama Bowl.

Davis was third on the team in tackles with 94, including 56 unassisted. He had seven tackles for loss and one sack. He had double-digit tackles in six games and had a career-high 16 against Cincinnati.

"I think [Davis and Magee] are really good players," Bower said.

Junior **Chris Vaughn** (6-0, 213) will probably be Davis' backup, but must beat out redshirt freshman Dillon Checkler (6-1, 227) for the spot.

Freshman **Derrick Ducksworth** (6-2, 225) has the size and speed needed to make an impact at middle linebacker.

Vaughn played in all 11 regular-season games and started two. He played 63 snaps against Oklahoma and finished 13th on the team in tackles with 33, including 20 unassisted tackles. With his experience, Vaughn should have the edge over Checkler for the job.

Junior **Joe Henley** (6-0, 216) should take over the starting slot at strong-side linebacker. He played mostly special teams last season, but saw action in all 11 regular-season games.

Redshirt freshmen **Terry Anderson** (6-2, 218) and **Joe Scott** (6-1, 240) should also find their way into the linebacker rotation. Anderson starts the fall slotted as Henley's backup. Also vying for playing time will be redshirt freshman **Beau Maggio** (6-3, 202).

"We'll have a fast group at linebacker," Bower said. "We've got good speed and ability."

DEFENSIVE BACKS

Like the defensive line, the secondary is also going through a rebuilding phase. Gone is rover back Leo Barnes, the team's second-leading tackler with 104. Barnes was a first-team All-C-USA player last season.

Also gone are cornerbacks Raymond Walls and Keon Moore. Walls was chosen to the All-C-USA second team and was taken by the Indianapolis Colts in the fifth round of the NFL draft.

Senior **Chad Williams** (5-10, 201), who started at free safety last season and earned second-team All-C-USA honors, moved to rover back in the spring. Williams led the team in tackles last season with 114, including 78 unassisted tackles, 11 tackles for loss and eight sacks. He also knocked down five passes and forced a team-high four fumbles, recovering one.

"We've played some numbers [in the secondary] so it's not like we're playing some guys that haven't played before," Bower said. "I feel better about that area. I think we've got good ability at that area. I feel pretty good about that. Chad Williams is a really good player at safety for us. I'd expect us to be pretty good there."

Sophomore **Alex Ray** (5-11, 198) will probably be Williams' backup, but will be pushed by sophomore **Karone Champagne** (5-10, 192) and redshirt freshman **Larry Crayton** (6-1, 195). Ray played in 11 games last season and finished with five tackles. Champagne played in three games, mostly on special teams.

Sophomores **Etric Pruitt** (6-0, 181) and **Corey Hosey** (6-0, 185) will battle for the free safety job. Pruitt, slotted as the starter entering fall practices, earned the spot during the spring. He played in 10 games last season and had nine tackles, seven unassisted.

Hosey moved from wide receiver to safety in the spring. The Golden Eagles' coaches gave Hosey the most improved defensive player award in the spring, and they're expecting his improvement to continue this season.

Redshirt freshman **Carsha Stromas** (6-2, 206) may be in the free safety mix.

At one cornerback spot, junior college transfer **Carmus Haynes** (5-9, 170) is slotted as the starter but must fend off the challenge of senior **Daryon Brutley** (5-11, 183), the second string field corner after spring workouts.

Junior college transfer **Leroy Johnson** (5-11, 180) will give the Golden Eagles depth at the cornerback spot.

Junior **Corey Yates** (5-10, 170) and redshirt freshmen **Pierre Hutchins** (5-8, 171) and **Seth Cumbie** (5-11, 177) will battle for the other cornerback job. Yates was slotted as the starter in the spring.

PUNTERS

Junior **Mark Haulman** (6-0, 175) returns as the starting punter. He averaged 41.3 yards on 76 punts last season and had 15 downed inside the opponent's 20-yard line. Ten more of his punts rolled into the end zone.

"Mark had a good year for his first year punting," O'Shea said. "He worked hard this spring and I believe he will have an excellent fall season. We need to develop a backup punter for depth purposes."

Hanna enters preseason practices as Haulman's backup.

SPECIAL TEAMS

Johnson doubles as a wide receiver and punt returner, and his speed gives the Golden Eagles a threat at both spots. Last season, Johnson returned 24 punts and averaged 13.9 yards. His long return was 42 yards.

Williams, the safety, will be Johnson's backup as a punt returner. He returned only four punts last season but averaged 23.5 yards and ran one back 63 yards.

Woods and Blackwell will be the kick returners. Woods returned nine kicks for a 24.3-yard average last season and had an 82-yard return.

"We were excited about the job that Kenneth Johnson did last year," O'Shea said. "There is no doubt that he can be a major force. This was an area that we worked hard on in the spring, trying to find capable punt returners behind Chad Williams."

Raymond Walls, the top kick returner last season, was a senior. He returned 16 kicks for a 20.6-yard average.

"Dawayne [Woods] has proved that he is more than capable of handling the kickoff return duties," O'Shea said. "I believe that Timmy [Blackwell] will be an oustanding returner with his speed and running ability."

Haulman is the holder and junior **Scott Croley** (6-0, 244) is the long snapper. Both were starters last year at those positions.

The Golden Eagles had three punts blocked last season while blocking two. Hanna had one field-goal attempt blocked.

"We've got to be a better special teams football team than we were last year," Bower said.

RECRUITING CLASS

Bower isn't one to boast about his recruits. Not until they prove themselves.

"Who knows?" Bower said of his 2001 class of recruits. "I think it was pretty good. All the guys we signed, we wanted to sign them. We'll see what they turn out to be like. It takes three or four years to determine how you did recruiting."

Southern Miss signed 31 players, including six junior college transfers.

The class consisted of one quarterback, four offensive linemen, six defensive backs, three linebackers, three defensive ends, six wide receivers, three running backs, and four defensive linemen. One player, **Karlin Riley** (6-2, 195) of Opelousas, La., was recruited as an athlete.

Perhaps the most heralded recruit was Ducksworth (6-2, 225), the freshman linebacker from Mize (Miss.) High School. He chose Southern Miss over Tennessee and Mississippi State. He made 119 tackles last season and helped Mize to the Class 1A state championship.

Freshman quarterback **Dustin Almond** (6-1, 185) of Orange Park (Fla.) High School threw for 2,012 yards and 18 touchdowns last season.

Bower will be looking for some help from his recruits at the receiver spots. Look for freshmen **Thomas Hosey** (6-2, 200) of R.H. Watkins High in Laurel, Miss., **Chris Johnson** (5-10, 185) of Lutcher High School in Gramercy, La. and junior **Todd Devoe** of Itawamba (Fla.) Community College to get into the mix at receiver.

"We've got to get some help from some incoming freshmen or juco players [at wide receiver]," Bower said.

Freshman defensive end **Chris McNair** (6-4, 215) of Gulfport (Miss.) High School may also earn playing time in his first season. McNair, an all-state player, came from the same high school that produced Golden Eagle standouts Cedric Scott and Rod Davis.

Including in the 2001 class were two junior college transfers who were redshirted last year. They are defensive tackles Crusoe and Jones.

BLUE RIBBON ANALYSIS

OFFENSE	B+
SPECIAL TEAMS	B
DEFENSE	C+
INTANGIBLES	A

Southern Miss must replace a number of top-notch defensive players, particularly on the front line and in the secondary. Still, the Golden Eagles never enter a season without plans of contending for the C-USA title.

"I think we've got a chance," Bower said. "I don't know if we'll be as talented as we've been on the defensive side of the ball but we've got some athletic ability there. It's whether or not some of our young kids or kids who haven't played much grow up and be productive."

Offensively, however, the Golden Eagles appear to be in pretty good shape, even though Bower says he is thin at wide receiver.

Nine starters return to an offense that ranked fourth in C-USA in scoring last season. It will be run by Kelly, an experienced quarterback with plenty of smarts.

The bulk of the offensive line returns, but Bower must settle on a center before the season begins. That won't be a problem if Hicks can make a good recovery from his knee injury and the surgery.

Bower is counting on a healthy return of running back Nix, whose kidney problems from the 2000 season carried into the off-season. Nix took part in spring practices, but was still on medication at the end of the spring semester.

"We need to get [Nix] back," Bower said. "He can do so many things and he does them all well. He's a good runner, good blocker, good pass receiver, smart player, consistent, a good leader for us. We need him to get healthy."

Southern Miss has traditionally had one of the best defenses in the league, and despite the heavy losses from the 2000 team, that shouldn't change.

Bower's biggest challenge will be replacing Scott at defensive end and Stewart and John Nix at tackles, plus three of the four starting defensive backs.

Injuries caused what could potentially have been a great 2000 season to be merely a good one, and it ended with an impressive victory over TCU in the GMAC Mobile Alabama Bowl. It was a great way for the Golden Eagles to end the season and start the off-season.

Now, Bower wants to keep the momentum going into the preseason and 2001.

"If we play hard and do it with a good attitude, I think we'll have a chance to have another pretty good year," Bower said.

If there's one coach in this league who can get his players to play hard with a good attitude, it's Bower. Count on the Golden Eagles to be pretty good again this year.

(D.L.)

2000 RESULTS

Tennessee	L	16-19	0-1
Alabama	W	21-0	1-1
Oklahoma State	W	28-8	2-1
Memphis	W	24-3	3-1
South Florida	W	41-7	4-1
Tulane	W	56-24	5-1
Houston	W	6-3	6-1
Louisville	L	28-49	6-2
UAB	W	33-30	7-2
Cincinnati	L	24-27	7-3
East Carolina	L	9-14	7-4
TCU (Mobile Bowl)	W	28-21	8-4

Texas Christian

LOCATION	**Fort Worth, TX**
CONFERENCE	**Conference USA**
LAST SEASON	**10-2 (.833)**
CONFERENCE RECORD	**7-1 (t-1st WAC)**
OFFENSIVE STARTERS RETURNING	**4**
DEFENSIVE STARTERS RETURNING	**5**
NICKNAME	**Horned Frogs**
COLORS	**Purple & White**
HOME FIELD	**Amon G. Carter Stadium (46,000)**
HEAD COACH	**Gary Patterson (Kansas St. '83)**
RECORD AT SCHOOL	**0-1 (First year)**
CAREER RECORD	**0-1 (First year)**
ASSISTANTS	
	David Bailiff (Southwest Texas '81)

Assistant Head Coach/Defensive Line
Mike Schultz (Sam Houston State '79)
Offensive Coordinator/Running Backs
Chuck Driesbach (Villanova '75)
Defensive Coordinator/Linebackers
Dan Lounsbury (Arkansas '74)
Quarterbacks
Eddie Williamson (Davidson '74)
Offensive Line
Jarrett Anderson (New Mexico '93)
Wide Receivers
Dan Sharp (Texas Christian '85)
Tight Ends
Willie Mack Garza (Texas '93)
Cornerbacks
Chad Glasgow (Oklahoma State '95)
Safeties
TEAM WINS (last 5 yrs.) 4-1-7-8-10
FINAL RANK (last 5 yrs.) 89-102-65-59-22
2000 FINISH Lost to Southern Miss in GMAC Mobile Alabama Bowl.

COACH AND PROGRAM

One week after Dennis Franchione left for Alabama last December, TCU completed its search for a new football coach.

Gary Patterson, who had been Franchione's defensive coordinator at TCU for three seasons, was the 11th and last candidate to be interviewed for the vacated job.

TCU's search committee made a unanimous decision. Patterson, a college assistant for 18 years, had his first head-coaching job.

His task will be to carry the momentum that Franchione generated the last three seasons. TCU is coming off its first 10-win season since 1938 when it won a national championship. The Horned Frogs have posted three straight winning seasons for the first time since the 1950s.

When the Horned Frogs play Nebraska on Aug. 25 in the Pigskin Classic, it won't be Patterson's debut as their coach. Patterson coached the team in the GMAC Mobile Alabama Bowl loss to Southern Miss.

His second game as the main man won't be much easier.

"My head coaching debut is different than most," Patterson told the *Horned Frog Sports Report* in the spring. "First it was a bowl game, then Nebraska in Lincoln. There were several reasons why we felt we needed to take the [Nebraska] game. Number one, we felt it was important for the image of TCU to step out.

"For us to keep climbing and building the program here, at some point in time we were going to have to answer the challenge. Whether we are ready or not as a young football team by that time, I don't know. It has helped our football team already, in that by scheduling that game, there is a lot more of a sense of urgency among our players and our coaches to become a better football team quicker."

There was indeed some restructuring to do after Franchione left for Alabama, taking all but one member of his staff with him. Offensive coordinator Mike Schultz was the only assistant who stayed at TCU.

Patterson, however, quickly assembled a staff and had it firmly in place for spring practices. One of his top hires was getting David Bailiff, now TCU's assistant head coach. Considered one of the best recruiters in Texas, Bailiff came from Southwest Texas State, where he served as assistant head coach and defensive coordinator.

Despite the loss of 27 lettermen and 13 starters—seven offensive, six defensive—Patterson isn't approaching his first full season as a head coach with rebuilding as the theme.

"No, I would not call this a rebuilding year," Patterson said. "But we do need to gain some experience to be successful in the fall. **Casey Printers** has an 18-4 record as our starting quarterback, and we return a large group of players that was on a defense that ranked number one in the nation.

"The key will be how quick our young players mature into their roles. If they raise their level of play, then we have a chance to be a very good football team."

Last season, the Horned Frogs relied on a staunch defense and the running of LaDainian Tomlinson, who finished fourth in the Heisman Trophy race. Tomlinson, who was the 2000 Doak Walker award as the nation's top running back, was the San Diego Chargers' first pick in the NFL draft and the fifth pick overall.

Patterson knows Tomlinson can't be replaced by one player, and he'll look for several players to fill his shoes. Likewise, Patterson knows several key defenders are gone, and some backups must play more prominent roles if the Horned Frogs are to match last year's top-rated defense.

Since he started coaching, Patterson has been a defensive coach, and his focus will continue to be defense. Before his job as TCU's defensive coordinator, he had the same title at New Mexico under Franchione from 1996-97.

Despite the losses from the 2000 team, the Horned Frogs are still a talented bunch.

"There is no question that our team speed is our biggest strength," Patterson said. "Individually, anytime you return a starting quarterback who has won 18 games in two seasons, then you have to be excited.

"We have a big playmaker returning in [wide receiver] **LaTarence Dunbar**, plus we also return four tight ends. Defensively, linebacker Chad Bayer returns after leading our team in tackles last season.

"We also return four of the five defensive ends that were part of our rotation last season. Although we lost our two safeties, we do have four cornerbacks returning who have started games in their career."

Patterson looks forward to playing in Conference USA. It's a good move for TCU and the league. The Horned Frogs played their last season in the Western Athletic Conference in 2000.

Four seasons after it won only one game, TCU is on solid football ground. It has won 25 games in the last three years and gone to three straight bowl games for the first time in school history.

In 2000, TCU was ranked every week of the season and got as high as ninth—its highest ranking since the 1959 team was seventh.

As his team enters C-USA, Patterson plans to continue what Franchione helped start at TCU.

"We have a tradition now," Patterson said. "This team has an understanding of what it takes to be a winning program. We have won back to back [WAC] titles, gone to three straight bowl games, and it was because of hard work. I believe this team understands that for us to keep winning, we have to continue to have a strong work ethic.

"This team has a great attitude, and they are determined to continue the tradition."

2001 SCHEDULE

Aug.	25	@Nebraska (Pigskin Classic)
Sept.	1	@North Texas
	8	@SMU
	15	Marshall
	22	Northwestern State
	29	@Houston
Oct.	13	@Tulane
	20	Army
	30	East Carolina
Nov.	10	@UAB
	24	Louisville
	30	@Southern Miss

QUARTERBACKS

With the departure of Tomlinson, Printers (6-3, 208), a junior, will become the focal point of the Horned Frogs' offense. There will be an increased emphasis on the passing game.

It won't be too much of a burden for Printers, who has started since he was a freshman in 1999. That year, Printers became the first first-year TCU player to start at quarterback since Chance McCarty started one game in 1993.

Printers finished his freshman year as the most valuable player in the Mobile Alabama Bowl.

As a sophomore in 2000, Printers had no slump. He finished fourth in the nation in passing efficiency, completing 58 percent (102-of-176) of his passes for 1,584 yards in the regular season. He threw 16 touchdowns and was intercepted six times.

Printers also rushed for 265 yards and scored four rushing touchdowns.

In the 28-21 loss to Southern Miss in the GMAC Mobile Alabama Bowl, Printers completed 10-of-22 passes for 115 yards and one touchdown, but was intercepted twice.

As a freshman, Printers was 28th in the nation in passing efficiency, completing 57.3 percent for 1,213 yards and eight touchdowns. He took over the starting job for Patrick Batteaux in the third game of the season and led the Horned Frogs to a 24-21 victory over Arkansas State.

After his freshman season, Printers showed great improvement as a runner. He had 32 carries for minus-69 yards as a freshman, and last season ran for 265 yards, averaging 3.2 yards per carry, and four touchdowns as the team's fourth-leading rusher.

Printers, a native of DeSoto, Texas, will take on more of a leadership role this season, and Patterson is glad to give him that responsibility. Printers is 18-4 as the starter.

In the spring, junior **Sean Stilley** (6-5, 234) solidified his position as the backup quarterback. Stilley played in six games last season and completed 3-of-6 passes.

Freshman **Zack Moore** (6-2, 172) came to the Horned Frogs out of Weatherford, Texas as a quarterback but may be moved to another position to utilize his athleticism.

Redshirt freshman **Brandon Hassell** (6-1, 191) is more of an option quarterback, but will probably be the third-stringer.

RUNNING BACKS

Nobody needs to remind Patterson or anybody else that the Horned Frogs won't be able to replace Tomlinson.

Tomlinson had one of the most remarkable seasons in TCU history in 2000, rushing for 2,158 yards in the regular season, averaging 5.8 yards per carry, and scoring 22 rushing touchdowns.

In the bowl loss to Southern Miss, Tomlinson ran for 118 yards on 28 carries and scored on runs of 7 and 33 yards.

As a junior, Tomlinson won the national rushing title with 1,850 yards, averaging 6.9 yards per carry and 168.18 yards per game. In the NFL draft, Tomlinson was the first running back chosen and the first TCU player chosen in the first round since Norm Bulaich in 1970.

Senior **Andrew Hayes-Stoker** (5-8, 194) may be the starter at tailback, but plenty of others will share the carries.

Hayes-Stoker was fourth on the team in rushing last season with 178 yards, averaging 4.4 yards per carry. He began the spring as the starter, but by the end, Patterson had doubts that the senior would start.

Several others made their bids for the job during the spring. Sophomore **Ricky Madison** (5-9, 193), who played in seven games last season and had 20 carries for 86 yards, showed glimpses of big-play abilities in the spring, and sophomore **Corey Connally** (5-11, 187) also had a good spring.

"The two leading candidates right now are Ricky Madison and Corey Connally," Patterson told the *Horned Frog Sports Report*. "Andrew Hayes-Stoker is the guy that has the experience at the position, but he doesn't have the overall 'go' speed that those guys have.

"They ran 10.3 and 10.4 [as] sprinters coming out of high school and it's their time to step up."

Although Connally has good potential, he has little college experience, playing only with the practice squad in 2000.

Junior **Reggie Holts** (6-0, 230), a transfer from Blinn (Texas) Junior College, may step into the starting job at fullback. In two years of junior college, Holts rushed for 1,200 yards, including 700 last season. As a senior at Langham Creek High School in Houston, Holts was among the leading rushers in the Greater Houston Area with 1,700 yards and 26 touchdowns.

George Layne, who would have been the starting fullback, opted to pass up his senior season and enter the NFL draft. Layne, drafted in the fourth round by Kansas City as the 108th pick overall, was the team's second-leading rusher with 279 yards last season, but had the best rushing average, 6.1 yards per carry. He also scored six rushing touchdowns.

Layne was also a receiving threat; he caught eight passes, averaging 18.9 yards per catch, and had two touchdown catches. His 3-yard touchdown catch in the bowl game gave the Horned Frogs a 6-0 lead.

Redshirt freshman **Mohammad Shittu** (5-11, 231) was slotted as the No. 1 fullback in the spring, but that may not be the case during fall practices. Junior **Jon Muther** (6-2, 230) was the second-string fullback when spring workouts began. Muther worked with the scout team last season.

Senior **Matt Schobel** (6-5, 257) could even play some fullback in passing situations, but he is listed on the roster as a tight end.

WIDE RECEIVERS/TIGHT ENDS

In the spring, Patterson said the wide receivers provided the biggest surprise, and it's a good thing. The top two receivers from last season, Tim Maiden and Cedric James, were seniors. Both caught 19 passes, and they combined for 658 receiving yards and seven touchdowns.

James was chosen by Minnesota in the fourth round of the NFL draft. He was the 131st overall pick.

Dunbar (5-11, 187), a junior, appears to be the go-to guy this season. Dunbar was the team's third-leading receiver last year with 17 catches for 251 yards and four touchdowns. He added two catches for 42 yards in the bowl game.

In the second scrimmage of the spring, Dunbar had four catches for 76 yards and two touchdowns, leading all the receivers in the scrimmage.

"LaTarence Dunbar has emerged as our offensive leader," Patterson told the *Horned Frog Sports Report* at the end of spring. "He was the No. 1 kickoff returner in the nation and can be a running back or wide receiver. The emergence of **Reggie Harrell** and **Reuben Randle**, who are big, tall receivers, made a difference this spring. They have a lot of ability.

"**Shane Hudnall** also stepped up. The biggest thing with them is that they are young and they need to mature and get stronger because wide receivers around here need to block."

Patterson will try to get the ball to Dunbar in any way possible, whether it's as a running back or receiver.

Harrell (6-3, 209), a redshirt freshman, was slotted as the starter at the "H" receiver position when spring started and he retained the position heading into fall practices.

Randle (6-4, 212), also a redshirt freshman, was Harrell's backup. Sophomore **Tremaine Butler** (6-0, 187) was the third-string H-back receiver.

Randle and Harrell both caught one pass for nine yards in the second spring scrimmage.

Junior **Terran Williams** (5-10, 166) will be Dunbar's backup at the "X" receiver spot. Williams, who had four catches for 78 yards last season, caught three passes for 65 yards and a touchdown in the second spring scrimmage.

Sophomore **Bruce Galbert** (6-4, 198) will also play the "X" receiver.

At the "Z" receiver, junior **Kevin Brown** (5-10, 180) has the most experience, but he may not be the starter when fall practices start. Brown played in all 11 regular-season games last season and finished with 11 catches for 157 yards and a touchdown.

Hudnall (6-0, 193), a sophomore, and redshirt freshman Anthony Gilliam (5-11, 170) will also vie for playing time. Hudnall is a good possession receiver.

Starting tight end **B.J. Roberts** (6-3, 237) returns for his senior season. Roberts was used primarily as a blocker. He had seven catches, averaging 15.3 yards per catch.

The versatile Schobel will probably be Roberts' backup at tight end.

OFFENSIVE LINE

The nucleus of last year's offensive line, nicknamed the "Big Uglies," has departed, making room for the "Big Uglies II." This new bunch may eventually be just as good, but it lacks the experience of its predecessors.

Gone are three All-WAC first-team players, tackles David Bobo and Mike Keathley and guard Jeff Millican. Another one of the Big Uglies, Jeff Garner, was also a senior last season.

Their departures left a big, ugly hole in the Horned Frogs' offensive front. Several players who were groomed as their replacements should fill those spots.

They are junior guards **Josh Harbuck** (6-6, 322) and **J.T. Aughinbaugh** (6-6, 323), junior center **Jamal Powell** (6-3, 322) and junior tackle **Brady Barrick** (6-5, 303).

Senior guard **Victor Payne** (6-1, 305) will start in front of Harbuck on the left side. Payne, who started last season, is the lone returning Big Ugly and with his experience will be a team leader.

Barrick will probably be the starter at right tackle with sophomore **John Glud** (6-6, 332) and redshirt freshman **Anthony Alabi** (6-6, 318) battling for the starting job at left tackle.

Glud has made a good adjustment after being moved from the defensive line.

Sophomore **Jonathan Morgan** (6-4, 327) was the second-string right tackle at the start of the spring.

Redshirt freshman **Zach Bray** (6-4, 314) will probably be behind Aughinbaugh at right guard. Redshirt freshman **Chase Johnson** (6-2, 291) will battle Powell for the starting job at center. Entering preseason practices, Johnson will probably be the No. 1 center, thanks to a very good spring.

Patterson says the offensive line needs to jell to be successful.

"The offensive line is a big key for us and they came a long way in 15 [spring] practices," he told the *Horned Frog Sports Report*. "[They are] probably just as talented, or more talented, in some positions than the group that left here. The difference is that they don't have four years of starting experience. It's our job to grow them up. The last time they had to start that early in age, they went 1-10, and I would prefer not to go through that again for them to learn those kinds of lessons.

"There are probably eight guys that are battling hard for positions, and that's deeper than we felt we were last year. This is the first year we have played six straight games without an open date, and two are against bowl teams. It's going to be very important that we establish two deep. We have always rotated a lot of players on defense anyway, but it will be important for us to have the second offensive line play a couple of series, at least one each half, to make sure we keep bringing them along."

2000 STATISTICS

Rushing offense	275.6	4
Passing offense	145.5	107
Total offense	421.1	23
Scoring offense	37.3	11
Net Punting	37.6	16
Punt returns	10.3	44
Kickoff returns	28.8	1
Rushing defense	84.4	7
Passing efficiency defense	91.2	3
Total defense	245.0	1
Scoring defense	9.6	1
Turnover margin	+10	13

Last column is ranking among Division I-A teams.

KICKERS

It's going to be a competitive fall for the starting job as place-kicker with the departure of Chris Kaylakie, who had a solid senior year. Kaylakie made 16-of-18 field-goal attempts and 50-of-51 PAT kicks.

Sophomore **John Braziel** (6-3, 206), who will also compete for the punting job, will be in the hunt for the starting kicker's job, along with freshman **Mike Wynn** (5-10, 195) and sophomore **Tommy Taylor** (5-9, 144). Taylor worked with the practice squad last season.

Braziel was used as a punter last season when starter **Joey Biasatti** (5-11, 196) suffered a leg injury, but wasn't used as a kicker.

Wynn is the Horned Frogs' likely kicker of the future, and he has a very good chance of being the guy this season. He was the starting kicker and punter for Midland (Texas) Lee High School, the Class 5A state champion and *USA Today*'s national champion. Wynn, who chose TCU over Tennessee and Oklahoma, made 9-of-12 field-goal attempts last season and converted 63 PAT kicks. He was selected by his teammates as their special teams player of the year.

DEFENSIVE LINE

Patterson has concerns about depth on the defensive front entering the 2001 season. Gone are All-WAC defensive tackle Shawn Worthen and starting nose tackle Stuart Ashley and starting tackle Donald Burrell.

Worthen had 51 tackles, including 12 tackles for loss and 2 1/2 sacks. Burrell had 28 tackles, including three for loss, and Ashley, who played in nine games, had 28 tackles and three tackles for loss.

The only returning starter on the line is senior end **Chad McCarty** (6-2, 255), who had 30 tackles, including seven for loss and three sacks. He beat out sophomore **Bo Schobel** (6-5, 254) for the starting job last season and will have to do the same this year.

Although McCarty was the starter, Schobel had better numbers—54 tackles (seventh best on the team) in the regular season. He was second on the team in tackles for loss with 14 and led with 6 1/2 sacks.

When spring started, McCarty was at the top of the depth chart, but it wouldn't be surprising to see Schobel in the lineup for the season opener.

Sophomore nose tackle **Chad Pugh** (6-3, 277) is an all-star of the future, and he will probably be slotted ahead of redshirt freshman **Brandon Johnson** (6-2, 292). Pugh played in all 11 regular-season games and had 27 tackles, five for loss.

Johnson had one of the best springs of any defender, and Patterson will give him ample playing time.

At tackle, junior **John Turntine** (6-2, 267) will battle for the starting job with sophomore **Richard Evans** (6-3, 279).

Senior **Joe Hill** (6-4, 238) and **Robert Pollard** (6-3, 255) are also expected to be prominent players at defensive end. Pollard had a great spring.

One of the team's strengths will be its speed on the ends, particularly with Hill and McCarty being backed up by Schobel and Pollard. The Horned Frogs can go two deep on the ends without losing much at all.

LINEBACKERS

In the spring, junior **LaMarcus McDonald** (6-1, 217) really pushed senior **Chad Bayer** (5-11, 231) for the starting job at strong-side linebacker. That was no easy task.

Bayer led the team in tackles in 2000 with 103 and had 13 tackles for loss and three sacks. McDonald played in 10 regular-season games and had 30 tackles. Their competition will make both players better.

At middle linebacker, senior **Adrian Lewis** (6-2, 210) may have the edge over sophomores **Josh Goolsby** (6-2, 236) and **Devon Davis** (6-2, 240). Davis is a transfer from Tennessee.

DEFENSIVE BACKS

Both starting cornerbacks return, with backup Greg Walls as the only departed senior. Walls started 10 games at cornerback as a junior, but two juniors, Jason Goss (5-9, 182) and **Bo Springfield** (5-10, 183), managed to pin down the starting jobs last season. Springfield started four games late in the season.

Senior **Kendrick Patterson** (5-11, 180) and sophomore **Tyrone Sanders** (5-10, 170) will be the backup cornerbacks.

"At corner, we bring back everyone but Greg Walls," Patterson told the *Horned Frog Sports Report*. "Jason Goss did not go through spring practice, but he is bigger and faster than he's ever been. I think he benched 450 pounds as a 180-pound corner."

The Horned Frogs, who employ five defensive backs, return one of the three starting safeties in junior **Charlie Owens** (6-0, 188). Owens should retain his starting job and will be backed up by junior **Nathan Roach** (6-1, 198).

Junior **Kenneth Hilliard** (6-1, 198), moved from cornerback to free safety, should get the start at his new position. He will probably be backed up by a senior, **Jason Higham** (5-10, 183).

Russell Gary, who had 36 starts at strong safety, has departed, and that left a big void. It will be filled by junior **Jared Smitherman** (6-10, 210), redshirt freshman **Marvin Godbolt** (6-0, 195), or sophomore **Brandon Williams** (6-2, 188).

Smitherman may be the starter heading into fall workouts, but if Godbolt continues the improvement he showed in the spring, he could bump Smitherman in the depth chart.

"There is a lot of chemistry that is missing right now that we are working to get back Kenneth Hilliard, who we moved from cornerback," Patterson told the sports report. "And his backup, Jason Higham, will be a key at free safety because that position is like the defensive quarterback. At strong safety, Marvin Godbolt has come a long way. Athletically, he is probably more talented than the three seniors who left here. The problem is that he doesn't have the game experience they had.

"... Godbolt made drastic improvement from practice one to practice 15 [in the spring]. He benched 435, squatted 615 and his vertical was 36 inches. [Departed senior Curtis] Fuller was a great player and leader [at free safety] who had a settling effect on our defense. Hilliard may be a better athlete, but the key will be how well he can mature as the quarterback back there, telling everyone what is going on and what needs to happen."

PUNTERS

Biasatti, a junior, should be back from his leg injury and able to compete with his replacement, sophomore Braziel (6-3, 206).

Last season, Biasatti averaged 41.6 yards on 26 punts and had eight inside the 20-yard line. Five went for touchbacks and four for fair catches.

Braziel averaged 37.5 yards on 17 points and had two inside the 20, two fair catches and one touchback. Chris Kaylakie, the departed kicker, had four punts for a 38.3-yard average.

SPECIAL TEAMS

Dunbar, the nation's leading kick returner last season, will retain the job this season. Dunbar averaged 33.7 yards on 15 returns and ran two back for touchdowns.

Three other kick returners—Cedric James, B.J. Roberts, and George Layne—have departed. James had four returns last season and Roberts and Layne one each.

The Horned Frogs will also look to replace punt returner LaVar Veale, who averaged 10.3 yards on 34 returns. He had an 85-yarder returned for a touchdown.

Goss, the cornerback, is the most likely replacement to return punts. He had three returns for a 10-yard average last season.

Also gone is deep snapper Brian Edmondson, who had the job the last four seasons. Junior **Brady Barrick** (6-5, 303) enters the fall with at the top of the depth chart for deep snappers.

RECRUITING CLASS

Patterson signed 17 players in his first TCU recruiting class, and he got a little bit of everything.

He signed four offensive linemen, three defensive backs, two linebackers, one defensive lineman, one wide receiver, one quarterback, one running back, one tight end, one defensive end and one place-kicker.

"We met the position needs that we were looking for—offensive linemen, safeties and a kicker," Patterson said. "We lost four offensive linemen from the 2000 team, so it was important to sign a solid group of linemen. We graduated five safeties, so we needed to sign some more defensive backs. We have placed a high priority on signing defensive backs in each of the last two classes that fit our scheme. Plus, with the loss of Chris Kaylakie, we needed to sign another kicker, and we found a great one in Mike Wynn."

Tye Gunn (6-4, 200) of LaGrange High in Texas could be the Horned Frogs' quarterback of the future. Gunn led LaGrange to the Class 3A state title last season and was one of the state's Top 100 players as chosen by the *Dallas Morning News*, *Fort Worth Star-Telegram*, *Houston Chronicle*, *Lubbock Avalanche* and *Waco Tribune*.

Gunn was chosen as the Class 3A player of the year by Dave Campbell's Texas Football/Fox Sports Net.

As a senior last year, Gunn put up some amazing numbers—running for 2,216 yards and 37 touchdowns and passing for 1,401 yards and 13 touchdowns. For his career, Gunn piled up more than 9,100 total yards offense and ran or threw for 127 touchdowns. He committed to TCU in July of 2000 and chose the Horned Frogs over Arizona, Baylor, Houston, Purdue and Texas Tech.

Holts, the junior college transfer, may well be the starting fullback in 2001. As a high school senior at Langham Creek in Houston, Holts was a finalist for the Houston Touchdown Club Player of the Year award.

Aside from Holts, the rest of the signees are freshman, many of whom will be redshirted.

One of the top defensive signees is linebacker **Shawn Brooks** (6-0, 200), rated as the sixth best linebacker in Texas as a senior at Jersey Village High in Houston. He ended his career with 200 tackles and was the Houston Touchdown Club's defensive player of the year. He chose TCU over Baylor, Kansas, Houston and Iowa State.

Flander Malone (6-0, 190) was one of the state's top running back prospects after his senior year at Skyline High in Texas, but he may move to defensive back at TCU. Despite splitting time with two other backs, Malone led the district with 846 yards on 116 attempts. He ran a 10.5-second in the 100-meter dash as a junior and chose TCU over Michigan State, Oklahoma, SMU and UCLA.

The new linemen are **Ben Angley** (6-5, 280) of Earth High in Springlake, Texas; **Stephen Culp** (6-3, 305) of Tyler High in Lee, Texas; **Shane Sims** (6-3, 300) of High High in Tomball, Texas; and **Michael Toudouze** (6-6, 280) of East Central High in San Antonio, Texas.

"In addition to Tye, we signed five or six top-100 players that we are excited about joining our program," Patterson said. "The rest of the group is a great evaluation class, similar to the senior class that took us to three straight bowl games. ... There is no doubt that our success last season had a big impact on this signing class. It was not just the 10-2 record and the national ranking, but I think playing on television every week played a big role.

"Players know that with us moving to Conference USA and playing on television every week, that they will gain a lot of exposure while they are at TCU. Playing on television probably helped us get some early commitments. We have gained a lot of national prominence over the last several years. I think players recognize that this is one of the top programs not only in Texas, but also in the country."

BLUE RIBBON ANALYSIS

OFFENSE	B-

SPECIAL TEAMS	B
DEFENSE	B-
INTANGIBLES	B-

Patterson has a plan for winning football games in 2001. It's not all that different from the previous three years when he was defensive coordinator for the Horned Frogs.

"I think the reason we have been successful at TCU is good defense and special teams, not making mistakes and having a really good running back," Patterson told the *Horned Frog Sports Report*. "The keys for our success [in 2001] are to still play that strong defense, be good on special teams and being able to move the ball, but still control the clock.

"Conference USA is more of a one-back league, and we have the capability on both sides of the line to do those things. I still think the most physical teams are the ones that win games on Saturday."

The first-year coach will rely on a stern defense, like last year when the Horned Frogs ranked first in the nation in total defense, allowing 245 yards per game, and first in scoring defense, allowing 9.6 points per game.

TCU posted two shutouts and held six teams to seven points or less.

However, Patterson faces the daunting task of replacing six starting defenders, including five who were All-WAC first-team players last year: defensive end Aaron Schobel, tackle Shawn Worthen, strong safety Russell Gary, free safety Curtis Fuller and linebacker Shannon Brazzell.

Offensively, the Horned Frogs will try to utilize the passing of Printers. Look for them to throw first, run second, and move the football with possession passing.

"Our philosophy in the passing game will be the West Coast philosophy of taking what the defense gives you," Patterson told the sports report. "Then pick your spots and throw downfield when they start creeping in. It's a little bit like Oklahoma when I saw them play Nebraska. They had a drive of about nine minutes and I think they only had two or three running plays.

"They were controlling the clock, playing throw and catch, and going about their business. Right now, we have a lot more in our offense, but with our young offensive line, until we improve in that aspect of the game, we are not putting them in a situation where they can't achieve. I would say we will throw to run, which is different than what we have done in the past."

Patterson enters the fall with several key positions needing to be filled. The offensive line must mature quickly. Defensively, the Horned Frogs will have three new starters on the line, and they will have new starters at free safety and strong safety.

"We have several positions that we are anxious to see who will take over," Patterson said. "We need to gain some experience on the offensive line since we have only one starter returning. We need to find a starter and establish some depth at strong safety.

"Offensively, we need to find a go-to tailback and a fullback."

It all adds up to plenty of work for Patterson and his staff before the opener at Nebraska in the Pigskin Classic. Their first year in C-USA should be much tougher than their days in the WAC. They might not win the league this year, but watch out for the Horned Frogs in the future.

(D.L.)

2000 RESULTS

Nevada	W	41-10	1-0
Northwestern State	W	41-14	2-0
Arkansas State	W	52-3	3-0
Navy	W	24-0	4-0
Hawaii	W	41-21	5-0
Tulsa	W	17-3	6-0
Rice	W	37-0	7-0
San Jose State	L	24-27	7-1
Fresno State	W	24-7	8-1
UTEP	W	47-14	9-1
SMU	W	62-7	10-1
Southern Miss (Mobile)	L	21-28	10-2

Tulane

LOCATION New Orleans, LA
CONFERENCE Conference USA
LAST SEASON 6-5 (.545)
CONFERENCE RECORD 3-4 (t-5th)
OFFENSIVE STARTERS RETURNING 5
DEFENSIVE STARTERS RETURNING 5
NICKNAME Green Wave
COLORS Olive Green & Sky Blue
HOME FIELD Louisiana Superdome (69,767)
HEAD COACH Chris Scelfo (NE Louisiana '81)
RECORD AT SCHOOL 10-13 (2 years)
CAREER RECORD 10-13 (2 years)
ASSISTANTS
Giff Smith (Georgia Southern '91)
Associate Head Coach/Recruiting Coordinator/Defensive Line
Frank Scelfo (Northeast Louisiana '81)
Assistant Head Coach/Offensive Coordinator/Quarterbacks
Pete McGinnis (Jacksonville State '77)
Defensive Coordinator/Inside Linebackers
Garratt Chachere (Tulane '92)
Outside Linebackers
Greg Davis, Jr. (Nicholls State '94)
Running Backs
Joey Houston (Gardner-Webb '95)
Secondary
Don Mahoney (Marshall '92)
Offensive Line
David Oliver (Northern Colorado '94)
Tight Ends/Special Teams
Trooper Taylor (Baylor '92)
Wide Receivers
TEAM WINS (last 5 yrs.) 2-7-12-3-6
FINAL RANK (last 5 yrs.) 68-54-13-81-71
2000 FINISH Beat Memphis in regular-season finale.

COACH AND PROGRAM

Chris Scelfo took on a monstrous task in 1999 when he took over for Tommy Bowden on Dec. 7, 1998.

Scelfo, who turns 38 on Sept. 30, had never been a head coach. He inherited a team that was 11-0 and headed to the Liberty Bowl. Bowden, who left for Clemson, had engineered a season for the ages at the New Orleans school. He was the toast of the town. Enter Scelfo, who had been the assistant head coach at Georgia from 1996-99.

After coaching the Green Wave to a 23-20 victory over Brigham Young in the Liberty Bowl, Scelfo started getting his program in place.

Coming off Tulane's first undefeated season since 1929, Scelfo was facing almost a no-win situation. It's pretty tough to beat an unbeaten season.

So when Scelfo went 3-8 in 1999, he was more disappointed than anybody. Tulane is a dream job for Scelfo, a native of New Iberia, La. His first season was a huge letdown.

It's no wonder Scelfo is more upbeat about things these days. While the Green Wave barely pulled off a winning season in 2000, going 6-5, it had a strong finish and won the last three games against Houston, Navy and Memphis.

Scelfo is far from satisfied, but he's certainly feeling better than a year ago.

"There's been a lot of progress made," Scelfo said. "We're still a long way from being in the upper echelon of our league on a consistent basis but I think we've attracted some good players in our program, and keeping them three or four years before they have to play is a key in any program.

"Hopefully in the next year or two we're going to see that."

With that in mind, Scelfo hopes to establish the same stability in personnel that Bowden had during his last two seasons with the Green Wave. Scelfo knows depth is crucial in producing a consistent winner.

"I think the quality of our first units are very consistent in all phases," Scelfo said. "A big concern is the depth that we have on our football team. That's something we've got to try to develop with some of these incoming players that we've recruited this year, to help us out in that area."

Scelfo enters the 2001 season after some reassignments in his coaching staff.

Frank Scelfo, Chris' older brother and a five-year veteran of Tulane's staff, takes over as the Green Wave's offensive coordinator. Frank Scelfo becomes the team's first offensive coordinator under Chris Scelfo. Frank coached wide receivers, tight ends and quarterbacks in his previous five seasons. He will also be assistant head coach.

David Oliver, the tight ends coach, will coordinate special teams and defensive line coach/recruiting coordinator Giff Smith was promoted to associate head coach.

"I have tremendous confidence in our entire offensive staff and Frank has been an integral part of that staff and in the success of our offense the last two years," Chris Scelfo said.

Frank Scelfo and Oliver were at Tulane with Bowden, while Smith came in 1999 from Georgia Southern.

"David has been very instrumental in our success in many different areas," Chris Scelfo said. "He's a very enthusiastic and organized coach who will pay close attention to detail. Special teams is an important area to me and this move gives it proper emphasis."

2001 SCHEDULE

Sept.	1	@LSU
	8	East Carolina
	22	Central Florida
	29	Southern
Oct.	6	@Cincinnati
	13	TCU
	20	@UAB
	27	@Army
Nov.	3	Louisville
	10	@Navy
	17	@Southern Mississippi

QUARTERBACKS

Record-setting quarterback **Patrick Ramsey** (6-3, 228) returns for his senior season and Scelfo will build the offense around him. Ramsey, a native of Ruston, La., is perhaps the most prolific passer in Tulane history. The Green Wave will employ a wide-open attack that will utilize his passing abilities.

In little more than two years, Ramsey has set 20 school passing records. He holds the top four single-game passing performances and is the only player to throw for more than 400 yards in a game. He's done that three times.

Amazingly, Ramsey has some competition for the job. Sophomore **J.P. Losman** (6-3, 195) is being groomed as Ramsey's replacement.

"I think they will continue to battle," Scelfo said. "I think we have two excellent quarterbacks."

Last year, Ramsey completed 58.9 percent of his passes for 2,833 yards and 24 touchdowns. He was intercepted 14 times.

Ramsey, who led the league with 283.3 passing yards per game, shared second-team all-conference honors with East Carolina's David Garrard last season. Ramsey also led C-USA in total offense (288.6), and ranked eighth nationally.

"Ramsey is on pace to break a lot of records," Scelfo said. "He has a chance to be a really good player for us."

Ramsey, who was the C-USA player of the week three times in 2000, threw 12 touchdown passes in Tulane's last three games. He missed the Sept. 16 East Carolina game and the last quarter of the Oct. 28 Louisville game because of minor injuries.

In 1999, Ramsey started all 11 games and set single-season records for passing yards (3,410), yards per game (310), and attempts (513).

His 25 touchdowns ranked second on the all-time list. On Sept. 21, 1999 against Army, Ramsey set the single-game record for passing yardage when he threw for 447 yards. His five touchdown passes and 37 completions in a game against Louisiana-Lafayette is also a single-game record.

Losman played in 10 games last season and started one. He completed 58-of-115 passes for four touchdowns and was intercepted twice.

In 1999, Losman sat out the year after transferring from UCLA. Losman was a standout in the 2001 spring scrimmage, completing 11-of-20 passes for 155 yards and two touchdowns and one interception. Ramsey was held out of the scrimmage.

RUNNING BACKS

Sophomore **Mewelde Moore** (6-1, 198) didn't miss a beat from his senior year at Baton Rouge (La.) Belaire High School to his freshman year at Tulane. Moore finished second in C-USA in rushing last season, gaining 890 yards and averaging 5.1 yards per carry. He scored two touchdowns.

It was the highest rushing total by a Tulane player since 1970 and the best rushing season ever by a freshman. He had five 100-yard rushing games and barely missed a sixth with 99 yards against Navy. He had three straight 100-yard games against East Carolina, SMU and Cincinnati in September.

Slowed by a high ankle sprain in October, Moore missed almost two entire games and played hurt in two more. He also caught 33 passes for 350 yards as the team's fourth-leading receiver. He led Tulane in all-purpose yards with 124 per game, which ranked fourth in C-USA.

With six catches for 101 yards against Army on Oct. 21, Moore became the first Tulane running back since 1988 to have a 100-yard receiving day.

Moore, who signed with the San Diego Padres in August of 2000, spent the summer playing minor-league baseball.

Junior **Brant Hocke** (5-8, 187) will be Moore's backup. Hocke was the team's second-leading rusher last season with 232 yards, averaging 3.6 yards per carry, and led the backs with three touchdown runs. He played in all 11 regular-season games, starting three, and caught nine passes for 71 yards in the regular season.

Freshman **Jeff Kirven** (5-11, 200) and senior **Gee Reshard** (5-6, 195) will provide depth at running back.

Starting fullback/tight end Mike Truax, who started eight games, was a senior last season. He had only five carries for 27 yards and caught three passes for 28 yards.

His replacement should be sophomore **Kris Coleman** (6-0, 240), with junior **Marcus Williams** (5-10, 220) as his backup. In the Green Wave's system, the fullback is used primarily as a blocking back. Coleman, who started two games last season, had 14 carries for 35 yards and a touchdown. Williams played in two games and had one carry.

"We've got a pretty good mixture of running backs that have been game tested," Scelfo said. "Obviously that's a key for us."

WIDE RECEIVERS/TIGHT ENDS

Most noticeably absent from the 2000 offense are starting wide receivers Adrian Burnette and Kerwin Cook, who combined for 122 catches, 1,699 receiving yards, and 20 touchdown catches.

Burnette, chosen to the All-C-USA first team, was second in the league in catches with 74 and led the league in receiving yards with 1,075. He led all C-USA players in touchdowns with 14.

Cook was third on the team in catches with 48 and third in receiving yards with 624. He had six touchdown catches.

"We lost Adrian Burnette, which was a big blow for us, and Kerwin Cook, but I feel like we've got some guys who have the potential to be good players there and a chance to catch a lot of balls," Scelfo said.

Senior **Terrell Harris** (5-10, 197) is the top returning receiver. Harris caught 64 passes for 694 yards and one touchdown last season.

Red-shirt freshman **Chris Bush** (6-1, 189) will be Harris' backup at the "H" receiver position.

Sophomore **Roydell Williams** (6-2, 171) is the probable starter at the "X" receiver spot. Williams played in all 11 games in 2000 and started one. He was fifth on the team in catches with 26 and in receiving yards with 338. He also caught two touchdown passes.

Sophomore **Chino Fontenette** (5-10, 198) is slotted as Williams' backup.

Two sophomores are the probable starters at the "Y" and "Z" receiver positions. **James Dunn** (5-8, 162), who caught one pass for 36 yards last season, is slotted as one starter and **Nick Narcisse** (6-0, 174) as the other.

Senior **Zander Robinson** (5-9, 173) could bump one of the starters, however. Robinson started two games last season and was sixth on the team in catches with 18 and receiving yards with 266. He also caught three touchdown passes.

Junior **Derrick Joseph** (5-11, 181), who played in five games last season and made one catch, will be a backup receiver.

The Green Wave must replace Truax, who doubled as a fullback and tight end. Sophomore **Eddie Robinson** (6-3, 240) ended the spring as the starter but must beat out sophomore **Tim Pinter** (6-5, 253) and junior **Kayne Lagraize** (6-3, 248) in fall workouts.

Robinson and Pinter lettered last season. Pinter, who played in six games, caught one pass for 11 yards. Robinson didn't catch a pass.

OFFENSIVE LINE

Scelfo will have a new starting tackle and two new starting guards on his offensive line this season.

The biggest loss will be tackle Bernard Robertson, an All-C-USA first-team player last season. He started since his freshman year when he was chosen to the league's all-freshman team. He was also chosen to the all-conference first team as a sophomore.

Robertson was chosen by the Chicago Bears in the fifth round of the NFL draft. He became the first Tulane offensive lineman drafted in 17 years and was the 138th pick overall. He's projected to play guard or center in the NFL.

Also gone is starting guard Bryan Wesbrook. Senior guard **Charles Caldwell** (6-3, 07) returns after being slotted as the starter in the 2000 preseason.

"That's a huge concern for us right now, our offensive line," Scelfo said. "We lost some really good players there."

Returning starters are senior center **Torie Taulli** (6-0, 272) and senior right tackle **Corey Sewell** (6-2, 281).

Sewell will undoubtedly be the anchor of the line. He was chosen to the All-C-USA freshman team in 1999 and has started since that season.

Senior **Chrys Bullock** (6-3, 313) is the probable starter at left tackle and will be backed up by junior **Derick Bugg** (6-3, 282).

Sophomore **Brendon Drysdale** (6-1, 281) enters the fall as the probable starter at left guard with junior **Seth Zaunbrecher** (6-4, 282) as his backup.

Caldwell should start at right guard, but could be pushed by sophomores **Joe Mitchell** (6-3, 324) and **Renzi Sandras** (6-2, 283).

Jimmy Kosienski (6-7, 245), who was red-shirted last season, will be Sewell's backup at right tackle.

Scelfo says some of his younger linemen will need to mature in a hurry.

"The quality of our depth isn't where we want it," Scelfo said. "There's going to be unfortunately some freshmen that are going to have to come in and contribute [on the line]."

2000 STATISTICS

Rushing offense	129.1	77
Passing offense	324.5	3
Total offense	453.5	7
Scoring offense	29.9	39
Net Punting	40.3	3
Punt returns	8.4	74
Kickoff returns	20.5	34
Rushing defense	180.5	83
Passing efficiency defense	118.7	57
Total defense	436.7	104
Scoring defense	31.5	86
Turnover margin	-2	69

Last column is ranking among Division I-A teams.

KICKERS

Junior **Seth Marler** (6-0, 178) will start for the third straight year as the place-kicker. Last season, Marler led the Green Wave in scoring with 85 points, making 16-of-21 field-goal attempts and 37-of-39 PAT kicks.

Marler made all 10 of his field-goal attempts from inside 39 yards, and was 6-of-8 from 40-49 yards and missed all three of his tries from beyond yards. His long field goal was 48 yards.

DEFENSIVE LINE

Two starters return to the defensive line in juniors **Floyd Dorsey** (6-0, 248) and **Roxie Shelvin** (6-2, 272), and Scelfo is confident the backups from 2000 can get the job done.

"We're based out of an eight-man front," Scelfo said. "We're to the point now where I think our defensive line, most of those guys have been in the program for a year or two or three and they've been fighting through the freshman and sophomore years. I feel good about that position."

Dorsey, one of the defensive ends, was fifth on the team in tackles with 54 and second in tackles for loss with nine. He had five sacks.

Shelvin, a tackle, had 35 tackles and six tackles for loss.

Sophomore **Alex Battard** (6-2, 245) and senior **Derrick Elzy** (6-4, 235) are Dorsey's backups. Sophomore **Lonnie Crayton** (6-3, 280) and redshirt freshman **Alvin Smith** (6-3, 303) will be behind Shelvin in the depth chart as fall practices begin.

Defensive end **Kenan Blackmon** (6-5, 250), a junior who started last year, faces a battle to retain his starting job. At the end of spring practice, senior **Glenn Lemoine** (6-3, 252) was the starter.

Blackmon had 39 tackles and nine tackles for loss last season. Lemoine had 24 tackles and five tackles for loss.

At tackle, junior **Marlon Tickles** (6-1, 298) is slotted as the starter after playing in all 11 games last season. He had 16 tackles and two sacks.

Sophomore **Terrence Tarver** (6-1, 269) and junior **Percy Branon** (6-1, 275) also play the tackle position. Branon played in three games last season.

LINEBACKERS

Perhaps the heaviest loss on the defensive side was the departure of middle linebacker Jerry Phillips, who led the Green Wave in tackles with 104 and ranks among the top 10 career tacklers at Tulane.

Phillips, who had eight tackles for loss and two sacks last season, was on the All-C-USA second team.

Noel Ellis, who also started during the 2000 season, must also be replaced. Ellis was third on the team in tackles with 87. He had 12 tackles for loss and five sacks.

The Green Wave will be young at the middle linebacker position. Sophomore **Daniel Nevil** (6-1, 213) is the probable starter with redshirt freshmen **Edgar Algere** (5-11, 225) and **Blake Baker** (5-10, 220) as the backups.

Senior **David Dorsey** (6-1, 224) should start at strong-side linebacker. He played in 11 games last season and had 36 tackles and four tackles for loss.

Dorsey will be backed up by junior **Chris Washington** (6-2, 225).

Sophomore **Wesley Heath** (6-0, 195) finished the spring as the starting weak-side linebacker. Heath played in 11 games last season and had 16 tackles. Juniors **David Dunlap** (6-3, 208) and **Preston Curtis** (5-11, 214) will also play weak-side linebacker.

"We lost two inside linebackers, Jerry Phillips and Noel Ellis, both to graduation," Scelfo said. "That's a position that I have concern about."

DEFENSIVE BACKS

Left cornerback **Lynaris Elpheage** (5-9, 156) and free safety **Quentin Brown** (5-9, 160) return as starters in the defensive backfield.

Elpheage, a sophomore, was an impact player as a true freshman last year. Chosen to the All-C-USA freshman team, Elpheage led the Green Wave in interceptions with three, including two against Cincinnati. He also led the team in pass break-ups with 14, which ranked third in the conference. He scored the Green Wave's first defensive touchdown of the year when he returned a fumble 23 yards for a touchdown against Navy on Nov. 11.

After joining the team late in preseason practices, Elpheage didn't move into the starting lineup until the fifth game, but still had 44 tackles, seventh best on the team.

Against Navy, Elpheage had four pass break-ups, seven tackles and two fumble recoveries.

Elpheage ended spring practices second on the depth chart behind junior **Trey Godfrey** (5-9, 166), but look for him to work his way back into the starting lineup during the preseason.

Brown, a junior, was fourth on the team in tackles and had four pass break-ups.

Junior **Adrian Mitchell** (5-10, 193) and senior **Meldon Barnes** (5-11, 193) are also free safeties.

Terry Fontenot (5-11, 203), a junior who played in all 11 games last season, should move into the starting lineup at strong safety. Also battling for the job will be sophomore **Darlvon Bracy** (5-10, 191).

Junior **Jeff Sanchez** (5-10, 169) should start at right cornerback, a spot also played by senior **Jamal Jones** (5-11, 189) and redshirt freshman **Lyneal Strain** (5-8, 170).

"I feel good about our secondary going into fall camp," Scelfo said. "We've got some guys back there with some experience and talent. Outside linebacker and strong safety are very interchangeable, and those are two positions where we need some younger players to step in that haven't played a whole lot. They'll need to raise their level of play."

PUNTERS

Senior **Casey Roussel** (6-1, 223) is back after another outstanding season with the Green Wave. Another good one should land Roussel in the NFL.

Roussel was C-USA's leading punter, averaging 44.2 yards on 59 punts, and was chosen to the all-conference first team. His long punt was 72 yards, and he had 10 for touchbacks, three for fair catches, and 13 downed inside the 20. He didn't have a punt blocked.

As a sophomore, Roussel also averaged 44.2 yards per punt, which was the third-highest average ever for a Tulane player.

SPECIAL TEAMS

The Green Wave must replace kick returner John Wilson, who averaged 20.8 yards on 33 tries. Zander Robinson appears to be the guy to replace Wilson. Robinson returned 13 punts last season, averaging 20.3 yards per return.

Elpheage, who returned two punts for 31 yards, will also get a shot at returning kicks.

Wilson was also the top punt returner, averaging 8.6 yardson 37 returns. Robinson will be in the hunt for the punt returner's job, but Scelfo will take a look at several others in the fall.

RECRUITING CLASS

In his first full recruiting class, Scelfo signed 21 players. The Green Wave staff concentrated on linemen and defensive backs. Nine of the signees were offensive or defensive linemen and five were defensive backs. All will be freshmen.

"We are excited about this group of players," Scelfo said. "They bring a lot of depth and quality to our overall team, and we have increased both our speed and our size with this class."

The Green Wave signed six players from Florida and six from Texas; five from Louisiana, two from Mississippi and one from Georgia and one from Alabama.

Offensive lineman **Chris McGee** (6-4, 255) of Ozen High in Beaumont, Texas, was rated as one of the top 66 players in Texas and was an honorable mention selection on the Texas Super Team, which consists of players from all classifications. He was rated as the 13th best offensive lineman in the state.

Linebacker **Antonio Mason** (6-0, 200) earned first team all-state honors last season at Mobile (Ala.) Murphy High. As a senior, he had 148 tackles, including 87 solo tackles.

One of the top athletes of the class is **Cletus McGee** (6-1, 190) of John Tyler High in Tyler, Texas. The *Dallas Morning News* listed McGee as a first team all-state player in Class 5A. He was one of 11 players chosen to the All-East Texas first team.

"I think there's going to be a chance for several of them to contribute," Scelfo said. "What roles they play depends on how fast they can make the jump."

Scelfo doesn't enter the fall with plans of redshirting any of his recruits.

"We don't redshirt anybody unless they ask to," Scelfo said. "Everybody's going to get an opportunity to play. I'm a guy that believes in playing talent over experience. If they can come in and make the jump then they're going to play."

BLUE RIBBON ANALYSIS

OFFENSE	B
SPECIAL TEAMS	B-
DEFENSE	C-
INTANGIBLES	C

Tulane had perhaps the most explosive offense in C-USA last season, leading the league in passing offense with 324.5 yards per game and total offense with 453 yards per game. It was third in scoring offense with 29.9 points per game, one-tenth of a point behind East Carolina.

Piling up the yardage and pouring on the points won't be the problem for the Green Wave. Not with Ramsey running the offense and Moore running the football.

It's the defense that must step to the forefront. That appears to be no small task with the departures of several key defenders, including linebackers Phillips and Ellis.

Scelfo admits he has concern about the linebacking corps.

Last season, the Green Wave ranked seventh in C-USA in pass efficiency defense and eighth in rushing defense and total defense. Obviously, the defense must improve before the Green Wave becomes a contender in C-USA.

By winning its last three games, Tulane ended the season on a positive note, and the Green Wave carried the momentum into the spring.

"I think we came out of spring feeling good about ourselves," Scelfo said. "We had good carryover on both sides of the ball. We got some ideas as far as who's able to step in [the lineup] going into fall camp. I think there's going to be some competition in a lot of places."

Unfortunately, the Green Wave's schedule isn't an easy one. While it opens with three of its first four games at home, those games are against East Carolina, Central Florida and Southern. And those come after the season opener at LSU.

Tulane finishes with five of its last seven on the road, and the two home games in that stretch are against TCU and Louisville. Not an easy task, either.

"We start out in Baton Rouge against LSU, which really came on strong last year, and then we play East Carolina," Scelfo said. "Those are two really quality teams to start out."

Scelfo's goal is to consistently challenge for the C-USA title, but the often-underrated league seems to only be getting better. TCU makes it even stronger.

"From top to bottom in our league, you've got four or five teams that are very mature in the fact that they've had some continuity there," Scelfo said. "They're proven winners year in and year out and they're consistent in what they've done. We're trying to get to that level.

"It will be interesting to see if we can stay healthy. We open up at home with three out of our first four, then we go on the road for five out of our last seven. That's always a tough draw."

(D.L.)

2000 RESULTS

Mississippi	L	20-49	0-1
East Carolina	L	17-37	0-2
SMU	W	29-17	1-2
Cincinnati	W	24-19	2-2
Louisiana-Lafayette	W	38-37	3-2
Southern Mississippi	L	24-56	3-3
Army	L	17-21	3-4
Louisville	L	32-35	3-5
Houston	W	41-23	4-5
Navy	W	50-38	5-5
Memphis	W	37-14	6-5

UAB

LOCATION **Birmingham, AL**
CONFERENCE **Conference USA**
LAST SEASON **7-4**
CONFERENCE RECORD **3-4 (5th)**
OFFENSIVE STARTERS RETURNING **6**
DEFENSIVE STARTERS RETURNING **10**
NICKNAME **Blazers**
COLORS **Forest Green & Old Gold**
HOME FIELD **Legion Field (83,091)**
HEAD COACH **Watson Brown (Vanderbilt '73)**
RECORD AT SCHOOL **31-35 (6 years)**
CAREER RECORD **63-112-1 (16 years)**
ASSISTANTS
Rick Christophel (Austin Peay '75)
Defensive Coordinator
Larry Crowe (UAB '94)
Special Teams
Pat Donohoe (Wayne State '76)
Defensive Line
Woodrow Lowe (Alabama '76)
Linebackers
Richard Moncrief (Clemson '93)
Receivers
John Neal (Brigham Young '80)
Pass Defensive Coordinator/Secondary
Toby Neinas (Missouri '94)
Running Backs
Pat Sullivan (Auburn '72)
Offensive Coordinator/Quarterbacks
Larry VanDerHeyden (Iowa State '62)
Offensive Line
TEAM WINS (last 5 yrs.) **5-5-4-5-7**
FINAL RANK (last 5 yrs.) **85-80-79-69-64**
2000 FINISH **Beat Army in regular-season finale.**

COACH AND PROGRAM

In a state that's crazy about its football, UAB's program continues to evolve with veteran coach Watson Brown as its leader.

The Blazers have grown up in a hurry. Just 10 years ago, UAB started playing football as a Division III program. It went to Division I-AA status two years later. In 1996, it grew to Division I-A, and Brown was on board to engineer the move.

Now in his seventh season at UAB, Brown is pleased to report his team's successes in two years of Conference USA. The Blazers are one of four teams that have posted a combined winning record in the league for the 1999 and 2000 seasons.

UAB, 7-6 in the league the last two years, joins Southern Mississippi, East Carolina and Louisville as programs with winning C-USA records over the two-year span. For the Blazers, that's good company to hang with.

"It's really, truthfully been quicker than I thought," Brown said of his program's success. "I didn't think we could be as competitive in this league as we've been when we started this, and then we lucked out in the early years.

"We stayed around the .500 mark, around five and six [wins], right in there while we were playing a brutal schedule. We've just been lucky."

The Blazers may have been lucky in the early years, but Brown figures his luck turned some in the last couple of seasons.

As the new member of C-USA, and because of the odd number of teams in the league, the Blazers had to play non-conference opponents that were designated to count toward its C-USA schedule.

Despite finishing in a four-way tie for second with a 4-2 record, UAB's 1999 team was left out of the bowl picture because of its 5-6 record. A loss to Wake Forest proved costly.

Last season, it was the same story with different characters.

"We finished second two years ago and had to drop a team to pick up Wake Forest for the league, and Wake Forest had a great team that year and [UAB] ended up 5-6," Brown said. "That game really hurt us. And then last year we had Kansas designated as a conference game on the road and lost on a 51-yard field goal in the last minute and that cost us one of [C-USA's] four bowl spots.

"So we've kind of been a little bit snake bit, but I think we've been really pleased with where we've been in the league the first two years and we've got most of our kids back. We should have a good football team."

After the 23-20 loss at Kansas in the second game of the season, UAB went on the road the next week and beat LSU, 13-10. "If we had beaten Kansas and lost to LSU, we would have been in a bowl," Brown said. "I'm not sure I'd want to make that switch, but if that had happened, we would have gotten one of the four bowl spots. We've just really been near snake bit the last two years in getting one of these bowl invitations."

If the LSU game had counted toward its C-USA record instead of the Kansas game, UAB would have tied Southern Miss for fourth in the league. Both would have had 7-4 overall records, and the GMAC Mobile Alabama Bowl could have chosen the Blazers over the Golden Eagles. Instead, Southern Miss finished 4-3, UAB was 3-4, and the Golden Eagles went to the Mobile Alabama Bowl where they beat 13th-ranked TCU, 28-21.

Brown wasn't happy about having to play at Kansas as the designated C-USA game, but he can also look back at two November losses as bowl breakers. The Blazers lost at Cincinnati, 33-21, on Nov. 4 before losing at home to Southern Miss, 33-30, in overtime in Birmingham on Nov. 11.

Still, you have to admire the Blazers' ability to be in contention for a bowl spot the last two years, even if they didn't make it. It hasn't been that long since UAB wasn't even playing football.

Brown has never backed away from a challenge, and you can check his resume as proof. He was the head coach at Vanderbilt for five years, Rice for two years and Cincinnati for one year. If you win five or six a year at those places, you're a genius.

"This [job has] been so different," Brown said. "We started this one from scratch, no scholarships. We got to 85 scholarships when we went into this league two years ago. It's been something different than I've ever done. Just go sign 25 a year and see what you can do. We had to build all the facilities. We didn't have anything when we got here, no coaches offices, dressing rooms, nothing."

Brown, who was Oklahoma's offensive coordinator before taking the UAB job, knew there would be some growing pains when he came to Birmingham. It's a program that is still evolving and Brown is glad to be part of it.

"This has been a totally different deal than anything I've ever done," he said. "But I think it's a really good job and there are some things we still need to do. I think we have an opportunity, because of the recruiting base we have, to stay in the upper echelon of the conference."

Brown signed a two-year contract extension through the 2005 season in January. His base salary was boosted from $140,000 to $200,000.

2001 SCHEDULE

Aug.	30	Montana State
Sept.	8	@Florida State
	15	@Pittsburgh
	22	Army
	29	@Southern Mississippi
Oct.	6	@Central Florida
	13	Cincinnati
	20	Tulane
	27	@Memphis
Nov.	10	TCU
	17	@Houston

QUARTERBACKS

Brown plans to open up the offense and he has just the quarterback for such a move. Senior **Jeff Aaron** (6-3, 205) started the last six games and went 4-2 after taking the job. In eight games, Aaron threw for 1,135 yards and five touchdowns, and he should be even more comfortable as the Blazers look to throw first and run second.

"Jeff is that style," Brown said. "He's more of a wide open kind of guy, working from the gun, free him up a little, run a faster pace. I think it fits Jeff to a tee. I think that's how he's a better player. He's a very talented young man."

Brown finally has the personnel at UAB needed to run more of a wide-open passing attack. It not only fits Aaron's style, but also Brown's.

"We have seven starters back [on offense], but I think for the first time I can do what I want to do," Brown said. "I want to throw the ball more than I run it and I want to be probably, if you had it 70 plays, throw it 40 and run it 30. I still want to be a good mix, but I want to be pass first. We've gone to a lot of [shotgun]. I've always been a no-huddle guy when we were capable of doing it.

"We've worked real hard on our no-huddle package this spring, so you're going to see us be a lot more wide open."

Last season, Aaron completed 100-of-182 passes (54.9 percent) with three interceptions. Daniel Dixon, the starter in the first five games, threw for 507 yards with two touchdowns and five interceptions. Dixon was a senior last season.

Junior **Thomas Cox** (6-2, 190) will be Aaron's backup. Cox, who was impressive in the spring, has game experience. Sophomore **Matt Johnson** (6-8, 214), who missed the last half of spring practice with a shoulder injury, completed 7-of-11 passes in the first spring scrimmage. He will be the third-string quarterback. His shoulder injury did not require surgery.

"Thomas Cox has been our backup here for a couple of years," Brown said. "He won the East Carolina game two years ago when our starter was out, so he's got some experience. We think we have two quarterbacks who we think can get this style of stuff done for us."

In the third and final spring scrimmage, Aaron completed 12-of-19 passes for 183 yards and two touchdowns. In three spring scrimmages, Aaron didn't throw an interception.

Cox completed 13-of-21 passes for 141 yards and one touchdown in the scrimmage.

RUNNING BACKS

Senior **Jegil Dugger** (5-11, 212) was held out of contact during spring practices, but he should be the No. 1 guy in the backfield come Aug. 30 when the Blazers open the season against Montana State.

Dugger, the Blazers' leading rusher last season, had off-season shoulder surgery. He rushed for 852 yards, averaging 4.8 yards per carry, and scored five touchdowns. Dugger wasn't used much as a receiver, catching just eight passes for 34 yards.

Dugger, who earned second team all-conference honors last season, has the speed to get around the corners and the strength to run inside.

It's no secret that Dugger will be the starter, but the job as his backup is up for grabs. Gone are the four backs who trailed Dugger in rushing yardage last season: Percy Coleman, Carl Fair, Cedric Thatch and Cory Conley. Those players combined for 815 yards last season.

"We've got to find one more man there and we'd rather it not be one of these freshmen coming in," Brown told the *Birmingham News* early in spring workouts.

"The freshmen are highly touted and well thought of but they don't know their right from their left as far as this offense."

You can bet at least a couple of them will know by the start of the season.

Two players most likely to emerge as backups for Dugger are juniors **Bernard Anderson** (6-1, 225) and **Dedric Hardrick** (6-2, 230). Both are bigger, power-type backs.

Anderson played mostly in the short-yardage package, rushing for 22 yards on four carries and scoring two touchdowns. In winter workouts, Anderson bench-pressed more than 400 pounds, a feat that caught Brown's eye.

Hardrick, a converted linebacker, played mostly special teams last season, but his surprising speed certainly makes him a contender for quality playing time.

With the added emphasis on the passing game, the Blazers may not have to go much deeper than Dugger, Anderson and Hardrick. Look for Dugger to have his best season.

"We've got three really bona-fide offensive football players: Jeff Aaron, Jegil Dugger and **Willie Quinnie** at wide receiver," Brown said. "We're going to build things around them. I think we've got really good people to go with them at these other positions, but you're going to see us build a package around those three guys."

WIDE RECEIVERS/TIGHT ENDS

Quinnie (6-2, 180), a junior, is the big-play man in the offense and on special teams. The Blazers are pinning much of their offensive hopes on a healthy Quinnie, who missed six games because of a knee injury. He was hurt in the season opener against Chattanooga, and although playing in just five games, Quinnie managed18 catches for 308 yards and a touchdown.

His knee injury was not serious, only very bothersome. It was a bruise to a tendon that often caused swelling and discomfort. He will be full speed by the opener.

Starting at flanker, Quinnie has the speed and moves that make him a breakaway threat whenever he touches the football. Now, Brown wants to keep him healthy the entire season.

"Willie's fine," Brown said. "He played the last two games. He missed [most of] eight games, but he finished the year playing the last two, against Southern Miss and Army."

In the third spring scrimmage, Quinnie burned cornerback Mario Stanley on a sideline route and caught a 55-yard touchdown from Aaron.

Senior **Leron Little** (6-6, 212) caught a 45-yard touchdown pass from Aaron later in the scrimmage. Little, who has been criticized for dropping passes in the past, was fifth on the team in catches last season with 11 for 199 yards and two touchdowns.

"Our receivers are playing great right now," Aaron told the *Birmingham News* after the second spring scrimmage. "Compared to last year, they've come a long way in the spring. They've come a long way as far as getting the right depth on their routes and their timing and being patient. They're taking their time going through everything instead of rushing their routes."

Sophomore **Charles Griffin** (6-2, 170) and senior **Royd Williams** (6-2, 205) will back up Quinnie at flanker. Both saw action last year. Williams caught seven passes for 78 yards and a touchdown. Griffin caught only one pass, a 35-yarder.

The probable starter at split end will be Little, who has been a part-time starter each of the last two seasons. Little caught a touchdown pass against LSU—the Blazers' only touchdown of the game—and another against Army. With a particularly good spring, Little seemed to have shaken his habit of dropping passes.

Two veterans will probably be Little's backups. They are fifth-year senior **Travis Johnson** (6-3, 195) and junior **T.J. Simmons** (6-3, 205). Johnson was fourth on the team in catches with 14 for 247 yards last season, while Simmons caught five for 98 yards and one touchdown.

Simmons, whose touchdown catch was against East Carolina, sat out spring practice because of a knee injury, but Brown expects him to be full speed when practice resumes in the fall.

Junior **Kenny Borders** (6-3, 190) is the probable starter at the wide receiver position. Borders got off to a slow start in 2000 because of an injury during preseason workouts and managed only five catches for 66 yards and a touchdown.

"Kenny Borders is what we call our wingback or our inside receiver," Brown said after spring practice. "He's the starter there now and he made some big catches for us last year."

His backups will be sophomore **Andrae Ollie** (5-11, 200) and senior **Maurice Gallery** (5-11, 180). Ollie is a converted running back. Gallery missed parts of the 2000 season and was limited in the spring because of a knee injury.

After last season, Brown hopes the injury bug doesn't hit his receiving corps again in 2001.

"We had so many hurt," Brown said. "We had nine wide receivers miss games. We've got a lot of experience there. We're a three-wide team now, so we're playing a lot of wide receivers. I think we've got good depth there."

At tight end, three young players must try to fill the large void left by the departures of seniors Undrae Crosby and Johnni Arrington, who dominated the position for more than two seasons. Crosby was used much more than just a blocker; he was the third on the team in catches last season with 17 for 176 yards.

Sophomore **Jeff Tippetts** (6-3, 220) and redshirt freshmen **Shane Pearson** (6-7, 260) and **Cory Nix** (6-4, 255) will vie for the starting job. Look for all three to get some playing time. Tippetts is a converted quarterback.

Although none have much experience, all three tight ends are very good athletes with good speed and size. Blocking will be their primary responsibility, but in the new system, the tight end could be even more of a factor than before. The guy who displays an ability to make catches in possession situations will probably win the starting job.

OFFENSIVE LINE

When spring practices started, developing the offensive line was at the top of the Blazers' to-do list. That will probably still be the case when preseason practices start in the fall.

"That's the key to our team," Brown said. "We're going to have three new starters there."

All-conference tackle Tony Dollison will be one of the key departures, along with tackles Kevin Grace and Philip Gambrell and guards Tim Medders and Kevin Ford.

Gambrell took over as the starter for Grace when Grace was injured at mid-season. Medders and Ford were both starters at times during the 2000 season.

Another player in the front-line rotation, **Artavious Williams**, suffered a severe injury to his hamstring on the last play against LSU and did not return. Williams (6-5, 340), a sophomore, did some work in the spring but was held out of contact.

Senior **Preston Fray** (6-5, 325) will start at left guard, but he didn't take part in spring practices after having shoulder surgery in the off-season. Fray will be backed up by sophomore **Allen Branch** (6-4, 320).

Only one starter on the line, junior center **Kirk Tuck** (6-1, 300), took part in spring practices.

That might not be all bad. With those veterans out, Brown was able to take a good, long look at several younger linemen.

Sophomore **Wilbert Hamilton** (6-4, 295), a third-string defensive tackle last season, should be the starter at left tackle. After making the move to offense, Hamilton solidified his spot on the starting front line with an impressive spring. He will be backed up by senior **Brad Spencer** (6-5, 295).

Redshirt freshman **Andy Galloway** (6-5, 310) will start at right tackle. Galloway was so impressive as a true freshman last season that he almost did not redshirt. Williams, who will be Galloway's backup, should be fully recovered from the hamstring injury in time for the season.

Junior **Larry Coachman** (6-1, 340), who saw limited playing time in 2000, also had a very solid spring and will start at right guard. Sophomore **Eddie LaFavour** (6-4, 290) and redshirt freshman **Barker White** (6-4, 290) will battle for the job as Coachman's backup.

"I think we're more talented than we were a year ago, but that will be the key to our team, how quickly our offensive line gets some experience and plays up to their potential," Brown said.

2000 STATISTICS

Rushing offense	163.7	36
Passing offense	153.2	103
Total offense	316.9	94
Scoring offense	21.6	82
Net Punting	34.6	57
Punt returns	9.0	68
Kickoff returns	17.9	94
Rushing defense	83.5	6
Passing efficiency defense	107.3	28

Total defense	290.9	11
Scoring defense	17.5	9
Turnover margin	+1	56

Last column is ranking among Division I-A teams.

KICKERS

Nobody will be able to wrestle the place-kicking job from senior **Rhett Gallego** (6-0, 185), coming off his best season. As a freshman, Gallego handled short- and medium-range kicks, making 7-of-7 with a long of 38 yards, but lost the job as a sophomore to Jake Arians.

Last season, Gallego had a great year, making 19-of-24 field-goal attempts with a long of 47 yards. He kicked game-winning field goals against LSU and East Carolina and earned second-team all-conference honors. His 32-yarder beat LSU and his 43-yarder beat East Carolina. He was 5-of-6 from 20 to 29 yards; 6-of-7 from 30 to 39 yards; and 8-of-11 from 40 to 49 yards.

Redshirt freshman **Nick Hayes** (6-1, 180) will be Gallego's backup and will handle the kickoffs. Hayes, who has a stronger leg than Gallego, may also kick some of the longer field-goal attempts.

DEFENSIVE LINE

Brown calls his defensive front "The Steel Shield" and it's a tough wall for opponents to bend, much less break. Three of the four starters on the defensive front return, and a couple of them, senior defensive end **Bryan Thomas** (6-4, 255), and senior tackle **Eddie Freeman** (6-6, 300) have been projected as potential first-round NFL draft picks next year.

Thomas, chosen to the all-conference second team, led the Blazers in sacks last season with 10 and was seventh in tackles with 45. He had 16 tackles for loss.

Freeman had 34 tackles, 10 for loss, and 5 1/2 sacks. He was held out of contact during spring practices after undergoing surgery to place a pin in his second toe of his right foot, a procedure done to straighten out a curvature. He is expected to be full speed in the fall.

Senior nose guard **Rodney Jones** (6-2, 290) started the second half of the 2000 season when the lineup was shuffled because of an injury to senior defensive end **Marlon Bush** (6-3, 280) in the LSU game.

Bush, who was playing as well as any defensive lineman before the injury, has moved from tackle to end. He was full speed for spring practices.

"We've really had five starters because [Bush] got hurt in the LSU game and another one had to start, so really we didn't even lose a starter there," Brown said. "We were playing five guys all the time there and really playing about nine guys on our defensive line.

"That is our strength, no doubt about it. We play about eight or nine guys, and only one of those guys [end Otis Leverette] is gone."

Backups include senior tackle **James Malone** (6-3, 285), junior defensive end **Hassan McKeithan** (6-2, 265), senior defensive end **Ryan Meeks** (6-3, 235), and redshirt freshman nose guard **Shamar Abrams** (6-2, 330).

LINEBACKERS

Senior **Adrian Abrams** (6-1, 235) leads a linebacking corps that is experienced and deep at the two positions. Abrams missed spring practice because of a disciplinary suspension, but is expected to be back for preseason practice.

Last season, Abrams was second on the team in tackles with 79 and had 15 tackles for loss and two sacks.

Senior **Nick Stewart** (5-11, 217) will share playing time with Abrams.

At the 'Mike' linebacker, senior **Rod Taylor** (6-2, 245) should be the starter and will be backed up by senior **John Humphries** (6-2, 250). They were teammates two years ago at East Mississippi Junior College, where they earned first-team all-conference honors.

"Rod Taylor and Nick Stewart have probably been our two steadiest players [at linebacker]," Brown said. "We play four guys there though. We also play John Humphries and Adrian Abrams, so we really play four guys and don't play any of them over 40 plays apiece. Again, depth is very good, but I think Rod Taylor and Nick Stewart have been our two best, solid players."

The Blazers will substitute often at the linebacking spots, and that should give redshirt freshmen **Nigel Eldridge** (6-2, 217) and **Gaylon Black** (6-1, 205) a chance to get into action. Both are promising young players.

DEFENSIVE BACKS

UAB uses five defensive backs, and all five starters return.

Senior free safety **Adrian Singleton** (6-2, 210) is a three-year starter and probably the best of the bunch. Last season, Singleton led the team in tackles with 85, including 55 unassisted tackles. He tied for the team lead with three interceptions.

Junior **Sentell Winston** (6-2, 197) will be Singleton's backup, and he helped his cause for more playing time with an outstanding spring. Brown said Winston was one of the team's most improved players in the spring.

"Singleton is probably our best player [in the secondary]," Brown said. "We play five defensive backs all the time. ... All five of those guys are back and I think four of our five backups are back."

Starting at strong safety will be senior **Torrey Hale** (5-9, 185), who began the 2000 season as a cornerback. He made the move to safety at mid-season and flourished at his new spot.

Backing up Hale will be senior **Andrew Kopecky** (5-11, 180), co-captain of the Blazers' special teams. Kopecky has earned a reputation as a fearless, aggressive player on special teams.

Senior **Avery Warner** (6-2, 205) will be the starter at weak safety. Warner has also been a big-time player on the Blazers' special teams the last three seasons. He made a crucial interception against LSU last season and blocked punts in successive games at the end of the year.

Backing up Warner will be senior **Wes Foss** (6-1, 195), who has also made some big plays in the past. Foss intercepted a pass in overtime against Cincinnati in 1999 that secured the victory and returned an interception 72 yards for a touchdown that sealed the win over Army last season.

Starting cornerbacks will be junior **Chris Brown** (6-2, 190) and senior **Pat Burchfield** (5-9, 185). Brown's interception in the last minute of the LSU game set up the winning field goal. His speed and strength make him an outstanding cover corner.

Burchfield came from East Mississippi Community College last season and earned a starting job. He returned a fumble 42 yards for a touchdown against Kansas in the second game.

Brown will be backed up by sophomore **Mario Stanley** (5-10, 185), one of the team's better athletes. Stanley is also a talented kick returner.

Sophomore **Dio Hill** (5-10, 185) will be Burchfield's backup. Hill signed with UAB out of New Smyrna Beach (Fla.) High School and sat out last season to concentrate on academics. Hill is also an outstanding athlete who could return kicks.

PUNTERS

Junior **Ross Stewart** (6-0, 180), a former quarterback at Susan Moore High School in Blountsville, Ala., returns as the starting punter after averaging 40.1 yards on 58 punts last season. He had 21 of his punts downed inside the opponent's 20-yard line.

His long punt went for 66 yards.

Redshirt freshman **B.J. King** (6-5, 195) will be the backup punter. Like Stewart, King is a former quarterback at Guntersville (Ala.) High School and could be listed low on the depth chart as a quarterback.

SPECIAL TEAMS

All of the Blazers' returners are back this year, and they should get a big boost with the return of a healthy Quinnie.

Last season, Hale led the Blazers in punt returns, averaging 9.7 yards on 13 returns. Coleman returned three punts for 20 yards, while Thomas and Warner each returned one punt.

Thatch was the top kick returner last year. He averaged 24.1 yards on nine returns. Stanley averaged 17.4 yards on eight returns.

Look for Quinnie to return punts and kickoffs as Brown tries to get him the football as many ways as possible.

"Our kicking game should be better," Brown said. "It's an experienced bunch back there."

Stewart will be the holder for field goals and PAT kicks. The Blazers must replace long snapper Chad Ferraez, who finished his career last fall. Not only was Ferraez a steady snapper, but also an aggressive player who often made tackles after punts.

Redshirt freshman **John Newton** (5-10, 210) was listed as the starting long snapper at the end of spring practice, and sophomore **Mark Pettus** (6-2, 225) was the backup. Pettus was Ferraez' backup the last two seasons.

RECRUITING CLASS

The 2001 recruiting class may be the best in the short history of the UAB program. At least that's what the Blazers' coaches are saying.

"This is a really solid class," recruiting coordinator John Neal told the Birmingham News. "A lot of the players that signed with us we feel are equivalent to the same player Alabama and Auburn signed that got a lot more publicity. The players in this class have a chance to be three- or four-year starters for us. A number are the best we've ever signed at their positions."

Brown and his staff have focused on recruits who fit their new pass-oriented philosophy. That means the UAB coaches went after fast, big-play receivers, athletic linemen and power running backs.

The Blazers signed 33 players, including 25 from Alabama.

UAB's class consisted of four offensive linemen, a quarterback, five running backs, four tight ends, two receivers, nine defensive linemen, four linebackers and four cornerbacks. Several recruits are listed as both offensive and defensive players.

"We're very pleased with this group," Brown said. "I think our classes have improved every year. We really recruited needs this year. We've done that the last two years. We were able to do even better this year than last, I think. This is a future class, with mostly freshmen."

In past years, the Blazers have signed as many as seven junior college players, but this year had just one, junior defensive end **Marvin Nickson** (6-5, 265) of East Mississippi Community College.

Cedric Hampton (6-2, 247), a tight end from Courtland, Ala., was headed to South Carolina before deciding on UAB. South Carolina may have backed off on Hampton because his eligibility was in question.

Darrell Hackney of Douglass (Ga.) High could be the quarterback of the future for the Blazers. Hackney (6-2, 230) threw for more than 4,000 yards and 50 touchdowns in three seasons. One of his teammates, wide receiver **Tavarus Thomas** (5-10, 180), also signed with the Blazers. Thomas caught 15 touchdown passes last season.

Twin brothers **Kendal** (5-11, 233) and **Randal Gibson** (6-0, 265) of Aliceville, Ala. were also among the signees. Kendal Gibson was the Class 3A back of the year.

With the defensive line gone after the 2001 season, this year's recruiting class should fill some of those holes, but several of the defensive line recruits could make the move to offense.

"We took a lot of defensive linemen who will be offensive linemen," Brown told the News. "The game has changed. It's not as power oriented. Everyone has to be quick for the position they play and we want to make sure our linemen have quick feet."

Brown will continue to search talent-rich Alabama for players. Of the 33 players signed, 25 are from Alabama. "That was our original plan, to live and die in the state of Alabama," Brown told the *News*.

BLUE RIBBON ANALYSIS

OFFENSE	C+
SPECIAL TEAMS	B
DEFENSE	A-
INTANGIBLES	B+

If the Blazers can survive the first half of the season, they might be OK. That's a big if, though.

After the season opener at home against Montana State, the Blazers face a rugged schedule of road games four of the next five weeks against Florida State, Pittsburgh, Southern Miss and Central Florida.

"I think this team is 10 points better than last year's right now," Brown said in the spring. "Our problem is that our non-conference schedule and our early schedule is so tough. Four of our first six are on the road. ... We could be a better team and not know it because basically we've replaced Florida State for LSU and [Louisiana-Lafayette] and Middle Tennessee have been replaced by Central Florida and Pitt, so there's no doubt our non-conference schedule is much tougher and our early schedule is much tougher."

UAB should have one of C-USA's better defenses this season, thanks to the return of 10 starters and 23 lettermen. It was a strong unit last year, ranking 11th in the nation in total defense. Opponents averaged 290.1 yards per game on the Blazers.

The Blazers lost defensive coordinator Bill Clay to Oklahoma State in January. Clay was the architect of the defense for four seasons. With most of the same personnel returning, Brown promoted veteran assistant Rick Christophel to the coordinator's spot and gave secondary coach John Neal the job as pass defense coordinator.

"With 19 kids back, I just didn't feel like we could change defenses," Brown said. "I thought that would be crazy. If you go try to get a really good outside guy, they want to do their systems, so I took Rick Christophel, who had been a defensive coordinator for me at Vanderbilt (in the late 1980s), and moved him to the defensive side of the ball to coordinate it and named John Neal our passing game coordinator. Then we brought Woodrow Lowe from the Oakland Raiders as our linebacker coach.

"I feel good about it, but I felt it was important that we kept the same system with so many players returning. If this happened a year from now, when I have a lot of new players, I wouldn't have the same problem."

There is plenty of experience on offense, too, with six starters and 19 lettermen coming back. However, the development of several newcomers on the offensive line will be crucial, as will the offense's ability to adjust to the new pass-first, run-second philosophy.

The Blazers will be counting heavily on Aaron, Dugger, and Quinnie, so keeping them healthy will be a key.

"Last year, we played to our defense," Brown said. "We were conservative, we played field position, we ate the clock, and this year I think we're deep enough to really—in our league—try to make the games longer and try to make other teams play a lot of plays and try to use our depth as a plus."

If the Blazers' new offense comes around, and the defense plays like it did last season, they could give Brown the bowl bid he's been seeking. But the Blazers must survive the rigorous early schedule without losing their confidence or any key players to injury.

"I'm very excited about our team, but also realistic, and I know for us to even reach the [7-4] record we had last year, we're going to have to beat some better teams," Brown said.

(D.L.)

2000 RESULTS

Chattanooga	W	20-15	1-0
Kansas	L	20-23	1-1
LSU	W	13-10	2-1
Louisiana-Lafayette	W	47-2	3-1
Louisville	L	17-38	3-2
Memphis	W	13-9	4-2
Middle Tennessee	W	14-9	5-2
East Carolina	W	16-13	6-2
Cincinnati	L	21-33	6-3
Southern Mississippi	L	30-33	6-4
Army	W	27-7	7-4

Akron

LOCATION	**Akron, OH**
CONFERENCE	**Mid-American (East)**
LAST SEASON	**6-4 (.545)**
CONFERENCE RECORD	**5-1 (t-1st)**
OFFENSIVE STARTERS RETURNING	**7**
DEFENSIVE STARTERS RETURNING	**6**
NICKNAME	**Zips**
COLORS	**Navy & Gold**
HOME FIELD	**Rubber Bowl (35,202)**
HEAD COACH	**Lee Owens (Bluffton '77)**
RECORD AT SCHOOL	**25-41 (6 years)**
CAREER RECORD	**25-41 (6 years)**
ASSISTANTS	**Luke Fickell (Ohio State '97)**
	Defensive Line
	Doug Geiser (Cornell '92)
	Tight Ends
	Greg Gillum (Ohio State '83)
	Wide Receivers/Recruiting Coordinator
	Bob Morris (Colorado '77)
	Defensive Coordinator/Defensive Backs
	Tom Stacy (Bowling Green '81)
	Quarterbacks
	Mike Williams (Iowa State '77)
	Linebackers/Special Teams
	Paul Winters (Akron '80)
	Offensive Coordinator/Running Backs
TEAM WINS (last 5 yrs.)	**4-2-4-7-6**
FINAL RANK (last 5 yrs.)	**103-111-107-93-96**
2000 FINISH	**Beat Kent State in regular-season finale.**

COACH AND PROGRAM

Akron was a football graveyard just a few years ago. The Zips program was so decrepit that even the nicest guy in the whole state of Ohio, former Notre Dame head coach Gerry Faust, couldn't turn it around.

Things hit bottom at the end of the 1994 season when Akron faced Ohio in a season-ending game in front of an intimate crowd of a couple thousand. After that battle of then-winless teams, both schools fired their coaches. Ohio chose Jim Grobe and Akron chose Lee Owens.

Until last year, folks making that obvious comparison about the two squads had no choice but to pick the Bobcats as ahead in the race back to respectability.

But a funny thing happened last year. The Zips beat Ohio for the second year in a row after four straight losses to the Green and White. Akron put together a second consecutive winning season. The gang at the Rubber Bowl beat their peers in the East, Miami and Ohio. And, if not for this year's All-MAC quarterback Byron Leftwich marching the Herd down the field in the final two minutes to win on the road, Akron would have won the East outright for the right to play Western Michigan in the MAC title game.

All those things were good. All those things meant progress. All those things happened in spite of having one of the MAC's worst defenses again in 2000. And that was including the presence of the best defensive back in the conference.

Departed cornerback Dwight Smith—headed to the NFL after getting picked in the third round of the draft by Tampa Bay—swept all the league's defensive and senior awards, and rightfully so, as he spearheaded a Zips defensive backfield that gave up only nine touchdowns. Smith was one of the best corners in the country—he turned in 10 interceptions and three fumble recoveries and even caught three passes for almost 100 yards. His 13 takeaways put Akron in the plus column for turnover ratio, and kept things from being any worse.

The Zips gave up more than 400 yards per game and more first downs than anyone but hapless Central Michigan. Akron also led the league in penalty yardage against.

Speaking of CMU, the Zips lost to the Chippewas in week two. Central may have been the league's worst team. The Zips also displeased the home folks with consecutive losses to dominant Northern Illinois and soon-to-be Division I-A school Connecticut. NIU destroyed the Zips, 52-35, at the Rubber Bowl; All-MAC tailback Thomas Hammock hit them for 174 yards and five touchdowns. The Zips couldn't stop a UConn team that Eastern Michigan did in week one, and lost again, 38-35.

So we do this dance again. Which Akron team is it? In '99, it won a lot of games, didn't have to play Marshall and beat few teams of any substance. In 2000, the Zips won the games that counted and couldn't stop anyone in the games that didn't. The defensive problems are still here, the best defender gone. And will one of the league's best rushing attacks be enough to protect a brand-new quarterback over the first few weeks?

We'll just have to play the games and find out. They can hang a banner at the Rubber Bowl displaying "2000 MAC East Regular Season Champs (tied)." Can they really hang with the big boys?

2001 SCHEDULE

Sept.	8	@Ohio State
	15	Eastern Michigan
	22	@Purdue
	29	Ohio
Oct.	6	@Western Michigan
	13	@Miami (Ohio)
	20	Bowling Green
	27	@Marshall
Nov.	3	@Central Florida
	10	@Buffalo
	17	Kent State

QUARTERBACKS

This is one of the three positions where Owens has real questions on this offense. A very productive unit was led last fall by departed quarterback Butchie Washington, a starter for virtually all of his four years in uniform. Washington threw for 2,319 yards and 17 touchdowns in his final season, most effectively to fellow departed senior wideout Lavel Bailey (44 catches, 876 yards, eight touchdowns). Those two gaps and a hole at left guard are the places the staff must begin to patch.

Sophomore **Nick Sparks** (6-3, 206) may be just the guy to take over what Washington started. And with Sparks' more impressive physical tools, coaches think he can take them further than the player he succeeds.

Sparks is fiery on the sideline and fast on the grass. Owens calls him "one of our two or three fastest guys on the field." The Flint, Mich., native transferred from West Virginia before last season, and while he would be a great fit for the new spread offense in Morgantown, folks in Akron are glad he is here.

Sparks will probably be asked to do a lot of what Tavares Bolden did for Toledo last year—hand off the ball to an excellent back and make smart throws off of bootlegs and rollouts. Sparks is much more mobile and eager to head upfield than Washington, and is a competitor on every down. In the Zips' second spring scrimmage, Sparks threw a pass that was tipped for an interception inside the defense's 20-yard line. After being blocked, Sparks recovered to chase down the offending safety 65 yards behind the play near his own 25-yard line. Faster than the rest of the team? Absolutely.

Look for the Zips to run a little outside option stuff with his ability to turn the corner.

Senior **Ryan Uhlenhake** (5-11, 205) has been the backup for parts of the last three seasons, and had a fine effort in the spring game. But despite his efforts there, it's hard to see the Zips winning many games with anyone but Sparks at the wheel.

Sophomore **Micah Faler** (6-2, 176) completed a couple passes last year in very limited action, mainly as the holder on kicks and in gimmick plays. Akron occasionally would line him up in a slot to set up gadget play throws to the departed Washington or Smith. Neither lefty sophomore **Jonathan Gill** (6-2, 221) nor freshman **Charlie Frye** (6-4, 200) should get into the mix this year barring injury. Gill has a very strong arm throwing the out.

RUNNING BACKS

If quarterback is the land of new faces, running back is like an old comfortable pair of slippers that just keeps getting better.

Junior **Brandon Payne** (5-10, 197) has a great first burst and field vision, and is a smart runner who can take what he is given. Payne will rarely get hit for a loss, and that thinking again made him one of the MAC's top rushers in 2000. Payne rushed for 1,062 yards last fall and scored 13 touchdowns for the second consecutive year. He was also the team's third-leading receiver with 22 catches and three touchdowns.

Payne led everyone with 105 more rushing yards in a low-scoring Zips spring game. He was the MAC's third-leading rusher last fall.

Sophomore **Bob Hendry** (5-10, 193) emerged in the spring as a stronger backup to Payne. Hendry looks more like a fullback and seems ready to run through walls as he tries to make contact with defenders. It is a lot like watching Ohio's Chad Brinker work, when Hendry runs wide on a sweep and looks for someone to put his helmet on. He was twice an All-Ohio player at Hoover High School in North Canton.

Third right now is junior **Junior McCray** (5-5, 160), who is an ideal small target as a punt or kick returner, but will have a hard time cracking the lineup ahead of Payne. McCray is very fast, but must have space to work his skills with the ball.

There are potentially five more backs in the new recruiting class. The best is reportedly

MID-AMERICAN

BLUE RIBBON FORECAST

East Division
1. Marshall
2. Ohio
3. Akron
4. Miami (Ohio)
5. Bowling Green
6. Kent State
7. Buffalo

West Division
1. Toledo
2. Western Michigan
3. Northern Illinois
4. Ball State
5. Central Michigan
6. Eastern Michigan

ALL-CONFERENCE TEAM

OFFENSE

POS. PLAYER SCHOOL HT. WT. CL.

WR Darius Watts, Marshall, 6-2, 177, So.
WR David Bautista, Bowling Green, 6-0, 186, Sr.
OL Steve Sciullo, Marshall, 6-5, 315, Jr.
OL Dennis Thompson, Ohio, 6-4, 284, So.
OL Konrad Dean, Akron, 6-4, 297, Sr.
OL Matt Brayton, Central Michigan, 6-7, 320, Sr.
OL Nick Glowacki, Ohio, 6-6, 310, Sr.
QB Byron Leftwich, Marshall, 6-5, 225, Jr.
RB Thomas Hammock, Northern Ill., 5-10, 218, Jr.
RB Chester Taylor, Toledo, 5-11, 205, Sr.
TE Mobolaji Afairiogun, Western Mich., 6-4, 228, Jr.

DEFENSE

POS. PLAYER SCHOOL HT. WT. CL.

DL Ryan Terry, Miami, 6-2, 315, Jr.
DL Anthony Allsbury, Western Mich. 6-2, 254, Jr.
DL Brandon Hicks, Bowling Green, 6-2, 250, Sr.
LB Terrell Jones, Miami, 5-10, 220, So.
LB Max Yates, Marshall, 6-2, 225, Sr.
LB Ken Philpot, Eastern Michigan, 6-2, 238, Sr.
LB Larry Williams, Northern Ill., 6-0, 236, Jr.
DB Demerist Whitfield, Northern Ill., 5-11, 182, Jr.
DB Ronald Rogers, Western Mich., 5-8, 174, Sr.
DB Bop White, Ohio, 6-0, 190, Jr.
DB Tedaro France, Central Michigan, 6-0, 183, Sr.

SPECIALISTS

POS. PLAYER SCHOOL HT. WT. CL.

PK Todd France, Toledo, 6-3, 185, Sr.
P Dave Zastudil, Ohio, 6-4, 225, Sr.
RS Josh Bush, Western Michigan, 5-9, 150, Sr.

OFFENSIVE PLAYER OF THE YEAR

Chester Taylor, RB, Toledo

DEFENSIVE PLAYER OF THE YEAR

Max Yates, LB, Marshall

NEWCOMER OF THE YEAR

Stafford Owens, RB, Ohio

MAC NOTEBOOK

There has been some confusion about the league's version of a postseason in 2001. Allow us to clarify: The champions of each division are determined by a team's record in games against division opponents only. For teams in the East, that means the league season is six games long. For teams in the West, it's five. Teams also play two teams from the opposite division, though these games can only count for or against a school should it be tied for the division lead and can act as one of the tiebreakers. These inter-division games occur on a rotation basis, with the exception of the game between Bowling Green and Toledo, which is played every year as a rivalry and was a condition of those two nearby schools (20 miles apart) being placed in different divisions. ... The winners of each division will meet in the nationally televised MAC Championship, this year to be played at the home field of the MAC West champion. The MAC Champion has gone on to the Motor City Bowl the last four years, but the new GMAC Bowl in Mobile, Ala. will get first selection from the MAC this year and this year only. The Motor City Bowl granted that to help sell the deal in Mobile in year one. Mobile could possibly lock up one MAC team before the MAC Championship game. The opponent will be a Conference USA team. ... The deal with Mobile is a two-year contract, with a clause that if the SEC has more bowl-eligible teams than bowl slots (more than seven teams), the GMAC Bowl can drop the MAC and pick up the extra SEC team. Then the MAC contract would extend for an extra year. The Motor City Bowl would then have its pick of the other team from the MAC Championship game, and it's assumed it would take a team from the West if Marshall stays true to form and wins the game. ... Don't be surprised if the long-rumored offer to Central Florida to become the MAC's 14th member, in football only, is forthcoming. Expect any potential move by Marshall to Conference USA or any other league to be a longer process, at least until 2003 or later.

Thomas Plummer (6-1, 215) from Etobicoke, Ontario. Plummer is a legitimate national recruit according to many of the scouting services, and some list him as the No. 1 recruit from Canada. He could be an impact player, though beating out a healthy Payne would be tough for any MAC back. Neither have the size to be fullbacks in Akron's offset-I offense, so getting them both to the field would be difficult.

Ditto for a pair who sat out last fall because of academics, **Matt Carter** (5-9, 176) and Je**ssie Scott** (5-10, 167) from nearby Copley and Massillon, Ohio.

At fullback, senior **Matt Zuercher** (6-0, 241) is used primarily as blocker and had just 11 carries for 25 yards. Sophomore **Dan Basch** (6-0, 228) had five carries last fall at this non-glamour position.

WIDE RECEIVERS/TIGHT ENDS

Bailey led the squad in catches with 44, but senior **Jake Schifino** (6-1, 205) was a close second with 42 and might be the better home run threat. Schifino scored four touchdowns, averaged more than 18 yards per catch and had a long play of 85 yards en route to his best season. Schifino is a hyper-athletic jump ball specialist who needs to learn to be an every down pass catcher and go-to guy. He missed spring sessions because of academics, but should return in August.

Behind him, it's anyone's guess. This was not a deep position last fall, as no returning non-starter has more than five catches at any position. The depth problem is made more serious by the fact that the cornerback Smith was the team's de facto third receiver, even garnering an occasional start.

Sophomores **Matt Cherry** (6-2, 186) and **Bates Szakos** (6-3, 187) are competing for the start at flanker, opposite Schifino. Cherry led the team with five spring game catches and Szakos caught the game-winner from Uhlenhake. But neither have any meaningful experience or official catches.

Senior **Andrew Wilson** (5-11, 191) is listed as the backup at split end behind Schifino. Can anyone help? Owens has some speed to burn with a pair of new faces; junior Lester Gill (5-11, 197) transferred last year from Laney (Calif.) Junior College, and redshirt freshman **Morris Ellington** (5-11, 179) stretched the field some in spring workouts. There is a desperate need for a possession receiver.

The starting tight end is senior **Tim Ritley** (6-3, 243), who was a good third-read target underneath for Washington and will make Sparks' development a little easier. Ritley was exceptional academically and his play has caught up to his books. Coaches said he really improved his blocking last fall, en route to 16 catches and a touchdown.

Behind him, you will see junior **Nick Fortener** (6-1, 249) and sophomore **Mike Brake** (6-4, 252) when the Zips go to a goal-line or short-yardage package. Each had but one catch in 2000.

OFFENSIVE LINE

Even if the Zips can't pass a lick, this line should let them do almost whatever they want on the ground. They did it last year, and there is no reason it should change. Like Northern Illinois last fall, Akron is one of the few teams in the MAC that will just line up and try to run over you. They have the tanks to do it.

They do miss graduated Jeremiah Danielson at left guard, but the rest of the group is senior and giant, and has a couple of potential All-MAC players.

The tackles are both seniors, with Temple transfer **Konrad Dean** (6-4, 297) at left and **Jeff Grzeskowiak** (6-5, 309) at right. It is a toss-up as to who is better, but both could end the year on all-star teams depending on just how many miles Payne and company put on the odometer.

The guards are senior **Paul Ondrusek** (6-2, 309), who can play any position on the line, and apprentice sophomore **Bryan Shaw** (6-3, 304). And center **Scott Smith** (6-3, 275) is a senior starting for his second full season.

The next generation is coming, and ready to play. The second unit has four redshirt freshmen—**Aaron Conley** (6-3, 300), **Jim Borrieci** (6-3, 289), **Aaron Feller** (6-4, 289) and **Mike Grzeskowiak** (6-6, 315)—and a sophomore to compete with Smith at guard—**Jud Cummings** (6-4, 303). Owens thinks this group can swap out and lose very little over the starters. Stockpiling linemen has become a key to making this program go.

That continued this year with two more freshman signees and **Mike Piccirillo** (6-2, 299), who sat out last year as a non-qualifier. This big group gets bigger, and opponents wonder if they will ever get to the Zips quarterbacks after managing only ten sacks in 2000.

2000 STATISTICS

Rushing offense	206.6	19
Passing offense	210.5	61
Total offense	417.2	27
Scoring offense	30.3	34
Net Punting	34.8	49
Punt returns	7.5	91
Kickoff returns	19.2	69
Rushing defense	196.8	97
Passing efficiency defense	109.1	34
Total defense	403.5	83
Scoring defense	26.8	72
Turnover margin	+7	23

Last column is ranking among Division I-A teams.

KICKERS

Senior **Zac Derr** (5-8, 155) was consistent last fall, and made 11-of-16 field goal tries, with four of his five misses from beyond 40-yards. He was the team's second-leading scorer with 71 and should cross the 200-point barrier for his career this fall.

DEFENSIVE LINE

The offense has the potential to be pretty good. The defense has nowhere to go but up, it would seem. Owens selected new defensive coordinator Bob Morris to try to right the ship. The coaches think they have some answers in the 4-4 front, starting with defensive end **Dwayne LeFall** (6-3, 248).

One of Owens' imports from northern California, LeFall was the best lineman the Zips had last year, leading the team with 4 1/2 sacks. But more important, he pursued well to the run on the outside, so much that teams had to change their game plans. Plus, as a former prep high jumper, he makes athletic plays that make Akron fans remember Jason Taylor.

"He is special," Owens said. "He showed by the end of last season what he is capable of doing. Since then, he's added about 20 pounds. He's got a chance to be a dominant pass rusher."

Special or not, LeFall— like Schifino—sat out spring drills for failing to take enough credit hours in the spring. Not a good sign for two of the team's top four or five players.

The other end is junior **Ryan Gargasz** (6-5, 250). Senior tackle **Chris Smith** (6-3, 280) splits the middle with **Ryan Schulz** (6-3, 250). But none of the players in the one-deep or the next group had more than a couple sacks or 26 tackles last year. The Zips need some impact players to show up here soon.

Converted linebacker **Marques Hayes** (6-1, 240) has a chance to be that guy at end.

There are four end or tackle signees in the new class, and while Owens likes the depth here, a difference-maker could see the field with very little trouble.

LINEBACKERS

The linebackers are experienced on one side, but are looking for help at rover and one of the inside spots. Seniors **Ed March** (5-11, 223) and **Eric Culberson** (6-3, 207) will be the rushers from the whip position on the weak side. Those two are experienced, and combined for 41 tackles and three sacks.

Senior **Terrell Colbert** (6-2, 237) and junior **Ryan Myers** (6-1, 226) return at the weak inside linebacker slot after combining for more than 60 tackles a year ago. Myers is a former Division II transfer from Ashland (Ohio) College.

The strong side is just a mess, with the undersized senior **Mike Young** (5-8, 186) trying to fight off huge guards at inside linebacker. He is the team's second-leading tackler with 41. His backup is the untested sophomore **Robert Jackson** (6-1, 207). One guy who might step in here is Prop 48 sophomore **Joe Radich** (6-1, 230), an extraordinary tackler from nearby Massillon.

At rover, senior **Brad Detwiler** (5-9, 192) is the incumbent player and has been a stalwart for three years. But junior college transfer **Marcus Suber** (6-1, 185), a junior, was brought in to play immediately and will get his shot over the summer. Suber, from Sacramento (Calif.) City College, had 50 tackles, 20 pass breakups and an interception last year. He's originally from Montery, Calif. and was recruited by several Division I-A schools.

Top prep recruit **Brendon Banks** (6-0, 190) will also get a shot at time at either of these outside spots. He starred as a prep for WPIAL powerhouse Woodland Hills High School near Pittsburgh. Banks was highly decorated, showing up on the *Pittsburgh Post-Gazette* Fabulous 22, *Pittsburgh Tribune-Review* Terrific 25 and *Pennsylvania Football News*' second-team all-state list.

DEFENSIVE BACKS

How do you replace the league's best defensive back, possibly ever? You don't, and Dwight Smith's presence here masked even more of what ailed the Zips defense last fall.

Junior **Corvin Amos** (5-9, 187) returns as a provisional starter on the other side, but he was abused by NIU and Marshall repeatedly last fall and may be in trouble when sophomores **Maurice Taylor** (5-11, 179) and **Rickey McKenzie** (6-0, 184) get going. Taylor played as a freshman and was one of the best young corners in the league after starring at Harding High School in Warren, Ohio. He played in the Big 33 All-Star game the prior summer and was a legitimate Big 10-level recruit. Taylor played in eight games, mainly on special teams, but has athletic gifts he has not yet even begun to discover. McKenzie also played in seven games last fall as a freshman. Amos is a vocal leader who has the swagger to do his job even after getting burned.

Junior college transfer **Kris Williams** (5-11, 178) will probably earn the nod at free safety, after redshirting last fall, ahead of redshirt freshman **John Fuller** (6-2, 192).

Potentially five players in the new class could see time at safety or corner, though it seems the needs for athletes are greater at the outside linebacker positions. **Greg Williams** (5-10, 195) from Glen Oak High School is the most highly touted of this cadre.

Akron needs to find tacklers and playmakers all over the place on defense.

"If we can get settled at rover and free safety," Owens said. "I think we have a chance to be pretty good on the defensive side of the ball."

Owens and Morris plan to show a little more flexibility in their defensive fronts, dropping out of the 4-4 or the eagle look that they've shown in recent years. Getting pressure from somewhere is a need.

PUNTERS

Sophomore **Andy Jerdon** (5-11, 199) returns for his second year of punting and made 52 kicks for nearly 40 yards an attempt (39.7). In his first year, he had none blocked and dropped 14 inside the opposing 20-yard line. The backup punter is Payne, who, if sent out to punt, would probably face the other team's defense calling an audible back into a base set.

SPECIAL TEAMS

Jerdon and Derr are both consistent if not spectacular. The loss of Smith really steals an element of athleticism from several units, both returning and blocking or covering punts.

Ritley and Smith are the long snappers. Faler is the holder for kicks.

Payne will reprise his role returning punts; he averaged more than eight yards a return a year ago. And the tiny McCray and junior defensive back **Ty Washington** (5-8, 178) will return kicks.

RECRUITING CLASS

Owens continues to bring in classes with skill levels beyond the current MAC average. There isn't the northern California flavor of recent classes, but plenty of northern Ohio, western Pennsylvania and a taste of Canada. Like Ohio and now Ohio State, Akron has made a point of trying to get all the in-state players it can.

It seems Akron has won the battle with Kent and now is getting its pick of the second-tier recruits in northern Ohio. It doesn't sound glamorous, but that's a group of players you can win with in the MAC.

BLUE RIBBON ANALYSIS

OFFENSE	C
SPECIAL TEAMS	C-
DEFENSE	D
INTANGIBLES	C

There was nothing in the spring to make you believe this defense has changed its stripes at all. Maybe after 29 July and August drills, this group will be ready to fight? Who knows? But the track record certainly isn't there.

Akron will be behind the proverbial eight ball from the start of this one. They throw an inexperienced quarterback to the Bobcats in game one, and then head down Interstate 71 to Ohio State and new head coach Jim Tressell. No matter what sort of disrepair the Buckeyes have been in the last few years, better Miami and Ohio teams came out of the Horseshoe with losses and this should be no different. The other home games are all probable wins, but road games at Western Michigan, Miami, and Marshall will be difficult. Not to mention that Akron plays all three non-MAC games away from home this fall (including at Purdue and Central Florida). It's hard to put together a great season with just four home games on the schedule.

Miami went through the same schedule last fall and came out fairly close (tied for third) with no cigar. Look for Akron to do something similar with about six wins, as the Zips again lose a couple games in which they score 30 or more.

(R.C.)

2000 RESULTS

Virginia Tech	L	23-52	0-1
Central Michigan	L	7-17	0-2
Central Florida	W	35-24	1-2
Ohio	W	23-20	2-2
Miami (Ohio)	W	37-20	3-2
Bowling Green	W	27-21	4-2
Northern Illinois	L	35-52	4-3
Connecticut	L	35-38	4-4
Marshall	L	28-31	4-5
Buffalo	W	49-14	5-5
Kent State	W	34-6	6-5

Ball State

LOCATION	**Muncie, IN**
CONFERENCE	**Mid-American (West)**
LAST SEASON	**5-6 (.455)**
CONFERENCE RECORD	**2-3 (t-3rd)**
OFFENSIVE STARTERS RETURNING	**8**
DEFENSIVE STARTERS RETURNING	**9**
NICKNAME	**Cardinals**
COLORS	**Red & White**
HOME FIELD	**Ball State Stadium (21,581)**
HEAD COACH	**Bill Lynch (Butler '77)**
RECORD AT SCHOOL	**26-41 (7 years)**
CAREER RECORD	**26-41 (7 years)**
ASSISTANTS	**Bob Bartolomeo (Butler '77)**
	Defensive Coordinator/Inside Linebackers
	Rich Spisak (Miami '73)
	Offensive Coordinator/Tackles/Tight Ends
	Ted Huber (Miami '74)
	Centers/Guards/Assistant Head Coach
	Keith Otterbein (Hillsdale '79)
	Running Backs/Recruiting Coordinator
	Scott Pethtel (Adrian '76)
	Outside Linebackers/Special Teams
	Brent Baldwin (Ball State '96)
	Quarterbacks
	Shannon Griffith (Ball State '91)
	Wide Receivers
	Larry McDaniel (Indiana '93)
	Defensive Line
	Dennis Springer (Ball State '92)
	Defensive Backs
TEAM WINS (last 5 yrs.)	**8-5-1-0-5**
FINAL RANK (last 5 yrs.)	**86-104-108-113-107**
2000 FINISH	**Beat Connecticut in regular-season finale.**

COACH AND PROGRAM

Which is more unlikely? A head coach keeping his job after a 21-game losing streak? Or that same coach surviving the streak and running off five wins in the last seven games of the 2000 season?

Things had gone nowhere but downhill for Ball State and head coach Bill Lynch after a MAC crown in 1996. That was the final year before the league added Marshall and went to divisional play, and the Cardinals were a competent bunch led by a future NFL punter who was the league's best player—Brad Maynard.

After a mediocre '97, things slapped bottom in '98 as the recruiting gap between Ball and the league's other top teams got too wide. Marshall fans still remember the beating the Cardinals took in Huntington in '98, and how the opposition could do nothing behind a cadre of 250-pound offensive linemen. The Cards lost the last six that fall, every game in '99, and suffered a brutal 0-4 beginning in 2000 to the likes of Kansas State and Florida. There was no sign of immediate progress and the vultures seemed to be circling in Muncie.

The 43-14 home loss in game four to Northern Illinois was the final straw. The next week, Lynch turned the team over to a redshirt freshman quarterback, **Talmadge Hill** (5-11, 198), and lightning struck at rival Miami. The more-mobile Hill replaced junior **Brian Conn** (6-2, 211), and led Ball State to a 15-10 win over the RedHawks.

That week at Yager Stadium, the Cards found their quarterback of the future in Hill, and the porous Miami defense gave confidence to a pair of running backs who would combine for more than 1,500 yards in 2000. Ball State went on to score 29 or more points in four of its next six games, all wins. And except for predictable losses to Toledo and Western Michigan, the Cards were competitive the rest of the way.

Hill showed impressive poise for a first-year player. He directed a come-from-behind victory against Central Michigan, passing for a touchdown with just more than five minutes to play and running for the winning touchdown with 57 seconds to play. Ball had been down 12 points, thanks in part to a mistake made by Hill. It was his ability to put that mistake out of his mind that Lynch singled out in his post-game praise of his new quarterback.

"The key to the game was after Hill threw an interception for a touchdown, he got back in the huddle and kept his composure and led a successful drive," Lynch said.

This year, the Cardinals have a taste of success behind them, the first for anyone on the roster. And virtually everyone returns or upgrades on both sides of the ball. Is it enough to pass any of the prohibitive top three in the West yet?

Lynch isn't sure. But he's glad to have a little momentum on his side—for a change.

"Winning five of our final seven games and posting a 4-3 mark in the Mid-American Conference were two of the most positive signs we can build on," Lynch said.

The schedule is substantially easier, as the two "collect-a-check" games are against less-than-top-10 competition (at Auburn and Kentucky), and the other games against I-AA laggard Southern Illinois and at Connecticut should both be wins.

But the games at Western and Northern are where the rubber meets the road. A win in either gets them marginally into the West race. Matching last season's win total is possible, but improving on it much would be difficult.

2001 SCHEDULE

Sept.	1	@Auburn
	8	@Kentucky
	15	Southern Illinois
	22	@Western Michigan
	29	Miami (Ohio)
Oct.	13	@Eastern Michigan
	20	Toledo
	27	@Connecticut
Nov.	3	Central Michigan
	10	Kent State
	17	@Northern Illinois

QUARTERBACKS

Hill added a new dimension to the Ball State

offense and took virtually every snap the rest of the way after taking over at Miami. In just under seven games, Hill threw for 1,455 yards and 13 touchdowns, on a completion percentage better than 61 percent. He did throw 12 interceptions.

From River Forest High School in suburban Chicago, the first-year player also ran for 256 yards when he was pushed outside the pocket and on designed rollouts. Though he didn't start a full season, Hill was selected as the MAC's freshman of the year and was the first freshman in BSU history to be the team's most valuable player.

"Talmadge had an outstanding season," Lynch said. "He was an integral factor in us winning football games. He is a very gifted student-athlete who has worked extremely hard to put himself in position to help lead our team."

Conn returns after starting much of '99 and the first four games of 2000. He passed for 249 yards and five interceptions against the early non-conference schedule and mop-up minutes against Western Michigan. Conn is a fairly accurate short-range passer.

Two other quarterbacks were on the spring roster, sophomore **Andy Roesch** (6-4, 228) and redshirt freshman **Steve Sutherland** (6-3, 180). Roesch is an excellent pocket passer, though may not fit the spread look on offense as well as Hill.

Kenny Sanders (6-3, 190) was one of the best players in the state in '99 at Broad Ripple High School in Indianapolis and sat out last season as an academic non-qualifier. Had he been eligible, he was considered by some to have savior potential. If he is ready to go this fall, he will be apprenticing to fight Hill for the starting gig in 2002. He threw for almost 8,000 yards in his prep career.

Freshman **Eric Hooks** (6-0, 190) was signed from North Central High School in Indianapolis.

RUNNING BACKS

In their third year of the conversion to a more spread-out passing offense, the Cardinals finally found the running backs who could succeed in the single-back set.

Fifth-year senior **Anthony Jones** (5-10, 192) has seen the bottom and helped lead BSU back to the middle last fall. He ran for 515 yards, though he had trouble keeping his average over three yards a carry. Jones was the hero of the Miami game, with 187 yards on a school-record 46 rushes. And he caught seven passes, including one for a touchdown.

But Lynch was looking for a guy with a better burst once he hit that hole and junior **Marcus Merriweather** (6-1, 215) took back the job in the weeks after Miami, running for 100 yards or more in four of the last five games. The elusive Merriweather went for 1,004 yards and eight touchdowns on the year, with 257 of those yards in a dominant 600-yard offensive performance versus Central Michigan. Merriweather is a difference-maker who should be an All-MAC candidate next season, once Chester Taylor is off the MAC rolls.

He also caught eight passes, and will try to expand that role as a safety valve and receiver on screens this fall.

Ball State still lists a fullback on the depth chart, though junior fullback Scott Volk (5-11, 225) saw nary a carry last fall and caught nine passes in limited duty. Look for even less of the two-back sets this fall, as the Cards work more with three wideouts.

Senior **Jason Teeters** (5-7, 174) had carries in every game last year and is a slippery, smaller change-of-pace back. He totaled 107 yards and a score.

Other backs will have a hard time seeing the field in 2001, but freshman signee **Otis Shannon** (5-9, 195) may already be good enough to break in for an occasional carry and work on the return teams.

Shannon was Indiana's Mr. Football last fall at Cathedral High School in Indianapolis. He ran for almost 8,000 yards in his high school career, with 2,394 last fall, and turned down some late Big 10 offers. He scored 93 touchdowns in four seasons.

WIDE RECEIVERS/TIGHT ENDS

For a team spreading the field, the Cards need to have more pass completions. Hill did a good job with percentages, but sheer volume will make things easier for everybody.

Last year's leading pass-catcher was junior **Sean Schembra** (5-10, 186), who came down with 40 grabs for 484 yards. Schembra is not going to stretch the field, but is the possession guy that so many of the MAC's spread offense teams seek out. He scored only one touchdown, but helped the Cards retain possession, earn first downs, and stay in the league's top half in time of possession.

Hometown hero **David Westbrook** (6-3, 201) is a senior from Muncie, and led the team with six touchdowns on just 27 catches. His 422 yards were second on the team, and he is the bigger play threat outside who can out-jump corners deep at split end.

Senior **Jamar Cottee** (5-10, 180) never really broke a big one last year in his 21 grabs for 165 yards. Cottee is another player like Schembra who runs smart, shorter routes and makes good catches. He's limited but effective.

Fellow senior **Corey Parchman** (6-3, 187) had 16 catches and a touchdown in just nine games.

Senior **Billy Lynch** (5-9, 160) is the son of the coach and was the point guard for the Cards' hoops team the last two years. A pesky little fly in the ointment of defensive backs, the younger Lynch had 12 catches and a score last fall and is pretty good at sitting down in open spots in a zone defense.

Three other receivers caught touchdown passes last fall, though they will have a hard time outpacing the bevy of seniors at the top of the depth chart. Incoming freshman **Ryan Hahaj** (6-4, 190) is a gigantic target who could make Hill's life much easier in the pocket. Hahaj is an All-Indiana player from Fort Wayne and the tallest BSU skill player in a while.

In the spread, the tight end is much like the fullback in that opportunities are few and far between. A senior starter is done here, but junior returnees **Jon Eckert** (6-5, 247) and **Tim Streit** (6-4, 246) bring back seven catches and a couple touchdowns.

OFFENSIVE LINE

Though you remember the Cards' lack of success over the last couple seasons, the two-deep that takes the field this fall is thick with seniors. Is this group peaking? The offensive line returns three-of-five starters.

"Our offensive line is relied upon heavily to protect our passer and open holes for the running backs," Lynch said. "This group is the true cornerstone of our offense. Add to the returning starters five more lettermen and we look for good things."

Junior **Colin Johnson** (6-1, 285) returns at center, with senior **Nathan Boyd** (6-1, 298) behind him and in the depth at guard.

Junior **David Miller** (6-3, 321) is the anchor inside and is a powerful run blocker. Junior **Travis Barclay** (6-4, 294) and senior **LaVar Charleston** (6-3, 301) from Detroit's Cass Tech High School are in the battle at right guard on the other flank.

The tackle position lost a pair of four-year lettermen, but returns the experienced **John Moore** (6-6, 280), a fifth-year senior from near Dayton, Ohio. He will start at right tackle, backed by redshirt freshman **Jeff Ramsey** (6-5, 275), stolen out of Miami's backyard in Fairfield, Ohio.

At blindside left tackle, sophomore **Kris Berry** (6-4, 278) led going into spring but was being pressed by fellow sophomore letterman **Joel Hofmann** (6-7, 282).

At tackle, the Cards also have redshirt freshman **Ty Knisley** (6-6, 285) to go along with big guard depth from fellow redshirt freshmen **Nick Tabacca** (6-5, 285) and **Travis Saylor** (6-4, 285).

Ball State signed three more prototype guards or tackles in the new freshmen class. The Red and White are finally back up to size and speed in this unit.

2000 STATISTICS

Rushing offense	164.8	34
Passing offense	154.9	101
Total offense	319.7	90
Scoring offense	19.2	91
Net Punting	27.9	111
Punt returns	7.5	93
Kickoff returns	15.3	112
Rushing defense	169.7	75
Passing efficiency defense	123.0	73
Total defense	369.4	62
Scoring defense	31.7	89
Turnover margin	-14	108

Last column is ranking among Division I-A teams.

KICKERS

The Cards return two kickers who have scored and still will have decisions to make come August. Senior **Thomas Pucke** (5-10, 205) scored just 14 points last season on 3-of-7 field goals. Pucke attempted field goals in all the wins, and was the starter the final four games.

Behind him, sophomore **Mike Langford** (5-9, 152) made 3-of-5 field goals and the bulk of the teams' PATs (13-of-16).

DEFENSIVE LINE

The numbers on defense from 2000 aren't very positive in most columns. But if you subtract the embarrassing results of the first four weeks, things look a little better for the longer term. Forget about the 183 points allowed in the first month and the picture shifts considerably.

Even with those numbers, Ball State still finished in the top half of the MAC in rushing, passing and total defense. The Cardinals have only two starting holes to fill on the starting defense, one on this front line.

League radio announcers are glad to see Sunungura Rusununguko gone, though Cards fans remember this hard-working tackle as one of the few bright spots during the depths of the losing streak. He was seventh on the squad in tackles with 41—10 for losses.

Senior **Mark Zackery** (6-0, 283) does return in the middle, with 42 stops and three sacks last fall. Sophomore **Greg Pagnard** (6-2, 276) and redshirt freshman **Jerome Tilmon** (6-3, 245) will do battle for the new starting spot alongside Zackery. Pagnard saw action in eight games last fall.

At the ends, Ball needs to develop more pressure at a position where no player had more than one quarterback sack in 2000.

Senior **Evan Triggs** (6-3, 266) starts at the left

side, back with 55 tackles to lead returning linemen. Youngsters **Paul Starbavy** (6-2, 233), a sophomore, and redshirt freshman **Martin Ferrill** (6-4, 225) are the depth here and need to get bigger and stronger.

At the far side, senior end **Rachman Crable** (6-4, 260) should be the best rusher of the down linemen, but he missed four games last fall with injuries. As a pure bull rusher, he should have a big senior season if he can rebound.

Junior **Jonas Williams** (6-0, 252) saw some action in seven games filling in last fall. Ball State brought in five players in the new class who project to nose or defensive end, and any of them who can impact now will skip a redshirt season. Pass rush is something that needs improved from the front four.

LINEBACKERS

The Cards return four linebackers who played starters' minutes last fall to these four positions. Much like the rest of the league that plays the 4-4, the inside guys are run stoppers, the outside are overgrown safeties, one who drops into pass coverage or blitzes off the weak side; the other stays over the strong side and picks up the tight end.

Inside, Ball has two of the league's best. Senior **Shaka Johnson** (6-0, 230) was to be the only bright spot on last year's defense, before the season turned around. Johnson led the squad in tackles as a junior, but dropped to 73 last year when freshman **Lorenzo Scott** (6-2, 195) sprouted up beside him to make 96 stops and a pair of interceptions.

Johnson played hurt some of last year, but Scott earned all his tackles. Recruited to play receiver out of metro St. Louis, Scott was the league's second-best freshman linebacker from that city (Miami's Terrell Jones was All-MAC). Scott missed the spring drills to play on the BSU baseball team, which was again one of the MAC's best.

With the athletic Scott covering all sorts of ground from the inside, it frees the outside backers for the pass rush. Two other fifth-year seniors are the backups here, though they will not often see the field if the starters stay injury free. **Allen Lidy** (6-0, 225) and **Brent Walker** (6-3, 218) combined for 34 tackles last year.

Ball's other lost starter was four-year letterman Nate Andrews, the team's fourth-leading tackler. Seniors **Cornelius Bowick** (6-2, 221) and **Vernard Alsberry** (6-0, 211) combined for 61 stops and three sacks from the strong outside spot. That slot will be locked down with these two experienced players. Bowick scored a touchdown last fall when he fell on a fumble in the end zone at Florida.

The other side is open, and senior **Alger Boswell** (5-8, 201) is the incumbent right now. But this is a spot that may be being held open for an impact recruit.

Linebacker and running back recruit **Donta Smith** (6-1, 205) is the perfect size to play at outside, and is the other big celebrity in the Cards' excellent class, along with Shannon. He made 183 stops as a senior at Central High School in East Chicago, Ind., and was an Associated Press All-Indiana selection.

This is the most experienced and skilled unit on a top-five MAC defense.

DEFENSIVE BACKS

As with all the 40-front defensive teams, this is a smaller unit, and one that often has to worry about playing more man-to-man coverage.

Junior **Jade Winchell** (5-10, 196) is an absolute vacuum cleaner at free safety and has two years of starting experience behind him. Winchell was the third-leading tackler last fall with 72. He had no interceptions. This team and position do need to work on getting some takeaways, and were minus-14 in turnover ratio last season.

Sophomore **Doug Owusu** (5-10, 171) played in just three games last fall and will be the apprentice here for another year.

At the corners, sophomore **Jesse Avant** (5-10, 182) was a revelation in his first year to start. He had 34 stops and a pick. Avant is backed up by his brother **Charles Avant** (5-10, 176), a junior, and senior **Chickaro Martin** (5-10, 170).

On the other side, junior **Steve Monson** (5-8, 169) is smaller, but has good make-up speed. He did collect 24 tackles last fall and broke up eight passes. Sophomore Quentin Manley (6-1, 172) has better physical tools and will press the issue here. He could be the fifth defensive back and scored a touchdown on a punt block versus Buffalo in 2000.

PUNTERS

Sophomore **Reggie Hodges** (6-1, 225) had plenty of chances to punt last fall, especially in September. In 64 punts, Hodges stopped only one inside the opponent's 20-yard line and averaged 36 yards per kick. This facet of the game must improve to get the young offense some better field position throughout a game.

Sophomore **Phil Cunningham** (6-2, 200) is next on the depth chart.

SPECIAL TEAMS

Neither of the kicking units knocked anybody out last fall, and the Cards need more distance from their punts and to settle on a consistent kicker.

Ball State returns its top returners, though Lynch did have one of the lowest averages (4.6 yards per) as a punt returner in the MAC. He is small and quick and needs to hit a big one early in 2001 to keep this spot. Look for Shannon or one of the other young players to get a shot here, or at returning kicks.

Schembra, Cottee and Jesse Avant returned most of the kicks last fall, none with longer than a 26-yard effort.

RECRUITING CLASS

This is definitely a top-half of the MAC recruiting effort on first glance, possibly for the third year in a row. Ball State has done a good job with getting in-state recruits who didn't fit the plan at Purdue and see the fairly negative writing on the wall at Indiana.

Players like Shannon, Hill, Scott and Sanders are big pickups. Ball has also done well in western Ohio and Michigan and the Chicago area, and is joining Miami in venturing into the St. Louis market for some quality recruits.

It's almost as if Lynch is trying to make up for the physical frailties of the '97-'99 teams by getting so many large athletes on both sides of the ball. Both lines appear to be set. Depth from this class needs to fit in at linebacker and corner, along with a speedy young receiver.

Ball State got off track a few years ago with some poor recruiting and stopgap dips into the junior college ranks. Lynch is lucky he's gotten this "second-chance," and appears to be making the most of it.

BLUE RIBBON ANALYSIS

OFFENSE	C-
SPECIAL TEAMS	D
DEFENSE	C
INTANGIBLES	C-

We expected to be talking to a new staff this spring in Muncie. But Lynch and his players put on a courageous performance last season, and one of the league's best programs on the academic side turned things around out of the classroom.

The Cards have at least two solid backs, plus whatever Shannon can add. And they have a huge line behind which to run. How much Hill grows as a passer will determine just how good this offense can be. This team still needs to find a game-breaker at receiver and some consistency. A lot of guys caught passes last fall, but no one caught very many. A star needs to emerge.

Special teams could be well below average, and there are no numbers that suggest otherwise.

The defense was pretty special for half a year, against the pass and run. They are very similar to Ohio in their need for a better pass rush and some more takeaways. Improved turnover margin would go a long way to keeping this unit fresh.

There are a lot of seniors here, and if this group is truly peaking, they've picked the wrong year to do it. In the "old" MAC, this would be a team competitive at the top of the league, which could sneak into a high finish as in '96. This year, the Cards would have to be better than Toledo and Northern and Western. That's a tall order. Look for a similar mark to last year, though they will sneak up on nobody.

Anything more than about six wins would represent a huge step forward. Kentucky is a winnable game. Mid-season games against Miami and at Eastern Michigan will determine whether this team stays near .500 or falls back some.

(R.C.)

2000 RESULTS

Florida	L	19-40	0-1
Western Illinois	L	14-24	0-2
Kansas State	L	0-76	0-3
Northern Illinois	L	14-43	0-4
Miami (Ohio)	W	15-10	1-4
Eastern Michigan	W	33-14	2-4
Buffalo	W	44-35	3-4
Central Michigan	W	38-34	4-4
Western Michigan	L	3-42	4-5
Toledo	L	3-31	4-6
Connecticut	W	29-0	5-6

Bowling Green

LOCATION	**Bowling Green, OH**
CONFERENCE	**Mid-American (East)**
LAST SEASON	**2-9 (.182)**
CONFERENCE RECORD	**1-5 (6th)**
OFFENSIVE STARTERS RETURNING	**8**
DEFENSIVE STARTERS RETURNING	**6**
NICKNAME	**Falcons**
COLORS	**Orange & Brown**
HOME FIELD	**Doyt Perry Stadium (30,599)**
HEAD COACH	**Urban Meyer (Cincinnati '86)**
RECORD AT SCHOOL	**First Year**
CAREER RECORD	**First Year**
ASSISTANTS	

Tim Beckman (Findlay '88)
Defensive Coordinator
Gregg Brandon (N. Colorado '78)
Offensive Coordinator
John Bowers (James Madison '79)

Linebackers/Recruiting Coordinator
Stan Drayton (Allegheny '93)
Running Backs/Special Teams
John Hevesy (Maine '94)
Offensive Tackles/Ends
Dan Mullen (Ursinus '94)
Quarterbacks
Greg Studrawa (Bowling Green '87)
Offensive Guards/Centers
Mike Ward (Georgetown '84)
Defensive Line
Tommie Thigpen (North Carolina '94)
Defensive Backs

TEAM WINS (last 5 yrs.)	**4-3-5-5-2**
FINAL RANK (last 5 yrs.)	**105-108-102-104-110**
2000 FINISH	**Lost to Toledo in regular-season finale.**

COACH AND PROGRAM

Things had gotten stale in the flatlands of northwest Ohio, and a change had to be made after six consecutive losing seasons. So 10-year head coach Gary Blackney was shown the door this off-season, taking two MAC championships and 60 career wins with him.

Athletic director Paul Krebs had been considering a move for a couple years and went back to his Buckeye roots to hire Notre Dame receivers coach Urban Meyer to lead the Falcons. Meyer is one of the youngest coaches in Division I-A and brings experience from previous stops at Ohio State, Cincinnati and Colorado State.

Meyer already has his players excited about taking the field, but he has a lot of work to do. No punches will be pulled. Everything is being tried as the new coach tries to hammer home the commitment required for Division I-A success.

"Seven or eight guys have left already, who didn't have that desire needed to play here now," Meyer said. "But the players who remain have taken the lead and are really flying around the ball now."

Instead of trying to pound the MAC with an offense that lacked enough beef up front, Meyer will try to make the Falcons competitive sooner with the spread passing offense that is now in vogue. Four-receiver sets with lots of motion, and even some empty backfields will be the rule on 90 percent of the downs.

Just as Jim Grobe tried to make up for lack of size and athletes with the option offense at Ohio, Meyer thinks this spread-passing look will close the gap to the front of the MAC quicker than smash-mouth football.

Meyer lists new West Virginia coach Rich Rodriguez as a friend and will try to emulate his offense that worked so well at Clemson and Tulane.

"We're all trying to learn about each other—players and coaches," Meyer said. "[The prior staff] left us some guys with ability."

On defense, Bowling Green showed a thus-far vanilla 4-3 in the spring and needs to find depth in the line and better athletes in the linebacker group at the second level.

"The essence of coaching—which consumes my mind and life more than anything right now—how far can you push them?" Meyer told the Toledo Blade. "Because we're pushing them extremely hard and extremely far right now."

This is a program that needed a push, and Meyer is more than willing to give it.

"Since 14 years ago when I decided to be a coach, I've watched the Earle Bruces, the Sonny Lubicks, the Lou Holtzes, the Bob Davies—every step they take and move they made," he told the Blade. "Then I'd say if I ever get in that situation, I would do this. If you are going to be successful, you have to analyze these sorts of things and this spring I've done that."

2001 SCHEDULE

Sept.	1	@Missouri
	8	Buffalo
	15	@South Carolina
	22	Temple
	29	@Marshall
Oct.	6	Kent State
	13	@Western Michigan
	20	@Akron
Nov.	3	Miami (Ohio)
	10	@Ohio
	23	Toledo

QUARTERBACKS

If you watched any of the Falcons' spring scrimmages, you saw that quarterback might be this team's most obvious strength. But it's not necessarily the QB you might think who has stepped to the fore.

Junior quarterback **Andy Sahm** (6-6, 220) looks like a prototype pocket passer. But that may be a poor fit for the new offense, as Sahm was a slow-moving backfield target most of 2000. With the exception of a shocking 40-plus yard run to help beat Kent, the signal caller from Indianapolis had virtually no luck running with the ball. And playing behind a porous line, Sahm made little progress throwing the ball, going from seven touchdown tosses in limited duty in '99 to just eight last fall against nine interceptions.

But he can still be a factor.

"I thought Andy Sahm had a great spring," Meyer said in April. "I was told Andy couldn't play [in this offense], and from looking at last year's film, I'd almost made the decision that he wouldn't be our quarterback."

There will be one set of play calls when Sahm is in the game, plays more suited to the cutting-up of zone coverages, which is his strength.

The other set of calls will belong to a pair of impressive youngsters who may better fit the all-around needs of this spread offense.

Sophomore **Josh Harris** (6-3, 205) put on an absolute show all spring and will be the starter here if he can improve his touch in the passing game. Harris got some limited minutes last fall, playing in six games as a rusher, passer and even kick returner. He scored twice and totaled 629 all-purpose yards but was a man without a real position under the old staff.

In the spring game, Harris twice had scoring runs of more than 50 yards and showed a burst to the open field as fine as any back in the league. He ended up with six carries for 133 yards, but it was his 5-of-14 passing that Meyer needs him to improve.

"We saw today a fast quarterback," Meyer said at the end of the day. "I told him running off the field today, 'Too bad you can't throw or you'd be a heck of a quarterback.' But I don't want him to have that reputation. The kid can flat throw and now he needs to get more consistent and make better throws."

The second-year player from Westerville North High School near Columbus has a chance to be very special if he can keep defenses honest with his arm. Like option quarterback Dontrell Jackson at Ohio, Harris is a guy who other coaches agree has difference-maker potential.

Bowling Green will have one set of play calls for Sahm and another for Harris and redshirt freshman **David Azzi** (6-2, 195). Azzi is a similar player to Harris, with excellent straightaway speed. He might not be quite as shifty. Recruited as a quarterback and punter, the Ottawa, Ontario native could be a candidate for the occasional trick play if he doesn't outright win the job behind center in this shotgun-happy offense. He's just that good and could be a real revelation at the spot.

"He may well be the most talented of the three; we'll just need to give him some time," Meyer said.

There was just one quarterback in the new recruiting class—**Cole Magner** (6-2, 180) who could also move to wideout. Magner played his prep ball in Palmer, Alaska.

RUNNING BACKS

The quarterbacks made a great first impression on the new staff, but the coaches would like to see some more depth at running back. Demands will be different here, as the shotgun offense will need a good mix of blocking and quick hands and feet from the single back.

Junior **Godfrey Lewis** (5-9, 190) is another of the Canadians of whom the prior staff was so fond and is the top back coming out of spring. Lewis was one of the scads of Bowling Green backs cut down last fall with injuries, a situation that saw the Falcons scramble defensive backs and freshmen as part of the "six-deep" roster in the Kent State game. Lewis would have been the No. 1 guy in 2000, but was injured after playing in only the first two games against Pitt and Michigan. He is a shifty back with a great burst who showed some talent running behind a very veteran line in '99.

Fifth-year senior **John Gibson** (5-10, 215) risks being ignored by the new staff as he missed the entire spring with injury. He was Bowling Green's top runner last fall with 514 yards and four touchdowns, but averaged only 3.3 yards per carry. That won't be good enough, though an effective spread offense should guarantee a big year for the running back who gets the most reps.

Junior **Joe Alls** (5-10, 191) also returns from an abbreviated eight-game season in which he added 291 yards and a touchdown, but this spot is wide open for immediate help. Players who can play now will. There are at least three backs in the early group of signees.

Fullback also saw some work in the spring sessions, though to little effect. Running a slower back on a mis-direction from shotgun depth will be near impossible against a good defense.

The fullbacks are led by redshirt freshman **Todd DiBacco** (6-1, 225), who played his high school ball at highly regarded Monaca High School in Western Pennsylvania. But like the tight end, the number of snaps this position sees the field may be very limited.

WIDE RECEIVERS/TIGHT ENDS

If you're going to go to four-wide or five-wide and run a no-huddle or speed-up attack, you need lots of bodies. Having 10 receivers is a minimum. So when two of your projected four starters get hurt to open spring practice, it retards the development for everybody.

Senior **Kurt Gerling** (6-2, 195) was the MAC Freshman of the Year back in '98 after a 660-yard season and had 53 catches in '99. Absolutely a difference-maker over the middle, Gerling went there once too often last year en route to a broken collar bone at Michigan. But he still managed 324 yards in limited duty last fall after missing the first month and trying to play hurt.

Then, with a clean slate this spring, Gerling tore an ACL and had surgery just a week into the new drills. He told a local paper that he plans to miss "zero games." But it will be tough to make the Sept. 1 opener at Missouri.

"I've watched him on tape," Meyer said. "And

from what folks around here say, it won't be a surprise if he can go this fall."

Fellow fifth-year wideout **Aaron Alexander** (6-0, 195) caught only six passes last fall in five games before a kneecap injury ended his season and a subsequent surgery took his spring.

The one returnee that was 100 percent landed on his feet last fall and made the best of a tough situation. Now senior **David Bautista** (6-0, 180) starts the year as an All-MAC candidate after catching everything thrown his way in 2000. The Cerritos Community College transfer caught 69 passes as a possession receiver and led the Falcons in catches, yards (915) and receiving touchdowns (three).

The other certainty is that junior **Robert Redd** (5-10, 195) is back and ready to be a MAC star again. Redd debuted with Gerling as a freshman in '98 and was definitely the speedier of the two. But the flashy Redd only worked hard in spurts and had differences with the prior coaching staff.

Those differences resulted in an aborted transfer to Louisville. But the Dayton native returned last year and was eligible for spring practice. He was dynamite in the spring game, catching two long scoring passes from Sahm. He is a speedy slot receiver who can create tremendous mismatches in the spread offense.

A lot of balls will be whizzing out of the Bowling Green backfield, but Redd is truly the home run threat, though the coach says he still has much to learn in the new offense.

Meyer also has high hopes for Prop 48 sophomore **Cornelius McGrady** (6-3, 194) who's been on campus a year after a successful career at Reynoldsburg (Ohio) High School. He will be the taller spilt end who should eventually take over as the top perimeter threat.

Freshmen **Chris Dodd** (5-11, 160), **Kevin Poindexter** (6-3, 175), and **Brittney Davidson** (6-3, 200), and sophomores **Austin Holman** (6-0, 195) and **Andre Pinchem** (5-9, 175), a former defensive back recruit with 12 catches in 2000, had auditions in the spring. They failed to win Meyer's attention.

"After those top couple, we are really hurting at wide receiver," Meyer said. "We need some guys to step up and that hasn't happened. We need to have 12 guys on scholarship here and be able to play eight."

At least five prep pass catchers are in the group of signees, and that number may grow by August. Meyer has expressed a desire to fill his open scholarships if he can find talented players this summer who qualify late academically.

Tight ends also did little to earn more time on the field in the off-season. Canadian sophomore **Jason Van Dam** (6-6, 260) has the right look, but still needs to work on hands after no catches in 2000 behind junior **Ross Durham** (6-6, 260), who caught three passes. Freshman **Jon Culp** (6-6, 245) joins the fray here, arriving from the excellent program at Mason High School near Cincinnati.

OFFENSIVE LINE

"This was the worst offensive line in the league," said the new head coach, more shocked than angry about the condition of a group who needed to be bigger and stronger to run the smash-mouth scheme of the last staff. "It was the weakest offensive line I've ever been around."

The first group responded well to spring coaching, and the new staff has high hopes for the two-deep as they start fresh with the younger guys.

You still have to block in the spread offense, but there is less of the size-intensive drive blocking and less movement in pocket protection due to the quick throws. This will make things a little easier on the line.

Two senior starters are gone at center and left tackle, and returning junior right guard **Greg Kupke** (6-3, 285) would have been a leader if not for a leg injury that ended his spring. He "may" be back for fall, which makes the search for protectors all the more imperative.

The Falcons will try to get by, starting in the middle with sophomore **Ryan Lucas** (6-4, 265) at center. Almost every snap in the new offense will be a "long" snap, and Lucas was up to the challenge all spring.

The coaches hope to get Kupke back at one of the guard spots and will get leadership from him and senior **Mike Bodnar** (6-3, 290). Things get bigger outside with a pair of veterans—senior **Malcolm Robinson** (6-4, 290) has experience in the trenches on both sides of the ball and mammoth junior **Dennis Wendel** (6-7, 303) was one of last year's bright spots.

Junior **Ryan Yeager** (6-4, 275) provides the depth at the inside spots. Redshirt freshman **Scott Mruczkowski** (6-4, 295) has a good future at tackle. The incoming freshman class only includes two potential players here—**Rob Warren** (6-6, 265) of Mentor, Ohio, and **Mike Thaler** (6-1, 290), the younger brother of Miami lineman Paul Thaler.

2000 STATISTICS

Rushing offense	98.4	101
Passing offense	163.7	95
Total offense	262.1	110
Scoring offense	15.8	104
Net Punting	34.6	52
Punt returns	8.3	77
Kickoff returns	17.0	91
Rushing defense	132.3	38
Passing efficiency defense	122.4	70
Total defense	351.9	48
Scoring defense	26.3	69
Turnover margin	+4	46

Last column is ranking among Division I-A teams.

KICKERS

Kicking was just plain lousy last fall, as a pair of now-departed players combined to bat .500 (10-of-20) on field goals.

Untested sophomore **Phil Messer** (6-1, 170) did the majority of kicking in the spring and might be joined by another of last year's Canadian recruits in **Shawn Suisham** (6-0, 180). This group is a complete wild card and cannot yet be counted on for big results.

Scholarship kicker **Nate Fry** (5-10, 200) arrives from just 25 miles down the road at Findlay High School and will be looking to win the job in August. He got plenty of practice kicking PATs in '99 as new Miami quarterback **Ben Roethlisberger** set Ohio's single-season record for passing touchdowns at Findlay.

DEFENSIVE LINE

All three defensive units have a star or two, but not nearly enough depth to stand up to ever-stronger MAC offensive lines.

Up front there are two stars, one inside and one out. And those two fifth-year seniors will have to be productive again to keep opposing quarterbacks from tearing up the secondary. **Brandon Hicks** (6-2, 250) seems a little small to be playing inside, but he produces good pass rush numbers and seems to be a guy counted on to reach well laterally against the run. Hicks started every game the last two seasons as a nose guard in the offset 4-3.

Hicks was chosen first-team All-MAC by *The Sporting News* and second team by the league's coaches.

The other veteran is defensive end **Ryan Wingrove** (6-3, 250), a solid pass rusher who needs to work hard against being snowed under by bigger tackles. The former high school tight end does well at getting off blocks and will be counted on to keep the perimeter off-limits to opposing runners.

D.J. Owchar (6-3, 273) is a junior who contributed frequently at tackle last fall, along with the Glantzis brothers from Mentor, Ohio. **Chris Glantzis** (6-4, 260) is a fifth-year senior who played well at end in the spring. The bulkier junior **Alex Glantzis** (6-4, 280) may help give a breather to Hicks further inside and is the biggest of the prospects here.

Sophomore **James Williams** (6-5, 260) was stolen out of Miami's backyard (Trenton, Ohio) and will be a future star when he improves against the run. Fellow sophomore **Jared Butts** (6-2, 265) also got a good long look in spring.

Depth at end is a concern with only a couple of the signees projecting to play line.

LINEBACKERS

Fifth-year senior **Khary Campbell** (6-2, 215) is the guy that Meyer will rely on in the middle of the field. Bowling Green's leading returning tackler, Campbell is one of the best in the MAC at pursuing the run inside-out. Getting him free of blockers will be one of the main responsibilities for the four down linemen, as he should be the hero of this 4-3 defense.

Junior **Marcus Allen** (6-0, 195) is a little undersized, but pursued very well in spring action and may be half a step quicker than Campbell. He had a game-high nine tackles in the spring finale.

While the tackles funnel to Campbell at middle linebacker, juniors **Geno Burden** (6-1, 212) and **Garry Fisher** (5-10, 218) will try to play over top of much bigger opposing tight ends at the strong side.

Meyer needs to find bigger guys long term at this slot. Redshirt freshman **Andy Grubb** (6-4, 255) has the prototype size defensive coordinators want here, along with sophomore **Rich Mauer** (6-3, 240) from suburban Cleveland. With the exception of the middle, look for a gradual overtaking process this fall on the outside, trading experience for size and youth.

Junior **Chris Haneline** (6-1, 215) was a star stopper at national high school power St. Ignatius in Cleveland, and projects well at weak-side or to provide more depth in the middle. He had an excellent spring.

Also having a good spring at weak-side was redshirt freshman **Jovan Burkes** (6-1, 220) out of Detroit Central High School, who had eight stops and 1 1/2 sacks in the spring game. Junior **Frank Garofalo** (5-10, 230) missed spring with an injury and may get caught behind a young numbers game.

DEFENSIVE BACKS

The biggest worry Blackney had going into last fall was the play of his secondary. This was a bad unit bad in '99 and it didn't improve a whole lot in 2000. But Meyer has already managed to find a future star in sophomore **Janssen Patton** (6-0, 180).

"This kid will play for awhile," Meyer said. "And by that, I mean that his career will go well beyond this campus and four years if he wants it to."

Patton has an eye for the ball and is one of the few corners in the league a coach can feel safe playing straight-up man-to-man coverage. He played in the City League at Columbus' Independence High School. Patton had an interception in the spring game to go along with four last fall, which was tied for third in the MAC. He also made 42 tackles, 35 unassisted. Patton will start at the "wide" or "field" corner spot.

Two sophomores will try to earn the job on the other side. **Michael Malone** (5-10, 180) played better against the run and could even project over to safety. **Jason Morton** (6-0, 180) is a virtual twin of his high school teammate Patton, and just needs more reps to improve.

The versatile **Darnell Bond-Awls** (5-8, 175) is a sophomore from nearby Toledo who played some in nickel packages and even as a running back when depth there disappeared in the Kent State game. He worked a little at receiver in the spring because of the lack of depth there and will get on the field somewhere in 2001.

Seniors **Sergio Lund** (6-0, 185) and **Chad Long** (6-0, 195) are veteran incumbent safeties but combined for only one interception and did nothing to really distinguish themselves last season. Lund is decent in coverage at free safety as a former corner.

Meyer said, "we need to get our best players out there," and these guys will need to work hard to be out there for the season opener.

Backup sophomore **Andrew Heers** (6-0, 190) missed the spring with injury and could help here, along with fellow sophomore **Andre Davis** (6-2, 190).

Senior **Karl Rose** (6-0, 185) fell out of favor last fall at "short" corner and might see the field as a nickel back along with junior **Jerry Wagner** (5-10, 185). There are at least four defensive backs in the new class, though needs at receiver could see them all slotted there in August.

PUNTERS

Junior **Pat Fleming** (6-2, 190) is like his backup Azzi in that he's from Ottawa. But Fleming has two solid years of punting under his belt and is "just killing the ball," Meyer said in the spring. He averaged 40 yards per punt on 59 attempts last year, and would have had more chances if not for a mid-season injury. None were blocked after three blocks in '99 and he set 12 down inside the opposing 20-yard line.

Azzi is supposed to be a solid punter as well, but has more of a future taking the shotgun snaps right now. Opposing coaches would be wise to watch personnel when Bowling Green sends the punt unit on the field this fall.

SPECIAL TEAMS

Kicking is still anybody's guess, though the punting is above average. But the Falcons have a difference-maker back if Redd is the guy to return punts and kicks. He led the MAC in punt return average when he last played here and could very well do it again with Justin McCareins gone from Northern Illinois.

Long averaged only six yards a return in the same spot last fall.

Redd will probably be joined by Alls or Lewis on the kick return package. Both of those running backs had success there in their first year at Bowling Green. Alls averaged just a shade under 20 yards a return last season.

RECRUITING CLASS

Meyer signed 20 players in time for the announcement of the new class this spring. But with at least seven defections since, the new coach has a handful of scholarships he can try to fill over the summer. Look for some new faces in August.

"The ones that left didn't want to make a real commitment to what we're going to do here," Meyer said.

This team had decent linemen who just needed serious weight room and blocking technique help, so Meyer signed lots of skilled backs and athletes. He also grabbed a kicker on whom he thinks he can depend for four years.

Bowling Green is not considered a garden spot in the league or nationally. But good facilities and a tradition of winning help.

"It's hard to sell this place in January," Meyer said, "but show it to kids when it's sunny and tell them the ratio of girls to guys is [about 2-1] and you can get them excited about coming here."

The last staff dipped into Canada after swinging and missing repeatedly in the traditional power prep programs in the Rust Belt. Guys like Fleming, Azzi and Van Dam are successes from those trips.

The new group is back in Ohio, especially looking toward Meyer's college home of Cincinnati. Meyer's staff is trying to make footholds in Georgia and join Kent State in suburban Maryland.

One late spring signing was that of mammoth offensive tackle **Jeff Wailand** (6-8, 310) from Bradenton, Fla. He and Bryant should step in to play immediately, giving the Falcons potentially two excellent freshman contributors in the trenches.

BLUE RIBBON ANALYSIS

OFFENSE	C
SPECIAL TEAMS	D+
DEFENSE	C-
INTANGIBLES	C+

If you just walked in off the street and watched the spring game at Doyt Perry Stadium, you'd have been blown away by the difference. Players were excited, parents were excited, and folks were genuinely happy to be there. There was enthusiasm at a place that had been like a funeral home in recent seasons.

The coaching change has led to that excitement, plus the fact that Meyer's version of the spread looks as crisp as a couple of big-name programs making the same switch this spring.

Even if these guys don't win a game, things are changing here. But they will win some games; it's just too bad this schedule will make it hard to get a good toe hold early.

Bowling Green may be facing one of the league's toughest schedules given the non-conference games: at Missouri and at South Carolina in the first three weeks, then a home game against much-improved Temple.

In the East, the games against pacesetters Marshall and Ohio are on the road. And in the two games against the West (which don't count toward the championship standings), the Falcons play at Western Michigan and are locked into a "rivalry pact" game every year with conference favorite Toledo. Ouch.

Any more than three wins will be difficult, but no matter the win total at the end of the year, this group will be ahead of Buffalo and Kent State. And, depending on whether Miami and Akron can stop anybody, Bowling Green could be the sexy surprise pick to move up in the East.

There is room on the front of the Doyt Perry press box for two more MAC Championship banners. They won't be placed there in 2001, but this program is finally moving forward again.

(R.C.)

2000 RESULTS

Michigan	L	7-42	0-1
Pittsburgh	L	7-42	0-2
Temple	L	14-31	0-3
Buffalo	L	17-20	0-4
Kent State	W	18-11	1-4
Akron	L	21-27	1-5
Miami (Ohio)	L	10-24	1-6
Eastern Michigan	W	20-6	2-6
Marshall	L	13-20	2-7
Ohio	L	21-23	2-8
Toledo	L	17-51	2-9

Buffalo

LOCATION Buffalo, NY
CONFERENCE Mid-American (East)
LAST SEASON 2-9 (.182)
CONFERENCE RECORD 2-4 (5th)
OFFENSIVE STARTERS RETURNING 7
DEFENSIVE STARTERS RETURNING 5
NICKNAME Bulls
COLORS Royal Blue & White
HOME FIELD UB Stadium (31,000)
HEAD COACH Jim Hofher (Cornell '79)
RECORD AT SCHOOL First Year
CAREER RECORD First Year
ASSISTANTS
Bill Lazor (Cornell '94) Quarterbacks
Tom Jones (Temple '80) Defensive Line
Roy Istvan (So. Connecticut '90) Offensive Line
Clayton Carlin (Juniata '87) Defensive Backs
Andrew Dees (Syracuse '92) Tight Ends
Brian Polian (John Carroll '97) Running Backs
Doug Socha (Cal State-Northridge '99) Wide Receivers
Thurmond Moore (San Jose State '77) Defensive Coordinator
Antonio Goss (North Carolina '89) Linebackers
TEAM WINS (last 5 yrs.) NA-NA-NA-0-2
FINAL RANK (last 5 yrs.) NA-NA-NA-114-114
2000 FINISH Lost to Miami (Ohio) in regular-season finale.

COACH AND PROGRAM

Two years into the MAC wars means new coaches for both major men's sports for the University at Buffalo. Syracuse assistant Jim Hofher is the guy charged with taking an infant Division I-A football program and making it credible. Players and folks around the MAC were surprised by the quick hook given former head man Craig Cirbus, an alumnus who had taken this program forward through Division I-AA and a too-soon switch upward in competition.

But new athletics director Bob Arkeilpane seems eager to put his own stamp on the show at UB, firing a basketball coach after the university self-reported NCAA violations and a football coach who pre-dated his tenure.

Buffalo has yet to prove very credible at the Division I-A level, but the talent pool left for Hofher isn't bad. The recruiting and strength programs were already improving, and the new coach thinks he can find a niche on the recruiting trail. He's worked for two of the most similar programs in the country, geographically and academically, and knows that the things he learned at Syracuse and Cornell are more applicable here than anywhere else.

"There are 90 high schools we can start with in the western New York area, and we need to make sure those kids come here," Hofher said.

The coach realizes that in his own backyard, players and prep coaches know Buffalo's reputation as the flagship of the state university system, and that it's the only public top-division football program there.

Sure, places like Cornell, Syracuse and Buffalo are cold and have tough academics; but Hofher's been part of success at the first two and thinks it can come at the third. The similarities among the three schools are striking.

The coach likes the developmental character of this program and league.

"In the MAC, players do it," he said. "And right now we are in a developmental stage here, with only two years in Division I. Coaching for us is a two-way street too, in that we need to learn and teach."

Trying to position Buffalo as a respectable option for top recruits from the northeast, Hofher has put together a staff with ties that will help in some recruiting areas not normally entered by MAC schools.

"Our defensive coordinator [Thurmond Moore] was at Syracuse, Bill Lazor [quarterbacks] played for me at Cornell, Brian Polian [running backs] grew up around the game here, Andrew Dees [tight ends] worked for a SUNY program and Clayton Carlin [defensive backs] is from Villanova."

Hofher wanted a staff with proven backgrounds and "good men who want to be here. If you have to beg them to come here, you need to move on to someone else."

Hofher will continue to try to poach recruits out of western Pennsylvania and Ohio, but looks to upstate New York, northern Pennsylvania and untapped Long Island and Philadelphia to be full of quality players who go unnoticed because of the lack of Division I-A programs in the northeast. Until Rutgers becomes credible long-term, there are only two high-level programs in the east that are north of the Pennsylvania turnpike—Syracuse and Boston College. And West Virginia's shift out of Pennsylvania and New Jersey will mean more high-ceiling players for all these schools. This is an opportunity for UB.

2001 SCHEDULE

Aug.	30	Rutgers
Sept.	8	@Bowling Geen
	15	@Army
	22	@Connecticut
	29	Central Michigan
Oct.	6	@Miami (Ohio)
	13	Marshall
	20	@Kent State
	27	@Eastern Michigan
Nov.	3	Ohio
	10	Akron

QUARTERBACKS

The buzzword of the spring when it came to quarterbacks was "communication," or more likely, the lack thereof as the candidates all struggled to take control in learning the new system. Hofher tried to get as much live action behind his quarterbacks and on film in the spring so that his staff would better be able to plan for summer practices.

The Bulls ran 372 plays from scrimmage during spring sessions, spent mainly at the Buffalo Bills' indoor facility to which UB has access much of the year.

The team also made it through the spring almost injury free. Dings have hampered the throwers in past years, but the top three made it through unscathed. Hofher thinks the three have similar skill sets, but senior **Joe Freedy** (6-2, 194) is the only one with any game action at the Division I-A level. Now a starter in 22 consecutive games, Freedy hurdled the rest of the depth chart because of injuries in '99 and has not looked back.

Freedy became just the fourth UB quarterback to top 2,000 yards in a season, and made the passing game one of the few bright spots in last year's offense. His completion percentage was good in 2000 (54.4 percent), but his decision-making (18 interceptions, 14 touchdowns) will have to improve some.

"They are similarly mobile and all have good throwing arms," Hofher said of his quarterbacks. "The difference will be how they deal with the new terms and language [of the offense], and how hard they work on their own to get there."

Freedy is the guy right now, but the future is probably a local redshirt freshman who impressed in the spring. **Randall Secky** (6-5, 215) has great feet to go along with great size and played high school ball locally at Maple Grove High School. While there, he was twice the state's Class D player of the year and threw for a record 33 touchdowns his junior year.

Secky seemed to catch on to the new offense fairly well in the spring and is listed even with Freedy on the post-spring depth chart.

Junior college transfer **Adam Johnson** (6-5, 210) showed up early as a sophomore last fall and redshirted in football before helping out the short-handed UB hoops team over the winter. Now a junior, the Chaffey (Calif.) Community College transfer is competent, but may not be in the long-term plans of the new staff. He was brought in as insurance last year based on the previous injury problems of recent Bulls quarterbacks. He has the strongest arm of the bunch and is a good decision-maker in the pocket.

There is little room for injuries here, with only three quarterbacks on the roster. UB did out-recruit Western Michigan for freshman **Jeff Powell** (6-3, 215) from Roosevelt High School in Wyandotte, Mich. Powell went through his 1,500-yard senior season without throwing an interception.

RUNNING BACKS

Though quarterback has the most experience, Hofher likes his talent at running back in the new offense. Though the group was ineffective over the first half of 2000, the backs averaged more than 196 yards per game in the last six games. This sort of production can continue with the budding depth at offensive line and the pack of backs trying to get on the field.

Sophomore **Marcus Dwarte** (5-6, 165) was the first freshman to lead the Bulls in rushing since 1994 and ran for 611 yards on an average of 4.7 yards per carry. The elusive Dwarte went for 329 of those yards in the final two games against Akron and Miami.

"He's very small, and shifty and excellent in the broken field," Hofher said.

But when the Bulls need more punch at the point of attack, Hofher can turn things over to the flashy senior skills of **Albert Grundy** (6-3, 230). Grundy was a junior college transfer from Valley Forge Junior College near Philadelphia, who scored four times on just 80 carries and totaled more than five yards per tote last fall.

Buffalo returns its top five ground gainers and will try to work in junior college transfer **Maurice Bradford** (5-11, 185), who got eligible over the winter after signing with the Bulls last season and practiced this spring. He is a former JUCO All-America pick and has excellent size and speed. To get him on the field, the coaching staff had Bradford work this spring at split end along with former running back **Bam McDonald** (5-9, 177).

Now a junior, McDonald was this team's starting tailback and fastest offensive player through the early season. But a game six injury against Bowling Green cut short his year. He takes his speed to the perimeter as well and ended the spring in the depth chart at receiver.

Senior **Derrick Gordon** (5-8, 203) will be in a battle for time at tailback or fullback after a 204-yard season last year. He is a compact, slashing runner who is also effective catching the ball.

"We have at least three pretty good backs, from big name schools," Hofher said.

Potentially, there are as many as three future tailbacks in the new class (not including Bradford). Odds are against any of them contributing this fall because of existing depth.

The Bulls have two very large fullbacks. Sophomore **Tom Shaughnessy** (5-11, 240) is the brother of last year's senior tight end Brandon Shaughnessy and tops the list of blockers here ahead of fellow sophomore **David Harvey-Bowen** (5-8, 232), a transfer from Division I-AA power Western Kentucky. Last year's top fullback has been moved to tight end.

WIDE RECEIVERS/TIGHT ENDS

Ten of the eleven most prolific pass-catchers from last year are back for 2001, with 167-of-189 receptions returning.

Hofher is so confident in this unit that he moved his second-leading receiver over to play free safety on the Bulls' defense.

Leading junior wideout **Andre Forde** (5-10, 206) is back with team highs in yards (590), touchdowns (six) and yards per catch (16.4). He tops the after-spring depth chart at split end. Forde was slowed in the spring by a pair of jammed thumbs, but he remains probably the strongest of the receiver group.

Behind him is sophomore **Rob Barber** (6-0, 199), who was invisible (five receptions, 45 yards) in 2000, but showed talent as a guy who could stretch the field this spring. The two refugees from running back, Bradford and McDonald (11 receptions in 2000) are here as well. McDonald could fill a role as a slot guy or third receiver like the similarly sized Ed Tillitz at Miami or Keith Warren at Ohio.

On the other side at flanker, sophomore **Zeke McKine** (5-9, 170) was a revelation last season whenever he touched the ball. The Hollywood, Fla., native suffered through three different injuries to put up 632 all-purpose yards and 32 catches in just nine games played. He scored twice through the air and will almost certainly return punts and kicks after averaging 21-yards per punt return in limited duty.

Junior backup **Dan Lindsay** (5-10, 190) is a prep teammate of McDonald, and caught seven passes last year. Other returnees include junior **Al Broccuto** (5-11, 176) and converted tailback **Ruben Vargas** (5-8, 194), a senior transfer from Delaware who is now third at flanker.

"We've got some guys with some great track times and will be interested to see what they have this summer," said Hofher, who is anxious to get involved a couple of redshirt freshmen who apprenticed last year.

This group is deep enough that the 33 receptions and four touchdowns of senior flanker **Dahnel Singfield** (6-0, 171) are headed to play free safety.

Back on offense, **Alvin Jennings** (6-1, 192) played prep ball at Harding High School in

Youngstown, Ohio and was a late signee last summer after qualifying academically. **Vaughn Welch** (5-10, 188) played high-level prep football in the WPIAL at Berwick (Pa.) High School. Both should play considerable minutes, along with one or more of the new freshmen.

Gabriel McClover (6-2, 210) has the best pedigree and best shot of helping this fall. He played his high school football in the Ft. Lauderdale area, and is another one of those guys with a "great track time," Hofher said. He and **Matt Kneuven** (6-2, 200) out of Cincinnati's Catholic League at LaSalle High School are both very tall and fast for the MAC.

At tight end, the Bulls lose their only senior star from 2000 in Brandon Shaughnessy (21 catches), but plug in their designated blocker at that spot from last year, junior **Chad Bartoszek** (6-6, 251). Bartoszek—a "good anchor out there on the edge," Hofher said—was a short-yardage specialist last fall as a blocker and receiver (six catches, two touchdowns).

"He can be a good player. He's got experience under his belt, he's a big target and athletic," Hofher said.

The new backup here is former fullback **Marvin Brereton** (6-2, 237), a senior from Mississauga, Ontario who averaged more than five yards per carry at fullback last fall. The only other listed tight end is sophomore **Jason Smalarz** (6-3, 245) who lettered last fall on special teams.

OFFENSIVE LINE

The offensive line at Buffalo was size-intensive, and Hofher is looking to change that some. You can be big in a good way or in a bad way, and Hofher wants more of the former. He started to get it in the spring.

"In January, we had 11 guys over 300 pounds," Hofher said. "By April we had four and by August I hope we're down to two. What I'm talking about is conditioning, strength and explosion, and that's where we needed to make a move."

Though nine players missed chunks of spring because of winter surgery, there were no major new injuries in the 15 practice sessions. The coach thought that was a good sign of the work the team put into its off-season workouts. Twenty-five guys lost a total of 333 pounds going into spring drills. They were ready.

Lighter and faster, the coach hopes this line is ready for the season. Two senior starters have departed, but two return, along with another who missed all of last season. This line should be better than the one that was the nation's most experienced in '99.

Demonstrating the depth here, Hofher has listed two players at each starting spot and will have nothing settled about a starting lineup until the week before that season opener with Rutgers.

Senior **John Nolan** (6-3, 270) is a returning starter at center and should be an anchor here after starting the final eight games last fall. Nolan played in the basketball-centric Jayhawk Conference at Fort Scott (Kansas) Junior College before transferring here last year. Redshirt freshman **Eric Weber** (6-5, 300) would have played last year at center or guard before breaking a leg in August. He's a local, from Canandaigua, N.Y.

Sophomore **Kevin Dunn** (6-1, 269) is here, too, along with redshirt freshman **William Paris** (6-3, 324), who projects out to guard eventually.

The guards are very experienced at left side and less so on the right. Left guard is a battle between seniors **Tim Hedges** (6-5, 307) and **Josh Stello** (6-2, 309). Hedges started the last eight games last fall, while Stello is a fifth-year player who missed last season with a torn ACL. He can fill in at guard and center, and even did a year as defensive tackle.

The right side guys are younger, but with high ceilings. Sophomore **Jeff Mills** (6-6, 305) is "developing," Hofher said, and will be in a dog-fight with Canton, Ohio, redshirt freshman **Dan Minocchi** (6-3, 290). Minocchi was probably the Bulls' most decorated line recruit last fall and played in the annual Big 33 All-Star Game between Ohio and Pennsylvania preps.

Junior **Matt Baniewicz** (6-0, 260) is the guy at right tackle for now and will compete with the larger senior **Brian Johnessee** (6-6, 328) for time here.

The left side is in younger hands with sophomore **Andy Avery** (6-6-6, 263) and redshirt freshman **Erik Zeppuhar** (6-3, 288) from Shaler High School in Pittsburgh. Avery makes the move here from the defensive line.

"Right now, it's a very big group, a very square group," Hofher said. "We've got some pretty good young players."

The wild card here might be junior **Alex Alvarez** (6-5, 290), who arrived early from Glendale (Calif.) Junior College for the spring and may interject himself at that right tackle slot.

The new freshman class includes three more linemen on the offensive side. **Zach Love** (6-5, 285) was a first-team all-state performer in Pennsylvania, blocking Strath Haven High School to back-to-back state titles and a 30-0 record the last two seasons.

"The game is physical, no matter what scheme you run- you cannot be finesse no matter your scheme," Hofher said. "Great lineman have to be pretty damned physical. They need to be tough-minded."

2000 STATISTICS

Rushing offense	131.2	75
Passing offense	191.3	78
Total offense	322.5	88
Scoring offense	16.1	102
Net Punting	29.6	107
Punt returns	12.0	27
Kickoff returns	15.9	109
Rushing defense	210.6	104
Passing efficiency defense	152.3	110
Total defense	428.1	101
Scoring defense	41.1	114
Turnover margin	-18	114

Last column is ranking among Division I-A teams.

KICKERS

This might be a sore spot for UB, though right now Hofher is fairly happy with the hand he's been dealt.

Last year, Buffalo didn't get into scoring position enough, and when it did, former kicker Scott Keller managed only six makes in 13 field-goal attempts, and the Bulls had two blocked.

This spring, Buffalo went with sophomore **Dallas Pelz** (5-11, 176), who has a lively leg and can also punt. Hofher said he kicked well under pressure on PATs and field goals. But there will be competition come fall, from signee **Michael Baker** (5-11, 185) of nearby Jamestown (N.Y.) High School. He is western New York's single-season scoring record holder for kickers, and knocked more than half his kickoffs for touchbacks as a senior.

DEFENSIVE LINE

This has been a flexible roster over the last few seasons as players have switched positions and even offense for defense frequently. That's the case again this year as the new staff is looking to continue last year's excellent pass rush but get some new tacklers on the field to replace the top three players who have departed from the total tackles list.

This line returns real strength inside, but needs help on the ends where the changes have been made. Now at defensive end, how about senior honorable mention All-MAC linebacker **Duane Williams** (6-2, 240). The former junior college transfer led the squad with nine quarterback sacks and turned in 53 tackles as an outside rusher, to go along with three interceptions. Probably the team's best defensive player, the burly Williams joined Johnson in the winter on the UB hoops team, where he was listed as a 6-5, 250 forward. Despite being absolutely lousy on offense, he was the only player all year capable of truly deterring Ohio's All-MAC power forward Brandon Hunter from doing damage around the bucket. How much he'll get done against larger offensive tackles is unclear, but physically he looks the part.

Sophomore **Terrance Dawson** (6-4, 275) went west for a year to San Francisco Junior College before returning closer to his Youngstown roots. He could project down to tackle in the future if he can't get time playing time behind Williams.

At the other side, fellow linebacker **Chris Shelly** (6-1, 230) moves down to end in this off-set 4-3 defensive front. While undersized, Shelly was the "most exciting lineman of the spring," in Hofher's opinion after working in the past as a weak-side backer. Injuries hampered him to under 30 tackles after an outstanding year in '99 with 89 stops and three forced fumbles.

Prep school grad **Anthony Andriano** (6-2, 230) arrived early for spring drills from Milford (Conn.) Academy and will be right there behind Shelly to provide depth here, alongside former pass rush specialist **Jamie Guerra** (6-3, 246), who comes off of shoulder surgery in consecutive seasons. Sophomore **Lorenzo Jones** (6-0, 256) also projects to the depth at end.

Instant help might come from junior college transfer **Obadiah Harris** (6-3, 230), a talented edge rusher who ended up here after committing to Illinois and West Virginia, and doing prep school and junior college classes at Valley Forge. From Chillicothe, Ohio, Harris was a national Top 100 recruit a few years ago before falling off the recruiting radar.

Inside, senior **Bob Dzvonick** (6-1, 260) plays over the nose and is a guy who plays hard out of habit, much like former All-MAC tackle Andy Aracri at Miami. He doesn't have a lot of natural ability, but he never quits on a play.

Behind him is sophomore **Marcus Clarett** (6-1, 300)— another top athlete out of Harding High School in Youngstown—who was one of only two freshmen to play last year in Cirbus' redshirt-heavy plan.

At the defensive tackle spot, angling over an offensive guard, Williams' junior college teammate **Omari Jordan** (6-6, 316) should get the starts. The senior from Detroit played limited minutes last year, but is physically the equal of any MAC interior rusher except for Ryan Terry at Miami.

Redshirt freshmen **Casey Russell** (6-1, 285), **Michael Nguti** (6-0, 313) and **Craig Johnson** (6-1, 299) are all locals from Western New York looking for their first taste of playing time behind Dzvonick and Jordan.

LINEBACKERS

This must be a decent group if Hofher is willing to move Williams and Shelly down low. The faces are pretty new, with those two shifted and only senior **Brandon Jordan** (5-10, 210) back to his starting slot at outside. Jordan put up just 37 tackles last fall in ten games. His backup is walk-on junior **Jason Montanez** (5-11, 240) who really caught the attention of coaches in the spring and showed up in awesome condition.

Size is a concern for Hofher here.

"Small guys at linebacker aren't bad, if they're great tacklers and tough at heart," Hofher said. "But if you've got small guys, they'd better be awesome."

In the middle, the staff loves redshirt freshman **Rodney Morris** (6-0, 225) out of Pahokee, Fla. They think he will be their starter at middle linebacker and a defensive captain for four years, because he moves so well in space and changes direction like a back.

Freshman **Hank Pirowski** (5-11, 195) was listed as the backup in spring, though the injured sophomore **Lamar Wilcher** (6-1, 234) is the real depth here. Wilcher played more and more as the season got longer, with six of his 17 tackles being for losses.

At the other outside spot, sophomore **Demetrius Austrum** (6-1, 226) ended the spring at the front of the line, but has only three games of experience from 2000.

Former safety **Bobby Johnson** (6-1, 205) is a senior from California who may be mature enough to step right in this season after missing the spring with surgery. And junior **Ryan Buttles** (6-1, 228) had a "very busy spring," Hofher said, cleaning up messes at outside backer as well.

This is the least-experienced unit on a very young team and could be a year-long headache because this defense lost four of its top five tacklers. Buffalo needs Harris to be immediate help at an outside spot or hope for contributions from one of two linebacker signees from south Florida. Or Andriano could come back up to a two-point stance to help at outside.

DEFENSIVE BACKS

Hofher has some playmakers at corner, a veteran who could be All-MAC at free safety and a new face at strong.

From Cincinnati, senior free safety **Craig Rohlfs** (5-10, 192) is a candidate to lead the team in tackles again after missing most of the 2000 season. Persistent shoulder problems have hindered him considerably since he should have been an All-MAC safety in '99. He is now completely healthy, and may be the smallest backup long snapper in America.

Ex-receiver Singfield moves over from the offense for his senior year and is technically behind Rohlfs on the depth chart, though he will probably be the first guy off the bench in a nickel situation this fall. He is exceptionally fast, but how he reads the run would be a question.

At strong, the coaches like the progress of redshirt freshman **J.J. Gibson** (5-9, 175). From Buffalo, Gibson is not big enough, but is an exceptional one-on-one tackler who Hofher said could make up for a lot. Quebec junior **Youdlain Marcellus** (5-9, 196) is of a similar mold and both could be pretty good by year's end.

The corners were at least competitive last year, and were helped by en excellent pass rush. They may have a little longer to have to cover this fall, which could expose holes.

Sophomore **Mark Graham** (6-0, 184) has three years left, and is the Bulls' third-leading returning tackler with 38 and three interceptions. He has a nose for the ball, and put up those numbers while not starting until week eight.

Behind him is a pair of redshirt freshmen. **Terek Henderson** (5-9, 170) from New Jersey is looking for his first game experience. So is **Darren Hicks** (5-9, 165) from Columbus, Ohio, but he missed the spring with injuries.

At the other side, junior **Mike Lambert** (5-8, 195) has proven himself as the Bulls' second-best man-to-man player.

PUNTERS

Pelz is the punter right now, though he again has no game experience kicking or punting. UB got only 29.7 net yards per punt last fall. Pelz had better be ready to be busy. Buffalo punted 69 times last year. The only other punter on the roster is sophomore **Pras Narasimhan** (6-2, 195) from Moorestown, N.J. Receiver Barber is also listed here as an emergency punter.

SPECIAL TEAMS

Kicking and punting will both have completely new faces hitting the ball this fall. But there is good news on the return units. There's no doubting the speed of McKine or Singfield on the punt return; those two averaged a combined 15 yards per return in limited opportunities last fall.

Those two will combine with Forde and possibly Bradford to return kicks. While no one expects the numbers put up from '96-'99 by Drew Haddad, this part of the game should be better than the league average.

Hofher was very pleased with senior long snapper **Kevin McCarthy** (5-10, 206). Freedy and Barber will hold for field goals.

RECRUITING CLASS

UB moved quickly to hire Hofher and he paid quick dividends by putting together a quality staff and getting on the phones during the dead period in December. Needs were filled at several positions, though the need at linebacker is most pressing and how the freshmen fit here will be key.

There are a lot of places in the east that grow Division I-A-quality players who end up at places like Delaware or Villanova. Buffalo can cherry-pick some of these guys from the top levels of I-AA. Detroit, Philadelphia, Youngstown and central Pennsylvania appear to be the places UB will try to mine in addition to western New York.

"It's no different here than anywhere else," Hofher said, trying to deflect how hard building the program at UB may be. "You need guys [players and coaches] with a solid approach to school, a competitive and sound plan, and one that complements all three units on the field."

"Four years ago, Western [Michigan] was 2-9, and since they've had the best four years in the history of the school. [Ohio] was 0-11, and [Jim] Grobe and his staff did a great job of changing things there. It can be done here. There are goals and lofty goals. The next milestone is .500 for a year, then some consistent level of success, and after that, compete and win the league."

BLUE RIBBON ANALYSIS

OFFENSE	C-
SPECIAL TEAMS	D
DEFENSE	D+
INTANGIBLES	C-

A lot of folks in Buffalo think the rug got pulled out on Cirbus a little early. But that's a moot point now for Hofher, who gets to work with the players Cirbus has recruited the last few years. There are stars here and there at some positions, but just not enough depth to win the battle yet in the trenches. It's coming on the offensive line and is already there at running backs.

But it's going to be hard for this defense to be as good as last year's less-than-award-winning effort unless it can find linebackers or a strong safety to help make up for the hundreds of tackles that left with the senior class.

A former quarterback and head coach at Cornell, Hofher knows this neck of the woods and how to make it work for him. Like Syracuse, it's a cold place with great practice facilities. Like Cornell, he has to worry about academics.

Luckily, Hofher is not handicapped by a terrible schedule. Rutgers, Army and Connecticut will all be favored to beat UB. But they are games the Bulls should not be blown out of by any stretch. How they perform there will be key to whether this team has the confidence to steal games from lower-division MAC teams such as Eastern Michigan and Kent. Just like last year, getting two to four wins would be phenomenal.

(R.C.)

2000 RESULTS

Syracuse	L	7-63	0-1
Rutgers	L	0-59	0-2
Connecticut	L	21-24	0-3
Bowling Green	W	20-17	1-3
Marshall	L	14-47	1-4
Ohio	L	20-42	1-5
Ball State	L	35-44	1-6
Northern Illinois	L	10-73	1-7
Kent State	W	20-17	2-7
Akron	L	14-49	2-8
Miami (Ohio)	L	16-17	2-9

Central Michigan

LOCATION	**Mount Pleasant, MI**
CONFERENCE	**Mid-American (West)**
LAST SEASON	**2-9 (.182)**
CONFERENCE RECORD	**1-4 (6th)**
OFFENSIVE STARTERS RETURNING	**7**
DEFENSIVE STARTERS RETURNING	**9**
NICKNAME	**Chippewas**
COLORS	**Maroon & Gold**
HOME FIELD	**Kelly/Shorts Stadium (30,199)**
HEAD COACH	**Mike DeBord (Manchester ('78)**
RECORD AT SCHOOL	**2-9 (1 year)**
CAREER RECORD	**2-9 (1 year)**
ASSISTANTS	

John Milligan (Michigan '90)
Defensive Coordinator/Outside Linebackers
Butch Jones (Ferris State '90)
Offensive Coordinator/Running Backs
Jim Schulte (Central Michigan '74)
Defensive Line/Assistant Head Coach
George Ricumstrict (Central Michigan '90)
Inside Linebackers
Jason Carr (Michigan '95)
Wide Receivers
Plas Presnell (Michigan State '73)
Tight Ends
Harold Goodwin (Michigan'96)
Offensive Line
Scot Loeffler (Michigan '97)
Quarterbacks
Curt Mallory (Michigan '90)
Defensive Backs

TEAM WINS (last 5 yrs.)	**5-2-6-4-2**
FINAL RANK (last 5 yrs.)	**99-110-106-110-112**
2000 FINISH	**Lost to Northern Illinois in regular-season finale.**

COACH AND PROGRAM

You are not going to get too fancy with second-year Central Michigan head coach Mike DeBord.

In a league now inundated with the offensive flavor of the week, the "spread," DeBord last year tried to hunker down and bust you in the mouth with the run and mix in the occasional smart pass.

DeBord ran the offensive show at Michigan before getting the call from coaching legend and CMU athletic director Herb Deromedi. And he believes in playing the kind of mistake-free offensive ball the Wolverines did with guys like Brian Griese at the controls.

While the personnel may be a little different on the Happy Hill, DeBord knows what he wants to accomplish and how to get there.

"I had a great situation, probably the best you could have in the whole country without being a head coach," DeBord said. "But you come here, it's not a hard sell. They're committed to being serious about football and the situation is wonderful."

Ninety yards of indoor turf, a quality weight room and a refurbishing of Kelly/Shorts Stadium make the school 70 miles north of Lansing a pretty solid stop on the MAC tour. Other than the harsh winter that seems to afflict nearly every MAC campus, there's a lot to sell kids on being a Chippewa.

This program had stopped achieving the last few seasons, as rival Western Michigan and Toledo stepped to the front of the MAC line. And changes needed to be made. But the problems here are minor compared to programs like Kent State, Eastern Michigan and Buffalo. Getting the team back on track should take only a couple years.

In addition to a new commitment to weight training, DeBord has the fire back in his players. To quote graduated safety and top tackler Brian Leigeb, "we're fired up about being fired up!"

Being fired up wasn't enough in several games last year, as the Chips' lack of size in the defensive trenches made it tough to compete against the MAC's top rushing attacks at Ohio and Northern Illinois. But an exceptional effort in a home win over Western punctuated the final portion of the season with a glimpse at what could be, and kept the Broncos winless at Kelly/Shorts for a decade.

"We won that game in the fourth quarter," said DeBord, whose team led by 14-10 at the half. "I thought 'Here we go, they're gonna put it in high gear.' But then we put on a long drive and marched the field for a TD. And the defense finished well—we all played with responsibility."

The Chips hit this spring and hit a lot, taking as many full-contact practices as the NCAA allows in the 15 spring sessions. DeBord said it was time for fundamentals and hitting in large doses, to build mental and physical toughness.

"We're still lacking some things, and need to work on strength and size and conditioning," he said. "We're close but not there yet. But the key is to see some confidence, to create that team ego."

2001 SCHEDULE

Aug.	30	Eastern Kentucky
Sept.	8	@Michigan State
	15	@Boise State
	22	Toledo
	29	@Buffalo
Oct.	13	Ohio
	20	@Marshall
	27	Northern Illinois
Nov.	3	@Ball State
	10	Eastern Michigan
	17	@Western Michigan

QUARTERBACKS

Sophomore **Derrick Vickers** (6-1, 185) returns at quarterback after passing for 1,059 yards in 2000. From Florida, Vickers is very mobile and always a threat on the rollout. He will also have more chances to tuck it and run this fall if CMU runs some of the four-receiver sets seen in the spring.

"He is so much better than he was last fall," DeBord said. "If he improves maybe 10 percent more over the summer, and follows the plays, he can help us win. He needs to play smart, like a Griese, and not make mistakes."

The Chips are fairly short-handed behind Vickers. Junior **Derek Gorney** (6-2, 198) is a smart backup who saw very limited duty in 2000 (1-for-3 passing). Redshirt freshman **Jeff Perry** (6-1, 185), who's from California, was a late signee last summer.

The next CMU quarterback may be in the recruiting class.

Freshman **Kent Liddell-Smith** (6-5, 200) is the all-time passing yardage leader at Start High School in Toledo. His mix of size and mobility should work well with DeBord's versatile offensive look.

RUNNING BACKS

"We were terrible at running the football last year and we were terrible at stopping the run," DeBord said. "And we'll spend a lot of time working on those areas before next season."

Well said. Not only did CMU lack a 1,000-yard rusher, no Chippewa back cracked the 500-yard barrier. The Chips barely got into four digits as a team (1,016 yards) on the ground. Still, the top three rushers do return, starting with the injury-prone junior **Vince Webber** (5-9, 205), who managed 458 yards and three touchdowns, both team highs. Webber has broken his jaw twice in the last year, knocking him out of game and spring action.

Junior **Robbie Mixon** (5-11, 185) filled in for him part of 2000, running for 285 yards in only five games. DeBord said Mixon has gotten stronger in the off-season, though he still could be challenged by swift sophomores **Kenan Lawhorne** (5-11, 195) and **Terrence Jackson** (6-0, 210). From Florida and New Jersey, respectively, the two are powerful upright runners and can win playing time with a good summer. Jackson also has the build to play at fullback should the coaches want this pair to play together in the two-back sets.

"Our program is not at a point where we can say a guy is the starter after spring ball," DeBord said. "We're looking for competition at each position."

Behind Jackson at fullback is fellow sophomore **Kyle Tefelski** (6-2, 220). Freshman **Lance Gailliard** (5-11, 185) is a star of DeBord's second recruiting class and played Cass Tech in Detroit.

WIDE RECEIVERS/TIGHT ENDS

The top two outside receivers are gone, leaving sophomore **Steve Messam** (5-9, 175) as the most experienced pass catcher. He pulled in 22 catches last fall, but a post-spring look at the depth chart shows him second string at flanker. There is one junior, **Rob Turner** (6-3, 200), in the mix at wideout, and a gaggle of sophomores—**Dante McKnight** (5-10, 187), **Willie Hill** (5-11, 180) and **Rod Means** (6-3, 192).

All will be counted on to step in on a new-look CMU depth chart, which features three receivers and a tight end. Trouble is, this quartet was around for only 11 combined catches last fall.

Turner is the possession receiver who needs to take his great practice skills and turn them into performance. Hill is the speed merchant here, but DeBord will need help from some of the four receiver recruits in the new class, all of whom will have a chance to play.

At tight end, sophomore **Adam Supianoski** (6-3, 235) is the top candidate for playing time, despite the fact that neither he nor backup sophomore **Drew Donaldson** (6-4, 215) caught a pass last year. These guys will have to work hard not to be just placeholders for the three ends in the incoming group of freshmen.

Caleb Anthony (6-4, 255) was an all-state end at Ludington High School in Michigan. **David Kurzen** (6-5, 235) did the same at Tuslaw High School in Massillon, Ohio.

This offense will obviously be changing some, with a 12-man depth chart showing that the Chips will run from one- and two-back sets this time around.

OFFENSIVE LINE

Central might not have had any all-stars in its backfield in 2000, but the lessons learned in trying to make space for last fall's Chips should pay off in the trenches and on the stat sheet in 2001. What was a real weakness should now be a strength.

"They're a lot bigger and more physical than when we got here," DeBord said. "Now this will be a part of the real strength of our offense."

The listed sizes for these guys are enormous by MAC or any standards at 6-5, and 302 pounds on average for the 10 linemen on the two-deep roster.

Senior **Matt Brayton** (6-7, 320) is the anchor at left tackle and is a serious candidate for All-MAC honors. He'll need to improve as a run blocker to get there. His backup is mammoth sophomore **Tom Langton** (6-7, 315).

Left guard was a spring toss-up between sophomore **Derek McLaughlin** (6-5, 295) and junior **Paul Breiger** (6-4, 305).

The center, **Anders Hill** (6-5, 285), is the other senior in the deep group at offensive line. Redshirt freshman **Eric Ghiaciuc** (6-5, 290) is the snapper of the future and should be a fixture along with the rest of the youth on the right side of the line for a while.

Junior **Kyle Croskey** (6-3, 310) is being pressed at right guard by redshirt freshman, **Brandon Pitzer** (6-3, 285), and another first year player will start on the outside.

Redshirt freshman **Adam Kieft** (6-7, 300) "has not yet even scratched the surface of his talents," said his coach, and is the new rock at right tackle. Fifth-year senior **Eric Dumont** (6-6, 315) provides depth here, but could be pressed by another of the three prep line recruits arriving over the summer.

Freshman **Jeff Jenerou** (6-8, 290) is from Manistique, Mich., and projects very well at tackle.

2000 STATISTICS

Rushing offense	92.4	104
Passing offense	179.1	86
Total offense	271.5	107
Scoring offense	12.5	112
Net Punting	32.1	91
Punt returns	11.3	33
Kickoff returns	16.4	107
Rushing defense	267.6	114
Passing efficiency defense	108.4	33
Total defense	417.4	95
Scoring defense	34.2	102
Turnover margin	-8	87

Last column is ranking among Division I-A teams.

KICKERS

Central didn't score enough points last fall and the meager total of four field goals on the year made things a little hot under the seat of last fall's kickers. They combined to go-4-of-8 and are still on the roster, though DeBord spent the spring talking up redshirt freshman **Josh Ignace** (5-8, 170) from Grand Blanc, Mich.

But the coach spent a grant to get a full-time kicker and hopes freshman **Mike Gruzwalski** (5-8, 166) can step in this season after being an all-state player in Michigan at Eisenhower High School. He comes off an 80-point prep season.

DEFENSIVE LINE

Last fall, this unit was too small, too slow and not physical enough. Physical is a word you'll hear from DeBord or even opposing players who remarked of CMU players asking them to "ease up" late in games.

So, these guys got the brunt of the weight room work from conditioning coach Denny Starnes over the winter.

Playing the nose requires a player to be a team guy who knows he won't get many chances for glory. Junior **Marvin Smith** (6-1, 265) is a "great anchor for this line and a great student-athlete," DeBord said. Smith is a consistent player who plays over top the center in a "2" technique in this offset 4-4 defense.

Senior **Josh Skeel** (6-1, 265) is the backup at the nose and also needs to get bigger to handle the rigors of the MAC schedule.

With Smith at nose guard, junior **Dominic Mancini** (6-3, 270) moves over to defensive tackle. That's more of a one-gap position in the 4-3, and he will usually line up over the outside shoulder of an offensive guard and try to angle his way through the line. Sophomore **Jay Davidson** (6-4, 265) played at this spot last year as a freshman and turned in 16 tackles.

The ends must develop pocket pressure in a 4-4 and DeBord saw one of last year's bright spots, sophomore **Ike Ajoku** (6-2, 245), step up in spring and get to the top of the depth chart at end. The Brooklyn native passed up junior **Matt Reynolds** (6-3, 260) with a great spring; Reynolds is the team's No. 3 returning tackler.

At the other side, junior **Cullen Jenkins** (6-3, 245) continued his progress after a 49-tackle season with eight stops for a loss. Sophomore **Matt Wohlgemuth** (6-5, 240) played some in his first fall in Mount Pleasant and definitely has the frame to add more weight and contribute here. Central signed only two new defensive linemen over the winter; both ends who need to get bigger. **Morgan Sheppard** (6-4, 235) was another Michigan all-stater at Brandon High School in Ortonville.

LINEBACKERS

DeBord does have some good linebackers at his disposal, if that undersized line can keep the guards or center from getting off the blocks. Middle linebacker **Darvin Lewis** (6-3, 225) is a junior star-in-waiting from Detroit. Lewis is the team's top returning tackler with 113, and should improve on that total as this defense tries to shift more responsibility to the linebackers. Leigeb was the team's top tackler for four years from a safety spot, something the coaches don't want to see happen again if possible. Redshirt freshman **Anthony Tyus** (5-10, 215) is the apprentice here and played prep ball just more than an hour south near Lansing.

Senior **James Westrich** (6-1, 215) is probably the best Chippewa against the run and plays on the weak side of the formation. He gets to operate in a lot of space and is an excellent open-field tackler. Sophomore **Ed Hillery** (6-1, 205) is the backup here. He had 21 stops last fall to go with 55 for Westrich.

At the "drop" or cover linebacker spot, a converted safety resides on the strong side of the eight-man front. Senior **Finley Carter** (5-10, 180) had 41 tackles and an interception last fall and brings speed, if not enough size down to the box. Speedy redshirt freshman **James King** (6-1, 190) will try to learn the position but will have trouble winning playing time over Carter.

In reality, the safety spot formerly occupied by Leigeb (147 tackles) is much like the rover position in the Marshall defense and plays right up there with the linebackers. DeBord calls it the "Buck" linebacker. The replacement for some of the 242 stops of **Rodrico Epps** and Leigeb has enormous shoes to occupy and the expectations for redshirt freshman **Jon Nelson** (6-1, 195) have been set high.

"He's playing toward a higher level, because he knows what's been there before," DeBord said. "But we won't know for sure until we hit the field in August."

Nelson will be playing his first game when the season opens with Eastern Kentucky. Sophomore **Derrick Wallace** (6-0, 210) is the other part of this equation and had 17 tackles while playing in just four games in 2000.

DEFENSIVE BACKS

With two of the "linebackers" in the 4-4 look just being oversized safeties, the free safety will get pretty lonely back here and have the responsibility of making the play call for the defensive secondary.

This position is left to redshirt freshmen. Converted linebacker **Joe Ballard** (6-4, 205) and **Ron Bartell** (6-3, 190) both have zero game action in Division I-A and were alternating at this spot all spring.

Team speed here has been a worry, so look for immediate help from the 25-player recruiting class, which includes six defensive backs. Safeties are the "erasers" that make everyone else look good.

If there is a need for help at safety or outside linebacker, there isn't one in the starting lineup at corner.

Seniors **Tedaro France** (6-0, 185) and **Wayne Dudley** (6-0, 185) are both fifth-year players who will help make the job of the safety that much easier. Both appear on the front of the CMU spring media packet and are legitimate candidates for All-MAC honors again this fall. France had 30 tackles and a team-high five interceptions and is the best man-coverage player on the team.

Dudley is in a fight at left corner with former safety Epps (5-10, 180), yet another fifth-year player who notched most of his 95 tackles last fall at safety. Both would start for a majority of MAC teams. Epps is a former walk-on. Dudley added 46 tackles and an interception.

Redshirt freshman **Richard Kiel** (5-10, 180) is the apprentice at either corner spot. But he'll need to watch his back for those six new backs, two from Ohio, two from Michigan, one from Illinois and one from Quebec.

PUNTERS

Sophomore **Brian Brandt** (6-2, 200) punted well as a freshman, stopping 16 kicks inside the opposing 20-yard line and averaging almost 40 yards per punt. He did have plenty of opportunities (87 punts).

Backup quarterback **Grant Arnoldick** (6-4, 215) is listed as the second punter.

SPECIAL TEAMS

Special teams? They are certainly something of a question right now beyond the punter spot. DeBord is expecting a lot from a freshman kicker. Backup quarterback Gorney is the holder on kicks, along with Brandt. The long-snappers are also both untested redshirt freshmen—**Josh Reardon** (6-1, 220) and **R.J. Bentley** (6-0, 220)—which could be a recipe for problems.

The top two kick returners are departed, with Dudley and Messam having only 12 returns between them last year. Look for the running back Jenkins to get a look here. Punt return is very much up for grabs, with slot receiver Rob Turner as the only returnee with any real experience. One of the speedy athlete recruits in the defensive backfield could be the answer here.

RECRUITING CLASS

After Central Michigan brought in a 23-man class last season, more attrition opened things up enough for DeBord to sign 25 players this year. The class is local (15 from Michigan) and built for a purpose. In addition to the six defensive backs, CMU signed four receivers, three tight ends, three offensive linemen, three linebackers and two defensive ends.

This was a team that needed speed and added it. The only gap seems to be more size on the defensive line, which was a real issue last fall. But it matches nicely with last year's signees, who DeBord said have worked out well so far.

"It's a heck of a class [2000]," he said. "They have great chemistry, work well together, and are very tight. They want to do something special here."

"We went out and got skill kids this year [2001]. And we've started to build on the interior lines. I want to have a group that we can believe in and win with in years three through five. This program is in the process of getting back to where it was."

In addition to the spots of more glaring need, junior college recruit **Jovan Clarke** (6-3, 230) may be able to break into the rotation at linebacker. From Highland (Kansas) Community College, Clarke runs well and has better size than most of the Chips at those spots.

BLUE RIBBON ANALYSIS

OFFENSE	D+
SPECIAL TEAMS	D+
DEFENSE	C
INTANGIBLES	C+

The letter grades aren't negative, but just realistic. Programs that are in the rebuilding stage are not good on paper, because they either look bad in print or are unproven on the field. Coaches in this league have no doubt that DeBord will be the guy to bring CMU back to some prominence in the MAC West.

But right now, even with a solid offensive line, there's not yet a star to power that offense. Maybe he'll appear this fall. Ditto for a defense that is pretty good on the second and third levels, but still too small inside.

This program is growing, both in the weight room and in the win column. But like Joe Novak had to do, the Chips will have to enjoy their bright spots with pride and take some lumps again this fall. Good things come to programs that build with the long haul in mind, like at NIU and Ohio.

Right now, this group should beat out Eastern Michigan, and a stellar performance will have the

Chips fighting with Ball State and NIU to tug at the heels of the top three in the West.

How quickly the players adjust to the position changes on both sides of the ball will determine the level of success for 2001.

(R.C.)

2000 RESULTS

Purdue	L	0-48	0-1
Akron	W	17-7	1-1
Wyoming	L	10-31	1-2
Boise State	L	10-47	1-3
Toledo	L	0-41	1-4
Kent State	L	21-24	1-5
Ohio	L	3-55	1-6
Ball State	L	34-38	1-7
Eastern Michigan	L	15-31	1-8
Western Michigan	W	21-17	2-8
Northern Illinois	L	6-40	2-9

Eastern Michigan

LOCATION Ypsilanti, MI
CONFERENCE Mid-American (West)
LAST SEASON 3-8 (.273)
CONFERENCE RECORD 2-3 (t-3rd)
OFFENSIVE STARTERS RETURNING 5
DEFENSIVE STARTERS RETURNING 7
NICKNAME Eagles
COLORS Dark Green & White
HOME FIELD Rynearson Stadium (30,200)
HEAD COACH Jeff Woodruff (Kent '79)
RECORD AT SCHOOL 3-8 (2 years)
CAREER RECORD 3-8 (2 years)
ASSISTANTS
Pete Alamar (Calif. Lutheran '83)
Offensive Coordinator/Offensive Line
Cary Conklin (Washington '98)
Quarterbacks
Mike Cummings (Buffalo '94)
Defensive Line/Recruiting Coordinator
Bob Diaco (Iowa '95)
Running Backs
John Dignan (Michigan State '94)
Inside Linebackers
Billy Harris (Michigan '70)
Defensive Coordinator/Defensive Backs
Scott Schroeder (Iowa '91)
Offensive Tackles/Tight Ends
Mark Woodson (Wayne State '83)
Wide Receivers
Tommie Thigpen (North Carolina '94)
Defensive Backs
TEAM WINS (last 5 yrs.) 3-4-3-4-3
FINAL RANK (last 5 yrs.) 100-105-111-111-109
2000 FINISH Lost to Western Michigan in regular-season finale.

COACH AND PROGRAM

Jeff Woodruff is between a rock and the proverbial hard place. Everyone has to get that first head-coaching job to move up the ladder. But landing in Ypsilanti goes in the book as one of the toughest assignments in Division I-A. This program has one winning record in the last decade and one of the weakest fan and media followings anywhere.

Sure, they're in the Detroit environs, which you would think might help the coverage and recruiting. That might be true if the mighty University of Michigan wasn't more than a few miles down the road. Back when EMU was just a teacher's college, this wasn't a major consideration. But for a generally non-competitive Division I-A program to be in this big a shadow from Ann Arbor, suffice to say that makes it tough on a head coach.

So, Woodruff can hope to get this group back to adequacy and that's about it. Toledo and Western Michigan look like they will be the leaders in the MAC for a good while. But he can catch the rest of the West, and with some creative scheduling and imagination on offense, this can happen pretty soon.

Woodruff has a MAC pedigree in his family (he's the son-in-law of former Kent State and Washington coach Don James) and is used to the sometimes difficult climes of the league in weather and recruiting. He may not have been EMU's first choice last summer, but his understanding of the MAC may put him ahead of sexier candidates who didn't get the job.

The Kent State grad coached quarterbacks, then coordinated the offense for James at Washington en route to three Rose Bowls and a 1991 national title. After two years back on the high school circuit in Arizona, he went to work on the staff of Dick Tomey at the University of Arizona. His team will continue with a single back and will show more sets with three or even four wideouts, looking a little more like Marshall than last fall.

"As a staff, we only know of one way to do this," Woodruff said. "We wanted to improve a lot of things—a better team chemistry, academics, work in the eight room. This is to be a ground-up restoration of a program."

Eastern won its first game of the season at Connecticut, lost seven in a row and then won two of its last three at home over Central Michigan and Northern Illinois. Those two wins against MAC West teams occurred in front of a combined crowd of about 14,000, which first-hand attendees would describe as a very generous estimate.

"We just have to win, that's all there is to it," the coach said. "People will then jump on the bandwagon and say they've been there since day one. I've seen it, I've been there."

There is a lot wrong here, but there is less to fix than there was a year ago when Woodruff arrived to find too many undisciplined and weak players who weren't on pace to graduate—ever. He's working on those issues closer to the field. All he can do in this equation is try to win. The guys in suits who hired him need to find a way to make EMU sports relevant again for media, fans and television, or risk the rumbles about the MAC dropping a team or two becoming earthquakes in Washtenaw County.

2001 SCHEDULE

Sept.	1	Southeast Missouri State
	8	@Maryland
	15	@Akron
	22	Indiana State
	29	Western Michigan
Oct.	6	@Connecticut
	13	Ball State
	27	Buffalo
Nov.	3	@Northern Illinois
	10	@Central Michigan
	17	@Toledo

QUARTERBACKS

Woodruff had a senior who made the learning curve a little flatter last fall in senior star Walt Church. A starter for three seasons, Church gave the new head coach at least one part of the offense he could rely on when he arrived in Ypsilanti. Church graduated owning virtually every EMU passing record after taking over for Charlie Batch.

So who is left with experience? Well, virtually no one. Junior **Troy Edwards** (6-2, 199) is 36-of-59 for his career, but completed only seven passes last year and started his only game in '99. He's another smart quarterback in the Church mold who takes his time and goes through his reads very carefully. He won't hurt a defense with his feet, and can make good throws if he gets time. Arm strength might be a question, as there are a lot of hard outs and 6-yard inside slants to throw in this high-percentage passing offense.

Junior **Jeff Crooks** (6-3, 210) is a transfer from Fullerton (Calif.) Junior College and led all California junior college quarterbacks with 2,293 passing yards and 18 touchdowns. He adds the dimension of rushing, piling up more than 500 yards last season. He enrolled early and was with the team for spring drills.

"It's really a competition between those two," Woodruff said. "Both are mobile and can throw on the run, which is different than the situation we had with [Church]. Crooks does have more experience as a scrambling quarterback."

Redshirt freshmen make up the next level of the depth chart. **Collin Carey** (6-3, 193) needs to bulk up and work on his arm strength some. **Chinedu Okoro** (6-2, 190) played high school ball at Morgan Park High School in Chicago and was a nice surprise in the spring game, throwing the best deep ball and out pattern and even getting downfield to help block on running plays. His senior year he threw 22 touchdowns to just four interceptions and led his school to the city title game.

Only one other quarterback will be added in the fall. **Kainoa Akina** (6-1, 185) was an all-state pick in Arizona and the son of Arizona assistant coach Duane Akina. Tucson was Woodruff's last stop (running backs coach) before getting the call to EMU.

The quarterbacks coach is a good one with pretty fair name recognition. Cary Conklin led the University of Washington to much of its success while Woodruff was there before vesting his NFL pension with the Washington Redskins.

RUNNING BACKS

Eastern was one of the worst rushing teams in America before Woodruff got here last year (909 yards in '99). Things improved a little in 2000, but not enough—1,047 yards was the tally, thanks to the difficulty in finding a feature back on this roster and an offensive line plagued with injuries.

While the numbers weren't much better, the Eagles did find their feature back of the future in sophomore **Ashantti Watson** (5-11, 185). Recruited as an athlete and expected to play defensive back, Watson played all 11 games and gained 353 yards on 85 carries (4.2 yards per carry), scored four touchdowns, caught 16 passes and returned 10 punts and nine kickoffs. He is one of the few real difference-makers on the roster and will be on the field as often as possible this fall. He's a sparkplug and has a great first step like Michael Turner at Northern Illinois.

"He did very well for a true freshman," Woodruff said. "His 40 time and everything have improved, just like almost everyone on this squad."

Woodruff may add a late junior college qualifier over the summer, but after Watson, it's really anyone's guess. Junior **Rick Schutt** (5-9, 182) ended the spring as the No. 2 back, but has exactly two career carries in two years spent mainly on coverage teams. With the exception of a couple of full-time receivers who have slot reverses to their credit, no other running back who returns had a carry last year.

Junior **Ime Akpan** (6-0, 220) is a transfer from Youngstown State who did prep school at Fork

Union (Va.) Military Academy. He tore an ACL late in spring drills and will miss the season. Junior **Chris Reynolds** (6-0, 250) is sitting out this year after transferring from Indiana, where he was a fullback. Reynolds played his prep ball at Pershing High School in Detroit and is part of a trickle of Hoosier players heading to MAC teams; that might become a deluge if IU can't come up with a winning record this year and head coach Cam Cameron gets fired.

There is a need for immediate depth here, more than any other position on this team. Five of the recruits played some running back in high school and **Jerome Henderson** (5-8, 170) was stolen out of MAC rival Western Michigan's backyard at Kalamazoo Central High School. He is one of several Eagle recruits on the *Detroit News* "Fabulous 50" team and on that same publication's all-state dream team.

WIDE RECEIVERS/TIGHT ENDS

Last year, Eastern "ran" the ball by using the short pass. Outs, bubble screens and the occasional inside slant were the rule of the day and resulted in MAC-leading catch numbers for senior **Kenny Christian** (6-1, 198).

Christian caught 78 balls for 808 yards in just 10 games. Sure he only averaged 10.0 yards per catch, but that was a better alternative than actually running between the tackles. Christian got to the end zone just three times, but his yeoman work as a possession receiver opened things up on the other side of the field. He was in the midst of an NCAA appeal for a fifth season in late May.

Christian had catches in three games in both '96 and '98, redshirting with back injuries in '97, then started the last two years. Based on the results of another NCAA appeal by offensive lineman Craig Cipa, Eagles fans should not get their hopes up.

Junior **Kevin Walter** (6-3, 208) emerged as more of a home run threat, catching 55 passes. Walter then stretched the field, totaling 721 yards en route to five scores. Before last fall, Walter had made all of one reception in his career.

Junior **Jamal Stevens** (5-11, 182) had 14 catches last year and is the only other returnee with much experience. He is listed as the backup to Christian at flanker. Senior **Eric Ibom** (6-2, 202) is the backup to Walter at split end. Redshirt freshmen **James Stanford** (6-2, 193) and **Alonzo Harris** (6-2, 180) are next in line at receiver. Harris is a high school teammate of Okoro, while Stanford is the twin brother of backup running back **Gary Stanford** (6-2, 190).

The wild card in all this may be senior transfer **Chris Archie** (6-4, 207), who has tremendous size and speed. Archie began his NCAA career at Cincinnati before returning home to Michigan and getting eligible at Grand Rapids Junior College. Archie caught 11 passes as a freshman at UC in '97. He can out-run or out-jump a lot of folks, as he clearly showed in the spring. He just had trouble in the spring game coming down with the ball on the fly and timing lobs deep downfield.

"He is the one guy who can hit that home run ball," Woodruff said.

While EMU showed a lot of three wide sets in the spring, it still lists both a tight end and H-back on the depth chart. Junior **Brett Wells** (6-3, 238) is first in line at tight end. He started the first three games in 2000 before breaking a foot. Ditto for sophomore **Kevin Zureki** (6-3, 250), who started four more games before breaking his foot in week 10. Zureki did catch 12 passes for 112 yards in his limited time.

Redshirt freshmen **Sam Anderson** (6-5, 220) and **Adam Jacobs** (6-4, 195) could see the field when the Eagles go to a double- or triple-tight end look inside the 10-yard line.

EMU looks to be very multiple and can come at opponents from virtually any offensive look.

OFFENSIVE LINE

Last year, the offensive line was nearly as wretched as the running game, as each fueled the other's woes. Three senior starters return here, and a fourth, Cipa, will not after appealing to the NCAA for a medical redshirt and being denied. He played all of the first two games of the season and tore knee ligaments in the first series at South Carolina. That single series was reason enough for the denial, say the folks in Indianapolis.

Seniors **Cory Annett** (6-3, 296), **Rich Chorak** (6-2, 282) and **John Grabowski** (6-6, 300) started a combined 31 games last fall and are holding down the fort for now. Annett is a center, Chorak a guard and Grabowski a left tackle. After that, Woodruff has redshirt freshman **Dan Davis** (6-4, 250) penciled in at the other guard slot and juniors **Izaac Madril** (6-4, 290) or **Michael Johnson** (6-3, 287) slotted at right tackle.

This group is most likely to change when August arrives with a freshman class that has up to six prospects for the offensive line. Four are sized to play right now and probably will have to do so. EMU fans hope the football team at nearby Romulus High School is exceptionally good, because Woodruff and his staff signed seven players from this school within earshot of the Detroit airport.

Two are from an offensive line there called "The People Movers"—**Myron Mosby** (6-3, 355) and **Sam Estes** (6-7, 330). **Brian Booth** (6-5, 275) is from "Mad" Anthony Wayne High School in northwest Ohio, and **Brad Kegebein** (6-7, 290) played private school ball at Detroit Country Day High School. It's a big class and these are big guys.

"We are a lot bigger and stronger than we were last year," Woodruff said. "Though it may not yet reflect it in our listed sizes. When we started, only one guy on the squad could bench 400 pounds. Now we have a bunch, and we have 82 percent of the team who have cut back their body fat. Leaner, stronger, faster."

2000 STATISTICS

Rushing offense	95.2	103
Passing offense	218.8	50
Total offense	314.0	96
Scoring offense	19.0	94
Net Punting	33.1	80
Punt returns	9.5	56
Kickoff returns	17.0	104
Rushing defense	194.0	93
Passing efficiency defense	123.0	73
Total defense	404.5	84
Scoring defense	31.8	90
Turnover margin	+1	56

Last column is ranking among Division I-A teams.

KICKERS

Senior **Toller Starnes** (5-8, 197) is back after a quiet 2000. Had he kicked for a team with more scoring, he might have fought with Brad Selent and Steve Azar for the All-MAC honors he was forecast to win in the preseason. The team's leading scorer the last two years made 11-of-14 field goals and 22-of-23 PATs.

Junior **Eric Klaban** (5-10, 185) is a transfer from Ohio State and will provide backup help.

DEFENSIVE LINE

Seven starters return from last year's defense, and two of them are right up front in the 4-3 package. This group didn't finish higher than ninth in a league of 13 in any major defensive category. So returning seven isn't necessarily a huge blessing right now.

Senior **James Turner** (6-2, 272) and **Jari Brown** (6-4, 280) are the guys inside at defensive tackle and combined for 17 starts on the line last year on the way to 95 tackles and six sacks.

Junior **Elliott Daniels** (6-1, 231) started four games at end and came through with a couple of sacks in very limited minutes. He's penciled in at left end with senior **Antoine Hines** (6-5, 265) as the other bookend. The Eagles got the bulk of their sacks and pressure off the outside linebackers last year and have a lack of beef from this front four.

Nik Buckmeier would have been a senior starter after seven starts in 2000, but quit football after the season.

Woodruff is trying to beef up the trenches on both side of the ball and has five or six guys for the defensive front depending on who gets assigned to the offensive line. One from Romulus—**John Wester** (6-2, 240) projects to end or linebacker. Three from Canada—**Steve Kieffer** (6-4, 260), **Matt Kudu** (6-4, 255) and **Olivier Gagnon-Gordillo** (6-4, 240)—and one from Chicago—**Matt Lisek** (6-3, 250)—should start or letter.

LINEBACKERS

The defensive line may be rolling like the lines of a hockey team for a while, but the linebackers are almost set in stone.

Senior **Kenny Philpot** (6-2, 250) is an All-MAC performer at strong side and last fall led the team with 108 stops to go with five quarterback sacks. He is a vacuum cleaner strong enough to get off tight end blocks and stop the run.

At middle, senior **Scott Russell** (6-1, 244) nearly matched Philpot with 104 tackles and five more sacks. These guys will be on the field as much as humanly possible in 2001.

The weak-side loses its starter in the productive Jason Short and goes back to junior **London Lindsay** (5-10, 190), a former safety who started 11 games in '98 and '99. Lindsay was a great special teams player earlier in his career and runs very well to the ball. Getting his experience on the field here gives the defensive coaches more time to worry about that line.

Sophomore lettermen **Dave Lusky** (6-2, 220) and **Mike Salvatori** (6-2, 200) are apprenticing at strong side. The backups at the other two spots have virtually no experience. Redshirt freshman **Braden Feucht** (6-3, 200) is being groomed at middle linebacker after a stellar career at Worthington (Ohio) High School. Wester is very highly rated as a linebacker, but may start his career at line because of his size and the needs up front.

DEFENSIVE BACKS

The Eagles were supposed to have three starters back in the secondary for 2001, but two had already played their way into the second-string by the end of spring practice.

Senior **Maurice Ryland** (6-0, 186) is a junior college transfer and still has his starting gig while senior **Andrae Brooks** (6-2, 192) did not at spring's conclusion. Ryland had 43 tackles in 2000, while Brooks tied for the team lead with two interceptions.

Brooks had been passed by junior **Erick Middleton** (5-10, 182), who played just four games last fall. Middleton wins the job right now on flat-out speed in the 4.3 range. It lets him make up for with range what he lacks in technique.

Fellow junior **Terrence Dils** (6-1, 177) is pushing Ryland for time and also had a good early 2001, competing as a hurdler for EMU and grabbing an interception in the spring game.

Freshman **Rontrell Woodruff** (6-0, 185) is the best defender of the athlete/back recruits and was twice all-conference and all-city at Lathrup High School in suburban Detroit. He led his prep team with 115 tackles, five interceptions and nine sacks.

Woodruff and the staff also stole one out from under new Missouri coach Gary Pinkel by signing corner **Marvin Harris** (5-11, 198) from Hutchinson (Kansas) Junior College by way of Miami, Fla. Harris was second-team All-Jayhawk Conference at Hutchinson.

PUNTERS

Woodruff hopes he has an answer for his punting gap with junior college transfer sophomore **David Rysko** (6-1, 185) from Grand Rapids (Mich.) Junior College. Rysko spent just one year there before redshirting behind four-year starter Nick Avondet last fall. Rysko was up and down in the spring and might get a wild card challenge from redshirt freshman **Colin Wiltshire** (6-3, 265), an import from Melbourne, Australia. Starnes is also the emergency punter.

SPECIAL TEAMS

Ryland and Watson were taking most of the kickoffs by the end of spring, and the Eagles want the latter to get the ball as much as possible.

Watson also led the team in punt returns in 2000. It's possible that one of the talented freshman athletes like Harrison or wideout **Dominic McCollum** (6-2, 190), who returned four kicks or punts for scores as a high school senior, could see playing time here.

RECRUITING CLASS

It's a huge class, in numbers and in the sheer bulk of the signees in the offensive and defensive trenches. Considering the coaches didn't get going until Dec. 15 last winter, it's impressive in its breadth and depth, with more in-state recruiting than either of the other Michigan MAC schools. It also shows the Canadian dabbling that most of the northern programs in this league are trying, plus a couple of dips into western Ohio and Chicago.

"We had a mission statement when we took over here that we were taking back the state," Woodruff said. "Why go a thousand miles when you can the same talent within just 100 miles of campus? Plus Michigan kids cost us less to recruit and cost the team less money for in-state tuition when we hand out scholarships. It makes good sense."

EMU has some serious needs, but will go a long way toward protecting those skill players of the future by what they did this off-season. Next year, the Eagles will desperately need linebackers and still need quality athlete types on both sides of the ball.

That said, this class shows more progress than one would have expected for a first-year head coach who's not from Michigan. Now EMU needs some wins and better scoring numbers on offense to get the attention of even better prep players.

BLUE RIBBON ANALYSIS

OFFENSE	D+
SPECIAL TEAMS	C-
DEFENSE	D+
INTANGIBLES	C-

There are only a few games where the Eagles should be a non-factor this fall. Thanks to a more sensible schedule, the program should improve in the win column. Whether the quality of play actually advances is up to Woodruff and these players. Winning five games is not out of the question, though having two Division I-AA teams on the schedule smacks of what Toledo did in 2000 to pad out a win total. Still, wins are wins, and this is a program looking for absolutely anything positive on which to hang its hat.

Woodruff's guys are making progress this summer that they didn't in 2000.

"In the spring you have just 15 practices, but in the summer, if the kids are there and take charge, you can have five times that much time on the field," the coach said. "You can't get it done anymore with just two-a-days. You need to have players willing to make this commitment on their own. Last year we couldn't get 15 guys to stay around. This summer we have 55 to 60 on campus."

A quarterback must be found, and how well Edwards and Crooks perform early will determine whether the coaches have to worry about winning games or developing players like Okoro. Some decent blocking would go a long way toward preserving the jobs of those upperclassmen quarterbacks. The other big hole is at defensive line, where some new faces will have to jump in to provide some pass rush at end.

Because they hired coaches at the same time, Eastern and Central Michigan will be compared and put on the scales over the next few years to see who's developing critical mass more quickly. CMU coach Mike DeBord was part of the monolith in Ann Arbor just a couple years ago. Beating the Chips over the next few years would feel great for the folks at Eastern, who have to fight that Maize and Blue shadow every day.

Eastern won the first round last year, 31-15, and will try to go to Mount Pleasant and do it again on Nov. 10.

When you look at this schedule, there are a lot of winnable games. No longer cannon fodder, the Eagles can win (like Ohio in '97) at Maryland and have already proven they can beat Connecticut. EMU draws Buffalo and Akron from the East, two teams that are less than imposing. Things are lining up for a fair to middling season. And that would be a huge step forward.

(R.C.)

2000 RESULTS

Connecticut	W	32-25	1-0
Miami (Ohio)	L	17-34	1-1
South Carolina	L	6-41	1-2
Temple	L	40-49	1-3
Central Florida	L	10-31	1-4
Toledo	L	14-42	1-5
Ball State	L	14-33	1-6
Bowling Green	L	6-20	1-7
Central Michigan	W	31-15	2-7
Northern Illinois	W	39-32	3-7
Western Michigan	L	0-28	3-8

Kent State

LOCATION	**Kent, OH**
CONFERENCE	**Mid-American (East)**
LAST SEASON	**1-10 (.091)**
CONFERENCE RECORD	**0-6 (7th)**
OFFENSIVE STARTERS RETURNING	**6**
DEFENSIVE STARTERS RETURNING	**9**
NICKNAME	**Golden Flashes**
COLORS	**Navy & Gold**
HOME FIELD	**Dix Stadium (30,520)**
HEAD COACH	**Dean Pees (Bowling Green '71)**
RECORD AT SCHOOL	**3-30 (3 years)**
CAREER RECORD	**3-30 (3 years)**
ASSISTANTS	
	Mike Drake (Western Michigan '80)
	Offensive Coordinator/Quarterbacks
	Greg Colby (Illinois '75)
	Defensive Coordinator/Inside Linebackers
	Billy Gonzales (Colorado State '94)
	Defensive Backs/Recruiting Coordinator
	Kurt Barber (USC '92)
	Defensive Line
	Dan Kratzer (Missouri Valley '71)
	Wide Receivers
	Bill Mottola (Springfield '89)
	Centers/Guards
	A.J. Pratt (Capital '98)
	Offensive Tackles/Tight Ends
	Ben Sirmans (Maine '96)
	Running Backs
	Ron Wright (Findlay '81)
	Outside Linebackers
TEAM WINS (last 5 yrs.)	**2-3-0-2-1**
FINAL RANK (last 5 yrs.)	**111-109-112-112-115**
2000 FINISH	**Lost to Akron in regular-season finale.**

COACH AND PROGRAM

Last year in this space you read about a Kent State team with the defense to compete in the Mid-American Conference and whose coach hoped to get better production out of an abysmal offense and a new quarterback.

And while the defense was exceptional up front, the group playing in the space behind the front seven couldn't stop anybody.

So, with an offense that could only score more than 20 points once and a sieve in the defensive backfield, Kent made very little progress in the third year of coach Dean Pees' tenure in Portage County.

Sure, another bunch of young guys got plenty of playing time—to take their lumps without much pressure. But at some point, something has to change. And this school, whose other athletic programs are so very good, expects progress.

With the fourth year upon him, Pees will make changes on offense. Former offensive line coach Mike Drake moves over to run the show on offense and will probably be working with an inexperienced quarterback as he tries to find production. Three sophomores factor in there along with a freshman from the new class.

Rumors circulated of some option football rearing its head at Dix Stadium, but it was absent from public scrimmages other than a little orbit motion out of the running backs. No matter, this offense needs to be able to score, and running the ball out of traditional sets has not been the answer. If there is a strength on this team, it's at receiver.

Pees sees last year as a missed opportunity, starting with a confidence buster against local rival Youngstown State.

"We had one of our best defensive games of

the year and held them to 204 yards," Pees said. "But we threw a pick, they ran it back to the eight … they ended up with a couple cheap touchdowns."

That loss, and others at Pitt and Purdue, moved Kent to 0-3. A mid-season win over Central Michigan required overtime, and the Flashes closed the season by scoring just 42 points in the last five games. While the season was over long before, the game 10 loss at Buffalo was the breaking point.

"All day we're moving the ball, then suddenly, late in the fourth [quarter], we can't get a first down," Pees said. "Then, they just roll it down the field on us. They hadn't done that to anybody all year, ever."

Usually Kent plays great against Akron, but the UB loss was devastating and the Golden Flashes dropped the season finale to the Zips, 34-6.

It was a trying experience for everyone.

"I want to be the guy who changes this," said Pees, talking about the long-term habit of losing at Kent. "We came in here under the plan that we should treat this as if there'd never been football at Kent before. I've only been a part of three losing seasons in 27 years of coaching.

"We went to a bowl every year at Michigan State and Notre Dame. It doesn't have to be a 9-2 season; a winning season would be like the Super Bowl around here. It would get us over the hump. At some point, Kansas State was terrible and [Bill] Snyder changed that. I want to be that guy here."

2001 SCHEDULE

Sept.	1	@Iowa
	8	Bucknell
	15	Miami (Ohio)
	22	@West Virginia
Oct.	6	@Bowling Green
	13	Northern Illinois
	20	Buffalo
	27	@Ohio
Nov.	3	Marshall
	10	@Ball State
	17	@Akron

QUARTERBACKS

Drake has worked a lot of years around Pees, and the head coach had planned long term for him to take over the offense. But last year's abject failure to produce on the ground or in the air has forced a change.

The leading candidate to quarterback the new offense is sophomore **Ben McDaniels** (6-0, 175). McDaniels was a star at national prep power Canton McKinley High School who had gotten to the top of the depth chart last fall before suffering a fracture in his back in the Miami game. Although it sounds serious, it was a non-displaced break, which healed in time for McDaniels to see action at the close of the season.

In the spring game, McDaniels threw an accurate ball with plenty of air under it and seemed to have good touch. The key for him in this offense is to make good decisions and not throw the interceptions that lost games to YSU and Bowling Green last fall.

McDaniels might not have as strong an arm as the taller sophomore **Jeff Valentino** (6-3, 195), but probably makes better decisions. Valentino got his first start at Central Michigan and led the team to its only win in that overtime game. From Sharon, Pa., Valentino played prep football in Pennsylvania's storied WPIAL. He is a flashier player than McDaniel, looking to make the more spectacular play with his strong, if not always accurate arm. He completed 54-of-107 passes for four touchdowns and 545 yards.

The third quarterback, for now, is **Adam Frederick** (6-2, 205), a sophomore who is part of Kent State's five-player cadre from Pittsburgh's Shadyside Academy.

None of the veterans have a lock on the job if a freshman can come in and quickly grasp the play book. **Josh Cribbs** (6-1, 185) is a star from Washington D.C.'s Dunbar High School who was an All-Metro pick by the *Washington Post*. Cribbs brings his favorite receiver from Dunbar, **Darrell Downey** (5-11, 165), and looks ready to run or pass, as his 23 passing touchdowns and seven rushing last fall would suggest. He was intercepted just four times.

This spot could be wide open.

RUNNING BACKS

Last year, Kent needed to find a 1,000-yard rusher to show progress on the offense. That didn't happen. Senior tailback **Chante Murphy** (6-0, 210) totaled 800 yards, good enough for team honors as outstanding offensive player. Murphy and returning backup junior **Booker Vann** (5-11, 210) combined for nearly 1,200 yards, but neither are a real breakaway threat to get to the open field.

That breakaway guy could be sophomore **Mikal Lundy** (5-10, 185) or sophomore **David Alston** (5-9, 195). Those two made only 15 carries between them last fall, but the pair from New Jersey may be the difference-makers Pees needs.

Lundy is a bigger back who runs upright but has excellent open-field vision and is elusive. Alston is a new face the head coach compares to former Kent star back Astron Whatley, except that he's a little smaller and quicker.

"I like our depth," Pees said. "With three or four guys at tailback and fullback, we shouldn't have any trouble staying fresh."

Senior **DeMarlo Rozier** (5-9, 220) is the most recognizable name at fullback and the most experienced. But he was almost always a blocker in 2000, getting only 18 carries as an 11-game starter. Kent can go larger with a pair of youngsters—sophomore **James Ruggiero** (6-2, 240) is another from Shadyside Academy and redshirt freshman **Charles Newton** (6-1, 250) is a pure battering ram from Western Hills High School in Cincinnati.

WIDE RECEIVERS/TIGHT ENDS

Though the offense was ineffective most Saturdays, the returning wideouts and ends could play for most MAC teams.

Senior **Jurron Kelly** (6-0, 170) is a legitimate All-MAC candidate if someone can get him the ball. Another New Jersey native on a team whose recruiting in the Jersey/Delaware/Maryland corridor is growing, Kelly had 37 catches in just nine games to lead the squad. His stats (393 yards, two touchdowns) suffered with the loss of former star quarterback Jose Davis after the '99 season.

Kelly is the every down threat, while the other starter, senior **Matt Curry** (6-0, 180) is more a pure speed threat on the outside. Curry did step up with Kelly missing a pair of games, and added 511 yards on 35 catches.

The third receiver is more of a possession specialist. Junior **Josh Bostick** (6-2, 200) redshirted last year after 19 grabs in the '99 season. The three might spend some time together as the offense adds some "trips" looks.

Sophomores **Daryl Moore** (6-0, 195) and **Maurio Medley** (6-6, 210) are the next wave. Moore is a converted tailback; Medley is a long strider who can tower over most MAC cover men and reminds some coaches of Miami receiver Jason Branch.

Tight end was a bright spot and safety valve last season for the Kent quarterbacks. Coming out of the spring, sophomore **Neil Buckosh** (6-3, 245) had improved his blocking and was running as the top end. He had 18 catches last year to lead Golden Flash tight ends, ahead of the 17 grabs of junior **Ray Quinn** (6-3, 220). Quinn is the designated passing downs guy, though he too has improved his blocking.

Junior **Brycen Erbe** (6-4, 260) is the road grader here, replacing junior **Joel Reikowski** (6-5, 255). Last fall, Reikowski had 11 catches and a touchdown. He moves inside a spot to tackle.

OFFENSIVE LINE

Getting an experienced player with good feet outside will be key for a line that will be without three senior starters from 2000.

The returnees are solid. Senior right guard **Brian Hallett** (6-4, 295) is a fourth-year starter and an Academic All-MAC player for the second year. At the other guard, fifth-year senior **Vic Vrabel** (6-4, 300) is a good run blocker who has started at every line spot except center in his time at Kent State.

Beyond those two, the Flashes have size but not experience. Junior **Kevin Jamieson** (6-4, 295) got some spot duty last fall and projects to tackle now. Sophomore Steve Smith was McDaniels' center at McKinley High School and will be handing him the ball again.

Twins in size, newcomers **Jason Andrews** (6-5, 285) and **Mike Jenkins** (6-5, 285) are redshirt freshmen who will try to step in at the two tackle spots. Jenkins is from Maryland; Andrews played at prep power Henry Clay High School in Lexington, Ky.

Sophomore **Shawn Sarrett** (6-6, 285) will be the first line of depth at guard and is one of the many prep school recruits Kent State has signed from Fork Union (Va.) Military Academy. He's a little older and stronger as a 22-year old sophomore.

Junior **Deron Bowling** (6-3, 280) was in the two-deep at guard last year as well.

2000 STATISTICS

Rushing offense	111.6	90
Passing offense	156.4	99
Total offense	268.0	108
Scoring offense	11.6	113
Net Punting	33.4	77
Punt returns	6.4	101
Kickoff returns	18.1	88
Rushing defense	164.4	72
Passing efficiency defense	147.5	108
Total defense	408.5	90
Scoring defense	32.6	95
Turnover margin	-2	69

Last column is ranking among Division I-A teams.

KICKERS

It's too bad this team has had such a tough time scoring the last couple of years. Senior **Dave Pavich** (6-1, 170) was virtually automatic as a sophomore and was 37-of-37 on PATs before missing three last season. Off-season surgery limited him last season, though he was back to form for spring. In 2000, Pavich was just 6-of-10 on field goals and 12-of-15 on PATs.

DEFENSIVE LINE

How deep is this position? At season's end in 2000, the Kent State defense's two-deep showed only one departing senior in an eight-man group at defensive line. League-wide, coaches cited this front as one of Kent State's real strengths.

So of course, with a couple hot shot linebackers joining two of the MAC's best, you have to get them all on the field.

Now the line is part of a 3-4 defense, which means more double teams for star junior nose guard **Roy Attieh** (6-1, 305). Attieh anchors what is the East's best front seven, and just mauls opposing centers. His new backup is Florida sophomore **Alan Williams** (6-3, 255), who had a superior spring. Fifth-year senior **Aaron Mayer** (6-2, 275) is a two-year letterman who can also help at nose.

The ends are at least four-deep, starting with an All-MAC candidate at end in senior **Mark Strickland** (6-1, 240) and junior **Shawn Armstead** (6-4, 230) in the one deep, and junior **John Nurczyk** (6-4, 260) and sophomore **Delvin Barker** (5-11, 230) the next wave. Look for Nurczyk to gain the most playing time in this group, as the 3-4 set needs more bulk from its defensive lineman. Armstead got some spring work as rush linebacker as well.

"We had a situation when I was [defensive coordinator] at Michigan State where we had some injuries right before September and I was teaching this new deal right up to kickoff," Pees said. "It's easier this way and they've really taken to it well."

LINEBACKERS

Just who is good enough to force the coach to change schemes over the winter? Senior linebackers **Rashan Hall** (5-11, 220) and **James Harrison** (6-1, 240) both broke their share of chin straps last fall and both should grab some All-MAC honors of some sort again this fall. But their roles will change. Instead of both being on the outside, Hall will be the middle or "Mike" linebacker and the larger Harrison will be the strong-side backer playing over the opposing team's tight end.

The new weak-side linebacker is sophomore **Anthony Henriquez** (5-11, 220), who had to sit out last year as an academic non-qualifier. He was the best player on Pees' scout teams and will cut into the statistics of the two seniors as he cleans up against the run.

This new scheme looks a lot like the 3-4 Pees ran at MSU, with fairly deep drops by the linebackers away from blockers, and is similar to the 3-4 scheme that was so successful at West Virginia in past years.

That scheme needs a weak-side pass rusher who can also drop into coverage, and Kent has it in super-sized sophomore linebacker **Pierre Wilson** (6-4, 265). Wilson hails from Riviera Beach, Fla. and will be able to do some serious damage as an edge rusher in the MAC. That size at linebacker is only matched by former Steelers star Levon Kirkland. Wilson is a Michigan State transfer whom Pees recruited before coming to Kent State.

Veteran senior **Heath Hommel** (6-0, 225) adds depth at the middle if he returns from successful knee surgery, with junior **Justin Gatten** (6-2, 220) also plugged in at strong.

Sophomore **Brandon Richardson** (6-4, 235) is the apprentice behind Wilson at the "Rush" linebacker spot. Sophomore **Jeff Jensen** (6-4, 245) also has prototype size for the strong or rush position, but needs to overcome torn knee ligaments as well.

"We have tremendous depth anywhere along this front seven," Pees said. "And there are enough players working hard that this depth chart can really change."

DEFENSIVE BACKS

As good as Kent State's front was last year or could very well be this fall, the secondary often made it a pointless endeavor. This is a case where getting back seven of the top eight players might not necessarily be great news.

"All the starters are back," Pees said. "But that may be good or bad. I'm not particularly happy. We played them all since they were young but the improvement hasn't been there."

Statistically, the secondary didn't knock down enough passes or take the ball away often enough (six interceptions). And it was always a group in flux as coaches looked for the best mix.

Some guys don't understand the zone. Some don't have the speed. But the right combination is elusive here.

The most consistent is junior corner **Jacon Avery** (5-11, 170), who is the best mix of tackling and stopping the pass. But for just staying in another guy's pads, junior **Justin Baugham** (5-10, 185) is the guy to have in single coverage. Junior **Nashville Dyer** (5-10, 175) started six straight games to end last season and may team with his high school teammate sophomore **Ray Coley** (5-11, 195) as a corner pair.

Those two are from Riviera Beach, Fla., along with starting strong safety **Desmond Turner** (6-0, 190). A sophomore, Turner was a bright spot last year in coverage and is the team's fifth-leading returning tackler with 67 hits.

Junior **Robert James** (6-4, 200) has linebacker size at safety. The backups here are senior **Reggie Crook** (6-0, 195) and junior **Scott Booker** (6-2, 195), who combined for 30 stops.

This is a position where a freshman could certainly step in immediately, and there are a half-dozen athlete or defensive back recruits in the class.

PUNTERS

Junior **Jared Fritz** (6-2, 185) turned into the starter at punter last fall and went for an average of 40.4 yards per punt and stopped 13 punts inside the opponent's 20-yard line. He also serves as Pavich's holder on the field goal unit.

SPECIAL TEAMS

Kent uses two snappers for special teams work—sophomore **Lance Rudzinski** (6-4, 210) snaps on long situations like punts and sophomore **Jerami Hodgkinson** (5-8, 230) does the trick on field goals and PATs.

Top receiver Kelly should again be the main punt returner; Top back Murphy will get first call to return kicks and may be joined by Kelly, Vann or Alston.

RECRUITING CLASS

It's a hard job to recruit at Kent State. It's hard enough to have to show a recruit any MAC campus in winter, but selling a program that flat-out hasn't won in a kid's lifetime is near impossible. Pees will tell you a story about a top recruit in northeast Ohio who is having a good Division I-A career. The player wanted to go to Kent State, but couldn't face his friends and high school teammates and tell them he was going there. Being embarrassed is tough.

So, while there's a lot of talent in this corner of Ohio, the focus has shifted; not to junior college players, but to prep school guys from Fork Union, Hargrave and other fifth-year academies. And, to the sometimes under recruited mid-Atlantic region.

There are 10 offensive or defensive backs (athletes), five interior linemen, four linebackers, a quarterback and a kicker to take over for Pavich next year. Six are from these prep schools.

But is it a MAC-level class? The current defensive and offensive fronts on the field are big enough and up to the challenge. The gap at Kent State continues to be at the skill spots; Pees hopes, someone will answer the call this fall and help him immediately at defensive back.

BLUE RIBBON ANALYSIS

OFFENSE	D+
SPECIAL TEAMS	C-
DEFENSE	C
INTANGIBLES	D

He's a rough-and-tumble kind of coach, but most people would root for Pees to have some success here. He's trying to do things the right way, and has graduation rates and grade point averages going up every year.

"It's no longer a job, it's a quest," said Pees, who has had opportunities to go back into the world of being a big school coordinator again. But he wants to be the guy who transforms Kent State from punching bag to MAC contender.

But the problem is the same as last year. Sure, the defense will be better, but there are no real signs that the offense will be able to keep that beleaguered eleven off the field for long. Some new formations here and there will not change the fact that Kent does not have game breakers playing any of the offensive back positions. Unless they find that 2,000-yard passer or 1,000-yard rusher early this fall, the valiant efforts of stalwarts such as Hall, Harrison and Attieh will again be wasted.

(R.C.)

2000 RESULTS

Pittsburgh	L	7-30	0-1
Purdue	L	10-45	0-2
Youngstown State	L	20-26	0-3
Miami (Ohio)	L	14-45	0-4
Bowling Green	L	11-18	0-5
Central Michigan	W	24-21	1-5
Ohio	L	7-44	1-6
Marshall	L	12-34	1-7
Western Michigan	L	0-42	1-8
Buffalo	L	17-20	1-9
Akron	L	6-34	1-10

Marshall

LOCATION	**Huntington, WV**
CONFERENCE	**Mid-American (East)**
LAST SEASON	**8-5 (.615)**
CONFERENCE RECORD	**5-1 (t-1st)**
OFFENSIVE STARTERS RETURNING	**7**
DEFENSIVE STARTERS RETURNING	**5**
NICKNAME	**Thundering Herd**
COLORS	**Kelly Green & White**
HOME FIELD	**Marshall Stadium (38,000)**
HEAD COACH	**Bob Pruett (Marshall '65)**
RECORD AT SCHOOL	**58-9 (6 years)**
CAREER RECORD	**58-9 (6 years)**

ASSISTANTS

Mark Gale (Oklahoma State '81)
Inside Linebackers/Associate Head Coach
Kevin Kelly (Springfield '82)
Defensive Coordinator/Defensive Backs
Bill Legg (West Virginia '85)
Tight Ends/Recruiting Coordinator
Mark McHale (Shepherd '73)

Offensive Line
Dwayne Nunez (Lamar '92)
Wide Receivers
Ernie Purnsley (Wake Forest '90)
Running Backs
Bill Wilt (Eureka '77)
Defensive Line
Ed Zaunbrecher (Middle Tennessee State '72)
Offensive Coordinator/Quarterbacks
TEAM WINS (last 5 yrs.) NA-10-12-13-8
FINAL RANK (last 5 yrs.) NA-40-47-25-65
2000 FINISH Beat Cincinnati in Motor City Bowl.

COACH AND PROGRAM

Talking to Marshall head coach Bob Pruett, you would have almost no idea how tough a sesaon the Herd had in 2000. Sure, it ended predictably enough, with a MAC regular-season championship won in front of the home folks in Huntington and a trip to Detroit's Motor City Bowl to dispatch a mediocre team from a "name" conference.

"The high point of last year? Winning the championship," Pruett said. "Our goal every year is to be in that championship game here, and anything that comes after that is just gravy on top. For us it was great to take a team of young guys and watch them improve so much from September to the end."

But between the season-opening win over Division I-AA patsy Southeast Missouri State and the win over Cincinnati at the Silverdome, Marshall looked decidedly human.

Cut up by injuries and a defense that couldn't live up to its league-best numbers of the year before, the Herd had real trouble with quality opponents. There were no big wins out of league at North Carolina or Michigan State. And when faced by the other top tier teams of the MAC, Marshall had few answers in the regular season.

The Herd suffered its first home loss since its return to the MAC in '97, a 30-10 whipping by Western Michigan on national TV in week five. The scheduling genie then sent Marshall to another MAC city with a grudge, and the Herd came back from Toledo on the losing end of a 42-0 thrashing by the Rockets. If not for the generosity of former UT head man Gary Pinkel, the margin could have reached 60.

Marshall had fallen to 2-4 by this point and was watching the rest of the league's media get busy writing it off and crowning someone else champion. It didn't happen. And with the exception of a regressive performance at Ohio in the regular-season finale, the Herd won the rest of its East games and saw the Bobcats, Miami and Akron eliminate each other from the title hunt. Which brought us again to this predictable end.

Marshall was exposed as a team lacking depth, lacking a feature back for much of the year, unable to protect the passer and completely lost against the run. That final point remains an issue, and was borne out at Ohio, where the Herd gave up a ludicrous 401 rushing yards and five touchdowns on the ground. That defeat hit home for Pruett, who sat on the Peden Stadium field long after the game asking the producer of his televised show to "hurry up, or else they'll turn that scoreboard back on and start kicking our butts again."

Pruett pledges that version of Marshall football will not return.

In fact, it will be a real surprise to him and Marshall fans if the Herd does not return to its dominance of past seasons.

"I think we are a better football team, a more experienced football team, and all those injuries mean more experience for the guys now starting. The league's going to be the toughest it's been," said Pruett when asked about folks' misconceptions about his team and his thoughts on those top teams in the West. "But it won't be a good misconception to have if you think we can't win this thing. I hope we play them [Toledo and Western Michigan], because it means we've made our goal again this year [the MAC championship game]."

2001 SCHEDULE

Sept.	1	@Florida
	8	Massachusetts
	15	@Texas Christian
	29	Bowling Green
Oct.	6	@Northern Illinois
	13	@Buffalo
	20	Central Michigan
	27	Akron
Nov.	3	@Kent State
	10	@Miami (Ohio)
	17	Ohio

QUARTERBACKS

Things could not have been any more difficult for an inexperienced quarterback last fall. And despite the battering and bruising, junior **Byron Leftwich** (6-6, 240) proved durable enough to withstand 30 sacks and constant pressure. He not only withstood the firestorm, he put on a whirlwind effort of his own on the offensive statistics sheet. The Washington, D.C. native led the MAC in passing yards (3,441), accuracy (61.1 percent), total offense (286 yards per game) and touchdowns (21), while throwing just nine interceptions. All this behind a line that often included two or three first-year Division I-A players.

He put up those numbers for an offense that had the league's second-lowest average time of possession. He is the MAC's best quarterback, a pro prospect and may be the best in the NCAA, in Pruett's humble opinion.

"He's got a chance to be the best in the country," Pruett said. "He's got a major-league arm and makes great decisions."

Big words perhaps, but for a staff that developed pro quarterback Chad Pennington, they are ones you can take seriously. This team seems to change offensive coordinators every other year, but the results and success stay the same. For Leftwich, things should get easier this fall. He is the unquestioned leader of this unit and has earned every bit of it.

Leftwich passed for more than 200 yards in all but one game, and led Marshall on an 84-yard drive in the final minutes to win at Akron, the game that would decide the MAC East champion.

He never lost any meaningful time to injury, despite taking a beating in the pocket all year. But if Leftwich does miss time this year, the Marshall offense will look to an experienced senior, **Stephen Galbraith** (6-0, 198), for leadership. Galbraith is a transfer from Memphis who started some games there as a freshman. He is the son of former Marshall offensive coordinator Marty Galbraith, and last fall was 13-of-24 passing with three touchdowns in five games.

Galbraith is a competent backup and will be a solid caretaker, though he lacks Leftwich's get-away foot speed.

The future here lies in a pair of redshirt freshmen, **Stan Hill** (6-3, 190) and **Andrew English** (6-3, 224). They were in last fall's three-quarterback class (Kenny Irby transferred to Tennessee State in the off-season). Hill led in the spring and combines a solid arm with excellent speed. The Mississippi native played four years for his father's team at Tupelo High School and was the state's offensive player of the year in '99.

RUNNING BACKS

While Leftwich exceeded nearly every expectation, the Marshall running backs had their problems. Going into the season, the Herd expected to be deep at this position, with two quality returnees and a junior college transfer to challenge them.

But by week four, junior **Brandon Carey** (5-10, 185) was down with torn knee ligaments and the junior college transfer, Ernest Pitts, had already gone home to Mississippi for the fall. Two weeks later, junior **Chanston Rodgers** (5-10, 205) lost his starting job, as he was never fully recovered from a spring ACL tear. Both Rodgers and Carey want to be out of braces for the summer so that they can get into the battle for playing time with junior **Franklin Wallace** (5-11, 192).

Wallace was the only bright spot here, rushing for 555 yards on 100 carries and getting to the end zone seven times. He is the best blocker of the three and did well as a pass receiver (13 catches, 124 yards) out of the backfield. He is the most complete package here, and though he lacks true breakaway speed compared to a healthy Carey, his blocking more than made up for it, especially with the troubles on the offensive line last year. He started the last six games.

Wallace was a Prop 48 non-qualifier two years ago, but could get four years on the field if he graduates by the end of summer 2003.

Carey is a guy who does have that burst and some shake-and-bake ability in the broken field. But he lacks strength to run over tacklers. His best work may be as a third-down specialist or returning kicks. Carey reminds many of former Mississippi star John Avery in build and style. He played in just five games last fall, averaging six yards a carry (38 carries, 241 yards, one touchdown).

Rodgers is a stronger back who runs more upright and needs to improve his blocking. Last season he ran for 204 yards and five touchdowns on an average of just 3.1 yards per carry.

Marshall plays a single-back look almost exclusively, putting extra tight ends in at fullback in short-yardage situations. If a tough yard is needed, the Herd can call on senior running back **Trod Buggs** (5-11, 218). Buggs is a converted linebacker and special teams star who ran 16 times for two touchdowns last year.

Pruett said he has three healthy backs going into the summer and sees this position as a possible strength. Beyond the top three and the specialist Buggs, there are possibly three new recruits who could play here. Freshman **Kiel Angry** (5-9, 190) from Leesburg, Ga., was recruited by Clemson and South Carolina. **Wilbur Hargrove** (6-1, 180) is coming off a year at Hargrave (Va.) Military Academy and runs a 4.3 in the 40-yard dash. Marshall signed no freshman backs in the 2000 class.

WIDE RECEIVERS/TIGHT ENDS

The Herd has plenty of speed and young bodies at receiver, but very little experience. There are no seniors in the projected top 10 players at wideout, with just senior **Gregg Kellett** (6-3, 256) at tight end to represent the graduating class.

Sophomore **Darius Watts** (6-2, 177) is a difference-maker with awesome speed at split end. He was one of the MAC's most dangerous players on the outside, forcing safeties to double team him much of the year. Watts has a body like former Marshall star Randy Moss, in that he's exceptionally thin and muscular but seems to lack weight room strength. Not that he really needed it, though, as the Georgia native led the team in receiving yards (616) and yards per catch (17.1) on just 36 catches. Watts went for six touchdowns to lead the Herd despite being fifth on the team in catches.

If there is a question, it's whether Watts is ready to be the go-to guy when he was a second or third option much of last fall. He started four games before the bowl. The other wideouts only return 13 catches combined from last season.

Watts will be on the field a lot, with his backups being junior **Chris Ray** (5-11, 186)—a junior college transfer who redshirted last fall—and senior walk-on **Denero Marriott** (6-1, 178).

On the other side at flanker, Pruett wants big things from junior **Curtis Jones** (6-2, 195), who caught just 11 passes for 183 yards last fall, and got most of those on a season-long 76-yard grab. Jones has yet to scratch the surface of his abilities and must have a good year to help this offense.

Pruett likes the progress of redshirt freshmen **Josh Davis** (6-0, 191) and local prospect **Robby Isaacs** (6-2, 174) from nearby Portsmouth, Ohio. They will both push Jones after spending most of last season in the weight room.

The slot receiver is the safety valve for this offense, as Marshall runs a lot of inside slants and screens to take the pressure off the quarterback. Here as well, the Herd must look to its youth with redshirt freshman **Brad Bates** (5-10, 162) and sophomore **Chris Martin** (5-8, 177). Bates sat out last year like the group at flanker. Martin played half the season before an injury. He lacks breakaway speed, but has excellent hands and learned how to find the gaps in a zone as star wideout at Nitro (W.Va.) High School.

Someone other than Watts will emerge as a star at this position, and the most obvious candidate should arrive in August. Junior college transfer **Kendrick Starling** (6-1, 180) played last fall at Navarro (Texas) Community College and caught 113 passes in two years for more than 2,500 yards. He twice earned junior college All-America honors.

The speedy Starling was considered by some recruiting services to be the best junior college receiver in the country. He was being recruited by Kansas State and Pitt among others. Starling could plug nicely into the flanker position, provided he passes one class this summer in order to graduate with his two-year degree.

At tight end, Kellett caught 12 passes for 137 yards and two touchdowns. Backups **Eddie Smolder** (6-3, 238) and **Demetrius Doss** (6-4, 220) did not catch a pass last season. Redshirt freshman **Joe Deifel** (6-3, 231) caught several passes in the spring game and is working on trying to earn a scholarship this fall.

OFFENSIVE LINE

An absolute mess last fall thanks to injuries, offensive line is a position that can do nothing but improve for Marshall this season. The Herd took their lumps up and down the line, but now returns a group with a season's worth of starts at both tackles and center.

Junior **Jeff Edwards** (6-4, 275) from nearby Kenova, W.Va., started the last 11 games last fall at center, and should remain there, though both of the candidates to start at guard can also work here.

Senior **Steve Content** (6-2, 265) will get the nod for now at left guard after playing some center last year. Junior college transfer **Steve Perretta** (6-2, 285) arrived early in the spring and will almost certainly start at right guard after coming from Long Island's Nassau Community College.

Junior **Paul Hardy** (6-4, 298), sophomore **Joey Stepp** (6-1, 299) and freshmen **Nate Griffin** (6-5, 316), **Doug Gast** (6-5, 260) and **Ricardo Phillips** (6-5, 291) are the depth at the three inside spots.

Pruett also like in-state product **Dwayne Robinson** (6-3, 310) from Musselman High School and said the Herd's other junior college lineman, **Anthony Bonds** (6-4, 280), could play immediately inside.

Outside, things are a little more stable. At left tackle, junior **Steve Sciullo** (6-5, 325) is an All-MAC lineman and was Marshall's only truly dominant pass blocker last fall. He played at Shaler High School near Pittsburgh.

His backup is an intriguing prospect. Sophomore **Matt Zahn** (6-8, 375) hurt his shoulder and developed a "not tough" rep with the coaches at Ohio State two years ago. Now at Marshall, his coaches say he's tough enough, but needs to keep an eye on his girth to be mobile enough to play.

At right tackle, sophomore **Nate McPeek** (6-4, 313) had some tough moments as he learned to play as a freshman, but earned himself a starting job. The Russell, Ky., native lives nearly within sight of Huntington across the river. Junior **Joe Orsini** (6-7, 332) is another in-state player the Marshall coaches fished out the eastern panhandle on their normal recruiting trips to the Washington, D.C. area.

2000 STATISTICS

Rushing offense	113.5	88
Passing offense	298.7	10
Total offense	412.2	31
Scoring offense	28.5	44
Net Punting	36.3	30
Punt returns	10.1	46
Kickoff returns	18.3	84
Rushing defense	175.2	79
Passing efficiency defense	116.8	51
Total defense	355.7	52
Scoring defense	23.6	49
Turnover margin	+5	38

Last column is ranking among Division I-A teams.

KICKERS

This is not a strength—yet. Marshall went looking for a kicker last year, signed one, and then had him leave for his Georgia home during camp. So the Herd limped through the season, with senior walk-on **J.R. Jenkins** making 14-of-20 field goals and 40-of-41 extra-point kicks. Punter **Curtis Head** (5-11, 164) spent the spring kicking field goals, with walk-on freshman **Ben Lewis** (5-11, 188) and walk-on senior **T.C. Beaver** (5-11, 167) on the roster as well.

The Herd signed freshman **Sam Erny** (5-11, 190) from Louisville, Ky., and it is expected a graduate assistant will be stationed with him for much of August to keep him from disappearing as well. This is a serious need, especially with the sheer amount of points Marshall scores in a typical season. Nailing all those 20-yard extra-point kicks will be paramount; if someone can do that consistently, the coaches should have their blood pressure lowered considerably.

DEFENSIVE LINE

Marshall plays the 4-4, "40-front" defense that seems to be in vogue right now, though the Thundering Herd has been doing it for a while under defensive coordinator Kevin Kelly.

The ends are not huge, but they are experienced. Senior **Ralph Street** (6-0, 255) plays over the strong side and is the designated pass rusher of the group. He was fifth on the team in tackles with 74 and led the squad in sacks for a second year, with eight. Street has a motor that never stops. Last year, Street said in the Marshall media guide that his season goal was to "destroy anything that moves."

Sophomore **Maurice McKinney** (6-2, 215) is the backup here and needs to get bigger to play this spot permanently. There is a trio of prep end recruits in the new class who will be jumping into the action in 2002 with the loss of the seniors.

The other senior is **Kelvin Smith** (6-1, 240), who joined the program from Mississippi Gulf Coast Community College last fall. Smith is very fast, but only saw enough action in 12 games and had a mere 15 stops. Sophomore **Paul Sinclair** (6-0, 250) is the depth here.

Size may need to become more important at end, where the tackles from Toledo and Ohio seemed to dominate the Herd at the point of attack.

Street started every game last year at end, but at the other spots, every starter but one is gone.

Inside, Pruett has some young guys with great energy. Sophomore **Marlan Hicks** (6-3, 295) plays over the nose and has an All-MAC future if he continues to improve. Sophomore **Nathan Leslie** (6-4, 250) played well here in the spring and will not go back to tight end. Ditto for a local recruit, redshirt freshman **Josh Cordell** (6-4, 288), who already has great size for this spot.

At defensive tackle, junior **Orlando Washington** (6-2, 255) is an in-state recruit who just does not stop and seems to be in on every play. He had one start here last fall and will help anchor the center.

Behind him is a pair of space-fillers—junior **Richard Rodgers** (6-4, 277) and sophomore **Toriano Brown** (6-0, 281). Rodgers is a transfer from Virginia and could very well pass Washington with a good August; he could be the league's impact transfer.

Two of the three defensive end recruits are from prep schools, and Pruett has never held back in playing freshmen if they can help immediately.

LINEBACKERS

While the down guys may lack some age, the next level of the Herd defense does not. All four of the starters at the linebacker spots are seniors, headed up by All-MAC inside linebacker **Max Yates** (6-3, 228). Yates has a nose for the ball, hits very hard and has excellent lateral speed. He is hard to fool and pursues very well against the run. Combining size and fundamentals, he is the best inside linebacker in the league. Yates turned in 115 tackles last fall, to go with a pair of sacks and interceptions. He was busy with Marshall's trouble against the run last year, and sometimes had trouble getting off the blocks of opposing guards or centers. But he should rebound this fall.

Junior **Duran Smith** (6-0, 224) is the backup here and had just seven tackles in minimal time last year.

The other inside linebacker is senior **Alonzo Jones** (6-0, 201), who split time here with fellow senior **Sam Goines** (6-0, 203). They combined for 53 tackles while backing up the graduated George Miller. Like the guys outside, this is a small, quick position that is susceptible to bigger offensive lines.

Outside, senior **Larry Davis** (6-0, 190) is the starter at the weakside or "whip" position and returns 25 tackles. The backup is sophomore **Charlie Tynes** (6-0, 194), who had 42 stops last year and could very easily win back more time this season. Both could put up some good pass rush numbers if the coaches decide to loose this position to rush more like in the similar defenses at Virginia Tech or Toledo.

The other side is the "rover," which senior **Michael Owens** (5-10, 210) plays a lot like strong safety. Owens might be the league's leader in broken chinstraps. The Logan, W.Va., native is a mighty hitter against the run and was third in team tackles with 81 last fall. Owens led the squad with five interceptions.

There are four true linebacker recruits in the new class. But with the seniors inside and the smaller safety types outside, it's unclear where they might fit in this fall.

Pruett thinks he has All-MAC players in Yates, Owens and Street, and may have one or two more in the backfield.

DEFENSIVE BACKS

Last fall, Marshall opened the year with a pair of senior All-MAC corners, and the coaches thought there were no questions here. But Maurice Hines got hurt and coaches and fans figured out that he and Danny Derricott weren't as fast as they thought. So, while the Herd trades out three longtime starters back here (Doug Owens is gone at free safety), its gets bigger and faster on the outside.

Juniors **Terence Tarpley** (5-10, 174) and **Yancey Satterwhite** (5-11, 175) make this backfield more athletic right now. That duo got three starts last fall and combined for 46 tackles. Tarpley is probably a little ahead of Satterwhite, but both are excellent and would start for any MAC squad.

The starters will be on the field a lot the next two seasons, unless some of the four freshmen backups can really make an impression. All four are on the smaller side, like the departed Hines and Derricott: **Dorian Williams** (5-7, 154), **Roberto Terrell** (5-8, 176), **Renaldo Williams** (5-8, 184) and **Jimmy Tyson** (5-7, 160).

At free safety, junior **Chris Crocker** (5-11, 183) is the last line of defense and should be one of the league's best.

"He's just a hitter, pure and simple," Pruett said. "He can bring a lot of physicality and got a lot of playing time the past couple years when we've had people banged up."

Crocker had 56 tackles and three interceptions in filling in for Hodges and Owens, and started eight games. Senior **Fardan Carter** (5-9, 183) is excellent on special teams and is the primary backup here.

There are at least five potential defensive back recruits in the new class, but this should be a position where not many of them should have to see the field this year.

PUNTERS

If he doesn't have to kick, Head should be one of the league's top punters. He was second in the league at nearly 41 yards per punt, and suffers the fate of being behind Ohio's potential All-America punter Dave Zastudil for much of his career. Head kicked the ball 60 times last year, with two being blocked.

SPECIAL TEAMS

Looking for a kicker, Marshall at least returns experience at snapper and holder. Senior captain **Chris Massey** (5-11, 232) is back at snapper and either Martin or Head will be the holder.

Watts and Jones should be dynamite as kick returners and Bates will step into the roll of punt returner.

RECRUITING CLASS

It's hard to judge most Marshall recruiting classes immediately, as the Herd will take its share of chances on players who need to improve academically. But this class looks to be one of the best here in recent history.

The running backs are excellent, and Leftwich-to-Starling will be an exciting combination if it happens. But the bigger concerns were on defense.

"We needed some more defense," Pruett said. "We got some really good linebackers, and a lot of guys who can run and be a factor for us in the future."

What does the class look like? Like any other Marshall class, it looks south in a big way. Lots of Virginia, especially the Tidewater-area where Pruett used to coach preps, and basically the entire southeast is fair game most years. The Herd fills its roster in D.C., Mississippi, Virginia and Florida most often. Marshall's presence seems to be growing in Kentucky and Louisiana. The loss of assistant coach Jay Hopson could hurt the team's pipeline to Mississippi, where the Herd found nine players currently on the roster.

A big key this year is getting production from the three junior college signees; the three signed last season didn't end up helping much.

It has been said that the Herd just takes a big bus south and picks up all the kids who can play and then waits to see if they can make it at school. For the most part, that strategy has worked well for the league's best program.

BLUE RIBBON ANALYSIS

OFFENSE	B-
SPECIAL TEAMS	C-
DEFENSE	C
INTANGIBLES	A

Last year, Marshall experienced something it hadn't before in the MAC—bumps in the road. And not just little bumps. Marshall was beaten by three of the teams that had been chasing the Herd the last few years. Is the MAC catching up? Is Marshall's recruiting sinking to the level of the rest of league? Or was it just some injuries at the wrong times?

There is still no reason to believe this group will stop the run, and no matter how athletic, the new defensive backs can't be that much better than last year's. And the offense lacks experience at all three receiver spots. Will potential league MVPs Yates and Leftwich be enough to lead the Herd back to the MAC Championship game, no matter where it's played?

Sad as it may be for the rest of the league, we have to say yes. A lot of writers have lost a lot of face betting against these guys the last four years. Somehow, Marshall always manages to make it work. The Herd does have more athletes than anyone else in the league and has a consistent system on both sides of the ball that hasn't changed in years. And, the Herd has the confidence of Pruett, who will be more than happy to tell you anytime what Marshall football means.

"What's the biggest challenge?" the coach said. "I always think that the next year is the biggest challenge. Repeating is the biggest challenge."

If Marshall makes it through Florida without too much collateral damage, the Herd can do it again. The schedule falls just right again, as in '99. Akron and a Jim Grobe-less Ohio have to come to Huntington, and the game at Northern Illinois shouldn't count unless there's a tiebreaker situation in the East. And going 10-1 should guarantee ranking and a bowl bid for the Herd again. This time, the MAC has designs on sending the Herd to Mobile for the GMAC Bowl. Do they really want these guys to opening recruiting lanes in Alabama as well?

(R.C.)

2000 RESULTS

Southeast Missouri State	W	63-7	1-0
Michigan State	L	24-34	1-1
North Carolina	L	15-20	1-2
Buffalo	W	47-14	2-2
Western Michigan	L	10-30	2-3
Toledo	L	0-42	2-4
Kent State	W	34-12	3-4
Akron	W	31-28	4-4
Bowling Green	W	20-13	5-4
Miami (Ohio)	W	51-31	6-4
Ohio	L	28-38	6-5
W. Mich.(MAC Champ.)	W	19-14	7-5
Cincinnati (Motor City)	W	25-14	8-5

Miami (Ohio)

LOCATION	**Oxford, OH**
CONFERENCE	**Mid-American (East)**
LAST SEASON	**6-5 (.545)**
CONFERENCE RECORD	**4-2 (t-3rd)**
OFFENSIVE STARTERS RETURNING	**6**
DEFENSIVE STARTERS RETURNING	**6**
NICKNAME	**RedHawks**
COLORS	**Red & White**
HOME FIELD	**Yager Stadium (30,012)**
HEAD COACH	**Terry Hoeppner (Franklin '69)**
RECORD AT SCHOOL	**13-9 (2 years)**
CAREER RECORD	**13-9 (2 years)**

ASSISTANTS

Shane Montgomery (North Carolina State '90)
Offensive Coordinator/Quarterbacks
Jon Wauford (Miami '93)
Defensive Coordinator
Brian George (Ohio '94)
Defensive Line
Taver Johnson (Wittenberg '94)
Linebackers
Joe Palcic (Miami '98)
Defensive Backs
John Peterson (Ohio State '91)
Offensive Line
Jim Wachenheim (North Central '78)
Assistant Head Coach/Running Backs
Brian Von Bergen (Illinois '92)
Receivers/Recruiting Coordinator

TEAM WINS (last 5 yrs.)	**6-8-10-7-6**
FINAL RANK (last 5 yrs.)	**94-74-69-88-92**
2000 FINISH	**Beat Buffalo in regular-season finale.**

COACH AND PROGRAM

When Miami head coach Terry Hoeppner took over the program, he said he had "some strong ideas about offense." And those strong ideas included a lot of what we've seen at Purdue the last few seasons. It's been a strange turn for Miami fans used to the between-tackle antics of Travis Prentice and Deland McCullough.

With graduated quarterback Mike Bath at the controls the last two seasons to ease the learning curve, the guys in Red and White have made progress. But this spread offense needs a star to make it work. And instead of a halfback, that guy will have to be a quarterback.

Hoeppner has a choice between a couple very good ones. The winner of the August battle for playing time between a pair of second-year quarterbacks will have the weight of the program on his shoulders.

Last year, Miami may have over-achieved en route to a 6-5 record on only a quartet of home games. The RedHawks had their usual

"Tomahawk Win" to open the season at Vanderbilt; this time with even more drama then usual as Bath hit tailback Calvin Murray with a touchdown pass on fourth-and-goal to win, 33-30.

After winning at Eastern Michigan, Miami put up a great fight at Ohio State before three Bath interceptions in the final quarter. Poor decision making in the pocket and a blown chip shot field goal and PAT doomed the Hawks to a 27-16 loss.

"Did we overachieve early on?" Hoeppner said. "Maybe, but our biggest problem was inconsistent play."

The best half of the season was the 35-0 margin at the break in the home opener against Kent, on the way to a 45-14 win. But the next two weeks would bury Miami's confidence and put it behind the proverbial eight ball for the MAC East race.

A 37-20 loss at Akron put the RedHawks down a break to the rest of the East, with that division's winner only decided by a team's record in its six games versus the rest of the division. And then came a turn in the glare of the spotlight when Miami dropped one of its only four home games to national punch line Ball State.

Coming off a nation's-longest 21-game losing streak with a 15-10 win at Yager, Ball State exposed Miami as a team which had trouble consistently producing on offense or stopping anybody on defense.

"That's when we bottomed out (versus Akron and Ball)," said Hoeppner, who saw his team give up nearly a half-mile of offense in those two weeks (861 yards). After a win against Bowling Green and its worst loss in 30 years at arch rival Cincinnati (45-15), Miami rebounded to 4-4 with its best game of the season, a come-from-behind win over Ohio.

"We had to persevere," Hoeppner said. "Ohio was the best team we played, they were playing for a championship and we played with purpose and came back and won."

With Miami trailing 24-13, two long touchdown passes in the final 8:27 from Bath to wideout Jason Branch and a forced fumble sealed a made-for-television win.

But the same on-again, off-again gremlins kept Miami from playing for that MAC title again, with a three-point first half and 28-point second half in the 51-31 loss at Marshall, and the 17-16 close-shave win at Buffalo.

"We had a lot of dominant halves," Hoeppner said, though his team often needed them more in pairs. "But we told the guys during the half at Huntington (Marshall) that they could be part of the greatest comeback in Miami history and they made a good run at it."

Hoeppner is a former defensive coach who's been on the watch as the once-vaunted Miami defense has faded. The 1999 and 2000 seasons were marred with injuries to the defensive front and not enough help from a Miami defense that lacked an All-MAC defensive back for the first time in a decade.

Those gaps on defense and the change of offensive system make the coach's first two seasons look fairly good at 6.5 wins per. But now, with fans expecting excitement and production, he must turn the reins over to a bundle of new faces on both sides of the ball—only six returning starters are seniors and only a couple more figure to see meaningful playing time.

While the coach refused to complain about last year's road trip-oriented schedule, he might wonder about this season. Things start rough with four of the first five games on the road. Then come two MAC West games against Western Michigan and resurgent Ball State. The year ends with Marshall and a throwaway game 12 at Hawaii. Don't forget that this happens on 12 consecutive weekends.

It's going to be hard for Miami to contend given the youth on this squad, but a win over Ohio or Marshall would again make the RedHawks a late-season player in the run to the MAC Championship game.

2001 SCHEDULE

Sept.	1	@Michigan
	8	@Iowa
	15	@Kent State
	22	Cincinnati
	29	@Ball State
Oct.	6	Buffalo
	13	Akron
	20	@Ohio
	27	Western Michigan
Nov.	3	@Bowling Green
	10	Marshall
	17	@Hawaii

QUARTERBACKS

The choice Hoeppner will have to make seems like an easy one if you like statistics. But other qualities count for something, too. That why this position will still be a battle in August, and the coach says he will battle to make sure neither of these guys "spends much time wearing a cap" on the sideline.

The numbers guy is redshirt freshman **Ben Roethlisberger** (6-5, 210), who brings a pedigree as fine as any quarterback ever to snap on a helmet in the MAC. In just a single season as quarterback at Findlay (Ohio) High School, the former wideout broke the state's single season marks for yards and touchdowns (54) working from a spread passing attack. But his only experience at the Division I-A level is wearing out a scout team last fall and 15 practices in the spring of 2001.

The other half of Miami's future at quarterback is sophomore **Ryan Hawk** (6-2, 195) from nearby Centerville, Ohio. Hawk also ran his share of the scout offenses last year, but was called on against Ohio to run some option and try to change the pace of the offense in that critical MAC East game. While his numbers were minimal, Hoeppner said his team could not have won without Hawk's contribution. Whether that proves a worthy use of Hawk's freshman year will be determined in the future.

"Ben and Ryan are both the real deal," Hoeppner said. "They have different strengths, but both are established as winners. They both have such great intangibles and both can throw the ball or run."

Roethlisberger showed that in last summer's Big 33 All-Star game and Hawk displayed it with 38 rushing touchdowns in his prep days. Both should play, and it would be no surprise if they were on the field at the same time.

The third guy at quarterback is not expected to play: freshman **Josh Betts** (6-3, 210) from Butler High School in nearby Vandalia, Ohio. Like Hawk before, he was 2000's Southwest Ohio Player of the Year—passing for more than 2,800 yards. Betts had a 5:1 ratio of touchdowns to interceptions.

Last year's third quarterback recruit, redshirt freshman **Jeremy Thompson** (6-4, 200), is trying to add strength in the weight room as he moves to defensive end.

RUNNING BACKS

Adding some bulk at the running back spot may be just what Miami needs. Injuries chewed up the two speed guys there last year—senior **Steve Little** (5-10, 206) and sophomore **Cal Murray** (5-10, 175). Little has the reputation as a guy with great moves, even in close quarters; Murray showed himself to be a shifty runner as well, and a safety valve catching the ball out of the backfield.

Little missed the spring with recurring back problems, but led the team with 986 rushing yards last fall, punctuating that total with 222 to close the year at Buffalo. It was the first time Miami went without a 1,000-yard rusher since 1993.

Murray also wore down as the season went on, but had his moments en route to his nearly 500 yards of total offense. He had 113 yards and four touchdowns against Kent and a 90-yard kick return at Ohio State. He is in his third year in the program after entering in 1999 as an academic non-qualifier. But Murray is on pace to graduate in four years or less and should be able to play a fourth season in 2003.

Sophomore **Luke Clemens** (5-10, 195) was the hero of the spring practices and may force Hoeppner's hand when it comes to playing time. Another local player from Dayton, Clemens got some special teams work last fall and stepped into the void created by injuries in the spring. He had no Division I-A offers before walking on at Miami and is now on scholarship. Clemens was one of only four freshmen to play last season, though that time was spent at safety and special teams.

"It's not a scientific process," Hoeppner said. "I'm not sure in cases like this whether to feel sorry that we didn't recognize a guy like him in high school or silly that no one else did."

Defenders never seem to have a clean shot at Clemens. He becomes one of at least 75 Miami players to go from walk-on to scholarship in the last decade. The RedHawks are proud of their program of strength training that has made numerous walk-ons into All-MAC players, including six of the defensive starters on the Miami team that went 10-1 in 1998.

While adequate, this is a position where a superb freshman could earn some playing time. A larger player who can block in the single-back shotgun look would help; two are in the new class, **Derek Rehage** (6-1, 225) a fullback-type from Saint Leon, Ind., and **Mike Smith** (6-0, 183) from Twinsburg, Ohio.

Sophomore **Andy Dooley** (6-3, 220) had a goal-line touchdown last year in limited duty and former defensive end **Julian Goodman** (6-2, 242), a senior, had 20 carries in a similar short-yardage role.

Fullback is a position spending less and less time on the field in the spread offense, but redshirt freshman **Andy Capper** (6-2, 245) may be good enough to play. The highly touted freshman broke his leg his senior year at Springfield's Kenton Ridge High School and was not completely healed until this spring after re-injuring it in last summer's Big 33 Game.

"They shouldn't have let him play," Hoeppner said. "It really set him back."

WIDE RECEIVERS/TIGHT ENDS

Will the RedHawks have enough receivers to make the offense work? Coach Hoeppner knows he has a few, but he needs to find more depth. Three of the top five receivers in total yardage from 2000 are gone.

Hoeppner has his share of niche receivers—a tall guy, a fast guy, some little guys who can sit down in a zone. But who will step forward to be the every down player that Miami has had in past years with Trevor Gaylor, Jay Hall or Sly Johnson?

Junior **Jason Branch** (6-6, 218) looks a lot like Gaylor in terms of build, and last year broke the hearts of the guys in Green with his two late scores against Ohio. He scored four touchdowns and gained 465 yards on 31 catches last fall.

"He's tall, but needs to play stronger and bigger," Hoeppner said.

Junior **Ed Tillitz** (5-9, 175) is that slot guy who can go and sit down in the middle of a zone or go deep. The sometime-punt returner is also a pinch runner and defensive replacement for Miami's baseball team. He was second-team Academic All-America last season and averaged 12.2 yards per punt return and nearly 10 yards per catch on 39 grabs. He had two punt returns for touchdowns against Eastern Michigan.

With 10 catches for 157 yards in 2000, junior **Chauncey Henry** (6-1, 202) is a Florida import and designated speed merchant who played well in the spring and just needs to improve his hands to help stretch things for the other receivers underneath.

Another junior, **Randy Stegman** (5-10, 187), had a couple grabs last fall, and beyond that Miami will look to some new faces. Redshirt freshman **Mike Iriti** (6-0, 170) was Roethlisberger's favorite prep target at Findlay High School and Hoeppner hopes those two can again develop some chemistry.

Diminutive freshman **Michael Larkin** (5-7, 160) is another familiar local name from Xavier High School in nearby Cincinnati and will turn some heads if Miami quarterbacks can get him the ball.

Sophomores **Calvin Blackmon** (6-4, 200), **Nick Braun** (6-1, 190), **Jamie Cooper** (6-3, 185) and **Korey Kirkpatrick** (6-1, 190) all will have to at least take the field if new offensive coordinator Shane Montgomery gets into the eight- or nine-man rotation you always hear from spread offense coaches.

Two receivers are in the freshman class. Miami has had good luck with assistant coach Bobby Johnson getting the school into the St. Louis market, and he brought home a potential impact player in ball-hawk **Martin Nance** (6-4, 190) from Pattonville, Mo. Nance led his school to 22 wins his last two years and had six interceptions to go with his 42 catches on offense.

Tight end may have gone under-used last fall when Mike Sullivan was touted as All-MAC and wound up catching just 18 passes. There was so little depth at this spot last fall that RedHawk coaches used backup defensive ends to run decoy routes late in the Ohio game.

With two seniors gone, senior **Robert Frazier** (6-4, 253) is the only tight end on the roster with a catch last season.

Blocking edge rushers will be key with a new set of quarterbacks, so this spot become very important. Former quarterback **Matt Brandt** (6-5, 225) is a sophomore from Toronto, Canada who will have to get a look here. Then again, depending on how many more four- and five-receiver sets the RedHawks run the tight end and fullback positions may not be needed.

OFFENSIVE LINE

With those new signal callers, you want protection. Miami will get it, with the only real hole at right tackle. Sophomore **Jacob Bell** (6-5, 285) moves from there over to the left side and will man the backside left tackle. He played prep ball at the storied St. Ignatius High School in Cleveland.

Inside, the core is very experienced and very good. **Paul Thaler** (6-3, 281) anchors at center, flanked by fellow seniors **Phil Hawk** (6-5, 313) and high school teammate **Joe Costello** (6-6, 314).

Miami strength coach Dan Dalrymple is the league's best, and just got a new state-of-the-art strength center on the hill above Yager Stadium in May. Hoeppner gave him the instruction last year to make his guys more sleek, but the size and strength still seem to be there.

The unit is bigger and deeper. Redshirt sophomore **Ben Herrell** (6-7, 270) and redshirt freshman **Zac Elcess** (6-5, 275) are top candidates to fill the spot at right tackle, and fellow redshirt freshman **Ben Hartings** (6-4, 260) is working his way into the depth chart at guard.

The brother of NFL linemen Jeff Hartings, Hartings just needs to get a little bigger and is a "flat-out technician," Hoeppner said. "He will tear somebody up. His brothers are teaching him well."

Miami may be close to legitimately being 10-deep in this unit once you add redshirt freshman **Dave Rehker** (6-5, 305), a Big 33 All-Star from the Cleveland-area, and one of the five potential offensive linemen in the new class.

Freshman **Ryan Fisher** (6-4, 300) from Henry Clay High School in Lexington, Ky., is "good enough to play right now and may be the first guy off the bus when we play Michigan," Hoeppner said.

2000 STATISTICS

Rushing offense	154.9	48
Passing offense	232.2	37
Total offense	387.1	43
Scoring offense	24.7	64
Net Punting	34.3	63
Punt returns	12.3	23
Kickoff returns	20.1	45
Rushing defense	213.1	108
Passing efficiency defense	120.8	63
Total defense	405.0	85
Scoring defense	26.0	67
Turnover margin	-14	108

Last column is ranking among Division I-A teams.

KICKERS

Junior kicker **Andy Brumbergs** (6-5, 225) has to get more consistent. Though he has a decent leg, Brumbergs' misses last year seemed to happen at inopportune times en route to a 12-for-17 season kicking field goals. He was 30-of-33 on PATs. He missed a PAT and a 21-yard field goal attempt at Ohio State.

The long snapper is junior **Scott Sagehorn** (6-3, 220), who has started there the last two years.

DEFENSIVE LINE

Hoeppner said this unit is better, if for no other reason than the absence of health problems. Two starters return from the end-of-2000 depth chart, with four of the top eight linemen back.

Junior **Ryan Terry** (6-2, 315) gets the nod at right tackle in the 4-3 look. A starter in 19 games his first two years, Terry is potentially the best and biggest down lineman in the MAC. He had 68 stops, including 11 at Ohio State and 11 tackles for loss.

"He needs to step it up," Hoeppner said. "He can be that guy [All-MAC], he just needs to know that it's time."

Senior **Bob Petrovic** (6-5, 252) returns at defensive end and is a very smart player whose production dipped some in 2000. But with sophomore **Phil Smith** (6-1, 258) at the other end, this unit should be fine. Smith played much of last season as a stop gap linebacker when that unit was cut down with injuries.

The other tackle should be senior **Gino Digiandomenico** (6-4, 282), who tries to return to 100 percent from a broken leg. Redshirt freshmen **Will Rueff** (6-4, 255) and **Larry Burt** (6-4, 305) will be part of the next wave at end and tackle, respectively. Junior **Kurt Mester** (6-4, 263) has seen substantial minutes the last two seasons at end as well. Any of the rest of the cast of youngsters and walk-ons will have to get bigger to get into the mix at defensive line.

The best of the freshmen is **Marcus Johnson** (6-3, 265) from Ursuline High School in Youngstown. He should be in the two-deep and on the field with a good summer.

LINEBACKERS

This position was racked with injuries a year ago. But the starting group that returns combined for 273 stops in a character-building season.

Outside, junior **Matt Robillard** (6-3, 220) is a converted safety who came up with 104 tackles last fall and junior **Eddie Price** (5-11, 221) is one of the more consistent parts of this crew.

In the middle was a wonderful surprise for Hoeppner and Miami fans. Sophomore **Terrell Jones** (5-10, 220) arrived from the St. Louis area, forced the coaches to dispatch his redshirt in game four and led the nation's freshmen with nearly 12 tackles a game for the rest of the year.

"He's not big, but he knows exactly where he has to be," Hoeppner said. "It's like he's small enough the blockers can't always find him. He knows stuff you shouldn't know as a freshman; he's always learning, suggesting how we change our plays and sets."

His coach called him the epitome of the student athlete, with a grade-point average better than 3.25 last semester. But MAC foes know that he's a terror on the field.

Behind this group, depth is still questionable. Juniors **Cortt Cousino** (5-10, 220) and **Matt Edwards** (6-2, 240) and sophomore **Nate Clayton** (6-2, 229) have all been in the two-deep the last couple of years but have suffered major injuries.

"Both Matt and Nate were unable to help much a year ago," Hoeppner said. "But they've made strides and we hope they can make a difference."

Three linebackers highlight the new class, including **Tyler Vogel** (6-3, 220), who helped Coldwater High School twice get to the state finals in football in Ohio.

DEFENSIVE BACKS

Miami has gone a while without a big star in the secondary.

Junior **Milt Bowen** (6-2, 213) is the top returnee here and moves over from corner to play some safety. He is well known as a stopper on special teams and runs very well for a run-stopping strong safety. He returns the teams only interceptions from last fall (two).

Redshirt freshman **Matt Pusateri** (5-11, 190) had a great spring to lock down the job at free safety.

Outside, senior corner **Michael Adams** (5-9, 186) returns and could get another year if he completes graduation requirements.

Potentially, the better cover corner is redshirt freshman **Alphonso Hodge** (5-11, 185) from Cleveland's St. Edwards High School. He is the best pure man coverage player at Miami and could have the same impact freshman Janssen Patton did last fall for Bowling Green.

Senior **Rod Clark** (5-8, 190) will probably be the first guy off the sideline as a nickel safety or corner. Sophomore **Ryan Sprague** (5-10, 175) provides depth at corner along with redshirt freshman **Van Monroe** (6-3, 175) and former junior college transfer junior **Paul Tripp** (6-0, 180).

There are two potential defensive backs in the new class. **Ryan Redd** (5-10, 170) was an athlete recruit for Illinois until Illini defensive coordinator left the school for Ohio and Miami swooped in. Redd averaged nearly nine yards per carry as a running back and had 17 deflections and 80 tackles as a defender.

PUNTERS

McCullough is gone after a very solid four-year run. With no punter in the recruiting class, Hoeppner will turn duties over to redshirt freshman **Michael Wafzig** (6-4, 200), a walk-on from nearby Germantown, Ohio.

Wafzig punted very well in spring, though Brumbergs is the insurance policy here. Wafzig is also listed as a receiver should Miami desire some fourth-down trickery.

SPECIAL TEAMS

Tillitz set school records in punt returns last year with his two-touchdown showing at EMU and an excellent average at 12.2 yards per return.

Bowen will return as a kick returner, and probably will be flanked by Murray. Bowen is remembered for his touchdown return in the '98 win at North Carolina.

RECRUITING CLASS

"I have a penchant for big guys, and want to stockpile them," Hoeppner said. "We don't get a lot of finished products like some bigger conference schools, but we do a good job developing them."

And so that's what the Miami staff did, dotting the 22-man class with interior line prospects.

This is an excellent MAC class, with Fisher and Johnson probably ready to contribute this fall. But needs still exist for receiver and tight end depth. Ditto for that defensive backfield.

Miami has done a very good job controlling the southwest Ohio recruit and keeping him at home. With staff changes at Ohio and Bowling Green, it's unclear how long the RedHawks will be able to keep this backyard to themselves.

BLUE RIBBON ANALYSIS

OFFENSE	C
SPECIAL TEAMS	D+
DEFENSE	C
INTANGIBLES	B

Despite inconsistent play, Miami had a shot to steal the MAC East title very late in the season after beating Ohio.

Roethlisberger will make this team fun to watch if he wins the starting quarterback job, and this entertainment value will keep Miami fans from noticing that this team is not there—yet. Next year it could be. The players keep getting bigger, graduating and winning enough. But could this team have a breakout year like the 10 wins in '98? Absolutely not.

The defense will be on the field a lot and inexperience in the defensive backfield will take its toll.

There could be surprises, but this team will be hard-pressed to improve on last year's finish and could have real problems if it doesn't get at least two wins in September.

Right now, this is a team like the rest of the MAC—still chasing Marshall.

"We could just get an all-star team together and go down there and take it from them," Hoeppner said. "But the championship goes through them right now."

Where the Bulldogs finish in the middle of the MAC East with Bowling Green and Akron will determine just what they have to look forward to for 2002.

(R.C.)

2000 RESULTS

Vanderbilt	W	33-30	1-0
Eastern Michigan	W	34-17	2-0
Ohio State	L	16-27	2-1
Kent State	W	45-14	3-1
Akron	L	20-37	3-2
Ball State	L	10-15	3-3
Bowling Green	W	24-10	4-3
Cincinnati	L	15-45	4-4
Ohio	W	27-24	5-4
Marshall	L	31-51	5-5
Buffalo	W	17-16	6-5

Northern Illinois

LOCATION	**DeKalb, IL**
CONFERENCE	**Mid-American (West)**
LAST SEASON	**6-5 (.545)**
CONFERENCE RECORD	**2-3 (t-3rd)**
OFFENSIVE STARTERS RETURNING	**7**
DEFENSIVE STARTERS RETURNING	**5**
NICKNAME	**Huskies**
COLORS	**Cardinal & Black**
HOME FIELD	**Huskie Stadium (31,000)**
HEAD COACH	**Joe Novak (Miami '67)**
RECORD AT SCHOOL	**14-41 (5 years)**
CAREER RECORD	**14-41 (5 years)**
ASSISTANTS	
	Scott Shafer (Baldwin-Wallace '90) **Defensive Coordinator/Defensive Backs**
	Dan Roushar (Northern Illinois '84) **Offensive Coordinator/Offensive Line**
	Matt Canada (Indiana '93) **Quarterbacks**
	Pat Narduzzi (Rhode Island '90) **Linebackers**
	Sidney McNairy (Purdue '93) **Wide Receivers**
	Frank Kurth (Ball State '84) **Tight Ends**
	Mike Priefer (Navy '89) **Defensive Tackles**
	Mike Sabock (Baldwin-Wallace '77) **Defensive Ends/Recruiting Coordinator**
	DeAndre Smith (SW Missouri State '92) **Running Backs**
TEAM WINS (last 5 yrs.)	**1-0-2-5-6**
FINAL RANK (last 5 yrs.)	**109-112-110-108-93**
2000 FINISH	**Defeated Central Michigan in regular-season finale.**

COACH AND PROGRAM

It's been a long wait for fans in DeKalb, but the patience shown by folks in the stands and the Northern Illinois administration began to pay off in 2000.

Last season, the first winning record of coach Joe Novak's regime followed the first winning league record (1999). And now the Huskies look for the first back-to-back years over .500 since 1990.

But hold on just a second. Sure, NIU looked like a world-beater as that huge offensive line graded roads from Auburn to Akron and everywhere in between. A quick look at the depth chart shows a bevy of missing blockers and All-MAC performers who made this engine go last fall.

Going into a sixth season, Novak experienced the sort of success a rebounding program should in years four and five. But it happened on the backs of a lot of seniors.

Massive 6-9 tackle Ryan Diem heads to the pros, a fourth-round NFL draft choice of the Indianapolis Colts. He was the symbol of what the Huskies have accomplished on offense the last few years. Not only was he bigger and stronger than anyone he faced across the line of scrimmage, he was meaner and didn't quit even when his man was on the ground.

Along with guard Kyle Jakubek and center McAllister Collins, Diem leaves a giant gap on the NIU line that powered the No. 12 rushing (228 yards per game) and scoring offenses (37.2 points per game) in the nation. He and Collins were two of eight Huskies to earn All-MAC honors from the league's coaches.

The Huskies again showed themselves capable of putting up huge numbers on offense, but could not yet handle the very elite teams—Toledo and Western Michigan—of the MAC West. Eliminate those two games and NIU outscored the opposition, 363-190, for the year.

"We didn't play well at Western," Novak said. "That was absolutely our worst performance."

And that loss came in week seven, as NIU had just pounded Akron at the Rubber Bowl and folks thought the game in Kalamazoo had title implications.

The Huskies played better against Toledo, but were knocked off track with an injury to star tailback **Thomas Hammock**.

"We haven't really competed yet with those top teams, but now we should be as good as anybody," Novak said. "It was hard early, hard to take the losing. It was hard to walk in every week and take it when we started here."

Northern may have turned the corner last fall, as new school records were set on offense in points, touchdowns, total yards and first downs. If the Huskies can stop anybody at all, that firepower will keep them in their share of games.

2001 SCHEDULE

Aug.	30	South Florida
Sept.	8	@Illinois
	15	@Wake Forest
	22	Sam Houston State
	29	@Toledo
Oct.	6	Marshall
	13	@Kent State
	20	Western Michigan
	27	@Central Michigan
Nov.	3	Eastern Michigan
	17	Ball State

QUARTERBACKS

Senior **Chris Finlen** (6-3, 205) is the ringmaster who must balance the passing element with one of the nation's best running games. He was the first Huskie elected team captain since the Franklin Roosevelt administration, and has appeared in 30 games en route to being second in NIU's all-time passing yards category with 4,515.

The fifth-year player took a medical redshirt in '98 after being pressed into emergency service as a freshman. He's dropped 13 pounds since last fall and is running and throwing better this spring.

"He's always been a hard worker, and we don't ask him to go out and have to win games for us," Novak said. "We want to put him in the positions where he can make the decisions to help us win and not have to do things he doesn't do well."

Finlen completed his passes at a 57 percent clip for 11 touchdowns and 1,857 yards. He may have more to do if NIU shows more of the one-back look it worked on in the spring. The Huskies look a lot more like Toledo of the last couple seasons when they go to that style, which they used effectively in the season-ending win over Central Michigan.

Behind Finlen there are real questions. One of last year's backups, Craig Harmon, transferred, and junior **Dan Urban** (6-1, 195) spent the spring playing baseball for the Huskies. Urban may have a pro future in that sport, but has lost ground if he comes back for football in August. Urban passed for more than 300 yards in limited duty last fall, including a school record 99-yard touchdown pass against Ball State.

Novak calls junior college transfer **Kyle Padia** (6-3, 220) his insurance policy. The junior was the first to pass for more than 3,000 yards at West Valley (Calif.) Community College.

Redshirt freshman **Josh Haldi** (6-2, 192) is also in the mix here. Quarterback recruit **Joe Stamm** (6-2, 185) played in a pair of state title games for Metamora (Ill.) High School and led an offense which averaged more than 44 points per game.

RUNNING BACKS

Northern had superlatives by passers, receivers and runners in 2000. But the last group was the key, with a pair of rushers who combined for more than 2,000 yards and 23 touchdowns.

The better numbers belong to Hammock (5-10, 218), a junior who did his damage in just nine games (1,083 yards, 16 touchdowns) before getting dinged against Toledo. But even if his ankle is back to top form, the challenge from sophomore **Michael Turner** (6-0, 219) may make who starts irrelevant as these guys have to share time at tailback.

Turner added 983 yards and seven touchdowns in relief of Hammock and is actually more of a breakaway threat in the opinion of his coaches. He was a little timid in his spotlight debut against Toledo, but then put up monster games against Eastern and Central Michigan. His 281 yards on 52 carries in the finale was the eighth-best rushing game in Division I-A last fall and a MAC season-high.

Then again, Hammock is the country's No. 4 returning rusher. This is an awesome pair.

"We were really good at not fumbling," said Novak, who was pleased Hammock and Turner combined to give the ball away just three times in 2000. That works out to a fumble every 138 carries.

These two will need to work on their pass catching skills as NIU adds more single-back looks and the swing passes which accompany them.

Behind Hammock and Turner there is still more depth on the bench. Sophomore **DuJuan Johnson** (6-1, 196) sat out last year for academic reasons and is good enough to contribute immediately. Just where is unclear, but he is just as strong and fast as the incumbents. He ran a 10.6 100-meters as a prep.

Redshirt freshman **Jason Hawkins** (6-2, 225) will find a place to play somewhere. Originally recruited out of high school as a linebacker, Hawkins turned in an unreal season rushing the ball as a senior. How about first-team all state with the No. 2 single-season effort in Illinois history (2,794 yards and 41 touchdowns)? He was considered a Big Ten-level recruit coming out of Chicago suburb Schaumburg. He was an All-Area selection by the *Chicago Sun-Times*, just like Johnson.

Fullbacks will see less time on the field based on spring drills and what we saw at the end of the 2000 season, but senior **Alan Rood** (6-0, 246) is still the top guy there for now. Junior college player **Al Charles** (6-2, 226) comes from Lincoln (Ill.) Community College and will press for time here. Junior **Matt Dunker** (6-4, 253) has twice lettered and could appear here or as a tight end. He caught nine passes, including two touchdowns, last year.

WIDE RECEIVERS/TIGHT ENDS

Along with Dunker at end, senior **Joey Reed** (6-6, 240) brings some more blocking help on the edge. Last year's class included a pair of tight end recruits—**Brad Cieslak** (6-4, 239) and **Aaron Anderson** (6-5, 229)—and so does this year's group with **Ben Blonn** (6-3, 225) and **Matt Ohmen** (6-6, 225).

So tight end will have to pick up some of the slack with the loss of nearly half the teams' catches. Those left with the NFL draft and star flanker Justin McCareins, a fourth-round pick of the Tennessee Titans. McCareins was the league's special teams player of the year with a 19.1-yard average returning punts. Then there were his 66 receptions for 1,168 yards and 11 touchdowns.

So, who will be the answer as the guy who can keep opposing defense from trying a nine- or 10-man front? Former walk-on **Keith Perry** (6-3, 222) is the first candidate at that flanker position. A year ago the sophomore had 35 catches for 462 yards and a touchdown.

Junior **P.J. Fleck** (5-10, 175) returns from a shoulder injury that pared four games from his season after he had caught 17 passes.

Those numbers are all somewhat pedestrian, but came from an offense that didn't always have to pass the ball to win. Although the stats weren't that prodigious for any one returnee, NIU does have 10 of its top 11 receivers back. Completing 12-to-15 passes with no interceptions did the trick. Without the star McCareins as a safety valve, Novak needs someone to step forward. He might be a senior.

Darrell Hill (6-3, 197) has exceptional size and track speed, but last year connected with Finlen only six times in two games before a broken hand put him on the shelf.

"He is the fastest kid on the team and can just run and run," Novak said. "Yes, [Hill] has more speed than [McCareins], but he still has to learn. Right now he's still a track guy playing the football. He just needs to learn some nuances of receiving. The [NFL] scouts know; they're interested."

Hill, who has run a 4.37 40-yard dash, caught 32 passes in '99, with six touchdowns. A healthy Hill will also add splash to the NIU kick return effort.

OFFENSIVE LINE

The skill spots are filled to the brim with returning talent, but the question remains as to whether last year's gaudy numbers were a function of that skill or of the immense beef up front.

"I've seen some great backs make an average line look good," Novak said. "Last year there were some holes you could have gotten a truck through. We may have to throw the ball quicker this time."

There are holes at all three line positions as the Huskies said goodbye to a trio of four-year lettermen who combined for 106 starts.

Junior tackle **Tim Vincent** (6-6, 275) returns at one side, along with junior guard **Greg Clemens** (6-5, 299), who started nine games last fall. Vincent played for perennial Illinois prep power Galena High School.

Along with Clemens, there is some guard depth with senior **John Pedersen** (6-6, 296) and junior **Graham Sleight** (6-3, 310), who has started 10 times.

But the openings at any spot will have to be filled by some younger kids. Sophomore tackle prospect **Mark Orzula** (6-7, 318) is a giant, and redshirt freshmen **Jake Verstraete** (6-4, 283) and **Gary Young** (6-5, 310) also have the size to play now. Long term, this group may be better than the guys they replace, but you can't gauge anything without real game action.

Sophomore **Todd Ghilani** (6-3, 280) is in a war with redshirt freshman **Matt McGhghy** (6-4, 284) to replace Collins in the middle.

Guard prospects behind the three returnees include redshirt freshman **Ben Lueck** (6-4, 308) and a pair of sophomores in **Joel Ellis** (6-5, 310) and fellow Iowan **Shaun Schroeder** (6-2, 284). No matter who comes out in the two-deep, it will be a large group ready to spur the run in DeKalb.

Five tackles and guards highlight the new recruiting class, though it will be the coaching staff's prerogative to redshirt as many as possible as this program takes the next step toward consistent winning.

2000 STATISTICS

Rushing offense	228.1	12
Passing offense	199.7	69
Total offense	427.8	19
Scoring offense	37.2	12
Net Punting	31.0	100
Punt returns	16.2	6
Kickoff returns	20.6	30
Rushing defense	151.2	60
Passing efficiency defense	127.7	90
Total defense	360.8	53
Scoring defense	25.5	60
Turnover margin	+8	19

Last column is ranking among Division I-A teams.

KICKERS

For some reason, sophomore **Steve Azar** (5-7, 193) showed up unannounced in DeKalb a couple seasons ago. He was uninvited and without a scholarship. Novak says Azar just sort of walked in his office, looking like anything but a football player, and told him he'd like a chance to kick.

He got that chance. The prep soccer and football player from Colorado Springs apprenticed in the '99 season before winning the job in 2000. Azar has tremendous leg strength and kicked in the final nine games, making 14-of-15 field goals and 38-of-40 PATs en route to an 80-point season. He scored a record 10 PATs in the win over Buffalo.

Azar was a national all-freshman pick by *The Sporting News* and *Football News* and got honorable All-MAC honors from the league's coaches.

DEFENSIVE LINE

As decorated as much of the offense was, the defense was a little less storied. And the group with the least to write home about may have been the defensive linemen. While there were individual honors for both safeties and a linebacker, the defensive line combined for just 13 sacks. To get pressure, the Huskies often had to bring heat from linebackers.

"We're concerned about our size here and how small we've gotten right now," Novak said. "We spent the spring trying to get tougher and maybe a little bigger with the weights."

Novak called his guys a "yo-yo" on defense, and that was true. In all five losses, the Huskies gave up more than 410 total yards, including 503 to usually hapless Eastern Michigan. The main bright spot that kept NIU in the other games was this defense's propensity to steal the ball—27 turnovers helped the Huskies to second place in turnover margin in the MAC.

Half the line starters come from the successful parochial school program at Wahlert High School in Dubuque, Iowa. Senior **Trent Clemen** (6-3, 245) is a three-year starter who led the front in tackles (54) and pass deflections (six); junior prep teammate **Eric Didesch** (6-5, 278) plays over the center from his slot at nose guard and started seven times last fall.

The defensive tackle should be junior **Anthony Falbo** (6-5, 263), who contributed 19 tackles in 2000. The depth at the tackle spots right now comes from seniors **Rashad Walker** (6-0, 263) at nose and **Jon Peters** (6-3, 273) at defensive tackle.

Senior tackle Darian Tate will miss the fall with academic ineligibility and the search is on for a new starter and depth at end behind Clemen. Sophomore letterman **Jason Frank** (6-5, 240) is penciled in at left end, along with fellow sophomore **Lundy Swilley** (6-2, 244).

Wild cards are a pair of converted fullbacks, juniors **Sean Hopson** (5-10, 263) and **James Johnson** (5-10, 244).

This is a spot where Novak wants a recruit to help now. He had two large loads to move in at tackle in **Charles Johnson** (6-3, 270) and **Justin McIntyre** (6-1, 310). Johnson was recruited by Iowa while a prep in that state. McIntyre is nicknamed "Big Mac" and was voted his high school team's best *offensive* lineman at Evangelical Christian High School in Shreveport, La. That school is of course best known for high-powered offenses led by former national record-setting quarterback Josh Booty.

LINEBACKERS

The pick of the litter is one of the best juniors in the league, weak-side linebacker **Larry Williams** (6-0, 236). Strong enough to take on blockers but fast enough to play in space on the weak side, Johnson was a first team All-MAC selection by the league's coaches.

"He was our best defensive player last year, as only a sophomore," Novak said.

Williams has 181 tackles in 21 career starts and led the team last year in tackles for loss (13) and sacks (four).

Sophomore **Nick Duffy** (6-1, 231) played a lot for a first-year guy last fall, and is the signal caller in the middle after a 30-tackle season as a part-timer.

Senior **Ryan Laurenti** (6-2, 228) holds down the strong side coming out of spring. Some depth comes from sophomores **Vinson Reynolds** (6-2, 227) and **Wyatt Thomas** (5-11, 193), who moved over from tailback only to break his ankle in the spring.

Beyond them, depth is a real problem and experience is lacking. There are only two recruits at this spot in the new class. Both have the pedigree to help out soon. **Jason Hutton** (6-2, 232) played at Whitney Young High School in Chicago and was the 13th-best prospect in the Chicago area as rated by recruiting guru Tom Lemming. He was also a two-time All-Public League selection.

Javan Lee (6-3, 215) is the son of former Indiana State star and Pittsburgh Steeler Willie Lee. He was a two-sport (football and track) all-state athlete in Indiana after playing at Michigan City High School.

The other player who could help here is the sometime-running back Hawkins. An early August injury drove him from third to off the tailback depth chart in 2000, and he will be hard pressed to pass up the Turner/Hammock tandem there.

DEFENSIVE BACKS

Safeties are the last line of defense, hence their name. But it is to be seen whether Novak and NIU fans will feel safe with a new group of caretakers closest to the goal.

Jermaine Hampton and Buster Sampson were both All-MAC picks and both are done in DeKalb. They shared 119 tackles, which Novak hopes to find in a group of four lettermen at safety.

Sophomore strong safety **Akil Grant** (5-10, 188) had one of four punt blocks in the group last year and notched 16 stops in 11 games. He is a former prep linebacker and Novak thinks he is the guy who will blossom. Junior **Justin Dole** (6-0, 197) had eight stops and a fumble recovery.

At free, senior **Jon Pendergrass** (6-0, 206) is a better run-stopper, but played in only seven games last fall. Speedy **Gerard Taylor** (5-9, 182) is a sophomore backup here.

"The two last year were very good," Novak said, noting that Hampton's run support will be missed.

As for corners, Novak said, "We've got three good ones." **Demerist Whitfield** (5-11, 182) is just a junior and is the best athlete and all-around performer on the perimeter. Fellow junior **Vince Thompson** (5-11, 169) is a more blue-collar and less spectacular player, but found five interceptions last fall when teams tried to avoid Whitfield.

But halfway through spring, Novak had sophomore **Randee Drew** (5-10, 181) ahead of Whitfield on the depth chart. Drew is an all-purpose athlete who started on offense twice as a receiver, and once as a nickel back on the defense. He is a state high hurdles champion from Wisconsin and can be a difference maker with the "length" he can use in mid-air.

Redshirt freshman **Devron Francis** (5-10, 175) is a Florida import (like Whitfield) Novak really likes, but he will be hard-pressed to get time with the three top returnees. These corners have the ability to play a lot of man coverage on the outside, letting the safeties play closer to the line of scrimmage to break the run.

Three defensive backs are in the new class, including more insurance at corner in junior college transfer **Richard Pickens** (5-9, 180). A tremendous all-around athlete, Pickens can return punts and was an excellent running back at Robeson High School in Chicago. Novak is more interested in his five interceptions last fall and his play on a nationally ranked JUCO team at Joliet (Ill.) Community College.

PUNTERS

Junior **Jimmy Erwin** (6-2, 215) managed only about 38 yards per punt last fall, with a net of just more than 30. Novak needs him to be deeper and more consistent, though he doesn't have many other options. Novak likes to work with the special teams guys during practice and will make improving the punt game his personal project for the season. Erwin did go without a blocked punt in 44 attempts.

SPECIAL TEAMS

Azar is a potential star, at least as much of a star as any kicker could be. With his strong leg on the front end of kickoffs, Huskie tacklers had time to get downfield and kept every opposing kick return short of its own 40-yard line. He's also made 14 straight field goals.

The loss of McCareins takes away the league's top punt returner. For now, Whitfield is the guy to bring back punts. Receivers Hill and Fleck will get first shot at returning kickoffs.

Junior Steve Richenberger (6-3, 227) is the long snapper, with the punter Erwin and baseball-playing Urban holding for kicks.

Those new faces in the starting secondary showed a good knack for the ball, blocking four punts.

RECRUITING CLASS

Recruiting at Northern is an interesting exercise, but Novak's improvements with the program are opening more doors that used to be closed to MAC programs.

The biggest problem in mining some of the top inner-city programs in nearby Chicago is academics. A lot of the top City League prospects have more than their share of trouble qualifying academically, and unlike some MAC schools, Northern doesn't have as many majors or classes to hide kids who can't make it in the classroom.

"You've got to take some chances," Novak said. "We don't have a kid here that Illinois wanted, but we're getting better. It's like there are two [parts of] Illinois—Chicago and everywhere else, and I think we can do well in both. It's all about changing attitudes with some of these folks in the suburbs."

Some parents and kids don't want to go to a school with any compass directions in the name, but wins can make that stigma hogwash in DeKalb.

NIU had the league's best "on-paper" class in 2000 and followed it with 19 signees in this year's line-heavy group. Nine of the nineteen are on the interior lines, with at least a couple who should play as soon as they show up in DeKalb.

In addition to both parts of the home state, the Huskies are making inroads in places like Wisconsin and Iowa, and have tried to join Miami in getting into St. Louis. They have also had luck like Ohio in getting kids from northern Indiana who don't want to stay home at Ball State or Indiana.

BLUE RIBBON ANALYSIS

OFFENSE	B-
SPECIAL TEAMS	B-
DEFENSE	C-
INTANGIBLES	B-

Northern gave Novak an extension to 2005 and he continued his team's climb toward winning last year. But the success in 1999 and 2000 happened on the backs of too many guys who had to play their football in just four consecutive seasons. Novak is ready for the next step up where redshirting is the key to the future. A veteran NIU bunch played well at Northwestern and Auburn, and Novak knows that scheduling low-end teams from the big leagues can earn big notice when the MAC wins.

But redshirting and building from within means a possible spinning of wheels for a season or two, much like Ohio went through in '98 and '99. This is a very young team, with great skill guys and a lot of untested size in the trenches on offense. Things won't be so easy for the tailbacks this fall, but the glimpses of what's to come on both sides of the ball should keep the fans content with a mark about one game above .500

But with a schedule like Toledo's from 2000 (two I-AA teams set for Huskie Stadium), this team may end up looking better in the record book than it actually is. A "tomahawk win" is possible against former Ohio coach Jim Grobe at

Wake Forest in week three, but any hopes of breaking into the conference race hinge on games at Toledo and against Western Michigan. Luckily, the MAC Championship format will not count the game with Marshall on Oct. 6. There are a lot of tests to pass, but six wins sounds about right. With only 12 seniors in the Huskie pen, this program is far from a crescendo.

(R.C.)

2000 RESULTS

Northwestern	L	17-35	0-1
Illinois State	W	52-0	1-1
Auburn	L	14-31	1-2
Ball State	W	43-14	2-2
Central Florida	W	40-20	3-2
Akron	W	52-35	4-2
Western Michigan	L	22-52	4-3
Buffalo	W	73-10	5-3
Toledo	L	24-38	5-4
Eastern Michigan	L	32-39	5-5
Central Michigan	W	40-6	6-4

Ohio

LOCATION	**Athens, OH**
CONFERENCE	**Mid-American (East)**
LAST SEASON	**7-4 (.636)**
CONFERENCE RECORD	**4-2 (t-3rd)**
OFFENSIVE STARTERS RETURNING	**9**
DEFENSIVE STARTERS RETURNING	**9**
NICKNAME	**Bobcats**
COLORS	**Hunter Green & White**
HOME FIELD	**Peden Stadium (24,000)**
HEAD COACH	**Brian Knorr (Air Force '86)**
RECORD AT SCHOOL	**First Year**
CAREER RECORD	**First Year**
ASSISTANTS	
	Ron Antoine (Colorado State '97) Wide Receivers
	Pete Germano (Ohio Wesleyan '82) Tight Ends/Recruiting Coordinator
	Greg Gregory (Richmond '80) Offensive Coordinator/Quarterbacks
	Tim Kish (Otterbein '76) Defensive Coordinator/Inside Linebackers
	Steve Russ (Air Force '95) Outside Linebackers
	Everette Sands (Citadel '93) Running Backs
	Mike Sullivan (Army '89) Defensive Backs
	Mike Summers (Georgetown, Ky.'78) Offensive Line
	Eric Washington (Grambling '93) Defensive Line
TEAM WINS (last 5 yrs.)	**6-8-5-5-7**
FINAL RANK (last 5 yrs.)	**98-89-92-94-83**
2000 FINISH	**Beat Marshall in regular-season finale.**

COACH AND PROGRAM

Was it a huge surprise when former Ohio head coach Jim Grobe packed up and headed south last December for Wake Forest? No, not to folks who really knew the Ohio program. Grobe had done what he came to Athens to do; make respectable the worst program in the nation. Building something out of nothing was what Grobe and his staff did after landing from Air Force.

It's not as if this Bobcats team had peaked and Grobe knew it was time to go. But the head coach knew that even a MAC title in 2001 would not make him much hotter for a major conference school athletic director's list than he was after 2000. Still, Ohio lost only five starters in a tiny senior class and would be a favorite to finally topple Marshall in the East had he remained.

New coach Brian Knorr would be more than happy to sneak up on everybody and win this thing, not that he would be able to sneak up on too many folks.

League coaches are nearly unanimous in agreement that the Bobcats' offense is the league's hardest for which to prepare. Opposing teams can't run the option well enough with their scout teams and Ohio can come to the line in three or four different formations and run the same plays, making film scouting a nightmare.

Knorr was the defensive coordinator under the Grobe administration and was picked to stay and continue what started in '95. When hired, he was the nation's youngest Division I-A coach at 36. He is a former option starting quarterback at Air Force, who switched sides of the ball at Ohio. Under Knorr, the Bobcats will continue to show the service academy spread, wishbone and power running sets like the I. But don't be surprised this year to see Ohio throw out of the spread or even go to some shotgun under new offensive coordinator Greg Gregory. Like opposing graduate assistants didn't have enough tape to cut already.

Knorr also has avoided the pratfall that so often will undermine young coaches—the urge to hire too many of their inexperienced friends. The new staff differs from the old in that most of the guys don't have service academy backgrounds. But it is an experienced staff, which will be key in the transition. Defensive coordinator Tim Kish was at Illinois last fall, for example.

Things are changing in Athens. The stadium expansion adds 4,000 seats this fall by dropping the field and eliminating the track, and terraced end zone seating (similar to that at Virginia) for students and general admission will increase capacity still more in 2002. The new coaching staff kept up a common theme all spring: "There's a good thing going here. Let's not screw it up."

2001 SCHEDULE

Aug.	30	@Akron
Sept.	8	@West Virginia
	13	@North Carolina State
	22	Iowa State
	29	@Akron
Oct.	6	Toledo
	13	@Central Michigan
	20	Miami (Ohio)
	27	Kent State
Nov.	3	@Buffalo
	10	Bowling Green
	17	@Marshall

QUARTERBACKS

Is there a better pure option quarterback in the country than junior **Dontrell Jackson** (5-10, 175)?

Not that many folks are running the option every down, and Ohio looks to be moving the same way. But in terms of pure quickness and decision-making while reading the defense, you will be hard-pressed to find someone better suited to run this offense.

A year ago, Jackson led the diverse Bobcat offense in rushing (864 yards), passing (861) and total offense (1,725).

He ran for only two scores in his 155 carries, but averaged 5.5 yards per carry and stretched defenses laterally so that the Ohio backs could stab through for more than 2,700 additional rushing yards.

Jackson is the part of the option for which opposing coaches have no real answers. The concern for Ohio comes when the Bobcats get behind and have to try to score through the air. The last two years, that's been a fairly difficult assignment, as opponents tee off on or block the passes of the undersized Jackson. In order to throw the ball effectively, Ohio blockers must clear big passing lanes or roll Jackson out. Another strategy may be the one tried in spring—the shotgun.

Ohio showed a lot of shotgun along with its usual three running sets in April. This is similar to what has been tried recently at Indiana with Jackson's high school teammate—Antwan Randle-El. Randle-El, Jackson and redshirt freshman Ohio back **Stafford Owens** (5-8, 180) were the last three starting quarterbacks at Thornton High School near Chicago. All were winners of the area's prep player-of-the-year honors while there.

Jackson is a third-year starter. Last year, he was backed up by junior **Freddie Ray** (6-2, 200), who is not proficient at running the option but bears a similarity in playing style to Toledo quarterback Tavares Bolden. Ray is a pinpoint thrower with excellent size and some decent escapability in the bootleg.

Ray played in seven games last fall, including some in important passing situations. He led a touchdown drive to help put away Marshall in the season finale, but was also on the field to fumble in the final moments where Ohio trailed at Miami. He is a former Prop 48 player who could potentially earn back a fourth season—by graduating in four years—after playing his first ball in 2000 as a sophomore.

Third-string quarterback **Rashad Butler** (6-0, 190) is a redshirt freshman from Georgia who operates more in the mode of Ray. Taller than Jackson, he also has a credible arm and runs very well in the broken field. He could even see the field some this fall as a running back, say Ohio coaches. That potentially could put three option quarterbacks on the field at the same time, with him, Owens and Jackson.

RUNNING BACKS

Is it possible to have too many backs? That is a question that Ohio and Northern Illinois may have to answer this fall. (We suspect the answer is no.)

Northern had two backs combine for more than 2,000 yards and Ohio's returnees put up more than 2,200 en route to the league's top rushing attack and the league's third-best scoring number on offense (343 points).

Junior **Chad Brinker** (5-11, 210) is one of the league's strongest backs, and is more likely to try to go through you than around you. Brinker is powerful, but deliberate, and takes his share of shots over the course of the season. He is sometimes almost too intense. After a 734-yard season in which he averaged five yards per carry and scored 12 touchdowns rushing and receiving, Brinker missed the spring with minor surgery to correct a long-time shoulder problem.

Brinker is an all-purpose threat, catching two touchdown passes last year, and was the hero of the win at Minnesota. At the Metrodome, he ran for a score, threw for a score, and caught a touchdown pass in the victory.

Senior **Jamel Patterson** (6-1, 200) is just as good as Brinker. He is a big-play back who has the potential to make you miss in a phone booth because of his tremendous ability to change direction. Patterson went for 660 yards on just 114 carries (5.8 yards per), and scored seven touchdowns in more limited duty. The North

Carolina native will be looking to hit a home run in game two at North Carolina State, and is one of the few Bobcats in another small senior class who played when the 'Cats lost there in '98.

This year, Patterson will work some more at receiver or the former Z-back position held by all-purpose graduate Raynald Ray. Bobcats coaches think they can exploit his big-play potential by getting him the ball through the air a couple yards up field and letting him make something of it.

The departed Ray is the only Bobcat loss of note from the skill positions. Last year, he led the team in catches (15), receiving yards (308) and was fourth in rushing with 481 yards (8.3 per carry) and five touchdowns. His replacement at Z-Back has giant shoes to fill, but seems like he will be up to the challenge.

Stafford Owens (5-10, 180) is smaller than Ray, but this position will probably see the ball less as a true halfback out of the I formation or wishbone and spend more time on the perimeter. The redshirt freshman made the traveling squad last fall, but the coaches preserved his four seasons of future action and the guy the players call "Snake," should be the league's top freshman newcomer.

Recruited by Colorado, Indiana and other power conference schools, Owens, an option quarterback, led the state of Illinois in rushing touchdowns with 30, rushed for 1,850 yards on only 152 carries for an astounding 12.2 yards per carry and passed for 874 yards and 14 touchdowns. Thus he was responsible for 44 touchdowns in his senior year.

Owens was selected player of the year in the Chicago area by six different newspapers, including the *Sun Times* and *Tribune*. He was also the second-leading scorer on the Thornton High School basketball team behind a junior seven-footer named Eddy Curry, an NBA lottery pick this summer. His speed is somewhere in the high 4.3s. Owens is one of the league's best athletes right now and should be a true impact player.

At fullback, Ohio is also stacked, returning junior **Joe Sherrill** (6-0, 230), who ran for 323 yards in just nine injury-riddled games and did not lose a yard all season. His backup is another star redshirt freshman, **Ray Huston** (6-1, 200), from the ultra-successful Centerville High School program near Dayton.

Huston has gotten lighter and stronger since arriving in Athens and may topple Sherrill by the end of August. He is an excellent pass catcher and similar straight-ahead runner. He was highly recruited by many MAC schools and started at fullback in the Big 33 All-Star game between Ohio and Pennsylvania preps in 2000.

Keland Logan (6-1, 270) is a sophomore who started three games when Sherrill was hurt, and had Ohio's long run of the year, a 67-yard near-touchdown at Minnesota. Coaches are concerned about his conditioning and off-field disciplinary issues. He may not be welcomed back from the doghouse this summer.

The bulldozer from Youngstown ran for 254 yards at a clip of 5.4 yards a carry, but had a couple untimely fumbles that cut into his contributions as the season closed. If he isn't back, sophomore **Tony Rozzoni** (6-0, 226) is another Sherrill look-alike who got 82 yards in very limited carries in five games last fall.

WIDE RECEIVERS/TIGHT ENDS

Receivers will see more action this year. It has been a popular refrain the last few years in Athens, but you almost get the feeling they mean it this year under new coordinator Gregory.

Junior **Joe Mohler** (6-3, 200) is the leading returning receiver with 13 catches for 251 yards and three touchdowns. Mohler is a heady player with excellent speed and leaping ability. He will help stretch the field as the starting split end. Senior **Mareion Royster** (6-1, 186) moves over here after three years backing up Ray at Z-Back.

Junior **Tierra Pought** (6-0, 175) is the next player here, and will see the field a lot as Ohio often alternated receivers as they brought in plays from the sideline in recent years. Pought caught only one pass last year, but can also run well and is an excellent option blocker after playing a similar offense at Thornton High School with Jackson and Owens. Fellow Thornton grad **Brian Ingram** (6-2, 185) also joins the squad at wideout after sitting out last year because of academics.

When Owens is in at Z-Back, that will be more of an all-purpose position. But when he is out, more typical receiving duties will fall to a pair of vets. Junior **Jason Caesar** (5-9, 170) is a pure speed guy and returner who sat out last season to work on books and run for the Ohio track team. Now he's back and has worked enough on his hands to get back in the two-deep.

Junior **Keith Warren** (5-7, 180) is a waterbug type with the biggest biceps of any non-lineman on the squad. Warren has good hands and a great first step and can line up at Z-Back or tail-back. He is a Columbus native who transferred home from Morgan State after being its top special teams player two years ago.

Sophomore **Justin Halada** (6-1, 209) impressed again this spring by making tough catches in traffic and showing more speed than expected. He also can play at flanker or in the slot.

Senior **Chris Knaack** (6-3, 253) is a converted fullback who caught six passes at tight end last fall. He is an excellent blocker, while junior **Randy Pennington** (6-3, 250) is a little better receiver and should seriously improve his contributions this year with an expanded passing game. He played only three games last fall because of an injury. Sophomore **Derek Gandy** (6-3, 286) usually saw the field only in short-yardage or goal-line situations, and is an emergency tackle because of his size.

OFFENSIVE LINE

This is one of the league's best, and a major reason for the mountain of rushing statistics Ohio has put up in the last five years—the five best on the ground in Bobcat history.

Ohio lost one starter from last year's group—Zach Holt at guard— and played well last year while breaking in two brand-new players in the rotation at tackle.

Inside, senior **Taylor Ketchum** (6-2, 295) split time with junior **Doug Wooten** (6-1, 290) at center. Both had starts and played well in spurts. Ketchum is a junior college transfer from Glendale (Calif.) Community College. Wooten played just 30 miles down the road from Athens in rural Jackson, Ohio.

The guards are gigantic, and senior **Nick Glowacki** (6-5, 312) has a lot to prove after missing most of last year with a broken arm. That followed All-MAC honors his sophomore season. He is probably the best straight-ahead run blocker in the MAC when healthy. The other guard is mammoth senior **David Patton** (6-9, 320), who has the size of last year's top MAC lineman (Ryan Diem at Northern Illinois) but needs to learn to be just as mean to have a shot at the next level.

The depth at guard is very untested, at best. Junior **Paul Stanko** (6-4, 260) is a converted defensive end and offensive tackle who would need to get bigger to play guard here. Senior **Khalid Johnson** (6-1, 315) played for a Pennsylvania state champion team at Woodland Hills High School near Pittsburgh but missed last year with knee problems and has been seriously out of condition for two years. And sophomore **Tim Givens** (6-5, 290) has yet to make the progress coaches have expected of the Columbus native.

Givens could well be passed by either of the two redshirt freshmen, **Eric McCrady** (6-2, 300) and **Dave Williams** (6-4, 270), a pair of highly touted signees from Pennsylvania. McCrady probably will stay at guard; Williams probably will go to tackle.

At tackle, sophomore **Dennis Thompson** (6-3, 280) was one of only two true first-year players to see the field for Ohio, and turned out to have the highest performance grades for the season from his position coaches. Thompson started eight games, including the opener, and was dominant after spurning larger programs to attend the school where his father and grandfather also played. He was a prep star at Walsh Jesuit High School in suburban Akron.

Thompson got his starts at left tackle, giving up three to junior **Chris Jackson** (6-3, 280), who also started six times on the right side. Jackson is the swing guy on this versatile unit and can play any spot on the line but center. **Erik Grahovac** (6-3, 278) got the other starts at the right side and his coaches said he's "always thinking football."

After these three, there is some depth. Sophomore **Steve Lawrence** (6-4, 264) saw some very limited minutes last fall. Junior **Eric Brown** (6-3, 296) arrived early in the spring of 2000, along with Ketchum, from a junior college, but never got his conditioning or books in order last season and did not play.

The Bobcats signed two linemen in their small freshman class, though neither should have to play this fall, barring some sort of major catastrophe.

2000 STATISTICS

Rushing offense	323.0	2
Passing offense	95.1	113
Total offense	418.1	25
Scoring offense	31.2	29
Net Punting	39.7	4
Punt returns	11.9	29
Kickoff returns	19.5	64
Rushing defense	129.4	36
Passing efficiency defense	118.9	59
Total defense	349.3	43
Scoring defense	18.9	19
Turnover margin	+4	39

Last column is ranking among Division I-A teams.

KICKERS

Junior **Kevin Kerr** (6-0, 176) has one of the league's stronger kicking legs, though his numbers slid a little last fall to just 12-of-18 on field goals. All but one of Kerr's misses were beyond 44 yards. Kerr led the squad with 75 points, adding 39-of-42 PATs.

DEFENSIVE LINE

A year ago, the Bobcats were one of the league's best scoring defenses (18.9 point-per-game, third in MAC), but they did it with turnover margin (+4) and rushing defense (third in MAC). Ohio could not stop the pass, most of the time for lack of pressure created by the 3-4 defensive front.

Now, the front three aren't expected to deliver big sack numbers, but they are expected to tie up a lineman or two each to let the blitzing linebackers get to the passer. The Bobcats lose a nose guard and backup end off this front line, but think they can be better this fall.

Starting junior nose man **Lamar Martin** (6-1, 286) told folks in the spring that he was going to be "an All-MAC tackle this year." Trouble was, this proclamation came on the sideline of the Ohio spring game, as Martin stood on crutches recovering from minor knee surgery. He was jogging again by May and should be completely healthy. He is one of the real leaders on this defense and should live up to his bold prediction if he plays as well as he did last year in full-time minutes.

Burly sophomore **Andre Parker** (6-1, 285) impressed last year at defensive end, starting six games and falling on a couple of fumbles as a big-play rusher. He will move inside to the nose, and should be improved as a tackler, considering he played most of last year with a broken hand in a cast. Junior **Eli Kiener** (6-0, 258) is a transfer from Division II Glenville State (W.Va.), and got significant minutes here in the spring with the injury to Martin in the second week. As a former wrestler, Kiener is excellent out of a four-point stance.

After spring, senior **Mike Fox** (6-4, 264) and sophomore **Keith Adamson** (6-2, 255) are penciled in to start at the defensive ends. Those two combined for 77 tackles and four sacks last fall. Ohio notched 20 sacks in 2000.

Senior **Art Adams** (6-4, 252) will play this fall for his fourth year—if he completes graduation requirements over the summer. He is a former Prop 48 recruit from nearby Chillicothe. Though he often over pursues and seems to wear a sign that says "Draw Me, Trap Me," Adams is an excellent third-down bull rusher and special teams kick blocker.

Redshirt freshman **Garrett Bush** (6-4, 272) was often the Bobcats' best defensive lineman last fall, but the commitment had been made to retain his redshirt, so he stayed on the scout team. Bush played his prep ball for the legendary program at McKinley High School in Canton and will be a real impact player this fall. He's probably the best pursuer and pass rusher of this front three.

LINEBACKERS

Right now, this is a group in flux. Ohio coaches were not happy with the pass rush they got from their outside linebackers last year. So designated senior pass rushers **Greg Baskin** (6-1, 238) and **Trendale Perkins** (6-1, 239) were moved to the right side in the spring, as the staff hoped those two similar players can push each other to new heights. The two projected top rushers at outside linebacker combined for only 2 1/2 sacks last fall, and that just won't do.

The leading sack artist from last year is senior **Matt Weikert** (6-1, 225), with 5 1/2 sacks. Weikert's is a tremendous story. He is a former walk-on who played himself into the two-deep only to see his dreams shattered at EMU in '99 with an ACL tear. But Weikert rehabbed his way back onto the team and into the lineup and became Ohio's best outside backer last year. No one works harder or plays harder. But he is hardly the prototype pass rusher the staff has been looking for.

Ohio has tried to sign some more guys who look like rushers. Sophomores **Hugh Grant** (6-3, 220) and **Willie Sherman** (6-3, 242) may be the future here after very limited duty last year.

Inside, things are a little more confused. Top inside run-stuffer **Tom Weilbacher** (6-0, 230), a senior, is awesome against the run but moved from weak to strong-side for the spring, along with top backup **Demetri Taylor** (6-4, 220). Taylor played last year as a freshman. Weilbacher led the 'Cats with 92 tackles. Odds are that Weilbacher would move back to weak-side for the fall, if Taylor can figure out the strong-side berth vacated by senior Matt Spitler.

Senior **Shawn Murphy** (6-1, 220) and sophomore **Rich Constantine** (6-0, 230) are listed at the weak-side, but if some new faces make it to campus for summer drills, it's doubtful either will get a start this fall.

Last season, Ohio signed one of the MAC's best freshman classes of linebackers. Trouble was, other than Taylor and Kentucky-native **D.T. Boon** (6-3, 210), none fully qualified academically. This year, all those guys are hoping to be on campus full-time after getting their academics in order. All have the pedigree to start this year or next, and could be the linebacker counterparts to Owens and Bush.

Ricky Cherry (6-0, 220) is a Durham, N.C. native and projects to outside linebacker. A four-time all-league player at Durham's Northern High School, Cherry was recruited by all the in-state ACC schools after winning four league titles.

Evan Curry (6-5, 218) and **Mike Henry** (6-1, 215) started at outside and inside backer, respectively, for Ohio in the 2000 Big 33 All-Star game and didn't look out of place against the numerous Penn State and Ohio State recruits there. Curry played his prep ball in the Cleveland area. Henry was an All-Ohio player at nearby Ironton High School. These three, plus Taylor, should get to play together for a long time. How much they and the other highly touted new faces play will determine a lot about whether this team gets over the hump in Huntington.

DEFENSIVE BACKS

Junior **David "Bop" White** (6-0, 190) might be the league's best man-to-man cover corner. He spent the off-season getting stronger so that he can make more than an occasional tackle as well. In 2000, White had 41 tackles and a team-high three interceptions. Bop will take some occasional chances, but has the make-up speed to occasionally bait an opposing quarterback.

Sometime-Bobcat hoops point guard **Thomas Stephens** (6-0, 175) is sophomore who played a lot in nickel situations last fall. Stephens was a four-sport star in high school, and jumps for the Bobcat track team as well. He's one of the squad's finest athletes.

On the far side, Bop's brother Donnie finished up his eligibility, leaving the boundary corner slot to senior **Arden Banks** (5-9, 195). Banks is confident and a little better against the run than White. He had 39 stops last year in limited duty.

Redshirt freshman **Rahman Shavers** (6-0, 189) is another of last year's excellent recruiting class and will push for a starting job. Banks and Stephens saw substantial time last year, as the 'Cats often put in their top four corners in lieu of a nickel package against passing teams.

Special teams star **Aaron Hall** (5-10, 175) is a junior speedster who can sub at corner and plays on the outside of the Bobcat punt coverage unit. He's the brother of former star fullback Sid Hall.

At safety, senior **Chris London** (5-10, 200) is the most "cut" Bobcat from the weight room and has just the attitude to be a great run-stopper at strong safety. He is a highlight-reel player and the leader of the secondary. He was third on the team with 78 stops in 2000, and he also snared a pair of interceptions. His backup is Henry's prep teammate, **James Taylor** (6-0, 190), a sophomore making the move over from wide receiver, where he caught eight passes last fall.

The free safety right now is former corner recruit **Bashawnta "Joe" Sellers** (5-10, 190), who added 33 tackles in nine games (an injury limited his time) while sharing the position with the departed Duffer Duffy. Sellers wants to make the big hit like London, but sometimes misses his zone responsibilities to help the corners and gets stuck in no man's land.

Redshirt freshman **Roy McCullough** (6-2, 180) is a similarly converted corner who will push for serious playing time and should be the first guy off the sideline if Ohio does play a true nickel this fall. McCullough and Shavers are the best of five defensive back recruits signed last year.

PUNTERS

Punting in the MAC begins and ends with All-America candidate **Dave Zastudil** (6-3, 230). The fifth-year player is looking to lead the MAC in punting average for the fourth consecutive season, and was fifth in the country last fall with his 44.3 yards-per-punt average.

Zastudil is a former prep quarterback, and film review of the last few Ohio seasons forces opposing teams to always take note of the fake. Kerr is the backup here; he had to punt once last fall.

The Bobcats signed a scholarship punter in **Matt Miller** (6-1, 185) from Westerville North High School near Columbus.

SPECIAL TEAMS

Brinker and Patterson are an exceptionally physical duo to return kicks in the MAC. The pair both averaged more than 22 yards per return and have game-breaking ability in the broken field.

Caesar also might see some time here. He will be the primary punt returner, though Owens could also break into that rotation if his hands improve.

Sophomore **Brandon Swiger** (6-3, 250) replaces four-year snapper Jay Roden, and he will be snapping to Zastudil to set up for Kerr's kicks.

RECRUITING CLASS

It's a tiny class, and not that highly touted, even for MAC standards. But it's probably a good thing Ohio didn't have many scholarships to have to fill in a year where the head coach had to spend more time recruiting a new staff than new athletes.

Ohio got its punter of the future, four athletic offensive or defensive back recruits, two big linemen, and a future rush end or linebacker in local signee **Ike Simmons** (6-2, 210) from nearby Gallipolis, Ohio.

The Bobcat staff still has a grant or two to burn over the summer on a key late qualifier, or could take an impact transfer if one became available.

To be honest, the development of last year's class and the signees from that group just joining the team this spring or fall will be far more important. Owens, Bush and McCullough will be very important, along with those new linebackers. Throw in Indiana transfer Jade Pruitt (5-8, 180), a speedy junior receiver and returner in the Owens mode, and you have a full boat of guys who can help now.

Watch for Ohio to try to rebuild ties to Ohio from the old staff, especially in Columbus with defensive coordinator Tim Kish. But the new staff has more ties south to the Carolinas, Georgia and Florida that they will try to exploit.

BLUE RIBBON ANALYSIS

OFFENSE	B
SPECIAL TEAMS	A-
DEFENSE	C+
INTANGIBLES	C+

It would be easy to pick Ohio to win the East if

Grobe and his veteran staff remained. But between a new staff and a rough preseason schedule, you have to go with the sure hand at Marshall.

The Bobcats are very talented and should be one of the top rushing teams in the NCAA again this fall. But the key will be diversifying the offense and finding a guy as electric as the graduated Ray. Owens should be that player.

Defense is the concern. Good in the red zone, the Bobcats need a lot more pressure up front to make things easier on those defensive backs. The special teams are the league's best right now.

The hard part is the season. Getting Akron in week one instead of week five is a good trade for the Bobcats. But stacking the N.C. State game just five days after West Virginia is a big risk. The two teams may be similar to prepare for on offense, but two big road games in a week are rough. That does give the 'Cats extra time going into the big home opener with Iowa State. Oh, and Toledo comes to town the next week on the way to 11-0. It's the roughest first five or six weeks in the league, except for perhaps Bowling Green's. Not to mention the season ends at Marshall. Ouch. Then again, the Herd started badly, tripped repeatedly and still swept its East games. And that's all the Bobcats need to do: beat Akron in the opener, hold serve the rest of the way, and it's green against green for the title on November 17.

(R.C.)

2000 RESULTS

Iowa State	L	15-25	0-1
Minnesota	W	23-17	1-1
Tennessee Tech	W	52-14	2-1
Akron	L	20-23	2-2
Western Michigan	L	10-23	2-3
Buffalo	W	42-20	3-3
Kent State	W	44-7	4-3
Central Michigan	W	52-3	5-3
Miami (Ohio)	L	24-27	5-4
Bowling Green	W	23-21	6-4
Marshall	W	38-28	7-4

Toledo

LOCATION	**Toledo, OH**
CONFERENCE	**Mid-American (West)**
LAST SEASON	**9-2 (.818)**
CONFERENCE RECORD	**4-1 (t-1st)**
OFFENSIVE STARTERS RETURNING	**8**
DEFENSIVE STARTERS RETURNING	**8**
NICKNAME	**Rockets**
COLORS	**Midnight Blue & Gold**
HOME FIELD	**Glass Bowl (26,248)**
HEAD COACH	**Tom Amstutz (Toledo '77)**
RECORD AT SCHOOL	**First Year**
CAREER RECORD	**FirstYear**
ASSISTANTS	**Rob Spence (Iona '81)** **Offensive Coordinator** **Lou West (Cincinnati '77)** **Defensive Coordinator** **Dino Dawson (Wayne State '91)** **Wide Receivers** **Doug Downing (Purdue '88)** **Running Backs** **Joe Gilbert (Hamilton '87)** **Offensive Line** **Chris Hedden (Ashland '94)** **Tight Ends** **Dennis Winston (Wayne State '91)** **Inside Linebackers** **Paul Randolph (Tennessee-Martin '87)** **Defensive Line** **Dave Walkosky (Toledo '92)** **Outside Linebackers**
TEAM WINS (last 5 yrs.)	**7-9-7-6-10**
FINAL RANK (last 5 yrs.)	**97-91-100-89-41**
2000 FINISH	**Lost to Bowling Green in regular-season finale.**

COACH AND PROGRAM

It's simply a matter of respect. The Mid-American Conference doesn't get much. Former Toledo head coach Gary Pinkel had done everything one could do in the MAC, or so it seemed. Consider these accomplishments: fifty wins in the last six seasons (ninth best winning percentage in Division I over that span), NFL draft picks, a parade of graduating players and All-MAC honorees, two division titles to begin the MAC's divisional era.

The Rockets even put up a 10-win season last fall. But it wasn't enough. It's never enough in the MAC. Like Miami in '98, Toledo became the second team in modern I-A history to stay home in the postseason with double-digit wins.

After flirting with the job at Washington (where he was once an assistant to former Kent State coach Don James) a couple seasons ago and seeing it go to the southern California recruiting connections and TV-anchor hair of Rick Neuheisel, Pinkel took the first train out that he could at year's end—to Missouri on Nov. 30.

He tried to take his entire staff with him, but it only took a few weeks for the folks at UT to call home favorite son and alum Tom Amstutz to take his first job as a head coach.

Amstutz played guard for the Rockets in the mid-70s and since has spent 21 of his 24 years in coaching on the Toledo staff. That includes the last seven as defensive coordinator, overseeing the change to the turnover-happy 4-4 defense in 1995.

"Missouri is the second-best place I've ever been," Amstutz said upon his return to Ohio's north coast. "But you know what's first. I was working hard for them, but my heart is still in Toledo and I'm happy to come back. I've prepared for this 21 years and I'm ready. There's no doubt about it."

To be honest, it's hard to decide which is the better story for the Rockets this fall—the fact that they return eight starters on each side of ball and an All-MAC kicker, or the fact that Amstutz has told the second-ranked rushing and scoring offense in the league to tear up its old play books.

That's right. Toledo too will spread the field and throw the ball around the yard this fall. And Amstutz has got some experienced help to make it happen. Coordinator Rob Spence was most recently on the staff at Louisiana Tech, which used star quarterback Tim Rattay and four or five receivers on every down to twice defeat UT in recent seasons.

"I know from playing [Louisiana Tech] that I'm very impressed with that kind of offense," Amstutz said. "It really tests an opposing defense and is good at getting guys into one-on-one situations with tacklers."

It's a fresh start for everyone, especially fifth-year senior running back **Chester Taylor** (5-11, 205) who will get more chances to show the NFL scouts he can block and catch the ball. He could go for 2,000 yards if this offense has any success at all.

The Toledo defense led the MAC in scoring and rushing defense, and turnover margin (+2.0 per game). That group also gets a new coordinator in former Virginia Tech assistant Lou West. He and West Virginia coordinator Phil Elmassian built a similar 4-4 attack package in Blacksburg that will put more pressure on opposing passers and their own cornerbacks. There will be a star made this season in Toledo at the Whip linebacker position.

Oh, and by the way, this Rockets team has more than just a simple MAC West title in mind. If you believe last season's results and what the various polls and computers say, this team is headed for a national ranking. Toledo ended the fall at No. 27 in both the Associated Press and *USA Today* polls and in the top 25 of five of the computer rankings used to derive the Bowl Championship Series.

Just as Marshall broke into the national spotlight in '98 and '99 to get some top 25 votes, Toledo is counting on it. The Rockets made a statement last fall in destroying Penn State, 24-6, in State College, and have a chance to grab national attention early if they beat Minnesota. After that, UT should be a hefty favorite in every game except perhaps the Oct. 6 date at Ohio. Going 11-0 is not a pipe dream; it's a serious expectation this year at the Glass Bowl.

2001 SCHEDULE

Aug.	31	Minnesota
Sept.	8	@Temple
	15	Youngstown State
	22	@Central Michigan
	29	Northern Illinois
Oct.	6	@Ohio
	20	@Ball State
	27	Navy
Nov.	6	Western Michigan
	17	Eastern Michigan
	23	@Bowling Green

QUARTERBACKS

Senior **Tavares Bolden** (6-1, 205) was last year's All-MAC quarterback in a vote of the league's coaches. It's hard to quarrel with the choice, as he led the league's winningest team and threw just four interceptions in a full season of action. He also gave up just one fumble and was sacked only three times.

Bolden's job was to go out and not keep the Rockets from winning. His modest numbers through the air (1,597 yards and 13 passing touchdowns) were a function of his sometimes caretaker role. Just like Chris Finlen at Northern Illinois, Bolden knows his limitations and stays within them, though he has a little more getaway speed (390 rushing yards).

Odds are that Bolden will not be an NFL prospect like the more decorated Byron Leftwich at Marshall. But his team won more than Marshall, more than any team in the league last fall, and that's how the MAC coaches made their votes. He's known for his feet and was deadly in '99 and 2000 on bootlegs and rollouts.

"He's got a stronger arm than folks think," Amstutz said.

Now, Bolden *will* be put in a position where he could lose a game. And that will be the test for the Rockets, for a defense used to spending less time on the field and an offense not used to the quick developing throws of the spread. Decision-making will be critical.

Bolden missed the spring game after a minor concussion at the end of spring drills. The new offense has as many as 40-50 sets to be learned. The quarterback remarked that it was like being "all freshmen again."

"I couldn't have asked for a bigger challenge in my career," Spence told the *Toledo Blade* in the spring. "This is the first place I've been where the change was so dramatic and different. It's like the world's turned upside-down for these players."

The cast of characters to whom Bolden will be throwing is broad and new, much like the other quarterbacks behind him. Sophomore **Keon Frazier** (6-1, 190) took most all the snaps for both offenses in the spring game and was maybe the most improved Rocket in the spring. Junior **J.R. Winchester** (5-10, 190) is a converted defensive back and probably will be passed in the fall by one of the three new recruits.

Junior college signee **Brian Jones** (6-2, 215) from Shasta (Calif.) Junior College is the mature insurance policy if Bolden or Frazier goes down. Jones played in a spread offense the last two seasons.

Two quarterbacks from last year's class—Travis Atwell and Andre Thomas—opted to leave after the change in coaching staff and offense.

RUNNING BACKS

MAC running backs begin and end with Taylor. And if he weren't so darned healthy, folks would know that the group here is as deep as any in the league, Northern Illinois and Ohio included.

But Taylor is the bell cow, and if the potential Heisman candidate graduates this summer as expected (he began his college career as an academic non-qualifier), he'll be in position to lead the Rockets, MAC and possibly the nation in rushing, not to mention begin work on his masters degree.

Superlatives? There are too many to mention, but here's a sampling: MAC highs in rushing yards per game, touchdowns and total scoring. Consecutive 1,000-yard seasons. Twice All-MAC. Doak Walker Award candidate. Seventeen 100-yard rushing games in a career.

Taylor had 141 yards and two scores in that win at Penn State last fall, and is the second-leading returning ground gainer in the NCAA, at nearly 5.9 yards per carry. He had 1,470 yards rushing in 11 games, and was seventh in the NCAA in rushing and scoring.

After Taylor carved up Penn State, Nittany Lion coach Joe Paterno called him "as good a running back as we'll see all season." In a season where Penn State had Pitt's Reggie Barlow and Michigan State's T.J. Duckett on the bill of fare, that's pretty fair praise.

The new offense could cut into Taylor's numbers by forcing him to spend more downs blocking or running routes. But, then again, as well as Taylor ran through eight- and nine-man fronts in the past, what he could do against just five or six guys in the box might be amazing.

"[Taylor is a] guy who really wants the ball in his hands, and we really had to talk seriously with him this spring about how his role might change," Amstutz said.

If for some reason the plan breaks down over the summer, Toledo would still be in good hands. Senior **Antwon McCray** (6-0, 205) is a Taylor clone who'd be more than happy to pick up some carries this fall. McCray picked up 567 rushing yards in limited duty a year ago.

Third-stringer **William Bratton** (5-11, 220), a senior, played backup minutes in '99 when he notched 486 rushing yards. Coaches said he was the best back in spring drills.

Two more backs are on the roster already, sophomore **Adam Cuomo** (5-9, 195) and redshirt freshman **Webster Jackson** (5-11, 200), from Central Catholic High School in Toledo. Freshman back **Trinity Dawson** (5-10, 180) is one of five current Rockets from the less-than-typical MAC recruiting territory of Oklahoma.

WIDE RECEIVERS/TIGHT ENDS

If the backs are proven, the receivers certainly are not. The old Toledo depth chart had 12 positions on the offense, including a fullback and an H-back. The new one has 12 as well, though it will be the tight end and a fourth wideout who will spend time switching in and out of the game. A single back will have far more responsibilities than just taking the ball, picking a gap and heading north or south.

"We're going to spread the field and attack at all times," Amstutz said. "We'll use multiple formations, go no-huddle, and throw the ball a lot."

Only two of the four receiver spots list a returning starter. Top senior legacy Mel Long, Jr. finished his career in 2000 with a team-high 51 grabs in setting a UT career mark of 175.

The top returnee is a former slot receiver, junior **Donta Greene** (5-7, 180), who caught 31 passes last fall (and 30 as a freshman) but whose size will keep him a zone-buster in the slot or catching the inside screen. He is not the prototype outside stretch receiver this offense needs. He did catch two touchdown passes last fall. No one else who remains caught more than 15 balls last fall.

Junior **Manny Johnson** (5-7, 155) is currently listed as a starter at one of those outside spots, but he may also be better suited to the inside. He played his prep football at River Rouge (Mich.) as a teammate of Taylor.

On the other side, experienced junior **Carl Ford** (6-1, 170) is listed as a prohibitive starter at the X-receiver spot on the outside.

The new offensive staff really likes redshirt freshman **Terrance Hudson** (6-1, 180) from Cleveland. He has the highest ceiling of all the new faces.

Beyond those four, there are a lot of bodies, but separating the wheat from the chaff will be a process still going on well into the season. The coaches who run this sort of offense always talk about the need for at least 11-12 receivers on scholarship to make it work.

Though there are still too many walk-ons in the depth chart, there are at least five big-time athletes already in camp.

Redshirt freshman **Corterris Reese** (6-2, 175) is a prospect for the outside and set a Kentucky prep record his junior year with 1,663 receiving yards on 84 catches. Detroit-area sophomore **Drake Wilkins** (5-10, 173) missed last fall as an academic non-qualifier. Junior **Miquel Irvin** (6-2, 180) played sparingly last fall after ending spring at the top of the depth chart, and was an all-state player in Ohio at Akron St. Vincent High School. Sophomore **Jason Freeman** (6-3, 205) also has good size and jumping skills, and is one of 10 players from the Pittsburgh area on the team. Sophomore **David Mentlow** (5-10, 175) is a converted cornerback from Kent, Ohio, who played in the Big 33 All-Star game as a prep.

There are possibly a couple more receivers in the new class. What is certain is that some stars must be found at this position. There will need to be at least two 50-catch receivers and eight guys with at least 10 to 12. Receivers coach Dino Dawson comes north from Bowling Green, where his duo of Kurt Gerling and David Bautista last fall were the only watchable facets of Falcons football.

The Toledo staff might have found one of its big-play guys late in the recruiting game. Junior college transfer **Delano Scott** (5-9, 175) from Sacramento (Calif.) City College signed with the Rockets on May 9. Scott, a junior, had 73 receptions in his junior college career. As a sophomore, he averaged 28 yards per catch and scored 10 touchdowns. He was team captain last season and helped lead the Panthers to a 9-2 record. Scott has "legitimate 4.3 speed," said his coach at Sac City, Lamonte Love.

At tight end, this could finally be the year that junior **Greg Grothous** (6-6, 240) breaks through. Recruited by some far more famous programs out of nearby Delphos St. Johns High School, he's been hampered by ankle and back maladies. In terms of prep pedigree, he should be one of the MAC's best if he can have a healthy year. His blocking will also be even more important to the outside if Taylor is going to run without a fullback.

Redshirt freshman **Chris Holmes** (6-5, 259) out of Whitney Young High School in Chicago may have more of a future in running situations and double tight end sets at the goal line. Senior **Jason Speice** (6-2, 230) started the last two games of 2000 for Grothous. Unlike Bowling Green, Toledo has excellent tight ends and will run some double sets out there in non goal-line situations.

OFFENSIVE LINE

This unit was just flat dominating in 2000. There's no way a starting quarterback is sacked just three times and backs run for 254 yards per game if this group isn't getting it done.

The question will be if the road-graders of the past are ready to zone block for this quick release passing game.

Three guys with starters' minutes return for 2001, though Amstutz is looking for some tackles. He also will stay with the strong-side/weak-side switching of his linemen despite the change in the offense. The two who are gone, by the way, were also All-MAC first-teamers.

Senior center **Nick Otterbacher** (6-1, 280) is anticipated back for the fall after missing the spring with shoulder problems. Amstutz called him the "toughest player on the team" before his spring shoulder problems. He started 10 games last fall en route to All-MAC honorable-mention honors from the coaches. Until fall, junior **Chris Tuminello** (6-3, 282) was the guy here.

The guards return experience, albeit with a position switch. Junior **Noah Swartz** (6-5, 302) moves from left tackle to strong-side guard after starting 11 games outside last year. Senior **Matt Comer** (6-3, 283) has 14 starts at guard in his career and stays put after starting eight last fall. He can play anywhere on the line and is the star-to-be on the line.

Redshirt freshman **Wael Jarbou** (6-5, 285) and sophomore **David Odenthal** (6-2, 292) are the next wave inside. Jarbou is from the Detroit area and Odenthal is a long Delta flight from there. The 22-year-old is from Cologne, Germany and played for the European high school American FB champions (Irmgardis) in '97 and '98. He played as a true freshman here last fall. A great preseason by Odenthal could solidify things enough to send Swartz back outside.

At tackle, junior **Archie Godfrey** (6-5, 281) must be ready to step up and earn a starting job. From the Columbus suburb of Gahanna (Lincoln High School), he has improved every year. Sophomore **Darric Randolph** (6-3, 272) is behind Godfrey at the left spot. The strong-side tackle should be sophomore **Tim Dirksen** (6-4, 285) from Marion, Ohio. Behind him area a pair of giant freshmen, **Erik Faasen** (6-8, 335) from Michigan and **Nick Kaczur** (6-6, 300) from Brantford, Ontario.

The new tackles will have to perform more zones blocks and less of the straight-ahead running game push from past years.

2000 STATISTICS

Rushing offense	253.8	9
Passing offense	150.7	105
Total offense	404.5	37

Scoring offense	36.4	13
Net Punting	32.6	84
Punt returns	8.3	76
Kickoff returns	20.3	41
Rushing defense	81.5	5
Passing efficiency defense	100.5	15
Total defense	269.0	3
Scoring defense	11.4	3
Turnover margin	+22	1

Last column is ranking among Division I-A teams.

KICKERS

Senior **Todd France** (6-3, 185) is reliable and has gotten All-MAC mention of every sort (first team, second team, honorable mention) his first three seasons in the league. France was also second-team Academic All-America last fall while hitting 15-of-19 field goals and all 49 PATs. His career-long field goal is 51 yards. He holds a grade point average of better than 3.9 in engineering.

DEFENSIVE LINE

Only one senior is missing from last year's group, but end Dejuan Goulde goes in the book as one of the best ever at Toledo. He was one of three departed Rockets on the All-MAC first team and was the runner-up for the league's defensive player of the year with nine sacks and 73 tackles.

Now, Amstutz says that he returns enough depth to rotate his lines almost wholesale. Five players combined for the 33 starts on defensive line that didn't belong to Goulde.

Toledo allowed just 11.4 points per game, and that started up front.

Senior **Leo Frierson** (6-3, 245) started 10-of-11 games at the end opposite Goulde and had three sacks as a defensive co-captain.

Fellow senior **David Bockmore** (6-4, 249) moves back outside after seven starts at tackle in 2000. He recovered a pair of fumbles, grabbed an interception and collected three sacks inside.

Behind them, Amstutz is happy with the progress of one of his Oklahoma imports, redshirt freshman **Don Gaines** (6-3, 226) and fellow second-year freshman **Phil Alexander** (6-3, 230) from Chicago. Sophomores **Frank Ofili** (6-3, 240) and Canadian end **Didier Ormejuste** (6-4, 245) have more experience here. Ofili did get a start last fall at end and had six sacks in 2000 as a more situational pass rusher.

LINEBACKERS

Just like Goulde, All-MAC linebacker Kevin Rollins won't be there to clean up all the tackles in the middle of the field. Rollins had 95 stops last year and 300 for his career, and led the team with 10 sacks from inside backer.

But three returnees have meaningful experience, and junior **David Gardner** (6-2, 231) put up tremendous numbers in only nine games as the other half of that inside tandem (82 tackles, 12 for losses). Another one of the Pittsburgh-area recruits, Gardner picked up two fumbles last year and started four games as a freshman. He will make all the play calls and adjustments for the defensive front.

Junior **Tom Ward** (6-1, 236) brings back 70 stops from last fall and should start alongside after starting twice in 2000.

Senior **Jason Manson** (6-1, 226) has some experience, but the coaches would like to develop sophomores **Anthony Abron** (6-2, 220) and **Ray Turner** (6-0, 205).

Redshirt freshman **Quennen Burdine** (6-1, 215) is one of three additions to the team from Santa Fe High School in Edmund, Okla. last year. He blocked three punts as a prep senior and will be important on special teams this fall.

The outside backers in this 4-4 may be closer to safeties than linebackers in size. It's the typical rover/whip look, with the former like a strong safety who comes up to the line of scrimmage and usually lines up over the tight end. The latter will set up on the weak side of the formation and often rush the passes from the edge, hoping to outrun a tackle around the end of the line. Safety-sized Corey Moore (drafted by the Buffalo Bills) made this an art form at Virginia Tech. This position is susceptible to being run over by a power rushing team.

Senior **Corey Morris** (6-0, 208) is a returning starter at the whip and is a three-year letterman who added 75 tackles and six sacks last fall. He gets help from fellow senior **Sid Daniels** (5-10, 190), who added 55 more stops and four sacks.

At rover, two sophomores will battle for the time after the loss of another All-MAC player—Ira Singleton. **Paul Dye** (6-2, 206) had 13 tackles last year in relief and **Dorian Goulde** (5-10, 192), the younger brother of defensive end Dejuan, added 17 stops, mainly on special teams. Another sophomore, **Olanzo Jarrett** (6-2, 200), is making the move here from free safety. He's from Toronto, Ontario.

DEFENSIVE BACKS

In this system, there are only three defensive backs. Senior free safety **Andy Boyd** (6-2, 203) stayed home after attending Toledo's Whitmer High School and is now in position to notch an All-MAC type of year. Boyd topped the squad with parts of 95 stops and three interceptions, bringing his career total to nine.

Junior **Demetris Simms** (6-2, 196) returns as the backup here, and is from Ross High School in nearby Freemont, Ohio—the same school that gave the football world All-Pro cornerback Charles Woodson.

The corners both return to make the secondary one of the defense's strengths. **Brandon Hefflin** (6-1, 170) is only a sophomore and has a chance to be one of the very special young corners in the league. Hefflin started every game as a true freshman, stole three interceptions and had a fumble return and punt block for touchdowns. He should be ticketed for All-MAC honors next year if not sooner after prepping at Penn Hills High School in Pittsburgh.

"He can be the best corner in this league and is the kind of person with an NFL future," Amstutz said.

Junior **Jehu Anderson** (6-1, 186) had 64 stops and an interception last fall and improved considerably after starting as a freshman.

Sophomore **Brandon Carter** (5-9, 170) is another local talent from in Toledo. Juniors **Tony Miller** (5-9, 179) and **James Stanley** (6-1, 185) are the depth here, along with sophomores **Keith Dandridge** (6-0, 190) and **Derrick Hobbs** (5-8, 200). Carter was the first player off the sidelines last fall when the Rockets faced nickel type passing situations.

PUNTERS

Sophomore **Brandon Hannum** (6-3, 222) is a former walk-on from suburban Columbus power Westerville North High School. He earned a grant after putting up 38 yards per punt last fall. There are no other punters on the roster, making France the backup or emergency punter.

SPECIAL TEAMS

Though Long is gone, there is still plenty of speed and experience to get the Rockets through at the return and snapping spots. Hefflin averaged nearly 8.5 yards on 19 punt returns, and backup corner Miller is next in the depth here.

Miller and wideout Ford will return kickoffs this fall.

Bolden holds for kicks and he'll be catching those snaps from the backup center Tuminello.

RECRUITING CLASS

If you're wondering why this group hasn't been mentioned much to this point, it's not just because of the depth of this team. While experienced, the Rockets lost very few players last fall in a small senior class and gave out only 12 new grants last February. Those grants included three quarterbacks, but otherwise were just spread here and there around the depth chart. Scott became signee No. 13 on May 9.

Virtually none of these guys save Scott will play or will need to play. It was a good thing Toledo had so much returning talent—the new staff lost a step as Amstutz spent the dead recruiting period in December trying to hire fresh bodies. Universally, this is not considered a very strong class compared to prior Toledo efforts. But luckily, in that case, it is small and will not be of any harm in the longer term.

Some observers like the two defensive linemen signed, **Ballard Winbush** (6-4, 260) from Westerville North High School and **Chris Wakeman** (6-5, 250) from the wilds of Michigan's Upper Peninsula. And the continued mining of Oklahoma by linebackers coach David Walkosky seems like a good idea considering the lack of talent in his more traditional assigned areas of southeast Ohio and West Virginia. Ditto for grabbing quarterback **Terrance Matthews** (6-2, 180) from east Texas.

Toledo has a good mix of talent from Ohio, Michigan and western Pennsylvania and is a strong enough MAC program to succeed in those traditional areas. It will be curious to see where this new staff develops contacts. Amstutz said that Florida, Georgia and the Texas/Oklahoma corridor would be additions to the core areas. That is not something the rest of the league needed to hear.

The Rockets are in a good spot, both in terms of on-field tradition and geography. They are dead center in the middle of MAC Country—300 miles from Northern Illinois or Buffalo, 200 miles from Central Michigan or Miami.

BLUE RIBBON ANALYSIS

OFFENSE	B
SPECIAL TEAMS	C+
DEFENSE	B+
INTANGIBLES	B+

It's a huge risk, changing this power offense which has done the Rockets so proud in recent seasons. But Amstutz remembers Louisiana Tech laying the lumber to some of his best defenses and thinks that the spread is the future. To be honest, a lot of coaches agree right now.

The learning curve is a very steep one, but Amstutz is sure he has the brains and the brawn on board to make this new system work.

When the curtain goes up on Aug. 31 against Minnesota at the Glass Bowl, it will be a very early midterm for the progress of this offense and staff against a Minnesota team that is gutted on defense. That's because after this game, there really aren't too many tests ahead. An angry Temple bunch and Ohio on the road won't strike fear in too many hearts nationally, though the Rocket coaches will have to have their best game plan for both. And the Rockets get the duo of top teams in the West—Western Michigan and Northern Illinois—at home. This is the perfect schedule to run the table.

The defense is back with similar talent up front and improved protection on the corners. It's odd, how some teams in this league have switched to 4-4s to fight the run in a league that seems to be passing more. But Toledo has run it for years, and has confidence. The new "Virginia Tech" flavored version of this defense will be even more intense.

The 10-1 season set school marks with most points (400) and fewest turnovers (nine) and gave up the fewest rushing yards in the MAC or in school history at only 897. Toledo scored 50 touchdowns. Just as there was no denying Marshall a 13-0 season in '99, this should be Toledo's year. If it can beat a mediocre big conference squad in week one on ESPN2, the world is its oyster.

And if they do run the table, the MAC West champ plays host to the league's championship game at a Glass Bowl that averaged 104 percent of listed seating capacity last season. After years of complaining about locker rooms and having to go to Huntington every year, the Rockets should get to say, "Detroit here we come!"

(R.C.)

2000 RESULTS

Penn State	W	24-6	1-0
Weber State	W	51-0	2-0
Eastern Illinois	W	31-26	3-0
Western Michigan	L	14-21	3-1
Central Michigan	W	41-0	4-1
Eastern Michigan	W	42-14	5-1
Marshall	W	42-0	6-1
Navy	W	35-14	7-1
Northern Illinois	W	38-24	8-1
Ball State	W	31-3	9-1
Bowling Green	L	17-51	9-2

Western Michigan

LOCATION Kalamazoo, MI
CONFERENCE Mid-American (West)
LAST SEASON 9-3 (.750)
CONFERENCE RECORD 4-1 (t-1st)
OFFENSIVE STARTERS RETURNING 5
DEFENSIVE STARTERS RETURNING 7
NICKNAME Broncos
COLORS Brown & Gold
HOME FIELD Waldo Stadium (30,200)
HEAD COACH Gary Darnell (Oklahoma St. '70)
RECORD AT SCHOOL 31-15 (5 years)
CAREER RECORD 34-20 (6 years)
ASSISTANTS
Brian Rock (Bowling Green '85)
Offensive Coordinator/Wide Receivers
Jim Knowles (Cornell '87)
Defensive Coordinator/Defensive Line
Wally Ake (William & Mary '72)
Safeties
Dan Enos (Michigan State '91)
Quarterbacks
Keith Flynn (North Carolina '83)
Running Backs
Guy Holliday (Cheyney '87)
Tight Ends
Kyle Nystrom (Michigan State '88)
Linebackers/Special Teams
Dave Voth (Central Arkansas '82)
Offensive Line
Joe Woods (Illinois State '92)
Cornerbacks
TEAM WINS (last 5 yrs.) 2-8-7-7-9
FINAL RANK (last 5 yrs.) 106-90-97-87-70
2000 FINISH Lost to Marshall in MAC championship game.

COACH AND PROGRAM

Head coach Gary Darnell reportedly told his assistants not to buy any property when they landed in Kalamazoo in 1997. For the star coordinator with stops at Texas, Florida, Wake Forest, Notre Dame and Kansas State, a long stay wasn't expected. Darnell pushed the Broncos to the nation's most-improved record in '97, going from 2-9 the previous year to an 8-3 season. After a 31-7 loss that year at Ohio, Western won six straight to end the year and is 29-12 ever since that turning-point game at Peden Stadium.

In the meantime, the real estate situation has settled down, and despite a few flirtations with other jobs the last two seasons, Darnell looks to be here for the long haul. Like Toledo, the Broncos have had their share of win streaks and great regular seasons only to have to end the year with a regularly scheduled loss at Marshall in the MAC title game.

On Oct. 5, the Broncos made league history on national TV by being the first MAC team to win at Marshall since the Herd rejoined the league. The score was 30-10 as Western did what no one else had been able to do in Huntington. Panned by the preseason prognosticators, the Broncos were just as good as the '99 team that lost a MAC title game at Marshall in the final 30 seconds to the departed pro Chad Pennington. Even with the loss of long-time starting quarterback Tim Lester and tailback Robert Sanford, the defense more than did its part in beating Toledo in the regular season and getting back to another MAC title game.

Marshall got its revenge at home in that season finale, which ended Western's season and sent Marshall fans again to wintry Detroit for Christmas.

But what's been built in Kalamazoo is special. Darnell presides over the most successful four years in the modern era of the program and that success is a catalyst for one of the league's best complexes of weight rooms, offices and luxury suites at Waldo Stadium. This entire west Michigan community is starting to see this team as its own and it shows in the burgeoning attendance numbers.

The success in and out of conference is proven. The Broncos got a win at Iowa last fall, a near miss at Wisconsin and have set sights high again at Michigan and Virginia Tech this fall. Western will take on any challenge, and for the last three years has handled it well as anybody. Just like Toledo, this team has enough "juice" with the youngsters to go into Detroit and Chicago and come out with far better than the usual MAC-level recruit. The true measure of respect for a MAC team is here; that's when mediocre big conference schools won't schedule you anymore.

2001 SCHEDULE

Aug.	30	Illinois State
Sept.	8	@Virginia Tech
	15	@Michigan
	22	Ball State
	29	@Eastern Michigan
Oct.	6	Akron
	13	Bowling Green
	20	@Northern Illinois
	27	@Miami (Ohio)
Nov.	6	@Toledo
	17	Central Michigan

QUARTERBACKS

The shadow of Lester loomed very large last year for now-veteran senior **Jeff Welsh** (6-3, 215). But the two-year backup from the Chicago area answered the call with a 2,537-yard season on 59 percent completions. Welsh threw for 15 scores and 12 interceptions, but made fairly good decisions. He was better early in the season when opposing teams still hadn't caught on to the limitations under which he was playing.

Opposing coaches say Welsh seemed to have instructions to make no more than two passing reads and then take off running. That would very easily explain how he was third on the team in carries with 72. It also explains how an inexperienced quarterback running a sometimes three- or four-wide offense didn't make too many mistakes. Another thing that helped was having an All-MAC tight end as one of those two primary reads on almost every play.

Welsh scored twice on the ground and had a season-long rush of 35 yards on one of his frequent scrambles. Not a game breaker like Josh Harris at Bowling Green, Welsh is fast enough to force defenses to have a spy or rover keep an eye on him. Consistency was the name of the game, as he passed for more than 300 yards just once (against Ohio) and never completed more than 23 in a game. His numbers in that role still convinced the league's coaches to vote him an All-MAC honorable mention player.

Senior **Ryan Harris** (6-1, 192) is the backup and saw action in seven games in 2000. The Idaho native was a junior college transfer last fall and was 14-of-27 for 246 yards and two touchdowns in his first season at Western.

No other quarterbacks saw action last year. The future at the position is probably freshman **Mitch John** (6-3, 182) from La Jolla High School in San Diego. **Blayne Baggett** (6-2, 205) is from the north Detroit suburbs and threw for 1,400 yards and 14 touchdowns last fall at Central High School in Walled Lake.

RUNNING BACKS

Toledo got another year for All-MAC back Chester Taylor. And Western wishes it could have gotten a fifth year for departed senior Robert Sanford. Sanford scored 18 touchdowns last fall en route to being the MAC's Offensive Player of the Year and winner of the Vern Smith Award, given to the league's top overall player. Sanford was the NCAA's eighth-leading rusher at 1,571 yards and went for 100 yards in seven consecutive games, including 203 in the win at Marshall. Sanford was the MAC Freshman of the Year in '97 as a 1,000-yard fullback.

So who is the star-to-be in this one-back offense? Senior **Charles Woods** (5-10, 194) is from south Florida like Sanford and got nearly 300 yards and six scores in mainly mop-up duty in 10 games last year. He's evasive, not as likely to try to run through you like Sanford. Sophomore **Phillip Reed** (5-10, 198) had carries in just four games last year and is fairly unproven.

Luckily though, running back is one of the easiest positions to learn. So if one of the three freshmen can get up to speed quickly on the blocking scheme, one of them will try to be the next Sanford.

The speedy favorite is **Daniel Marks** (6-0, 207) from Miami Beach. An all-state second-teamer in Florida, Marks ran for 3,500 yards in two seasons.

Freshman **Trovon Riley** (5-11, 190) ran sprints in track and is an area Top-100 selection by the *Chicago Sun-Times* after playing in

Kankakee, Ill. Western needs to find depth here now, with no other credible halfbacks on the roster after signing zero in the 2000 freshman class.

WIDE RECEIVERS/TIGHT ENDS

Western comes to the line with a spread offensive look. Single-back, three wideouts and a tight end are the usual personnel. As is the case at running back, an All-MAC player is finished after 2000. Wideout Steve Neal was first-team All-MAC three times and caught 67 passes for 848 yards last fall—good for fourth in the league in yards and catches. But his game-breaking speed made other things possible for every other receiver on the squad.

Now, the chances and the catches should fall to senior receiver **Josh Bush** (5-9, 150). Bush is at his best on special teams, but is the top returning pass-catcher with 40 grabs and four receiving touchdowns. Bush has been fairly durable despite his size, but whether he can be a primary receiver in this sort of offense in unclear. There's no question he can be productive.

Another Florida native, Bush will start as the slot receiver in the Western offense, ahead of fellow senior **Marco Wolverton** (5-10, 183). Wolverton was one of six Broncos with double-digit catches last year (12).

Outside, the Broncos want players who are a little taller and were ready to start a couple seniors by spring's end. **Micah Zuhl** (6-0, 191) and **Darnell Jennings** (6-3, 195) combined for 20 catches and two touchdowns last year but will be battling juniors **Kendrick Mosley** (6-0, 178) and **Brandon Johnson** (6-3, 207) all summer.

Mosley had his season abbreviated at just two games with injury last year after being a projected starter. Johnson has the chance to be excellent sitting down against zone defenses.

Redshirt freshman **Ty Walker** (6-3, 188) is from Lansing and sat out last fall. All will be pushed by a group of receiver recruits who are collectively the league's best.

With only one wideout in last year's class, Darnell signed four this winter. **Greg Jennings** (6-1, 190) stayed home near Kalamazoo's Central High School to play for Western. He is No. 10 in the *Detroit Free Press* Fabulous 50 rankings and was an all-state player in football and hoops.

Osborn Curtis (6-1, 175) is one of the top 50 recruits this year from the Chicago area. **Tony Scheffler** (6-5, 223) is the big possession receiver Western has lacked and **Pat Graham** (6-0, 180) was a finalist for Indiana's Mr. Football award after averaging 28 yards per catch at Broad Ripple High School in urban north Indianapolis.

The Broncos also signed a pair of quality tight ends, but this position belongs to junior **Mobolaji Afairiogun** (6-4, 228). Afairiogun was so good as a pass catching tight end that he rarely came off the field for a fourth wideout. He caught 32 passes for 365 yards and three touchdowns, earning All-MAC first-team honors from almost everyone. The Detroit native has sophomore **Anthony Kiner** (6-5, 297) as a backup, though he usually only sees the field in goal-line and short-yardage situations. He might as well be another tackle out there.

Former quarterback recruit **Josh Nycz** (6-5, 220) is also a tight end hopeful as a sophomore. New recruit **Walter Stith** (6-8, 236) is from Atlanta and has size reminiscent of NFL All-Pro Tony Gonzalez or an air-traffic control tower. He could also help coach Robert McCallum's Bronco hoops team in the high post.

OFFENSIVE LINE

Western returns three senior starters to the offensive line that was one of the league's most effective at both facets of the offense. But there are new faces at perhaps the most important spots. At center, junior **Jake Gasaway** (6-3, 285) takes over after being the team's long snapper for all of 2000. He's a converted defensive tackle.

Junior **Kevin Kramer** (6-4, 296) should be the backup here again.

At guard, it is a pair of returning seniors, **Adam Cones** (6-5, 280) and **Jeff Hinson** (6-2, 279) who provide experience for now. Both are exterior linemen who have moved inside since arriving at Western. Sophomore **Ed Boness** (6-4, 326) has the size the coaching staff prefers here and could move up over the summer. He was an all-state pick by the *Chicago Sun-Times* and Chicago Tribune as a prep senior in '98.

At tackle, the size is there, but that's where competition from the new freshman could be the hardest. Senior **Matt Stover** (6-4, 302) is the returning starter at right tackle and added 20 good pounds last year while moving over from center.

Sophomore **C.R. Moultry** (6-6, 333) is a one-man-band over on the island at left tackle and is light on his feet. He will need to work on technique but can overpower folks.

Behind them are junior **Fred McCants** (6-6, 343) at left and sophomore **Jon Garcia** (6-5, 339) at right. McCants is an early spring arrival from Grand Rapids (Mich.) Community College whose size may push him to the front of the line at guard by the first of September.

Darnell signed five top linemen in the winter and like Bob Pruett at Marshall, seems to have no real qualms about playing his best talent, no matter the age. Freshmen **Mike Weaver** (6-7, 317) from Mississauga, Ontario and **Shawn Wiza** (6-7, 293) from Wisconsin could plug in now at tackle or guard. Wiza also could get into the act around the goal line as an extra tight end.

2000 STATISTICS

Rushing offense	168.5	32
Passing offense	232.1	38
Total offense	400.6	38
Scoring offense	29.9	38
Net Punting	32.2	89
Punt returns	15.3	10
Kickoff returns	20.4	40
Rushing defense	105.3	20
Passing efficiency defense	108.2	31
Total defense	283.3	9
Scoring defense	11.6	4
Turnover margin	-4	78

Last column is ranking among Division I-A teams.

KICKERS

Graduated senior Brad Selent was the answer here for so long, finishing 2000 as the school's all-time scoring leader and the MAC's most prolific kicker as well with 307 points.

Darnell has to turn things over to a completely new face. Sophomore **Byungwoo Yun** (5-11, 195) spent a year at Fullerton (Calif.) Junior College kicking and punting with a long field goal of 47 yards. Yun is originally from Korea, though has lived the last eight years in Orange County, Calif. Redshirt freshman **Robert Menchinger** (5-10, 150) is the only other kicker on the roster.

DEFENSIVE LINE

This Broncos' defensive line is the pride and joy of new coordinator Knowles and the pressure they delivered in 2000 was the root of the team's success on this side of the ball. Darnell is a former lineman himself and won't stand for anything less than top-notch performance here.

Western was fourth nationally in scoring defense (11.6 points per game), ninth in total defense, and in the top 20 in passing and rushing defense. The Broncos have All-MAC selections from last fall at both bookends and will need an even stronger performance from the tackles to keep offensive guards off of the new inside linebackers.

Junior **Anthony Allsbury** (6-2, 254) was first-team All-MAC at right end and is a great story after beginning his career as a walk-on. Allsbury tied for fifth in the league with eight quarterback sacks, including two at Wisconsin.

Quickness at these defensive end spots is what made last year's rushing defense so good as teams tried to avoid Western's pair of All-MAC inside backers. Even option and power-sweep teams like Ohio and Northern Illinois had trouble running against this group, and the ends were key in making that happen.

Fellow junior **Chris Browning** (6-2, 248) plays at the left end—the side away from the nose guard in this offset 4-3—and grabbed second-team All-MAC attention from the coaches. He started the last six games and totaled five sacks and 31 stops.

A pair of second-year players, redshirt freshman **Nick Melcher** (6-3, 230) and sophomore **Jason Babin** (6-3, 239) are the depth at end. Babin totaled 34 tackles in playing all 12 games. Melcher is a converted linebacker; Babin played last year as a freshman after failing to qualify academically in '99 and being re-recruited. He last played a full season in '97 as a prep junior. He averaged more than 20 tackles a game for Paw Paw (Mich.) High School.

At tackle, senior **Brian Pinder** (6-1, 260) is ahead of junior **Jeff Westgate** (6-5, 266). The pair combined for 39 tackles and will need to improve those numbers and their lateral quickness. Westgate moves in from end.

Over the nose, senior **Larry King** (6-4, 268) moves in to the starting lineup and has the size to take up space here. He also broke up a couple passes last fall, showing his versatility and skill in dropping off into an occasional zone look.

Sophomore **Chad Wangerin** (6-4, 305) is the backup here and will be hard to move; he slides over a gap from tackle.

Redshirt freshman **Ernest Osborne** (6-5, 218) is a developmental project from Dillard High School in Fort Lauderdale, Fla. Timed at 4.5 in the 40 in high school, Osborne was second-team all-state in only his first year playing football. He projects to end if he can get stronger.

A pair of last fall's recruits at line are no longer on the roster, so the coaches had to find some more gap-stuffers.

Joe Alvarez (6-2, 240) from Naperville, Ill. is the highest rated by the various recruiting services and was first-team all state. **Jack Gitler** (6-2, 245) was all state in Michigan and state champ in the discus.

LINEBACKERS

All three of the linebackers may be brand new and are an obvious target for opposing coordinators early in the season.

Garrett Soldano and Mario Evans were the two top tacklers on the team last fall, combining for 216 tackles and eight sacks at the inside linebacker positions. Outside, senior **Terrence Moore** (6-2, 200) was third with 63 stops and is petitioning the NCAA for an extra year of eligibility. But the Broncos can't count on him to be back for the fall.

So where does that leave Western? With a pair of juniors in **Jason Malloy** (6-1, 232) and **Bryan Lape** (6-3, 211) who can only try to occupy the open shoes left behind. The two combined for only parts of 37 tackles last year and lack much experience beyond special teams and mop-up time. Lape is a former walk-on.

Outside, the Broncos will pencil in senior **Carlos Smith** (6-4, 216) for now as they await word on Moore. A Dearborn native, like Malloy, Smith started five games at free safety in '99 and made 29 stops last fall. Junior **Jermaine Foreste** (5-10, 200) is the backup at the more pass coverage-oriented outside spot.

Inside, the depth will come from a pair of redshirt freshmen, **Erik Oleson** (6-3, 233) and **Willie Miller** (6-2, 230).

There's only one new face in the freshman class and he will almost certainly need to play this fall. **Josh Behrens** (6-2, 250) is giant for the position and played through an ankle sprain his senior year to still collect more than 100 tackles. He was honored by the *Detroit News* as a member of its "Fabulous 50."

DEFENSIVE BACKS

Though the second level of the Broncos' defense has some serious questions, the defensive backs are a strength, with two returnees who grabbed All-MAC honors last year.

Senior corner **Ronald Rogers** (5-8, 174) is the team's top returning tackler (54) and had four interceptions for a second straight year. He is one of the league's best and would get serious pro interest if he were just a bit taller. Despite his lack of size, Rogers is excellent against the run and is a great leaper, a talent he uses to add a vertical component to his coverage. Man-to-man, Rogers is excellent and is one of three starters from Florida in this unit.

At the other corner is fellow senior **Joe Ballard** (6-0, 191), who had 47 tackles and broke up six passes last year. He's another player from Dillard High School in Fort Lauderdale and has played every game in three seasons without an interception.

The safeties are junior **Jermaine Lewis** (6-4, 194) at free and senior **Brandon Brown** (5-10, 185) at strong. Lewis was also second-team All-MAC in 2000 and had 46 tackles and three quarterback sacks. He is a transfer from Wisconsin-Oshkosh and ran a 10.59-second outdoor 100 before competing at the Penn Relays for the Bronco track team. Brown is the second-leading returning tackler with 53.

This is probably the MAC's most experienced and speedy unit of defensive backs. The four reserves behind this unit combined for 49 stops last fall and don't figure to see the field often. Senior **Wes Dodson** (5-10, 180) is the first safety off the bench and junior **Sam Reynolds** (6-1, 182) is the nickel package corner. **Scott Robinson** (6-0, 178) and **Clay Powell** (6-2, 193) are backs who redshirted last year. Powell is the cousin of former Northern Illinois star Deon Mitchell.

The new class includes two freshmen from in-state—prep high jumper Kevin Ford (5-11, 185) and **Kip Paul** (6-1, 218), an all-state second-teamer at running back who's from Grand Rapids.

PUNTERS

Junior **Matt Steffen** (6-1, 195) is back for his third season, though he hasn't been that busy. Steffen had only 45 punts last fall, and two were blocked. Steffen punted in the '99 season opener at Florida and successfully got five kicks away there. He was one of just two freshmen to letter that season.

Kim should be the backup/emergency punter.

SPECIAL TEAMS

Though Selent is gone, the Bronco special teams are still some of the league's best just based on the quick-strike threat of their return teams.

The receiver Bush is already the school's all-time leader in punt return yardage (628 yards) and was second in the league behind NIU's Justin McCareins with 15 yards per punt return. He had touchdown returns in consecutive games against Eastern and Central Michigan. Voted Western's permanent special teams captain, he should be the league's best all-purpose offensive back this fall. Mosley is the listed backup here.

Bush does not return kicks. As good as the Broncos' defense was, there weren't many kicks to return. Western had only 20 returns last year, the bulk of which went to senior **Rashad McDade** (5-10, 172). McDade is listed as a corner but rarely sees the field there, instead serving as the featured kick returner. He averaged better than 21 yards per on 14 returns. Rogers also had three returns last year for 83 total yards.

Current center Gasaway will stay on the field for the long snaps. The safety, Dodson, is the holder on kick attempts.

RECRUITING CLASS

This very well could be the league's best class depending on who gets eligible by August or qualifies academically at Marshall.

It's a group heavy with five offensive linemen, one from a junior college (McCants), two tall timbers (Weaver and Wiza), and the best may be **Mark Ottney** (6-5, 270) from Troy, Mich., whose brother plays line at Michigan State.

There are answers for immediate needs at every position but linebacker, and Behrens should be excellent there.

Much like Toledo, Western has shown the ability to go get some of the best in the Midwest. Darnell's staff stayed home to sign 12 from the state, eight of those on the *Detroit News* "Fabulous 50" list.

But the difference is that the Broncos have the best ties to players in Florida who come in just below the SEC nets, and have parlayed those players into some great performers. The strength of this program, Darnell said, is that these players all could play now, but the team is good enough that most won't have to.

BLUE RIBBON ANALYSIS

OFFENSE	C
SPECIAL TEAMS	D+
DEFENSE	B-
INTANGIBLES	B+

It's remarkable just how little the MAC's media and few prognosticators thought of this team going into the 2000 season. The consensus pick was second or third in the West with a significant drop-off in performance.

But the defense persevered and Welsh proved more than competent in getting the ball to Sanford, Neal and Afairiogun and this team again won the West. Last year's team was great enough on offense not to need a superstar under center. This year will be a real test for the senior quarterback. Without being able to fall back on 30-40 carries by Sanford, his decision-making will be that much more critical. This offense will be effective but mid-pack in the MAC.

On defense, Western simply has no linebackers on whom they can rely—at least not yet. The new guys could be great. They will get a chance to show it at Michigan and Virginia Tech. The athletes in this secondary are big-league.

But no matter how far this program has developed, the odds are against the Broncos this fall. The automatic kicking of Selent is gone. It will come down to a couple games again this fall to win the West. And those games are being played in DeKalb, Ill. and Toledo, not at Waldo Stadium.

Western will run the table at home, but what it does on the road will determine whether there is a postseason in Kalamazoo. Then again, we all said they were taking a step back last year, too. Toldeo's Rockets need to watch their backs and the calendar for that Tuesday night game on ESPN on Nov. 6 or they will be home again at 9-2 or 10-1, watching the Broncos again on national TV.

(R.C.)

2000 RESULTS

Wisconsin	L	7-19	0-1
Iowa	W	27-21	1-1
Indiana State	W	56-0	2-1
Toledo	W	21-14	3-1
Ohio	W	23-10	4-1
Marshall	W	30-10	5-1
Northern Illinois	W	52-22	6-1
Kent State	W	42-0	7-1
Ball State	W	42-3	8-1
Central Michigan	L	17-21	8-2
Eastern Michigan	W	28-0	9-2
Marshall (MAC Champ.)	L	14-19	9-3

Air Force

LOCATION Colorado Springs, CO
CONFERENCE Mountain West
LAST SEASON 9-3 (.750)
CONFERENCE RECORD 5-2 (2nd)
OFFENSIVE STARTERS RETURNING 3
DEFENSIVE STARTERS RETURNING 4
NICKNAME Falcons
COLORS Blue & White
HOME FIELD Falcon Stadium (52,480)
HEAD COACH Fisher DeBerry (Wofford '60)
RECORD AT SCHOOL 135-72-1 (16 years)
CAREER RECORD 135-72-1 (16 years)
ASSISTANTS Richard Bell (Arkansas '59)
Defensive Coordinator/Inside Linebackers
Dean Campbell (Texas '72)
Running Backs
Dick Enga (Minnesota '63)
Tight Ends
Tim Horton (Arkansas '90)
Receivers
Tom Miller (Cortland State '69)
Special Teams/Outside Linebackers
Jappy Oliver (Purdue '78)
Defensive Line
Chuck Peterson (Air Force '85)
Offensive Coordinator
Vic Shealy (Richmond '84)
Defensive Backs
Ed Warinner (Mount Union '84)
Offensive Line
Jeff Hays (Air Force '84)
Kickers
TEAM WINS (last 5 yrs.) 6-10-12-6-9
FINAL RANK (last 5 yrs.) 71-75-30-78-40
2000 FINISH Beat Fresno State in Silicon Bowl.

MOUNTAIN WEST

BLUE RIBBON FORECAST

1. Colorado State
2. UNLV
3. BYU
4. Utah
5. San Diego State
6. Air Force
7. New Mexico
8. Wyoming

ALL-CONFERENCE TEAM

OFFENSE

POS. PLAYER SCHOOL HT. WT. CL.

WR Ryan Fleming, Air Force, 6-5, 225, Sr.
WR Pete Rebstock, Colorado State, 5-9, 182, Sr.
OL Doug Kaufusi, Utah, 6-6, 308, Sr.
OL Adam Goldberg, Wyoming, 6-7, 315, Jr.
C Jason Scukanec, BYU, 6-2, 282, Sr.
OL David Moreno, San Diego State, 6-2, 285, Sr.
OL Ben Miller, Air Force, 6-4, 270, Sr.
QB Jason Thomas, UNLV, 6-4, 230, Jr.
RB Adam Tate, Utah, 6-1, 230, Sr.
RB Cecil Sapp, Colorado State, 6-1, 218, Jr.
TE Jose Ochoa, Colorado State, 6-3, 255, Sr.

DEFENSE

POS. PLAYER SCHOOL HT. WT. CL.

DL Brian Johnson, New Mexico, 6-3, 275, Sr.
DL Anton Palepoi, UNLV, 6-4, 275, Sr.
DL Jerome Haywood, San Diego State, 5-9, 280, Sr.
DL Peter Hogan, Colorado State, 6-3, 255, Jr.
LB Jason Kaufusi, Utah, 6-3, 250, So.
LB Jomar Butler, San Diego State, 5-11, 205, Sr.
LB Justin Ena, BYU, 6-3, 261, Sr.
DB Justin Gallimore, Colorado State, 5-10, 198, Sr.
DB Kevin Thomas, UNLV, 5-11, 180, Sr.
DB Stephen Persley, New Mexico, 5-9, 175, Sr.
DB Will Demps, San Diego State, 6-0, 215, Sr.

SPECIALISTS

POS. PLAYER SCHOOL HT. WT. CL.

PK Dillon Pieffer, UNLV, 5-11, 175, So.
P Aaron Edmonds, BYU, 5-11, 192, Sr.
RS Dallas Davis, Colorado State, 5-10, 181, Sr.

OFFENSIVE PLAYER OF THE YEAR

Jason Thomas, QB, UNLV

DEFENSIVE PLAYER OF THE YEAR

Brian Johnson, DE, New Mexico

NEWCOMER OF THE YEAR

Junior Mahe, WR, BYU

MOUNTAIN WEST NOTEBOOK

Twenty Division I-A coaches have been at their jobs longer than six years. Of that total, four are from the Mountain West: Fisher DeBerry of Air Force (17 years on the job), Ron McBride of Utah (11), Sonny Lubick of Colorado State (eight) and Ted Tollner of San Diego State (seven). The MWC is the only conference to have more than three coaches with seven or more years at their respective schools. ... Only one new coach joins the league this year, Gary Crowton, who has the unenviable task of replacing a legend at BYU. LaVell Edwards stepped down last season after 29 years and a 257-101-3 record in Provo. A native of Orem, Utah, the 43-year-old Crowton spent the last two years as the offensive coordinator for the Chicago Bears. His offense was third in the NFL in passing yardage in 1999, so he'll fit right in at BYU. Before going to the Bears, Crowton was the head coach at Louisiana Tech from 1996-98. He compiled a 21-13 record there. ... The MWC has two bowl-game arrangements this season. The league's champion will play in the Liberty Bowl and the No. 2 pick will go to the Las Vegas Bowl. ... Mountain West teams were undefeated in the postseason last year. Air Force won the Silicon Valley Football Classic, Colorado State the Liberty Bowl and UNLV the Las Vegas Bowl. In its two-year existence, the MWC has sent five of its eight teams to bowl games. The conference has a 4-2 record in those games. ... Rematches from two 2000 bowl games are set for the regular season. UNLV, which played Arkansas in the Las Vegas Bowl, travels to Arkansas on Sept. 1. And Colorado State and Louisville, the Liberty Bowl opponents, play at Louisville on Oct. 4 in an ESPN-televised game. ... Nearly half of the 56 league games played in the MWC's two years were decided by seven or less points. ... The annual Colorado State-Colorado game will be played this season in Denver at the new Invesco Field at Mile High. ... The MWC's averaged attendance last year was 32,257, ranking it seventh among the 11 Division I-A conferences.

COACH AND PROGRAM

When Air Force coach Fisher DeBerry was recently asked when he was going to retire, he took a little bit of umbrage at the question and replied, "Why, do you think I'm getting old?"

Well, at 63, DeBerry is just two years away from the standard retirement age. But as far as DeBerry is concerned, he isn't about to retire any time soon, at least not until he's not wanted any more.

And that certainly shouldn't be the case any time soon, not after the success DeBerry has enjoyed since taking over the program in 1984. He has compiled a winning record in all but two of his 17 seasons with a 135-72-1 overall mark and 77-48-1 conference record. He's taken his team to 11 bowl games and won six, including last year's Silicon Valley Bowl, where the Falcons defeated Fresno State, 37-34.

A year ago, the Falcons were picked for the middle of the pack in the Mountain West Conference, only to finish second. They were the only team to defeat league champion Colorado State. Air Force had just seven starters returning, but that is normal at the Academy, where most players work their way up the depth chart and mostly play as juniors and seniors.

That will be the case again this year as the Falcons have just eight starters returning from last year's 9-3 team. But the senior class has been very successful so far, compiling a 27-9 record over the last three years and winning three Commander-in-Chief trophies. If they win another this year, they will become just the third class to win four CIC trophies.

In May, DeBerry and his seniors visited Washington D.C., where they were presented with the Commander-in-Chief Trophy by President Bush. The new president praised DeBerry, saying, "I love Coach DeBerry's motto: faith, family and Falcons. This is a man who has his priorities straight. And they must be, because he's not just recruiting football talent, he's recruiting character. He's not just recruiting to win football games, he's recruiting to win our nation's wars, if we have one."

Bush also joked about the Falcons dominating the CIC Trophy. "Winning this trophy is supposed to be a struggle, not a hobby. And the truth is, if you spend any more time in Washington, the folks back in Colorado Springs are going to start saying you're out of touch," Bush said.

Last year, the Falcons promised before the season started that they would pass the ball a lot more and put the "Air" back in Air Force under new offensive coordinator Chuck Peterson.

They kept their promise in producing the most passing yards in a season in 28 years and the sixth highest total in school history. Quarterback Mike Thiessen is gone and the Falcons will have to hope they can find a replacement to run the offense as effectively as effectively.

DeBerry says his team wants to challenge for the Mountain West Conference title, but is just as interested in winning the Commander-in-Chief title, which the program has done 12 times under DeBerry in 17 years, compiling a 28-6 record against Army and Navy.

Of course the Falcons will play their annual games against Army and Navy, and for the third straight year, the Falcons will play a Division I-AA team as Tennessee Tech pays a visit to Colorado Springs. The Falcons open the season with none other than defending national champion Oklahoma and conclude the season with a trip to Hawaii. They may not be picked to win the Mountain West title, but they should be in the think of the race as usual.

2001 SCHEDULE

Sept.	1	Oklahoma
	15	Utah
	29	@San Diego State
Oct.	6	@Navy
	13	Wyoming
	20	@Brigham Young
	27	@New Mexico
Nov.	3	Army
	8	@Colorado State
	17	UNLV
	24	@Hawaii

QUARTERBACKS

How important is the quarterback position at Air Force? "The whole season depends on our quarterback and how our new quarterback matures," DeBerry said. "We're no better than the quarterback position."

The quarterback position has always been vital to the Falcons' offense because the quarterback is the guy who makes the option work. That's still the case, but now there's more the quarterback must do in the Falcon system besides run the option. Now, he has to be able to throw.

Passing became a critical part of the Air Force offense last year under Thiessen, whose passing totals were the most in 30 years and the third most in school history. He also led the team in rushing with 713 yards and scored 10 touchdowns.

DeBerry lists three quarterbacks who could take over for Thiessen, but says that senior **Keith Boyea** (5-10, 190) is the favorite heading into the fall. Boyea was actually ahead of Thiessen two years ago before running into problems and having to sit out the 1999 season while serving an academy suspension.

Boyea backed up Thiessen last year, but completed only 3-of-8 passes for 27 yards and rushed for 26 yards and a touchdown. In the spring game, he rushed for 51 yards and completed 8-of-18 passes, but he also fumbled and threw two interceptions. Still, he heads into fall as No. 1, although the coach says he will keep an open mind with a couple of talented underclassmen to consider.

"Keith didn't get any playing time for us last year," DeBerry said. "He has a good arm and good option skills—he can do it all. He certainly has the skills, but now he needs to show it in the games."

Junior **Bryan Blew** (5-11, 190), who rushed three times last year for 56 yards and completed his only pass attempt last year, is the logical backup. However, sophomore **Chance Harridge** (6-0, 180) beat him out for the No. 2 spot after Blew didn't have a very good spring and Harridge played well.

Harridge was so impressive he actually moved ahead of Boyea midway through the spring, before Boyea emerged as No. 1 before practices ended.

"We're really excited about Chance—he's going to be very good," DeBerry said.

A fourth quarterback who is a long shot heading into fall is sophomore **Travis Thurmond** (5-9, 175). He played well in the spring, including the Blue-Silver game, but he isn't likely to pass up the other three quarterbacks.

DeBerry said he will make a final decision on this year's quarterback two weeks into fall camp, but for now, the Falcons' fortunes appear to rest on Boyea, who seems to have all the skills necessary to be a successful quarterback for Air Force. Without any measurable experience, however, the question is how long it will take him to feel comfortable as the Falcons' main man.

RUNNING BACKS

For most college teams, the fullback position is mostly an afterthought, a position that many teams don't even employ in these days of one-back offenses.

At Air Force, it is very important, second perhaps only to the quarterback in the Falcon offense. That's true not only because the fullbacks are expected to run the ball, but because their blocking skills are vital to the wishbone. Because AFA lost Nathan Beard and Scott Becker, who combined for just under 1,000 yards last year, DeBerry is more than a little concerned.

"Two critical areas of our football team are quarterback and fullback," DeBerry said. "At fullback we lost two really fine players and we have to have a dominant inside game."

Sophomore **Dan Shaffer** (5-8, 195) looks to be the starter heading into fall despite his size. He doesn't look much like a fullback. But Shaffer beat out two more experienced players in senior **Jimmy Burns** (5-11, 210) and junior **Anthony Kelley** (5-9, 205).

In 2000, Kelley played in three games and rushed for 65 yards, while Burns played in four games and rushed for 48 yards. Someone else who could see time is sophomore **Todd Leslie** (5-9, 200).

Another small player, junior **Leotis Palmer** (5-8, 175), should be one of the starting halfbacks heading into the fall, after the Falcons lost Oualario Brown and Scotty McKay, who rushed for 496 and 494 yards, respectively. Palmer is the top returning rusher on the team after playing in 10 games last year and rushing for 260 yards on 44 carries.

Senior **Tom Heier** (5-9, 180), set to be a starting halfback last year until being felled by a knee injury, will probably be the other starter in the backfield. In 1999, he played in seven games and rushed for 105 yards.

The backups will be junior **Brandon Brown** (6-0, 170), who has been switched from the defensive backfield, and junior **Michael Fieberkorn** (6-2, 195).

Two others on the list of reserves are junior **Don Clark** (6-0, 200) and sophomore **Nate Baldwin** (5-8, 165). Baldwin was impressive during last winter's workouts when he set an Air Force record in the three-hop leap of 36 feet, 4 inches and just missed the 40 yard dash record with a time of 4.31.

DeBerry also said there were a couple of incoming freshmen he was "excited about," but he isn't allowed to name any names until the players actually show up at Air Force.

WIDE RECEIVERS/TIGHT ENDS

Last year, the Falcons were worried about replacing Matt Farmer, who finished his career as one of the top receivers in Air Force history. But senior **Ryan Fleming** more than made people forget about Farmer as he put together one of the best seasons a receiver has ever had at the Air Force.

The 6-5, 220-pound Fleming caught 52 passes for 930 yards. That was the second-best receiving total in AFA history and the fourth-best total for receptions. Because he caught only eight passes for 169 yards as a sophomore, Fleming has almost no chance to catch the career totals of Ernie Jennings, who caught 148 passes for 2,362 yards from 1968-70.

Backing up Fleming are junior **Brian LaBasco** (5-9, 175) and junior **Ricky Amezaga** (5-11, 180). LaBasco caught 15 passes for 165 yards, while Amezaga caught three passes for 47 yards and a touchdown. **Anthony Park**, a 5-9, 155-pound junior, "will turn some heads," DeBerry said.

"This could be the strongest part of the team," DeBerry said. "We've got Fleming back, LaBasco and Amezaga, who had a really good spring. We'll play all three."

At tight end, three players are competing for the job. Senior **Keith Runyon** (6-4, 230) came out of spring as No. 1 on the depth chart after moving over from linebacker the year before. The other two expected to compete for the top job are junior **Andy Lueckenhoff** (6-2, 230) and sophomore **Adam Strecker** (6-5, 220).

OFFENSIVE LINE

Like most other positions on the team, the Falcons lost most of their starters on the offensive line. Gone are their center, two guards and a tackle. The one returning starter is a gem, however, a player DeBerry says "may be the best we've had here at the academy."

DeBerry is talking about senior tackle **Ben Miller** (6-4, 270), who was a strength on the Falcon line a year ago. Miller missed spring ball with shoulder and thumb injuries, but is expected to be back in the fall.

The offensive line is vital to the Falcons' option attack, so the Falcons hope some of their seniors who have been waiting in the wings will step up this year.

Senior **Matt Mai** (6-3, 270) is penciled in at the center position, with senior **Matt Joseph** (6-5, 280) and senior **Brian Strock** (6-3, 265) at the guards. At the right tackle position, senior **Joseph Pugh** (6-3, 265) emerged as the starter.

Backups on the line include sophomore **Blane Neufeld** (6-3, 250) and junior **Scott Meyer** (6-3, 240) at tackle, senior **Brett Huyser** (6-3, 240) and sophomore **Jesse Underbakke** (6-3, 240) at guard and senior **Paul Cansino** (6-1, 260) at center.

Also providing depth on the offensive line will be junior **Randy Gibbs** (6-1, 260), junior **Wayne Southam** (6-2, 250) and junior **Nate Olsen** (6-6, 250).

"After 29 days [in August], our offensive line is going to be good," DeBerry told the *Colorado Springs Gazette*.

One player who could have been a senior starter this season, 6-3, 300-pound guard Terrance Barreau, was dismissed from the academy for an honor code violation.

2000 STATISTICS

Rushing offense	294.9	3
Passing offense	157.0	98
Total offense	451.9	9
Scoring offense	34.9	16
Net Punting	33.1	81
Punt returns	7.9	84
Kickoff returns	21.4	23
Rushing defense	159.5	69
Passing efficiency defense	126.9	88
Total defense	373.0	65
Scoring defense	25.3	59
Turnover margin	+7	23

Last column is ranking among Division I-A teams.

KICKERS

The Falcons are hopeful senior **Brooks Walters** (6-0, 185) will fill the shoes of Dave Adams as well as Adams did for Jackson Whiting a year earlier.

Adams converted on 19 of his 24 field goals, including a 54-yarder, and 37-of-39 PATs last year, only a slight dropoff from Whiting's numbers of the year before.

Walters backed up Adams last year but never got a chance to kick in a game. However, DeBerry was impressed with Walter's kicking through the month of spring practice. In one scrimmage he kicked a 52-yard field goal.

"Our kicking game will be all right," DeBerry said. "Brooks Walters had a really impressive spring."

Adam Thornton, a 5-9, 190-pound junior who kicked a 49-yarder in a spring scrimmage, is listed as Walters' backup.

DEFENSIVE LINE

DeBerry is all smiles about his defensive line, which he says might be as good as any he's had at the academy.

"Probably the strength of our team is the defensive front," DeBerry said. "Those three are as good as we've had here. They will be as physical and athletic as any we've ever had."

"Those three" are senior left tackle **Dan Probert** (6-4, 270), senior right tackle **Justin Pendry** (6-6, 285) and nose guard **Zach Johnson** (6-3, 265).

Pendry and Johnson are returning starters from last year when Pendry ranked fifth on the team with 48 tackles, while Johnson was eighth with 34 tackles and also recorded one sack.

"Pendry had a great spring," DeBerry said. "Zach Johnson will be as good a player as there is at middle guard in our conference."

Probert didn't play as much, but was very effective when he did play, recording five sacks and eight tackles for losses among his 16 tackles.

Backups include senior **Nate Osborne** (6-5, 255) at left tackle, junior **John Hicks** (6-2, 265) at nose guard and junior **Eric Thompson** (6-2, 245) at right tackle.

AFA defensive line coach Jappy Oliver concurred with his coach when he told the *Colorado Springs Gazette*, "Our line should be the strength of our defense, if not our entire team. I expect it."

LINEBACKERS

What was the strength of the defense a year ago could be a question mark this year with little returning experience. The Falcons lost three of their four top tacklers in C.J. Zanotto, Matt Pommer and Corey Nelson.

Senior **Matt McCraney** (6-2, 220) has the most experience with one start as a sophomore, but a serious knee injury kept him out most of last year and slowed him again this spring, causing him to miss all of practice. Still, he should be a starter on the outside come fall.

At the other outside spot, sophomore **Ryan Carter** (6-2, 210) has emerged as the starter after a superb spring. DeBerry told the *Colorado Springs Gazette* Carter "was one of those guys who came out of the woodwork this spring."

Carter beat out senior **Tre Cage** (6-2, 215), who will push for the starting job in the fall. Cage had 10 tackles last year, mostly on the special teams.

Backups on the outside besides Cage are sophomore **Adrian Wright** (6-0, 212) and sophomore **Monty Coleman** (6-2, 225). Wright had an outstanding spring game where he made 11 tackles, including one sack, made two pass deflections and recovered a fumble.

On the inside four players were pretty evenly matched during the spring and all could see significant action this season. Seniors **Jamie Arthur** (5-9, 215) and **Andy Rule** (6-2, 230) are listed as the starters, but senior **Jon Eccles** (6-2, 235) and **Marchello Graddy** (6-2, 220) are close behind.

Because of the lack of depth at the linebacker position, DeBerry will look at some freshmen to help out in the fall.

DEFENSIVE BACKS

The Air Force secondary looks solid with three players who saw a lot of starting experience last year, led by senior strong safety **Sam Meinrod** (6-1, 200). Meinrod was sixth on the team in tackles last year with 43, including 2 1/2 sacks and also came up with an interception, a fumble recovery and five pass deflections. DeBerry calls Meinrod "a smart player."

At free safety, sophomore **Jeff Overstreet** (6-0, 170) takes over for Wes Glisson after seeing quite a bit of time for a freshman. He intercepted a pass and made 13 tackles last year. DeBerry compares him to a pair of former Falcon All-Americans.

"Jeff Overstreet is a lot like [former Air Force all-Americans] Scott Thomas and Carlton McDonald," he told the *Colorado Springs Gazette*. "He takes a lot of pride, doesn't mind working and can cover a lot of ground. And he's so smart."

"I feel real good about the safety positions. We're pretty set there."

At the strong cornerback, junior **Paul Mayo** (5-10, 170) showed rapid improvement at the end of last year and looked good in the spring game.

"He has a chance to be a real good one," DeBerry said. "He makes plays."

The weak-side corner position has experience with junior **Wes Crawley** (6-0, 190) being pushed by junior **Joel Buelow** (6-1, 195) and sophomore **Trent Zinn** (5-9, 175). Crawley made 28 tackles last year and led the team with two fumble recoveries. Buelow registered 22 tackles and intercepted a pass.

Zinn may play the other corner position, where he is listed as a backup to Mayo. Other reserves include seniors **Larry Duncan** (5-8, 200) and **Erik Svendsen** (6-2, 205) at strong safety, senior **Adam Hanes** (6-0, 195) and junior **Joe Brazier** (6-1, 190) at free safety and sophomore **Matt Terry** (5-8, 175) at weak corner.

PUNTERS

As with their place-kickers, the Falcons are pretty much on a year-to-year basis with their punters as players rarely holding the starting spot more than a year.

Last year, the Falcons had to replace Scott Gribben and came up with Dallas Thompson, who averaged a respectable 40.8 yards with 15 of his 50 punts ending up inside the 20.

Now that Thompson has graduated, the Falcons were searching anew again but seem happy with junior **John Welsh** (6-3, 190), who backed up Thompson a year ago. He earned the job in the spring ahead of senior **John Cortney** (5-11, 180). Two years ago, Welsh was the punter on the junior varsity team.

"I'm very pleased with the punting of John Welsh," DeBerry said.

SPECIAL TEAMS

When you say special teams at Air Force, the first thing you think of is blocked kicks. The Falcons have developed a remarkable kick-blocking reputation over the years, which has resulted in a few extra wins.

Last year the Falcons blocked nine kicks, which brings the number of kicks blocked since 1990 to 68. During the 1990s, only Virginia Tech blocked more kicks than the Falcons among all the teams in Division I-A.

The Falcons often use their front-line players on special teams and each of this year's starting defensive linemen, Pendry, Johnson and Probert, blocked kicks last year.

Air Force will have different players handling the kicking chores this year as Walters will take over the place kicking duties, while Welsh will be the punter. Sophomore **Howard Turner** (6-3, 225) and Miller will be the deep snappers.

Several players will be looked at to return kicks, with Palmer having the most experience. Palmer returned six kickoffs for a 22.0-yard average and three punts for a 12.7-yard average. Amezaga returned seven kickoffs last year for a 22.7-yard average and returned a kickoff 100 yards in the spring game. DeBerry also said receiver Park may get a chance to return kicks.

RECRUITING CLASS

There's no official news about the Falcons' recruits because they don't release names of recruits until mid-summer when appointments to the Air Force Academy are officially made. Still, DeBerry knows who he recruited, and he's happy with his new players.

"We've had a real good recruiting year and I'm excited about it," DeBerry said. "That's if they all come. Some players make an easy transition and others don't. Our hope would be that there will be a freshman who will come in and surprise us."

Freshmen rarely play at Air Force and most end up on the junior varsity team. Also there is no redshirting at Air Force, so players rarely get more than three years experience on the varsity.

Although no players' names were released by the Academy, some commitments were reported by the hometown newspapers of the newcomers in early February.

Among the players who committed to Air Force were two Texans—**Cole Coan**, a 6-3, 255-pound defensive end and **Colin Allred**, a 6-2, 225-pound linebacker.

BLUE RIBBON ANALYSIS

OFFENSE	C+
SPECIAL TEAMS	B
DEFENSE	B+
INTANGIBLES	B+

With only eight starters back and a new quarterback operating the option, the last thing the Falcons need is a tough season opener. So what team did they go and schedule for Sept. 1? None other than defending national champion Oklahoma.

At least the game will be at home, but it's not the way to get started with an inexperienced team featuring an entirely new backfield and almost new offensive line.

The other non-league games won't be nearly as challenging with Division I-AA Tennessee Tech, Navy, Army and Hawaii rounding out the schedule. But the Oklahoma game will certainly test the Falcons in a hurry and expose whatever holes exist.

"Our team has to grow up fast," DeBerry said. "We're going to have a lot of young players with very little game experience at some positions."

The Falcons are known for their offense, but this year, at least in the early going, the defense will be the strength of the team. The Falcons think they have the best defensive front in the MWC with two returning starters and a third who played a lot last year and a strong secondary with three players who saw substantial playing time.

The strength of the offense is the receiving corps—of all things—but that won't make a difference if there isn't a quarterback to deliver the ball. The offensive line only has one returning starter and must open the holes better than it did in the spring to make the Falcons' option game effective.

Except for the opener against Oklahoma, the Falcons should pad their non-conference record, which is a gaudy 15-2 over the past four seasons. One of the only losses was the overtime defeat to Notre Dame last year and the Irish aren't on the schedule this year. They may be hard-pressed to get four wins in the Mountain West Conference unless their offense gets in gear by mid-season. Regardless if they win the MWC title, the Falcons should add another Commander-in-Chief's Trophy to their collection and with seven or eight wins overall could find themselves in another bowl game.

(M.S.)

2000 RESULTS

Cal State-Northridge	W	55-6	1-0
Brigham Young	W	31-23	2-0
Utah	W	23-14	3-0
UNLV	L	13-34	3-1
Navy	W	27-13	4-1
Wyoming	W	51-34	5-1
New Mexico	L	23-29	5-2
Notre Dame	L	31-34	5-3
Army	W	41-27	6-3
Colorado State	W	44-40	7-3
San Diego State	W	45-24	8-3
Fresno State (Silicon)	W	37-34	9-3

Brigham Young

LOCATION	Provo, UT
CONFERENCE	Mountain West
LAST SEASON	6-6 (.500)
CONFERENCE RECORD	4-3 (t-3rd)
OFFENSIVE STARTERS RETURNING	7
DEFENSIVE STARTERS RETURNING	6
NICKNAME	Cougars
COLORS	Blue & White
HOME FIELD	Cougar Stadium (65,000)
HEAD COACH	Gary Crowton (BYU '83)
RECORD AT SCHOOL	First Year
CAREER RECORD	21-13 (3 years)
ASSISTANTS	Lance Reynolds (BYU '80) Offensive Line
	Mike Borich (Western Illinois '88) Offensive Coordinator/Receivers
	Ken Schmidt (Utah '64) Defensive Coordinator/Linebackers
	Mike Empey (BYU '94) Tight Ends
	Paul Tidwell (Southern Utah '79) Running Backs/Kickers
	Robbie Bosco (BYU '86) Quarterbacks
	Tom Ramage (Utah State '57) Defensive Line
	Brian Mitchell (Purdue '95) Cornerbacks
	Barry Lamb (Oregon '78) Special Teams/Safeties
TEAM WINS (last 5 yrs.)	14-6-9-8-6
FINAL RANK (last 5 yrs.)	22-81-56-56-76
2000 FINISH	Beat Utah State in regular-season finale.

COACH AND PROGRAM

For the first time since 1971, BYU won't have the familiar presence of LaVell Edwards on the sideline. Edwards announced before the end of last season that 2000 would be his final year. It almost turned out to be his worst, too, as the Cougars struggled with a tough schedule and some gaping holes, in the offense in particular.

They went into the last game against Utah with a 5-6 mark and no chance for a conference title or bowl game. After blowing a 16-point lead, they found themselves trailing, 27-26, with less than a minute to go and facing a fourth-and-13. That's when **Brandon Doman** completed a long pass to Jonathan Pittman out to midfield. Three plays later, Doman scored on a 4-yard run, giving BYU a miraculous victory.

It was storybook ending for Edwards and though it wasn't a great season, he went out on a winning note and a record that included only one losing season (1973). He also left as the sixth winningest coach of all-time with 257 victories.

In December, the school hired one of its own, BYU grad Gary Crowton, as the head coach. He came from the Chicago Bears, where he was the offensive coordinator. Before spending two years with the Bears, Crowton was the head coach at Louisiana Tech, where he compiled a 21-13 record—including 9-2 record in '97—in three seasons.

"I have always dreamed of coaching at BYU," Crowton said. "To be able to follow in the footsteps of a legend like LaVell Edwards is incredibly humbling and challenging. I pledge to BYU that I will devote my energy to continuing BYU's football tradition."

The 43-year-old Crowton moved up the coaching ladder in a hurry after serving as a student assistant coach under Edwards in '82. He spent time at small programs such as Snow (Utah) Junior College, Western Illinois and New Hampshire before moving to a couple of bigger schools, Boston College and Georgia Tech, in the early 1990s. Then he moved to Louisiana Tech as the offensive coordinator in '95. After one year in that position, Crowton moved up to head coach for three years before going to the Bears.

Most new coaches clean house and bring in their own guys, but Crowton opted to retain seven of Edwards' nine assistants and added just two coaches—Mike Borich as the offensive coordinator and receivers coach and Paul Tidwell as the recruiting coordinator and coach of the running backs and kickers. Ken Schmidt, a 20-year veteran of the Cougar staff, remains the defensive coordinator and linebackers coach.

Crowton should bring new energy to a program that many believe has become a bit stagnant in recent years. The question is whether Crowton will have the same magic that Edwards has enjoyed for most of the last 30 years in Provo.

Edwards left behind a solid nucleus with 50 returning lettermen, including 27 on offense and 23 on defense. BYU returns seven starters on offense and six on defense, including seven All-MWC players.

"We feel like we have a lot to work with in terms of personnel," Crowton said. "We will be using as much time necessary to evaluate the players we have and identify our strengths. The philosophy won't be all that different. We'll have a few different looks, but the key will be to adapt to the talent we have and go from there."

2001 SCHEDULE

Sept.	1	Nevada
	8	@California
	15	@Mississippi State
	29	@UNLV
Oct.	5	Utah State
	13	@New Mexico
	20	Air Force
	27	@San Diego State
Nov.	1	Colorado State
	10	@Wyoming
	17	Utah
Dec.	1	@Hawaii

QUARTERBACKS

In the late 1970s and 1980s, the Cougars had one All-America quarterback after another, from Gifford Nielsen to Marc Wilson to Jim McMahon to Steve Young to Ty Detmer, who won the Heisman Trophy in '90.

It has been a few years since the Cougars have had an All-American quarterback. And they are not likely to have one this year. Three home-grown quarterbacks who have yet to put together more than a few games apiece will compete for the job.

Doman (6-1, 195), a senior who saw limited action his first two-and-a-half seasons, is No. 1 heading into the season after leading the Cougars to two victories at the end of last year.

Brett Engemann and **Charlie Peterson** shared the job through the first eight games, until Doman was given the chance after nearly three seasons of waiting.

Doman got the start against New Mexico in Edwards' home finale and directed the Cougars to a 37-13 victory. In passing for 349 yards and rushing for 51, he became the first BYU player since Steve Young to pass for 300 yards and rush for 50 in a game.

For the season, Doman completed 55.4 percent of his passes for 782 yards and two touchdowns. During his first two seasons he threw only four passes and actually played more at receiver, catching nine passes in '99.

"Since Brandon finished last season as the starter, he'll be the No. 1 guy," Crowton said before spring practice.

By the time spring practice finished, Doman was still the No. 1 guy. But he wasn't far enough ahead that Crowton won't look at the others in the fall.

Engemann started the '00 season as No. 1, and after struggling in his first game against Florida State, looked like the latest great Cougar quarterback when he engineered a come-from-behind, 38-35, victory over Virginia, passing for 447 yards on 34-of-41 attempts.

However he sprained his knee against Air Force and after seeing limited action against UNLV, he went out for the season with a shoulder injury against Syracuse. The 6-4, 224-pound junior is the brother-in-law of talk-show host Larry King, who is married to Engemann's older sister, Shaun. King has bragged about Engemann in his *USA Today* columns.

Peterson (6-1, 198), a senior, took over for Engemann when he went down and had his best games against Utah State when he completed 24-of-37 passes for 324 yards and a touchdown and against San Diego State, when he threw for 376 yards, completing 34-of-58. In one stretch of the season, Peterson went 164 pass attempts without an interception, breaking the record Jim McMahon set two decades earlier. He went down with a partial shoulder separation in a big loss to Colorado State and lost his job to Doman for the final two games.

The fourth BYU quarterback will be redshirt freshman **Todd Mortensen** (6-4, 215), who passed for nearly 5,000 yards in his prep career in Arizona before leaving on an LDS Church mission for two years.

Crowton isn't opposed to a friendly competition for the starting job continuing into fall practice.

"Nothing is set in stone," he said. "We have four very talented guys who are going to be competing for the starting job. And once we make our decision, that's who we plan to go with. We'll just have to see what happens."

RUNNING BACKS

The Cougars are happy with their top two running backs —junior **Luke Staley** (6-1, 218) and senior **Brian McDonald** (5-10, 210), who gained most of the team's rushing yards last year.

Staley finished with 479 yards on 130 carries, which was slightly more than the 432 yards he gained the previous year on just 92 carries, when he was voted MWC Freshman of the Year. Both seasons Staley was slowed by injuries. He missed four games as a freshman and underwent shoulder and knee surgery after the season. He was questionable for 2000 but was in the starting lineup against Florida State, only to suffer a concussion and miss the next game. He played against Air Force and suffered a knee injury that required surgery. He bounced back to rush for 167 yards in his next game against UNLV.

McDonald, who transferred from Cerritos (Calif.) Junior College, played in every game last year and started twice and led the team with eight touchdowns. His 464-yard rushing total was just behind Staley, and he had a much better yards-per-carry average at 4.6.

"Both are very good players," Crowton said. "Luke has good speed and good hands, while Brian has good balance and quickness. Both are strong and have great size and bring a great deal of experience. We just need to keep them healthy. There's no question Luke and Brian will play a very important role in our offense."

Staley and McDonald both proved they can catch the ball, something they will do a lot of in Crowton's offense. Staley made 28 receptions for 327 yards, while McDonald caught 15 passes for 79 yards.

Kalani Sitake, who started every game at fullback last year, gained 100 yards while mainly being used as a blocking back. He is gone. Senior **Mike Nielson** (6-2, 232), a transfer from Utah State, had the edge at fullback going into spring drills. He and senior **Ned Stearns** (6-0, 215) will fight it out for the top spot.

Nielsen caught one pass two years ago and mainly played on the special teams last year. Stearns has seen action all three of his previous years and done it all—rushing the ball, catching passes and returning punts and kickoffs.

Others who could see action in the backfield are senior **Paul Peterson** (5-8, 196), who was the team's top kickoff returner last year, redshirt freshman **Logan Deans** (6-0, 220) and newcomer **Dustin Gabriel**, a 6-1, 190-pound freshman from Allen, Texas.

Marcus Whalen—who showed great promise with 209 yards last year, including a team-high 91 in 10 carries against Utah State—was dismissed from the team during the winter for two alcohol-related arrests.

WIDE RECEIVERS/TIGHT ENDS

Last year the Cougar coaching staff thought they had one of their finest groups of receivers ever with the likes of Margin Hooks, Jonathan Pittman and Ben Horton, along with tight end Tevita Ofahengaue. That foursome accounted for more than half of the 272 completed passes last year with Hooks and Pittman combining for nearly half of the 3,295 receiving yards. With all that talent graduated, the Cougars will have a difficult time finding replacements.

The leading returning receiver is actually a running back, Staley. The top returnee who plays receiver is senior **Mike Rigell** (5-7, 175), who caught 21 passes for 220 yards and three touchdowns. The only other receiver with any experience is senior **Soren Halladay** (6-1, 195), who played in just five games, catching five passes for 86 yards in 2000 after catching nine passes for 95 yards a year earlier.

"I've really been pleased with the progress of the receivers," Crowton said. "There is a lot for us to look at. We have some speedy guys who have shown some nice things. This position is going to be very competitive."

The best receiver may turn out to be **Junior Mahe** (5-11, 190), who is back at BYU after sitting out a year because of an honor code infraction and then playing a year at junior college. As a freshman at BYU in '98, Mahe rushed for 481 yards and averaged 4.9 yards per carry with six touchdowns.

Last year at Dixie (Utah) Junior College, Mahe earned JC Gridwire second-team All-America honors after leading the nation in receiving with 57 receptions for 1,387 yards and 19 touchdowns.

"I'm excited about him," Crowton said. "He can hold his head high because he's done everything he's been asked as far as getting back into good standing with this university. He's grown a lot through the whole experience."

Two young receivers in the program who may get a chance to play a lot this year are sophomores **David Christensen** (5-9, 185) and **Toby Christensen** (5-11, 188), who aren't related. Toby, the son of former Oakland Raider All-Pro Todd Christensen, saw limited action last year, while David saw extensive action on the special teams, returning six kickoffs and two punt returns.

Other receivers in the program are redshirt freshman **Zac Collie** (5-11, 171), redshirt freshman **Brian Cusick** (6-0, 200), junior **Pat Williams** (6-0, 191), sophomore **Jason Kukahiko** (6-1, 184) and freshman **Breyon Jones** (5-11, 180).

Despite losing Ofahengaue, who received some notoriety as the final selection of the NFL draft, the Cougars think they have three excellent candidates for the tight end job.

Senior **Doug Jolley** (6-4, 241) and junior **Gabriel Reid** (6-3, 246) both saw extensive action last year and they are in a fight with **Spencer Nead** (6-4, 260), a transfer from Ricks (Idaho) Junior College. Jolley caught 14 passes for 213 yards and a touchdown, while Reid had four receptions for 50 yards.

"This will be a key position for us," Crowton said. "We have size, speed, depth, good hands and guys who can block. With any one of these guys in the lineup, we have some options."

OFFENSIVE LINE

Last year's inexperienced offensive line has matured into an experienced group that should be one of the strengths of the team. All five starters from 2000 return.

Senior center **Jason Scukanec** (6-2, 282) earned second-team All-MWC honors last year and is the preseason favorite to be the first-team All-MWC center this year. Three other returning starters who earned All-MWC honorable mention honors are junior tackle **Ben Archibald** (6-4, 303), senior guard **Aaron McCubbins** (6-3, 295) and junior tackle **Dustin Rykert** (6-7, 301). The fifth starter is senior guard **Teag Whiting** (6-3, 298), who may face disciplinary action because of an after-hours incident at a Salt Lake City bar in June.

Two junior college transfers, **Quinn Christensen** (6-6, 295) and **Ryan Keele** (6-4, 296), are good enough to supplant one or two of last year's starters and both should see a lot of action this year. Sophomore **Scott Jackson** (6-4, 287), who saw limited action last year because of an ankle injury, will back up Scukanec. Junior **Issac Herring** (6-4, 306) and sophomore **Vincent Xanthos** (6-3, 284) will also play backup roles.

Xanthos has been around. He lettered as a freshman at Maryland and transferred to Minnesota before going on an LDS mission and transferring to BYU.

"The offensive line will be very competitive," Crowton said. "Without a solid offensive line, a team is really limited. Our depth and experience along the offensive line will definitely be one of the strengths of this team."

2000 STATISTICS

Rushing offense	99.4	99
Passing offense	274.6	16
Total offense	374.0	55
Scoring offense	23.3	73
Net Punting	37.5	20
Punt returns	7.0	100
Kickoff returns	20.1	50
Rushing defense	121.7	30
Passing efficiency defense	140.6	103
Total defense	345.0	40
Scoring defense	25.8	66
Turnover margin	-9	91

Last column is ranking among Division I-A teams.

KICKERS

For the last four years, the Cougars haven't had to worry about their place kicking, which has rested on the reliable foot of Owen Pochman. But with Pochman gone after becoming the all-time leading field-goal kicker and scorer at BYU, the Cougars need to find a replacement.

Pochman was taken by the New England Patriots in the seventh round of the NFL draft. He was the first kicker drafted from BYU since Lee Johnson was selected in the fifth round by the Houston Oilers in 1985 and the first BYU player drafted by New England since Jason Andersen was selected in the seventh round of the 1998 draft.

BYU first looked to replace Pochman with senior **Aaron Edmonds** (5-11, 192), who also handles the punting for the Cougars. However, freshman **Matt Payne** (6-4, 247) won the job in the spring and will be backed up by Edmonds.

DEFENSIVE LINE

The Cougars lost the meat of their line with the graduation of Hans Olsen, Chris Hoke and Setema Gali and will have a challenge to produce another strong line, which has been a tradition at BYU over the years.

Senior **Ryan Denney** (6-7, 275) returns at right end after starting 11-of-12 games last year and finishing sixth on the team in tackles with 47. He also had four sacks, a fumble recovery and two blocked kicks. He will be backed up by his younger brother, **John Denney** (6-6, 250), who will be a sophomore after playing one season at Ricks (Idaho) Junior College.

The other end spot will probably be filled by senior **Brett Kiesel** (6-5, 269), who played in every game, making 22 tackles, including 10 for losses with five sacks. Redshirt freshman **Brandon Stephens** (6-5, 258), who has been converted from tight end, is expected to back up Kiesel. Another converted tight end, junior **Jeff Cowart** (6-4, 259) will provide depth at the end position.

"We have some quickness and good size along the defensive line," Crowton said. "Specifically, the guys we have lined up at defensive end are big and fast. They're going to be good."

Sophomore **Ifo Pili** (6-3, 315) is back from a church mission and could move right into a starting tackle slot. As a freshman before his mission, Pili shared starting duties and registered 17 tackles and a sack.

"We're excited about having Ifo back," Crowton said. "With his experience and leadership on the field, he will be a major factor on the defensive line."

Two others who will be looking to grab a starting tackle spot are junior **Chris Watkins** (6-2, 285) and sophomore **Ryan Gunderson** (6-3, 280), while redshirt freshman **Michael Marquardt** (6-4, 260) is slated to back up Pili. Watkins is coming off off-season back surgery, while Gunderson played in just three games last year, where he made three tackles.

Defensive line coach Tom Ramage, who has coached football for 44 years, including 30 at BYU, has announced that this will be his final year of coaching.

LINEBACKERS

Unlike their inexperienced defensive line, the Cougars have a wealth of experience at linebacker with all three starters returning from a year ago.

In senior **Justin Ena** (6-3, 261), the Cougars have a solid anchor on the linebacking corps. Ena was a first-team all-league selection last year after starting all 12 games and leading the team with 107 tackles, including 11 for losses and three sacks.

Senior **Issac Kelley** (6-4, 240) also started every game at the strong-side linebacker position and ranked third on the team with 63 tackles, including 14 for losses with four sacks. The year before he had 34 tackles after switching from quarterback.

The third returning starter is sophomore **Paul Walkenhorst** (6-5, 248), who was pressed into action as a first-year freshman last season when injuries put Jeff Holtry and Josh Lowe out for the year. He was sixth on the team with 48 tackles and forced two fumbles and blocked a kick that made a difference in a three-point win over UNLV.

"There's no question our linebackers are going to be good," Crowton said. "These three guys are experienced and bring a lot to the defense. Our linebackers, including some of the younger guys, are going to get a lot of action this year. We expect they will be the key strength to our defense."

The young players Crowton is talking about include sophomores **Bill Wright** (6-2, 220), **Colby Bockwoldt** (6-1, 218), **Brent Carlson** (5-9, 227) and **Ammon Mauga** (6-0, 215). Another player to keep an eye on is freshman **Brady Poppinga** (6-3, 237), who has already moved to a backup position behind Ena.

DEFENSIVE BACKS

The Cougars are loaded at the cornerback positions with both starters and two key reserves returning, but will be hurting at safety. Both of last season's starters, Tyson Smith and Jared Lee, have graduated.

Sophomore **Jenaro Gilford** (6-1, 180) returns at a corner position after missing last season because of a suspension for an off-the-field incident at the BYU campus. In '99, he played backup and came up with an interception, and is expected to be a solid contributor this year.

"Jenaro is big and strong and can cover exceptionally well," Crowton said. "It will be good to have him back and not have to worry about that side of the field."

Three seniors will battle for the other corner spot, with **Michael Lafitte** (5-6, 160) having the edge coming out of spring ball. Last year, he started three games and made 12 tackles, broke up three passes and recovered a fumble.

Derrus Wilson (5-8, 182) also started three games and registered 19 tackles, while intercepting a pass and recovering a fumble. **Danny Phillips** (6-0, 194) actually played more than any of the other corners last year, starting eight games and coming up with 25 tackles and breaking up two passes. Don't be surprised to see different starters throughout the season with all four earning significant playing time.

At safety, senior **Dustin Staley** (5-11, 178) is back after playing cornerback most of last season. He started seven games, produced 18 tackles, four pass breakups and one forced fumble. Staley, the older brother of Cougar running back Luke Staley, made 25 tackles the previous year and also intercepted a pass when he played safety.

Junior **Michael Madsen** (6-1, 195), whose father was an all-conference player at BYU, saw action in six games and intercepted a pass against Wyoming.

Sophomore **Levi Madrieata** (6-2, 210), who transferred from the University of Washington and sat out last year, is penciled in as the starter at free safety. Another sophomore, **Kurt Elliott** (5-11, 190), who saw action on the special teams, will be the backup free safety.

"I think our safeties will be pretty good," Crowton said. "We have some experience there and they have shown some good things early on. They have good size and range."

Others who will provide depth in the backfield are sophomore **Alex Farris** (5-11, 195), Air Force transfer **Brandon Heany** (5-10, 180), a sophomore, and redshirt freshman **Jon Burbidge** (6-0, 201).

Isiah Joiner, who would have added depth at the corner position, was dismissed from the team in May for violation of unspecified team rules.

PUNTERS

Edmonds came in from Ricks (Idaho) Junior College last year and performed like a veteran. He led the Mountain West and was 10th in the nation with a 43.6-yard average with no blocks and 17 kicks inside the 20. He also had 19 punts of more than 50 yards with a best of 61 against Mississippi State.

Payne, who will handle the placekicking duties for the Cougars, will be the backup punter. Also, tight end Jolley, who punted once in 1999, can also be called on to punt if needed.

SPECIAL TEAMS

Edmonds is solid as the punter, while place kicking could be a bit shaky as Payne gains experience. Senior **Anthony Ward** (6-3, 253) is the deep snapper.

Rigell will be the main kick returner again this year after returning 29 punts for 195 yards and nine kickoffs for 143 yards. Peterson actually handled the bulk of the kickoffs last year, returning 24 for 516 yards. Christensen, who returned two punts and six kickoffs last year, including a team-best 45-yarder against New Mexico, will also be one of the main returners. Stearns and Nielsen also have experience as kick returners.

RECRUITING CLASS

The top recruit among the 17 signees is actually a retread. Mahe saw significant action as a freshman running back in '98, left the team for breaking the school honor code, attended Dixie Junior College, where he starred as a receiver, and was signed again to play this year.

Another Dixie player, Christensen, is expected to push for a starting spot on the offensive line. Three other junior college transfers, defensive lineman Denney, offensive lineman Keele and tight end Nead, will all provide immediate help.

Of his junior college signees, Crowton said, "Those are national recruits. They could have gone anywhere they wanted. They will have an immediate impact."

Besides the two junior college offensive linemen, the Cougars also signed **Travis Bright** (6-5, 310) from Queen Creek, Ariz., and **Jeff Rhea** (6-4, 275) from South Jordan, Utah.

"When I looked at our list of players, I felt we didn't have a lot of depth at offensive line," Crowton said. "So we went a after a few offensive lineman. These are guys who will help us immediately and in the future."

The biggest need was at wide receiver, where the Cougars signed five players—four high schoolers, plus Mahe.

They included **Saia Hafoka** (5-9, 165) from Kahuku, Hawaii, **Bryce Mahuika** (5-10, 185) from Vancouver, Wash., **David Tafuna** (6-1, 195) from Mesa, Ariz. and **Breyon Jones** (5-11, 180) from Round Rock, Texas.

One freshman who could make an immediate impact is running back Dustin Gabriel, a 6-1, 190-pounder from Allen, Texas.

BLUE RIBBON ANALYSIS

OFFENSE	B-
SPECIAL TEAMS	C+
DEFENSE	B
INTANGIBLES	B

At least the Cougars don't open with the defending national champion as they did a year ago when they faced Florida State in the Kickoff Classic. Crowton should get off on the right foot with a home game against Nevada for the season opener. If the Cougars don't win, it will be a long season. After that it gets tougher with road games at Cal and Mississippi State before the Mountain West Conference season begins.

BYU has built a strong tradition under Edwards, with no losing seasons in nearly 30 years, but the Cougars did have to rally last year to finish with a 6-6 record. They lost a lot of talent at the wide receiver spots and almost their entire defensive line, along with a record-setting kicker. The quarterback situation is anything but solid, with a starter who has basically played in two games in his career. There is talent in the offensive backfield, the entire offensive line returns and a solid group of linebackers and defensive backs return.

Crowton should bring some new excitement to Provo, although it will be hard to improve much on the passing game that has been such a big part of BYU football the last 30 years under Edwards. Watch for Crowton to get his career off to a winning start, but it may be tough to win a conference title. An 8-4 record might be as good as it gets.

(M.S.)

2000 RESULTS

Florida State (Pigskin)	L	3-29	0-1
Virginia	W	38-35	1-1
Air Force	L	23-31	1-2
Mississippi State	L	28-44	1-3
UNLV	W	10-7	2-3
Syracuse	L	14-42	2-4
Utah State	W	38-14	3-4
San Diego State	L	15-16	3-5
Wyoming	W	19-7	4-5
Colorado State	L	21-45	4-6
New Mexico	W	37-13	5-6
Utah	W	34-27	6-6

Colorado State

LOCATION	**Fort Collins, CO**
CONFERENCE	**Mountain West**
LAST SEASON	**10-2 (.834)**
CONFERENCE RECORD	**6-1 (1st)**
OFFENSIVE STARTERS RETURNING	**6**
DEFENSIVE STARTERS RETURNING	**6**
NICKNAME	**Rams**
COLORS	**Green & Gold**
HOME FIELD	**Hughes Stadium (30,000)**
HEAD COACH	**Sonny Lubick (W. Mont. '60)**
RECORD AT SCHOOL	**67-29 (8 years)**
CAREER RECORD	**88-48 (12 years)**
ASSISTANTS	

John Benton (Colorado State '87)
Co-Offensive Coordinator/Offensive Line
Mick Delaney (Western Montana '64)
Running Backs
Tom Ehlers (Colorado State '85)
Defensive Line
Dan Hammerschmidt (Colorado State '87)
Co-Offensive Coordinator/Quarterbacks
Larry Kerr (San Jose State '75)

Defensive Coordinator/Linebackers
Brian Schneider (Colorado State '94)
Tight Ends/Special Teams
Jesse Williams (Sonoma State '92)
Defensive Line
Matt Lubick (Colorado State '95)
Wide Receivers
Marvin Sanders (Nebraska '90)
Defensive Backs

TEAM WINS (last 5 yrs.)	**7-11-8-8-10**
FINAL RANK (last 5 yrs.)	**70-32-63-48-28**
2000 FINISH	**Beat Louisville in Liberty Bowl.**

COACH AND PROGRAM

Since Sonny Lubick took over the Colorado State program in 1993, the Rams have won five conference titles and played in five bowl games while becoming one of the most respected college programs in the West.

Besides winning Western Athletic Conference titles in 1994, '95 and '97, the Rams have two Mountain West Conference titles to their credit, tying for first in the inaugural MWC season in 1999 and winning outright last year with a 6-1 mark. They ended up with an overall 10-2 record and capped off the season by defeating Louisville, 22-17, in the Liberty Bowl. Lubick was also selected Mountain West Conference Coach of the Year for the second straight year.

Since 1994, only 10 teams in the nation have won more games than Colorado State and only one, Florida State, has won more conference titles (seven) than the Rams' five. Lubick is already the winningest coach in school history with a .698 percentage (67-29).

The 64-year-old Lubick served as an assistant coach at CSU in the early 1980s before going to Stanford as an assistant for four years. Then it was off to Miami, where he was the defensive coordinator for four more years and was part of the Hurricanes' national title teams in 1989 and 1991. After arriving at Fort Collins in 1993, it took him just one year to turn around the Ram program, which in 1994 went 10-2 and earned a berth in the Holiday Bowl. While Lubick has had the chance to return to Miami and opportunities to go elsewhere, he has opted to stay at Colorado State, where he's likely to end his career.

After going 8-4 the previous year, the Rams were picked behind Utah and BYU by many experts before the 2000 season. But the Rams opened the season with another victory over rival Colorado, survived three early-season wins against Mountain West Conference opponents by less than a touchdown apiece and then routed San Diego State, BYU and Wyoming later in the year. They capped off the season with the comeback win over Louisville in the Liberty Bowl. Only close losses to Arizona State by three and Air Force by four prevented the Rams from having a perfect season.

The Ram coaching staff has stayed intact for the most part under Lubick, but when two coaches left after last season, another Lubick was added. That would be Matt Lubick, Sonny's oldest son. The 29-year-old was the secondary coach at Oregon State, which completed its best season ever with a Fiesta Bowl win over Notre Dame. He'll coach the wide receivers at Colorado State. The other new coach is Marvin Sanders, who will coach the secondary.

This year's schedule is similar to last year's, with games against Colorado and Nevada and a rematch against Louisville on the road on Oct. 4. The other non-league game is against Fresno State, a team that beat the Rams handily two years ago.

2001 SCHEDULE

Sept.	1	@Colorado
	8	Nevada
	14	@UNLV
	22	San Diego State
	29	@Wyoming
Oct.	4	@Louisville
	13	Fresno State
	27	Utah
Nov.	1	@Brigham Young
	8	Air Force
	17	@New Mexico

QUARTERBACKS

Replacing Matt Newton, who has led the Rams to an 18-8 record and two league championships as well as a pair of bowl berths over the last two seasons, won't be easy. Newton passed for 2,609 yards last year and finished his career with 5,223 yards.

The Rams have two main candidates and a third coming in this fall to compete for the job.

Sophomores **D.J. Busch** (6-4, 203), Newton's little-used backup last year, and Michigan State transfer **Bradlee Van Pelt** (6-3, 217) went into spring drills fighting for the job and when drills ended in mid-April, nothing had changed. CSU coaches called it a draw and said the issue will be decided in fall camp and if not, they may even institute a two-quarterback system.

Busch, a former prep all-America from Santee, Calif., has experience in the program though limited action in games (11-of-18 completions for 104 yards in three games). He is more of a prototypical drop-back quarterback, while Van Pelt, the son of former NFL standout Brad Van Pelt, is an athletic type who likes to scramble and run with the ball.

"He makes plays, he's athletic, and the defense has to defend both his running and passing, and that's a big-time threat," Busch said of Van Pelt.

The spring scrimmage, where both players played equally with the first and second units, didn't solve anything. Busch completed 12-of-20 passes for 140 yards, while Van Pelt completed 8-of-15 for 176 yards and also rushed for 12 yards.

After the Green-Gold scrimmage, Lubick said he was as confused as ever.

"Right now I am looking for suggestions and won't make a call," he said." I got excited about one guy and then the other guy came in and I got excited about him. I am looking for suggestions and I might let the media vote."

Said co-offensive coordinator and quarterbacks coach John Hammerschmidt, "Right now, we'd have a tough time deciding. They both made a lot of improvement. It's just who runs the club and gets consistent drives together, that'd probably be the decision."

While Busch and Van Pelt are expected to battle it out in August, another highly touted quarterback may enter the fray. **Justin Holland** (6-3, 190) was a *Parade* All-American who broke state high school records in Colorado for passing yards with 10,567 and touchdown passes with 108. Holland has said he intends to compete for playing time right from the start.

"We're going to give him opportunities as soon as he comes in for the fall," Lubick said. "I know Justin is not going to back down from anything."

Two other quarterbacks in the program who competed in spring drills are sophomore **J.W. Morgan** (6-3, 220), who completed 3-of-5 passes for 40 yards and a touchdown in the spring game, and junior **Cory Hess** (6-3, 219), who went 3-for-3 for 22 yards.

RUNNING BACKS

Going into last season, there was much concern about how the Rams would replace Kevin McDougal, who had rushed for more than 1,100 yards in 1999. **Cecil Sapp** (6-1, 218) was barely a blip on the radar screen of possible replacements, but by the end of the year, the Rams were wondering how they could have survived the season without him.

The year before Sapp, a junior, had rushed for just 40 yards, but Lubick still expected big things from him, declaring before the season that Sapp "doesn't know how good he can be."

Given the chance to play full-time, Sapp exploded for 841 yards and 10 touchdowns, which doesn't include the 160 yards and one touchdown he rushed for in the Liberty Bowl, where he was voted the offensive MVP. Sapp's 841 yards led the Mountain West Conference and he is a preseason choice for all-league running back.

Unfortunately, Sapp suffered a broken leg midway through spring drills, which was expected to sideline him until summer and could even extend into fall camp. While Sapp's injury is very disappointing to the Rams, the silver lining is that it gave a couple of other players the opportunity to step up and show what they can do.

Junior **Rahsaan Sanders** (6-0, 212), second on the team behind McDougal in 1999 with 468 rushing yards, was the top running back in the spring game with 51 yards on seven carries. He rushed for 524 yards and four touchdowns last year—including a 116-yard game against Nevada—and should play a big part in the Rams' offense this year.

Junior **Henri Childs** (6-2, 217) is a transfer from Kansas who impressed some people when he ran for 40 yards and a touchdown in the spring game. Lubick praised the play of Childs, saying he "played very well this spring."

Having both Sanders and Childs should make the Rams coaches feel a lot better in case Sapp is slow coming back from his injury.

Also back are senior **Duan Ruff** (5-9, 187) and sophomore **Jeff McGarrity** (6-0, 225), who rushed for 205 and 101 yards, respectively, last year. Junior **Chad Dixon** (6-0, 189), who redshirted the year before, played a lot in the spring and gained 22 yards on eight carries in the spring game.

WIDE RECEIVERS/TIGHT ENDS

The receiving position may turn out to be the deepest on the team with three experienced pass catchers back, along with several talented newcomers. The tight end position is also solid with a returning all-league performer.

The receiving corps is led by senior **Pete Rebstock** (5-9, 182), who earned first-team All-MWC honors after catching 46 passes for 768 yards and six touchdowns. His best performance of the year came against Air Force, when he pulled down nine catches for 168 yards and three scores.

Then there's **Dallas Davis** (5-10, 181), who led the Rams in receiving in 1999 with 51 receptions for 665 yards and three touchdowns, but had to sit out in 2000 because of an injury. His absence allowed Rebstock to shine, but this year Rebstock and Davis give the Rams a potent 1-2 punch assuming they're healthy. Davis underwent shoulder surgery in the spring, while Rebstock sat out part of the spring with a thigh injury.

Junior **Joey Cuppari** (6-1, 175), was a consistent receiver for the Rams last year, grabbing 31 passes for 438 yards and five touchdowns. The previous year he caught 20 passes for 308 yards.

Perhaps the biggest eye-opener of spring drills was the splendid play of sophomore wide receiver **Eric Hill** (6-0, 185).

Hill was impressive all through spring practice and he capped it off by catching 10 passes for 159 yards and two touchdowns in the spring game. Last year Hill played in just three games, catching five passes for 55 yards.

"I knew Eric Hill had potential," Lubick told the *Denver Post*. "He is probably as good a young receiver as there is in the conference."

Hill is poised to have a breakout year.

"The coaches have faith in me, and I believe in myself," Hill said. "I'm full of confidence right now. I know I can go out and make plays, against CU, Air Force, whoever it may be."

Other receivers to keep an eye on are sophomore **Chris Pittman** (6-1, 185), who caught six passes in the spring game after catching three passes for 31 yards last year, and sophomore **Russell Sprague** (6-4, 204), the younger brother of defensive back **Aaron Sprague**.

"Pittman and Sprague are solid," Lubick said. "Those three (including Hill) are as good as we've recruited at Colorado State."

Another revelation this spring was the play of redshirt freshman **Joel Dressen** (6-6, 235), who jumped from No. 3 on the depth chart to starter at the H-Back position vacated by two-year starter Cory Woolstenhulme.

"He's probably the most pleasant surprise of the entire spring," said Lubick of Dressen.

Senior **Brad Svoboda** (6-1, 174), and sophomore **Matt Baldischwiler** (6-3, 230), who each caught one pass last year, will be ready to take over should Dressen falter.

Returning All-MWC tight end **Jose Ochoa** (6-3, 255), who has started 24 straight games, is back for his senior season. Last year he was fifth on the team in receptions with 22, three of them going for touchdowns. He'll be backed up by sophomore **James Sondrup** (6-6, 251).

OFFENSIVE LINE

Three starters and one former starter return on the offensive line that will be looking to fill holes at the center and strong side tackle positions.

Senior **David Shohet** (6-6, 315) has started 24 straight games at weak side tackle and should be a candidate for all-league honors this year. He'll be backed up by junior **Aaron Green** (6-5, 270).

Senior **Broc Finlayson**, (6-5, 315) finally overcame foot injuries that had plagued him for a couple of seasons and put in a full season at the strong side guard position. He is backed up by senior **Broderick Lancaster** (6-4, 315), who has plenty of experience; he's started 19 games during his career.

Junior **Morgan Pears** (6-8, 309) took over at the weak side guard spot five games into the season and started the final seven games and should return as a starter this year.

Erik Pears, a 6-8, 300-pound redshirt freshman and the younger brother of Morgan, is a top candidate to take over the center position vacated by Justin Borvansky, a first-team All-MWC selection last year. He is vying with sophomore **Mark Dreyer** (6-4, 281), who was among the spring's pleasant surprises.

At the strong side tackle position where the Rams must replace Tim Stuber, sophomores **Terrell Gardner** (6-6, 347), the largest player on the team, and **Kelly Wall** (6-4, 300) are vying for the starting spot.

2000 STATISTICS

Rushing offense	137.3	67
Passing offense	247.0	28
Total offense	384.3	48
Scoring offense	31.0	31
Net Punting	39.1	26
Punt returns	16.0	7
Kickoff returns	22.2	16
Rushing defense	145.8	53
Passing efficiency defense	113.1	44
Total defense	328.1	31
Scoring defense	18.9	19
Turnover margin	+0	59

Last column is ranking among Division I-A teams.

KICKERS

With the graduation of two-year starter C.W. Hurst, who led the team in scoring each of the last two seasons, the place-kicking job is wide open. Senior **Kent Naughton**, a 6-0, 185-pound former walk-on, is listed as the starter, but he didn't do enough in the spring to sew up the job heading into fall.

He'll be challenged in the fall by another walk-on, redshirt freshman in **Jeff Babcock** (5-10, 180) and incoming freshman **Kevin Mark** (6-1, 165).

Mark comes all the way from Coral Springs, Fla., where he was a second-team all-state selection at Douglas High School. In his high school career, Mark set records for PATs in a season with 35 and for the longest field goal (52 yards).

DEFENSIVE LINE

Besides quarterback, the biggest question mark on the team is the defensive tackle position, where the Rams lost Jamie Bennett, a first-team All-MWC selection and Mike Mackenzie, an honorable mention pick.

Senior **Lucas Smith** (6-4, 280) has played every game the last three seasons without a start, but finally has the opportunity to play full time this fall. As a freshman, Smith recorded 22 tackles and a sack, but fell off to 10 tackles as a sophomore. Then last year, Smith finished with 25 tackles, including a career-best five against Arizona State.

The other tackle spot is up for grabs with sophomore **Bryan Save** (6-2, 265), **Josh Steward** (6-2, 271) and redshirt freshman **Patrick Goodpaster** (6-3, 277) all battling. Steward, a converted linebacker, has the most experience with six tackles and a sack last year, while Save, who had three tackles, had a productive spring. Then there's Goodpaster, who made a good impression on coaches during spring drills.

"Our first (defensive line) unit should be very good," Lubick said after the spring game. "We had a couple tackles come through that were big for us. I thought Patrick Goodpaster did a good job, as well as Josh Steward, and those are two guys we were hoping would come through."

Junior **Peter Hogan** (6-3, 255) and senior **Geoff Graue** (6-4, 247) are the returning starters at end, although senior **Chad McGuckin** (6-4, 263) will push Graue for the right-end position.

Graue started 10-of-12 games last year and made 43 tackles, including three for loss and three sacks. McGuckin started two games and came up with 20 tackles and three sacks.

Hogan is the top returning lineman after starting 11 games and registering 52 tackles and four sacks.

Backups include junior **Wallace Thomas** (6-3, 239), who filled in for Hogan when he sprained an ankle, redshirt freshman **Jonathon Simon** (6-6, 251) and sophomore **Andre Sommersell** (6-3, 210) at the end positions and **Kelsio Howard** (6-3, 294) at tackle.

LINEBACKERS

Three-time all-conference performer and 2000 MWC Defensive Player of the Year Rick Crowell is gone, drafted in the sixth round by the Miami Dolphins, but two other starters return to give the Rams stability in the middle of the defense.

Junior **David Vickers** (6-0, 208) was third on the team with 91 tackles. He made 10 or more tackles in four games and earned honorable mention all-league honors. He'll man the middle this year.

Junior **Doug Heald** (6-2, 215) started eight games last year at weak-side linebacker, made 52 tackles and came up with a key 48-yard interception return for a touchdown in a come-from-behind win over Utah. However, sophomore **Eric Pauly** (6-4, 215) may get the starting nod in the fall. He played mostly on special teams last year and in 1999 he was defensive scout team player of the year.

Sophomore **Adam Wade** (6-1, 210) is slated to take over for Crowell at strong-side linebacker, but he is coming off major knee surgery and may not be 100 percent at the start of fall drills. He started the first three games before going out with an injury. Senior **Rocky Martin** (6-2, 217), who started two games, including the Liberty Bowl game and made 13 tackles on the season will be ready to take over if Wade's knee isn't better.

Senior **Tony Colacion** (6-2, 230) who started three games in 1999 and played in all 12 games last year, is another capable backup at linebacker.

DEFENSIVE BACKS

Two starters are gone, Terrance Gibson and John Howell, who was drafted by Tampa Bay in the fourth round of the NFL draft, but two starters return in senior cornerback **Justin Gallimore** (5-10, 198) and senior strong safety Aaron Sprague (6-2, 220).

Both players are talented enough to contend for all-league honors this year and will be counted on to help the younger players fill in the holes left by Gibson and Howell.

Sprague was an honorable mention all-league pick after making 83 tackles, fourth-best on the team, and grabbing two interceptions.

Gallimore has started the last two years and led the team with three interceptions, including a 63-yard touchdown return against Wyoming. Gallimore was fifth on the team in tackles with 59, the same total he had as a junior. He also came up with two quarterback sacks from his cornerback position.

Gallimore's twin brother, Jason, is expected to start at the free safety position after backing up Howell last year and playing nickel back. Jason, a 5-10, 200-pound senior, made 22 tackles last year after getting 26 the year before and came up with two quarterback sacks both years. Against Wyoming, he joined his brother in the end zone by picking up a fumble and racing 52 yards for a touchdown.

The left cornerback position is being contested by junior **Rhett Nelson** (6-1 194) and sophomore **Dexter Wynn** (5-9, 165). Nelson is coming back from a shoulder injury after playing in eight games and making 16 tackles and one interception. Wynn has been a special teams standout who has the skills to be an outstanding cornerback but needs experience.

Among the backups in the defensive backfield are senior **Thai Woods** (6-0, 180), a two-year reserve at cornerback, senior **Ameer Lowe** (6-1, 180) and sophomore **Lenzie Williams** (6-1, 204) at strong safety and **Guy Porter** (6-1, 180), a junior college transfer from Fullerton (Calif.) Junior College and redshirt freshman **Landon Jones** (6-2, 222). Lowe is the most experienced with 11 starts in 1999 and seven last year.

PUNTERS

Junior **Joey Huber** (6-4, 223), a former walk-on out of Arapahoe High School in Littleton, Colo., took over punting duties last year and did a commendable job. His 39.1 average wasn't great, but good enough that he was voted honorable mention All-MWC by the league coaches.

His best game came against Air Force, where he booted a season-best 59-yarder and averaged 42.5 per kick. Twelve of his punts were downed inside the 20-yard line.

SPECIAL TEAMS

One of the keys to the Rams' success in recent years has been the play of their special teams.

The top returners from last year's team are back, along with Dallas Davis, who returned two punts for touchdowns in 1999 before sitting out most of last year with an injury.

The Rams' fine receiver, Rebstock, averaged 16.8 yards on 28 punt returns and scored on a 66-yard punt return against Nevada. He also returned 12 punts for a 24.5-yard average.

Wynn, a backup defensive back, set a school record with a 31.8-yard average on 12 kickoff returns, including a 100-yard return against San Diego State. He also averaged 22.7 yards on seven punt returns.

Punting should be solid with Huber having a year behind him, but place-kicking could be a concern with two walk-ons, Naughton and Babcock trying to beat out freshman Mark.

RECRUITING CLASS

The Rams signed 21 players, but to show the strength of the program, only one of them is a junior college player. That's typical of the Rams under Lubick—last year just one of the Rams' 15 recruits was a junior college transfer.

If possible, Lubick will redshirt all the freshmen, but a handful could end up playing this fall. One of the most likely is place-kicker Mark from Florida. Also highly acclaimed quarterback Holland from Bear Creek H.S. in Lakewood, Colo., could compete for a starting spot.

The one junior college transfer is Porter, a defensive back from Fullerton (Calif.) College. Porter was voted the Mission Conference Central Division Defensive Player of the Pear after intercepting six passes and registering 69 tackles.

"Guy Porter is the best all-around athlete we've had in my eight years here," Fullerton coach Gene Murphy said.

Among the players who may be making their mark for CSU in the future are **Jason Anderson**, a 6-7, 250 defensive lineman from Encino, Calif.; **Albert Bimper**, a 6-2, 300-pound lineman from Arlington, Texas; **Jair Brown**, a 5-11, 170-pound wide receiver from San Diego; **Uldis Jaunarajs**, a 5-11, 190-pound running back from Lakewood, Colo.; and **Frostee Rucker**, a 6-4, 215-pound linebacker from Tustin, Calif.

BLUE RIBBON ANALYSIS

OFFENSE	B
SPECIAL TEAMS	B+
DEFENSE	B
INTANGIBLES	A-

For two straight years, the Rams have knocked off in-state rival Colorado in the season opener in Denver. That's caused some embarrassment for the Buffaloes, who feel superior playing in the prestigious Big 12 Conference, but to many folks it shows that the Rams have taken over as the best college team in the state.

The Rams and Buffs meet again in this year's opener, and if the Rams can prevail again, they could be on their way to another 10-win season.

Their other non-league games are at home against Nevada and Fresno State of the WAC and a road game at Louisville, which will be looking for revenge after last year's Liberty Bowl loss.

With no dominant teams in the Mountain West this year, the Rams are as likely as anyone to finish first. A big test will come Sept. 14 when the Rams travel to Las Vegas to play up-and-coming UNLV, which a lot of folks are picking to challenge for the title. That game is scheduled for a Friday night and the Rams also have three Thursday night games on their schedule.

Even though they lost their quarterback and offensive coordinator along with nine starters, you can't count the Rams out of the championship race for 2001. In fact, after their success of recent years, how can you pick anyone else to win the MWC championship?

(M.S.)

2000 RESULTS

Colorado	W	28-24	1-0
East Tennessee State	W	41-7	2-0
Arizona State	L	10-13	2-1
Nevada	W	45-14	3-1
New Mexico	W	17-14	4-1
UNLV	W	20-19	5-1
Utah	W	24-17	6-1
San Diego State	W	34-22	7-1
Brigham Young	W	45-21	8-1
Air Force	L	40-44	8-2
Wyoming	W	37-13	9-2
Louisville (Liberty Bowl)	W	22-17	10-2

New Mexico

LOCATION	**Albuquerque, NM**
CONFERENCE	**Mountain West**
LAST SEASON	**5-7 (.417)**
CONFERENCE RECORD	**3-4 (t-5th)**
OFFENSIVE STARTERS RETURNING	**8**
DEFENSIVE STARTERS RETURNING	**5**
NICKNAME	**Lobos**
COLORS	**Cherry & Silver**
HOME FIELD	**University Stadium (30,000)**
HEAD COACH	**Rocky Long (New Mexico '74)**
RECORD AT SCHOOL	**12-23 (3 years)**
CAREER RECORD	**12-23 (3 years)**
ASSISTANTS	**Dan Dodd (Drake '78)** **Offensive Coordinator** **Bronco Mendenhall (Oregon State '88)** **Defensive Coordinator** **Jeff Conway (NW Missouri State '81)** **Special Teams Coordinator/Tight Ends** **Blake Anderson (Sam Houston State '92)** **Running Backs** **Bob Bostad (Wisconsin-Stevens Point '89)** **Offensive Line** **Gerald Bradley (Weber State '89)** **Receivers** **Curtis Modkins (TCU '93)** **Cornerbacks** **Lenny Rodriguez (San Diego '77)** **Linebackers** **Grady Stretz (UCLA '96)** **Defensive Line**
TEAM WINS (last 5 yrs.)	**6-9-3-4-5**
FINAL RANK (last 5 yrs.)	**83-61-101-84-82**
2000 FINISH	**Lost to Brigham Young in regular-season finale.**

COACH AND PROGRAM

A second straight tie for fifth in the Mountain West Conference doesn't seem like much of a season, but for a team that was picked to finish at the bottom of the league, it was a pretty good outcome for New Mexico.

In fact, heading into November, the Lobos were in first place with their destiny in their own hands, only to lose back-to-back heartbreakers to San Diego State and UNLV before finishing off with a big loss at BYU.

"I thought we were going to do something really special, but we fell short of that, which was really disappointing," said coach Rocky Long, who completed his third season at his alma mater. "So that is kind of a sour taste left in our mouth. We need to get over that hump."

Despite the struggle to the finish line, Long was pleased with the improvement his team made after a start that looked like it would have trouble winning any games. The Lobos started off with three straight losses, then ran off five wins in six games—the only loss being a three-pointer to league champion Colorado State—before the final three losses.

"I thought we made great strides and improved dramatically from the year before," Long said. "We played a lot more competitive football against a lot of good football teams. If you look over the whole season and consider the quality of our schedule, I would say it was a pretty good season because we showed dramatic improvement."

Indeed, the Lobos' first three losses were to eventual bowl teams, including a close one to Oregon State, which went 11-1 and won the Rose Bowl, and Boise State, which finished 10-2.

"The past two years, we have shown in most games that we can compete with not only everybody in our league, but with everyone on our schedule," Long said.

Three years earlier, Long took over for Dennis Franchione—who went to TCU and later to Alabama—and since then has been trying to rebuild a senior-dominated team that went 9-3 in 1997. Long's initial team won three games, followed by a four-win season in 1999 before the Lobos moved up to five wins last year. Similar improvement this year would give New Mexico only its fourth winning season since 1982.

For that to happen, the Lobos will have to see marked improvement from their offense—which averaged less than 300 yards per game and ranked 109th out of 115 teams in the nation in passing—and no fall-off from the defense, which carried the team much of last season.

The Lobos lost 13 seniors, but return 45 lettermen, about half of whom played extensive minutes for the Lobos last season. Eight starters return on offense, but only five on defense.

The program received a big boost late last year when ground was broken at the north end of University Stadium for the construction of an additional 5,700 seats to increase stadium capacity to more than 37,000.

"I know our confidence is very high right now, especially with stadium expansion underway," Long said. "There's no doubt that kids are really impressed by the improvements we are making to our facilities. It shows there is a commitment to making our program better."

2001 SCHEDULE

Sept.	1	UTEP
	8	@Texas Tech
	15	New Mexico State
	22	@Baylor
	29	@Utah
Oct.	6	@Wyoming
	13	Brigham Young
	27	Air Force
Nov.	3	@San Diego State
	10	UNLV
	17	Colorado State

QUARTERBACKS

Last year, Long caused a bit of controversy when he pushed senior quarterback Sean Stein out the door, urging him to transfer after spring practice even though Stein was the logical starter after leading the Lobos to three victories the year before.

Long wanted a younger, more athletic quarterback to direct his offense and had two junior college transfers he wanted to try. The first, Jeremy Denson, started two games, but after a pair of defeats where the offense sputtered with an average of just 223 yards of total offense in each game, the Lobos made the switch to **Rudy Caamano**.

Caamano, a 6-1, 185-pound junior, came from Mt. San Antonio Junior College with three years of eligibility remaining. Once he took over as quarterback, the Lobos' fortunes rose. In his first game, the Lobos led future Top 10 team Oregon State, 20-14, going into the fourth quarter before the Beavers scored twice to pull out a win. Then came three straight victories over Northern Arizona, New Mexico State and Wyoming, before the close loss to CSU.

For the season, Caamano's numbers weren't that great yardage-wise with 1,270 yards passing, but he did complete 55.7 percent of his passes for 11 touchdowns. He was intercepted just seven times.

"Rudy Caamano played a lot of football last year and got a lot better," Long said.

Caamano's improvement was evident in the spring game, when he threw a pair of touchdown passes in the Cherry team's 27-0 victory over the Silver. Caamano completed 14-of-24 passes for 176 yards.

"Rudy has started where he ended last year," Long said after the spring game. "I think he's getting better and he is getting a lot more comfortable with the offense. He's performing at a better level."

Denson would have been a junior this year with a medical redshirt, but he decided to transfer to Florida A&M in May after deciding he didn't want to compete for a backup job in the fall. Last year he completed just 34.4 percent of his passes for 105 yards with no touchdowns and two interceptions and he was slowed in the spring by a broken right (throwing) hand suffered in a winter pickup basketball game.

With Denson gone sophomore **Casey Kelly** (6-3, 190) moved up the depth chart to No. 2, followed by senior **Ken Stopka** (6-2, 200) and redshirt freshman **Jeff Grady** (6-2, 205).

"We have two young guys [Kelly and Grady] in the program that show potential of being really good quarterbacks," Long said.

While Long says Caamano will be the starter heading into the fall, he expects the other three to compete and be ready to take over should Caamano falter or get injured.

"I think it's always harder to lose a job than to take somebody else's over," he said. "But I don't think that will deter the other three quarterbacks from trying to compete and win the job."

Kelly sat out the spring game with lacerations to his face, while Stopka was 2-of-9 for 12 yards and Grady was 0-for-4 passing.

"The quarterback position is the most critical for us to be better on offense," Long said. "We showed some improvement on offense during the season, but we have to improve dramatically at that position."

RUNNING BACKS

The backfield should be one of the strongest positions on the team with several experienced players back, led by seniors **Jarrod Baxter** and **Holmon Wiggins**.

Wiggins (6-0, 210) led the Lobos in rushing for the second straight year with 727 yards and also led the team with five touchdowns. He was seventh in the MWC with 60.6 yards per game and also caught eight passes for 53 yards and a touchdown. The year before he rushed for 618 yards and five touchdowns and with another comparable season to the last two, he will move into the top 10 list of all-time rushers at UNM.

Baxter (6-1, 250) is a homegrown product who rushed for 570 yards last year and 434 the year before. With his size, he mostly plays fullback and is known as a devastating blocker who led the running backs with 44 knockdown blocks last year.

"We've got two quality guys coming back in Jarrod Baxter and Holmon Wiggins," Long said. "Both of them have proved they can play at this level and be successful."

Senior **Javier Hanson** (6-1, 195) came in as a junior transfer from El Camino (Calif.) College and started five games, scoring three touchdowns and rushing for 201 yards. In the spring game, Hanson had the big offensive play of the night when he ran 66 yards for a touchdown. He finished the game with 72 yards on five carries and scored two touchdowns.

Another top backup is junior **Quincy Wright** (5-10, 185), who saw limited action last year (three carries for six yards), but looked impressive in the spring game in leading the Silver squad with 60 yards on 11 carries, going against the first-team defense.

Other backups in the backfield are sophomore **Adrian Boyd** (6-0, 175) at tailback and red-shirt freshman **Landrick Brody** (5-11, 240) at fullback.

Freshman **Dontrell Moore** (5-11, 203), a Parade All-American from Roswell, N.M., might be one freshman who could see playing time.

WIDE RECEIVERS/TIGHT ENDS

When your top receiver is your fullback with just 28 receptions, you know there are problems with your passing game. Lobo receivers caught only 66 passes last year, a number that UNM coaches would like to at least double this year.

Top receiver Rob Caston (22 receptions) has graduated, but most of last year's receivers return for the Lobos.

Senior **Kirk Robbins** (5-11, 185), who caught 16 passes for 224 yards and a touchdown, and sophomore **Dwight Counter** (6-2, 172), who caught 13 passes for 147 yards a touchdown, are the top two returnees. Neither has a starting job locked up. Counter came out of spring listed as No. 1 at one spot, while Robbins was listed as a backup at the other behind sophomore **Rashaun Sanders** (6-2, 200).

Sanders, who was a track star in high school in the 100-meter dash and long jump, impressed coaches all spring and made two catches in the spring game. Other returnees who will compete at wide receiver are junior **Joe Manning** (6-0, 180), sophomore **Terrence Thomas** (6-2, 180), junior **Jake Farrel** (6-4, 200) and senior **Joel Baker** (6-0, 190). Thomas led all receivers in the spring game with four catches for 60 yards.

The best receivers on this team may turn out to be a pair of junior college transfers.

Junior **Michael Brunker** (6-2, 175) was an all-conference receiver at Grossmont (Calif.) College, where he caught 40 passes for 800 yards and eight touchdowns. He transferred at mid-year and participated in spring drills.

Scheduled to come in this fall is junior **Derrick Shepherd** (6-1, 181), who made 31 catches for 786 yards at Fort Scott Community College in Kansas.

"One of the reasons we recruited two junior college wide receivers is because we don't think our receivers performed very well last year," Long said.

At tight end, three-year starter Jonathan Burrough is gone and the only player with any experience is junior **Joe Fiola** (6-3, 270). He started four games last year but was used mostly as a blocker and didn't catch any passes.

"Joe got a lot of playing time last year and has a lot of experience," Long said.

Three new players who will get a look are red-shirt freshman **Michael Augustyniak** (6-5, 247), sophomore **Bryan Penly** (6-2, 235) and freshman **Brian Beaty** (6-3, 246). Penly was the only first-year freshman to letter in 2000.

OFFENSIVE LINE

Three-year starter Jon Samuelson is gone, but the Lobo line should be stronger as a whole this year with the other four starters returning.

Junior center **Rashad McClure** (6-3, 295) has started the last two years and participated in 93 percent of the Lobos' offensive plays in 2000. He ranked second behind Samuelson in knockdown blocks with 83.

Senior **Jeremy Sorenson** (6-4, 290) returns at left guard after starting all 12 games and registering 81 knockdown blocks. Senior left tackle **B.J. Long** (6-5, 290) has 15 career starts to his credit, while sophomore **Jason Lenzmeier** (6-5, 305) started seven straight games before suffering a broken leg against BYU, which kept him from being full speed during spring drills.

There is good depth behind those four with senior **Jon Oliver** (6-6, 280), junior **Brian Choi** (6-5, 315), sophomore **Derek Watson** (6-3, 283) and sophomore **Justin Colburn** (6-4, 275). Redshirt freshmen who could earn a lot of playing time are **Steve Fahnert** (6-5, 295), **Nate Hembree** (6-5, 280) and **Claude Terrell** (6-3, 320).

Oliver, who started five games as a sophomore and six last year mostly at guard, could take over Samuelson's old spot at the right tackle spot. Choi tore the medial collateral ligament in his left knee in and missed much of spring practice, while Fahnert also missed spring practice with an injured shoulder.

Eric May, the Lobos' largest lineman at 6-6, 320 pounds who would have been a junior, won't return to the team in the fall.

2000 STATISTICS

Rushing offense	148.0	56
Passing offense	118.6	110
Total offense	266.6	109
Scoring offense	19.1	93
Net Punting	35.5	40
Punt returns	9.4	57
Kickoff returns	21.2	25
Rushing defense	115.3	29

Passing efficiency defense	105.7	25
Total defense	309.4	17
Scoring defense	20.8	36
Turnover margin	+8	22

Last column is ranking among Division I-A teams.

KICKERS

Vladimir Borombozin (5-10, 164) came in from West Hills (Calif.) College last fall to improve a woeful kicking game and did a decent job in converting 10-of-15 field goals. However, he was a little shaky on PATs in making just 21-of-25. Lobo coaches believe he will be much better in his senior season.

"Vladimir has a great work ethic and great confidence in his ability as does the coaching staff," Long said. "I think after a year of kicking at the Division I level, he will be much better this year."

Sophomore **Ben Shankle** (5-8, 165), a walk-on from Arkansas, is the backup and can also play receiver.

DEFENSIVE LINE

With senior **Brian Johnson** (6-3, 280) back after a sterling junior season when he averaged 9.5 sacks per game and was a first-team All-MWC selection, the Lobos have someone to anchor the defensive line. The question is, who will step up to help Johnson on the defensive line this year?

With Jeff Macrea and Henry Stephens graduated, senior **Antonio Manning** (6-2, 265) and junior **Adrian Terry** (6-1, 258) are slated to take their spots on the defensive line.

Manning made the switch to defensive line from linebacker—where he played sparingly last year—to earn the starting defensive end position. Sophomore **D.J. Renteria** (6-2, 270) backed up Johnson last year and saw a lot of action for a freshman, posting 10 tackles and three sacks. He will challenge Manning.

Terry moved over to nose guard from end, where played in every game with one start and made 20 tackles and 1 1/2 sacks. Against Air Force, he forced a key fumble in the second half that led to an upset victory.

He will be backed up by senior **Tony Mazotti** (6-4, 290), who had 11 tackles in 11 games, and redshirt freshman **Kyle Coulter** (6-1, 260). Sophomore **Guillermo Morrison** (6-3, 265), who might be the only defensive lineman in America with a 37-inch vertical leap, is scheduled to back up Johnson, who has come a long way since joining the Lobos as a 195-pound walk-on running back.

Players who will provide depth on the defensive line include junior college transfers **Hebrews Josue** (5-11, 180) and **Daniel Kegler** (6-3, 260).

LINEBACKERS

It may look like the Lobos are hurting here after losing two starting linebackers in Mike Barnett and David Mauer, but the linebacker position could be one of the strongest and deepest on the team with several players with experience and some younger players with potential.

Senior **Mohammed Konte** (6-2, 225) finished fifth on the team in tackles after starting nine games and also came up with an interception, a sack and two fumble recoveries. Senior **Gary Davis** (6-0, 230) started five games and was seventh in tackles with 59 and is known for his speed. The third starter is expected to be either junior **Charles Moss** (6-0, 215), who played significant minutes in registering 53 tackles, or **Shannon Kincaid** (6-2, 225), a sophomore who saw minimal action last year.

Senior **Amos Wilson** (6-2, 230) was slated to start last year, but sat out as a redshirt. His return will give the Lobos needed depth at the position along with redshirt freshmen **Chrishone Harris** (6-2, 225), **Domingo Villarruel** (6-3, 220), **Frank Rodgers** (6-2, 230) and **Nick Speegle** (6-5, 207).

"All of our young linebackers have shown real good ability in practice," said Long, who hopes that translates in to good performances in games.

DEFENSIVE BACKS

The Lobos use five players in the secondary, counting the lobo back position, which was up undecided coming out of spring ball. Defensive coordinator Bronco Mendenhall tried several players there during the spring. He hinted that the defense could switch to a four-linebacker set if the coaches weren't satisfied with anyone to play the position that Brian Urlacher filled so well before he went on to become the NFL Defensive Rookie of the Year last year.

Senior **Scott Gerhardt** (6-0, 185), who started a few games at lobo in place of Rantie Harper when he was injured in midseason, is the top candidate to play the lobo spot. Gerhardt, who also started seven games at free safety last year, finished eighth on the team with 53 tackles with two interceptions. His backup will be redshirt freshman **Kevin Walton** (6-0, 193), who is coming off a broken leg.

Sophomore **Brandon Ratcliff** (6-0, 200) came from nowhere to become the MWC Freshman of the Year in 2000 and he'll be back as the starting strong safety. He tied for third on the team in tackles last year with 71 and is the top returning tackler for the Lobos. He also came up with four sacks and a fumble recovery and caused two fumbles. He sat out of spring drills to focus on academics. His backup will be senior **Edwin Garrett** (5-9, 180), who has moved over from cornerback.

A third returning starter in the backfield is senior cornerback **Stephen Persley** (5-9, 175), who started all 12 games and earned second-team All-MWC honors, after getting five starts the year before. He led the team with 12 pass breakups, had two interceptions for 27 yards and also registered 39 tackles. He also blocked two punts and scored a pair of touchdowns off the blocks.

The question marks for the Lobos come at the other cornerback position and at free safety. Sophomore **Terrell Golden** (5-10, 195) played in every game and started five at free safety, and made 35 tackles and 2 1/2 sacks and led the team with three interceptions. But he came to spring camp overweight, which slowed him somewhat.

Junior college transfer **David Hall** (5-10, 185), who was also tried at lobo, will challenge Golden along with redshirt freshman **Joe Henderson** (5-11, 185).

The other cornerback position looks like a dog-fight, with junior college transfer **David Crockett** (5-10, 175) having the edge over **Desmar Black** (5-9, 180)—who missed spring drills recovering from a shoulder injury after starting two years ago and playing little in 2000—and senior **Dante Childress** (5-8, 185), who had 13 tackles last year.

Redshirt freshmen **Curtis Flakes** (5-10, 153) and **Brandon Gregory** (5-9, 172) are likely to back up Persley at the other corner position.

PUNTERS

The Lobos suffered a blow late in the spring when starting punter Cort Moffit decided to leave the team. He had started the two previous seasons and improved significantly in his second year, averaging 39.7 yards per punt with 20 kicks dropped inside the 20-yard line and a 78-yarder to his credit. The fact that he left after spring football was completed left the Lobo coaches scrambling.

Borombozin, who punted once last year and has high school experience, is the most likely candidate to be the starter. But the coaches would prefer not to overload Borombozin, who already handles place kicking and kickoff chores. Three other players who may be tried at punter in the fall are backup quarterback Grady, tight end Augustyniak—who punted in high school—and redshirt freshman **Norbert Gabaldon** (5-10, 179), a walk-on punter.

SPECIAL TEAMS

With Borombozin returning, the Lobos' place kicking looks solid, but Moffit's abrupt decision to leave the team puts a big question mark on the punting game.

The Lobos lost long snapper Joe Maese, who was actually chosen by the Super Bowl champion Baltimore Ravens in the sixth round of the NFL draft, but tight end Fiola should be an adequate replacement. Caamano will be the holder with Moffit as his backup.

Wiggins, who fielded 46 punts last year for an 8.5-yard average, will be back again as the main punt returner, while several players will try to fill the kickoff returner spots, including Ratcliff, who had eight for a 22.1-yard average, Sanders, Counter, Robbins and Wiggins.

RECRUITING CLASS

Like a year ago, the Lobos are bringing in nine junior college transfers, four of whom participated in spring drills, along with 17 freshmen, one more than last year.

Among the transfers most likely to challenge for starting positions right away are wide receiver Brunker, safety Hall and cornerbacks Crockett and Gregory.

The jewel of the recruiting class could be **Dontrell Moore**, a 5-11, 203-pound running back from Roswell, N.M., who was a *Parade* All-American.

How could Long and his staff pull off signing a *Parade* All-American who was recruited by, among many others, Notre Dame? Through hard work. The New Mexico staff stayed on Moore's trail.

"I felt throughout this recruiting process, they showed they wanted what was best for me," Moore told the *Roswell Daily Record*. "Maybe it was a recruiting spiel, but I felt they were concerned about me a little bit more."

Moore also was intrigued by the chance to go to a program that's on the rise and have a chance to be the go-to guy right away. But he won't rest on his prep laurels when he arrives on campus in August.

"I have the potential to be the feature back, but that doesn't mean anything if I go in there and not work," he told the *Daily Record*. "I can be sitting on the sidelines just like anyone else. But if I work, which I am going to do, then I look forward to being the feature guy."

Among the other 17 high school recruits are running backs **Aaron Brack** (5-11, 196) out of Austin, Texas; **Tony Frazier** (5-6, 180) from Houston, Texas; and wide receiver **Hank Baskett**, a 6-4, 205-pound multi-sport standout from Clovis, N.M. Baskett is the state record holder in the high jump, where he has cleared seven feet.

The only quarterback among the recruits is **Kyle Krystick**, a 6-3, 217-pounder from Fountain Hills, Ariz. The biggest player among the recruits is **Terrance Pennington**, a 6-7, 314-pound offensive lineman from Compton, Calif., who was heavily recruited by Washington, Oregon and Colorado.

Like most coaches, Long expects all the freshmen to redshirt, but says that can change if "one of them turns out to be a great player."

Besides Pennington, the Lobos signed two junior college transfers who weigh more than 300 pounds—6-4, 340-pound **Calvin McDonald** from Fort Scott (Kansas) Community College and **Danny Perez**, a 6-3, 300-pounder from Mt. San Antonio (Calif.) College.

"I want to look like Colorado State and BYU and Utah when we walk out there," Long told the Associated Press. "I'm tired of walking out thinking we've got big guys and all I see is shadows when the other team is on the other sideline."

While Long called this recruiting class the best in his three years at New Mexico, he knows the proof won't come for a while.

"We're finally starting to win some battles," he told the Associated Press, "but we'll find out how well we did in a year or two."

BLUE RIBBON ANALYSIS

OFFENSE	B
SPECIAL TEAMS	C+
DEFENSE	B-
INTANGIBLES	B

Last year's schedule turned out to be tougher than expected as Oregon State ended up a Top 10 team and Boise State and Texas Tech both went to bowl games. This year, the Lobos face a more palatable schedule. Two of their first three games are home games against rivals UTEP and New Mexico State and the other two non-league games are against Texas Tech and Baylor of the Big 12 Conference. The Texas Tech game on the road will be a challenge, but the Lobos should be favored to win the other three games, which would get them off to a fast start before they open league play at Utah.

New Mexico's offense can't be much worse than last year when it averaged a paltry 266.6 yards per game. Caamano has a year behind him at quarterback and both of last year's top running backs, Wiggins and Baxter, are back, along with most of the receivers and four starters on the line. Questions come at several positions on the defensive side and in the punting game, where the Lobos have no experience.

The Lobos should be competitive in the Mountain West Conference and win some games, but without the strong defense that has carried them so well the last couple of years, they aren't likely to get over the hump and produce a winning record or challenge for the MWC title.

(M.S.)

2000 RESULTS

Texas Tech (Hispanic)	L	3-24	0-1
Boise State	L	14-31	0-2
Oregon State	L	20-28	0-3
New Mexico State	W	16-13	1-3
Northern Arizona	W	35-28	2-3
Wyoming	W	45-10	3-3
Colorado State	L	14-17	3-4
Air Force	W	29-23	4-4
Utah	W	10-3	5-4
San Diego State	L	16-17	5-5
UNLV	L	14-18	5-6
Brigham Young	L	13-37	5-7

San Diego State

LOCATION	**San Diego, CA**
CONFERENCE	**Mountain West**
LAST SEASON	**3-8 (.273)**
CONFERENCE RECORD	**3-4 (t-5th)**
OFFENSIVE STARTERS RETURNING	**11**
DEFENSIVE STARTERS RETURNING	**10**
NICKNAME	**Aztecs**
COLORS	**Scarlet & Black**
HOME FIELD	**Qualcomm Stadium (71,400)**
HEAD COACH	**Ted Tollner (Cal Poly '62)**
RECORD AT SCHOOL	**40-40 (7 years)**
CAREER RECORD	**66-60-1**
ASSISTANTS	**Ulima Afoa (San Diego State '82) Tight Ends Damon Baldwin (San Diego State '90) Offensive Line Fred Bleil (Westmar '71) Secondary George Booker (Western Washington '93) Defensive Line Charlie Camp (Arizona '96) Linebackers Ken Delgado (San Jose State '83) Defensive Coordinator Wayne Dickens (Rutgers '73) Wide Receivers/Special Teams Dave Lay (San Diego State '64) Offensive Coordinator Dave Schramm (San Diego State '87) Running Backs**
TEAM WINS (last 5 yrs.)	**8-5-7-5-3**
FINAL RANK (last 5 yrs.)	**84-84-68-60-78**
2000 FINISH	**Lost to UNLV in regular-season finale.**

COACH AND PROGRAM

When you talk about San Diego State football, you usually think of talented players, a tough schedule and an underachieving team.

Every year, the Aztecs seem to have a bunch of all-league players who go on to play professionally, yet they don't rack up the bowl games and league titles like other teams in their conference do.

Last year a half dozen top players were lost for the season by the second game, which crippled the Aztecs for the Mountain West portion of the schedule. A lot of that had to do with the tough early season games against Arizona State, Illinois, Arizona and Oregon State, which beat up San Diego State's young players before the league season rolled around.

Ted Tollner, who begins his eighth season with his record at exactly .500, 40-40, believes in playing games against tough opponents. The tough non-conference schedule he insists on playing every year hurts his overall record, but in seven years, his teams have only one shared title, a WAC Pacific Division co-championship in 1998. Tollner acknowledges there is a risk of injuries in playing top-notch teams, but he sees other advantages.

"It helps us in recruiting and gives us TV exposure and also helps the program financially," he said. "It's difficult, but I like it and our players like it. It's challenging."

Tollner has always been known as a brilliant offensive mind, going back to his days at Brigham Young in the early '80s when he was the quarterback coach while Jim McMahon and Steve Young played there. Yet last year, his team struggled offensively because of the youth of his players and several devastating injuries. He vows to turn that around this year with an offense that returns 12 starters if you count all-league tight end **Gray McNeil**, who sat out with an injury last year.

Tollner coached at USC in the 1980s, and inconsistency was a problem that eventually cost him his job. In just his second season with the Trojans, his team made it to the Rose Bowl and he was voted Pac-10 Coach of the Year. But he lasted only four years before heading to the NFL, where he coached with three different teams before landing at San Diego State in 1994.

Since compiling back-to-back eight-win seasons in '95 and '96, the Aztecs have had just one winning season since. They've fallen off with 5-6 and 3-8 records the last two years after a Las Vegas Bowl appearance in a 7-5 season in 1997. Those kinds of numbers would make a lot of coaches uneasy, but Tollner doesn't act too nervous about his future. He still has a lot of time left on a 10-year contract extension he signed in 1997. Perhaps that's one reason Tollner is not afraid to schedule prominent opponents every season.

With all but three starters back from last year, the pieces appear to be in place for the Aztecs to make a title run this year, if they can avoid the injuries of recent years.

Besides having most of their players back from last year, the Aztecs also retained the services of all nine assistant coaches, giving the team even more stability.

"If we can stay healthy, we can compete with anyone in the league," Tollner said.

2001 SCHEDULE

Aug.	30	Arizona
Sept.	8	@Arizona State
	15	@Ohio State
	22	@Colorado State
	29	Air Force
Oct.	6	Eastern Illinois
	13	@UNLV
	27	Brigham Young
Nov.	3	New Mexico
	10	@Utah
	17	Wyoming

QUARTERBACKS

It hurt the Aztecs last year when returning starter and senior Jack Hawley went down with an injury in the second game and was lost for the season. But that gave young **Lon Sheriff** the chance to be thrown into the fire and gain valuable experience.

That experience will pay off for Sheriff (6-3, 215) heading into his junior season. He passed for 2,163 yards, completed 53.4 percent of his passes and led the Aztecs to a pair of come-from-behind victories. On the other hand, he was also the quarterback for seven Aztec losses. And he threw just six touchdown passes while being intercepted 11 times.

"We didn't plan on Lonnie being the quarterback last year," Tollner said, "but he came in and did a nice job for us."

While Sheriff is the incumbent, he'll be pushed for the top job by University of Texas transfer **Adam Hall** (6-2, 205), who looked good during spring drills.

Sheriff improved incrementally as the season progressed after a couple of rough outings in the early going. His best games came late in the season (such as the 30-of-46, 393-yard performance against Colorado State and a 17-of-32, 328-yard outing in the season-finale against UNLV).

As a redshirt freshman, Sheriff completed 11-of-22 passes for 113 yards in spot duty. He missed spring practice in 2000 because of shoulder surgery.

The injury bug bit him again this spring in a most bizarre way when he sprained a finger doing a "touch the line" drill. That forced him to miss eight days of practice and gave Hall a chance to show his stuff.

Hall, a sophomore, was one of the nation's most sought-after quarterbacks coming out of high school. Last year, he spent his redshirt season guiding the Aztecs' scout team. He left Texas after one year because he didn't foresee much playing time with Major Applewhite and Chris Simms in the Longhorn program.

"Adam did very well with the first team and he showed he's ready to play and compete," Tollner said after spring practice.

Tollner even said he would consider playing both Sheriff and Hall in early games if neither emerged as a solid No. 1 in fall practice.

Backing up Sheriff and Hall are a pair of highly touted quarterbacks who sat out as redshirts last year. **Danny Armstrong** (6-0, 210) passed for 2,283 and 17 touchdowns as a senior at La Quinta (Calif.) High School, while **Jon Stoner** (6-1, 205) was the 4A Player of the Year at Cactus High School in Glendale, Ariz.

With those four, Tollner said he has never felt better about his quarterback situation.

"Everyone will get an opportunity to play," he said. "They play alike, but each person has his own unique style."

RUNNING BACKS

Larry Ned (5-11, 210) expected to have two senior seasons because of an NCAA rule that allows a player to who enters school as a partial qualifier and stays on track to graduate can make up for his lost freshman year.

He'll be a senior again this year, but his first senior year didn't turn out the way he expected. Because of an assortment of injuries last year, Ned played in only six of his team's games and produced less than half as many yards as each of the previous two seasons.

Ned finished with 357 yards, best among the Aztecs, but that wasn't saying much for a team that finished 107th out of 114 teams in rushing last year with a 77.6-yard average.

The previous two seasons, Ned had rushed for 762 yards and 894 yards, despite splitting time with departed Jonas Lewis. Ned earned second-team All-Mountain West honors in 1999 with his best game coming against Utah when he rushed for 203 yards.

"Larry had two good years, but last year was a very frustrating year for him," Tollner said. "Larry is capable of being as good a runner as the conference has. He has over 2,000 yards of rushing in his career and is a veteran quality player. He appears to be totally recovered from his injuries."

Backing Ned up in the Aztecs' one-back offense will be senior **James Truvillion** (5-10, 195), who started four games last year and finished with 255 yards rushing on. The year before he saw only limited action in rushing for 68 yards on 21 carries and a as a freshman played in all 12 games, mostly on the special teams.

Other returnees who should see action at running back include junior **Garric Simmons** (6-0, 225), who rushed for 215 yards last year and sophomore **Jason Van** (5-10, 190), who rushed for 113 yards and two touchdowns. Also, the Aztecs are excited about redshirt freshman **Justin Green** (6-0, 225) a homegrown product from San Diego High School.

"We feel we have real good depth at running back," said Tollner, who knows the running game must be improved over last year for the Aztecs to succeed.

WIDE RECEIVERS/TIGHT ENDS

A year ago the Aztecs didn't know how they could replace Damon Gourdine, but **Derrick Lewis** and **J.R. Tolver** stepped up to have outstanding seasons, even with a rookie quarterback.

After catching just eight passes the previous year, Tolver (6-1, 205) hauled in 62 passes for 808 yards and a touchdown to earn second-team all-league honors. Heading into his junior season, Tolver, a converted high school quarterback, is expected to be one of the premier receivers in the conference.

Tollner said that statistics can be misleading and points out that over the last seven games, Tolver was especially effective when he made 46 of his 62 catches.

"He should be one of the better receivers we've had here," Tollner said.

Lewis, a 6-2, 185-pound senior who never played high school football, was more of a big-play receiver, catching half as many passes (31) as Tolver for nearly as many yards in averaging 25.2 yards per reception with three touchdowns. The year before, he posted similar numbers with 26 catches for a 21.2-yard average and four touchdowns.

"I like his athleticism—he can run and jump and has good hands," Tollner said. "But we've got to get him the ball more."

Tollner would like to find more depth at receiver.

"We've got a real solid twosome in Tolver and Lewis," Tollner said. "[but] we have real question marks after that."

He's excited about **Ronnie Davenport**, who played two years for Cal, starting as a sophomore, before deciding to transfer. The 6-2, 190-pound Davenport will be a junior after sitting out last year as a student at San Francisco City College.

Senior **Deric Martin** (6-2, 185) is listed as the starting H-Back, a position that featured four different starters a year ago. Martin caught just three passes for 18 yards in five games. He'll be backed up by **Justin Stewart**, a 6-1, 200-pound senior.

Among the players who will provide depth are senior **Thomas Howard** (6-1, 205), who caught 14 passes for 155 yards last year, senior **Craig Mitchell** (5-9, 175), junior **Paul Nelson** (6-0, 210), a transfer from UCLA, and redshirt freshmen **Lonnel Penman** (6-2, 200) and **Adam Gray-Hayward** (6-1, 185).

The tight end position should be strong with two returning players with significant starting experience.

McNeil (6-2, 250), a senior, was an all-conference performer in 1999 but was lost for the 2000 season in the second game against Illinois with a torn ACL. He had gotten off to an impressive start with seven catches for 42 yards in the opener against Arizona State. In 1999, McNeil was third on the team in receptions with 22 for 283 yards.

Senior **Brian Gelt** (6-3, 240) took over for McNeil last year and filled in nicely. He started nine games and caught 15 passes for 112 yards and a touchdown.

"I expect to play both [McNeil and Gelt]," Tollner said.

The Aztecs actually have seven tight ends on scholarship, including sophomore **Raleigh Fletcher** (6-4, 260), who started a game last year, and junior **Jason Dion** (6-4, 265). Both should see action this year.

OFFENSIVE LINE

A year ago, the Aztec offensive line was very young, so young that only one senior played any significant amount of time.

"We're better for it now," Tollner said. "We have everybody back, eight of our top nine guys."

To show how much the young line has progressed, the only SDSU player who was a returning starter last year may not even start in 2001.

Senior **Mike Houghton** (6-6, 315) was a part-time starter in 1999 and he started the first nine games at center last season. Then junior **Raul Gomez** (6-3, 295) moved over from the guard spot to center.

But coming out of spring, the starting center spot was grabbed by junior **Johnathan Ingram** (6-2, 290), who started eight games at guard last year. Gomez moved to guard and will battle with senior **Zach LaMonda** (6-2, 300), who sat out with an ankle injury last year after being projected as a starter.

Meanwhile Houghton has moved over to the strong tackle spot, where he is battling sophomore **Brendan Darby** (6-7, 290), who came on strong in his freshman season. Darby started six games and graded out at 86 percent for the season.

Two other solid starters heading into fall are senior **Chester Pitts** (6-4, 305) at quick tackle and senior **David Moreno** (6-2, 285) at strong guard.

Moreno was the only 11-game starter on the offensive line and most consistent player as he earned second-team All-MWC honors in his first season.

Other backups include senior **David Mayhew** (6-2, 275) at center and redshirt freshman **Mike Kracalik** (6-9, 315) at quick tackle, while senior **Sikoti Uipi** (6-3, 290), who saw limited action last year after transferring from Mt. San Antonio (Calif.) College, will compete at the guard positions.

2000 STATISTICS

Rushing offense	77.6	108
Passing offense	227.4	41
Total offense	305.0	103
Scoring offense	15.5	106
Net Punting	32.9	82
Punt returns	7.4	94
Kickoff returns	18.0	93
Rushing defense	145.6	52
Passing efficiency defense	121.6	68
Total defense	350.2	45
Scoring defense	24.8	57
Turnover margin	-5	82

Last column is ranking among Division I-A teams.

KICKERS

SDSU will miss Nate Tandberg, who provided the margin of victory in wins over BYU and New Mexico and made 12-of-19 field goals on the year. He also converted all 18 of his extra point tries.

Junior **Brian Simjanovski**, who at 6-3 and 230 pounds is built like a linebacker, handled kickoffs and punts last year and is the top candidate to replace Tandberg. Simjanovski didn't play football until he was a senior at Escondido (Calif.) High School, but he became an All-Valley pick as a kicker.

Tommy Kirovski, a 6-1, 195-pound transfer from Palomar (Calif.) Junior College, will challenge for the starting position. As a sophomore he was 11-of-12 and perfect outside 40 yards and was also a perfect 50-of-50 on PATs.

DEFENSIVE LINE

No one on the team has more experience than

senior **Jerome Haywood** (5-9, 280), who has started 34 straight games at nose tackle. He's been a second-team all-league selection for three straight years and should be one of the premier defensive linemen in the MWC this year.

Haywood made 40 tackles last year after 35 and 30, respectively, the previous two seasons. As a sophomore he was selected by *Sports Illustrated* as one of the nation's "best little men," a reference to his height, not his weight.

"Jerome has been a mainstay for us for three years," Tollner said. "He's a dynamite player inside who gives us leadership and experience."

Backing up Haywood will be senior **Jared Ritter** (6-3, 255), who had six tackles in seven games last year and redshirt freshman **Sagan Atuatasi** (6-3, 320), who signed with USC out of high school before moving to San Diego.

Senior **Akbar Gjaba-Biamila** (6-5, 270), who missed most of last season with an Achilles heel injury, earned the other defensive tackle spot in the spring. In 1999 he played in seven games and started two at defensive end alongside his brother, Kabeer, making 14 tackles and one sack. Then last year he started the first game before going out with his injury.

Redshirt freshman **Marcus Levi** (6-4, 280) is listed as a backup, but he can play outside also.

"We have some players at (the tackle) position," Tollner said. "This group represents better size and experience than maybe we've ever had."

Heading into spring the projected starter at tackle was sophomore **Anthony Foli** (6-4, 265), who started six games as a freshman when he made 34 tackles, including six for loss and two sacks. However he was moved to the outside, where he'll go into the fall as a backup defensive end behind junior **Ryan Iata** (6-4, 270). Iata, known for his quickness as well as his power, started eight games last year, making 24 tackles with two sacks. He missed the 1999 season because of a knee injury.

At the other end spot, senior **Andrew Brigham** (6-3, 305) and junior **Amon Arnold** (6-4, 265) will battle for the starting position, although it really won't matter who starts because both will play a large chunk of minutes. Last year, Arnold started six games and Brigham four as both played a lot. Brigham finished with 25 tackles and a pair of sacks, while Arnold had 16 tackles and four sacks for negative 23 yards. Redshirt freshman **Jason Perry** (6-3, 225) will be a backup at defensive end.

LINEBACKERS

The Aztecs think they have perhaps the best linebacker corps in the conference with two starters back, plus some top-notch junior college players and redshirt freshmen.

Senior **Jomar Butler** (5-11, 205) was one of just five players in the league to record double-figure tackles with 112, including 89 unassisted. What makes the tackle totals so impressive is that Butler plays outside linebacker instead of middle linebacker, where most of a team's tackles usually come. Butler also grabbed an interception, recovered a fumble and came up with two sacks.

Butler had played in 1998 before going out with a hernia. Then he left the team for personal reasons in 1999 before returning for his amazing 2000 season when he was selected as the team's MVP.

Dylan Robles, a 6-1, 225-pound senior, is back at the other outside spot where he made 63 tackles, including 10 for loss and five sacks, last year.

Middle linebacker Bryan Berg was one of just two defensive starters lost from last year and he'll be replaced by sophomore **Beau Trickey** (6-1, 235), who saw a lot of action last year when he registered 26 tackles.

The backups are redshirt freshman **Stephen Larsen** (6-1, 230), senior **Jay Kos** (6-3, 215), redshirt freshman **Kirk Morrison** (6-0, 230) and junior college transfer **Lou Heather** (6-2, 235).

"We have a quality group with seven linebackers who can run, but five of seven haven't played much for us," Tollner said. "We have a more athletic group this year."

DEFENSIVE BACKS

Three starters return, led by senior safety **Will Demps** (5-11, 200), an All-MWC performer a year ago. Demps was second on the team in tackles with 97 and led everyone with 15 tackles for loss. He also tied for the team lead in interceptions with two, including one for a touchdown, recovered a fumble and broke up five passes.

Senior **Garret Pavelko** (6-0, 200) started at free safety last year after coming from Palomar Junior College and was a pleasant surprise with 62 tackles and three sacks. He was also an All-MWC academic selection.

Ricky Sharpe, a 6-1, 185-pound junior, came on strong last year to start all 11 games and earn second-team All-MWC honors. He made a 57-yard interception return for a touchdown against Colorado State and recovered three fumbles in addition to making 65 tackles.

Senior **Donte Gamble** (5-8, 160) has the inside track to replace Brian Russell at the other corner spot. He'll battle redshirt freshman **Marviel Underwood** (5-10, 200), of whom big things are expected in the future.

"We have three guys in the secondary who have played at a pretty good level for us," Tollner said. "The rest of it is going to have to shake down. We have several players to look at and some we think are ready to make a contribution. They are young, but we may need them now."

Demps' backup will be sophomore **Shane Johnson** (6-0, 190), while redshirt freshman **Josh Dean** (6-0, 210) will be the backup behind Sharpe. Sophomore **Jeff Shoate** (5-11, 180) and junior **Greg Taylor** (5-8, 165) are backups at cornerback.

PUNTERS

After joining the team as a walk-on the year before, Brian Simnjanovski took over as the punter and performed as well as anyone could have expected. He averaged 42.8 yards on 55 punts to rank second in the MWC and 14th in the nation.

"That was impressive because he averaged more than 42 yards without altitude like the other punters in the league," Tollner said.

He had nine punts more than 50 yards, including a 60-yarder, and averaged 43.8 yards in conference play.

Kirovski, who is challenging Simnjanovski for place kicking duties, will be the backup punter.

SPECIAL TEAMS

Simnjanovski could end up doing all the kicking for the Aztecs, although the coaches would prefer it if he just had to worry about punting and kickoffs. It all depends on how well newcomer Kirovski performs as a place-kicker.

Redshirt freshman **Casey Naylor** (6-2, 220) is slated to be the long snapper, while another redshirt freshman, backup quarterback Stoner, will be the holder.

Tollner said the return men are a "question mark" with Sean Pierce gone. Lewis had the most kickoff returns last year, but he's listed as the punt returner. Last year he returned five punts for an 11.2-yard average.

Gamble, who had five kickoff returns for a 25.2-yard average last year, will be one of the main kickoff returners along with Truvillion, who had 10 returns for a 17.1-yard average and Lewis, who returned 14 kicks for a 21.1-yard average.

RECRUITING CLASS

The Aztecs signed 22 players, 14 from high school and eight from junior college. Three of the JC transfers participated in spring drills. Unlike a year earlier when several junior college transfers stepped in and saw a lot of action, it's unlikely that many of the newcomers will make an immediate impact in 2001.

Among the junior college transfers most likely to play this year are linebacker Heather and wide receiver Davenport. With experience at every position, it's likely the Aztecs will be able to redshirt most of their freshmen.

The Aztecs concentrated on defense in their freshman class with four defensive backs, three linebackers and two defensive linemen among the 14 signees.

One of those defensive backs is **Marcus Demps** (6-0, 185), the younger brother of SDSU's All-MWC safety Will Demps.

BLUE RIBBON ANALYSIS

OFFENSE	B+
SPECIAL TEAMS	B-
DEFENSE	B+
INTANGIBLES	C+

Lately the Aztecs have been in kind of an every-other-year mode where they have a bunch of returning senior starters one year and a young team the next. This year, the Aztecs enjoy one of those senior-dominated teams with 23 starters returning after fielding a young team with only eight returning starters a year ago.

The question is, will the Aztecs be able to take advantage of the situation, at least better than they did two years ago when they returned a bunch of players off a Las Vegas Bowl team, only to struggle to a 5-6 mark?

Once again the schedule won't be any help as the Aztecs must play Arizona and Arizona State of the Pac-10 the first two weeks followed by Ohio State of the Big Ten the next week. Then they start the MWC season against defending champion Colorado State and Air Force, one of three victorious MWC bowl teams last year, before finally getting a breather of sorts against Eastern Illinois.

The Mountain West Conference race looks wide open and the Aztecs should win their share of games in the league. However with another tough non-conference schedule, the Aztecs will be hard-pressed to emerge with a winning record again this year.

(M.S.)

2000 RESULTS

Arizona State	L	7-10	0-1
Illinois	L	13-49	0-2
Arizona	L	3-17	0-3
Oregon State	L	3-35	0-4
Wyoming	W	34-0	1-4
Utah	L	7-21	1-5
Brigham Young	W	16-15	2-5
Colorado State	L	22-34	2-6
New Mexico	W	17-16	3-6
Air Force	L	24-45	3-7
UNLV	L	24-31	3-8

UNLV

LOCATION	Ls Vegas, NV
CONFERENCE	Mountain West
LAST SEASON	8-5 (.615)
CONFERENCE RECORD	4-3 (t-3rd)
OFFENSIVE STARTERS RETURNING	8
DEFENSIVE STARTERS RETURNING	6
NICKNAME	Rebels
COLORS	Scarlet & Gray
HOME FIELD	Sam Boyd Stadium (36,800)
HEAD COACH	John Robinson (Oregon '58)
RECORD AT SCHOOL	11-13 (2 years)
CAREER RECORD	115-48-4 (14 years)
ASSISTANTS	John Jackson (New York '56)
	Assistant Head Coach/Running Backs
	Rob Boras (DePauw '92)
	Offensive Coordinator/Offensive Line
	Ken Niumatalolo (Hawaii '89)
	Tight Ends
	DelVaughn Alexander (USC '95)
	Wide Receivers
	Mike Bradeson (Boise State '81)
	Defensive Coordinator/Secondary
	Steve Leach (Troy State '91)
	Defensive Backs
	Craig Wederquist (Drake '82)
	Defensive Line
	Steve Johns (Occidental '91)
	Linebackers
	Joe Hubbard (UC San Diego '82)
	Offensive Assistant/Recruiting Coordinator
TEAM WINS (last 5 yrs.)	1-3-0-3-8
FINAL RANK (last 5 yrs.)	107-99-103-97-49
2000 FINISH	Beat Arkansas in Las Vegas Bowl.

COACH AND PROGRAM

It didn't take John Robinson long to turn around the moribund UNLV program and transform it into a bowl-winning one ready to challenge for a Mountain West championship. Just two years removed from a winless season, the Rebels produced an 8-5 record last year and concluded their season with a 31-14 victory over Arkansas in the Las Vegas Bowl.

Robinson, who turns 66 in July, is already a hero in Las Vegas, where in April he was rewarded with a contract extension that runs through the 2005 season. He'll receive $150,000 base salary with a total of $500,000 per year.

"My goal is to keep John Robinson for life," said UNLV president Dr. Carol C. Harter, who was behind the hiring of Robinson two years earlier. "If at the end of five years he wants to continue coaching, he can have a new contract."

Robinson will be 70 by that time, and who knows, maybe he'll want to keep coaching. The UNLV job seems to have rejuvenated the former USC coach, who appeared washed up when he was fired in 1997, despite winning three bowl games in five seasons in his second go-around at USC.

"The last month of the season was stuff for storybooks," Robinson said. "There were some moments that were as much fun as I have experienced in my career. It was amazing when you remember that we had the injury to (quarterback) **Jason Thomas** and then a disastrous loss to Utah but then won out.

"I was very proud. I was particularly proud of our seniors, who had come from as low as you can go to as high as you can go. That was rewarding to me. The look in their faces after how they played the bowl game against Arkansas was enough to keep me going in this business for a long time."

After taking a year off, Robinson signed on at UNLV, the same school he had defeated in 1997 for his 100th career victory. He vowed he was "here to win now," and not be content with a five-year rebuilding plan.

In 1999, he started with a bang, winning the first two games, before falling back to win just one more the rest of the way and finish with a 3-8 mark. Last year, the Rebels showed marked improvement with three wins in their first five games, all by large margins, including a 34-13 thrashing of Air Force.

Unlike a year earlier when the Rebels lost five home games by 28 points or more, the losses in 2000 were usually close, a one-pointer to MWC champion Colorado State, a three-pointer to Brigham Young and a three-point loss at Mississippi in overtime. The only big losses came in the opener at Iowa State and to Utah when Thomas was out with an injury.

In Robinson's two years, the Rebels have won five more games than Rebel teams of the previous five seasons combined. With his bowl victory, he improved his record as the winningest bowl coach in NCAA Division I history (with a minimum of eight games). He has compiled a sparkling 8-1 bowl record, including a perfect 4-0 in the Rose Bowl.

How has Robinson been so successful so quickly? To the veteran coach, there's no secret to his success.

"You just come in and start flailing away and hope something good happens," Robinson told the Associated Press. "We've been able to recruit a few players who have made an impact, and I think that has been the key."

Last year's success seems to have given the program instant credibility, as evidenced by the fact that the Rebels' first three games will be televised by ESPN. They open with Arkansas, the same team they defeated in the Las Vegas Bowl with a Thursday night game in Little Rock on Aug. 30, then play Northwestern and defending champion Colorado State the following two Fridays.

2001 SCHEDULE

Sept.	1	@Arkansas
	7	Northwestern
	14	Colorado State
	22	@Arizona
	29	Brigham Young
Oct.	6	@Nevada
	13	San Diego State
	27	@Wyoming
Nov.	3	Utah
	10	@New Mexico
	17	@Air Force

QUARTERBACKS

The Rebels really only have two quarterbacks, but they couldn't be happier with the pair they've got.

Junior Thomas (6-4, 230) is being touted for all-America honors and even the Heisman Trophy after a stellar sophomore season. Backing him up will be redshirt freshman **Kurt Nantkes** (6-4, 215), a former minor-league baseball pitcher.

Thomas transferred from USC after his freshman season with high expectations and met most of them, despite sitting out a couple of games with a foot injury. He was voted MWC Newcomer of the Year after completing 53 percent of his passes for 1,708 yards and 14 touchdowns and rushing for 599 yards and 11 touchdowns. In the Las Vegas Bowl, he completed 12-of-17 passes for 217 yards and three touchdowns. His 599 yards rushing are already a career record for a UNLV quarterback.

"Jason Thomas may be the most gifted athlete I've ever coached," Robinson said.

That's saying a mouthful for a man who has coached the likes of Marcus Allen, Charles White and Anthony Munoz.

"The best thing about Jason is his competitiveness," Robinson said. "He wants to do whatever it takes. For someone who hasn't been on the field much, he is surprisingly advanced."

To show how important Thomas was to his team, when he was out with an injury, the Rebels were beaten handily at Utah, 38-16. That was the Rebels' only bad loss of the year. After Thomas returned to the lineup the next week, the Rebels ran off four straight victories.

As good as Thomas was last year, his coach is expecting a lot more from him in 2001.

"Jason has to be more efficient than last year," Robinson said. "He was certainly brilliant, but like every quarterback, efficiency and consistency become the big issues. We owe it to everyone to give this man the opportunity to reach his potential. I expect him to double last year's passing yardage."

One potential wrench in the works is the fact that Thomas underwent surgery on his throwing shoulder in early May. But Robinson called the procedure "very minor" and said Thomas was expected to be back to full strength within six weeks.

As for Nantkes, he is the quarterback of the future, unless Thomas really bombs (not likely) or gets injured this year. Rebel coaches think so much of Nantke that they weren't willing to sacrifice his redshirt season last year when Thomas got injured.

"Kurt has impressed us tremendously," Robinson said. "He's an older (20 years old), mature freshman and has shown us that he is a really big-time competitor and will do really well."

If Thomas and Nantkes both happen to go down, the Rebels could be in trouble. The only other available quarterbacks are sophomore **Ryan Hanson** (6-2, 220), who lettered as a long-snapper last year and played for the UNLV baseball team in the spring, and prep signee **Tyler Arciaga**, who has the size of Thomas at 6-3, 230.

RUNNING BACKS

You can't get much better production out of your running game than the Rebels got last year when they ranked 13th in the nation in rushing with an average of 228 yards per game.

But the Rebels lost three players who were responsible for nearly 2,000 yards, including Jeremi Rudolph (1,005), Kevin Brown (798) and James Wofford (189).

The top returnee is junior fullback **Steven Costa** (6-1, 225), who rushed for just 132 yards on 22 carries, with the majority of the yards coming in a win over Air Force. Costa's numbers won't go up dramatically this year because he plays fullback and is responsible mostly for blocking.

The guy the Rebels are counting on to take over for Rudolph and Brown is senior **Jabari Johnson** (5-11, 200), a transfer from the University of Washington. Last year he saw only mop-up duty with 58 yards in 17 carries, but he'll shoulder a huge load for the Rebels this year.

"I'm sure Jabari was disappointed with the amount of time he got a year ago, but he did manage to get back into football after missing a year," Robinson said. "I expect him to be solid at the beginning and develop into an outstanding runner by the end of the season. He's a very serious, very intense runner who has the physical power and instincts."

Junior **Joe Haro** (5-10, 190), who missed half of last season with an injury, returns to the offense after spending last year in the defensive backfield. His best game came three seasons ago when he ran for 59 yards on four carries against BYU.

Two others who will look for time at the tailback spot are junior **Johnnie Graham** (6-0, 215) and sophomore **Royce Boone** (5-10, 210). A couple of freshmen who could end up seeing a lot of action are **Dyante Perkins** (6-1, 220) from Las Vegas and **Dominique Dorsey** (5-8, 165), a record-setting back from Tulare, Calif.

Senior **George Gordon** (6-0, 250) will be the backup at fullback.

"We need to be able to run the ball," Robinson said. "We were 13th in the nation in rushing last year, but lost three of the men who were most responsible for that ranking. I don't think we can get the same return as last year, but we must be a good running team."

WIDE RECEIVERS/TIGHT ENDS

Of the 129 passes caught by Rebels last year, more than half were snagged by Nate Turner, whose 947 receiving yards were also more than half of UNLV's total. Turner caught 10-of-16 touchdown passes thrown by Rebel quarterbacks.

The production of Turner will be difficult to replace, but the Rebels think they have some talented young players ready to pick up the slack.

Junior **Troy Mason** (5-10, 170) is the top returning receiver after catching 27 passes for 492 yards and one touchdown (with a team-leading 18.2 yards per catch) a year ago. Mason, also a first-team MWC punt returner, is known for his blazing speed and big-play ability. He caught three passes for 89 yards in the Las Vegas Bowl.

The other wideout slot is likely to be filled by senior **Bobby Nero** (6-1, 180), who had a disappointing season after transferring from Oregon. After missing much of preseason camp with an injury, Nero caught just eight passes, although three were for touchdowns.

Others who should be in the wide receiver mix are senior **Charles James** (6-2, 185), who had just two catches last year before getting sidelined for most of the season with an injury, and sophomore **Michael Johnson** (5-10, 180), who has shown toughness and receiver instincts despite not playing much.

The Rebels may also end up using one of the four high school receivers signed in February—highly touted **Earvin Johnson** (6-3, 195), **Erik Elkington** (6-2, 180), **Marcus Maxwell** (6-4, 190) and **Mike Freund** (6-2, 215).

"It's an interesting group," Robinson said. "Everyone needs to upgrade. Last year, Troy Mason made one of those dramatic improvements from a freshman to sophomore. The key is continuing that."

The tight end position has been mostly an afterthought in the Rebel offense the last couple of years (just eight catches last year), but the Rebels plan to upgrade the position this season.

Junior **DeJhown Mandley** (6-4, 250), who caught six passes for 98 yards and one touchdown as a sophomore, is the incumbent at tight end but is expected to be challenged by junior **Trevan Sorensen** (6-4, 245) and junior **Brad Osterhout** (6-4, 245).

"We're going to try to make the tight end a bigger part of the passing game," Robinson said. "DeJhown has come on from a rookie who played a lot to a solid player to someone who should emerge as a big factor. We need to feature him more."

OFFENSIVE LINE

The line lost its best player in all-league tackle John Greer, but a lot of experience returns, making this a much deeper position this year.

"John Greer led our offensive line into real respectability," Robinson said. "That was an amazing group and all but one is back. More than any other position in sports, the offensive line must play together. This group really did it and now has a look in its eye that you want to see."

Junior **Tony Terrell** (6-4, 310), an All-MWC honorable mention pick last year, is back at right guard, while another honorable mention pick, senior **Peter Tramontanas** (6-5, 285) is back at center.

At the left guard spot, senior **Greg Hulett** (6-3, 300) is back, but being challenged closely by senior **Shane Wagers** (6-5, 310). Senior **Brandon Bair** (6-6, 300) will man the left tackle spot, while redshirt freshman **Jimy Zoll** (6-6, 290) will battle junior college transfer **Matt Williams** (6-6, 300) for the tackle spot formerly occupied by Greer.

Among the lettermen serving as backups are sophomore **Dominic Furio** (6-2, 285) at center, junior **Eddie Freas** (6-2, 315) at left tackle and freshman **Marcus Johnson** (6-1, 300) at right guard. Also, Rutgers transfer **Sheddrick Mitchell**, a 6-7, 325-pound junior, and sophomore **Matt Parkhurst** (6-3, 290), a returned LDS missionary, will also provide depth.

"We have the potential to be as good as last year, but I'm worried about the effect of losing John Greer will have on us," Robinson said.

2000 STATISTICS

Rushing offense	227.8	13
Passing offense	159.2	97
Total offense	387.1	44
Scoring offense	28.2	45
Net Punting	36.1	33
Punt returns	15.4	8
Kickoff returns	20.7	28
Rushing defense	141.2	49
Passing efficiency defense	121.5	67
Total defense	351.2	47
Scoring defense	21.8	41
Turnover margin	-4	78

Last column is ranking among Division I-A teams.

KICKERS

One of the surprises of last year's team was the emergence of sophomore **Dillon Pieffer** (5-11, 175) as the starting place-kicker. He joined the team as an invited walk-on and took over for Ray Cheetany, who had struggled to make just 13-of-18 PATs, in the seventh game. Pieffer made 19-of-20 extra points the rest of the season and six of seven field goals.

"Dillon Pieffer was a lifesaver for us last year," Robinson said. "Where we were hurt early with low kicks and slow leg time, now we have a guy that kicks it really hard and has great swing time."

DEFENSIVE LINE

This could be the strongest position on the team with eight of nine lettermen returning from last year, including all five players who played the ends.

Leading the way is senior defensive end **Anton Palepoi** (6-4, 275), who came in as a junior college transfer a year ago and finished second in the league in sacks with eight. Palepoi had 37 tackles on the year, including 11 for loss.

Junior **Ahmad Briggs** (6-3, 230) is expected to start again on the right side. Although he isn't that big, he makes up for it with his speed and quickness. He saw extensive action last year when he made 33 tackles six for loss and 4.5 sacks.

Three seniors expected to see a lot of time at the end postion are **Steve Newton** (6-3, 235), **Adrian Watson** (6-3, 240) and **Scott Parkhurst** (6-3, 245), although Parkhurst may be moved to linebacker. The three had almost identical statistics last year as Parkhurst had 23 tackles, Watson 22 and Newton 20. Parkhurst had a pair of sacks, while Newton had 1.5 sacks and an interception.

"We have five defensive ends that are all fast and play with great intensity," Robinson said. "Anton Palepoi, who is outstanding on the edge, is an All-American, no question about it. But the others are all very fast and talented and will be even better."

At the nose guard position, where Anthony Suggs has graduated, it looks like a three-way battle is shaping up in the fall among junior college transfer **Garrett Brassington** (6-2, 285), a junior, sophomore **Dietrich Canterberry** (6-4, 290) and junior **Phil Reed** (6-3, 265). Dietrich has the edge going into fall coming off an impressive freshman season when he came up with 18 tackles, including two for loss and two sacks.

Of Brassington Robinson said, "He's a power player. He's done well and is improving. He's getting his body level lower and doing much better."

The tackle spot will be filled by senior **Ahmad Miller** (6-4, 295), who was ninth on the team in tackles with 38 last year and also came up with a sack. Reed will be his backup unless he ends up winning the nose guard job.

"Ahmad Miller has quietly developed into a really solid player and one of the big surprises on our team last year was Dietrich Canterberry," Robinson said. "We have the size in the middle, but not much depth."

LINEBACKERS

The Rebels suffered a setback in the spring when senior **James Sunia** (5-10, 240) re-injured a leg that forced him to sit out half of the 2000 season. Sunia suffered a torn MCL/ACL after making 22 tackles and two sacks in five games. And how did he injure his knee this spring? Would you believe moving a box at his home?

While the Rebels expect Sunia to play this year, he may not be at full strength at the start of the season. He's on the verge of becoming the Rebels' all-time leading tackler. He has 260 and only needs 35 more to take over the No. 1 spot

The guy who replaced Sunia in the middle last year, **Ryan Claridge**, is back after being thrust into a starting role as a true freshman. The 6-3, 240-pound sophomore, who finished fourth on the team in tackles last year, is a two-sport athlete with an unusual combination for a football player—he also plays for the Rebel tennis team.

Redshirt freshman **Adam Seward** (6-2, 235) will also compete for time in the middle.

"Adam Seward has come on and had a big-time spring," Robinson said.

Parkhurst will compete on the strong side along with senior **LaMar Owens** (6- 2, 235). Senior **Shanga Wilson** (6-1, 225) and junior **Tosh Burrus** (6-0, 210) are the top candidates on the weak side.

"The young linebackers were a pleasant surprise last year," Robinson said. "Ryan Claridge is on his way to becoming a really outstanding player."

DEFENSIVE BACKS

There's more than one Thomas on the UNLV

team who is being promoted for postseason honors.

Senior cornerback **Kevin Thomas** (5-11, 180) has been a first-team all-conference selection each of the last two years. Thomas has already smashed the UNLV record for career pass breakups with 45, 18 more than the No. 2 player on the list. He has seven career interceptions.

Thomas' best season was in 1999, when he came up with five interceptions, 24 pass breakups and 52 tackles, all season bests. Last year his numbers weren't as impressive, perhaps because most opposing quarterbacks tried to avoid him. Thomas finished with two interceptions, 14 pass breakups and 46 tackles.

"Kevin Thomas comes back after having in my opinion an outstanding year," Robinson said. "He didn't have as much success as his sophomore year, but still played at a high level. I think he can become an All-American this year."

Senior free safety **Sam Brandon** (6-3, 195), a converted receiver, was the defensive MVP last year. He led the team with 82 tackles, including 52 unassisted. He also came up with a key interception in the regular-season finale against Hawaii and blocked a field goal against Mississippi.

"Sam Brandon is one of the two or three biggest keys to our team," Robinson said. "After learning to play pass coverage last year, he is just a tremendous attack safety."

Two players who will have to be replaced are strong safety Randy Black and cornerback Amar Brisco. Several players will be candidates to take their places this fall.

The strong safety position is up for grabs with junior **Ross Dalton** (6-3, 205) battling with sophomore **Derek Olsen** (6-3, 200). Dalton had 11 tackles in a backup role, while Olsen made 14 tackles as a standout on the special teams. Others who could vie for the strong safety spot are junior **Toby Smeltzer** (5-10, 185) and three redshirt freshmen—**Jamaal Brimmer** (6-1, 205), **Ashley Subingsubing** (5-11, 195) and **Zach Bell** (6-2, 215).

Junior college transfer **Chamelon Sutton** (5-11, 195) could be a factor when he joins the team for fall drills.

As for the other cornerback spot, junior **Jamal Wynn** (6-0, 180) is the frontrunner after getting 13 tackles and a pass deflection last year.

Two redshirt freshmen, **Joe Hunter** (6-0, 175) and **Ruschard Dodd-Masters** (5-11, 175), and sophomore **Sean Mackey** (6-1, 190) will be among those challenging for the cornerback job.

"Jamal Wynn is going to be one of the key guys on our team," Robinson told the *Las Vegas Review Journal*. "He has to step up, much like Amar Brisco did last year. ... (Wynn) gives evidence that he can do that."

PUNTERS

Ray Cheetany started last year as the Rebels' punter, place-kicker and kickoff man. He didn't last the year as the place-kicker, but he was a solid punter, averaging 41.3 yards per punt, although his average was down considerably from the previous year when he averaged 45.4 yards and was fourth in the nation.

That year he took over for **Ryan McDonald**, three games into the season. McDonald, a 5-10, 185-pound sophomore, sat out in 2000, but is back this year as the starter.

"Replacing Ray at punter is going to be hard," Robinson said. "Ryan McDonald does not have the range that Ray had, but he punts the ball very fast and is able to get height. Our gross punting will be down, but our net should hold steady."

SPECIAL TEAMS

The Rebels hope Pieffer can match last year's performance when he missed only two kicks over the last five games after taking over as the starter. The Rebels will miss punter Ray Cheetany and hope Ryan McDonald will be adequate in his place.

Mason will be back as a punt returner after averaging 16.4 yards per punt, seventh in the nation, highlighted by an 84-yard touchdown return against New Mexico. He also handled most of the kickoffs the last two seasons, averaging 17.5 yards last year after a 23.1-yard average in 1999. He is expected to be the main man on kickoffs again this year.

Nero has experience returning punts and kickoffs, with a 21.4-yard average on five kickoffs last year.

Hanson, who also plays catcher on the Rebel baseball team and is a backup quarterback, returns as the long snapper.

RECRUITING CLASS

The Rebels signed 20 players, including four junior college transfers and three transfers from four-year schools. Offense was the focus as 12 offensive players were signed, including four running backs, along with five defensive players and three listed as "athletes."

The two transfers from Division I-A schools are **Deon Burnett**, a 5-11, 210-pound running back from Washington State and **Tyrone Tucker**, a 6-2, 240-pound linebacker fro m Iowa State. Burnett will be junior, while Tucker will be a senior. Andrew Faga, a 6-0, 240-pounder fullback from Idaho State, will be a sophomore when he becomes eligible.

Among the players who could make an immediate impact are offensive lineman Williams, already listed as a starter at the right tackle position, and Brassington, a defensive lineman who will challenge for the starting nose guard position.

The only quarterback in the recruiting class is Arciaga, from Bonita Vista High School in Bonita, Calif. The biggest recruit is 6-7, 325-pound offensive tackle Mitchell from Butte (Calif.) College.

"It's as good a class as we've had here," said Robinson. "We are getting more people who are not down-the-road players, but guys that will compete for playing time in their first season."

BLUE RIBBON ANALYSIS

OFFENSE	B
SPECIAL TEAMS	B-
DEFENSE	B+
INTANGIBLES	B+

If the Rebels can survive their first five games, they could be on their way to an exceptional season. If they start something like 1-4, it could set the tone for a tough year.

The Rebels open with Arkansas, a team that will be looking for a little revenge for last year's Las Vegas Bowl when the Rebels travel to Little Rock. The following week Northwestern of the Big Ten comes to town for a Friday night encounter, and then the Rebels get defending MWC champ Colorado State. Next up is UNLV's first-ever matchup with Arizona on the road, followed by another MWC game, this one against perennial MWC power BYU. "It's going to be an exciting September around here," Robinson said. "When you first see the schedule, you have to see it as a negative for us. But our program has had to play the long odds a lot. If we win four or five at the beginning, we're nationally prominent. We can't shy away from that now."

It's unlikely the Rebels will win all five of those games before the end of September, but if they win the majority and knock off CSU and BYU in Las Vegas, they could be on their way to the MWC championship.

(M.S.)

2000 RESULTS

Iowa State	L	37-22	0-1
North Texas	W	38-0	1-1
Brigham Young	L	7-10	1-2
Air Force	W	34-13	2-2
Nevada	W	38-7	3-2
Colorado State	L	19-20	3-3
Wyoming	W	42-23	4-3
Mississippi	L	40-43	4-4
Utah	L	16-38	4-5
New Mexico	W	18-14	5-5
San Diego State	W	31-24	6-5
Hawaii	W	34-32	7-5
Arkansas (Las Vegas)	W	31-14	8-5

Utah

LOCATION	**Salt Lake City, UT**
CONFERENCE	**Mountain West**
LAST SEASON	**4-7 (.364)**
CONFERENCE RECORD	**3-4 (t-5th)**
OFFENSIVE STARTERS RETURNING	**11**
DEFENSIVE STARTERS RETURNING	**6**
NICKNAME	**Utes**
COLORS	**Crimson & White**
HOME FIELD	**Rice-Eccles Stadium (45,634)**
HEAD COACH	**Ron McBride (San Jose St. '64)**
RECORD AT SCHOOL	**75-53 (11 years)**
CAREER RECORD	**75-53 (11 years)**
ASSISTANTS	**Kyle Whittingham (BYU '84)** **Defensive Coordinator/Linebackers** **Craig Ver Steeg (USC '83)** **Offensive Coordinator/Quarterbacks** **Don Eck (Utah '83)** **Offensive Line** **Jugi Hogue (San Jose State '73)** **Cornerbacks** **Steve Kaufusi (BYU '94)** **Defensive Ends** **Gary Andersen (Utah '86)** **Defensive Tackles/Special Teams** **Vincent White (Stanford '84)** **Wide Receivers/Running Backs** **Alex Gerke (Utah '88)** **Tackles/Tight Ends** **Bill Busch (Nebraska Wesleyan '88)** **Safeties**
TEAM WINS (last 5 yrs.)	**8-6-7-9-4**
FINAL RANK (last 5 yrs.)	**73-76-72-55-77**
2000 FINISH	**Lost to BYU in regular-season finale.**

COACH AND PROGRAM

After tying for the first-ever Mountain West Conference title in 1999 and enjoying a run of nine straight non-losing seasons with five bowl games in the 1990s, last year was supposed to be the big one for Utah football.

With several key players returning from a 9-3 Las Vegas Bowl-winning season, huge things were expected from the 2000 Utes. Heck, some folks were even talking about an undefeated season with three seemingly beatable Pac-10 opponents to open the season and home games against the best MWC teams.

Instead, the season turned into a disaster for the Utes right from the get-go. They ended up losing those opening three games to middle-of-the-pack Pac-10 teams—Arizona, Washington State and California—and kept getting worse once league play began. The Utes lost at home to Air Force before finally getting a win at Utah State in a non-league game and another at San Diego State. But another home loss to eventual league champion Colorado State—when Utah blew a seven-point fourth-quarter lead—ended any title hopes. And a 10-3 loss at New Mexico showed the ineptitude of the Ute offense.

The Utes finally played like they were expected to with convincing wins over UNLV and Wyoming and they seemed to have a victory in the bag against BYU, only to see the Cougars drive 80 yards in the final minute to pull out a 34-27 win in the finale.

After that disappointing season, many were calling for a change at the top, despite Ron McBride's success over the previous decade with no losing seasons since his first year in 1990 and an overall mark of 75-53. Instead, changes were made at the next level down and four assistants either left or were shoved out the door, including a couple of longtime coaches. Special teams coach Sean McNabb had been with the program 24 years while offensive coordinator Tommy Lee, who was the scapegoat for the Utes' offensive problems, had been at Utah for six years. Longtime coach Fred Graves accepted a job with the Buffalo Bills after 19 years with Utah.

Brought in to resurrect the Ute offense is former USC quarterback Craig Ver Steeg, who came from Illinois after stops with the Chicago Bears and Cincinnati. Ver Steeg promises to bring innovation to the Ute offense, which was viewed as stagnant and unimaginative by many Ute fans in recent years.

The other new coaches are Stanford graduate Vincent White, who will be in charge of running backs and receivers, Alex Gerke, a former Ute player who will coach the tackles and tight ends, and Bill Busch, who will coach the safeties.

Unfortunately, the Utes don't have a battle-tested experienced quarterback in the program with **Lance Rice**, who played in the last four games, joined by two quarterbacks who show a lot of potential but have no experience. The Utes appear stocked with good running backs and have several top offensive linemen back. With Steve Smith gone, the receiving corps could be a little thin. More players are gone from the defense, which carried the team for most of last season

The Utes face a tough game Sept. 8 against Oregon, which is likely to be ranked in the top 20, or even the top 10, but otherwise their non-conference schedule isn't overpowering with the likes of Utah State, Indiana and South Florida. What concerns the coaching staff is a three-game stretch in September when the Utes must play Oregon, Air Force and Indiana all on the road. Three losses there could result in a loss of confidence as the Utes head into the meat of their conference season, which includes road games at Colorado State, UNLV and BYU, three of the league favorites.

McBride, who at 61 doesn't have a lot of years left, has never worried about any pressure from unhappy fans. But this could be a make or break year for McBride. Ute fans as well as McBride's superiors may not tolerate another losing season.

2001 SCHEDULE

Sept.	1	Utah State
	8	@Oregon
	15	@Air Force
	22	@Indiana
	29	New Mexico
Oct.	6	South Florida
	20	Wyoming
	27	@Colorado State
Nov.	3	@UNLV
	10	San Diego State
	17	@Brigham Young

QUARTERBACKS

With two senior quarterbacks who had extensive starting experience behind them, the quarterback position looked solid last year. The only problem was the Utes couldn't decide between Darnell Arceneaux and T.D. Croshaw, and neither performed well at all.

The Utes went back and forth between the two before finally giving up and turning to redshirt freshman Rice, who played most of the final four games.

Rice, a 6-2, 193-pound sophomore, would appear to be the logical starter heading into this year after performing admirably with 42-of-86 completions for 625 yards and four touchdowns. However, the Utes are keeping the job open until fall because of a couple of heralded quarterbacks who sat out last year and played on the scout team.

Sophomore **Ryan Breska** (6-4, 209) is a big left-hander who transferred from Purdue because he didn't want to play behind All-American Drew Brees. Then, there's redshirt freshman **Brett Elliott** (6-3, 193), considered one of the top quarterback recruits in school history after passing for 2,970 yards and 32 touchdowns his senior year at Lake Oswego High in Oregon.

"We like all three quarterbacks a lot," McBride said. "Rice will be No. 1 when the team reports in August, but Breska and Elliott both came on so strong at the end of spring that nothing is cast in stone."

Each of the three quarterbacks brings something different to the table. Rice is known for his athletic ability and making good decisions. Breska has size and is known for his strong arm and quick release, while Elliott has been called a hybrid of the other two.

"Lance has proven in game situations to be very intelligent decision-maker," McBride said. "We really like Breska's arm strength and at 6-foot-4, he sees the field well. Elliott is a playmaker. He has confidence that when he's behind the center, something good will happen."

Any of the three could end up directing the offense this fall, but one thing the Ute coaches don't want is a repeat of last year when Arceneaux and Croshaw shared the top spot. Breska may end up winning the job because his style seems to fit the offense Ver Steeg has brought to the program.

RUNNING BACKS

Like the quarterback position, the running back spot was in disarray for much of last season until **Adam Tate** was given the opportunity. The Utes started off with DeShaun Crockett, who turned out to be too small to fit the Utes' system. Then they tried Nick Morgan, who had been in the program for several years without getting much of a chance. They also gave an opportunity to **Dameon Hunter**, a junior college transfer.

After those three combined for a mere 167 yards in three games, the Utes turned to Tate, a junior college transfer who had arrived after the August training camp because of what the university referred to as "some late academic paperwork issues."

Tate, a 6-1, 229-pound senior, is a big, powerful back in the mold of a couple of former Ute backs now starring in the NFL, Jamal Anderson and Mike Anderson. In his first start against Air Force, he picked up 112 yards on 21 carries with one touchdown. He followed that with a 133-yard effort against Utah State and 104 yards against San Diego State.

By the end of the season, Tate had rushed for 660 yards on 160 carries, scored seven touchdowns and earned All-MWC second-team honors. Hunter, a senior who is nearly the same size (5-11, 231) as Tate, finished with 339 yards and a touchdown in 2000.

Hunter is listed as Tate's backup at halfback, but he may have a tough time beating out junior **J.R. Peroulis** (6-1, 205), a transfer from Arizona State. He is the fastest of the running backs and third fastest on the team (4.41 in the 40), and as McBride says, "if he gets past the line of scrimmage, he can take it all the way home."

Another halfback to keep an eye on is sophomore **Edwin Benton** (5-10, 203), who came from virtually nowhere in spring ball to impress the coaches and was called "the surprise of the spring," by McBride.

"We feel like we need four guys at halfback, but they're all deserving of playing time," McBride said. "It won't be easy keeping them all happy, but it's a good problem to have."

Another forgotten man found new life when the Utes changed to a two-back set and added a fullback to the offense for the first time in years.

Senior **Thomas Fortune** (6-3, 253) hasn't seen much action in his career, rushing for 34, 47 and 17 yards, respectively, each of the last three seasons. Although the Utes will use his big body for blocking, he should also get more chances to run the ball this year.

Fortune will be backed up by redshirt freshman **Rob Sirstins** (6-2, 208) and sophomore **Brandon Bliss** (5-11, 205), who are both adept at catching the ball.

"If we went back to a one-back set, we'd have an awful lot of good players on the sideline," McBride said. "Four tailbacks and three fullbacks took a ton of reps in the spring and we loved them all."

WIDE RECEIVERS/TIGHT ENDS

With a strong backfield, the Utes won't have to rely on their passing game as much, which is good because they don't have much experience at the wide receiver position. Still, Utah plans to pass the ball a lot this year with the new offense and will have to rely on a bunch of newcomers, along with a couple of talented veterans.

Senior **Cliff Russell** (6-0, 184) is the fastest player on the team and could be the fastest ever to play at Utah (he was once clocked at 4.25 in the 40). Last year he led Utah with 37 receptions, despite missing four games with a broken arm, and was also second on the team in receiving yards with 517 and with three touchdowns.

Also returning is junior **Josh Lyman** (6-0, 196), a former walk-on who was fourth on the team last year with 17 receptions for 245 yards. He will be the starting split end heading into fall, while Russell is the flanker. Unfortunately, both players had to miss spring practice with hamstring pulls.

However, their absence gave some youngsters the chance to step up and show what they could do.

Freshman **Morgan Scalley** (5-10, 188) just returned from a two-year church mission and impressed in the spring with his speed and ability to break tackles. McBride compares him to Bryan Rowley, one of the top receivers in Ute history from a decade ago.

Sophomore **Justin Walterscheid** (5-9, 169) is another who was able to show his skills in spring ball. He hasn't played in a game yet, but has good bloodlines as the son of former Chicago Bear Lenny Walterschied.

Three highly recruited receivers will join the mix in the fall, including freshman **Jaun McNutt** (6-1, 185) and junior college transfers **Paris Jackson** (6-3, 190) and **Devin Houston** (5-10, 175).

"The JC guys have to play," McBride said. "Jackson is a big athletic receiver with good hands. Houston is an exciting player and a deep threat. I also expect McNutt, who is a speed receiver, to play his first year."

Another blue-chip freshman receiver, Lynzell Jackson (6-3, 180), will not be eligible this year while completing NCAA academic requirements.

The tight ends will be expected to catch more passes than in the past, when they were mostly counted on for blocking. Senior **Michael Richardson** (6-2, 271) is known as Mr. Do-Everything for the Utes. Last year he started six games at right guard, three at center and one at tight end. The year before he started four games at guard and two at tight end. He should be a full-time tight end this year, where he should catch more than the two passes he caught last year.

Backing up Richardson are senior **Scott Price** (6-4, 251), senior **Dennis Smith** (6-3, 217) and sophomore **Matt Hansen** (6-5, 251).

"Our tight ends need to be more versatile," said McBride, who expects them to do more than just block.

OFFENSIVE LINE

As a former offensive line coach, McBride pays special attention to his offensive line and this year he is well pleased with the talent and experience he has.

Four starters return—actually five if you count two part-time starters at center—and McBride believes three of his upperclassmen are good enough to eventually play in the pros.

Senior left tackle **Doug Kaufusi** (6-6, 311) was a first-team All-MWC selection last year, while right tackle **Jordan Gross**, a 6-5, 306-pound junior, was an honorable mention selection. Senior left guard **Ed Ta'amu** (6-2, 320) is a converted defensive lineman who is perhaps the strongest player on the team, yet also has an incredible 34-inch vertical leap.

"We have three guys—Gross, Kaufusi and Ta'amu—who are the cream of the crop in this league," McBride said. "They're great players who have taken a ton of reps. I expect them to play beyond college."

At center, sophomore **Dustin McQuivey** (6-3, 254) returns after starting most games last year in place of senior **Steve McKane** (6-0, 281), who missed most of the season with a knee injury. McKane expects to receive a medical redshirt from the NCAA. If he does return, he may have a hard time beating out McQuivey.

The other starter will be sophomore **Sean Souza** (6-5, 279), who played with the first unit all spring. Souza will be backed up by junior **Tevita Vakalahi** (6-1, 299).

Other backups on the offensive line are senior **Kevin Wilson** (6-7, 309) and redshirt freshman **Makai Aalona** (6-5, 283) at tackles, and redshirt freshmen **Sione Pouha** (6-3, 275) and **Max Peterson** (6-2, 276) at guard and center, respectively.

2000 STATISTICS

Rushing offense	133.1	71
Passing offense	203.9	67
Total offense	337.0	80
Scoring offense	21.3	84
Net Punting	34.4	61
Punt returns	9.2	60
Kickoff returns	21.9	19
Rushing defense	128.2	35
Passing efficiency defense	107.8	30
Total defense	288.3	10
Scoring defense	18.8	18
Turnover margin	-11	101

Last column is ranking among Division I-A teams.

KICKERS

Mention the word "kicker" around McBride and he may start twitching.

McBride has always been wary of kickers and some of their quirky behavior, but the last two years the inconsistent Ute kicking game has been a source of agitation for McBride and has cost the Utes the chance to win a few more games.

It all started back in 1998 when senior **Ryan Kaneshiro** (5-10, 190) missed a 32-yard field goal that would have defeated arch rival BYU in the final game. The next year, senior **Golden Whetman** (6-0, 201) took over, but when he started missing he was replaced by Cletus Truhe, who had been the kicker before Kaneshiro. Truhe finished off the '99 season decently, but last year the team's kicking woes really plummeted.

Whetman beat Kaneshiro out in fall camp, but kicked horribly during the season, missing nine of his first 10 field-goal attempts. So Kaneshiro took over for rest of the season and made 6-of-8 field goals and all of his PATs.

But guess what? A newcomer, **Brian Lewis** (6-2, 220), came in this spring and beat out both veteran kickers. Lewis, a junior, is originally from St. George, Utah, but was the starting punter at Oklahoma before leaving for a two-year church mission. He's also a talented place-kicker and may keep the job in the fall.

DEFENSIVE LINE

The Utes lost Andy Bowers, but have everybody else back on the defensive line, which should be a strength of the team. The bodies are the same, but during the spring the Utes played musical chairs and moved nearly all the front-line players to new positions.

MWC Freshman of the Year **Jason Kaufusi** (6-3, 249), a sophomore, has been moved from his rush end position to stud linebacker where the Utes had a hole to fill. That opened the way for junior **Marcus Jones** (6-2, 243) to play more.

"We had to find a way to get Marcus on the field without taking Jason out of the lineup," McBride said.

Senior **Ma'ake Kemoeatu** (6-5, 309) was moved from nose guard, where he started last year, to end in the spring before being moved back. Junior **Garrett Smith** (6-3, 270), who had 10 sacks and 72 tackles last year, slid over from tackle to end, while senior **Lauvale Sape** (6-2, 290) started the spring at nose guard, but moved over to a tackle position.

Behind those talented upperclassmen, the Utes have several newcomers waiting their turns, including junior **Kasey Jackson** (6-3, 281), who transferred from Cal; junior college transfer **Elia Laeli** (6-3, 275); and freshmen **Steve Fifita** (5-11, 274) and **Chris Kemoeatu** (6-4, 315), a highly recruited player from Hawaii who is the younger brother of Ma'ake.

LINEBACKERS

Replacing Kautai Olevao, who was a four-year starter and three-time all-league player, won't be an easy task for the Utes. But they've come up with a pretty good solution by moving Jason Kaufusi over from defensive end. Kaufusi, the MWC Freshman of the Year, will still play on the outside, just a little farther back than he did last year.

Junior **Sheldon Deckart** (6-2, 239) was the Utes' second leading tackler last year, playing the middle linebacker position, but he was moved outside to rover during spring ball.

"Sheldon is the guy," McBride said. "He has great speed and lateral movement and is the team leader on defense along with Ma,ake [Kemoeatu]."

Moving to the middle will be senior **CR Dwinnell** (6-1, 228), who had 30 tackles as a backup last year. Dwinnell was a walk-on last year who quickly caught the coaches' eyes because of his aggressive style and football savvy.

Backing up Dwinnell in the middle will be redshirt freshman **Zach Tune** (6-3, 247), who came on strong during spring drills. Other backups at linebacker include junior **Jeremy Lyman** (6-2, 230), senior **Stan Moleni** (6-2, 254) and junior **Brooks Bahr** (6-3, 219). The latter two were slowed by injuries last year, while Lyman transferred from Nebraska.

Two newcomers who could see action this year are junior college transfer **Dominic Payne** (6-4, 205) and freshman **Steven Thompson** (5-10, 212).

DEFENSIVE BACKS

The Utes no longer have any Dysons or Christiansons and Brandon Dart has finally used up his eligibility, which stretched to an unbelievable seven years.

Utah is basically starting over in a secondary where both Andre and Patrick Dyson are gone as well as Kimball Christianson, whose twin brother started at linebacker, and Dart who was granted three medical redshirt years by the NCAA. Also gone are Jason Potter and Jeff Ray, who both started several games last year.

The only player with any starting experience is sophomore **Arnold Parker** (6-2, 210), who started a few games at safety and was the Utes' main nickel back last year. He will be the strong safety this year and the coaches are expecting big things from him.

"I expect Arnold Parker to be the best safety in the league," McBride said. "He's big, tough and can flat out run (4.32 speed in 40)."

The rest of the secondary is inexperienced and will have to grow up in a hurry in the pass-happy MWC.

Sophomore **Anthony White** (5-9, 201) is penciled in as the free safety and he will be pushed by junior college transfer **Antwoine Sanders** (6-3, 200) and walk-ons **Dave Revill** (5-11, 205) and **Aaron Bryant** (6-3, 212), who are both sophomores.

The cornerback and nickel positions are undecided, with several players vying for the open spots. Junior **Airabin Justin** (5-11, 177) and senior **Yohance Scott** (6-0, 192) are the top candidates at corner, while redshirt freshman **Bo Nagahi** (5-9, 177) will be the likely nickel back.

Junior **D'Shaun Crockett** (5-8, 184), who began last season as he starting tailback, is still learning to play defense and could end up starting at one of the corners.

Others who could figure in the cornerback competition are juniors **Cody Weight** (5-11, 179) and **Desmond Davis** (5-7, 178) and freshman **Antonio Young** (5-11, 185), a highly touted recruit from Carson, Calif.

"We need to get some separation at cornerback," McBride said. "This position scares me because we still don't know who our four best guys are."

PUNTERS

Whetman was an adequate, though not outstanding punter last year with a 38.6 average on 63 punts after being a second-team all-American punter for Ricks (Idaho) College. He was challenged in the spring by Lewis, who started for Oklahoma before his LDS mission and finished 21st in the nation with a 41.9-yard average.

Lewis came out of spring ball ahead of Whetman, but if the Utes decide they would rather have him handle the place kicking and kickoff duties, Whetman may keep the punting gig.

SPECIAL TEAMS

One of the Utah's biggest problems last year was the play of its special teams. As a result, McNabb, who had coached special teams for the last 24 years, became the scapegoat and moved to another job.

Oklahoma transfer Lewis turned heads in the spring with his various kicking talents and Ute coaches hope he will make everyone forget about last year's kicking woes.

"Brian Lewis was our best field goal kicker and punter in the spring and was right there on kickoffs," McBride said. "But nobody will do all three."

It looks like Lewis will handle kicking chores and Whetman will remain the punter, although Lewis is capable of doing the punting also. Kaneshiro, an off-and-on starter the last three years, provides depth at place-kicker.

The Utes have big holes to fill on the return teams, replacing Steve Smith, who returned one punt for a touchdown in 2000 after getting three the year before, and Patrick Dyson, who returned a kickoff for a touchdown last year.

The two players most likely to handle punt returns and kickoff returns are Crockett and freshman Nagahi, who have speed but no experience.

RECRUITING CLASS

The Utes signed 25 players, including 18 high school players and seven junior college transfers.

The biggest catch was defensive lineman Chris Kemoeatu, widely considered the best player in Hawaii. The 315-pounder chose Utah over Washington and Nebraska.

Freshman defensive lineman **Bernard Fano** (6-2, 260) was originally committed to Arizona State before switching to Utah, while freshman linebacker **Marques Ledbetter** (6-3, 220) is a top athlete from Mississippi who has baseball scouts after him.

Other top recruits include wide receivers Paris Jackson, McNutt and Lynzell Jackson, linebackers Payne and Thompson and cornerbacks Young and **Shayne Scruggs** (5-10, 185). Scruggs is a sophomore who played at Santa Ana Junior College in Honolulu.

"This class more than fills what we need," McBride said. "It's very athletic and all of these guys have proven they can play the game the way it's supposed to be played."

BLUE RIBBON ANALYSIS

OFFENSE	B
SPECIAL TEAMS	B-
DEFENSE	B-
INTANGIBLES	C+

The Utes' success this year could rest on the shoulders of their quarterback. Who will play the position? The Ute coaches think they have three good choices in returnee Rice, Purdue transfer Breska and former prep sensation Elliott, but the decision on the starter may not come until late in fall drills. The rest of the team looks solid with several fine running backs, experienced lines on both sides of the ball, solid linebackers and a transfer who may solve the kicking woes. The Utes have good athletes at receiver and defensive back, but inexperience could be a problem at those positions.

Last year, the Utes were favored to win the league only to fall flat on their faces and limp home with a 4-7 record. This year, there won't be high expectations for Utah, which should be picked to finish in the middle of the standings. With no dominant teams in the MWC, the Utes have the talent to beat any team in the league and with a little luck could even sneak away with a championship. But they have had a penchant for beating themselves in recent years and must avoid that habit to have any chance at a title. Still they should end up with a winning record overall and in league play.

(M.S.)

2000 RESULTS

Arizona	L	3-17	0-1
California	L	21-24	0-2
Washington State	L	21-38	0-3
Air Force	L	14-23	0-4
Utah State	W	35-14	1-4
San Diego State	W	21-7	2-4
Colorado State	L	17-24	2-5
New Mexico	L	3-10	2-6
UNLV	W	38-16	3-6
Wyoming	W	34-0	4-6
Brigham Young	L	27-34	4-7

Wyoming

LOCATION Laramie, WY
CONFERENCE Mountain West
LAST SEASON 1-10 (.091)
CONFERENCE RECORD 0-7 (8th)
OFFENSIVE STARTERS RETURNING 8
DEFENSIVE STARTERS RETURNING 6
NICKNAME Cowboys, Pokes
COLORS Brown & White
HOME FIELD War Memorial Stadium (33,500)
HEAD COACH Vic Koenning (Kansas St. '82)
RECORD AT SCHOOL 1-10 (1 year)
CAREER RECORD 1-10 (1 year)
ASSISTANTS
Matt Wallerstedt (Kansas State '87)
Defensive Coordinator/Inside Linebackers
Bryan Bossard (Delaware '89)
Defensive Secondary
Tom Turchetta (Miami '73)
Defensive Line
Rusty Burns (Springfield '78)
Offensive Coordinator/Quarterbacks
Justin Byleveld (Wyoming '92)
Tight Ends
Rob Phenicie (Memphis '89)
Wide Receivers
Lawrence Livingston (Weber State '86)
Offensive Line
David Arnsparger (Florida '87)
Secondary
Mick McCall (Southern Colorado '78)
Running backs
TEAM WINS (last 5 yrs.) 10-7-8-7-1
FINAL RANK (last 5 yrs.) 53-87-81-53-103
2000 FINISH Lost to Colorado State in regular-season finale.

COACH AND PROGRAM

After being hired as the 29th head coach at Wyoming last year, after three years serving as the defensive coordinator, Vic Koenning knew he'd have a challenge matching the win totals of the previous six seasons.

The Cowboys had averaged nearly eight victories per season, while never suffering through a losing record. Koenning wasn't expecting eight wins, but he had no idea his team would end up with just one victory in his initial season and go winless in conference play.

Koenning was left with just nine starters and 35 lettermen after Dana Dimel became the latest Cowboy coach to bolt the plains of Laramie when he went to the University of Houston after just three years. Before that, Joe Tiller departed in 1996 to accept the job at Purdue and prominent coaches such as Dennis Erickson, Pat Dye, Fred Akers and Bob Devaney all left Wyoming for more high-profile jobs.

Not only was Koenning left with a fairly thin roster, several injuries to key players decimated the Cowboys and left them with their worst season since 1939 when they went 0-7-1. The Cowboys did have three one-win seasons since '39, including a 1-9 record in 1970, but none as bad as 1-10.

The day after the dreadful season ended last November, Koenning had a meeting with his coaches and players and vowed to not forget how bad it felt to finish 1-10 and to make goals for big improvements in 2001.

"We met the night after the Colorado State loss and established some goals," Koenning said. "We decided we wanted to be the most improved team in the country and we decided that there were things we had to do to accomplish that."

Among the improvements were to improve overall team speed, increase strength on both of the lines, increase flexibility and athleticism, to develop an attitude and to become fundamentally sound in all aspects of the game.

"We needed to regain the Cowboy attitude," Koenning said. "In short, we wanted to do what we do a whole lot better."

After spring practice, Koenning thought his team was on its way to achieving those goals.

"I think we became much better fundamentally at every position," he said. "I think we have accomplished that because we are a little more mature, we have better leadership and everyone is in the second year of the system."

The Cowboys have a likely win to open the season against Division I-AA team Furman and possible wins against Kansas and Utah State, both on the road. However, a Thursday night ESPN2 game against perennial power Texas A&M will be tough, even if it is at home. Then the Cowboys must open the Mountain West Conference season against two-time defending champion Colorado State.

2001 SCHEDULE

Sept.	1	Furman
	6	Texas A&M
	15	@Kansas
	22	@Utah State
	29	Colorado State
Oct.	6	New Mexico
	13	@Air Force
	20	@Utah
	27	UNLV
Nov.	10	Brigham Young
	17	@San Diego State

QUARTERBACKS

Last year the Cowboys had Jay Stoner, the top returning quarterback and a preseason favorite to win offensive player-of-the-year honors in the league. But he didn't come close to getting MVP honors or even all-league as injuries kept him out of two games and limited him in others. Stoner ended up passing for just 1,552 yards and 10 touchdowns with 12 interceptions as the Cowboys' offense struggled as a whole.

Going into the season, Stoner had looked like a shoo-in to become the school's all-time leader in passing and total offense yards, but came up just short of the totals of Tom Corontzos, who played from 1988-91. As it turned out, Stoner didn't even match his passing totals from each of his first three seasons.

Sophomore **Casey Bramlet** (6-4, 203) quarterbacked the Cowboys when Stoner went out and was decent, completing 24-of-57 passes for 288 yards and a touchdown with one interception. He looks like the No. 1 guy heading into fall camp.

"Casey has all the physical tools, but he has only five games of experience under his belt," Koenning said. "He needs to continue to work on his reads, getting the ball away on time and getting it to the right people. He has the opportunity to be an outstanding quarterback at this school. The pre-fall session will be important to him."

Senior **Matt Swanson** (6-2, 200) has the most experience in the program as he started two games in 1999 when Stoner was injured and ended up completing 56 percent of his passes for 886 yards and six touchdowns. Last year he completed just 6-of-12 passes for 106 yards and a touchdown.

A couple of things working against Swanson are the fact that he missed spring drills with an injury and he's a senior. If it's close between him and Bramlet, the coaches are likely to go with the younger player, looking ahead to the future. Swanson will likely be the backup punter again, as he was last year.

"It will be a great positive to get Matt Swanson back with us," Koenning said. "He missed the spring due to injury, but he has made a great deal of progress on his rehabilitation. He lends a lot of stability to the position because of his leadership and experience."

Behind Bramlet and Swanson, the Cowboys have little experience. Walk-on redshirt freshman **J.J. Raterink** (6-1, 195) gained some valuable experience in the spring backing up Bramlet. Two freshmen, **Cory Bramlet** (6-4, 195), Casey's younger brother, and **Matt Belshe** (6-2, 213) will most likely redshirt this year unless injuries press one of them into service.

RUNNING BACKS

The Cowboys have little depth at this position, but at least they have some experience, something they had little of last year.

Senior **Nate Scott** (6-1, 193) led the Cowboys in rushing in 2000 with 645 yards and five touchdowns, including a 95-yard touchdown. He sat out the year before after suffering the double whammy of a hernia and ankle injury.

Sophomore **Derek Armah** (5-10, 193), a former high school quarterback, was a solid addition to the backfield, rushing for 515 yards, although he didn't score a touchdown.

Scott and Armah were also used as receivers as Scott caught 14 passes for 113 yards and a touchdown, while Armah caught eight passes for 56 yards.

"Scott and Armah could be a great combination for us," Koenning said.

Redshirt freshman **Kit Bradshaw** (6-1, 193) had an excellent spring and is listed as the No. 3 tailback heading into fall. Koenning calls him the "back of the future."

Other young backs who will provide depth are freshmen **Kevin Fulton** (5-9, 184), **Lewis James** (5-10, 200), **Phillip Drakes** (5-10, 185) and **C.R. Davis** (6-1, 180).

"I would imagine that maybe one of those guys will be in the starting mix," Koenning said.

Several players are in the mix at the fullback position, where most of the top candidates were injured during the spring, including returning starter **Garth Tesinsky** (6-0, 238). The only healthy fullback in the spring was senior **Antwan Floyd** (6-2, 229), a converted linebacker who hasn't seen any action carrying the ball yet.

Despite being a starter, Tesinsky carried the ball only 12 times for 56 yards and a touchdown. He's expecting to get more chances during his senior season. Seniors **Marcus Ford** (6-1, 220) and **Aaron Frude** (5-10, 204) were also injured in the spring, but may challenge in the fall along with junior **Tyler Scharman** (6-2, 196).

It looks like the Cowboys will have plenty of bodies at the tailback and fullback this year. The guy to keep an eye on, though, is Scott.

"I think Scott is on the verge of becoming a tremendous back," Koenning said. "There is no doubt he can make a difference."

WIDE RECEIVERS/TIGHT ENDS

Over the years, Wyoming has earned a reputation for developing outstanding receivers. Because of receivers such as Marcus Harris (1994-96) and Ryan Yarborough (1991-93), who rank 1-2 on the NCAA career receiving yards list, and Jay Novacek, who went on to star for the Dallas Cowboys, it's no wonder Wyoming calls itself "Receiver U."

Sophomore **Ryan McGuffey** (6-1, 196) appears to be the latest star to emerge in the Cowboys' tradition of great receivers. Last year as a freshman, he caught 63 passes for 696 yards and four touchdowns. To show how much he is respected by his teammates, he became the first sophomore in Cowboy history to be selected as a captain.

Joining McGuffey at receiver are sophomore **Malcom Floyd** (6-6, 206), who caught 43 passes for 360 yards and a touchdown, and junior **Brock Ralph** (6-3, 182), who caught 30 passes for 425 yards and three scores.

Koenning is excited about three players who played well in the spring and should provide the Cowboys with solid depth this fall—sophomore **Leonard Jones** (5-9, 150), redshirt freshman **Sean Bowman** (6-2, 200) and junior **Scottie Vines** (6-2, 190). Koenning calls Jones "a major playmaker. When we got the ball in his hands, he made things happen."

Vines has moved over from the basketball team, where he struggled last year after coming from Eastern Utah Junior College.

"He has a tremendous amount of ability," Koenning said. "He catches the ball better than anyone we else we have. He can get so much better, but he really needs the repetitions."

Another listed on the three-deep chart is junior **Sean Brennan** (6-1, 208), a walk-on who was yet to see much action for the Cowboys.

"I like this group," Koenning said. "We have good size and ability. McGuffey is as good as there is and with the addition of Jones and Vines, we have a couple of game-breakers."

The tight end position is a different story with several guys in the mix, but no standouts. Last year's starter, Arlen Smith, caught only one pass all year.

Sophomore **Kolby Drube** (6-3, 220) has the most experience after catching five passes for 40 yards last year and is the likely starter. Others who will challenge him include redshirt freshman **Chris Cox** (6-7, 240), a returned Mormon missionary, junior walk-on **Scott Sorensen** (6-4, 235) and sophomore **Joe Anderson** (6-3, 232), who moved over from linebacker.

Two freshmen, **Dan Fisher** (6-6, 273) and **Brian Majcen** (6-4, 245) will get a look in the fall, but probably won't see a lot of action this year.

"We have a chance to be five deep at this position," Koenning said. "None of them are all-conference yet, but they are all very young and have great futures."

OFFENSIVE LINE

In junior **Adam Goldberg** (6-7, 315), the Cowboys think they have a tackle as good as any offensive linemen in the conference. He started every game as a freshman at left tackle and was moved to right tackle for his sophomore year. He played both sides in the spring, but is expected to play left tackle this fall. Koenning calls him "the kind of guy you can win a championship with."

Junior **Rob Kellerman** (6-6, 291), who started every game in 1999 as a freshman, was limited last year because of knee problems. He's the obvious choice to play the other tackle position, but if he can't return to his earlier form, senior **Bill Bullert** (6-6, 293) will fill the spot, as he did last season. Bullert played a lot of snaps in the spring and has experience.

The top guard is sophomore **Rano Sasa** (6-2, 310), a strong player whom the Cowboy coaches would like to see drop a few pounds to improve his mobility. He's scheduled to play left guard with redshirt freshman **Tim Riley** (6-2, 285) backing him up. Riley improved steadily during spring practice as he recovered from an injury.

The right guard position has come down to a battle between sophomore **Henry Randle** (6-3, 281) and junior **Anthony Stannard** (6-2, 280). Koenning said they may both end up playing about 50 percent of the time.

Junior **Mike Irvin** (6-3, 280) returns as the starter at center, but the Cowboys are keeping an open mind and looking at redshirt freshman **Trenton Franz** (6-3, 275) as well as Stannard and incoming freshman **Jeff Warren** (6-5, 295).

Redshirt freshman **David Gough** (6-6, 261) is a little light, but he'll be a backup at tackle. A couple of players who could see action after sitting out much of the spring with injuries are redshirt freshmen **ER Wolf** (6-5, 280) and **Kyle Huseby** (6-6, 265), while incoming freshmen **Brandon Avery** (6-5, 260), **Isaac Morales** (6-6, 280) could make their mark this year.

Pat Hutchinson started at guard last year and has eligibility remaining, but he isn't able to continue playing because of an injury.

2000 STATISTICS

Rushing offense	106.2	93
Passing offense	190.1	80
Total offense	296.3	104
Scoring offense	15.5	106
Net Punting	32.9	83
Punt returns	7.5	92
Kickoff returns	18.2	90
Rushing defense	183.2	85
Passing efficiency defense	154.6	114
Total defense	400.7	81
Scoring defense	35.7	106
Turnover margin	-9	97

Last column is ranking among Division I teams.

KICKERS

The Cowboys will have a difficult time replacing Aaron Elling, a three-year starter who made 67 percent of his field goal tries and 68-of-70 PATs. Sophomore **Jarvis Wallum** (5-11, 195), a walk-on from South Dakota who was impressive during spring drills, will probably replace Elling.

"We certainly felt good about how Jarvis Wallum did during spring training," Koenning said. "He was accurate and was able to hit from distance."

Sophomore **Justin Graham** (5-10, 170) displayed a strong leg in the spring with the ability to make 40-yard-plus field goals. Either Graham or Wallum could end up handling kickoffs, although the Cowboys aren't likely to match Elling's ability to kick the ball out of the end zone, which he did about one-third of the time last year.

DEFENSIVE LINE

The best player for the Cowboys last year was Patrick Chukwurah, who made 100 tackles, including 19 for losses, seven sacks, 15 quarterback hurries and was an All-Mountain West Conference first-team selection.

There's no doubt the Cowboys will miss having Chukwurah play "Bandit," a combination defensive end/linebacker position. Not only did the Cowboys lose Chukwurah, they also lost nose guard Jeff Boyle and defensive tackle Pat Hirsch.

The only returning starter on the defensive line is junior **Brandon Casavan** (6-5, 254), but he was injured during spring drills and hardly played.

Still Koenning is upbeat about his defensive line, saying "we have some battlers in there who are battle-tested."

Many of last year's injuries hit the defensive line, so several youngsters saw playing time sooner than expected.

Senior **Damon Roark** (6-3, 280) will start at tackle after coming off a knee injury, which healed better than anyone expected. The Cowboys wanted to try Casavan inside, but his injury prevented that plan, although he could still be moved in the fall.

Because of Casavan's injury, junior **Josh Rollins** (6-3, 260) was given more opportunity to play in the spring and made great strides.

Junior **Chad Buehler** (6-2, 260) has moved into the nose guard spot and although Koenning likes his athletic ability, he says Buehler must put on weight to be more effective in the middle. Junior **Tam Pruitt** (6-3, 279), coming off a major injury, will back up Buehler.

The biggest hole to fill will be at Chukwurah's bandit spot and Koenning is excited about the play of senior **Tim Glynn** (6-4, 240), who had 29 tackles as a backup last year after playing sparingly his first two seasons.

"Tim Glynn had a very special spring at bandit," Koenning said. "I thought he'd play well, but he was really special. He has shown he can really be a dominating player."

Among the other players who are likely to play a lot on the defensive line are senior **Daniel Gibson** (6-4, 295), sophomore **Casey Adams** (6-5, 250), junior **Jon Aimone** (6-4, 233) and redshirt freshman **Anthony Jones** (6-5, 240).

LINEBACKERS

All three starters, including leading tackler Kwabena Peprah, are gone from the linebacker corps, although senior **Leo Caires** (6-1, 218), who was projected to be a starter before going down with a knee injury, is back.

"He is an outstanding player and a great leader," Koenning said of Caires, who was selected a captain last year.

Senior **Jason Jones** (5-11, 212) nailed down another starting spot in the spring, which wasn't a surprise because he was sixth on the team in tackles last year (45) despite playing in just seven games.

Junior **Herman White** (6-0, 217) was expected to be the other starter, but went down with an injury in the spring. He should be ready by fall, but senior **Matt Klotz** (6-1, 212) will go into fall practice as a starter after a productive spring.

Although sophomore **Tyler Gottschalk** (6-4, 219) is listed as a backup on the two-deep charts, don't be surprised if he ends up playing significant minutes. Last year the Cowboys planned to redshirt him, but he ended up playing enough to finish fourth on the team in tackles with 75, including five for loss.

Junior **John Wilson** (6-3, 234) got extra reps in the spring because of injuries and will be a valuable reserve.

Two newcomers who could work their way into the lineup are sophomore **Jeremy Davis** (6-1, 245), a transfer from Kentucky, and freshman **Chris Jordan** (6-1, 210).

"This is another area where the competition is outstanding and that will only make us better," Koenning said. "I'm excited about what's happening here."

DEFENSIVE BACKS

Last year, the secondary situation was so dire that Koenning went out and recruited six junior college transfers to provide immediate help.

It's a different story this year as the secondary should be the strength of the defense with all four starters returning, plus several experienced reserves.

Heading the list is senior **Al Rich** (5-11, 200), who had to sit out with an injury last year after two outstanding seasons. In 1998 he was selected all-conference after making 75 tackles and three interceptions. He had similar numbers in 1999 despite playing with an injured shoulder and wrist that later required surgery.

Last year, the Cowboys moved the talented Rich to running back, but he played in only one game, rushing for 35 yards and catching a pass. This year he's back at his usual safety position, where he performed well in the spring.

"It means everything in the world to have Al Rich return for us," Koenning said. "He is a great leader, a great player. What a great captain."

Senior **Lamar James** (6-0, 202) returns at the other safety position after finishing third on the team in tackles with 84 and recovering two fumbles. He'll be closely challenged by sophomore **Jacque Finn** (6-3, 188), who saw plenty of action as a freshman last year. Finn finished sixth in tackles with 49 and led the team with two interceptions. Senior **Pete Merrill** (6-1, 193) will be the backup at the other safety behind Rich.

Senior **Eric Lee** (5-11, 175), last year's starting cornerback and one of the six junior college transfers from a year ago, missed spring drills, but that gave freshman **Gary Wright** (5-9, 158) the chance to show what he could do.

Another one of last year's transfers, senior **DeShawn Abram**, is one of the tallest cornerbacks in the country at 6-4 and 203 pounds. He ranked fifth on the team with 57 tackles last year and came up with one of the team's five interceptions.

Backups at the corners, besides Wright, are sophomore **Roderick Jackson** (5-11, 164) and junior **Ryan Calahan** (5-11, 184).

The Cowboys hope sophomore **John Levingston** (6-2, 202) can return from an injury that kept him out last season after he was projected to contend for the starting free safety position. Others who could battle for time in the secondary are redshirt freshman **Tom Vincent** (6-2, 188) and incoming freshmen **Guy Tuell** (6-1, 190) and **Chad White** (6-3, 196).

"It's so much fun to have depth where we had very little a year ago," Koenning said.

PUNTERS

Tom Waring adequately handled the punting chores for the last two seasons when he averaged 41.6 yards as a junior and 42.4 yards last year. Heading into the fall, this is one of the positions that concern the Cowboy coaches the most.

Sophomore **Luke Donovan** (6-0, 185), who hasn't punted since he played for Spearfish High School in South Dakota, is No. 1 going into the fall, but a shaky No. 1.

Matt Swanson, who backed up Waring for the second straight year, punted 10 times for a 35.2 average. He may end up as the regular punter unless he wins the quarterback job.

"It is definitely a concern for us heading into two-a-day practices," Koenning said of the punting situation. "Luke Donovan has shown a very strong leg. But he needs to work on mechanics and he has not done anything under fire."

SPECIAL TEAMS

With the Cowboys trying out a new punter and a new place-kicker as well as new kickoff returners, the special teams will be a question mark at least through the early part of the season.

McGuffey gives Wyoming some experience at punt returner, where he averaged 7.9 yards on 17 returns last year. Wright will also help out returning punts.

The punting job will go to either Donovan or Swanson, while Wallum and Graham are the top candidates for place-kicker.

Swanson will handle holding duties, while Glynn will be back as the long snapper with redshirt freshman **David Gough** (6-6, 261) backing up.

RECRUITING CLASS

Often when a team goes 1-10, the coaches panic and look for immediate help in the junior college ranks. Yet the Cowboys showed their commitment to the future by signing just two junior college players to go along with 25 freshmen.

"Last year we did not have a choice but to fill our needs with older guys," Koenning said. "This year we emphasized high school players. We identified some very definite needs, and I think we were able to fill those needs."

Wyoming was especially searching for linemen and defensive backs, positions where the Cowboys lacked numbers a year ago.

"Our depth was poor in the secondary and in both lines," Koenning said, "so our goal was to sign a lot of student athletes in both areas. We wanted to establish more numbers in those positions."

The two junior college transfers, Randle and Rollins, will both challenge for starting spots. Randle played at Coffeyville (Kansas) Community College, where he allowed just one quarterback sack from his right tackle position. He enrolled at Wyoming for the spring semester and has three years of eligibility remaining.

Rollins, from Ricks (Idaho) College, was an honorable mention NJCAA All-American and a NJCAA Academic All-American. He had 78 tackles and 13 sacks last season.

Like most coaches, Koenning would like to redshirt as many freshmen as possible, but after a down year like 2000, he may be forced to play some newcomers right away.

In the secondary, freshmen Guy Tuell and Chad White will compete for playing time. Both are talented athletes. Tuell, from Yuma (Colo.) High School, was ranked second in the state in wrestling and also competed in the triple jump and relays in track. Tuell also played running back, toughing it out in a state semi-final game for 200 yards despite suffering a broken hand.

White, from Grapevine (Texas) High School, brings good size to the secondary. He too was a track star and a two-way player on his football team. White caught 56 passes for 1,000 yards his senior year.

BLUE RIBBON ANALYSIS

OFFENSE	B-
SPECIAL TEAMS	C-
DEFENSE	C+
INTANGIBLES	C

After last year's rough beginning, Koenning has nowhere to go but up. A lot of folks are rooting for Koenning, who is popular with fans and media, but because of Wyoming's long tradition of football excellence, he can't get by with any more 1-10 seasons.

Koenning is encouraged by the program's progress and the effort his players have given.

"The good thing about our team is that many who have sat out during spring training will be ready in the fall, and most, if not all, of those individuals will help us," Koenning said after spring practice. "We're very pleased with the way everyone has responded. We're not there yet, but we are getting closer. Their work ethic has brought us closer."

Unfortunately, significant improvement will be hard to come by this year after the Cowboys lost their four-year starter at quarterback as well as all but one of their front seven on defense and both their punter and place-kicker. A lot of young players will have to step up for the Pokes.

"We have a ways to go, but we are in a much better situation now than we were a year ago," Koenning said.

The Cowboys should definitely win more than one game this year. But it's unlikely they'll get back on the winning side of the ledger and they'll probably finish near the bottom of the MWC again.

(M.S.)

2000 RESULTS

Auburn	L	21-35	0-1
Texas A&M	L	3-51	0-2
Central Michigan	W	31-10	1-2
Nevada	L	28-35	1-3
New Mexico	L	10-45	1-4
San Diego State	L	0-34	1-5
Air Force	L	34-51	1-6
UNLV	L	23-42	1-7
Brigham Young	L	7-19	1-8
Utah	L	0-34	1-9
Colorado State	L	13-37	1-10

PAC-10

BLUE RIBBON FORECAST

1. UCLA
2. Oregon
3. Washington
4. USC
5. Oregon State
6. California
7. Stanford
8. Arizona State
9. Washington State
10. Arizona

ALL-CONFERENCE TEAM

OFFENSE

POS. PLAYER SCHOOL HT. WT. CL.

WR Kareem Kelly, USC, 6-1, 185, Jr.
WR Keenan Howry, Oregon, 5-10, 170, Jr.
OL Scott Peters, Arizona State, 6-4, 290, Sr.
OL Chris Gibson, Oregon State, 6-3, 280, Sr.
C Brandon Ludwig, California, 6-4, 285, Sr.
OL Steven Grace, Arizona, 6-3, 290, Sr.
OL Eric Heitmann, Stanford, 6-4, 295, Sr.
QB Joey Harrington, Oregon, 6-4, 220, Sr.
RB Ken Simonton, Oregon State, 5-8, 195, Sr.
RB DeShaun Foster, UCLA, 6-1, 215, Sr.
TE Jerramy Stevens, Washington, 6-7, 260, Jr.

DEFENSE

POS. PLAYER SCHOOL HT. WT. CL.

DL Kenyon Coleman, UCLA, 6-6, 280, Sr.
DL Terrell Suggs, Arizona State, 6-3, 230, So.
DL Larry Tripplett, Washington, 6-1, 300, Sr.
DL Kurt Wallin, Arizona State, 6-2, 270, Sr.
LB Lance Briggs, Arizona, 6-1, 230, Jr.
LB Scott Fujita, California, 6-5, 250, Sr.
LB Robert Thomas, UCLA, 6-2, 235, Sr.
DB Dennis Weathersby, Oregon State, 6-1, 200, Jr.
DB Jameel Powell, California, 6-1, 185, Jr.
DB Tank Williams, Stanford, 6-3, 215, Sr.
DB Billy Newman, Washington State, 5-10, 195, Sr.

SPECIALISTS

POS. PLAYER SCHOOL HT. WT. CL.

PK Ryan Cesca, Oregona State, 5-8, 175, Jr.
P Nate Fikse, UCLA, 5-9, 180, Jr.
RS Bobby Wade, Arizona, 5-11, 190, Jr.

OFFENSIVE PLAYER OF THE YEAR

Ken Simonton, RB, Oregon State

DEFENSIVE PLAYER OF THE YEAR

Robert Thomas, LB, UCLA

NEWCOMER OF THE YEAR

Shaun Cody, DL, USC

PAC-10 NOTEBOOK

Two new head coaches join the Pac-10 in 2001 after the Arizona schools both cleaned house after last season. John Mackovic takes over at Arizona and Dirk Koetter at Arizona State. ... Talk about a tough crowd. The Pac-10 is so loaded with quality running backs—Oregon State's Ken Simonton, UCLA's DeShaun Foster—that a 1,000-yard gainer from 2000, Maurice Morris, doesn't get a sniff of preseason All-Pac-10 recognition. Morris was second in the conference in yards rushing per game (100.5) a year ago. And what of poor Joe Igber of Cal? All he did was gain 900 yards last season, but he has no hope of any first-team All-Pac-10 honors. ... Two offensive coordinators with big-time reputations have switched locales. Norm Chow, after a one-year sojurn to the East Coast (at North Carolina State), has relocated to USC, and Al Borges left UCLA for Cal. Before heading to the ACC last season, Chow was the long-time offensive coordinator at BYU. ... A defensive coordinator who will make an impact this season is Larry Mac Duff, the man who helped create Arizona's double-eagle flex in the early 1990s. He's returning to the school after four years with the New York Giants. "The double-eagle flex defense is different from what most people play," Mackovic said. "That gives us a ready advantage. Opponents have to spend time identifying what roles our people play and where they'll be at any given time. It's a defense built in the style of guerilla warfare. It hits you at one spot, then hits you at another spot. It's difficult to tell where our players are going to come from." ... Several key players who were injured a year ago—such as UCLA's Kenyon Coleman, Arizona's Steven Grace and Cal's Langston Walker—are back and should make major contributions this season.Coleman, a defensive end, and offensive lineman Grace were injured early enough in the season to claim a red-shirt year. ... The Pac-10 was loaded with quality tight ends in 2000, but this season, Washington's Jerramy Stevens stands out as the only star at that position.

Arizona

LOCATION	Tuscon, AZ
CONFERENCE	Pac-10
LAST SEASON	5-6 (.454)
CONFERENCE RECORD	3-5 (t-5th)
OFFENSIVE STARTERS RETURNING	6
DEFENSIVE STARTERS RETURNING	7
NICKNAME	Wildcats
COLORS	Cardinal & Navy
HOME FIELD	Arizona Stadium (56,002)
HEAD COACH	John Mackovic (Wake Forest '65)
RECORD AT SCHOOL	First Year
CAREER RECORD	85-64-3 (13 years)

ASSISTANTS

Steve Bernstein (Occidental '67)
Secondary
Jay Boulware (Texas '96)
Tight Ends
Charlie Dickey (Arizona '85)
Offensive Line
Rick Dykes (New Mexico '82)
Offensive Coordinator
Rob Ianello (Catholic '86)
Wide Receivers
Bobby Kennedy (Northern Colorado '89)
Running Backs
Marty Long (Citadel '86)
Defensive Line
Larry Mac Duff (Oklahoma '70)
Defensive Coordinator
Scott Pelluer (Washington State '81)
Linebackers/Special Teams

TEAM WINS (last 5 yrs.)	5-7-12-6-5
FINAL RANK (last 5 yrs.)	46-31-7-40-46
2000 FINISH	Lost to Arizona State in regular-season finale.

COACH AND PROGRAM

Coach John Mackovic has landed in Tucson, but the big question is whether he had a quarterback stuffed in his pocket when he arrived.

The Wildcats lost Ortege Jenkins to graduation and local fans are worried that the cupboard is bare in terms of quarterbacks. Junior **Jason Johnson** (6-2, 210) is going to get the call and his elevation has come almost unopposed. Whether he can handle the job will be determined, but one thing is for sure. If anything happens to Johnson, it could be a long year for the Mack attack.

"I would say that our quarterback development was average for the total group," Mackovic said of the Wildcats' spring drills. "Johnson is clearly ahead of the others. He showed that he has been in a college football program, and that he has the experience and a real good understanding of how things work. After that, it is far more difficult to determine who is in the position to play at the No. 2 or No. 3 spots. If you look at the numbers, sophomore **Cliff Watkins**' (6-3, 215) numbers are likely to be second best."

Obviously, the Cats have some work to do.

"At the quarterback position, the biggest disadvantage was having six players," Mackovic said of trying to evaluate his new personnel. "It was impossible to be totally fair to each one of them by giving them the same number of plays. In the limited amount of time that we had, we had to be sure that Johnson was getting at least half of the work. We learned a lot about Jason, and he learned a lot about us and what we are trying to do."

Whether the rest of the Wildcats learned the offense while Johnson was doing the same remains to be seen. Six starters return from the 2000 squad that finished with five straight losses after a 5-1 start. That collapse cost long-time coach Dick Tomey his job.

Mackovic was hired to rejuvenate a program that was always pretty decent under the previous coach. The word is that the Wildcats will be showcasing a much-improved passing attack under Mackovic, but it was only a couple of years ago that Arizona's offense was putting up incredible numbers.

"I am pleased that we learned as much as we did in the amount of time we had [in spring drills]," Mackovic said. "We put so much more on the players' shoulders to learn the new offense. Our quarterbacks had to find out what they could do and learn a whole new offense. They had to see what they could handle, and they really didn't have a lot of time.

"Today, defenses are so talented and so well-schooled that you must have a lot of offense. We have to expose our guys to different things, which we did. Now, we have to build on that for the fall. It doesn't mean that we won't move the ball, but it is going to take one complete year to feel comfortable with everything on offense."

Eventually, Mackovic hopes to sport a high-powered passing attack. But right now he has to concentrate on improving an offense that was last in the Pac-10 last season in third-down conversions (28.1 percent).

Mackovic says a more aggressive philosophy should help.

"I call it a multiple pro offense because it is an offense that shows a team is more willing to throw the ball," he said. "The kind of offense where you run and throw only when you have to has gone by the wayside. We will have a series of formations, lots of shifts and movements. We will incorporate both one-back and two-back looks. Our immediate goal is offensive improvement. Arizona finished at or near the bottom [of the Pac-10] in most offensive categories last season. The passing game was the most dramatic in its fall-off. We will put emphasis on a quality passing game.

"I call the plays. The value in play calling is not so much what you call but when you call a play and why. You have to have a sense of the ebb and flow. To me that's the art of the game. Offense has to have a certain strategy, how you start, what your intentions are."

Mackovic, who says he will get the Wildcats to win immediately, might have to suffer a bit in 2001 as he sorts everything out.

If Arizona administrators were unhappy with 5-6 last season, they might have to close their eyes this year. It's not going to be easy.

"I was concerned [about the coaching change] because this is going to be my senior season," senior center **Steven Grace** (6-3, 290) said. "I was pretty comfortable with the coaches we had. But the calls are being kept the same and we all have to go in with an open attitude. I'm very happy now.

"I'm excited about our whole team. Personally, I think we're going to be very good in the offensive line and that's where the offense is made, in the trenches. I think we're going to be a little more aggressive offensively this season."

Grace said the new staff has paid a lot of attention to the team's failure to capitalize in the red zone last season. UA scored touchdowns only 52 percent of the time it penetrated the opponent's 20.

"That was a little weak," Grace said. "And we've also been concentrating on special teams, the kicking game, trying to put everything together."

Is Grace worried it won't come together this season? "People say you need three years to rebuild," he said. "Coach Mackovic says 'Screw that.' He came in and said he doesn't expect anything less than a Pac-10 championship. So we've got 80 guys staying here in Tucson this summer going through repetitions."

Of course, the ultimate goal is to get the Wildcats to the Rose Bowl, something that has never happened.

If Arizona is to make any kind of move in 2001, it probably will have to rely on its defense. Whether the days of Desert Swarm defense have passed remain to be seen.

"Nothing can stay the same," Mackovic said. "Everything has to be better. The defense has shown that it is active, and that it gets to the football quickly. We did a good job of trying to challenge the defense as much as we could with our offense's passing attack. And, as the spring progressed, I was pleased with the way the defense was able to call up the adjustments."

While some things will change, the defense won't have a new look. New defensive coordinator Larry Mac Duff, the man who helped create UA's double-eagle flex in the early 1990s, is back after four years with the New York Giants.

"The double-eagle flex defense is different from what most people play," Mackovic said. "That gives us a ready advantage. Opponents have to spend time identifying what roles our people play and where they'll be at any given time. It's a defense built in the style of guerilla warfare. It hits you at one spot, then hits you at another spot. It's difficult to tell where our players are going to come from. It's not like lining tanks up in a row and whoever has the most tanks wins. It's an overload system where you can attack in any given area.

"I believe we have good players who are familiar with this defense and who will give us a chance to continue its performance and reputation. It was not very difficult for me to decide to keep this scheme for 2001. We were fortunate to have Larry Mac Duff join the program because he knows and helped design this defensive system."

After recording 113 tackles last season, junior linebacker **Lance Briggs** (6-1, 230) is happy the double-eagle flex has remained intact.

"Coach Mac Duff knows what he is doing," Briggs said. "And he has added his extra attitude and his own touch."

Like Grace, Briggs said he was a bit unsure of what would happen at Arizona.

"But coaching change is part of the business," he said. "We didn't have the year we hoped for last season. They changed coaches and we all understand that. We've got to learn to finish games. We got defeated a lot in the fourth quarter last season. Many times, aside from the Oregon State game, we pretty much led all of our games into the third quarter. In the fourth quarter, we lost it."

Briggs can't point to a few specific problems to correct.

"You can't narrow it down to one cause," Briggs said. "It was a team effort. We win as a team, and we lose as a team. It comes down to the fact that if we didn't win in the fourth quarter, then we didn't work hard enough. The new staff has come in and established a discipline level and maybe that's good. I'm very comfortable with the team chemistry now—that's never been better. Our mind is right."

With seven starters returning on defense, Mackovic is hoping a great attitude and discipline translate in a winning season.

"Our defensive unit has no new players, and it really has the chance to be a better unit than it was a year ago," Mackovic said. "Coach Mac Duff has helped raise the intensity."

If the Cats can raise their intensity on defense, they could be pretty good. Only four teams rushed for more than 100 yards against Arizona last season and the Cats allowed just 88.5 yards rushing a game. The Wildcats had 38 sacks and forced 33 turnovers, the second most of any team in the nation.

Still, they go into the 2001 season trying to break a team-record five-game Pac-10 losing streak. Arizona certainly should be primed to get off to a fast start regardless of whether its offense is ready. San Diego State, Idaho and UNLV are the three non-conference opponents, and if the Wildcats don't win at least two of those, it figures to be a long season.

2001 SCHEDULE

Sept.	1	@San Diego State
	8	Idaho
	22	UNLV
	29	Washington State
Oct.	6	Oregon
	13	@Oregon State
	20	@Washington
	27	Southern California
Nov.	3	@California
	10	Stanford
	23	@Arizona State

QUARTERBACKS

The big question in Tucson this season has nothing to do with the coaching change.

Simply stated, "Who the heck around here can play quarterback?"

It seems that while Tomey left the cupboard full at many positions, the program seems void of depth at quarterback. Of course, whether that is true will be determined early in Arizona's 2001 season. Johnson won the spring competition by a wide margin, probably a good thing for a team implementing a new system. Johnson goes into summer camp as the guy who will get the lion's share of snaps instead of having to split them evenly with his competition.

Johnson won't be able to draw upon experience because he has thrown only six passes in major college competition, completing three. He has played in parts of four games and he did take most of the practice snaps as the No. 2 quarterback last season behind Jenkins. Watkins was in the battle for backup work last season, but he couldn't match Johnson in the spring.

After that, there are bodies, and hope. Redshirt freshman **John Ratay** (6-3, 200) is the brother of former Louisiana Tech star Tim Ratay. Whether he can match his brother's considerable talent remains to be seen. Ratay started his career at Tennessee, but after enrolling early in Knoxville, he quickly decided fellow freshman Casey Clausen would be tough to beat out and transferred west.

The other redshirt freshmen are **Steve Fleming** (6-6, 220), a big guy who has yet to impress the coaching staff, and **Erik Garcia** (6-0, 190).

Sophomore **Kyle Slager** (6-1, 200) is billed as a mobile quarterback.

On the way is freshman **Nic Costa** (5-11, 195), who was one of Oregon's top high school players last season.

"Developing quarterbacks is a key for us," Mackovic said. "There were six quarterbacks on the spring roster, but we haven't seen any of them play. The good news is there is some talent. We need at least two of them to emerge as players in whom we'll be confident."

RUNNING BACKS

Sophomore **Clarence Farmer** (6-0, 225) put together a 666-yard freshman season that included three games over 100 yards and five touchdowns. Those numbers would usually guarantee a tailback a long career as the No. 1 man. However, Arizona has three very talented tailbacks, so Farmer will have to earn his time every step of the way.

It might be time for junior **Larry Croom** (5-10, 210) to step to the plate as one of the conference's top tailbacks. Two years ago, Croom was considered one of the nation's outstanding prep tailbacks and it was thought he would make an immediate impact. Last season, Croom gained 257 yards and averaged 4.0 per carry. Those aren't great numbers, but Mackovic loves his ability to catch the ball, a must in his offensive system.

Sophomore **Anthony Fulcher** (5-11, 200) doesn't have very much experience, but the feeling in Tucson is that if he gets a chance, he could develop into a star.

Redshirt freshmen **Chris Harris** (5-10, 175) and **Tremaine Cox** (5-11, 190) also will be pushing for time.

Senior **Mike Detwiler** (6-2, 230) is the only experienced player at fullback because senior **Eli Wnek** (6-3, 245) was moved back to his original position at defensive end. It will be interesting to see if Detwiler can hold down the job now that Mackovic will be introducing his style of fullback play where the position does a lot more than block. Detwiler had only one carry last season.

Freshmen **Sean Jones** (6-1, 210) and **Antoine Singfield** (6-1, 230) might receive a golden opportunity to play right away.

"Our running backs didn't get to put on much of a show this spring because we had people hurt," Mackovic said. "And, we didn't have much of an offensive line to block for them. I think there are some good players who will get their hands on the ball in the fall. Fulcher didn't get to practice very much during the last few weeks, but he looked very good early on. Farmer just loved being out there, and I am very pleased that he was out there every day and doing whatever he could to show that he is ready to keep his position."

Mackovic also noted a change of philosophy at fullback.

"Fullback is not just a slugger position," he said. "Detwiler, for example, has to be a runner, a receiver, and he has to be able to block."

WIDE RECEIVERS/TIGHT ENDS

Junior **Bobby Wade** (5-11, 190) is the featured performer among the wideouts, coming off a season in which he caught 45 passes for 626 yards.

Mackovic has to deal with a logjam of players here, including seniors **Malosi Leonard** (6-2, 210) and **Brandon Marshall** (5-11, 195) and sophomores **Andrae Thurman** (6-0, 180), **Gary Love** (5-9, 180) and **Lance Relford** (6-0, 195), who all played last season.

Thurman had 14 catches for 145 yards. Marshall caught 11 passes for 175 yards. Leonard had 10 catches for 127 yards and he also completed a pass after throwing on a trick play.

Others hoping to impress Mackovic are senior **Nick Fleury** (6-2, 200), juniors **Michael Hairgrove** (6-2, 210) and **Burke Eiteljorg** (5-10, 185), sophomore **Russell Dokken** (6-2, 180) and redshirt freshman **Ricky Williams** (6-2, 205).

At tight end, starter Brandon Manumaleuna graduated, so a host of raw players will be competing with junior **James Hugo** (6-6, 270), who saw considerable playing time last year. Hugo was primarily a blocker and he didn't make a catch in 2000.

The inexperienced crew includes senior **Peter Hansen** (6-8, 245), junior **Jeff Wilk** (6-3, 250), sophomore **Justin Levasseur** (6-5, 245) and redshirt freshman **Tyrone Brown** (6-3, 240). Arizona has placed three tight ends (Richard Griffith, Roderick Lewis, Mike Lucky) in the NFL over the last 10 years so it will be interesting to see if Mackovic can develop another NFL player in a hurry.

"Wide receiver should be a position that we can count on," Mackovic said. "We dropped a lot of passes early in the spring, but we improved dramatically by the end. We didn't get to see Wade [who sat out spring drills because of an injury], but Thurman had a terrific spring and Leonard and Marshall are veterans who understand the game. I am confident that we will be able to put receivers on the field who can help us, and it is a group that should not hold us back."

Mackovic said anyone who wants to start at tight end has to be versatile, just like Arizona's fullbacks.

"We are going to use two tight ends quite a bit," he said. "We threw a lot of balls to the tight ends, more than they're used to, but we want to get the maximum out of that position. Hugo doesn't drop any balls, and Hansen, Levasseur and Brown really came on during practice. Hansen catches like a basketball player, and his size gives him an advantage over a lot of people.

"He is someone I really felt strongly about as having moved up. He did some good things during the spring. I was concerned that all he was doing was blocking kicks. But he is becoming a total football player."

OFFENSIVE LINE

Medical woes might ultimately determine how effective this unit becomes.

Senior left tackle **Makoa Freitas** (6-4, 305) had off-season foot surgery and missed spring camp. Freitas, who earned freshman All-America honors from *The Sporting News* after the 1998 season, missed eight games last season because of his injury.

Grace was a second-team All-Pac-10 guard in 1999 who played only one game last season because of a shoulder injury. Senior guard **Kevin Barry** (6-5, 330), sophomore guard **Reggie Sampay** (6-3, 275) and junior right tackle **Darren Safranek** (6-7, 280) were all starters last season.

With junior guard **Aaron Higginbotham** (6-5, 260), a key reserve last season, also returning, Arizona seems to have plenty of talent if the frontline players stay healthy.

Seeking time along the line are redshirt freshmen **Conan Crum** (6-6, 270), **Keoki Fraser** (6-2, 320), **Chris Johnson** (6-3, 310) and **Perry Thompson** (6-6, 310) and sophomore **Brandon Phillips** (6-7, 285).

Phillips made a big move in camp, so none of the returning starters' jobs are completely safe. And the fact Arizona allowed 41 sacks last season points toward change.

"Where we are right now, our pass blocking is not good enough to win games," Mackovic said bluntly. "It was important for us during the spring to put the players in the position to where they had to compete one-on-one. I thought that we let down outside, but we were playing with young players at tackle because Safranek and Makoa had to sit out because they were recovering from injuries. It may not have been fun all of the time, but the young players on the line gained invaluable experience."

That experience helped Phillips.

"Phillips was voted the most improved offensive player [of camp]," Mackovic said. "He has such a bright future if he continues to work the way he has been working. He moved from the defense, and he came a long way during the spring from where he started."

2000 STATISTICS

Rushing offense	154.1	50
Passing offense	154.2	102
Total offense	308.3	101
Scoring offense	23.1	75
Net Punting	34.6	56
Punt returns	12.0	27
Kickoff returns	21.9	18
Rushing defense	88.5	8
Passing efficiency defense	108.4	32
Total defense	317.5	21
Scoring defense	21.5	40
Turnover margin	+10	13

Last column is ranking among Division I-A teams.

KICKERS

Junior **Sean Keel** (6-0, 200) is back to handle the place kicking. He hit 13-of-17 field-goal attempts last season, his 76.5 percent average the second best among conference kickers. He also made 25-of-26 extra points with the miss being blocked.

He was 9-of-10 on field goals inside the 40 and he made 4-of-5 kicks from 40-to-49 yards.

Redshirt freshmen **Doug Jones** (5-9, 190) and **Ramey Peru** (6-1, 165) both hope to get a look, as does junior **Chris Gray** (6-1, 195).

"I think that Keel can be as good as anyone in the Pac-10," Mackovic said. "He has excellent timing and he understands himself, and he has a nice attitude about the game. He works to correct things, and he is very stable."

Mackovic said he will work to develop complete football players, starting with the kickers.

"We'll develop a program for them to follow," Mackovic said. "It will be all-encompassing, and we'll make them feel like football players first and specialists second. They'll be involved in practice and involved in drills, and not standing around. This will give them more confidence as football players and the team more confidence in them as players."

DEFENSIVE LINE

Losing defensive ends Joe Tafoya and Idris Haroon leaves a big gap for Mackovic to fill. The hope is that senior **Johnny Jackson** (6-3, 260), a junior college monster who was hampered by injuries last season, will live up to the promise he showed at Sacramento City College. He had just eight tackles last season.

Wnek, who had five sacks as a freshman, figures to land one of the starting spots after returning to his old position. Senior **Alex Luna** (6-0, 230) has seen time at the position and he should push Jackson and Wnek. Luna had 22 tackles last season, including five for losses.

Inside at tackle seniors **Keoni Fraser** (6-1, 280) and **Anthony Thomas** (6-2, 290), sophomore **Young Thompson** (6-2, 295) and junior **Ben Alualu** (6-1, 275) all return as players who have considerable experience. Thomas had 26 tackles, including 11 for loss. Fraser had 10 tackles for loss among his 24 tackles last season. Young Thompson had three tackles for loss.

Junior **Aaron Huisman** (6-4, 230) and senior **Tony Thompson** (6-0, 250) also return. Redshirt freshman **Fata Avegalio** (6-2, 225) impressed the coaching staff during camp and he might be ready to make his move.

Others vying for time are seniors **Dusty Alexander** (6-1, 290) and **Austin Uku** (6-1, 240), junior **Robert Ramsey** (6-3, 260) and redshirt freshmen **Vince Feula** (6-1, 280) and **Matt Perry** (6-2, 275).

"I think our defensive tackles need to become better pass rushers, but we have a lot of good run stoppers on the defensive front," Mackovic said. "Six defensive linemen are seniors out of the top eight to 10 players. One thing that I need to keep my eye on is that we are going to have a lot of holes to fill after the season, and recruiting defensive lineman will be a high priority on the recruiting list."

LINEBACKERS

The unit is led by Briggs, the leading returning tackler in the conference. Briggs recorded double-digit tackles in seven games in 2000 and was a first-team All-Pac-10 selection a season after playing fullback as a redshirt freshman.

Briggs also knocked down seven passes and had two interceptions. He had 11 tackles for loss.

"Briggs could start for any team in the country," Mackovic said. "He makes the tackles, and he flies to the ball. He is very good in man-to-man coverage, he's smart, and he is just that talented."

The other inside spot is a toss-up with senior **Shelton Ross** (6-0, 225) one of the main candidates. Ross had 19 tackles last season in spot duty. The outside linebacker spot might go to sophomore **Joe Siofele** (6-1, 240), who played in all 11 games last season with 17 tackles, including four for loss.

Redshirt freshmen **Patrick Howard** (6-0, 235) and **Andy Nuessle** (6-3, 230) and junior **Ray Wells** (6-0, 220) all sat out last season and will be in the mix. Seldom-used junior **Scott McKee** (6-3, 225) and sophomore **Matt Molina** (6-2, 220) hope to increase their time.

"Wells, who we recognized as the most improved defensive player, was someone we were looking at when the spring started, and he was a player the coaches knew something about," Mackovic said. "He really had a terrific spring, and he moved up significantly at the end.

"We also recognized Eli Wnek for his hustle. He is rejuvenated for the chance to play on the defense again, and he is a significantly different player on defense. He shows ingenuity, and he does a great job of using his quickness and pass rush moves. Siofele did a nice job during the spring. He never says anything. He just plays hard when he's on the field."

DEFENSIVE BACKS

Sophomore cornerback **Michael Jolivette** (5-9, 180) and senior strong safety **Brandon Nash** (6-1, 215) are honors candidates who anchor the secondary.

Jolivette had five of his unit's 16 interceptions last season and he finished 19th in the country in interceptions per game. He was the fourth-leading tackler on the team with 42 and he led the team with 14 passes defensed. Nash, a first team All-Pac-10 academic pick, had 40 tackles last season, including seven for loss. He also had two interceptions and broke up seven passes.

Junior free safety **Jarvie Worcester** (6-0, 195) and senior cornerback **Jermaine Chatman** (5-11, 180) also saw substantial action last season. Worcester, who had 26 tackles and broke up five passes, was the starter until the final two games of the season when he sat out with a shoulder injury. Chatman had three interceptions and 34 tackles last season.

Other cornerbacks returning who had starting experience are senior **Anthony Banks** (6-0, 170), junior **David Laudermilk** (6-2,170) and sophomore **David Hinton** (5-11, 170). Adding depth are sophomore free safety **Clay Hardt** (6-1, 195) and senior strong safety **Zaharius Johnson** (6-0, 195). Sophomore **Danny Perry** (5-9, 185) showed a lot of ability on special teams last season and he might be a factor.

"Jolivette is for real," Mackovic said. "He's a good cover man, and he plays his position very well. It's great to see our receivers work hard to try to beat him. He has a good sense of the ball in the air and the receiver."

PUNTERS

Mackovic is putting pressure on incumbent senior **Chris Palic** (6-3, 205) to produce more height on his punts. Palic averaged 37.1 yards per punt last season.

The team's net punting average was just 34.6. Peru is a backup at punter as well.

"Punting will get a lot of attention," Mackovic said. "We have a returning starter and some other candidates. We owe a certain respect to guys who have performed in the past. But Palic was very inconsistent during the spring. As a senior, he should be someone that we can count on. He got a lot of push from Peru this spring, and they both have similar styles, which is interesting. It is more of a race at that position right now."

SPECIAL TEAMS

Wade handled punt returns last season and will do so again this year. He returned 26 punts for a 10.1 average, including a 60-yard touchdown return. Wade had fumbling problems in 2000, so the pressure will be on him to show improvement in that area.

Senior **Anthony Banks** (6-0, 170) also handled some punts last season with similar woes. Love, Croom and Thurman are expected to handle kickoff duties. Love averaged 21.2 yards per return last season on 15 attempts. Mills returned four kickoffs for 113 yards, a 28.2 average.

Four-year snapper Nate Campbell is gone, so Arizona needs to find a long snapper. Redshirt freshman **Ben DalMolin** (5-11, 190) is a candidate.

Arizona does have Hansen returning. He's a kick-block specialist who was voted to the All-Pac-10 second team last season. Hansen has blocked seven field goal and point-after kicks during his career.

Mackovic again stressed the importance of convincing everyone on the team the importance of special teams.

"One of the things we have to keep in mind is the balance between the actual kickers and everyone else around them," he said. "Special teams are units that have to work in concert, and the opposite when your special team is trying to break down the opponent's unity. These plays can cost a season."

RECRUITING CLASS

All eyes will be on incoming freshman quarterback Nic Costa, who was a SuperPrep, PrepStar and Prep Football Report All-American out of Aloha, Oregon. He is being compared to former Arizona quarterback Keith Smith.

"I don't think there is any way that he could come in and be ready to start the season," Mackovic said. "There is so much to be learned, and we will be moving twice as fast in the fall as we were in the spring. It is highly unlikely that a freshman could do it. Costa is smart, and he learns, and we will just have to see how that plays out."

Arizona landed some other high-profile recruits. Tailback **Mike Bell** (6-1, 205) out of Tolleson High School in Phoenix, was a *Parade*, *SuperPrep* and *PrepStar* All-American. He rushed for 2,484 yards as a senior, averaging 8.7 yards per carry. Bell became the second player in state history to rush for 2,000 yards in consecutive seasons after having 2,038 and 22 touchdowns as a junior.

PrepStar All-America tight end **Brad Brittain** (6-5, 261) out of Torrey Pines High School in California might have a chance to make an immediate impact.

BLUE RIBBON ANALYSIS

OFFENSE	C-
SPECIAL TEAMS	B
DEFENSE	B
INTANGIBLES	C

The Wildcats are going to see a lot of nine-man defensive fronts until they prove they can throw the ball effectively. Johnson will be blitzed from every angle and will be under fire from the opening snap of the season. Whether Arizona's offensive players can digest a new system and break in a new quarterback at the same time remains to be seen.

Along with other offensive problems to be solved, another question begs to be asked. What happens if Johnson is injured or turns out to be a lemon? The chance for Arizona to completely collapse this season certainly exists.

On the other hand, a veteran defense should keep Arizona in a number of games. Desert Swarm might still live in Tucson. With a very weak preseason schedule, Arizona could put together a 3-0 start and not even play that well. However, a solid start might be crucial in terms of developing confidence. The players are aware of their five-game losing streak to close last season, and they are hoping the new coaching staff takes them in a new direction.

The call here is that Arizona's offense sputters and the Wildcats miss the bowl picture.

(J.H.)

2000 RESULTS

Utah	W	17-3	1-0

Ohio State	L	17-27	1-1
San Diego State	W	17-3	2-1
Stanford	W	27-3	3-1
USC	W	31-15	4-1
Washington State	W	53-47	5-1
Oregon	L	10-14	5-2
UCLA	L	24-27	5-3
Washington	L	32-35	5-4
Oregon State	L	9-33	5-5
Arizona State	L	17-30	5-6

Arizona State

LOCATION	**Tempe, AZ**
CONFERENCE	**Pac-10**
LAST SEASON	**6-6 (.500)**
CONFERENCE RECORD	**3-5 (t-5th)**
OFFENSIVE STARTERS RETURNING	**7**
DEFENSIVE STARTERS RETURNING	**7**
NICKNAME	**Sun Devils**
COLORS	**Maroon & Gold**
HOME FIELD	**Sun Devils Stadium (73,379)**
HEAD COACH	**Dirk Koetter (Idaho State '81)**
RECORD AT SCHOOL	**First Year**
CAREER RECORD	**27-10 (3 years)**
ASSISTANTS	**Ron English (California '90)** **Cornerbacks** **Dan Fidler (Arizona State '81)** **Safeties** **Jeff Grimes (UTEP '91)** **Offensive Line** **Brent Guy (Oklahoma State '83)** **Defensive Coordinator** **Mark Helfrich (Southern Oregon '96)** **Quarterbacks** **Darryl Jackson (San Diego '92)** **Wide Receivers** **Ted Monachino (Missouri '90)** **Defensive Line** **Tom Nordquist (Oregon State '93)** **Running Backs** **Tom Osborne (Washington State '83)** **Tight Ends/Special Teams**
TEAM WINS (last 5 yrs.)	**11-9-5-6-6**
FINAL RANK (last 5 yrs.)	**4-15-33-35-43**
2000 FINISH	**Lost to Boston College in Aloha Bowl.**

COACH AND PROGRAM

The age-old question will again be addressed at Arizona State during the 2001 football season. How many wins is enough?

Bruce Snyder won 58 games in nine seasons as head coach of the Sun Devils and went to bowl games five of the last six seasons. In 1996, his 11-1 team was nipped in the Rose Bowl, 20-17, by Ohio State and narrowly missed winning a national championship.

All that just wasn't enough for the administration, which gave Snyder the boot even though he took the team to the Aloha Bowl last season. ASU said Aloha to Snyder.

In his place comes Dirk Koetter, a guy who has the task of living up to the administration's lofty ambitions in a conference that includes programs such as former powerhouse USC, which has failed to crank out national championship contenders on a yearly basis the way it once did.

Perhaps the Pac-10 is simply too balanced for any program to expect domination on a yearly basis. Oregon, Washington State and Stanford all have broken lengthy Rose Bowl droughts in the last 10 years. Oregon State has rejuvenated a program that was dead and gone. Perhaps bowls in four of the last five seasons wasn't so bad.

Nonetheless, the Sun Devils have landed a new man.

"We had high expectations here last year because we had serious talent," said ASU senior center **Scott Peters** (6-4, 290), a Lombardi Award candidate. "We just didn't get any wins. Every year, we put guys in the NFL. In my opinion, we have underachieved here. Coach Koetter has overachieved wherever he has been."

Certainly, Koetter was a monster overachiever at Boise State, where he went 25-10 in three seasons. Before he arrived, Boise State never had a winning season in Division I-A. He had three, including the school's first two bowl wins as a Divison I-A team.

And besides just winning, the Broncos were a kick to watch. They were first in Division I-A football last season in scoring (44.91 points a game). They were No. 2 in the nation in total offense (496.27 yards per game).

Koetter, who developed high-powered offenses at Oregon when he was offensive coordinator there in 1996-97, knows how to move a football. Now the question is whether he can develop a consistent big winner in the Pac-10.

"We're so close to being where we should be," said Peters, who believes Koetter might be able to push ASU over that edge. "We were up 28-0 in the second quarter against UCLA and we lost. Against Washington, we played horrible and we only lost, 21-15. We had some bad calls against Oregon and we lost in overtime."

For whatever reason, the old Sun Devils seemed to fall into a rut at times.

"We didn't have the enthusiasm when we played poorly," Peters said. "We had a tough time getting out of the tank. The biggest issue was our character.

"I think this has been a positive change for us, a new start. We have a fresh attitude. Coach Koetter is different. Everything is more focused. The detail is the thing that is amazing to me. Just watching our receivers run their routes. He gets on guys if they make a mistake.

"I was worried at first because this is my senior year. But the coaches have made it much easier. I'm as happy as I could be."

Obviously, one thing that makes Peters smile is Koetter's offensive expertise. But Sun Devils senior safety **Willie Daniel** (6-0, 205) said he also is impressed with the new ASU coach.

"Something was missing for us chemistry wise," Daniel said. "This school has put a lot of players into the pros. Guys like Todd Heap and Adam Archuleta and J.R. Redmond. It always has produced pros. Something was missing chemistry wise. It just wasn't there so they changed coaches. That decision is out of the players' hands."

It would be hard not to feel sorry for Snyder, and the Sun Devils in general last season. They lost three of their final four games after lightning hit their plane (blowing a hole in the tail) after the Washington State game.

"I tore my MCL that game," Peters said. "Our plane getting hit by lightning just topped it off. We had stewardesses crying and guys praying. I thought we might be going down."

The plane didn't go down, but the Sun Devils did. Besides the lightning strike, other misfortune hit the Sun Devils. A spate of injuries crippled the offense.

"We can't try to make excuses about what happened to us," Daniel said. "Players play the game and we didn't make enough plays. A coach can motivate you, but players have to play. I think now we should be more confident and more disciplined, and maybe we needed that. It's probably a good thing."

The good news for Koetter is that he has 14 starters back (seven on both offense and defense) from a team that reached a bowl game last season.

Although Koetter needs to develop a quarterback, he has some dynamic tailbacks and a solid offensive line.

"We have a good run package," Peters said. "The difference [from last season] will be our passing game. I don't want to say we looked great in the spring, because we had quarterbacks battling for No. 1, but we should be pretty good. We have four guys coming back on the offensive line."

Could the Sun Devils pound the ball at teams even though Koetter is known for his passing offense?

"If I had my way, I would like to run more," Peters said. "Then you get to pound people more."

ASU might have to pound people more if the passing game doesn't improve from the spring workouts.

"I think the coaches would have liked us to look better in the spring," Peters said. "But we had a new play book and a new system."

Koetter understands that everything isn't going to come together in one spring session.

"We said going into spring ball that we had some definite goals we wanted to accomplish," Koetter said. "And I think we are headed in the right direction on those goals. We wanted to find the best 22 players and identify who our playmakers are. We wanted to recommit to team football and the special teams aspect of team football.

"As far as identifying the players, the picture cleared up at some positions and not so much at others. The other extremely positive thing coming out of spring ball was that we got a lot of work done without anybody getting seriously injured which would prevent them from being ready in the fall."

Besides trying to get a new offensive scheme ready, Koetter also has installed a new defensive scheme. New defensive coordinator Brent Guy utilizes a defensive system with five defensive backs and two linebackers.

"We laid out a schedule for the whole spring and hoped we could stay on schedule," Guy said. "We were able to do that. We even installed a couple of things in the last days of spring practice that we hadn't planned on doing.

"Our defense has a lot of movement and we give a lot of different looks, pre-snap looks with the guys moving around. We want to try to be as deceptive as we can. That's one of the harder things to learn. Right now our players are concentrating on knowing where to be and exactly what to do."

Koetter said he wasn't surprised the defense came along so quickly.

"In that respect, the defense learned their system faster than the offense, which they should," Koetter said. "It doesn't have to be that way, but in our system, our defense is based on letting the players play. In our offensive system, while we want to let the players play, there tends to be more thinking involved. I was very impressed with the percentage of guys who bought in and how quickly they bought into what we are doing.

"You're always nervous when you go into a program about whether your guys are going to come out and work hard every day. Whether it was in winter conditioning, the weight room, our running program or in spring football, we never had that issue. Those guys worked hard, and that will pay dividends for us down the road."

Interestingly, Daniel somewhat disagreed with Koetter's description of his defense as one that "lets the players play."

Daniel said last year's philosophy was more

geared to allowing the players to react.

"This defense is more structured," Daniel said. "It's a team defense where everyone has a specific job. If everyone does their job, it will work. Our defense last year was more about playmaking and using your natural ability.

"But the change hasn't really affected me that much other than I have to learn a new defense. My position has only changed a little bit. Football is football."

Looking at his experienced teammates, Daniels expects the Sun Devils to have a solid defensive year.

"As a whole, our defense will be good," he said. "We've picked the new defense up fast and we have people who are talented and who can play their spot. We have experience and confidence."

That experience is something Koetter is relying on to help ASU through a season of transition.

"I think that we have some good, established leaders on our team," he said. "Our leadership will continue to grow into the fall. I think back to other teams I've been on, where you talk to our coaching staff and ask who our leaders are, and nobody says anything. That's not the case here. We have players everyone can identify as leaders. There are guys who aren't afraid to wear that hat."

2001 SCHEDULE

Sept.	8	San Diego State
	15	@UCLA
	22	@Stanford
	29	San Jose State
Oct.	6	Louisiana-Lafayette
	13	@USC
	20	Oregon State
	27	Washington
Nov.	3	@Oregon
	10	Washington State
	23	Arizona

QUARTERBACKS

Despite minor injuries and a bout with mononucleosis, sophomore **Jeff Krohn** (6-2, 185) managed to start 10 games last season while setting school single-game records for a freshman with 432 yards and five touchdown passes against Oregon. He threw for 1,751 yards and 12 touchdowns.

Junior **Matt Cooper** (6-5, 240) appears to be making more of an impression on the new staff than he was able to do and the former staff. Cooper appeared in just five games last season, but did throw a touchdown pass in the Aloha Bowl.

Redshirt freshman **Andrew Walter** (6-5, 230), a highly recruited prep out of Grand Junction, Colo., might also be ready now.

"All three returning guys showed enough at one time or another [in the spring] that we thought he could be the guy," Koetter said. "But nobody set himself apart enough that we wanted to say this is the one we are going to live and die with in the fall. Cooper was the most consistent quarterback of the spring. Krohn showed at times why he was the guy who was counted on last year. I can see why they went with Jeff. He's a very smart, athletic guy. Coming off collarbone surgery in the Aloha Bowl, he just needs more time in the weight room.

"Walter is everything he was advertised to be from a talent standpoint. Like any guy who is a redshirt freshman, he experienced his growing pains in learning a second offense in less than a year."

RUNNING BACKS

It might finally be time for senior **Delvon Flowers** (5-11, 195) to shine after he went down with a torn ACL in his left knee that wiped out his 2000 season.

After averaging 6.4 yards a carry in 1999 with 512 yards rushing and six touchdowns, Flowers was expected to vie for national honors and was added to the Doak Walker watch list until he blew out his knee. If he returns without losing a step, he is a tremendously fast game-breaker. If he doesn't return to his previous form, ASU does have other talented tailbacks.

Senior **Tom Pace** (5-10, 190) was a walk-on until his play last season convinced the coaching staff he deserved to be on scholarship. He rushed for 720 yards, scored six rushing touchdowns and caught two touchdown passes.

Also in the mix is sophomore **Mike Williams** (6-0, 190), who started three games as a freshman last season and finished with 514 rushing yards and five touchdowns.

"Tailback is probably the deepest position on our offensive team," Koetter said. "We have three guys who have started at different times in their careers and who have proven to be successful runners at this level. I think we can win with any of the three. Delvon was not quite 100 percent this spring, but close to it. I was very impressed with his work habits. He never turned down a rep in the spring and always wanted more. Even though some days I thought he was favoring that leg, he never came out. I think he got his confidence back almost to a fault.

"Pace got off to a great start, and it's easy to see why he is such a solid player. He can do everything—run, catch, block. A groin pull limited the second half of spring ball for him, but we saw enough to know he is going to play a lot of football for us. Williams is another guy who I am excited about. He has gotten stronger and faster and he has a great attitude."

Adding depth are sophomores **Derick Arnold** (6-1, 205) and **Jermaine McKinney** (5-11, 220).

Sophomore **Mike Karney** (6-0, 260) leads the group at fullback after playing in 11 games last season as a freshman backup to graduated starter Stephen Trejo. Karney's experience with the ball was limited as he carried just 14 times for 42 yards and caught four passes for 42 yards.

Sophomore **Steve Hoppe** (6-2, 200) moved to fullback from linebacker and he hopes to make an impact at his new position. Junior **Darrel Turner** (6-0, 260) adds depth.

"Karney is what every college team is looking for in a fullback," Koetter said. "He doesn't mind doing the dirty work. He sees himself as a blocker first, is an excellent receiver and has fine hands."

WIDE RECEIVERS/TIGHT ENDS

With All-America tight end Todd Heap and talented wide receiver Richard Williams gone, the Sun Devils will be hard-pressed to replace them. Fortunately for Koetter, it would appear he has plenty of talent left.

Senior wide receiver **Donnie O'Neal** (6-2, 180) led the team with seven touchdown catches in 2000 and he finished with 39 catches for 661 yards. Sophomore **Sean McDonald** (5-9, 170) caught 22 passes for 358 yards and he figures to improve. Junior **Justin Taplin** (6-0, 190) might finally live up to his promise after a 13-catch, 169-yard season. Senior **Ryan Dennard** (6-4, 220) hopes to build on his Aloha Bowl performance in which he caught the first touchdown pass of his career.

"I think this is a solid group," Koetter said. "There are some playmakers and we have good depth. Probably the most consistent receiver day in and day out in spring ball was Dennard. I am very pleased with the things he did as a receiver, a route runner and a blocker. Taplin is a guy I know has play-making ability in him. He is a good blocker and an experienced tough guy who we will use as a return man."

Other players hoping to break into the lineup are sophomore **Skyler Fulton** (6-2, 200) and red-shirt freshman **Mike Smith** (6-2, 200).

The situation at tight end is much different than last season when Heap dominated. His backup, junior **Mike Pinkard** (6-3, 250), caught six passes for 100 yards last season and might get the call as the 2001 starter. Sophomore **Frank Maddox** (6-3, 250) is challenging for the spot while freshman **Lee Burghgraef** (6-5, 230) might get an immediate chance to play.

"Tight end is our least experienced position on the team," Koetter said. "Pinkard is definitely good enough on the line of scrimmage as a blocker and we would like him to continue to develop as a receiver. One of our biggest disappointments of the spring was that Maddox didn't get to play much because of a hamstring strain. From what we can tell, he is exactly what we are looking for."

OFFENSIVE LINE

Peters is the dominant figure on the ASU line, a Lombardi candidate who was a first-team All Pac-10 selection last season. He had off-season knee surgery and missed full-contact drills in spring camp, but he expects to be ready by the time summer camp rolls around.

At left guard, ASU returns senior **Marquise Muldrow** (6-3, 320), who started nine games last season. Last year's starting right guard, senior **Kyle Kosier** (6-6, 290), moves to right tackle. Senior **Levi Jones** (6-6, 315) is back at left tackle, where he earned second team All Pac-10 honors last season.

The only new member on the line will be sophomore right guard **Regis Crawford** (6-3, 320), who has the versatility to play either guard or tackle. Senior **Travis Scott** (6-6, 310), sophomores **Tony Aguilar** (6-3, 310) and **Damien Niko** (6-4, 325) and red-shirt freshmen **Adrian Ayala** (6-4, 325) and **Drew Hodgdon** (6-3, 325) are trying to break into the lineup.

"I think our offensive line will be the strength of our offense," Koetter said. "In the few days Peters was able to do limited things during the spring, you could really see his ability. Because of our lack of depth, some of our underclassmen got a lot of work in the spring, which even though was frustrating at times, will be a good thing for us in the long run.

"We're really excited about three guys who did not play as much last year in Scott, Crawford and Hodgdon. Because of injuries, they had to play multiple positions in the spring."

2000 STATISTICS

Rushing offense	114.2	87
Passing offense	266.8	20
Total offense	381.0	50
Scoring offense	26.9	49
Net Punting	36.1	31
Punt returns	8.8	70
Kickoff returns	20.1	47
Rushing defense	167.3	74
Passing efficiency defense	112.3	42
Total defense	401.4	82
Scoring defense	25.5	56
Turnover margin	+11	10

Last column is ranking among Division I-A teams.

KICKERS

Junior **Mike Barth** (6-0, 210) returns after hitting 15-of-23 field goals and 32-of-34 extra points. He won two games (Colorado State and Washington State) on late, 48-yard field goals. He missed most of spring ball because he had his appendix removed.

Junior **Greg Pieratt** (6-1, 180) is putting the pressure on Barth and redshirt freshman **Travis Cloyd** (6-0, 190) might be ready to compete for the starting job.

DEFENSIVE LINE

This could be the year sophomore defensive end **Terrell Suggs** (6-3, 230), last season's Pac-10 Freshman of the Year, generates some national attention.

Suggs burst on the scene in 2000 with 16 tackles for loss and 10 sacks. He became just the second player in school history to start the season opener as a freshman.

Besides his tackles for loss, he also forced four fumbles. Considering ASU has another impact player on the line in senior tackle **Kurt Wallin** (6-2, 270), who returns at right tackle after registering 12 tackles for loss in 2000, Mackovic has to feel great about his defensive line. Another defender who can separate an offensive player from the ball, Wallin forced three fumbles last season. Joining Wallin at the other tackle position will be a combination of seniors **Tommy Townsend** (6-3, 295), **Paul Glass** (6-6, 335) and **Danny Masaniai** (6-2, 315).

"At defensive tackle, we have a lot of depth with guys who have played a lot of games," Guy said. "They were very productive for us in the spring. It's hard to play down there in the trenches. We like to call them 'War Dogs', because it is hand to hand combat every snap. You've got to have tough veterans."

Playing opposite Suggs at the other defensive end will be sophomore **Brian Montesanto** (6-5, 250), who earned four starts last season and played in all 12 games.

Backups at end are sophomores **Chad Howell** (6-4, 240), who had two starts last season but tore his ACL against Stanford, and **Ben Fox** (6-2, 260).

Fighting for time on the line will be junior **James Beal** (6-1, 290) and redshirt freshmen **Jared Wolfgramm** (6-5, 220) and **Jimmy Verdon** (6-3, 260). Guy said he is excited about his young defensive linemen.

"We have talent there that I think will grow with us and grow with the defense," Guy said. "Suggs is a very exciting player with the types of plays he can make. He can go in there and sack the quarterback on any snap and he runs plays down even when they are going away from him. Most offenses don't count on having to block that guy. You have to contend with him on every snap because of his speed."

LINEBACKERS

The Sun Devils not only have to replace Pac-10 Defensive Player-of-the-Year Adam Archuleta, they are using a new system that utilizes only two linebackers.

One of those positions figures to be held by senior **Eric Fields** (6-3, 235), who started every game at outside linebacker last season. He had 11 tackles for loss and two forced fumbles. Junior **Solomon Bates** (6-2, 260) is a good fit at the other linebacker position as he had 99 tackles last season and was an honorable-mention All-Pac-10 pick. He forced four fumbles and had 12 tackles for loss, including three sacks. Bates showed his athleticism by deflecting eight passes and intercepting two passes.

Junior **Mason Unck** (6-2, 235) also will see a lot of time after he showed remarkable recovery from a torn ACL last season by playing in six games.

Pushing for snaps will be senior **Jamall Anderson** (6-1, 250), junior **Josh Amobi** (6-2, 215) and redshirt freshmen **Connor Banks** (6-2, 240) and **Zack Mims** (6-2, 220).

"We have almost as much depth at linebacker as we do at defensive tackle," Guy said. "We had to restructure because both of our linebackers play off the line of scrimmage where Fields and Unck had been on the line of scrimmage. Bates has big-play ability and Fields and Unck will play a lot. I like to rotate those guys around a lot to keep them fresh because they are involved in special teams. Amobi and Banks made a lot of progress in the spring."

DEFENSIVE BACKS

It will be an interesting time to utilize a five-man defensive backfield considering the Sun Devils are a bit short on experience in the secondary. Daniel (6-0, 205) is the guy who might have to hold everything together.

Joining him is junior **Alfred Williams** (6-1, 200), who will play another of the safety positions. Daniel finished fourth on the team in tackles last season as the starting strong safety. Williams was the starting free safety and he finished third on the team in tackles, forced two fumbles and had an interception.

A key position switch puts former tailback **Davaren Hightower** (6-1, 210) at safety. Hightower, a senior, was the team's third-leading rusher last season. Others challenging to win the third safety position are senior **Monte Franks** (6-1,205) and juniors **Patrick Wilson** (5-10, 200) and **Brandon Falkner** (6-0, 200).

"Our safeties have to be big-play guys," Guy said. "They have the opportunity to make a lot of tackles. We blitz some and bring them off the edges, so they have to be guys who have the ability to make open-field tackles. Hightower showed a lot of progress toward the end of spring ball."

Other safeties vying for time are redshirt freshmen **Mike Holloway** (6-0, 200) and **Ricardo Stewart** (5-11, 200). Guy praised both his redshirt freshmen and said he wouldn't be surprised if they found their way into the lineup.

At cornerback, ASU is starting from scratch, as both starters are gone. Redshirt freshmen **R.J. Oliver** (5-9, 170) and **Emmanuel Franklin** (5-11, 185) impressed Guy in the spring and are considered to be front-runners for the starting jobs.

Junior **Josiah Igono** (5-10, 180) started two games last season and is the only returning player with experience at the position. Others trying to crack the lineup are junior **O.J. Hackett** (5-10, 165) and sophomore **Adrian Thomas** (6-0, 185). Guy might eventually have to look at incoming freshmen to help out at the position.

"Our two [redshirt] freshmen did a good job in the spring," Guy said. "Those guys had to get better because they were forced to take all the reps. Cornerback is probably the thinnest position we have. Igono has started a couple of games, but other than that, we don't have anyone who has played in a game. We have talented kids, so we are excited about that."

Daniel said he will do what he can to help out his inexperienced corners.

"Our corners are young and they have never played a down of college football," Daniel said. "But they are eager and I love to go to bat with guys like that."

PUNTERS

Senior **Nick Murphy** (6-0, 185) returns after being an All Pac-10 honorable mention pick last year. That might not sound like much, but the conference was stacked with great punters. Murphy, who is handling the punting duties for a third consecutive year, was a semifinalist for the Ray Guy Award last season when he averaged 41.3 yards a punt.

Backing up Murphy is junior **Brian Biang** (6-0, 205).

"Murphy did a great job in the spring," special teams coach Tom Osborne said. "I was concerned because we changed some of the things that he has done. Nick adapted and accepted that very well. He did the best job of any of the specialists in the spring. He was consistently awesome. I just hope we can cover him now."

SPECIAL TEAMS

Flowers should bring excitement to the kickoff return unit after averaging 22.3 yards a return in 1999.

"Delvon is a shake-and-bake guy," Osborne said. "He has the ability to make people miss and obviously he got healthy and more confident in the spring. You could see he demonstrated some great skills."

Pace, who led the nation in return yards at Idaho before transferring to ASU, will also help out on kickoff returns along with Williams. McDonald and Taplin split the punt return duties last season and will again in 2001. McDonald returned 28 punts for a 9.4 average.

Taplin had a 6.7 average on 24 tries. Osborne arrived from Oregon to rejuvenate the Sun Devils special teams units.

"Our players' attitudes about the importance of special teams in winning games has improved," he said. "They have to understand how hard they have to play on special teams."

The Sun Devils are fortunate to have quite a few long snappers. Senior **B.J. Miller** (6-2, 210) and junior **Jay Breckenridge** (6-2, 225) both can snap on punts while Peters handles the short snapping duties.

RECRUITING CLASS

The marquee signing was tailback **Hakim Hill** (6-0, 210) out of City High School in Iowa City, Iowa. The son of former Arizona State and Buffalo Bills star J.D. Hill was a USA Today All-American. He accumulated 3,585 yards and 57 touchdowns during his prep career. He rushed for 1,820 yards and 28 touchdowns as a senior. He picked ASU over Nebraska, Notre Dame, Washington and Iowa.

With 27 recruiting days after he was hired, Koetter concentrated on in-state recruits, landing eight of them. He was most happy about his class' overall speed. Of his 17 recruits, 10 had sprinter's speed.

One of the speedsters is **Lamar Baker** (5-11, 190) a cornerback from Agua Fria High School in Avondale, Ariz. *Student Sports Magazine* listed Baker as the No. 3 cornerback recruit in the country. He had 126 tackles as a senior and rushed for 1,100 yards as a tailback. He runs a 10.6 in the 100 meters.

Another speedster is tailback **Cornell Canidate** (5-9, 175) out of Alhambra High School in Phoenix. Canidate is the younger brother of former Arizona star Trung Canidate, who now plays for the St. Louis Rams. He scored seven touchdowns on returns as a senior. He averaged more than 10 yards a carry his senior year.

The only junior college player signed was junior defensive back O.J. Hackett. Hackett, from Chaffey (Calif.) College, had 20 pass breakups last season. He's known as a big hitter for his size and also has good speed and coverage skills.

BLUE RIBBON ANALYSIS

OFFENSE	B-
SPECIAL TEAMS	B
DEFENSE	B
INTANGIBLES	B

You get the feeling that everything Koetter touches turns to gold, so there might be some magic in Tempe this year. Koetter will need some breaks. Although his non-conference schedule is easy—games against San Diego State, San Jose State and Louisiana-Lafayette—the Sun Devils have to open Pac-10 play the second week of the season on the road at conference favorite UCLA.

If Koetter's systems are going full bore, his team could get drilled in that one. Worst yet, the conference schedule makers played a joke on ASU this season. Its first three conference games are on the road against UCLA, Stanford and USC.

Certainly, the cake non-conference opponents will keep ASU in the bowl picture and therefore Koetter's team should grow in confidence even if it stumbles in Pac-10 play.

If ASU does have trouble in the first half of conference play, it will be interesting to see if Koetter can hold the troops together. A minor bowl appearance would be a good place for Koetter to start in Tempe. Of course, that's exactly the result that got Snyder fired a year ago.

(J.H.)

2000 RESULTS

San Diego	W	10-7	1-0
Colorado State	W	13-10	2-0
Utah State	W	44-20	3-0
UCLA	L	31-38	3-1
California	W	30-10	4-1
Washington	L	15-21	4-2
Washington State	W	23-20	5-2
Oregon	L	55-56	5-3
USC	L	38-44	5-4
Stanford	L	7-29	5-5
Arizona	W	30-17	6-5
Boston College (Aloha)	L	17-31	6-6

California

LOCATION	**Berkeley, CA**
CONFERENCE	**Pac-10**
LAST SEASON	**3-8 (.273)**
CONFERENCE RECORD	**2-6 (t-8th)**
OFFENSIVE STARTERS RETURNING	**8**
DEFENSIVE STARTERS RETURNING	**7**
NICKNAME	**Golden Bears**
COLORS	**Blue & Gold**
HOME FIELD	**Memorial Stadium (75,028)**
HEAD COACH	**Tom Holmoe (BYU '83)**
RECORD AT SCHOOL	**15-29 (4 years)**
CAREER RECORD	**15-29 (4 years)**
ASSISTANTS	**Al Borges (Cal State-Chico '81)**
	Offensive Coordinator
	Keith Borges (Sacramento State '92)
	Tight Ends
	Bill Dutton (Cal '54)
	Defensive Line
	Ron Gould (Oregon '88)
	Running Backs
	Ken Margerum (Stanford '80)
	Wide Receivers
	LeCharls McDaniel (Cal Poly-S. L. Obispo '81)
	Special Teams
	Lyle Setencich (Fresno State '69)
	Defensive Coordinator
	Randy Stewart (Boise State '80)
	Defensive Backs
	Ed White (Cal '68)
	Offensive Line
TEAM WINS (last 5 yrs.)	**6-3-5-4-3**
FINAL RANK (last 5 yrs.)	**56-50-46-49-59**
2000 FINISH	**Lost to Stanford in regular-season finale.**

COACH AND PROGRAM

Cal center **Brandon Lugwig** noticed a different attitude among has teammates as they prepared for this season. For the first time in several years, the Bears don't just think they can be good.

They know it.

"There is a difference between believing and knowing," Ludwig said.

Huh? Is the burly offensive lineman just playing semantics or does he have a point?

Certainly, that will be determined by the outcome of the 2001 season. Cal hasn't had a winning regular season since Steve Mariucci spent his lone season in charge in 1997.

It might have been different last year if the Bears didn't invent ways to lose close games. Two blocked punts in the Stanford game led to an overtime loss. A porous defense that allowed 23 fourth-quarter points doomed them in a 36-24 loss at Washington.

Ludwig's theory is that the Bears lacked the confidence they now have as a veteran unit that has been through the wars. They know now.

Well, as long as we're playing semantics, try these. Gone. History. Outta here. Fired.

Yup, those all could apply to Cal head coach Tom Holmoe if he doesn't produce a winner in the fifth year of his contract. He has made it well known in Berkeley that he won't stay if the team has another losing season, so there is plenty of pressure to go around, from the head coach, to the staff, to the players.

Suffice to say that Cal simply has to get off to a fast start or the program could come apart at the seams.

"There's a real urgency about this coming season, but all the pieces are in place," Holmoe said. "Our personnel is the best since I've been here. We've played some younger guys the past few years, but now they're veterans with experience in big games. Plus, we now have a coaching staff that I wouldn't trade for any staff in college football. Now we just need to go out and win some football games.

We expect success."

In Berkeley, that seems to be the consensus. Confidence is high for several reasons. The first, and perhaps most important, is that Cal's schedule gives the team a fighting chance to develop into a bowl participant. Although BYU and Illinois are not patsies by any means, they are two programs coming off sub-par seasons that will be playing the Bears at Memorial Stadium in Berkeley.

The Cougars, who were 6-6, will be sporting a new coach (Gary Crowton) for the first time in 30 years. That in itself could lead to a little adjustment period.

Cal's lone non-conference road opponent in 2001 is Rutgers, a team that was truly awful last season despite having a quarterback (Mike McMahon) who was drafted. Scarlet Knights head coach Terry Shea got the axe in favor of Greg Schiano, who should have his hands full trying to rebuild a sorry program.

Certainly, Cal should have a fighting chance to win all three of those games, or at worst, two of the three.

The Pac-10 season then begins with a road trip to Washington State, a team that hasn't lost to Cal at home since 1979. Even so, if Cal expects to reach a bowl, it must be able to beat WSU, a squad that has won three conference games the last two seasons.

From there it becomes the usual knock-down, drag-out battle of the Pac-10, but if Cal can start the season 3-1 or 4-0, a 3-4 record the rest of the way will be good enough for bowl eligibility. Is that too much to ask?

Cal fans think not, especially because of another major factor now in Cal's favor. During the off-season, Holmoe convinced Al Borges to leave his offensive coordinator job at UCLA to take over the same position in Berkeley. Cal's offense, which finished at the bottom of the Pac-10 the last three seasons in points scored, got an instant injection of coaching genius.

Borges has worked wonders wherever he has stopped, his last two stints at Oregon and UCLA. In six years at those two schools (the last five at UCLA), his offenses averaged 31 points per game. If he can breathe some life into a lethargic Bears' offense (that averaged just 22 points a year ago), perhaps Cal fans will be reintroduced to a word that has become foreign—victory.

"The big difference in this team is personnel," Holmoe said. "We go into the season with the best group we've had since I've been here. We have good, experienced players and pretty good depth. It's encouraging."

2001 SCHEDULE

Sept.	1	Illinois
	8	BYU
	15	@Rutgers
	22	@Washington State
	29	Washington
Oct.	13	Oregon
	20	@UCLA
	27	@Oregon State
Nov.	3	Arizona
	10	USC
	17	@Stanford

QUARTERBACKS

The general feeling is that junior **Kyle Boller** (6-4, 210) has been hindered—as well as being beaten to a pulp—the last two seasons by Cal's general lack of talent. It would be hard to argue such a notion, especially because the Bears scored the fewest points in the Pac-10 both seasons.

Boller did raise his completion percentage from 38.6 percent his freshman year to 46.7 percent last season.

"I'm very happy with Kyle's progress," Borges said. "He has been just a sponge and a guy who I think just needed a little more kicking in the pants. But he is a guy who can handle it. He has taken his lumps and he is ready to take it to the next step."

Borges said he is concentrating on Boller's fundamentals, such as footwork.

"It is no different than coaching linebackers," Borges said. "We talk so much about reads, we forget all about the other things that matter. If you can't get your feet set, you can't play the position."

Boller, who last season completed 163-of-349 passes for 2,121 yards and 15 touchdowns, said he appreciates the knowledge that Borges brings.

"I feel more comfortable, even more so than in the past," Boller said. "I'm not sure why. I guess I understand more than I did."

So does Boller believe the Bears will finally break their bowl drought?

"We're looking forward to the season," he said. "It's been too long (since Cal had a winning season). But I really don't like talking about it, because guys talk about it every year. We have to go out and prove it."

Backing up Boller will be untested senior **Eric Holtfreter** (6-2, 230) and redshirt freshman **Reggie Robertson** (6-2, 185). Holtfreter is a strong, physical, drop-back style quarterback while Robertson could be utilized as a roll out passer. In an emergency, Holtfreter would get the call, but Robertson might be worked into games later in order to prepare him for the future.

RUNNING BACKS

Coaches from around the Pac-10 have stated that Cal has a load of talent at running back, yet the Bears have struggled with their rushing offense.

Borges will do what he can to change that as he tries to establish a running game that will keep opposing defenses from concentrating on pass coverage. Borges loves play-action, but that has little meaning when a team is averaging 3.4 yards a rush as Cal did last season.

Leading the way at tailback is junior **Joe Igber** (5-8, 200) a shifty, quick runner who has no peer in the Pac-10 in terms of changing direction while on the move. Igber's problem has been that he has been knocked off his feet by arm tackles. But Borges said his diminutive back has improved his strength in the off-season to combat that problem. Igber averaged 81.9 yards a game last season and he figures to improve that statistic as long as he remains healthy.

Borges said he has no problem running Igber 25 times or more a game because he doesn't take a lot of direct hits because of his elusiveness.

"He is as good a stop-and-go runner as I've coached," Borges said of Igber. "He has an uncanny ability to come out of piles. And now we want to get him more involved in the passing game."

Perhaps Borges' toughest task will be to keep backup tailbacks **Joe Echema** (5-11, 215), a junior, and **Saleem Muhammad** (6-0, 210), a senior, content. Muhammad started against Stanford last season and ran for 99 yards. He believes he deserves a shot at being the starter. Echema, whose top effort was a 72-yard performance against Fresno State, knows he is running out of time.

"I love that position," Borges said of his depth at tailback. "Anyone we line up can play the position. But football is about role playing. Not everyone can be the star."

Another task for Borges will be to work senior **Marcus Fields** (6-2, 220) into the equation. Fields, who sat out last season with a shoulder injury, is one of the few players on the team with breakaway speed. He has run for 1,525 yards during his career as a tailback and is expected to line up at fullback, H-back and tight end this season.

"Fields is a willing blocker and he can catch a lot of passes," Borges said. "He has a lot of skill. I'm constantly trying to figure out ways to incorporate him into the offense."

The more traditional fullbacks on the roster are junior **Ryan Stanger** (6-2, 245) and **Pana Faumuina** (6-0, 235), who will called upon to clear the way for Igber.

WIDE RECEIVERS/TIGHT ENDS

Cal's wide receiver unit is now serviceable, which is light years ahead of the situation in 1999. Holmoe cleaned house and recruited a horde of wideouts before last season and most contributed in one way or another.

Leading the group is junior **Derek Swafford** (5-10, 175), the old-man river of the team at 26. The former minor leaguer in the Pittsburgh Pirates' organization missed the first half of the season with a back injury, but caught 25 passes in the final six games for 335 yards (a 13.4 yards-per-catch average) and three touchdowns. Swafford's best attribute is his ability to be a playmaker, a guy who is hard to corral after the catch. Although he doesn't possess true breakaway speed, he is shifty and quick. Borges will try to work Swafford into short routes, such as middle screens, in order to showcase his athleticism.

Swafford and fellow junior college transfer **Charon Arnold** (5-11, 175), a senior, were expected to be starters for Cal last season, but each suffered an injury. Swafford was out the first half while Arnold was out the second half with a stress fracture of the lower leg. Arnold had 12 catches and two touchdowns in the first four games before being hindered the rest of the way.

Those injuries forced sophomores **Geoff McArthur** (6-1, 200) and **Chase Lyman** (6-4, 200) into duty. McArthur showed his big-play capability with 56- and 63-yard receptions. He had the most receiving yards (336) of any Cal player. Lyman finished the season with 19 catches for 313 yards and two touchdowns.

Besides those four, Cal has solid possession receivers in seniors **Sean Currin** (6-1, 190) and **Chad Heydorff** (6-1, 185).

"Our wide receivers are steady and dependable," Borges said. "And they are faster than I imagined."

At tight end, Cal has very little proven talent. Junior **Terrance Dotsy** (6-4, 280) lost weight in the off-season in an effort to improve his quickness and make himself a more viable receiver.

Backups **Tom Swoboda** (6-4, 235) and **Matt Schafer** (6-4, 245) don't appear ready for Pac-10 play. Incoming freshmen **Jordan Hunter** (6-6, 235) and **Brett Bischofberger** (6-3, 235) will be given every opportunity to win playing time. Borges likes to incorporate the tight end into his attack, but he might not have the personnel to do much with the position this season. However, Fields did see time at tight end in the summer, so he might end up there if no other player asserts himself.

OFFENSIVE LINE

Can this group stay healthy? That's the big question that might ultimately decide Cal's fate in 2001. Four starters return who have a combined 75 starts behind them, but other than sophomore offensive tackle **Mark Wilson** (6-6, 295), they have had their share of aches and pains.

Starting left tackle **Langston Walker** (6-8, 335) broke his ankle midway through last season and had to work his way back into playing shape during spring drills. Senior center Ludwig (6-4, 285) made the move from guard during the spring and has been plagued by minor injuries that have forced him to miss games in each of the last three seasons. Junior guard **Scott Tercero** (6-5, 295) got off to a slow start last season after knee surgery but he appears to be fully recovered. If those four players remain healthy, Cal should be in good shape.

Ludwig was a second-team All Pac-10 selection last season and Wilson was a third team freshman All American. Tercero was a freshman All American in 1999 before being slowed by injuries last season. The open position is right guard, where sophomore **Nolan Bluntzer** (6-4, 265) leads a group of candidates who are vying for the job. Bluntzer is a tough, active player who is a bit small for the position.

Former walk-on **Ryan Jones** (6-4, 270), a junior, is pushing Bluntzer. A wild card is sophomore guard **David Hays** (6-3, 285) who missed the 2000 season because of knee surgery after going into summer camp as a starter. If Hays returns healthy in the summer, he would complete a very talented unit.

Depth appears to be a major problem here. Backups on the line include senior **Nofoaalii Tuitama** (6-7, 285), redshirt freshman **Erik O'Brien** (6-8, 295), sophomore **Chris Murphy** (6-6, 300) and sophomore **Nick Shaeffer** (6-5, 295).

2000 STATISTICS

Rushing offense	123.9	80
Passing offense	193.5	76
Total offense	317.5	93
Scoring offense	22.4	80
Net Punting	35.0	46
Punt returns	9.7	51
Kickoff returns	20.2	44
Rushing defense	110.8	24
Passing efficiency defense	126.8	87
Total defense	365.4	57
Scoring defense	26.8	72
Turnover margin	-4	80

Last column is ranking among Division I-A teams.

KICKERS

After playing musical place-kickers in 1999, Holmoe decided to stick with sophomore **Mark Jensen** (6-2, 185) last season. Jensen responded by hitting 11-of-16 and 10 of his final 12. He made 11-of-13 attempts from 40 yards or less.

Those numbers have convinced Holmoe to stick with Jensen unless something goes wrong. Sophomore **Jeremy Hershey** (6-0, 205) has a strong leg and redshirt freshman **Anthony Fassero** (6-1, 200) has looked good in practice, but the job is Jensen's to lose.

DEFENSIVE LINE

All America defensive end Andre Carter and rock-solid defensive tackle Jacob Waasdorp are gone, so Cal fans, if not the coaches, panicked. How can the Bears make up for the loss of those two players? Defensive coordinator Lyle Setencich wrapped up the answer easily.

"We can't replace them," he said. "We might coach another 50 years and not see another Andre Carter." Carter gets to stay in the Bay area after the San Francisco 49ers made a trade to be able to draft him in April. A deal with the Seattle Seahawks enabled the 49ers to take Carter as the seventh pick in the first round.

Clearly a talent the likes of Carter will be missed, but Setencich believes he can field a respectable line that will do its job and allow a very deep linebackers and secondary corps to do their job.

"I like this defense," Setencich said. "There is something charismatic about them and their work ethic."

Perhaps the one sure thing on the line this season is junior **Tully Banta-Cain** (6-4, 250), a rush end who showed considerable improvement over the course of the 2000 season. He finished eighth in the conference with six sacks and he had 13 tackles for loss. He finished the season with five tackles for loss against Stanford.

Other than Banta-Cain, the rest of the line is up for grabs. Junior college transfer **Tom Canada** (6-3, 265), a junior, made a big push during spring drills to win a defensive end slot. Canada played last season at Hancock (Calif.) Junior College, where he made 16 sacks for California's top-ranked junior college defense. Canada was a first-team all-league pick and honorable mention All-America selection.

After quitting school a year ago, junior defensive end **Jamaal Cherry** (6-4, 260) is back and looking very fast. Junior **Daniel Nwangwu** (6-4, 290) and sophomore **Josh Beckham** (6-2, 280) lead the group for candidates to start at the two inside tackle slots. Redshirt freshman **Jonathan Giesel** (6-2, 285) is slightly behind those two.

When summer camp opens, senior **Tim Pompa** (6-3, 275) and junior college transfer **Josh Gustaveson** (6-3, 250) will join the mix at defensive end. And All America freshman **Lorenzo Alexander** (6-3, 280) will be given a chance to start somewhere on the line.

Pompa is back after sitting out last season for failing a steriod test. Gustaveson, a junior, had 18.5 sacks last season at Snow Junior College in Utah. Alexander had 17 sacks for St. Mary's High in Berkeley.

Adding to the depth are redshirt freshmen **Tom Sverchek** (6-3, 290), **Chris Linderman** (6-3, 245) and **Louis-Phillippe Ladouceur** (6-5, 260).

"We're going to be young and inexperienced on the line," Setencich said. "But they have dramatically improved since the first day of spring.

LINEBACKERS

The impact player of this group is senior outside linebacker **Scott Fujita** (6-5, 250), a guy who just a year ago was pondering retirement because of a neck injury. Doctors took care of the problem and Fujita went on to record 13 tackles for loss in 2000. Now completely healthy, Fujita has been able to bulk up with 10 more pounds and Setencich predicts he'll have a huge season.

"He looks a lot better than I thought he could be," Setencich said.

Backing up Fujita will be junior **Calvin Hosey** (6-4, 235), a quick player who might eventually be used elsewhere because of his talent.

Setencich uses linebacker by committee to handle the other two inside positions. Junior **John Klotsche** (6-0, 240), junior **Matt Nixon** (6-1, 220) and senior **Chris Ball** (6-3, 220) all have proven they can be effective at the Pac-10 level. Nixon had 15 tackles for loss last season and Ball has tremendous quickness that makes him a threat to blitz on every play.

Senior **J.P. Segura** (6-0, 235) and senior **Jason Smith** (6-0, 230) have seen lots of action and could step into the lineup without a drop in the level of play.

Junior **Marcus Daniels** (6-1, 230), redshirt freshman **Eli Thompson** (6-2, 230) and redshirt freshman **Brian Tremblay** (6-1, 230) will be vying to win playing time.

DEFENSIVE BACKS

The sky is the limit. Junior cornerback **Jemeel Powell** (6-1, 185) has very quickly become one of the nation's top defensive backs. Despite missing three games during his sophomore season, he had 16 pass deflections to go with a team-high four interceptions. He is a confident, athletically gifted difference maker.

Consider the impact three of Powell's four interceptions had in Cal's three wins. Against Utah, Powell picked off a pass in the corner of the end zone at the end of the first half to stop a Ute threat to take the halftime lead. In the third overtime against UCLA, he out-jumped Bruin receiver Brian Poli-Dixon for an interception in the end zone to give Cal the victory. Powell's fourth-quarter interception at USC prevented any Trojan comeback attempt and helped preserve another Cal win.

On the other side, junior **LaShaun Ward** (6-1, 195) offers the same kind of athletic talent as Powell, but he has to show he has developed the saavy to dominate at the position. Ward has suffered lapses at times in terms of his decision making, and those can lead to big plays for the opposition. If Ward becomes consistent, pro scouts will take notice.

Cal should have some depth at cornerback as sophomores **Atari Callen** (5-9, 190) and **James Bethea** (5-11, 190) have both seen considerable action. Junior college transfer **Ray Carmel** (5-11, 185) is expected to step right into the rotation. Carmel, a junior, was a triple threat at Moorpark (Calif.) Junior College, playing tailback and returning kicks in addition to his defensive duties. Carmel had 1,300 all-purpose yards a year ago, 19th among California junior college players.

At free safety, Cal has an honors candidate in junior **Nnamdi Asomugha** (6-2, 210), a big hitter who started all 11 games last season. A year ago, Asomugha led Cal with 76 tackles, 48 of them unassisted. He ranked fourth among returning Pac-10 defensive backs in tackles.

In the off-season, some extensive weight-room work added 10 pounds to Asomugha's frame.

The question for Cal is strong safety, where junior **Bert Watts** (6-1, 210) and senior **Dewey Hale** (6-0, 205) split time last season. Hale had 50 tackles and Watts made 36, but neither showed the consistency that would make the coaching staff happy. Because no one appears ready to step in front of those two, either Watts or Hale will have to make a big step up.

Redshirt freshman **Perron Wiley** (6-0, 210) and sophomore **James Smith** (6-1, 190) don't appear ready to handle significant time, although both have bright futures.

PUNTERS

With Nick Harris, the NCAA's all-time record holder for most punts and yardage in a career, off to the Denver Broncos, the Bears will be experimenting to find a capable replacement.

Sophomore **Tyler Fredrickson** (6-3, 205) came out of spring drills as No. 1 on the depth chart. Hershey looked good at times, but was inconsistent. Redshirt freshman Fassero also was in the mix. To add to the competition, Holmoe said he recruited two walk-on punters to join the fray in August.

"I've got to remind myself at times that this is going to be different," Holmoe said. "For four years, we had NFL quality punting. Most teams are like the way we are now."

SPECIAL TEAMS

Trying to find long snappers has taken on the look of a casting call for a Broadway play. Line up and show your stuff. During spring drills, no one looked capable of handing the punt-snapping chores. Balls were all over the field.

Fortunately for Cal, Nixon will be able to snap in a pinch. Nixon broke a bone in his hand during spring drills and wasn't available to snap. Holmoe didn't mind because he wanted to find another capable snapper because Nixon holds down a key blocking position (just in front of the punter) on the punt team. The punt blocking was nightmarish last season as blown assignments turned into lost games.

Special teams coach LeCharls McDaniel, the former Washington Redskins special teams coach, was hired this season to straighten out the problems.

"We have a coach now who can pinpoint what we need to do," Fredrickson said. "He has us on film, and he goes over and dissects it."

McDaniel should have some ammunition to work with on the kickoff return and punt return teams. Powell was fifth in the country with an 18.2 yards per punt return average, a mark that was a Cal record. Powell had 83- and 38-yard punt returns and was chosen second-team All-Pac 10 as a return specialist. Besides Powell, Ward, Callen, Bethea and Carmel are capable return specialists.

"I'm just getting acclimated to the environment and what the guys can and can't do," McDaniel said. "We,re looking for consistency right now, that's the main factor."

RECRUITING CLASS

Once again, Holmoe said his recruiting class was solid even if deemed unspectacular by those who rate such things.

The highest profile prep signed by Holmoe was St. Mary's-Berkeley defensive lineman Lorenzo Alexander (6-3, 280). He was the Bears' only *Parade* and *SuperPrep* All-American. PrepStar rated him as the No. 2 defensive line prospect in the West. He had 17 sacks and 25 tackles for loss for St. Mary's in his senior season. Most of the other signees were a notch below Alexander's status, although the Cal coaching staff was just as high on several of them.

Safety **Ryan Foltz** (6-2, 195) out of Westlake (Calif.) High School is considered a diamond in the rough. He has great speed and was an all-league volleyball player.

In terms of playing right away, tight end Jordan Hunter probably has the best shot among the high school signees. As far as the future goes, tailback **Terrell Williams** (6-0, 195) of Hoover-San Diego was recruited away from USC, LSU, Texas A&M and ASU. He has been clocked in 10.8 for the 100 meters.

Quarterback **Richard Schwartz** (6-4, 205) should help solidify the depth at his position. *PrepStar* rated him as the ninth-best quarterback recruit in the West. Among the junior college transfers, Canada and Gustaveson are players who are expected to compete for a starting spot on the defensive line. Carmel adds much needed depth at defensive back.

BLUE RIBBON ANALYSIS

OFFENSE	B-
SPECIAL TEAMS	C-
DEFENSE	B
INTANGIBLES	B

Cal has a lot of players walking around who have been through the mill. If you indeed learn from your mistakes, experience should be a factor pushing Cal toward a bowl berth.

Holmoe took major steps to correct problems by hiring Borges as his offensive coordinator and McDaniel as his special teams coach. If Cal's offensive and defensive lines hold up, this could be the surprise team of the Pac-10.

Cal's schedule sets it up for a fast start, and if Boller gets a little confidence, a bowl should be expected. What kind of bowl probably will be determined by injuries. While Cal's starters can compete with just about any Pac-10 team, Holmoe doesn't have the depth to survive significant losses.

(J.H.)

2000 RESULTS

Utah	W	24-21	1-0
Illinois	L	15-17	1-1
Fresno State	L	3-17	1-2
Washington State	L	17-21	1-3
Arizona State	L	10-30	1-4
UCLA	W	46-38	2-4
Washington	L	24-36	2-5
USC	W	28-16	3-5
Oregon State	L	32-38	3-6
Oregon	L	17-25	3-7
Stanford	L	30-36	3-8

Oregon

LOCATION	**Eugene, OR**
CONFERENCE	**Pac-10**
LAST SEASON	**10-2 (.833)**
CONFERENCE RECORD	**7-1 (t-1st)**
OFFENSIVE STARTERS RETURNING	**8**
DEFENSIVE STARTERS RETURNING	**4**
NICKNAME	**Ducks**
COLORS	**Green & Yellow**
HOME FIELD	**Autzen Stadium (41,698)**
HEAD COACH	**Mike Bellotti (UC-Davis '73)**
RECORD AT SCHOOL	**49-22 (6 years)**
CAREER RECORD	**72-47-2 (11 years)**
ASSISTANTS	**Nick Aliotti (UC-Davis '76)** Defensive Coordinator
	Gary Campbell (UCLA '73) Running Backs
	Dan Ferrigno (San Francisco State '75) Wide Receivers
	Mike Gillhamer (Humboldt State '76) Secondary
	Steve Greatwood (Oregon '80) Defensive Line
	Don Pellum (Oregon '84) Linebackers
	Robin Ross (Washington State '77) Special Teams/Tight Ends
	Jeff Tedford (Fresno State '83) Offensive Coordinator
	Neal Zoumboukos (UC-Davis '68) Offensive Line
TEAM WINS (last 5 yrs.)	**6-7-8-9-10**
FINAL RANK (last 5 yrs.)	**36-38-29-17-10**
2000 FINISH	**Beat Texas in Holiday Bowl.**

COACH AND PROGRAM

The numbers at Oregon get downright scary.

Senior quarterback **Joey Harrington** (6-4, 220) led the Pac-10 in total offense last season with 256.3 yards a game. He's back.

Senior tailback **Maurice Morris** (6-0, 205) was second in the conference in rushing last season at 100.5 yards per game. He's back.

In all, eight members of the Ducks' potent offense that put up 408.9 yards a game are back.

Most of all, head coach Mike Bellotti, the guy who has transformed Oregon into the Pac-10's most consistent powerhouse, is back. Bellotti was getting all kinds of feelers last season from programs that wondered if he could work the same magic in their town that he has done in Eugene, Ore. When the dust cleared, Bellotti stayed at home and started preparing for 2001.

It should be a fun and rewarding season for Ducks fans, who are accustomed now to bowl appearances. Last year it was the Holiday Bowl, a game in which the Ducks beat Texas, 35-30.

Lest you forget, Oregon was the Pac-10 tri-champion (7-1) last season. Washington got the Rose Bowl berth and Oregon State got all the money by participating in the Fiesta Bowl, while Oregon had to settle for the Holiday and a 10-2 overall record.

A narrow 27-23 loss at Wisconsin in the second week of the season and a 23-13 loss at Oregon State were the only things separating the Ducks from an amazing season.

Now 2001 is here and Harrington and company would like to do something really special. In case you haven't heard, the Rose Bowl this season is operating as the national championship game. In order to get to that game, the Pac-10 champion probably needs to go undefeated.

Nobody knows that more than the Ducks, who play host to Wisconsin in the season opener. In past years, such a game would work more as preparation for the tough Pac-10 schedule. But these days, the Ducks are dreaming big.

"The next step up for us would be to go undefeated," said Harrington, 14-2 as a starting quarterback. "A lot of it has to do with timing, getting the right break, putting ourselves in a position to go undefeated.

"I think this year we have a better chance of doing it because of our experience and our talent. This is the most talented team we've had here. The guys who we will have out there who are making contributions have been out there for two or three years. We know how to win close games. If you look at the numbers, I think we've gone 10-1 in games the last two seasons that have come down to the last series."

Downright scary.

Harrington attributes much of that success to the atmosphere—created by the coaching staff—at Oregon.

"Personally, I think it has a lot to do with the relationship of the players," he said. "It might sound hokey, but we are a family here. Ninety to 95 percent of the players stay here in the summer. We have barbecues, we go rafting, we learn each other's ins and outs. We learn how each person will react in certain situations. We know each and every player is our friend and that they will watch our back."

Bellotti surely knows his team is going to score a lot of points this season. But he's got something else on his mind. Oregon lost seven defensive starters from the 2000 squad. Of the four returning players, three are in the defensive backfield. There will be lots of points scored in Eugene this season, but by what team? Last year's defense was a huge part of the Ducks' success story, holding opponents to 19.9 points a game, the second-lowest total of any Pac-10 team.

Senior cornerback **Rashad Bauman** (5-8, 180) says not to worry.

"Things went well in the spring," he said. "I think we answered the questions we needed to answer. I really think our front seven is going to be our strength. We have linebackers who have been here since we were freshmen and they have the knowledge for the game. They just weren't starters."

Harrington isn't worried that the Ducks will be involved in shootout after shootout.

"I have a lot of confidence in our defense," he said. "Yeah, we graduated a lot of starters, but we also have guys like [sophomore] **Kevin Mitchell** (5-10, 210) and [senior] **Wesly Mallard** (6-2, 215) who are starters that they aren't counting as starters. We've got a lot of guys on defense who have played a lot of significant minutes.

"I thought our defense made significant strides in the spring. They were fast and the played hard. Our backers especially—and we've had some great linebackers the last few years—were fast. I haven't seen that kind of speed here at linebacker."

The head coach agrees with Harrington's assessment. In fact, he says Oregon has speed everywhere.

"This could be the fastest team we've ever had," he said. "But I still want to see that translated to performance on the field. You can talk about speed, you can talk about strength, but what I want to talk about is performance on the football field. I would like to believe that by us being a step faster as a team, we can be as good or better than we were last year."

Bellotti knows that if his team is going to be ranked among the best in the nation, he has some holes to plug. Not only did he lose a lot of defensive starters, he lost some excellent special teams players, including both his main return men, his punter and place-kicker. He knows pollsters that rate his team in the top 10 probably aren't examining his problems.

"I don't worry very much about what people say in the early-season or preseason polls," he said. "The only poll I'm interested in is the final one.

"I do think that it's exciting for athletes, our boosters and alumni that Oregon is mentioned with the best programs in the nation, and I certainly think we deserve to be there because we've earned that right. But I think you have to earn it every year. Preseason publications are just that. It gives us some positive fuel for the first, but it's something that you've got to live up to, and you've got to do it every Saturday in the fall when it counts."

And while his offense seems primed to make every snap count, Bellotti knows the other areas are just as important.

"The number one priority in the spring was the kicking game because we have a new punter, three new people competing for the place-kicking job, a new special teams coordinator and a new long snapper," he said. "Obviously, I have huge concerns at this point about the traditional excellence of our kicking game.

"The second major question is our defense. We lost some key people there. We need to create opportunities to discover who are going to be the players there, especially at the linebacker positions."

Of course, Bellotti has faced similar problems in the past and usually has found a way to keep his team in the bowl picture.

"Last year there were several seniors who stepped up," he said. "Which you would expect from someone who had been in the program for four or five years. This year, we're faced with some younger players needing to be ready, but I think that's all right. It isn't as much a question of whether they are physically ready to compete, it's more a mental mind-set. What we have to do as coaches and as a team is prepare some young players to be ready for their opportunity."

After the tough opener with Wisconsin, the Ducks play host to Utah, a team that fell on its face in 2000. The Pac-10 season opens a week later with a home game against USC, followed by the final non-conference game against Utah State.

Oregon never will be accused of having a killer non-conference agenda. Just like last season, when the conference title couldn't be decided because Oregon and Washington didn't play each other, the two teams miss each other again in 2001. Oregon's two biggest games really are its final two, an away date at UCLA and a home finale against rival Oregon State.

One thing is certain: Every opponent will gear up for the Ducks, who no longer are considered a surprise team when they creep into the national rankings.

"Some people are starting to notice us," Bauman said. "But I think some people still have doubts about us. There are people out there who call us the Oregon Beavers. We just want to let our actions do the talking."

2001 SCHEDULE

Sept.	1	Wisconsin
	8	Utah
	22	USC
	29	@Utah State
Oct.	6	@Arizona
	13	@California
	20	Stanford
	27	@Washington State
Nov.	3	Arizona State
	10	@UCLA
	17	Oregon State

QUARTERBACKS

Besides leading the conference in total offense, Harrington was No. 1 in passing yardage (247.3) and touchdown passes (22). Only Danny O'Neal (1993 and Bill Musgrave (1989) had better numbers at Oregon than Harrington as a nonsenior. Harrington completed 212-of-405 passes (52.8 percent) last season for 2,967 yards with 14 interceptions. He piled up 3,091 yards of total offense.

Besides being so effective as a passer, Harrington also proved he was effective on an occasional run. He scored six rushing touchdowns last season and finished with 125 rushing yards.

"The one thing I know about Harrington is that he is not going to rest on his laurels," Bellotti said. "He has the team's ultimate performance as his barometer for what he wants to do. I'm excited about that. The combination of his ability to perform and his ability to lead are the most exciting aspects of his play."

Harrington expects the offense's level of play to be very high. Asked how the Ducks' spring drills went in terms of offense Harrington answered, "Great. We didn't miss a step. Usually the guys have to get acquainted in the spring, but we brought so many guys back. We stepped right in and picked it up."

As usual at Oregon, there seems to be no shortage of quarterbacks. Although he has no experience, sophomore **Jason Fife** (6-4, 215) had a super spring and appears capable to run the attack if anything happens to Harrington. Also available is redshirt freshman **Scott Vossmeyer** (6-3, 220) and freshman **Chris Lombardo** (6-1, 210).

RUNNING BACKS

Morris is the story here. He came from Fresno City Junior College and lived up to his reputation as the nation's No. 1 junior college recruit. He showed his toughness by pounding inside to pick up yards, and also displayed his explosiveness (his long was 66 yards). He scored eight touchdowns an averaged 4.2 yards a carry.

"Morris takes a lot of pressure off me," Harrington said. "In the games I was going 9-for-21 and wasn't on top of my game, we would give it to Mo and he would run for 160. He is the kind of guy who can take over a game with one big run or just pound away. He is tough, quick, a great competitor."

Even though Harrington is the top returning quarterback in the conference, opponents have to prepare for Morris.

"Mo is such a threat," Harrington said. "A good example was last season against USC. I hadn't had a great start, so they put eight or nine guys in the box [to stop Morris]. We threw for 350 yards on them."

Junior **Allan Amundson** (5-9, 185) had 235 yards as Morris' main backup last season. Amundson averaged 3.8 yards a carry and scored two touchdowns.

Sophomores **Onterrio Smith** (5-11, 200), **Kenny Washington** (6-0, 195) and **Ryan Shaw** (5-11, 195) all hope to get into the picture in the future. Washington gained 50 yards on 11 carries and Shaw had eight carries for 30 yards last season. Smith is a transfer from Tennessee who sat out last season.

Senior fullback **Josh Line** (6-2, 240) is the returning starter who concentrates mostly on blocking. Line had 13 carries for 32 yards last season. Sophomore fullback Josh Rogers (6-3, 255) had some good moments in spring camp when Line sat out with a shoulder injury and he is hoping to win some snaps.

WIDE RECEIVERS/TIGHT ENDS

Keenan Howry (5-10, 170) in two years has become an awesome weapon. The junior caught 52 balls for 780 yards last season with five touchdowns. Now that Marshaun Tucker has graduated, Howry becomes the focus of Oregon's passing game. He had a long gain of 66 yards last season and he is a threat to go all the way every time he touches the ball. Harrington said he has developed a special bond with Howry.

"I've been throwing to him since the first day he stepped on the field," Harrington said. "I feel confident I know where he is going to be. And he has gotten so much faster since he came here. He is running 4.3, 4.4 now."

It will be an interesting battle to see who emerges as Oregon's No. 2 wideout. Redshirt freshman **Keith Allen** (6-1, 205) had a big spring and he might be ready to play. Junior wide receiver **Jason Willis** (6-1, 190) is back after catching 21 balls for 204 yards last season. Sophomore **Samie Parker** (5-10, 165) returns after an 11-catch, 201-yard season.

Others trying to win snaps are redshirt freshmen **Keith Allen** (6-1, 205), **Joey McCollum** (5-10, 175) and **Paris Warren** (6-1, 210) sophomore Gary Daniels (6-2, 175) and junior **Cy Aleman** (6-3, 200). Aleman had two catches for 34 yards in 2000.

At tight end, senior **Justin Peelle** (6-5, 245) is a returning starter who caught 24 passes for 388 yards and five touchdowns in 2000. Filling out the depth chart are redshirt freshmen **Willie Walden** (6-6, 270) and **Aaron Trimm** (6-3, 250).

OFFENSIVE LINE

Three starters return from the 2000 line, but Bellotti isn't quite sure where they are going to be lining up in 2001. Sophomore **Joey Forster** (6-4, 295) will again be a right guard, that much is known. Coming out of spring, it appears that senior **Ryan Schmid** (6-4, 280) will handle the center duties with senior **Jim Adams** (6-4, 295) at left guard.

That would put junior **Phil Finzer** (6-5, 300) at right tackle and junior **Corey Chambers** (6-4, 320) at left tackle.

If any of that doesn't work out, Bellotti might add sophomore **Dan Weaver** (6-4, 295) to the equation and shift everyone else around. Adams is versatile enough to play guard or center, so he could move over a spot. In that scenario, Schmid would slide over to play guard.

One of the factors that make the lineup somewhat questionable is that Chambers missed almost all of spring ball with a shoulder injury. Also out for the spring was junior **Josh Jones** (6-2, 285), who had an ankle injury.

Others trying to break into the lineup are redshirt freshmen **Josh Atkins** (6-5, 320), **Michael Delagrange** (6-6, 330), **Robin Knebel** (6-5, 315), **Adam Snyder** (6-4, 300) and **Nick Steitz** (6-4, 295), juniors **Mike Belisle** (6-5, 320) and **Pat Fields** (6-1, 265) and senior **Jesse Wallace** (6-6, 280).

"The big question for us on offense is which group of five offensive linemen will be the best group for us to play with," Bellotti said.

2000 STATISTICS

Rushing offense	151.2	52
Passing offense	257.7	25
Total offense	408.9	34
Scoring offense	29.5	42
Net Punting	37.7	14
Punt returns	7.7	88
Kickoff returns	22.5	14
Rushing defense	124.0	31
Passing efficiency defense	103.0	17
Total defense	331.1	32
Scoring defense	19.9	31
Turnover margin	+3	46

Last column is ranking among Division I-A teams.

KICKERS

Last year's place-kicker, Josh Frankel, didn't have a real solid year as he made 13-of-25 field goals. But while he might not have been stellar, it always is uncomfortable for a team when the incumbent leaves.

Freshman **Jared Siegel** (5-10, 170) and juniors **Navid Niakan** (6-1, 180) and **David Rosenberg** (6-0, 195) have never kicked in a Division I-A game and they are currently the main players competing for a very important job. Niakan transfered from Chabot College in Hayward, Calif., and Rosenberg is a transfer from Eastern Michigan.

DEFENSIVE LINE

Replacing impact player Saul Patu, who had 19 tackles for loss and 11 quarterback sacks in 2000, is the main goal. Patu and graduated defensive linemen Jed Boice and Jason Nikolao combined for 34 tackles for loss last season, so there is a lot of replacing to do.

Junior defensive end **Seth McEwen** (6-5, 255) is the lone returning starter and he had the fewest numbers of the starting linemen last year with 16 tackles, including four for loss. Senior defensive tackle **Zack Freiter** (6-3, 280) started the final four games of last season and he will hold down one of the interior positions. Freiter had 23 tackles and four for loss last season.

Junior defensive end **Quinn Dorsey** (6-4, 255) had a big spring and appears to have taken the lead for the other defensive end job. He saw limited action in 2000 and finished with two tackles.

"I thought he did some good things in the spring," Bellotti said. "We've know that he is athletically gifted. There are some technique things and some intensity things that he needs to work on, but I thought he made some strides."

Redshirt freshman **Igor Olshansky** (6-6, 290) might be ready to assume a starting spot at defensive tackle.

Others trying to win a job on the defensive line are seniors **Mac Russell** (6-6, 310) and **Chris Tetterton** (6-0, 275), juniors **Craig Dukes** (6-3, 250), **Adam Isfeld** (6-0, 255), **Eric Johnson** (6-3, 250), **Kai Smalley** (6-2, 270) and **Ed Wangler**

(6-4, 260) and redshirt freshmen **Kevin Mack** (6-2, 240) and **David Toomey** (6-1, 270),

LINEBACKERS

One of Oregon's huge losses was middle linebacker Matt Smith, another tackling machine that Bellotti seems to produce on a yearly basis. Smith had 90 tackles last season, including 11 for loss. Also gone is inside linebacker Michael Callier and outside linebacker Garrett Sabol. Sabol was Oregon's second-leading tackler last season with 58 stops, 11 for loss. Callier produced 54 tackles and had nine for a loss. That's a lot of tackles to replace.

Trying to nail down this season's starting positions are a trio of players who all have played limited roles, junior **Garret Graham** (6-4, 235), Mallard and Mitchell. Mitchell made the biggest impact last season with 39 tackles, including four for loss. Mallard (perfect name for a Duck) turned in 26 tackles with three for loss. Graham had 13 tackles.

They will be pushed by juniors **David Moretti** (6-1, 235) and **John Harris** (6-0, 235) and redshirt freshman **Ryan Loftin** (6-3, 230) and **Jerry Matson** (6-0, 210).

Junior college transfer **David Martin** (5-11, 205) is arriving in summer camp and he will get a long look.

DEFENSIVE BACKS

Bauman, who had four interceptions last season to tie for the team lead with the departed Smith, registered 32 tackles in 2000. He said he will do what he can to help out his inexperienced teammates this season.

"I will do my part," Bauman said. "But I'm not really a vocal leader. We'll let the young guys speak for us. They bring all kinds of new stuff with them, new lingo."

Bauman said if the defense can be consistent, the Ducks should win a lot of games.

"Joey [Harrington] and Mo [Morris] can put up 40 points a game," he said.

Senior **Steve Smith** (6-1, 190) starts at the other cornerback spot. He had 38 tackles last season, but 32 of them were unassisted.

At free safety, junior **Rasuli Webster** (6-0, 210) was an impact player last season with 59 tackles. Sophomore **Keith Lewis** (6-1, 190) has made a huge impression and it appears he will take over at strong safety. The coaching staff might ultimately decide to swap Lewis and Webster at the two safety positions.

Backing up at cornerback are sophomores **A.K. Keyes** (5-9, 170) and **Steven Moore** (5-9, 170). The backups at safety are redshirt freshman **Stephen Clayton** (5-11, 190) and senior **Gary McGraw** (5-9, 180).

PUNTERS

Kurtis Doerr averaged 40.7 yards a punt last season and has moved on. That has to be disturbing to Bellotti because Oregon led the conference in net punting at 37.7 yards a kick. Junior college transfer **Jose Arroyo** (5-11, 185) is the bet to replace Doerr. Last year at Pasadena (Calif.) City College, Arroyo averaged 37.5 yards per punt while downing 14 of his 38 tries inside the 20-yard line. He had a long punt of 70 yards.

SPECIAL TEAMS

New special teams coordinator Robin Ross returns to the program after two years as an assistant with the Raiders, and he hopes to continue the good work done by Tom Osborne, who left to take the special teams job at Arizona State.

Oregon's return teams should again be in good shape. Amundson averaged 23.9 yards per return and the team was 14th in the country in that category with a 22.54 average. Howry averaged eight yards a punt return and is a danger to score every time he touches the ball.

The coaching staff thinks Lewis is an exceptional return man and he will be worked into the mix this season.

The Ducks were also good in other areas. They led the Pac-10 in kickoff coverage, holding teams to a 16.1-yard average.

RECRUITING CLASS

With the defense losing so many bodies, as well as a punter, Bellotti went for the quick fix in the junior college market, signing six players. All are juniors.

Defensive linemen **Junior Siavii** (6-5, 335) and **Darrell Wright** (6-3, 235), Martin and cornerback **Countney Miller** (6-1, 190) all will get a shot at earning significant snaps immediately. Siavii comes from Butte (Calif.) College, where he had 58 tackles and nine sacks as a nose tackle. Wright is out of Reedley College in California, where he registered a school record 17 1/2 sacks last season. Martin had 91 tackles last season at Los Medanos (Calif.) College despite missing three games. Miller arrives from Fort Scott Community College in Kansas, where he broke up eight passes last season.

The marquee signee from the high school class was **Kellen Clemens** (6-2, 190) out of Burns, Ore. The *Parade* and *USA Today* All-American was ranked as the third best quarterback in the country by PrepStar. Clemens threw for 3,226 yards and 37 touchdowns his senior season.

The Ducks will get help at wide receiver from **Demetrius Williams** (6-1, 160) from Pittsburg (Calif.) High School. He was a *SuperPrep* All-American and a unanimous pick on the *Long Beach Telegram*'s Best in the West team. He had 34 catches for 829 yards last season. He was a member of the *Contra Costa Times*' Cream of the Crop team.

BLUE RIBBON ANALYSIS

OFFENSE	A+
SPECIAL TEAMS	C
DEFENSE	C+
INTANGIBLES	A

Fans will be looking at offense at its finest this season in Eugene and Harrington and company should have plenty of firepower to handle almost every challenge that comes their way.

However, those one or two games that will decide the conference championship probably won't go Oregon's way this season because of its defensive inexperience.

Replacing Patu might be one big headache that Bellotti won't be able to overcome. Having a big-play guy on the defense is essential in those last couple of minutes that decide games. Teams can't always survive by sending linebackers blitzing to the quarterback. And if Oregon doesn't find some effective defensive linemen, it will be hard pressed to compete with teams such as UCLA with tailback DeShaun Foster, USC with tailback Sultan McCullough and rival Oregon State with tailback Ken Simonton.

It appears to be the year of the tailback in the Pac-10 and opponents will have to find a way to stop that rushing attack or watch with its offense standing on the sideline. The best way to beat Oregon is to keep its offense off the field, so opposing coaches should be content to blast away at the middle of the line, especially if the Ducks are soft up front.

Of course, that's a nice thought for opponents, but Bellotti always seems to find people to come through, and this season might not be any different. Another Pac-10 championship certainly is a possibility, but the bet here is that the Ducks fall just a bit short. A return to the Holiday Bowl wouldn't be a huge surprise.

(J.H.)

2000 RESULTS

Nevada	W	36-7	1-0
Wisconsin	L	23-27	1-1
Idaho	W	42-13	2-1
UCLA	W	29-10	3-1
Washington	W	23-16	4-1
USC	W	28-17	5-1
Arizona	W	14-10	6-1
Arizona State	W	56-55	7-1
Washington State	W	27-24	8-1
California	W	25-17	9-1
Oregon State	L	13-23	9-2
Texas (Holiday Bowl)	W	35-30	10-2

Oregon State

LOCATION	**Corvallis, OR**
CONFERENCE	**Pac-10**
LAST SEASON	**11-1 (.917)**
CONFERENCE RECORD	**7-1 (t-1st)**
OFFENSIVE STARTERS RETURNING	**4**
DEFENSIVE STARTERS RETURNING	**5**
NICKNAME	**Beavers**
COLORS	**Orange & Black**
HOME FIELD	**Reser Stadium (35,362)**
HEAD COACH	**Dennis Erickson (Montana State '69)**
RECORD AT SCHOOL	**18-6 (2 years)**
CAREER RECORD	**131-46-1 (15 years)**
ASSISTANTS	**Craig Bray (UNLV '75)** Defensive Coordinator
	Dan Cozzetto (Idaho '79) Running backs
	Michael Gray (Oregon '83) Defensive Line
	Tim Lappano (Idaho '80) Offensive Coordinator
	Jim Michalczik (Washington State '89) Special Teams
	Greg Newhouse (Nevada-Reno '76) Linebackers
	Al Simmons (Hayward '83) Secondary
	Greg Smith (Idaho '69) Offensive Line
	Eric Yarber (Idaho '95) Wide Receivers
TEAM WINS (last 5 yrs.)	**2-3-5-7-11**
FINAL RANK (last 5 yrs.)	**72-60-41-67-5**
2000 FINISH	**Beat Notre Dame in Fiesta Bowl.**

COACH AND PROGRAM

They have been to the promised land. What now?

One of the NCAA's longest running jokes only a few years back, Oregon State followed coach Dennis Erickson's lead and raced to the top of the charts in 2000.

The Beavers' amazing 11-1 season was capped by a 41-9 blowout of Notre Dame in the Fiesta Bowl that had to shock fans in every corner of the United States, except for those in Pac-10 cities.

It was evident on the West Coast that the Beavers were for real. Even so, college football fans could be forgiven if they watched the rout of Notre Dame with their jaws dropped to the coffee table. Even the Beavers were surprised by the outcome.

"It was so great," Oregon State senior quarterback **Jonathan Smith** (5-11, 200) said. "So many things were going through my head in that game against Notre Dame. There were so many guys on that team that I just enjoyed being around. But I guess my favorite memory from the season was just hanging out on the sidelines at the end of the Fiesta Bowl, taking pictures and enjoying the moment.

"We were garbage and we came full circle."

Smith, who didn't have any major bowl aspirations when he came to Oregon State, and who actually would have laughed at such a thought, doesn't mind admitting that he was shocked to be playing Notre Dame in a major bowl.

"No way," he said. "Not in my wildest dreams did I think we could be playing in that game. I was hoping that maybe we could go to some bowl game, that maybe we could have a winning season."

Oregon State broke a 28-year losing streak in 1999 and until the Fiesta Bowl, Smith's favorite moment in the program had been the day his team beat Cal in Corvallis in 1999 to seal its winning season (7-5).

"It was two different emotions," Smith said. "It was the ultimate high when people stormed the field after we beat Cal [in 1999]. People were crying. But then we lost in the Oahu Bowl, and that put a damper on the season."

There was no damper put on last season. In fact, it could have been argued that Oregon State deserved some consideration as being the nation's best team.

"We were the top of the top," Smith said.

Not everyone was as surprised by Oregon State's rise as Smith. Junior right cornerback **Dennis Weathersby** (6-1, 200) said he hadn't been around for OSU's ugly seasons, so he expected to win.

"I know last season meant a lot more for the program, the ex-players and the fans," said Weathersby, who enters his third season as a starter. "I didn't have to experience the losing seasons that they had to experience. My ambition was to get to the Rose Bowl. I thought we would have a shot, and it was up to us to take advantage of that shot."

Erickson got the Beavers to the top by rising them from trash can ashes.

"I've got the utmost respect for him," Smith said of Erickson. "It is a mystery to me how he pushes the buttons, gets guys to all go in the right direction. He is a genius."

Yeah, but what have you done for us lately?

Erickson will have to use every bit of that coaching genius to forge a repeat for Oregon State. He lost a ton of talent from the 2000 team and although he's got key personnel returning at running back and quarterback, he's got a lot of holes to plug with only 10 returning starters, fewest of any Pac-10 team.

"You don't lose guys like DeLawrence Grant, LaDairis Jackson, Darnell Robinson, Terrence Carroll and Keith Heyward and not be hurt," Erickson said. "We have some areas of concern. We lost some starters from last year who were very good players, so we have to fill those voids. The biggest thing we have to do is find out who the replacements will be in those areas."

Erickson's defense, which led the conference by allowing just 18.5 points a game and in fewest yards at 314.4, was especially hard hit.

"We lost both our defensive ends and we lost an outside linebacker," he said. "We also lost a cornerback and a safety."

Weathersby said the Beavers just need a little seasoning on defense.

"We have a lot of depth and we have a lot of speed," he said. "We do lack size. But it shouldn't be too hard as long as team chemistry is clicking, and it is. We have a lot of talent, a lot of young talent. It comes down to a lot of study and preparation."

Study and preparation are Erickson's specialties.

"He has done a lot for us," Weathersby said of his head coach. "He has given us perspective on what it takes to win. He has taken everything step by step. I don't worry about too much here. It is a laid-back atmosphere right now."

Weathersby doesn't have to answer to his friends anymore who used to tease, "Where is Oregon State at? Are they in the Pac-10?"

As Weathersby says, "It's cool."

But isn't there huge pressure to prove that last year wasn't a once-in-a-lifetime accomplishment?

"I don't look at it like pressure for us," Weathersby said. "It's all about doing our assignments. If we do our assignments, everything will take care of itself. As long as the defense plays consistent, we feel we will be successful."

Erickson says there is a little more to it than that. He said the offense has some holes to plug, too.

"Offensively, we lost all three starting receivers," Erickson said. "We lost our top two tight ends and some people on the offensive front. Really, the only area where we are in good shape is at running back and quarterback on offense."

Yeah, but in those areas he is in great shape. Erickson has enough gifted athletes returning that he should be able to hold off any full-blown collapse. After all, he does have one of the nation's top running backs returning in senior **Ken Simonton** (5-8, 195).

Simonton is trying to become the first player in Pac-10 history to run for 1,000 yards in four seasons. His 1,474 rushing yards last season were just short of the 1,486 yards he had as a sophomore. He rushed for 1,028 yards as a freshman. His first two seasons he set Pac-10 records for most yards by a freshman and a sophomore. Besides all those yards, Simonton scored 18 touchdowns last season.

Although Simonton will go into this season billed as a Heisman candidate (Terry Baker was Oregon State's last winner in 1962), his chances probably aren't good considering the Beavers could well be in a rebuilding mode.

Nonetheless, he has many records to eclipse. He needs 79 points to become the Pac-10's all-time leading scorer. His 4,073 yards rushing leaves him fifth all-time in the Pac-10. While he probably won't catch No. 1 Charles White (USC) who piled up 6,245 yards, No. 2 Marcus Allen (USC) at 4,810 is well within his sights.

To consider what he has done already, Anthony Davis and Charles White of USC, Darrin Nelson of Stanford, Russell White of Cal and Napoleon Kaufman of Washington are the only players ever to rush for 1,000 yards in three seasons. Only four players in Division I-A ever had four 1,000-yard seasons—Tony Dorsett, Amos Lawrence, Denvis Manns and Ron Dayne.

With 21 100-yard games to his credit already—including a 234-yard game against USC last season—it should be fun to watch Simonton pile up the yardage again this season.

If that's not enough, Erickson has at his disposal a tremendous backup tailback in senior **Patrick McCall** (5-10, 190), who proved last year he can be just as dangerous as his prolific teammate. McCall ran for 633 yards and seven touchdowns in 2000. His 5.3 yards per carry average were just short of Simonton's 5.5.

"Obviously our strengths are returnees at quarterback and our running game with Ken Simonton and Patrick McCall," Erickson said. "That is the type of team we are probably going to be this year. Our strength has to be running the football. I don't know that you will ever have a better one-two punch than Simonton and McCall.

"[To complement that] we need to have some development at wide receiver and we need guys who will make big plays. That has to happen for us."

Smith, who has started 27 consecutive games over the last three seasons, said his offensive teammates should come through just fine.

"We have quite a few starters graduating," he said. "But I think we can replace them. We have some guys who will have to step up even though they have a lack of experience. It doesn't mean they can't do it. It's just going to be a little different. We're going to have some new faces."

Unfortunately for Smith, he missed spring practice so he could start smoothing over some of the rough edges.

"I had surgery in January on my fractured [left, non-throwing] wrist," he said. "It wasn't healing right. I had a graft from my pelvis put into my wrist. They wanted to kick-start the healing."

Smith said he is confident he will be 100 percent when summer camp begins. When that camp begins, Oregon State will set its sight on repeating its 2000 performance.

"Our expectations are the same as when I came here three years ago," Erickson said. "Our goals are to win the Pac-10 championship and go to a bowl game. That is what our goals are every year and that is what they always will be here."

It doesn't seem likely, though, that Oregon State can surpass last season's amazing finish.

"Obviously it would be tough to take [another step]," Smith said. "I don't know that overall we're as talented as we were last season. But we might be a little tougher mentally, and we might realize what it takes to win. Again, it will come down to the ball bouncing the right way."

Erickson said he won't know too much about his team until it takes the field in the season opener at Fresno State. "I don't know you really find out what your true personality is until the season starts," he said.

Oregon State probably won't learn a lot about its personality until its Pac-10 opener on Sept. 29 when UCLA visits Corvallis. The Bruins certainly have the look of the Pac-10 favorite, so the Beavers will have to come out of the box hot.

The three non-conference games that precede UCLA aren't horribly tough. Fresno State is a tough place for any team to play, but the other two games are at New Mexico State and at home against Montana State.

Now that Oregon State has lost its reputation as one of the weak sisters of college football, Erickson will have to upgrade the schedule if he expects to get respect from the pollsters.

The Beavers' conference schedule in 2001 appears to be more than fair as they face UCLA and Washington, expected to be two of the tougher teams, at home.

2001 SCHEDULE

Sept.	1	@Fresno State
	8	North Texas
	15	Montana State
	29	UCLA
Oct.	6	@Washington State
	13	Arizona
	20	@Arizona State

	27	California
Nov.	3	@USC
	10	Washington
	17	@Oregon

QUARTERBACKS

He is not big enough. His arm isn't strong. He won't be a high choice in the NFL draft. Go ahead. Knock Smith. He is the guy who has led the Beavers to two consecutive bowl games, the guy who led the route of Notre Dame in the Fiesta Bowl. He is the guy who always seems to come up with the big plays at crunch time.

Smith holds team records for passing yardage (3,053 in 1999) and touchdown passes (20 in 2000). He is second in career passing yardage with 7,253 and second in total offense at 6,923. Against Notre Dame in the Fiesta Bowl, he completed 16-of-24 passes for 305 yards and three touchdowns. In his career, he has 41 touchdown passes to 19 interceptions.

After Smith's wrist surgery, the Beavers are hoping he is not only accurate but healthy.

Senior **Nick Stremick** (6-2, 200) is the only other OSU quarterback to have played in a college game. He has played in two. The hope of the future is sophomore **Shayne House** (6-5, 220), who is coming off shoulder surgery.

Also at quarterback are redshirt freshmen **Ryan Kanekeberg** (6-4, 200) and **Adam Rothenfluh** (6-3, 200).

"Stremick completed the spring as the backup and I felt he had an extremely good spring," Erickson said. "House's shoulder is still bad and that's a problem. Kanekeberg and Rothenfluh played well at times."

RUNNING BACKS

It seems almost unfair that the Beavers can give Simonton a breather and then come right back with McCall, a Michigan transfer who is an extremely talented back as well.

Of course, Simonton still is the man.

"We expect a big year from Kenny," Smith said. "He will have a great leadership role and we will go as Kenny goes. I know he makes my job easier. When you send Kenny out there, you know you will be facing a lot of eight man fronts."

Erickson summed up the position by saying, "At tailback we have Simonton and McCall. What else do you need to say?"

There are other guys who will be able to find a run as the clock is ticking down in the final quarter. Among them are red-shirt freshmen **Dwight Wright** (5-8, 195) and **Riley Jenkins** (6-0, 190).

WIDE RECEIVERS/TIGHT ENDS

The Beavers lost their top four pass catchers from last season's team so Erickson will have to find some stars in a hurry.

At the slot, sophomore **James Newson** (6-1, 210) and senior **Mike Payton** (5-9, 185) both played in a handful of games last season with one catch between them.

Newson made the biggest move in spring ball and looks like he will be the starter on opening day.

"We thought Newson had a tremendous spring for us," Erickson said. "We knew he has had a lot of potential, and he began to show that potential."

At split end, junior **Shawn Kintner** (6-3, 205) comes out of spring as the starter. He has one career start and has seen action in 23 games. He has 13 career catches for 148 yards.

The only other player who has seen any game time is sophomore **Aaron Hill** (6-2, 190), who has played in three games with two catches. Redshirt freshman **George Gillett** (6-1, 195) hopes to make a move in summer camp.

At flanker, junior **Seth Trimmer** (6-5, 201) had three starts in 21 games. However, in two seasons, he has caught just three balls for 26 yards. Walk-on sophomore **Nate Brentano** (5-11, 175) played in three games last season and redshirt freshmen **Ron Monteilh** (5-11, 195) and **Ryan Petersen** (6-4, 180) both are trying to win time.

"It is a group that is inexperienced in some ways, but isn't in other ways," Smith said. "Kintner and Trimmer have both played a lot and they now must step up and play. Shawn is a tremendous player and now it is his time. The same thing can be said of Seth."

Erickson said his wide receivers have a lot of progress to make.

"We have to have people come through for us at wide receiver," he said. "We are not going to make a living throwing the ball as our strength, but we will throw it successfully and adequately."

At tight end, senior **Mark Walsh** (6-3, 260), junior **Tyler Ross** (6-3, 250) and sophomore **Tim Euhus** (6-5, 240) all have played in games but none has earned a start.

Walsh, by far, is the most experienced, but Euhus looks like the eventual starter.

Junior college transfers **Jermaine Jackson** (6-3, 240) and **Travon Magee** (6-7, 25) will get an opportunity to win the starting job in summer camp.

"We thought tight end was a very questionable position going into the spring," Erickson said. "It still is to a degree. Euhus grew up and had a good spring, along with Jackson. Ross and Walsh had their moments. Tim and Jermaine were the two that ended up playing the best. It is an area where we have a lot of people, but somebody needs to step up."

OFFENSIVE LINE

Although the Beavers lost three starters from the 2000 offensive line, they should be able to put together a unit that can clear some holes for Simonton to achieve his records.

Senior **Chris Gibson** (6-3, 280) returns at center, where he earned All America and All-Pac-10 honors in 2000. Senior **Vincent Sandoval** (6-4, 300) moves from left tackle to right tackle. Sandoval had started 12 games at left tackle.

Senior **Keith DiDomenico** (6-5, 305), who didn't play last year, returns at right guard, where he had been a two-year starter. DiDomenico has 22 career starts under and was an honorable mention All-Pac-10 center in 1999.

The question marks are on the left side of the line. Junior **Lee Davis** (6-3, 310), who played in four games last year, will have the opportunity to play left tackle. Junior **Mike Kuykendall** (6-6, 320), who played in all 12 games last season, leads the battle for left guard.

Also in the fight for the left guard job are redshirt freshmen **Kanan Sanchez** (6-4, 330) and **Jarvez Hall** (6-0, 335), senior **Tyler McClaughry** (6-4, 285) and sophomore **Jason Haas** (6-5, 270).

Fighting for the left tackle spot is sophomore **Brian Kilkenny** (6-4, 280). Other line backups are seniors **Dustin Janz** (6-3, 295) and **Paul Davidian** (6-4, 285), sophomore **Matt Davis** (6-4, 310) and redshirt freshmen **Matt Brock** (6-1, 300) and **Doug Nienhuis** (6-5, 280).

"Our strength is our running backs and our offensive line," Erickson said. "I feel very good at where we are with our running game. The key for us will be finding our left guard in the [summer camp]. It was a heck of a battle in the spring between Kuykendall, Sanchez and McClaughry. That won't be resolved [until the season begins]."

2000 STATISTICS

Rushing offense	186.1	28
Passing offense	225.4	44
Total offense	411.5	32
Scoring offense	32.6	19
Net Punting	36.0	35
Punt returns	8.1	82
Kickoff returns	20.7	29
Rushing defense	93.1	10
Passing efficiency defense	103.5	18
Total defense	314.4	20
Scoring defense	18.5	16
Turnover margin	+16	4

Last column is ranking among Division I-A teams.

KICKERS

Last season's All-Pac-10 kicker, junior **Ryan Cesca** (5-8, 175) returns, so the job is locked up. Cesca has made 83-of-84 PATs the last two seasons and made 16-of-19 field goals last season. His 94 points in 2000 were a team record. His 152 points in two seasons rank fifth all-time.

Sophomores **Mike White** (6-1, 190) and **Kirk Yliniemi** (6-0, 185) are the backups.

DEFENSIVE LINE

Putting pressure on the opposing quarterback could be a big headache for Erickson if the Beavers don't find some adequate defensive ends in a hurry. At right end, senior **Kyle Rosselle** (6-5, 255) has played in 35 games but has only one start. He is leading senior **Brian Tulikihihifo** (6-4, 280), who has seen action in nine games.

Also trying to win time at right end are juniors **Jayson Jean-Baptiste** (6-4, 245) and Peter Gregg (6-0, 240). Baptiste is a junior college transfer who won't participate until summer camp. At left end, sophomore **Dan Rothwell** (6-7, 250) is listed as the starter ahead of junior **Alvin Steen** (6-2, 260). Rothwell saw limited action in four games last season. Steen is a junior college transfer who won't compete until summer camp.

The interior would seem to be in better shape with the return of junior **Eric Manning** (6-1, 300), who has 12 starts in his career. He has excellent speed for a big man and is expected to pull down some post-season honors. Another junior college transfer, junior **James Lee** (6-3, 300), arrives in summer camp and he will get a long look.

Senior **Daniel Torres** (6-3, 255) and redshirt freshman **Mike Havens** (6-5, 270) will be backups.

At right defensive tackle, sophomore **Dwan Edwards** (6-3, 285) is listed as the top guy after spring drills. He played in all 12 games last season.

Sophomore **David Lose** (6-2, 295) and redshirt freshman **Paul Soto** (6-1, 290) will be competing for time.

"I thought our tackles had a very good spring," Erickson said. "Manning has a chance to be as good as anyone in our conference. Edwards played well as a backup last year and he had a solid spring. We still need to find another tackle.

"Soto and Lose, a pair of young players, have a chance to help. We will take a good look at Lee this fall. We really haven't resolved who our defensive ends will be. Rosselle and Rothwell were solid. We need to find a third and fourth guy. Steen and Tulikhihifo are possibilities and Jean-Baptiste is a guy we need to take a good look at."

LINEBACKERS

Erickson said the strength of his defense is at

linebacker. Sophomore middle linebacker **Richard Seigler** (6-3, 215) returns after starting all 12 games and earning freshman All-America honors last season. He was the Beavers' second-leading tackler with 72 stops.

At weak linebacker is senior **James Allen** (6-3, 230), who has 18 career starts. He was selected a *Playboy* preseason All-American.

Junior **Nick Barnett** (6-2, 200) has five career starts and has seen action in 24 games.

The backups at linebacker are junior **Jason Lowe** (6-3, 230), sophomores **Jason Jacobs** (6-1, 205) and **Noah Happe** (6-5, 220) and redshirt freshmen **Seth Lacey** (6-1, 220), **Jonathan Pollard** (6-1, 235) and **Trent Bray** (6-1, 215).

"Seigler had a tremendous spring in the middle and Pollard emerged as his backup," Erickson said. "Jacobs came on strong behind Barnett at the outside linebacker spot. This is a very good group of players."

DEFENSIVE BACKS

Weathersby is the premier player on Oregon State's defense, a guy who could end up on some All-America teams if OSU has a big year. The *Playboy* preseason All-American also is a two-time All-Academic Pac-10 pick.

"I just want to be a complete player in covering, stopping the run and making the extra effort," Weathersby said.

At the other corner is junior **Calvin Carlyle** (6-0, 185) who has 23 career starts at free safety. He made the move to cornerback in the spring and the coaching staff still might move him back to safety in the summer.

If Carlyle remains at corner, senior **Jake Cookus** (5-10, 190) could claim the free safety job. Cookus has four career starts and has played in 35 games. He had five interceptions last season, including three against Oregon.

Senior **Eric Mobley** (5-10, 195) is also fighting for the position. He has played in 28 games but hasn't earned a start yet.

At strong safety, redshirt freshman **Mitch Meeuwsen** (6-2, 210) made a big impression in spring camp and is listed as No. 1 on the depth chart going into the summer.

Close behind Meeuwsen is junior **Terrell Roberts** (5-10, 200), who has played in 22 games during his career.

Backups at cornerback are junior college transfer **D.J. Coote** (6-1, 195), sophomore **Shamon Jamerson** (5-11, 180) and redshirt freshmen **Aric Williams** (5-11, 165) and **Johan Thomas** (5-8, 170). Backups at safety are senior **Brad Gerry** (5-9, 180) and junior **Luke Scott** (5-10, 180).

"Our secondary is an area where we must identify our corners," Erickson said. "Dennis had a great spring and he has been All-Pac-10 and All-American. We moved Carlyle out from safety and he probably will play both positions. Coote improved a great deal in the spring.

"A real surprise for us was Aric Williams. At safety, we had a couple of players emerge this spring in Meeuwsen and Roberts who should really help us."

PUNTERS

Mike Fessler, who handled the punting duties the last four years, is gone. Sophomore walk-on **Carl Tobey** (6-1, 220) will battle with incoming freshman **Ryan Cozzetto** (6-0, 195) for those duties during summer camp.

"The punter is up for grabs at this point," Erickson said. "Tobey had the best spring, but we have Cozzetto coming in the [summer] and he is outstanding. We will see what happens when they compete against each other."

SPECIAL TEAMS

Kickoff return man Ricky Walker, who averaged 22.2 yards a return, is gone. So is punt return specialist T.J. Houshmandzadeh, who averaged nine yards a return.

Erickson will be testing a number of players during summer camp to come up with his specialists.

Gillett has the lead on punt return duties and Newson and McCall are good bets to return kickoffs. Kuykendall handles long snaps and Trimmer is the holder.

RECRUITING CLASS

With heavy losses, Erickson went after eight junior college players for immediate help. If they pan out, it will be considered a terrific class. If not, perhaps a bomb.

Jean-Baptiste, out of San Jose (Calif.) City College; Coote of Ventura (Calif.) College; Jackson of Mt. San Antonio (Calif.) College and Steen of Los Angles Harbor College will have a solid shot at making an immediate impact.

Jean-Baptiste is known for his 4.6 speed so he could be a big-time pass rusher. Coote is a 4.5 guy who was rated the 16th best player in the nation by *JC Gridwire*. Jackson is a blocking specialist who could be used to clear the way for Simonton. And Steen set the career record for sacks (24) at Los Angeles Harbor despite playing in only seven games last season because of injury.

"We believe our junior college transfers have a chance to make a tremendous impact," Erickson said. "All of them have an opportunity to come in and contribute this year, and that is a big key for us."

Among the preps, quarterback **Derek Anderson** (6-6, 230) out of Scappoose High School in Oregon was the major haul. Anderson was a *SuperPrep* All-American who was ranked by that publication as the No. 2 prospect in the nation at the position.

The wide receiver corps might get immediate help from **Jayson Boyd** (6-4, 190), a *SuperPrep* All-American out of John North High School in Riverside, Calif. He caught 54 passes for 834 yards his senior season.

Cozzetto, out of Mountain Pointe High School in Phoenix, Ariz., averaged 40.3 yards a punt last season.

"It is a class with great speed and we are excited about them. We have a couple of guys who have a chance to play early and have an impact," Erickson said.

BLUE RIBBON ANALYSIS

OFFENSE	A
SPECIAL TEAMS	B
DEFENSE	C
INTANGIBLES	B

The Beavers have a great coaching staff and some tremendous offensive talent. However, it will be interesting to see how quickly Erickson can plug some of the many holes that were left by graduation. Replacing an entire wide receiver corps or most of a defensive line isn't the easiest thing to accomplish.

And one thing the Beavers have had going for them the last couple of years is great continuity on the offensive line. Replacing three starters might disrupt the flow.

Even with those problems, the Beavers play a soft non-conference schedule, and they have enough rushing talent to finish at least .500 in the conference. That alone is enough to point them toward a bowl. How major a bowl is the question. The view from here is that the experience of winning won't be enough to overcome a rebuilding type of season. Opponents might well line up 11 deep on the line of scrimmage to see what the OSU receiver corps has to offer. And if they don't hit some big plays early, Simonton and company will have to fight for every yard.

(J.H.)

2000 RESULTS

Eastern Washington	W	21-19	1-0
New Mexico	W	28-20	2-0
San Diego State	W	35-3	3-0
USC	W	31-21	4-0
Washington	L	30-33	4-1
Stanford	W	38-6	5-1
UCLA	W	44-38	6-1
Washington State	W	38-9	7-1
California	W	38-32	8-1
Arizona	W	33-9	9-1
Oregon	W	23-13	10-1
Notre Dame (Fiesta Bowl)	W	41-9	11-1

Southern California

LOCATION	**Los Angeles, CA**
CONFERENCE	**Pac-10**
LAST SEASON	**5-7 (.417)**
CONFERENCE RECORD	**2-6 (t-8th)**
OFFENSIVE STARTERS RETURNING	**8**
DEFENSIVE STARTERS RETURNING	**6**
NICKNAME	**Trojans**
COLORS	**Cardinal & Gold**
HOME FIELD	**L.A. Memorial Coliseum (92,000)**
HEAD COACH	**Pete Carroll (Pacific '73)**
RECORD AT SCHOOL	**First Year**
CAREER RECORD	**First Year**
ASSISTANTS	**Norm Chow (Utah '68)** **Offensive Coordinator** **Nick Holt (Pacific '86)** **Inside Linebackers** **Lane Kiffin (Fresno State '98)** **Tight Ends** **Wayne Moses (Washington '77)** **Running Backs** **Ed Orgeron (Northwestern State '84)** **Defensive Line** **Kennedy Pola (USC '87)** **Outside Linebackers** **Keith Uperesa (BYU '84)** **Offensive Line** **DeWayne Walker (Regents College '86)** **Secondary** **Kirby Wilson (Eastern Illinois '89)** **Wide Receivers**
TEAM WINS (last 5 yrs.)	**6-6-8-6-5**
FINAL RANK (last 5 yrs.)	**48-25-39-43-53**
2000 FINISH	**Lost to Notre Dame in regular-season finale.**

COACH AND PROGRAM

Whoops! Student body right was no longer a sweep at USC last season. It was the chase after a fumble.

Although the Trojans led the Pac-10 in total offense in 2000 at 415.9 yards a game, they threw away games with reckless abandon. Thirty-six turnovers, the team's most since 1977, doomed what could have been an impressive season.

Those turnovers cost Paul Hackett his job as head coach, and in his place comes Pete Carroll, whose fate won't be much better if he can't get his players to hang on to the ball.

This much is known. Carroll inherits one very fine offense that has a plethora of weapons. USC is going to put some points on the board. Whether that is enough depends on the defense and whether USC can stop coughing up the ball at its 15-yard line.

"Our overall philosophy is very simple," Carroll said. "It's all about the football. When we're on offense, we've got to hold onto it and control it. And when we're on defense, we've got to go get it. It's really as simple as that.

"The initial philosophy of our program is about possession of the football. In our first team meeting we talked about it. All our guys have been instructed on how to put it away. We are very strict about it and very tough and demanding. They can get in trouble even if they don't carry the ball right. They don't have to turn it over to get into trouble with us. It's a huge issue and I just believe philosophically that possession is one of the critical aspects that you can control."

Carroll can also control his offensive game plan, but that is something he will shy away from doing.

"Offensively, we want to control the ball with the passing game, while still being balanced," he said.

Why not? The John Robinson days of the sweep at USC are long gone. Carroll has hired offensive guru Norm Chow, the longtime master of all those tremendous BYU offenses, to run the show at the Coliseum. Chow left BYU to take the offensive coordinator's job at North Carolina State, and having rejuvenated the Wolfpack's offense, found Carroll's high-dollar offer much too lucrative to turn down.

Trojan boosters are willing to go into their pockets to hire the best because they long for the days when USC was a regular member of the Top 10 club. Of course, that is no longer the case. The power of the Pac-10 has headed north, to such places as Eugene, Ore., Corvallis, Ore., and Seattle.

USC no longer has to maintain its tradition. It has to dig itself out of a hole. Chow is the quick-fix solution, a guy who can squeeze offense out of a plastic kicking tee. He has been handed junior quarterback **Carson Palmer** (6-5, 220), the league's top wide receiver in junior **Kareem Kelly** (6-1, 185) and an outstanding tailback in junior **Sultan McCullough** (6-0, 185), and told to produce—now.

"Coach Chow is an awesome guy," said Palmer, who said he is working hard to reduce his interceptions. "I really didn't know much about him or the BYU offense. I just knew they threw the ball a lot. I saw them throwing the ball 40-to-45 times a game. You've got to love it."

Carroll has no doubt that USC is going to be blasting down football fields all over the West Coast with a dynamic short passing game.

"That's what Norm has been a master of," Carroll said. "It's an offense that is designed around precision, which means the system has to be quarterback-friendly. It is set up so the quarterback really can be successful. Our goal is to complete 63 percent of our passes.

"And with this offense, we can attract highly skilled quarterbacks, receivers and running backs, and spread the field so we can use their talents. When we put all the ingredients together, we can have an extraordinarily effective offense. When we spread the defense out with our formations, it also will open up the running game. Draws and traps and counters should allow our running backs to split the defense and get into the secondary in a hurry with nobody around them. I think our runners are well suited to that style.

Carroll said he wants to bring out the best of what he inherited on offense.

"And that's some quality athletes," he said. "We have a number of skill players who have proven to be productive. Now, we must build up the offense around their special talents. Our plan is to expand the offense to highlight a wide-open attack."

Chow was offensive coordinator for 27 years at BYU before coaching at North Carolina State last season. At BYU, he coached six of the top 12 NCAA career passing efficiency leaders. Eleven of his BYU teams ranked among the top 30 single-season passing yardage leaders in NCAA history.

"I've been able to assemble what I feel is a dream-team staff," Carroll said. "Our new coaches left very good jobs to come here. We're all here to do something special. The key, of course, was getting Chow. He is arguably the best offensive coordinator in the history of college football, certainly in terms of championships and wins and people he has coached. He is not only a great attraction for us in recruiting and a great asset as a coach, but he allows me to do what I want to do, which is to focus on the defense."

Nobody is going to be focusing on the defense much in Los Angeles unless it starts losing games for the team. The eyes will focus on Palmer, who appears ready to have a breakthrough season, with or without Chow. He is fifth all-time on the team's completion (397) and total offense (5,050 yards) charts.

"It's a new offense and I'm going to be throwing a lot of quick stuff off three-step drops," Palmer said. "We're going to get rid of them quick, hit them short and once a quarter, let one of them go long."

At Palmer's disposal will be McCullough, the fastest Trojan ever with a 10.17 in the 100 meters. He ran for 1,163 yards and six touchdowns last season, so don't expect Chow to forget who is in the backfield with Palmer. McCullough's yardage total from last season was the most yards by a USC running back since 1990. He had seven games of more than 100 yards rushing.

Add Kelly to the mix and opponents are going to have a rough time making defensive plans. Kelly has caught a pass in every game he has played for USC and he is ninth on USC's career reception list. He had 55 catches for 796 yards last season. Besides everything else, he can stay with McCullough in a foot race. He holds the American collegiate and world junior 50-meter record of 5.67l.

Chow down on that.

"Offensively, we really didn't lose anybody except for a couple of offensive linemen and we can replace them," Palmer said. "We still have a lot of work to do at learning the offense, but we got off to a real good start in the spring.

"The West Coast offense [which the Trojans ran last season] is five times more complex than this offense. Our new offense has a lot of different looks and formations, but it really is a lot of the same plays."

Palmer said he has enjoyed working with Chow.

"He is one of those guys you have to respect," Palmer said. "Besides from football, you respect him for what he has done, the type of person he is, the type of family he has raised. I'm scared to let him down. The last thing I want to do is let him down."

Unfortunately for Carroll, he couldn't find another Chow out there for his defense, so he is going to serve as his own defensive coordinator. He spent spring ball going over takeaway tactics, especially because the team forced just 17 turnovers a year ago.

"I've always coached a very aggressive, attacking style of defense," Carroll said. "It starts up front with how we attack the line of scrimmage with our defensive linemen. But we'll make our opponents defend all our defenders because they will all be part of our blitz package. They'll all pressure. We will mix man-to-man with zone-blitz pressure. We will keep people off balance and force the kinds of errors that allow us to change the game with turnovers.

"We'll have a pro-style defense. It will be an attacking, up-the-field approach for our front seven and an aggressive, bump-and-run style of play in the secondary. We will run a four-three scheme but with three-four personnel."

Personnel is the key word for Carroll, who won't have the kind of impact players on defense he is blessed with on offense. He will need to develop some defensive stars in a hurry, or get ready for 42-41 shootouts.

His defensive line was devastated by graduation and two of last season's linebackers might be starting in the NFL next season. There are plenty of holes to fill. And those holes have to be plugged in a hurry.

Kansas State has come aboard to face USC in its second game at the Coliseum. The Trojans open Pac-10 play against one of the conference favorites, Oregon. That game will be played in Eugene, Ore. and could put USC in a hole early. The usual tussle with Notre Dame will be played Oct. 20. Nothing should come easy in Carroll's first season.

"I'm not going to make any bold predictions," Carroll said. "We're going to be very competitive and very aggressive. We're in the process of putting this team together. We'll be good. The strength of this club will come from its team attitude and willingness to play together and to play hard. That will give us the best chance to reach our potential. I've already seen that in the good work ethic this group has developed in the off-season. The players look to our approaches for the team."

Palmer said if USC had to make a change, Carroll seems to be the guy for the job.

"He is an awesome guy," Palmer said. "He has so much enthusiasm. You can tell he loves the game because he is fired up all the time. I'm excited."

2001 SCHEDULE

Sept.	1	San Jose State
	8	Kansas State
	22	@Oregon
	29	Stanford
Oct.	6	@Washington
	13	Arizona State
	20	@Notre Dame
	27	@Arizona
Nov.	3	Oregon State
	10	@California
	17	UCLA

QUARTERBACKS

Palmer is the complete story here, a guy who could develop into a Heisman candidate under Chow. He should fit right into Chow's system, too, because he has always shown the ability to complete a high percentage of his passes. In nine of his 20 starts, he has completed at least 60 percent of his passes. Last season he had 1,914 yards passing as he racked up the second most completions and yards in school history.

All was not good, though. Palmer also tossed 18 interceptions, a statistic that could kill USC if repeated.

"He has really good mobility," Carroll said.

"When we looked at the tapes, we saw a strong-armed kid, a playmaker. We also saw voids and inconsistencies in his play. He has been top flight throughout our camp, though. He's thrown the ball with great accuracy and he's picked up the offense very well.

"He didn't have a bad play during the spring. We like him on the move, going in and out of the pocket. He is very much in command of the offense."

Palmer said he knows what to focus on going into the season.

"We're going to improve on our turnovers by me not making so many stupid decisions," he said. "I need more concentration this season."

Of course, Palmer understands that he isn't to blame for every interception.

"Some were just bad luck," he said. "Some balls would hit off a receiver. But there were a couple bad decisions, too."

The Trojans probably will have to live and die with Palmer because no other quarterback on the roster has thrown a pass in a game. Redshirt freshman **Matt Cassel** (6-5, 215) is a highly recruited player who should move into the back-up role. The other quarterbacks all are walk-ons—sophomores **Taylor Talt** (6-3, 185) and sophomore **Richie Wessman** (6-1, 185) and red-shirt freshman **Matt Harris** (6-4, 210).

The calvary is coming. All-America prep quarterbacks **Billy Hart** (6-3, 200) and **Matt Leinart** (6-6, 220) join the program in the fall and could be elevated quickly should anything happen to Palmer.

RUNNING BACKS

Although the emphasis will be on the passing game, USC is loaded with talent at tailback. McCullough should put up monster numbers if given the carries.

However, the talent doesn't stop with him. Backup **Malaefou MacKenzie** (6-0, 215), a senior, has rushed for 765 yards and has 37 receptions during his career so Chow will be thinking of ways to get him involved. Last season MacKenzie gained 284 yards on 41 carries. With MacKenzie and McCullough getting the lion's share of the work, the other tailbacks don't figure to see much playing time. And Chow is thinking about playing them together.

"We've experimented with that combination and we really like it," Carroll said. "Malaefou has tremendous versatility catching the ball out of the backfield and lining up as an outside receiver. And he's a good blocker and can carry the football. I'm pleased with what he has shown us.

"Sultan has done a very nice job catching the ball as well, but we've used him more running the ball out of the backfield than Malaefou. We're moving those guys around and I think it gives us a good combination of threats."

Senior walk-on **Mark Gomez** (5-10, 205), junior **Miguel Fletcher** (5-11, 195), sophomore walk-ons **Jeffery Hill** (6-0, 215) and **Brien McMullen** (5-9, 180) and redshirt freshman **Chris Howard** (5-11, 180) will simply have to wait. Former Michigan tailback Justin Fargas has transferred to USC, but he will have to sit out this season.

There is plenty of good news at running back for Chow because starting senior fullback **Charlie Landrigan** (6-0, 225) also returns. Landrigan had eight carries for 34 yards last season and eight catches for a 5.9 average. But carrying the football isn't his specialty. He will be clearing the way for McCullough.

Backup fullback **Chad Pierson** (6-1, 240), a junior who had 133 rushing yards and 147 receiving yards last season, is also back. Senior **Sunny Byrd** (6-1, 225) doesn't figure to see much time.

WILD RECEIVERS/TIGHT ENDS

Kelly will make a run at major national awards this season, especially with Chow turning the offensive focus toward him. Why not? He has caught a pass in every game he has played for USC. He had 55 catches for 796 yards last season.

Opponents won't be able to concentrate solely on Kelly because junior **Marcell Allmond** (6-1, 190) figures to have a big year as well. He averaged 15.2 yards a reception before breaking his leg in the fifth game in 2000. A hurdler and decathlete on the track team, he is back to full speed.

Joining those two is sophomore **Keary Colbert** (6-1, 185), whose 33 receptions last season were the second most ever by a USC freshman.

"The emergence of Colbert has been impressive," Carroll said. "I think he was one of the most improved players in the spring. He just looks stronger and more confident.

"He's run away from our defense a few times, catching short passes and making them long gains. Hopefully we can build on that."

Adding depth is junior **Steve Stevenson** (6-2, 200), who has caught 21 passes during his career, including 15 catches last season with an 18.9 average.

Senior **Ryan Kaiser** (6-1, 190), sophomores **Sandy Fletcher** (6-1, 185) and **D. Hale** (6-0, 185) and redshirt freshmen **Ryan Haden** (6-0, 200) and **Forrest Mozart** (6-1, 195) probably won't see much time. Joining the fray is freshman **Frank Candela** (5-9, 180), a 22-year-old who played four years of minor league baseball before deciding to go to college.

It will be more difficult for Carroll to find a tight end. The big surprise of spring camp was the successful move to tight end by senior linebacker **Kori Dickerson** (6-4, 230), who is a 6-8 high jumper for the track team.

"I think it has worked out terrific for us," Carroll said. "He's given us a real good boost down the field catching the football. He's picked things up quite well and caught the ball well. He's really a target and I like his attitude. He brings a real upbeat, positive outlook and gives us a nice spark. If we need him to come back to defense because of injuries, we could still do that."

Four-year starter Antoine Harris is gone and that's why Dickerson was forced to make the switch. Dickerson will be competing with sophomore **Alex Holmes** (6-2, 295), who had seven catches last season. The rest of USC's tight end candidates have five career catches between them. Juniors **Doyal Butler** (6-3, 245) and **Scott Huber** (6-3, 250), sophomores **Chad Cook** (6-4, 225) and **Alex Bottom** (6-4, 220) and redshirt freshman **Gregg Guenther** (6-8, 265) will all try to make their move during summer camp.

OFFENSIVE LINE

The middle of the line appears to be in great shape as junior guard **Zach Wilson** (6-5, 315), senior guard **Faaesea Mailo** (6-4, 330) and center **Lenny Vandermade** (6-4, 270) all are returning starters.

Wilson is a two-year starter on the right side. Mailo was a starting tackle last season and had six starts at guard two seasons ago. He has been used as a short-yardage fullback. Vandermade was a first-team freshman All American last season.

That leaves a host of candidates to work their way into starting tackle roles. Sophomore **Norm Katnik** (6-5, 280) made the biggest move during spring drills and has apparently nailed down one spot. Sophomore **Eric Torres** (6-5, 310) is first on the depth chart at left tackle going into summer drills.

Junior **Phillip Eaves** (6-6, 320), sophomores **Jacob Rogers** (6-6, 275), **Nate Steinbacher** (6-6, 320) and **Justin Brown** (6-6, 310) and redshirt freshman **Joe McGuire** (6-5, 280) are vying for the final opening.

"Katnik has done a nice job for us," Carroll said. "He is real athletic. In college football, there is a trend to put smaller, speedy pass rushers on the outside to try to get that athleticism that helps you in the pass rush. [To combat that] Norm is a mobile kid and very light on his feet. He's made a nice impression. He didn't do a whole lot last year, but now he is a 280-pound kid and he is moving well.

"We're finding that tackle is a competitive spot and it is still unsettled. That will be an issue in summer camp. We have three or four guys who can fill in there, but Norm is ahead."

Also trying to get into the mix on the line are redshirt freshmen **Blair Jones** (6-7, 265), **Travis Watkins** (6-3, 296) and **Spencer Torgan** (6-1, 265), junior **Derek Graf** (6-4, 275) and sophomore **Joe Boskovich** (6-4, 240).

2000 STATISTICS

Rushing offense	153.6	51
Passing offense	262.3	24
Total offense	415.9	28
Scoring offense	25.8	58
Net Punting	28.4	110
Punt returns	9.2	63
Kickoff returns	19.5	62
Rushing defense	125.8	33
Passing efficiency defense	124.0	77
Total defense	343.0	39
Scoring defense	28.1	79
Turnover margin	-19	113

Last column is ranking among Division I-A teams.

KICKERS

As the Pac-10 has become more balanced from top to bottom, head coaches know that close games are a fact of life. That's why Carroll will be concentrating on his team's field-goal kicking unit. Last season, USC missed eight field goals and 10 extra points. That is far too many gifts for the other team.

Those kinds of statistics won't allow Carroll to rest easy.

USC did get a big kick last season, but David Bell, who beat UCLA with a field goal nine seconds from the final bell, is gone. Returning is senior **David Newbury** (5-9, 170) who is 15-of-29 for his career. No coach is going to be happy sending a 50 percent place-kicker on the field, so the competition begins.

Sophomore **John Wall** (5-8, 175), who hit all five of his field goals last season but was 9-of-14 on extra points, is questionable for this season because of knee surgery. All of Wall's extra-point misses were blocked and he sat out USC's final three games last season with a groin injury and a torn right knee ligament.

Carroll made it clear after spring drills that no one has the job wrapped up and the competition would probably continue right until the opening game. Redshirt freshman **Drew Thomas** (6-3, 200) is also waiting for a chance.

DEFENSIVE LINE

The Trojans have holes to fill. Tackle Ennis Davis, who had 146 tackles (36 for loss) during his career, is gone. So is Sultan Abdul-Malik (22.5 career sacks) and Shamsud-Din Abdul-Shaheed, who had 74 career tackles, and two-year starting defensive end Matt Childers.

USC will be depending on several part-time players from last season's team to handle jobs on a full-time basis. Players such as senior **Ryan Nielsen** (6-5, 275), who has 76 career tackles and split time last season with junior **Bernard Riley** (6-3, 305). Riley had 20 tackles last season at tackle.

"I thought our defensive line came along nicely in the spring," Nielsen said. "The learning process easily came together. Coach Carroll is a player's coach and he is more hands-on than I am used to. You know that he is calling the shots. He will take control."

However, as Carroll inserts his system, he tries to keep the channel of communication open with the players. Nielsen said the players have a committee to offer Carroll suggestions.

"He wants feedback from us," Nielsen said.

Besides giving suggestions, senior defensive end **Lonnie Ford** (6-3, 250)—who has 16 tackles for loss during his career—needs to become an impact player for the Trojans this season. Sophomore **Omar Nazel** (6-5, 215) will have to prove he can be an every-down player at defensive end. Junior college transfer **Daniel Pryor** (6-4, 245) of Compton (Calif.) College has a shot of seeing major time at defensive end.

The nose tackle spot should go to Riley, with redshirt freshmen **Malcolm Wooldridge** (6-2, 300), **Nathan Goodson** (6-5, 270) and **Kenechi Udeze** (6-3, 320) competing for time.

Backing up at end will be senior **Bobby DeMars** (6-4, 250), redshirt freshman **Jamaal Williams** (6-4, 260) and redshirt freshman walk-on **Jay Bottom** (6-2, 215).

Carroll said the Trojans have the right personnel to handle the job, especially because he likes to emphasize speed on the outside.

"Right now we are starting Ford and Nazel on the ends, which gives us additional speed," he said. "It will be a hallmark of our defense that we fly to the football."

Nielsen said that people who think USC's defense is going to be weak might be surprised.

"I think the defense is going to make the statement for our team," he said.

LINEBACKERS

The one-two punch of Zeke Moreno (285 tackles during his career with 33 for loss) and Markus Steele (152 career tackles, 29 for loss) is gone.

Dickerson, who had 32 tackles, has been moved to tight end. To say the position is wide open would be putting it mildly.

Junior **Aaron Graham** (6-1, 225) started four games last season and made 26 tackles. It looks like he will nail down an inside spot. Inexperienced junior **Mike Pollard** (6-0, 230) is listed as No. 1 at one outside position. Sophomore **Chris Prosser** (6-2, 225) and senior **Darryl Knight** (6-3, 225) have each started two games during their careers and they are potential starters inside. Senior **Henry Wallace** (6-2, 210) will get a long look.

Others include senior **John Cousins** (6-2, 200), who redshirted last season with a finger injury, junior **Anthony Daye** (6-1, 260), who was a defensive end last season, and redshirt freshmen **A.J. Single** (6-3, 255), **Lee Webb** (5-11, 240), and walk-on **Aaron Orndorff** (6-1, 235).

"Linebacker is a spot that is very competitive," Carroll said. "We've moved guys around and into different spots trying to find the right mix. Graham has been in the lead position. He's the one who has had the most playing experience. Prosser and Cousins have done nice jobs. Pollard has played well.

"We moved Webb from fullback to linebacker even though he has very little background playing the position. He's made a lot of big hits and made a positive impression. I really can't tell you who is going to play in the opener."

DEFENSIVE BACKS

The steadying force on defense should be junior strong safety **Troy Polamalu** (5-10, 210), who returns after being the second-leading tackler last season with 83. He also had seven deflections.

Free safety should be in good hands with senior **Frank Strong** (6-1, 220), who had 20 tackles last year, and junior **DeShaun Hill** (6-0, 195), who had 39 tackles, three for loss, and two interceptions while splitting time.

A newcomer coming into the picture is redshirt freshman **Matt Grootegoed** (5-11, 205), who sat out last year with mononucleosis. Also trying to win time are redshirt freshmen **Jason Leach** (5-11, 200), **Kyle Matthews** (6-0, 170) and **Matt Lemos** (5-10, 165).

With so much depth back from last season, the Trojans should be able to withstand the loss of Ifeanyi Ohalete, who had 168 career tackles and five interceptions.

Back at one corner is senior **Kris Richard** (6-0, 180), who has 77 tackles and six interceptions during his career.

Competing for time at cornerback will be junior **Darrell Rideaux** (5-9, 175), who made 21 tackles last season. He is a sprinter who has run 10.30 in the 100 meters. Rideaux and senior **Chris Cash** (5-11, 170), who had 39 tackles and two interceptions, both saw starting time last season.

Junior cornerback **Kevin Arbet** (5-11, 175), who made 31 tackles last year, and senior **Eric Reese** (5-11, 215) add depth.

The wildcard in the defensive backfield is senior cornerback **Antuan Simmons** (5-10, 190), who has 175 tackles, seven interceptions and six blocked kicks in three years as a starter. He was hospitalized for six weeks with a benign abdominal tumor that threatened his life last season and kept him from playing. He returns in the hope of garnering national honors.

"Antuan has been a positive for us," Carroll said. "The team understands where he has come from in a short period of time. He's an inspiration and a big boost to the corner position. He's got some big plays in him.

"I think the cornerback position has been a pleasant surprise. We have five guys who are competing. We feel like our level of play is up. I think the guys have taken to DeWayne Walker and his coaching style and our bump and run style that we like. That to me isn't an area of question other than who is going to start and who will get the bulk of playing time."

PUNTERS

Senior **Mike MacGillivray** (5-10, 205), who has averaged 39.4 yards a punt over his career, is a three-year starter, so he will handle the punting duties.

"We've punted the ball pretty well for the most part," Carroll said of MacGillivray's work in the spring.

Sophomore **Tommy Huff** (6-1, 225) is the backup.

SPECIAL TEAMS

Carroll won't have to go searching for return men. Strong was the team's top kickoff return man with a 21.6 average last season and he should handle those duties again this season. Candela, MacKenzie and Grootegoed also will get a look.

Richard handled punts last season and will vie with Candela and Kelly for those duties this season.

Carroll said USC has to improve all its special teams units if it expects to compete for the conference title.

"The performance of our special teams will be a focal point," he said. "We must be efficient and effective in our special teams play. We had 12 kicks and punts blocked with two of the punt blocks being returned for touchdowns last season. We blocked only four punts or kicks ourselves. We finished last in the Pac-10 in net punting (28.4) and that was the fifth-worst average in the country. We were ninth in the Pac-10 in kickoff returns at 19.5."

RECRUITING CLASS

The marquee star of a small recruiting class was defensive end Shaun Cody (6-5, 255), who was honored by *USA Today* as its National Defensive Player of the Year as well as being a *SuperPrep*, *PrepStar* and *Parade* All American. At Los Altos High in Hacienda Heights, Calif., Cody had 105 tackles and 22 sacks.

As a tight end on offense, he caught 50 passes for 850 yards. Considering USC's defensive line woes, Cody might move up the depth chart quickly when he arrives for summer camp.

The other huge picks were Leinart and Hart. Leinart was a *Parade*, *PrepStar* and *SuperPrep* All-American. At Mater Dei High in Santa Ana, Calif., Leinart threw for 2,870 yards and 28 touchdowns. He threw for 411 yards and four touchdowns against national champion De La Salle. Hart attended Mission Viejo (Calif.) High School and threw for 1,800 yards and 14 touchdowns on his way to *SuperPrep* and *PrepStar* All-American honors.

The tailback in the group is **Darryl Poston** (5-11, 185), who ran for 1,619 yards and 20 touchdowns at Edison High in Huntington Beach, Calif.

Linebacker **Austin Jackson** (6-4, 230) is expected to play his freshman season after registering 130 tackles at Serra High in Gardena, Calif.

A player who could make a huge impact down the road is wide receiver **William Buchanon** (6-4, 175), the son of former NFL cornerback Willie Buchanon. Buchanon caught 30 passes for 553 yards and five touchdowns as a senior and earned PrepStar and *SuperPrep* All-America honors.

BLUE RIBBON ANALYSIS

OFFENSE	A
SPECIAL TEAMS	B
DEFENSE	C
INTANGIBLES	C

The question at USC is whether Carroll can do the kind of job that Dennis Erickson did at Oregon State, taking a team and getting immediate results.

Certainly, Carroll has more offensive weapons on hand than Erickson did at OSU. However, Carroll has some major work to do on defense. Defense is Carroll's forte, so he should be able to get things pointed in the right direction quickly.

The schedule is fair enough, so there is no reason to think the Trojans won't at least get to a minor bowl.

Unfortunately for Trojan fans, the team might not be able to develop quickly enough to make a run at a Pac-10 championship. After facing San

Jose State in the opener, Carroll's inexperienced defense will have to handle the Kansas State offensive machine at the Coliseum. That's a tall order for a team using so many new defensive linemen and linebackers. And if the Trojans do step up to that task, they have to come right back against offensive juggernaut Oregon in Eugene the following week.

It is quite possible the Trojans could drop a couple of games early, and then everyone will get a good look at Carroll's ability to hold everything together. That was a problem for the Trojans under Hackett as they tended to fall into some ugly funks and couldn't pull out of them.

(J.H.)

2000 RESULTS

Penn State (Kickoff)	W	29-5	1-0
Colorado	W	17-14	2-0
San Jose State	W	34-24	3-0
Oregon State	L	21-31	3-1
Arizona	L	15-31	3-2
Oregon	L	17-28	3-3
Stanford	L	30-32	3-4
California	L	16-28	3-5
Arizona State	W	44-38	4-5
Washington State	L	27-33	4-6
UCLA	W	38-35	5-6
Notre Dame	L	21-38	5-7

Stanford

LOCATION	**Stanford, CA**
CONFERENCE	**Pac-10**
LAST SEASON	**5-6 (.455)**
CONFERENCE RECORD	**4-4 (4th)**
OFFENSIVE STARTERS RETURNING	**9**
DEFENSIVE STARTERS RETURNING	**7**
NICKNAME	**Cardinal**
COLORS	**Cardinal & White**
HOME FIELD	**Stanford Stadium (85,500)**
HEAD COACH	**Tyrone Willingham (Michigan State '77)**
RECORD AT SCHOOL	**35-33-3 (6 seasons)**
CAREER RECORD	**35-33-1 (6 seasons)**
ASSISTANTS	
	Kent Baer (Utah State '73) Defensive Coordinator
	Mike Denbrock (Grand Valley State '86) Offensive Line
	Bill Diedrick (Eastern Washington '70) Offensive Coordinator
	John McDonell (Carroll College '81) Offensive Line
	Trent Miles (Indiana State '87) Wide Receivers
	Buzz Preston (Hawaii '82) Running Backs
	Denny Schuler (Oregon '69) Defensive backs
	Dave Tipton (Stanford '71) Defensive Line
	Phil Zacharias (Salem College '81) Special Teams
TEAM WINS (last 5 yrs.)	**7-5-3-8-5**
FINAL RANK (last 5 yrs.)	**31-42-44-23-34**
2000 FINISH	**Defeated California in regular-season finale.**

COACH AND PROGRAM

The search hadn't been going on that long when Stanford coach Tyrone Willingham found a player during spring drills he hopes will inject a little explosiveness into his offense. That player is sophomore **Teyo Johnson**, a 6-foot-6, 250-pound former quarterback who has decided his best chance to play on The Farm will be as a wide receiver.

Unhappy with his team's ability to hit the home run on offense a year ago, Willingham has made it clear that players who show the ability to produce the big play will be worked into the offense. Johnson, who doubles as a key reserve for the Cardinal basketball team, has the ability to go sky high to make the catch.

The possibility of throwing to a 6-6 wideout is exciting to senior quarterback **Randy Fasani** (6-4, 235). "Teyo is an amazing athlete," Fasani said. "He is a great athlete and he has very good anticipation. Just imagine throwing to a guy who is 6-6 instead of a wide receiver who is 5-7.

"But we have to remember he only has been playing football about two weeks."

Johnson's lack of experience doesn't bother Willingham, who knows a home run hitter could be the final ingredient to give Stanford perhaps the top offense in the conference.

"We need to regain the mantle of being an explosive football team," Willingham said. "The lack of that ingredient, I believe, effected our overall team play last season. We simply did not have the one or two players who could be counted on to provide that threat. We need to regain that type of player. We need that explosiveness to be a component of our offensive football team."

After catching a pair of touchdown passes in Stanford's final spring scrimmage, Johnson has the Stanford faithful confident that the offense will have enough weapons to get the team back into the top half of the Pac-10 in 2001. It was a rather quick fall from grace last year as Stanford followed its Rose Bowl season of 1999 with a 5-6 dud.

Making matters worse, Stanford was one rather embarrassing effort from reaching a bowl game. Consider that for the second consecutive season, Stanford lost to San Jose State, this time 40-27. Considering the Cardinal snapped back the next week to beat Texas, 27-24, it seems Willingham's team has some strange mental block when it comes to facing the commuter school across the bay.

Willingham will have to figure out that block—Stanford plays at San Jose State the second game of the 2001 season. If the Cardinal can overcome that challenge, it bodes well for the future.

Stanford plays host to Boston College, a very average East Coast team, in the opener, then tries to overcome its jinx against San Jose State, which has a new coach this season in Fitz Hill. Then Stanford plays host to Arizona State, which has a new coach in Dirk Koetter. Then the Cardinal plays at USC, which has a new coach in Pete Carroll.

If programs do indeed have trouble adjusting to a new staff and new system, Stanford could capitalize big-time in 2001. With 16 starters back from last season's 5-6 team, a few minor adjustments could, indeed, put Stanford back in a bowl.

"There really wasn't a whole lot of difference between last year's team and our Rose Bowl team," senior Stanford linebacker **Coy Wire** (6-1, 215) said. "We were just as good a team. We lost three games by 11 points and two of those games came down to final minute. Two years ago, the ball bounced our way. Last year we had a lot of tough games and tough breaks. But we had a lot of character."

Wire said his teammates are confident they can be back on top if they get a few breaks.

"We have all the tools we need as far as players," he said. "We have the best head coach in college football. We know what it will take, a strong group of leadership, guys who will step up and take the team by hand and lead us. There is no reason we shouldn't [challenge for the title].

"I know it was tough for me last season. I knew we had a good team and that the guys were trying hard. We just lost a lot of close games. But adversity builds character and we have 16 starters coming back, guys who all went through that."

One thing the Cardinal shouldn't have to go through this season is a quarterback controversy. It appears Fasani will be a solid No. 1 with talented sophomore **Chris Lewis** (6-3, 205) ready to step into the lineup if Fasani is injured or if Willingham wants to try a change of pace. Both were somewhat suspect last season as they had little or no previous experience going into the season. However, Fasani proved there were reasons he was one of the nation's top-ranked quarterbacks coming out of Del Oro High School in Granite Bay, Calif.

Lewis also showed he could perform well in a pinch, leading Stanford to two last-minute comeback victories.

Whether there is enough savvy at quarterback to produce the big plays so desired by Willingham remains to be seen.

Stanford goes into the season with solid quarterbacking, a wealth of talent returning at running back and an experienced offensive line. The question for Willingham is whether he can find a wide receiver who can go deep. Willingham knows it is tough to be successful in the Pac-10 grinding out first downs on a weekly basis.

Everyone will be keeping their eyes on Johnson's development, but at least early in the season, junior flanker **Luke Powell** (5-8, 165) will have to provide the fireworks. Powell showed his tremendous athleticism last season by averaging 27.9 yards a catch with 18 grabs for 502 yards. He also returned a punt 51 yards for a touchdown. However, Powell will have to increase his amount of catches if he expects to become Stanford's top wide out.

"Powell is electrifying," Fasani said. "He jokes about winning the Heisman this year. Actually, that's a real good thing to joke about. But he has to be more determined and I think he is. He has had real good off-season workouts."

After three knee operations, Fasani knows he has to do as much work as possible in the off-season as well. He believes he is actually getting faster and hopes to continue being a threat to scramble on almost any play.

That would give Stanford another big-play dimension that Willingham is seeking. Of course, most Stanford fans knew Fasani would be successful.

"I knew I could go out there and perform," said Fasani, who played some tight end in 1999 while he waited for his opportunity to start at quarterback.

"I absolutely hated playing tight end when I wanted to play quarterback and get out there and lead the team, but I had to get on the field somehow."

Fasani was confident he would make the most of his shot if Willingham put him behind center.

"I wanted to prove it to everyone else," he said. "You can do all the talking in world, but you have to prove it."

Fasani knows Stanford has a lot to prove so fans won't think that 1999 was a one-season fluke.

"Personally, I think we were a couple plays away from being a bowl team last season," he said. "Our level of talent was about the same as our Rose Bowl team. But that team got a couple of calls to go its way. We got some bad calls last year.

"But I don't believe in excuses. The tide just

didn't go our way. There were a couple of calls here and there, a couple of lucky plays for the other team, a couple of plays we didn't make. We were so close to being a 7-3 team.

"We've already begun fixing it. We have a lot of returning starters coming back. And we have [senior] **Brian Allen** (5-10, 200) and [junior] **Kerry Carter** (6-2, 235), two of the best running backs in the conference. Our offensive line has been jelling as a unit. Everyone on our team expects to win the Pac-10 championship."

Even if the offense does come around, Willingham also has some worries on defense. In Wire, who led the team in tackles last season after converting from running back the previous year, he has one star. But does he have any others?

Gone from last season's team are defensive end Riall Johnson, who led the Pac-10 in sacks with 15, and All Pac-10 defensive tackle Willie Howard. Those players were difference makers and will be very tough to replace.

"Replacing Howard and Johnson will be very difficult," Willingham said. "But we feel good about the players we have on defense, especially Wire and [senior free safety] **Tank Williams**. Those two young men have a love and zest for football and play it at a high level both emotionally and physically."

Willingham's contention is that Stanford has the talent and that if it can get everyone to play with the emotional zealousness of Wire or Williams, it will be just fine.

"We need to realize what we can become," Willingham said. "We need to realize how close we were last year to having a sound and solid season. If we can realize that and play hungry every week, we have a chance to be a good football team.

"Our disappointment from last season is that we did not get to a bowl game. That is the major focus of our team this year. With the Pac-10 being such a tough conference on the national level, if we can improve on our finish from a year ago, then I believe we can put ourselves in position to be one of the better teams in the country."

2001 SCHEDULE

Sept.	8	Boston College
	15	@San Jose State
	22	Arizona State
	29	@USC
Oct.	13	Washington State
	20	@Oregon
	27	UCLA
Nov.	3	@Washington
	10	@Arizona
	17	California
	24	Notre Dame

QUARTERBACKS

Fasani and Lewis give the Cardinal two players who would handle starting assignments at most Division I-A programs. Fanani finished 93-of-180 for 1,400 yards and 11 touchdowns last season. He threw six interceptions. However, he did have trouble staying healthy and missed three games and parts of two others. A sprained ACL and turf toe sent him to the sideline.

After three knee surgeries since arriving at Stanford, Fasani said he is just about 100 percent, even though his turf toe continued to give him some problems during spring drills. He said that lingering ailment will be healed by the time the 2001 season opens. If it is, he predicts a big offensive year for the team.

"We have a bunch of guys who have to step it up this season and I think they will," he said. "If they do, we will have a lot of weapons. I think the ball will be distributed evenly."

The snaps probably won't be distributed evenly at quarterback as Fasani appears to be the main man, but Lewis has shown he is a viable option if needed. Last season he led Stanford to last-minute victories over Texas and USC. He threw for 1,179 yards and eight touchdowns.

Backing up those two will be sophomore **Ryan Eklund** (6-7, 205), who doesn't figure to see much time this season.

"Quarterback play will, as always, dictate the success and failures of our football team to a large degree," Willingham said. "In Randy and Chris, we have two players who gained some experience and confidence from last year, but the question now is whether they can take it to the next level. And in taking themselves to another level, can they take our football team to another level?"

RUNNING BACKS

Stanford's running game by committee figures to be a team strength, although it is questionable whether the Cardinal would have more success by sticking with one tailback. As it stands, Allen and Carter figure to offer a substantial two-pronged attack.

Allen has started the last 17 games at tailback and he has rushed for 1,218 yards in his career. He had 117 rushes for 460 yards last season with a long run of 71 yards. He didn't score a touchdown. Carter rushed 179 times for 729 yards last season with six touchdowns.

Trying to win playing time are junior **Junior Faust** (6-0, 200), sophomore **Brandon Royster** (6-0, 195) and sophomore **Kenneth Tolon** (6-1, 190). Faust had three carries for 11 yards last season.

At fullback, senior **Casey Moore** (6-2, 240) returns. Moore rushed 50 times for 224 yards last season with three touchdowns. Junior **Eran Landry** (6-2, 235) and sophomore **Jared Newberry** (6-2, 230) are waiting their turn.

WIDE RECEIVERS/TIGHT ENDS

Powell leads this group and is the only returning starter with more than 250 yards receiving. He scored three touchdowns in 2000 and had a long grab of 76 yards.

"Over the last two years we've had to replace the two most prolific wide receivers in Stanford history in Troy Walters and DeRonnie Pitts," Willingham said. "That poses a major challenge to our football team to see if our receiving corps can be one of those areas where we can develop a breakaway player. Hopefully, there is a guy in this group who can step out and be that kind of player for us."

Johnson would love to become that player. It beats standing around on the sidelines.

"I'm still a quarterback in their eyes, but they need me on the field this year," Johnson told the *San Jose Mercury News*. "I won't do us any good standing on the sideline with a clipboard."

Johnson is far too good an athlete to waste.

"He's a tremendous athlete and we want him on the field," offensive coordinator Bill Diedrick told the *San Francisco Chronicle*. "But we don't want him too far away from what's happening at quarterback."

Senior **Ryan Wells** (6-0, 195) actually caught more balls than Powell last season (19 to 18) but had only 201 yards to Powell's 502. His ability to raise his 10.6 yards per catch average might determine if he wins a starting role in 2001. Also back is senior **Jamien McCullum** (6-0, 190), who caught 14 balls for 250 yards as a junior. Of McCullum's 250 yards, 75 came on one play. Senior **Caleb Bowman** (6-1, 185) caught 11 balls for 155 yards in 2000 and he is vying for time.

Senior **Evan Combs** (5-9, 17), sophomore **Nick Sebes** (5-11, 175) and sophomore **Greg Camarillo** (6-2, 195) are trying to work their way into the lineup.

At tight end, Stanford suffered a tough loss with the graduation of three-year starter Russell Stewart. However, Stewart (eight catches for 174 yards) wasn't a big part of the Cardinal offense in terms of pass catching. Perhaps juniors **Brett Pierce** (6-6, 245) and **Darin Naatjes** (6-7, 240) can make more of an impact in that area. Pierce had seven catches for 41 yards last season and Naatjes had six catches for 65 yards.

Senior **Matt Wright** (6-5, 260) and sophomore **Alex Smith** (6-5, 220) also are vying for the spot.

OFFENSIVE LINE

All five starters return, but they will have to show some improvement if the Cardinal expects to get into a bowl game. Stanford scored 23.7 points per game last season, averaged a decent 138.9 yards a game rushing and 375.7 yards in total offense. However, all those numbers will have to improve for Willingham's club to jump to the next level.

The line is anchored by senior guard **Eric Heitmann** (6-4, 295) who was a second-team All Pac-10 player a year ago. He has started the last 23 games at right guard.

Senior **Zach Quaccia** (6-4, 290) has started the last 20 games over two seasons at either left guard or center. Willingham will have to decide between Quaccia and junior **Mike Holman** (6-3, 285) as the starting center. Holman started six games last season, including five at center.

Senior **Paul Weinacht** (6-5, 280) started eight games at left guard last season and he might return there depending on whether Quaccia wins the starting job at center. Senior **Greg Schindler** (6-6, 310) started 22 of the last 23 games at right tackle, although Willingham is toying with the idea of switching him to guard. Sophomore **Kirk Chambers** (6-7, 295), last season's starting left tackle, also returns.

Add to the mix sophomore **Kwame Harris** (6-7, 320), the nation's top offensive line recruit in 2000, and it is obvious the Cardinal will have a lot of tough decisions to make about starters come September.

"We must receive improved productivity from our offensive line to be successful this season," Willingham said. "I believe we have the talent and experience to be much improved."

2000 STATISTICS

Rushing offense	138.9	65
Passing offense	236.8	34
Total offense	375.7	54
Scoring offense	23.7	70
Net Punting	32.0	92
Punt returns	9.2	61
Kickoff returns	20.2	46
Rushing defense	146.7	55
Passing efficiency defense	118.9	58
Total defense	365.8	58
Scoring defense	26.7	71
Turnover margin	+0	59

Last column is ranking among Division I-A teams.

KICKERS

Senior **Mike Biselli** (5-10, 195) took on the punting responsibilities last season and it might have hindered his field goal kicking. He did hit seven of his 12 attempts, but missed two tries inside the 30.

Whether his 37.2-yard punting average hindered Biselli's place-kicking is a matter of speculation, but Willingham might eliminate Biselli's double duty this season by giving the punting chores away.

DEFENSIVE LINE

Howard is gone and that leaves a huge void for the Cardinal. He was taken in the second round of the NFL draft by the Green Bay Packers.

"What is before us on the defensive line is a challenge," Willingham said, "a challenge to have some players or player step forward and be a better player than Howard. We have some young men returning who might be able to fill that role."

Senior **Austin Lee** (6-6, 270) has starting experience at defensive end and he figures to be a leading contender to start there this season. Lee had four tackles for loss in 2000. Another defensive end with starting experience is senior **Marcus Hoover** (6-4, 265), who had 30 tackles last season with four tackles for loss.

At tackle, senior **Matt Leonard** (6-4, 290) and senior **Craig Albrecht** (6-5, 295) have a good shot at landing a starting berth. Leonard had 21 tackles a year ago with six for loss while Albrecht had just four tackles.

Also battling for an inside tackle spot are senior **Travis Pfeifer** (6-4, 270) and senior **Trey Freeman** (6-3, 310).

Trying to win time are sophomores **Will Svitek** (6-7, 235) and **Scott Scharff** (6-5, 245). Junior **Cooper Blackhurst** (6-4, 245) moved from linebacker to defensive line for depth.

LINEBACKERS

Although Johnson, who spent much of his time on the line of scrimmage, is gone—drafted by the Cincinnati Bengals in the sixth round—Stanford is lucky to have big-play Wire back. Wire led the team with 81 tackles and he had 14 tackles for loss with eight sacks. Wire is a former running back who was moved to inside linebacker last season.

"It was tough for me," Wire said. "I was basically playing off instincts, just kind of flying around in seek-and-destroy mode. As the season went on, I learned more and now spring ball has helped me a lot. It gave me a chance to sit down and learn the defense. I was thrown in there last season.

"Now I am in a better position to help out the team because I know what the defensive line is doing and I can be more of a leader in terms of getting guys in the right position."

Wire admits that Stanford has some questions to answer on defense.

"It's going to be exciting watching our defense," he said. "We have a lot more speed and our defensive backs and linebackers are going to be a lot more involved in our schemes."

That means Wire might be turned loose.

"It's like the ball carrier is my prey," he said. "I'm like a lion hunting for meat."

Willingham likes to turn Wire loose.

"He helps us to be a better defensive football team," Willingham said. "In addition to his play making abilities, he provides energy and leadership. Having more knowledge of his position will make him even better next year."

Seniors **Anthony Gabriel** (6-3, 240) and **Matt Friedrichs** (6-1, 240) both started games at linebacker last season. Gabriel had 17 tackles, including four for loss, and he missed the second half of the season because of injury.

Friedrichs started seven games and had 42 tackles. Juniors **Brian Gaffney** (6-2, 230), **Jake Covault** (6-3, 225), **Pat Jacobs** (6-2, 225), and **Cooper Blackhurst** (6-4, 245) and sophomore **Amon Gordon** (6-4, 280) are in the mix.

DEFENSIVE BACKS

Williams (6-3, 215) is the definite leader of this group. He was a second-team All Pac-10 player last season and he could make a run at national honors in 2001.

"I think we have the ability with Tank to have one of the better players in the country," Willingham said.

Williams started every game at free safety last season and had 66 tackles and three interceptions. His backup is senior **Jason White** (6-0, 185).

Other returning starters are senior cornerbacks **Ruben Carter** (5-8, 170) and **Ryan Fernandez** (5-11, 175). Carter, who has started 24 games over the last three seasons, had 39 tackles last season with an interception. Fernandez finished with 48 tackles and three interceptions.

Seniors **Simba Hodari** (6-1, 200) and **Colin Branch** (6-0, 200) and junior **Jim Johnson** (5-10, 180) are trying to win the starting strong safety position. Of the three, Hodari had the most tackles last season with 24.

Adding depth are seniors **Brian Taylor** (5-11, 180), **Chijioke Asomugha** (5-11, 185) and **Garry Cobb** (5-11, 180) along with sophomores **Stanley Wilson** (6-1, 175), **Leigh Torrence** (6-0, 175) and **O.J. Atogwe** (5-11, 180).

"I'm excited about the secondary," Willingham said. "I think we're getting closer to having better depth. It should allow us to play at a higher level and increase the competitiveness in practice."

PUNTERS

Biselli averaged 37.2 yards and junior **Eric Johnson** (5-11, 175) averaged 34 yards per punt last season. Obviously, the Cardinal has a lot of room for improvement in this very important area. Willingham said Johnson had a solid spring and he is looking for him to handle those duties so Biselli can concentrate on place kicking.

"We think Eric Johnson is poised and ready to assume that responsibilty on a full-time basis," Willingham said.

SPECIAL TEAMS

Pitts handled most of Stanford's punt return duties last season but Powell also returned nine punts, including his 51-yard touchdown return.

Willingham is hoping Powell can concentrate on those duties this season and recreate those big plays more often. Wells averaged 22.5 yards per kickoff return last season and he should again handle those duties, with Powell adding help.

RECRUITING CLASS

It will be interesting to see how long it takes defensive end **Mark Anderson** (6-7, 260) from Fergus High School in Lewistown, Mont., to develop. Anderson ranked in 2000 as the 11th best player in the country, was the *SuperPrep* National Player of the Year.

Other top recruits for Stanford were linebacker **Michael Craven** (6-1, 220) from La Quinta, Calif., quarterback **Kyle Matter** (6-3, 195) from Hart High School in Newhall, Calif., and running back **J.R. Lemon** (6-1, 215) from Sandy Creek High in Fayetteville, Ga.

Craven was a Parade All-American and was ranked by *SuperPrep* as the second-best linebacker in the nation. Matter threw for 7,528 yards and 81 touchdowns in two season's as Hart's quarterback. Lemon was a consensus All-American despite missing five games his senior season because of an injury.

BLUE RIBBON ANALYSIS

OFFENSE	B-
SPECIAL TEAMS	C+
DEFENSE	C+
INTANGIBLES	B

By no means does Stanford have the look of a great team. It has few impact players and depth would seem to be a question. However, Willingham is going to have a lot of seniors in his starting lineup, and inexperienced or not, that sometimes translates to success.

Remember, too, that when Stanford reached the Rose Bowl after the 1999 season, the Cardinal didn't have a 'great' team that season, either. What Willingham and company did was take advantage of a down year in the Pac-10 by winning its close conference games. That is something Stanford didn't do last season, win its close games.

Fortunately for the Cardinal, it does have that stretch early in the season when new head coaches will be trying to get familiar with personnel. Three consecutive games against new coaches could prove to be a windfall for a squad with a lot of seniors and a veteran coach.

Eventually, teams like USC and Arizona State figure to get things rolling, but 2001 is a year that those teams look susceptible early, when Stanford gets them.

Eventually, the Cardinal's fate might be determined by its ability or inability to come up with a few quality wide receivers. Stanford could see the effect of a crummy wide receivers corps first hand by looking across the bay at rival Cal, which has taken years to dig out of a hole caused by a poor recruiting year at wideout.

Stanford really has the look of a 5-6 or 6-5 team with a few breaks one way for the other moving a game for the better or worse. No championship this year, but a lower bowl berth is not out of the question.

(J.H.)

2000 RESULTS

Washington State	W	24-10	1-0
San Jose State	L	27-40	1-1
Texas	W	27-24	2-1
Arizona	L	3-27	2-2
Notre Dame	L	14-20	2-3
Oregon State	L	6-38	2-4
USC	W	32-30	3-4
Washington	L	28-31	3-5
UCLA	L	35-37	3-6
Arizona State	W	29-7	4-6
California	W	36-30	5-6

UCLA

LOCATION	**Los Angeles, CA**
CONFERENCE	**Pac-10**
LAST SEASON	**6-6 (.500)**
CONFERENCE RECORD	**3-5 (t-5th)**
OFFENSIVE STARTERS RETURNING	**8**
DEFENSIVE STARTERS RETURNING	**8**
NICKNAME	**Bruins**
COLORS	**Blue & Gold**
HOME FIELD	**Rose Bowl (91,136)**
HEAD COACH	**Bob Toledo (San Fran. St. '68)**

RECORD AT SCHOOL 35-23 (5 years)
CAREER RECORD 64-59 (11 years)
ASSISTANTS
Gary Bernardi (Cal State-Northridge '76) Tight Ends
Ron Caragher (UCLA '89) Receivers
Marc Dove (Texas Tech '73) Linebackers
Don Johnson (Jersey City State '76) Defensive Line
R. Todd Littlejohn (Fresno State '70) Quarterbacks
John Pearce (East Texas State '70) Quarterbacks
Kelly Skipper (Fresno State '89) Offensive Coordinator
Phil Snow (Cal State-Hayward '78) Defensive Coordinator
Mark Weber (Cal Lutheran '80) Offensive Line
TEAM WINS (last 5 yrs.) 5-10-10-4-6
FINAL RANK (last 5 yrs.) 44-11-8-61-52
2000 FINISH Lost to Wisconsin in Sun Bowl.

COACH AND PROGRAM

With 16 starters returning from last season's 6-6 Sun Bowl team, along with the starting punter and place-kicker, UCLA seems poised to make a run at the Pac-10 championship.

The Bruins have impact players at all the key positions and a load of depth behind them.

"We lost very few starters," head coach Bob Toledo said. "Just three guys on offense—although one of them was (NFL bound wide receiver) Freddie Mitchell—and three guys on defense.

"This is the biggest senior group we've had since I've been there. I feel good about this football team. It is very similar to last year's team, only it's a more experienced group."

Last year's team suffered some key injuries early, and then never was able to pull out the big games as it stumbled to a 3-5 record in the Pac-10. Ten of UCLA's 12 games were decided by eight points or less and five of those were losses.

"Not only do we have pretty much the same group we started with last year, but because of injuries, we started three freshmen in the Sun Bowl," said Toledo, who is hoping that all that experience allows the Bruins to finish games better than it did a year ago.

One huge factor in UCLA's favor is that it will have senior defensive end **Kenyon Coleman** (6-6, 280) coming after the quarterback late in games. Coleman, considered an All-America candidate, suffered a knee injury in UCLA's third game of 2000 and sat out the rest of the season. Because he didn't play after that third game, he was able to utilize his redshirt year and return.

"Being here at UCLA has been a great experience for me and you only go through college once, so I decided to come back," said Coleman, who would have gotten major attention in the NFL draft. "Hopefully the NFL will still be there when I get done this season.

"I haven't accomplished everything I want to accomplish. I am grateful to still be at UCLA. I have too many positives going for me now and I am a year wiser and stronger. I want to prove I can be a dominant college player, something I haven't proven yet."

Last season, Coleman thought he was going to miss out on a magical year. UCLA was 3-0 when he got hurt, with wins over Alabama, Fresno State and Michigan. But then the season turned mediocre, perhaps heading on a downward trend in part because of his injury. He believes that magic could be realized this season.

"The expectations are high here," he said. "Looking at our team, we have six to eight people who can make NFL rosters. We have an awful lot of talent."

Putting together that talent will be a couple of new coordinators. Last year's defensive coordinator, Bob Field, was fired after spending 22 years with the program. Toledo needed to make room for the hiring of ASU defensive coordinator Phil Snow, who was left without a job when ASU head coach Bruce Snyder was fired.

Toldeo also lost offensive coordinator Al Borges, who quit to take the same position at Cal. In his place will be Kelly Skipper, who handled running backs last season.

Snow's arrival probably should be considered an upgrade. He has been considered one of the Pac-10's top coordinators for some time. Toledo doesn't expect Snow to require much of an adjustment period.

"Having been in the Pac-10 is an advantage," Toledo said. "Phil does know the teams. He has been doing it for years. And he ran a similar defense to what we were running."

As Toledo said, Snow knows the Pac-10. He's coached in the league for the last 14 seasons, the last nine at Arizona State and from 1987-91 at Cal. His units ranked among the top three in scoring defense in the Pac-10 in three of the last five seasons. Snow's 1996 group finished first in the conference in rush defense (98.0), pass defense (104.2) and total defense (306.2). Last season, the Sun Devils ranked first nationally in fumbles recovered and third in the country in number of turnovers created.

Selecting Skipper as the offensive coordinator kept a familiar face at a key position, even if Skipper doesn't have as much authority as Borges. The offensive-minded Toledo figures to handle a lot of those duties himself.

"We're doing the same thing on offense that we've done for years," Toledo said. "We haven't had to change."

Not that Toledo hasn't placed his faith in Skipper.

"I feel that Kelly has a great understanding of our offense," Toledo said. "He is just as familiar with the nuances of the passing game as he is with the running game. He comes from a coaching family (his father, Jim, was offensive coordinator and assistant head coach for the New York Giants in 1999 and is currently head coach of the XFL's San Francisco Demons).

"Kelly and I have worked very well together over the past three seasons. We share the same offensive philosophies, utilizing a balance between the running and passing games, and I know our offense will continue to flourish under Kelly's guidance."

Junior starting quarterback **Cory Paus** (6-2, 215) said he doesn't notice much of a difference from when he was taking orders from Borges.

"I think there was a smooth transition," Paus said. "There really isn't much difference. We're running the same offense. But Bob does have tenfold more input now. As far as I know, he will be calling the plays."

Known to be a gambler, Toledo's play calling should offer some fun surprises for UCLA fans, if not unpleasantness for opponents.

Of course, with so much returning talent, Toledo probably won't have to rely on tricks to get the job done.

"I think we have a chance to be pretty good," he said. "If we stay healthy, we've got a chance to be a very good team."

Paus, who has missed time because of injuries the last two seasons, is trying to remain cautiously optimistic.

"I don't want to count on anything before it happens," Paus said. "But everything seems to be in order."

Although the schedule is tough as usual with non-conference games against Alabama and Ohio State, if the Bruins can have success early, they could make a run at a big, big year. After road games at rebuilding Alabama and Kansas, four of the next five games are at home, including conference games against Arizona State, Washington and Cal.

2001 SCHEDULE

Sept.	1	@Alabama
	8	@Kansas
	15	Arizona State
	22	Ohio State
	29	@Oregon State
Oct.	13	Washington
	20	California
	27	@Stanford
Nov.	3	@Washington State
	10	Oregon
	17	@USC

QUARTERBACKS

No longer is there any dispute about who will be the No. 1 quarterback. Paus solidified his standing with a big year in 2000. He was the third sophomore to throw for more than 2,000 yards passing at UCLA and he completed 134-of-241 passes (55.6 percent) for 2,156 yards and 17 touchdowns. His 17 touchdowns tied him for fifth most in a season at UCLA. His efficiency rating of 145.8 would have led the Pac-10 if he had appeared in enough games.

"I am much more confident and knowledgeable," Paus said. "I have much better footwork, reads, touch."

Paus was asked if he is ready to have a big year.

"As far as I am concerned, I had a big year last year," he said. "If I hadn't missed two games, I would have led the conference in passing."

He might have reason for being a bit touchy. After a successful freshman season that was ended prematurely by a broken collarbone, Paus found himself in a heated battle for the starting job in the spring of 2000. Eventually, he won the job.

"There is no question that he is the starting quarterback," Toledo said. "But there are some areas where he needs to improve. He had a great season last year, but he made about a half dozen real bad plays that hurt us"

Maturity and experience might cure those ills, so the Bruins should be in good shape if Paus doesn't get hurt again. If he does fall to injury (he missed almost four full games last season), his backups won't be completely inexperienced.

Junior **Ryan McCann** (6-4, 210), who gave Paus a run for the starting job last season, and senior **Scott McEwan** (6-3, 200) have both been thrown into the fire before. McCann led the Bruins to a season-opening win over Alabama after Paus was injured on the opening series and then started the next three games, including wins over Michigan and Fresno State. He completed 60-of-120 passes for 688 yards and four touchdowns.

Paus came back and reclaimed his job and McCann didn't play again, eventually undergoing surgery for a torn labrum in his left throwing shoulder. McEwan played in two games, including the entire second half of UCLA's 21-20 Sun Bowl loss to Wisconsin. He completed 17-of-28 passes (60.7 percent) for 164 yards.

Waiting in the wings is redshirt freshman **Roman Ybarra** (6-2, 175), last year's scout team quarterback.

"Ryan did a nice job stepping in when Cory

was injured early in the season," Toledo said. "He did the things necessary to win some big games and he demonstrated he has very good athletic ability. He will compete with Cory for playing time. Scott didn't see as much action as either Cory or Ryan, but he did well in both his opportunities. The coaching staff was a lot of confidence in him."

RUNNING BACKS

It appears senior tailback **DeShaun Foster** (6-1, 215) will battle with Oregon State tailback Ken Simonton for offensive player-of-the-year honors in the Pac-10. He figures to be a contender for the Doak Walker Award that goes to the nation's top running back, and if UCLA rolls up a lot of wins early, he could get into the Heisman hunt.

Foster is a strong inside runner who has breakaway speed once he gets through the line. He has scored 31 touchdowns and 188 points and has rushed for 2,085 yards during his career to rank 11th in school history.

Despite missing a game and a half with a broken bone in his right hand, Foster gained 1,037 yards last season, including 187 in the season opening win over Alabama. He also had 159 yards rushing against Stanford, 140 against Fresno State and 107 against Wisconsin in the Sun Bowl. He scored 13 touchdowns and was voted to the All-Pac-10 first team. His 16 receptions ranked third among the Bruins.

"You can see how much he does for us when he is healthy," Paus said of Foster. "It's going to be a big added bonus for us if he can stay healthy all season. He is real good at everything. He can catch passes, he can run hard. He can do it all."

Although Toledo won't mind going to Foster 25 times a game (he carried 42 times against Alabama) or more, sophomore **Akil Harris** (6-0, 210) gives UCLA a very strong backup when needed. He gained 201 yards last season and averaged 4.5 yards a carry. Against Arizona State, he rushed for 100 yards and two touchdowns on 13 carries.

Toledo is considering ways to sneak redshirt freshman **Manuel White** (6-3, 240) into the lineup as well. Actually, at his size, people are going to notice when White takes the field. Toledo said he will use White and Foster in the same backfield. White was UCLA's scout team player of the year last season and he appears ready to go. He was a high school All-American at Valencia High School in 1999, rushing for more than 2,500 yards with 38 touchdowns. He scored 78 touchdowns during his high school career.

Blocking for the tailbacks will be senior fullbacks **Ed Ieremia-Stansbury** (6-2, 260) and **Matt Stanley** (6-3, 245). Ieremia-Stansbury started six of the final nine games of the season after switching over from linebacker the season before. Ieremia-Stanbury caught three touchdown passes but carried the ball just five times for 24 yards.

Stanley started two games and played in eight. A dislocated right shoulder against Michigan limited his playing time the rest of the season. The former walk-on caught three passes for 24 yards last season.

Both Ieremia-Stansbury and Stanley had shoulder surgery in the off-season, so expect Toledo to get a good look at junior **Chris Jackson** (6-3, 265) who made the switch from linebacker last season, and redshirt freshman **Pat Norton** (6-1, 240).

"We feel we have a number of talented running backs," Toledo said. "DeShaun is a complete performer. He possesses great vision and size to go along with breakaway speed. He was on his way to a super season last year when he got hurt, yet still ended up with over 1,000 yards. Akil is an exciting young tailback with a bright future. We got a glimpse of his vast potential last season.

"Manuel was a very solid performer on our scout squad and is capable of helping us. At fullback, both Ed and Matt did a good job a year ago. Chris is waiting in the wings."

WIDE RECEIVERS/TIGHT ENDS

For the entire puzzle to come together, senior **Brian Poli-Dixon** (6-5, 220) has to prove he can be a No. 1 wideout on an every game basis. As the second guy behind Mitchell, Poli-Dixon proved he had plenty of big-play capability, finishing with 53 catches for 750 yards and five touchdowns. Now he will be facing each opponent's top defensive back.

Poli-Dixon is the second receiver at UCLA to catch at least 44 passes in a season twice (Kevin Jordan is the other) and he also is only the second player in UCLA history to have 712 receiving yards or more in two seasons (J.J. Stokes is the other). He had 165 yards receiving against Washington last season, the 11th-best game in UCLA history. He is eighth on UCLA's career reception list with 115 and 11th in receiving yards with 1,712.

Poli-Dixon had 44 catches for 712 yards and 10 touchdowns in 1998, but had to sit out 1999 because of a broken right wrist in the third game.

"He needs to be our No. 1 guy and I believe he can be," Paus said of Poli-Dixon. "He has the talent."

Toledo agrees.

"Brian has proven he is one of the most productive and dependable receivers in school history," he said. "He became a much more consistent player last season and he is primed for a big year. We also look for him to continue in a leadership role with this inexperienced group."

Whether Toledo has depth in his receiving corps remains to be seen. Mitchell and Poli-Dixon were an impossible duo to defend and it might be up to sophomore **Tab Perry** (6-3, 228) to take the heat off Poli-Dixon this season. Toledo said Perry, who set UCLA records for kickoff returns (29) and kickoff return yards (598) last season, has looked outstanding in workouts.

"Tab did a nice job as a freshman and we feel he has the size, speed and overall talent to be a major contributor this year," Toledo said. "And it was shock to us when he came in at 228 pounds. A guy who runs the 40 in 4.4 at his size."

Senior **Jon Dubravac** (6-4, 215) is another big body who should be tough for smallish defensive backs to handle. However, Dubravac caught only 14 balls last season, so he needs to prove he can be more consistent. Senior **Cody Joyce** (6-2, 200) was a special teams player last season who is trying to win more snaps.

Untested sophomores **Jerry Owens** (6-3, 185) and **Ryan Smith** (6-3, 200) and freshman **Craig Bragg** (6-1, 180) will be vying for time. Owens and Bragg are former high school All-Americans.

"I expect Craig to contribute this year," Toledo said. "He is a receiver with speed and he displayed plenty of big-play ability with the scout team last season."

UCLA is loaded at tight end with the return of senior **Bryan Fletcher** (6-5, 235) and junior **Mike Seidman** (6-5, 240). The two combined for 16 catches and three touchdowns last season and both are solid blockers. Fletcher caught 10 balls for 144 yards and two touchdowns last season and he figures to get the nod as the starter. Seidman had one touchdown catch last season.

Sophomore **Blane Kezirian** (6-6, 240) and senior **Dennis Fox** (6-4, 230) are trying to win time at the position.

"The performance of the tight end is critical in our offensive scheme and we have two players capable of making major contributions," Toledo said of Fletcher and Seidman. "I would expect to throw more to our tight ends this season because of their talent and experience levels."

OFFENSIVE LINE

Three-year starting guards Oscar Cabrera and Brian Polak are gone. However, the Bruins have a solid, three-man nucleus returning in senior center **Troy Danoff** (6-5, 310) and junior tackles **Mike Saffer** (6-5, 305) and **Bryce Bohlander** (6-6, 290).

Danoff has started 21 games over the last two seasons while Saffer has 19 starts and Bohlander has 14 consecutive starts. Backing up Danoff will be redshirt freshman **John Ream** (6-4, 290), who is coming off knee surgery.

Senior **Ed Anderson** (6-6, 280) and redshirt freshman **Steven Vieria** (6-6, 295) are trying to win backup jobs at tackle.

Junior **Blake Worley** (6-6, 310), who started 10 games at tackle in 1999, is trying to win the starting job at left guard. Redshirt freshman **Paul Mociler** (6-5, 295) appears to be the main competition. Mociler had knee surgery before last season and decided to sit out the year.

At right guard, sophomore **Shane Lehmann** (6-5, 285) is battling redshirt freshman **Eyoseff Efseaff** (6-3, 285) for starting honors.

"Our tackles gained valuable experience last season and performed well," Toledo said. "We have just one starting senior, and we are trying to replace a couple of three-year starters. I expect the competition at guard to be intense. We know this is a gifted group and we are confident that it will come together and be able to turn that talent into a high level of performance."

2000 STATISTICS

Rushing offense	98.7	100
Passing offense	264.0	23
Total offense	362.7	63
Scoring offense	30.3	34
Net Punting	37.5	18
Punt returns	6.3	102
Kickoff returns	19.7	54
Rushing defense	186.0	88
Passing efficiency defense	120.8	64
Total defense	411.7	92
Scoring defense	31.5	87
Turnover margin	+7	23

Last column is ranking among Division I-A teams.

KICKERS

Junior **Chris Griffith** (6-2, 200) was second-team All-Pac-10 last season after he made 11-of-14 field-goal attempts and 44-of-46 point-after attempts. In the last two seasons, he has made 18-of-22 field-goal attempts inside the 40.

Redshirt freshman **Chris Kluwe** (6-5, 200) is a talented young kicker who is waiting for his turn to either punt or do the place-kicking.

DEFENSIVE LINE

Make room for Coleman. He figures to be one of the most dominating defensive ends in college football, as he was expected to be last season before the injury. Some thought Coleman would try the NFL draft, but he has decided to come back for some unfinished business. As a junior in 1999, he had 50 tackles with nine tackles for loss. He also broke up eight passes. He started the first three games of last season before being injured.

"Kenyon has grown into a dominating player

with a rare blend of size, strength and speed," Toledo said. "He can be a force in the Pac-10."

Junior **Rusty Williams** (6-4, 270), who missed the Sun Bowl as well as spring practice because of shoulder surgery, will start at the other defensive end position. Williams, whom Toledo says has a non-stop motor, had started the previous 22 games before the Sun Bowl.

Williams and Coleman will be pushed by sophomore **Dave Ball** (6-6, 265) and sophomore **Mat Ball** (6-6, 265), twin brothers who had a combined seven starts last season. Mat had an interception return for a touchdown against Oregon State last season.

In the middle, senior **Ken Kocher** (6-4, 320) is back in full health. Kocher's time was limited to nine games last season with just one start because of minor injuries. He started nine games in 1999. "I don't see anyone comparing to him at 320 pounds," Coleman said. "He is an athletic specimen. He never was healthy last season, but people aren't going to believe what he can do."

Sophomore **Rodney Leisle** (6-4, 295) should start at the other tackle slot after coming off a freshman season in which he led Bruin linemen with 36 tackles. He earned a spot on *The Sporting News* Freshmen All-America team.

Also in the mix at inside tackle will be senior **Anthony Fletcher** (6-4, 295) who had 28 tackles last season. He started seven games last season but tailed off toward the end of the year because of minor injuries.

Giving the Bruins depth are juniors **Sean Phillips** (6-6, 300), **Steve Morgan** (6-3, 290) and **Saia Makakaufaki** (6-3, 290) along with sophomore **Asi Faoa** (6-4, 270).

"We had more than our share of injuries (on the defensive line) last season," Toledo said. "On the plus side, we were able to get some of our talented young players on the field for experience. It is very exciting to realize we return virtually everyone from last year. I expect our run defense and our ability to pressure the quarterback to be much improved."

Toledo believes UCLA's defensive line is ready to make a statement.

"Coleman coming back is huge and Kocher and Fletcher are very good," he said. "Throw in Leisle, a freshman All-American. If there is a strength on this team, it is the defensive line."

Because of that strength, Coleman said Snow will require the linemen to get sacks without help from blitzing linebackers. Coleman said Snow's defense will do more stunting up front than the Bruins did last year while the linebackers "sit back and cover."

LINEBACKERS

Senior **Robert Thomas** (6-2, 235), a Butkus semifinalist, returns as the main man in the middle for the Bruins. Going into his third season as a starter, Thomas is expected to make a solid run at All-America status.

"We have one of the nation's most gifted linebackers," Toledo said. "He is a big-time player and he will be a high draft choice."

Thomas led UCLA in tackles last season with 88 and also had nine tackles for loss. He also led the Pac-10 with six forced fumbles and was a second-team All-Pac-10 selection.

"Robert has natural linebacker instincts," Coleman said. "He could have gone in the draft this season if he wanted."

At weak-side linebacker will be senior **Ryan Nece** (6-3, 225), who had 78 tackles last season. He has started the last 21 games.

"Ryan is a three-year starter who brings a steadying influence to the team," Toledo said.

Toledo will keep an eye on Nece, who had surgeries on both shoulders during the off-season.

At strong-side linebacker, sophomore **Brandon Chillar** (6-3, 230) is making a run at a starting berth after playing as a backup and special teams performer in 2000.

Senior **Stephen Sua** (6-2, 270) was used as a defensive end last season but has switched to strong-side linebacker. He had two sacks in 2000.

Toledo will have to find room for junior **Marcus Reese** (6-2, 210), who had 34 tackles last season.

"Marcus possesses big-play potential," Toledo said. "He will see the field extensively."

Other backups at linebacker are sophomore **Dennis Link** (6-2, 210), junior **Audie Attar** (6-0, 205) and redshirt freshmen **Ray Cassaday** (6-1, 250) and **Tim Warfield** (6-2 235).

DEFENSIVE BACKS

The anchor in the secondary is strong safety turned free safety **Marques Anderson** (6-0, 205), a senior who had 73 tackles last season and forced 10 turnovers.

"He creates turnovers and he hits people," Toledo said. "He is the guy who needs to make more plays for us."

Anderson led the Bruins with 11 tackles for loss and he recovered four fumbles, including one for a touchdown against USC.

The other returning starter is junior cornerback **Ricky Manning Jr.** (5-9, 180), who was selected to the All-Pac-10 first team last season. Manning has started 22 consecutive games for the Bruins, Last season, he had 65 tackles and four interceptions.

"In Manning and Anderson, we have two of the best secondary performers in the college game," Toledo said. "However, the unit as a whole must be ready to show overall improvement. We have a lot of youngsters who will challenge for playing time. We need several of them to step up their game and be ready to contribute despite their lack of experience."

Junior **Joe Hunter** (5-11, 170) and sophomore **Keith Short** (5-9, 165) are vying for the other starting cornerback slot. Sophomores **Kevin Braunt** (6-0, 190), and **Ryan Wikert** (6-2, 185), redshirt freshman **Ben Emanuel** (6-3, 202) and senior **Jason Stephens** (6-2, 190) are trying to claim the starting strong safety berth. Stephens has the most experience of the bunch, starting seven games in 1998 with 58 tackles.

"We have no idea about (the players other than Anderson and Manning)," Toledo said. "We might go with true freshmen."

PUNTERS

Junior **Nate Fikse** (5-9, 180) averaged 43.3 yards (13th in the nation) on 75 kicks last season and he could become the conference's top punter now that Cal's Nick Harris has left for the NFL.

Fikse had 19 punts of 50 yards or more last season and 17 of his punts were downed inside the 20. He also handles the kickoff duties. Kluwe is the backup here.

SPECIAL TEAMS

Toledo should sleep well at night because senior **Jeff Grau** (6-4, 250) enters his fourth season as the team's long snapper for both punts and place kicks. A former walk-on, Grau's value was apparent so Toledo awarded him a scholarship.

Also valuable is Perry, who made a huge splash on kickoff returns last season. He average 20.6 yards per return. Manning handled punt returns, and he averaged 6.7 yards on 18 returns.

"Special teams is an important part of every football team," Toledo said. "Griffith and Fikse have outstanding credentials. In Manning and Perry, we also have dependable return specialists who will give us good field position."

RECRUITING CLASS

The concentration was on defensive backs and offensive linemen and UCLA appears to have done an excellent job in those areas.

Five UCLA players—offensive linemen **Collin Barker** (6-8, 300), from Wortham (Texas) High School and **Robert Cleary** (6-7, 285), from Temescal Canyon (Calif.) High School, safety **Matt Ware** (6-3, 195), from Loyola (Calif.) High School, running back **Tyler Ebell** (5-9, 175) from Ventura (Calif.) High School, and wide receiver Junior Taylor (6-2, 185), from Mesa (Ariz.) High School—were members of *PrepStar*'s Dream Team. Eleven other Bruins were *PrepStar* All-Americans.

Although Ebell was one of the most decorated of UCLA's recruits—*Parade* All-American, *USA Today* California Player of the Year—he probably won't get a chance to play as a freshman with Foster handling the tailback duties.

Ebell set national records with 4,495 yards rushing and 64 touchdowns. He rushed for 300 yards or more in 10 games as a senior.

Fellow *Parade* All-American Ware has a better shot of playing right away in UCLA's defensive backfield.

BLUE RIBBON ANALYSIS

OFFENSE	A-
SPECIAL TEAMS	B+
DEFENSE	A-
INTANGIBLES	B

Everything is in place for the Bruins to charge to the top of the Pac-10. If Kocher plays as well as advertised and Coleman stays healthy, this could be UCLA's best defense in years.

However, Toledo is going to have to find some cornerbacks in a hurry because Pac-10 teams tend to go through a lot of them during a season. An injury to a player like Manning could lead to a disaster.

On offense, Paus should blossom because Foster is going to be getting all the attention. That play-action freeze that will stifle defenses should allow Paus that extra split second to find his second and third receivers and avoid the huge errors that plagued him his first two seasons.

The line looks OK, but UCLA needs to find a couple of dependable receivers to perform behind Poli-Dixon and Perry.

All in all, UCLA has very few weak spots. In a conference where all the teams seem to have a couple of problem areas, the Bruins have the look of the most complete team. If Toledo can handle the burden of calling the plays himself while running the team at the same time, it could be a huge year for UCLA.

The Bruins' biggest two games in terms of national attention will come back-to-back on Sept. 22 at home against Ohio State (fourth game of the season) and then at Oregon State on Sept. 29 (fifth game). If the Bruins can find a way to start the season 5-0, they will have a shot at keeping a Pac-10 team in the Rose Bowl, which hosts the national championship game this season.

(J.H.)

2000 RESULTS

Alabama	W	35-24	1-0

Fresno State	W	24-21	2-0
Michigan	W	23-20	3-0
Oregon	L	10-29	3-1
Arizona State	W	38-31	4-1
California	L	38-46	4-2
Oregon State	L	38-44	4-3
Arizona	W	27-24	5-3
Stanford	W	37-35	6-3
Washington	L	28-35	6-4
USC	L	35-38	6-5
Wisconsin (Sun Bowl)	L	20-21	6-6

Washington

LOCATION	**Seattle, WA**
CONFERENCE	**Pac-10**
LAST SEASON	**11-1 (.917)**
CONFERENCE RECORD	**7-1 (t-1st)**
OFFENSIVE STARTERS RETURNING	**6**
DEFENSIVE STARTERS RETURNING	**6**
NICKNAME	**Huskies**
COLORS	**Purple & Gold**
HOME FIELD	**Husky Stadium (72,500)**
HEAD COACH	**Rick Neuheisel (UCLA '84)**
RECORD AT SCHOOL	**18-6 (2 years)**
CAREER RECORD	**51-20 (6 years)**
ASSISTANTS	
	Tony Alford (Colorado State '92) Running Backs
	Steve Axman (C.W. Post '69) Quarterbacks/Wide Receivers
	Keith Gilbertson (Central Washington '71) Offensive Coordinator
	Randy Hart (Ohio State '70) Defensive Line
	Bobby Hauck (Montana '88) Safeties/Special Teams
	Chuck Heater (Michigan '75) Cornerbacks
	Tim Hundley (Western Oregon '74) Defensive Coordinator
	Brent Myers (Eastern Washington '82) Offensive Line
	Tom Williams (Stanford '92) Outside Linebackers
TEAM WINS (last 5 yrs.)	**9-8-6-7-11**
FINAL RANK (last 5 yrs.)	**17-14-36-32-7**
2000 FINISH	**Beat Purdue in Rose Bowl.**

COACH AND PROGRAM

Just call him Doc Neuheisel.

In the aftermath of a tremendous Rose Bowl-winning season, Washington coach Rick Neuheisel has seen his team devastated by graduation and injuries. Now it's up to Neuheisel and his staff doctors to put the pieces back together.

When Neuheisel went into spring practice, he knew he would have a lot of work to do after the Huskies lost 10 starters from their No. 3-ranked team that went 11-1. That was enough of a challenge in itself.

That challenge expanded big-time when the team doctor turned in the following report: sophomore tailback **Rich Alexis** (6-0 215) would miss spring drills because of shoulder surgery. Shoulder surgery? Oh, by the way, sophomore wide receiver **Justin Robbins** (6-0, 180) and senior defensive tackle **Marcus Roberson** (6-4, 260) also would be out with shoulder surgery. Redshirt freshman cornerback **Sam Cunningham** (6-0, 180) and senior outside linebacker **Jafar Williams** (6-0, 230) also would miss spring because—you guessed it—shoulder injuries.

But shoulder injuries didn't hog all the attention of the team doctors. Sophomore offensive tackle **Nick Newton** (6-4, 315) missed spring with an ankle injury, redshirt freshman nose tackle **Josh Miller** (6-3, 280) was out with a wrist problem, sophomore cornerback **Derrick Johnson** (6-0, 175) had a foot ailment and junior tailback **Paul Arnold** (6-1, 200) had a sore back.

Those were all injuries expected to heal.

Then consider that senior defensive end Ryan Julian had to retire because of knee injuries. He started all 12 games last season. And senior reserve offensive guard Rock Nelson also had to quit because of back problems.

Another blow was the fact first-team All-Pac-10 free safety Hakim Akbar decided to declare early for the NFL draft and was taken by the New England Patriots in the fifth round. He had 97 tackles last season.

Injuries and the draft weren't the only reasons for loss of personnel. Cornerback Anthony Vontoure, who saw substantial time, was dismissed from the team.

There was no truth that Neuheisel had to suit up his relatives just to get through spring drills.

"You know, it was one of those years where everyone gave their blood, sweat and tears every game," senior nose tackle **Larry Tripplett** (6-1, 300) said. "Everyone was laying it on the line, regardless of injury, and now people are seeing the aftermath.

"But no way would anyone trade what has happened. And it is good to know you have teammates who will do whatever it takes to win. Right now, though, we've been thin, and guys are missing time."

Tripplett, a second-team All American last season, is expected to be one of the nation's top defensive players, but he isn't sure exactly who will be around him after going through a spring with Washington missing so many excellent players.

"It's hard at times, because you don't get a good idea how good your team is," he said. "A lot of guys who will play this season didn't play in the spring. We've missed an opportunity to grow as a team. But even so, I thought it was a good spring. We had young guys who were put into leadership roles who learned a lot."

This season will offer some huge leadership challenges to the Huskies, who lost their heart-and-soul quarterback Marques Tuiasosopo to graduation. Battling to fill Tuiasosopo's cleats are sophomore **Cody Pickett** (6-4, 205) and junior college transfer **Taylor Barton** (6-2, 205).

Barton was previously paired with Neuheisel at Colorado and has reunited with him after spending one year at City College of San Francisco.

Neuheisel said Washington needs leaders to step up like Tuiasosopo did last season.

"Last season was a wonderful memory and something we all ought to cherish," Neuheisel said. "Now it's 'What have you done for me lately?' We come into this season with a completely new persona. The Washington Huskies are the Pac-10 champs, or at least the co-champs, and are the Rose Bowl champions and a national player.

"Everyone is going to be gunning for the Dawgs. That carries with it a heavy responsibility. The leadership of this team will be even more important than the leadership of last year's team. It is important if you enjoyed last year, and you enjoy that ride and that climb and culmination, then you really ought to set your sights on not just duplicating it, but going above and beyond it."

Finding leaders is just one problem for Neuheisel.

While replacing Tuiasosopo might seem like the No. 1 priority to fans, Neuheisel might have ever bigger troubles when he tries to replace four-fifths of his offensive line. Tackles Elliot Silvers and Wes Call and guards Chad Ward and Matt Fraize are all gone along with key reserves Matt Rogers and Dominic Daste. Those players helped the Huskies lead the Pac-10 in rushing at 211.7 yards a game.

"Our top priority is the offensive line," Neuheisel said. "I think quarterback gets too much attention, regardless if there is competition there or not. That is the nature of the game and the position. To be in the paper and deal with the press on a daily basis will probably be good for our quarterbacks."

Washington also has troubles on the defensive line, where Julian and rush end Jeremiah Pharms are gone. Pharms had 41 tackles for loss during his career. Gone at linebacker is Derrell Daniels, who was voted the team's defensive MVP last season after registering 97 tackles.

Topping it off is the graduation of punter Ryan Felming, a three-year starter.

"One thing we haven't lost is heart and determination," Tripplett said. "We are going to make strides. Being Huskies, we are taught young in our careers that no matter what the score, you fight to the end. No matter what happens here, we are always going to fight. It's a never-say-die attitude. Now it's the responsibility of our senior class to teach our young guys that. I hope and pray they get the message."

Neuheisel has some huge questions to answer if the Huskies are to become the first Pac-10 team to repeat as champion since Washington did it in 1990-92. But in his second season, he did exactly what he was hired to do—get the Huskies back to the Rose Bowl.

Tripplett said he knew when Neuheisel showed up at Washington that things would go in a positive direction.

"I knew when I first met him," Tripplett said. "He recognized what we needed to do to develop. Team chemistry is terribly important and I think what he has done is testimony that if you bring 125 guys together, you can do anything.

"There are no words to recap last season. It had just about everything in it. We had close games and we had blowouts. It was like we were living in a movie. We went through everything and we had a storybook ending. It was the highlight of my life so far. It was so incredible, and yet, as good as it was, it makes you more hungry. We want to get back there again."

Getting back there won't be easy.

Adding to the challenge is a ferocious non-conference schedule that includes a home game against Michigan to open the season on Sept. 8 and a road game at Miami on Sept. 15. That's not exactly good news for a team trying to get healthy and with a host of new starters. But Neuheisel said his players will enjoy every challenge.

"I think we made a good point last year," he said. "And certainly this is a thought that dominated my free time. This isn't just about winning, it's about proving. It is about competition. I had made the point early last season, after the Oregon loss, that if we could press a button and all of a sudden we would be instantly in the Rose Bowl, how many players would press it?

"That isn't what you play for. If someone gives you the trophy, it doesn't mean as much as if you earned it. Earning it is the bottom line and earning begins now. In our locker room is a sign that says Rose Bowl Champions 2001, question mark 2002. It's important we understand we are going to decide where we fall in terms of the finish line."

Fall probably isn't a good term to use around the Washington campus these days. Neuheisel has enough injured players. Tripplett, however, tells his fans not to worry. He says all the first-line players will be healthy by the time the Michigan game rolls around. In fact, he said, they're all pretty healthy already.

"Hey, we're headed out to play some basketball right now," he said.

Now that should make Neuheisel nervous.

2001 SCHEDULE

Sept.	8	Michigan
	15	@Miami
	22	Idaho
	29	@California
Oct.	6	USC
	13	@UCLA
	20	Arizona
	27	@Arizona State
Nov.	3	Stanford
	10	@Oregon State
	17	Washington State

QUARTERBACKS

Pickett forged a bit of a lead over Barton in the spring, but the battle for the position was still too close to call.

"There is a very good possibility that two guys could share the position," Neuheisel said.

Neither has extensive major college experience, so whoever wins the battle will be learning on the job.

"Cody has a stronger arm than I do," Barton said. "I try to beat people with my head."

Certainly, Pickett is the more physical of the two but Barton is a mobile quarterback who said his decision-making skills after reading the defense is one of his strengths.

Pickett had just six pass attempts last season with one completion in three regular season games as Tuiasosopo dominated the action. He did play one series—completing two passes—in the Rose Bowl when Tuiasosopo went down with an injury. Other than that moment, Pickett's most important role was as the holder on place kicks.

Barton led City College of San Francisco to the mythical junior college national title last season. He threw for 2,059 yards and 24 touchdowns while splitting time in a two-quarterback system. Barton was recruited to Colorado by Neuheisel and he was there for the 1998 and '99 seasons before leaving.

A step behind Pickett and Barton is **Ryan Porter** (6-3, 190), another junior college transfer who redshirted last season while serving as Washington's scout team quarterback.

Neuheisel said Pickett's brief Rose Bowl experience should help him.

"I think Pickett's confidence grew immensely given the Rose Bowl situation and the performance he gave," Neuheisel said. "That can do nothing but make you feel good about yourself. And he's had great off-season work."

Neuheisel is, of course, familiar with Barton.

"Taylor Barton is as advertised," Neuheisel said. "He's a very confident player. I've had personal experiences before with him on the practice field, so I know what I am getting. Having watched the game film from City College, I think he's a very, very talented kid."

Eventually, Neuheisel expects Porter to join the fray. "Porter also has grown as a player," he said. "I'm anxious to see if that growth can continue and if he can become a guy who we can count on in tough situations."

Whether any of the three quarterbacks can come close to matching Tuiasosopo remains to be seen. Tuiasosopo is Washington's all-time leader in total offense with 6,875 yards. Of that total, 1,374 were rushing yards.

None of Washington's current quarterbacks appear to have Tuiasosopo's running ability, but Neuheisel said Husky fans will continue to see the option as part of his team's offense.

"We're not throwing the baby out with the bath water," he said. "Option football is one of the reasons we were successful in our conference."

RUNNING BACKS

Washington is solid at tailback as long as Alexis' shoulder heals in time for the opening game. Last season, Alexis gained 738 yards, a Washington freshman record. He also led the team with nine touchdowns and averaged 6.3 yards a carry. He showed his explosiveness with an 86-yard touchdown run against ASU and a 50-yard touchdown run against Miami. He had a 50-yard gain in the Rose Bowl.

If Arnold is able to recover from his back injury, Washington will be stacked at tailback. He was the starting tailback for the Huskies the first half of last season until he hurt himself. He averaged 5.1 yards a carry with 296 yards in all. He also caught 10 passes and averaged 13.8 yards a catch.

Dependable senior **Willie Hurst** (5-10, 200) will be available if anything happens to Alexis or Arnold. Hurst averaged 6.1 yards per carry last season and accumulated 402 yards in nine games. He missed the last two regular season games with a broken collarbone, but returned to run for 53 yards and a touchdown in the Rose Bowl.

The tailback depth keeps going as senior **Braxton Cleman** (6-0, 215) returns as well. He averaged 5.1 yards a rush with 246 yards last season. He gained 105 yards against Washington State in last year's Apple Cup game. Cleman can play fullback as well.

Trying to win time at tailback is sophomore **Sean Sweat** (5-9, 200).

Fullback possibilities for the Huskies are senior **Ken Walker** (6-1, 230), senior **John Hart** (6-1, 235), converted junior nose tackle **Spencer Marona** (6-2, 250) and junior **Matthias Wilson** (5-11, 215).

"We have a lot of very talented players and they have demonstrated the ability to work together and to share the spotlight," Neuheisel said of his running backs.

WIDE RECEIVERS/TIGHT ENDS

Wide receiver again is a suspect position for Washington, which is seeking big-play type receivers. Senior **Todd Elstrom** (6-3, 200) returns after a 47-catch, 683-yard season, and he anchors the group.

Robbins caught 22 passes for 267 yards and four touchdowns, including a 22-yard touchdown in the final minutes to beat Stanford. If he improves as expected, he could be an impact player.

Junior **Wilbur Hooks** (6-0, 190), who caught 11 passes for 151 yards, has to show he can be more consistent.

A wild card in the group is junior **Chris Juergens** (6-3, 210), who had 42 receptions for 516 yards in 1999 but sat out last season with a knee injury.

Neuheisel is hoping seniors **Terry Tharps** (5-10, 175) and **Patrick Reddick** (5-10, 190) evolve into the speed receivers his team so badly needs. Neither has shown much to this point.

Redshirt freshman **Rayshon Dukes** (6-0, 185) will get a long look because of his speed.

Whether those players translate into a solid group remains to be seen. Still, Neuheisel gives them his stamp of approval.

"A year ago, wide receiver was a major concern and now it's a major strength," he said.

Whether wide receiver becomes a strength for the Huskies might be determined by the impact the incoming freshman have on this group.

Right now, the major strength as a receiver is junior tight end **Jerramy Stevens** (6-7, 260), who will probably end up in the NFL before his senior season rolls around. He set a Washington tight end record with 43 catches for 600 yards and three touchdowns last season.

"Jerramy is the consummate tight end," Neuheisel said of the former high school quarterback. "I don't think he dropped a ball all year. He catches the ball very well and he's able to get open. He could certainly get a lot better in his route running and understanding how defenses play. In terms of a guy getting down the field and being able to catch the ball, he is just a real asset for a quarterback in the middle of the field."

Senior **Joe Collier** (6-7, 260), who caught two passes in the Rose Bowl, heads the backup tight ends along with junior **Kevin Ware** (6-3, 275) and **John Westra** (6-5, 250). Ware, who didn't catch a pass last season, might be switched to offensive guard.

Redshirt freshman **Graham Lasee** (6-5, 245) also is trying to win time at tight end.

"Tight end is a strength and we need to capitalize on that," Neuheisel said. "We have some talented players there and it is going to be a big part of the offense."

OFFENSIVE LINE

Wipe out.

No, the Huskies didn't go surfing. They just had a lot of seniors playing key roles last season.

Consequently, Neuheisel will hope that his backups have learned their jobs well. If not, his brand new quarterbacks are going to take their lumps while they learn the offense.

"We lost six of our top seven guys," Neuheisel said. "I think we are plenty talented, but of all the positions on the football field, the one that requires experience the most is offensive line. It is going to get the lion's share of attention."

Fortunately for Neuheisel and the Huskies, they have an experienced man making the line calls in senior center **Kyle Benn** (6-3, 300), who has 25 career starts. Benn is going to be required to run the show as the players around him develop.

Sophomores **Todd Bachert** (6-4, 305) and **Nick Newton** (6-4, 315), junior **Elliott Zajac** (6-4, 315) and junior college transfer **Francisco Tipoti** (6-5, 295), a junior, are leading contenders to fill guard spots.

"We're going to play inside with guys like Zajac and Newton," Neuheisel said. "I think both those guys are ready to play. They just need to get skinned up a bit and get it done. Bachert probably will go inside as well and I think he is ready to play. He's been in our program now two years and I think he's anxious to get his playing time increased. Tipoti is someone we hope can fill one of the guard positions.

"Then we will play three young guys: [redshirt freshman] **Khalif Barnes** (6-5, 285), [red-shirt freshman] **Ryan Brooks** (6-6, 300), [sophomore] **Andre Reeves** (6-5, 320) at tackle. It might be that their inexperience will show so we will move one of our inside guys out, but my hope is that they'll be talented enough and athletic enough for them to handle it."

2000 STATISTICS

Rushing offense	211.7	16
Passing offense	196.2	74
Total offense	407.9	35
Scoring offense	32.1	23
Net Punting	33.3	78

Punt returns	7.3	95
Kickoff returns	21.2	24
Rushing defense	141.5	50
Passing efficiency defense	111.9	41
Total defense	349.5	44
Scoring defense	22.4	42
Turnover margin	-3	74

Last column is ranking among Division I-A teams.

KICKERS

Junior **John Anderson** (6-2, 185) has kicked 25 field goals during his career and scored 147 points. He is solid, so Neuheisel can turn his attention to other areas.

DEFENSIVE LINE

It all starts with Tripplett, who will make a run at all the national awards. He had 11 tackles for loss and 6 1/2 quarterback sacks, tremendous numbers for a nose tackle.

"Larry Tripplett is an explosive player," Neuheisel said. "It's difficult to block him with just one guy. I would say most teams scheme to try to take him out with two people, and in doing so, they create seams and gaps for other players to get home to the quarterback or make the tackle. He's just one of those game-altering type players when he's playing at his best.

"The consistency is what's got to happen. He's got to become as consistent as he can be. He got nicked with some injuries toward the end last year and didn't have the same kind of numbers he had at the beginning. If we can get him start to finish the way he started last season, we'll have a heck of a player."

Tripplett is smart enough to understand that opponents will be concentrating on him this season because Washington will be starting rookies on the defensive line.

"My job is to cause havoc in the backfield and try to make plays," he said. "As long as I do my job, that's the only thing I am concerned about, that and getting victories."

Tripplett said Washington looked good along the defensive line during spring drills, but he thinks his unit needs to improve to get the Huskies back to the Rose Bowl.

"We have to become a better run stopping team,"

Tripplett said. "We were a good running team last year and that caused our opponents a lot of trouble because we controlled the clock. We don't want to let our opponents do that to us this year."

Tripplett said two new members of the Washington defensive line this season, junior college transfer **Kai Ellis** (6-3, 245), a junior, and redshirt freshman **Zach Tuiasosopo** (6-2, 235), the brother of Marquess, will eventually be Pac-10 stars at defensive end.

"I am just thankful that Mr. Tuiasosopo had another son," Tripplett said. "Zach is an awesome athlete and he will do great things for us. Kai is a transfer who has looked impressive. Physically, Kai is incredible. And Zach has the heart and determination that comes in the Tuiasosopo blood. I wouldn't be surprised that in the end, Kai and Zach get more attention than I do."

Vying for spots at the other defensive tackle spot are sophomore **Jerome Stevens** (6-3, 300), Roberson (eight tackles for loss, six sacks last season) and junior **Ossim Hatem** (6-3, 280), who had six tackles for loss in 2000.

"We feel good about our situation on the defensive line," Neuheisel said. "But we would have felt better if Roberson was back during the spring. He had to sit out due to his shoulder surgery. I'm excited to see Kai and Zach on the field and to watch some of our redshirt players start to fill into positions."

LINEBACKERS

If Williams doesn't have any more ankle injuries, Washington should be fine at linebacker. Williams is an experienced player who had 21 tackles last season before going down with the injury.

Also back is junior **Ben Mahdavi** (6-2, 235), who started eight games and the Rose Bowl. He had 52 tackles and a 35-yard fumble return for touchdown against Idaho.

Coming on strong is senior **Anthony Kelley** (6-2, 220), who saw a lot of time last season because of Williams' injury. Also, sophomore **Marquis Cooper** (6-4, 210) looks like a good bet to fill one spot at inside linebacker.

Seniors **Jamaun Willis** (6-2, 245) and **Sam Blanche** (6-1, 220), sophomore **Tyler Krambrink** (6-1, 210) and redshirt freshmen **Tim Galloway** (6-1, 230) and **Matt Lingley** (6-2, 225) are trying to break into the lineup.

"We are going to be more athletic at linebacker," Neuheisel said. "Daniels was outstanding in terms of productivity, but I think we could get a little faster than Derrell was."

DEFENSIVE BACKS

Senior cornerback **Omare Lowe** (6-1, 205) leads this group and sophomore cornerback **Chris Massey** (5-11, 170) is the other returning starter in the defensive backfield.

Of course, replacing Akbar will be Neuheisel's toughest duty. Junior strong safety **Owen Biddle** (5-10, 190), who got a start in the Rose Bowl, will get the first look at the position. Senior **Nick Olszewski** (5-10, 180) will also get to compete for playing time. Sophomore **Greg Carothers** (6-2, 205), who had 27 tackles last season, is also fighting for a starting job at strong safety.

Trying to earn a starting berth at free safety is senior **Roderick Green** (5-11, 185), a former starting cornerback who redshirted last season to concentrate on academics.

Players adding to the depth of the defensive backfield are sophomore free safety **Jimmy Newell** (6-1, 195) and senior free safety **Wondame Davis** (5-11, 170). Davis played as a flanker last season.

Neuheisel will attempt to increase his depth in the secondary by moving two former offensive players, senior **Lenny Haynes** (5-10, 195) and junior **Jelani Harrison** (6-1, 205), back there.

"When I first arrived here, defensive back was an area of real concern," Neuheisel said. "I think that in a couple of years, we've developed into a very confident defensive backfield. It would be a little short sighted to say 'We're there' because we're playing with so many young players. There are a lot of guys who need to get better and their great days are ahead of them.

"When you've got Carothers coming back at safety, having had the experience he had last year, I think you feel good he will be able to play well. The other safety spot remains a question mark. Newell was unable to play [all year] because of a broken wrist, but I'm confident he will have an impact there. With the early departure of Akbar, we're going to have to see how things develop. Biddle played a couple of series in the Rose bowl and did fine."

PUNTERS

Ryan Fleming graduated, so Anderson and freshman **Derek McLaughlin** (6-2, 190) will be fighting to handle the punting duties.

Senior **Jim Skurski** (5-11, 200) had a strong spring punting and he could take over if Anderson and McLaughlin don't pan out.

SPECIAL TEAMS

Sophomore **Derrick Johnson** (6-0, 175) handled the kickoff duties last season and led the Pac-10 with a 24.2 yards per attempt average, so the Huskies have that position in good hands. Johnson could be joined by one of the highly recruited freshmen who will arrive in the fall.

Johnson was expected to return punts in 2000, but he had problems handling the ball and was removed from that duty. He could return if a season of experience has helped.

Toure Butler handled most of the punt returns last year, but he graduated, so Neuheisel will be looking at his prized freshmen to fill the position. Arnold would be another possibility.

Both long snappers return. Mahdavi handles snaps for punts and Zajac for place kicks.

RECRUITING CLASS

Washington had its usual strong haul of preps, but the focus of this year's class will rest on transfers Ellis and Barton, who both managed to get into school in time to participate in spring drills.

Among the high school players, Husky fans are hoping *Parade* All American **Charles Frederick** (6-0, 190) out of Boca Raton, Fla., can help out right away. Frederick caught 29 touchdown passes as a senior at Pope John Paul High School. *Student Sports* magazine ranked him as the nation's top high school wide receiver. A tremendous all-around athlete, he is expected to play point guard on Washington's basketball team in the winter. If Frederick meets all his academic requirements during the summer, Washington also will gain a tremendous return man.

The other recruiting coup was **Reggie Williams**, a 6-4, 215-pound wide receiver out of Tacoma, Wash. A consensus (*Parade*, *USA Today*, *SuperPrep*, *Prepstar*) All-American, he was *Prep Football Report*'s top wide receiver in the country.

Among the other top recruits is defensive lineman **Tui Alailefaleula**, a 6-4, 270-pounder out of Anchorage, Alaska who had 38 sacks his final two years. He was a *SuperPrep* and *PrepStar* All-American.

Another *PrepStar* All-American was safety **Evan Benjamin** (6-0, 200) out of Redmond, Wash. He was a consensus pick as the best defensive back to come out of Washington last recruiting season.

The other huge local signee was **Will Conwell** (6-4, 220), a linebacker from Kent, Wash. who also was the state's shot putting champ.

BLUE RIBBON ANALYSIS

OFFENSE	C
SPECIAL TEAMS	B
DEFENSE	C
INTANGIBLES	A

This might be a year that Washington has to get by on pure coaching. Certainly, the Huskies have tons of athletic talent based on their top-ranked recruiting classes season after season. But they lost far too many big-time players.

Breaking in a new quarterback against national powerhouses like Michigan and Miami is just one of Neuheisel's many headaches. But that task pales in comparison to building an entire offensive line. Certainly, the Huskies have lots of bodies to fill the void, but just consider if each of the new starters makes one mistake a game.

Four sacks. That would be hard to live with over the course of a season.

It's no sure bet that is going to happen, but you would have to expect some kind of learning curve. Besides everything else, the Pac-10 is so balanced these days that experience teams tend to win the close games, something that Washington accomplished last season.

It wasn't that long ago that Washington State and Stanford won Rose Bowls, then fell to the second division of the Pac-10 the next season. It doesn't take too many straws to break the camel's back these days in the Pac-10.

Washington does have one nice little factor in its favor in that it doesn't play Oregon this season, and the Ducks figure to be an offensive nightmare for most teams. However, the Huskies do have to play Pac-10 favorite UCLA in Pasadena and Oregon State in Corvallis.

Washington appears to be far too stable a program to fall completely off the map this season, but a minor bowl seems the likely target.

(J.H.)

2000 RESULTS

Idaho	W	44-20	1-0
Miami	W	34-29	2-0
Colorado	W	17-14	3-0
Oregon	L	16-23	3-1
Oregon State	W	33-30	4-1
Arizona State	W	21-15	5-1
California	W	36-24	6-1
Stanford	W	31-28	7-1
Arizona	W	35-32	8-1
UCLA	W	35-28	9-1
Washington State	W	51-3	10-1
Purdue (Rose Bowl)	W	34-24	11-1

Washington State

LOCATION	**Pullman, WA**
CONFERENCE	**Pac-10**
LAST SEASON	**4-7 (.364)**
CONFERENCE RECORD	**2-6 (t-8th)**
OFFENSIVE STARTERS RETURNING	**9**
DEFENSIVE STARTERS RETURNING	**10**
NICKNAME	**Cougars**
COLORS	**Crimson & Gray**
HOME FIELD	**Martin Stadium (37,600)**
HEAD COACH	**Mike Price (Puget Sound '69)**
RECORD AT SCHOOL	**63-73 (12 years)**
CAREER RECORD	**109-117 (21 years)**
ASSISTANTS	**Robb Akey (Weber State '88)** **Defensive Line** **Chris Ball (Missouri Western '86)** **Defensive Backs** **Bob Connelly (Texas A&M-Commerce '94)** **Offensive Line** **Bill Doba (Ball State '62)** **Defensive Coordinator** **Kasey Dunn (Idaho '92)** **Running Backs** **Mike Levenseller (WSU '78)** **Offensive Coordinator** **Aaron Price (WSU '94)** **Quarterbacks** **Mike Walker (WSU '82)** **Defensive Line** **Jim Zeches (Cal State-Northridge '73)** **Tight Ends**
TEAM WINS (last 5 yrs.)	**5-10-3-3-4**
FINAL RANK (last 5 yrs.)	**58-12-50-76-61**
2000 FINISH	**Lost to Washington in regular-season finale.**

COACH AND PROGRAM

If experience is indeed a huge factor in the Pac-10, Washington State should vastly improve upon its three combined conference wins over the last three seasons.

But does a year of learning really make all that much difference?

As more than one coach has noted in the past, "The good news is that we have experience. The bad news is that we have everyone coming back."

Washington State coach Mike Price isn't worried that the 19 starters he has returning went 4-7 last season. He knows the Cougars were only a few points from a successful season after losing three overtime games in a four-game span.

"The kicking game hurt us in all three overtime losses last year," Price said. "In one it was a missed extra point, in another a blocked field goal and in a third a missed field goal. We needed to make those kicks. Had we made a couple of those kicks, we would have been looking at victories."

Price is hoping that a couple of kicks won't keep his team from a bowl berth this season. He has a defense made up of returning players who have started 150 games. His offensive starters have a combined 93 starts behind them. He has reserves who have started 22 games. Even his kickers have started 11 games.

Still, all that experience doesn't mean the Cougars don't have something to prove. Remember, they went out meekly last season with a 51-3 loss to Pac-10 co-champion Washington.

Certainly the WSU offense has a lot to prove. It averaged 121.3 yards rushing a game last season and whether those same players have a year of experience, they have to improve that mark if they expect to score more than the 25.5 points a game the Cougars mustered.

Putting together the offense will be new coordinator Mike Levenseller, and he has some talent to work with in returning junior quarterback **Jason Gesser** (6-1, 195), the Pac-10's most elusive signal caller, along with former Marine tailback, senior **Dave Minnich** (6-0, 220).

Although the defense allowed 174.3 rushing yards a game and 412.6 yards of total offense last season, Price believes that unit will be his team's strength in 2001.

Early in the 1990s, WSU often built its fortunes upon its defense, such as the 1994 Palouse Posse that led the nation in total defense.

Price said his current defense has that kind of potential. He said his back seven (three linebackers and four defensive backs) is the most solid of any he has coached.

"I think we're going to be outstanding (on defense)," Price said. "**Raonall Smith** and **James Price** are veteran four-year linebackers. **Billy Newman** and **Lamont Thompson** have the same experience in the secondary. **Lamont started as a freshman and so did (junior) Marcus Trufant**. I am very excited about that group of players and so is (defensive coordinator) Bill Doba. We're doing some things defensively that I think will make us very exciting to watch."

If Gesser can go from exciting to effective, WSU's offense might give its defensive unit enough support to lead to a winning season. The big question for the Cougars early is whether they will get much help from a wide receiver corps that lost its top two threats, Milton Wynn and Marcus Williams.

The biggest question mark on defense is the line, but Price is confident his more experienced unit will fare better this season.

If WSU can make the step to the upper division of the Pac-10, it could join Washington, Oregon and Oregon State as Pac-10 powerhouses.

"We would have liked to have won an overtime game or two last year and it would have been a solid sweep in the Northwest," Price said. "We were close."

Close, but no cigar.

"We need to not make as many mistakes and penalties," Minnich said. "In the Oregon [loss], two penalties in overtime hurt us a lot. It was nice to hang with Oregon, but it would have been better to beat them. Coach is working on that."

Very little separates the top of the Pac-10 from the bottom, so Price doesn't think it is impossible that the Cougars will be a contender for the title in 2001. That being said, Price also said the conference rates with any other in the country.

"I think it's obvious the Pac-10 is back with the best people in the country," he said. "We've had six different teams win or share the title over the last four years and nine of 10 teams have won or shared the championship over the last eight years, so that tells you the balance in our league. Anybody can win it at any time. It doesn't seem to matter how you did last year, it's what's up this year.

"I have no idea who the favorite will be. I know the sports writers will pick someone, but it's not going to be us. We're just trying to take one game at a time and not project how we're going to do and what I think might happen. I just think we're going to be better. We improved this spring and we're a better football team now than we were a year ago."

Price has his players convinced they can correct the flaws of 1999 and 2000.

"If everyone plays the way we can, we will be real solid," said senior strong safety Newman (5-10, 200), who has been one of the Pac-10's best defensive backs the last two seasons. "There is no question we have good leaders on this team, guys who have been here before. The younger guys will follow suit. This year it's not a matter of the coaches riding us. The players have been taking care of business on their own. There is a lot of enthusiasm, and I haven't seen that in a long time."

Although he was a redshirt freshman when Washington went to the Rose Bowl after the 1997 season, Newman said the Cougars benefit by the presence of players such as Thompson (6-2, 215) and senior linebacker Price (5-11, 215), guys who played on that team.

"Those guys know what it takes," Newman said.

Thompson's case is special. He suffered a serious neck injury last season that forced him to miss what would have been his senior year. In a way, it worked out well for him and the program and he gets a chance to lead a very impressive looking defense.

Ironically, Price has almost all of his players back but has added two new coaches—Aaron Price and Bob Connelly—and switched Levenseller to offensive coordinator. So it will be interesting to see if everyone is on the same page early in the season.

"We'll have to see how two new coaches and a new offensive coordinator change the look of WSU football," Price said. "It may not change a lot, but I do think it's been kind of refreshing with two younger guys joining us, Aaron Price and Bob Connelly. Mike Levenseller has taken over as offensive coordinator and he is an outstanding teacher. I think you have to play with what you have, so we may not be as spectacular or flashy on offense. We may be a more disciplined unit that runs the ball a little better."

The schedule certainly is favorable for the

Cougars to make a run at a bowl berth. WSU's three non-conference opponents are Idaho, Boise State and Colorado, with the Idaho and Colorado games in Pullman. Of course, Idaho and Boise State are the kind of programs that often produce solid clubs, but if the Cougars deserve to be in a bowl, they should beat those two. Colorado is coming off a poor season, so the Cougars have a shot in that game, too.

Washington State's fourth game of the season is against Cal in Pullman, the conference opener for both teams. That game probably will tell WSU's fate for the rest of the season. The Cougars haven't lost to Cal at home since 1979 and two of their three conference wins over the last two seasons have come against the Bears. However, Cal is expected to be much improved this season, so the winner of this game might be for real.

The rest of the conference season is favorable for WSU with home games against the top three conference favorites, Oregon State, Oregon and UCLA.

2001 SCHEDULE

Aug.	30	Idaho
Sept.	8	@Boise State
	15	Colorado
	22	California
	29	@Arizona
Oct.	6	Oregon State
	13	@Stanford
	27	Oregon
Nov.	3	UCLA
	10	@Arizona State
	17	@Washington

QUARTERBACKS

An indication of Gesser's importance to the Cougars might have come in last season's finale against Washington. With Gesser watching from the sideline with a broken leg, the Cougars managed just three points. In the nine games he played last season, Gesser completed 128-of-246 passes for 1,967 yards. He threw 16 touchdowns and had 10 interceptions.

But it isn't his arm that drives opponents nuts. Gesser is perhaps the most elusive quarterback in the Pac-10. He gained 200 yards rushing last season, a number that was offset by 153 yards in losses because of sacks. If he didn't possess uncanny escapability, those sack totals would have been much higher. His escapability should allow his untested wide receivers a little extra time to maneuver this season.

Gesser finished as the top-rated quarterback in the Pac-10 in 2000 and was fourth in passing and total offense. He threw a school-record six touchdown passes against Arizona and in one stretch threw 130 passes without an interception.

Behind Gesser will be sophomore **Matt Kegel** (6-5, 230), who led Washington State to a victory over USC after taking over for the injured Gesser. On the season, Kegal completed 40-of-91 passes for 535 yards, one touchdown and one interception. If Price decides to switch to Kegal on occasion, it certainly will allow the Cougars to change looks from the scrambling Gesser to a more traditional drop-back type passer.

"I think we're real solid at the quarterback position," Price said. "With the emergence of Kegel and the job that he's done, especially in the spring game, we have two battle-savvy quarterbacks who already have proven they can win in the Pac-10.

"I don't think Matt thinks of himself as a backup to Jason. He's still on the "A" team. Jason showed last season he is a dangerous quarterback and leader who will be even better this season. When something breaks down, Jason has the ability make a big play because he is so athletic. Gesser and (senior wide receiver) **Nakoa McElrath** can be the big-play type guys we need."

RUNNING BACKS

Minnich eventually earned the starting tailback job after the sixth game last season. He finished with 754 yards on 165 carries to go with four touchdowns. Those numbers should increase now that Minnich has a year on the football field after four years in the Marine Corps.

Price said his tailback came to spring camp in much better football shape than he was in last season. Minnich ran a 40-yard dash in 4.5 during the spring, which means he also has gotten a bit quicker.

Senior **Jeremy Thielbahr** (6-2, 230) and senior **John Tippins** (6-1, 220) back up Minnich. Both are seldom-used players who will be suspect should anything happen to Minnich. Thielbahr had two carries last year for no yards and Tippins didn't carry the ball. A void was created when former starting tailback Deon Burnett (405 rushing last year) quit the team at the end of last season. Price might have to go to an incoming freshman if Minnich is hurt.

"I am very high on Minnich," Price said. "He had a great winter and spring and is now in tip-top football shape. He was in tip-top Marine Corps shape when he came here last fall, but that didn't parlay into football shape. In the spring, after winter conditioning, Dave ran a 4.5 for the pro scouts. He has the full package now because he can catch the ball, block, run inside and run outside. If he stays healthy he'll be one of the best backs in the conference.

"Thielbahr also had a good spring. He is a very smart back who knows all the assignments, where to run, who to block and where to run on pass assignments. He is going to be very valuable, both as a back and on special teams.

"Tippins is another young man who improved in the spring. We'd like to see him quit dancing behind the line of scrimmage Saturday afternoons and save his dancing for Saturday night after the game. He's at the point now where he can step into a game and help us if he will attack the line. We are also going to look at all the freshman running backs and give everyone a shot during fall camp to see who can step forward."

WIDE RECEIVERS/TIGHT ENDS

In the search for an impact wide receiver, Price turned toward the basketball team where tremendously athletic junior **Mike Bush** (6-6, 200) was showing how high he could go up for the ball. Now Bush will be skying high for footballs, as he proved in a short amount of spring practice work that he can make an impact on the football field.

The Cougars have to experiment with an inexperienced player like Bush because they lost their top two wideouts from last season—including Milton Wynn, picked by the St. Louis Rams in the fourth round of the NFL draft. WSU appears to lack the big-play performer needed to keep a defense honest. The Cougars return six wide receivers who have experience, but none goes into the season commanding double coverage.

Bush's size will demand extra attention if he proves he can be a consistent target. If Bush can provide half the contributions he did for WSU's basketball team, he'll be a real find. Last season, Bush played in 17 games, starting 14, and led the Cougars in scoring (15.9 points per game) and was second in rebounding (5.2). Admittedly a contact sports junkie, Bush has also played rugby.

If Bush develops, it could provide the Cougars with an excellent one-two combo if senior McElrath (6-2, 195) shows the explosiveness he did in WSU's spring game in which he caught 10 passes, three for touchdowns. McElrath had 14 catches for 303 yards last season.

"He has the ability to be a dominant receiver in this league," Price said. "If he can discipline himself."

Along with McElrath, junior **Collin Henderson** (6-1, 188) figures to start at wideout. Henderson, who caught 14 passes for 150 yards last year, has 12 career starts but will move from slot to flanker. Junior **Curtis Nettles** (5-7, 158) is expected to be one of the starters when the Cougars use three wideouts. Nettles had nine catches for 93 yards last season.

"If there's a question mark on our team it's at the wide receiver positions," Price said. "One of the players who may help alleviate that question mark is Bush, the top player on our basketball team who joined us in the spring. Mike has great height, can jump and make plays and is super competitive.

"Henderson is very steady. McElrath has the ability to be a big time receiver. All he needs is more consistency and discipline. Nakoa has the ability to make us a winner in the Pac-10. How dedicated he is this summer will go a long way toward making him the great player he can be, or just an average player. He has the ability to perform at that level [as he did in the spring game] every game. It will be a matter of dedication. While we have good depth at the receiver positions, we need a couple of them to really jump to the top next fall."

While WSU lost its top wide receivers, both tight ends from last year, junior **Russell Mizin** (6-4, 240) and senior **Mark Baldwin** (6-6, 245), are back. Mizin is a two-year starter who has started 17 games. Baldwin transferred from junior college last season and was limited by a shoulder injury in 2000. But Price said he is ready to make an impact. Mizin caught 12 passes for 79 yards last season.

OFFENSIVE LINE

It remains to be seen if Price's enthusiasm for a group that struggled mightily last season is well founded. The head coach said his starting five offensive linemen compare favorably to the 1997 group that helped the team reach the Rose Bowl.

"I have not coached an offensive line as athletic as this group," Price said. "We are bigger and stronger than last year and obviously we have experience, something we didn't have in abundance last year. This line will be as good as any I have coached."

Washington State started a junior, three sophomores and a freshman last season. Now a senior, guard **Joey Hollenbeck** (6-4, 277), is a former defensive lineman who switched over after being a starter in 1998. The other guard slot will be held by either junior **Phil Locker** (6-5, 303), junior **Derrick Roche** (6-6, 281) or sophomore **Billy Knotts** (6-7, 285). Locker and Roche were both starters last season.

Going into summer camp, the starters at tackle will be sophomore **Josh Parrish** (6-6, 288), a returning starter, and redshirt freshman **Sam Lightbody** (6-9, 300), who was projected as a starter in 2000 but suffered a hand injury that ended his season.

Redshirt freshman **Calvin Armstrong** (6-7, 315) is close to breaking into the lineup and is also expected to see significant playing time. And if Knotts doesn't win a job at tackle, he could help at guard.

Junior **Tyler Hunt** (6-4, 280) returns at center.

"I think our line is ready to step up in the Pac-10," Price said. "Bob Connelly has done a nice job in simplifying some of our schemes and allowing us to be athletic. We have, by far, the most athletic offensive line we have had in my 12 years at WSU. While they may have been a little inexperienced last year, that is not the case now. The nucleus of our line has made a collective 53 starts over the last two years.

"Parrish, Lightbody, Knotts, those guys are athletic and they are going to be great offensive linemen, as good as we've had. I think this will be a better offensive line than our Rose Bowl team. They have dedicated themselves to the weight room.

"A perfect example is Hunt. He played every down last year, but at about 260 he was undersized. He has dedicated himself to the weight room and now he is over 280 and his weight room stats have improved greatly. Hollenbeck and Roche are in the same mold, athletic and with experience. We also have some younger players like Armstrong who have benefited from a year in the weight room and will see a lot of playing time."

2000 STATISTICS

Rushing offense	121.3	84
Passing offense	241.5	31
Total offense	362.7	63
Scoring offense	25.5	60
Net Punting	33.5	76
Punt returns	7.3	97
Kickoff returns	19.6	57
Rushing defense	174.3	77
Passing efficiency defense	122.7	71
Total defense	412.6	94
Scoring defense	32.2	91
Turnover margin	-1	65

Last column is ranking among Division I-A teams.

KICKERS

The Cougars hope they have shored up their place kicking output with the addition of two newcomers. Junior college transfer **Adam Holiday** (6-3, 223), a junior, appears to have won the kickoff duties after a strong spring performance. Holiday, who doesn't kick field goals, put a high percentage of his kickoffs into the end zone during spring practice, something WSU kickers could not do last year.

Who wins the job of kicking field goals and extra points probably will not be known until the first game. The contenders returning from last year are senior **Nick Lambert** (5-11, 200) and sophomore **Drew Dunning** (5-10, 170), plus freshman **Graham Siderius** (6-2, 195), a highly touted newcomer from Reno, Nevada

Last year Lambert won the kicking chores going into the first game, but suffered a leg injury three games into the season. In the spring Dunning took a slight edge in the battle, pending a renewed rivalry in the fall.

"Poor kickoffs were a problem for us last season so the addition of a kickoff specialist improved that aspect of the game in the spring," Price said. "Last year I think we had two kickoffs in the end zone that were not returnable, but Holiday showed this spring he can get them deep into the end zone.

"I also think our place-kickers did a better job in the spring. Bringing in a high school All-American [Siderius] in the fall should also improve our kicking. We also spent more time in the spring working on what we will do in overtime games. That's not something you usually spend a lot of time on in practices."

WSU was 11-for-19 in field goals last season.

DEFENSIVE LINE

Washington State's fortunes might be determined on the defensive line, where three starters from last season will be attempting to do a better job stopping the run. WSU also has four other players returning who saw considerable action.

Anchoring the line are junior defensive end **Fred Shavies** (6-1, 240) and junior tackles **Tomasi Kongaika** (6-1, 290) and **Rien Long** (6-7, 280). Shavies had 29 tackles last season, including six for loss and two sacks. Kongaika also had 29 tackles with six tackles for loss and one sack. Long had 15 tackles with five for loss and one sack.

Obviously, those numbers will have to increase for all three if the Cougars expect to move to the top of the Pac-10.

Trying to win a starting position at the other defensive end position will be sophomore **Isaac Brown** (6-3, 220) and senior **Tupo Tuupo** (6-3, 270). Sophomores **Tai Tupai** (6-4, 320) and **Jeremy Williams** (6-4, 280) are vying for playing time at tackle. They might get that time, too, because Kongaika missed spring drills because of a leg injury. Tuupo, Tupai and Williams all had two tackles for loss last season. Brown had three sacks.

"We will begin the season with a veteran line, which is huge when you mix them in with our deep seven," Price said. "The experience our line gained last year and with the additional year of strength and weight gain, we should more than hold our own up front.

"We're going to get pressure on people. The strength of our defense is going to be the deep seven, but the strength of our team is going to be our total defense. We have depth on the line now and we have size. Inside we have two big guys in Long and Tupai, both close to 300 pounds.

"Williams had an excellent spring and will see a lot of action. Both Kongaika and junior tackle **Ing Aleaga** (6-3, 285) were injured in the spring, but they are experienced veterans with 18 starts between them. While they may not be 100 percent when we start the season, they should be ready by the fourth or fifth game when other people are starting to get worn down. We also have junior **Nate Mallory** (6-3, 285), who joined us in January out of junior college."

Price said the Cougars have four athletic guys who can play at the end positions.

"Tuupo and Shavies are both converted linebackers now playing defensive end," he said. "Tuupo has really improved his strength since last fall. The two guys behind them are sophomore **Isaac Brown** (6-3, 220) and redshirt freshman **D.D. Acholonu** (6-3, 240). Both are speed-type defensive ends who can really run and can track you down from sideline to sideline."

LINEBACKERS

All three starting linebackers return. Seniors Price (5-11, 215) and Smith (6-2, 241) and junior **Melvin Simmons** (6-1, 210) are primed to have big years. Price was second on the team with 72 tackles last season, including eight for loss. Smith was third with 71 tackles, including 12 for loss. Simmons had 59 tackles, fourth best among the Cougars, and seven tackles for loss including four sacks.

"How many teams can return three starters?" Price said. "We've got talented starters and depth. The three veterans from last year, Smith, Price and Simmons, are very strong, very fast and very experienced. They know how to play in this league."

WSU's top three backups from 2000 also return: sophomore **Mike Isaacson** (5-11, 210), sophomore **Al Genatone** (6-0, 220) and senior **Serign Marong** (6-2, 235).

DEFENSIVE BACKS

Thompson (22 career starts) was expected to be an All-America candidate last season at free safety but had to sit out the year because of his neck injury. He is tied for first on the team's career interception chart with 14.

Price expects Thompson, Newman at strong safety and junior cornerback Trufant (6-0, 188) to earn national honors this season. Newman, who has started 23 games, led the team in tackles the last two seasons with 100 in 1999 and 105 in 2000. The All Pac-10 second-team performer had four interceptions. Trufant had three interceptions last season, his second as a starter. He had 16 pass defenses and 58 tackles.

WSU's key backups also return. Sophomore **Erik Coleman** (5-10, 195) has moved to No. 1 on the depth chart at the cornerback opposite Trufant.

Sophomore **Jason David** (5-8, 160) and senior **Mike Freeman** (5-10, 180) will see lots of time when opponents go to multiple wide out sets.

"Coleman and David played a lot last year as true freshmen, so they're not new to the game," Price said. "Trufant has had two good solid years behind him, so he's ready to have an outstanding junior season. It is not a stretch to compare our starters to the secondary of 1994 when we had guys like John Rushing and Torey Hunter. We also have outstanding depth with young guys like David, who will be our fifth defensive back. Freeman played last year as a junior college transfer and he played well at cornerback in the spring."

Trying to break into the lineup are redshirt freshman cornerback **Karl Paymah** (6-0, 190) and junior cornerback **Virgil Williams** (6-1, 195).

Seeing time at safety will be sophomore **Ira Davis** (6-0, 205) and redshirt freshman **Hamza Abdullah** (6-2, 215).

PUNTERS

WSU's top punter from a year ago, senior **Alan Cox** (6-2, 190), returns after averaging 38.4 yards a punt. He was the only player to punt for the Cougars in 2000 and will handle the duties again this season, even though his numbers weren't overwhelming.

SPECIAL TEAMS

Henderson returned 15 punts for 91 yards last season and he probably will get the call most of the time this season. But Price would like to get a little more explosiveness out of his return game and Henderson's long return last season was 19 yards. Of the other seven punts last season handled by somebody else, four were returned by Newman, who managed just three return yards.

Nettles averaged 17.3 yards per kickoff return last season, Newman averaged 21.2 and Coleman 25.4. All three are expected to get a shot at that duty again.

"We have a host of good returners," Price said. "Henderson has been our punt returner for two years, but he's going to be challenged by Trufant and David. Coleman was outstanding returning kickoffs last year until he got hurt. Newman also did a fine job. We're putting more emphasis on our return game this year, trying to make more big plays."

Henderson holds for extra points and field

goals.

RECRUITING CLASS

Washington State's monster recruit was **Dwayne Wright** (6-1, 185) out of Lincoln High in San Diego. Wright earned nine of 10 votes in the *Long Beach Press Telegram*'s Best in the West poll. He rushed for 2,323 yards as a senior with 39 touchdowns. Wright is one of WSU's few recruits who appears ready to make an immediate impact.

Another Best in the West pick was quarterback **Chris Hurd** (6-2, 185) out of Deer Valley High School in Antioch, Calif.

Price said Hurd, who threw for 1,800 yards and 25 touchdowns as a senior, has a "rocket arm."

Siderius not only is a place-kicker, he led McQueen High to the Nevada state championship as a quarterback. He made 74-of-75 extra points and hit 11-of-14 field goals. Four were more than 50 yards.

BLUE RIBBON ANALYSIS

OFFENSE	C
SPECIAL TEAMS	C
DEFENSE	B-
INTANGIBLES	C

Sure, the Cougars have plenty of players back and, yes, they were close to turning the corner last year if they had only won a couple of the overtime games they lost. Even so, this is a team that hasn't yet proven it knows how to win close games, and sometimes that can be an impossible hump to get over.

Worst of all, WSU doesn't really have a strength to hang its hat on, something that creates an identity. Gesser, indeed is elusive, but an apparently weak wide receiver corps could wipe out any substantial passing attack.

Minnich is a solid tailback, but he is no Ken Simonton. The defense has some impact players, but it is arguable whether it has any All-America candidates.

The line seems to lack a dominant pass rusher. Of course, Washington State has surprised all the so-called analysts before and Price has a magical way of squeezing wine from prunes. Certainly, there is no dominating foe in the Pac-10, so the Cougars figure to be competitive in most of the games.

But to pick this team to finish anywhere in the top division would be folly.

(J.H.)

2000 RESULTS

Stanford	L	10-24	0-1
Utah	W	38-21	1-1
Idaho	L	34-38	1-2
California	W	21-17	3-1
Boise State	W	42-35	4-1
Arizona	L	47-53	4-2
Arizona State	L	20-23	4-3
Oregon State	L	9-38	4-4
Oregon	L	24-27	4-5
USC	W	33-27	5-5
Washington	L	3-51	5-6

SOUTHEASTERN

BLUE RIBBON FORECAST

Eastern Division
1. Florida
2. Tennessee
3. South Carolina
4. Georgia
5. Kentucky
6. Vanderbilt

Western Division
1. Mississippi State
2. LSU
3. Arkansas
4. Alabama
5. Auburn
6. Ole Miss

ALL-CONFERENCE TEAM

OFFENSE

POS. PLAYER SCHOOL HT. WT. CL.

WR Jabar Gaffney, Florida, 6-1, 202, So.
WR Josh Reed, LSU, 5-11, 200, Jr.
OL Mike Pearson, Florida, 6-7, 292, Jr.
OL Terrence Metcalf, Ole Miss, 6-3, 305, Sr.
C Ben Claxton, Ole Miss, 6-3, 281, Jr.
OL Fred Weary, Tennessee, 6-4, 301, Sr.
OL Tommy Watson, Mississippi State, 6-4, 303, Sr.
QB Eli Manning, Ole Miss, 6-4, 205, So.
RB Dicenzo Miller, Mississippi State, 5-10, 202, Sr.
RB Cedric Cobbs, Arkansas, 6-1, 228, Jr.
TE Derek Smith, Kentucky, 6-6, 265, Jr.

DEFENSE

POS. PLAYER SCHOOL HT. WT. CL.

DL Alex Brown, Florida, 6-3, 264, Sr.
DL Will Overstreet, Tennessee, 6-4, 260, Sr.
DL John Henderson, Tennessee, 6-7, 290, Sr.
DL Kindal Moorehead, Alabama, 6-4, 293, Jr.
LB Mario Haggan, Mississippi State, 6-3, 243, Jr.
LB Trev Faulk, LSU, 6-3, 225, Jr.
LB Kalimba Edwards, South Carolina, 6-6, 262, Sr.
DB Sheldon Brown, South Carolina, 5-10, 192, Sr.
DB Lito Sheppard, Florida, 5-10, 196, So.
DB Pig Prather, Mississippi State, 6-3, 191, Sr.
DB Todd Johnson, Florida, 6-1, 194, Jr.

SPECIALISTS

POS. PLAYER SCHOOL HT. WT. CL.

PK Jeff Chandler, Florida, 6-2, 219, Sr.
P Damon Duval, Auburn, 6-0, 184, Jr.
RS Ray Perkins, Vanderbilt, 5-10, 191, So.

OFFENSIVE PLAYER OF THE YEAR

Jabar Gaffney, WR, Florida

DEFENSIVE PLAYER OF THE YEAR

John Henderson, DT, Tennessee

NEWCOMER OF THE YEAR

Kelley Washington, WR, Tennessee

SEC NOTEBOOK

The SEC won't play football on Friday nights, even though the NCAA has allowed its schools to do so. "The SEC respects the tradition of high school football on Friday night," assistant commissioner Charles Bloom told the Associated Press. "The only reason to do that is for television, but I don't think you'll see our teams move their games to Friday for that." League coaches echoed those thoughts. "Fridays are for high schools, Saturdays are for colleges and Sundays are for pros," Auburn coach Tommy Tuberville told the AP. "Friday night high school football is kind of like a religion." ... Forty players from the SEC were taken in the NFL draft in April. The SEC and the Big Ten each had 40 players drafted, which led all conferences. The Big 12 had 30 players selected and was followed by the Pac-10 with 24, ACC with 21 and Big East with 18. Among SEC schools, Georgia led with six players chosen, followed by Tennessee with five and Florida, Mississippi State and Vanderbilt with four. Alabama, Auburn, Kentucky, LSU and Ole Miss each had three players selected while Arkansas had two players picked. South Carolina did not have a player chosen in the draft. ... *The Sporting News* has ranked Tennessee's Neyland Stadium the No. 1 college football stadium in the country. Florida's Florida Field was picked third. In its rankings, *TSN* used four criteria—setting, structure, fans and history. Neyland ranked high in all areas. In terms of setting, *TSN* said, "There's not a better view in college football. On one side of the stadium is the Tennessee River, where fans arrive by boat and tailgate hours before kickoff and hours after the game. On the other side is The Hill, the historic center of UT's old campus." Neyland Stadium is the nation's second-largest facility with a seating capacity of 104,079.

Alabama

LOCATION	**Tuscaloosa, AL**
CONFERENCE	**Southeastern (Western)**
LAST SEASON	**3-8 (.273)**
CONFERENCE RECORD	**3-5 (t-5th)**
OFFENSIVE STARTERS RETURNING	**6**
DEFENSIVE STARTERS RETURNING	**5**
NICKNAME	**Crimson Tide**
COLORS	**Crimson & White**
HOME FIELD	**Bryant-Denny Stadium (83,818) Legion Field (83,091)**
HEAD COACH	**Dennis Franchione (Pittsburg State '73)**
RECORD AT SCHOOL	**First Year**
CAREER RECORD	**138-65-2 (18 years)**
ASSISTANTS	**Ron Case (Carson-Newman '73) Safeties Stan Eggen (Moorehead State '77) Defensive Line Lee Fobbs (Grambling '73) Running Backs Jim Bob Helduser (Texas Lutheran '79) Offensive Line Les Koenning Jr. (Texas '81) Offensive Coordinator/Quarterbacks Kenith Pope (Oklahoma '76) Assistant Head Coach/Receivers Chris Thurmond (Tulsa '75) Cornerbacks Mark Tommerdahl (Concordia College '83) Tight Ends/Special Teams Carl Torbush (Carson-Newman '74) Defensive Coordinator/Linebackers**
TEAM WINS (last 5 yrs.)	**10-4-7-10-3**
FINAL RANK (last 5 yrs.)	**12-41-32-9-54**
2000 FINISH	**Lost to Auburn in regular-season finale.**

COACH AND PROGRAM

When Dennis Franchione shows up as your football coach, you know something has gone terribly wrong.

For example, take Alabama. In 1999, it beat Florida twice, finished eighth in the country and won its first SEC championship in seven years. It was a popular top-five preseason pick (No. 3 by *Blue Ribbon*) and an overwhelming favorite to win the SEC West in 2000. Then, something went terribly wrong.

The team that beat Florida twice the year before suddenly couldn't beat Central Florida. It lost on the road to UCLA and at home against Southern Mississippi. It lost its opener and its finale.

So for the fifth time since Bear Bryant retired after the 1982 season, Alabama was in the market for a new coach. More specifically, it was in the market for a coach with a reputation for rebuilding.

Enter Dennis Franchione, a 50-year-old Kansas native with 18 years head-coaching experience. Based on his track record, he was an obvious choice to clean up the mess coach Mike DuBose left behind. Franchione already had three successful rebuilding projects on his resume.

Southwest Texas State had suffered five consecutive losing seasons when it hired Franchione in 1990. His first team went 6-5 and his second went 7-4. New Mexico hadn't had a winning season since 1982 when Franchione was hired as head coach in 1992. Five years later, New Mexico went 9-4, won the WAC Mountain title and played in a bowl. TCU was 1-10 in 1997, the year before Franchione was hired. His TCU teams went 7-5, 8-4, and 10-1.

Next stop: Alabama.

"We have found, what I believe, is the coach most capable of guiding this team into the future," Alabama athletic director Mal Moore said in announcing Franchione's hiring last December. "His success has been impressive at every level."

Franchione won big at Southwestern (Kansas) College (14-4-2). He won bigger at his alma mater, Pittsburg (Kansas) State (53-6), where he was the NAIA coach of the year. But he didn't hit the jackpot until he went to TCU.

After his first TCU team went 7-5, Franchione's bosses were so impressed they almost doubled his financial package of $450,000.

"Hopefully this makes a statement that TCU wants us to be here and we want to be at TCU," Franchione said after the hefty pay raise. "We look at this as a long-term agreement."

Long-term turned out to be two years. The lure of more money and tradition-rich Alabama proved irresistible to Franchione, who plans to take the same approach at this established football power as he did at all the lesser stops along the way.

"You can't change a team physically a great deal (when you first arrive)," he said. "But you can change them mentally."

Franchione's first order of business is to create a family atmosphere. During two-a-days in his first season at TCU, Franchione put his philosophy to music. After nightly meetings, he had players sing the school fight song and alma mater.

"We tried to get them to be proud of who they are and where they are," Franchione said at the time. "We try to do things as a team to build a togetherness that you are afraid may have splintered for a team that just went through a 1-10 season."

Alabama football has just a tad more history behind it than TCU. But after the misadventure of 2000, the Tide has psychological scars of its own. After all, losing eight games at Alabama can be considerably more painful than losing 10 at TCU.

Franchione will realize that soon enough. He was in a bigger media market in Fort Worth, Texas, but has never been subjected to the kind of scrutiny that accompanies the Alabama job. He was surprised at the large contingent of media that showed up for Alabama's spring game and assumed it was because there was a new coach on board. No, he was told, that was just an average spring-game media turnout for Alabama football.

There's more scrutiny to come.

2001 SCHEDULE

Sept.	1	UCLA
	8	@Vanderbilt
	15	Southern Miss
	22	Arkansas
	29	@South Carolina
Oct.	6	UTEP
	13	@Ole Miss
	20	Tennessee
Nov.	3	LSU
	10	Mississippi State
	17	@Auburn

QUARTERBACKS

After one spring workout, Franchione announced he was moving senior walk-on **Jonathan Richey** (6-1, 208) to the top of the depth chart. What does that tell you?

You could write that off as a psychological ploy to motivate veterans **Andrew Zow** and **Tyler Watts**, or you could take it as an assessment of the Tide's mediocrity.

"I don't send messages that way," Franchione told the *Birmingham News* last spring. "Jonathan wasn't wonderful in the first scrimmage. He kind of won it by default."

A week after Richey's sudden ascent up the depth chart, he was back at No. 3, behind Zow and Watts. Deciding between those two won't be so easy.

Zow (6-2, 222), a senior, reclaimed the No. 1 position by completing 6-of-8 passes for 120 yards in the second scrimmage. He was 3-of-7 for 103 yards and threw an interception in a defense-dominated spring game, but that didn't change the quarterbacks' ranking. It could change this fall, however.

Zow has passed for 5,329 yards in his career and helped lead the Tide to its conference championship in 1999. But his inconsistency has contributed to Alabama's erratic offense. Last year he completed only 48.2 percent of his passes and threw only six touchdown passes, compared to 14 interceptions.

Despite Zow's problems, Watts (6-3, 217), a junior, wasn't good enough to win the job last fall. He completed 31-of-56 passes for 303 yards and one touchdown. Watts gives the Tide a running threat but can't stretch a defense with his arm as well as Zow.

Alabama fans are as excited about the arrival of freshman **Brodie Croyle** (6-2, 185) of Rainbow City, Ala., as they once were about Watts. Croyle graduated from Westbrook Christian High School in Rainbow City, Ala., in December and enrolled at Alabama a month later.

Croyle, who missed his senior season with a knee injury, passed for 2,838 yards and 38 touchdowns while throwing only seven interceptions as a junior.

Despite not playing as a senior, he passed for 9,323 yards and 105 touchdowns in his career, which began in the eighth grade. Some recruiting services considered him the No. 1 quarterback prospect in the country.

"When he catches up mentally with his physical assets, he is the total package," Franchione told the *Mobile Register.* "And I am not going to try and hold him back. Of all our quarterbacks, he comes closer to being the total package."

Offensive coordinator Les Koenning Jr. said there was no plan to alternate quarterbacks.

"We'll play the best guy," he said. "If the guy that starts is making plays, he'll keep playing. We run three huddles in practice. So three quarterbacks are going to get lots of reps."

RUNNING BACKS

Shaun Alexander established himself as one of Alabama's greatest running backs in his senior season of 1999. His greatness was magnified in 2000.

Alabama's myriad of problems couldn't all be attributed to the loss of Alexander. Nonetheless, you couldn't ignore how the offense unraveled without him, despite the return of so many players from the SEC championship season of 1999.

Alexander could make the tough yards and break the big plays. He provided confidence as well as yards. In a pinch, the Tide knew it could put the ball in his hands.

The offense is still adjusting to life without Alexander. Junior **Ahmaad Galloway** (6-1, 228), sophomore **Brandon Miree** (6-2, 233) and sophomore **Santonio Beard** (6-1, 207) will share the running load.

Galloway ended last season as the starting tailback and held the No. 1 job through the spring. A hard-nosed runner, Galloway rushed for 659 yards on 137 carries for a 4.8-yard average. A former blue-chip prospect from Millington, Tenn., Galloway began to assert himself in the spring of 2000. He gained 65 yards on the first play of the spring game and finished the day with 114 yards on only eight carries.

Miree came back from a broken leg in spring practice of 2000 to rush for 426 yards on 94 carries last fall. Miree, who has run a 10.6 100 meters, rushed for 2,455 yards and scored 31 touchdowns his senior year of high school.

Beard, a two-time Mr. Football in Class 4A in Tennessee, missed last season with knee and shoulder injuries after playing mainly on special teams in 1999 as a freshman. He showed no effects of the injuries in spring practice. In one scrimmage, he rushed for 98 yards on 17 carries. "Santonio is very rough around the edges but shows some flashes," Franchione said. "He can be a real ball carrier."

Freshman **Marquez Dupree** (6-0, 215) could be a factor in the running game. He's the son of former Oklahoma star Marcus Dupree. Marquez, a three-time all-state pick, rushed for 1,305 yards and 17 touchdowns last year at Philadelphia (Miss.) High School, the same school for which his father played. He excelled in baseball and track as well, setting a school record for home runs and running a 10.3-second 100 meters.

Sophomore **Donnie Lowe** (6-2, 247), a converted linebacker, won the starting fullback job in the spring. Lowe was a high school star in LaVergne, Tenn., where he had 150 tackles and rushed for 900 yards as a senior. One recruiting service ranked him as the fifth-best prospect in the state. He showed why in the spring, impressing his new coaches with his blocking, receiving and running.

"I think he's got all the components to be a really good fullback," Franchione said. "The good thing about Donnie is he is a good listener. He listens in the meetings and he applies it to his individual drills. You can tell him something one time and he has it."

Redshirt freshman **Nick Signaigo** (6-3, 231) showed promise in the spring after taking on his third position. He started as a linebacker, then moved to tight end before Franchione's staff made him a running back.

"He's a tough kid," Koenning said. "He broke his hand during the spring but was able to keep practicing."

WIDE RECEIVERS/TIGHT ENDS

Freddie Milons' drop off from 1999 to 2000 speaks volumes for the Tide's offensive decline. He caught 65 passes for 733 yards, rushed for 178 yards on only 15 carries and averaged almost 10 yards per return on 29 punt returns in 1999.

Last year, he caught only 32 passes for 287 yards, gained 39 yards on 12 carries and lost his job as a punt returner. Milons (5-11, 191) quit speaking to the media last year; there was speculation that he had a bad attitude. Dabo Swinney, his former position coach, defended him.

"I've heard all (the rumors)," Swinney told the *Birmingham-Post Herald* last November. "That he had a fight with coach DuBose. That he wouldn't get off the bus. That he skipped a team meeting. That he's a racist. That he's not a team guy. I've heard all of it and none of it's true.

"I think the big mistake Freddie made was not talking to the media. He got frustrated, and his personality—he's not comfortable in a role as a spokesman for this team. He wants to play, then go home and play video games."

Milons' new coaches were satisfied with his work ethic and attitude in the spring. Having seen Milons on tape in both 1999 and 2000, Koenning attributed it more to a team malaise than a decline in one player.

"It was a tough situation for them last year," he said. "If it hadn't been a tough situation, we wouldn't be here."

After last season, Milons is grateful for the positive attitude Franchione's staff has brought to the program.

"The coaching staff does a great job of keeping everybody positive," Milons told the *Mobile Register*. "Last year nothing was going right, no matter what we did. We had team meetings, trying to fix whatever was wrong and we couldn't get it done. Now we have another chance to get it right. We need to spark a spark in somebody. We don't want what happened last year to happen again."

When Milons faltered, **Antonio Carter** emerged as the Tide's No. 1 receiver. Carter, a 5-9, 195-pound junior, caught 45 passes for 586 yards. Carter's biggest game—eight catches for 157 yards against Ole Miss—came when Milons was out of the lineup with a knee injury. Now, some observers think Carter, not Milons, might be Alabama's best pure receiver.

Senior **Jason McAddley** (6-2, 199) gives Alabama a third experienced wide receiver. He had 27 catches for 413 yards and three touchdowns last year. He also had 24 catches in 1999. McAddley has size and speed but drops too many passes.

Less experienced receivers like junior **Joel Babb** (6-0, 186), sophomore **Triandos Luke** (6-0, 190) and junior **Sam Collins** (6-1, 181) also figure in the receiver rotation.

Junior tight end **Terry Jones** (6-4, 265) was headed for an outstanding season when he suffered a torn anterior cruciate ligament in his left knee against South Carolina. Jones, who missed the last six games, caught six passes for 123 yards in the first five games.

"He's working through the injury," Koenning said. "I don't think he played as well as we predicted because of the knee surgery and getting over the injury. He got better as the spring went along."

Junior **Theo Sanders** (6-3, 248) and sophomore **Casey Gilbert** (6-4, 286) will back up Jones. Sanders is fast for his size, having run a 10.9 100 meters at Shades Valley High School in Birmingham. Gilbert is making the transition from offensive guard to tight end.

OFFENSIVE LINE

Based on Alabama's sack attack in the spring, it will have the best pass rush in the SEC this fall. Unfortunately for Alabama, the offensive line was an accomplice.

After the first scrimmage, Franchione said: "Our ends ran past our tackles so fast at the line of scrimmage, we couldn't even get in position to grab them and hold them.

In defense of the offensive line, it was having to adapt to a new system. Moreover, it wasn't that experienced to begin with.

Tackle **Dante Ellington**, a 6-6, 354-pound junior, and sophomore guard **Dennis Alexander** (6-6, 339) are the only returning starters. The probable new starters are junior center **Alonzo Ephraim** (6-4, 288), junior guard **Marico Portis** (6-3, 308) and freshman tackle **Wesley Britt** (6-8, 304).

"We're rough around the edges, obviously," offensive line coach Jim Bob Helduser told the *Mobile Register*. "They're going to get better and I'm going to keep pushing them to get better and they're going to keep pushing themselves."

Pushing wasn't always easy last spring. Ellington and Alexander had trouble carrying their weight.

"We'd like to see (Ellington) in the 320 to 325 range," Koenning said. "When he was a freshman and sophomore, that's the range he played in. We'd love to see Dennis get down a little, too. We tell kids strength is an important part of our program, but we want it to be a lean strength.

"Dante has talent. I hope he gets in shape. Ephraim played a little last year. He's a good, intelligent kid. Dennis Alexander fits in well at guard. Portis has been around a long time. He has had to bounce back and forth between center and guard."

Although the line was overwhelmed at times in the spring, Koenning believes it will benefit from the adversity.

"They were getting a multitude of different looks," he said. "I think it will pay dividends for us in the fall."

All of the starting positions aren't set. Junior college transfer **Atlas Herrion** (6-4, 299) will push Britt, and redshirt freshman **Justin Smiley** (6-3, 292) will compete with Portis for a starting job.

"(Herrion has) got really good movement skills," Helduser told the *Huntsville Times*. "Junior College players are a little more physically mature, and he's got good strength."

2000 STATISTICS

Rushing offense	137.6	66
Passing offense	171.7	91
Total offense	309.4	100
Scoring offense	20.7	86
Net Punting	38.4	11
Punt returns	12.1	26
Kickoff returns	18.3	86
Rushing defense	125.4	32
Passing efficiency defense	122.7	71
Total defense	337.0	35
Scoring defense	22.4	42
Turnover margin	-8	96

Last column is ranking among Division I-A teams.

KICKERS

Senior **Neal Thomas** (5-11, 183) returns to handle the place-kicking chores. He made 9-of-13 field-goal tries and all 27 of his extra-point kicks last season, his first as a starter. He proved himself right away, hitting a 50-yarder in his first game at Legion Field.

Thomas first demonstrated his leg strength in high school at Clinton, Miss., where he kicked a 53-yarder. He made 31-of-39 field-goal tries in two years at Hinds (Miss.) Community College.

DEFENSIVE LINE

The Tide didn't have to wait until September to suffer a setback. It lost defensive end **Kindal Moorehead** to a season-ending Achilles tendon injury in August. His return was one of the bright spots of the spring.

"Overall, he was probably the best defensive player we had in the spring," defensive coordinator Carl Torbush said of Moorehead, who had eight tackles in one spring scrimmage. "He played at defensive end and tackle and responded very well. He's a big guy that has athletic skills. Right now, we would like to use him at defensive end but there's no question we could move him inside."

Moorehead, a 6-4, 293-pound junior, was a first-team All-SEC pick in 1999. In 22 career starts, he has 70 tackles, 24 tackles behind the line, 10.5 sacks and 34 quarterback pressures.

If **Kenny King** (6-5, 277) is healthy, he will give the Tide another proven starter at defensive end. He missed the last five days of spring practice after complaining of numbness in his left leg. Doctors held him out for precautionary reasons but later gave him clearance to participate in preseason drills. He also missed practice time in the spring with a bruised knee.

King, a Freshman All-SEC pick in 1999, was hampered by a shoulder injury last year but still managed 42 tackles and a team-high 27 quarterback pressures in eight games. In 1999, he had 19.5 tackles behind the line (including sacks).

Senior **Aries Monroe** (6-4, 231) has experience as a backup at defensive end. He had 24 tackles, including five for losses and three sacks last year.

Sophomore **Nautyn McKay-Loescher** (6-4, 240) also should compete for a starting position.

"Monroe had a really good spring," Torbush said. "He's a combination outside linebacker/end. He can stand up and drop back in pass coverage if you need him to."

McKay-Loescher, who played sparingly last year, was ranked as the No. 1 prospect in Canada after his senior year. His speed and intensity drew praise from the coaches in the spring. He was the winner of the Dwight Stephenson Most Valuable Lineman Award in the spring game.

Junior **Shawn Oglesby** (6-6, 216) had a big spring, capped by two sacks and another sack for a loss in the spring game. Oglesby, a former junior college All-American, was redshirted last season.

Junior **Jarrett Johnson** (6-4, 281) and senior **David Daniel** (6-0, 264) will man the tackle positions. Johnson led the Tide in tackles for losses (14) and sacks (7) last year. He had 64 tackles overall.

"Jarret reminds me of an old-time football player," Torbush said. "He's a good athlete, not necessarily a great one. He has an instinct for being around the ball."

The Tide has little experience among the other tackle candidates. Daniel and junior **Derek Sanders** (6-5, 283) had 12 tackles between them last year.

Sophomore **Anthony Bryant** (6-3, 349) has plenty of size and potential. He was a consensus first-team high school All-American at Newbern, Ala. He had 178 tackles and 11 sacks as a senior. As a tight end, he caught 15 passes for 441 yards and eight touchdowns.

"This is an area that concerns us because of depth," Torbush said. "As physical as this league is, you've got to make sure you've got enough players there."

Because of the questionable depth at tackle, it might be more tempting to move Moorehead inside, particularly if the young ends continue to play as they did in the spring.

LINEBACKERS

Matching up the best linebackers with the right position was a priority of spring practice, which ended with junior **Saleem Rasheed** (6-3, 227) in the middle and sophomore **Brooks Daniels** (6-2, 205) and senior **Victor Ellis** (6-3, 232) on the outside.

In 1999, Rasheed became the first freshman in Alabama history to lead the team in tackles. He had 84 tackles, eight tackles for losses and three sacks and was selected the SEC's Freshman Defensive Player of the Year. Last year, Rasheed had 81 tackles, four tackles behind the line and eight quarterback pressures.

"He had a great freshman year and not as good of a sophomore year," Torbush said. "But I was very impressed with him in the spring."

Rasheed, who moved from outside to middle linebacker in the spring, had eight tackles and a sack in one scrimmage. He had seven more tackles in the spring game.

Like Rasheed, Daniels made a positive impression on Torbush right away. He won the starting job at rover back, which requires the qualities of a strong safety, linebacker and defensive end.

"He may be the most consistent player we have," Torbush said. "He reminds me of Jackie Walker (a former All-America linebacker at Tennessee). He's got tremendous acceleration and is an explosive hitter."

Daniels, who had 14 tackles last year in a reserve role, was rated as the No. 4 linebacker prospect in the Southeast as a senior at Hamilton County High School in Jasper, Fla. Not only did he have 115 tackles as a senior, he also played quarterback and returned kicks.

Ellis is the team's leading returning tackler. He had 94 tackles, including nine for losses, last year. He also forced a fumble and blocked two kicks.

"He started at inside linebacker and did pretty well there," Torbush said. "But we got him where he needs to be. He's a very smart player. The last four or five spring practices he was really solid."

The Tide also has solid backups at linebacker. Senior **Darius Gilbert** (6-3, 253), a former starter, had 60 tackles last year. He will spell Rasheed at middle linebacker.

Sophomore **Cornelius Wortham** (6-1, 211) might unseat Ellis at strong-side linebacker in preseason practice. Wortham, who had 14 tackles last year as a freshman, was an all-state player in high school at Calhoun City, Miss.

Redshirt freshman **Jason Rawls** (6-0, 215) is listed behind Daniels. Rawls of Statesboro, Ga., is just getting started as a linebacker. He was switched from running back in the third game of his senior season.

The Tide's linebacker depth took a hit in the spring when junior middle linebacker **Marvin Constant** (6-1, 245) had to give up football. Constant underwent three knee surgeries after injuring his knee on the final play of the LSU game in 1999. He played in only five games last year after starting eight games as a redshirt freshman in 1999.

"That was our biggest disappointment," Torbush said. "He was a prototypical middle linebacker. He had a chance to be a special guy."

DEFENSIVE BACKS

Based on spring practice, Alabama should have three new starters in the secondary. Junior cornerback **Gerald Dixon** (5-11, 182) was the lone returning starter listed No. 1 on the depth chart. A high school quarterback, Dixon won a starting job at cornerback midway through his freshman year in 1999.

There's not much experience elsewhere, with the exception of senior **Reggie Myles** (6-0, 184), who fell behind sophomore **Charles Jones** (6-0, 175). Jones sparkled in the spring game, but Myles will have a chance to win back his starting job in the fall. Myles had 38 tackles, two interceptions and broke up seven passes last year. Those numbers were a drop off from 1999, when he led Alabama with five interceptions and also had 59 tackles and two sacks.

Junior **Hirchel Bolden** (6-0, 196) was ahead of sophomore **Carlos Andrews** (6-0, 200) at the other corner. Andrews is the first backup at both corners.

Bolden, who played quarterback and tailback in high school, played the last two years as a backup. Andrews, of Tallahassee, Fla., played in nine games last year.

Senior **Shontua Ray** (5-11, 212), a heavy hitter who had an impact on special teams in the past, leads the way at strong safety. He is followed by walk-on **Waine Bacon**, a 5-10, 195-pound junior who impressed coaches with his competitiveness in the spring.

"The secondary is one of our biggest worries," Torbush said. "A lot of guys are untested here.

"I think we improved during the spring. But we do have some concerns because not many of them have played a lot in real ball games."

PUNTERS

Junior **Lane Bearden** (6-2, 198) is back for his second year as Alabama's punter. He averaged 40.7 yards on 60 punts last year. He had a long punt of 62 yards and landed 12 punts inside the 20.

Bearden contributed in 1999 as a kickoff specialist. After Bearden became the kicker, Tide opponents averaged starting at their 18-yard line. Eleven of his kicks were not returned.

In high school, Bearden was an all-state punter at Helena, Ala. He was selected as most valuable player of the Alabama-Mississippi all-star game as a punter.

SPECIAL TEAMS

The Tide must replace Arvin Richard as a kick returner, but Milons, Ray and McAddley all have experience. Milons returned nine kicks for an 18.3-yard average last year. In 1999, he averaged 21.5 yards on 11 kickoff returns.

Milons and Carter give Alabama two experienced punt returners. Milons had a 71-yard return for a touchdown last year against UCLA.

RECRUITING CLASS

After signing one of the best classes in the country in 2000, Alabama dropped off considerably in 2001. No one should have been surprised.

Changing head coaches is a surefire method for disrupting recruiting. Speculation about NCAA violations didn't help either. Meanwhile, arch-rival Auburn picked up momentum under second-year coach Tommy Tuberville.

That was a lot to overcome.

"For a staff in transition we did a good job," Franchione said. "Obviously, our coaches had a number of unique issues to deal with. We're anxious to get a whole year and develop deeper relationships with recruits."

Despite its obvious disadvantages, Alabama had its recruiting successes, the most obvious of which was Croyle.

Alabama signed another highly regarded quarterback, **Spencer Pennington** (6-4, 215), who led his Fayette County High School team to the Class 4A state championship. He passed for 2,433 yards and 20 touchdowns as a senior. He's also an outstanding baseball player. He had 15 home runs in 112 at-bats and hit .430 as a junior.

The Tide revisited its 2000 class in signing defensive tackle **Mac Tyler** (6-6, 335). A first-team All-American last year, Tyler failed to qualify academically and enrolled at Milford Academy, where he played both tackle and end last season. He had 75 tackles and 13 sacks at Milford.

Two huge all-state offensive **linemen—Von Ewing** (6-6, 297) and **Mark Sanders** (6-7, 305)—signed with the Tide. Ewing gave up only one sack in his last 21 games; Sanders was a two-time all-stater. **J.B. Closner** (6-4, 290) of San Antonio, Texas, was another offensive line signee. He made all-district and all-city as a junior and senior. He played both offense and defense in high school.

Alabama hopes tight end **Donald Clark** (6-6, 260) of Fort Scott (Kansas) Community College can help right away. He was an all-conference pick in junior college after playing high school football at Spanish River in Boca Raton, Fla.

The Tide signed two other tight ends. **Mark Anderson** (6-6, 215) of Tulsa, Okla., is credited with running a 4.5 40. He played offense and defense at Booker T. Washington High School. In one game, he had two blocked punts, three sacks and 20 tackles. Clint Johnston (6-4, 235) of Wetumpka, Ala., was a two-time all-stater.

Quentin Bowers (6-0, 265) played tight end and defensive end at East Central (Miss.) Community College but was recruited as a fullback. His half-brother, linebacker **Freddie Roach**, also signed with the Tide. Roach is a 6-2, 225-pound linebacker. Roach, from Brooks High School in Killen, Ala., rushed for 1,277 yards and 18 touchdowns as a senior. He had 194 tackles, including 23 stops behind the line and caused six fumbles.

Roach was rated the No. 2 linebacker in the state. He was a two-time All-State pick and was the American General Back of the Year as a senior. Roach was a Super Senior selection by the *Birmingham News* and was No. 5 on the *Tuscaloosa News* Sweet Sixteen.

Wide receiver **Bryan Bass** (6-1, 180) played high school football at Fayette County, Ala., and at Westminister Academy in Fort Lauderdale, Fla. Bass also played baseball in high school and in June was chosen by the Baltimore Orioles with the 31st pick in the draft. A switch-hitting shortstop, he batted .500 with 12 home runs and had 14 stolen bases as a junior.

Brandon Brooks, a wide receiver from Shades Valley High School in Birmingham, is an intriguing signee. He's only 5-4 and 152 pounds but makes up for size with speed. He won the state championship in the 55-meter sprint as a junior and senior with times of 6.43 and 6.51. He returned seven punts for touchdowns his last two years of high school. Last year, he rushed for 725 yards, caught 13 passes for 325 yards and intercepted six passes.

Alabama might have helped its kicking game with the signing of **Mike McLaughlin** (6-1, 190), a high school All-American at Gautier (Miss.) High

School. McLaughlin made 12-of-16 field-goal attempts, including five of more than 40 yards. His longest field goal was 49 yards.

Linebacker **Todd Bates** (6-4, 220) of Heflin, Ala. was one of the top defensive signees. He was honored as the state's Class 4A Lineman of the Year after making 119 tackles, recovering five fumbles, causing five fumbles and intercepting three passes as a senior. He also caught 10 passes as a tight end.

BLUE RIBBON ANALYSIS

OFFENSE	C
SPECIAL TEAMS	B-
DEFENSE	B
INTANGIBLES	A-

A new coaching staff surely will be a morale booster. The schedule will help, too. Alabama's four toughest conference games—against South Carolina, Tennessee, LSU and Mississippi State—will be at home.

The strength of this team, like so many of its predecessors, should be the defensive front seven. Moorehead, King and Rasheed are All-SEC candidates.

Wide receiver also could be a plus, providing Milons returns to his 1999 form. There's no single running back in Alexander's class, but a healthy Santonio Beard will give Alabama more backfield depth than last year.

Questions abound in the secondary, offensive line and at quarterback.

If the Tide's pass rush is as effective in the fall as in the spring, the secondary's inexperience will be minimized. But if it is vulnerable to the pass, it will be exploited during a three-game stretch against Eli Manning of Ole Miss, Casey Clausen of Tennessee and Rohan Davey of LSU.

The weakness in the offensive line is more glaring. The two returning starters were overweight and out of shape in the spring. How's that for leadership?

Zow or Watts? That question won't be answered until preseason, if then. Although Zow is a better passer, Franchione might be more comfortable with Watts, who is less apt to make the kind of blunders that have plagued Zow. A stickler for protecting the football, Franchione won't likely forget Zow's drive-killing interception in the spring game.

After what happened last year, Alabama can ill afford another shaky start. That's why September non-conference games against UCLA and Southern Mississippi will be so important. Both the Bruins and Golden Eagles beat Alabama last year and they're capable of doing it again.

In the SEC race, Alabama can be encouraged by the topsy-turvy nature of the West Division. Auburn finished fifth in 1999 and won the division in 2000. Mississippi State finished fourth in 1997 and won the division in 1998.

Arkansas finished fourth in 1994 and first in 1995.

Given that history, you can make a case for Alabama going from worst to first. It more likely will fall somewhere in between.

(J.A.)

2000 RESULTS

UCLA	L	24-35	0-1
Vanderbilt	W	28-10	1-1
Southern Miss	L	0-21	1-2
Arkansas	L	21-28	1-3
South Carolina	W	27-17	2-3
Ole Miss	W	45-7	3-3
Tennessee	L	10-20	3-4
Central Florida	L	38-40	3-5
LSU	L	28-30	3-6
Mississippi State	L	7-29	3-7
Auburn	L	0-9	3-8

Arkansas

LOCATION	**Fayetteville, AR**
CONFERENCE	**Southeastern (Western)**
LAST SEASON	**6-6 (.500)**
CONFERENCE RECORD	**3-5 (t-5th)**
OFFENSIVE STARTERS RETURNING	**8**
DEFENSIVE STARTERS RETURNING	**6**
NICKNAME	**Razorbacks**
COLORS	**Cardinal & White**
HOME FIELD	**Razorback Stadium (72,000)**
HEAD COACH	**Houston Nutt (Okla. St. '81)**
RECORD AT SCHOOL	**23-13 (3 years)**
CAREER RECORD	**59-35 (9 years)**
ASSISTANTS	**Bobby Allen (Va. Tech '83)** **Defensive Line** **David Lee (Vanderbilt '75)** **Quarterbacks** **Mike Markuson (Hamline '83)** **Offensive Line** **Danny Nutt (Arkansas '85)** **Running Backs** **George Pugh (Alabama '76)** **Wide Receivers** **James Shibest (Arkansas '88)** **Tight Ends** **John Thompson (Central Arkansas '82)** **Defensive Coordinator/Linebackers** **Chris Vaughn (Murray State '98)** **Outside Linebackers** **Dave Wommack (Missouri Southern '78)** **Secondary**
TEAM WINS (last 5 yrs.)	**4-4-9-8-6**
FINAL RANK (last 5 yrs.)	**40-39-15-19-51**
2000 FINISH	**Lost to UNLV in Las Vegas Bowl.**

COACH AND PROGRAM

Arkansas had lost three consecutive games when it took the field at Tennessee's Neyland Stadium last October. A bad stretch was about to become historically bad.

Tennessee scored 35 points in the first quarter and added 21 more in the third quarter en route to a 63-20 victory. That was the most points given up by the Razorbacks in 82 years.

After the embarrassing defeat, the Hogs took their four-game losing streak to Starkville, Miss., where the Bulldogs were still in contention for the SEC championship. How could their fans not expect the worst?

But the worst of times have brought out the best in Houston Nutt's Arkansas teams. Last year was no exception. Nutt promoted assistant John Thompson to defensive coordinator, then rallied his team to consecutive victories over nationally ranked Mississippi State and LSU.

"I love the way we came back from the Tennessee game," Nutt said. "It's a matter of believing in the players, staying positive and not giving up and pointing the finger. Coming back from the dead when everybody writes you off—that's probably the best thing we've done. That's what life is all about."

That wasn't the first time Nutt's motivational prowess helped revive the Razorbacks in his three years as head coach. In 1998, after the Hogs lost back-to-back games in the last minute to Tennessee and Mississippi State, they played one of their best games of the year in beating LSU, 41-14. In 1999, they rebounded from a 38-16 loss to Ole Miss to upset Tennessee the following week.

Nutt's relentlessly positive outlook was tested more than once last year. The Hogs couldn't stay healthy. They lost their two best running backs and their starting quarterback to season-ending injuries. They lost fullback Adam Daily to a career-ending injury. The injuries started in preseason and continued through December's bowl preparation.

"We had five shoulder injuries, three broken ribs—on and on," Nutt said. "Dean Webber has been a trainer for almost 30 years and he said he'd never seen anything like it.

"We are hopefully going to get a lot healthier. We won't have as many as 10 surgeries in a long time. Dean says it comes around like this every 10, 12 or 15 years. I'm holding him to that."

Injuries figured prominently in Arkansas' 6-6 season, its worse under Nutt, who coached the Razorbacks to an 8-0 start in his first year and 17 victories in his first two years. Last year's record, capped by a 31-14 loss to UNLV in the Las Vegas Bowl, was a step down. But you don't keep Nutt down for long. His goals haven't changed a bit since he returned to the program he followed as a child in Little Rock. He returned to Arkansas intent not just on winning a conference title, but winning a national championship as well.

"I still believe that," Nutt said. "But we're in one of the toughest conferences in the country. You got to have a little luck. With the facilities we have and the recruiting classes we have, I think we're going to get there."

Arkansas' most obvious facility this season will be the expanded and renovated Donald W. Reynolds Razorback Stadium in Fayetteville. Not only will the stadium be expanded from 51,000 to 72,000, it will include new suites, club seating on the east side and chair-back seats and club seating on the south side. Moreover, another expansion plan is already in the works to increase stadium capacity to more than 80,000.

A bigger stadium isn't the only change. Nutt's staff has undergone a makeover, with the departure of Fitz Hill, Joe Ferguson and Bill Johnson, and the addition of Dave Wommack, George Pugh and John Lee.

Wommack, who was the defensive coordinator at Southern Mississippi, will be reunited with Thompson. They first worked together as graduate assistants at Arkansas and years later as assistants at USM. You could characterize their defense with two words—"multiple" and "unconventional"—but Womack has two words of his own: "organized confusion."

"When we talk about it, I get excited about our package," Thompson said. "That's not to say we've got the greatest (scheme) out there. We just believe in it and where it can go."

Arkansas' offense also will have a different twist. The Razorbacks worked on the option in spring practice and plan to use it as a change of pace this fall. Lee, an assistant at Arkansas from 1984 through 1988, was the offensive coordinator and quarterbacks coach the last seven years at Rice for former Arkansas head coach Ken Hatfield.

2001 SCHEDULE

Sept.	1	UNLV
	8	Tennessee
	15	North Texas
	22	@Alabama
	29	@Georgia
Oct.	13	South Carolina
	27	Auburn
Nov.	3	@Mississippi
	10	Central Florida
	17	Mississippi State
	24	@LSU

QUARTERBACKS

Sophomore **Zak Clark** (6-2, 195) made significant gains in the spring while returning starter **Robby Hampton** was sidelined after shoulder surgery.

"He has gotten better," Nutt said of Clark. "His mechanics have gotten better. David Lee has done a good job with his footwork. His decision-making has gotten better. I think last year he really got introduced to the big leagues. I'm real proud of him and how far he has come."

Clark, who started two games last year after Hampton was injured, completed 28-of-68 passes for 321 yards for one touchdown and was intercepted six times as a freshman. His accuracy was markedly better in the spring.

In the final spring scrimmage, Clark completed 7-of-9 passes for 125 yards and two touchdowns. Part of Clark's improvement could be attributed to his improved health. He was hampered by an ankle injury last fall.

"Just to see him limping around the last six or seven games last fall, he had probably lost a little confidence," Nutt told the *Arkansas Democrat-Gazette*. "The ball is traveling better, stronger."

Clark, who grew up in Fayetteville, knows the high expectations of being an Arkansas quarterback. He has tried to harden himself to the inevitable criticism.

"It's just one of the things that comes with the territory and you have to deal with it," he told the *Northwest Arkansas Times*. "You just experience it and try to block out the bad things and not get too high when good things happen and people say nice things about you."

Hampton, a 6-2, 220-pound junior, completed 145-of-261 passes for 1,548 yards, 13 touchdowns and eight interceptions in his first year as a starter.

Hampton, 25, spent four years in the Toronto Blue Jays organization as an outfielder after playing both sports in high school at Mt. Pleasant, Texas. Although Clark improved significantly in the spring, Nutt still considers Hampton his starter.

"I don't think you can lose a position by being hurt," he said.

Hampton was able to lift weights in the spring but still hadn't started passing. He watched the spring workouts from the sideline.

"Zak looks good," Hampton said. "He has put on weight and is stronger, throwing the ball really well and accurately and was very impressive with his feet."

No matter how the quarterback competition plays out in preseason, the friendship between Hampton and Clark will be a plus.

"We have a great relationship," Clark told the *Northwest Arkansas Times*. "He is a great guy and a good quarterback. When he comes back—whatever happens on whether I'm the guy or he's the guy—we will support each other and the team first and foremost."

The Razorbacks tried another option at quarterback in the spring. Wide receiver **Gerald Howard**, a 5-7, 186-pound junior, moved to quarterback and ran an option package. His option pitch to **Steven Harris** resulted in a 12-yard touchdown run in the spring game.

RUNNING BACKS

If **Fred Talley** makes a full recovery from a knee injury, Arkansas will have more depth at tailback than any other team in the SEC. Talley, Cedric Cobbs and Brandon Holmes all rushed for more than 100 yards in at least one game last year.

Cobbs, a 6-foot-1 228-pound sophomore, was being promoted as a Heisman Trophy candidate before last season after a dazzling freshman season. Said Nutt: "I've been around some great ones. I was at Oklahoma State when Barry Sanders and Thurman Thomas were there. You can mention Cedric Cobbs in the same sentence with those guys at this stage of his career. He should be a legitimate Heisman candidate. We plan to give him plenty of opportunities with the ball in his hands."

True to their word, the Hogs gave Cobbs the ball 34 times in the second game against Boise State. The former high school All-American from Little Rock responded with 174 yards. A week later, he suffered a season-ending shoulder injury against Alabama.

"We are excited to get him back on the field," Nutt said. "He has shown what he can do when he is healthy. He can make something happen when he gets around the corner, and he can make people miss."

Cobbs rushed for 668 yards and averaged 5.8 yards a carry as a freshman. He became only the third freshman in Cotton Bowl history to win the most valuable player award, rushing for 98 yards on only 15 carries, scoring on a 37-yard pass play and adding 27 yards on kick returns.

Although Cobbs went through spring practice, he said his right shoulder still didn't feel 100 percent. He had two carries for 21 yards and gained 18 yards on a screen pass before a hip pointer cut short his final spring scrimmage.

"I asked for more work (in the spring) and I got it," Cobbs told the *Arkansas Democrat-Gazette*. "I've gotten better. I've gotten faster and stronger."

When Cobbs was injured last fall, Talley showed what he could do when healthy. The 5-9, 180-pound junior led the Razorbacks with 768 yards rushing despite playing in only seven games. He had three consecutive plus-100 yard games against Auburn (161), Ole Miss (214) and Tennessee (142). The 517 yards in three consecutive games was a school record.

"He showed tremendous breakaway speed and he got better as the year went on," Nutt said. "He has a great ability to make the first guy miss."

Talley also has an ability to outrun everybody. He won the state 100-meter championship with a time of 10.43 seconds at Long View (Texas) High School, where he also ran a 47.8 leg on the 1,600-meter relay team.

Talley began running full speed in May and was expected to be ready for preseason contact. If he isn't at top form, a redshirt year would be an option because Holmes and Cobbs are there to share the running load.

Holmes doesn't have the speed of Cobb or Talley, but he sustained the Hogs' rushing attack after they were injured. In the final two games of the season, he rushed for 238 yards and three touchdowns. He gained 143 yards on 42 carries in the Hogs' upset of 24th-ranked LSU and scored the game-winning touchdown in an overtime victory over No. 13 Mississippi State.

"Brandon did a great job for us down the stretch," Nutt said. "He is a big, physical back that should only get better. Brandon is a versatile back and has the ability to line up at fullback or tailback."

Holmes finished strong in the spring. He rushed for 68 yards on just six carries and had a 31-yard run and 1-yard touchdown run.

Arkansas can also use Holmes at fullback. When the Razorbacks ran their option package in the spring, it was most effective with Holmes at fullback and Cobbs at tailback because Holmes gives them more of an inside running threat.

Senior **Alvin Ray** (5-9, 196) was listed as the No. 1 fullback in the spring but that is apt to change in the fall. A former Texas all-stater, Ray was moved from tailback, where he rushed for 259 yards the last three years as a backup.

Former defensive lineman **Sacha Lancaster**, a 6-4, 255-pound senior, is the likely starter. After bulking up to more than 300 pounds as a defensive linemen, Lancaster hopes to play fullback at 250 next fall.

Last fall, sophomore Daily looked like the Hogs' fullback of the future. Daily, a 6-0, 250-pounder, was diagnosed with a career-ending spinal-cord injury last December.

WIDE RECEIVERS/TIGHT ENDS

The Razorbacks lost a 6-4, go-to wide receiver in Boo Williams, but have a couple of other big targets returning in juniors **Sparky Hamilton** (6-4, 210) and **Sam Breeden** (6-4, 226).

Hamilton, a high school All-American from Lufkin, Texas, played in 1999 as a freshman and caught 16 passes for 205 yards last year. Breeden, a junior college transfer, caught only two passes last year. He was an all-conference player at Butler County (Kansas) Community College.

"Sam Breeden has really come on," Nutt said. "The guy continues to improve. He understands the offense and isn't frustrated at all."

Sophomore **Richard Smith** (5-10, 175) gives the Hogs a proven receiver at flanker. He set a school freshman record by catching 33 passes for 320 yards last year.

"Richard is a great route runner," Nutt said. "He has great hands and has a special ability to catch the deep ball."

Smith, who made the All-SEC Freshman team, was highly recruited out of Evangel Christian High School in Shreveport, La. He caught 84 passes for 1,700 yards and 20 touchdowns as a senior. Max Emfinger's recruiting service ranked him as the top slotback in the country. As a junior at Evangel, Smith won the state championship in the long jump and the triple jump.

A less heralded sophomore might have an impact at receiver this year. **George Wilson** (6-1, 205), was a two-time Kentucky all-stater who came to Arkansas on an academic scholarship. He suffered a season-ending shoulder injury in the third game. Wilson, who thrives as a possession receiver, had two receptions for 37 yards and one touchdown in the final spring scrimmage.

Sophomore **Correy Muldrew** (6-2, 200), who had two catches for 50 yards and one touchdown in the final scrimmage, will also compete for playing time at wide receiver. He's a two-time all-stater from Hope, Ark. Sophomore Harris (6-0, 180) is another candidate, as is Howard, who worked at both quarterback and receiver in spring practice. Howard caught eight passes for 84 yards last year.

Junior **Marcellus Poydras** (6-5, 256) started five games at tight end last season but was listed behind junior **Nathan Ball** (6-4, 281) in the spring.

Ball split time between tight end and the offensive line last year. Each caught four passes in 2000, but the Hogs want a strong blocker at this position. Sophomore **J. Strain** (6-4, 260), who has been bothered by injuries throughout his career, will also get a shot at playing time. Strain, a native of Fayetteville, was ranked as one of the top five college prospects in the state by most of the recruiting services.

OFFENSIVE LINE

A potentially outstanding stable of running backs is only one of the reasons Arkansas should be encouraged about its rushing attack. It not only has the runners. It has the blockers.

The Hogs will return four of five starters from last season. Their only loss was starting tackle Gary Hobbs, who was dismissed from the team last January. Hobbs, who left the team in 1998 and returned a year later, started nine games last year at right tackle.

Sophomore **Mark Bokermann** (6-5, 308) is expected to replace Hobbs. The returning starters are junior center **Josh Melton** (6-5, 288), senior right guard **Kenny Sandlin** (6-3, 319), senior left guard **La'Zerius White** (6-4, 328), and senior left tackle **Shannon Money** (6-4, 309). Those four have combined for 89 starts in their career. Sandlin, Money and Melton are all being promoted as All-SEC candidates.

Money is regarded as the most physically gifted of the linemen and has exceptional footwork. A converted guard, he made second-team All-SEC last year despite missing two games with an ankle injury.

Melton, a former freshman All-American, has started 19 consecutive games. Concussions might be a concern for him, however. He suffered one concussion in the South Carolina game last October, then suffered a second one during spring practice. He didn't participate in the last three workouts of the spring and is expected to play with extra padding in his helmet next season.

Sandlin has started 24 consecutive games. He is one of the team's most emotional players.

"He can dominate you at the line of scrimmage," Nutt said. "He is always blocking and pushing until the whistle blows."

Like Sandlin, White has started 24 consecutive games and is another reason three different Arkansas running backs had 100-yard games last year. White started out slowly with the Razorbacks after being redshirted in 1997. He didn't even letter in 1998 and was ticketed for backup duty the following year. But he won the starting job in preseason and has been in the lineup ever since.

Bokermann's development is a key to the offensive line.

"He's dropped bad weight and put on good weight," offensive line coach Mike Markuson told the *Arkansas Democrat-Gazette*. "He gets better in the weight room every day, and he does more than what's required. That's what wins."

Jim Peters (6-3, 285) lettered last year as a backup at offensive guard. The sophomore is a former walk-on who impressed the coaches with his work ethic, and has been on scholarship since January of 2000. Sophomore guards **Scott Davenport** (6-2, 307) and **Caleb Perry** (6-4, 296) also have playing experience. Sophomore **Dan Doughty** (6-2, 285), a former noseguard, backed up Melton at center in the spring.

Sophomore **Bo Lacy** (6-4, 286) lettered last year at tackle. Sophomore **Jerry Reith** (6-3, 298), a former defensive lineman, also will get a shot at tackle, as will freshman **Brian Hill** (6-6, 297). Hill redshirted last year after being one of the top recruits in the state at Harrison, Ark.

2000 STATISTICS

Rushing offense	150.3	53
Passing offense	174.2	89
Total offense	324.5	86
Scoring offense	24.0	68
Net Punting	36.5	24
Punt returns	6.0	104
Kickoff returns	19.5	63
Rushing defense	139.1	46
Passing efficiency defense	102.8	16
Total defense	292.1	12
Scoring defense	23.5	48
Turnover margin	-9	97

Last column is ranking among Division I-A teams.

KICKERS

Sophomore **Brennan O'Donohoe** (6-0, 220) made 4-of-6 field-goal tries and 20-of-21 extra-point kicks last year but had a couple of big misses—one in a two-point loss to Auburn and another in the bowl game when it was still close. Arkansas needs a solid season from him because there is no other proven place-kicker.

O'Donohoe, who is also the backup punter, was an Arkansas all-stater as a senior. He kicked a 52-yard field goal as a high school junior in El Dorado.

DEFENSIVE LINE

Senior defensive end **Carlos Hall** (6-4, 261) and senior nose guard **Curt Davis** (6-3, 282) are the two returning starters on the front four. The Razorbacks also expect big things from junior defensive end **Raymond House** (6-3, 266), and tackles **Jermaine Brooks** (6-3, 295) and **Jason Peters** (6-5, 311).

Hall, a former Arkansas all-stater, began his career at linebacker, then switched to defensive end in the spring of 1998. His speed (a reported 4.42 40) and athleticism (a 42-inch vertical leap) got Arkansas' attention right away. He has had 13 tackles for losses the last two years. But based on his size, quickness and experience, he should be more productive.

House, who split time with Randy Garner last year, had 28 tackles, including four for losses last year. He impressed Nutt by repeatedly making big plays in the spring.

"He's very disciplined and he's gotten stronger," Nutt told the *Arkansas Democrat-Gazette*.

House first flashed his potential at McClellan High School in Little Rock, where he distinguished himself as an all-around athlete. He played on a championship AAU team in basketball, was a state weightlifting champion and played fullback, defensive end and defensive tackle in football.

Sophomore **Jayson Johnson** (6-3, 313), redshirt freshman **Elliott Harris** (6-4, 266), sophomore **Keith Turner** (6-4, 245) and sophomore **Justin Scott** (6-2, 253) will provide depth.

Davis returns for his third year as a starter. He combines experience and great technique. He had 37 tackles, including four for losses last year. Redshirt freshman **Arrion Dixon** (6-4, 273) was listed as his backup in the spring.

Brooks, a junior, had 24 tackles, including three for losses, last year. Peters, a redshirt freshman, was impressive in the spring.

"He's a playmaker," Thompson said of Peters. "We found out some things by moving him around in the spring. We started him out inside and he's OK, and then we moved him outside and 'wow.' "

Peters was rated as the 18th best prospect out of Texas by Max Emfinger's recruiting service. Peters, who excelled in the shot put and basketball at Queen City High School, is credited with a 4.8 40.

"I feel like I'm getting ready to be a force in this league," Peters told the *Northwest Arkansas Times*. "But I know I have a lot to learn to do that."

Brooks is the likely starter, but Peters could fill in anywhere on the line—at end, nose guard or tackle. Red-shirt freshman **Pat Winn** (6-4, 295) provides more size but no experience.

"We've got some SEC-size bodies," Thompson said. "But we're so young. The key is how quickly these guys mature."

LINEBACKERS

This is the mystery position for Arkansas, which lost linebackers Quinton Caver, J.J. Jones and Jim Ed Reed. Caver, an All-SEC pick, will be the hardest to replace. He had 96 tackles, including 10 for losses, last year.

The new linebacker corps is small but fast. Not one of the starters weighed as much as 220 pounds at the end of spring.

Sophomore **Shane Collins** (6-2, 215), a standout running back and linebacker in high school, was the No. 1 middle linebacker at the end of spring drills.

Sophomores **Tony Bua** (5-11, 212) and **Caleb Miller** (6-3, 213) will start on the outside.

"Collins is a 4.4 (in the 40) guy," Thompson said. "He's a tough playmaker."

Senior **Jermaine Petty** (6-2, 261), No. 2 on the depth chart, gives the Razorbacks size at middle linebacker. He had 24 tackles each of the last two years but his tackles for losses dropped from eight in 1999 to four last year. He was a junior college All-American at Butler County Community College.

Bua had 42 tackles, including three for losses, last year. A former Louisiana all-stater, Bua has been tried at free safety and rover back.

Jimmy Beasley (5-11, 191) has experience as a backup. Sophomore Miller (6-3, 213), who backed up Caver at middle linebacker last year, was shifted to outside linebacker in the spring and adapted well.

Miller, who first proved himself at Arkansas on special teams, had 21 tackles, including four for losses last year.

Gavin Walls (6-2, 217), a transfer from Coffeyville (Kansas) Community College, also had a good spring. He was listed as a backup at outside linebacker but has the size and hitting ability to play several positions.

"Our linebackers are kind of throwbacks," Thompson said. "(The starters) are all in the 215-pound range but they're really fast and active. They're all strong, but there's not a lot of bulk there. The biggest concern is their wearing down."

DEFENSIVE BACKS

With sophomore free safety **Ken Hamlin** (6-2, 193) leading the way, the secondary should be the strength of the defense. Hamlin made freshman All-American in a sensational first season. He led the team with 104 tackles, intercepted two passes and broke up seven others.

"He's the leader of our team," Thompson said. "He can do a lot of different things."

Hamlin drew comparisons to former Arkansas star safeties Steve Atwater and Kenoy Kennedy after becoming the first Hog to lead his team in tackles as a freshman. He had 16 tackles against Alabama and 13 in back-to-back games against Ole Miss and Tennessee.

"When he is playing center field, everyone knows he will pop you," Nutt said. "He can break on the ball extremely well and he has excellent football smarts."

Hamlin, who was redshirted his first year, first made a name for himself as a running back/defensive back at Frayser High School in Memphis. He rushed for 1,276 yards and had 96 unassisted tackles as a senior.

Senior **Corey G. Harris** (5-10, 200) provides experience at strong safety. He ranked fourth on the team last year with 50 tackles and was second with eight passes broken up. Harris had nine interceptions in 1999 at Butler County (Kansas) Community College. Senior **D'Andre Berry** (5-9,

180), a former cornerback, will add depth at strong safety. Berry had 38 tackles and two interceptions last year.

"Corey is a natural playmaker," Thompson said. "He has speed and good feet. He didn't lead the nation's junior colleges in interceptions because they just threw it to him. He made plays.

"Corey Harris (at strong safety) can be the same thing. He has a great burst to the football. He will be an NFL safety."

Sophomore **Eddie Jackson** (6-0, 186), a sprinter on the Arkansas track team, is a returning starter at cornerback. Senior **Harold Harris** (5-11, 191), who suffered a season-ending injury in the first game last year, will compete with sophomore **Lawrence Richardson** (5-11, 174) at the other corner. Senior Orlando Green was dismissed from the team after spring practice for disciplinary reasons.

Richardson, a high school All-American at Galveston (Texas) Ball High School, sat out last year while becoming academically eligible and missed the first six spring practices as a part of a suspension for a March 7 arrest for shoplifting. But once he got on the field, he impressed everyone with his speed, coverage skills and knack for breaking on the ball.

PUNTERS

Junior **Richie Butler** (6-1, 222) returns as one of the top punters in the country after a stellar 2000 season. He ranked 12th nationally and third in the SEC last year with a 42.8-yard average. He also dropped 17 punts inside the opponents' 20-yard line. He hit five inside the 20 against LSU. He capped his season by averaging 46.1 yards per punt against UNLV in the Las Vegas Bowl.

"Not only can he kick the ball a long way, but he can also land it in a spot that helps us win the field-position battle," Nutt said. "He did an outstanding job of keeping opponents backed up deep in their own territory."

SPECIAL TEAMS

Junior **Steadman Campbell** (5-8, 166) and sophomore Steven Harris (6-0, 170) return to handle the return chores.

Campbell returned 16 punts for 103 yards and a 6.4-yard average last year. He missed the bowl game and all of spring practice after suffering a broken ankle in a post-season practice last December. He's expected to be ready for preseason workouts.

Harris averaged 21 yards on 20 kickoff returns, with a long one of 44. Talley, Cobbs and Howard also have experience as a kick returner, and Richardson could be used as a punt returner or kick returner.

RECRUITING CLASS

On a bad day, Nutt is optimistic. On a good day, he's really optimistic. Signing day was a good day.

"I think it's our best class," Nutt said. ""There's not one guy you'd say, 'Er, that's a reach.' Not one."

The headliner of the class is Atlanta's **Ahmad "Batman" Caroll**, a defensive back who earned his nickname by leaping over center in youth-league football. Not only is Carroll an All-American, he also joins a team that needs help in the secondary.

Carroll set a Georgia high school record in the 100-meter dash (10.41 seconds) and was second in the 200-meter dash (21.24). He won the national AAU championship in the 100 meters with a 10.38 time.

Credit the Razorbacks with creative recruiting in Carroll's case. A man dressed in a Batman costume drove into the Broyles Center parking lot in a Batmobile when Carroll made his official visit in January.

Carroll should play as a true freshman, most likely in the secondary.

Junior **Jimarr Gallon** (5-11, 195) also could help out right away. He was selected the Jayhawk Conference Defensive Player of the Year at Butler Community College, where he had 10 tackles for losses, three sacks and two interceptions.

Arkansas' other *Parade* All-American signees didn't have to travel as far as Carroll. Offensive lineman **Shawn Andrews** (6-6, 330) is from Camden, Ark., and linebacker **Jeb Huckeba** is from Searcy, Ark.

Andrews, who averaged 16.3 pancake blocks per game, was limited to six games as a senior because of a back injury. Emfinger ranked him as the fourth best offensive guard in the country.

Huckbea (6-4, 210) excelled as an outside linebacker and wide receiver in high school. He had 163 tackles, five interceptions and 44 pass receptions as a senior. He should be an immediate contributor on Arkansas' defense.

Running back **De'Arrius Howard** (6-0, 205) was another prominent in-state signee. Howard scored 55 touchdowns his last two seasons at West Memphis High School. He was rated as the nation's No. 13 running back by Rivals100.com.

"When he carries the ball, defenders just fall off of him," Nutt told the *Arkansas Democrat-Gazette*. "You can see why he ran for 400 yards in a high school game."

Nutt has made speed a priority in recruiting, and this might be his fastest class yet. Fifteen of his 24 recruits list their 40 times as 4.5 seconds or better. One of the fastest is defensive back **Marvin Jackson** (5-9, 165) of Navarro College in Galveston, Texas. Jackson, who is credited with a 4.3 40, was a JC Gridwire All-American. Last year, he had nine interceptions, two fumble recoveries and scored five defensive touchdowns.

The Razorbacks signed three quarterbacks—**Tarvaris Jackson** (6-3, 215), **Cole Barthel** (6-2, 205) and **Matt Jones** (6-5, 215). Despite his size, Jones is credited with a 4.4 40. Jones, who is also an outstanding basketball player, was rated as the No. 13 quarterback/super athlete nationally by Emfinger. He rushed for 939 yards, passed for 830 and ranked in the top five in the state in punt returns as a senior at Northside High School in Fort Smith, Ark.

BLUE RIBBON ANALYSIS

OFFENSE	B
SPECIAL TEAMS	C+
DEFENSE	C
INTANGIBLES	B

Almost two years after Clint Stoerner's last game, quarterback is still a question mark at Arkansas. Hampton was accurate enough last year and Clark had his moments, but you still have to wonder if these guys are capable of leading the Hogs to a division championship.

Certainly, Hampton and Clark would be further along if not for injuries. When Clark was able to stay healthy in the spring, he made tremendous strides. Nonetheless, Hampton likely will begin the season as the starter.

Either way, Arkansas' quarterback will be blessed with complementary talent. The Razorbacks have a salty offensive line and proven running backs. The wide receivers are OK, although there's no obvious big-play guy.

The running game isn't just good, it's versatile. Cobbs and Talley have game-breaking speed but also can make the tough yards, as the power-running Holmes did down the stretch last year. Hampton and Clark won't have to be great passers, just competent enough to keep the pressure off the running game.

Arkansas' running attack also should make it easier for the defense, which is apt to get some welcome breaks while the Hogs are driving the ball down the field 4, 5, and 6 yards at a time.

Having Thompson as the defensive coordinator from the get-go should be a big plus for the defense. The addition of Wommack is another plus. They will help make the most of Arkansas' defensive talent. The defense needs someone to step up at linebacker and also could use a big year from Hall at defensive end.

Arkansas has been to three consecutive bowls under Nutt and this year should make No. 4. But if it's going to challenge LSU and Mississippi State for the SEC West title, it needs a big September.

In the first month of the season, the Razorbacks will play three teams—Georgia, Tennessee and UNLV—that beat them by an average of 30.3 points last season.

(J.A.)

2000 RESULTS

Southwest Missouri State	W	38-0	1-0
Boise State	W	38-31	2-0
Alabama	W	28-21	3-0
Georgia	L	7-38	3-1
Louisiana-Monroe	W	52-6	4-1
South Carolina	L	7-27	4-2
Auburn	L	19-21	4-3
Mississippi	L	24-38	4-4
Tennessee	L	20-63	4-5
Mississippi State	W	17-10	5-5
LSU	W	14-3	6-5
UNLV (Las Vegas Bowl)	L	14-31	6-6

Auburn

LOCATION	**Auburn, AL**
CONFERENCE	**Southeastern (Western)**
LAST SEASON	**9-4 (.672)**
CONFERENCE RECORD	**6-2 (1st)**
OFFENSIVE STARTERS RETURNING	**6**
DEFENSIVE STARTERS RETURNING	**5**
NICKNAME	**Tigers**
COLORS	**Burnt Orange & Navy Blue**
HOME FIELD	**Jordan-Hare Stadium (85,214)**
HEAD COACH	**Tommy Tuberville (S. Ark. '76)**
RECORD AT SCHOOL	**14-10 (2 years)**
CAREER RECORD	**39-30 (6 years)**
ASSISTANTS	**Don Dunn (ETSU '76) Defensive Tackles Eddie Gran (California Lutheran '87) Running Backs/Special Teams Greg Knox (Northeastern State '86) Wide Receivers/Recruiting Coordinator John Lovett (C.W. Post '73) Defensive Coordinaotr/Defensive Backs Noel Mazzone (New Mexico '80) Offensive Coordinator/Quarterbacks Phillip Lolley (Livingston '73) Outside Linebackers Hugh Nall (Georgia '82) Offensive Line Terry Price (Texas A&M '93) Defensive Ends Joe Whitt (Alabama State '72) Linebackers**
TEAM WINS (last 5 yrs.)	**8-10-3-5-9**
FINAL RANK (last 5 yrs.)	**25-9-37-27-21**

2000 FINISH Lost to Michigan in Citrus Bowl.

COACH AND PROGRAM

Auburn coach Tommy Tuberville had two running backs on his mind last December. One was Auburn junior Rudi Johnson, the leading rusher in the Southeastern Conference. The other was **Carnell "Cadillac" Williams**, a *Parade* All-American from Etowah, Ala.

Tuberville guessed there was a 50-50 chance Johnson would go pro early. But he couldn't recruit Williams full-bore until he knew for sure. So he waited.

While Tuberville waited, Alabama, Tennessee and others took their best shots at one of the best running backs in the country. Finally, Williams committed to the Vols. But the recruiting wasn't over. In fact, it was just getting started for Auburn.

"We kind of rolled the dice," Tuberville said. " We let him know we wanted him but we waited until after the bowl game to make our big sale.

"I'm waiting in December because I didn't know about Rudi. I'm going to have a different game plan (in the recruitment of Williams) depending on whether Johnson goes or stays."

Once Johnson decided he was leaving, Tuberville opted for Plan A, convincing Williams that he would be "the guy" in Auburn's running game. The strategy worked. Williams backed off his commitment to the Vols and signed with Auburn.

One of the South's foremost salesman had struck again.

Ask Tuberville about coaching, and the subject invariably turns to selling. He's now in his second year of selling Auburn football, and apparently loving every minute of it.

When Butch Davis left the University of Miami for the Cleveland Browns' head-coaching job, Tuberville's name popped up on the speculation list. He quickly said he wasn't interested. As he put it, "I've got the best job in the world right here."

Tuberville got the best job in the world by doing a heckuva job at Ole Miss, winning 30 games in five years, then breaking the Rebels' hearts by switching to the side of another SEC West rival. Ole Miss' loss was Auburn's gain. In Tuberville's second year, the Tigers—picked to finish in the second half of their division—won the West.

Auburn fans can't expect another division title, but they can expect Tuberville to keep the Tigers competitive while building toward bigger things. The come-from-behind recruitment of Williams gives them a reason for optimism. And whatever optimism Auburn supporters have, Tuberville fans it. He can sell Auburn, Ala., like a War Eagle native.

"There's a lot more that goes into a job than coaching on the field," he said. "Will you get the support from the fans? Will you get the support from the administration. Do you have a good recruiting base? We probably have six and seven million people in a 100-mile radius."

Tuberville believes he has everything he needs to win big at Auburn. All that and no traffic.

"I lived in Miami nine years," he said. "You could spend 45 minutes or more in a traffic jam driving home from work. And you're gone so much anyway.

"Here, (all the coaches) live about five minutes from the office. This is a place where your children have an opportunity to grow up in a community, play Little League baseball and football. One of the reasons I left Miami in the early '90s was my family."

After working with Tuberville for seven years, Noel Mazzone feels like part of the family. The coaches became friends after they met during a football camp in Greely, Colo., in 1984. When Tuberville became the head coach at Ole Miss in 1994, he hired Mazzone as his offensive coordinator and quarterbacks coach. Mazzone was one of seven assistant coaches who left Ole Miss and joined Tuberville at Auburn.

"I think I work for the best guy in the country," Mazzone said. "He's always been up front with us about things. We've got a lot of faith in Tubs."

After last year, so should Auburn.

2001 SCHEDULE

Sept.	1	Ball State
	8	Mississippi
	15	@LSU
	22	@Syracuse
	29	@Vanderbilt
Oct.	6	Mississippi State
	13	Florida
	20	Louisiana Tech
	27	@Arkansas
Nov.	10	@Georgia
	17	Alabama

QUARTERBACKS

Mazzone already has a great reputation for developing quarterbacks. It will be even better if the Tigers come up with a capable successor to Ben Leard.

Mazzone, a quarterback himself at the University of New Mexico in the late 1970s, has been a quarterbacks coach at Colorado State, TCU, Minnesota, Ole Miss and now Auburn. His most recent successes are Leard and Stan Patridge at Ole Miss.

Who's next?

On the last day of spring practice, the answer was senior **Daniel Cobb** (6-4, 228). He completed 8-of-12 passes for 216 yards and a touchdown. That carried him past junior **Jeff Klein** (6-3, 222) and redshirt freshman **Jason Campbell** (6-5, 213).

"The thing Daniel brings to you is that he's been behind the center a lot in college football, whether it's junior college or whatever," Tuberville told the *Birmingham News* after the final game. "I'm not saying he's going to be the starter. But it shows by his mannerisms on the field, the way he handles the huddle, about how he handles the pressure—when we made him third team, it didn't bother him. He just hung in there and waited his time and moved his way up."

"As the Quarterbacks Turn" was the recurring offensive theme in spring practice. Cobb went from third to first in one scrimmage. Sophomore **Allen Tillman** (6-2, 209) went from quarterback to wide receiver.

Cobb was lagging behind Klein and Campbell at the start of spring before soaring to the top of the depth chart with an impressive scrimmage. He completed 6-of-10 passes for 83 yards.

Cobb, a former *SuperPrep* All-American, began his career with the Georgia Bulldogs. He was medically redshirted in 1997 and 1998 after a blood clot developed in his throwing shoulder in 1997. Cobb underwent surgery in 1998 and spent the rest of the year in recovery and rehabilitation. He then transferred to Butler County Junior College, which he led to a national title. He completed 112-of-250 passes for 2,315 yards, 24 touchdowns and 10 interceptions at Butler.

Klein started four games as a redshirt freshman in 1999 when injuries decimated the quarterback corps. He completed 19-of-31 passes for 270 yards against Central Florida and was 19-of-39 for 245 yards against Florida.

Klein, who suffered a torn anterior cruciate ligament in the spring of 2000, played in only three games last year as a backup to Leard.

"I'm sure all the quarterbacks think they are the guy to beat," said Klein, who threw three interceptions in one scrimmage. "That's what makes the competition fun. I probably have a jump on the other guys because I have been around longer and know the offense."

Campbell, a *Parade* All-American, is the most athletically gifted of the quarterback candidates. Redshirted in 1999, Campbell was a two-time all-stater at Taylorsville (Miss.) High School. He also was selected to the *Clarion-Ledger*'s Dandy Dozen and made all-state in basketball as a junior. He gave up basketball his senior year to concentrate on football.

The Tigers received a scare during the spring when Campbell suffered a knee injury a week and a half before the annual A-Day Game. They were relieved when an MRI showed no structural damage to the knee.

Unlike Klein and Cobb, Campbell is an outstanding runner. He rushed for 45 yards on six carries and had one run of 28 yards in a scrimmage.

"Campbell is probably the best athlete of the three," Mazzone said. "Dan and Jeff are more mature because they're older. I expect more of them because of their experience, so I coach the guys a little differently. Jason has a ton of ability. He's just scratching the surface of what he's got to know in this offense."

Tuberville said he planned to decide on a starting quarterback early in preseason drills. That means Klein and Campbell will have to make up ground in a hurry. Klein threw only two passes—one an interception—in the spring game. Campbell completed 8-of-20 passes.

"I just can't tell myself I've won it yet," Cobb said. "I don't think it would be right for me to say that."

RUNNING BACKS

The battle for the starting tailback slot should be just as interesting as quarterback once Williams reports for preseason practice. Williams (5-11, 185) apparently lacks only experience. He's fast, athletic and productive.

Williams rushed for more than 6,000 yards in high school. As a senior, he rushed for 1,729 yards, scored 23 touchdowns and averaged close to 10 yards per carry. On defense, he had 78 tackles and six interceptions. As you might guess, he made quite an impression on his high school coach.

"He's a combination of Gale Sayers, Walter Payton and Barry Sanders," Etowah High School coach Raymond Farmer said. "He went to a Nike camp in Georgia and had the highest vertical jump of 37 inches and ran a 4.42 (second) 40.

"(Georgia coach) Mark Richt said he's the best he's seen in 15 years. Carnell will play right away wherever he goes; he's not your normal 17-year-old kid."

A chance to start right away was a huge factor in Williams' decision to attend Auburn. He thought he would have less competition there than at Tennessee, which signed two other high school All-America running backs.

"With them (UT) signing three, four or five backs, I didn't want to go in a situation like that," Williams told the *Knoxville News-Sentinel.*

There is s no experienced competition at Auburn. Sophomore **Casinious Moore** (6-0, 219) rushed for 61 yards on 23 carries last year; freshman **Ronnie Brown** (6-1, 226) was redshirted last season; sophomore **Chris Butler** (5-11, 207) sat out last season after transferring from Nebraska.

Moore, a high school star in Anniston, Ala., was redshirted in 1999 after suffering a knee injury. He was selected to the *Birmingham Post-Herald's* "10 Most Wanted" list as a high school senior.

"He is finally 100 percent from his knee surgery," Tuberville said. "I thought he had a good first season but he has a lot to learn."

Brown, whom Tuberville says reminds him the most of Rudi Johnson, was the Georgia 2A Player of the Year at Cartersville High School, where he gained 1,931 yards and scored 25 touchdowns as a senior. Butler, a standout hurdler in high school, rushed for more than 3,000 yards his last two years at Hoover (Ala.) High School.

Auburn didn't waste time checking out its new backs in the spring. In the first scrimmage, the three tailbacks carried the ball 57 times. Butler led the way with 84 yards on 29 carries while Brown had 66 yards on 17 carries. Moore gained 42 yards on 11 carries.

Auburn also was in the market for a new fullback, after the loss of Heath Evans. Sophomore **Brandon Johnson** (6-0, 231) won the job in the spring, and junior Michael Owens (6-0, 220) will back him up.

"Brandon has good hands and probably will end up being a better blocker than Heath," Mazzone said. "He doesn't have Heath's speed but he'll be a solid player. He's one of our toughest kids."

Owens, who rushed for more than 2,000 yards as a high school senior, played in seven games last year, mostly on special teams. He's also a good receiver out of the backfield.

WIDE RECEIVERS/TIGHT ENDS

The Tigers lost leading receiver Ronney Daniels but return **Tim Carter**, **Marcel Willis** and **Deandre Green**.

Carter, an All-American sprinter on Auburn's track team, had 21 catches for 271 yards and rushed 15 times for 116 yards last year. The 6-0, 197-pound senior also gives the Tigers a big-play kick returner.

Green, who didn't compete in the spring for personal reasons, made the All-SEC freshman team last year after catching 23 passes for 240 yards.

Green (6-2, 210) also had four catches for 49 yards, including a 21-yard touchdown reception, against Michigan in the Citrus Bowl.

"Deandre is a member in good standing of our football team," Tuberville told the *Birmingham News.* "Over the course of the football season, he really grew as a person and a player. We look forward to his return this summer."

Willis, a 6-1, 182-pound junior, caught 27 passes for 352 yards last year. He had five more catches for 69 yards in the Citrus Bowl.

Joe Walkins (5-9, 173) will get his first shot at playing time after redshirting last year. He caught 55 passes for 1,012 yards as a senior at Dillard High School in Fort Lauderdale, Fla.

"Receiver is my concern," Mazzone said. "The starters are solid, but we have to have freshmen come in and help."

The Tigers are well fortified at tight end with sophomore **Robert Johnson** (6-6, 271) and junior **Lorenzo Diamond** (6-3, 248). Johnson made the Rivals.com True Freshman All-American team after catching 12 passes for 168 yards and three touchdowns. Johnson, a high school All-American from Montgomery, Ala., suffered a broken bone in his wrist against Georgia but played with a protective cast against Alabama and in the SEC championship game against Florida. Johnson didn't practice in the spring because of a foot injury but is expected to be at full speed for preseason practice.

Like Johnson, Diamond sat out spring practice after undergoing minor knee surgery. He will also be ready for preseason practice. Diamond, who is an adept blocker, had 16 catches for 172 yards last year and caught a career-high four passes in the SEC championship game. He had three catches for 59 yards against Alabama.

Auburn also expects a contribution from signee **Jay Ratliff** (6-5, 230) at tight end. Ratliff, a former Georgia all stater, played at Hargrave (Va.) Military Academy last year.

OFFENSIVE LINE

The Tigers will return four of five starters in the offensive line, including All-SEC tackle **Kendall Simmons**, a 6-3, 319-pound senior. Simmons started all 13 games at left tackle after moving from guard to tackle during the preseason. He graded higher than 90 percent in six games last season.

"Kendall has really become a leader for us," Mazzone said. "He's big and strong and can run. He's one of the best offensive linemen I've ever been around."

The returning starting guards are seniors **Mike Pucillo** (6-4, 315) and **Hart McGarry** (6-5, 289). Pucillo worked at center in the spring because starter **Ben Nowland** (6-2, 306) was out with a broken hand. Pucillo already has 27 career starts, including five as a redshirt freshman in 1998. In 1999, he started six games at guard and three at center. McGarry has 18 career starts. Nowland has 11 career starts.

"Pucillo is a solid guy at right guard," Mazzone said. "At left guard, Hart has played a lot of games. He may not be as talented athletically as some of our guys, but he understands where he's supposed to be and how to get there."

Nowland's absence in the spring created an opportunity for freshman **Danny Lindsey** (6-2, 295), who enrolled at Auburn in January. Lindsey, who had 97 snaps in one scrimmage, was No. 2 on the depth chart after spring. He was a first-team all-state selection at Coffee High School in Douglas, Ga., and was ranked as one of the top 50 offensive linemen in the country by Rivals.com.

There is a question mark at right tackle, which Colin Sears manned last year. Sophomore **Mark Pera** (6-6, 295), a two-time all-state selection from Memphis, Tenn., played sparingly last year at tackle. Redshirt freshman **Nate French** (6-2, 297) moved from the defensive line to the offensive line the last week of spring practice. He was a two-time Georgia all-stater in high school.

Redshirt freshman **Ryan Broome** (6-6, 298) is another tackle candidate. *SuperPrep* ranked Broome as one of the top 50 players in Georgia his senior year. He lived in Barbados until his senior year of high school.

Sophomore **Monreko Crittenden** (6-5, 344) began the spring at right tackle but was switched to right guard. Crittenden, a former Alabama all-stater, played almost exclusively on special teams last year.

"We're hurting for depth," Mazzone said. "At the spring game, we didn't have enough linemen to have two full offensive lines. We'll bring in three or four freshmen and at least one of them will have to step up and play for us."

2000 STATISTICS

Rushing offense	163.3	38
Passing offense	193.3	77
Total offense	356.7	70
Scoring offense	24.0	68
Net Punting	37.6	15
Punt returns	7.6	90
Kickoff returns	20.1	52
Rushing defense	98.3	15
Passing efficiency defense	114.8	46
Total defense	303.3	14
Scoring defense	19.6	28
Turnover margin	+1	58

Last column is ranking among Division I-A teams.

KICKERS

Junior **Damon Duval** (6-0, 184) gained most of his recognition as an All-SEC punter but didn't fare badly as a place-kicker. He made 14-of-18 field-goal attempts, including 6-of-9 from more than 40 yards.

Duval first demonstrated his strong leg at Central High School in Chattanooga, Tenn., where he kicked a 57-yard field goal and four 55-yard field goals. He also ranked as one of the top soccer players in the country in the Olympic Development Program.

In two years at Auburn, Duval has made all 57 of his extra-point attempts. He is s 23-of-33 on field-goal tries.

Redshirt freshman **Phillip Yost** (6-1, 180) gives Auburn another promising kicker. Yost, who pushed Duval for the starting job in the spring, was a first-team USA Today All-American at Auburn High School in 1999. He made 11-of-15 field-goal attempts, with a long one of 52 yards. Yost kicked a 61-yarder to win the field-goal competition at the National Kicking Service Camp.

DEFENSIVE LINE

Sophomore **DeMarco McNeil** (6-1, 301) heads up a solid defensive front. McNeil, a former Mr. Football in Alabama, didn't take long living up to his high school billing once he got his chance.

McNeil, who was redshirted in 1999, started all 13 games last year. He led the team with 13 tackles for losses and five sacks and ranked second on the team with 67 total tackles. Nobody else on the team had half as many tackles for losses.

"He made some plays last year," Tuberville said. "As of yet, he's not a Warren Sapp, Russell Maryland or Jerome Brown (defensive linemen whom Tuberville coached as an assistant at Miami). But he's got a chance. He's not as quick as those players at this time, but he's young."

McNeil isn't the only All-SEC candidate on Auburn's defensive front. Senior defensive end **Javor Mills** (6-4, 271), a former junior college transfer, led the team with quarterback hurries and tied for second behind McNeil in tackles for losses. He had his best game against Alabama, with nine tackles, two tackles for losses, a sack and two quarterback hurries.

Sophomores **Reggie Torbor** (6-3, 238) at end and **Spencer Johnson** (6-3, 273) at tackle are also returning starters. Torbor, a former second-team Louisiana all-stater, made the SEC All-Freshman team last year. Johnson, who made the Rivals.com True Freshman All-American team, was second on the team with 10 quarterback hurries and three sacks last year. He was one of the state's top prospects two years ago at Southern Choctaw High School in Silas, Ala.

"I don't think there's any question he can be a great one, really something special," defensive coordinator John Lovett told the *Huntsville Times.* "Last year, he came in, he'd played linebacker his whole life, and we threw him right in there at defensive tackle.

"He was undersized and playing a new Auburn spring football position against some of the best football in the country. He's up to 275 or so, he's still got room to grow, and he moves so well."

Tuberville is looking for help on the line.

"We need to find some depth behind (the starters)," Tuberville said. "I think we have four players, but we need to find others to play behind them. The front four has a chance to be very good if they get some help behind them."

Senior **James Callier** (6-0, 246) has plenty of experience, although at linebacker. A former All-SEC freshman pick, Callier was moved to defensive end and had an immediate impact.

"That's been really good for us," Lovett told the *Huntsville Times.* "He can just use his motor and go. Initially, he fought it, but once he got out there running around he said 'Hey, this is fun.' It took some pressure off him. I think that is one of the best things we did (in the spring)."

"That really shows our younger players something," Tuberville said of Callier's switch. "Here's a guy who's been here for four years and he's willing to sacrifice for the team."

Senior defensive end **Alton Moore** (6-7, 263) has experience as a backup. A two-time junior college All-American, Moore had 19 tackles and four tackles for losses last year.

The Tigers are counting on freshman **Marcus Johnson** (6-2, 283) and sophomore **Dexter Murphy** (6-2, 268) for more depth. Johnson, who was redshirted last year, was rated as one of the top 50 players in Florida by *SuperPrep* magazine. He had 85 tackles and 10 sacks his senior year at Ed White High School in Jacksonville, Fla. Murphy played in eight games at tackle last year.

Redshirt freshman **Bret Eddins** (6-5, 255) should help out at defensive end. Eddins, who had 10 tackles in one spring scrimmage, had 196 tackles his senior season at Trinity High School in Montgomey, Ala. His full name is Jordan Bret Eddins. He was named in honor of the late Shug Jordan, who coached Bret's father, Liston, at Auburn in 1973-75.

LINEBACKERS

While senior **Tavarreus Pounds** (6-1, 245) was recuperating from shoulder surgery in the spring, sophomore **Dontarrious Thomas** (6-3, 225) emerged as one of Auburn's best defensive players.

"He came in here at 190 pounds and now he's 225," Tuberville said. "He's going to be an excellent linebacker."

After replacing the injured Pounds last fall, Thomas finished third on the team with 62 tackles and made the All-SEC Freshman team. He had 10 tackles against Arkansas and eight against Florida in the SEC championship game.

Pounds, who will enter fall drills as No. 2 on the depth chart, was leading the team in tackles when he was injured last season. He also was hampered by injuries in 1998 and 1999. A shoulder bruise curtailed his playing time near the end of the 1998 season and he missed the Florida game with a hip flexor in 1999.

Redshirt freshman **Victor Horn** (6-0, 231) backed up Thomas in the spring. Horn was a star running back at Huntsville High School.

Junior **Mark Brown** (6-1, 239) has starting experience at the other inside linebacker slot. Brown, who had four starts last year, was listed ahead of redshirt freshman **Mayo Sowell** (6-1, 220) and sophomore **Phillip Pate** (6-3, 212) in the spring. Sowell is a former Alabama all-stater. Pate played mainly on special teams last year.

Junior **Rashaud Walker** (5-9, 206) returns as a starter at outside linebacker. Walker led the team with seven tackles and a sack in the Citrus Bowl.

Former walk-on **Roderick Hood** (5-11, 192) is the other starter. Hood, who earned a scholarship before last season, finished the year with 44 tackles and five pass deflections. He showed his versatility and speed by returning kicks. Utilized as a kick returner the last three games, Hood averaged 27 yards.

Sophomore **Roshard Gilyard** (5-9, 208) and junior **Damien Postell** (6-0, 215) are the backups. Gilyard made the All-SEC Freshman team last year, starting seven games as a free safety. A *SuperPrep* All-American from Jacksonville, Fla., Gilyard was moved to linebacker in the spring. Postell didn't play last season after being switched from offense to defense in the spring of 2000. He rushed for almost 4,000 yards at Baldwin (Fla.) High School.

DEFENSIVE BACKS

Stanford Simmons, a 6-2, 198-pound junior, is the only returning starter at the three secondary positions. Simmons, a former *Parade* All-American, started seven games last year at free safety after playing as a backup in 1999. Freshman **Corey Hicks** (6-2, 210), who enrolled at Auburn in January, will serve as a backup.

Although cornerbacks **Travaris Robinson** and **Ronaldo Attimy** didn't start last year, they saw playing time as reserves. Robinson, a 5-10, 187-pound junior, had 30 tackles and an interception last year. He also returned 10 kickoffs for 164 yards. Robinson was switched from wide receiver after the 1999 season.

Attimy (5-10, 188) played in eight games last year after transferring from Northeastern Oklahoma A&M Junior College. He's a former all-state running back from Spring Valley, N.Y.

Redshirt freshman defensive back **Donnay Young** (6-0, 191) had a good spring, which should surprise no one who saw him at North Clayton High School in College Park, Ga, where he played wide receiver and defensive back, punted, kicked, and returned kicks.

"We're looking for Donnay Young, **Junior Rosegreen** and **Brian Henderson** to really step up and compete because we really don't have very much experience at cornerback," Tuberville said.

Rosegreen, a 6-0, 180-pound redshirt freshman, was a first-team Florida all-stater in high school. *SuperPrep* magazine rated him as one of the top 25 players in the state.

PUNTERS

Duval demonstrated both strength and finesse as a punter. He finished 11th in the country and second in the SEC with a 43.3-yard average and also punted 11 balls inside the 20.

In 1999, Duval made the All-SEC Freshman team by finishing second in the conference and 18th nationally with a 42.9-yard average. He landed 14 punts inside the 20. He was similarly effective in high school, where he averaged 44.7 yards as a senior and 43 for his career.

RECRUITING CLASS

Williams and linebacker **Lemarcus Rowell** were the crown jewels of a consensus top 20 recruiting class that was ranked as high as ninth nationally.

Tuberville credited the recruiting success to success on the field.

"I don't think there's any doubt our success this year helped us," said Tuberville, who led Auburn to nine victories and the SEC Western Division championship. "The one thing I learned from Jimmy Johnson, you go out and recruit as hard as you want, send out letters and do all the things in recruiting. But the one thing that is going to help you the most is winning football games.

"I'm really pleased with the speed we've got, and the size. We did sign quite a few linemen, mostly offensive linemen. There had only been six offensive linemen signed at Auburn the last three years, so we definitely needed offensive linemen. We filled those needs."

Aside from Williams, Rowell (6-3, 220) of Opelika, Ala., was Auburn's most celebrated recruit. A consensus All-American, he had 339 tackles the last two years. He was ranked as the top linebacker in the South by BorderWars.com and the sixth best linebacker in the nation by Rivals.com.

Tuberville also was enthused about the addition of five defensive backs.

"I thought probably the most urgent need we had was defensive back," Tuberville said. "We're really running short of defensive backs, especially corner. I think we got some guys who can come in and play."

Dee Durham (5-9, 175) of Atlanta was rated as one of the top six defensive backs in the country by *PrepStar.* He had 15 interceptions the last two years. Auburn signed two defensive backs from Hargrave (Va.) Military Academy—**Rodney Mars** (6-0, 190) and **Carlos Rogers** (6-1, 175).

Antarrious Williams (6-1, 185), the Georgia 4A Defensive Player of the Year, played defensive end at Shaw High School in Columbus, Ga., but was recruited as a defensive back. He had 19 tackles for losses, eight sacks, four fumble recoveries and two interceptions as a senior. He was ranked as one of the top five athletes in the Southeast by *PrepStar.*

Auburn's defense also should benefit from the signing of highly recruited Birmingham defensive tackle **Antwarn Franklin** (6-4, 310). Franklin had 90 tackles and seven sacks last year and was an all-state offensive lineman as well.

Steven Ross (6-5, 265) was rated as the No. 2 defensive lineman in the Southeast by *PrepStar* and one of the top 100 players in the country by Rivals.com. **Wayne Dickens** (6-2, 273) was a first-team all-state selection and a USAToday.com All-American at Lake Gibson High School in Lakeland, Fla.

One of Auburn's most intriguing signees was Louisiana running back Brandon Jacobs, a 6-5, 240-pounder with exceptional speed. He didn't qualify academically and planned to enroll at Coffeyville (Kan.) Community College.

Jacobs rushed for 3,022 yards and 38 touchdowns as a senior at Assumption High School in Napoleonville, La. He also returned eight kickoffs for touchdowns.

BLUE RIBBON ANALYSIS

OFFENSE	C
SPECIAL TEAMS	B+
DEFENSE	C
INTANGIBLES	B

Tuberville learned a lesson last year during Auburn's unexpected run to the SEC West title.

"It taught me that if you have good chemistry, leadership and guys who believe in what you're doing, you can accomplish a lot," Tuberville said. "We weren't overly talented but we had great chemistry and played from the starting gun to the end without ever letting up."

This year's team has more talent but less experience, and Tuberville is concerned about the latter.

"If I had my druthers, I'd rather have more experience and less talent," he said. "You win with experienced players."

The schedule doesn't bode well for a young team. After opening against Ball State and playing Ole Miss at home, Auburn will play three consecutive road games at LSU, Syracuse and

Vanderbilt. Then, the Tigers return home to play Mississippi State and Florida, two of the best teams in the league. In a division as balanced as this one, that combination of schedule and inexperience will be difficult to overcome.

"If we could work our way back into the top 25, I'd consider it a good year," Tuberville said.

He's selling himself short. That would be a great year.

How different it would have been if Johnson, Evans and Ronney Daniels hadn't jumped to the NFL early. The Tigers still would have to break in a new quarterback, but they would have been able to surround him with experienced talent. Moreover, the Tigers would be promoting Johnson for the Heisman Trophy.

Now, they will have to wait for another star running back to come along. If Williams is as good as predicted, the wait won't be long.

(J.A.)

2000 RESULTS

Wyoming	W	35-21	1-0
Ole Miss	W	35-27	2-0
LSU	W	34-17	3-0
Northern Illinois	W	31-14	4-0
Vanderbilt	W	33-0	5-0
Mississippi State	L	10-17	5-1
Florida	L	7-38	5-2
Louisiana Tech	W	38-28	6-2
Arkansas	W	21-19	7-2
Georgia	W	29-26	8-2
Alabama	W	9-0	9-2
Florida (SEC Champ.)	L	6-28	9-3
Michigan (Citrus Bowl)	L	28-31	9-4

Florida

LOCATION Gainesville, FL
CONFERENCE Southeastern (Eastern)
LAST SEASON 10-3 (.770)
CONFERENCE RECORD 8-1 (1st)
OFFENSIVE STARTERS RETURNING 8
DEFENSIVE STARTERS RETURNING 9
NICKNAME Gators
COLORS Orange & Blue
HOME FIELD Ben Hill Griffin Stadium (83,000)
HEAD COACH Steve Spurrier (Florida '67)
RECORD AT SCHOOL 112-25-1 (11 years)
CAREER RECORD 132-38-2 (14 years)
ASSISTANTS
Buddy Teevens (Dartmouth '79) Tight Ends/Receivers
Jon Hoke (Ball State '80) Defensive Coordinator/Secondary
Jimmy Ray Stephens (Florida '77) Centers/Guards
Ricky Hunley (Arizona '84) Defensive Line
Jim Collins (Elon '74) Recruiting Coordinator/Special Teams/Outside Linebackers
Dwayne Dixon (Florida '85) Receivers
Lawson Holland (Clemson '76) Running Backs
John Hunt (Florida '84) Offensive Tackles
Jerry Odom (Florida '91) Inside Linebackers
TEAM WINS (last 5 yrs.) 12-10-10-9-10
FINAL RANK (last 5 yrs.) 1-4-4-11-9
2000 FINISH Lost to Miami in Sugar Bowl.

COACH AND PROGRAM

In the realm of Florida football, it's understood that the Gators compete for championships every year.

The Southeastern Conference title, which Florida has won six times since 1991, is certainly one of those prizes that everyone in Swamp land eyeballs at the beginning of each fall.

But as the Gators prepare for the 2001 season, the stakes may be as high as they've been since Steve Spurrier returned to his alma mater as head coach in 1990.

The returning talent, wealth of depth, dizzying expectations and key games at home make Florida as good a pick as any to win the national championship.

By Florida standards, it's been a while.

The Gators last won college football's top prize in 1996, which happens to be their only national title. Before last season, 1996 was also the last time Florida won an SEC championship.

"Nobody much talks about SEC championships anymore," says Spurrier, who's finished first in the SEC eight of his 11 years in Gainesville.

The 2000 season drew mixed reviews. Despite one of his younger teams, Spurrier was able to steer the Gators back to Atlanta for the SEC Championship game, where they smothered Auburn, 28-6.

The SEC title helped to ease the sting of losing to fierce rival Florida State two weeks earlier. It was the Gators' third consecutive loss to the Seminoles, a bitter pill for Spurrier to swallow. Just as nauseating, though, was getting pushed around in the Sugar Bowl by Miami, which ran off and left Florida for a 37-20 victory.

It was the second year that the Gators had closed the season with a whimper. They lost their last three games in 1999 and two of their last three last season.

SEC championship or no SEC championship, Spurrier wasn't sitting pat. When spring practice opened in March, he showed a side that few had seen during spring drills. The Gators hit, hit and hit some more.

Coaches and players alike called it the most physical and most intense spring practice of the Spurrier era, a stark contrast to the days when Spurrier was hesitant to allow his players to beat up on each other.

"I didn't think we competed as hard as we should last year," Spurrier said. "We need to learn to compete harder."

In every scrimmage, Spurrier made sure he devised some type of system to keep score. There were some memorable wars between the offense and defense.

Senior strong safety **Marquand Manuel** (6-0, 208) took it upon himself to huddle his mates for a pep talk.

Spurrier cut one scrimmage short after the defense had its way. Senior defensive end **Alex Brown** (6-3, 264) later accused the offense of quitting, to which Spurrier told him to zip it up.

"Some of our scrimmages felt like a Florida-Florida State game," Brown said after the Gators' spring game.

Suffice to say that Spurrier has his club's attention, which coupled with the talent on this team, could be bad news for everybody else.

The Gators return eight offensive starters and 16 of their top 22 players from a unit that led the SEC in scoring offense with an average of 37.3 points per game.

The only thing unsettled offensively coming out of the spring has a familiar ring to it in Gator Land: Who will start at quarterback?

Spurrier said it's a dead heat between sophomores **Rex Grossman** (6-1, 218) and **Brock Berlin** (6-1, 209).

On defense, the Gators will be ridiculously deep just about everywhere. Junior cornerback **Lito Sheppard** (5-10, 194) may be the best all-around player in the league. He's part of a defense that returns nine starters and 18 of its top 22 players from a year ago. But Sheppard will miss at least one game after failing a random drug test in May. Sheppard tested positive for marijuana, and as a first-time offender, he would be required to miss only one tenth of his athletic season, or one game. Sheppard has appeal options, but could be suspended for two or more games at the discretion of the university.

The Gators, who led the nation with 40 forced turnovers, had 25 different players start a game last season on defense—and 20 of those players are back.

"The team we coached in the spring is only part of the story," Spurrier said. "What our players accomplish on their own from now to August will have a bigger bearing on what sort of team we will have next season. Hopefully, we will be an improved team when fall camp begins."

Look for a few streaks to continue.

The Gators can set an SEC record by winning nine or more games this season. That would be 12 straight nine-win seasons.

Also, Florida State and Florida are the only two schools in the country to play in a January bowl game in each of the last eight seasons.

"Every year, we have high goals around here," Sheppard said. "This year's no different. If anything, they're higher, and that's the way we like it."

2001 SCHEDULE

Sept.	1	Marshall
	8	Louisiana-Monroe
	15	Tennessee
	22	@Kentucky
	29	Mississippi State
Oct.	6	@LSU
	13	@Auburn
	27	Georgia (at Jacksonville)
Nov.	3	Vanderbilt
	10	@South Carolina
	17	Florida State

QUARTERBACKS

It just wouldn't be Florida football without a little intrigue at the quarterback position. This season, there figures to be more than a little intrigue. But such is life when you're the trigger man (or trigger men) for Spurrier.

Grossman and Berlin were neck and neck coming out of the spring. Spurrier's not budging, either, if there is a favorite. Those who know the "ball coach" best think he wants it to be Berlin, the steady, straight-laced kid who from the time he arrived in Gainesville has been compared to Danny Wuerffel.

But Berlin threw all of 27 passes last season as a true freshman, while Grossman started the final eight games after stepping in for Jesse Palmer. Grossman earned first-team All-SEC honors while tossing 21 touchdown passes, the second most by a freshman in league history.

And yet, it's not his job.

"Obviously, I would have liked to have separated myself, but I'm not really worried about the situation too much," Grossman told the *Orlando Sentinel*. "I'm not going to comment on it a whole lot."

Spurrier didn't sound thrilled with either of his quarterbacks upon the completion of the spring. But then, when is he thrilled?

"The quarterback play has been decent,"

Spurrier said. "Brock has made a lot of strides. I don't know how much Rex has made. He's been here one year longer. Hopefully, both of them can get a lot smarter."

The only trace of a surprise in all this was that Grossman was better than good a year ago. He has that knack for making plays, no matter how unorthodox they might look.

Remember the shotgun snap over his head last season and Grossman scrambling back to get the ball and firing a touchdown pass to sophomore receiver **Jabar Gaffney**? That memorable sequence was Grossman at his best. For the season, he completed 61.8 percent of his passes for 1,866 yards and was intercepted just seven times.

"With all the situations Rex has played in, and doing as well as he did, he's got the experience over Brock," Gaffney told the *Orlando Sentinel*.

Perhaps so, but Grossman didn't enjoy a stellar spring, one that got off to a rotten start when he was suspended for the first week by Spurrier for academic reasons.

Grossman didn't throw a touchdown pass in the first five scrimmages and was intercepted four times. Berlin had four touchdowns and just two interceptions during those same scrimmages.

Then again, Grossman has never been a practice player. His high school coach noted as much when Grossman headed south to Florida from South High in Bloomington, Ind.

Grossman's strengths are his ultra-quick release and strong arm. He's not afraid to take a few chances, either. Berlin, on the other hand, is more the textbook quarterback. He typically does it exactly the way Spurrier draws it up, and not all of his passes are bullets. Some even tend to float, again reminiscent of the Wuerffel days when he knew the offense every bit as well as Spurrier.

"[Berlin] brings this awareness of the game," junior receiver **Reche Caldwell** told the *Orlando Sentinel*. "He is very smart out there. He knows what's going on. He can read defenses very fast and get it to the right place."

Berlin even wears the No. 7 jersey that Wuerffel made famous. Moreover, he hasn't lost a game in which he's started since grade school. Berlin was 45-0 as a starter in leading Evangel Christian High in Shreveport, La., to three straight state titles.

"We'll see who improves the most between now and September, who seems the most ready to play," Spurrier told the *Florida Times-Union*. "Quarterbacks can really improve between now and September. Shane Matthews comes to mind as a guy that came in [fourth] team to start with and really prepared through the summer and became our starter back in '90.

"We'll see how Rex and Brock do as far as preparation and so forth going into preseason. Hopefully we'll have one guy and we'll let him go until he can't go anymore."

If history holds true, they both will play. And chances are that the one who does end up starting the season won't necessarily be the one who finishes it.

Who knows? In the early going, Spurrier could decide to rotate them on every play. It wouldn't be the first time. He did it with Doug Johnson and Palmer in the 1998 Tennessee game.

While Spurrier may not have written the job description for playing quarterback, he knows exactly what he wants—and what he demands.

"Playing quarterback is a game of decisions, smart playing, getting from bad plays to good plays," Spurrier told the *Florida Times-Union*. "We're not at that level right now. We're going to keep pitching 40, 50 times a game. We've got to get to that level somehow. Both of them have a lot to learn.

"Playing quarterback nowadays is more decision-making, more thinking, than it is who can throw the hardest pass."

RUNNING BACKS

The Gators are mortal at running back, but that doesn't mean they're hurting back there. There's just nobody like Fred Taylor in the lineup.

Senior **Robert Gillespie** (5-9, 190) and junior **Earnest Graham** (5-9, 220) shared the tailback position last season, and both return.

Gillespie is more of a slasher who will bounce it outside, while Graham tends to have that bowling ball effect between the tackles. They combined for 1,354 of the 1,453 yards the Gators amassed at tailback last season.

They also both catch the ball effectively coming out of the backfield, a must in Spurrier's system. Gillespie led all running backs with 26 receptions last season, while Graham had 19 catches. Graham ended the season with a flourish. He rushed for 169 yards in the SEC Championship, a record in that game, and he followed that with 136 yards in the Sugar Bowl loss to Miami. Gillespie missed both of those games after suffering an injury to his left knee.

The Gators ran the ball 43.7 percent of the time last season and threw it 56.3 percent. That's the lowest run percentage in the Spurrier era, a trend that caught up with Florida against Florida State.

Spurrier went away from the run early, and the Gators painted themselves into a pass-only mode.

The running back having the best spring was sophomore **Ran Carthon** (6-0, 213), but he suffered a shoulder injury midway through spring drills and missed the rest of practice. Carthon is expected to return to the practice field by the latter part of August. He was voted the Gators' most improved running back in the spring.

Redshirt freshman **Willie Green** (5-8, 215) also showed flashes, but missed all of last season after undergoing surgery on both knees. Green, *USA Today*'s Player of the Year in Florida as a high school senior, didn't go unnoticed by Spurrier.

"Willie Green showed the coaches that he is ready to jump in there and play some this season," Spurrier said. "We look for him to alternate with Earnest Graham and Robert Gillespie."

That rotation could include as many as four people. No Florida running back has ever averaged 20-25 carries a game over a season under Spurrier. Only three have done that since 1955—Larry Smith (1967), Neal Anderson (1985) and Emmitt Smith (1989).

If Green stays healthy, the Gators will have an overflow of options. His knees seemed to hold up during the spring, and he received a ton of work. Green came to Florida as a high school legend from Osceola High in Kissimmee, Fla., where he earned Parade All-America honors as senior. For his career, Green rushed for 7,947 yards and scored 107 touchdowns—second best in Florida prep history behind only Emmitt Smith.

At fullback, the Gators will need to replace dependable Rod Frazier, who started 26 games.

Senior **Rob Roberts** (6-2, 252) is expected to be back for the start of the season after injuring his knee late in spring practice and undergoing surgery. Roberts has moved from tight end to fullback several times during his career. He's a bruising blocker.

After Roberts' knee injury, redshirt freshman **Ray Snell** (6-0, 223) emerged as the top fullback in the spring. A walk-on, Snell is the brother of sophomore offensive tackle **Shannon Snell** (6-5, 308).

WIDE RECEIVERS/TIGHT ENDS

One thing's for sure about the Gators' quarterback controversy. Whoever's pulling the trigger is going to have a dynamic set of playmakers to throw to at receiver.

And experienced, too.

Gaffney (6-1, 202) and Caldwell (6-0, 198) accounted for 1,944 yards between them last season, making them the second most prolific receiving duo in the nation. Gaffney, given a second chance by Spurrier, responded by having a dream season. He set NCAA Division I freshman records for most receiving yards (1,184) and touchdown receptions (14).

He was selected the national freshman of the year by *The Sporting News* and was a consensus first-team All-SEC pick. His 71 receptions set the SEC freshman record. Not bad for a guy who started last season without a scholarship.

That was one of the conditions Spurrier imposed on Gaffney if he wanted to re-join the team. Gaffney was kicked off after his no contest plea to petty theft stemming from a December 1999 incident at the Swamp during the Class 5A state championship game. Gaffney was accused of entering the locker room and stealing cash and jewelry from players and coaches while they competed in the game.

It wasn't until June of last year before Spurrier agreed to let Gaffney return—but only if there were no more slip-ups.

This past off-season, Gaffney was involved in another incident when the mother of a 15-year-old boy accused Gaffney of beating up her son when Gaffney caught the boy trying to steal his scooter.

University police investigated and decided not to press charges, and the state attorney's office is still investigating.

The cloud of those probes obviously didn't sit well with Gaffney, who didn't have the best of springs. He seemed to disappear at times and even dropped a pass in the spring game.

As good as Gaffney was last season Caldwell wasn't far behind. He finished with 49 catches for 760 yards and six touchdowns.

The emphasis in the spring was to develop more balance at receiver, and the Gators think they've done that. Gaffney and Caldwell combined for 120 catches last season. The remainder of the Florida receiving corps combined for just 59.

Junior **Taylor Jacobs** (6-0, 190) could help change that ratio. He drew rave reviews and probably had the best spring of any of the Gators' receivers. Jacobs started in five games last season, catching 17 passes for 198 yards.

More importantly, Jacobs caught the eye of Spurrier with his route running and understanding of the offense. Jacobs caught touchdowns in two of the Gators' last three scrimmages.

"Taylor might be as good as Reche right now," Spurrier said. "Reche's had a so-so spring."

Jacobs said he allowed the pressure of his first year at Florida to weigh on him.

"I came in my first year and played as a true freshman, and there was a lot of pressure to come in last year and play a lot," Jacobs told the *Orlando Sentinel*. "I came from a small high school and coming into this big program, that was a really big jump and I didn't handle it well.

"It's all about doing things and making plays and forgetting about people in the stands."

Sophomore **Carlos Perez** (5-11, 204) vaulted into the top four at receiver with a solid spring. He was selected the team's most improved receiver during the spring.

"Carlos Perez has jumped ahead of the other

guys," Spurrier told the *Orlando Sentinel*. "He's caught the ball, run good routes, so he's probably in the top four right now."

Senior **Brian Haugabrook** (6-2, 200) injured his knee during the spring and had surgery. He's hopeful of returning early this season. He caught 18 passes for 249 yards and two touchdowns last season.

Others who could contribute include sophomore **Matt Jackson** (5-10, 190), sophomore **Kelvin Kight** (6-0, 192), redshirt freshman **O.J. Small** (6-1, 211) and redshirt freshman **Reggie Vickers** (5-10, 170).

Just when you thought Spurrier's offensive system was about to become a little more predictable, he throws in a new wrinkle.

This season, that wrinkle could involve throwing to the tight end more. Junior **Aaron Walker** (6-6, 254) caught a pair of touchdown passes in the spring game. Walker started in eight games last season and caught three touchdown passes.

Don't be surprised if that figure increases this season.

"We've got a few [plays for the tight ends] in the playbook, but it's hard to get it to us sometimes because you've got Jabar Gaffney and Reche running great routes," Walker told the *Tampa Tribune*. "When we get a chance to get the ball, we need to take advantage of the situation."

Spurrier was also impressed with the development of sophomore **Ben Troupe** (6-4, 250) during spring drills. He was voted the team's most improved tight end.

The third tight end is junior **Kirk Wells** (6-4, 222). He had 12 catches for 167 yards and two touchdowns a year ago.

OFFENSIVE LINE

The biggest void up front was left by the early departure of right tackle Kenyatta Walker, who went in the first round of the NFL draft. The Gators hope to replace him with the largest player in Florida history.

Sophomore **Max Starks** is listed at 6-7 and 362 pounds. But he's still growing, and doctors think he may be closer to 7-foot and 400 pounds by the time he stops.

Already, Starks has surpassed the 6-8 mark and won't say what he weighs. It's obviously too much for Spurrier.

"If we could get about 20 pounds off of him, he would have a chance to be a really good offensive lineman," Spurrier said.

The Gators are set at left tackle, where junior **Mike Pearson** (6-7, 292) returns after starting in 20 games his first two years at Florida. Pearson was one of four Gators to start in every game last season.

Pearson was a first-team All-SEC selection by the coaches last season and a second-team selection by the Associated Press.

In many respects, he's fortunate to be playing football after a freak automobile accident in July of last year when he fractured his skull. Pearson cracked his head on the overhead in a parking garage.

The interior of the Gators' offensive line had its problems last season, but should be strengthened with the return of senior center **Zac Zedalis** (6-3, 280).

Zedalis injured his knee in the 1999 season opener and has not played since. Though he hasn't played in a game in nearly two seasons, Zedalis looked sharp and healthy this spring.

Granted an extra year of eligibility by the NCAA, Zedalis should bring some stability to the middle of the Gators' offensive line, not to mention some leadership. He's started in 14 career games, including 11 at center and three at guard.

Junior **David Jorgensen** (6-4, 290) started every game at center a year ago. He played most of last season with a wrist injury. He had surgery in January and missed all of spring drills.

Jorgensen, though, will have a difficult time keeping his job, especially if Zedalis doesn't incur any setbacks with his knee.

Senior **Thomas Moody** (6-3, 321) is the third starter back in the offensive line. He started all 13 games at left guard last season but will shift to right guard this year.

Moody accomplished every offensive lineman's dream last season when he caught a 7-yard touchdown pass against South Carolina off a deflected pass.

The departed Leon Hires will be missed at the other guard spot. **Shannon Snell** exited the spring as the starter at left guard. He played in 10 games last season for 161 plays, the most of any freshman offensive linemen for the Gators.

Senior **Erik Strange** (6-4, 311) will also push for the starting job at left guard. He was one of the team's top guards last season before injuring his knee against LSU and missing the rest of the season. Strange started two games a year ago.

Every starter on the offensive line this season, with the exception of Starks, will have started at some point.

Spurrier was encouraged by the progress this spring of redshirt freshman offensive tackle **Bobby Williams** (6-4, 270). And at guard, junior **David Kearley** (6-4, 295) is back after playing in six games a year ago. Kearley didn't see any game action in 1998 or 1999 because of back and knee injuries.

Center Aaron Deal, who would have been a backup this season, left the team at the end of spring practice and plans to transfer.

A pair of freshmen could provide immediate depth. **Jonathan Colon** (6-7, 280) is back after a year at prep school and could play tackle or guard. **Mike Degory** (6-6, 320) is another who probably won't redshirt and could wind up at center.

2000 STATISTICS

Rushing offense	110.5	91
Passing offense	308.2	8
Total offense	418.7	24
Scoring offense	37.3	10
Net Punting	34.3	64
Punt returns	15.0	13
Kickoff returns	19.2	70
Rushing defense	133.1	39
Passing efficiency defense	98.6	12
Total defense	346.0	42
Scoring defense	19.7	29
Turnover margin	+19	3

Last column is ranking among Division I-A teams.

KICKERS

Senior **Jeff Chandler** (6-2, 219) went into last season as a senior, but was granted an extension of his eligibility in November by the NCAA. He played just one play in the second game as a freshman in 1997.

Thus, one of the premier kickers in the nation is back for another season.

Chandler, the Gators' all-time scoring leader, was 16-of-19 on field goals last season. His 54-yarder against Georgia tied for the third longest in Florida history. The only glitch last season for Chandler was that he missed four extra points.

His best season came in 1999 when he was voted second-team All-America and first-team All-SEC. He tied for the best field-goal percentage in the nation by hitting 21-of-24 attempts.

Chandler was chosen as the Gators' MVP for the 1999 season, demonstrating his worth as an offensive weapon.

A former walk-on, Chandler has the leg strength to connect from 50 yards on in, and he's never missed more than four field goals in a season. For his career, Chandler has made more field goals (48) than any kicker in Florida history.

"He's been in a lot of big games and made a lot of big kicks," Spurrier said.

DEFENSIVE LINE

It's a good thing that the Gators forced so many turnovers last season because they had their moments when they couldn't stop anybody on the ground.

Tennessee's Travis Henry shredded the Florida defense for 175 yards, with more than 130 of those coming on missed tackles. The Gators were able to drive the length of the field, though, in the final minutes and steal away with the win in Knoxville.

A few weeks later, the Gators weren't as fortunate. The Mississippi State tandem of Dicenzo Miller and Dontae Walker combined for 339 rushing yards, and the Bulldogs cruised, 47-35.

The problems stopping the run came with Gerard Warren in the lineup, too. Warren is no longer around after going third overall in the NFL draft to the Cleveland Browns.

Two of his cohorts at tackle, Derrick Chambers and Buck Gurley, are also gone.

The Gators gave up 133.1 rushing yards per game last season, which ranked them 39th nationally in rushing defense—the worst in the Spurrier era.

Suffice to say this will be a pivotal year for defensive coordinator Jon Hoke, who's entering his third season at Florida. The only place Hoke doesn't have just about everyone returning is at tackle.

Florida is counting heavily on junior college transfer **Bryan Savelio** (6-2, 288), a junior who is expected to shore up the middle. Savelio, the likely starter at left tackle, went through spring practice with the Gators and was chosen their most improved defensive lineman. He was a junior college All-American at Mesa (Ariz.) Community College.

Sophomore **Ian Scott** (6-2, 304) enters the fall as the starter at right tackle. Scott was the top backup at tackle last season and played in nine games. He missed four games midway through the season with a knee injury.

With his build and tenacity Scott reminds some of Tampa Bay Buccaneers star defensive tackle Warren Sapp.

The Gators will rotate four tackles into the game, meaning juniors **Tron LaFavor** (6-2, 278) and **Arpedge Rolle** (6-1, 270) will see considerable action.

Favor has played both end and tackle. He was a starter at tackle until he sprained his ankle early in spring drills and missed the last two weeks.

None of the top four tackles will be as dominant as Warren, but they're all solid. Scott probably has as much potential as any of them.

Sophomore **Kenny Parker** (6-2, 293) missed all of spring because of back surgery. He was moved to offensive line last season after a rash of injuries. Junior **Chris Reynolds** (6-1, 269) will provide some depth.

If Brown returns to his sophomore season form at defensive end, this line has a chance to be spectacular. He dropped off to 7 1/2 sacks last season after recording 13 in 1999 to set a Florida single-season record.

Brown has earned All-America honors each of the last two years, but there seemed to be something missing a year ago. Spurrier said more than once that Brown needed to start playing like an All-American and berated him for some of his bulletin board comments before the Tennessee game.

Sophomore **Clint Mitchell** (6-7, 254) is the starter at left end. He was a second-team freshman All-American by *The Sporting News* last season. He finished with 3 1/2 sacks.

Pushing Mitchell will be sophomore **Darrell Lee** (6-4, 257). He had an outstanding spring after playing in all 13 games a year ago.

The fourth end in the rotation will be senior **Kennard Ellis** (6-2, 244). He sprained a ligament in his wrist midway through the spring and missed the last two weeks. Ellis started in two games last season and finished with 2 1/2 sacks.

Sophomore **Bobby McCray** (6-6, 235) played sparingly in 2000, but was selected the club's most improved defensive end this spring.

"We have more guys who can play in the defensive front than a year ago with about five ends and five or six tackles who are making good progress," Spurrier said.

LINEBACKERS

If there is a transition period up front with some of the Florida defensive tackles, the Gators certainly have the linebackers to pick up the slack. It's the second-deepest position on the team, behind only the secondary.

All three season-ending starters return, as well as eight of the top nine from the two-deep last season. Seven linebackers who started a game in 2000 are back.

That doesn't even count senior middle linebacker **Andra Davis** (6-1, 254). He missed all of last season after suffering a knee injury in the opener against Ball State.

The type of linebacker that devours opposing running backs, Davis should vastly improve Florida's run defense. He was second on the team with 109 tackles in 1999 and was selected the Gators' most outstanding linebacker.

Davis is 10-to-15 pounds heavier than he was two years ago and could have trouble staying on the field on passing downs. But he looked like he was back to his old self in the spring.

Senior **Travis Carroll** (6-4, 263) ended last season as the starter at middle linebacker and played well. He missed the spring after undergoing shoulder surgery.

Carroll, who transferred from Alabama, was voted the Gators' most outstanding linebacker last season. It's conceivable that Carroll could be moved to the outside so Florida can get him and Davis on the field together.

Junior **Mike Nattiel** (5-11, 225) emerged as the starter at strong side linebacker last season. He led the Gators' linebackers with 61 tackles and made eight starts.

The weak-side linebacker spot will be manned by the junior tandem of **Byron "Bam" Hardmon** (6-1, 221) and **Marcus Oquendo-Johnson** (6-3, 213). Both missed a large chunk of spring practice with injuries—Hardmon suffered a stress fracture in his foot and Oquendo-Johnson a fractured forearm.

Hardmon has played in every game of his Florida career. His 632 snaps last season led all Florida linebackers and were sixth best on the team. Oquendo-Johnson has also played some defensive end in his career. His 11 "Big Plays" were best among the Gators' linebackers a year ago.

Sophomore **Travis Harris** (6-2, 240) proved last season that he can play inside or outside. He moved to strong side linebacker during the spring after the injuries to Hardmon and Oquendo-Johnson. But he also played some in the middle.

A freshman All-SEC selection a year ago, Harris was chosen the Gators' most improved outside linebacker in the spring.

Sophomore **Matt Farrior** (6-1, 224) will provide depth at weak-side linebacker. He started in three games. Sophomore **Dwright Jackson** (6-1, 209) is also back after moving from strong safety to linebacker during fall drills last year.

DEFENSIVE BACKS

The Gators' depth at linebacker is stunning. That is, until you take a look at the secondary. The entire two-deep from last season is back, and it's the same unit that produced 24 interceptions.

His off-the-field troubles notwithstanding, Sheppard may be the country's best and most accomplished cover man at cornerback. He has track speed and the kind of reaction the pro scouts covet.

If he weren't playing cornerback, he would probably be the Gators' best receiver. He played a few snaps there last season.

Only the fourth sophomore in Florida history to earn first-team All-America honors, Sheppard tied for the league lead with six interceptions last season.

He returned one of those for a touchdown against Tennessee to turn that game completely around.

Any time Sheppard gets his hands on the ball, it's almost as if he's destined to score. That's how dynamic he is, be it covering receivers or racing back the other way with a loose football.

"I have a knack for being around the ball," Sheppard told Cox News Service. "Somehow, plays just always come to me, and I'm able to make plays on the ball."

"Lito just knows how to turn the game around," Florida cornerback **Keiwan Ratliff** told the *St. Petersburg Times*. "He is always around the ball when big plays need to happen."

"He can make things happen," Auburn coach Tommy Tuberville told Cox News Service. "He's a very good defensive player, and he's a very good punt returner. He can turn a game around."

The other starter at cornerback is senior **Robert Cromartie** (5-8, 192). He has 24 career starts at cornerback after missing the first four games last season with an ankle injury.

Making the biggest move in the spring was sophomore Ratliff (5-10, 181). Switched from receiver to cornerback last fall, Ratliff played in all 13 games last season. His 375 snaps were the third most for a defensive freshman.

Senior **Bennie Alexander** (5-9, 182) is the fourth cornerback and has started in 24 games, the most of any Florida cornerback. But with the likes of Sheppard, Cromartie and Ratliff, Alexander could be relegated to backup and nickel situation duty.

In 1999, Alexander led the team with five interceptions. He started in six games last season.

Junior **Todd Johnson** (6-1, 194) is the starter at free safety and Manuel the starter at strong safety.

Johnson was a first-team All-SEC selection last season. He started the first four games at strong safety and the final nine at free safety. He led the Gators with 102 tackles a year ago and was second with 13 "Big Plays."

In eight of the 12 regular-season games last season, Johnson recorded a turnover.

Manuel is among the Gators' most experienced defensive players. He has started in 24 career games and had 83 tackles a year ago to finish second on the team behind Johnson.

During the 1999 season, Manuel led the Gators with 118 tackles.

Sophomore **Guss Scott** (5-10, 194) was the top backup at safety last season and really came on in the spring. He will spell Manuel some at strong safety. His 533 snaps last season led all Florida freshmen defenders.

Also back is senior **Lester Norwood** (6-2, 188). He will back up Johnson at free safety.

"Probably the highlight of what the defense was able to accomplish this spring was how the linebackers and safeties played their assignments and zone coverages," Spurrier said.

PUNTERS

The one glaring weakness for Florida can be found at punter. Gone is Alan Rhine, who led the SEC and ranked ninth nationally a year ago with an average of 43.3 yards per game.

The odds-on favorite to win the job is freshman **Matt Leach** (6-0, 180) of Sarasota, Fla., especially given the Gators' problems during the spring.

Redshirt freshman **Matt Piotrowicz** (5-10, 202) struggled with his consistency. Sophomore **Matt Morton** (6-2, 172) could also factor into the equation after transferring from Northwestern.

Spurrier said the job won't be decided until well into fall practice.

SPECIAL TEAMS

The Gators, with Chandler returning, should be as good as anybody in the league at placekicker. Chandler will also kick off. The punting situation stands at the opposite end of the spectrum. It was a real source of concern for Spurrier coming out of the spring, and it's never ideal to throw a true freshman back there.

Speedy Bo Carroll is gone, but few are better than Sheppard when it comes to returning kicks. He led the SEC in punt returns last season with an average of 14 yards and returned two for touchdowns.

On any other team, Ratliff would be the top return specialist. He averaged 16.1 yards on seven punt returns a year ago.

Sheppard, Ratliff, Gillespie, Jackson and Jacobs are all possibilities to return kickoffs. The Gators would love to get Sheppard's hands on the ball as much as possible, but they don't want him tiring in the fourth quarter, either. He averaged 22.9 yards on 13 kickoff returns last season.

Florida's net punting was poor last season. The Gators were tied for 10th in the SEC with a 34.3-yard average.

Roberts, when he's not blocking from his fullback position, will be the snapper for punts and field goals.

RECRUITING CLASS

What a difference a year can make. The Gators signed a recruiting class in 2000 that was hailed as the best in the country by just about everybody. But the 20001 incoming class was rated as low as 35th nationally by one recruiting service. Skim through the different lists of Top 25 players nationally and you won't find a single Florida signee.

The bottom line is that Florida is stacked with talent. Thus, many prospects were steered away when they saw all the freshmen and sophomores backing up junior starters on the Gators' depth chart.

"A year ago we stood up here with all the ideas we had the consensus No. 1 class in the country, and we didn't put much stock in it at the time," Florida recruiting coordinator Jim Collins told the *Florida Times-Union* on national signing day. "And we're not going to put that much stock in where we're ranked right now."

Making matters worse was that in the final hour, Florida lost three players who had previously committed to the Gators.

Running back Lydell Ross of Tampa, Fla., chose Ohio State. Junior college defensive lineman Torran Williams opted for LSU, while receiver Fred Gibson signed with Georgia.

The Gators did manage to stock up on offensive and defensive linemen, a definite need. Savelio is expected to play right away at defensive tackle.

On the offensive line, Colon and Degory could be good enough to play right away. Colon, originally from Miami, was a prep All-American in 1999 and started practice with the Gators last fall. But his ACT score was challenged by the NCAA, and he spent last season at Bridgton Academy.

Degory, who's from Palm Bay, Fla., was ranked among the Top 10 prep offensive linemen nationally last season by SuperPrep.

BLUE RIBBON ANALYSIS

OFFENSE	A
SPECIAL TEAMS	B+
DEFENSE	A
INTANGIBLES	A

In the dreary aftermath of the Sugar Bowl loss to Miami last season, Gaffney made a bold proclamation.

"I see us going to Pasadena," Gaffney said, referring of course to the Rose Bowl, which will host this year's BCS national championship game. "The only team that will be able to beat us is ourselves."

The timing of those comments was a bit curious, given the way the Hurricanes handled the Gators. But in retrospect, Gaffney may have been prophetic.

Nobody in the country returns more experience or more talent across the board, and Florida gets its two toughest games at home—Tennessee on Sept. 18 and Florida State on Nov. 17.

Defensively the Gators will have to improve, no question. They were eighth in the SEC and 42nd nationally in total defense a year ago, not the kind of stuff of which national championships are made.

"I'm happy with what our defense did this spring, but the real key is can they take it forward into the season and continue to improve," Spurrier said.

The quarterback quandary will also be interesting to watch. In 1996, Wuerffel was in a similar position entering that season as Berlin is entering this season.

Florida fans can only hope it all comes together that well. It's Pasadena or bust for the Gators.

(C.L.)

2000 RESULTS

Ball State	W	40-19	1-0
Middle Tennessee	W	55-0	2-0
Tennessee	W	27-23	3-0
Kentucky	W	59-31	4-0
Mississippi State	L	35-47	4-1
LSU	W	41-9	5-1
Auburn	W	39-7	6-1
Georgia	W	34-23	7-1
Vanderbilt	W	43-20	8-1
South Carolina	W	41-21	9-1
Florida State	L	7-30	9-2
Auburn (SEC Champ.)	W	28-6	10-2
Miami (Sugar Bowl)	L	20-37	10-3

Georgia

LOCATION	**Athens, GA**
CONFERENCE	**Southeastern (Eastern)**
LAST SEASON	**8-4 (.666)**
CONFERENCE RECORD	**5-3 (t-2nd)**
OFFENSIVE STARTERS RETURNING	**6**
DEFENSIVE STARTERS RETURNING	**7**
NICKNAME	**Bulldogs**
COLORS	**Red & Black**
HOME FIELD	**Sanford Stadium (86,117)**
HEAD COACH	**Mark Richt (Miami '82)**
RECORD AT SCHOOL	**First Year**
CAREER RECORD	**First Year**
ASSISTANTS	**Neil Callaway (Alabama '78)**
	Offensive Coordinator/Offensive Line
	Brian VanGorder (Wayne State '67)
	Defensive Coordinator/Linebackers
	Rodney Garner (Auburn '90)
	Defensive Line/Recruiting Coordinator
	John Fabris (Mississippi '80)
	Defensive Ends
	Willie Martinez (Miami '86)
	Secondary
	John Eason (Florida A&M '69)
	Receivers
	Tony Pierce (Montclair State '89)
	Running Backs
	Mike Bobo (Georgia '97)
	Quarterbacks
	David Johnson (West Virginia '83)
	Tight Ends
TEAM WINS (last 5 yrs.)	**5-10-9-8-8**
FINAL RANK (last 5 yrs.)	**39-8-16-16-16**
2000 FINISH	**Beat Virginia in Oahu Bowl.**

COACH AND PROGRAM

It was about this time last year that Jim Donnan uttered the infamous words that would ultimately come back to haunt him. He proclaimed to the college football world that he had waited his entire career to coach a team the caliber of last season's Georgia club. The result was not what anybody expected.

The Bulldogs, oozing with talent, rode a wave of inconsistency all season. They managed to win eight games, but the ones they lost were what got Donnan his ticket out of town.

South Carolina ambushed Georgia in the second week of the season, followed by losses to Florida, Auburn and Georgia Tech.

So despite 40 wins in five seasons and four bowl victories, Donnan was fired as Georgia's coach, taking with him a severance package in excess of $2.3 million.

Michael Adams, Georgia's president, was clearly behind the move, even after athletic director Vince Dooley had given Donnan a vote of confidence during the season. But in the end, the record that mattered was Donnan's 6-14 mark against Georgia's four biggest rivals—Auburn, Florida, Georgia Tech and Tennessee.

Another factor in Donnan's demise: The Bulldogs haven't won an SEC championship since 1982. How long has it been? Dooley was still coaching the Bulldogs, and Herschel Walker was breaking tackles and setting records between the hedges.

Suffice to say that dry spell hasn't gone over too well with Georgia fans.

That's where Mark Richt comes in. As Georgia's new head coach, he knows precisely what is expected. The Bulldogs not only need to win, but they need to start evening out some of those series with their rivals. And most of all, they need to re-enter the SEC championship picture.

"Georgia is one of those places where you can compete for a championship every year," said Richt, who learned his craft under Bobby Bowden at Florida State. In fact, there was a time when Richt thought he would never leave Florida State. One of the driving forces in the Seminoles' high-powered offenses, Richt spent 15 years on the FSU staff, the last seven as offensive coordinator.

Known for his innovative offensive styles, Richt developed two Heisman Trophy quarterbacks—Chris Weinke and Charlie Ward—and has sent six quarterbacks to the NFL.

It was a given that Richt, 40, was going to be scooped up by somebody. Virginia was interested, and so was Missouri. But he was determined to be selective. Seeing the opportunity at Georgia emerge, he came to the conclusion that it was simply one he couldn't ignore.

"We wanted a place to raise our family, have a chance to win at the highest level and become part of a community where we can live for a long time," Richt said. "We found all those things in Athens and the University of Georgia."

The most excruciating thing for Richt was parting ways with Bowden, who had been a football father to him. Richt's agreement to take the Bulldogs' job was contingent upon being allowed to remain with Florida State through last season's Orange Bowl national championship matchup against Oklahoma.

Even though Richt didn't have any previous head coaching experience, Dooley said it was an easy choice.

"I do think there are some advantages to having been a head coach, but, at the same time, someone has to get the chance to have that opportunity," said Dooley, who had no head coaching experience when he was hired in 1964.

"I'm thoroughly convinced that of the people we had interviewed and talked to that there's no one more qualified to step into the position as the head football coach at Georgia from an assistant's position than coach Richt. I'm thoroughly convinced that the man and hour have met."

The trick now for Richt is squeezing more out of the Bulldogs in the games that count. They wore the underachiever label well a year ago. Georgia had five players selected in April's NFL draft, including four in the first two rounds, yet lost games to Georgia Tech and South Carolina—a pair of teams that had no players drafted.

The touted defensive tackle tandem of Richard Seymour and Marcus Stroud has bolted to the NFL ranks, as has quarterback Quincy Carter. Of course, it was Carter's inconsistent play a year ago that played a key role in last season's upheaval.

The quarterback situation will be a central theme for the Bulldogs this season. Junior **Cory Phillips** (6-1, 214) and redshirt freshman **David Greene** (6-3, 222) ended spring practice in a battle for the job. The health of sophomore tailback **Musa Smith** (6-1, 212) will also be crucial for the Bulldogs. He was hurt for part of last season and missed the spring after undergoing foot surgery.

The defense has a chance to be one of the top units in the league despite the loss of Seymour and Stroud. Senior cornerback **Tim Wansley** (5-9, 172) led the SEC in interceptions last season with six.

Richt spent much of the spring installing his system and his philosophy. The Bulldogs didn't merely ease into it, either, and lost more than a few players to injuries.

"You've got to put in your system and teach the fundamentals of blocking and tackling," Richt said. "The only way to teach it is to block and tackle. It's typical that you're going to get some people banged up."

Overall, Richt said the headway the Bulldogs

made in the spring was promising.

"I think [the players] know we're coming in and expecting certain things from them athletically and academically," said Richt, the backup quarterback to Jim Kelly at Miami in the early 1980s. "I think they like the way we're pushing them hard on both ends. The morale has been outstanding."

The only holdover from Donnan's coaching staff is recruiting whiz Rodney Garner, who will continue to coordinate the recruiting and coach the defensive line.

Garner is perhaps the SEC's premier recruiter and has attracted top players everywhere he's been—Auburn, Tennessee and Georgia.

Richt brought in former Alabama offensive coordinator Neil Callaway to be the offensive coordinator and offensive line coach for the Bulldogs. But Richt will be the one calling the plays, just as he did at Florida State. What's more, Callaway knows his way around the league. He spent 11 years as the offensive line coach at Auburn under Pat Dye from 1981-92 and was Garner's position coach there.

The Bulldogs' defensive coordinator is an SEC neophyte. Brian VanGorder ran the defense last season at Western Illinois and held the same title at Central Michigan for the previous two seasons.

VanGorder and Richt met when VanGorder was coaching high school football in Boca Raton, which is Richt's hometown.

The only position coach with Florida State ties hired by Richt was John Eason, who will coach the receivers and serve as assistant head coach. Eason was the receivers coach at Florida State from 1981-94 and followed Brad Scott to South Carolina as assistant head coach and offensive coordinator from 1995-98.

Eason, 56, is the senior statesman. The average age of Richt's staff is 40, and he hired coaches from seven different colleges, as well as one from the NFL and one from the CFL.

2001 SCHEDULE

Sept.	1	Arkansas State
	8	South Carolina
	15	Houston
	29	Arkansas
Oct.	6	@Tennessee
	13	@Vanderbilt
	20	Kentucky
	27	Florida (at Jacksonville)
Nov.	10	Auburn
	17	@Mississippi
	24	@Georgia Tech

QUARTERBACKS

Phillips started five of the last six games a year ago for the injured Carter and passed for 400 or more yards in two of those five games. Nonetheless, Phillips failed to nail down the job in the spring. Greene closed the gap considerably during the final few scrimmages, and Richt simply wasn't ready to pick a starter.

"They both had their moments," Richt said. "After reviewing tape of all the scrimmages, they are basically even and we'll have them go into the fall as co-No. 1s and let them battle it out."

The obvious advantage for Phillips is that he has SEC experience. In his first start against Kentucky last season, he passed for 400 yards and four touchdowns. Against Georgia Tech, he passed for 413 yards and tied a school record with 36 completions. He finished with 1,093 yards, eight touchdowns and six interceptions.

But learning Richt's offense wasn't a snap for Phillips in the spring. He isn't a great athlete and has some limitations. At times, he almost looked confused.

"Cory is the guy who believes in himself the most," Richt said. "David gained confidence as the spring went on. Cory seems to also have a little more leadership ability right at this moment, but we felt David closed the gap in many areas."

The survivor will obviously be the one who makes the best decisions. That's what Richt's offensive system is predicated upon—a quarterback who makes things happen with very little time to think about it.

It would have been interesting to see Carter in Richt's system, but last season was such a forgettable experience for Carter that he gladly gave up his final year of college eligibility to enter the draft.

Greene, who passed for 2,102 yards and 19 touchdowns as a senior in high school, has the athletic ability to do a few more things than Phillips. But he also occasionally got himself in trouble in the spring with one too many ill-advised passes.

There's no substitute for playing in a game, which Greene hasn't at the college level.

"Quarterback is a slow process, and it's a process you have to work on," Greene told the *Athens Daily News* after a spring scrimmage. "I'm learning a lot of things. I kind of left it hanging up a little too long (on the interceptions). One of those I probably shouldn't have thrown. I have to get to the point where I'm making better decisions."

Greene is the first left-handed quarterback Richt has coached and the first for the Bulldogs since 1956.

There are still several different ways Richt could go with the offense, depending on who wins the job.

"We've used a lot of different formations, and I can't say which one we will use the most," Richt said. "It depends on the quarterback and what he does. We're still going to run out of the I-formation.

"We're also not counting out our four-receiver sets we used over the years at Florida State. It just all remains to be seen what these quarterbacks can handle."

It's not out of the question that a third quarterback candidate could enter the picture in the fall. Freshman **D.J. Shockley** (6-1, 175) of College Park, Ga. was a *Parade* All-American and has the kind of run-pass dimension Charlie Ward made famous at Florida State.

"He's got the ingredients it takes to compete (for the job)," Richt said after signing Shockley in February. "You are always looking for a quarterback who can, No. 1, make great decisions and has the arm to hit those targets. If you can add athletic ability to that, you have the chance to have something special. D.J. falls into that category."

RUNNING BACKS

Spring drills took a heavy toll on the Bulldogs' running back corps. The list of injuries just kept growing. The most serious was to redshirt freshman Albert Hollis (5-11, 194). He dislocated his right knee, tearing three of the four ligaments, and will miss the entire season.

Hollis' injury was enough of a concern in itself. The Georgia coaches had high hopes for him this fall. But Smith's healthy return will be vital if the Bulldogs are going to field a potent running attack. He was their most promising runner last season as a freshman, combining speed, strength and power. His next mission is to prove that he can avoid injuries. Smith broke a bone in his right foot during the second day of spring workouts and missed the remainder of spring practice.

"It's just [that he's not] getting the work and learning and gaining the confidence with the first team that you need to get," Richt told the *Athens Daily News*.

Smith started the final two games a year ago, rushing for 144 yards against Mississippi. He led all Georgia running backs with five touchdowns. But a knee injury caused him to miss two games, while a shoulder injury also hampered him.

The Bulldogs' leading rusher last season was the departed Brett Millican. Senior **Jasper Sanks** (6-1, 237) wasn't too far behind with 352 yards and four touchdowns. Sanks was moved to fullback by Richt heading into the spring, but had to move back to tailback after the rash of injuries.

A highly acclaimed prospect coming out of high school, Sanks has never really lived up to the hype, although he did have 896 yards during the 1999 season.

Georgia opted for Sanks over Jamal Lewis during the 1997 recruiting process, a move that backfired. Lewis went on to star at Tennessee and wound up being the fifth overall pick in the 2000 NFL draft. Sanks, who also hurt his knee during the spring, is slated to return to fullback assuming Smith makes it all the way back.

"My heart is at [tailback], but we discussed fullback and I have no problem playing it," Sanks told the *Athens Daily News*. "I'm prepared to play both. I just want to play football."

Sophomore **Kenny Bailey** (5-11, 191) will also be in the mix at tailback. He spent most of the spring as the Bulldogs' first-team tailback after carrying the ball just eight times for 49 yards last season.

Bailey was moved to cornerback during the latter part of last season, but he requested to be moved back to tailback when Richt took over for Donnan. Bailey rushed for 1,552 yards as a senior in high school.

Senior **Verron Haynes** (5-11, 223) played in all 12 games, including two starts, last season at fullback. But Haynes was arrested for simple assault and stalking of the alleged mother of his child in February.

Richt has said he may take disciplinary action against Haynes, depending on the outcome of Haynes' court proceedings.

Looking for a surprise?

Don't count out freshman **Tony Milton** (5-11, 195) making a bid for some playing time at tailback, especially should some of the injuries linger. Sophomore **Bruce Thornton** (5-11, 193) was moved to cornerback during the spring.

WIDE RECEIVERS/TIGHT ENDS

The Bulldogs return their top six pass catchers from last season, including junior **Terrence Edwards** (6-1, 165). Edwards led the team with 53 catches for 704 yards and four touchdowns. He was the MVP of the Oahu Bowl victory over Virginia.

In that game, Edwards caught eight passes for 79 yards and also had a 57-yard run for a touchdown. He's capable of hurting teams in a variety of ways, and Richt will look to get him the ball as much as possible. Edwards' 4.82 receptions per game ranked fifth best in the SEC a year ago.

Edwards lined up at quarterback on a few occasions last season, but Richt said he wants to see Edwards first master the system at receiver before expanding any further.

Sophomore **Damien Gary** (5-11, 176) is back after leading the Bulldogs with five touchdown catches last season. He finished with 36 catches, including 11 for 126 yards against Georgia Tech.

Junior Durell Robinson (6-1, 216) had his moments in the spring and has the potential to be the most complete receiver of the bunch. But

Robinson has been suspended from the university for the summer and fall semesters and won't be eligible to return until spring 2002. Robinson admitted to five violations of university conduct policies last March, and was originally suspended by Richt for four games. The longer suspension was handed out when Robinson failed to comply with sanctions necessary to maintain his standing as a Georgia student.

Sophomore **Reggie Brown** (6-2, 184) also has tons of ability and is the fastest of the Bulldogs' receivers, but he tends to drop too many passes. The former *Parade* All-American didn't have near the impact many had expected last season after sitting out the 1999 season when he was academically ineligible.

"I feel more confident in my game right now and my skills as a wide receiver because [after] that year off that I had I was a little rusty," Brown told the Athens Daily News. "I'm not going to blame that for how I played, but I feel like I'm more in the rhythm as a wide receiver so I should play better."

Also back is senior flanker **LaBrone Mitchell** (6-2, 201). He started in 10 games last season and finished with 11 catches for 116 yards. Mitchell has also been used some at quarterback.

Redshirt freshman **Tavarus Morgan** (5-10, 190) had an impressive spring and looks ready to contribute.

No position on the team is as deep as tight end, prompting Richt to devise more ways to get those guys the ball. The tight end wasn't a huge part of the offense at Florida State.

Junior **Randy McMichael** (6-4, 228) returns as the starter after catching 32 passes for 475 yards last season. McMichael was outstanding at times last season, but also suffered through some concentration lapses. He dropped a touchdown pass against Florida. But he also caught 12 passes for 156 yards against Georgia Tech.

Right on McMichael's heels is junior **Ben Watson** (6-3, 253). One of the strongest players on the team, Watson sat out last season after transferring from Duke. There's also junior **Jason Radar** (6-4, 240), who played extensively a year ago.

"Our tight end situation is intriguing enough to where we will probably get into some two tight end sets because of the talent we have there," Richt said.

OFFENSIVE LINE

Richt knew that grooming the offensive line to his liking would take time, and he said so at the beginning of spring practice. But as the opener approaches, questions still hover.

Lack of depth is the most glaring problem. The Bulldogs lost starting tackle Jonas Jennings and starting guard Brady Pate to graduation and began the spring with only 10 offensive linemen.

Their returning starting guard, senior **Kevin Breedlove** (6-4, 311), missed spring practice with a cut hand. Breedlove was voted to the SEC's All-Freshman team two years ago. But he struggled at times last season.

Junior **Alex Jackson** (6-4, 337) is a candidate to start at the other guard spot. He was one of the Bulldogs' top reserves last season. Teams are sure to test Georgia at the guard positions this fall.

Making a big move in the spring was sophomore **Chris Hewitt** (6-6, 281). He's a converted defensive lineman who moved to offense early last season.

"I was just starting to get a grasp on the system last year," Hewitt told the *Athens Daily News*. "I've got a good ways to go, but I'm pretty comfortable with this system. It's not instinctive yet, but I'm getting there."

Hewitt will provide what little bit of depth the Bulldogs will have at guard, and he could end up beating out Jackson for the starting job.

Junior **Jon Stinchcomb** (6-6, 278) is a returning starter at tackle. He was a second-team All-SEC selection last season. And while Stinchcomb drew most of the accolades, the best lineman on the team was probably senior center **Curt McGill** (6-4, 274).

"He's as good a college center as you're going to find," Richt said.

The other starting tackle spot could end up being a toss-up between junior **George Foster** (6-6, 321) and junior college newcomer **Kareem Marshall** (6-6, 350), a junior. Foster missed most of the spring with a sprained knee.

Richt was pleased with Marshall's progress in the spring after he joined the Bulldogs from Mississippi Gulf Coast Community College.

"We may rotate them all around, all three tackles," Richt said.

Despite the All-SEC honor, Stinchcomb was anything but dominant at tackle last season. The Bulldogs need him to take that next step and approach the level his older brother, Matt Stinchcomb, reached on his way to All-America honors at Georgia.

There were some obvious growing pains in the spring. But again, Richt expected as much.

"These guys are learning new terminology," Richt told the *Athens Daily News*. "To expect them to be sharp immediately is going to be asking an awful lot. The offensive line will probably be the last thing to jell."

2000 STATISTICS

Rushing offense	131.9	72
Passing offense	215.0	55
Total offense	346.9	75
Scoring offense	26.7	51
Net Punting	39.5	7
Punt returns	8.1	81
Kickoff returns	19.3	68
Rushing defense	111.1	25
Passing efficiency defense	104.4	21
Total defense	313.5	19
Scoring defense	18.0	12
Turnover margin	-1	65

Last column is ranking among Division I-A teams.

KICKERS

It was a whirlwind of a season last year for sophomore **Billy Bennett** (5-8, 159). He showed up at Georgia as a freshman walk-on from nearby Athens Academy, but found himself handling the Bulldogs' kicking chores before the calendar had flipped to October.

Bennett earned the starting job in the third game of the season and was awarded a scholarship about that same time. By the time he was finished, he was the school record holder for season field-goal percentage.

Bennett connected on 13-of-14 field-goal attempts (92.9 percent). To put that accomplishment in perspective, three former Georgia kickers who went on to play in the NFL never attained that kind of success rate in one season.

Rex Robinson made 15-of-17 in 1978, Kevin Butler 23-of-28 in 1984 and Todd Peterson 13-of-16 in 1992.

The ironic thing with Bennett was that he was barely even a blip on the radar screen when last season began. Junior **Brett Kirouac** (6-2, 198) came out of the spring as the Bulldogs' kicker, but was quickly nudged aside in the fall by Bennett.

Bennett, selected to *The Sporting News* freshman All-America team, averaged 1.44 field goals per game last season, which was third best in the SEC and 14th nationally.

The only miss by Bennett last season was a 50-yarder against Tennessee. Not known for having great leg strength, Bennett nonetheless kicked a 49-yarder against Mississippi. He also tied a school record with four field goals against Auburn.

On extra points, Bennett hit 24-of-26 and finished with 63 total points.

Kirouac could still be used for longer field goals. He made his only attempt a year ago, a 21-yarder, but missed two of his first eight extra-point attempts—clearing the way for Bennett to take over the job.

DEFENSIVE LINE

Losing a pair of tackles that go in the first round of the NFL draft is never ideal. Their departure compounds an already thin defensive line ranks. But there could be a star in the making. Sophomore **Johnathan Sullivan** (6-4, 280) is primed for a breakout season. He played in 10 games last season as a true freshman and showcased his vast potential.

Sullivan finished with 34 total tackles, including a sack, and played in the shadows of Seymour and Stroud. But the thinking coming out of the spring was that he has a chance to be better than both of them. Having spent the 1999 season at Hargrave (Va.) Military Academy, Sullivan played last season without having gone through a spring practice at Georgia. This was his first spring, meaning there's still plenty of upside to his development.

"He shows flashes and teases you, but then he brings me back to the reality that he's a [sophomore]," Garner told the *Athens Daily News*.

The other starter at tackle will be junior **David Jacobs** (6-4, 265). He's a little under-sized, but recorded 25 tackles a year ago and started in one game. Jacobs came to Georgia as a defensive end.

The Bulldogs are thin enough at tackle that a pair of freshmen may have to play. **Darrell Holmes** (6-3, 260) of Atlanta and *Darrius Swain* (6-4, 295) of Decatur, Ga., were both big-time prospects coming out of high school.

Sophomore **Shedrick Wynn** (6-3, 267) played sparingly last season, but could provide some depth at tackle. Sophomore **Ken Veal** (6-2, 297) also has minimal experience and was limited in the spring with a shoulder injury.

Needing bodies at tackle, Richt moved junior offensive lineman **Ben Lowe** (6-4, 280) to that position this spring.

The situation is considerably better at end, where the Bulldogs return four players who have starting experience.

The most accomplished is junior **Charles Grant** (6-4, 267). He started nine games last season and finished with 40 tackles, including two sacks. Grant missed a few practices in the spring with knee problems.

Senior **Terin Smith** (6-3, 248) is the likely starter at the other end. He started three games a year ago and recorded 5 1/2 tackles for loss. Senior **Josh Mallard** (6-2, 263) may be the quickest player on the Bulldogs' defensive line. His three sacks led the Bulldogs a year ago.

The most improved defensive lineman going into last season was senior **Bruce Adrine** (6-4, 275). He started in two of the first three games before suffering a season-ending knee injury in practice the week of the fourth game.

Junior college transfer **Nic Clemons** (6-6, 259) will also jump into the rotation at end. He went through the spring after signing early from Georgia Military College. Clemons didn't play high school football.

LINEBACKERS

Bell developed into an outstanding player last season. But even without him, the Bulldogs return four of their top five tacklers. The linebacker corps will be the strength of the Bulldogs' defense, and it starts in the middle with junior **Tony Gilbert** (6-1, 246).

The Bulldogs' leader with 96 tackles last season, Gilbert is making the move to middle linebacker after starting 10 games a year ago at strong-side linebacker.

"He's a guy that's so instinctive and just runs through blockers," Richt said.

Gilbert moved into the starting lineup after starter **Boss Bailey** (6-4, 218), a junior, was injured in the season opener. There wasn't much of a transition period for Gilbert, who had 16 tackles in the win over Kentucky. Gilbert has the same type of big-play potential as Bell.

Bailey's return from knee surgery is a huge bonus. He was third on the team with 66 tackles in 1999, but was hurt on the opening kickoff in the season opener last year against Georgia Southern.

The starter on the weak side is senior **Will Witherspoon** (6-2, 217). He started 10 games last season and was the club's third leading tackler with 85. His six tackles for loss ranked second best on the team.

If all three stay healthy, the Bulldogs will have one of the most athletic groups of linebackers in the conference.

If all three stay healthy, the Bulldogs will have one of the most athletic group of linebackers in the conference.

And there's some depth, too. Senior **Adrian Hollingshed** (6-2, 232) is the backup at middle linebacker. He started there in 1998, but missed most of the 1999 season with a shoulder injury. Hollingshed played in nine games last season and led the team with 12 tackles in the Oahu Bowl.

Senior **Ryan Fleming** (6-2, 222) will play behind Witherspoon on the weak side. Sophomore **Chris Clemons** (6-3, 208) will play behind Bailey on the strong side. Clemons played as a freshman and started in the opener after Bailey was injured on the opening kickoff.

VanGorder, who will coach the linebackers, has brought a little different style to the defense. He hasn't been afraid to get in a few players' faces, whereas Donnan's defensive coordinator, Gary Gibbs, was much more laid back.

"[Gibbs] wanted the intensity, but he just took a little bit different approach to it," Witherspoon told the *Athens Daily News*. "He was not as vocal as coach VanGorder is out there. They both have great minds, but the approach is a little bit different, and I think that's the biggest change for us."

DEFENSIVE BACKS

Wansley is the type of cornerback opposing offensive coordinators try to avoid. You don't want to throw it in his direction. Of his league-leading six interceptions last season, he took two back for touchdowns.

"Wansley dominated the spring at the cornerback position, more than anybody I've seen in my years of coaching," said Richt, who's been around his share of quality cover men at Florida State. "We couldn't find a receiver that could whip him. He's a great cover guy, but tough as nails and will come up and take on a guy."

There was one off-the-field glitch this spring, however. Wansley was suspended for the opener by Richt for academic reasons. Wansley also missed the bowl game last season for failing to adhere to the university's class attendance policy.

Thornton's transition to cornerback went well this spring. He was a playmaker at running back and as a return specialist and demonstrated those same qualities on defense.

"He's done everything we expected him to do to hold on to that spot," Richt said. "I think he's got a great future as a cornerback."

The nickel back will be junior college transfer **Brandon Williams** (5-10, 171), a junior. Williams had a solid spring after coming over from Mississippi Gulf Coast Community College.

Sophomore **Dantra Clements** (5-10, 188) played in all 10 games last season and gives the Bulldogs good depth at cornerback. Redshirt freshman **Ronnie Powell** (5-11, 191) also impressed during the spring.

At strong safety, junior **Terreal Bierria** (6-3, 205) is back for his third season as a starter. Bierria tied for second on the team last season with three interceptions. He was fifth on the team in tackles with 83.

VanGorder's system calls for a rover, where senior **Jermaine Phillips** (6-2, 211) is the man. It's basically the same position as free safety, and Phillips is a head hunter. His 85 tackles last season were third best on the team.

Phillips, who came to Georgia as a receiver, is the first partial qualifier Georgia ever signed. He sat out the 1997 season, but has since received that year back after graduating in four years.

The Bulldogs have experienced backups at both safety spots. Sophomore **Kentrell Curry** (6-2, 191) played in all 11 regular-season games last season and will back up Bierria at strong safety. He recovered a fumble for a touchdown in the bowl game.

Junior **Cap Burnett** (6-1, 223) will play behind Phillips at rover. Burnett started three games last season, but he's been bothered by concussions and a shoulder injury.

Safety Regan Torbert (6-3, 200), a sophomore, left the team this spring. He had already been suspended by Richt for the first four games of the season.

PUNTERS

Junior **Jonathan Kilgo** (6-2, 198) returns to give the Bulldogs one of the league's top weapons at punter.

Last season, Kilgo ranked fourth in the SEC and 19th nationally with an average of 42.2 yards per punt. He had 13 punts that traveled 50 yards or longer, including a long of 67 yards against Auburn. He also had a 64-yard punt in the Oahu Bowl.

Kilgo was equally accurate. He had 15 punts downed inside the 20-yard line and didn't have any punts blocked.

SPECIAL TEAMS

Richt has pledged to upgrade the Bulldogs' special teams, although they appear set at placekicker with Bennett and at punter with Kilgo.

The coverage units weren't bad a year ago. In fact, Georgia led the SEC in net punting, although much of the credit there goes to Kilgo and his ability to place the football.

On kickoff returns, Georgia's opponents averaged just 18.8 yards per return and didn't take any back for touchdowns. South Carolina, though, did have a 53-yard return in the second game of the season.

The Bulldogs' shortcoming a year ago was in the return game. They were ninth in the SEC in punt returns, averaging just 8.1 yards per return with a long of 20 yards and no touchdowns.

Gary is the most likely candidate to handle the punt return duties and has some elusiveness. He was the main man back there last season.

On kickoff returns, Thornton, Gary and Smith split those duties last season. Thornton received the bulk of the work and averaged 18.4 yards. The Bulldogs didn't have a kickoff return longer than 36 yards.

With Thornton moving to cornerback, he could see his duties as a return man decrease. One to watch, though, is Brown. He wasn't used as a deep man a year ago, but could get a chance this season.

Kirouac returns as the Bulldogs' kickoff man. He booted 13 into the end zone for touchbacks last season.

Fleming and Phillips starred on the coverage units a year ago and led the team with 12 special teams tackles apiece.

RECRUITING CLASS

Richt knew he had to have a quarterback to build his system around, which made Shockley a must. One of the main schools Georgia had to beat out for Shockley was Florida State.

If Shockley doesn't enter the Bulldogs' picture this season, it's only a matter of time before he does. Give him a spring in Richt's system, and look out.

The *Parade* All-American passed for 1,861 yards and 11 touchdowns last season, while also rushing for 864 yards and eight touchdowns. He's the ideal athlete to run Richt's fast-break offense.

Shockley's father, Don, who coached him in high school, says he can throw the ball 80 yards, run a 4.4 40-yard dash and long jump 23 feet, 7 inches.

It's no wonder that the first in-home visit Richt made in January after taking over at Georgia was to see Shockley, who attended the Florida State quarterbacks camp as a high school freshman. Richt had a feeling then that Shockley was headed for greatness.

With his quarterback of the future secured, Richt was also able to address the Bulldogs' more pressing need. Of the 25 signees, 11 were linemen (six defensive and five offensive).

That's after Donnan failed to sign any offensive linemen in last year's class and only three in his last two classes.

"We wanted to make sure we didn't get out of this class without enough big people up front," Richt told the *Athens Daily News*.

Holmes was rated as one of the top defensive ends in the country and could also play tackle. He finished with 64 career sacks in high school, including 25 as a senior.

Two of the three junior college signees were also linemen, while defensive end **Robert Geathers** (6-4, 225) of Georgetown, S.C., was a late surprise. The nephew of former NFL pass-rushing specialist Jumpy Geathers, Robert Geathers signed with Georgia a few days after national signing day. He was also considering South Carolina, Florida State and Tennessee.

The top two high school offensive line signees were **Russ Tanner** (6-4, 260) of Wrightsville, Ga., and **James Redmond** (6-7, 260) of Atlanta. Tight end **Andre Zellner** (6-4, 225) of Forsyth, Ga., was a *SuperPrep* All-American.

One of the most interesting catches was Milton, who was recruited by Florida State, Florida, Miami, Ohio State and Georgia when he came out of North Florida Christian High in Tallahassee, Fla., two years ago. Milton, however, was an academic long shot and wound up signing with Syracuse. He hasn't played football in two years, but is qualified academically and ready to go.

Garner was the MVP of this class, rated by most of the services among the top 15 in the nation. He held things together during the Donnan-to-Richt transition, and as usual, closed the deal on some of the bigger name recruits.

He was instrumental in holding on to *SuperPrep* All-America linebacker **Marquis Elmore** (6-3, 220) of Folkston, Ga., and in landing receiver Fred Gibson (6-4, 180) of Waycross, Ga., after he had initially committed to Florida.

"It's like the quarterback, sometimes he can get too much credit, sometimes he can get too much blame," Garner told the *Athens Daily News*.

There were a few disappointments. Cornerback Ahmad Carroll of Atlanta signed with Arkansas on national signing day, while offensive lineman Maurice Mitchell of Fork Union (Va.) Military Academy signed with Florida.

The top running back in the state, Jabari Davis of Stone Mountain, Ga., opted for Tennessee. Davis committed to the Vols soon after reports surfaced that the NCAA might be looking into former Memphis prep star Albert Means and his recruitment by Georgia.

BLUE RIBBON ANALYSIS

OFFENSE	A-
SPECIAL TEAMS	C-
DEFENSE	B
INTANGIBLES	B+

The Bulldogs' defense dominated the spring, which Richt—even with his offensive background—seemed to expect.

"In Tallahassee, I can't tell you how many times we got shut out in the spring game," he told the Athens Daily News. "There have been some 3-0 spring games over there. If your one offense is running through your one defense, you've probably got a problem. It's good when the defense plays well."

The Bulldogs' defense needs to be better than good if they're going to contend in the Eastern Division. Florida is being picked by many to win the national championship, and Tennessee is a consensus Top 10 national pick.

The good thing for Georgia is that the schedule allows some time for the offense to evolve. The first four games are at home—against Arkansas State, South Carolina, Houston and Arkansas—and it's conceivable that the Bulldogs could come out of that stretch 4-0.

They also get Auburn at home this season, but have to travel to Tennessee.

Richt has been around offensive excellence his entire career. Even with the uncertainty at quarterback, it's a given that his offense, in time, will be productive. If Smith comes back 100 percent from his foot surgery, that will ease the burden at quarterback.

The worst-case scenario would be for Phillips and Greene to get in a situation where there was no running game and they were having to throw 35 times a game.

All in all, it looks like another seven- or eight-win season, but no better than third in the East. It's a familiar (and frustrating) procession for Bulldog fans and one Richt knows must change if he wants to put down roots in Athens. Just ask Donnan.

(C.L.)

2000 RESULTS

Georgia Southern	W	29-7	1-0
South Carolina	L	10-21	1-1
New Mexico State	W	37-0	2-1
Arkansas	W	38-7	3-1
Tennessee	W	21-10	4-1
Vanderbilt	W	29-19	5-1
Kentucky	W	34-30	6-1
Florida	L	23-34	6-2
Auburn	L	26-29	6-3
Mississippi	W	32-14	7-3
Georgia Tech	L	15-27	7-4
Virginia (O'ahu Bowl)	W	37-14	8-4

Kentucky

LOCATION	**Lexington, KY**
CONFERENCE	**Southeastern (Eastern)**
LAST SEASON	**2-9 (.181)**
CONFERENCE RECORD	**0-8 (6th)**
OFFENSIVE STARTERS RETURNING	**8**
DEFENSIVE STARTERS RETURNING	**7**
NICKNAME	**Wildcats**
COLORS	**Blue & White**
HOME FIELD	**Commonwealth Stadium (67,530)**
HEAD COACH	**Guy Morriss (TCU '73)**
RECORD AT SCHOOL	**First Year**
CAREER RECORD	**First Year**
ASSISTANTS	**Rick Smith (Florida State '71)** **Asst. Head Coach/Secondary/Recruiting** **John Goodner (SW Oklahoma State '67)** **Defensive Coordinator/Linebackers** **Brent Pease (Montana '90)** **Offensive Coordinator/Quarterbacks** **Wesley McGriff (Savannah State '90)** **Running Backs** **Tom Adams (Rice '82)** **Defensive Tackles** **Larry Hoefer (McMurry '73)** **Safeties** **Chris Lancaster (Clemson '89)** **Defensive Ends** **Harold Jackson (Jackson State '68)** **Wide Receivers** **Mark Nelson (E. Central Okla. State '80)** **Special Teams/Tight Ends**
TEAM WINS (last 5 yrs.)	**4-5-7-6-2**
FINAL RANK (last 5 yrs.)	**45-37-26-54-69**
2000 FINISH	**Lost to Tennessee in regular-season finale.**

COACH AND PROGRAM

The easy part for Kentucky's football team will be playing a game again. In many ways, it should be soothing.

Last season was a forgettable one for the Wildcats, who were 2-9 and lost their last eight games. But the off-season was even worse.

The day before national signing day, head coach Hal Mumme resigned amid allegations of NCAA violations within his program. The school subsequently submitted an internal report to the NCAA on Feb. 28 acknowledging more than three dozen violations.

The NCAA has since responded with a preliminary letter of inquiry and has begun a preliminary investigation. An official letter of inquiry could be next, making for what will surely be an anxious next few months for the Wildcats.

Already, Kentucky has suggested certain penalties, including the loss of scholarships. Of course, the NCAA will have the final say.

At the root of the scandal was former recruiting coordinator Claude Bassett, who admitted to sending money orders to the high school coach of several Memphis prospects.

One of the most serious charges in Kentucky's internal report was that Bassett wrote an English paper for a player.

Mumme, who took the Wildcats to bowl games in two of his final three seasons at the school, has declined to discuss the allegations. He issued a statement upon resigning, however, saying he had no knowledge of any NCAA rules being broken and was unaware of any transgressions by his assistants. Bassett is now coaching high school football in Texas.

Mumme walked away with a nice little $1 million settlement from the university, which includes the use of two cars and the payment of all legal fees.

Left to clean up the mess was Guy Morriss, the offensive line coach under Mumme and one of the most respected coaches on that staff. Morriss was selected Kentucky's head coach on Feb. 6 and given a one-year contract.

His challenge is immense.

Florida, Georgia and Tennessee are perennial bullies in the SEC's Eastern Division. And suddenly, Lou Holtz has reinvigorated South Carolina.

Throw in the threat of potential NCAA probation at Kentucky, and it makes for a dizzying proposition for a first-year head coach.

"Our focus has been on this football team and doing what we need to do to improve as a team, nothing else," Morriss said. "We expect to be successful this fall."

Morriss, who played 15 years in the NFL and went to two Super Bowls, hasn't come in and made sweeping changes. But he's made it clear to everyone associated with Big Blue football that he does expect a certain attitude change.

In short, he expects a tougher breed of Wildcat this fall.

It started in the winter with 6 a.m. workouts four days a week. The Wildcats also hit with regularity during spring practice, something that was unheard of under Mumme.

Morriss has also emphasized the running game, while not forgetting about the passing game, and has made the weight room a priority for all his players.

"I think it's been a long time coming," sophomore offensive tackle **Antonio Hall** (6-5, 300) told the *Louisville Courier-Journal*. "Last year that's what we lacked. We lacked intensity, we lacked physical-ness. We lacked the whole football intuition. You can't play football without being physical ... and that's what's being instilled in us right now."

The firepower in the passing game that defined Mumme's system isn't going anywhere, Morriss said. The only difference is that he will pay as much attention to the running game, defense and special teams.

"We're going to bang a little bit," Morriss said. "We need to be able to run the football a little better and we're going to have to tackle a little bit better. I don't know how you do those types of things if you don't have some collisions out on the field."

The offense is now under the direction of Brent Pease, who loves to pass—Montana won the 1995 Division I-AA title throwing nearly 50 times a game under Pease's direction—but like his boss believes in establishing the run.

"We're able to do a lot of different packages now," Pease told *The Cats' Pause*. "A mixture of run and pass and screens and play-action. You don't have to establish a balance between run and pass, but you hope you have that as your arsenal."

Morriss sees no reason Kentucky's defense—known under Mumme for yielding points and yardage at the speed of light—can't be as electrifying as the offense.

New defensive coordinator John Goodner will employ an eight-man front similar to the scheme Joe Lee Dunn uses at Mississippi State. Goodner, previously the defensive coordinator at Texas Tech, will go with two inside linebackers and five safeties. The idea is to clamp down on the run and adjust to the pass.

"I've sat and watched several hours of John Goodner's game tapes that he has brought, and it is exciting for me to watch how those guys get after you," Morriss said. "I think the fans will really appreciate what he is trying to do."

The Kentucky players have seemed to appreciate Morriss. And more than anything else, they appreciate the new start.

2001 SCHEDULE

Sept.	1	Louisville
	8	Ball State
	15	@Indiana
	22	Florida
	29	Mississippi
Oct.	6	@South Carolina
	13	LSU
	20	@Georgia
Nov.	3	@Mississippi State
	10	@Vanderbilt
	17	Tennessee

QUARTERBACKS

Mumme was a one-quarterback coach. He proved that last season when he surprisingly decided to go with **Jared Lorenzen** (6-4, 275) instead of Dusty Bonner, who led the SEC in six different offensive categories in 1999.

Morriss, though, obviously doesn't mind a little drama at quarterback.

Lorenzen, a sophomore who looks more like an offensive tackle than he does a quarterback, was second nationally last season in total offense. He averaged 347.9 yards per game and led the SEC with 335.2 passing yards per game. But heading into the fall, Lorenzen is still fighting to keep his job.

Redshirt freshman **Shane Boyd** (6-2, 239) was on Lorenzen's heels all spring. A pitching prospect, Boyd has put his baseball career on hold to concentrate on football. He's given Morriss a few things to consider over the summer.

"If there's no clear-cut winner at any position, we'll go into two-a-days," Morriss told the *Lexington Herald-Leader*. "Why hurry? If it takes until the Friday before we play Louisville, so be it. Somebody eventually will come out of it as the top dog."

It's obvious the Kentucky coaches were trying to get Lorenzen's attention this spring. Morriss laid down the law that Lorenzen would need to lose some weight. He was somewhere around the 300-pound range when last season ended, but was closer to his listed weight of 275 this spring. Nobody's really saying what Lorenzen's target weight is, at least until he gets there.

"It's kind of weird," Lorenzen told the *Lexington Herald-Leader*. "For the first time in a while, my jersey feels a little big on me. Coach Morriss has really been pushing me and challenging me to lose weight, and I feel a whole lot better and have more energy out on the field."

Lorenzen has one of the strongest arms in college football. The hefty lefty broke six NCAA single-season freshman records last season. But he also tied a school record with 21 interceptions as compared to 19 touchdowns.

Morriss hopes to take some of the pressure off Lorenzen by establishing some semblance of a running game. The Wildcats won't run the shotgun nearly as much as they did under Mumme.

"We're still going to throw the ball a ton," Lorenzen said. "We'll be under center more and have more of a power attack, but it's still a wide-open offense."

Lorenzen says he doesn't mind the competition. He and Boyd have pushed each other.

"If you're the best man, then you shouldn't mind it," Lorenzen said.

Boyd signed a minor-league baseball contract with the Minnesota Twins last summer, but backed out before fall practice. He also decided not to play baseball at Kentucky this spring.

Similar to Lorenzen, Boyd is a bigger quarterback capable of putting up big numbers.

"The main thing was getting back into the flow of football," Boyd said. "That's why the spring was so important for me. Everybody has to adjust."

RUNNING BACKS

The main cogs in the running game are back, and Morriss is serious about wanting Kentucky to be able to move the ball on the ground. The Wildcats were 11th in the SEC last season in rushing offense and particularly had trouble running the ball near the goal line. It's a concern Morriss worked overtime on in the spring.

"We feel like you've got to be able to run the football to help out your passing game," Morriss told the *Louisville Courier-Journal*. "I know that's kind of been the reverse around here the last few years, but I think if nothing else it's a mental attitude, that you can line up and hammer and be effective with the running game."

Sophomore **Chad Scott** (5-10, 178) returns at tailback after starting as a freshman and rushing for 611 yards and four touchdowns. Lorenzen led the Wildcats in rushing touchdowns a year ago with five.

The question with Scott is whether he's big enough and durable enough to be an every-down back. But he's certainly versatile enough. He totaled 872 rushing and receiving yards last season, more than any other freshman running back in the SEC. He will have help. Junior **Artose Pinner** (5-11, 218) is back after rushing for 188 yards in six games. His average of 4.8 yards per carry led the team.

The third back in the equation could be junior **Martez Johnson** (5-10, 186), who has been around and knows the system. Chances are the Wildcats will split the carries among all three backs.

Another one of Morriss' touches was introducing a true blocking back into the offense. Senior **Joel Bryan** (5-10, 210) left the spring as the starter. He's a transfer from Texas A&M.

But freshman **Ronald "Rock" Johnson** (6-0, 246) will be given a chance to win the job when he arrives on campus this summer. Johnson, who's from Cleveland, was an April signee who rushed for 579 yards and nine touchdowns as a senior in high school.

"Rock is a prototype fullback," Morriss said. "He was a power runner and blocker in high school. He could come in and help us immediately."

WIDE RECEIVERS/TIGHT ENDS

The Wildcats need a few big-play receiving targets to develop this fall, or Lorenzen and Boyd could have trouble keeping defenses honest. The leading returning pass-catcher is junior tight end **Derek Smith** (6-6, 265). He missed the spring after undergoing shoulder surgery, but caught 50 passes for 716 yards and five touchdowns last season.

Smith will be used as more of a true tight end this season, meaning he will be asked to block more.

Kentucky's other tight end, Bobby Blizzard, was apparently not real crazy about that idea and elected to transfer to North Carolina. Junior **Chase Harp** (6-4, 246) returns after an injury-plagued sophomore season.

The real question is who will make the bulk of the plays on the perimeter for the Wildcats. Their top playmaker out there, Quentin McCord, has moved on to the NFL.

Senior **Dougie Allen** (5-10, 174) returns as one starter. He played well during the 1999 season before tearing up his knee. He struggled last season and was really never the same player. Should Allen return to his 1999 form, that would be a huge boost for the Wildcats.

The other starter coming out of the spring was senior **Anthony "Champ" Kelly** (5-11, 191). Kelly played in all 11 games last season and caught eight passes for 64 yards.

Junior college transfer **Aaron Boone** (6-3, 210) was impressive during the spring with his ability to make something happen after the catch. Boone is not particularly fast, but catches the ball well and has good instincts. Boone, a junior, was a junior college All-American last year at Snow College in Fillmore, Utah.

Sophomore **Derek Abney** (5-10, 170) missed the final part of spring with a bruised shoulder. Abney, anything but a big target, has great speed and is ferocious for such a small player.

Junior **Ernest Simms** (5-8, 165) is another diminutive speedster. But his hands are questionable, and he still needs work on his route running.

Junior **Brad Pyatt** (6-0, 199) has returned to the team after leaving last season because of injury problems. Pyatt, a starter in 1999, underwent off-season foot surgery.

Providing depth will be redshirt freshman **Tommy Cook** (6-0, 192) and junior **Neal Brown** (6-0, 181). Cook was the leading receiver in the spring game.

"We've got to find five or six receivers who want to attack the football," Morriss said. "When their time comes, they've got to be go-to type guys and they have to want the football, and we're waiting for some guys to step forward and fill that role."

OFFENSIVE LINE

The offensive line should be the strength of the team and could be one of the better units in the conference if everyone returns healthy in the fall.

Four full-time starters are back, along with a fifth player who has started off and on for the last couple of years. All five are either juniors or seniors.

Junior left guard **Kip Sixbery** (6-4, 320) and right tackle Hall give the Wildcats a pair of legitimate NFL prospects. Sixbery bench presses in the 500-pound range, and Hall turned down the likes of Ohio State and Tennessee to come to Kentucky.

Hall started every game last season as a true freshman, and Sixbery has also started since he was a true freshman. Senior **Nolan DeVaughn** (6-5, 321) will start at center if his surgically repaired knee holds up. He started two years ago but injured his knee in the first game of last season. He missed parts of spring practice with swelling in his knee.

There is a contingency plan at center, and a proven one at that. Junior **Keith Chatelain** (6-5, 306) started in 10-of-11 games last season and will step in again if DeVaughn isn't ready.

Senior **Matt Brown** (6-5, 312) has started the last two years at left tackle. He was held out of contact drills in the spring after undergoing off-season shoulder surgery.

The right guard spot will be manned by senior **Josh Parrish** (6-6, 332). He started in every game in 1999 and was a part-time starter last season. Morriss said the Wildcats need to be good up front early in the season while the rest of the offense evolves.

How some of the Wildcats heal will play a major role.

DeVaughn is probably the most serious question mark. The shoulder rehabilitation needs to continue to go well for Brown, while Parrish has also been bothered by a knee injury.

"I think we can be a good line without them (Brown, DeVaughn and Parrish)," Sixbery told the *Louisville Courier-Journal.* "But with them, we'll be that much better because experience counts for a lot."

The Wildcats do have some depth. **Jason Rollins** (6-5, 272) and **Matt Huff** (6-5, 296)—a pair of promising redshirt freshmen—are backups at the tackle position.

There's also the advantage of having more offensive variety this season.

"It's balanced," Boyd said. "Last year it was throw, throw, throw, run, throw, throw, throw. Now you don't know what we're going to do. We've got play-action. We've got passes. We've got runs. We've got screens. We'll get guys playing more honest against us."

2000 STATISTICS

Rushing offense	110.5	91
Passing offense	335.4	2
Total offense	445.5	11
Scoring offense	23.1	75
Net Punting	34.3	66
Punt returns	1.1	114
Kickoff returns	19.2	72
Rushing defense	163.2	70
Passing efficiency defense	153.2	112
Total defense	405.9	87
Scoring defense	34.8	104
Turnover margin	-12	104

Last column is ranking among Division I-A teams.

KICKERS

Senior **Seth Hanson** (6-2, 197) returns to do the place-kicking, and, it appears, only the place-kicking. He kicked and punted for the Wildcats last season, but was pulled from his punting duties by Mumme after one too many short punts.

A steady place-kicker, Hanson's made 30-of-39 field goals during his career. He doesn't have great range, but is pretty close to automatic inside 40 yards. He was 15-of-17 last season with a long of 40 yards. His 88.2 percent accuracy set a school record. A semifinalist for the Lou Groza Award, Hanson was 23-of-24 on extra points.

Hanson sat out the 1999 season after injuring his leg in August. He was chosen to the SEC's All-Freshman team in 1997.

DEFENSIVE LINE

Is this finally **Dennis Johnson**'s year?

Johnson (6-7, 261) thinks so, and so do the Wildcats' coaches. The junior defensive end came to Kentucky as *USA Today*'s national defensive player of the year after a stellar career in Harrodsburg, Ky.

But in the opener last season against Louisville, Johnson suffered a season-ending high ankle sprain. He was granted a medical hardship redshirt and still has two years of eligibility.

"People are still doubting Dennis Johnson," Johnson told the *Lexington Herald-Leader.* "So I've got to prove myself. I think sitting out last year was a blessing from God. I got to get stronger and sit back and watch, and now I feel like I'm in high school."

Johnson lost 12 pounds in the spring after a case of food poisoning. He would like to play this fall at 275 pounds.

"Dennis looks good to me," Goodner told *The Cats' Pause.* "He had a good spring, and I think he feels good about where he is right now."

The three other starters on the defensive line are back from last season, including sophomore tackle **Dewayne Robertson** (6-3, 315). Robertson was a consensus freshman All-SEC selection last season. He had 13 1/2 tackles for loss, including three sacks, and forced three fumbles. His second forced fumble against Indiana resulted in the game-winning touchdown.

Robertson quickly bought into Morriss' approach.

"I remember last year, practices were usually dead," Robertson told *The Cats' Pause.* "(No one) even acted like they wanted to be out there. Now everybody's motivated, everybody's up. We're learning to practice with a great tempo, and that's one of the things we're really working on."

Robertson also has great admiration for Goodner, whose job it is to improve Kentucky's porous defense.

"I look at him like he's my grandfather—he's a great role model, he comes out to work hard every day, and he's the same person every day," Robertson told *The Cats' Pause.* "He's a great man. And he can coach some defense, too, so we'll all right with him."

Sophomore tackle **Jeremy Caudill** (6-3, 296) also started as a freshman last season. One of the strongest players on the team, Caudill had 6 1/2 tackles for loss, including a pair of sacks.

"I think our front four is the strength of our football team, especially those two tackles up there," Goodner told *The Cats' Pause.* "Jeremy and Dewayne have got a chance to be something really special, as young as those guys are and as good players as they are. We've just got to continue to build around them."

At the other end, the Wildcats are hopeful that junior **Otis Grigsby** (6-4, 250) can make if back from a broken leg and ligament damage in his ankle after being injured in winter conditioning. He didn't go through the spring.

Senior **Chris Demaree** (6-4, 250) worked with the first team in the spring and will battle Grigsby for that other end spot.

The Wildcats feel good about their front four starters. The concern is the depth. There's none to speak of, at least in terms of any player who has contributed.

LINEBACKERS

If there's one key on defense for the Wildcats, it has to be senior linebacker **Jamal White** (6-3, 223). Morriss says White is the best athlete on the team, but that didn't necessarily translate into production the last few years.

White never caught onto what the Wildcats were trying to do defensively under former coordinator Mike Major. The different schemes and blitzes kept him constantly thinking—and not playing.

Goodner, with an assist from Morriss, is determined to change that.

"Jamal's one of the guys who has to be good for us to be good," Goodner told the *Louisville Courier-Journal.* "He's got play-making ability. What we've got to do as a coaching staff is put him in a position where he can make plays and let him play, because he's one of those guys who's got to be good for us to be good."

White, who's recorded just 32 career tackles, made his only start during the first game of the 1999 season. He grew increasingly frustrated over the last two seasons and saw his playing time diminish. He said the simplified defense has made his life easier.

"Last year was a struggle," White told the *Louisville Courier-Journal.* "This year, we're just out there playing ball, having fun. ... I don't have to think a lot. We're just out there playing. I'm pretty much free and coach Goodner's going to put us in a position to be successful."

Senior linebacker Ryan Murphy (6-2, 240) would have been back as the team's leading returning tackler after making 65 stops last season, but he was declared academically ineligible in June and is career is over. Ryan had started the last two years at middle linebacker.

Senior **Ronnie Riley** (6-2, 231) started the last five games a year ago at outside linebacker. During the off-season he concentrated on adding weight and strength to aid his move to the inside.

Junior **Morris Lane** (6-1, 206) has seen most of his action on special teams the last few years, but is braced to jump into the linebacker rotation this fall.

DEFENSIVE BACKS

The most unique feature of Goodner's scheme is the pair of safeties (or hybrid outside linebackers) that typically crowd the line of scrimmage.

Senior **Chris Gayton** (6-2 205) and junior **David Johnson** (6-0, 203) came out of the spring as the starters at the two outside safety positions. But sophomore **Octavious Bond** (6-1, 209) could wind up being the best of the bunch.

Senior **Patrick Wiggins** (6-0, 200) is also pushing for playing time. Gayton, who's from Montreal, started the first four games last season at outside linebacker, but sprained his knee and played sparingly the rest of the way.

Johnson was the Wildcats' strong safety last season and was fourth on the team in tackles with 44. Wiggins, a former quarterback, made one start at strong safety last season. He played in all 11 games and finished with 26 tackles.

Senior **Anthony Wajda** (6-4, 185) returns as the free safety. Wajda had five interceptions two years ago and earned second-team All-SEC honors. But he suffered through an inconsistent junior season.

Wajda is a good leaper and can go get the football, but he's not a great tackler. He will be pushed by junior **Quentus Cumby** (6-1, 204). It was a tight race coming out of the spring.

Similar to last season, teams will go after the Wildcats' cornerbacks, especially now that Eric Kelly is gone. Sophomore **Leonard Burress** (5-11, 184) and senior **Jeremy Bowie** (5-10, 187) are the probable starters and neither has ever been a full-time starter.

Bowie has the most experience, but didn't play last season. He was suspended after a DUI arrest. He started for half the season in 1999 and also played a lot as the nickel back.

"I think he pushed himself; he had more intensity," Kentucky secondary coach Rick Smith told the *Louisville Courier-Journal.* "I think he had something to prove because he let the team down with the DUI, and now he's back and he's trying to show everybody that he is more dedicated and isn't going to screw it up again."

Junior **Derrick Tatum** (6-0, 187) saw spot duty at cornerback last season and started three games late in the season. He figures in as the nickel back.

The Wildcats hope to get some depth from sophomore **Brandon Doggett** (5-9, 180) and redshirt freshmen **Earven Flowers** (5-10, 178) and **Claude Sagaille** (5-10, 183).

Whereas the old defensive blueprint at Kentucky left the cornerbacks in constant, man-to-man press coverage, the new philosophy is to play more zone mixed in with man principles.

"If you're going to play true man and really isolate those guys out there, you better be pretty special to be able to hold up out there," Morriss said. "It's nothing against our kids, but let's do it wisely and give them some help when we can."

Kentucky had fewer interceptions (five) than any team in the SEC last season. The Wildcats also surrendered the second-highest completion percentage and allowed the most passing yards and touchdown receptions.

PUNTERS

Junior **Glenn Pakulak** (6-3, 228) handled the punting in the Wildcats' final three games last season. He will likely take on those responsibilities full time this season. Hanson did the placekicking and the punting during the first eight games. But the Wildcats finished 11th in the league in punting average, and the thinking was to allow Hanson to concentrate solely on his place-kicking.

Pakulak, a walk-on, punted 12 times during his trial run a year ago, averaging 37.8 yards. He had a long punt of 47 yards.

SPECIAL TEAMS

Mumme frequently cracked jokes about special teams, which probably explains some of the Wildcats' struggles in that area the last few years.

Morriss is committed to placing more emphasis on special teams. In fact, he's made one of his assistants, Mark Nelson, the special teams coordinator.

One of Morriss' promises to Nelson is that he can have anybody he wants from the offensive and defensive units. In other words, there won't be a bunch of third-teamers and walk-ons covering kicks and blocking.

Morriss has also said that Kentucky won't gamble (fake punts) nearly as much on special teams.

Simms, who averaged 21.8 yards last season, and Martez Johnson each have experience returning kickoffs.

The Wildcats also desperately need to find a punt returner. They finished last among Division I-A teams last season with an average of 1.1 yards per return.

Sophomore **Clint Ruth** (6-1, 188) will probably kick off and could also be brought in for some of the longer field goals. Senior walk-on **Stephen Scaldaferri** is also a candidate to kick off.

RECRUITING CLASS

When word began to spread that Kentucky could be in trouble with the NCAA, this year's class was all but lost. And with Mumme resigning on the eve of national signing day, it became an impossible situation.

All told, Kentucky lost seven commitments after the university launched its internal investigation into possible rules violations. One of those was highly acclaimed receiver Montrell Jones of Louisville. Jones' about-face was especially painful because he chose bitter rival Tennessee.

Still, the Wildcats managed to sign 21 players. At the head of the class were linebackers **Chad Anderson** (6-2, 240) of Canton, Ohio and **Dustin Williams** (6-4, 250) of Channahan, Ill. Both will get a chance to play right away.

Williams could end up being moved to defensive end, especially once he gets into the Wildcats' weight program.

At running back, Johnson might not carry the ball too much, but he has the ability to clear the way for some people. He was the blocking back for tailbacks last season in high school that combined for 2,400 yards and 33 touchdowns.

Boone, the lone junior college signee, enrolled in January and went through spring practice. He jumped right into the mix at receiver.

Another newcomer to watch is defensive lineman **Ellery Moore** (6-3, 260) of Massillon, Ohio. His last year of high school was 1999, and he originally signed with Penn State. He didn't qualify academically out of high school, though, and attended a prep school last year that didn't have a football team.

Morriss and his staff were still busy recruiting in the spring. In addition to signing Rock Johnson in early April, Kentucky signed freshman quarterback **Dan Lumley** after spring practice concluded later in the month. Lumley (6-1, 170), from Windsor, Ontario, was a first-team All-Canada quarterback his senior season at Herman High School. In three seasons as a starter, Lumley led Herman to a 38-1 record and three Ontario championships.

"I like Dan's mobility and athleticism," Morriss said. "He has a strong arm and can throw the deep ball with a lot of touch. He's very bright and I'm impressed with his academic performance and maturity."

BLUE RIBBON ANALYSIS

OFFENSE	B-
SPECIAL TEAMS	C
DEFENSE	D
INTANGIBLES	B+

Morriss is determined to bring a certain toughness to the Wildcats, the likes of which they lacked under Mumme. He's hoping it pays off most during the latter stages of games. The Wildcats wilted in too many critical situations a year ago. They lost four games by six or fewer points.

Morriss has placed a premium on being able to run the ball in short-yardage situations, tackling better on defense and doing more than just showing up on special teams. The players have taken to his approach.

"Nothing against coach Mumme or any of the other coaches because they did a good job with the program, but when you have coaches you really want to go out and play for, it makes all the difference," Murphy said.

As many as 13 players who've started in the last two seasons return on defense. The offensive line is also laden with experience. But as is usually the case with Kentucky, avoiding injuries and any setbacks in rehabilitation from off-season surgeries will be critical. There simply isn't much depth anywhere. The Wildcats desperately need to get off to a good start. They open at home against Louisville and face Ball State at home the next week. Then comes a road trip to Illinois.

Besting last season's 2-9 nightmare shouldn't be overly difficult. But a winning record? That could be a stretch.

(C.L.)

2000 RESULTS

Louisville	L	34-40	0-1
South Florida	W	27-9	1-1
Indiana	W	41-34	2-1
Florida	L	31-59	2-2
Mississippi	L	17-35	2-3
South Carolina	L	17-20	2-4
LSU	L	0-34	2-5
Georgia	L	30-34	2-6
Mississippi State	L	17-35	2-7
Vanderbilt	L	20-24	2-8
Tennessee	L	20-59	2-9

LSU

LOCATION	Baton Rouge, LA
CONFERENCE	Southeastern (Western)
LAST SEASON	8-4 (.667)
CONFERENCE RECORD	5-3 (2nd)
OFFENSIVE STARTERS RETURNING	7
DEFENSIVE STARTERS RETURNING	10
NICKNAME	Tigers
COLORS	Purple & Gold
HOME FIELD	Tiger Stadium (91,600)
HEAD COACH	Nick Saban (Kent State '73)
RECORD AT SCHOOL	8-4 (1 year)
CAREER RECORD	51-30-1 (7 years)
ASSISTANTS	Derek Dooley (Virginia '90)
	Tight Ends/Recruiting Coordinator
	Jimbo Fisher (Samford '87)
	Offensive Coordinator/Quarterbacks
	Pete Jenkins (Western Carolina '64)
	Defensive Line
	Stan Hixson (Iowa State '79)
	Wide Receivers
	George Yarno (Washington State '78)
	Offensive Line
	Will Muschamp (Georgia Tech '94)
	Linebackers
	Charlie Harbison (Gardner-Webb '82)
	Defensive Backs
	Michael Haywood (Notre Dame '86)
	Runnning Backs/Special Teams
	Gary Gibbs (Oklahoma '75)
	Defensive Coordinator
TEAM WINS (last 5 yrs.)	10-9-4-3-8
FINAL RANK (last 5 yrs.)	13-16-35-41-15
2000 FINISH	Beat Georgia Tech in Peach Bowl.

COACH AND PROGRAM

If you thought Nick Saban's first season at LSU was one long joy ride, you should have heard the local talk shows the week after LSU lost to UAB in Tiger Stadium.

One Saturday later, Saban's Tigers rebounded to upset Tennessee, 38-31, in overtime. They went 6-2 over the last eight games, including a come-from-behind victory against Georgia Tech in the Peach Bowl.

What happened next is more surprising than the post-UAB turnaround—unless you know Saban's history. Four assistants left and not necessarily for better jobs. The departees included assistant head coach Rick Trickett and defensive coordinator Phil Elmassian.

The season and postseason enhanced Saban's reputation as a good coach who is hard to work for. One year was enough for Trickett, Elmassian, Sal Sunseri and Mel Tucker.

After little more than a year as LSU's head coach, Saban already had hired three defensive coordinators, the most recent of whom is Gary Gibbs, the former Oklahoma head coach who served as Jim Donnan's defensive coordinator at Georgia last year.

The defensive coordinator's title might be a misnomer at LSU, where Saban is basically in charge of the defense. Saban coached the secondary at West Virginia, Ohio State, Navy, Michigan State and the Houston Oilers. He was a defensive coordinator with Michigan State and the Cleveland Browns.

This isn't the first time LSU has had success with a former NFL defensive coordinator. Bill Arnsparger, who coordinated the Miami Dolphins' Super Bowl defenses in the 1970s, won 26 games and one conference title in his three years as LSU's head coach from 1984-86.

Also, like Arnsparger, Saban is a defensive-minded head coach who is comfortable with a wide-open offense. He proved that in five years as Michigan State's head coach and again last year at LSU.

Unlike Arnsparger, Saban has a gift for recruiting. He recruited one of the top classes in the country in 2001. The coaching attrition didn't affect recruiting, and Saban minimizes the effect it had on the Tigers in spring practice.

"We'd all like to have continuity because it's beneficial in terms of your relations, in how you teach the players, in recruiting and everything else," he said. "But when you have turnover and are able to attract quality people, the new ideas and enthusiasm they bring in are beneficial.

"I've been really pleased with the way the new people came in. Their experience and knowledge has been beneficial. Gibbs is an outstanding coach with a tremendous amount of experience. The players have responded very well to him. He's done a good job of taking our system and running with it."

Amidst all the coaching changes, LSU had little turnover in personnel. The Tigers will return 17-of-22 starters from an 8-4 team. But they've lost the element of surprise.

"We're not going to sneak up on anybody this year," Saban said. "Our psychological disposition has to be in taking one step up in our standards."

If last year is any indicator, the Tigers should be up to the challenge. They started out 2-2, losing 34-17 to Auburn and 13-10 to UAB. The offensive line suffered numerous injuries, and the quarterback situation was on shaky ground with injuries to both Rohan Davey and Josh Booty.

Given their recent history—the Tigers had lost 15 games the previous two seasons under Gerry DiNardo—they seemed on the brink of another collapse. Instead, they rebounded to upset Tennessee. But that wasn't the end of the adversity. The next week, Florida waylaid the Tigers, 41-9, in The Swamp.

Again, LSU responded positively, reeling off four consecutive victories in the SEC. By then, the UAB loss was forgotten. So were the consecutive losing seasons in 1998 and 1999.

A late-season loss to Arkansas only temporarily curbed the enthusiasm. LSU rebounded to defeat favored Georgia Tech, 28-14, in the Peach Bowl. The ending was reminiscent of the 1995 season when DiNardo, in his first year at LSU, led the Tigers to a 7-4-1 record, capped by a rousing 45-26 victory over Michigan State.

Five years later, the Tigers are counting on that losing Michigan State coach to finish what DiNardo started.

2001 SCHEDULE

Sept.	1	Tulane
	8	Utah State
	15	Auburn
	29	@Tennessee
Oct.	6	Florida
	13	@Kentucky
	20	@Mississippi State
	27	Mississippi
Nov.	3	@Alabama
	10	Middle Tennessee
	24	Arkansas

QUARTERBACKS

Few teams have ever had so much reason to be excited about a senior quarterback with four career starts. But few senior quarterbacks have had so many big games in so few opportunities. **Rohan Davey** (6-3, 239), whose career has been thwarted by knee and ankle injuries, has put together four dazzling games in his limited playing time the last two years.

In LSU's last game in 1999, Davey came off the bench to complete 10-of-12 passes for 224 yards and three touchdowns. In the 2000 opener against Western Carolina, he went 11-of-11 for 194 yards and three touchdowns. During the course of the two games, he completed 17 consecutive passes, which tied for third most in SEC history.

In his third career game, Davey completed 23-of-35 passes for 318 yards and a school-record-tying four interceptions in a 38-31 overtime victory against 11th-ranked Tennessee. He accomplished all that despite playing on a badly sprained ankle that often had him limping away from defenders.

His fourth great game was off the bench in relief of Josh Booty in the Peach Bowl. Davey completed 17-of-25 passes for 174 yards and three touchdowns as the Tigers rallied for 25 second-half points to upset Georgia Tech.

In the spring, Davey picked up where he left off. Just as important, he stayed healthy.

"Rohan Davey really had an outstanding spring in terms of his consistency and helping the other players play well," Saban said. "We've been very encouraged by him."

Saban doesn't hide his affection for Davey, who has suffered knee, ankle and hamstring injuries yet bounced back from each setback with great play. In 2000, Davey suffered a severe knee injury in February and missed all of spring practice. Then, he overcame an ankle injury to lead LSU past Tennessee, only to be sidelined again by a hamstring injury.

"To go through the circumstances he went through (last year)," Saban said. "And still, he never put himself ahead of the team. I think that's the most phenomenal thing about him, being unselfish and putting the team first."

Keeping Davey healthy will be crucial to this year's offense. The Tigers have no experienced backups. Walk-on **Marcus Randall**, a 6-2, 220-pound redshirt freshman, was the leading candidate for the backup job after spring drills. He completed 8-of-13 passes in one scrimmage and was 10-of-19 in the spring game.

"I think he kinda solidified himself as the backup quarterback," Saban said. "I think he had the best spring of all our backup quarterbacks, but I don't think he's where he needs to be as a solid backup. We're going to continue to work with all three backups."

Other possibilities are redshirt freshman **Matt Mauck** (6-2, 210) and freshman **Rick Clausen** (6-2, 180).

Clausen, the younger brother of Tennessee quarterback Casey Clausen, was one of LSU's earliest commitments. He completed 264-of-430 passes for 3,361 yards and 38 touchdowns as a senior at Taft High School in Woodlawn Hills, Calif.

RUNNING BACKS

Sophomore **LaBrandon Toefield** (6-0, 224) will be the focal point of the LSU rushing game for the second consecutive season. He made first-team freshman All-America last year when he rushed for 682 yards, the third-highest total ever for an LSU freshman. He accomplished that despite suffering an ankle injury, which knocked him out of the last three quarters of the Ole Miss game and all of the Arkansas game.

Toefield, who runs with quickness and power, had 100-yard-plus rushing games against Tennessee and Mississippi State. Against Tennessee, he scored on a 74-yard run. His outstanding first season is more noteworthy when you consider he hadn't played for two years. He was redshirted as a freshman after missing his senior year at Independence (La.) High School with a knee injury. As a junior, Toefield rushed for 2,800 yards and 45 touchdowns. He rushed for 1,800 yards and 32 touchdowns as a sophomore.

LSU has another experienced tailback in junior **Domanick Davis** (5-10, 207), who rushed for 274 yards as a freshman and 445 more last fall. Davis, one of the conference's best return men, moved to defense in the spring and played well at cornerback. Saban plans on using him at both positions this fall.

Davis first demonstrated his versatility in high school, where he was an all-state player at Breaux Bridge, La. As a senior, he averaged 41.2 yards on kickoff returns and 25.8 yards on punt returns. He also rushed for 1,242 yards and had nine interceptions and 104 tackles on defense.

Sophomore **Devery Henderson** (6-1, 180) is the fastest of LSU's running backs. Henderson, credited with a 4.3 40, is a sprinter on the LSU track team. Last year, he rushed for 116 yards on 23 carries. He scored a pair of touchdowns in the season opener against Western Carolina.

Freshman **Shyrone Carey** (5-8, 190) could give the backfield a boost. He was an all-state selection at Shaw High School in New Orleans two years ago when he starred as a running quarterback. He originally signed with Tennessee but failed to qualify academically.

Carey has "special ability," Saban told *The Morning Advocate*. "Should he gain his eligibility, we'll certainly try to create a role for him."

No matter who starts at fullback, he won't have the size of former starter Tommy Banks, a 6-1, 275-pound offensive lineman masquerading as a running back.

The new fullback candidates aren't just smaller, they're fairly new to the position. Junior **Elice Parker** (5-11, 228) is a former tailback. Junior **Solomon Lee** (6-1, 225) is a former tight end. Junior **Ryan O'Neal** (6-0, 221) is a former linebacker. Parker is the frontrunner after an impressive spring. He scored three touchdowns on short runs in the first spring scrimmage.

"Elice has good running skills and he's a hard runner," Saban told the *New Orleans Times-Picayune*. "He's probably undersized to be a jackhammer fullback like Banks, but we're going to need him to play well in the fall."

Parker earned a look at fullback after distinguishing himself on special teams last year. He forced a Kentucky fumble with a flying tackle on a kickoff. Parker said he planned to gain another five or 10 pounds before preseason drills. He's already the strongest running back on the team, with a bench press of 415 pounds.

WIDE RECEIVERS/TIGHT ENDS

Junior **Josh Reed** (5-11, 200) looks like a wide receiver until he catches the ball. Then he looks like the running back he once was. Reed was converted from running back to wide receiver in Week 9 of the 1999 season. He finished the year with eight catches for 134 yards, a 16.8-yard average. He was just getting warmed up.

Last fall, Reed emerged as an All-SEC wide receiver, catching 65 passes for 1,127 yards and 10 touchdowns. He averaged 17.3 yards per catch. Reed, who tied an LSU record with six 100-yard receiving games, was at his best in the games that mattered most. He caught 53 passes for 861 yards and nine touchdowns in eight SEC games. He had eight catches for 173 yards against Ole Miss, seven catches for 146 yards and three touchdowns against Tennessee and 10 catches for 113 yards against Mississippi State. He capped his season with an LSU-bowl- record nine catches for 96 yards against Georgia Tech in the Peach Bowl.

Reed is the star, but the Tigers have other experienced receivers in junior **Jerel Myers** (5-11, 180) and senior **Reggie Robinson** (6-2, 196). Myers had 29 catches for 347 yards after leading the Tigers in receiving with 64 catches for 854 yards in 1999. Robinson has averaged 25.7 receptions per season the last three years. He ranked second to Reed last year with 31 catches for 391 yards and two touchdowns, including an 80-yard touchdown catch on the second play from scrimmage against Western Carolina. Robinson had four catches for 65 yards in the Peach Bowl.

Sophomore **Jack Hunt** (6-0, 188) had just three receptions last year, but one of them gave the Tigers a crucial first down on a fourth-quarter drive against Alabama. He's not the fastest of LSU's receivers, but he has good hands and runs exact routes.

Senior **Ed Dangerfield** (6-5, 212), the cousin of former Florida star Ike Hilliard, will give the Tigers a big target if he can stay healthy. He suffered a severe knee injury in April of 2000 and played in only four games last year. He was bothered by injuries again in the spring.

LSU has another weapon in tight end **Robert Royal**, a 6-5, 231-pound senior who made first-team All-SEC last year. Royal is an outstanding blocker with exceptional speed for a tight end. He caught 22 passes for 340 yards and set an LSU single-season record with five touchdown receptions as a tight end. He caught game-winning touchdown passes against Alabama and Tennessee.

Royal, who was a standout defensive end in high school, also made a contribution in 1999, catching 19 passes for 143 yards and playing on special teams.

Senior **Joe Domingeaux** (6-5, 256) is an experienced backup at tight end. Domingeaux, who has 11 career starts, is such a good blocker LSU has used him at fullback in goal-line situations. Sophomore **Eric Edwards** (6-5, 244) gained experience as a backup last year, catching five passes for 127 yards. He had a 34-yard catch against Kentucky.

OFFENSIVE LINE

The Tigers will return three starters in the offensive line, but they won't be starting at the same positions. Junior **Rob Sale**, who started the last half of 2000 at guard, went through most of the spring at his old position before being switched to center.

Sale (6-2, 319) will try to fill the void left by first-team All-SEC center Lou Williams. He planned to lose between 10 and 20 pounds in the off-season.

"It always helps to be quick, but the most important thing is taking the right angles," Sale told the *Times-Picayune* in the spring. "I've got to learn what blitzes can come out of defensive packages. But I was put at center because I'm older and more experienced. It's a challenge, but I'm up for it."

LSU's other returning starters in the offensive line are senior guard **Dwayne Pierce** (6-3, 316) and sophomore tackle **Rodney Reed** (6-4, 284). In his first year as a full-time starter, Pierce was one of LSU's most consistent players last year. Reed won a starting position before the Tennessee game and held it the rest of the year. He first started at guard, then moved over to tackle because of injuries.

Junior **Brad Smalling** (6-7, 305) will probably start at the tackle opposite Reed. Smalling, a former second-team *USA Today* All-American from West Monroe, La., started five games last year. Junior **Jason Baggett** (6-6, 283), who played as a freshman at tight end, started five games at tackle in 1999 and played in all 11 games last year as a backup.

Junior **John Young** (6-3, 290), who has played sparingly the last two years, was the other starter at guard after spring practice. Redshirt freshman **Kade Comeaux** (6-6, 305), a former Louisiana all-stater, will provide depth at guard. Junior **Terry Phillips** (6-6, 294), who played defensive tackle last fall, switched to offense in the spring and could help out at guard or tackle.

2000 STATISTICS

Rushing offense	131.1	73
Passing offense	245.3	29
Total offense	376.4	53
Scoring offense	26.5	54
Net Punting	34.6	55
Punt returns	11.0	35
Kickoff returns	20.4	39
Rushing defense	134.8	41
Passing efficiency defense	112.5	43
Total defense	351.0	46
Scoring defense	20.1	32
Turnover margin	-1	65

Last column is ranking among Division I-A teams.

KICKERS

Junior **John Corbello** (5-11, 216) returns for his third consecutive year as a starter. He was 8-of-11 from inside 40 yards last year but struggled beyond that. For the year, he was 10-of-18 after going 9-for-12 as a freshman in 1999. He has missed only two extra-point attempts in his career. Corbella made the conference's all-freshman team two years ago.

DEFENSIVE LINE

With three of four starters returning, the Tigers expect improvement in their defensive front.

"Last year, our whole goal was to be part of the solution, not part of the problem," veteran line coach Pete Jenkins said. "It's now time for us to be helpful in the results.

"They all made progress as the season went along. They worked hard and got better. We made some progress. By the end of the bowl game, we were decent."

End Kareem Mitchell is the only departed starter. Junior **Kenderick Allen** (6-6, 290) filled his position impressively in the spring.

"He's got size and speed," Jenkins said of Allen, a former high school All-American. "He's really a gifted athlete. We were excited about the way he played in the spring."

Senior **Jarvis Green** (6-3, 259), a returning starter, also encouraged the coaches by the way he finished the spring.

"He was a guy that I really hadn't been able to help as much as I should have," Jenkins said. "But the last two scrimmages of the spring, he really took some steps forward. He's just getting accustomed to the scheme we run. By the end of the spring, he told me he was starting to react to things without having to think so much."

Green, who was a freshman All-American in 1998, will be a fourth-year starter. Bothered by nagging injuries last year, Green had one only sack after registering 15 in his first two years, including an LSU freshman record of eight.

Senior **Kyle Kipps** (6-4, 261) will back up both Green and Allen. Kipps, an All-SEC freshman tight end in 1998, made the transition to defense in 2000, starting seven games. Sophomore **Bryce Wyatt** (6-4, 237), who played on special teams last year, could help as a backup.

Senior **Muskingum Barnes** (6-2, 269) returns for his third year as a starter at tackle. Barnes, who began his career as a backup to All-American Anthony McFarland, has started 19 games. He battled through injuries last fall, finishing the year with 44 tackles, including four for losses. The season took its toll as Barnes had both of his elbows and a knee repaired through arthroscopic surgery in the off-season. His spring work was limited.

"We feel better about tackle," Jenkins said. "Sophomore **Chad Lavalais** (6-3, 280) had a really good spring. We're extremely proud of him. He's got outstanding ability. And junior **Byron Dawson** (6-2, 289) has made as much improvement as anybody on defense since last year."

Lavalais, a third-team freshman All-American last year, made eight tackles in his first college start against Alabama. He started the final three games of the regular season and the Peach Bowl.

Lavalais, a Class 3A all-state tight end in Marksville, La., is one of the most versatile players in the conference. In high school, he played tight end, running back and linebacker and also returned kicks and punted.

Dawson has logged playing time as a backup and occasional starter the last two years. He not only has worked hard to improve, he has worked to drop weight. Dawson weighed 340 pounds as a freshman.

Senior **Howard Green** (6-2, 310), a transfer from Southwest Mississippi Junior College, had 39 tackles, including eight for losses, while starting eight games last year. He will share playing time with Lavalais at one tackle.

LINEBACKERS

As a defensive coordinator at Georgia last year, Gibbs had two of the best tackles in the country in Richard Seymour and Marcus Stroud. A year later at LSU, he's got two of the best linebackers—juniors **Bradie James** (6-3, 228) and **Trev Faulk** (6-3, 225), who combined for 123 tackles last season.

"Trev and Bradie have been leaders in the past," Gibbs said. "They continue to grow. They really stepped up in the spring."

So did junior linebacker **Jeremy Lawrence** (6-2, 230), an experienced, steady player who sometimes gets overlooked in the midst of Faulk, a first-team All-SEC pick and James, a second-team All-SEC selection.

"Jeremy had a good spring, too," Gibbs said. "His technique got better, and he became a little more aware of his responsibilities and how he fits into the overall scheme.

"Those three guys played well last year. As a group, they're bigger, stronger and more knowledgeable."

Lawrence, the strong-side linebacker, had 42 tackles and four for losses while starting nine of 11 games last year. Faulk's 113 tackles were the most by an LSU player in 15 years; James wasn't far behind with 110. Faulk had nine tackles for losses and recovered four fumbles. James had eight tackles for losses and five sacks. LSU's three starting linebackers have a combined 43 starts entering their junior years.

"They were active and played a lot of plays last year," Gibbs said. "We'd feel a lot better with quality backups. One of our goals in the spring was to try and develop as many quality backups as we could. I think we're improved."

Senior **Walter Moreham** (6-0, 220) played in all 12 games last year as a backup. He had a fumble recovery in the victory over Houston. A couple of promising redshirt freshmen—**Marcus Yanez** (6-0, 210) and **Lionel Turner** (6-3, 225)—could give LSU needed depth. Both are former Louisiana all-staters.

DEFENSIVE BACKS

Senior free safety **Ryan Clark** (5-11, 185) is a great guy to build a secondary around. The second-team All-SEC pick has made 209 tackles, intercepted five passes and had six tackles behind the line the last two years.

Clark, who has started 23 consecutive games, was selected the team's outstanding defensive player twice last year, against Tennessee and UAB. He had 14 tackles against Auburn.

Senior strong safety **Lionel Thomas** (6-0, 196), a converted linebacker, complements Clark well in the secondary. He had 71 tackles and broke up five tackles last year. He had 13 tackles against Auburn and nine against Mississippi State.

Senior **Robert Davis** (5-10, 184) started the last three regular-season games and the Peach Bowl at cornerback. He also saw considerable playing time in 1998 and '99.

Junior **Domanick Davis** (5-10, 207) quickly demonstrated his defensive skills when he moved from offense in the spring.

"I had never seen him play defense, but a lot of people told me what a good one he was in high school," Saban told the *Times-Picayune*. "I can see why, the way he moved around out there (in the spring). Some guys have ability but don't have instinct. Domanick has instinct. As a defensive back, you have to make judgments quickly, and it's hard to teach that."

Senior **Norman LeJeune** (6-0, 188), a valuable special teams player last year, might start at cornerback after making progress in the spring. Davis will be a backup corner and play the nickel back whenever the Tigers go to a five-man secondary.

PUNTERS

Sophomore **Donnie Jones** (6-3, 217) is the returning starter but averaged only 38.1 yards last year. He did manage to land 17 punts inside the 20-yard line. He had his best game against Kentucky, averaging 43 yards on four punts, including a season-long 69-yarder.

Jones was an all-state selection, averaging 43.4 yards as a senior at Catholic High School in Baton Rouge.

SPECIAL TEAMS

LSU's return game consists of Davis and more Davis. He averaged 23.8 yards on kickoff returns to rank third in the SEC and 25th nationally last year. He was also third in the SEC in punt returns with an 11-yard average. He achieved those numbers without breaking a run longer than 48 yards on a kickoff and 30 on a punt return.

RECRUITING CLASS

Saban proved at Michigan State he could recruit talented players. But he never recruited a class as roundly praised as this one.

"I don't care what anybody says, LSU's class this year rivals any from the SEC within memory," said Jamie Newberg of the Border Wars recruiting service.

Said longtime recruiting analyst Bill Buchalter of the *Orlando Sentinel*: "They have locked the walls around New Orleans and Baton Rouge, and that was the key."

LSU signed the top four players in the state, and the top player in the state last year, quarterback **Shyrone Carey** (5-8, 190), who signed with Tennessee but never enrolled. Carey played at Shaw High School in Marrero.

Saban didn't just capitalize on the recruiting riches of Louisiana. He scored significant victories elsewhere, particularly in Texas, where his signees included Hemphill's **Ben Wilkerson** (6-4, 265), rated as the No. 1 center in the country; Houston running back **Joe Addai**, a 6-0, 195-pounder who rushed for more than 500 yards in one game; and all-state wide receiver **Bennie Brazell** (6-2, 180), rated the No. 1 high school hurdler in the country.

The Tigers also signed highly rated players from California, Maryland, Florida and Alabama. Their 13 out-of-state signees marked the highest total since the 15 signed by Mike Archer in 1988.

David Jones (6-4, 240) was selected Mr. Football for the state of Maryland. The tight end had 30 catches for 480 yards as a tight end and had seven sacks on defense.

In Alabama, LSU picked up defensive end **Brandon Washington** (6-4, 275) from Tuscaloosa. Washington had 17 sacks and 30 quarterback hurries as a senior.

Tim Pope (6-2, 225) was rated the No. 2 linebacker in Florida by the *Florida Times-Union*. He had 115 tackles as a senior.

"We believe we have filled a lot of needs," Saban said. "We got quality big people, a few guys who are playmakers on defense and skill on offense. And we have a lot of speed in this class.

You can file Carey in the speed department.

"He's fun to watch," Saban told the *New Orleans Times-Picayune*. "He's short, but he's strong, and he has more power than he shows."

The Tigers might have further bolstered their offense with the signing of Parade All-Americans **Michael Clayton** (6-4, 210), a wide receiver, and **Marcus Spears** (6-2, 270), a tight end. Wilkerson (6-4, 275) is also a *Parade* All-American.

Clayton played wide receiver, quarterback and defensive back in high school. He was a first-team all-state selection in basketball. Spears (6-5, 280) caught 28 passes for 435 yards, rushed for 245 yards and had 22 tackles for losses and four fumble recoveries on defense. He was all-state as both a tight end and defensive end.

Junior college tackle **Torran Williams** (6-4, 295) of Dodge City (Kansas) and end **Marquise Hill** (6-7, 290) could provide immediate help on defense. Hill was a consensus All-American at De La Salle High School in New Orleans, where he had 92 tackles as a senior.

Recruiting good players to LSU isn't unusual. Former coach Gerry DiNardo also received rave reviews for a couple of his classes. And DiNardo's predecessor, Curley Hallman, had the No. 1-ranked class in the country in 1992. Unfortunately for DiNardo and Hallman, too many of their much-touted signees either didn't pan out or failed to qualify academically.

Twenty-three of Saban's 27 recruits had qualified academically by the time they signed.

BLUE RIBBON ANALYSIS

OFFENSE	A-
SPECIAL TEAMS	C-
DEFENSE	B
INTANGIBLES	B+

Based on last year's resurgence and the talent returning, LSU should be the consensus favorite to win the SEC West. But remember, this is LSU.

The Tigers consistently have done less with more than any other team in the conference. They have a tremendous recruiting base, rabid fans and storied Tiger Stadium. They also have a history of failure that belies their assets.

Since Charles McClendon was forced out as head coach in 1979, LSU has hired seven coaches. Of the seven hires, DiNardo lasted the longest—five years. Except for Curley Hallman, all those coaches had some success. They just couldn't sustain it.

At least Saban is off to a good start. His team rallied to win five of its last six games, and most of the key players return. Davey, Reed, Toefield and Royal give the Tigers plenty of playmakers on offense. The rest will be up to the offensive line, which has been wracked by injuries the last two years.

The Tigers are similar on defense. They have several All-SEC-caliber players who provide a strong nucleus. They just need more support from the complementary players.

LSU will have to overcome a scheduling disadvantage to win the West. Outside its division, LSU must play Tennessee and Florida. Worse yet, it has to play them on consecutive Saturdays.

Before LSU takes on the best of the East back-to-back, it has an opportunity to build momentum with three consecutive home games, followed by an open date before the Tennessee game. The schedule is also conducive for a strong finish. Three of the last four games are at home, and the Tigers have two weeks to get ready for Arkansas.

It's way too early to determine whether Saban is the long-term answer for a program that has repeatedly underachieved. But short-term, he has LSU in position for its first divisional championship.

(J.A.)

2000 RESULTS

Western Carolina	W	58-0	1-0
Houston	W	28-13	2-0
Auburn	L	17-34	2-1
UAB	L	10-13	2-2
Tennessee	W	38-31	3-2
Florida	L	9-41	3-3
Kentucky	W	34-0	4-3
Mississippi State	W	45-38	5-3
Alabama	W	30-28	6-3
Ole Miss	W	20-9	7-3
Arkansas	L	3-14	7-4
Georgia Tech (Peach)	W	28-14	8-4

Mississippi State

LOCATION Starkville, MS
CONFERENCE Southeastern (Western)
LAST SEASON 8-4 (.667)
CONFERENCE RECORD 4-4 (t-3rd)
OFFENSIVE STARTERS RETURNING 9
DEFENSIVE STARTERS RETURNING 5
NICKNAME Bulldogs
COLORS Maroon & White
HOME FIELD Scott Field (40,656)
HEAD COACH Jackie Sherrill (Alabama '66)
RECORD AT SCHOOL 67-48-2 (10 years)
CAREER RECORD 172-93-4 (23 years)
ASSISTANTS Jim Tompkins (Troy State '62)
Assistant Head Coach/Linebackers
Glenn Davis (Delta State '82)
Running Backs
Joe Lee Dunn (UT-Chattanooga '68)
Defensive Coordinator
Terry Lewis (Southern '70)
Offensive Tackles/Tight Ends
Carroll McCray (Gardner-Webb '83)
Centers/Guards
John Hendrick (Pittsburgh '81)
Defensive Line

Melvin Smith (Millsaps '82)
Secondary
Craig Stump (Texas A&M '87)
Wide Receivers
Sparky Woods (Carson-Newman '76)
Offensive Coordinator

TEAM WINS (last 5 yrs.) **8-10-8-7-5**
FINAL RANK (last 5 yrs.) **43-33-19-12-24**
2000 FINISH Beat Texas A&M in Indep. Bowl.

COACH AND PROGRAM

Mississippi State hadn't enjoyed back-to-back winning seasons in 10 years when athletic director Larry Templeton began the search for a head coach to replace Rockey Felker after the 1990 season.

"We had reached a point where we had to get a proven winner and a guy that would change the expectations of our fans," Templeton said.

Easily said.

But Templeton delivered. He hired Jackie Sherrill, who already had helped build championship programs at Texas A&M and Pittsburgh. Some critics cited Texas A&M's problems with the NCAA when Sherrill was the athletic director and head football coach. Others speculated Sherrill would merely use Mississippi State as a stepping stone to another job.

Yet 10 years later, only Florida's Steve Spurrier has more tenure among SEC football coaches. In the SEC West, Arkansas, Auburn and Ole Miss each have had four coaches since Sherrill was hired at Mississippi State. LSU and Alabama have had three apiece.

In a volatile division, Mississippi State has become Mr. Steady. The Bulldogs have averaged better than eight victories per season for the last four years and played in four consecutive bowl games.

This isn't the first time Mississippi State has succeeded by hiring a former Texas A&M coach. Emory Bellard led the Bulldogs to nine- and eight-win seasons in 1980-81, but he couldn't sustain the success. Sherrill's teams have been to seven bowls in 10 years.

Winning is nothing new for Sherrill, who won 50 games in five years at Pittsburgh and coached the Aggies to three consecutive conference championships. But his work at Mississippi State qualifies as his greatest accomplishment.

"When I was at Pittsburgh, we were winning a lot of games, but I wasn't a good coach," Sherrill said. "I got lucky at Pittsburgh and recruited some good players. "Here (at Mississippi State), I've been able to do something that hadn't been done."

Example: Mississippi State has had seven winning seasons in 10 years under Sherrill; it also had seven winning seasons in the previous 33 seasons.

Don't expect the Bulldogs to drop off this season. Never mind that they have lost more of their defense. They have reloaded by recruiting a number of junior college standouts. That's hardly a shocker.

No other coach in the SEC has capitalized on junior college recruits like Sherrill. Junior college recruits don't just sign with Mississippi State; they graduate, which Sherrill obviously uses as a selling point in recruiting.

"There are two schools in the country with the ability to make (junior college recruiting) work," Sherrill said. "Mississippi State and Kansas State. The difference is the ability to graduate them."

Sherrill's successful track record with junior college recruits predates his time at Mississippi State. In fact, he has been recruiting them since he was a graduate assistant at Alabama in 1967. He has expanded his junior college recruiting at Mississippi State, which benefits from having one of the most competitive junior college conferences in the country in its home state.

"We realized everybody else—Miami, Florida, Penn State—came in here and recruited junior college players awfully heavily," Sherrill said. "We knew more about those players. We also started placing a lot of junior college players (who didn't qualify academically out of high school). We were able to get those guys back."

Mississippi State's recruiting classes often turn out better than the recruiting services predict.

"There's two types of recruits," Sherrill said. "One is the alumni's recruit; the other is the player's recruit. Throughout my career, I've had the ability to pick the kid that's not a superstar that ends up being a superstar."

The Bulldogs' success on the field and in the draft backs Sherrill up. In the last three years 12 Mississippi State players have been drafted into the NFL.

Sherrill has recruited more than players. He also has put together an outstanding coaching staff that includes two former head coaches—Sparky Woods (offense) and Joe Lee Dunn (defense)—as coordinators.

"I love working for Jackie," said Woods, the former head coach at South Carolina. "He wants you to be sound and he wants to understand your plan of attack, but he's not a second-guesser. I also think he's a great player's coach. He really cares about his players."

Not only does Sherrill give his coordinators plenty of leeway, he lets his other assistants coach as well.

"He doesn't micromanage," secondary coach Melvin Smith said. "I'm not a traditional DB coach. He allows me to teach the way I need to."

2001 SCHEDULE

Sept.	1	Memphis
	15	Brigham Young
	22	South Carolina
	29	@Florida
Oct.	6	@Auburn
	13	Troy State
	20	LSU
Nov.	3	Kentucky
	10	@Alabama
	17	@Arkansas
	22	Mississippi

QUARTERBACKS

Sherrill has had outstanding players at almost every position in his 10 years at Mississippi State, but quarterback is one glaring exception. **Wayne Madkin** is trying to change that.

Madkin, a 6-4, 216-pound senior, returns for his fourth year as a starter. He improved significantly between his sophomore and junior seasons but still has a ways to go in the opinion of Woods.

"If he continues to work, he has the potential to be an all-conference player," Woods said. "I still think he misses some opportunities that are there. One of our goals for him is to not have any more throw away plays, where he discharges the ball because he didn't think anything was there. He needs to understand more clearly where all the eligible receivers are; what happens if the defense does such and such, where should I go now?"

His interception-touchdown pass ratio (eight of each) reflects that shortcoming. But as much as Madkin has already improved, who's to say he won't be even better as a senior?

He was plagued by inconsistency early in his career. In two games as a freshman, he was 7-of-19 passing. As a sophomore, Madkin went 5-of-18 with four interceptions against Oklahoma State. In Mississippi State's 10-2 season in 1999, backup quarterback Matt Wyatt—not Madkin—rallied the team for two of its come-from-behind victories. But last year, Madkin completed 56.1 percent of his passes for 1,908 yards. He also became a more effective runner, gaining 310 yards before you subtract what he lost in sacks.

Most of Madkin's rushing yards come when a defense gives him too much daylight. Although he's not particularly adept at breaking tackles, he has great speed for a quarterback.

Behind Madkin is sophomore **Kevin Fant** (6-2, 204), who gained experience last year as a backup, completing 18-of-34 passes for 210 yards. Although he's not as fast as Madkin, Fant has running ability.

"He has a great toughness about him," Woods said. "He's a real competitor. That gives him a chance. He has some fundamental things he needs to improve on. He has to protect the ball better."

If anything happens to Madkin or Fant, the Bulldogs would have to count on freshman **Kyle York** (6-2, 200) of Spring, Texas. York, who threw 31 touchdown passes as a senior, was rated as one of the top 100 prospects in Texas.

"It would be great if we could redshirt him," Woods said. "He's like Fant, a real bright kid that can throw the ball."

RUNNING BACKS

Senior **Dicenzo Miller** (5-10, 202) emerged as one of the best running backs in the SEC last season as a junior, averaging 6.3 yards per carry while gaining 1,005 yards. And he was the team's second-leading pass receiver with 24 catches for 344 yards.

"He has great acceleration," Woods said. "He's probably not as fast as **Dontae (Walker)** or **Justin (Griffith)** if you lined up and raced them. But like a lot of good backs, he's got another gear. And he has great balance. "

Those skills enable Miller to make the tough yards between the tackles and break big plays as well. He also has the ability to shift out of the backfield as a wide receiver.

Based on the Bulldogs' success last year, Miller will continue splitting time with Walker, a 5-10, 221-pound junior who began living up to his pre-college expectations last year after a somewhat disappointing freshman season during which he struggled to shake off an early-season ankle injury. Rated as the No. 1 high school running back in the country by several recruiting services, Walker gained 384 yards and returned four kickoffs for 76 yards in 1999. Not bad for a freshman but not nearly what he might have delivered on healthy legs. The ankle injury, which occurred in two-a-day workouts, continued to thwart him during the regular season.

Healthy as a sophomore, Walker averaged 5.4 yards per carry and rushed for 795 yards. He led the Bulldogs with a 26.7-yard average on 11 kickoff returns.

"I don't know anybody in the SEC who plays the whole year with one tailback," Woods said. "We'll keep playing both of them unless one steps way ahead of the other one."

Griffith (5-11, 221), a junior, has tailback experience and running ability, but the Bulldogs need him more at fullback, where he is the only experienced returnee. He has caught 56 passes the last two seasons and rushed for 332 yards.

Redshirt freshman **Darnell Jones** (5-11, 242), who is more of the prototypical I-formation fullback, could challenge Griffith for the starting position. Jones was ranked as the No. 4 fullback in the South by Pigskin Preps Recruiting. As a senior at Greenwood (Miss.) High School, he averaged 8.9 yards per carry and rushed for 1,054 yards and 17 touchdowns.

WIDE RECEIVERS/TIGHT ENDS

The Bulldogs have room for improvement. Junior **Terrell Grindle** (5-10, 177) had a team-leading 31 catches for 436 yards, an average of only 14.3 yards per reception; Larry Huntington, the team's next best wide receiver, has graduated.

"We've got about eight good athletes who can all run," Woods said. "Hopefully out of that group, a couple of them will emerge."

Grindle, senior **Harold Lindsey** (6-1, 211), and senior **Clarence Parker** (6-3, 203) would be the top three based on experience. Lindsey had 10 catches for 89 yards, and Parker caught eight for 143 yards. Darius Tubbs (6-2, 194) played sparingly and had one catch. Sophomore **Justin Jenkins** (6-1, 208) played just enough last year to show he has big-play potential. He caught seven passes for 160 yards (a 22.9-yard average) and rushed six times for 46 yards. An outstanding spring moved him into the starting lineup.

Help is on the way from several promising redshirt freshmen: **Antonio Hargro** (6-4, 185), **Ray Ray Bivines** (6-0, 165) and **McKinley Scott** (6-2, 185).

Hargro, who is also an outstanding track athlete, might have played last year if he hadn't suffered an ankle injury. A former first-team all-stater at Gautier (Miss.) High School, he was ranked as the No. 4 receiver in the Southeast by *Prep Star.*

Bivines, who was the star quarterback on Hargro's high school team, was a first-team all-stater as a quarterback and kick returner. With his strong arm and game-breaking ability as a runner, Bivines could help the Bulldogs at quarterback in a pinch.

"He doesn't have (sprinter) speed like Hargro, but he's fast and can change directions," Woods said. "We'd like him to be a kick and punt return guy, too."

Scott, another first-team all-stater, averaged 24.9 yards on 28 catches as a high school senior in Tunica, Miss.

"Scott is another big receiver like Hargro," Woods said. "He's tough and smart. I think he's going to be a good player."

Junior **Donald Lee** (6-4, 248) is another solid tight end for the Bulldogs, who have put two tight ends—Reginald Kelly and Kendell Watkins—in the NFL under Sherrill. Lee caught 19 passes for 204 yards last season.

The Bulldogs are more concerned about developing another tight end. Lee's backup, sophomore Aaron Lumpkin (6-4, 253), needs to gain strength and improve his blocking.

OFFENSIVE LINE

You needed a scorecard to keep track of all the comings and goings in the offensive line during the spring.

The biggest change was at the top. Offensive line coach Jerry Fremin retired for health reasons; Sherrill promptly hired two assistants to replace him, then moved tight ends coach David Wilson to recruiting coordinator full-time. Wilson served as both a coordinator and on-the-field coach last season.

The new line coaches are Carroll McCray (guards and centers) and Terry Lewis (tackles and tight ends).

The next big change was at center, where the Bulldogs needed to find a replacement for Michael Fair. Midway through spring practice, they moved starting guard **Tommy Watson**, a 6-4, 303-pound senior, to center. Watson will be backed up by junior **Kevin Sijansky** (6-2, 278) and sophomore **Blake Jones** (6-4, 283).

Watson, who combines good technique with great effort, is the likely leader of this line whether he's at center or guard. He and fellow junior college transfer **Courtney Lee** (6-4, 346) stepped right in and filled two starting positions when they arrived on campus last year. Lee, who runs well for his size, returns as a starter for his senior season.

With Watson moving to center, that created an opening at guard. Freshman **Brad Weathers** (6-5, 320), sophomore **Donald Tucker** (6-4, 321), or junior college signee **Michael Allen** (6-3, 340) of Northwest Mississippi Community College should be able to fill the vacancy.

Weathers, 20, joined the Bulldogs after serving a two-year Mormon mission. Tucker has experience as a backup at guard and tackle. Recruiting analyst Max Emfinger ranked Allen as the third-best junior college lineman; J.C.

Gridwire made him a second-team All-American. **At the end of April, it was still a question whether Allen would be academically eligible to join the Bulldogs in the fall.**

The Bulldogs also signed center **Chris McNeil** (6-4, 280) of Petal, Miss. He was rated as one of the top five centers in the country by *USA Today.com.*

"I would hate to think he would be the guy," Woods said of McNeil. "That's not fair to put a freshman in that situation."

Sherrill isn't so sure about that. With a need for more depth in the line, he doesn't believe the Bulldogs can afford to redshirt McNeil.

When Floyd "Pork Chop" Womack was injured last season, sophomore **Derrick Thompson** (6-6, 304) stepped in for the All-SEC tackle and played well. He and returning starter **Kenric Fairchild**, a 6-foot-4, 318-pound senior, give the Bulldogs two experienced tackles.

Junior **Carl Hutchins** (6-5, 306) has experience as a backup tackle. Junior **Kyle Wallace** (6-5, 326), a first-team all-stater in high school, was the first backup at both guard positions last year.

Sophomore **Eric Thompson** (6-6, 334), Derrick's twin brother, should compete for playing time after suffering a knee injury last year. Redshirt freshman **David Stewart** (6-7, 285), a first-team Alabama all-stater in high school, is another possibility.

"Our deal here is kind of like receiver," Woods said. "We've got some people who can help us if they develop."

2000 STATISTICS

Rushing offense	193.8	25
Passing offense	192.5	78
Total offense	386.4	46
Scoring offense	31.5	25
Net Punting	38.0	12
Punt returns	9.9	48
Kickoff returns	21.5	21
Rushing defense	97.5	13
Passing efficiency defense	105.9	26
Total defense	339.5	36
Scoring defense	24.1	53
Turnover margin	+9	17

Last column is ranking among Division I-A teams.

KICKERS

Mississippi State will miss Scott Westerfield, though not as much as it might have anticipated after his junior season in 1999. Westerfield, another junior college success story, hit on 18-of-24 field-goal attempts—including two game-winners—in 1999. Last year, he was 12-for-18 but missed four between 30 and 40 yards.

Westerfield's likely successor is sophomore **John Michael Marlin**, a 5-8, 155-pounder. He handled the kickoff chores last year while backing up Westerfield on field goals. Thirteen of his 59 kickoffs resulted in touchbacks.

Marlin was a second-team, all-state kicker at Tupelo (Miss.) High School in 1999. He made 16-of-34 field-goal attempts his last two seasons in high school. Marlin hit 50- and 51-yard field-goal attempts as a junior and had a 54-yarder wiped out by a penalty as a senior.

DEFENSIVE LINE

Two years ago, when Mississippi State led the nation in defense, Dunn rotated eight to 10 linemen with little drop off in quality. Those days are long gone.

When the Bulldogs began spring practice, Dunn said, "Most of the guys we've got are not big enough to play and win in the SEC. I'd just play one defensive line if we started tomorrow."

Tackle **Dorsett Davis**, a 6-6, 314-pound senior, is the only sure thing on the defensive front. Davis figured prominently in the Bulldogs' No. 1-ranked defense in 1999 and continued to improve last season.

"He probably should be better than any (defensive linemen) we've had if he improves as much as he already has," Dunn said. "He's huge, can run and is very physical."

Davis, Toby Golliday, Willie Blade and Ellis Wyms gave the Bulldogs a stout defensive front last season. But unlike 1999, there wasn't as much bench support. Now, Dunn is even uncertain about his starters.

Redshirt freshman **Demotto Youngblood** (6-4, 240) worked as the No. 1 nose guard in the spring. Sophomore **Lenny Day** (6-3, 248) played sparingly last year as a backup. Sophomore **Ifem Ezekwe** (6-3, 265) was listed as a third-string tackle last season.

"There are so many unproven players. If we don't get help from guys coming in, we're going to have our work cut out for us," Dunn said. "I think the guys coming in will help."

The Bulldogs added five defensive linemen.

Freshman **Ronald Fields** (6-3, 293) originally signed with the Bulldogs last year, then enrolled at Hargrave (Va.) Military Academy. He had 97 tackles as a high school senior in Bogalusa, La.

Junior **Kahlil Nash** (6-4, 265) was a first-team NJCAA All-American at Arizona Western College. Nash, who signed with Ole Miss out of high school but never enrolled, also played at Milford (Conn.) Academy.

Juniors **Michael Oyefesobi** (6-4, 285) and **Dannie Snyder** (6-3, 285) were teammates of Nash's at Arizona Western College. At Miramar (Fla.) High School, Oyefesobi was a 230-pound tight end. Snyder was a second-team All-Arizona Junior College selection last year.

Sophomore **Tommy Kelly** (6-6, 280) will have three years of eligibility after transferring from Hinds (Miss.) Community College. Although he played only one year of high school football, he was a second-team all-state selection as a defensive lineman his senior year at Provine High School in Jackson, Miss.

LINEBACKERS

All-SEC middle linebacker **Mario Haggan**, a 6-3, 243-pound junior, and senior **Conner Stephens** (6-4, 250) make this the strength of the Bulldogs' defense.

Haggan, who moved from the outside to inside

last year, made 132 tackles, the most by a Bulldog in four years. He led the SEC in tackles with an average of 12 per game and made second-team All-American. He still didn't satisfy Dunn.

"He's got to be a little more consistent," Dunn said. "He played good early in the year but didn't play as good in the middle of the year."

Dunn now second-guesses a decision to have a different position coach work with Haggan during the course of the season.

"We thought a change might help," Dunn said. "But it took (Haggan) a while to get acclimated."

Dunn also expects more from Stephens this season.

"If he would ever wake up and reach his potential, he probably would be as good as anybody in the country," Dunn said. "He's a little bit on the lazy side. I'm hoping he wakes up. He can run like a deer and is big and strong."

Senior **Dwayne Robertson** (6-0, 219) is the leading candidate to start at the other outside linebacker spot. A former junior college All-American, Robertson is credited with running a 4.5 40. Robertson was redshirted in 1999 after suffering an elbow injury. He played as a backup last year.

Behind the starters are sophomore **Jason Clark** (6-2, 236) at middle linebacker and junior **Ivan Billie** (6-2, 233) and freshman **Robert Spivey** (6-3, 220) at outside linebacker. Clark, who was one of the top high school recruits in Mississippi in 2000, played last year as a backup. So did Billie, another former blue-chip recruit from Mississippi. Spivey, who was redshirted last year, was an all-state defensive end at Clarksdale, Miss., as a high school senior.

"We'll be real deep at linebacker," Dunn said. "We've got two guys from junior college who will help."

Corey Brown (6-1, 225) and **Kamau Jackson** (6-1, 238) were the marquee linebacker signees. Brown, who is credited with a 4.5 40, was a consensus junior college All-American at Butler (Kansas) Community College. He helped lead his Jacksonville Raines High School team to the Florida 4A state championship. Jackson was a first-team NJCAA All-American at Copiah-Lincoln (Miss.) Community College, where he had 135 tackles in nine games last year despite playing with a torn anterior-cruciate ligament in his knee.

Brandon Downing (6-2, 225), another linebacker recruit, was a first-team all-state selection at Clarksdale (Miss.) High School.

DEFENSIVE BACKS

The Bulldogs lost three of their five starters, including All-America cornerback Fred Smoot and underrated safety Eugene Clinton. That doesn't mean they won't field another strong secondary.

"I anticipate it being as good as it's ever been," said Smith, who is building an impressive resumé as a defensive backfield coach.

All-SEC senior safety **Pig Prather** (6-3, 191) already has established himself as a playmaker. The defense took a huge hit when he suffered a season-ending knee injury in the second quarter of the Arkansas game.

"We probably win the Arkansas game and the Mississippi game (with Prather)," Smith said. "He was as important to our defense as anybody. He can cover anybody and tackle anybody. He's as good as any (defensive back) we've had, probably a combination of Ashley Cooper, Tim Nelson, Fred Smoot and Eric Brown."

Prather, who had 11 tackles for losses and five sacks last year, didn't participate in spring practice but was expected to be at full speed for the beginning of preseason workouts.

Junior **Josh Morgan** (6-1, 188), a returning starter at free safety, played much of last season with an injured shoulder, but still finished second on the team with 95 tackles. Morgan underwent postseason surgery to repair his shoulder, which was first injured in the last game of the 1998 season.

"Josh basically played the whole season with one arm," Smith said. "He struggled in the middle of the year against some really good players. Our goal for him this year is to make All-SEC."

Junior **Shawn Byrdsong** (5-9, 188), a former cornerback, is a likely starter at the other safety position. He became a starter late in the 2000 season because of injuries and finished with two interceptions and 38 tackles.

Senior **Anthony Bryant** (5-10, 191), a special-teams standout, should be a factor. Also, the Bulldogs have redshirt freshmen **Gabriel Wallace** (6-0, 185) and **Slovakia Griffith** (5-11, 180) for secondary depth. Both were first-team all-staters in high school.

The Bulldogs have to replace both cornerbacks. Given their track record, that might not be as tough as it sounds. The Bulldogs have a history of delving into the junior college ranks and coming up with the likes of Smoot and Robert Bean.

"We signed six DBs," Smith said. "I call them a fleet. They're as good as we've ever signed."

Demetric Wright (6-0, 180) of Northwest Mississippi Community College was one of the most celebrated signees, partially because of his position and partially because of his personality. That combination has fostered comparisons to All-America cornerback Smoot.

"I can see it and I'm cool with (the comparison)," Wright told the Jackson Clarion-Ledger after signing with the Bulldogs. "We play the same in a lot of situations on film. We're both aggressive, we both like to run our mouths and we both love to play the game.

"I respect him. We're kind of close. And we've got the same mentality in a lot of ways."

Both Wright and Smoot were junior college All-Americans, Wright at Northwest Mississippi and Smoot at Hinds. Wright was No. 9 on this year's top 25 junior college recruits list; Smoot was No. 8 on the 1999 list.

Sherrill signed two other junior college defensive backs who were ranked in the top seven nationally. **Korey Banks** (5-11, 172) of Garden City (Kansas) Community College signed in December and went through spring practice, where he excelled.

"There's no question Demetric was the best at his spot in the state," said Sherrill, who said the defensive side of his class was the best he has ever signed.

Smith puts Banks in the same class. "I think he's special," Smith said. "He reminds me of the bunch that just left—Smoot and Bean."

Smith also thinks senior **Marco Minor** (6-4, 205) could be in the same category if he puts his mind to it. Minor played sparingly until injuries forced him into the starting lineup for the Independence Bowl, where his fourth-quarter interception set up a game-tying touchdown.

"He's got enough tools to do whatever he wants to," Smith said. "He played receiver in junior college. I think he came in here still thinking he might be a receiver."

PUNTERS

Jared Cook, a 5-10, 185-pound redshirt freshman, will replace Prentiss Cole, who averaged 41.3 yards in his only season as the No. 1 punter.

Cook had an outstanding career at Jordan High School in Columbus, Ga. He averaged 45.6 yards per punt as a senior and 43.4 yards as a junior. He made all state both seasons.

Cook is a good all-around athlete. He was a three-year starter at quarterback and batted .462 in baseball his junior season.

SPECIAL TEAMS

Mississippi State's return game might not be much different from its running game. It's Miller and Walker.

Walker averaged 26.7 yards on 11 kickoff returns last year. Miller averaged 7.8 yards on 13 punt returns.

Bivines also could contribute as both a kick and punt returner.

RECRUITING CLASS

The Bulldogs' heralded recruiting class was marred by tragedy. Defensive tackle Paul Broussard was murdered in Baker, La., last March. Broussard was ranked as the top junior college defensive tackle in the country by Rivals.com and one of the top 50 prospects in Texas his senior year at LaPorte.

Broussard was one of 11 junior college signees, and most of them play defense.

Wright and Banks aren't the only defensive back prospects. The "fleet" also includes **Richard Ball** (5-11, 185), a first-team, All-Jayhawk Conference player at Fort Scott (Kansas) Community College, and **Walter Burdett** (6-1, 215), who played cornerback and safety at Middle Georgia Community College after starring as a high school running back in Atlanta.

A couple of freshman recruits—**Clarence McDougal** (6-1, 205) and **Rico Bennett** (6-1, 190)—also could contend for playing time in the secondary.

McDougal is an exceptional all-around athlete who already is being compared to Prather. After starting last season at wide receiver, he switched to running back to help his Clinton, Miss., team and rushed for 1,400 yards while averaging 8.0 yards per carry. Bennett, who is credited with a 4.47 40, was listed as one of the top five prospects in the state by *Jeff Whitaker's Deep South Football Recruiting Guide*. Bennett was a first-team all-state cornerback.

Coco Hodge (6-1, 235) of Clinton, Miss., figures in the Bulldogs' future fullback plans. Rated as one of the top 12 prospects in the state, Hodge rushed for more than 1,000 yards despite suffering a broken leg at mid-season as a senior. He's credited with a 405-pound bench press and a 4.6 40.

Jeff Billings (6-2, 250) is another fullback prospect. He was a two-time All-Central Texas selection at Rayburn High School in Pasadena, Texas. A powerful blocker, Billings also excelled at linebacker in high school.

Allen and McNeil weren't the only offensive line signees. **Johnny Wadley** (6-4, 345) was a first-team all-stater at Hernando (Miss.) High School. **Avery House** (6-5, 285) was an all-state selection as a junior and senior at Springville (Ala.) High School. *SuperPrep* ranked him as the No. 14 prospect in Alabama.

BLUE RIBBON ANALYSIS

OFFENSE	B
SPECIAL TEAMS	C
DEFENSE	B
INTANGIBLES	B+

You know what to expect from the Bulldogs under Sherrill and his staff. The Bulldogs will gamble more on defense than offense and will field big, physical lines on both sides of the ball.

You also know they will be tough to beat at home. The Bulldogs have gone 16-1 their last three years at Scott Field, and they will play seven home games in 2001.

And one more thing: You know better than to judge them by how many starters they lost.

The Bulldogs suffer key losses, yet continue winning. For example, take last year. The Bulldogs returned only three starters on defense and five on offense from a 10-win team. They responded by winning eight games, despite losing key players to injury.

They will continue that success, especially if their junior college recruits come through on defense. After all, the Bulldogs already have a great defensive nucleus with Haggan, Stephens, Prather, Davis and Morgan. Keeping those guys healthy will be crucial.

Breaking in two new cornerbacks isn't as scary as it sounds, even though the Bulldogs will have to cope with Spurrier's high-flying passing game in The Swamp. There's nothing complicated about the Bulldogs' defense if you're a cornerback. You play man to man.

The Bulldogs will be better offensively if they can continue to run the ball as they did last year, plus expand their passing game. Madkin gives them the most experienced quarterback in the SEC; Miller and Walker will provide a great one-two punch at running back; the influx of new receivers is promising. The rest will be up to an offensive line that will have two new starters.

The Bulldogs have won 26 games, including two bowls, the last two years. They've become accustomed to winning.

So don't make too much of last year's attrition. The Bulldogs should battle LSU for the SEC West championship.

(J.A.)

2000 RESULTS

Memphis	W	17-3	1-0
Brigham Young	W	44-28	2-0
South Carolina	L	19-23	2-1
Florida	W	47-35	3-1
Auburn	W	17-10	4-1
LSU	L	38-45	4-2
Middle Tennessee	W	61-35	5-2
Kentucky	W	35-17	6-2
Alabama	W	29-7	7-2
Arkansas	L	10-17	7-3
Mississippi	L	30-45	7-4
Texas A&M (Independence)	W	43-41	8-4

Ole Miss

LOCATION Oxford, MS
CONFERENCE Southeastern (Western)
LAST SEASON 7-5 (.583)
CONFERENCE RECORD 4-4 (3rd)
OFFENSIVE STARTERS RETURNING 6
DEFENSIVE STARTERS RETURNING 5
NICKNAME Rebels
COLORS Cardinal Red & Navy Blue
HOME FIELD Vaught-Hemingway/ Hollingsworth Field (50,577)
HEAD COACH David Cutcliffe (Alabama '76)
RECORD AT SCHOOL 16-9 (2 years)
CAREER RECORD 16-9 (2 years)
ASSISTANTS Richard Bisacci (Yankton '86)
Assistant Head Coach/Running Backs
Marion Hobby (Tennessee '89)
Defensive Ends
John Latina (Virginia Tech '79)
Offensive Coordinator/Offensive Line
Don Lindsey (Arkansas-Monticello '65)
Defensive Coordinator/Linebackers
Mike MacIntyre (Georgia Tech '89)
Defensive Backs/Recruiting Coordinator
Ron Middleton (Auburn '85)
Tight Ends
Rick Petri (Missouri-Rolla '76)
Defensive Tackles
Kurt Roper (Rice '95)
Quarterbacks
T.D. Woods (Tennessee '90)
Receivers
TEAM WINS (last 5 yrs.) 5-8-7-8-7
FINAL RANK (last 5 yrs.) 52-28-31-24-42
2000 FINISH Lost to West Virginia in Music City Bowl.

COACH AND PROGRAM

It's amazing that West Virginia led Ole Miss, 49-9, before the end of the third quarter in last year's Music City Bowl. It's more amazing that Ole Miss fans can smile at the memory.

The last quarter of a dreadful game marked the beginning of a new era in Ole Miss Football. Call it "Manning II."

With Ole Miss trailing by 40 points, redshirt freshman quarterback **Eli Manning** came off the bench to complete 12-of-20 passes for 167 yards and three touchdowns. By game's end, Ole Miss fans were already looking forward to 2001.

Archie made the Manning name famous at Ole Miss more than 30 years ago. He was a two-time first-team All-American, a first-round NFL draft pick and an all-pro with the New Orleans Saints. He was arguably the most exciting player in the storied history of SEC football.

Ole Miss didn't win an SEC championship with Manning at quarterback, but it often played like a champion, repeatedly upsetting superior teams. Eli revived the magic with the fourth-quarter comeback against West Virginia.

Eli can't scramble like his father. But his passing and poise remind Manning followers of his older brother Peyton, the former Tennessee All-American now starring with the Indianapolis Colts in the NFL.

In the midst of the Manning hoopla is coach David Cutcliffe, Peyton's quarterback coach and offensive coordinator. Peyton thrived under Cutcliffe; Eli is apt to do the same.

When you consider what Archie did for Ole Miss and what the Cutcliffe-Manning combination did for Tennessee, you can understand the Rebels' optimism. Cutcliffe has picked up where former Ole Miss coach Tommy Tuberville left off before taking the head-coaching job at Auburn. The Rebels won eight and seven games in Tuberville's last two years as head coach, then matched that in the first two years under Cutcliffe.

Bottom line: Ole Miss has had four consecutive winning seasons for the first time since 1968-71.

No one questions Cutcliffe's football savvy. In addition to Peyton, Cutcliffe developed quarterback Heath Shuler into a first-round draft pick after only three years. He also helped the Vols win a national championship in Tee Martin's first year as a starting quarterback.

Cutcliffe might have gotten a head-coaching job sooner if not for his low-key personality. He refrained from self-promotion while his Tennessee offenses were piling up huge numbers. While Cutcliffe received high marks for coaching, you couldn't help but wonder if he could handle the other aspects of a head-coaching job in one of college football's most competitive conferences. He was a major player in the recruitment of a number of big-time college prospects at Tennessee, but that was at an established national power. Ole Miss would be a tougher sell.

Moreover, he would be compared to Tuberville, a super salesman who quickly upgraded Ole Miss' level of talent.

So far, so good. Five members of Cutcliffe's 2000 recruiting class are expected to start this season; the 2001 class is even better, according to recruiting services.

Cutcliffe's biggest challenge is improving the defense, especially against the run. Perhaps the hiring of Don Lindsey will help. Lindsey, who began his coaching career under Bear Bryant, joined Ole Miss after spending the last two years as the defensive coordinator with the British Columbia Lions of the Canadian Football League.

2001 SCHEDULE

Sept.	1	Murray State
	8	@Auburn
	15	Vanderbilt
	29	@Kentucky
Oct.	6	@Arkansas State
	13	Alabama
	20	Middle Tennessee
	27	@LSU
Nov.	3	Arkansas
	17	Georgia
	22	@Mississippi State

QUARTERBACKS

Manning (6-4, 205) made the most of his first spring as the No. 1 quarterback. Taking twice as many snaps as last spring, he improved significantly.

"He was more in tune with what we were doing," Cutcliffe said. "He was good with his decision-making. He really improved in a lot of ways.

"Athletically, he was a different guy—stronger and quicker. He's got a very strong arm and a quick release. He's got a great deep ball. He can lay the ball in (a receiver's hands) well down the field. He can throw the deep comebacks, the crossing routes."

In other words, by the time Eli starts his first game, he's apt to be one of the best quarterbacks in the league. He showed what he could do in the bowl game. He showed it again in the spring game when he threw for four touchdowns.

"The thing about Eli, he didn't waste any time," Cutcliffe said. "He has made every practice count."

Cutcliffe still sees room for improvement, but it's more fine-tuning than anything else.

"He's got to continue to work on his accuracy," Cutcliffe said. "When I say accuracy, I'm talking about pinpoint accuracy."

Junior **David Morris** (6-1, 181) was the only other scholarship quarterback on the Rebels' spring roster. He backed up Romaro Miller in 1998 and 1999 and was redshirted last year. When Miller was injured in 1998, Morris started the final regular-season game against Mississippi State's heralded defense, completing 11-of-28 passes and throwing three interceptions.

Morris, who passed for 1,750 yards as a senior in Mobile, Ala., was bothered by arm and back injuries his first two years but made progress the last two springs.

Cutcliffe believes he signed a couple of capable quarterbacks in **Seth Smith** and **Michael Spurlock**.

"I'm really excited about them," Cutcliffe said. "Both are very athletic with extremely strong arms. We had them both in camp, so we know a lot about them."

Spurlock (5-11, 190) of Indianola, Miss., was a second-team all-state quarterback and first-team all-state punter. Spurlock set 5A state records of 3,348 yards passing and 35 touchdown passes as a senior. He also rushed for 1,161 yards and scored 10 touchdowns. He's expected to play baseball as well as football at Ole Miss.

Spurlock had a couple of incredible games as a senior. Against Ruleville Central, he passed for 544 yards and nine touchdowns and rushed for 146 yards. Against Jackson Murrah, he passed for 457 yards, ran for 157, kicked a 42-yard field goal and had a 61-yard punt.

Smith (6-3, 190), of Hillcrest Christian in Jackson, is also expected to play baseball at Ole Miss. He completed 121-of-206 passes for 1,950 yards and 21 touchdowns as a senior. He passed for 56 touchdowns in his high school career.

"We've got two quarterbacks coming in who are outstanding players," Cutcliffe said.

RUNNING BACKS

Senior **Joe Gunn** (5-10, 200) has been overshadowed much of his career by Deuce McAllister, yet he still ranks fifth all-time on Ole Miss' career rushing list.

Bothered by injuries last year, Gunn rushed for 382 yards on 125 carries. The year before, he gained 951 yards and averaged 5.2 yards per carry.

"He was back healthy in the spring," Cutcliffe said. "He had the kind of spring I hoped he would have.

Gunn, who is also a receiving threat out of the backfield, arrived at Ole Miss after an illustrious high school career in Amory, Miss. As a senior, he set a state rushing record by gaining 2,608 yards on 244 carries. He averaged 10.7 yards per carry and scored 28 touchdowns.

"He's a power-packed runner," Cutcliffe said. "He's a 400-pound-plus bench presser."

A couple of juniors, **Robert Williams** (5-10, 180) and **Tremaine Turner** (5-10, 197), will back up Gunn. Williams, a former Alabama all-stater, rushed for 161 yards the last two years as a backup. He had touchdown runs of 31 and 33 yards. Turner, who has 69 rushing yards in his career, played even less.

Cutcliffe has high hopes for Williams.

"Robert has definitely improved his quickness," Cutcliffe said after the spring game. "He is faster, stronger and in really good shape. He is an explosive player who can do a lot of things for us. He has really good hands. He can get us the tough yards, and his added strength has made a significant difference for him."

Senior **Charles Stackhouse** (6-2, 240) gives Ole Miss a solid blocker and receiver at fullback. He rushed for 182 yards on 37 carries (a 4.9-yard average) and caught 11 passes for 88 yards last year despite playing with an injured left knee, which has since been surgically repaired.

"He's big and fast and can do a lot of things," Cutcliffe said. "He will be instrumental in our passing game."

Cutcliffe likens Stackhouse to Shawn Bryson, who played for Cutcliffe at Tennessee and now plays for the Buffalo Bills.

Junior **Toward Sanford** (5-10, 217) and redshirt freshman **Rick Razzano** (5-11, 230) will also contribute at fullback. Sanford, a former Mississippi all-stater, has rushed for 167 yards in his career and caught 12 passes for 147 yards. Razzano, a second-team all-stater from Milford, Ohio, was redshirted last year.

"Toward was our most improved offensive player in the spring," Cutcliffe said. "He's a very talented player."

WIDE RECEIVERS/TIGHT ENDS

"Speed" is the key word here. Cutcliffe believes he has assembled a cast of receivers with comparable speed to the ones he had at Tennessee.

"This is the fastest group we've had by far (at Ole Miss)," Cutcliffe said. "We're faster and more physical."

The fastest of the bunch is sophomore **Chris Collins** (6-1, 190), who set the Mississippi high school record when he ran a 21.90 200 meters at Amite County High School in Liberty, Miss. He had 12 catches for 168 yards and added 74 yards on four kickoff returns as a freshman.

"Chris Collins has electrifying speed," Cutcliffe said.

Collins earned a starting position in the spring opposite former junior college transfer **Omar Rayford**, a 6-1, 198-pound senior. Rayford, who had 66 catches his last year at Northwest Community College, finished strong last year.

"He had 26 catches in the last six games, counting the bowl game," Cutcliffe said. "And he had a great spring."

Redshirt freshmen **Bill Flowers** (6-0, 180) and **Trey Fryfogle** (6-1, 185) also performed well in the spring, further encouraging Cutcliffe about his wide-receiving corps.

Flowers is the son of Richmond Flowers, who was a star wide receiver and All-America hurdler at the University of Tennessee. Like his father, Bill is an accomplished hurdler. He won the state championship in the 300-meter hurdles and the 55-meter high hurdles at Pelham (Ala.) High School. He also made a name for himself as a pass receiver, catching a state-record 174 passes in his career. As a senior, he had 75 receptions. He was honored as the Gatorade Athlete of the Year in Alabama.

Fryfogle also starred in football and track in high school, in Lucedale, Miss. Fryfogle ran the 100 meters in 10.79 and finished second in the state with a 49.4 clocking in the 400 meters. He was a member of the *Clarion-Ledger*'s Dandy Dozen after catching 77 passes his last two seasons.

The Rebels might get a boost from their incoming freshmen. Wide receiver Mike Espy (6-0, 180) was rated as the No. 2 prospect in the state by *SuperPrep*, which ranked him as the No. 6 wide receiver prospect in the country. The two-time all-stater caught 114 passes and scored 31 touchdowns in his high school career.

The Rebels signed three other promising wide receiver prospects: **Jason Armstead** (5-9, 160), **RaTavious Biddle** (6-1, 180) and **Mario Hill** (6-1, 200). Armstead, one of three junior college signees, played wide receiver and quarterback at Gulf Coast (Fla.) Community College.

"We have to get it done on the field, but there's no doubt we've upgraded our speed at receiver," Cutcliffe said. "This group should be outstanding."

Junior **Doug Zeigler** (6-4, 250) is a returning starter at tight end. He had 15 catches for 173 yards last year. Zeigler, who was switched from quarterback to tight end after joining the Rebels, passed for more than 3,000 yards at Wilmington (Ohio) High School.

Zeigler will be backed up by senior **Mitch Skrmetta** (6-4, 250) and sophomore **Eric Rice** (6-3, 220). Skrmetta has played in 22 games as a backup the last two years.

OFFENSIVE LINE

Senior **Terrence Metcalf** (6-3, 305), a preseason All-American, returns to anchor a line that returns three other starters—senior guard **Matt Koon** (6-4, 297), junior center **Ben Claxton** (6-3, 281) and junior tackle **Belton Johnson** (6-5, 290).

Metcalf, who was a first-team All-SEC tackle last year, began his college career at guard. The former *Parade* All-American started 12 games as a freshman.

He was given a medical redshirt in 1998 after suffering a season-ending ankle injury in the third game. In 1999, he returned to earn second-team All-America honors.

Metcalf, who has exceptional speed for his size, was switched from guard to tackle in the spring of 2000 and thrived at the new position. The Rebels gave up only seven sacks, the fewest in the SEC.

Like Metcalf, Claxton has been thwarted by injuries. He suffered a fractured ankle in the season opener against Tulane and missed four games. Until then, he had made 13 consecutive starts, including 12 in 1999 when he made *The Sporting News'* Freshman All-America team.

"He can be one of the better centers in this league," Cutcliffe said. "He had the kind of spring we had hoped for."

With Claxton healthy, Koon returns to guard. He started six games at center last season after Claxton's injury. Koon played the previous two seasons as a backup. Koon's strength is his versatility. He has played several line positions and tight end.

Johnson started every regular-season game after coming back from a serious injury. He suffered a fracture of the lower left leg and ankle during the first week of spring practice. He underwent ankle surgery and returned to win a starting job in preseason.

Junior **German Bello** (6-2, 307) was the leading candidate to win the other starting job. He will be pushed at left guard by redshirt freshman **Doug Buckles** (6-4, 285). Bello played in 18 games, including one as a starter, the last two years. Buckles has a glossy resume from his days at Madison (Miss.) Central High School. He started 43 consecutive games and was rated as the No. 1 college prospect in the state by the *Clarion-Ledger*. He also made several All-America lists.

The Rebels have little experience behind their starters. Sophomore center **Justin Sawyer** (6-3, 288) played in 10 games last year as a backup. Freshman **Cliff Woodruff** (6-6, 284), who was redshirted last year, will back up Metcalf. **James Campbell** (6-5, 290), another redshirt freshman, is behind Johnson at the other tackle slot. Redshirt freshman **Marcus Johnson** (6-6, 330) is behind Koon at right guard.

2000 STATISTICS

Rushing offense	146.8	58
Passing offense	200.2	68
Total offense	347.0	74
Scoring offense	28.5	43
Net Punting	35.0	45
Punt returns	11.9	30
Kickoff returns	18.6	83
Rushing defense	178.3	80
Passing efficiency defense	96.2	9
Total defense	365.9	59
Scoring defense	25.5	60
Turnover margin	+7	23

Last column is ranking among Division I-A teams.

KICKERS

Sophomore **Lee Rogers** and freshman **Jonathan Nichols** will vie for the place-kicking job after the loss of Les Binkley.

"They are two talented youngsters and hit the

ball very well (in the spring)," Cutcliffe said. "They probably have more range than what we had with Les, but their challenge is being able to show and display that consistency that Les did."

Rogers (5-11, 175) made 9-of-12 field-goal attempts at Lamar High School in Meridian, Miss. Nichols (6-0, 185), who was redshirted last year, was a first-team all-stater at Pillow Academy in Greenwood, Miss. He made 98-of-100 extra points and 27-of-42 field goals in high school.

DEFENSIVE LINE

A defense that gave up 4.6 yards rushing per carry last year is an obvious concern, and it starts with the front line, which is the smallest and one of the least experienced in the SEC.

Senior tackle **Anthony Sims** (6-3, 268) is the only returning starter. The rest of the front four—senior tackle **Kenny Jackson** (6-3, 315) and sophomore ends **Charlie Anderson** (6-4, 225) and **Josh Cooper** (6-4, 230)—doesn't have a single start.

"I felt (Anthony) had a good spring," Lindsey said. "Anthony Sims gets as much out of his weight and size as he could. He's a fine technician and plays hard.

"(Anderson and Cooper) are young players who have played very little. They're just not very experienced football players. But I feel they're potentially good players."

Cooper had 16 tackles and led the team with nine quarterback hurries in limited playing time last year. Anderson played even less. Together, they will form the smallest defensive end tandem in the SEC.

"Gaining weight and strength is one of the priorities for the defense, period," Lindsey said. "I looked at the other defenses in the division last year. We were by far the lightest."

Jackson is the exception. The transfer from Hinds County College needs to lose weight; Lindsey wants him to drop about 25 pounds for next season.

"At his weight, he doesn't have any endurance," Lindsey said. "Some people can carry 300 pounds. He's not a 315-pound body type."

The Rebels have even less experience on their backup line of ends **Brian Lester**, a 6-2, 226-pound redshirt freshman, and junior **Justin Blake** (6-2, 263).

Lester was redshirted last year and Blake has been bothered by injuries while playing in 18 games the last two years.

Junior **Yahrek Johnson** (6-23, 263) and sophomore **Jesse Mitchell** (6-3, 267) are the backup tackles. Johnson played in all 11 games and had two starts when Sims was injured last year. He's a former All-Metro player in Atlanta, where he started three years at Henry Grady High School.

Mitchell, a former Mississippi all-stater, had 22 tackles and 2.5 quarterback sacks as a backup last year.

LINEBACKERS

The return of junior middle linebacker **Eddie Strong** (6-3, 235) is a huge boost for the linebacking corps. Strong, who was a preseason All-SEC pick in 2000, missed the entire season after suffering a stress fracture in his left foot during preseason drills. The injury was devastating for a defense that was already spread thin.

A consensus high school All-American, Strong first had an impact on the Ole Miss defense as a freshman in 1998 when he made six starts and finished third on the team in tackles. As a sophomore, he made second-team All-SEC and led Ole Miss in tackles while playing all three linebacker positions.

"Eddie probably hasn't come close to realizing what he's capable of," Lindsey said. "He's a big, tall linebacker that's making the transition from the outside to inside. He's proven he has the skills and ability to be a top performer.

"He felt a little rusty in the spring but didn't have any repercussions from the injury. He went out and got back in the groove."

Strong is glad to be back and thinks the Ole Miss defense will be improved.

"We are going to be different this year," Strong said after the spring game. "We have learned a new system, and I think we are starting to get the hang of it. We are going to stop the run this year. We have worked hard, and the defense is starting to come together."

Like Lindsey, Cutcliffe was pleased with Strong's performance in the spring.

"It was good to have Eddie back on the field and leading our linebacker corps," Cutcliffe said. "He's a proven player in this league. It was great to see his physical play and his leadership and playmaking ability during spring drills."

Junior **Lanier Goethie** (6-0, 210) is a returning starter at one of the outside linebacker positions. He started nine games last season and finished third on the team in tackles. He also had four tackles for losses and two fumble recoveries. He played as a backup in 1999 as a freshman.

The Rebels hope junior college transfer **L.P. Spence** (6-2, 210) can help right away at the other outside linebacker. He has taken a circuitous route to Oxford. Spence, ranked No. 7 on the *Jackson Clarion-Ledger*'s Top 25 Mississippi Junior College list, originally signed with Ole Miss but wound up at Valley Forge Military Academy in Pennsylvania. In his first game at Valley Forge, he suffered two broken bones in his lower leg and had to undergo four surgeries. He sat out the 1998 season, enrolled at Arkansas State, then transferred to Northeast (Miss.) Community College.

If Spence doesn't come through, Ole Miss still has senior **Kevin Thomas** (5-9, 190), who was listed as Goethie's backup after spring practice. Thomas first made an impression on special teams as a freshman walk-on in 1998. He continued to excel on special teams the following year while earning playing time at linebacker as a backup. He won a starting job last year and responded with 59 tackles, two forced fumbles, two interceptions and three tackles for losses.

Junior **Germain Landrum** (6-3, 225), a transfer from Butler (Kansas) Community College, was No. 1 at the other outside linebacker after going through his first spring practice. He originally signed with Minnesota, then enrolled in a junior college.

Junior **Ryan Hamilton** (6-1, 220), sophomore **Justin Wade** (6-3, 230), junior **Ian Bass** (6-0, 220) and redshirt freshman **Rob Robertson** (6-2, 215) are also in the linebacker picture. Hamilton has the most playing experience. Robertson was redshirted last year. Bass played in seven games last season after being switched from running back to linebacker in the fall.

DEFENSIVE BACKS

Junior strong safety **Syniker Taylor** (6-0, 205) and senior cornerback **Justin Coleman** (5-11, 175) are the returning starters in the secondary. Sophomore free safety **Von Hutchins** (5-11, 180) and junior **Desmon Johnson** (5-10, 160) held the lead on the other starting positions after spring practice.

Taylor, who made second-team All-SEC last year, is one of the premier athletes in the conference. He was a solid contributor for the Ole Miss basketball team his first two seasons, but decided not to play last season so he could concentrate on football. Taylor finished second on the team with 67 tackles last year and also had three interceptions, two fumble recoveries and 19 passes defensed.

Taylor, who played as a true freshman and started as a sophomore, had a phenomenal athletic career at Gulfport (Miss.) High School. He played wide receiver, wingback, running back, defensive back and outside linebacker while making all-state in football. He averaged 27.8 points per game as a senior in basketball and twice won the state championship in the long jump.

"Syniker is a much-improved player," Cutcliffe told *Ole Miss Sports News*. "I do not think people realized how injured Syniker was a year ago. He struggled to get through the year, but he pushed through and made some big plays. He has a chance to be a great football player, and I would not trade him for any other safety man in the league. He is an All-SEC and maybe even an All-American type player in the secondary."

Coleman, who has 17 career starts, has speed and experience at corner but was being pushed in the spring by junior college transfer Chris Knight, a 5-foot-10, 165-pound junior.

"Justin doesn't have the position just because he's a returning starter," Lindsey said. "He hasn't won it outright yet."

Johnson had a good spring after backing up Ken Lucas at corner last year. He forced a fumble and intercepted a pass in his limited playing time.

Hutchins, who was bothered by injuries in the spring and fall of 2000, played sparingly as a backup.

Several other players will have a chance to compete for jobs in the fall. Sophomore **Marcus Woodson** (6-0, 185) at strong safety and sophomore **Travis Blanchard** (5-11, 175) at free safety both impressed Lindsey in the spring.

So did sophomore **Jerry Johnson** (6-3, 193), whom the Rebels first tried at receiver and quarterback, and sophomore **Tavarius Horne** (5-11, 200), who was moved from safety to cornerback the last half of spring practice.

PUNTERS

Redshirt freshman **Cody Ridgeway** won the punting job in the spring. He was a first-team all-stater at Central-Merry High School in Jackson, Tenn., where he averaged 41.1 yards on 50 punts. Ridgeway never had a punt blocked in high school.

"He's a very talented youngster," Cutcliffe said. "I'm anxious to see how he responds in game situations."

SPECIAL TEAMS

The Rebels lost a game-breaker in McAllister. Nonetheless, with all the speed on their roster, they should be able to find capable return men.

Williams returned 12 kicks for 274 yards last year. He will handle both kickoff and punt returns this season.

Collins will be the second choice on kickoff returns, with Rayford available for punt-return duties. Collins returned three punts for touchdowns as a junior in high school.

RECRUITING CLASS

As a longtime assistant coach at Tennessee, Cutcliffe was aware Mississippi produced good football players. He wasn't aware it produced so many. Now, he's trying to capitalize on that.

Of the 24 signees in Cutcliffe's third recruiting class, 17 are from Mississippi. He didn't go far to get the others, signing five from Alabama and two from Georgia.

"We've done very well in-state, and we're going to continue to do everything we can to build on that because of the outstanding talent available," Cutcliffe said. "The message is that we've gotten better recruiting the state each year we've been here.

"That doesn't mean we can't do well when we can go out of state. I think it sends a message that we can go out and compete. I know that we can go out and compete anywhere, particularly in the southern part of the country."

Ole Miss signed five players on the *Jackson Clarion-Ledger*'s Ten Most Wanted list. By comparison, Mississippi State signed two, and Southern Mississippi signed one.

Two of the Rebels' most touted recruits were offensive linemen—**Chris Spencer** and **Tre Stallings**.

Spencer (6-4, 315) was rated the top prospect in the state by the *Clarion-Ledger* and was a consensus first-team All-American. An accomplished weightlifter, he holds the Class 5A state record of 755 pounds in the squat. Stallings (6-5, 300) was rated No. 7 on the Most Wanted list and was a first-team all-stater.

The Rebels signed three other big linemen, **Bobby Harris** (6-4, 306) of Decatur, Ga.; **Tony Bonds** (6-3, 290) of Russellville, Ala; and **Mike Gibson** (6-2, 280) of Gadsden, Ala.. Harris earned all-county honors in 5A. He didn't give up a sack his senior year. Bonds was a two-time first-team all-stater. He allowed only two sacks his last two years and had 86 tackles on defense. Gibson was the Alabama Class 3A Lineman of the Year and a first-team all-stater. He had 145 tackles and 16 quarterback sacks.

McKinley Boykin (6-2, 270) is another all-state lineman signee from Alabama. He made all state for all-classifications at McAdory High School in Bessemer. He was a second-team All-South selection by BorderWars.Com. **Michael Bozeman** (6-2, 260) of Hawkinsville, Ga., made all-region as an offensive guard and linebacker. He was credited with 180 tackles as a senior. **Jimmy Brooks** (6-4, 260) of Ripley, Miss., made second-team all-state as a defensive lineman. He had 130 tackles as a senior.

The Rebels signed several productive running backs: **Sylvester Brown** (5-10, 215) of Madison Central in Madison, Miss.; **Vashon Pearson** (6-1, 206) of Ripley; and **Kelvin Robinson** (6-2, 215) of Jackson, Miss. Brown had a 5A state record 7,130 yards rushing in his career. He was selected to the Max Emfinger *USA Today.com* All-America first team and was also honored as the 5A Offensive Player of the Year in Mississippi. Pearson, the Class 3A Player of the Year, rushed for 2,607 yards as a senior and 1,931 yards as a junior. Robinson rushed for 1,410 yards last year.

Jeremy Ruffin (6-2, 200) was a first-team all-stater as a linebacker and defensive end at Meridian (Miss.) High School. **Bryant Thomas** (6-1, 190) had 2,363 yards total offense as a quarterback at Louisville (Miss.) High School. He was a second-team all-state selection.

Matt Grier (6-, 200) of Itawamba (Miss.) Community College has outstanding credentials in the secondary. He was a second-team junior college All-America selection by J.C. Gridwire. He had 71 tackles and four interceptions. He also returned 11 kickoffs for a 29.2-yard average.

Travis Johnson (6-1, 190) of Shannon, Miss., and **Eric Oliver** (6-2, 200) of Jasper, Ala., both made all-state. Johnson played safety, wide receiver and quarterback. Oliver had 90 tackles as a cornerback and safety.

BLUE RIBBON ANALYSIS

OFFENSE	B
SPECIAL TEAMS	C
DEFENSE	C-
INTANGIBLES	B

Ole Miss has a potentially outstanding offense and potentially porous defense. The schedule will help both.

The non-conference schedule consists of Murray State, Middle Tennessee State and Arkansas State. The SEC schedule includes Vanderbilt and Kentucky, the worst teams in the East. Aside from its game at Kentucky, Ole Miss won't have to travel farther than Auburn, Ala.

The hiring of Lindsey and the return of Strong to middle linebacker will help the defense. But that won't be enough when the schedule turns tougher in the second half of the season, and the Rebels have to line up against strong run-oriented teams like Alabama, Arkansas, Georgia and Mississippi State.

The offense will miss McAllister, who contributed so much as a runner, receiver and kick returner. But if Gunn stays healthy, Ole Miss' defense won't be the only one with problems. Metcalf ranks with the best offensive linemen in the conference, there's speed at wide receiver, and Eli Manning is a star waiting to happen. Moreover, Cutcliffe knows what to do with those kinds of weapons.

Ole Miss can't expect to match its eight victories of Cutcliffe's first season. In fact, the Rebels will be hard-pressed to match its seven victories of last year. But with a Manning at quarterback, six victories and a fifth consecutive bowl could be a lot of fun.

(J.A.)

2000 OLE MISS RESULTS

Tulane	W	49-20	1-0
Auburn	L	27-35	1-1
Vanderbilt	W	12-7	2-1
Kentucky	W	35-17	3-1
Arkansas State	W	35-10	4-1
Alabama	L	7-45	4-2
UNLV	W	43-40	5-2
Arkansas	W	38-24	6-2
LSU	L	9-20	6-3
Georgia	L	14-32	6-4
Mississippi State	W	45-30	7-4
West Virginia (Music City)	L	38-49	7-5

South Carolina

LOCATION	**Columbia, SC**
CONFERENCE	**Southeastern (Eastern)**
LAST SEASON	**8-4 (.666)**
CONFERENCE RECORD	**5-3 (t-2nd)**
OFFENSIVE STARTERS RETURNING	**9**
DEFENSIVE STARTERS RETURNING	**8**
NICKNAME	**Gamecocks**
COLORS	**Garnet & Black**
HOME FIELD	**Williams-Brice Stadium (80,250)**
HEAD COACH	**Lou Holtz (Kent State '59)**
RECORD AT SCHOOL	**8-15 (2 years)**
CAREER RECORD	**224-110-7 (29 years)**
ASSISTANTS	**Skip Holtz (Notre Dame '86)**

Assistant Head Coach/Offensive Coordinator
Charlie Strong (Central Arkansas '82)
Defensive Coordinator/Defensive Line
Dave Roberts (Western Carolina '69)
Recruiting Coordinator/Outside Linebackers
Chris Cosh (Virginia Tech '82)
Inside Linebackers
Todd Fitch (Ohio Wesleyan '86)
Receivers
Dave DeGuglielmo (Boston University '90)
Offensive Tackles/Tight Ends
Buddy Pough (South Carolina State '75)
Running Backs
John Gutekunst (Duke '66)
Secondary
Paul Lounsberry (Simpson College '73)
Offensive Guards/Centers

TEAM WINS (last 5 yrs.)	**6-5-1-0-8**
FINAL RANK (last 5 yrs.)	**24-35-57-71-18**
2000 FINISH	**Beat Ohio St. in Outback Bowl.**

COACH AND PROGRAM

Who says Lou Holtz isn't a miracle worker?

What his South Carolina football team accomplished last season certainly bordered on the miraculous, and the pieces are in place to have an even better year in 2001.

Holtz, the charismatic 29-year coaching veteran, engineered one of the more memorable turnarounds in college football history. The Gamecocks went from a nightmarish 0-11 record in 1999—Holtz's debut in Columbia—to an 8-4 record last season that was close to being 9-3 or even 10-2. Remember, too, that South Carolina began last season dragging the nation's longest losing streak at 21 games and counting.

Suffice to say the USC fans were worked into a frenzy, and with good reason. Nowhere in the country are the fans more loyal or more rabid, and finally, they had tasted the big time.

The highlights were too many to count:

• The Gamecocks closed the season with a 24-7 spanking of Ohio State in the Outback Bowl. It was just their second bowl victory in school history and the first time they had even been to the postseason since closing the 1994 season with a victory over West Virginia in the Carquest Bowl.

• For the first time in 14 years, South Carolina finished the season nationally ranked, 19th in the Associated Press poll and 21st in the ESPN/*USA Today* coaches poll.

• The 5-3 SEC record was the Gamecocks' first winning record since joining the league in 1992. In fact, South Carolina went into the Florida game with the Eastern Division title on the line, but the Gators prevailed, 41-21, in Gainesville.

• The second week of the season, South Carolina shocked then-No. 9 Georgia, 21-10, intercepting five Quincy Carter passes in the process. The fans stormed the field afterward and ripped down the goal posts for the second straight week. The goalposts also came down after the season-opening 31-0 victory over New Mexico State ended the 21-game losing streak.

It was truly a season to remember, but one Holtz and his players insist needs to be left in the past if the Gamecocks are going to push full steam ahead this season.

"I told the players after the bowl game, that while we're pleased with the progress we've made, we can't sit back and try to maintain what we've done," said Holtz, selected the SEC Coach of the Year last season. "Expectations will be higher. Standards will be greater, and the ante has risen. If they come to understand that, then we have a chance to take it to another level—and that's what we want to do."

While nobody in the South Carolina camp seems to be resting on his laurels, the Gamecocks whipped through spring practice with a certain swagger in their step. They expect to be good this season, expect to be in title contention and expect to go into tough environments and win.

That's a far cry from this time a year ago, when

Holtz was drawing on everything in his vast bag of tricks to give his team a reason to believe. Twenty-one consecutive losses represent an eternity in football speak.

"It was a matter of rallying around each other, and that's what coach Holtz made us realize," senior quarterback **Phil Petty** (6-3, 208) said. "Going through that made us stronger. I don't think this will be a team that rattles easily."

As successful as the Gamecocks were a year ago, the disappointment of losing the three games in a row to Tennessee, Florida and Clemson lingers. Holtz is confident there will be no such lulls this season.

The Gamecocks return eight starters on offense and nine on a defensive unit that led the SEC in scoring defense and was sixth nationally last season.

"Talent-wise, we'll be good," Holtz said. "We can be competitive in the SEC. We can win and will win, and it's not going to be an up-again, down-again thing. We were a Top 20 team, and I see no reason why we can't be there again.

"I'm expecting the seniors to play the best football of their careers, and when the seniors leave, there won't be very much talent drop-off, if any at all."

The other thing the Gamecocks have going for them is experience. This will be their most experienced team in years. There's also some quality depth, the kind in which Holtz could only crack jokes about a year ago.

"We could never get on Noah's Ark ... we don't have two of anything," Holtz quipped entering the spring of 2000.

But that was then, and this is now.

Coming out of the most recent spring workouts, the defense—which will again be the strength of the team and one of fiercest in the league—featured seven senior starters and three junior starters. Nine of the top 22 players on defense are juniors.

"I like to have a senior-dominated defense," South Carolina defensive coordinator Charlie Strong told the *Greenville (S.C.) News*. "Each year, that's the class I want that dominates and then just keep rolling.

"You're going to lose some guys, but you've still got guys coming. So it's not like all of a sudden when they're going, the cupboard's bear."

Strong, one of the country's hottest up-and-coming defensive coordinators, is a head coach in the making. Even during the winless season, his defense finished fifth in the SEC in total defense and 20th nationally.

"The standard has been set," said Strong, who coached the defensive line at Notre Dame before joining Holtz at South Carolina. "We've gained a reputation for playing good defense around here, and I think this team has a chance to be just as good as the defense last year."

Offensively, the Gamecocks were dramatically better last season than they were in 1999 when they ranked 114th nationally in total offense and were equally woeful in scoring offense, averaging just 7.9 points per game.

According to the spring depth chart, six of the starters will be seniors and four juniors.

"When you take a look at the number of people we having coming back on this year's football team, you get encouraged," said Holtz, who spent a week in May speaking to troops in the Middle East. "But let me assure you, you can take nothing for granted because the chemistry of the team can be completely different."

Already, there's been a major distraction during the off-season, one that flared last season before the Gamecocks' bowl trip.

Junior running back **Derek Watson** (6-1, 212) has been in and out of trouble off the field and heads into the fall indefinitely suspended by Holtz. Every indication, though, is that Watson—who led the SEC with 166.7 all-purpose yards per game last season—will be given a chance to return to the team.

His latest run-in with the law came after a female student accused him of punching her in the arm after the two argued in April. Watson was arrested, and she later took out a restraining order against Watson, who faces a June 27 court date on the assault charge.

In February, Watson was accused of shoving a referee to the floor and threatening him during an intramural basketball game. Holtz disciplined Watson, who later publicly apologized to the referee.

Watson also missed the Outback Bowl when he was suspended after a December wreck that happened while he was driving a teammate's car. Watson was given a ticket for driving with a suspended license and driving too fast.

Holtz said Watson has certain things he must do to re-join the team. He doesn't sound like a coach who's about to abandon his star player.

"What this axe murderer has done is push one student referee and grab a woman by the arm," Holtz said facetiously back in May. "Now that's serious, but everybody else makes out like he goes around beating everybody up.

"But once again, there are different people with different agendas."

Holtz has been vague about when Watson might return and the specifics surrounding his potential return. But the door is clearly open.

"At the present time, it's my understanding that he's willing to do these things and if he does them, we'll have to see," Holtz said.

With or without Watson, Holtz has proven time and time again that he's a master molder of football teams. He certainly has this team's attention, and in turn, the Gamecocks are a team who could command their share of attention by season's end.

"He's pretty much as advertised," Petty said. "He's very tough on us, and he coaches us very hard. He wants us to be as close to perfection as possible. And that's what we try to do day in and day out."

2001 SCHEDULE

Sept.	1	Boise State
	8	@Georgia
	15	Bowling Green
	22	@Mississippi State
	29	Alabama
Oct.	6	Kentucky
	13	@Arkansas
	20	Vanderbilt
	27	@Tennessee
Nov.	10	Florida
	17	Clemson

QUARTERBACKS

Petty isn't spectacular when it comes to any one thing, but he does several things well. Most of all, he did the things necessary last season for the Gamecocks to win.

A starter since his sophomore season, Petty finished fifth in the SEC a year ago in total offense. He passed for 2,285 yards and eight touchdowns, but also had 10 interceptions.

Holtz would like to see Petty improve that touchdown-to-interception ratio, something Petty was much better at during the spring.

As a sophomore, Petty threw one touchdown as opposed to seven interceptions, but missed five games with a knee injury. He also had no pass protection. His protection was better last season and will be even better this year.

Generally, Petty is the kind of quarterback who plays within himself and doesn't try to do too much.

"Phil Petty is so confident," Holtz said. "He's very accurate, has a nice quick release and throws on time. He's very cool out there and had an excellent spring."

Once again, the Gamecocks will run their share of four wide receivers, with Petty making quick decisions and quick throws. That's what he does best, getting the ball to the right places.

Petty's best game last season came against Mississippi State, when he passed for a career-high 305 yards and two touchdowns. He enters this season sixth on USC's all-time passing list with 3,730 yards.

Holtz entered the spring saying he wanted to play two quarterbacks this season. The other one he had in mind was redshirt freshman **Dondrial Pinkins** (6-3, 215). The multi-dimensional Pinkins brings a certain athleticism to the position that Petty doesn't offer, and Pinkins had his moments in the spring. But he also threw five interceptions in the spring game.

"That's the worst game I've had in my entire life," said Pinkins, who was 13-of-32 for 152 yards in the spring game.

Nonetheless, Pinkins is still the Gamecocks' future at quarterback. It's just unclear how much he'll play this season. When there's any opportunity, expect to see him out there. He has the strongest arm of the quarterbacks, gets rid of it in a hurry and can escape pressure. But he's still working on reading defenses and making the right decisions.

Pinkins actually played in three games a year ago. He suffered torn cartilage in his knee during preseason camp, which stunted his progress. He applied for a medical hardship to the get the extra year.

Coming out of Camilla, Ga., Pinkins was frequently compared to Quincy Carter. As a senior, he passed for 1,210 yards and 11 touchdowns and also rushed for 950 yards and 19 touchdowns.

The No. 2 quarterback on the depth chart coming out of the spring was junior **Erik Kimrey** (6-1, 200). A walk-on, Kimrey passed for 120 yards and two touchdowns and wasn't intercepted in the spring game.

Until Pinkins learns to protect the ball better, Kimrey will remain the backup, Holtz said.

"I feel good with my mental progress (during spring drills)," Kimrey told the *Greenville News*. "I really was able to grasp the offense and really come up with a frame of mind where I really felt like I went out each play and knew exactly where I needed to go with the ball."

Kimrey is best remembered by South Carolina fans for throwing the game-winning touchdown pass last season to beat Mississippi State. Pressed into duty when Petty injured his ankle in the final minutes, Kimrey responded by throwing a perfectly executed 25-yard fade route to Jermale Kelly on a do-or-die, fourth-and-10 play.

The Gamecocks also like the potential of redshirt freshman **Rod Wilson** (6-3, 203). The only question is where Wilson will end up—quarterback or receiver?

There was growing speculation that Wilson, who ran the wishbone and wing-T in high school, might be moved over to help the receiving corps in the fall.

"Rod Wilson will be a quarterback here, no doubt about it," Holtz said. "I also think it's obvious that he could help us at wide receiver. He catches the ball well and runs well with it afterward. But he doesn't want to do that. I recruited him as a quarterback and told him he would not move unless it was his decision."

RUNNING BACKS

Holtz's comment regarding Watson a year ago is ringing as ominously as ever as the 2001 season approaches. Holtz said Watson would either be sweeping out or selling out stadiums some day.

It's been a turbulent ride for the junior running back, one of the most explosive threats in the country. Watson, who last season became USC's first 1,000-yard rusher since Duce Staley (1,116 in 1996), is awaiting his fate after being suspended indefinitely by Holtz. Charged in May with assaulting a female student, Watson can't seem to stay out of trouble off the field.

To contend for the SEC title, the Gamecocks definitely need Watson on the field. Without him, their offense becomes real average in a hurry. Holtz, though, hasn't sounded like a coach who's about to part ways with Watson, who rushed for 1,066 yards and 11 touchdowns last season.

The prototype tailback, Watson is the total package. He has it all—speed, power, change of direction and the ability to cut back and go the distance.

Watson, who comes from an impoverished home life, probably doesn't have many more lives remaining with Holtz, who says Watson has made considerable advances off the field despite his troubles.

"On the field, Derek Watson, his attitude, his work habits, his toughness, his durability, his love for the game, is exceptional," Holtz said. "You're not talking about a moody guy who sulks around.

"Off the field, he has made some bad decisions, but he is making progress. As long as a guy is making progress, moving in the direction we want him to go, then I feel comfortable."

The Gamecocks have several other options in the backfield, but none as electrifying as Watson. The bruiser is junior **Andrew Pinnock** (6-0, 248). A Jerome Bettis clone, Pinnock was the team's second-leading rusher last season with 406 yards. He squashes defenders with his straight-ahead running style.

Pinnock and Watson complement each other well when they're in the same backfield. Pinnock, though, isn't as much of a natural in the one-back set as Watson. A terror in short-yardage situations, Pinnock scored seven touchdowns last season.

The other way the Gamecocks could go is with junior **Ryan Brewer** (5-10, 210), the star of the Outback Bowl. Brewer teed off on his home state Ohio State Buckeyes by totaling 214 all-purpose yards and scoring three touchdowns.

Brewer started at tailback in the bowl game after Watson's suspension. He rushed for 109 yards and two touchdowns and also had 92 yards receiving and a touchdown.

A throwback, Brewer will again be used this season at both running back and receiver. He also returned some punts last season. Brewer rarely goes down on the first hit and always seems to find the right holes. He's also the Gamecocks' best receiver out of the backfield.

Senior **Travis Lewis** (6-0, 250) will back up Pinnock at fullback. He was moved from defensive end last year. The Gamecocks have a jumbo package on the goal line where Lewis lines up at fullback and Pinnock at tailback, giving them a pair of 250-pounders in the backfield.

Redshirt freshman **Gonzie Gray** (6-0, 180) had a good spring and is one of the fastest players on the team.

WIDE RECEIVERS/TIGHT ENDS

Holtz said repeatedly during the spring that the receiver position was one of his greatest concerns.

"I am greatly concerned about our receivers against man coverage," Holtz said.

Indeed, the Gamecocks don't appear to have that one real burner, the guy who can consistently get behind defenses or turn a short toss into a long touchdown. They also need a go-to receiver to emerge in the mold of the departed Kelly. The most likely candidate is senior **Brian Scott** (6-2, 210). He was the team's third-leading receiver last season with 35 catches for 560 yards and two touchdowns.

Not blessed with great speed, Scott is a big target who runs good routes. He led all receivers in the spring game with seven catches for 126 yards. Scott said he's not interested in becoming the next Kelly, but rather carving his own niche in the Gamecocks' offense.

"I'm going to play Brian Scott's game. I'm going to do what I do," Scott said. "Jermale is gone. I'm Brian Scott. I'm not trying to fill anybody's shoes. If nobody fills his shoes, then nobody fills his shoes. I'm going out to play my game."

The other starting outside receiver will be senior **Carlos Spikes** (6-0, 200). The former quarterback had 12 catches for 149 yards last season. A year ago, he lined up at quarterback for a few snaps.

After starting the 2000 season with a four-receiver set about 80 percent of the time, the Gamecocks were closer to 50-50 when the season ended. The top slot receiver is Brewer, who caught 36 passes for 418 yards and two touchdowns last year. He's not known for his speed, yet took a pass over the middle against Tennessee and raced 78 yards for a touchdown.

Brewer, who also has the best hands of the receivers, missed the last week of spring practice after fracturing his wrist. He underwent surgery and is expected to be ready for the start of fall practice.

The other slot when the Gamecocks go to four wideouts is senior **Corey Alexander** (5-9, 182). A junior college transfer last season, Alexander did very little, although he did have a 58-yard touchdown catch against Mississippi State. The Gamecocks are hoping that Alexander can become more of a big-play threat this season.

The other receiver South Carolina needs to have a breakout season is senior **James Adkisson** (6-4, 215). He has all the tools to be a great one, but tended to drift in and out of games last season. He ran a 4.38 40-yard dash in the spring.

Adkisson dropped a touchdown pass against Alabama and never really seemed to recover. A junior college transfer last season, he finished with 17 catches for 227 yards—but no touchdowns.

"He has tremendous potential, but he hasn't reached it yet, not because he hasn't worked at it and not because he doesn't want to," Holtz said. "He just hasn't let it loose."

Others who could contribute are speedy redshirt freshman **Andrea Gause** (6-9, 175), as well as junior **Willis Ham** (6-3, 205). Ham played in nine games last season and started against Vanderbilt. He came on this spring.

A pair of junior college newcomers could also help. Junior **Ricky Ricks** (6-3, 215) is from Gulf Coast (Miss.) Junior College, while junior **Chavez Donnings** (5-11, 185) was a late signee from Butler County (Kansas) Community College.

The starting tight end coming out of the spring was senior **Rod Trafford** (6-4, 260). But sophomore **Hart Turner** (6-4, 240) is the better receiver of the two.

OFFENSIVE LINE

This will be Gamecocks' best offensive line since Holtz has been on the job. Physically, South Carolina has made considerable progress in the trenches. Nine of the 10 offensive linemen on the two deep coming out of the spring weighed 290 pounds or more. More importantly, those nine also have playing experience or have started in a game.

The only player gone from last season's two deep is center Scott Browne, but he will be replaced by senior **Larrell Johnson** (6-1, 300). Browne was undersized, and the Gamecocks took a beating a year ago from teams with dominant defensive tackles. But Johnson started at center in the Outback Bowl, and South Carolina rushed for 218 yards.

After starting at guard last season, junior **C.J. Frye** (6-3, 290) moved to center in the spring and will back up Johnson there. Junior **Cedric Williams** (6-3, 295) is the starting left guard. He was a first-team All-SEC selection last season by the Associated Press. A former defensive lineman, Williams played some at tackle as a redshirt freshman.

The starting right guard is junior **Shane Hall** (6-6, 300) after he moved over from tackle. Hall will be challenged by senior **Kevin Rivers** (6-3, 300). It's been a frustrating last two seasons for Rivers. He was academically ineligible a year ago and battled a knee injury two years ago. But as a redshirt freshman, Rivers started eight games at guard and was chosen second-team freshman All-America by *The Sporting News*.

Phillip Jones, who had started at both center and guard the last two seasons, was forced to give up football after problems with his feet and toes worsened.

Even though he's only a sophomore, left tackle **Travelle Wharton** (6-4, 300) is probably the best all-around offensive linemen the Gamecocks have. He was freshman All-SEC and freshman All-America last season.

Senior **Melvin Paige** (6-5, 300) is back as the starter at right tackle. He's been a starter ever since his redshirt freshman season.

The top backup at tackle is junior **Watts Sanderson** (6-4, 295), who made a couple of starts during his redshirt freshman season. Holtz was also pleased with the progress this spring of sophomore **Jeff Barnes** (6-4, 275).

"At tackle, I don't think there is as much difference," Holtz said. "Watts Sanderson has closed the gap tremendously between him and Travelle Wharton, and Jeff Barnes has closed the gap on Melvin Paige. I feel pretty good there. In the interior, losing Philip Jones hurts us."

The Gamecocks need to get better at lining up and knocking people off the ball. Last season, they had trouble mustering a running game against some of the better defenses. They were held to less than 100 yards rushing against Mississippi State, Tennessee, Alabama and Florida.

2000 STATISTICS

Rushing offense	157.0	47
Passing offense	210.9	60
Total offense	367.9	60
Scoring offense	23.5	72
Net Punting	34.2	68
Punt returns	8.4	75
Kickoff returns	19.6	58
Rushing defense	115.2	28

Passing efficiency defense	98.0	11
Total defense	308.2	16
Scoring defense	15.8	6
Turnover margin	+3	46

Last column is ranking among Division I-A teams.

KICKERS

One of the continuing trouble spots during Holtz's time at South Carolina has been the place kicking. The Gamecocks have done more than struggle. They've been downright bad.

Last season, they made just 11-of-19 field-goal attempts. Six of those misses came inside 40 yards and could have made a difference in some games. Included were misses from 29 and 21 yards in the 27-17 loss to Alabama. It wasn't any better in 1999 when the Gamecocks were just 10-of-18.

When walk-on kicker **Joey Bowers** made a field goal in one of the spring scrimmages earlier this year, the fans in attendance stood and roared.

The top kicker coming out of the spring was sophomore walk-on **Dan Weaver**. But he will get plenty of competition in the fall from incoming freshman **Josh Brown** (6-2, 185) of Clarksburg, Md. Brown's signing marked the first time since Holtz has been at South Carolina he gave a scholarship to a place-kicker.

Making the kicks from inside 40 yards is a must if the Gamecocks are going to pull out the close ones this season.

DEFENSIVE LINE

The Gamecocks want to evolve into more of a four-man front team and hope to use more of that set this season. The lack of players on the defensive line simply didn't allow them to play four up front the last two seasons.

Still, their base will remain three down linemen, three linebackers and five defensive backs.

Cleveland Pinkney and Cecil Caldwell were the anchors of the defense last season. Strong called Pinkney the Gamecocks' best defensive player. Caldwell wasn't far behind with 11 tackles for loss, including seven sacks.

"Overall, I worry about depth in the defensive line," Holtz said. "Are we strong enough when people run right at us? I think we are fast enough. I think we tackle well."

Replacing Pinkney at nose guard will be junior **Langston Moore** (6-1, 290). A starter at offensive guard as a freshman, Moore is a more active player than Pinkney and could develop into more of a big-play artist when it comes to sacks and tackles for loss.

Moore had a pair of sacks last season in a reserve role. But he's just not that immovable force in the middle that Pinkney provided for the Gamecocks.

Senior **Willie Sams** (6-5, 280) will back up Pinkney at nose guard. He played in all 12 games last season, including one start.

Exiting the spring, senior **John Stamper** (6-4, 265) was the starting left end and senior **Dennis Quinn** (6-4, 265) the starting right end. But when fall camp begins, all eyes will be on junior college newcomer **Shaun Smith** (6-3, 308), a junior from Butler County (Kansas) Junior College. Smith was rated by some analysts among the top 10 junior college prospects in the country. He broke the Butler County record last season with 20 sacks.

The Gamecocks were excited about the progress of redshirt freshman **Jonathan Alston** (6-5, 265) in the spring. He will also be in the rotation at end.

"It was important that we got John Stamper back from the baseball team as I expect him to be a starter on the defensive line with Langston Moore and Dennis Quinn," Holtz said. "I think those three are very solid, but I am concerned about the backup players in that area."

When South Carolina does go to four linemen, the extra pass rusher will be senior **Kalimba Edwards** (6-6, 262), who will almost certainly be a defensive end in the NFL. He has the ideal build and the quickness off the corner to gobble up quarterbacks.

LINEBACKERS

The SEC is loaded with great linebackers, but South Carolina's group is as good as any. And that's despite losing Andre Offing, who led the team in tackles last season.

All three of the Gamecocks' starters are seniors, and all three have their unique styles. Edwards, chosen to *Playboy*'s preseason All-American team and a consensus All-SEC selection last season, is a can't-miss NFL prospect. With another productive season, he could push himself into the top 10-or-15 picks of next year's draft.

He's versatile, as evidenced by the fact that he can play outside linebacker or defensive end, and is relentless when it comes to getting to the quarterback.

Edwards was third on the team in tackles last season with 74 and tied for the team lead in sacks with seven. In the bowl game, Edwards had three sacks. Even with his great size, he showcased his athletic ability to return an interception 81 yards for a touchdown against Tennessee.

The other starter on the outside is senior **Shannon Wadley** (6-1, 235). He's not as big as Edwards, but pound for pound is the best hitter on the team. His nickname is "Body Bags."

When the pile is moving backward, you know Wadley is the one delivering the blow. He's also the fastest of the linebackers and finished last season with 64 tackles.

The middle linebacker is senior **Kenny Harney** (6-2, 252). He's back after fracturing his leg last season against Mississippi State. A starter since his freshman season, Harney has put on about 10 pounds. He's the best combination linebacker of the three and calls all the signals. He can make plays from sideline to sideline and moves extremely well for a middle linebacker. He finished with 45 tackles despite missing five games last season.

The top two reserve linebackers inside are sophomore **Jeremiah Garrison** (6-1, 218) and redshirt freshman **Brian Brownlee** (6-3, 235). The Gamecocks see Brownlee as their middle linebacker of the future. Garrison played some last season as a freshman and is capable of rushing the passer or dropping into pass coverage.

Edwards' backup will be redshirt freshman **Jack Johnson** (6-2, 220). Johnson broke his foot his senior year in high school and wasn't heavily recruited. He's a pure speed rusher coming off the corner.

At the end of spring practice, another of the Gamecocks' backups, junior Pat Fleming, was dismissed for a violation of team rules.

DEFENSIVE BACKS

Depth won't be a problem in the secondary, where the Gamecocks return a bundle of players who have SEC experience. All five starters return from last season, including All-SEC cornerback **Sheldon Brown** (5-10, 192). Brown, a senior, rates up there with Florida's Lito Sheppard and Georgia's Tim Wansley as the premier cover men in the league. He's fast, smart and productive. His four interceptions last season led the team. He also had 15 pass deflections and 67 tackles.

Brown, the leadoff hitter on the USC baseball team, didn't participate during much of spring practice. But he's clearly ahead of everybody else in the Gamecocks' secondary and is the kind of player who can shut down star receivers.

Flanking Brown at the other cornerback will be senior **Andre Goodman** (5-10, 188). He's spent most of the last two years fighting back from a wicked injury that saw him rip his knee apart as a freshman. Goodman appears to be back to his old self after running a 4.32 40-yard dash in the spring, the fastest on the team. But he said the true test will come on the field.

"I think my psychological boost probably will come from my on-field activity more than running the 40," Goodman told the *Greenville News*. "Just being able to have the reaction, the break-up speed, the catch-up speed, coming out of your back-peddle quicker—those are the things as far as the on-the-field activities."

The third cornerback in the equation will be senior **Kevin House** (5-11, 178). He had three interceptions last season and was a starter in nine games in 1999.

Junior college newcomer **Isaac Stackhouse** (5-10, 180), a junior out of Jones County (Miss.) Junior College, could also get a shot at cornerback.

The Gamecocks are equally stocked at free safety, where sophomore **Deandre Eiland** (6-0, 178) was listed as the starter coming out of the spring. Eiland, voted to the SEC's All-Freshman team last season, didn't participate in the spring because he was running track. Eiland started the last five games a year ago after senior **Antione Nesmith** (6-0, 215) injured his knee against Arkansas. In those five games, Eiland intercepted four passes.

Nesmith will also play extensively after coming back from knee surgery with a strong spring. He started his career at South Carolina as a running back.

The most competition in the spring was at the two spur safety spots, the Gamecocks' version of part-linebacker and part-safety. Senior **Rashad Faison** (5-9, 188) is the club's leading returning tackler at one spur safety. He had 99 tackles last season, including a team-high 13 for loss. Faison's five sacks placed him behind only Caldwell and Edwards. A former cornerback, Faison can also cover. He started some as a freshman at cornerback and provides invaluable flexibility in the secondary.

Senior **Willie Offord** (6-1, 218) wrapped up the spring as the other starter at spur safety. He had 59 tackles a year ago but will be pushed by junior **Jonathan Martin** (5-10, 215).

In the fall, junior college newcomer **Jermaine Lemon** (6-2, 215), a junior out of Georgia Military Academy, is expected to do some catching up. He was the only one of the junior college signees who went through the spring.

Junior **Jamie Scott** (5-10, 218) was listed as the backup to Faison, while sophomore **Dunta Robinson** (6-1, 170) wasn't even listed in the two deep despite playing in nine games as a true freshman. Redshirt freshman **Jamacia Jackson** (6-2, 195) also showed some promise in the spring.

"They competed well," Strong told the *Greenville News*. "They're all packed together at that (spur) position. One guy might be a little bit better, but not much."

PUNTERS

Junior **Tyeler Dean** (5-9, 189) returns as the punter. He finished with an average of 39.4 yards, ninth in the SEC. Dean did improve as the season wore on and punted well in the bowl game. He punted four times for a 46.8-yard average against the Buckeyes. His long punt was 56 yards against Arkansas.

Dean had 14 punts downed inside the 20-yard line, and he also had one blocked.

SPECIAL TEAMS

It goes without saying that the Gamecocks need to kick the ball better, both place kicking and punting. But, then, that's why Holtz signed Brown, the Maryland high school state record holder with 12 made field goals during his junior season.

Brown is also accustomed to kicking off the ground, which can be a headache for kickers making the transition to college. He also played quarterback, leading Urbana High School to the Class 2A title and an undefeated season.

"We have certain things that were mandatory in this kicker," Holtz said. "The No. 1 mandatory thing was he had to have played football. I don't mean kick the football, play football. He wanted to play quarterback (at USC). I said, 'You aren't going to play quarterback. You're going to punt and kick.'

"We think he's very good. I don't know where he's rated nationally. I don't care. We watched him on film."

Holtz handles the special teams and is committed to seeing them improve. The coverage units were decent last season, and the Gamecocks also have several possibilities on the returns. Brewer was the top punt returner a year ago and also returned a few kickoffs.

Donning also has experience as a return specialist, while Watson is the most dynamic of the Gamecocks' kickoff return men. Alexander is another one to watch there.

One area that needs improvement is net punting, where South Carolina finished last in the league a year ago.

RECRUITING CLASS

The most intriguing of the 2001 signees was junior **Corey Jenkins** (6-2, 215) of Garden City (Kansas) Junior College. A former first-round draft pick in baseball by the Boston Red Sox, Jenkins could wind up at any number of positions. He's that kind of athlete.

His first stop will be at quarterback. He was a two-time junior college All-American who rushed for 10 touchdowns and passed for eight more. There's also the chance that Jenkins could play some at receiver or safety. In the end, it will be where the Gamecocks need him the most, which will likely be receiver.

Jenkins, 24, signed with South Carolina out of high school, but never enrolled and went the baseball route. He's sure to make an impact somewhere.

The Gamecocks signed six junior college players. Smith is the type of dominant defensive lineman that doesn't come along every year and was a real catch for South Carolina.

Donnings will be another one to watch at receiver. He originally signed with Florida State out of high school before going to junior college. He caught 42 passes for 851 yards and 12 touchdowns last season at Butler.

The top high school signee for the Gamecocks was freshman defensive end **George Gause** (6-5, 223) of Conway, S.C. Gause was generally considered the top defensive prospect in the state.

Defensive line help was a priority, especially with the graduation of Pinkney and Caldwell. Offensive lineman **Josh Malloy** (6-5, 365) of Shelby, N.C. is massive and may have a chance to play early.

Bringing in Brown filled a pressing need at place-kicker. Now, if only he can consistently make them from inside 40 yards.

The Gamecocks missed out on all the state's top receivers, and making it worse, all three went to rival Clemson. Roscoe Crosby, Airese Currie and Tymere Zimmerman—three of the top 10 receiving prospects nationally—chose the Tigers over the Gamecocks.

South Carolina also had a commitment from receiver Dallas Baker of New Smyrna Beach, Fla., but he wound up signing with Florida. Baker's uncle, Wes Chandler, was a star receiver at Florida.

"We did not get the game-breaker that we need at wide receiver," Holtz said. "They tell me maybe we have one. But I don't know. I don't think we have it on our team."

The other disappointment was losing out on defensive end Robert Geathers of Georgetown, S.C., to Georgia. Once again, several of the highest rated prospects in the state went elsewhere.

Nonetheless, Holtz called it his best class at South Carolina.

"Everybody says, 'Did you have a good year?' " Holtz said on national signing day. "I think it's the best class we've brought in. But it's like giving birth to a baby. Is it a lawyer? Is it a doctor? Is it going to discover a cure for AIDS? Is it going to end up in prison? You don't know. You've got to grow. You've got to develop it."

BLUE RIBBON ANALYSIS

OFFENSE	B-
SPECIAL TEAMS	C
DEFENSE	B+
INTANGIBLES	B+

Maybe this really is "next year" for the Gamecocks.

Their rabid fans are bursting at the seams with anticipation. They're on track to sell 55,000 season tickets, more than South Carolina has ever sold.

Holtz is the ultimate poor-mouther, but even he hasn't been able to refrain from talking about how good this team could be. The key word there is "could."

Everything needs to work out with Watson, and he needs to be less of a distraction off the field and more of one on the field for opposing defenses.

The Gamecocks also need the likes of Scott and Adkisson to come on at receiver.

Once again, the defense will carry this team, and it's a unit that should be Strong's best yet at South Carolina. Edwards, Harney, Wadley, Faison and Brown are All-SEC caliber players. Moore has a chance to be that type of player.

Holtz, 64, certainly hasn't shown any signs of slowing down, not until his job is complete at South Carolina.

"You ask what keeps you in coaching," he said. "As long as you have dreams ... you have energy to get up and go do this.

"I still believe we can build a top 10 program. We can build a program as good as any in the country. I think we're on a firm foundation. That's our goal and that's our objective."

Reaching that goal this season could be a tall order, especially with the schedule. The Gamecocks have to go to Georgia, Mississippi State, Arkansas and Tennessee and get Florida at home.

One thing's for sure, too. They aren't going to sneak up on anybody this season, especially not Georgia during the second week of the season.

Even so, it's the kind of team—buoyed by Holtz's legendary ability to motivate—that could easily give the Bulldogs and the Tennessee Vols something to think about when it comes to that second spot in the East.

(C.L.)

2000 RESULTS

New Mexico State	W	31-0	1-0
Georgia	W	21-10	2-0
Eastern Michigan	W	41-6	3-0
Mississippi State	W	23-19	4-0
Alabama	L	17-27	4-1
Kentucky	W	20-17	5-1
Arkansas	W	27-7	6-1
Vanderbilt	W	30-14	7-1
Tennessee	L	14-17	7-2
Florida	L	21-41	8-2
Clemson	L	14-16	8-3
Ohio State (Outback)	W	24-7	9-3

Tennessee

LOCATION	**Knoxville, TN**
CONFERENCE	**Southeastern (East)**
LAST SEASON	**8-4 (.666)**
CONFERENCE RECORD	**5-3 (t-2nd)**
OFFENSIVE STARTERS RETURNING	**8**
DEFENSIVE STARTERS RETURNING	**8**
NICKNAME	**Volunteers**
COLORS	**Orange & White**
HOME FIELD	**Neyland Stadium (104,000)**
HEAD COACH	**Phillip Fulmer (Tennessee '72)**
RECORD AT SCHOOL	**84-18 (9 years)**
CAREER RECORD	**84-18 (9 years)**
ASSISTANTS	
	John Chavis (Tennessee '79)
	Assistant Head Coach/Defensive Coordinator
	Randy Sanders (Tennessee '87)
	Offensive Coordinator/Quarterbacks
	Dan Brooks (Western Carolina '76)
	Recruiting Coordinator/Defensive Line
	Mike Barry (Southern Illinois '69)
	Offensive Line
	Doug Marrone (Syracuse '86)
	Offensive Tackles/Tight Ends,
	Steve Caldwell (Arkansas State '77)
	Defensive Ends
	Woody McCorvey (Alabama State '72)
	Running Backs
	Larry Slade (Shepard College '71)
	Secondary
	Pat Washington (Auburn '87)
	Receivers
TEAM WINS (last 5 yrs.)	**10-11-13-9-8**
FINAL RANK (last 5 yrs.)	**8-5-1-10-19**
2000 FINISH	**Lost to Kansas State in Cotton Bowl.**

COACH AND PROGRAM

Only three short years ago, Tennessee reached the pinnacle in college football with its first national championship in nearly 50 years. The talent was there to certainly contend for another one, maybe even two. But the Vols contracted a bad case of NFL-itis in 1999 and put on a clinic in how to underachieve.

Then last season, hamstrung by early defections to the NFL, coach Phillip Fulmer took a young team in what was clearly a rebuilding year and managed to win eight games. Of course, all anybody remembers was the deflating finish.

Tennessee suffered a 35-21 Cotton Bowl whipping at the hands of Kansas State, a loss that put a serious damper on a second consecutive season. It was also the second straight year that Tennessee had been physically pushed around in a bowl game, something Fulmer reminded his players of often in spring practice. Nebraska did the honors in the 2000 Fiesta Bowl.

"Our focus was becoming more physical and getting tougher," Fulmer said. "I feel good about the gains we made in those areas."

He'll feel even better if the Vols take it a step further this fall, a season that presents a crossroads of sorts for a program that isn't accustomed to riding in the middle of the SEC pack.

"It's time we get back to where Tennessee is supposed to be, in the hunt for championships," said senior defensive tackle **John Henderson** (6-7, 290), who won the Outland Trophy last season as the nation's top interior lineman and is *Blue Ribbon*'s national and SEC preseason defensive player of the year.

The Vols are talented enough to jump back into the national title chase, but serious questions persist. And with the schedule, it's entirely possible that Tennessee could be a better football team this season and have the same record.

The harrowing thing for Fulmer and Co., though, is that another eight-win finish will go over in these parts about as well as FBI Appreciation Day would at Tony Soprano's mob hangout.

The grumbling will be significant if the Vols don't re-join the country's elite this season. They were left out of the final Associated Press Top 25 poll last season, breaking a string of five straight Top 10 national finishes.

In their last 16 games—dating to the 1999 upset by Arkansas—the Vols are just 10-6. But senior defensive end **Will Overstreet** (6-4, 260) said he and his mates are committed to steering the Big Orange back into the limelight, and more importantly, back onto the path most observers thought the Vols were headed coming off the 1998 national championship.

The players donned camouflage "Preparing for Battle" shirts this off-season while working out. They said it's the most physical spring they can remember at Tennessee.

And tucked away in their collective memory banks were the disappointments of the 2000 season, one that saw fans at LSU and Georgia tear down the goal posts after rare victories over the Vols.

"You remember the whole season, people tearing down goal posts and junk like that and people rushing the field on you," Overstreet said. "This year, our motto is going to be: We're not going to let anybody tear the goal posts down on us. ...

"We're going out there to win, going out there to take names and going out there to play like Tennessee ought to play."

To do that, the defense may have to carry the offense early. The Vols will count on a host of freshman running backs and receivers this fall, never an ideal situation in the SEC. Gone is all-time leading rusher Travis Henry, and the receiving corps was average at best during spring practice.

Making it even more difficult to gauge for the Vols was that so many of the skill players missed spring workouts with injuries and other conflicts. Tennessee was so depleted that in one scrimmage, senior fullback **Will Bartholomew** (6-0, 248) operated out of a one-back set.

Help is on the way in the form of *Parade* All-America running backs **Jabari Davis** (6-0, 230) of Stone Mountain, Ga., and **Cedric Houston** (6-0, 205) of Clarendon, Ark. Also arriving are multi-purpose threat **Derrick Tinsley** (6-0, 180) of Marietta, Ga., and highly acclaimed receiving prospect **Montrell Jones** (6-2, 185) of Louisville, Ky.

"If those guys come in and are the type of players we think they can be, we can be a pretty good offense," offensive coordinator Randy Sanders said. "If not, we'll be somewhat limited like we were last year. But we'll make it work."

There was also a gift of sorts last December when minor league baseball player **Kelley Washington** (6-3, 220) decided he wanted to play football again and walked on at Tennessee. The 21-year-old freshman was the hit of spring practice. He started out at quarterback, where he threw and ran for touchdowns, and then showed his versatility by catching a few touchdown passes at receiver. Suffice to say he's going to be on the field somewhere.

"He reminds me of another No. 15 who used to be around here," said Fulmer, referring to former Vols' great Carl Pickens.

There were both good and bad off-season developments for the Vols, who return eight starters on each side of the ball. Henderson decided to return for his final season instead of entering the NFL draft. He's a consensus All-American and college football's most dominant defensive lineman.

"I saw the big picture," Henderson said. "I wanted to enjoy college and enjoy being out there and having fun. The next level is basically money and business, and I wasn't ready for that."

The bad news came after spring practice in May, when sophomore offensive tackle **Michael Munoz** (6-6, 310) underwent his second knee surgery in six weeks. He will sit out this season and attempt to come back for the 2002 season.

Munoz has a degenerative condition in his left knee and had a fragment of decaying articular cartilage replaced. He missed all of spring practice, allowing the Vols to plan without him. But his loss will nonetheless be felt. When the 2000 season ended, the coaches thought Munoz was probably their best offensive lineman.

What Fulmer likes best about this team is the leadership. Henderson, especially, has become a strong leader who has always led by example. But now, he's becoming more vocal.

Even though he sat out the 1998 season as a partial qualifier, Henderson remembers vividly the tone linebacker Al Wilson set for that team.

"That's what we ask of them, the best players to be the best leaders," Fulmer said. "That's when you have a chance to be a really good football team."

Fulmer did make one coaching change in the off-season when he fired tight ends coach Mark Bradley, the first position coach Fulmer has ousted since he took over as head coach. Replacing Bradley was Doug Marrone, who was the offensive line coach at Georgia last season and the offensive line coach at Georgia Tech before that. Marrone will coach the tight ends and offensive tackles for the Vols, while Mike Barry will work with the centers and guards.

2001 SCHEDULE

Sept.	1	Syracuse
	8	@Arkansas
	15	@Florida
	29	LSU
Oct.	6	Georgia
	20	@Alabama
	27	South Carolina
Nov.	3	@Notre Dame
	10	Memphis
	17	@Kentucky
	24	Vanderbilt

QUARTERBACKS

This time last year, the Vols were going in blind at the quarterback position. None of the combatants had any significant college experience. It didn't take long for sophomore **Casey Clausen** (6-4, 210) to make his presence felt. He came to school early last year and went through spring practice and burst onto the scene as a starter against Alabama.

The Northridge, Calif., product completed 62 percent of his passes for a Tennessee freshman record 1,473 yards and 15 touchdowns. He led the Vols to six straight wins to close the regular season, although he bombed in the Cotton Bowl loss to Kansas State.

"When I came here, I expected to compete for the starting job," Clausen said. "It's no different now. I've got to get better every practice and every game."

Blessed with a big-time arm and a quick release, Clausen has all the tools. He also showed uncanny poise for a freshman throughout much of last season. His direction of the offense in the game-winning drive against South Carolina was masterful.

Never short on confidence, Clausen helped the Vols to open up their offense last season with his ability to get the ball down the field. And he also brought a certain swagger that had been missing.

"Casey added a spark last year from an intensity and leadership standpoint," Fulmer said. "It is very unusual to see a freshman take on that much responsibility, but last year we had no choice. He took advantage of a very tough situation and made it a positive."

Clausen seemed to pick up steam, too. He threw for five touchdowns against Arkansas and for four touchdowns against Kentucky. But in the wintry conditions of the Cotton Bowl and against the Kansas State defense—the best one he faced all season—he was reduced to a 7-for-25 performance for 120 yards and three interceptions.

Equally troublesome was Clausen's performance in the spring. He had good days and bad days, and at times appeared to be unmotivated with many of his offensive weapons on the shelf.

"I don't think Casey has put his stamp on the offensive team just yet," Fulmer said after a so-so performance by Clausen in the spring game. "He competes, but he still needs to improve. There's no doubt that he can."

Sanders was even more blunt.

"The timing and continuity of the passing game is nowhere near where it needs to be," he said.

Fulmer monitored Clausen closely over the summer and has made it clear that he thinks there's "another level" Clausen can reach. An All-SEC freshman selection a year ago, Clausen certainly has the physical makeup to do it. But he still has to prove it mentally.

Washington will probably spend most of his time at receiver this season. But there's just something about a mobile quarterback who can break down defenses and make plays that intrigues Fulmer.

Consequently, expect Washington to stay involved in the Vols' quarterback equation. He's not ready to play there on every down, but given a full season and another spring, who knows?

"He's going to be on the field somewhere, and I could envision him getting snaps at both places," Fulmer said.

Washington increased his chances for making major contributions by deciding in late May to stay in Knoxville for the summer instead of reporting to the Florida Marlins' minor league organization. Washington had played in the Marlins' system the last four years and has three years left on his contract.

By not reporting, Washington goes on the

Marlins' restricted list. He plans on resuming his baseball career in 2002.

"Staying here in Knoxville to work out with the football team is something I really need to focus on this summer," Washington said. "This will give me an entire summer to get more comfortable with the offense and to define my role on this football team. It is also important for me to be around the guys who will be my teammates this fall."

Suffice to say Fulmer was pleased with Washington's decision.

Junior **Joey Mathews** (6-3, 215) exited the spring as Clausen's backup and had several nice touchdown throws in scrimmages. Mathews started the opener last season against Southern Miss, suffered an injury and was replaced by A.J. Suggs two weeks later against Florida. Suggs played the rest of the way until Clausen moved into the starting role at mid-season.

Suggs, not thrilled about the demotion, left the team following the Cotton Bowl and is transferring to Georgia Tech.

RUNNING BACKS

The names roll off the tongue like the alphabet. The number of star running backs who've come through Tennessee the past 10 years is staggering. Chuck Webb. Reggie Cobb. Charlie Garner. James "Little Man" Stewart. Aaron Hayden. Jay Graham. Jamal Lewis. Travis Henry.

Suddenly, though, they're all gone. Henry put the finishing touches on a school-record 3,078 career rushing yards last season. He was taken in the second round of the NFL draft by the Buffalo Bills. His value last season was immense. He made so many yards on his own, which is even more amazing when you consider how limited the Vols were in the passing game for much of the season.

Senior **Travis Stephens** (5-9, 185) will get first crack at Henry's tailback job. Stephens played a reserve role last season with 359 yards and seven touchdowns. He agreed to redshirt during the 1999 season so he wouldn't waste a year behind Lewis and Henry.

Quick and elusive, Stephens' strength is making people miss, and he runs bigger than he looks. He started some games during the early part of the 1998 season after Lewis hurt his knee, and most Tennessee fans still remember him dragging Georgia defenders on his back in that game.

"It's my job to lose, and I like it that way," said Stephens, who was slowed by a hamstring injury in the spring and missed a lot of contact work. "Competition is only going to make you better."

The concern with Stephens is whether he's big enough to be an every-down back. Can his body stand up to 24 or 25 carries a game?

Either way, Fulmer said during the spring that he anticipates playing as many as two or three tailbacks this season. The others he had in mind were still finishing up their senior year of high school at the time. Davis, Houston and Tinsley will be on campus this summer and will be thrown into the fire right away.

The Vols have shown in the past that they're not afraid to lean on freshman running backs, and they've been successful, too. Stewart, Hayden and Lewis all come to mind.

"Obviously, we've recruited to our concerns, and hopefully, those guys will come [here] in shape and fill some needs," Fulmer said. "You don't count on that being the whole answer. We'll be all right. But those guys who've been here have got to play well."

Davis has been compared by some to Lewis with his size and powerful running style, although he's not as fast. The one to watch, though, is Houston. He has clocked a 4.4 40-yard dash, runs with power and speed and cuts with the best of them. Tinsley, also a track standout, is more of a speed back who has exceptional footwork.

While the anticipation of getting all three on campus was high this spring, it's still a bit of a gamble to be counting on so many freshmen.

"I'm sure these next few months I'll be a little antsy," Sanders said. "I would sleep a little better if I knew exactly what these freshmen are going to be able to come in here and do."

The Vols are stocked at fullback where Bartholomew had an outstanding spring. He bulked up close to 250 pounds and looked more agile. He got plenty of reps with all the injuries and looked good in the one-back set.

"I feel better than I've felt, faster, stronger and more powerful," Bartholomew said. "I'm happy with where we are, especially the offensive line, fullbacks and tight ends."

Sophomore **Troy Fleming** (6-2, 220) was sidelined the whole spring with a foot injury, but he's shown glimpses of being the kind of fullback who can do a little bit of everything. The hope is that he can provide Shawn Bryson-like contributions with his speed and ability to catch the ball out of the backfield.

Redshirt freshman **Corey Larkins** (5-8, 185) and sophomore **Michael Brewster** (5-6, 173) received most of the work in the spring at tailback. They provide an insurance policy in case the freshmen are slow to adjust.

WIDE RECEIVERS/TIGHT ENDS

Nobody can remember a time when the Vols entered a season with fewer established playmakers on offense than they will this season. The receiver position is in much the same shape as the running back position. The Vols are in need of some newcomers making instant contributions.

Moreover, they also need some of the players who've been around for a while to step up to the plate and deliver on a more consistent basis.

The rock of the Vols' receiving corps has taken his act to the NFL. Cedrick Wilson—chosen by the San Francisco 49ers in the sixth round of the draft—started from the time he was a freshman and caught 12 touchdown passes a year ago.

"I'd like to have Carl Pickens and Alvin Harper and those guys back, but they don't let us do it that way," Fulmer said. "Sure, I'd like to get into some free agency."

Washington is probably the closest thing to a free agent and every bit as athletic as past Vol greats such as Pickens and Harper. He certainly looked the part in the spring.

"It's always nice to have a guy with that kind of athletic ability when you're calling plays," said Sanders, who must now find different ways to get Washington the ball.

Though he took snaps at quarterback in the spring, Washington is needed most at receiver. He displayed the ability to catch the ball and make something happen after the catch during the spring. He also looked like a natural when it came to beating defenders off the line and catching the deep ball.

"I've always been a pure athlete and able to adapt," said Washington, who's originally from Stephens City, Va., and is playing football for the first time in four years. "I came here wanting to show people that I could play at this level, and I think I did that. I've gotten stronger, gotten mentally better as a football player and I've gotten tougher. I've just got to continue to grow."

The player the Vols really need to blossom is junior **Donte Stallworth** (6-1, 190). His problem has been inconsistency. He's been great in one game and a non-factor in the next two. He didn't have a good spring. Stallworth was hampered by a minor injury and also dropped far too many balls.

"He has the ability to be a great player," Fulmer said. "Now whether he'll ever let himself go and do that, we'll see."

Stallworth finished second on the team last season with 35 catches for 519 yards and two touchdowns.

"It's time for me to be the go-to guy," said Stallworth, who has the perfect blend of size and speed. "The team is counting on me to be that guy, and it's a goal I have. It was a little frustrating this spring, but I'm confident I'll get it done this season."

If it's not Stallworth, then maybe it's senior **Eric Parker** (6-0, 172) or junior **Leonard Scott** (5-11, 170). Parker has been dependable and catches the ball just about anywhere, but he's been unable to avoid injuries. Scott is an SEC sprint champion who can beat anybody deep. But his hands are average at best.

Redshirt freshman **Tony Brown** (6-2, 181) sat out the spring after recovering from back surgery. He could be the surprise of the receiving corps and has impressed coaches during informal workouts.

Senior **Bobby Graham** (6-0, 185) will also factor into the rotation. He's best remembered for his game-saving catch against Memphis two years ago.

During the off-season, Fulmer dismissed Eric Locke from the team after Locke admitted to the fraudulent use of a teammate's ATM card. Locke was never really a factor after transferring from Alabama and saw his playing time gradually decrease.

Of the incoming freshmen, Jones has the best chance to jump right in and play. He was chosen Mr. Football in Kentucky last season after catching 72 passes for 967 yards and 14 touchdowns.

Jones, who doesn't have great speed, will need to prove that he can separate from defenders at the SEC level. But he's the kind of player who always seems to come up with the ball.

The Vols seemingly added a weapon to their repertoire this spring in sophomore tight end **Jason Witten** (6-5, 265), who caught touchdown passes in several scrimmages. Fulmer thinks Witten will be an NFL tight end some day.

The tight end has been non-existent in the Vols' offense the last few seasons. But Fulmer said Witten is the first real pass-catching tight end they've had in a while.

"It's up to me to catch the ball and make something happen with it," Witten said. "If I show I can do that, then I'm going to get an opportunity."

Senior **John Finlayson** (6-4, 275) returns as the starter at tight end, but will be used more as a blocker. The Vols have completed just 17 passes to the tight end the last four seasons.

OFFENSIVE LINE

With questions hovering around the skill positions, the experience and depth on the offensive line has helped to ease those concerns. Even without Munoz, this has a chance to be one of the better offensive lines in the league.

There's never any substitute for being able to get three, four, or five yards when you need it. The Vols only wish they had that luxury last season on the failed third-and-2 play against Florida.

"Last year, at times, we really had a hard time just lining up and knocking folks off the ball, getting downhill on folks and bloodying their noses," Sanders said. "I think we are much closer to being able to do that at his point right now than we ever were last year."

The Vols also yielded a league-high 27 sacks

a year ago. Back are five players who started at some point last season, including senior left guard **Fred Weary** (6-4, 301). He's the Vols' best offensive lineman and a potential All-SEC performer.

Weary, who opened as the Vols' center last season, injured his ankle against Florida and missed the rest of the year. He returned in the spring after surgery and was the anchor of the line. An exceptionally strong player, Weary has been plagued by injuries and hasn't been able to completely develop. The Vols desperately need him to stay healthy for the whole season.

"Fred's presence makes an incredible impact, just from an attitude and leadership standpoint," Fulmer said. "He is an example-setter and calls on his fellow linemen and expects them to perform."

Junior **Anthony Herrera** (6-4, 300) started 11 games last season at left guard, but has moved to left tackle. The Vols like his footwork out there, although he had a rough outing in the spring game trying to block Overstreet.

"He (Herrera) brings an attitude of toughness to the offensive line and he's a little better athlete," Fulmer said. "Anthony is so physically gifted and has such a wonderful attitude. There's still another level, that with a few technical things, he can reach."

Senior **Reggie Coleman** (6-5, 315) was the starter at left tackle last season but was moved to right tackle near the end of spring. Fulmer wants to see Coleman become a little more physical.

The up-and-coming prospect at tackle is sophomore **Sean Young** (6-7, 305). He had elbow surgery and missed most of last season. The Vols expect him to push for playing time this season. Fulmer is looking for a certain tenacity at the tackle position he didn't think was there a year ago.

"I don't care who it is; Sean Young, Anthony Herrera, and hopefully, Reggie Coleman will reach those heights," Fulmer said. "We're going to have to be able to knock people off the ball better than we have at tackle in the last year or so."

Sophomore **Scott Wells** (6-2, 287) took over at center last season after the injury to Weary and played admirably. He's a little under-sized, but makes up for it with his smarts, toughness and willingness to battle on every play. Wells could have a fight on his hands to keep the job from sophomore **Jason Respert** (6-3, 305). Had Respert not sprained his knee toward the end of spring practice, he would have been bracketed as a starter at center along with Wells.

Respert was the Vols' most improved lineman during the spring and is a former prep All-American. He could also slide over and play guard.

The starter at right guard coming out of the spring was junior **Will Ofenheusle** (6-8, 320). He started the first five games there last season before being replaced by Toby Champion.

Fulmer is committed to getting the best five linemen on the field, which means there could still be some jockeying. If Young and Respert keep coming, they could be starting by season's end.

One change during the spring was sophomore **Chavis Smith** (6-3, 285) moving from defensive tackle to offensive guard.

The Vols' offensive line made considerable strides in the weight room during the off-season. All five projected starters maxed out at 400 pounds or more on the bench press. Weary led the way with 505 pounds.

2000 STATISTICS

Rushing offense	162.7	39
Passing offense	210.5	62
Total offense	373.2	57
Scoring offense	32.6	19
Net Punting	37.5	19
Punt returns	8.7	55
Kickoff returns	23.5	7
Rushing defense	74.3	3
Passing efficiency defense	119.5	62
Total defense	294.5	13
Scoring defense	19.3	23
Turnover margin	+4	39

Last column is ranking among Division I-A teams.

KICKERS

The place kicking job was wide open heading into last season, but junior **Alex Walls** (6-1, 190) burst onto the scene and had a dream season. A walk-on when the season began, Walls hit on 18-of-20 field goals and was selected one of three finalists for the Lou Groza Award as the top place-kicker in the country.

Walls made his first 14 attempts last season and didn't miss an extra point in 39 attempts. He tied the school record with five field goals against Florida. His strength is getting the ball up quickly, making his kicks difficult to block. He doesn't have great range, but did make all three of his field goals between 40 and 49 yards.

Whether it was a slump or bout with the shanks, Walls did not have a good spring. He was far too inconsistent and missed too many short field goals. It was enough of a concern that Fulmer mentioned senior **Christian Chauvin** (5-10, 195) more and more prominently as the spring progressed. Chauvin is a transfer from LSU.

"Alex really needs to have a great summer and get himself back into the groove," Fulmer said.

DEFENSIVE LINE

The strength of Tennessee's team will be on the defensive line. Three of the four starters return, and one of those is being displaced.

Junior defensive tackle **Albert Haynesworth** (6-6, 310) had a great spring and will team with Henderson to give the Vols the SEC's most imposing one-two punch in the middle.

The other good news is that Overstreet is back at defensive end after fighting through back and knee injuries last season.

The Vols led the SEC with 50 sacks last season. Henderson was the league's individual leader with 12.

"No doubt, we have the best D-line in the country," Haynesworth said. "With our defensive tackles and defensive ends, we're going to get so much push up the field that nobody's going to be able to stop us.

"We've got the same people from last year, more experience. It's like wine. It just gets better with time."

If Haynesworth is as good as he looked in the spring, his assessment could be right on. Terribly immature for most of his first two seasons, Haynesworth played his best football down the stretch a year ago. He picked right back up in the spring and made a living penetrating the offensive backfield.

"I want to be the kind of player that makes a couple of big plays every series, not just a couple every game," said Haynesworth, a consensus prep All-American coming out of Hartsville, S.C. "The coaches have pushed me, and I'm pushing myself."

The biggest difference, Henderson thinks, is that Haynesworth is listening better and absorbing coaching better.

"I've seen a big change in him, and I think you're going to see it on the field," Henderson said.

The other starter at defensive end is senior **Bernard Jackson** (6-4, 255), who has still yet to realize his vast potential. Jackson started in a couple of games last season and is the kind of talent that could break out at any time. But he's yet to do it and has just one more year.

"This is a big year for me and for the whole defense," said Jackson, who has just two career sacks. "There's going to be a lot riding on how we play this year."

Henderson is certain to attract loads of double teams, which means Haynesworth and blitzing linebackers should get plenty of chances. The Vols are deep at tackle, too.

Senior **Edward Kendrick** (6-4, 265) started last season but will open this season as Haynesworth's backup.

Sophomore Lynn McGruder had also shown tremendous promise, but in June he was arrested on drug charges and dismissed from the team.

Henderson never stopped pushing this spring. He senses something special about this team.

"One of the reasons I stayed is that I had a strong feeling about this team," Henderson said. "We're experienced and have a lot of guys who have played. I think we have a real good chance to win a lot of games."

Weary, who went up against Henderson during spring drills, said the best is yet to come from the guy most experts are predicting will be the first player chosen in next year's NFL draft.

"He's letting everybody know that it's time to get back to work, and him also," Weary said. "What he did last year is last year.

"It's going to be amazing to see how good he can be this year on that football field."

Overstreet dropped off to 4 1/2 sacks last season after recording 7 1/2 as a sophomore. But after a knee injury against Georgia, he wore a brace the rest of the season and was never the same.

"It was frustrating, knowing I was this close to making a play to help the team and getting there a second late," Overstreet said.

He underwent arthroscopic knee surgery in January and said his knee is once again healthy. He's still taking cortisone shots to his back. "I would say that 70 percent of the kids in the country wouldn't have been able to finish the season last year," defensive coordinator Johnny Chavis said. "That tells you something about Will."

Depth at end will come from junior **Omari Hand** (6-5, 255) and junior **Constantin Ritzmann** (6-4, 252). Hand improved his stock with a solid spring, while Ritzmann is one of the Vols' quickest pass-rushers.

The Vols signed a pair of junior college defensive linemen, with junior **Demetrin Veal** (6-3, 275) of Cerritos (Calif.) College being a guy who could possibly play end or tackle. The Vols will try him first at end, where he was rated No. 1 in the junior college ranks last season by *SuperPrep.*

Junior **Aubrayo Franklin** (6-2, 290) of Itawamba (Miss.) Junior College could help at tackle. He was a former linebacker in high school.

LINEBACKERS

The Vols lost a pair of big-play performers at outside linebacker in Eric Westmoreland and Anthony Sessions. They were the two leading tacklers on the team last season and combined for 14 1/2 sacks.

Westmoreland—drafted by the Jacksonville Jaguars in the third round—was also the leader of the defense, an extension of Chavis on the field. Their productivity will certainly be missed, but Chavis wasn't exactly fretting about his linebackers in the spring.

In fact, he was excited. "I've been here for 12 years, and we've never started spring practice with a group potentially as good as this group," Chavis said.

Potential can be a dangerous word, but Chavis likes what he sees in some of his young linebackers.

Sophomore **Kevin Burnett** (6-3, 230) has All-American written all over him. He played last season as a true freshman and looms as a bigger version of former Tennessee linebacker Raynoch Thompson. Burnett is projected to be the starter on the weak side. The only concern with him is whether he will be ready for the opener. Burnett separated his shoulder during spring practice and underwent surgery. His rehabilitation will keep him out of contact work during the preseason, and his availability come September is uncertain.

The Vols are set in the middle, where senior **Dominique Stevenson** (6-0, 225) returns for his third season as a starter. Stevenson was a partial qualifier as a freshman, but graduated in four years and regained his final year of eligibility. The top returning tackler on the team, Stevenson had 71 last season and also has the ability to move outside if the Vols need him there. Injuries slowed Stevenson in the spring, and he underwent arthroscopic knee surgery after spring workouts.

Gaining valuable experience in Stevenson's absence was sophomore **Robert Peace** (6-3, 230). Peace was among the most improved defensive players in the spring and made a push for playing time.

Junior **Keyon Whiteside** (6-2, 230) missed the entire spring while recovering from knee surgery. Chavis, though, said Whiteside was pushing Stevenson last season before injuring his knee against South Carolina.

The starting strong side linebacker is junior **Eddie Moore** (6-0, 220), who played in a backup role last season. Moore was also a force on special teams and is a big-time hitter.

The Vols also like sophomore **Tony Campbell** (6-3, 210), who came to Tennessee as a safety. If Burnett doesn't recover in time to be ready for the opener, Campbell could step in on the weak side. Otherwise, he will back up Moore on the strong side.

Chavis loved the competition at linebacker this spring.

"Nobody's got their card punched," Chavis said. "This isn't a union. We'll work our rear off to make sure we get the best out there. You don't play just because you've been there. You've got to be productive."

One of the Vols' most heralded signees was linebacker **Kevin Simon** (5-11, 225) of Concord, Calif. Simon is the highest rated linebacker prospect the Vols have signed in years and could help in the middle or outside. But like Burnett, Simon is also coming off surgery (he injured a knee in a postseason all-star game) and is a serious question mark for this season.

DEFENSIVE BACKS

The Vols caught a break when senior **Andre Lott** (5-11, 185) decided to return for another season after getting an additional year of eligibility for graduating in four years.

Lott, like Stevenson, was a partial qualifier and sat out his freshman season. He's started ever since, both at cornerback as a sophomore and free and strong safety last season.

Part of Lott's decision to come back hinged on being allowed to move back to cornerback, where he should rank among the league's elite. Lott feels more comfortable there.

Who starts at the other cornerback is still anybody's guess. Senior **Teddy Gaines** (6-0, 175) and sophomore **Jabari Greer** (5-10, 170) battled all spring.

Missing in action this spring was senior **Willie Miles** (6-0, 175), who was sidelined with a wrist injury. Miles and Gaines started every game at the two cornerback positions last season but had their troubles.

One problem with all the Tennessee defensive backs was how many potential interceptions they dropped. It was also a group that didn't play the ball in the air very well at times.

The Vols struggled all season to put teams away. The most glaring example came in the Florida game when the Gators drove 91 yards in the final minutes for the winning touchdown.

The biggest concern remains at safety. Sophomore **Rashad Baker** (5-11, 180) is back at free safety. He started during the middle part of last season, but missed the last couple of games with an ankle injury. Baker was also sidelined for much of spring practice. A former receiver, he's shown flashes of being a great one but just needs more time to develop.

The strong safety spot is up for grabs. Sophomore **Mark Jones** (5-9, 171) had a rousing spring after also moving over from receiver. He's fast and loves to hit.

Competing with Jones at strong safety was junior **Steven Marsh** (6-0, 180). He's also a big hitter, but struggles in pass coverage.

The Vols are hoping that junior college newcomer **Julian Battle** (6-3, 205) of Los Angeles Valley College can come in and win one of the safety jobs. Battle, originally from Royal Palm Beach, Fla., was regarded as one of the nation's top junior college prospects. He's played both receiver and defensive back in junior college and has some of the same instincts that Deon Grant had when it comes to going after the football.

Senior **Buck Fitzgerald** (5-9, 180) is an experienced backup at safety, while senior **Tad Golden** (6-1, 190) has also played extensively back there.

If Greer doesn't win one of the starting cornerback jobs, he will be the Vols' nickel back this season.

"The big emphasis has been on making plays, and we've had a couple of guys step up," secondary coach Larry Slade said. "Andre Lott and Jabari Greer have made several plays. Mark Jones and Rashad Baker are playmakers. Teddy Gaines had a real good spring, but we've got to get Teddy making plays."

The Vols were 10th in the league last season in pass defense and pass efficiency defense.

PUNTERS

David Leaverton, despite his forgettable debut as a freshman, developed into one of the better punters in the country. He was the second punter taken in the NFL draft when the Jacksonville Jaguars selected him in the fifth round.

Now the Vols are back to square one.

In the spring, the twosome of freshman **Dustin Colquitt** (6-2, 181) and junior **Seth Reagan** (6-2, 197) battled for the job. The left-footed Colquitt held a slight lead but was having some trouble with his drops. He certainly has the genes. His uncle, Jimmy Colquitt, ranks No. 1 in career punting at Tennessee. Dustin's father, Craig Colquitt, ranks No. 2 in career punting and played for several years in the NFL.

Neither Colquitt nor Reagan has ever punted in a college game. Reagan is also the holder for field goals and extra points.

"Dustin Colquitt stepped up at the end of the spring," Fulmer said. "He has the most talent, but Seth Reagan is hanging right in there."

A third possibility is incoming freshman **Justin Reed** (6-6, 240) of Punta Gorda, Fla. He was a second-team *USA Today* All-American last season and averaged 47.4 yards per punt. Reed is also a baseball prospect as a pitcher and has a 90-mph fast ball.

SPECIAL TEAMS

Assuming Walls gets his stroke back, the Vols should be OK here.

"Alex needs to have a great year again," Fulmer said. "He gives you the confidence that if you get inside the orange area, you are going to be able to score some points."

Of course, it's always scary to go into a season with an untested punter.

Steve Caldwell, who coaches the defensive ends, has been placed in charge of special teams. The return game has great potential. Scott will again return kickoffs. He was fourth in the SEC last season with a 23.6-yard average. Stephens may also get a chance, while Tinsley was a terror at returning kicks in high school.

The punt returner is Parker, who was also fourth in the SEC last season with a 10.1-yard average. Parker is fearless when it comes to catching the ball and rarely ever calls for a fair catch.

Baker filled in some last season for Parker when he was injured and could also get a chance this season to return a few punts.

The Vols' coverage units were generally pretty good last season, allowing just 18.2 yards on kickoff returns and 5.7 yards on punt returns.

Walls is the favorite to kick off. He stepped in for Leaverton last season after Leaverton was slowed with an injury.

RECRUITING CLASS

As usual, Fulmer pulled together one of the top-rated recruiting classes in the country. Most of the analysts agree that he has few peers in the head-coaching field when it comes to attracting the top players.

Since Fulmer became head coach in 1993, the Vols have perennially raked in as much quality talent as anybody in the country. Since 1994, NFL teams have drafted 50 Tennessee players. That's second in the country in that span (to Florida State's 56).

The close to the 2001 class was what was so impressive about this latest haul. The Vols picked up four of the top 40 rated players nationally in the final week, along with Jones. That final haul included three *Parade* All-Americans—Simon, Davis and Houston.

Davis, Houston and Tinsley were rated among the top 10 running backs in the country, while **Keldrick Williams** (5-9, 200) of Montgomery, Ala., was the fourth running back to sign.

"We had an awful lot of people across the country that were interested in coming to Tennessee because of the success we have had at that position," Fulmer said. "I think Jabari Davis, Cedric Houston, Derrick Tinsley and Keldrick Williams certainly give us some security that we can put a quality Southeastern Conference back on the field next fall."

The situation with Houston went right up to the very end. He wavered between Arkansas and Tennessee. Despite enormous pressure to stay in state, he eventually settled on the Vols.

"I think the run by Tennessee (in the final week) has to go down as one of the best in recent memory," national recruiting analyst Jeremy Crabtree said. "To pull off some of the surprises that they did, plus land All-America players like Kevin Simon and Jabari Davis, is amazing.

"We've always known that coach Fulmer could

recruit, but this has to be one of his best efforts yet."

Fulmer was equally pleased with the class, ranked as high as third by one service and among the Top 10 by everybody.

"It seems as if we signed a very athletic group of guys, if you try to just define the class," Fulmer said. "Some guys will fit immediate needs. But most of all, they added to the foundation that is already in place to hopefully have some very fine years here in the future."

The Vols needed playmakers at receiver. Joining Jones were **Michael Collins** (6-6, 215) of Nicholson, Ga., and **Jomo Fagan** (6-2, 175) of Plantation, Fla. Collins, who played quarterback as a high school senior, will also play basketball at Tennessee.

Simon was the plum of the linebacker class, but **Jason Mitchell** (6-1, 215) of Abbeville, La., was another one the Vols had right at the top of their list.

The Vols signed three junior college players, and all three will be counted on to play right away.

The only area the Vols came up short, said Fulmer, was in the offensive line. He wanted to sign one or two more. He also addressed the number of in-state players (at least 14) who signed with schools outside the state such as Texas, Oklahoma, Florida, Florida State and Nebraska.

"We try to be selective to our needs and at the level we think we have to compete at from a national standpoint and make those decisions accordingly," Fulmer said. "There are a lot of guys or several guys we would have liked to have signed in the state of Tennessee. But to be fair to them and us, we elected to pass."

BLUE RIBBON ANALYSIS

OFFENSE	B
SPECIAL TEAMS	A
DEFENSE	B
INTANGIBLES	B-

The biggest thing working against the Vols this season is their schedule. They open at home against Syracuse, and then, instead of getting the traditional week off leading up to the Florida game, travel to Arkansas the second week of the season. The Razorbacks are still smarting from last season's embarrassing 63-20 loss to the Vols.

The trip to Florida conjures up the same old story lines. Tennessee hasn't won at the Swamp in 30 years, and judging by how strong the Gators are this year, that losing streak might get a little longer.

LSU and Georgia come to Knoxville. But there's a trip to Alabama and a non-conference trip in November to Notre Dame. It's certainly not a schedule tailor made for a run at a championship.

Clausen's development will be key. He needs to take another big step and make the people around him better if the Vols' offense is going to fully evolve.

Counting on a bundle of freshmen is never how you draw it up, and it's still difficult to tell how much, if any, the secondary has improved.

On the flip side, the front seven on defense should be something to see, and the offensive line has a chance to be dominant.

Ultimately, though, if the Vols are going to climb back into the Top 10, they will have to do it with their defense.

"The coaches say things like, 'Defense wins championships,' and I believe that," Henderson said. "I think if we're as good as we should be on defense, we'll have a chance to go a long way."

Given the schedule, a BCS bowl might be a stretch—but not as far-fetched as winning at Florida.

Seeing is believing, which begs the question: Why will this year be any different?

(C.L.)

2000 RESULTS

Southern Mississippi	W	19-16	1-0
Florida	L	23-27	1-1
Louisiana-Monroe	W	70-3	2-1
LSU	L	31-38	2-2
Georgia	L	10-21	2-3
Alabama	W	20-10	3-3
South Carolina	W	17-14	4-3
Memphis	W	19-17	5-3
Arkansas	W	63-20	6-3
Kentucky	W	59-20	7-3
Vanderbilt	W	28-26	8-3
Kansas State (Cotton)	L	21-35	8-4

Vanderbilt

LOCATION	**Nashville, TN**
CONFERENCE	**Southeastern (Eastern)**
LAST SEASON	**3-8 (.272)**
CONFERENCE RECORD	**12-7 (5th)**
OFFENSIVE STARTERS RETURNING	**7**
DEFENSIVE STARTERS RETURNING	**7**
NICKNAME	**Commodores**
COLORS	**Black & Gold**
HOME FIELD	**Vanderbilt Stadium (41,448)**
HEAD COACH	**Woody Widenhofer (Missouri '65)**
RECORD AT SCHOOL	**13-31 (4 years)**
CAREER RECORD	**25-62-1 (8 years)**
ASSISTANTS	
	Ed Lambert (Cal-State Hayward '70)
	Assistant Head Coach/Running Backs
	Steve Crosby (Fort Hays State '74)
	Offensive Coordinator/Receivers
	Herb Paterra (Michigan State '62)
	Defensive Coordinator/Linebackers
	Bill Laveroni (California '70)
	Offensive Line
	Dino Folino (Villanova '71)
	Secondary
	Dennis Harrison (Vanderbilt '78)
	Defensive Line
	Bill Maskill (Western Kentucky '71
	Tight Ends/Special Teams
	Jeff Rutledge (Alabama '79)
	Quarterbacks
	Ray Zingler (Utah State '57)
	Recruiting Coordinator/Outside Linebackers
TEAM WINS (last 5 yrs.)	**2-3-2-5-3**
FINAL RANK (last 5 yrs.)	**47-46-70-39-63**
2000 FINISH	**Lost to Tennessee in regular-season finale.**

COACH AND PROGRAM

It had all the ingredients of a breakthrough season. But last year was not one to remember for Vanderbilt or head coach Woody Widenhofer.

The Commodores, after winning five games in 1999, fell off to three wins. They won only once in the conference, and that came against hapless Kentucky.

By the time the season-ending game against Tennessee rolled around, there were swirling rumors that Widenhofer was in trouble. There was even a report by ESPN Radio that he was gone.

Widenhofer, entering his fifth season at Vandy, wound up surviving. But his rope is a short one. He met with Vanderbilt chancellor Gordon Gee and athletic director Todd Turner last November. The gist of that meeting was clearly defined: There needed to be marked improvement in every aspect of the Vanderbilt program if Widenhofer is going to see a sixth year.

What's that mean?

The general feeling in Nashville is that Vanderbilt needs to make a bid for a winning season. And if the Commodores don't get to six wins, they need to at least come very close.

It's a tall order considering the school's football history.

Vanderbilt has suffered through 18 consecutive losing seasons and has finished with a losing record in 24 of the last 25 years.

"Woody knows that we are expecting improvement from his team," Gee said last November. "I am looking for some changes to be made in the off-season that will make us a more competitive team next year."

Turner said there were a number of variables involved.

"We put issues on the table that we think need to be addressed," Turner said. "It runs the gamut, from assessing your offense and your defense to looking at your recruiting to looking at your budget needs and your facilities and your staffing and your strength program and your academic support program.

"Every component that goes into a football program. ... What needs to be done in the next 12 months to help us be in position to win football games next year."

At Vanderbilt, that's never an easy proposition. The rest of the league dwarfs the Commodores when it comes to finances, facilities and football talent.

Vandy, with its pristine academic reputation, is almost an outcast in the SEC. More than once, the question has been raised as to whether the Commodores belong in the SEC.

Of course, that's the least of the worries right now for Widenhofer, whose contract runs through 2004. His only concern is showing more results.

"I think there has got to be an evaluation of each and every coach, including myself," Widenhofer said. "Then I need to create more of a sense of urgency and make sure that we don't have the same kind of collapse next year that we had this year."

To that end, Widenhofer implemented a three-part plan during the off-season. There was some talk that he might make some changes on his staff. While he did shuffle some things around, he didn't fire anyone. But Widenhofer has vowed to take a more "hands-on" approach this season with his staff and players.

"I'm going to get heavily back involved with the defense," Widenhofer said. "That's my strong suit. I've talked it over with (defensive coordinator) Herb (Paterra) and the defensive staff, and they're glad to have me back involved.

"I'll be involved in the scheme, game-planning and coaching on the field."

The second part of Widenhofer's plan involves spreading out the special teams responsibilities to every member of the coaching staff. Bill Maskill handled those chores last season by himself. He will still have a hand in special teams, as well as coaching the tight ends, but everybody else will also help coach special teams. Widenhofer has placed himself in charge of special teams, which broke down in key situations last season.

The third part of Widenhofer's plan centers around developing leadership among the players. He thought his team lacked leadership a year ago.

"I've always felt a leader is born, but I've changed my mind about that and I think a lot of kids are born with leadership characteristics and we need to help develop them," Widenhofer said. "Every Wednesday we'll have our leadership seminars and we'll have guest speakers come in and we'll talk about the importance of proper leadership.

"Plus, we have really upped the efforts in our winter conditioning and weight program in terms of them being more demanding. We've set them up to be individualized. We have four or five groups come in at different times of the day so that they can get the full benefit of our weight coaches."

The void in leadership was most glaring to begin last season. The Commodores' top two defensive players, linebacker Jamie Winborn and cornerback Jimmy Williams, were suspended for the first two games for receiving loans and investment advice from a Vanderbilt booster.

The season opener was equally disastrous. Vandy blew a lead late in the game and lost, 33-30, to Miami (Ohio). It was a sign of things to come, although Widenhofer was proud of the way his team kept fighting.

The Commodores rallied from a 21-3 deficit against Tennessee and nearly upset the Vols in the finale at Adelphia Coliseum.

"If you go out and play the way we did the last two weeks, you can win a lot of games," Widenhofer said. "It is a tough, tough league, and if you are not ready to play mentally, you are going to get beat."

There are two new faces on Widenhofer's staff. Bill Laveroni will coach the offensive line and replaces Mike Deal, who resigned to become the offensive coordinator for the NFL Europe's Scottish Claymores. Laveroni was at Rutgers last season, but was without a job after head coach Terry Shea resigned at the end of the season.

The Commodores also have a new recruiting coordinator in Rahim "Rock" Batton, who will also work with the outside linebackers. Batten took over for Ray Zingler, who moved into a football administration job with the Commodores.

Batten was a safety at Vanderbilt in the late 1990s and had been working as a graduate assistant.

An assistant that nearly got away was quarterbacks coach Jeff Rutledge, who accepted the offensive coordinator's position at Virginia and then reconsidered.

Rutledge, who's been on the Vandy staff since 1995, didn't want to separate from his family for more than a year.

"People who hear about what I did in the coaching profession will say I am nuts," Rutledge said. "Career-wise, it was the right thing to do. But in the end, it was a decision that was not based on my career. It was based on what is best for my family."

The Commodores return seven starters on each side of the ball. But the loss of Jared McGrath and Elliott Carson on offense and Winborn and Williams on defense can't be overlooked. Winborn was chosen in the second round of the NFL draft by the San Francisco 49ers and Williams went in the sixth round to the Buffalo Bills.

New playmakers need to emerge. And above all, Vanderbilt needs to do a better job of running the ball and stopping the run if it's going to improve on last season's 3-8 finish. The Commodores were last in the league in rushing offense (96.5 yards) and tied for last in rushing defense (178.3 yards).

2001 SCHEDULE

Aug.	30	Middle Tennessee
Sept.	8	Alabama
	15	@Mississippi
	22	Richmond
	29	Auburn
Oct.	13	Georgia
	20	@South Carolina
	27	@Duke
Nov.	3	@Florida
	10	Kentucky
	24	@Tennessee

QUARTERBACKS

Senior **Greg Zolman** (6-4, 208) is entering his fifth year in the program and coming off his most productive season. It's the kind of stability at quarterback Vanderbilt hasn't had much of over the years.

Zolman finished second only to Kentucky's Jared Lorenzen in passing yards per game last season. Zolman averaged 221.9 yards and had 2,441 for the season, the most by a Vanderbilt quarterback since 1988. He also moved into third place at Vanderbilt with 5,469 career passing yards and is on track to become the school's all-time passing leader.

Starting a season as the established No. 1 quarterback is quite different for Zolman, who spent the last few years looking over his shoulder. But now he's thrown for 2,000 yards in each of his last two seasons and has started 24 straight games.

Plain and simple, he's the man.

"I've gotten better every year since I've been here," Zolman said. "I think some of the bad things that happened overshadowed the improvements I made (last year).

"I got over the worrying by just playing. When I finally realized the coaching staff has confidence in me, it really helped."

While the left-handed Zolman has clearly made it his job, there's still room for improvement. He was not listed among the league's top 10 in passing efficiency last season and also threw 14 interceptions as opposed to 13 touchdown passes.

Having been in the same offense now for three years, Zolman should be better. He knows what offensive coordinator Steve Crosby wants and has a comfort zone with the plan.

Zolman, who passed for 250 or more yards in six games last season, has also taken on more of a leadership role, somewhat of a novelty at Vandy.

The Commodores haven't really had a quarterback who was a leader under Widenhofer because nobody was settled long enough to fill that role.

"You have to be able to throw the ball to win in the Southeastern Conference, and I think we improved in that area last year," Crosby said.

Zolman was hampered in the spring by a biceps injury in his throwing arm that has bothered him for nearly a year.

"When it flares up, it bothers me and it really does affect my throwing," Zolman said. "When I'm throwing it well that's when it's not bothering me."

The race this spring was for the backup job. Senior **Tim Olmstead** (6-2, 195) and sophomore **Benji Walker** (6-4, 212) each had their moments to keep the competition raging into the fall.

Olmstead, the transfer from Florida, played in three games last season in his first year of eligibility at Vanderbilt. Walker was a redshirt freshman last season and attempted just one pass.

I'm hoping to be the No. 2," said Olmstead, more of a drop-back passer. "If Greg goes down, I want to show them that I am ready to go."

Walker is a better runner than Olmstead and ran some option out of the shotgun during the Commodores' spring game.

"Benji, to me, is a guy that gives you certain things as a runner," Crosby said. "Olmstead, on the other hand, when it comes to being a pure thrower, he can be lethal. I really don't know (who is No. 2) at this point."

RUNNING BACKS

A year ago, the Commodores were last in the league in rushing offense, averaging just 3.1 yards per carry.

McGrath was the main cog in the rushing attack, and he's gone after moving to fourth on Vandy's all-time rushing list.

Not far behind McGrath last season, though, was sophomore **Ray Perkins** (5-10, 191). McGrath had 527 yards and Perkins 425 yards. More notably, Perkins averaged 4.9 yards per carry.

"We always thought Perkins was going to be an impact player," Widenhofer said.

Having gone through his first spring, Perkins figures to be only better his second time around. He did all of his damage last season as a freshman. Blessed with great speed, Perkins concentrated on becoming a more well-rounded back during spring drills. He wants to be a guy who can also effectively run between the tackles and doesn't have to always rely on his speed.

Perkins, despite 13 catches for 102 yards last season, also wanted to improve as a receiver out of the backfield.

Although listed as the No. 1 running back, Perkins heard some footsteps this spring.

Senior **Rodney Williams** (5-11, 208) made a stirring reappearance after falling off the radar screen last season. He gained just 141 yards after leading the Commodores in rushing as a redshirt freshman and sophomore.

There was some sentiment that Williams might go ahead and graduate and not even return for his senior season. But he put that notion to rest with a solid showing in the spring and seems eager to push Perkins.

"There is no way I could leave on the kind of note I made last season," said Williams, who scored eight touchdowns as a sophomore. "I came here to handle some things, and I haven't handled those things yet. I used the spring to get back on track."

Crosby said he would be comfortable with either Perkins or Williams in the backfield.

"Rodney is on a mission to play well," Crosby said. "With those two guys, we have two really good players—and we will need them both."

Redshirt freshman **Norval McKenzie** (5-11, 200) had a good spring game and will provide depth at running back. Senior **Lew Thomas** (6-0, 212) is also a possibility if something should happen to Perkins or Williams. Thomas played receiver last season, but rushed for 286 yards in 1998.

The Commodores used a fullback a little more than they did two tight ends as last season progressed. Junior **Chris Mitacek** (5-11, 208) is their top fullback. He carried the ball just one time a year ago.

Freshman **Matthew Tant** (5-11, 208) of Pegram, Tenn. could also play his way into some carries. He was the Commodores' most heralded signee in the class of 2001.

WIDE RECEIVERS/TIGHT ENDS

The offense will clearly be the strength of this team and has a chance to be one of the best Vanderbilt has had in some time. But for that to happen, the Commodores need a few receivers other than junior **Dan Stricker** (6-3, 201) to make some plays. Stricker is Zolman's favorite target, and the two are extremely close off the field. They've even been known to draw up plays on their own.

Last season, Stricker finished third in the SEC and 18th nationally with 90.4 receiving yards per game. An outstanding route runner, Stricker is also plenty fast enough, as evidenced by his touchdown receptions of 50, 44 and 35 yards last season. He's established himself as one of the league's most dependable go-to receivers and was voted second-team All-SEC a year ago.

"There is a difference between personal confidence and realizing that everyone else has confidence in you, too," Stricker said. "The second part is what I was missing. I definitely had confidence in myself, but I wanted to make everyone have confidence in me. When that happens, then you just elevate your game."

Stricker finished with 61 catches for 994 yards and five touchdowns. The only other Vandy receiver to finish with more than 14 catches last season was Carson at tight end, and he's gone.

The other two most experienced receivers are junior **Anthony Jones** (6-2, 172) and junior **M.J. Garrett** (6-3, 206). Jones, who missed time in the spring with a sprained left hip, led the team with an average of 21.3 yards per catch as a freshman. But he missed the 1999 season for academic reasons and caught just 13 passes for 260 yards last season.

Garrett is the prototype big target, but has struggled with drops and running the right routes. He did have two touchdown catches last season.

The Commodores have moved sophomore **Chris Young** (6-2, 178) to H-back. He played receiver as a freshman and caught just 14 passes for 119 yards and no touchdowns.

Young, Vanderbilt's top signee in the 2000 class, didn't have a particularly impressive spring and needs to show some of the same play-making ability that led to prep All-America honors as a senior in Batesville, Miss. In the spring game alone, Young dropped three passes.

"We can't do that," Crosby said. "We have to find some guys that want to catch the ball and secure the ball."

Sophomore **Ronald Hatcher** (5-10, 170) was moved from running back to H-back and split time with Young in the spring.

The Commodores also signed six receivers in February, and all six played receiver in high school. Widenhofer made it a point to sign players who were pure receivers as opposed to those who projected as receivers. All six will get a chance this fall, and not many of them are expected to redshirt, either.

The best of the bunch is **Jason Mathenia** (6-1, 180) of Copperas Cove, Texas.

Losing Carson will put a dent in the Commodores' short passing game that they've relied on so heavily. Carson had been their second leading receiver for three years in a row.

Junior **Tim Simone** (6-5, 236) will replace Carson in the starting lineup. Simone had 12 catches for 127 yards and a touchdown last season.

OFFENSIVE LINE

There was good news and bad news with the offensive line last season. Zolman's protection was good. He was sacked just 15 times in 11 games. But when it came to running the ball, the Commodores couldn't. They also had trouble scoring, which usually means an inability to knock people off the ball near the goal line.

"We moved the ball well last year, but we've got to score more points than we've been scoring," Widenhofer said. "To win and be in the hunt, you've got to score an average of 25 points."

Last season, Vanderbilt was last in the league and 97th among 114 Division I-A teams in scoring offense (17.5 points per game).

The first order of business this spring was finding replacements for left tackle Brian Gruber and guard Michael Saltsman. They were fixtures up front and had started off and on since their sophomore seasons.

The Commodores shuffled a few people around in the spring and came away with every position settled except for the all-important left tackle spot.

Redshirt freshman **Justin Geisinger** (6-4, 304) and sophomore **Jordan Pettit** (6-4, 284) waged a battle for a starting berth that will extend into fall camp. Widenhofer is excited about the development of Geisinger, who bench-pressed 415 pounds as a high school senior.

The three returning starters are junior center **Jamie Byrum** (6-4, 277), senior right tackle **Pat Green** (6-7, 335) and junior left guard **Jim May** (6-4, 303).

Byrum started all 11 games last season at center and is an excellent pass protector. He's bulked up 25 pounds since coming to Vandy. Backing up Byrum will be sophomore **Jason Tant** (6-3, 270). He's the older brother of touted signee Matthew Tant.

Green is the largest player on the team. He took a redshirt year in 1999 after injuring his ankle and still needs to improve his quickness against the multitude of speed pass rushers in the league.

May made the move from right guard to left guard, while senior **Duncan Cave** (6-1, 284) will take over as the starter at right guard. Cave was a part-time starter last season and is the strongest player on the team. He's a competitive weight lifter during the off-season.

"Duncan has lost some weight, and he's been moving around a little bit better," Widenhofer said. "He's always been strong enough, now he is more mobile."

The concern, an age-old problem at Vanderbilt, is depth. There's very little experience behind the starters. So much so that incoming freshman signee **Nigel Seaman** (6-5, 305) could get a shot at tackle.

The other thing the Commodores have to do is muster some semblance of a running game. They've gone 13 straight games without a 100-yard rusher.

"Ideally, you'd like to be able to run the ball to set up the pass," Crosby said. "But last year, it was more the opposite for us."

2000 STATISTICS

Rushing offense	96.5	102
Passing offense	224.2	47
Total offense	320.7	89
Scoring offense	17.5	97
Net Punting	36.4	27
Punt returns	8.6	72
Kickoff returns	22.0	17
Rushing defense	178.3	80
Passing efficiency defense	114.1	45
Total defense	390.9	78
Scoring defense	24.8	57
Turnover margin	-3	74

Last column is ranking among Division I-A teams.

KICKERS

Already looking for more scoring out of his offense, Widenhofer is banking on a freshman to fill the void at place-kicker.

Lance Garner (6-0, 175) of Kempner, Texas is the heir apparent to John Markham, who departed as the Commodores' all-time leading scorer. Markham, who made 14-of-18 field goals last season, was the second place-kicker taken in April's NFL draft, going to the New York Giants in the fifth round.

Sophomore walk-on **Chuck Folino** (6-0, 170) handled Vanderbilt's place kicking in the spring, but Widenhofer made it clear that it was Garner's job to lose.

As a high school senior, Garner connected on 5-of-8 field goals, including a 52-yarder and 50-yarder. Garner, one of the first players to commit to the Commodores, was voted all state as both a kicker and punter.

DEFENSIVE LINE

Defense had been a constant under Widenhofer. That is, until last season. The Commodores fell off in just about every area. They were 11th in the league in total defense, 10th in scoring defense and tied for 12th in rushing defense.

Seeing the slide, Widenhofer has pledged to be more active with his defense this season.

"My main focus is to get back involved with the defense," Widenhofer said. "It feels good to be working hands on with the players and the coaches again."

Good defense always starts in the defensive line, and the Commodores aren't loaded by any means in their three-man front. The first thing they must do is replace four-year starting nose tackle Ryan Aulds.

Widenhofer is extremely high on sophomore **Brett Beard** (6-3, 281), who came on in the spring. But Beard is untested, and there's even less experience behind him. A pair of redshirt freshmen, **Matt Clay** (6-2, 280) and **Aaron Carter** (6-3, 273), were listed as Beard's backups coming out of the spring.

The best defensive lineman on the team is senior end **Doyle Crosby** (6-4, 302). He had 50 tackles, including two sacks last season. Crosby has started since his redshirt freshman season and has nine career sacks. Crosby is talented enough that he could start for just about any other SEC team, but he's probably the only defensive lineman on the Commodores' roster you could say that about. Crosby, fast for his size, could still afford to drop some weight. He dislocated his shoulder during the first spring scrimmage and missed most of the spring workouts.

The other returning starter at end is senior **Wally Conyers** (6-7, 266). He had 24 tackles last season, but no sacks. Conyers is a rangy player who sometimes has trouble at the point of attack. The depth at end is decent, certainly better than it is at nose tackle.

Junior Ryan Nungesser (6-4, 260) will back up Crosby and Conyers and could even rotate in some as a starter. Nungesser had just one tackle a year ago.

LINEBACKERS

For the first time during Widenhofer's tenure at Vandy, he must replace two starting linebackers—Matt Stewart outside and Winborn inside.

Winborn didn't have a great junior season, and it started inauspiciously enough with his two-game suspension, but he was the kind of playmaker in the middle that Widenhofer's defense requires.

Physical problems weren't the only thing that plagued Vanderbilt on defense last season. There were also too many mental mistakes.

"We've got to get back to the days where we never made mistakes on defense, lined up in the right place all the time and didn't make mental errors," Widenhofer said.

With Winborn giving up his final year of eligibility and being scooped up in the second round of the NFL draft, junior **Mike Adam** (6-3, 240) will get the first chance fill Winborn's inside linebacker position.

Adam started for Winborn during his two-game suspension and struggled. Adam was even pulled out of the Alabama game for being out of position too many times. But in his defense, he was unaware until the very end that he would be stepping in for Winborn. The impending suspension was kept under wraps, and Adam simply wasn't mentally prepared.

"I have never been as excited as I am right now," Adam said. "Being able to watch Jamie the last couple of years was an incredible opportunity. To me, he was the best linebacker that I have ever seen and I'm glad I got to learn under him."

Adam will have to work to keep the job. On his heels is redshirt freshman **Pat Brunner** (6-3, 245).

"It's a pretty good battle," Widenhofer said. "They're both doing very well, and it will probably go on into two-a-day practices next fall. Adam has played some and that helps him, but Brunner is an instinctive guy who is big and strong at 245 pounds. He runs good and is a real tough guy."

Senior **Antuian Bradford** (6-0, 231) returns as the other starter inside. Bradford doesn't have Winborn-like ability, but he's solid. He had 75 tackles, including three sacks last season. His 10 quarterback pressures led the team, and his seven tackles for loss tied for second.

The leader of the defense will be senior outside linebacker **Nate Morrow** (6-4, 248). He had 71 tackles and 2 1/2 sacks last season. Morrow developed into a productive pass rusher as a sophomore after moving over from inside linebacker.

Stepping in for Stewart—a fourth-round pick by the Atlanta Falcons—at the other outside linebacker will be junior **Hunter Hillenmeyer** (6-4, 232). He played some last season and finished with six tackles, but made his strongest push in the spring. Backing up Hillenmeyer is sophomore **Libnir Telusca** (6-3, 225).

"I knew Hunter would play well. Last year's experience helped him," Widenhofer said. "And it's good to see Libnir is pushing him."

One of the biggest surprises of the spring was the rebirth of sophomore **Brandon Walthour** (6-3, 219). Dismissed from the team last season, Walthour came back to get some quality time with the first team this spring. He was filling in for Morrow, who was slowed by a groin injury. Walthour, one of the best athletes on the team, asked Widenhofer in January if he could re-join the team and agreed to pay his own way through school.

Walthour looked as good as any linebacker in the Commodores' camp during the spring and will almost certainly get his scholarship back.

"The coaches really didn't have to give me the chance to redeem myself, so I have to give them credit," Walthour said. "I figured since they gave me a chance I might as well pay them back."

DEFENSIVE BACKS

Three starters are back in the secondary, but gone is left cornerback Jimmy Williams. The team's top cover man, Williams—like Winborn—didn't have a great season last year.

Nonetheless, replacing him won't be easy. Junior **Aaron McWhorter** (6-1, 192) is the player the Commodores are counting on. McWhorter was the nickel back last season and finished with 15 tackles.

In Vandy's scheme, cornerback is perhaps the toughest position to play. The linebackers run free, meaning the cornerbacks get very little help. Teams are sure to test McWhorter right off the bat.

His backup coming out of the spring was sophomore **Ian Gaines** (5-11, 188). He moved over from running back and hopes to have the same success as Williams, who made a similar move.

"I would love to follow in his footsteps in that sense," Gaines said. "I have a chance to play over there speed-wise and agility-wise, so I might as well use it."

Junior **Rushen Jones** (6-1, 195) returns as the starter at right cornerback. The Vanderbilt staff thinks he's a rising star. Jones had seven pass breakups and one interception last season. Jones is big enough and physical enough to take on any receiver.

Jones' backup will be sophomore **Lorenzo Parker** (5-11, 182), who moved over from receiver in the spring.

The starting free safety is junior **Justin Giboney** (6-0, 195). He was sixth on the team in tackles last season with 52 and also had two pass breakups.

Junior **Jonathan Shaub** (6-1, 201) is behind Giboney at free safety. He had an interception last season and provides the only real depth at safety.

Senior **Harold Lercius** (5-11, 195) is the strong safety. He's improved his tackling tremendously and will be one of the better defensive players on the team this season.

Lercius, who began his career as a cornerback, has started 25 consecutive games. He led the secondary and was third on the team last season with 75 tackles. He was also second on the team with six pass breakups.

A trio of high school signees could also get immediate looks in the secondary. **Ben Koger** (6-1, 190) of Brentwood, Tenn., and **Moses Osemwegie** (6-0, 205) of Nashville may be counted on for depth at safety.

Dominique Morris (6-0, 180) is a promising prospect at cornerback and was a teammate of Osemwegie's at Montgomery Bell Academy.

PUNTERS

Senior **Joe Webb** (6-3, 214) is back to do the punting. Last season, Webb was 10th in the SEC with a 38.6-yard average. He had a long of 55 yards and 19 punts downed inside the 20-yard line.

Webb missed the 1999 season with a knee injury and took a redshirt year. He's worked at getting the ball off quicker but has yet to live up to his lofty high school billing coming out of Plano, Texas.

SPECIAL TEAMS

Widenhofer has put the special teams burden squarely on himself. He will oversee that part of the game this season, but with help from all of his assistants.

The Commodores weren't necessarily inept last season in special teams. But they broke down in crucial situations, whether it was a blocked kick here or a bad snap there.

Widenhofer didn't think it was fair to have one coach overseeing special teams and also coaching a position. That's why he assigned every coach on his staff a segment of special teams. For instance, secondary coach Dino Folino will coach the punt return team.

Widenhofer and Maskill will coach the punting team, while running backs coach Ed Lambert will coach the outside cover men on the punt team.

The return units are in good shape. Perkins led the SEC last season and was 15th nationally in kickoff returns with a 24.6-yard average. He had a long of 51 yards.

Hatcher will again return punts. He was sixth in the SEC last season with a 9.4-yard average.

Gone, though, is Jimmy Williams, who returned kickoffs and punts the last few years for the Commodores.

Garner will probably handle the kickoff chores and would be a candidate to punt if Webb struggles.

RECRUITING CLASS

Recruiting is never a snap at Vanderbilt, especially when you're competing against the likes of Florida, Tennessee, Georgia and Alabama. But the reality is that the Commodores don't get caught up in trying to go after the "who's who" prospects or the ones on all the prep All-America lists.

Occasionally, they may get a few national top 100 players. But with their lofty academic standards, it takes a special fit.

Widenhofer was especially pleased with the 2001 class because Vanderbilt was able to keep several players in the talent-rich Middle Tennessee area at home. The best of the bunch was Tant, the highest rated prospect the Commodores signed and one that could have gone just about anywhere.

Penn State, Tennessee, Notre Dame. Nebraska and Ohio State had all shown interest. But Tant committed back in June of 2000, following in the footsteps of his older brother, Jason Tant.

The only question with Tant is where he will play. The possibilities are running back, H-back and linebacker, although Widenhofer said on signing day that Tant would be a running back for the Commodores.

Tant bench-presses 350 pounds and has been clocked at 4.5 in the 40-yard dash. He's truly a physical specimen, the type Vanderbilt doesn't land every day.

"Everybody says that Vanderbilt can't win an SEC championship, but I think it can be done and that's one of my goals," Tant said. "I really like the players and coaches at Vandy, and I think this is the right time to be there. Vanderbilt is also the first school to show confidence in me by offering me a scholarship, so that meant a lot to me."

In addition to Tant, the Commodores didn't have to venture far to sign Morris and Osemwegie, both of Montgomery Bell Academy in Nashville. A fourth local product to join the Vanderbilt program was Koger, also a track standout.

"There was a really good, solid group of Middle Tennessee-area players this year and especially in the Nashville area," Widenhofer said. "We would have liked to have had a few more, but it didn't work out that way. I am really pleased with the four that we did get."

Always on the lookout for quality linebackers, Widenhofer was able to sign **Otis Washington** (5-11, 200) of Saginaw, Mich. Rated among the top 60 linebackers nationally, Washington canceled a visit to Notre Dame after committing to Vanderbilt.

Washington was a SuperPrep All-American and a finalist for the Michigan Athlete-of-the-Year award. He made 150 tackles, including 15 sacks, and had four interceptions last season. As a running back, Washington also rushed for more than 1,300 yards a year ago.

"The problem during his recruitment was that coaches didn't know which side of the ball they wanted him to play on," Saginaw High coach Don Durrett said. "He's the only player who ever started for the varsity team as a freshman at our school and we were awfully good while he was here. He doesn't know what losing is."

A third nationally rated prospect to choose the Commodores was quarterback **David Koral** (6-3, 215) of Malibu, Calif. Koral exploded onto the recruiting scene last season when he threw for 764 yards in a single game. That performance set a national high school record.

Koral finished with 4,068 yards, 44 touchdowns and just 13 interceptions. He attracted interest from Miami, Oklahoma, Washington, Kansas State and Duke.

One of Vanderbilt's priorities during this class was at receiver. The Commodores signed six, including the Texas twosome of **Jerrin Holt** (6-3, 210) of Grand Prairie and Mathenia of Copperas Cove.

The most intriguing of the Commodores' signees was Seaman. Vanderbilt beat out Ohio State for Seaman, who is originally from the island of Dominica and moved to the United States in 1988.

Vanderbilt wound up signing 26 players in February, one more than the NCAA limit of 25. But cornerback **Kelechi Ohanaja** (6-1, 185) of Arlington, Texas will wait until January of 2002 before accepting a scholarship.

BLUE RIBBON ANALYSIS

OFFENSE	C+
SPECIAL TEAMS	C
DEFENSE	C
INTANGIBLES	C

Notice that Widenhofer hasn't made any bold predictions this year. His only comment to the media before the start of spring practice in March was that he was "cautiously optimistic" about the 2001 season.

Obviously, Widenhofer learned his lesson about making predictions after the 3-8 finish last season and will let his team's play speak for itself.

It looms as a make-or-break season for Widenhofer. He probably doesn't have to manufacture a winning season to save his job. But he needs to show progress, which means five wins could be the magic number.

More than anything else, the Commodores need to get off to a good start to build some confidence. Five of the first six games are at home, and the opener against Middle Tennessee State is absolutely critical if Vanderbilt is going to improve on last season's results. That game has been shifted to Thursday night, Aug. 30, at Vanderbilt Stadium.

Then comes Alabama at home, followed by a road date at Mississippi, followed by home games against Richmond, Auburn and Georgia. Finding at least three wins in that stretch is a must because the last half of the schedule is a killer. The Commodores close the season with road dates at South Carolina, Duke, Florida and Tennessee. The only home game in that span is against Kentucky.

Widenhofer knows his team can't afford a repeat of last September.

"Once we got to 0-3, it really changed the attitude, especially on defense," he said.

Ultimately, these Commodores will need the type of defensive effort the fans in Nashville grew accustomed to during Widenhofer's first few years if there's any hope of a winning season. If not, even getting to five wins will be a stretch.

(C.L.)

2000 RESULTS

Miami (Ohio)	L	30-33	0-1
Alabama	L	10-28	0-2
Mississippi	L	7-12	0-3
Duke	W	26-7	1-3
Auburn	L	0-33	1-4
Wake Forest	W	17-10	2-4
Georgia	L	19-29	2-5
South Carolina	L	14-30	2-6
Florida	L	20-43	2-7
Kentucky	W	24-20	3-7
Tennessee	L	26-28	3-8

SUN BELT

BLUE RIBBON FORECAST

1. Middle Tennessee State
2. Idaho
3. North Texas
4. New Mexico State
5. Arkansas State
6. Louisiana-Lafayette
7. Louisiana-Monroe

ALL-CONFERENCE TEAM

OFFENSE

POS. PLAYER SCHOOL HT. WT. CL.

WR Kendall Newsom, MTSU, 6-1, 181, Sr.
WR Chris Lacy, Idaho, 6-0, 183, Sr.
OL Brandon Westbrook, MTSU, 6-6, 285, So.
OL Nick Zuniga, North Texas, 6-3, 319, So.
C Ian Hobbs, North Texas, 6-4, 285, So.
OL Tony Wragge, New Mexico St., 6-3, 3-5, Sr.
OL Garry Johnson, Arkansas State, 6-4, 309, So.
QB John Welsh, Idaho, 6-2, 213, Sr.
RB Dwone Hicks, MTSU, 5-11, 218, Jr.
RB Kenton Keith, New Mexico State, 5-11, 180, Sr.
TE Jerry Pegues, Arkansas State, 6-3, 245, Sr.

DEFENSE

POS. PLAYER SCHOOL HT. WT. CL.

DL Wil Beck, Idaho, 6-2, 310, Sr.
DL Brandon Kennedy, North Texas, 5-10, 325, So.
DL Derrick Marshall, La.-Lafayette, 6-3, 260, Sr.
LB Tanaka Scott, MTSU, 6-2, 266, Sr.
LB Brad Kassell, North Texas, 6-3, 241, Sr.
LB Anthony Hood, MTSU, 6-2, 235, Sr.
LB D'Wayne Taylor, New Mexico St., 6-0, 195, Sr.
DB Charles Tillman, La.-Lafayette, 6-1, 190, Jr.
DB Don McGee, North Texas, 5-11, 190, Jr.
DB Jordan Kramer, Idaho, 5-8, 155, Jr.
DB Joe McClendon, MTSU, 5-10, 182, So.

SPECIALISTS

POS. PLAYER SCHOOL HT. WT. CL.

PK Brian Kelly, MTSU, 6-0, 168, So.
P Grant Autry, Louisiana-Lafayette, 6-1, 200, Jr.
RS Hansford Johnson, MTSU, 5-8, 156, Sr.

OFFENSIVE PLAYER OF THE YEAR

Dwone Hicks, RB, MTSU

DEFENSIVE PLAYER OF THE YEAR

Wil Beck, DL, Idaho

NEWCOMER OF THE YEAR

David Akers, WR, Idaho

SUN BELT NOTEBOOK

The Sun Belt Conference begins its inaugural season with four teams that played in the Big West Conference and three teams that were Division I-A independents last season. Of the Big West teams, only Idaho finished with a winning conference record. The Vandals, 5-6 overall, finished third in the Big West at 3-2. ... The Sun Belt will send its inaugural champion to the New Orleans Bowl to be played the third week of December in the Louisiana Superdome. ... Last season, New Mexico State, North Texas and Arkansas State each finished 1-4 in the Big West and in a three-way tie for fourth. ... Idaho has posted winning records in 17 of the last 19 seasons. Before that run started in 1982, the Vandals had only four winning seasons in the previous 42 years. ... Tom Cable, in his second season as Idaho's coach, played for the Vandals under Dennis Erickson in the mid-1980s. ... Three Sun Belt teams, Louisiana-Monroe, Louisiana-Lafayette and Arkansas State, went 1-10 in 2000. ... In its second season of I-A football, Middle Tennessee was 6-5 in 2000; it was the program's first winning season since the 1996 team went 6-5. The Blue Raiders ranked 16th nationally in total offense. ... New Mexico State will look for just its third winning season since 1967, one coming when the 1999 team went 6-5. ... Louisiana-Lafayette's only victory of 2000 came on Nov. 4 when it beat Louisiana-Monroe, 21-18, but the Ragin' Cajuns may have played their best game in the Nov. 18 season finale when they pushed Middle Tennessee into double overtime before losing, 41-38, in Murfreesboro, Tenn. ... Arkansas State has posted only three winning seasons since it moved to Division I-A status in 1993 and has averaged less than three wins a season. Coach Joe Hollis improved the team's record in each of his first three seasons before going 1-10 last year. ... Louisiana-Monroe is coming off its worst season since 1964.

Arkansas State

LOCATION	Jonesboro, AR
CONFERENCE	Sun Belt
LAST SEASON	1-10 (.090)
CONFERENCE RECORD	1-4 (t-4th Big West)
OFFENSIVE STARTERS RETURNING	5
DEFENSIVE STARTERS RETURNING	4
NICKNAME	Indians
COLORS	Scarlet & Black

HOME FIELD Indian Stadium (33,410)
HEAD COACH Joe Hollis (Auburn '69)
RECORD AT SCHOOL 11-34 (4 years)
CAREER RECORD 15-39-1 (5 years)
ASSISTANTS
Jim Marshall (Tennessee-Martin '72)
Offensive Line
Larry Porter (Memphis '96)
Running Backs
Troy Rothenbuhler (Ohio State '95)
Receivers
Leon Burtnett (Southwestern College '65)
Defensive Coordinator/Inside Linebackers
Phil Davis (Wyoming '82)
Offensive Coordinator/Quarterbacks
Jeff Carter (Mississippi '92)
Defensive Secondary
Mike Conway (Olivet Nazarene '83)
Defensive Line
TEAM WINS (last 5 yrs.) 4-2-4-4-1
FINAL RANK (last 5 yrs.) 91-106-104-102-100
2000 FINISH Beat North Texas in regular-season finale.

COACH AND PROGRAM

It will be a season of change for Arkansas State.

First, the Indians switch from the Big West Conference to the new Sun Belt Conference. Coach Joe Hollis has also added several new coaches, including an offensive coordinator with a new philosophy (Phil Davis).

Arkansas State is also hoping for a change in luck. The Indians have lost eight games the last two seasons by a combined 38 points (4.8 points per game). Last year, ASU lost in double-overtime to North Carolina State by seven points, lost the home opener to Memphis by two points, its homecoming game against Richmond by three points and to New Mexico State in overtime by six points.

The Indians don't even have luck in their own stadium. In the last two years, ASU has gone 4-6 at home. Of those six losses, five were by a total of 20 points, two went into overtime and one was decided on 51-yard field goal as time expired.

When Hollis took over the program in 1996, he pledged to make ASU competitive. The next step is to make the Indians winners, and to help that he persuaded Davis to return to Jonesboro as offensive coordinator and quarterback coach. The former ASU quarterback coach came from Houston, where he served in a similar role.

"I am pleased that Phil has joined our coaching staff," Hollis said. "I was very impressed with him at our first meeting. I have heard only great things about him from people in the coaching profession who have worked with him or coached against him.

"He's extremely knowledgeable about the offensive side of the football, he is very competitive and he knows Arkansas State University. He's a perfect fit for our program."

This will be the third stint at ASU for the 42-year-old Davis, who served one year with ASU's quarterbacks in 1983 before returning to his alma mater, the University of Wyoming, for two seasons.

He then returned to ASU in 1987, where he remained for six years. During that time, he helped lead the Indians to the last of four NCAA Division I-AA playoff appearances.

"I am glad to be back at ASU," Davis said. "I am really looking forward to working with this offense and get things going. I still have friends at ASU and In Jonesboro, and have kept up with the school's progress."

Also added to the staff were Jim Marshall (offensive line) and Mike Conway (defensive line coach).

"Arkansas State has been able to attract quality people to our coaching staffs, and this time is no different," said Hollis, who also serves as the school's athletic director. "I am highly impressed with Jim and Mike. Both of them have been head coaches, which is attractive to me. And, they both want to be at ASU and both can add very positive things to our program."

Marshall comes to ASU from Wyoming, where he coached the offensive line last year. He was head coach at Tennessee-Martin for three years.

"Jonesboro is a beautiful town, and it's just the right size and has everything you want," Marshall said. "The campus is just beautiful, and I've known coach Hollis for a long time. I've never coached with him, but we've coached against each other and I've know him from clinics, conventions and meetings that both of us attended."

Conway was associate head coach at Geneva College in Beaver Falls, Pa., last year. He was head coach from 1997-99 at his alma mater, Olivet Nazarene University in Kankakee, Ill.

"I'm an on-the-field guy, getting into the lives of the players and getting to know them," Conway said. "I was missing some of that as a head coach. So I made a commitment to get back into coaching and I really enjoy that part of it more than anything."

Hollis and the Indians are looking forward to their first year in the Sun Belt Conference, which will feature a berth in the New Orleans Bowl in December for the conference champion.

"The people in the Sun Belt Conference office and the league membership have worked very hard to make Sun Belt football a reality," Hollis said. "They have done a great job putting this football league together. It's great for Arkansas State and our football program to have a more regional flavor with teams that our fans can identify with and fans can look forward to the New Orleans Bowl."

Six home games, including a visit from Ole Miss, highlight the Arkansas State 2001 football schedule.

"We have put together a quality schedule, a competitively balanced schedule," Hollis said. "It should be an exciting year for Indian fans with a six-game home schedule, a marquee game with Ole Miss and a chance for a bowl game with the start of Sun Belt Conference football.

"We're thrilled to have Ole Miss come to Jonesboro and Indian Stadium. I know our fans and players will be excited on Nov. 6, and with it being such a short drive, I'll be surprised if they don't bring a lot of fans as well."

Hollis came to ASU after spending five seasons as the offensive coordinator at Ohio State. A native of Lawrenceburg, Tenn., Hollis joined the Ohio State staff as offensive line coach in 1991 and was promoted to offensive coordinator in 1991. Before OSU, Holllis spent six years at Georgia as the offensive line coach. He also served as an assistant at Troy State, Auburn and Tulsa as well as one year as head coach at Jacksonville State.

2001 SCHEDULE

Sept.	1	@Georgia
	8	@Baylor
	15	Nicholls State
	22	Jacksonville State
Oct.	6	Mississippi
	13	Louisiana-Lafayette
	20	@North Texas
	27	Idaho
Nov.	3	@Middle Tennessee
	10	@New Mexico State
	17	Louisiana-Monore

QUARTERBACKS

Gone is four-year starter Cleo Lemon and his backup, Andy Shatley. Consequently, the Indians enter the 2001 season without a quarterback who has taken a snap in game action.

The battle at quarterback will be a competitive one with the likely starter redshirt freshman **Bryan Gauthreaux** (6-0, 184). He impressed ASU coaches in the spring by showing an ability to scramble and throw with great accuracy.

Also in the mix at quarterback are junior **Tommy Miller** (6-4, 205), redshirt freshman **Jerome Stegall** (6-0, 191) and sophomore **Tye Forte** (6-0, 200).

Miller has seen action only on special teams, but has pocket savvy, good size and an ability to read defenses.

Stegall practiced last fall at wide receiver, but will join the quarterback scramble. He played in a run-oriented system at Wynne High School in Jonesboro and should be a good fit for the option being installed by Davis.

Forte, from Fair High School in Little Rock, Ark., missed two seasons because academics. He was considered one of the state's top athletes coming out of high school and is a threat to run or pass the ball.

Hollis and his staff concentrated on installing the option during spring drills.

"I think it was one of those things that they were a little uncomfortable," Hollis said. "It's going to be a positive weapon for us though. It's very hard to defend. But still, we're working with four quarterbacks and I think you still struggle with continuity when you work with that many. But at this point in time, that's what we're going to continue to do."

In the spring, Hollis said he had no plans to switch any quarterbacks to another position. But he also said each candidate is talented enough to help elsewhere.

As if the quarterback situation wasn't competitive enough, it got even more so in April, when Arkansas State signed Diablo Valley (Calif.) College quarterback **Michael Clark** (6-1, 217). Clark, a junior, threw for 2,051 yards and 16 touchdowns last year in just eight games. He threw for 476 yards and four touchdowns in one game.

"Michael is a great addition for this team as far as skill, experience, talent and leadership goes," Hollis said. "His signing gives us instant experience in the fall at the quarterback position.

"He's a bright young man and adds another dimension to our offense. We were very fortunate that he was still available to be signed so late. We're extremely happy he chose ASU."

RUNNING BACKS

While the battle continues at quarterback, there is no doubt about who is the No. 1 tailback.

Senior **Jonathan Adams** (6-0, 217) rushed for 1,004 yards on 202 carries last fall and scored a team-leading six touchdowns. It was a breakout season for Adams, nominated in 2000 for the Doak Walker Award, given annually to the best running back in college football. Adams was the first running back in ASU history to be nominated for the award.

He has rushed 435 times in his three seasons at ASU and has lost only 166 yards. For every yard Adams loses, he gains 18.25. He is a punishing runner who could become the first running back in school history to reach the 1,000-yard mark in two different seasons.

Adams' backup for the second straight season will be senior **Danny Smith** (5-9, 169). He suffered a hamstring injury and missed two of the last three games last year. Smith rushed for 193 yards on 43 carries.

Also in the mix at running back are redshirt freshman **Quincy Williams** (6-0, 191), redshirt freshman **Tracey Whitaker** (5-10, 200) and sophomore **William Grandberry** (5-10, 201).

Williams received a medial redshirt last year after undergoing knee surgery before the season began. He is expected to be healthy this fall and could contend for a spot in the running back rotation.

Whitaker was impressive last fall with the scout team, and Grandberry redshirted last year after missing the previous year because of academic woes.

ASU lost fullbacks Jacquis Walker and Nick Brumfield, but senior **Sanchez Sherer** (6-0, 240) should fill the void. Sherer was a junior college transfer last year who spent most of his time on special teams. He is an intense player who enjoys the hitting involved with playing fullback.

Backing up Sherer will be sophomore **Frank**

Arritt (6-3, 236), who played "U-back" last year.

WIDE RECEIVERS/TIGHT ENDS

Gone is talented Robert Kilow and his acrobatic antics, but waiting to take over is junior **James "Hiccup" Hickenbotham** (5-10, 173). A speedster who played tailback in high school and prep school, Hickenbotham is the leading returning receiver from last season, when he caught 17 passes for 256 yards and one touchdown.

The other starter at wideout will be senior **Mark Hamilton** (6-3, 193), who caught 10 passes for 196 yards and a team-leading 19.6 yards per catch last year. Also scheduled to see plenty of playing time is senior **Alvin Powell** (6-1, 180), who played in both the slot and on the outside last year. He caught 10 passes for 88 yards.

Several redshirts will be in the battle for playing time at wideout, including freshman **Chuck Walker** (6-0, 171), sophomore **Jerry Mack** (6-1, 203), freshman **Paris Foots** (5-10, 165) and sophomore **Neil Bounds** (6-2, 197).

Junior **Jerry Pegues** (6-3, 245) brought outstanding blocking skillls to ASU from junior college last season and led the tight ends with 13 receptions for 104 yards and three touchdowns. He started eight games.

Sophomore Bob Lanaux (6-6, 260) was a designated blocker at tight end last year. Adding depth at tight end will be walk-on redshirt freshman **Brian Day** and junior college signee **Adam Lancaster** (6-4, 280). Big things are expected of Lancaster, who played at Fort Scott (Kansas) Community College.

OFFENSIVE LINE

The Indians lost three starters, but have two standouts returning in right tackle **Garry Johnson** (6-4, 306) and right guard **John Crossley** (6-2, 307).

Johnson, a junior, was a first-team All-Big West selection a year ago and has been compared to NFL stars Orlando Pace and Korey Stringer, players Hollis coached at Ohio State. Johnson graded out more than 90 percent in every game last season, and is ASU's first All-America candidate on the offensive line since 1987.

Crossley, also a junior, is one of the Indians' strongest players. Johnson and Crossley give ASU an imposing right side of the line.

Starting at center will be either junior **John Allison** (6-2, 275), a junior college transfer, redshirt freshman **Tab Slaughter** (6-2, 265) or junior **Andrew Tripp** (6-1, 297).

Allison was recruited out of Riverside (Calif.) College to bring experience to the center position. Slaughter improved during his redshirt season and Tripp is trying to battle back from several knee injuries.

While the right side of the line is set, the left side is up for grabs. The starters heading into spring practice were redshirt freshman **Brandon Crocker** (6-4, 329) at tackle and junior **Jesse Duncan** (6-4, 342) at guard. Also battling for spots are sophomore **Anthony Mitchell** (6-4, 288), junior **Burt Samples** (6-7, 290) and junior **Luis Nunez** (6-2, 290).

2000 STATISTICS

Rushing offense	128.9	78
Passing offense	183.9	82
Total offense	312.8	97
Scoring offense	22.5	78
Net Punting	32.5	88
Punt returns	12.9	20
Kickoff returns	24.2	5
Rushing defense	207.4	101
Passing efficiency defense	145.5	107
Total defense	453.1	111
Scoring defense	37.3	109
Turnover margin	-3	74

Last column is ranking among Division I-A teams.

KICKERS

Senior **Andy McPherson** (5-9, 166) is scheduled to handle the place kicking duties. He has shown promise in the past, but has not kicked the last two seasons while playing behind Nick Gatto.

DEFENSIVE LINE

Hollis and his staff are excited about the linemen in their 3-4 alignment.

The top two linemen are junior **Corey Williams** (6-4, 278) at tackle and junior **John Bradley** (6-2, 272) at end. Williams and Bradley played last year after sitting out 1999 because of academics. They both had to learn to play the defensive line and made first-year mistakes, but both showed signs of becoming stars.

Williams started out at linebacker, but now weighs 278 and runs a 4.6 in the 40. Bradley bulked up to 272 heading into spring drills. The duo will be tough for most opponents to handle in the Sun Belt.

Scheduled to start at nose tackle is junior **Mark Michaels** (6-3, 260), who came to ASU from Navarro (Texas) Junior College in the spring. He spent four years in the Marines before going to junior college and is a player with discipline and toughness.

Junior **Wayne Heath** (6-2, 275), who played with Michaels at Navarro, will add more experience to the defensive front.

Also trying to move up the depth chart and earn playing time will be sophomore **Brian Rucker** (5-11, 306), sophomore **Bryant Berry** (6-0, 290) and sophomore **Tyrone Jackson** (6-2, 297). Rucker played some last year as a freshman, while Berry is a player who could earn significant playing time this fall. Jackson should add depth at end after playing on the scout team last year.

LINEBACKERS

Senior **Tyshon Reed** (6-0, 205) is the only returning starter among the linebackers. He started on the outside last year and tied for team honors with six tackles for loss.

Sophomore **Brandon Rager** (6-3, 243) earned considerable playing time on the inside last season. He is a good run-stopper who played well as a freshman.

Also listed No. 1 on the depth chart at linebacker are sophomore **Reggie Everett** (6-0, 225) on the outside and senior **Eti Taula** (6-1, 240) on the inside. Everett, from Miami, Fla., was originally signed by Syracuse. He went to junior college after spending one season at Syracuse and joined the Indians during the spring. Taula saw limited playing time in 2000 because of a back injury.

Sophomore **Chris Hogan** (6-0, 238) should see playing time along with redshirt freshmen **Andre Covington** (5-10, 218) and **Aaron Thomas** (5-11, 220). Hogan played on the inside and outside last year.

Sophomore **Lee Echols** (5-11, 201) was scheduled to start at free safety but was shifted to linebacker in the spring.

"You always worry when you start spring ball with 24 total defensive players," ASU defensive coordinator Leon Burtnett said. "I think we'll have to be really smart and hope we don't get people hurt. Right now, we're sitting there with three inside linebackers and three outside linebackers, and that's a major problem in those areas."

DEFENSIVE BACKS

Returning at cornerback is junior **Terrance Fuller** (5-11, 191), who started seven games last season. He also played some safety, and ended the year as one of the best cover men for the Indians.

Sophomore **Chris Jones** (5-9, 169) is scheduled to start at the other corner. He was a wideout before being shifted to the secondary, and started the last two games last year.

Junior **Keith Headley** (6-1,196) should start at strong safety. Echols' move to linebacker may clear the way for junior **Casey Venters** (6-0, 200) to start at free safety.

Senior **Eniak Mpwo** (5-10, 182) is a speedster who should see considerable playing time at the corner.

PUNTERS

McPherson is also scheduled to handle the punting, even though he has never punted in a game before.

In the spring, Hollis signed junior **Brian Federmann** (6-2, 195) from Allan Hancock College in Santa Maria, Calif. Federmann punted 39 times as a sophomore there for a 40.6-yard average. He averaged 40 yards as a freshman.

"We were in need of another punter since Andy Shatley left us," Hollis said. "We are very pleased to add someone of Brian's caliber to our team, and he brings valuable experience that will help us immediately."

Federmann was voted second-team all-conference and was fourth in California in punting last season.

"He's a solid addition to our team in every way possible," Hollis said. "His father is a preacher, he is great in the classroom, and he is strong in the community, too."

SPECIAL TEAMS

Hickenbotham will return kickoffs and punts. He averaged 25.6 yards on kick returns last season, including a 99-yard return for a touchdown. For his career, Hickenbotham averages 25.9 yards on 28 punt returns.

Smith filled in some last year as the Indians' punt returner, and could be the main returner in the fall. Adams will offer help returning kicks.

RECRUITING CLASS

Arkansas State signed 27 players on national signing day.

"It was a team effort," Hollis said. "Our coaches did a great job of recruiting. My hat's off to our assistants. I keep saying this year after year, but once we get a youngster on campus, we have a great opportunity to sign him. We've got a great product to sell, we know how to present it, we've got a plan, we've got a direction, we've got a goal."

Arkansas State later signed a quarterback (Clark) and punter (Federmann) to push the total to 29 players.

"Our emphasis in recruiting this year was obviously character and obviously talent," Hollis said. "We did our homework on every signee. We wanted to make sure they fit in at ASU and fit in Northeast Arkansas.

"Academically, it's a sound group. We're very pleased. I'm excited about this group and what kind of flavor it will add to our football program and our football team."

The battle at quarterback will be joined in the fall by freshmen signees **Josh Driscoll** (6-2, 210) and **Elliot Jacobs** (6-2, 210).

Driscoll played at Southside high in Fort Smith, Ark., where he led his team to a state runner-up finish. He passed for 3,175 yards and 36 touchdowns on 291-of-457 passing and rushed for 810 yards and 10 more scores. Driscoll runs a 4.58 in the 40 and was chosen an Arkansas Top-12 by the *Forrest Davis Recruiting Annual* and one of the top prospects in *Jeff Whitaker's Deep South Football Recruiting Guide.*

Jacobs played at El Dorado (Ark.) High, where he rushed 259 times for 1,768 yards and 18 touchdowns while passing for 1,867 yards on 135-of-266 and 18 touchdowns as a senior. He was considered an "Arkansas Star" in the Deep South Guide.

Signees at tailback were freshmen **Antonio Warren** (5-11, 185) and **Andrae Rose** (6-0, 198). Warren played at Wynne (Ark.) High and was chosen to the Associated Press Super Team as a defensive back. He carried 200 times for 1,853 yards and 23 touchdowns as a senior. Rose played at Jonesboro (Ark.) High, where he ran for 1,441 yards on 241 carries as a senior. He scored 18 touchdowns, 16 on the ground.

An impact player at fullback could be **Beau Shrable** (6-0, 240), who played at Osceola (Ark.) High. He bench presses more than 400 pounds and squats more than 600.

Help at wide receiver could come from freshmen signees **Jason Boyd**, (6-4, 185), **Terrance Chavis** (6-2, 208), **Andy Auth** (6-1, 190), **A.K. Moulton** (5-10, 175) and Jason Wood (5-11, 175). Boyd played at Beaumont in St. Louis, Mo., where he caught 22 passes for 628 yards and five touchdowns. Chavis caught 32 passes for 1,021 yards and 12 touchdowns at Fordyce (Ark.) High. Auth played at Germantown (Tenn.) Houston, where he chosen All-Metro by the *Memphis Commercial Appeal.* Moulton caught 18 passes for 325 yards at Sam Houston High in Arlington, Texas

Coming in the fall to add depth in the offensive line are **Steve Gibbs** (6-3, 335) and **Michael Southern** (6-3, 275). Gibbs was a four-year starter on the defensive and offensive lines at Bartlett (Tenn.) High. Southern registered 16 "pancake" blocks at Northside High in Fort Smith, Ark.

Chavis may get a chance at linebacker, along with freshmen **Eddie Walker** (6-1, 200) and **Steve Tookes** (5-10, 235).

Walker made 150 total hits at Fordyce (Ark.) High.

Several signees could also move into the depth chart in the secondary. Tookes played at Stephenson High in Stone Mountain, Ga., where he made 136 total hits with 12 sacks.

Several other signees, as many as 18, could wind up on the depth chart.

BLUE RIBBON ANALYSIS

OFFENSE	A-
SPECIAL TEAMS	C-
DEFENSE	B
INTANGIBLES	B+

Arkansas State opens the season at Georgia and Baylor before a home dates against Nicholls State and Jacksonville State. Then comes the home game against Ole Miss before the new Sun Belt season opens with Louisiana-Lafayette.

Davis will bring more success to the offensive side of the ball in the future, and the Indians' luck will eventually change in close games. Still, this is a team with only nine returning starters and too many gaps to fill for a winning season in 2001.

Look for another season around 3-8 for the Indians, but don't be surprised if Hollis and his squad are ready to compete for a Sun Belt championship in the near future.

(S.C.)

2000 RESULTS

North Carolina State	L	31-38	0-1
Oklahoma	L	7-45	0-2
Memphis	L	17-19	0-3
TCU	L	3-52	0-4
Richmond	L	27-30	0-5
Mississippi	L	10-35	0-6
Idaho	L	25-42	0-7
New Mexico State	L	29-35	0-8
Utah State	L	31-44	0-9
Boise State	L	14-42	0-10
North Texas	W	53-28	1-10

Idaho

LOCATION	**Moscow, ID**
CONFERENCE	**Sun Belt**
LAST SEASON	**5-6 (.454)**
CONFERENCE RECORD	**3-2 (4th Big West)**
OFFENSIVE STARTERS RETURNING	**5**
DEFENSIVE STARTERS RETURNING	**5**
NICKNAME	**Vandals**
COLORS	**Silver and Vandal Gold**
HOME FIELD	**Martin Stadium (37,600)** **Kibble Dome (16,000)**
HEAD COACH	**Tom Cable (Idaho '86)**
RECORD AT SCHOOL	**5-6 (1 year)**
CAREER RECORD	**5-6 (1 year)**
ASSISTANTS	**Brett Ingalls (Idaho '84)** **Offensive Coordinator** **Ed Rifilato (California Coast '98)** **Defensive Coordinator** **Tony Crutchfield (BYU '91)** **Cornerbacks** **Tim Drevno (Cal State Fullerton '92))** **Offensive Line** **Rich Fisher (Colorado '92)** **Receivers** **Pat Fitzgerald (Northwestern '97)** **Linebackers** **David Hansburg (Amherst College '90)** **Safeties** **Todd Hoiness (Idaho '91)** **Running Backs** **Brian Thure (California '95)** **Tight Ends**
TEAM WINS (last 5 yrs.)	**6-5-9-7-5**
FINAL RANK (last 5 yrs.)	**93-97-74-86-91**
2000 FINISH	**Lost to Boise State in regular-season finale.**

COACH AND PROGRAM

After taking over the football program at his alma mater last season, Tom Cable watched his Vandals stumble early with three straight losses to Washington, Montana and Oregon.

Undaunted, Cable kept the Vandals focused, and they responded with five victories in their last eight games. The five wins left Cable and Idaho fans confident about the possibility of a winning season in 2001.

"We've done a lot of work this winter as coaches," Cable said. "We had to improve, too. We've done a lot of research and we visited a lot of people on both sides of the ball and had people come in here and help us.

"That's what my role is—to help my coaches get better with the players getting better. Together it will work. We certainly know that we were just as much, if not more, of the problem last year than the players we were playing with."

Before taking over the Idaho program, Cable was offensive coordinator in 1999 at the University of Colorado. He was the Colorado offensive line coach in 1998 after coaching the same position at California from 1992-97. Cable had previous jobs as an assistant at Nevada-Las Vegas and Cal State Fullerton.

A four-year letterman at Idaho, Cable started three years at guard and was voted All-Big Sky Conference in 1985. His coach was Dennis Erickson.

"The one person I'm most proud to be associated with is Dennis Erickson," Cable said. "He really got things going in 1982. I'm so thankful and so lucky and so blessed to be the first one who played for him to come back and do this."

Idaho moves from the Big West to the Sun Belt this season, where it joins Arkansas State, New Mexico State, North Texas, Middle Tennessee State, Louisiana-Lafayette and Louisiana-Monroe.

"I think the whole thing is a positive for us in our program right now," Cable said. "We're in the middle of growing as a program in terms of our facilities and the continued surge up the ladder in Division I. I think all of that helps us tremendously.

"Being in a conference is good for a couple reasons. One you're able to recruit to it. You're able to recruit to kids to still be all-conference, still have a chance to be All-American. You're playing for a championship; you're playing for a bowl opportunity."

Getting off to a better start will be a goal for the Vandals, who open against Washington State, Arizona, Montana Washington and Boise State.

"The first five, six weeks will be very, very important for us to stay healthy and get off to a good start," Cable said. "Then we start the league. We start right away with probably the two toughest teams in the league with Middle Tennessee State on the road. The next week we go to New Mexico State. If there are two preseason favorites, it's probably them."

After the first day of spring practice, Cable said he felt confident there is plenty of talent to sort through as he prepares the Vandals for the 2001 season.

"It was good to get back out there and get done with 5-6," said Cable, referring to last year's record. "I was excited to get started on the field again.

"This group of kids has really worked hard and had a great winter. It was fun to watch them today. They enjoyed it. They had fun. There's good tempo. Guys are hustling, working hard and they're pushing each other. That's what I want for this football team."

2001 SCHEDULE

Aug.	30	Washington State
Sept.	8	@Arizona
	15	@Montana
	22	@Washington
	29	Boise State
Oct.	6	@Middle Tennessee
	13	@New Mexico State
	20	Louisiana-Lafayette
	27	@Arkansas State
Nov.	3	Louisiana-Monroe
	17	North Texas

QUARTERBACKS

Senior **John Welch** (6-2, 213) threw for 3,171 yards last season after breaking his right ankle and missing six games in 1999. In 1998, Welch led the Vandals to their first bowl victory (Humanitarian Bowl) and was voted the game's most valuable offensive player.

Last year, Welch joined former Vandals greats John Fresz, Doug Nussmeier, Ken Hobart and Ryan Fein in the 3,000-yard club. He is fifth on the Vandals' career passing list with 5,186 yards

"Obviously, John is the starter now," Cable said. "What we've got to do is develop a backup quarterback."

Idaho's other quarterbacks are sophomore **Brian Lindgren** (6-4, 203) and redshirt freshman **Adam Mallette** (6-2, 213). Lindgren was redshirted in 1999 and was a backup last season. Mallette was redshirted last year after starting three years at Rocky Mountain High School in Fort Collins, Colo.

"Brian has really changed his work habits," Cable said. "I see his maturity getting better. If he can continue to do that, I think he's a good talent.

"We think very much of Adam. He had a tremendous fall as a redshirt. I think they're going to have one of the best battles in terms of competition on this football team."

In the spring game, Lindgren completed 8-of-14 passes for 99 yards for the winning team. He was intercepted once.

Mallette was 20-of-44 for 212 yards, but failed to lead his team to a score.

"You could see a noticeable difference out there," Cable said. "I thought Brian did a lot of really good things. I thought Adam could never get settled down and find his rhythm. We'll have to look at the film, but I'm sure this battle is going to go on into fall camp."

RUNNING BACKS

Senior tailback **Anthony Tenner** (5-9, 202), who missed the 2000 season with a broken finger, rushed for 100 yards on 14 carries and one touchdown in the spring game. He has a career average of 4.5 yards per carry.

"In Anthony we've got stability, leadership, maturity, a guy who's been in the game, a guy who's run for a bunch of yards already," Cable said. "He has proven he can do it at this level."

Sophomore **Zach Gerstner** (5-10, 195), Tenner's main competition for the starter's job, missed the spring scrimmage with a sprained ankle. He rushed 58 times for 304 yards and four touchdowns last season as a backup to Willie Anderson. He also caught seven passes for 72 yards and a touchdown.

"Zach was very, very valuable last year, very steady," Cable said. "He brings a sense of security to the coaches at that position."

Also in the chase for time at tailback is junior **Blair Lewis** (5-11, 205), who joins the Vandals from Pasadena City College in Arcadia, Calif. A powerful runner, Lewis had 235 carries for 1,525 yards at PCC and also returned kicks and punts.

Cable believes some depth at tailback will come from freshmen **Paul Ziegler** (6-0, 175) and **Leslie Lee** (5-8, 190).

Competing for the starting job at fullback will be senior **Laki Ah Hi** (6-0, 237), junior **Kevin O'Connell** (6-2, 238) and sophomore **Nate Griffin** (5-11, 229).

Ah Hi played running back as a freshman in 1997 before redshirting in 1999. He was moved to linebacker in 1999, but came back to the offensive side in 2000 primarily as a blocking back. O'Connell, a quarterback in high school, was moved to fullback last year where he started the final three games. Griffin started six games last year and carried three times for 27 yards.

"Fullback is nice because you've got a number of guys who were there," Cable said. "I think we're in great shape for the future as well as the immediate. We've got good runners, good ball catchers, good physical guys. That's going to be a strength of the offense."

Two redshirt freshmen—**Willie Sipoloa** (6-1, 231) and **Brian Yarno** (6-0, 224)—will also compete for playing time at fullback.

WIDE RECEIVERS/TIGHT ENDS

The Vandals were loaded at wide receiver last year, but the only proven returnee is senior **Chris Lacy** (6-0, 183). In 2000, Lacy led the Vandals with 45 catches for 776 yards.

"Chris is the one guy who has proven over time and big games that he can make plays at this level, but we have to find more guys like him," Cable said. "We have got to find playmakers."

Cable hopes two of those playmakers will be junior college signees **David Akers** (6-0, 179) and **Andrew Hill** (5-10, 160). Akers, a junior, joined the Vandals after two outstanding seasons at Chaffey (Calif.) College. He caught 59 passes as a freshman and 39 more last year in Chaffey's run-oriented offense. Hill, like Akers, is expected to make an immediate impact on the Vandals' offense.

"We went out and got David and Andrew to come in here and speed us up first of all," Cable said. "What I really liked about David is his playmaking ability. He's very elusive. He's very good after the catch."

Returning to the Vandals after a suspension will be sophomore **Orlando Winston** (6-0, 182). Junior **Josh Jelmberg** (6-1, 189) started five games at wide receiver last year and junior **Chris Belser** (5-11, 173) started three games. Jelmberg caught 44 passes and Belser had 15 catches.

"Orlando will add an element of play-making ability," Cable said. "He was very much on his way to being a starter before the suspension."

Also returning after a redshirt season will be senior **Rossi Martin** (6-0, 171). He was the Vandals' second-leading receiver with 33 catches for 483 yards and four touchdowns in 1999.

"In Martin, we're getting a playmaker back," Cable said. "Now all of a sudden (receiver) and the quarterback position really should be the best positions in our offense."

The starter at tight end will be senior **Geoff Franks** (6-4, 246), who backed up all-league performer Mike Roberg last year. Franks caught 16 passes for 175 yards.

"I think Geoff will be every bit as effective as Roberg," Cable said. "There are some things he does better than Mike; there are some things he doesn't do as well. I think he's going to give us a dimension blocking. The nice thing about Geoff is he can get down the field; stretch the field and he's proven."

OFFENSIVE LINE

Cable was pleased with the openings made by the Silver team offensive line during the spring game.

"I really saw nice things in that line," he said. "Any time a back can come out here and run for 100 yards behind a glued together, mismatched offensive line, that's good."

The only returning starter is sophomore tackle **Jake Scott** (6-5, 279), who originally walked on but later earned a scholarship. He started 11 games last season.

"Jake is a very excited young player who more than holds his own," Cable said. "I think you'll see him start to dominate in some games this year and then in the last two years of his career be a star. He's a great one to have in terms of starting a new project and a new offensive line and building around him. He is a good leader; has good character and loves to play the game."

Cable believes several other linemen are ready to break through this season, including sophomore **Matt Martinez** (6-2, 3-6), senior **Joel Barker** (6-4, 272), junior **Seann Mumford** (6-6, 199), redshirt freshman **Tony Kiel** (6-3, 315), sophomore **Jason Cobb** (6-4, 228) and sophomore **Kyle Stewart** (6-2, 307).

"There are a number of guys here you really feel like it's about their time now," Cable said. "So that issue of depth we had last year, even though we had a quality line, I think will be a little bit better this year."

Also joining the line will be junior college signees **Ray DeAnda** (6-9, 325), **Robert Mitchell** (6-1, 319) and **Ariel Bellofiore** (6-3, 342). All are juniors.

"All three of those guys bring you some maturity," Cable said. "I think that group, and with what we have here right now, we have a chance to be very strong in the offensive line."

2000 STATISTICS

Rushing offense	148.0	56
Passing offense	305.2	9
Total offense	453.2	8
Scoring offense	29.2	41
Net Punting	31.3	98
Punt returns	4.5	110
Kickoff returns	18.3	85
Rushing defense	166.5	73
Passing efficiency defense	145.4	106
Total defense	437.6	105
Scoring defense	34.3	103
Turnover margin	-12	104

Last column is ranking among Division I-A teams.

KICKERS

Junior **Keith Stamps** (5-10, 227) has been a backup at place-kicker and punter since walking on in 1998.

The kicker, however, will probably be signee **Brian Pope** (6-1, 210). A sophomore, Pope played one season at San Bernardino Valley College in Colton, Calif. He was 6-for-6 on field goals last year with his longest a 47-yarder. He missed only one point-after kick and averaged 49.5 yards per punt.

At Colton High School, Pope was 13-for-13 on field goals with his longest 51 yards. He didn't miss an extra-point kick in high school.

DEFENSIVE LINE

Senior **Will Beck** (6-2, 310) started every game last year at tackle as did senior **Ryan Knowles** (6-3, 252) at end. Junior **Mike Jones** (6-3, 278) started nine games at tackle and junior **Josh Jelinek** (6-4, 311) started two games.

Also back for the Vandals will be senior defensive end **Dennis Taeatafa** (6-3, 260), who missed the 2000 season to be with his mother, who died last fall. A key backup in '98 and '99, Taeatafa has 19 tackles and six tackles for loss in his career.

Two other linemen expected to compete for playing time are redshirt freshman **Brian Howard** (6-2, 261) and sophomore **Dan White** (6-2, 229).

"You start looking at them and you think 'wow.' You start to see something developing and now it's starting to happen," Cable said. "I'm excited about that group. They give us a chance to have a real dominant front seven."

LINEBACKERS

None of the starters return, but sophomores

Patrick Libey (6-2, 225), **Jordan Lampos** (5-10, 234) and **Jason Williams** (6-2, 225) saw plenty of action in 2000. Libey had 17 solo tackles and 11 assists, Lampos finished the season with 26 tackles and eight assists and Williams added 25 tackles and a quarterback hurry.

"Libey and Lampos are both growing up a lot," Cable said. "They're still young but they didn't play and act like young people. Jason was very valuable for us last year."

Cable expects immediate help from junior college transfer **James Staley** (6-1, 214), who played last year at Chaffey (Calif.) College. He is touted as one of the top signees for the Vandals after making 83 tackles and three quarterback sacks last year in earning all-conference honors.

"James was really about as fine a playmaker as I saw on defensive film," Cable said. "We were really lucky to get him."

Cable also made some roster changes by moving senior **Brad Rice** (6-1, 211) and junior **Jordan Kramer** (5-8, 155) from safety to linebacker.

"What it did, and you could already see it in winter drills, was speed us up on defense," Cable said. "We're more athletic in the front seven, we've got more speed in the front seven."

As a sophomore, Rice was the Vandals' second-leading tackler with 94 and he added 92 more last season. He played quarterback in high school. Kramer started nine games last year at free safety and was the team's leading tackler with 58 solo stops and 29 assists.

DEFENSIVE BACKS

Junior **Tim Sams** (5-9, 178), who started one game last year at cornerback, has been moved to safety. Senior **Ighe Evero** (5-11, 204) returns at safety and along with Sams will form the building blocks at the position.

Also expected to compete for playing time at safety are junior **Sergio Robletto** (5-10, 186), Redshirt freshman **Mike Wakefield** (5-11, 199) and prep star **Nate Nichols** (6-2, 205). Robletto played last year at Long Beach City College in Downey, Calif., and could play some safety. Wakefield played running back and punted at Durango High School in Durango, Colo. Nichols was a three-year starter for Walla Walla (Wash.) High School, where he was ranked on the second tier of the *Seattle Times* Top 100 players.

"Nate could come in here and play right now in terms of depth," Cable said. "He may not be a starter, but I think he could help us right away."

Returning at cornerback are senior **Duval Seaamster** (5-11, 174), sophomore **Antjuan Tolbert** (5-11, 164) and redshirt freshman **Simeon Stewart** (5-8, 161). Two junior college signees will also compete for starting positions—**Sammy Ruben** (5-9, 270) and **Ricky Crockett** (5-10, 190). Both are juniors.

"We've got some numbers and some guys who can come in and help us do this right away," Cable said.

PUNTERS

Returning as the Vandals' punter will be sophomore **Ryan Downes** (6-5, 184), who had 58 punts for a 35.9-yard average last season. He had 15 kicks inside the 20 and a long punt of 63 yards.

"Ryan really struggled the first half of last season," Cable said. "If we can get him to pick up where he left off and improve from there he will be spectacular. I think he's got a big-time future."

SPECIAL TEAMS

Lacy's career average of 25.6 yards per kickoff return is third best all-time at Idaho. He led the Vandals and was 31st in the nation in kick returns last year with 15 for an average of 23.3. His longest return was 45 yards.

Downes may be headed for an exceptional year as a punter while the place-kicking duties should be fine in the hands of newcomer Pope.

RECRUITING CLASS

Cable and his staff started the recruiting season by signing eight junior college players to scholarships in December, including four offensive linemen, two defensive backs, one receiver and one linebacker.

"The offensive line obviously was a need for us," Cable said. "It was really important for us to get four mid-year players.

"It's key having them come in in January because the longer an offensive line is together, the better they become."

When it came time to sign high school players, Cable and his staff didn't stray far from home.

"The neatest thing about this class, to me, is how we brought the University of Idaho back to the Northwest," he said. "We got 14 kids from right here in our backyard.

"That's pretty big. The fun thing for me is, not only are they from here, but they're good players. Our talent level went way up and our size went up and our speed went up."

Six Idaho high school players top the list of Cable's second recruiting class. Along with them came six from Washington, two from Oregon, two from Colorado and one from California.

"The high school list is very strong; very deep," Cable said. "It's got everything in it. I really like the depth of the class. There are a couple of steals in this class for us."

Cable was very pleased to sign Pasco (Wash.) High School defensive lineman **Brandon Kania** (6-3, 230) and Central Catholic High School quarterback **Michael Harrington** (6-4, 190) from Portland, Ore.

Kania was a three-year starter at tight end and defensive end for Pasco.

"He has a great work ethic both on the field and in the classroom," Pasco coach Steve Graff said. "He's very quick to the football. He's also very good at studying the opponent and figuring out what they're trying to do."

As a senior, Harrington completed 61 percent of his passes (186-of-302) for 2,900 yards. He had 38 touchdown passes and 11 interceptions. As a junior, he threw for almost 1,800 yards.

"He's really matured physically and probably more importantly, mentally," Central Catholic coach Joe Bushman said. "He's got a great work ethic."

Cable and his coaching had to scramble for recruits in his first season with the Vandals. It was different the second time around.

"I can't thank my coaches enough," Cable said. "Again, they've done an outstanding job of finding the best players to fit our needs. Recruiting is a long process and it takes them away from their homes and families. I'd like to express my gratitude to their families, too, for the support they've shown in helping us build the future of Vandal football."

BLUE RIBBON ANALYSIS

OFFENSE	B-
SPECIAL TEAMS	C
DEFENSE	B-
INTANGIBLES	B

Cable and his staff filled some needs with their recruiting class, but the key once again will be the first third of the season. Included in the stretch are an Aug. 30 home opener against Washington State and road trips to Arizona, Montana and Washington.

"Being able to play in August against Washington in a TV game is pretty neat," Cable said. "Motivation on both ends is good for both WSU and Idaho. Then we play another Pac-10 school in Arizona and they have been traditionally a defensive power.

"Montana had a great year, being runner-up in I-AA. I think that speaks to what their program has become and has been for a while now. Then Washington. When you get a chance to play the Rose Bowl champion, that's a neat thing for everybody involved."

If the Vandals can escape key injuries in the early part of the season, they could be a factor in the race for the Sun Belt championship. The offense should be fine after a finish of eighth nationally last year in total offense.

"I'd rather finish eighth in scoring," Cable said. "I think we've got to score more points. That means better in the kicking game as well as the red zone.

"In general, I think we have a chance to be very good on offense. I think the big question is how we rebuild the offensive line, if they're able to allow us to run the ball and protect the quarterback. If we can do those things, I think we can be a littler better on offense."

Nine players who started at least one game last season return on defense.

"My gut feeling is we're going to be a completely different defense than we were a year ago," Cable said. "Not maybe necessarily in how we look or what we're doing, but how we play.

"I don't care if you give up a million yards, don't give up points. The bottom line is points—how many you score, how many you give up. That's got to become our mentality. I expect us to be very good."

It will be difficult for Idaho to overcome Middle Tennessee and New Mexico State, but Cable isn't ready to concede a trip to New Orleans.

"I think what (commissioner) Wright Waters and the Sun Belt Conference have done by getting a bowl game in the Super Dome in New Orleans is really, really big time," Cable said. "Once this thing comes down, and hopefully we're fortunate to play in it, and people see it and spend a week in New Orleans will raise the level of excitement for this league and for the bowl game itself."

(S.C.)

2000 RESULTS

Washington	L	20-44	0-1
Montana	L	38-45	0-2
Oregon	L	13-42	0-3
Washington State	W	38-34	1-3
Montana State	W	56-7	2-3
West Virginia	L	16-28	2-4
Arkansas State	W	42-25	2-5
Utah State	L	14-31	2-6
North Texas	W	16-14	3-6
New Mexico State	W	44-41	4-6
Boise State	L	24-66	4-7

Louisiana-Lafayette

LOCATION	**Lafayette, LA**
CONFERENCE	**Sun Belt**
LAST SEASON	**1-10 (.091)**
CONFERENCE RECORD	**NA**
OFFENSIVE STARTERS RETURNING	**5**

DEFENSIVE STARTERS RETURNING 10
NICKNAME Ragin' Cajuns
COLORS Vermilion & White
HOME FIELD Cajun Field (31,000)
HEAD COACH Jerry Baldwin (Miss. Valley State '75)
RECORD AT SCHOOL 3-19 (2 years)
CAREER RECORD 3-19 (2 years)
ASSISTANTS Gary Bartel (Texas Tech '76)
Assistant Head Coach/Defensive Backs
Larry Edmondson (Texas A&M '83)
Offensive Coordinator/Quarterbacks
Tony Tademy (Louisiana Tech '83)
Defensive Coordinator/Linebackers
Cordell Bailey (Alcorn State '80)
Tight Ends
Mark Miller (LSU '95)
Offensive Backs/Assistant Recruiting Coordinator
Tucker Peavey (Southern Mississippi '86)
Offensive Line
Tyke Tolbert (LSU '91)
Wide Receivers/Recruiting Coordinator
Carey Bailey (Tennessee '92)
Defensive Tackles
Troy Wingerter (USL '93)
Defensive Ends
TEAM WINS (last 5 yrs.) 5-1-2-2-1
FINAL RANK (last 5 yrs.) 78-101-98-107-111
2000 FINISH Lost to MTSU in regular-season finale.

COACH AND PROGRAM

Most times it's difficult for a team that suffered through a 1-10 season to look back and find something positive to build on for the future.

That isn't the case with Louisiana-Lafayette.

Primed for its first season in the new Sun Belt Conference, Louisiana-Lafayette and the other teams in the new league realize the team to beat in 2001 is Middle Tennessee State University.

Flash back to Nov. 19, 2000: Middle Tennessee State 41, Louisiana-Lafayette 38 in double-overtime.

"The kids showed a lot of character to come back at Middle Tennessee, a team that was playing pretty well and predicted to beat you by four touchdowns," Louisiana-Lafayette coach Jerry Baldwin said. "To go out and lay it on the line showed a lot of heart and character.

"We got a glimpse into what Sun Belt Conference play is going to be like. That game tells me and our team that, if we continue to improve, we will be right in the mix as far as contending for the Sun Belt Conference title."

Forgetting about his team's one-victory 2000 season, Baldwin believes the Ragin' Cajuns should compete for the Sun Belt championship.

"That's our goal," he said. "Middle Tennessee was probably playing better than anybody in the league, and we should have beat them. We are right in the mix. There is no team in the Sun Belt Conference now that had a dominant year, except Middle Tennessee. We played them into double-overtime and had an opportunity to win the game. We just did not know how to close the deal."

The Ragin' Cajuns are excited about the 2001 season because they will be opening a new chapter in the history of the school. After five years as an NCAA Division I-A independent, Louisiana-Lafayette will move into the Sun Belt with a chance of earning a trip to the Louisiana Superdome—and the fledgling New Orleans Bowl—in December as league champion.

Sun Belt opponents must venture into "The Swamp," where the Ragin' Cajuns are 88-70-2 at Cajun Field since the stadium was completed in 1971. The field sits two feet below sea level in a natural bowl. The nickname came about because of that and the proximity to nearby wetland areas.

"We have far more to sell now than we did a year ago or two years ago," Baldwin said. "We still have a fine university with fine academics. The record has nothing to do with the quality of the school.

"We now have more to sell in that we are discussing conference play, an opportunity to play for a conference championship, an opportunity for a bowl and individual honors within the conference. I am excited about what we have to sell, so we will sell those as hard as we can."

Despite Baldwin's optimism, the Indians have won a total of six games the last four years. Still, Baldwin hasn't lost sight of what he was hired to do on Dec. 10, 1998—turn the program into a winner.

"We haven't lost any confidence," Baldwin said. "We feel we are on the right track. We're disappointed in the outcome of the 2000 season. We felt we should have won more games than we did, but that's behind us.

"Our goal is to win the Sun Belt Conference championship. We are in position to contend for that and we just have to continue to look forward. We can't look back."

Baldwin came to Louisiana-Lafayette after serving on the LSU staff for six years. He was the Tigers' defensive line coach in 1998 after working with the linebackers in 1993-94 and the defensive ends in 1995-97.

Baldwin was instrumental in developing LSU's defense that rose from last place in the SEC in 1993 to first in '94. He also helped guide the Tigers to an Independence Bowl berth in 1995 and '97 and a Peach Bowl bid in '96.

During his time at LSU, Baldwin coached Gabe Northern, a two-time first-team All-SEC selection and a second-round NFL draft selection by the Buffalo Bills in 1996; Kenny Mixon, a second-round draft pick by the Miami Dolphins in '88; and James Gilyard, who teamed with Northern to make up one of the nation's top defensive end tandems.

Another prominent LSU player tutored by Baldwin was nose guard Anthony "Booger" McFarland, who completed his LSU career in '88 after earning two All-SEC honors, being voted the defensive most valuable player in the Peach Bowl in '96 and the SEC Defensive Player of the Year in '95.

Before coaching at LSU, Baldwin served 10 years as a defensive coach at Louisiana Tech. He became assistant head coach, the first African-American in school history to hold that position.

Baldwin has a reputation for being a sound recruiter and in his career has coached three All-Americans and seven players who played in the NFL.

"We made tremendous progress this spring," Baldwin said after the spring game. "We are ahead of where we were a year ago. We are a better football team now that we were at any point last year.

"We've made some significant progress. It's really been good. We've improved in every area of the game. The attitude has been great and the enthusiasm has been good, so you want to keep that going."

2001 SCHEDULE

Sept.	1	Nicholls State
	8	@Minnesota
	15	@Central Florida
	22	Southern Mississippi
	29	Middle Tennessee
Oct.	6	@Arizona State
	13	@Arkansas State
	20	@Idaho
	27	Louisiana-Monroe
Nov.	10	@North Texas
	17	New Mexico State

QUARTERBACKS

Sophomore quarterback **Jon Van Cleave** (6-4, 232) threw for 199 yards and a touchdown in the spring game. He received the outstanding offensive back honors from the coaching staff and finished the night 17-of-35 with one touchdown pass.

Backup quarterback **Matt Lane** (6-0, 192), a redshirt freshman, was 16-of-32 for 172 yards and a touchdown pass.

"I was very pleased with both quarterbacks," Baldwin said. "They showed great leadership and poise and moved the ball."

In 2000, Van Cleave completed 60-of-132 passes for 687 yards and one touchdown. He was intercepted five times. In high school, Van Cleave was a three-year starter at Pantego Christian School in Arlington, Texas. He threw for more than 5,700 yards and 83 touchdowns during his prep career and was ranked No. 25 nationally and No. 3 in Texas by analyst Tom Lemming.

RUNNING BACKS

The No. 1 tailback on the depth chart is junior **Jerome Coleman** (6-1, 225), who ran for 416 yards on 114 carries last year. He scored four touchdowns. Coleman ran for 46 yards on 15 carries in the spring game.

Senior **Trikeith Miller** (6-0, 195), who gained 10 yards on 13 carries in the spring game, is also expected to see considerable playing time.

Sophomore **Ivan Taylor** (6-2, 185) thrilled the spring game fans with a 30-yard touchdown run.

In the Louisiana-Lafayette offensive scheme, there are four wideouts and no fullback.

WIDE RECEIVERS/TIGHT ENDS

The Ragin' Cajuns are loaded in the receiver corps. Leading the way are two returning starters and an all-star candidate who will be a full-time wide receiver this fall.

Both senior **Marcus Wilridge** (5-11, 195) and junior **Andre George** (6-0, 200) started last year for the Ragin 'Cajuns. Wildridge returns for his third season and should continue his rise among the Cajun receiving greats. He ranks among Louisiana-Lafayette's top eight career leaders in both receptions and receiving yardage. Last season, Wilridge had 38 catches for 524 yards and three touchdowns. George caught 24 passes for 404 yards and two touchdowns.

George was voted the outstanding wide receiver during spring drills.

Junior **Nick Dugas** (6-1, 185) is one of the top returning rushers and passers for the Cajuns, but is being moved into the full-time roll of receiver and punt returner for the 2001 season.

Last season, Dugas ran for 125 yards on 53 carries at quarterback. He also completed 10-of-25 passes for 76 yards.

The other starting receiver on the depth chart is sophomore **Frederick Stamps** (5-10, 165), who caught 21 passes for 151 yards last year. After one spring scrimmage, Stamps received praise from Baldwin.

"Offensively, Fred Stamps really stepped up and played well," Baldwin said.

Stamps caught 21 passes for 151 yards during a stellar career at Carver High in New Orleans.

The backups at wide receiver are juniors **Cory Scott** (6-3, 205) and **Elijah Mallery** (6-0, 160), redshirt freshman **B.J. Crist** and sophomore **Eric Bartel** (5-9, 160). Scott had four receptions last year for 24 yards.

Louisiana-Lafayette also returns its starting tight end in **Josh Joerg** (6-3, 235), a sophomore who caught only one pass for seven yards last year. Backing up Joerg will be junior **Blake Bourque** (6-1, 235) and redshirt freshman **Lawrence Johnson** (6-5, 237).

OFFENSIVE LINE

The only returning starter in the offensive line is junior tackle **Jonathon Raush** (6-7, 265), a tight end in high school who started 11 games in 1999. He was voted the most outstanding offensive lineman during spring drills.

Raush earned All-Louisiana honors in 1999 as the offensive line opened holes for tailback Darren Brister to become the school's all-time leading rusher among backs, trailing only quarterback and current Philadelphia Eagle Brian Mitchell in that category.

"The defense should be ahead of the offense right now," Baldwin said during the final week of spring practice. "The offensive is relatively young, particularly up front."

The other starters on the spring depth chart were sophomore **Marques Smith** (6-4, 348) at right tackle, sophomore **D'Anthony Batiste** (6-3, 273) at left guard, redshirt freshman **Paul Balensiefen** (6-2, 308) at right guard and senior **Garrett Charkalis** (6-3, 310) at center.

Backups in the offensive line will be sophomore **Chris Perrone** (6-5, 315), sophomore **Jay Smith** (6-1, 265), junior **Josh Newton** (6-3, 270), sophomore **Cory Monroe** (6-4, 300), and redshirt freshman **Demetrios Brooks** (6-4, 311).

2000 STATISTICS

Rushing offense	123.6	81
Passing offense	161.8	94
Total offense	285.5	105
Scoring offense	15.5	105
Net Punting	29.5	108
Punt returns	10.4	42
Kickoff returns	16.6	106
Rushing defense	150.8	59
Passing efficiency defense	131.3	95
Total defense	387.0	76
Scoring defense	32.3	92
Turnover margin	+2	51

Last column is ranking among Division I-A teams.

KICKERS

Junior **Jonathan Knott** (6-2, 190) will handle the place kicking duties. A signee from Northeastern Oklahoma A&M in Miami, Okla., Knott was an all-conference first-team honoree in the Southwest Junior College Football League.

He made 12-of-17 field goals and 56-of-62 point-after kicks in two years in junior college.

Knott was a four-year letterman as a kicker at Broken Arrow (Okla.) High. He helped lead the Redskins to one conference championship and four appearances in the state playoffs.

DEFENSIVE LINE

The Louisiana-Lafayette defense showed signs of brilliance at times in 2000 and 10 starters return.

Headlining the returnees in the defensive line is senior end **Derrick Marshall** (5-11, 220), who made 46 tackles last year with 11 tackles for loss and seven sacks en route to All-Louisiana honors.

"Derrick is having a great spring," Baldwin said. "His pass rush has really improved and he has shown a lot of leadership."

Other starters returning are sophomore end **Daniel Taylor** (6-1, 236), junior tackle **Charley Smith** (6-4, 275) and junior nose guard **Walter Sampson** (6-3, 240).

Sampson made 33 tackles last year, including seven tackles for loss and seven sacks. Smith finished the season with 15 tackles and Sampson had 33.

Sampson was listed on the spring depth chart behind senior **Chris Gistorb** (6-2, 280), who made 10 tackles last year.

Also in the hunt for playing time are sophomore **Derace James** (6-3, 255), senior **Darrell Cottonham** (6-2, 290) and sophomore **Emmitt Holiday** (6-3, 215).

LINEBACKERS

Returning starters at linebacker are juniors **Marrious Berry** (5-11, 220) and **Ricky Calais** (5-11, 212). Berry made 44 tackles last year while Calais was right behind with 43.

The starter at "Sam" linebacker will be junior **Ross Brupbacher** (6-1, 220), who was selected the most outstanding linebacker during spring drills. He made 29 tackles in 2000, including two sacks.

Brupbacher drew praise almost daily from Baldwin during spring practice.

"I saw a lot of aggressive play from Brupbacher and Calais," Baldwin said.

Berry is actually listed behind sophomore **Antonio Floyd** (6-2, 230) at "Mike" linebacker.

Calais is the "Will" linebacker, and will get relief help from junior **Marcus Malveaux** (5-11, 221). The backup for Brupbacher will be sophomore **Trey Randall** (6-1, 210).

DEFENSIVE BACKS

An all-star candidate for the Ragin' Cajuns is left cornerback **Charles Tillman** (6-1, 190), a junior.

A year ago, Tillman led the Cajuns with six interceptions, the highest total by a Louisiana-Lafayette player since Orlando Thomas, now with the Minnesota Vikings, made six in 1996. Tillman finished the 2000 season ranked No. 9 nationally with 0.55 interceptions per game and was voted to the first teams of both the All-Louisiana and *Football News* All-Independent teams.

Another all-star candidate, sophomore free safety **Kyries Hebert** (6-3, 205), wants to break the record held by Tillman and Thomas. Hebert, known for his hard hits, has led the Cajuns in tackles each of his first two seasons.

"I want to lead the team in interceptions this year with at least seven," Hebert said. "I don't know if he (Tillman) knows it, but I'm taking it this year. I'll be sure to remind him.

"I was also looking at Orlando Thomas' tackle record. I'm looking to go after that. It took him four years, but I'm going to do it in three."

Hebert was impressive during spring drills with his crushing tackles.

"Right now, it's about competitiveness," he said. "If you are a competitor, you are going to go out and treat it like a game situation. That's what we've been doing this spring."

Hebert's brashness is just fine with his coach.

"Kyries has shown some real leadership, Baldwin said."

Also returning in the secondary is strong safety **Peter Villia** (5-10, 190), a senior. He was voted the most outstanding defensive back during spring drills. The starting right cornerback will be either senior **Darien King** (5-8, 160) or senior **Brad Franklin** (6-1, 190).

PUNTERS

Junior **Grant Autrey** (6-1, 200) returns as the Cajuns' punter. Last season, Autrey punted 81 times for an average of 37.1 yards per kick. His backup will be reserve tight end Joerg.

SPECIAL TEAMS

Baldwin and his staff would like for Autrey not to punt 81 times again next year, and they believe Knott will be a good addition as the team's place-kicker.

Dugas will be the primary punt and kick returner, with backup help from Stamps and George.

The holder is sophomore **Eric Bartel** (5-9, 160) and the snapper is junior **William Delahoussaye** (6-2, 240).

RECRUITING CLASS

Baldwin and his staff signed 21 players on national signing day, including seven junior college players. One of the signees, Knott, will be the Cajuns' punter.

Two defensive backs are among the junior college players—junior **Quinton Boyd** (5-11, 195) and junior **Jamaal Sanders** (5-11, 190).

Boyd, who played at New Mexico Military Institute in Rosswell, N.M., is from Sidney Lanier High School in Montgomery, Ala. He helped his team to a combined 17-6 record the last two seasons. His high school team went 29-8 during his last three seasons.

Sanders also played last year at New Mexico Military. He earned four letters as a strong safety, cornerback and linebacker at Bayshore High School in Brandenton, Fla.

Offensive lineman signee **Antoine Grant** (6-4, 345) played last year at Jones County Junior College in Ellisville, Miss. He was a member of the 12-0 national championship team in 1998, and was an all-state honoree and an All-America second-team honoree in '99. He was voted the team's most valuable offensive lineman. Grant played at Quitman High School in Shubuta, Miss.

Another player from New Mexico Military, offensive lineman **Josh Newton** (6-3, 270), also signed with the Cajuns. Newton was an all-state honoree at Goddard High in Roswell, N.M.

The Cajuns signed a wide receiver in **Claude Whitaker** (6-1, 200) from Blinn Junior College in Brenham, Tex. He played running back at Clear Book High in Houston.

The final junior college signee linebacker is linebacker **Trey Randall** (6-2, 225), from Kilgore (Texas) Junior College. He also played at Clear Brook, where he posted more than 100 tackles one season and ended his prep career at Clear Brook's all-time leading tackler.

Among the high school all-stars signed by the Louisiana-Lafayette staff was quarterback **Ryan Lampton** (6-0, 205), from G.W. Carver High in New Orleans. He graduated early from high school and participated in spring drills with the Cajuns.

Lampton threw for 800 yards and six touchdowns as a senior. He also rushed for 300 yards and two touchdowns. A versatile athlete, he also caught 22 passes for 400 yards.

The Cajuns also signed a place-kicker in **Lucas Murphy** (5-11, 185), from St. Thomas More high in Lafayette. He made 46-of-50 extra-point kicks and 4-of-10 field goals. He had three field goals of more than 50 yards and also averaged 42.1 yards per punt. He also had 36 touchbacks on kickoffs and made a school-record 59-yard field goal and a 57-yarder.

Also among the high school signees were six

offensive linemen as the Ragin' Cajuns look to improve their scoring output in the future. Headlining the linemen was Nathan Roger (6-4, 265), who played at Thibodaux (La.) High School. He was chosen by the Thibodaux Quarterback Club as the city's most valuable offensive player. He was a member of the preseason *Louisiana Football Magazine* offensive first team and was on the list of its top 80 recruits.

Also on the offensive side, Baldwin and his staff signed wide receiver **Bill Sampy** (6-1, 175) from Carencro (La.) High. He helped lead his team to the 1996 state championship, and once caught five passes for 116 yards in a game.

The final five high school standouts are defensive specialists. Headlining the group is defensive back **Jerrell Carter** (5-8, 175) from Amite (La.) High School. Playing cornerback and wingback, Carter led his team to a 16-0 record and the state championship. He was a three-time all-district and two-time all-state honoree.

Another good catch was linebacker **Carlos Davis** (6-1, 215) from Fair Park High in Shreveport, La. He made 100 tackles and also came up with three sacks and three interceptions his senior season. Also a basketball standout, he helped lead Fair Park to a 34-5 record and a berth in the Top 28 Tournament as a senior.

BLUE RIBBON ANALYSIS

OFFENSE	C-
SPECIAL TEAMS	C-
DEFENSE	C+
INTANGIBLES	B

Baldwin put a lot of stock in the Ragin' Cajuns' close loss to Middle Tennessee State in the season finale. It was a good effort by Louisiana-Lafayette, especially because the Blue Raiders are the preseason choice to take the inaugural Sun Belt Conference football championship.

Still, it's hard not to look at the facts surrounding the Louisiana-Lafayette program. Things like five straight losing seasons.

Louisiana-Lafayette could make some noise in the new league, but the non-conference schedule includes Minnesota, Central Florida, Southern Mississippi and Arizona State.

"The pressure that I feel is not pressure, but motivation to get the job done," Baldwin said. "I don't need any outside entity to move me to do what I am supposed to do. I am self-motivated. I will work as hard now as I have ever worked."

It will take hard work, another good year from the veteran defense and a yeoman's effort from the young offense to get this program in the winning column in 2001.

(S.C.)

2000 RESULTS

Sam Houston State	L	14-21	0-1
Texas	L	10-52	0-2
Texas Tech	L	0-26	0-3
Northwestern State	L	21-23	0-4
UAB	L	2-47	0-5
Tulane	L	37-38	0-6
Louisiana Tech	L	14-48	0-7
North Texas	L	0-13	0-8
Louisiana-Monroe	W	21-18	1-8
Jacksonville State	L	14-28	1-9
Middle Tennessee	L	38-41	1-10

Louisiana-Monroe

LOCATION	**Monroe, LA**
CONFERENCE	**Sun Belt**
LAST SEASON	**1-10 (.091)**
CONFERENCE RECORD	**NA**
OFFENSIVE STARTERS RETURNING	**7**
DEFENSIVE STARTERS RETURNING	**8**
NICKNAME	**Indians**
COLORS	**Maroon & Gold**
HOME FIELD	**Malone Stadium (30,437)**
HEAD COACH	**Bobby Keasler (ULM '70)**
RECORD AT SCHOOL	**6-16 (2 years)**
CAREER RECORD	**84-50-3 (11 years)**
ASSISTANTS	**Mike Collins (ULM '83)**
	Defensive Coordinator/Linebackers
	Stan Humphries (ULM '87)
	Offensive Coordinator/Quarterbacks
	Darryl Mason (Arkansas '82)
	Wide Receivers
	Manny Michel (Tennessee Tech '84)
	Defensive Line
	Pat Murphy (ULM '83)
	Strong Safeties
	Kenneth Ray (Southern Miss '95)
	Running Backs/Tight Ends
	Tim Rebowe (LSU '87)
	Defensive Backs
	Chris Truax (LSU '92)
	Offensive Line
	Roger Carr (Louisiana Tech '84)
	Recruiting Coordinator/Administrative Assistant
TEAM WINS (last 5 yrs.)	**5-5-5-5-1**
FINAL RANK (last 5 yrs.)	**81-93-96-100-113**
2000 FINISH	**Lost to Wofford in regular-season finale.**

COACH AND PROGRAM

Injuries and a brutal early schedule in 2000 led to Louisiana-Monroe's worst season since joining the Division I-A ranks in 1994.

The 1-10 record included eight losses where the Indians scored 10 or fewer points. Three losses were shutouts and another was a 70-3 blowout at Tennessee.

The offensive breakdown led ULM coach Bobby Keasler to make the first coaching changes since taking over the program in 1998. Keasler promoted quarterbacks coach Stan Humphries to offensive coordinator. Humphries played quarterback on the Indians' 1987 I-AA national championship team.

Humphries will move the offense to a one-back set from the spread used in the past. The offense averaged just 242.3 yards per game last year, 112th among Division I-A teams. The Indians were 114th in I-A—that's dead last—with their average of 8.7 points per game.

Eight starters return to the offensive unit who started at least four games last year, including junior quarterback **Andy Chance**.

Also new to the offense is wide receivers coach Darryl Mason, who takes over for former wide receivers coach/offensive coordinator Roger Carr. Carr is now the Indians' recruiting coordinator.

In another coaching move, Kenny Ray will take over the running back coaching duties as well as coaching the tight ends. He coached tight ends and helped offensive line coach Chris Truax with the tackles last season.

On the defensive side, Tim Rebowe replaces Ray Richards as the secondary coach. A graduate of LSU, Rebowe served the last six seasons as the defensive backs coach at Nicholls State and the last three as recruiting coordinator there.

Another change this season for ULM will be joining the new Sun Belt Conference with Arkansas State, Idaho, Louisiana-Lafayette, Middle Tennessee State, New Mexico State and North Texas. The Indians have competed as a I-A independent the last seven seasons.

Keasler thinks the move to a conference will provide immediate benefits.

"I can see some rivalries right off the bat," Keasler said. "With North Texas and Louisiana-Lafayette being so close, those can be rivalry games and I can see us developing a nice rivalry with Middle Tennessee."

Middle Tennessee is the team ULM has to shoot for, Keasler thinks, as the new league begins play.

"In my opinion, not knowing too much about New Mexico State and not having seen North Texas for a few years, Middle Tennessee could be the team to beat in the Sun Belt."

Last season, ULM opened the season by playing at Minnesota, Memphis and Tennessee in the first four games. The 2001 season opener will be at Malone Stadium against Sam Houston State. Road games will follow to Florida and Cincinnati before the conference schedule begins. Also on the non-conference schedule are Central Florida and Troy State

"It's really important for us to open up at home," Keasler said. "It's always tough if you open up on a negative.

"Cincinnati, a Conference USA opponent, is a good test for us. Central Florida should also be a good test for us. It's a very competitive schedule."

The 1-10 season last year was just the fourth losing record in Keasler's 11 years as a head coach and just the second with less than five wins. The Indians lost 16 first- or second-team players for at least one game to injury last season and eight starters missed at least one game with injuries.

"We had a good spring and there's no question we're further along now than we have been in the past," Keasler said before the ULM spring game. "We're getting our numbers up and that's going to provide us depth into the program, the ones who will come in the fall and the Sun Belt Conference this fall, we're getting where we need to be as a football team."

During the off-season, 12 Louisiana-Monroe strength records were broken by nine different players representing practically all areas of the team. Also, five different Indians broke the 40-yard dash record for their positions.

In nine years as the head coach at McNeese State, Keasler posted a 78-34-2 record and his Cowboy teams won at least nine games in six of his last seven seasons. In 1991, '94 and '95, Keasler was voted Louisiana Collegiate Coach of the Year and he was twice chosen the American Football Coaches Association Regional Coach of the Year.

Five times, Keasler was the Southland Football Coach of the Year and in 1997 he finished third for the prestigious Eddie Robinson Award as the national coach of the year.

Under Keasler, the Cowboys won Southland Conference titles in 1990, '91, '93, '95 and '97 and his teams advanced in the I-AA playoffs in seven of his final eight seasons. In 1997, McNeese advanced to the I-AA championship game where the Cowboys lost to Youngstown State, 10-9.

In his final season at McNeese, the Cowboys spent much of the season ranked No. 1 and finished 9-3 after yet another I-AA playoff appearance.

Keasler was 5-6 in his first season at ULM before last season's 1-10 nightmare.

2001 SCHEDULE

Sept.	1	Sam Houston State
	8	@Florida
	15	@Cincinnati
	22	Middle Tennessee
	29	New Mexico State
Oct.	6	North Texas
	20	@Central Florida
	27	@Louisiana-Lafayette
Nov.	3	@Idaho
	10	Troy State
	17	@Arkansas State

QUARTERBACKS

This year's ULM team features two quarterbacks who rank in the top 10 on the Indians' career passing list. Senior **Andre Vige** (6-3, 200) ranks No. 8 all-time, and Chance (6-2, 207), a junior, is No. 10.

When Chance went down with a concussion the fourth game last season, Vige stepped in and completed 54.3 percent of his passes inn three games as a starter. The offense sputtered, however, so Chance again heads the depth chart heading into the 2001 season.

Two years ago, Chance passed for 1,327 yards and ran for 438.

Vige started in 1998 as a freshman, but didn't play much when Chance was shining in 1999.

In the chase for the No. 2 spot behind Chance is redshirt freshman **Adam Gatlin** (6-1, 184), rated one of the nation's top 15 drop-back passers in the nation by recruiting analyst Max Emginger. Gatlin, out of Alexandria (La.) High School, has exceptional arm strength.

Another quarterback is junior **Daniel Peterson** (6-3, 190), who is also the Indians' long snapper.

Chance completed 8-of-17 passes for 58 yards in the spring game, but went down late in the scrimmage with a back injury when he was hit after releasing a pass. Doctors later determined he had a bulging disc in his lower back.

"It was just a bum deal," Chance told the *Monroe News-Star*. "It was just bad timing. I think that the biggest thing for me is I didn't expect it to happen. It kind of frustrated me when it did happen."

Team doctors were confident Chance could play in the fall.

The injury to Chance didn't help Humphries' opinion of the spring game.

"We had probably our worst day of the spring today," Humphries said after the game. "We weren't ready to play offensively and it showed, but that doesn't take away from the great spring that we head."

RUNNING BACKS

ULM averaged only 57.5 yards per game rushing last year and gone is leading rusher Mark Henderson (88 carries for 436 yards).

Junior **Keith Thomas** (5-11, 190), who was ULM's third leading rusher in 1998 before sitting out the 1999 season, ran for 186 yards on 56 carries last year. He started two games and also caught 11 passes for 80 yards.

Junior **Bryant Jacobs** (5-7, 179) will back up Thomas. He ran for 164 yards on 43 carries last year and is a breakaway threat. During the offseason, Jacobs established ULM tailback records for bench press (400), squad (560) and 40-yard dash time (4.39).

Redshirt freshman **Trey Patterson** (5-10, 185) is the No. 3 tailback. He was rated the No. 3 tailback in Louisiana after his senior season at John Curtis High School in Kenner.

The No. 1 fullback is freshman **Ivory Brown** (6-0, 225). Because the Indians are a one-back team, Brown could see playing time elsewhere. In the spring game, Brown rushed six times for a game-high 87 yards. He had runs of 19, 18 and 45 yards and also caught a 1-yard touchdown pass from Gatlin.

"Ivory hadn't played in a long time after redshirting, so it was good to see him back into the flow," Keasler said.

WIDE RECEIVERS/TIGHT ENDS

Louisiana-Monroe's hopes for the 2001 season suffered a serious setback in late June when junior receiver John M. Floyd (6-4, 215) was charged with attempted second-degree murder and receiving stolen items.

Floyd, 22, was charged with firing four shots at a woman, striking her car three times. Floyd, who transferred to Louisiana-Monroe last year after he was dismissed from Southern Mississippi, was dismissed from the ULM football team after his arrest.

Shira Steele said the May 23 shooting occurred after Floyd allegedly became angry while she attempted to use his computer.

"I was trying to use the Internet," Steele said. "While I was trying to use his computer, he said a few obscene words to me and I said a few back to him and then he asked me to leave his apartment."

Floyd was dismissed from the Southern Mississippi football team for violating team rules. He enrolled at ULM in August 2000 and sat out the football season as required by NCAA rules.

Floyd was expected to be a key player in the ULM offense this season. ULM coaches thought he would be a quick fix for an offense that scored just 96 points during a 1-10 season in 2000.

Floyd caught nine passes for 97 yards as a freshman in 1999 at Southern Mississippi.

With Floyd missing, taking over at the "Z" receiving position will be junior **Sean Brown** (5-9, 166), who returns for his third season after catching 59 career passes.

The "X" receiver will be sophomore **H.J. Adams** (5-10, 185), who caught 18 passes last year and set a ULM record for kickoff returns. Also expected to see plenty of playing time is sophomore **Brooks Greer** (5-10, 163), who had 14 catches last year.

"Both of those guys [Adams and Greer] are doing well and both will play a lot," Humphries said before the spring game. "But right now we're trying to find out which one is going to be the most consistent."

Sophomore **Mark Vincent** (5-11, 197) is expected to start at the "F" receiver. He had 15 receptions last year, but was slowed by an ankle injury.

The new offense will feature the tight end and junior **Ben Wright** (6-2, 250), who played center and offensive tackle in the past when injuries decimated the offensive line. He will be backed up by sophomore **B.J. Welch** (6-2, 230).

Wright caught four passes for 46 yards in the spring game.

"Ben Wright had a heckuva spring game and did a great job today," Keasler said. "He's a warrior."

OFFENSIVE LINE

The offensive line was thin during spring drills, but help is on the way with when the recruiting class arrives in the fall. Only nine offensive linemen were on hand for spring drills.

"We've got great competition right now at each position in the offensive line," offensive line coach Truax said. "Plus, we have five new guys coming in the fall and they are going to be able to help us."

Senior **Larry Pink** (6-3, 277) started last year at left guard and has been moved to left tackle. Sophomore **Kenny Ordeneaux** (6-4, 286) will back up Pink.

At left guard will be senior **Juan Parra** (6-3, 304) who started five games last year at center. Behind him is sophomore **Ben Zapata** (6-2, 310), who started one game at right guard and two at left guard last year. He nursed a knee injury in the spring.

Sophomore **Robert Aguirre** (6-3, 305), who started two games at center last year before breaking his leg against Memphis, will start at center. He could be pushed by redshirt freshman **Hayden Wadsworth** (6-2, 255).

At right guard, sophomore **Shane Luna** (6-2, 290) returns for his second season. His is listed head of sophomore **Bruce Hampton** (6-2, 255).

At right tackle, sophomore **Josh Wade** (6-4, 270) is listed at No. 1 after making one start last year.

"I've got to find someone to step up at right tackle," Truax said during spring drills. "Josh Wade is working there right now and Parra is one of the swing guys we're working at both guard and tackle. We don't have the numbers we would like right now, but we're having great competition at each position. The line is giving a great effort and they're a tough, gritty bunch."

2000 STATISTICS

Rushing offense	57.5	114
Passing offense	184.8	81
Total offense	242.3	112
Scoring offense	8.7	114
Net Punting	26.8	113
Punt returns	5.7	107
Kickoff returns	17.7	98
Rushing defense	163.7	71
Passing efficiency defense	143.1	105
Total defense	353.6	50
Scoring defense	37.7	110
Turnover margin	-17	112

Last column is ranking among Division I-A teams.

KICKERS

Sophomore **Daniel Francis** (5-10, 186) made 3-of-4 field goals and 4-of-4 extra-point kicks last year before suffering a broken ankle in the fifth game.

With Francis injured, senior **Justin Mink** (5-8, 155) made 2-of-3 field goals and 3-of-4 extra points. Sophomore **Tyler Kuecker** (6-0, 195) handled some of the kickoff duties.

Francis, No. 1 on the depth chart, made 3-of-5 field goals in the spring game.

DEFENSIVE LINE

ULM returns both defensive ends in sophomore **Corey Conde** (6-4, 240) and junior **Brennan Bertrand** (6-4, 238). Conde, however, was moved to tackle during spring drills and Bertrand ended spring drills behind sophomore **John Thompson** (6-2, 245), a transfer from South Carolina.

Conde started 10 games last year on the left side and finished with 32 tackles, 23 unassisted. Bertrand led the linemen in tackles with 56 last year. He also led the team in quarterback sacks (three) and tied for the team lead in tackles for lost yardage (6-26). His nine quarterback hurries were also a team-best.

Redshirt freshman **Maynard Johnny** (6-3, 318) will probably start at end, ahead of freshman

Mabrae Wilson (6-2, 220), who was a dominant end and linebacker at Amite (La.) High School.

Also expected to play at end will be sophomore **Justin Ebersole** (6-4, 260), who played in eight games and made 18 tackles last year.

Senior tackle **Donald Malveaux** (6-2, 290) returns as a starter for the third straight year. He had 35 tackles last year while splitting time between tackle and nose tackle. Freshman **Michael Holmes** (6-2, 270) is No. 2 at tackle after suffering a season-ending knee injury in the opener last year at Minnesota.

The projected starter at nose tackle is sophomore **Michael Anthony** (6-2, 260), who appeared in all 11 games last year and made 27 tackles. Behind him are freshman **Marvin Taylor** (6-2, 284), junior **Bobby Bell** (5-11, 311) and sophomore **Ryan Norris** (6-2, 257).

"Because we had new guys coming in in January that gave us more speed at end, we were able to move some guys inside and give us more depth," defensive coordinator Mike Collins said. "Conde is an inside player and over the long run he will add more for us at defensive tackle. Thompson has been everything we had hoped for and more at defensive end."

LINEBACKERS

Injuries depleted the linebacker corps last year, but that allowed sophomore **Maurice Sonnier** (6-2, 210) to see plenty of playing time. He made 67 tackles and could become a dominant player at "Will" linebacker.

Behind Sonnier will be sophomore **David Higgins** (6-0, 223), redshirt freshman **John Winchester** (6-4, 205), sophomore **Mark Miller** (5-10, 210) and freshman **Chester Thompson** (5-11, 215).

Senior **Otis Robinson** (5-10, 213), who suffered a season-ending knee injury last year against Memphis, will start at "Mike" linebacker. He won team defensive player-of- the-week honors three times last season and has 203 career tackles.

Behind Robinson will be junior **Chris Brantley** (6-0, 215), redshirt freshman **Matt Latino** (6-2, 220), junior **Carlos Hughes** (6-2, 255) and sophomore **Darwin Roberts** (6-0, 210).

Hughes, who also suffered a knee injury last year against Memphis, has 37 career tackles.

"We have been able to establish great competition in a lot of areas defensively," Collins said during spring drills. "At linebacker, we've got tremendous depth and in the secondary we've got better depth at all five positions and that has allowed us to make some moves there."

DEFENSIVE BACKS

Senior **Dedrick Buckles** (5-11, 215) and sophomore **Seneca Lee** (5-11, 170) both return after starting last season, but both spent the spring adjusting to new positions. Buckles, who led the Indians in tackles in 2000, has moved from strong safety to free safety. Lee, last year's starter at free safety, is now the first team right cornerback.

Buckles made 103 tackles last year, 61 unassisted. He also broke up four passes, forced a fumble and recovered a fumble. Lee made 69 tackles last year and returned an interception 41 yards for a touchdown.

The other starters in the secondary during spring drills were senior **Karlton Washington** (5-8, 177) at left cornerback, sophomore **Courtney Joiner** (5-10, 188) at strong safety, and junior **Derrick McGill** (5-9, 192) at right strong safety.

Washington led the team last year with three interceptions and has seven interceptions and seven pass breakups over the last two years.

PUNTERS

The punter will once again by sophomore **Steven Hunnicutt** (6-3, 209), who averaged 35.0 yards per punt last year. He had a vision problem diagnosed in the off-season that ULM coaches thought slowed down his mechanics.

This is an area the coaching staff would desperately love to improve, and if it doesn't with Hunnicutt, the coaches could turn to Chance, who punted in high school.

SPECIAL TEAMS

Patterson and Jacobs will handle most of the kickoff returns with help from Brown and Greer.

Handling punt returns will be Adams, Lee, Floyd and freshman **Travin Moore** (5-11, 180).

Adams is second in kick-return yards in ULM history with 860 yards. He trails Kevin Washington (1991-94) by 100 yards.

RECRUITING CLASS

Keasler and his staff signed 26 athletes with a goal of getting bigger and better in the offensive line.

"I think the team is much improved after today," Keasler said after signing day. "Some can make an immediate impact, and some are expected to. Our main focus was depth. We needed to get some big play guys in here with some athletic ability, guys that can help us now.

"There's no doubt that the Sun Belt made a difference in recruiting. They now know there is something to play for and with the bowl affiliation, kids are giving us a look."

Keasler said **Leo Pruneda**, **Zack Sims** and **Will Watkins**, three of ULM's five junior college recruits, could provide immediate help in the offensive line.

"We wanted to bring some maturity into the program," he said. "I think we did that, along with bringing some size and athletic ability up front."

Pruneda (6-5, 315) was an honorable mention All-American at Blinn (Texas) College last year. Sims (6-4, 335) played defensive tackle at Northwest (Miss.) Community College. A strong player, Sims should have no trouble switching to offense. Watkins (6-5, 320) did not allow a sack in 442 pass attempts last season at Highland (Kansas) Community College.

Also among the signees were Floyd, a receiver, and Brown, a fullback. Both played at Southern Mississippi.

With ULM playing a 4-2-5 on defense, Keasler and his staff were looking for speedy linebackers on national signing day.

Alnecco Shine (6-2, 225) is an all-around athlete who also competed in track and basketball. He made more than 150 tackles his senior season at Jonesboro-Hodge High School in Jonesboro, La.

KaRon Mohammed (6-4, 225), who was coached at Arkansas Baptist High by his father, Alfred D. Mohammed, a former Arkansas standout who played with the Buffalo Bills, made all-state with 113 tackles and 11 sacks.

LaKeith Robinson (6-2, 215), who runs a 4.5 in the 40-yard dash, was a standout at Destrehan (La.) High, where he made 102 tackles and 24 sacks.

BLUE RIBBON ANALYSIS

OFFENSE	C-
SPECIAL TEAMS	C
DEFENSE	C
INTANGIBLES	C

The promotion of Humphries to offensive coordinator should pay off for the Indians, who were pathetic offensively last season.

As it is with most teams, the offensive line must come through. It will be crucial for the junior college signees to add depth.

The defense dominated in the spring game with the Maroon team limiting the Gold to only two touchdowns that came from the second-team offense against the second-team defense. That kind of effort will be needed during the regular season.

It would be a great lift if ULM could open the season with a home victory over Sam Houston State. A loss there could lead to disaster because the next six games are against Florida, Cincinnati, Middle Tennessee State, New Mexico State and Central Florida.

Don't expect another 1-10 season by the Indians, but it will be a surprise if they finish above .500.

(S.C.)

2000 RESULTS

Minnesota	L	10-47	0-1
Memphis	L	0-28	0-2
Nicholls State	W	27-21	1-2
Tennessee	L	3-70	1-3
Southwest Texas State	L	7-27	1-4
Arkansas	L	6-52	1-5
Middle Tennessee	L	0-28	1-6
Central Florida	L	0-55	1-7
Louisiana-Lafayette	L	18-21	1-8
Louisiana Tech	L	19-42	1-9
Wofford	L	6-24	1-10

Middle Tennessee

LOCATION	**Murfreesboro, TN**
CONFERENCE	**Sun Belt**
LAST SEASON	**6-5 (.545)**
CONFERENCE RECORD	**NA**
OFFENSIVE STARTERS RETURNING	**7**
DEFENSIVE STARTERS RETURNING	**6**
NICKNAME	**Blue Raiders**
COLORS	**Royal Blue & White**
HOME FIELD	**Horace Jones (30,788)**
HEAD COACH	**Andy McCollum (Austin Peay '81)**
RECORD AT SCHOOL	**9-13 (2 years)**
CAREER RECORD	**9-13 (2 years)**
ASSISTANTS	
	Larry Fedora (Austin College '85)
	Offensive Coordinators/Wide Receivers
	Steve Davis (Livingston '75)
	Defensive Coordinator/Defensive Backs
	Alex Robins (Maryville College '69)
	Quarterbacks
	Joe Wickline (Florida '83)
	Offensive Line
	Floyd Walker (Middle Tennessee State '89)
	Tight Ends
	Darin Hinshaw (UCF '93)
	Running Backs
	Howard McMahan (Louisiana Tech '92)
	Outside Linebackers
	Kacy Rodgers (Tennessee '91)
	Defensive Line
	Kevin Fouquier (USL '89)
	Linebackers
TEAM WINS (last 5 yrs.)	**NA-NA-NA-3-6**
FINAL RANK (last 5 yrs.)	**NA-NA-NA-106-86**
2000 FINISH	**Beat Louisiana-Lafayette in regular-season finale.**

COACH AND PROGRAM

With three outstanding recruiting classes in the house and the system of coach Andy McCollum entrenched, Middle Tennessee State football fans are ready to make reservations for a trip to New Orleans on Dec. 18.

That's because MTSU fans believe their Blue Raiders can win the Sun Belt Conference championship in their first year in the league and play in the New Orleans Bowl, which will match the league champion against the third pick from the Mountain West Conference. The game, which received approval from the NCAA in late April, will be played in the Louisiana Superdome and will be televised by ESPN2.

"This is a great challenge for this program and an even better opportunity after two years as a I-A Independent," McCollum said. "The league will be highly competitive despite this being the first year of play, but I definitely feel we have a chance of being there at the end.

"We work every day to improve and now we hope to take another stride in the right direction after last season."

After taking over the MTSU program two years ago, McCollum guided the Blue Raiders to a 3-8 record. Known as a premier recruiter, McCollum continued to bring in top-notch talent and Middle Tennessee went 6-5 last season with an offense that ranked 16th nationally and a defense that improved 31 spots in the NCAA's total defense rankings from 1999 to 2000.

Last year's winning record was even more impressive because the Blue Raiders played a monster schedule with road games at Illinois, Florida, Maryland, Mississippi State and UAB.

"I have always instilled in my players that Middle Tennessee will back down from no one," McCollum said. "Last year we didn't. We went toe to toe with some of the top teams in the country and I think we grew from the experience.

"We will continue playing a challenging schedule because that is how you become better and win championships."

Other than league games this year against Louisiana-Monroe, Louisiana-Lafayette, Idaho, North Texas, New Mexico State and Arkansas State, MTSU will play Vanderbilt, Troy State, Mississippi, LSU and Connecticut.

Last season, MTSU beat Murray State, Louisiana-Monroe, Connecticut, South Florida, Louisiana-Lafayette and Louisiana Tech.

"We will have to be at our best every game and every down if we expect to compete for a championship," McCollum said. "I believe we have a strong nucleus returning, but we have to execute, win the takeaway-giveaway department and stay away from injuries if we have any hopes of playing past Nov. 17."

McCollum brought in what was determined to be the best recruiting class in MTSU history in 1999, then followed that a year later with a class rated among the top half of the 114 Division I-A programs. The 2001 class was rated the best in the Sun Belt.

"The bottom line is that we try to improve a little each year," McCollum said. "Hopefully, we will be able to continue doing that.

"Obviously we are very ambitious for the 2001 season, but that is the case every year. We are always positive and believe strongly in what we do."

McCollum changed his staff for the 2001 season, hiring Steve Davis as the Blue Raiders' defensive coordinator. Davis will also coach the MTSU secondary.

Former Central Florida standout Darin Hinshaw will coach the running backs and Kevin Fouquier will direct the linebackers. Offensive coordinator Larry Fedora, who spent the last two years coaching the running backs, will now take over the wide receivers.

"I am truly excited about the knowledge and enthusiasm these three additions bring to our staff," McCollum said. "All three have great reputations as top-notch recruiters throughout the country, which is very big to us at Middle Tennessee. They have a genuine care about our kids both on and off the playing field. I could not be happier than to have these guys a member of our family."

Davis, who has been a part of two undefeated regular seasons over the last six years, was most recently the defensive back coach for Southern Miss in 1999. A 1975 graduate of Livingston (now the University of West Alabama), Davis spent the 1999 season as the defensive backs coach for Southern Miss, where he helped lead the Golden Eagles to a Conference USA and Liberty Bowl championship. Davis sat out the 2000 campaign because of family obligations, and while off the college sideline he volunteered at Petal High School in Petal, Miss., and guided it to a 9-3 mark.

Hinshaw, a four-year starter for UCF at quarterback, spent the 2000 season as the quarterbacks coach for the Golden Knights, making him the first person other than UCF head coach Mike Kruczek to coach the quarterbacks since 1985.

Fouquier makes his way to Murfreesboro after spending the 2000 season as the defensive coordinator for Central Arkansas. This will not be the first time Fouquier has been on a staff with McCollum. While at UTEP in 1990 and '91, Fouquier was a graduate assistant working with the wide receivers and McCollum was the Miners' linebackers and special teams coach.

McCollum and his staff were pleased with the spring practice that concluded April 7.

"We've had a good spring," McCollum said. "We had a physical spring. There were a lot of young guys playing out there and a lot of mental mistakes. But those are things we work on all the time and that's just something we'll get better at."

New defensive coordinator Davis is simply happy to be coaching with McCollum in Murfreesboro.

"I like it here. I like it here a lot," Davis said. "The coaching staff here is a great bunch of guys and a great bunch of people. They're probably as good a group as I've been with in a long time and that makes it fun.

"I'm not sure what's gone on here in the past, but I'm not really concerned with what's happened here in the past. What I'm concerned about now is the future and putting in a good scheme that's sound and simple enough to follow to where we don't make mistakes."

2001 SCHEDULE

Aug.	30	@Vanderbilt
Sept.	8	Troy State
	22	@Louisiana-Monroe
	29	@Louisiana-Lafayette
Oct.	6	Idaho
	13	@North Texas
	20	@Mississippi
	27	New Mexico State
Nov.	3	Arkansas State
	10	@LSU
	17	Connecticut

QUARTERBACKS

Middle Tennessee will stick with its platoon system at quarterback that led to an offense that last season produced an average of 433 yards a game and 32 points.

Record-setting quarterback **Wes Counts** (6-1, 187), a senior, is a master with the short passing game. He owns 15 school records and is the most accurate passer in Blue Raider history with a 63.2 career completion percentage. Counts, a lefthander, passed for 1,536 yards last year and had four touchdown passes against South Florida.

Counts started nine games, but gave way twice to senior **Jason Johnson** (6-2, 210), whose expertise is throwing the long ball. Johnson also threw for more than 1,000 yards last season. He rallied the Blue Raiders to a season-ending victory over Louisiana-Lafayette that secured a winning record.

"We have two very experienced quarterbacks," Fedora said. "It's a luxury not a lot of teams have. If one is having an off day, then we can bring the other one in to hopefully add some spark.

"They are both very competitive and push each other every day in practice, which only helps make our team better."

Battling for the spot behind Counts and Johnson are senior **Lance Phillips** (6-2, 206) and redshirt freshman **Kevin Searcy** (5-11, 182). Phillips hasn't played much since transferring from Ole Miss in 1999. A native of nearby Smyrna, Tenn., Phillips is comfortable with the offense.

Searcy sat out last season after a high school career at Banneker in College Park, Ga. A talented athlete with superb playmaking ability, Searcy become more knowledgeable of the offense and stronger during his redshirt season.

RUNNING BACKS

MTSU is billing junior **Dwone Hicks** (5-11, 218) as an All-America candidate after his 1,277 rushing yards set a school record in 2000. He has rushed for more than 100 yards nine times and has an average per rush of 6.9 yards.

Hicks, a Doak Walker Award candidate, gained national attention last year by rushing for 311 yards and six touchdowns in the victory over Louisiana Tech.

During the spring game, Hicks was limited to only two carries for 7 yards as McCollum worked extensively on the passing game while looking at younger players. Hicks did catch a 16-yard pass.

Behind Hicks will be sophomore **Don Calloway** (5-7, 179), who ran for 108 yards and three touchdowns and added 136 yards and a touchdown through the air against Louisiana-Lafayette when Hicks was injured.

Also back is senior **Jamison Palmer** (6-0, 206), who led the Blue Raiders in rushing in 1999. He suffered a season-ending knee injury in the opener last year at Illinois. He is also a good receiver with 28 career receptions.

In the mix will be sophomore **Rashard Lee** (6-0, 217), who has yet to make in impact at MTSU after a stellar career at Brunswick (Ga.) High School. He was a USA Today All-American and was rated the No. 1 athlete in Georgia by several recruiting services.

"We set out to really improve our running game a year ago because we knew it was the only way to win football games," Fedora said. "The emphasis started in the spring and carried over last fall.

"Now we have to build on that success, which I think we can do. Everybody knows what Dwone did last year and we have three more behind him that are capable of doing the same thing. I'm excited about this bunch because they are very talented, all athletic, can catch the football and are all very coachable."

Two candidates will compete for the fullback

position, but don't expect them to get many carries. Only twice in the 22 games McCollum has been MTSU's coach has there been a fullback in the starting lineup.

Senior **Jason Spray** (5-10, 227) had six carries and two receptions in 2001, but had several key blocks on long runs by Hicks. The other fullback is junior **Steve Ellison** (5-11, 264), who had only one rushing attempt last season.

WIDE RECEIVERS/TIGHT ENDS

The Blue Raiders are loaded at running back and the talent is just as impressive in the receiving corps.

"If the receivers are not performing, then our offense does not work," Fedora said.

Headlining the talent pool at wide receiver is another All-America candidate—senior **Kendall Newson** (6-2, 181). Newson is the school's all-time leading receiver with 173 catches in 32 games and the school's career leader in receiving yards with 2,278. He has caught at least one pass in 32 straight games.

"Kendall Newson is the most fierce competitor I have ever seen on the field," McCollum said. "He lines up every day to win, and most of the time he does. He possesses the mentality you want your entire team to have."

Behind Newson at the slot will be sophomore **Hashem Joyner** (5-10, 165). He sat out 2000 because of academic requirements.

The "X" position will be handled by junior **Tyrone Calico** (6-4, 215), the second all-time leading receiver at MTSU. Calico, who will switch from No. 27 to No. 7 (his old high school number), caught 47 passes for 752 yards last year. He beat Mississippi State All-America cornerback Fred Smoot for two scores last year.

Backing up Calico will be senior **Nick Payne** (6-4, 177), who made only two catches in 2000.

The starter at flanker will be senior **Hansford Johnson** (5-8, 156), who a year ago was third on the team in receptions with 31. Johnson was Middle's third-leading rusher with 245 yards and completed 3-for-4 passes for 89 yards. A busy guy, Johnson also returned punts and kicks and scored touchdowns by rushing, passing and receiving.

Junior **Sean Saylor** (6-0, 186), a former walk-on, will back up Johnson. He is considered one of the most effective blockers in the receiving corps. Junior **Rondell Newson** (6-0, 148), younger brother of Kendall, will also compete for playing time at flanker.

Expected to be the starter at "Z" is junior **David Youell** (5-11, 179), who caught 30 passes for 252 yards last year. He had at least one catch in each game. In the race for a starting position will be sophomore **Kerry Wright** (5-8, 165), who sat out last year for academic reasons. He was rated the No. 21 receiver in the nation coming out of Tri-Cities High School in East Point, Ga.

A battle is expected at tight end between junior **Lucas Frost** (6-3, 262) and sophomore **Brett Bucher** (6-5, 240). Frost played in all 11 games last year, and started three. Bucher is a transfer from North Carolina State.

OFFENSIVE LINE

With talent at quarterback, running back and receiver, the key to the Blue Raiders' success will be the offensive line, which will be nearly brand new because four of five starters from a year ago are gone. The MTSU coaches feel good about the linemen they recruited.

"We finished last year with one of the top offenses in the country and I feel we can be ever better in 2001," Fedora said. "If we can eliminate turnovers and stay healthy this offense has a chance to be better than a year ago."

Although four linemen graduated, the best one is back in left tackle **Brandon Westbrook** (6-6, 285), a sophomore who is a candidate for all-conference honors. Westbrook missed the last game of the 2000 season after suffering a broken leg against South Florida. He had 85 knockdowns a year ago and is expected to be 100 percent.

Backing up Westbrook will be junior **Jonathan Proby** (6-3, 276) and redshirt freshman **Seth Grabo** (6-4, 274).

The left guard position will be filled by either junior **Preston Portley** (6-4, 336), junior **David Coy** (6-4, 308) or senior **Jonathan Barry** (6-2, 310).

Portley was an all-conference player last year at Ft. Scott (Kansas) Community College. He played only one year of high school ball. Coy is the front runner to start at left tackle, but could see some time at guard. He played 262 snaps last season. Barry has been primarily a travel squad player in the past.

Three more players will battle for the start at center—junior **Glen Elarbee** (6-2, 260), junior **Nate Blasi** (6-2, 275) and sophomore **Josh Willoughby** (6-4, 341). Elarbee played a personal best 48 snaps last year. Biasi is a former junior college All-American who was rated the 12th best player in the Jayhawk Conference. Willoughby, who has been bothered with injuries during his career, moves from guard to center.

Junior **Kevin Pascoe** (6-3, 295) should get the start at right guard. He started four times last year. His competition will come from sophomore **Bill Brasch** (6-4, 330), a transfer from Northeast Oklahoma A&M.

Coy should start at right tackle, but must fight off a challenge from sophomores **Gary Sanders** (6-4, 280) and **Chris Scott** (6-5, 312).

2000 STATISTICS

Rushing offense	194.4	24
Passing offense	239.2	33
Total offense	433.5	16
Scoring offense	31.8	24
Net Punting	32.1	90
Punt returns	10.7	38
Kickoff returns	19.6	61
Rushing defense	151.5	61
Passing efficiency defense	127.2	89
Total defense	387.9	77
Scoring defense	28.7	80
Turnover margin	+0	59

Last column is ranking among Division I-A teams.

KICKERS

Sophomore Brian Kelly (6-0, 168) made 11-of-13 field goals last year and 39-of-44 extra-point kicks. Kelly, whose career long is 46 yards, made his first five field goals in 2000 and then ended the season on a positive by making the game-winning field goal against Louisiana-Lafayette in the second overtime.

DEFENSIVE LINE

New coordinator Davis will switch the Blue Raiders from a 3-4 scheme to the 4-3 this year. He should give MTSU new enthusiasm as the defense tries to catch up with the offense in terms of national attention.

"We have showed a lot of improvement from year one to year two, but we have to continue," McCollum said. "We have improved with size and speed and now need to work on our personality. And that's where our leaders have to step up. We should be better because now our talented freshmen from last year are sophomores."

The defensive line will be anchored by left end **Tanaka Scott** (6-2, 266), a senior who led the Blue Raiders last year in sacks, tackles for loss and hurries. He will be backed up by junior **Ray Miller** (6-2, 236), who struggled last year. MTSU coaches are hopeful he can have a breakout season.

Scott led his team in the spring game with six tackles and a sack.

"I thought we put a lot of pressure on the offense," Scott said. "I've got some great thoughts about our momentum as we head into the summer and then fall practice. We've just got to keep coming out and playing hard."

Redshirt freshman **Jerry Vanderpool** (6-3, 304) will start in the middle. The product of Brentwood Academy near Nashville picked up valuable strength during his redshirt season. He will be backed up by a couple of walk-ons and possibly some of the new recruits.

Junior **Curtis Daniely** (6-5, 256) will start at right end in the new alignment. He played in 10 games last year, but had only 13 tackles. Another local product, sophomore **Joe Moos** (6-2, 247) from Murfreesboro Riverdale High School, could see time behind Daniely.

LINEBACKERS

Three starters return as the Blue Raiders switch to the 3-4 scheme under Davis.

Starting inside will be 2000 starters **Scott Brown** (6-2, 222), a senior, and **Chris Gatlin** (6-2, 212), a junior, Brown started 10 games last year and was fourth on the team in tackles. Gatlin started eight games and was eighth in tackles despite nursing a nagging ankle injury. He and Brown should form a tremendous duo in the middle this season.

Brown will be backed up by senior **Billy Durham** (5-11, 210), who started two games last year. He played in 11 games and was a standout on special teams, playing a season-best 45 snaps at linebacker against Illinois. Also in competition will be another Nashville product, **Randy Arnold** (5-11, 220), a junior from Glencliff.

Gatlin's main competition will be senior **Louis Kemp** (5-8, 208), who moved over from fullback in the spring of 2000. He played in 10 games last year.

A starter at one of the outside positions will be senior **Anthony Hood** (6-2, 235), who started five games last year. He averaged more than 20 snaps per game and could be an all-conference player this season. He will be challenged by senior **Wes Stephens** (6-4, 248) from nearby Nashville McGavock High School.

The other outside linebacker should be redshirt freshman **Chris Hough** (6-1, 207), who sat out last year to get stronger. His competition will come from newcomers.

DEFENSIVE BACKS

Two of four starters return, led by senior **Jykine Bradley** (5-10, 180). He led MTSU last year in interceptions (three), pass breakups (12) and was sixth in tackles from his left cornerback position.

Bradley's backup will be sophomore **Wardell Alsup** (5-10, 160), who played receiver in 2000. A product of Murfreesboro Oakland High School, Alsup was recruited to play cornerback.

Sophomore **Brandon Lynch** (6-0, 172), will start at strong safety. Lynch has been voted the Blue Raiders' Special Teams MVP three seasons. His backup will be freshman **Shawn Allen** (6-1, 190), who enrolled at MTSU in January. He was rated the No. 2 safety in Georgia while playing for Troup County High in LaGrange, Ga. He runs a 4.4 in the 40-yard dash.

The starter at right cornerback should be sophomore **Muhammad Rashada** (5-11, 165), who had 17 tackles and an interception last year. Rashada is also the team's kickoff return specialist.

Fighting Rashada for a starting spot will be juniors **Kendall "Rod" Higgins** (5-10, 175) and **Chris Johnson** (5-10, 184). Higgins, a speedster, earned the most snaps on special teams for the Blue Raiders last year. Johnson has started nine times during his college career and usually enters the lineup in nickel situations.

Also returning is junior free safety **Kareem Bland** (6-1, 186), who started nine games last year. He was third on the team with 66 last year and is known as a big-play specialist. Bland will be pushed for playing time by sophomore **Joe McClendon** (5-10, 182), who made 13 tackles in his first career start last year against Mississippi State.

Sophomore **Michael Woods** (6-1, 196) is an outstanding athlete who should see time at free safety. He could play some linebacker as well.

PUNTERS

Returning to do the punting will be sophomore **Robert Billings** (6-0, 197), who averaged 37.5 yards per kick last year. He put 18 kicks inside the 20. Billings had a long punt of 62 yards against UAB.

SPECIAL TEAMS

Hansford Johnson returns for the third straight year to field punts for the Blue Raiders. He was rated 41st in the country a year ago with 10.4 yards per return and has two 100-yard return games in his career.

Alsup and Rashada will be returning kickoffs in 2001. Alsup led MTSU last year with 15 returns for 292 yards. Rashada had five returns for 136 yards last year against Mississippi State and averaged 23.8 yards per return.

The long snapper will be Matusek. Youell will hold for field goals.

RECRUITING CLASS

McCollum knows how to recruit. His 2001 recruiting class was rated the best in the new Sun Belt Conference.

One of the tops signees is Allen, who could wind up starting in the secondary. He anchored Troup County's 4 x 100 state championship relay team.

Among the other notables in the signing class are free safety **Larue Beck** (6-3, 185) from Marietta (Ga.) High School, who was rated the No. 30 prospect nationally by Rivals100.com; tight end **Quan Domineck** (6-44, 245) from Cedar Grove High School in Ellenwood, Ga., who was chosen to Fox Sports Net's Countdown to Signing Day All-South team; junior **Nate Blasi** (6-2, 275) from Butler County Community College in Wichita, a Gridwire JuCo All-American; linebacker **Alvin Fite** (6-1, 215) from Nashville Hillsboro, who was voted Class A Mr. Football Defensive Player of the Year; and quarterback **Andre Green** (6-3, 208) from Sandy Creek High School in Fayetteville, Ga., who was rated the No. 58 player in the country by Rivals100.com.

The Blue Raiders also signed **Andrico Hines** (6-2, 228), a quarterback at Southwest Mississippi Community College in Riverdale, Ga., who was chosen to the Mississippi JUCO All-Star team in 2000.

Help in the special teams area could come from **Reggie Jones** (6-3, 200) from Middle Georgia Junior College in Atlanta, who was the NJCAA All-America return specialist in 2000.

Another standout comes from Red Bank High School in Chattanooga in linebacker **Fletcher Williams** (6-1, 215). Williams led Red Bank to a 15-0 record and helped the Lions win the Class 5A state title at MTSU's Floyd Stadium.

BLUE RIBBON ANALYSIS

OFFENSE	B+
SPECIAL TEAMS	B+
DEFENSE	C
INTANGIBLES	B+

If the offensive line comes through, the Blue Raiders will be awesome on offense. They averaged 239 yards passing and 194 yards rushing last year.

Counts and Johnson are outstanding at quarterback and there is plenty of depth behind Hicks at running backs. The wide receivers should also be rated among the nation's best by the end of the season.

It will be interesting to see if the Blue Raiders can improve even more on defense under the direction of new coordinator Davis. The special teams are expected to be among the best in the conference as well.

McCollum has the MTSU program on the rise and a championship in the Sun Belt Conference is a possibility. A trip to New Orleans would be nice for the Blue Raiders and their fans. The only problem is that a Sun Belt championship could make McCollum a hot commodity for a head-coaching job in a bigger conference.

(S.C.)

2000 RESULTS

Illinois	L	6-35	0-1
Florida	L	0-55	0-2
Murray State	W	44-28	1-2
Maryland	L	27-45	1-3
Louisiana Tech	W	49-21	2-3
Louisiana-Monroe	W	28-0	3-3
UAB	L	9-14	3-4
Mississippi State	L	35-61	3-5
Connecticut	W	66-10	4-5
South Florida	W	45-9	5-5
Louisiana-Lafayette	W	41-38	6-5

New Mexico State

LOCATION	**Las Cruces, NM**
CONFERENCE	**Sun Belt**
LAST SEASON	**3-8 (.273)**
CONFERENCE RECORD	**1-4 (4th Big West)**
OFFENSIVE STARTERS RETURNING	**6**
DEFENSIVE STARTERS RETURNING	**5**
NICKNAME	**Aggies**
COLORS	**Crimson & White**
HOME FIELD	**Aggie Memorial (30,343)**
HEAD COACH	**Tony Samuel (Nebraska '79)**
RECORD AT SCHOOL	**14-30 (4 years)**
CAREER RECORD	**14-30 (4 years)**
ASSISTANTS	

Kendall Blackburn (William Penn '89)
Tight Ends
Ross Els (Nebraska-Omaha '88)
Secondary/Special Teams
Barney Cotton (Nebraska '83)
Assistant Head Coach/Offensive Coordinator
Michael Garrison (Nebraska-Omaha '84)
Running Backs
Gerry Gdowski (Nebraska '90)
Quarterbacks
Rich Glover (Nebraska '73)
Defensive Line
Mark Mauer (Nebraska '82)
Receivers
Richard Rodgers (California '84)
Secondary
Steve Stanard (Nebraska '89)
Defensive Coordinator/Linebackers

TEAM WINS (last 5 yrs.)	**1-2-3-6-3**
FINAL RANK (last 5 yrs.)	**108-107-105-83-106**
2000 FINISH	**Lost to North Texas in regular-season finale.**

COACH AND PROGRAM

Even with an offense that scored 30 or more points in a school-record seven consecutive games in 2000, New Mexico State managed only three victories. The problem? Defense.

Aggies coach Tony Samuel, whose defensive unit led the nation in total defense five times when he was an assistant at Nebraska, can't wait for his defense to catch up.

"Our defense was not very good last year because of injuries," Samuel said before spring practice. "Defense is especially a critical phase for us."

The offense is just fine. The Aggies have ranked among the nation's top 20 in total offense in two of the last three seasons, and have been among the nation's top 10 in rushing yards per game the last two seasons.

Since Samuel took over the New Mexico State program in 1992, the Aggies have been 2-9, 3-8, 6-5 and 3-8. All indications are that Samuel has the program ready to compete in the new Sun Belt Conference. Things have certainly changed since he arrived in Las Cruces.

"It's like night and day," Samuel said of the atmosphere surrounding the program. "The team effort in the off-season is a huge improvement. That jumps right out at you.

"The kids are putting in the time in the weight room, really working hard. They're working with a purpose, not just showing up to be seen. They're putting in the extra effort without having to be told to. They're coming early and leaving late."

Samuel, who enjoyed great success as a player and coach at Nebraska, took over a program at Mew Mexico State that was rated as one of the nation's worst. The 6-5 record in 2000 was only the school's second winning season since 1978.

During its 3-8 2000, New Mexico State posted three of the nation's top 10 single-game total offensive efforts, including a 660-yard performance at Idaho. The I-formation rushing attack installed by Samuel and his staff helped NMSU lead the Big West Conference in rushing in each of Samuel's four seasons in Las Cruces.

"Our offense will always be productive," Samuel said. "One of the critical things with our offense is ball control and the elimination of turnovers. We scored a lot of points last season and did some good things, but I thought we have too many turnovers and small penalties.

"We really need to work on limiting those problems and that will improve our whole team."

In his 19 years at Nebraska, Samuel was involved in a postseason bowl game every year and never experienced a losing season. During his tenure in Lincoln as a coach, his defensive unit led the nation in total defense five times, led the country in pass defense three times and posted the top defense in the country against the run on five occasions.

Samuel knows defense. He just hasn't been able to bring the same type of success to New Mexico State.

"We will be faster and bigger on the defensive

line than last season," Samuel said. "I think our defensive line wasn't as big last season and we had some young players trying to play as true freshmen."

Samuel will enter the 2001 season in a new conference—the Sun Belt—and with the support of the school's administration. He was awarded a contract last year through the 2004 season.

It was announced in April that New Mexico State would play Louisville in the John Thompson Foundation Football Challenge at Papa John's Cardinal Stadium on Thursday, Aug. 23, in Louisville, Ky.

The game will be the first NCAA Division I game of the 2001 season and will mark the first time NMSU has played a 12-game schedule in its history.

"To play the first game of the 2001 football season is a great opportunity for New Mexico State," Samuel said. "Louisville had a great season last year and this will be a chance for us to compete with a high-caliber team."

Louisville was 9-3 last year and won the Conference USA title with a 6-1 record. The Cardinals, who have played in three bowl games in the last four seasons, lost to Colorado State, 21-17, last year in the Liberty Bowl.

"This is a wonderful opportunity for a great institution like New Mexico State to participate in our inaugural John Thompson Foundation Football Challenge," said Hall of Fame basketball coach John Thompson. "There are hundreds of deserving young people who will benefit from this event."

NMSU defensive line coach Rich Glover was recently selected to the Sports Illustrated College Football All-Century Team.

Glover, who played at Nebraska, was chosen one of the greatest players of the 1900s. In 1972, Glover reached the pinnacle of college athletics when he was invited to the Downtown Athletic Club of New York for the Heisman Trophy ceremonies. Glover, a senior at the time, finished third in the Heisman voting behind teammate Johnny Rodgers and Oklahoma's Greg Pruitt.

2001 SCHEDULE

Aug.	23	@Louisville
Sept.	1	@Texas
	8	Oregon State
	15	@New Mexico
	22	@Kansas State
	29	@Louisiana-Monroe
Oct.	6	@Tulsa
	13	Idaho
	27	@Middle Tennessee
Nov.	3	North Texas
	10	Arkansas State
	17	@Louisiana-Lafayettte

QUARTERBACKS

Back for his senior season will be quarterback **K.C. Enzminger** (6-1, 204), who ranks in the top five in six career offensive categories at NMSU, including first in quarterback rushing (1,029 yards) and third in touchdowns (46).

As a junior, Enzminger was voted second-team All-Big West Conference. He has started 22 straight games and ranks second in Aggie history in interception percentage (.0318), third in touchdowns responsible for (46), fourth in passing efficiency (121.09), fourth in total offense (4,835 yards), fifth in passing touchdowns (33), sixth in yards per passing attempt (7.127), eighth in passing (3,806 yards) and is tied for eighth in 200-yard passing games (seven).

Gone are backups Damien Ocampo and Tony Howard. Returning is **Buck Pierce** (6-2, 190), a freshman who redshirted last year and signees **Te-Mon Wallace** and **Paul Dombrowski**. Pierce was a three-year starter for Del Norte High School in Crescent City, Calif., where he passed for more than 5,400 yards and 54 touchdowns in three years.

"K.C. is back for his senior season, but we have to establish ourselves at quarterback," Samuel said.

Wallace (6-0, 204), is a junior who played last year at West Hills Junior College in Coalinga, Calif. The left-hander participated in spring drills with the Aggies and is listed behind Enzminger and Pierce on the depth chart. Wallace was chosen first-team, All-Central Valley Conference last year when he threw for 1,576 yards and 11 touchdowns. He graduated in 1998 from Dillard High School in Fort Lauderdale, Fla., where he led Broward County in passing his senior year and was voted his team's offensive MVP.

Dombrowski (6-1, 205) played at Sultana High School in Hesperia, Calif., where he became the fifth player in San Bernadino County history to rush and pass for 1,000 yards in the same season. He set single-season school records for total offense (2,498 yards), touchdowns, points, rushing average and punt-return average. He started three years at three different positions (free safety as a sophomore, running back and backup quarterback as a junior, and quarterback as a senior).

"We have quality players at the quarterback position and they just need to learn the offensive system that we run," Samuel said.

RUNNING BACKS

Senior **Kenton Keith** (5-11, 180), who received honorable mention honors last year in the Big West, will take over for Chris Barnes at I-back. Last year, Barnes became just the eighth player in NMSU history to rush for 1,000 yards. Keith carried six times for 48 yards in the spring game.

The NMSU running attack has been one of the nation's best in recent years.

"I don't put much stock in rankings," Samuel said. "Our brand of offense should produce those types of yards. I expect us to tally some high numbers.

"The line will do a good job as usual and we have some good running backs, so this team should put up the same numbers as a year ago. But we have to find backups and depth at each position."

Listed behind Keith on the depth chart are junior **Walter Taylor** (5-9, 170) and sophomore **Tony Bostic** (5-9, 190). Bostic led all rushers with 66 yards on 11 carries in the spring game while Taylor gained 10.4 yards every time he touched the ball. He finished with 52 yards rushing.

The fullback will be senior **Keeon Johnson** (5-11, 215), who rushed for seven yards on seven carries in the spring game and scored on a 1-yard run. His backup will be junior **Kermit Okamura** (5-7, 195).

WIDE RECEIVERS/TIGHT ENDS

The strength of the offense will be the receiving corps with returning starters **Manwell Talbert** (6-2, 215), a senior, and **P.J. Winston** (6-0, 180), a junior. They combined last year for 60 receptions, 11 for touchdowns, and 1,013 yards.

Backing up Winston at the Z-receiver will be sophomore **Ronshay Jenkins** (5-7, 156), who had 108 yards receiving on eight catches in the spring game. He caught a 34-yard pass from Pierce as time expired in the game, which ended in a tie at 32. Behind Talbert at X-receiver will be junior **Leon Oloya** (6-2, 185).

Sophomore **Alex Davis** (6-4, 225) returns at tight end.

"All of our receivers are back and we will be strong in the offensive backfield," Samuel said. "I think our offense has some players coming back who I think are pretty good. Alex Davis played as a true freshman at tight end. He had a good year and you could see the improvement throughout his first season."

Davis' backups at tight end will be senior **Michael Bangs** (6-4, 218) and junior **Chris Gocke** (6-4, 250). Gocke participated in spring drills after playing last year at College of the Sequoias in Visalia, Calif. He caught 28 passes for 424 yards as a sophomore and is considered an outstanding run blocker.

OFFENSIVE LINE

The key returnee in the offensive line will be senior right guard **Tony Wragge** (6-3, 305), a two-time All-Big West selection who has started 23 consecutive games. Last year, he anchored an offensive line that helped NMSU rank sixth in the nation in rushing (274.2 ypg) and 17th in total offense (429.5 ypg).

Wragge helped the Aggies post four of the nation's top 35 rushing totals and three of the top 32 total offensive figures in 2000.

"Tony is the leader of the offensive line and will be a four-year starter for us," Samuel said. "We lost Matt Hancock and Mick Rodemeyer, but we have some players coming back."

Another returning starter in the offensive line is junior **Shalimar Jackson** (67-4, 310) at left guard. Listed behind Jackson is redshirt freshman **Steve Subia** (6-4, 320). The projected starters at tackle are senior **Jason Jewell** (6-5, 290) and junior **Terry Givens** (6-4, 330).

"We have redshirt Steve Subia, who has a lot of potential, but has been injured throughout his career," Samuel said. "Terry Givens also returns after playing quite a big last year."

Battling for the starting position at center will be sophomore **Andy Dale** (6-1, 280) and senior **Chad Kahlsdorg** (6-5, 290).

"I really want to see how the center position clears up," Samuel said. "The center is very important in our offense and I think we have two very capable guys that need to just learn the system."

2000 STATISTICS

Rushing offense	270.1	6
Passing offense	159.3	96
Total offense	433.5	17
Scoring offense	26.8	50
Net Punting	34.7	53
Punt returns	9.2	64
Kickoff returns	19.4	65
Rushing defense	198.9	99
Passing efficiency defense	137.5	102
Total defense	417.3	95
Scoring defense	32.5	94
Turnover margin	-5	82

Last column is ranking among Division I-A teams.

KICKERS

Returning as the Aggies' place-kicker will be sophomore **Dario Aguiniga** (5-11, 175). He made 9-of-19 field goals last year. He made kicks of 27, 38 and 18 yards against Arkansas State.

DEFENSIVE LINE

The Aggies are expected to be faster and bigger on the defensive line than they were last season. Samuel is high on sophomore tackle **Tommy Laborin** (6-3, 305).

"Tommy has a lot of potential and improved as the season went on last year," Samuel said. "If Tommy takes his level of play and focus up to where I think he can, he will be unstoppable."

Returning at nose guard is sophomore **Joe Olivo** (6-2, 240). The other projected starters are ends **Ryan Bakke** (6-2, 240), a senior, and **Jamar Cain** (6-2, 215), also a senior.

Junior **Hayward Findley** (6-3, 280) participated in spring drills after playing last year at Laney Junior College in Oakland, Calif. He started there at defensive end the last two seasons.

A high school player who could see playing time as a freshman is **Lionel Apineru** (6-1, 275) from Barstow (Calif.) High School. He was a star defensive lineman and also was the No. 1-ranked heavyweight wrestler in California.

LINEBACKERS

Seniors **D'Wayne Taylor** (6-0, 195) and **Jamar Lawrence** (6-2, 215) return at linebacker.

Taylor has started 33 consecutive games at linebacker. He led the team in tackles as a redshirt freshman (87) and as a junior (73). The two-time All-Big West selection tied for the league lead in tackles for loss (16) last year.

Taylor finished 11th in the Big West last year with his 87 tackles and tied for the league lead with two fumble recoveries.

"D'Wayne returns as a three-year starter at linebacker and we redshirted some players who can come in and compete at the other linebacker positions," Samuel said.

Also in the picture at linebacker are sophomore **Michael Winter** (6-2, 225), senior **Josh Watts** (6-0, 215), redshirt freshman **Rich Glover** (6-1, 225), redshirt freshman **Simon Ocampo** (5-11, 215) and sophomore **Julmar Howard** (5-10, 190).

Freshman signee **Torrence Price** (6-4, 210) could see some playing time next season. He played last year at Pontiac (Mich.) High School, where he served as team captain for two years. He was chosen the team's defensive MVP as a senior.

DEFENSIVE BACKS

Junior **Tyrone Gifford** (6-0, 198), a fresh face like Laborin, is expected to play well at free safety.

"Tyrone is a kid who played a lot last season," Samuel said. "He is like Laborin. If he ever decides to take his game to another level, he will be as good as any player in the country."

Senior **Corey Paul** (5-8, 170) will return to action in 2001 after suffering a fractured ankle before the 2000 season. He underwent surgery to place a pin in the ankle. As a junior in 1999, Paul made 44 tackles, intercepted three passes and broke up three more.

"We didn't use Corey much in the spring so his ankle could heal," Samuel said. "He will be back for the season, however."

Expected to compete for playing time at cornerback are seniors **Robert Canidate** (5-8, 175) and **Tony Lukins** (5-10, 185). Penciled in at strong safety after spring drills was junior **Siddeeq Shabazz** (5-11, 193).

PUNTERS

The Aggies signed junior **Brian Copple** (6-1, 195) out of Chabot Community College in San Lorenzo, Calif. Copple earned first-team All-Golden Gate Conference honors in 1999 and 2000. He had 145 punts with no returns for touchdowns, and also played defensive back in 1999.

SPECIAL TEAMS

Aguiniga will be back to handle the place kicking and Copple should be fine as the punter.

The Aggies also get Paul back as a punt and kickoff returner. Before his injury last season, Paul was the Aggies' top punt returner and was second in kickoff returns. He ran back 20 punts for 143 yards (7.2 average) and returned eight kickoffs for 194 yards (24.3 average).

Jenkins will also return punts.

"The kicking game really has to improve because it wasn't as good as it was two years ago," Samuel said. "It got better as the year went on, but the kickoff coverage wasn't what I thought it should be."

RECRUITING CLASS

Samuel and his staff signed eight junior college players and seven high school all-stars.

"You bring junior college players in to play," Samuel said. "But that isn't always the case because it takes a special person to goo from the junior college level and step in at the Division I level. We brought in some quality players and we're counting on some of them to come through."

Wallace at quarterback, Gocke at tight end, Findley in the defensive line and Copple at punter participated in spring drills for the Aggies. Four more junior college players will join the squad in the fall, including cornerback **Darrell Bernard**, defensive ends **Terrence Johnson** and **Curtis Robinson**, and linebacker **Tim Patrick**. All will be juniors.

Bernard (5-11, 180) played two years at West Hills Junior College in Coalinga, Calif. He started all nine games at cornerback as a sophomore and led the team with nine pass breakups. He also made 24 tackles.

Johnson (6-1, 270) also played at West Hills Junior College, where he started all nine games at rush end last year. He earned second-team All-Central Valley honors and was selected the team's MVP on defense. He led West Hills with 13 sacks and 52 tackles, eight for losses.

Robinson (6-3, 290) played at Scottsdale Community College in Chandler, Ariz. He made 60 solo tackles his sophomore season, 14 for losses. He was also credited with seven tipped passes, five quarterback hurries, three sacks and one fumble recovery. He originally signed with Scottsdale as a tight end.

Patrick (6-1, 220) played at Glendale Community College in Phoenix, Ariz., where he led his team to the junior college national championship his sophomore season. He had 35 tackles (30 solo), six quarterback sacks, two interceptions and two fumble recoveries.

Among the high school signees, Apineru is expected to compete for time in the defensive line and Price could be an impact player at linebacker. Dombrowski brings good numbers to the quarterback position.

Samuel is also high on linebacker **Jimmy Cottrell** (6-1, 210) from Douglas County High School in Castle Rock, Colo. Cottrell played nose guard as a sophomore before moving to linebacker his last two seasons. He was chosen Continental League Player of the Year as a senior and was honored as the county's defensive player of the year. He also made first team all state. A wrestler like Apineru, Cottrell was ranked as high as fourth in the state at 215 pounds.

"We have some players who can make an impact, but sometimes you never know because it is a different level of competition," Samuel said. "On paper we have some players that should be able to help us, like Apineru, who won the California state wrestling title at 275 pounds, which shows he is a good athlete.

"We have some linebackers, Jimmy Cottrell from Colorado and Torrance Price from Michigan, who can play and look the part as Division I football players."

The Aggies also signed an outstanding high school running back in **Tony Irons** (5-10, 185) from Lincoln (Neb.) Southeast High School. He played I-back on offense and linebacker and safety on defense. Irons earned all-state honors from the *Omaha World Herald* and the *Lincoln Journal* as a junior and senior.

He gained 992 yards on 132 carries as a senior after rushing for 1,345 yards on 145 carries as a junior. Irons led Southeast to a 13-0 record and the Class A state championship last fall. He also competed in track and field as a sprinter and long jumper.

Rounding out the recruiting class were offensive lineman **Justin Shopbell** (6-4, 303) and cornerback **Cameron Wright** (6-1, 173). Shopbell, who played at Woodbury (Minn.) High School, was a two-time all-state honoree. Wright, from Valley Christian High School in San Jose, Calif., was a three-year starter among the state leaders in interceptions (12) his senior year.

BLUE RIBBON ANALYSIS

OFFENSE	C
SPECIAL TEAMS	C
DEFENSE	C+
INTANGIBLES	B

After New Mexico State opens the 2001 football schedule on Aug. 23 against Louisville, the Aggies still must play an 11-game schedule that is being called the toughest in school history.

After the Louisville game, NMSU must play at Texas before playing host to Pacific-10 and Fiesta Bowl champion Oregon State at Aggie Memorial Stadium on Sept. 8. The Aggies then travel to New Mexico, Kansas State, Louisiana-Monroe and Tulsa for a grueling season-opening stretch with six of the first seven games on the road.

The Aggies could be competitive in the new Sun Belt Conference with their high-powered offense. Last year, NMSU beat Arkansas State, but lost to Idaho and North Texas. The defense should be better this year, but could be battered after Louisville, Texas, Oregon State, New Mexico and Kansas State.

If the Aggies are healthy for the Sun Belt stretch the second half of the season, they could make some noise. It will be tough for Samuel and his team to win the conference title and earn a berth to the New Orleans Bowl in the Louisiana Superdome on Dec. 18. If the defense keeps up with the offense, however, a 13-game schedule is a possibility for the Aggies.

(S.C.)

2000 RESULTS

South Carolina	L	0-31	0-1
New Mexico	L	13-16	0-2
Georgia	L	0-37	0-3
UTEP	L	31-41	0-4
Army	W	42-23	1-4
Tulsa	W	42-28	2-4
Arkansas State	W	35-29	3-4
Boise State	L	31-34	3-5
Utah State	L	37-44	3-6
Idaho	L	41-44	3-7
North Texas	L	23-30	3-8

North Texas

LOCATION	Denton, TX
CONFERENCE	Sun Belt
LAST SEASON	3-8 (.273)
CONFERENCE RECORD	1-4 (t-4th Big West)
OFFENSIVE STARTERS RETURNING	6
DEFENSIVE STARTERS RETURNING	6
NICKNAME	Eagles, Mean Green
COLORS	Green & White
HOME FIELD	Fouts Field (30,500)
HEAD COACH	Darrell Dickey (Kansas '84)
RECORD AT SCHOOL	8-25 (3 years)
CAREER RECORD	8-25 (3 years)
ASSISTANTS	
	Gary DeLoach (Howard Payne '76) Defensive Coordinator/Secondary
	Spencer Leftwich (Stephen F. Austin '88) Offensive Line
	Ramon Flanigan (SMU '97) Quarterbacks
	Bill Michael (Arkansas '59) Tight Ends/Offensive Line
	Mike Bugar (Florida State '69) Defensive Line
	Eric Russell (Idaho '91) Defensive Ends
	Kenny Evans (Northeastern Oklahoma '82) Linebackers
	Kelvin Martin (Boston College '87) Wide Receivers/Special Teams
	Rick Gailey (Texas Tech '00) Running Backs
TEAM WINS (last 5 yrs.)	5-4-3-2-3
FINAL RANK (last 5 yrs.)	92-100-95-109-104
2000 FINISH	Beat New Mexico State in regular-season finale.

COACH AND PROGRAM

When coach Darrell Dickey took over the North Texas football program in 1998, he brought in a game plan for success that included old-fashioned football values and a recruiting policy to sign the best players in Texas.

With the 2001 season begins, Dickey hopes his old-school tactics and ability to communicate with players pays dividends in the victory column.

"There is a lot of excitement among our players right now," Dickey said. "We were just three minutes away from winning six games last year. That's not to say that we should have won those games, but we were nearly able to do that with a very young football team. They have to understand that the key to our season is how much improvement they make from spring practice until two-a-days in August."

In 1998, Dickey and UNT finished in second place in the Big West Conference, the best finish in the school's five years in the league. In 1999, the Mean Green beat two teams that went to bowl games—Texas Tech and Boise State. Last year, as Dickey said, the mean Green came within a few minutes of six victories—losing in the fourth quarter to Utah State, Idaho and Texas Tech.

This season North Texas moves into the new Sun Belt Conference.

"There is some familiarity there and I think we will be better able to develop some rivalries," Dickey said. "Some of our guys were actually recruited by Sun Belt schools and that never happened in the Big West because we were so spread out. I think one thing that makes it exciting is that nobody really knows what to expect."

Dickey's three recruiting classes have been dominated by players from Texas high schools. His first in 1999 produced nine players who will enter August as projected starters in just their third seasons. The 2000 class included seven players who are either slated to be starters or made starts last year as freshmen. Some of the players in the 2001 class could also make an impact this fall.

"The biggest strength that we have is that for the first time since I've been here we have an experienced player at each position," Dickey said. "In past years we've had to deal with a lot of on-the-job training. We need to continue to upgrade our ability and depth at each position. People are having to earn their playing time rather than getting it by default."

Dickey was hired as the North Texas coach on Feb. 25, 1998. The 41-year-old Texas native was an outstanding quarterback at Kansas State, leading the Wildcats to their first bowl appearance in school history—the 1982 Independence Bowl.

Dickey played college football for his father, Jim Dickey, Sr., and his older brother, Jim Dickey, Jr., is the head coach at Crosby High School in Houston. He became a NCAA Division I-A offensive coordinator at age 28 at Memphis. He later became the offensive coordinator and assistant head coach at UTEP (1994-96) and in 1997 helped SMU to an outstanding season in his first year as head of the Mustangs' offense.

While playing at Kansas State, Dickey started all four seasons at quarterback (1979-82), throwing for 4,098 yards and 23 touchdowns. He finished with 4,526 yards of total offense and is the only player to lead Kansas State in total offense and passing offense all four years. He was voted the team's most valuable player in 1982, and was the team's outstanding freshman in 1979.

Dickey and the Mean Green will enter the 2001 season with two new coaches. Kelvin Martin has been hired to coach wide receivers and coordinate special teams and Rick Gailey has been elevated to full-time status and will coach running backs.

Martin served as wide receivers coach and special teams coordinator at Jacksonville. After finishing his career as the all-time leader in receptions (133) receiving yardage (2,377) and receiving touchdowns (28) at Boston College, Martin played in the NFL for 10 years—seven with the Dallas Cowboys.

"We are very excited to add Kelvin Martin to our coaching staff," Dickey said. "He brings a rare combination of experience both on and off the field. He will be helping us improve our passing game and our special teams, two areas that he excelled in as a player.

Said Martin, "I'm excited and it's a great opportunity for myself. My family is very excited about returning to the Dallas area. I think the fact that I played in Dallas for several years should be to my advantage in recruiting."

Gailey was a graduate assistant last year at UNT and coached defensive backs.

"He has done a nice job for us with everything we've asked him to do since he's been here and he deserves the opportunity," Dickey said. "It should be a smooth transition because he is already familiar with our players and our system."

In the Mean Green spring game, the White team took a 23-7 victory over the Green. Dickey liked what he saw.

"I was very pleased with the effort both tonight and all through the spring," Dickey said after the game. "We've got a lot of guys injured, but that gave some other players an opportunity. I am just pleased that the guys went out in this cold weather and the intensity level was good."

2001 SCHEDULE

Sept.	1	TCU
	8	@Oklahoma
	15	@Arkansas
	22	Texas Tech
	29	@South Florida
Oct.	6	@Louisiana-Monroe
	13	Middle Tennessee
	20	Arkansas State
Nov.	3	@New Mexico State
	10	Louisiana-Lafayette
	17	@Idaho

QUARTERBACKS

Sophomore **Scott Hall** (6-1, 211) started the last nine games last year and became the first freshman to lead UNT in total offense since 1987. He established himself as a quarterback who could run and pass equally in Dickey's offense, which is an option-oriented, I-formation set.

Backing up Hall will be senior **Richard Bridges** (6-3, 223), who threw for a team-best 85 yards in the spring game, completing 7-of-13 passes. Also behind Hall is junior **Spencer Stack** (6-2, 205). Both Bridges and Stack have led UNT to victories the last two seasons. Bridges has 10 career starts behind him.

It is possible that freshman signee **Andrew Smith** will be given a chance to battle for a starting job. Smith (6-0, 180) from Bay City (Texas) High School, led his team to the Class 4A Division I state championship. He threw for 2,281 yards and 23 touchdowns in his two seasons as a starter.

"Andrew will be given that opportunity," Dickey said. "Now the situation has changed a little bit. We had a freshman that played quite well last year. We have two young men behind him that have game experience. The quarterback situation is a lot better than when I first got here. We have some depth.

"Andrew will be brought in, just like Scott Hall, and if he's the best guy at moving the sticks, he'll play. If there are three or four guys ahead of him, then we'll determine what's the best situation for him."

Dickey said Smith is a gifted athlete and an intelligent young man.

"You watch the film, look into his character and he has high marks in everything," Dickey said. "He's the type of quarterback we want here, and he's the type of person we want here. We ask our quarterbacks to do a lot of things that may go unnoticed. We took all those things into account and feel very strongly about Andrew."

RUNNING BACKS

North Texas must replace the all-time leading rusher in school history in Ja'Quay Wilburn, who led UNT in rushing the last four seasons and finished with over 3,000 career yards.

Michael Hickmon rushed for 575 yards last year, scored three touchdowns and averaged 4.2 yards per carry the last two years but decided before the start of spring practice he didn't want to play football any more.

In the spring game, senior **Dustin Dean** (5-10, 221) ran for a game-high 61 yards on 20 carries.

"This was a lot of fun tonight," Dean said. "It is kind of a reward for all the spring practices we've had. The last couple of scrimmages were the determining factors on who played where. The game was really more for fun.

"I'm really excited about next fall. Our depth at receiver is good and we've got some guys who can catch and then run with the ball. We've got two or three players at running back who are looking good and Scott Hall had a good spring at quarterback. All around, it was a good spring."

To fill the void from losing Wilburn and

Hickmon, UNT brought in junior college transfer **Kevin Galbreath** (5-9, 190), who rushed for 626 yards in seven games last year for Northeast Oklahoma A&M and was the MVP of the Red River Bowl.

"There are no guarantees, but we recruit junior college guys because we feel like we need somebody to come in and have a legitimate chance to start right off the bat," Dickey said. "Kevin Galbreath is a quality running back."

The development of some of the high school signees will be crucial to the Mean Green's success in 2000. Among the signees is **Ja'Mel Branch** (5-7, 170), from Katy (Texas) High School. He rushed for 147 yards and a touchdown in the state championship game, leading his school to the Class 5A Division II title. Branch rushed for 1,665 yards on 221 carries and scored 10 touchdowns last year. He ran for 1,665 yards as a junior.

"We're going to start him off at tailback," Dickey said. "They don't measure you when you get into the end zone. Ja'Quay Wilburn is the all-time leading rusher in the history of the school and he's very similar in size to Ja'Mel. We feel like he will help us. If he's talented, he won't be sitting over there with me."

Dickey also brought in two more high school stars with impressive credentials in **Roy Bishop** (6-2, 207) from San Angelo (Texas) Central High School and **Patrick Cobbs** (5-9, 189) from Tecumseh (Okla.) High School. Bishop ran for 1,530 yards last year and Cobbs ran for 2,354.

The starting fullback will be senior **Robert Whitehead** (6-3, 226), who started four games last year. A former linebacker who started four games there as a freshman, Whitehead has been used primarily as a blocker. His backup will be redshirt freshman **Freddie Johnson** (6-2, 190).

WIDE RECEIVERS/TIGHT ENDS

UNT also lost its top two receivers in Byron Curtis and LaDarrin McLane, who combined for 34 catches and 515 yards last year.

Just as he did at tailback, Dickey brought in a junior college standout in **Michael Thrash** (6-2, 167), who had 32 receptions for 585 yards and four touchdowns last year at Northeastern Oklahoma A&M.

"We lost two receivers and we felt like we needed a guy who could make an immediate impact and we feel very good about Michael Thrash," Dickey said.

Returning from last year is junior **George Marshall** (6-1, 186), who had six catches for 55 yards in UNT's first three games, but didn't catch a pass in the next five. He rebounded and caught three passes for 108 yards and two touchdowns in the last three games. He had a 60-yard touchdown reception late in the game against Idaho that gave UNT the lead.

"We hope that we don't have to use a by committee situation at tailback and receiver," Dickey said. "We don't know right now. We would prefer to have one guy step up and be the go-to guy at those positions."

Also returning is senior **Corie Massey** (5-10, 167), who caught 10 passes for 130 yards last season. Nine of his receptions went for first downs.

Junior **Jeff Muenchow** (6-4, 240) returns at tight end along with sophomore **Randy Gardner** (6-4, 245). Muenchow has started 16 games and played some last year with a broken hand. Gardner started once last year. They combined for 12 receptions for 160 yards and a touchdown last year.

OFFENSIVE LINE

Four starters return in the offensive line, led by sophomore right guard **Nick Zuniga** (6-3, 319), who earned second-team All-Big West Conference honors last year.

Junior left tackle **J.R. Randle** (6-5, 294) has earned honorable mention all-conference honors each of the last two seasons. He has started 20 times.

Junior **Matt Turney** (6-3, 290) moved from defensive line to offensive line last August and started 10 games at left tackle. Sophomore center **Ian Hobbs** (6-4, 285) started 11 games as a redshirt freshman last year.

Look for depth from sophomore **Chris Land** (6-4, 320) and junior college transfer **Mark Molamphy** (6-3, 294). Land saw action last season and Molamphy started for Butler County (Kansas) Community College, which averaged 354 yards and 34 points per game last year.

Also returning is senior **Brad Woosley** (6-8, 352) and redshirt freshmen **Andy Brewster** (6-4, 247) and **Jonathan Jusiewicz** (6-4, 255).

2000 STATISTICS

Rushing offense	134.3	69
Passing offense	107.3	112
Total offense	241.5	113
Scoring offense	14.7	109
Net Punting	29.0	109
Punt returns	12.2	24
Kickoff returns	16.2	108
Rushing defense	182.8	84
Passing efficiency defense	117.5	55
Total defense	379.7	71
Scoring defense	27.3	75
Turnover margin	+4	39

Last column is ranking among Division I-A teams.

KICKERS

Senior **Jason Ball** (5-7, 160) played most of last season with a strained hamstring, but still made 6-of-10 field goals, including a career-best 52-yarder.

Ball's backup will be redshirt freshman **Brad Kadlubar** (5-11, 196) from Ennis, Texas

DEFENSIVE LINE

Unlike the 2000 season, most of the defensive line returns this year.

Sophomore **Brandon Kennedy** (5-10, 325) earned second-team All-Big West honors as a freshman last year. He made 33 tackles, 10 for losses and one quarterback sack. He also had nine quarterback hurries and forced two fumbles.

"I think the defensive line is the most improved part of our football team from a year ago," Dickey said. "It was a big question mark for us last year, but now we have some depth. We should have 10 guys on scholarship at defensive tackle and eight guys at defensive end. That's miles ahead of where we were when I first got here three years ago.

"We have got to put pressure on the quarterback with a four-man rush. We might blitz, but haven't yet proven to be a good man-to-man coverage team."

Joining Kennedy as a returning starter is senior end **Ron Paris** (6-3, 228) and junior tackle **Chris McIver** (6-1, 254). McIver was second-team All-Big West last year with 19 tackles. Paris led the defensive line with 43 tackles.

Other letter winners returning are junior **Eric Bridges** (6-2, 226), sophomore **Luke Conder** (6-3, 257), senior Gabe Haro (6-0, 266), sophomore **Chris Ridgeway** (6-4, 243), sophomore **John Ryan** (6-3, 270) and sophomore **Donovan Wright** (6-1, 250).

Also returning is former SMU standout **Alex Pahulu** (6-0, 290), a senior who saw limited playing time last year.

North Texas could get some immediate help from junior college defensive end **Darrell Daniels** (6-5, 230), who had 65 tackles last year, including eight sacks, in 10 games for Ft. Scott Community College in Kansas City, Kansas.

LINEBACKERS

The leader of the linebackers will be senior Brad Kassell (6-3, 241), who earned unanimous first team All-Big West honors last year after making 115 tackles. He had nine tackles for loss and two quarterback sacks, intercepted four passes and recovered four fumbles.

"Brad has a chance to be remembered as one of the top linebackers to have ever played here," Dickey said. "The sky is the limit. How good of a season he has will also depend on how good the rest of our defense performs."

UNT coaches hope sophomore **Taylor Casey** (6-3, 210) can turn into a player like Kassell. At outside linebacker he made 29 tackles last year.

Three sophomores are expected to make significant contributions at linebacker—**Justin Claborn** (6-2, 242), **Cody Spencer** (6-3, 230) and **Chris Hurd** (6-1, 220).

"We hope our linebackers can fill the gap left by the loss of three veterans from last year," Dickey said. "We lost some steady, solid players. Taylor Casey got some great experience last year and we're hoping a few more players can come in and make an impact."

DEFENSIVE BACKS

Junior **Don McGee** (5-11, 190) returns at cornerback. He tied Kassell for the Big West lead in interceptions with four last year. He also had 35 tackles and two blocked kicks, including one he returned for a touchdown.

Sophomore **Craig Jones** (6-0, 211) returns at safety after finishing second on the team with 73 tackles last year.

Sophomore **Ty Jackson** (5-7, 171) will start at the other cornerback position after being a standout last year on special teams.

Also returning at safety is junior **Robert Conrad** (6-1, 205), who had 29 tackles last season. The starter, however, may be redshirt freshman **Jonas Buckles** (5-11, 213), a consensus state top 100 player at Houston Yates High School.

"Jonas has the potential to be a guy who makes a difference on the defensive side of the ball," Dickey said. "We lost a steady player in Heath Moody. Jonas has a lot of potential and we are hoping that he can perform at this level the way he did in high school."

Redshirt freshmen **Dominque Mackey** (6-1, 192) and **Walter Priestley** (5-10, 178) will compete for playing time at cornerback and sophomore **Nathan Roberts** (6-1, 201) will see time at safety after two injury plagued seasons.

PUNTERS

Ball will also handle the punting. Last season, he averaged 38.2 yards per punt, and had 17 punts inside the 20. He also had 11 forced fair catches and no touchbacks in 75 attempts. Kadlubar could push Ball as the starting punter.

SPECIAL TEAMS

Jackson averaged 10.7 yards per return last year on punts, which led the Big West. However, North Texas had four punts blocked, two field goals blocked and averaged just over 16 yards per kickoff return.

The Mean Green led the Big West in punt returns (12.2), but was last in net punting (29.0).

Ball will handle UNT's kickoff duties.

"We had some areas last year where we were very strong," Dickey said. "Jackson led the league in punt returns. Our punt and kick protection struggled at times, but last year, we had a lot of young guys out there with no experience. Now they have that experience."

RECRUITING CLASS

Dickey was very pleased with his recruiting class.

"We feel this has a chance to be a very strong class," he said. "Some of these players have a chance to make an impact this season. It's becoming harder to do each year because we've got some players who have experience and we have a returning player at nearly every position.

"We wanted to recruit a football player at every position except punter and kicker. We've signed as many as three players at certain positions. We feel good about all of them. The key is not one or two guys. The key is that this group comes in, they all pan out, they develop and we get an impact player at every position on our team."

Dickey will need immediate help at running back, and Smith will get a quick look at quarterback.

"This group can run and that's the name of the game," Dickey said. "There is some good size in this group, but even the linemen in this group can run. We like to get size if we can, but we feel we really need speed and that's a need we looked to address. The large majority of the players we wanted, we got."

Bishop, from San Antonio Central, could help fill the void at running back.

"I expect to give him the ball a bunch," Dickey said. "He's a guy from day one that we really liked. He had a lot of offers from people down the stretch He had to deal with some questions about whether he made the right decision, and we're glad he's here. He probably has the potential to carry the ball 25, 30 times a game."

BLUE RIBBON ANALYSIS

OFFENSE	C
SPECIAL TEAMS	C+
DEFENSE	C
INTANGIBLES	B

Dickey appears to have the Mean Green on a track for success in the future, but the best chance for six wins came last year. It will be difficult for the Mean Green to get over the .500 mark this season.

UNT will play host to five games, four of those in Denton and one at Texas Stadium. The Mean Green will play six league games in the inaugural season of the Sun Belt Conference, and five non-conference games—including a game against defending national champion Oklahoma— and three others against teams that played in bowl games last season.

After playing TCU in the opener, UNT will then hit the road to play Oklahoma and then Arkansas. The Mean Green will return to host Texas Tech at Texas Stadium in Irving on Sept. 22. It will be the first game that UNT has hosted at Texas Stadium since facing the Red Raiders in 1998.

The Mean Green will then travel to Tampa to face Division I-A newcomer South Florida. The game will be played at the site of the 2001 Super Bowl, Raymond James Stadium.

UNT then plays its first ever Sun Belt game on the road against Louisiana-Monroe on Oct. 6. The first Sun Belt home game will be played on Homecoming Weekend against Middle Tennessee on Oct. 13.

It will be a tough road for the Mean Green. Even though six starters return on offense and defense, there are simply too many voids to fill with young, inexperienced players for a run at the Sun Belt championship. Maybe in 2002.

(S.C.)

2000 RESULTS

Baylor	L	7-20	0-1
Texas Tech	L	7-13	0-2
UNLV	L	0-38	0-3
Kansas State	L	10-55	0-4
Samford	W	41-6	1-4
Utah State	L	12-17	1-5
Boise State	L	0-59	1-6
Louisiana-Lafayette	W	13-0	2-6
Idaho	L	14-16	2-7
Arkansas State	L	28-53	2-8
New Mexico State	W	30-23	3-8

Boise State

LOCATION Boise, ID
CONFERENCE Western Athletic
LAST SEASON 10-2 (.833)
CONFERENCE RECORD 5-0 (1st Big West)
OFFENSIVE STARTERS RETURNING 7
DEFENSIVE STARTERS RETURNING 4
NICKNAME Broncos
COLORS Blue & Orange
HOME FIELD Bronco Stadium (30,000)
HEAD COACH Dan Hawkins (Cal-Davis '84)
RECORD AT SCHOOL First Year
CAREER RECORD 40-11-1 (5 years)
ASSISTANTS Chris Peterson (Cal Davis '88)
Offensive Coordinator/Quarterbacks
Bob Gregory (Washington State '87)
Defensive Coordinator
Chris Strausser (Cal State Chico '89)
Offensive Line
Kent Riddle (Oregon State '91)
Running Backs/Special Teams
Robert Prince (Humbolt State '89)
Wide Receivers
Romeo Bandison (Oregon '94)
Defensive Line
Ron Collins (Washington State '87)
Linebackers
Robert Tucker (Williamette '97)
Safeties
Kenny Lawler (Regents College '96)
Defensive Backs
TEAM WINS (last 5 yrs.) 2-4-6-10-10
FINAL RANK (last 5 yrs.) 110-95-91-64-57
2000 FINISH Beat UTEP in Humanitarian Bowl.

COACH AND PROGRAM

One of the best programs in the country over the last few years has quietly built its reputation in Boise, Idaho. In the last two seasons alone, Boise State has won 20 games, won back-to-back Big West titles and the first two Humanitarian Bowls. The 20 wins are the sixth most in the country since 1999.

The offensive production is even more impressive. Last season, the Broncos led the nation with 45 points per game, including a staggering 53 points per game during Big West play. Quarterback Bart Hendricks was the Big West Player of the Year and tailback **Brock Forsey** ranked sixth in the country in all-purpose yards.

Boise State's success and the Western Athletic Conference's need for another western team has brought the two together this season. Though the Broncos will be playing their inaugural season in the league, Boise is familiar with the territory, having beaten future bunkmate UTEP in the Humanitarian Bowl last year.

The WAC isn't a tremendously big step up in competition, but it is a higher level than Boise has seen in conference play. The move is a testament to the reputation the school has built, but it will also be a challenge. The league returns several key offensive standouts and may be as balanced this season as it has ever been.

Multiplying the challenge will be the fact Boise has a new coach in Dan Hawkins, who became the school's third head coach in the last five years after Dirk Koetter left for Arizona State. There is always a transition period for new coaches, but this one should take little time. Hawkins was on Koetter's staff for three years and has been a head coach before. From 1993-97, he coached at NAIA Williamette University in Salem, Ore. He went 40-11 in his five years, including reaching the 1997 title game.

Under Koetter, he was the tight ends and special teams coach and developed a reputation for being close to all Boise players, not just the ones he coached. He was instrumental in the Broncos ranking 10th in the nation in kickoff returns and helping Forsey turn into one of the most productive all-purpose players in the nation.

Hawkins' influence was seen elsewhere, too. Kicker **Nick Calaycay** finished 2000 as the most accurate kicker in the nation while Jeff Edwards finished his career with the best punting average in school history.

Hawkins has challenges ahead. His only head coaching experience is on the NAIA level and he has almost an entirely new staff. Only Kenny Lawler and Robert Tucker, who was a graduate assistant last year, remain from last year. Hawkins has to find a new quarterback and the defense is littered with holes.

"There are some definite story lines to this season," Hawkins said. "New quarterback, new defense, new coach, new league. We're making a jump up. Will it be business as usual? No. We're stepping up. Status quo isn't good enough any more."

The positive is that the team is fairly experienced and knows Hawkins and his style. In his tenure, he has encouraged off-the-field community participation, overseeing the teams' community service and public involvement program.

2001 SCHEDULE

Sept.	1	@South Carolina
	8	Washington State
	15	Central Michigan
	22	UTEP
	29	@Idaho
Oct.	6	@Rice
	13	Tulsa
	20	@Fresno State
	27	Nevada
Nov.	10	@Hawaii
	17	San Jose State
	24	@Louisiana Tech

QUARTERBACKS

There may not ever be another at Boise State

quite like Hendricks. He started for three years and was a two-time Big West Offensive Player of the Year selection. He holds 10 school records, and his evolution as a player mirrored the development of the Broncos' program.

Though he had a lot of offensive weapons a year ago, Hendricks' leadership and accuracy were the main reasons Boise led the nation in scoring and averaged more than 50 points per game in conference play. In Koetter's system, which will be very similar to the new one under Hawkins, the quarterback was easily the most important player on the field. A lot of responsibility was put in his hands. With a new offensive coordinator and a quarterback picture that is far from clear, some of those responsibilities will probably be reined in and fall on Hawkins.

"I'm not that concerned that we don't have a quarterback," Hawkins said. "When you lose a two-time player of the year, though, plugging that spot becomes an issue. Especially with us when we have a lot of other skill position players returning."

Sophomore **Ryan Dinwiddie** (6-0, 192) will be the starter in the season opener against South Carolina. Dinwiddie has a lot of the same characteristics as Hendricks, and Hawkins,—who saw Hendricks' three-year development up close—may be willing to hand Dinwiddie the keys to the offense. With the Broncos scoring so many points and often blowing teams out early, Dinwiddie played in eight games in 2000. But he has thrown only 19 passes in his career.

The concern is Dinwiddie's endurance. He is on the small side and could have trouble withstanding the pounding of a full season. If he gets time and moves around some, Dinwiddie has a strong and accurate arm. In high school, he started two years, throwing 56 touchdown passes and leading his team to a 27-1 record.

Hawkins will go with Dinwiddie, but he could be enticed with either redshirt freshman in **Michael Sanford** (6-4, 199) or junior **B.J. Rhode** (6-4, 230), who is beginning his fourth year in the program.

"We'll go with Dinwiddie," Hawkins said, "but that doesn't mean other people won't get snaps and a chance to show that they can move the football."

Rhode has the size and experience with the system, but he has attempted only 18 passes in two years and spent 2000 as a redshirt. Like Dinwiddie, though, he has a strong arm and produced massive high school numbers.

Sanford also produced the big prep numbers (including a school-record 25 completions in one game). His 6-4 frame would likely be ideal, but at just under 200 pounds, he needs to put on weight and get at least some game experience before he is a legitimate Division I-A starter.

Boise's only quarterback signee was **Sean Steichen** (6-0, 190), who is out of the Hendricks/Dinwiddie mold. He is headed for a redshirt season.

RUNNING BACKS

If Dinwiddie has problems adjusting to the system or to the rigors of being a starting quarterback, the running game will have to carry the offensive load, something that isn't normally done in the Broncos' attack.

With Hendricks as coach the last three years, the running game helped set up the pass and running the football was never a huge priority. That's the way Hawkins eventually wants it to be in 2001. Because of the quarterback situation, he may have to wait longer than he wants, though he says that isn't going to be the case.

"We are so far ahead of where we have been the last few years as far as Xs and Os go," Hawkins said.

Hawkins said that includes the quarterbacks, but their experience gap won't be bridged until they actually play in games. That's why the running game will play an increased and most likely more vital role. And if that's the case, the Broncos are in good shape. The top two rushers from a year ago are back as well as a stocked fullback stable.

Forsey (5-11, 198), a junior, will make the Broncos' offense tick. Hawkins was instrumental in turning Forsey into one of the most productive all-purpose players in the country. Last season, Forsey finished sixth in the country in all-purpose yards, averaging 183.0 per game, including three games of more than 200-plus yards. He set a school record with 292 yards last year against Northern Iowa and his 183-yard average was the second best in school history. He also ran for 914 yards and became a valuable threat in the passing game, catching 23 passes for 399 yards.

Forsey is a big back to be as shifty and as good at cutting back against the grain as he has become. He could be headed for a 1,000-yard season.

Forsey's running mate is sophomore **David Mikell** (5-10, 190), who is the flash to Forsey's workman-like style. Mikell averaged 5.5 yards per carry a year ago and scored three touchdowns in one game against North Texas. With 4.46 speed in the 40, he is among the fastest Boise players. Going with his belief that his best playmakers should be on special teams, Mikell is also a big contributor on the kick-return unit. Last season, Mikell finished third in the nation with an average return of almost 29 yards.

Even behind Mikell and Forsey there is talent, but little experience. Redshirt freshman **Donny Heck** (5-10, 188) and sophomore **David Word** (5-7, 172) will get carries, but the duo combined for only six carries a year ago.

Heck redshirted last season after running for almost 1,900 yards as a senior and being selected the Idaho Gatorade Player of the Year.

At fullback, junior **Matt Strofus** (6-2, 233) moves into the starting role after backing up the last two years. Strofus is an example of how good and how improved the strength and conditioning program at Boise has become. Since arriving in

WESTERN ATHLETIC

BLUE RIBBON FORECAST

1. Fresno State
2. San Jose State
3. Hawaii
4. Rice
5. UTEP
6. Boise State
7. Tulsa
8. SMU
9. Louisiana Tech
10. Nevada

ALL-CONFERENCE TEAM

OFFENSE

POS. PLAYER SCHOOL HT. WT. CL.

WR Lee Mays, UTEP, 6-3, 190, Sr.
WR Donald Shoals, Tulsa, 5-10, 175, Sr.
OL Joe Schey, Fresno State, 6-6, 315, Jr.
OL Vince Manuwai, Hawaii, 6-2, 296, Jr.
C Rodney Michael, Fresno State, 6-4, 300, Jr.
OL Chris Fe'easgo, San Jose St., 6-3, 324, Sr.
OL Matt Hill, Boise State, 6-6, 298, Sr.
QB David Carr, Fresno State, 6-3, 220, Sr.
RB Deonce Whitaker, San Jose St., 5-6, 175, Sr.
RB John Simon, Louisiana Tech, 5-9, 202, Sr.
TE John Hampton, SMU, 6-2, 235, Jr.

DEFENSE

POS. PLAYER SCHOOL HT. WT. CL.

DL Larry Brown, Rice, 6-2, 290, Sr.
DL Nick Burley, Fresno State, 6-4, 246, Jr.
DL Alan Harper, Fresno State, 6-2, 285, Sr.
LB Jorge Cordova, Nevada, 6-2, 235, So.
LB Dan Dawson, Rice, 6-2, 200, Sr.
LB Pisa Tinoisamoa, Hawaii, 6-1, 255, Jr.
LB Vic Viloria, SMU, 5-10, 225, Jr.
DB Crance Clemons, UTEP, 5-10, 160, Jr.
DB Vernon Fox, Fresno State, 5-10, 200, Sr.
DB Bobby Gray, Louisiana Tech, 6-1, 210, Sr.
DB D.J. Walker, UTEP, 6-3, 210, Jr.

SPECIALISTS

POS. PLAYER SCHOOL HT. WT. CL.

PK Derek Crabtree, Rice, 6-4, 210, Sr.
P Travis Hale, Rice, 6-3, 201, Jr.
RS Donald Shoals, Tulsa, 5-10, 175, Sr.

OFFENSIVE PLAYER OF THE YEAR

Deonce Whitaker, RB, San Jose State

DEFENSIVE PLAYER OF THE YEAR

Alan Harper, DL, Fresno State

NEWCOMER OF THE YEAR

Isaak Sopoaga, DL, Hawaii

WAC NOTEBOOK

After just one year as a nine-team league, the WAC has expanded to 10 for the 2001 season. Boise State and Louisiana Tech join the league just in time for the departure of TCU, which is bolting for Conference USA. Each WAC team will play an eight-game league schedule, missing one team for two years. ... WAC teams are guaranteed spots in two bowls this year. One team is bound for he Silicon Valley Football Classic in San Jose, Calif. The other will compete in the Humanitarian Bowl in Boise, Idaho. ... There are two new head coaches in the WAC this season. Dan Hawkins takes over at Boise State and Fitz Hill at San Jose State. ... Rice coach Ken Hatfield, beginning his 23rd season, is the fifth winningest active coach in Division I-A. His career record is 147-104-4. Hatfield has the most wins over WAC teams with 34 over the last eight years. ... Every team in the league returns at least 11 starters. SMU, Nevada and Rice all have 19 starters returning, tops in the league. Nevada has the most offensive starters back (10), while SMU has the most defensive starters returning (10). ... Of the 25 first-team All-WAC players in 2000, only seven return this season. Among the returning players are several statistical leaders from a year ago. San Jose State's Deonce Whitaker was fourth in the nation and tops in the WAC with 1,577 yards rushing (157.7 per game). Tulsa's Donald Shoals led the league in receptions with 80. UTEP's Lee Mays had the most receiving yards (99.8 per game).

1998, Strofus has put on 25 pounds and been a standout special teams player.

Sophomore **Greg Swenson** (5-10, 205) will get carries, but is better used as a blocker.

The Broncos signed junior college fullback **Clint Feminis** (5-10, 212), who will get a chance to step in and play significant snaps. He is a good blocker, but is more of a running threat. In two years at the College of the Siskiyous in Weed, Calif., where Hawkins once coached, Feminis gained more than 1,200 yards and scored 15 touchdowns.

WIDE RECEIVERS/TIGHT ENDS

With the amount of wide receiver talent Boise has returning, all Broncos quarterbacks need to do is get the ball in the air and in the general direction. Someone is likely to come down with the ball. Boise returns a receiver corps that goes eight deep and includes five players who caught at least one touchdown pass.

Junior **Lou Fanucchi** (5-11, 191), senior **Jeb Putzier** (6-5, 234) and junior **Jay Swillie** (6-3, 207) are the leaders of the bunch. Fanucchi is the big-play threat. Last season, he led the team in receptions, yards and touchdowns and averaged almost 20 yards per catch. He was the biggest beneficiary of the wide-open, high-powered offense and Hendricks's arm. Fanucchi's average was helped by 10 catches of more than 30 yards and a 37.6 yards average on his eight touchdowns.

Fanucchi is able to concentrate on the outside and big plays—and stay out of the middle of the field—because of Putzier. Putzier moved from tight end to receiver last season and responded with 35 catches for 592 yards. Both those totals were second on the team behind Fanucchi. Putzier's size creates space and keeps the smaller receivers from having to take a pounding. Though he has 4.55 speed in the 40, Putzier rarely catches balls outside the hash marks.

If there is a "possession" receiver, it's Swillie. Of his 66 career receptions, almost 80 percent have given Boise a first down. He is the underneath threat on both the outside and inside and the perfect complement to Fanucchi's big-play ability and Putzier's "big-body" ability in the middle. Swillie catches passes all over the field and may be the most versatile of all the Boise receivers.

In the three wideout set, junior **Andre Banks** (6-2, 177), senior **Brian O'Neal** (6-0, 189) and junior **Billy Wingfield** (5-10, 181) will all get balls thrown their way. Depending on how the quarterback situation shakes down, the three may play even more than expected.

The trio doesn't have an abundance of receptions among them, but the catches they have made have made a difference. Banks snagged 19 balls as a sophomore a year ago with four going four touchdowns. O'Neal has caught only 16 passes in his career, but three were for touchdowns. Wingfield, a junior who redshirted a year ago, is the fastest Boise receiver and the other likely deep threat in addition to Fanucchi.

Sophomore **Jerry Smith** (5-10, 171) and redshirt freshman **T.J. Acree** (5-10, 165), both local products, will also see time.

Sophomore **Kevin Louwsma** (6-4, 250) has big shoes to fill at a tight end position that has become a tradition at Boise. In each of the last three years, the Broncos have produced an all-conference tight end. Robby Snelling had 24 catches and five touchdowns a year ago. He was replacing Dave Stachelski, a two-time all-conference pick who now plays with the New Orleans Saints. Louwsma became a big part of the Broncos offense late last year. He missed the first four games with a knee injury, but showed no effects of the injury after the season.

Still, Louwsma will be pushed for snaps. Junior **Rocky Atkinson** (6-2, 247) moved over from the defensive side before last year. Because of his frame and his ability to block and catch short passes, many believe he compares favorably to Snelling, while Louwsma is the better blocker and overall tight end.

Redshirt freshman **Antoine Williams** (6-2, 234) and junior college transfer **Kuwese Walker** (6-3, 230) will both get extended looks in the fall.

OFFENSIVE LINE

Much like the rest of the offense, the offensive line returns experience and talent. Four starters are back as well as the top backup at tackle and two newcomers whom Hawkins said are ready to immediately contribute.

In Boise's system, the offensive line has to be athletic enough to keep up with the offensive pace. Because of the amount of throwing involved, the focus, like most offensive lines, isn't on run blocking but on how to have good balance and use leverage to throw defensive linemen off balance.

The best up front is senior right tackle **Matt Hill** (6-6, 298), who was a second-team all conference selection in his first year after moving over from defensive tackle. His frame will wear on WAC defensive ends, most of whom are in the small and fast mode.

The right side is in good shape with junior **Rob Vian** (6-5, 300) at guard. Though a better run blocker than pass blocker, Vian has become a decent pass blocker because, as one of the team's strongest players, he can use brute strength to overpower twisting ends and most tackles. Junior center **Scott Huff** (6-2, 292) is reason for the continuity of the offensive line. He has started 17 straight games and will be vital in the development of a new quarterback.

Senior left tackle **Peter Naumes** (6-3, 279), who started the final seven games last year, is the fourth returning starter. He took over for senior **Derek Olley** (6-5, 305), who started at left tackle as a sophomore in 1999. Olley will have a chance to compete for the job in the fall.

Olley's situation shows how deep the Broncos are up front. If Olley returns to his 1999 form, Naumes may switch to left guard, the only vacant spot on the line. If Naumes doesn't move over, either redshirt freshman **Russell Colburn** (6-4, 293) or junior college transfer **Jess Hernandez** (6-3, 284) will slide inside.

Senior **Jeff Cheek** (6-5, 293) and junior **Nick Lamalu** (6-6, 319) are solid backups, but both primarily are guards. Injuries at tackle could force some juggling or playing one or more of the three freshmen offensive linemen—**Darryn Colledge** (6-4, 269), **Kellen Wright** (6-3, 262) or **Micah Kormylo** (6-4, 270)—all of whom need redshirt years.

2000 STATISTICS

Rushing offense	174.7	30
Passing offense	321.5	5
Total offense	496.3	2
Scoring offense	44.9	1
Net Punting	34.8	48
Punt returns	9.3	59
Kickoff returns	22.9	11
Rushing defense	139.2	48
Passing efficiency defense	118.6	56
Total defense	367.5	61
Scoring defense	22.8	46
Turnover margin	+8	19

Last column is ranking among Division I teams.

KICKERS

Boise State immediately becomes one of the best special teams units in the WAC because of Calaycay (5-7, 168). A former walk-on, the junior was a Lou Groza Award nominee last season after making 15-of-16 field goal attempts and leading the nation in field goal accuracy at 93.8 percent. He set a school record with 104 points, which also led the Big West.

With two seasons left, Calaycay, a serious candidate for the Groza Award this year, is already Boise State's 10th leading all-time scorer.

DEFENSIVE LINE

New defensive coordinator Bob Gregory switched things up when he got to Boise. He eliminated a safety spot and added a linebacker. He must have watched film and decided to face some pretty ugly realities. There isn't much returning on defense and especially up front, where it will be essential in the pass-happy WAC to get a pass rush so the secondary doesn't get hung out to dry.

The linebackers and defensive backs may make more tackles than the Broncos want because of a depleted line that lost three starters, including ends Jeff Copp and Zach Weber, both of whom were first-team All-Big West selections a year ago. Junior **Tony Altieri** (5-10, 280) returns at tackle, but the rest of the line will be chosen among spare parts.

And even Altieri comes with questions. Thought strong and quick at 280 pounds, he is only 5-10. A taller lineman who may not be as strong can take him out of plays fairly easily simply by using leverage. Altieri's game is all about getting lower than the taller offensive linemen. That leaves him susceptible to double teams and often takes him out of providing a pass rush. Last season, Altieri made 30 tackles, but only three were for loss.

Junior **Bobby Hammer** (6-2, 263) will slide in next to Altieri. Hammer has played off and on the last two years, mostly in between setting records in the weight room. The strongest player on the team recently set position records in the squat, hand clean and bench press.

Sophomore **Paul Allen** (6-2, 273), who played in 12 games a year ago, and sophomore **Dane Oldham** (6-2, 259), who got into eight games in 2000, are the backups.

Just like last season, the end situation is a concern after the loss of two all-conference players. This year's fill-ins are seniors **Sky Dumont** (6-2, 238) and **Mike Phillips** (6-2, 241), junior **Marcus Purkiss** (6-3, 237) and redshirt freshman **Julius Roberts** (6-5, 225). Dumont and Phillips were the only players among the four to make a tackle in 2000 (19 combined) and the only two to play in every game. Purkiss, who will likely start opposite Philips, is the best returning pass rusher.

Roberts is going to get a shot because he will be able to out run most tackles in the WAC. He put on 25 pounds during his redshirt year and still ran a 4.75 40-yard dash in the spring. At 225 pounds, he is still small, but he is a good all-around athlete, having earned several basketball honors in high school in addition to excelling in football.

LINEBACKERS

The new linebacker spot has senior **Greg Sasser** (5-9, 206) with new letters beside his name on the depth chart, but probably has done little to change his duties. He finished third on the team in tackles and tied for second in tackles for losses. He was also involved in pass coverage. He will still be asked to provide secondary help, but, because of a depleted line, Sasser needs to be even more of a factor in the running game than he was a year ago.

Boise calls the position a "Sam" linebacker, but it won't be much different than the rover spot a lot of teams use.

After Sasser, there are no returning starters. Sophomores **LaGary Mitchell** (6-1, 244) and **Tarvis Burgher** (6-1, 204), both special teams standouts a year ago, will play, but Burgher will back up Sasser and Mitchell will likely end up backing up junior college transfers **Chauncey Ako** (5-11, 234) and **Kameron Merritt** (6-2, 228). The two were among five linebackers the Broncos signed.

Ako was one of California's top junior college linebackers. He has decent size and can hit. He is a prototypical linebacker with good speed and even better size. Merritt doesn't have the size (215 pounds,), but at 6-2 is three inches taller than Ako. Merritt led Shasta (Calif.) Junior College in tackles last year and was a two-time all-conference selection at strong safety.

With Merritt and Sasser not being the ideal size, Gregory is making it clear that he wants to be aggressive and expects his linebackers to be factors in all areas. Injuries could be a concern here as well. There isn't much depth behind the starters. Redshirt freshmen **Andy Avalos** (5-10, 213) and **Nick Stranberg** (6-1, 234) can back up any of the positions. But Avalos isn't that big, and Stranberg, who does have good size, is coming off a broken leg suffered a year ago.

DEFENSIVE BACKS

An attacking defense puts pressure on the defensive backs. It forces them to become playmakers in the running game and makes them get their jerseys dirty on tackles, which a lot of defensive players don't like to do. Boise State has a player who not only likes to stick his hat in the mix, but also is pretty good at doing so.

Junior free safety **Quintin Mikell** (5-10, 197) was the Big West Co-Defensive Player of the Year after leading the team in tackles with 118. He played a big role in the Humanitarian Bowl win over UTEP, making nine tackles, intercepting a pass and recovering a fumble. And, in his spare time, he returns punts. He is the unquestioned leader of the defense and a player who will have to become an even bigger part of the team in 2001 for the defense not to be a liability.

Sophomore **Wes Nurse** (5-10, 181) is Mikell's partner at safety with Sasser having moved up to give the Broncos an additional linebacker. Originally recruited as a wide receiver, Nurse has good enough speed, strength and coverage ability that he could play cornerback if needed. And that could be a possibility for the Broncos, who have little experience on the outside.

Senior **Greg Toomes** (5-9, 177) and sophomore **Julius Brown** (5-10, 184) played in every game last year, but neither is a set starter.

Redshirt freshman **Gabe Franklin** (5-10, 179), junior college transfer **Terrial Hall** (5-9, 170) and junior **Randy Sleden** (5-8, 151) could all play. Two prep signees, **Chris Carr** (5-10, 171) and **Lee Marks** (5-9, 167), will get a chance to see the field early.

PUNTERS

Junior college transfer **Keith Schuttler** (5-11, 191) arrived in Boise in the spring and was immediately handed the punting job. He replaces Jeff Edwards, who set a school record with a 42.5 yards-per-punt career average. Schuttler averaged 42.0 yards per kick a year ago at Glendale (Ariz.) Community College, which won a junior college national title.

Redshirt freshmen **Nicholas Jones** (6-1, 249) and **Sam Knopp** (5-8, 168) are on the roster, but neither are threats to Schuttler.

SPECIAL TEAMS

Having to replace punter Edwards is the only blemish keeping Boise State from immediately being the best special teams unit in the WAC.

Calaycay has some of the best numbers in the country. He is already among the top 10 scorers in school history and is a legitimate contender for the Groza Award.

Hawkins is the former special teams coach. He made his impression on former coach Koetter by taking his best athletes and asking them to make plays on special teams. Forsey ranked among the top 10 in the country in all-purpose yards thanks to averaging 21.5 yards per kickoff return. His return partner, Mikell, was third in the nation a year ago with almost 29 yards per return, including a 98-yard return for a touchdown.

The team's best defensive player, Mikell averaged 9.1 yards per punt return in 2000, with a long return of 43 yards.

The Broncos also have some of the best coverage units in the league because of Hawkins' philosophy of using speedy, aggressive athletes to make plays.

RECRUITING CLASS

Hawkins dipped into seven states for his first recruiting class. Three newcomers came from Washington and only one, Kormylo, from Idaho.

The 22-player class was loaded with seven junior college transfers, all of whom are expected to provide some sort of impact next season.

Schuttler is an immediate starter and Ako, Hall and Merritt are likely starters on a defense ravaged by graduation. Schuttler is the only one of the seven transfers not originally from California.

Of note, junior college transfer Feminis played at College of the Siskiyous in Northern California, where Hawkins was the offensive coordinator from 1988-91.

The class ranks in the middle of the pack in the WAC, but the Broncos got the immediate defensive help they desperately needed with the junior college transfers.

The only freshmen likely to contribute are Marks and Carr, who will both get looks at the two cornerback spots.

BLUE RIBBON ANALYSIS

OFFENSE	B+
SPECIAL TEAMS	A-
DEFENSE	D
INTANGIBLES	C-

Boise State has always put up points and will again this year. The running game is there as well as the protection up front. The question at quarterback—who will replace Hendricks?—and the fact Boise is making a significant jump in competition probably means the Broncos will miss out on a bowl game. But the Broncos have enough talent to show the folks in the WAC that there is a new threat at the top.

Boise State opens the year at South Carolina, but should be able to win its next two, both at home. The Sept. 22 game against UTEP is the Broncos' first WAC game and it comes against one of the league's defending co-champions. The WAC is thin enough that even with a slip against the Miners, Boise can finish in the top half of the conference.

The coaching change from Koetter to Hawkins will have some impact. However, Hawkins has been a head coach before and was a three-year assistant under Koetter before being promoted. The Broncos should be more worried about how they are going to replace three starters on the defensive line, both linebackers and a total of six players who earned All-Big West honors.

Playing six games at Bronco Stadium, including three of its first four, will give Boise much needed confidence early in the year. The Broncos have gone unbeaten the last two seasons at home and carry a 14-game home winning streak into 2001.

(C.M.)

2000 RESULTS

New Mexico	W	31-14	1-0
Southern Iowa	W	42-17	2-0
Arkansas	L	31-38	2-1
Central Michigan	W	47-10	3-1
Washington State	L	35-42	3-2
Eastern Washington	W	41-23	4-2
North Texas	W	59-0	5-2
New Mexico State	W	34-31	6-2
Arkansas State	W	42-14	7-2
Utah State	W	66-38	8-2
Idaho	W	66-24	9-2
UTEP (Humanitarian)	W	38-23	10-2

Fresno State

LOCATION	**Fresno, CA**
CONFERENCE	**Western Athletic**
LAST SEASON	**7-5 (.583)**
CONFERENCE RECORD	**6-2 (3rd)**
OFFENSIVE STARTERS RETURNING	**9**
DEFENSIVE STARTERS RETURNING	**6**
NICKNAME	**Bulldogs**
COLORS	**Red & Blue**
HOME FIELD	**Bullldog Stadium (41,031)**
HEAD COACH	**Pat Hill (UC Riverside '73)**
RECORD AT SCHOOL	**26-22 (4 years)**
CAREER RECORD	**26-22 (4 years)**
ASSISTANTS	
	John Baxter (Loras College '85)
	Associate Head Coach/Tight Ends/Special Teams
	Dennis Wagner (Utah '80)
	Assistant Head Coach/Offensive Line
	Dan Brown (Boise State '82)
	Defensive Coordinator/Linebackers
	Andy Ludwig (Portland State '87)
	Offensive Coordinator/Quarterback
	Kerry Locklin (New Mexico State '85)
	Defensive Line
	John Settle (Appalachian State '89)
	Running Backs
	Tim Simons (Fresno State '67)
	Wide Receivers
	J.D. Williams (Fresno State '90)
	Secondary
TEAM WINS (last 5 yrs.)	**4-6-5-8-7**
FINAL RANK (last 5 yrs.)	**95-85-87-80-74**
2000 FINISH	**Lost to Air Force in Silicon Valley Bowl.**

COACH AND PROGRAM

Pat Hill has been so much more to the Fresno State program than the coach who has won 20 games the last three years and put the Bulldogs' program on the map. He has given the program an attitude. Case in point is last year's Silicon Valley Bowl.

The Bulldogs fell behind Air Force, 34-7, before rallying to trail, 37-34, with 14 seconds left. They needed a 33-yard field goal to tie the game. Instead of kicking the ball, Hill, whose teams are always good on special teams, faked the kick and tried to give his offense a couple of cracks at the end zone. The fake fell short, but the message was delivered. Hill doesn't mind taking chances and putting his faith squarely on the shoulders of his players.

Under Hill, Fresno has become one of the more successful programs in the West. Over the last 30 games, the Bulldogs are 19-11. Only Air Force and Oregon have better records during the same stretch.

With 15 starters—many of them two-year starters—returning, improving on last year' seven wins is a possibility. The Bulldogs play 13 regular-season games and there are no cupcakes, also a trait of the program under Hill. The Bulldogs open against Colorado in the inaugural Jim Thorpe Classic and have Oregon State, which will be ranked in the top 10 of most preseason polls, coming to the Valley. A week later, the Bulldogs pack for a game at Wisconsin. And the non-conference schedule doesn't end there. On Oct. 13, Fresno plays former conference rival and Mountain West favorite Colorado State in Fort Collins.

Hill believes the tough schedule early in the year has always made his team better late. With the WAC balanced below Fresno, it could be the kind of springboard to going through the league unbeaten.

The non-conference schedule also helps in keeping fans in Fresno coming back. Last year, Fresno played in front of the four largest crowds in school history in its first four home games. The season average of 41,369 was more than 300 fans above Bulldog Stadium's capacity. In terms of capacity, Fresno finished second (Oregon State was first) among Western schools and in the top 25 in the nation.

This season, more than 30,000 season tickets have been sold, making the Bulldogs, and their high-powered offense, one of the Valley's toughest tickets. The crowd has helped make Bulldog Stadium one of the most difficult places to play in the nation. The Bulldogs beat SMU on Nov. 18, extending their home winning streak to 15 games. Only Florida State (36 straight) and Oregon (20 straight) have longer home winning streaks. Fresno hasn't lost at home since a 27-24 setback to Nevada in 1998.

In addition to taking care of teams at home, Fresno, under Hill, has become one of the most disciplined teams in the league. Much of that can be attributed to the emphasis the staff places on special teams. Since Hill took over four years ago, the Bulldogs have blocked 27 kicks, including 17 the last two seasons.

One of Hill's most enduring qualities, especially to the administration, is his involvement in the team's "Academic Gameplan," the brainchild of associate head coach John Baxter. Hill said he decided to take on the program not to satisfy the administration, but to make sure academics are the first priority.

In the fall of 1998, 16 football players were on the Dean's List with at least a 3.5 grade-point average. That same semester, 34 football players were above a 3.0 and 21 set academic personal records. Two years ago, 31 players had cumulative GPAs above 3.0 and senior Payton Williams became the program's first Academic All-American.

"We do this program because this is college football," Hill said, "not football college."

2001 SCHEDULE

Aug.	26	@Colorado (Jim Thorpe Classic)
Sept.	1	Oregon State
	8	@Wisconsin
	15	Utah State
	22	@Tulsa
	29	Louisiana Tech
Oct.	13	@Colorado State
	20	Boise State
	27	@Hawaii
Nov.	3	Rice
	10	@SMU
	17	@Nevada
	24	San Jose State

QUARTERBACKS

Hill's offenses have been outstanding in his four years because he has had the luxury of having an experienced leader each season. In his first two years, Billy Volek led the Bulldogs. Last season, Hill turned the reins over to senior **David Carr** (6-3, 225) and Fresno was even better. Carr avoided the interception trouble that plagued Volek and threw for 23 touchdowns on his way to being voted second team All-WAC. This season, Carr, who holds the school record for career completion percentage, should compete with San Jose State's Deonce Whitaker and UTEP's Lee Mays for WAC Offensive Player-of-the-Year honors.

Carr has prototype size and is one of the team's returning captains. Last season, he was forced to make plays early because of the Bulldogs' schedule and because of a litany of injuries in the Fresno backfield. The experience made the strong-armed Carr a better player even though he struggled early.

With a bevy of talent back at receiver and a backfield that is once again healthy, Carr should have an even better year that last season when he threw for 2,729 yards, the sixth most in school history.

Carr isn't a very mobile quarterback, but he is able to get by because he has the strongest arm in the league. Even when Volek was the quarterback, coaches said Carr had the strongest arm on the team. He has the ability to fire up his teammates and get them into the flow of the game early and the leadership to finish games. The Bulldogs scored 93 points in the first quarter, more than any other quarter, and 77 in the fourth quarter, Fresno's second most productive quarter.

Behind Carr, a situation is developing much like the one Carr was in two years ago. Junior **Jeff Grady** (6-2, 195) played in five games last year, but he may not play at all this season. If redshirt freshman **Nathan Ray** (6-0, 195) develops, Grady is headed for a redshirt year and the starting job in 2002. This is the same path Carr followed three years ago. He spent the 1999 season on the bench during Volek's senior year before stepping in to the starting role last year.

RUNNING BACKS

All the firepower is there for Fresno State. The receivers returning have impressive numbers. Three starters are back on the offensive line. Carr is headed for a breakout year. The only thing Hill has his fingers crossed on for his offense is the health and consistency of his running backs. Fresno has three of its top four rushers back, but none of them gained more than 400 yards. Of the five teams that featured the run in the WAC last year, the Bulldogs finished last. Overall, only SMU and Nevada had fewer rushing touchdowns.

Junior **Josh Levi** (5-7, 195), led the team with 397 yards, but he played only nine games and got in the end zone only twice on a team-high 92 carries. Levi is the smallest of the Bulldogs' backs, but despite his injuries has been the most consistent. Coaches would like him to become more of a receiving threat and a better blocker because he's not really an every down back.

If Levi continues to develop and senior **Paris Gaines** (6-1, 225) and junior **Derrick Ward** (6-0, 230) can rebound from knee injuries, Fresno will have one of the best backfield punches in the league.

Gaines had only 359 yards and one touchdown last season. Those numbers are deceptive because Gaines probably came back too soon from a knee injury suffered in the 1999 Las Vegas Bowl. The injury required major surgery and Gaines probably needed more than a year of rehab. He came back and played in every game, though he wasn't full speed until late in the year.

Ward, the best back the Bulldogs have when healthy, is the key to taking pressure off Carr and the receivers. He played in only six games a year ago, carrying 45 times for 189 yards. He injured his knee and had surgery in the off-season.

Though he may be rusty early in the year, Ward is still the best power and breakaway threat Fresno has. As a freshman in 1999, Ward averaged 6.0 yards per carry and scored seven touchdowns. He also has seven carries of more than 50 yards. That's the kind of punch the Bulldogs need if defenses begin relaxing, playing deep zones and bringing multiple blitz packages in at attempt to rattle Carr.

Even though 12 players got carries a year ago, Hill will give the bulk of the carries to Levi, Gaines and Ward and would like Ward to step up and become the back the Bulldogs can feature.

The only other player who may get time is junior **Tim Osborn** (6-2, 220), a converted tight end, who may still play some at the H-back/tight end spot.

WIDE RECEIVERS/TIGHT ENDS

UTEP's Lee Mays is the top receiver in the WAC. But no receiving corps in the league, as a whole, can touch the talent and overall depth Fresno has. The Bulldogs return their top eight receivers, including three who have been first or second-team All-WAC during their careers. In 2000, the eight combined for almost 2,800 receiving yards and 24 touchdowns. The concern, just like the running backs, is health.

Last year, seniors **Charles Smith** (5-9, 175) and **Rodney Wright** (5-9, 175), both of whom were All-WAC in 1999, were the top receiving duo in the country until an ankle injury to Wright in the fourth game of the season against Rice cost him six games. Before the injury, Wright was fourth in the nation in receptions. Still, he was the third-leading receiver on the team with 33 catches, 389 yards and two touchdowns. Smith also missed one game, but finished with 33 catches, 526 yards and a team-high six touchdowns.

When Wright went down, junior **Bernard Berrian** (6-2, 190) provided Carr with a bigger target on the outside. Carr must have like what Berrian was providing because Berrian finished the year as the team leader in yards (543) and catches (36). He was second with a 15.1-yard average and four touchdowns.

Wright and Smith, who also gets the ball on reverses and punt returns, are the starters, but only because the Bulldogs use a tight end and a hybrid running back/receiver/blocker. For the most part, Fresno stays in a three-wide receiver set with only one running back. In that formation, Wright, Smith and Berrian should provide the sort of punch that will have Fresno at the top of the WAC's offensive charts.

Smith and Wright are identical in size and almost identical receivers. Both can fly and both have good hands. Their size is a concern, especially considering some of the defensive backfields Fresno will see early.

Berrian is the big threat who can go over the middle, but at 190 pounds he can't sustain a lot of punishment either. Having depth allows Fresno to take chances and open up the offense in an attempt to pull upsets in its brutal non-conference schedule. Having as many as 10 players who will catch passes forces defenders to keep up with fresh players, allowing the Bulldogs' offense to keep its high-pressure, up-tempo offense on the field at all times.

The depth is solid, but it is also injury prone. Sophomore **Marque Davis** (6-0, 190) was expected to contribute last season. He did for the first two games before an abdominal injury sidelined him for the rest of the year. Had Davis been healthy, it would have been him instead of Berrian to replace Wright after the injury.

Sophomore **Deandre Gilbert** (5-10, 180) and senior **David Shabaglian** (6-0, 185) are the other threats on the outside. The two can back up at any of the receiving positions. Last season, they combined for 20 catches, 232 yards and two touchdowns.

None of the six receivers are tall, strong threats over the middle. But they all have big play ability. In fact, almost anyone who catches the ball at Fresno has the ability to make a big play. Of the 15 players who caught passes in 2000, only two didn't have a catch of at least 12 yards. Five had plays more than 30 yards and Berrian, Smith and Wright all had catches of at least 50 yards.

Tight end is another offensive weapon for the Bulldogs. Sophomore **Jeremy Johnson** (6-4, 205) isn't the blocking sort of end most teams have.

Redshirt freshman backup **Duncan Reid** (6-6, 220) could turn in to a prototype tight end, but Fresno doesn't really need that. This is the position that needs to make the catches over that middle to take the pressure and undue punishment off the small, speedy receivers on the outside.

Johnson, a second-team All-WAC choice last season behind UTEP All-American Brian Natkin, needs to continue breaking through after his 2000 when he caught 27 passes for 285 yards and two touchdowns.

When the Bulldogs aren't playing a three-wide receiver set, they have an H-back in the game. This is where the traditional tight end plays. Sophomore **Alec Greco** (6-3, 230) is a returning starter. He can block or catch passes. Last season he averaged 12 yards per catch on 11 receptions. Because of the running back depth, Osborn will play H-back as well. Redshirt freshman **Stephen Spach** (6-4, 220) will also be thrown into the mix.

OFFENSIVE LINE

There is no question that the Bulldogs have Cadillac-caliber offensive weapons. Every position on the field has all-conference capability. And that includes the big boys up front. Three starters and one part-time starter are back, but the spot protecting Carr's backside needs to be filled and depth needs to develop to help overcome a brutal early season schedule and to help a running game that has struggled with inconsistency and injuries.

Junior center **Rodney Michael** (6-4, 300) anchors an offensive line that will have five starters checking in at more than 300 pounds, the biggest front line in school history. One of the best centers in the WAC, Michael is a two-year starter and has been the glue of the offensive line for a while. He has started the last 23 games and was an honorable mention All-WAC choice as a sophomore.

Both guards are back beside Michael. Senior **Russell Harding** (6-2, 300) is at left guard and sophomore **Fitu Tu'ua** (6-5, 310), who started six games last season, is at right guard. Harding is the strongest player on the team and is one of the veterans Hill needs to help several younger players develop into vital backup roles.

Coaches have been high on Tu'ua since he arrived in Fresno. He is a fiery competitor who Hill is expecting to be entrenched at right guard for three years.

Junior right tackle **Joe Schey** (6-6, 315), who started 11 games last year, is another athletic lineman. Despite being 315 pounds, Schey can move and, like the rest of the Bulldog linemen, has to be in good shape to get up and down the field when Fresno is running its up-tempo offense. Considering how much the hurry-up could be in place this year, getting in shape early is a must up front.

Schey is also a product of the "Academic Gameplan" system. He was one of the top students on the team a year ago and was an academic all-district selection.

The biggest lineman on the team will protect Carr's blindside at left tackle. Junior college transfer **Victor Taifane** (6-5, 335) will have a learning curve early. That is going to put pressure on Harding and Michael to help keep the big linemen the Bulldogs will see against Colorado, Oregon State and Wisconsin off of Carr. Taifane, from West Hills (Calif.) College, was an honorable mention All-American selection by J.C. Gridwire.

Behind the starting five, there isn't much experience. No one has stepped forward to make a push at backup tackle, and the guard spots are still a question. Junior **Keith McKnight** (6-4, 315) can play center and did for much of the spring. He may be forced into duty elsewhere depending on injuries.

Sophomore guard **Ian Harper** (6-3, 295) played some last season. In time, Hill believes he can be the versatile guard the Bulldogs need.

Junior **Patrick Franene** (6-0, 285) is the only other player with significant experience. He is better suited at tackle, but can play almost anywhere.

2000 STATISTICS

Rushing offense	121.7	83
Passing offense	227.0	42
Total offense	348.7	72
Scoring offense	25.7	62
Net Punting	35.2	42
Punt returns	12.6	22
Kickoff returns	19.2	71
Rushing defense	147.6	57
Passing efficiency defense	104.4	23
Total defense	353.0	49
Scoring defense	19.5	27
Turnover margin	+2	51

Last column is ranking among Division I-A teams.

KICKERS

Fresno has both its place-kicker and kickoff specialist back. Junior **Asen Asparuhov** (6-5, 215) is a lanky kicker who was the team's leading scorer last year with 63 points. He was 36-of-37 on extra points, but he needs to become more consistent on field goals, making only 9-of-16 a year ago. His biggest problems came from long range, where he was 6-of-13 from 30 yards and beyond, including 2-of-6 from 40-49 yards.

Sophomore **Brett Visintainer** (6-0, 165) has a strong leg despite a small frame. He handled kickoffs a year ago and will again this season.

DEFENSIVE LINE

The Bulldogs' 4-3 scheme is built around quick defensive ends and senior **Alan Harper** (6-2, 285), one of the most dominating defensive tackles in the country. Harper, a two-time first-team All-WAC choice, is one of three returning starters on a line that has some young depth and, along with an experienced secondary, should help the Bulldogs be one of the top defenses in the conference once again.

Last season, Fresno finished second in total defense and scoring defense in the WAC behind TCU, which finished first in the nation. The success really showed against the run, where only the Horned Frogs allowed fewer rushing touchdowns, had a better average per carry or had more sacks. A lot of that credit goes to Harper, who despite double teams and playing inside, made 14 tackles for loss. Because teams have to commit more than one player to him, he can disrupt the continuity of a line like no other defensive player in the league.

A lot of Harper's success is because of junior end **Nick Burley** (6-4, 240). Burley is typical of the smaller and quicker ends that most WAC teams have. He is the beneficiary of the attention Harper receives, but Burley makes plays when he gets the chance. Last year, he had two sacks and nine tackles for loss in a year where he was getting used to the speed of the college game and size of the offensive linemen.

Opposite Harper, junior **Jason Stewart** (6-1, 280) is back after making 44 tackles, three tackles for loss and two sacks. Stewart isn't that involved in the pass rush, but he is almost as important as Harper against the run.

Senior **Jake Probst** (6-2, 240) is the other returning starter. He isn't as good a pass rusher as Burley, but he is solid against the run, making nine tackles for loss last year.

Fresno has seven linemen returning who played last season and the depth is spread fairly evenly. Sophomore end **Clarence Denning** (6-3, 250) played in 10 games in a limited role as a freshman. He had 11 tackles and one interception. Hill is high on Denning and thinks he may be able to put on even more weight and become a dominating end.

Fellow sophomore **Justin Woltz** (6-3, 250) and senior nose tackle **Grant Harrington** (5-11, 260) round out a rotation that needs to be good early against the big boys on the schedule to take pressure off a secondary that is going to be tested.

LINEBACKERS

The only area where Hill has to raise his eyebrows with concern is at linebacker. All three starters, all of whom earned some sort of All-WAC honor last season, are gone. Two of those starters, Orlando Huff and Tim Skipper, had more than 100 tackles and were the heartbeat of the defense. Of the three Hill expects to starts this year, only two played last year and the other missed the year with an ankle injury.

Fortunately for the Bulldogs, their secondary and defensive line are the best in the conference. The bad news is that the linebackers have to learn on the fly against a schedule that doesn't allow much room for error.

Senior **Justin Johnson** (6-3 220) is the player Fresno needs most to emerge to help a young crew. Johnson missed all last season with an ankle injury. In 1999, he led the team with six sacks. He takes over Huff's outside linebacker spot. Johnson has better speed than Huff and can cover backs, but he isn't as physical. If the defensive line plays like it should against the run, Fresno may be able to cover up that weakness in Johnson's game.

In the middle, sophomore **Marc Dailey** (6-1, 230) has large shoes to fill. He is stepping into a spot Skipper held for three years. Dailey did play last year and got big time experience when he subbed for Skipper against Ohio State and make seven tackles. He followed with five against UCLA and finished with 29 on the year.

The other outside spot is a battle between senior **Maurice Rodriguez** (6-2, 240) and junior **Sam Williams** (6-5, 240). Williams has nice size and speed, but Rodriguez is the better of the two against the run.

Senior **Terrance Hampton** (6-1, 220) is Dailey's backup and could play outside if needed.

DEFENSIVE BACKS

The Bulldogs have plenty of bright spots on this year's team. If there is one area Fresno can really beat its chest about, it's in the secondary. The Bulldogs return two All-WAC safeties and a bevy of depth and speed that will make Fresno one of the best pass defenses in the country.

Last year, the Bulldogs began building by finishing 23rd in the country in pass efficiency defense. Fresno allowed the fewest passing touchdowns in the league and had the third most interceptions. Only TCU and Tulsa gave up fewer yards.

The leaders are senior safeties **Anthony Limbrick** (6-1, 205) and **Vernon Fox** (5-10, 200). Both have been first-team All-WAC selections and are the most physical and imposing safeties in the league. Fox, the strong safety, finished last year with 68 tackles, eight for loss and had four sacks. That sack total could go up this year because of the depth in the defensive line and the potential need for an additional pass rush because of an inexperienced linebacker crew. A potential academic All-American, Fox makes the calls in the secondary and is the leader of the entire defense

At free safety, Limbrick has the potential to be one of the best in the country. Many thought he was going to be that last year before a thumb injury in the season opener against Ohio State kept him out the rest of the year. In 1999, Limbrick was a first-team all-conference choice.

At corner, senior **Tierre Sams** (5-9, 175) is the speed on the defense. The fastest player on the team, Sams led the Bulldogs a year ago with four interceptions. He could have a big year this season, knowing that he can be even more aggressive with the solid pass rush in front of him and Limbrick and Fox behind him.

Senior **Devon Banks** (5-11, 190) played strong safety last year, but could move to corner and give Fresno the physical presence opposite the speedy, but small Sams.

The depth is young. Sophomore **Bryce McGill** (5-10, 193) spent the spring in Limbrick's free safety spot. Redshirt freshman **Eric Lee** (6-2, 170) can play strong or free safety and corner if needed. Sophomores **Juan Bautista** (5-8, 192) and **Dee Meza** (5-8, 193) are backups on the corner.

Junior college transfer **Demorieux Reneau** (6-0, 195) played locally at Fresno City College and adds depth at almost any secondary position.

The pass-happy WAC will have its hands full with Fresno's defensive backfield, but those tables will be turned early in the year when Oregon State comes to Fresno and the Bulldogs go to Colorado. The secondary is good enough to carry the Bulldogs is a weak WAC, but a good performance in those games is needed to give Fresno confidence heading into a schedule that has 13 games and only one off week.

From a national perspective, if the Bulldogs want to lay claim to having one of the best defensive backfields in the country, those games are the chance.

PUNTERS

Junior **Jason Simpson** (6-1, 185) returns after averaging 38.0 yards on 67 kicks. Though his average wasn't as high as some of the top punters in the league, Simpson was accurate when he needed to be accurate. He put 18 of his 67 punts inside the 20, with only one touchback.

SPECIAL TEAMS

The kicking game is set with the return of leading scorer Asparuhov and Simpson at punter. Where the Bulldogs really make their mark on special teams is in creating havoc for other teams. In the last four years under Hill, Fresno has blocked 27 kicks, including seven last year.

Baxter, who developed the "Academic Gameplan" program, also runs one of the most successful special teams units in the nation. While the Bulldogs averaged 12.6 yards per punt return in 2000, opponents averaged less than half that at 6.1 yards per return. The figures were closer on kick returns where Fresno averaged 192 and opponents 19.1

The main cog in the coverage units is junior **Kevin Murphy** (6-0, 200), the deep snapper for punts, field goals and extra points.

To get back to the same kind of success blocking kicks that has become a trademark, the Bulldogs have to find a replacement for Terrence Brown, who was the kick blocking specialist.

The punt and kick returns are back with Berrian, Wright and Smith. Berrian had an 88-yard touchdown last year, but he needs to be more consistent. Despite that 88-yarder, he finished with only a 10.5-yard average. Smith also returns punts.

Wright and Berrian are the kick returners. Both averaged over 17 yards per return in 2000.

RECRUITING CLASS

The Bulldogs set attendance records last year, playing in front of school record crowds in each of their first four games of the season. The crowds show what kind of following the Bulldogs have developed in the Valley. The attendance figures, along with winning 15 games the last two seasons, have turned the heads of California players. The fertile Valley area, which used to be picked over by the Pac-10 schools, is now a battleground. Of the 24 players the Bulldogs signed, 21 are from California and only two are junior college signees. It's evident Hill is building a program and wants to do it with local players.

The player who will make the most impact is literally the biggest player in the class. Taifane immediately becomes Fresno's left tackle and the man responsible for keeping Carr upright.

Reneau is the other junior college product. Reneau played at Fresno City College and will step into the secondary rotation.

Because of the depth the Bulldogs have, most of the freshmen will be redshirted. And, for the first time in Hill's four years, Fresno will be able to take the majority of a class to five seasons.

The only signees outside of California came from the same high school in American Samoa. Defensive lineman **Michael Mapu** (6-4, 230) and nose guard **Lokeni Lokeni** (6-2, 285) are both from Fagaitu, American Samoa. Taifane is originally from Pago Pago, American Samoa.

BLUE RIBBON ANALYSIS

OFFENSE	B
SPECIAL TEAMS	A-
DEFENSE	A-
INTANGIBLES	B

Fresno State is the best team in the WAC. The Bulldogs return 15 starters, their leading scorer and four players who were All-WAC first-team selections. The offense, as long as the running game can become more consistent and avoid injuries, is high-powered and should put up the kind of balanced numbers that coach Pat Hill needs. Two offensive line starters are needed, including one at left tackle to protect Carr's blind side.

The strength is on defense where Harper, a Lombardi Award candidate, is one of the best in the country. He had 14 tackles for loss a year ago in a position that isn't expected to put up big numbers. Three secondary starters return, which gives the Bulldogs an advantage in a pass-happy league. The size at safety is something no other WAC team has.

Fresno has the nation's third-longest home winning streak, but the overall schedule will be the biggest test in 2001. Three games are against teams that won bowl games a year ago. Only the game against Oregon State, one of the top teams in the nation, is at Bulldog Stadium. A trip to Colorado and Wisconsin are sandwiched around the Oregon State game. The Bulldogs aren't likely to win any of those games, but they need to stay competitive in order not to lose confidence and lose a game in the WAC schedule early.

Fresno avoids both WAC co-champions from last year with TCU out of the league and UTEP not on the schedule.

If the Bulldogs can get through the early part of their schedule and avoid any slips as a result of the brutal schedule, a bowl game and a WAC title should await.

(C.M.)

2000 RESULTS

Ohio State	L	10-43	0-1
UCLA	L	21-24	0-2
California	W	17-3	1-2
Rice	W	27-24	2-2
Nevada	W	58-21	3-2
UTEP	L	13-23	3-3
Tulsa	W	34-12	4-3
Hawaii	W	45-27	5-3
TCU	L	7-24	5-4
SMU	W	14-7	6-4
San Jose State	W	37-6	7-4
Air Force (Silicon Valley)	L	34-37	7-5

Hawaii

LOCATION	**Honolulu, HI**
CONFERENCE	**Western Athletic**
LAST SEASON	**3-9 (.250)**
CONFERENCE RECORD	**2-6 (t-6th)**
OFFENSIVE STARTERS RETURNING	**9**
DEFENSIVE STARTERS RETURNING	**5**
NICKNAME	**Warriors**
COLORS	**Green & White**
HOME FIELD	**Aloha Stadium (50,000)**
HEAD COACH	**June Jones (New York State Regents)**
RECORD AT SCHOOL	**12-13 (2 years)**

CAREER RECORD 12-13 (2 years)
ASSISTANTS
George Lumpkin (Hawaii '72)
Associate Head Coach/Linebackers
Kevin Lempa (Southern Connecticut St. '74)
Defensive Coordinator
Vantz Singletary (Kansas State '89)
Defensive Line
Mike Cavanaugh (Southern Conn. St. '86)
Offensive Line
Dan Morrison (UCLA '71)
Quarterbacks
Wes Suan (Linfield '75)
Running Backs
Dennis McKnight (Drake '81)
Special Teams
Ron Lee (Williamette '67)
Wide Receivers
Rich Miano (Hawaii '87)
Defensive Secondary
TEAM WINS (last 5 yrs.) 2-3-0-9-3
FINAL RANK (last 5 yrs.) 102-103-109-65-90
2000 FINISH Lost to UNLV in regular-season finale.

COACH AND PROGRAM

The Hawaii program is June Jones' baby. It's the only job for which he said he would ever leave a promising NFL coaching career. He made good on that promise two years ago and endeared himself to the Island by winning nine games and taking a Warriors team that hadn't won a game the year before to its first WAC title since 1992 and a bowl game. He won several coach-of-the-year awards and the Hawaii program was suddenly on the national scene.

The Warriors struggled last season, dropping from nine wins in 1999 to only three. But the honeymoon in Honolulu is far from over for Jones' staff. He's there as long as he wants to be. This is his program.

And, once again, Hawaii could be a national, feel-good story. Not because of what will be an improved team, but because of the remarkable recovery Jones has made after a Feb. 22 car accident left him in critical condition. Jones was driving on H-1, Hawaii's main highway, toward the Honolulu airport when he lost control of his car and hit a pole.

"I honestly don't remember anything that happened," Jones said. "I was driving to the airport and then the next thing I remember is waking up in the hospital."

The Island rallied behind Jones, holding a candlelight vigil not long after the accident. Hawaii players promised anyone who asked that their coach might have had to miss spring practice, but they were sure he'd be ready for fall practice. From all indications, Jones will be back. He was released from the hospital within a month of the accident and was looking forward to 2001 not long after.

Jones should be looking forward to the year with anticipation. The Rainbows have nine starters back from an offense that was led by freshman quarterback **Timmy Chang**. One of the most highly recruited players ever to sign with the Warriors, Chang, the WAC Freshman of the Year, started nine games and set eight school passing records. He threw for more than 3,000 yards in only 10 games. And, he has his four leading receivers returning.

Second-year defensive coordinator Kevin Lempa struggled in his first season, but he didn't have much to work with. No defensive player started every game at the same position. Six starters missed at least one game.

The uncertainty on defense led to losses in seven of the Warriors' first eight games. The Hawaii fans, however, were patient. Jones has made Aloha Stadium a place to be on Saturdays with his entertaining offense. The Warriors led the WAC in attendance in 1999 and drew more than 30,000 to every home game a year ago.

In an attempt to make the team more than just a Honolulu experience, Hawaii opens this season against Montana on Maui.

"We are Hawaii's NFL franchise," Jones said. "We don't have any pro sports here. We want to be the pro team—so to speak—out here. Doing that means not just being Honolulu's team."

2001 SCHEDULE

Sept.	8	Montana
	15	@Nevada
	29	Rice
Oct.	6	@SMU
	13	UTEP
	20	@Tulsa
	27	Fresno State
Nov.	3	San Jose State
	10	Boise State
	17	Miami (Ohio)
	24	Air Force
Dec.	1	Brigham Young

QUARTERBACKS

When Jones took over in 1999, he had a team that hadn't won a game the season before, but it had a leader. Dan Robinson was a mature quarterback who was already married and older than most college players. He was the player Jones and the Warriors rode to national acclaim. When Robinson graduated, Jones was left with a freshman and a junior with no experience.

Jones started his more experienced quarterback, senior **Nick Rolovich** (6-1, 193) but found out quickly who was going to lead Hawaii for the next four years. Rolovich threw for 367 yards in the season-opening loss to Portland State. A game later, he was sitting on the bench watching Chang (6-1, 190) produce the kind of numbers Jones thought he would get from a veteran quarterback.

In only one season, Chang, the WAC Freshman of the Year, became the Warriors' eighth all-time leading passer. If he comes close to the 3,041 yards he threw for in 2000, Chang will be the all-time leader. He threw 19 touchdown passes, including at least one in every game he played, and set eight school records. He completed 52.2 percent of his passes and threw for more than 300 yards in six games. And, despite having minus-49 yards rushing, Chang was fifth in the country in total offense. He did have problems with throwing interceptions (19) and reading defenses, something that got better toward the end of the year but still needs improvement.

In Jones' run-and-shoot offense, the quarterback is going to get numbers. Being accurate and able to make plays outside the pocket is more important than the statistics. Chang has the numbers. He needs to improve on making plays with his feet and understanding when to run instead of forcing passes.

Chang, who played locally at the highly successful St. Louis School, is also a vital part of Hawaii's recruiting. He was one of Jones' first big targets. He was the first highly regarded Hawaiian player to stay on the Island and play for Jones. Chang's signing raised a lot of eyebrows and has helped the already popular Jones become even more effective in convincing players good enough to play on the mainland that leaving isn't always the best choice.

Rolovich, who will back up Chang this year, simply struggled a year ago. He had a hard time moving the team against Portland State. The next week against UTEP, he was 6-of-28 in the first half before Chang replaced him. In only four games, he did manage to throw for 815 yards. But he was erratic, completing only 46 percent of his passes.

Junior **Jared Flint** (6-5, 207) came to Hawaii from Orange Coast (Calif.) College last season, but did not play.

RUNNING BACKS

Strange as it seems, the running game is not an afterthought in Hawaii's run-and-shoot offense. In order for the offense to run smoothly, a back capable of breaking big runs has to be mixed in so the defense doesn't get comfortable. Last season, the Warriors had trouble finding that player.

Injuries forced Hawaii to make changes on the fly and nothing ever became settled. Afatia Thompson and Avion Weaver both got hurt, forcing walk-on James Fenderson into action. Fenderson was explosive, but had problems holding on to the ball.

This season, the running game starts with a clean slate. Weaver, Thompson and Fenderson, who led the team with 651 yards on 113 caries, are gone. Of the eight players Hawaii has at running back, only junior **Thero Mitchell** (5-10, 207) had a carry last season. Mitchell played in eight games, carrying 11 times for 79 yards and two touchdowns.

Mitchell will get carries, but the job belongs to junior college transfer **Josh Galeai** (6-2, 240). Galeai, a junior, is the punishing back who gets tough yards and catches the ball. Last season at Palomar (Calif.) Junior College, Galeai was part of a three-back rotation. He ran for 629 yards and eight touchdowns and was a key blocker for the other two backs. His speed and strength will be a welcome addition. He bench presses 225 pounds 21 times and runs a 4.6 40-yard dash.

Redshirt freshman **Chad Kapanui** (6-0, 226) is built like Galeai. He is the only returning back expected to get carries in addition to Mitchell.

Jones signed two highly recruited freshmen and won't be afraid to use either one. **Mike Bass** (5-6, 165) is small, but he is fast and could turn into a nice receiver out of the backfield. He was an explosive high school player, scoring 41 touchdowns in his career and setting school passing and rushing records.

Pesefea Fiaseu (5-11, 220) was the Hawaii Player of the Year. He scored more than 60 touchdowns and rushed for 4,039 yards in his career at the highly successful St. Louis School in Honolulu. He's another big time player who stayed on the Island.

WIDE RECEIVERS/TIGHT ENDS

John Jenkins, one of Jones' mentors in the run and shoot, once said, "the only thing better than four wide receivers is five wide receivers." Jones concurs. If he could find a way to split a lineman out, he would do it. And this season, Hawaii would have the talent to make it work. The Warriors return all four starting receivers. The four combined for almost 70 percent of the team's receptions and 22 of Hawaii's 25 receiving touchdowns.

The best of the four is junior **Ashley Lelie** (6-3, 178). The tall, speedy wideout plays on the outside and is one of the WAC's best playmakers. His 11 touchdowns last year were a school record. He finished with 1,110 yards—becoming only the third Hawaii receiver to have 1,000 yards in a season—on 74 catches and was a second-team All-WAC selection. He is already the school's fifth-leading receiver. He needs 1,238 yards to become the career leader.

Chang's security blanket is junior **Justin Colbert** (5-6, 155), who plays opposite Lelie. Though small, Colbert is a nice possession receiver. He averaged 12.6 yards per catch, but that was with a 74-yarder included. He needs to get stronger, though, because cornerbacks easily knock him off routes at the line of scrimmage.

The inside receivers are seniors **Channon Harris** (5-8, 153) and **Craig Stuzmann** (5-10, 203). Harris is pencil-thin, but he makes plays over the middle. Most of them are deep in the secondary after Stuzmann runs the underneath routes and occupies the safeties. In 2000, the duo combined for 90 catches, 1,212 yards and eight touchdowns.

Stuzmann and whoever takes over at running back have to be more productive in the middle of the field to keep Harris and Colbert from having to come close to linebackers and strong safeties.

The Warriors also reloaded in recruiting. **Omar Bennett** (6-1, 180) is a junior college transfer who will help out immediately. If his talent matches his credentials, the Warriors can expect big numbers. He originally signed with California, but spent last season at Laney (Calif.) Community College. He has great speed and is good kick and punt returner. He scored seven touchdowns last season on returns.

Jones said Bennett is good enough to be an immediate contributor, as evidenced by the scholarship offers he turned down to go to the Island. Michigan State, Ohio State, Wisconsin, USC, Arizona State and Arizona all offered.

Of the signees, **Justin Faimealelei** (6-1, 205) and **Kila Kamakawiwo'ole** (6-2, 200), both local products, are big targets expected to back up Stuzmann and help out in the middle of the field. In high school, Faimealelei played wide receiver, linebacker, safety, punter, and kicker in addition to returning kicks and serving as the backup quarterback.

OFFENSIVE LINE

Like almost every other position a year ago, the players on the offensive line took time to get to know one another. In the interim, the unit took its licks on the field. It didn't give up many sacks, but it never established the kind of consistency that is needed to run Jones' offense.

In the run and shoot, the offensive linemen have to be athletic. They have to be pass blockers first but not to the exclusivity of run blocking. The best run-and-shoot offenses always have at least one back that can gain yards. It keeps defenses honest because they aren't able to play seven defensive backs or become aggressive against the quarterback.

Hawaii did a good job of protecting Chang a year ago, but they didn't do a good job of moving the ball forward. The Warriors were the most penalized team in the league, setting a school record with 116. Most weren't for a lot of yardage. Three WAC teams had more penalty yards, meaning most of the Warriors' penalties were the short, false start kind that kill drives.

Jones expects the line to be better simply because of experience. Right tackle Kynan Forney is the only loss, but it's a big one. A first-team All-WAC selection, Forney was the leader of the entire offense.

Some other position needs to quickly pick up that role because there isn't much in Forney's vacated spot. Redshirt freshman **Uriah Moenoa** (6-3, 335) will get the first shot. He may have to drop some weight, though, to be an effective tackle. Sophomore **Mike Holt** (6-5, 300) and redshirt freshman Ryan Santos (6-3, 296) will both play and could end up forming a rotation with Moenoa.

The leader this season will be junior right guard **Vince Manuwai** (6-2, 296), who played alongside Forney a year ago. Coaches believe Manuwai could turn into one of the best to ever come off the Island. He had good speed and is almost as good a run blocker as he is a pass blocker. He started nine games at right guard last season and two at right tackle. If Moenoa has trouble, Mauwai could slide over.

"I'm not sure there's a better offensive lineman [in the country] than Manuwai," Jones said.

If that happens, junior **Shayne Kajioka** (6-3, 323) will step in at right guard. He started two games last year when Mauwai was at tackle.

Senior center **Brian Smith** (6-1, 276) is a quiet, steady leader. He started all 12 games last year and is a valuable special teams player. He has been the long snapper the last 36 games.

Senior right guard **Manly Kanoa** (6-5, 314), who has started 24 straight games, is back and gives the Warriors one of the biggest and best guard combos in the conference. Junior **Sione Tafuna** (6-0, 295) backs up Kanoa but can play either guard position. He also has the team's biggest appetite. At the end of spring practice, Tafuna won the team's pizza eating contest.

At left tackle junior **Lui Fuata** (6-3, 305) and sophomore **Keola Loo** (6-3, 302) provide a big rotation that isn't as agile as it needs to be. Fuata started nine games a year ago.

2000 STATISTICS

Rushing offense	73.8	109
Passing offense	322.9	4
Total offense	396.7	40
Scoring offense	24.5	65
Net Punting	35.3	41
Punt returns	9.8	49
Kickoff returns	19.4	67
Rushing defense	210.8	105
Passing efficiency defense	125.5	81
Total defense	405.2	86
Scoring defense	33.2	99
Turnover margin	-7	91

Last column is ranking among Division I-A teams.

KICKERS

The Warriors will be breaking in a new kicker after losing Eric Hannum and backup Jake Huggins. Redshirt freshman **Justin Ayat** (6-0, 198) will get first shot at replacing Hannum, who didn't have a great leg but was fairly consistent. A year ago, Hannum made 10-of-14 field goals.

Junior college transfer **Greg Kleidon** (6-0, 177) is a better punter, but he will have a hard time beating out incumbent **Mat McBriar**. Kleidon, who sat out last season with an ankle injury, could get a chance if Ayat struggles.

An interesting option could be junior college transfer **Tyrone Brown** (6-2, 225). Brown will play linebacker, but he also kicked field goals in high school.

DEFENSIVE LINE

Jones didn't think he was going to have to worry much about his defensive line a year ago. Things changed quickly. The Warriors got off to a slow start and the defensive line went right along with the rest of the team. There wasn't much of a pass rush and the run defense wasn't exactly the best, finishing 105th in the nation after giving up almost 211 yards per game.

The Warriors actually didn't surrender an inordinate amount of passing yards, but they didn't make any plays to keep teams from throwing against them. The line, though it had good size and will again this year, never established consistency. Players moved around. Injuries forced other movement. The result was one that puzzled Jones.

"You never know about the defense until you play a game," Jones said. "I thought we were going to be better on defense last year and look what happened."

Two starters and one experienced backup return along with a junior college prospect that has Jones thinking that the defensive line may be the most improved part of the defense. It needs to be to make up for only five returning starters on defense, only two of whom are in an inexperienced secondary.

Junior **Lui Fuga** (6-2, 305) is a big tackle who can make plays when he's healthy. He played 11 games a year ago, starting eight at tackle. He never was fully healthy and missed spring practice to take care of his injured shoulder. Fuga hurt so much that Jones wanted him to sit out later in the year, but he refused.

Alongside Fuga, is junior college transfer **Isaak Sopoaga** (6-4, 290), one of the most high-profile recruits the program has ever signed. Jones said Sopoaga turned down offers from Texas A&M and every Pac-10 team.

Last season, Sopoaga had 31 sacks and played every down on defense at College of the Canyons in California, where he was a junior college All-American. He shouldn't have any problems making the adjustment, especially with his size and athletic ability. He will be a welcome addition to a line that had trouble a year ago with the WAC's multiple offense.

Senior **Mike Iosua** (6-2, 282) started six games at tackle a year ago before missing the rest of the season with a shoulder injury. Iosua played end as a junior and could move outside is Sopoaga has the kind of year he is expected to have.

At end, junior **Laanul Correia** (6-2, 253) needs to provide a better presence against the run, especially because his counterpart on the opposite side hasn't played much. Correia played 11 games last season, but he made only 33 tackles. Of the 33, he had just three for loss.

On the other side, sophomores **Houston Ala** (6-1, 218) and **Wayne Hunter** (6-5, 286) play completely different styles. How Correia plays at the other end spot will determine who gets the majority of snaps.

LINEBACKERS

The Warriors needed help after losing two starters. Junior middle linebacker **Chris Brown** (6-1, 256) returns but needs help on the outside to cover receivers. Brown is fine when it comes to keying on one receiver over the middle or rushing the passer on a stunt. But he has trouble covering backs out of the backfield. He tied for the team lead in sacks with four and five more tackles behind the line of scrimmage.

He isn't as quick as senior **Bobby Morgan** (6-2, 220) or redshirt freshman **Watson Hoohuli** (6-0, 227). But neither have Brown's experience or ability to stop the run.

Of the weak side, junior **Pisa Tinoisamoa** (6-1, 255) played in all 12 games and started five at middle linebacker. He led the team with 10 tackles for loss and tied with Brown for the sack lead. Tinoisamoa is one of the few linebackers who can cover backs and has the size to make plays in the passing game. Those plays just need to come more frequently.

Senior **Joe Correia** (6-2, 246) and sophomore **Kevin Jackson** (6-4, 246) have the size to play opposite Tinoisamoa. But the two combined for only eight tackles a year ago. The "stub" spot in

Hawaii's 4-3 will probably go to junior college transfer **Tyrone Brown** (6-2, 225) or freshman **Ikaika Curnan** (5-11, 230).

Brown is already one of the fastest players on the team. He is a departure from Lempa's normal philosophy of playing big linebackers. But the Warriors need someone who can make plays. Hawaii finished among the worst in the country in turnover margin largely because of a struggling offense, but also because of a defense that didn't make many plays. Brown gives the defense its best chance of a playmaker among the front seven. Brown can also kick field goals and may get a chance if Aysat struggles.

Curnan was the Hawaii Defensive Player of the Year and a cornerstone of the local recruiting effort. As a senior, Curnan, who was also on his school's soccer team, had almost 100 tackles and seven sacks in 10 games.

DEFENSIVE BACKS

Get ready for this secondary to get a workout. Seniors **Nate Jackson** (5-10, 168) and **Jacob Espiau** (5-10, 190) are back at safety. However, the rest of the secondary is stocked with inexperience and opportunities for teams to do some testing.

A sophomore or freshman is expected to start at three of the four secondary positions. The inexperience could cause trouble early, especially if a defensive line that is mixing in several new players doesn't get some sort of pass rush to help out the backfield.

At left corner, sophomores **Gary Wright** (5-10, 191) and **Kelvin Millhouse** (6-1, 198) both have great size for corners. They just don't have experience, something Jones said is a must on defense.

"You just don't know about the defense until they've gotten out there and felt the contact of a game," Jones said. "It's guesswork before that."

On the right side, sophomore walk-on **Hyram Peters** (5-8, 182), who actually had a nice season a year ago, or redshirt freshman **Abraham Elimimian** (5-10, 175) will get first chance at replacing the steady Rinda Brooks. Peters had 53 tackles in 2000, but he had only three passes broken up and didn't have an interception.

All three secondary signees will play and could play at corner. **Lamar Broadway** (5-11, 175) played on both side of the ball in high school. **Cameron Hollingsworth** (6-0, 175), the best playmaker of the three, is the only true corner of the bunch. **Leonard Peters** (6-1, 162) was a local star in high school and was one of Hawaii's best defensive backs the last two years. All three could use significant weight room time and a redshirt year. But, the Warriors will have to play them.

If Jackson or Espiau doesn't slide over to free safety, sophomore **David Gilmore** (6-0, 178) or redshirt freshman **Matt Manuma** (6-1, 210) will get a shot. More than likely, Jackson, if he's recovered from a foot injury that hampered him all last season, will move over and let the bigger Espiau concentrate on making plays in the running game and be a part of the pass rush.

A year ago, Espiau and Jackson finished 1-2 on the team in tackles, combining for 227. They also combined for 11 interceptions. Jackson tied for the conference lead and was sixth in the nation with seven. Espiau set a school record when he had three of his four against Louisiana Tech.

PUNTERS

The punting game is in good hands. Sophomore McBriar (6-1, 189) had a nice freshman season, averaging 38.3 yards per kick. He put 10 punts inside the 20. His biggest strength is not allowing teams to return kicks. Of his 43 punts, only 10 were returned. And he didn't have a kick blocked. Much of that credit goes to deep snapper Smith, the starting center who has started 36 straight games at long snapper.

Junior Greg Kleidon transferred from junior college last season. He missed the year with an ankle injury. He could be used to kickoff or place kick if freshman Justin Ayat has trouble adjusting.

SPECIAL TEAMS

One of Hawaii's biggest losses came in its return game. Jamal Garland didn't have as good a 2000 as he did in 1999 when he was first-team All-WAC, but he still averaged almost 23 yards per kick return. Flex Armstrong averaged 11.0 yards per punt return and returned 19 kicks for almost 18 yards per return.

Sophomore **Clifton Herbert** (5-7, 163) and Colbert are the only returning players with more than two kickoff returns a year ago. Herbert is the only returning player who returned a punt.

Both jobs will probably fall to junior college transfer Bennett. Last season at Laney (Calif.) Community College, Bennett had seven touchdowns on returns.

RECRUITING CLASS

Hawaii got the running back it needed for this year, significant help on defense and continued Jones' focus of keeping the best players from the Island on the Island. Palomar (Calif.) Junior college transfer Galeai will start at running back. He is the big back that can grind out yards when the offensive line and receivers need a break from the run and shoot.

When the Warriors are running the up-tempo offense, junior college transfer Bennett will be part of the receiver rotation. He signed with Cal out of high school before playing a season at Laney (Calif.) Community College. He turned down several Pac-10 schools as well as Wisconsin, Ohio State and Michigan State to come to Honolulu. He is an explosive kick returner who will take over the kick and punt return duties.

Freshman wide receiver Faimealelei is the most versatile of the signees. In high school, the Oahu native played wide receiver, linebacker, safety, punter, quarterback and returned kicks. Hawaii's receiver depth makes him a candidate for a redshirt, but his size is enticing for the small receiver corps.

Sophomore Holt transferred after only one junior college season. He will play at right tackle and could start if red-shirt freshman Moenoa has trouble adjusting.

On defense, Jones thinks he got the run stopper and pass rusher the Warriors desperately need. Junior college transfer Issak Sopoaga is the starter at left tackle when he arrives in Honolulu. He gives Hawaii a nice, big tackle rotation with Lui Fuga on the right side. Last season, Sopoaga had 31 sacks and played every down on defense. He was a junior college all-American and one of the most high profile recruits the program has ever signed. Jones said Sopoaga turned down offers from Texas A&M and every Pac-10 team.

At linebacker, junior college transfer Brown and freshman Curnan will both play. Brown is already one of the fastest players on the team. He can also kick field goals and may get a chance if Aysat struggles.

Curnan was the Hawaii Defensive Player of the Year and a cornerstone of the local recruiting effort. The Warriors also signed the state's offensive player of the year in running back Fiaseu, who scored 63 touchdowns in high school.

Fiaseau's signing is also important because it continues to establish strong ties between the Hawaii program and Honolulu's St. Louis School, which has one of the most successful high school teams in the nation.

BLUE RIBBON ANALYSIS

OFFENSE	B
SPECIAL TEAMS	D
DEFENSE	C
INTANGIBLES	C

The Warriors are always going to be tough on the Island. On the mainland, they are always going to struggle. That's the reality of a program that has to travel more than 2,000 miles just to get to California. Last year, Hawaii went 0-4 away from Aloha Stadium and was never close in any game. The closest the Warriors came was an 18-point loss at Fresno State.

The defense is replacing six starters with a mix of junior college transfers, freshmen and players who have yet to feel what it's like to travel the way Hawaii has to travel. The offense, which is experienced, will need to carry the team early in the year while the defense adjusts to the rigors of early-morning practices and playing with new faces in new schemes.

The schedule actually helps out on that end. Hawaii opens the season on Maui, which will actually be a road game, but a very short trip in comparison. Then the Warriors go to Nevada. They have two weeks off before playing host to Rice and then going to SMU. All of Hawaii's first four games are winnable, as is the Oct. 13 game at home against UTEP, which suffered big graduation losses.

If Hawaii's defense has rounded into shape and the offense performs to the level Jones expects by Oct. 20, the Warriors could be looking good. On Oct. 20, Hawaii plays at Tulsa and then doesn't go back to the mainland the rest of the year. The final six games are at Aloha Stadium, including the last three WAC games, two of which are against league favorites Fresno State and San Jose State.

And, unlike most seasons, Hawaii isn't providing a cushy road trip for a giant late in the season. The last three games are non-conference games, but all three are winnable.

(C.M.)

2000 RESULTS

Portland State	L	20-45	0-1
UTEP	L	7-39	0-2
Tulsa	L	14-24	0-3
TCU	L	21-41	0-4
SMU	W	30-15	1-4
Rice	L	13-38	1-5
San Jose State	L	48-57	1-6
Fresno State	L	27-45	1-7
Nevada	W	37-17	2-7
Louisiana Tech	W	27-10	3-7
Wisconsin	L	18-34	3-8
UNLV	L	32-34	3-9

Louisiana Tech

LOCATION	**Ruston, LA**
CONFERENCE	**Western Athletic**
LAST SEASON	**3-9 (.250)**
CONFERENCE RECORD	**NA**
OFFENSIVE STARTERS RETURNING	**7**
DEFENSIVE STARTERS RETURNING	**8**

NICKNAME Bulldogs
COLORS Red & Blue
HOME FIELD Joe Aillet Stadium (30,600)
HEAD COACH Jack Bicknell (Boston Coll. '85)
RECORD AT SCHOOL 11-12 (2 years)
CAREER RECORD 11-12 (2 years)
ASSISTANTS
Ed Jackson (Louisiana Tech '83)
Assistant Head Coach/Defensive Line
Tom Masella (Wagner College '81)
Defensive Coordinator/Outside Linebackers
Conroy Hines (Louisiana Tech '89)
Offensive Coordinator/Quarterbacks
Randy Bates (Ohio State '83)
Defensive Backs
Todd Monken (Knox College '89)
Wide Receivers
Todd Howard (Texas A&M '91)
Inside Linebackers
Pete Perot (Northwestern State '83)
Offensive Line
Chris Vaszily (Albright College '90)
Tight Ends/Special Teams
Joe Robinson (LSU '85)
Running Backs/Recruiting Coordinator
TEAM WINS (last 5 yrs.) 6-9-6-8-3
FINAL RANK (last 5 yrs.) 90-68-61-50-97
2000 FINISH Lost to Hawaii in regular-season finale.

COACH AND PROGRAM

The WAC hasn't really ever seen anything like Jack Bicknell and Louisiana Tech. The league that made itself famous in the 1980s with high-powered passing attacks is about to see what a high-powered, 21st century offense looks like. Opponents may enjoy the Bulldogs' defense, but Tech is going to have some fun putting up numbers in its inaugural WAC season.

Though they are coming off one of their more disappointing seasons in the last 10 years, the Bulldogs are stocked with experience and could make it rough for some of their new bunkmates.

Bicknell runs an offense that has the fingerprints of current BYU coach Gary Crowten. Bicknell had spent his whole life in the Northeast before moving south to coach the Bulldogs' offensive line. Bicknell played center at Boston College while Doug Flutie was the quarterback. He played in three bowl games and was part of a high-octane offense in 1984 when Flutie won the Heisman.

Bicknell quickly picked up Crowten's system when he arrived in Ruston in 1997 to coach the offensive line. Under Bicknell, the Bulldogs allowed only 32 sacks in two years and won 15 games during that stretch. In addition to coaching the guys up front, Bicknell began learning Crowten's offense.

When Crowten left to become offensive coordinator for the Chicago Bears after the 1998 season, Bicknell, whose father coaches the NFL Europe's Barcelona Dragons, took over. In his first season, Tech, playing a tough, independent schedule, won eight games, including an upset of Alabama on the last play of the game.

Last season was the first true test for Bicknell. He lost several offensive weapons and had to deal with injuries. Still, he produced an offense that finished seventh in the nation in passing. But Tech also turned the ball over more than any other Division I-A team and put a suspect defense in difficult situations. The Bulldogs ran into, once again, one of the nation's toughest schedules, playing Kansas State, Penn State, Auburn and Miami.

This season Bicknell, still one of the youngest head coaches in the country, is hoping last year's tough road will make for a smooth turn onto the WAC highway. The conference is going to be a step up in play week in and week out, but the league doesn't have a team as good as the Kansas State, Penn State, Auburn and Miami foursome that was on the 2000 schedule. Those games made the school a lot of money a year ago and put the Bulldogs in much better position than fellow first-year member Boise State or even second-year member Nevada.

Tech knows how to go on the road and be competitive. It didn't happen much a year ago, but in the past the Bulldogs have been tough in hostile environments.

The travel is going to be different, but it's nothing Tech hasn't seen before. The Bulldogs have seven road games and play only three times in Ruston. The hometown fans won't get to see the team until the Oct. 6 game against San Jose State. The season opener is a conference game against SMU in Shreveport. The next three are on the road—two payday games at Oklahoma State and Kansas State and then at conference favorite Fresno State.

Having to play Fresno State and San Jose State, which has Heisman candidate Deonce Whitaker at running back, will initiate Tech into the WAC. It will test sophomore quarterback **Josh McCown** and a defense that should be improved with the infusion of several junior college transfers and signees.

The season is also a landmark year for the program. It is the 100th season of Tech football and features Ruston's newest building in The Charles Wyly Athletic Complex. The $2.5 million facility houses an all-sports training room, coaches' offices, conference rooms and a heritage hall.

2001 SCHEDULE

Sept.	1	SMU (Shreveport)
	8	@Oklahoma State
	15	@Kansas State
	29	@Fresno State
Oct.	6	San Jose State
	13	@Nevada
	20	@Auburn
	27	Rice
Nov.	3	@Tulsa
	10	@UTEP
	17	Boise State

QUARTERBACKS

Bicknell has his choice of experienced signal callers. Three have started. One is coming off an injury. Another is coming off an impressive freshman season. And the third is coming off a freshman season in which he didn't expect to play, much less start.

Going into last year, the Bulldogs had lost a lot of firepower. But, with James Jordan returning, Bicknell figured senior **Brian Stallworth** (6-0, 205) and Jordan would keep Tech atop the national passing leaders. The season started that way, but ended with sophomore McCown (6-4, 200) putting up the numbers and setting several school records on his way to a breakout freshman year.

Stallworth started the first three games, but suffered a season-ending knee injury in the fourth game. Before the injury, a torn left medial collateral ligament, Stallworth had completed 82-of-129 passes for 855 yards and seven touchdowns. But Tech wasn't moving the ball like it normally does.

Though he is likely to be a backup his senior season, Stallworth will always have a place in Tech fans' hearts. Against Alabama in 1999, he completed the pass on the final play of the game to give the Bulldogs the upset and a national ranking.

When Stallworth went out against Stephen F. Austin, sophomore **Maxie Causey** (6-4, 192) played the second half. He made his first career start the next week.

Then, McCown, whose two older brothers were Division I-A quarterbacks at Texas A&M and SMU, finally got his chance. Bicknell started him against Middle Tennessee and couldn't get him out the lineup. He set single game Division I-A freshman records for most completions (48 against Auburn), most attempts (72 against Miami), and most passing touchdowns (six against Louisiana-Lafayette).

In only eight games, McCown threw for 2,544 yards and 21 touchdowns on 244-of-369 passing. He had five 300-yard passing games and three 400-yard games, including 418 against Sugar Bowl champion Miami.

McCown did make freshman mistakes, throwing 15 interceptions. He needs to get better at making decisions outside the pocket. He will also have to be more of a leader this season with only one receiver returning that caught more than 10 passes a year ago and two new receivers expected to see significant time.

"I feel very good about the quarterbacks," Bicknell said. "Luke showed what he could do last year and he will continue to mature. Brian is a good quarterback that faced some very difficult situations last year. So much of our early troubles weren't his fault. There's going to be a lot of competition and that's good."

Tech signed two quarterbacks. One fits the system. The other is a head scratcher who could end up at another position. **Patrick McMahon** (6-1, 210) is a New Jersey native who is a pure drop back passer. **Matt Kubik** (6-3, 200), from Youngstown, Ohio, threw for 15 touchdowns and 1,470 yards as a senior. But he had 2,250 yards and 28 touchdowns rushing and was heavily recruited by Navy and Air Force, both of which are option heavy teams.

RUNNING BACKS

Tech only has one running back spot, but, like quarterback, there is a production machine and several other options. The other running back spot is used as another receiver position and senior **John Simon** (5-9, 202) does the job nicely. He started all 12 games last year, rushing for 565 yards on 109 carries.

More importantly, Simon led the nation's running backs for the second straight year with 72 catches for 711 yards and four touchdowns. He already ranks fifth on the school's career reception list with 191. He has caught a pass in 35 straight games and had at least three in every game last year. Miami found our first-hand how dangerous he is out of the backfield. Against the Hurricanes, Simon had 10 catches for 96 yards.

Simon also returns punts and kicks. If he has to provide the bulk of the offense, especially early, Bicknell may use someone else for returns so Simon doesn't wear out early in the year.

Juniors **Corey Addison** (5-11, 232) and **Arthur Jefferson** (5-7, 188) give Tech much-needed depth. The duo combined for 569 yards a year ago and may be used even more this year with Simon expected to carry a bigger offensive load. Jefferson is Simon's primary backup. Addison is a big, bruising back used primarily in short-yardage situations.

Junior-college transfer **Joe Smith** (6-3, 218) redshirted last season. He is another big back who can also catch passes.

The Bulldogs signed four "athletes." all of whom played some running back in high school. Bicknell likes to sign these kind of versatile players and then find a wide receiver, running back or defensive back slot for them. At least one of the four, if they aren't all redshirted, will end up at running back.

Shelton Sampson (5-11, 220) is the only true running back Tech signed. He ran for more than 4,300 career yards, including 1,820 as a senior.

WIDE RECEIVERS/TIGHT ENDS

Bicknell will get a test this year at Tech's most important position. The Bulldogs lost Jordan and the reliable Sean Cangelosi, who both have their names littered in the Tech record book.

Senior **Delwyn Daigre** (6-1, 205) has a chance to finish with those same accolades, but he needs several receivers to produce early to take defensive pressure off him. Daigre is the only receiver who caught more than 10 passes last season. The Bulldogs are stocked with players, but Bicknell doesn't know what most of them can do.

The offense is built around Simon, McCown and Daigre. Last year, Daigre caught 57 passes for 662 yards and a team-high eight touchdown.

Over the last three years, Daigre has been the Bulldogs' most steady receiver. He has two 100-yard games last year and eight in his career. He caught a season-high 10 passes against Miami and enters 2001 having caught a pass in 32 straight games. Daigre's 19 career touchdowns are fourth best in school history. He is seventh in career receptions and sixth in receiving yards. He plays in the slot and will be a hard matchup, because of his size and speed, for any WAC cornerback.

His biggest test will come early while the rest of the receiver corps tries to round into shape. The most productive of the other returning options are seniors **Frank Thompson** (5-9, 177) and **Allen Stark** (6-2, 193) and sophomore **D.J. Curry** (5-9, 171). The three are likely to fill in the other three receiver slots despite combining last season for only 26 catches.

Stark is the big option on the outside of Daigre. Thompson will play the slot on the opposite side. The speedy Curry is the outside receiver alongside Thompson.

After those four, there are a host of receivers that have to produce. **Freddie King** (5-7, 170) and **Ahmad Harris** (6-0, 175) are the two newcomers. King, a freshman, and Harris, a junior college transfer, both went through spring practice and will see plenty of opportunities coming their way. Harris will push Thompson for a starting spot, especially if he comes close to the 57 catches, 1,003 yards and seven touchdowns he had last year at Jones (Miss.) Junior College.

Sophomores **Damien Newton** (5-11, 182) and **Sam Washington** (6-1, 184), junior **Corey Berlin** (5-11, 176)—whose younger brother, Brock, is the Florida quarterback—and redshirt freshmen **Danny Wilson** (6-0, 193) and **Jerron Wishom** (6-0, 187) will all get chances. The group needs to impress early to take pressure off the defense and because Bicknell would like to have a rotation set before heading into the bulk of WAC play.

At tight end, junior **Major Richmond** (6-3, 209) is just a big receiver who happens to play on the line. He is taking over for three-year starter David Newman. Last year, Richmond didn't play much, catching only two passes. Despite his size, Richmond is a decent run blocker.

OFFENSIVE LINE

While the receivers mature and McCown adjusts to having new faces to throw to, an experienced offensive line needs to provide the time and protection for the transition. Left tackle Terrance Sykes, who started every game at left tackle, is gone, but Tech returns five players with starting experience.

Last season, the front five had a good season protecting McCown. The run blocking skills still aren't there, but the unit does have pass blocking ability and the starting five has a nice grasp on Bicknell's system.

Juniors **Shawn Murff** (6-3, 276) and **Damien Lavergne** (6-6, 344) and seniors **Thomas Coury** (6-4, 319), **Randy Richard** (6-4, 300) and **Logan Hulett** (6-5, 272) all started games a year ago.

Hulett is the only one who didn't start all season. He will move over to Sykes' left tackle spot.

The best of the bunch is Lavergne. He is big enough to play guard, but Bicknell, a former offensive line coach, likes him on the outside because he is so athletic. If Lavergne recovers well from off-season shoulder surgery, he is going to have success in the WAC, where most of the defensive ends, including those at Tech, are the small, speedy variety.

Richard and Coury are the guards. Both have good size, but they could have trouble early with the three early road games. Kansas State, Oklahoma State and Fresno State all have big, athletic tackles that will be a challenge to handle.

Murff came into his own last season. He needs to become a better blocker, but he is one of McCown's most calming influences.

Because of his background, Bicknell likes to have depth. He plays a lot of different linemen because Tech runs the field so quickly. Sophomore **Michael Gilmore** (6-4, 300) and junior **Kiso Aab** (6-1, 279) are the best of a group of five backups.

Tech signed five high school linemen. But with five linemen returning and experience behind those five, the entire group will redshirt.

KICKERS

Sophomore **Josh Scobee** (6-1, 174) arrived in Ruston last season with the reputation of having a strong leg. He was handed the kicking job as a freshman and performed well under the circumstances. He made 39-of-41 extra points and 10-of-17 field goals.

Scobee's field goal accuracy wasn't great, but Bicknell put him in difficult situations. Of the seven he missed, three were from 50 yards or beyond and three were blocked. His cannon-leg reputation proved well earned when he hit a 51-yard field goal in the loss to Miami.

DEFENSIVE LINE

Eight starters are back on a defense that had an interesting 2000. The Bulldogs ranked near the bottom of the nation in total defense, scoring defense and rushing defense, but the pass defense was 30th in the country and passing efficiency defense was 27th.

Part of the discrepancy came because teams ate up the clock by running the ball against an undersized defensive line and didn't have to try to do things through the air. The other part was because of an offense that turned the ball over more than any other team in the country. Tech gave up 44 touchdowns, but 14 were on drives of less than 50 yards. The Bulldogs were able to get the quarterback, but most of their sacks came against the weaker opponents on the schedule. Against the Miamis and Kansas States of the world, Tech was pushed around and left the secondary to make the tackles.

Tech is still going to be small up front this year. Senior end **Carlin Thomas** (6-3, 227) is the most productive lineman, but he gets pushed around when he's forced inside. He is quick and is good in pass coverage, but he needs improved production against the run.

As the other end, junior **Clint Elsworth** (6-4, 277) is a bigger option, but he isn't as good as Thomas at rushing the passer or either tackle against the run. Junior **Brandon Avance** (6-3, 250) will start at tackle and senior **Jamie Nichols** (6-3, 306), who combined with Avance for 65 tackles a year ago, will start on the nose. But both have stiff competition.

Freshmen **Travon Brown** (6-3, 228), a converted linebacker, and **Chris Van Hoy** (6-4, 277) and junior **A.D Vitto** (6-2, 216), another converted linebacker, back up Thomas and Elsworth.

Senior **Moses Love** (6-3, 272) and sophomore **Booker T. Washington** (6-3, 255) will challenge for Avance's tackle spot.

Junior **Quincy Myles** (6-2, 297), who played sparingly last season, is the only other option at nose tackle.

The Bulldogs signed five defensive linemen, but only one will see significant time. **Spencer Young** (6-3, 260), a transfer from Hudson (N.Y.) Junior College, can play tackle and end. He should push Elsworth or either tackle for a starting spot.

Tech was the only school Young visited in the South and he decided to stay. Last season, he played tackle and had 14 quarterback pressured and three forced fumbles.

LINEBACKERS

Tech lost two of its three linebackers, but has high hopes for a unit that will have to provide an additional run stopping presence in addition to being better against the pass than it was last year. Most WAC teams like to throw to backs, causing linebackers to make plays in the open field.

With Quincy Stewart and Brian Bradford—who combined for 133 tackles last year—having departed, junior **Gerome Wallace** (6-1, 239), the lone returning starter, is the captain of the defense.

Wallace came into his own last year with 70 tackles, but he needs to be a tackling machine this season to keep teams from grinding out drives.

On the outside, there is stiff competition. Bicknell moved junior **Curtis Randall** (6-2, 227) off the defensive line. Randall's pass rushing ability and experience against playing the run gives him the starting nod over sophomore **Jonte Price** (5-11, 209) and senior **Montoya Gipson** (6-1, 207), who was a backup free safety in 2000.

Antonio Crow (6-0, 223) went into the spring as the other starter, but he will have a hard time keeping his position. Junior college transfer **Chris Marshall** (5-11, 220) gives the Bulldogs a second important newcomer capable of starting.

Marshall had 10 sacks and 112 tackles in 10 games. He enrolled early and has impressed Bicknell.

"We have some possibilities at linebacker," Bicknell said. "We've got athletes there that we haven't had in the past."

One of those athletes is **Jeremy Hamilton** (5-11, 205) from Ruston High School. Hamilton looked all over the Southwest, but decided to stay in his hometown. He was rated as one of the top 20 linebackers in the nation in almost every recruiting publication.

DEFENSIVE BACKS

The one bright spot of the Tech defense in 2000 was the secondary. The unit finished 30th in the nation in pass defense and 27th in passing defense efficiency. The latter ranking means that even though the pass defense number was a result of teams grinding down the defense with the run, the secondary was making plays and getting turnovers.

The enforcers are back and have help from two corners who will be better in coverage once they don't have to make as many tackles.

Senior rover **Bobby Gray** (6-1, 210) thought about leaving school a year early. He led the team with 119 tackles a year ago despite missing two games with post concussion syndrome. He had 10 or more tackles in six games and had a career-high 18 in the season finale against now conference rival Hawaii. He has 287 tackles in his three years and is on the verge of breaking into the school's top five of all-time.

"Bobby is the type of athlete who can completely take over a game," Bicknell said. "He is definitely the anchor of our defense."

While Gray makes plays in the running game, junior **Michael John Lenard** (6-0, 202) keeps things under control in the middle of the field. He was second on the team in tackles but only one of the 81 tackles were for loss. He had at least five tackles in every game in 2000 and 11 against Miami. He had two interceptions, but needs to become a bigger playmaker.

Senior **Jason Olford** (5-10, 180), who had four interceptions a year ago, is set at one corner, but there is uncertainty on the other side.

Both junior **Willie Sheppard** (5-9, 197) and senior **Curtis Speller** (5-11, 188) played last season. Sheppard made 40 tackles and appeared to have the starting job under control. But Bicknell wants athletes and playmakers in the secondary. He thinks Speller or redshirt freshman **Corey Brazil** (5-8, 193) could be that player. Speller had a nice junior college career, but he had only 10 tackles last season.

PUNTERS

Sophomore **Dustin Upton** (5-11, 204) is back after handling punting duties as a freshman. He averaged only 35.9 yards per punt, a number that would have been last in the WAC by two yards per kick.

Upton's short, low kicks also didn't do any favors for a coverage unit that had trouble making plays downfield. Tech was 112th in the nation in net punting with only a 27.4-yard average. That needs to improve to help what again will be a suspect defense.

If Upton struggles, walk-on sophomore **Tommy Hebert** (5-10, 171) will get a chance.

SPECIAL TEAMS

The return units are in decent shape, but the kick coverage teams have to improve. John Simon is the only returning player who returned a kick last season. He will also handle punt returns. Last year, Simon had 11 punt returns, but he averaged less than 7.0 yards per return. As a team, the Bulldogs averaged only 7.1 yards per return, 99th in the country.

Simon was better on kickoff returns. He returned 18 for a 19.2-yard average. He also had a 56-yard return that was Tech's longest return of the year.

With Simon expected to carry an even bigger offensive load, Bicknell may look for additional options. Signee **Jamie Spigener** (6-4, 240) is a tight end who returned kicks in high school. As a senior, he returned 19 for a 30.2-yard average. Classmate **Freddie King** (5-7, 170), who graduated early and went through spring practice, may get time as a punt returner.

To help in field position, Bicknell may have to use more starters on the coverage teams. The Bulldogs were 112th in net punting, giving up more than 15 yards per return. Tech allowed 21.0 yards per kickoff return.

RECRUITING CLASS

Recruiting coordinator Joe Robinson normally has a simple plan—compete hard for the Louisiana players and then snag several athletes from the Dallas and Houston areas. This year, Robinson and staff stayed close to home for its most high profile signing and then branched out all over the country to bring in a class that is heavy on linemen and players who are expected to contribute right away.

Of the 25 signees, 10 are linemen, five apiece on offense and defense. With five offensive linemen returning and experience behind those five, the offensive line signees will redshirt.

Most will on defense with the exception of Young, a junior college transfer from Hudson (N.Y.) Junior College. Tech was the only school Young visited in the South and he decided to stay. Last season, he played tackle and had 14 quarterback pressures and three forced fumbles. He could start on a defensive line that was undersized a year ago. That was a big reason the Bulldogs had one of the worst rushing defenses in the country.

On the local front, linebacker Hamilton looked all over the Southwest but decided to stay in his hometown. He was rated as one of the top 20 linebackers in the nation in almost every recruiting publication. He had more than 100 tackles his junior and senior seasons. He was also a three-time all-state pick. He had offers from Baylor, Texas A&M and Arkansas, but picked Tech because he will probably start from the moment he steps on campus.

Junior college transfer Marshall will give the Bulldogs two new and much-needed faces in the linebacker corps.

On offense, wide receivers King and Harris will help a receivers unit that has only one player back that caught more than 10 passes a year ago. In Tech's four wide receiver set, there are always plenty of opportunities. King, a freshman, and Harris, a junior college transfer, both went through spring practice and will see plenty of those opportunities coming their way. Harris is a likely starter, especially if he comes close to the 57 catches, 1,003 yards and seven touchdowns he had last year at Jones Junior College.

In Tech's system, Bicknell believes that he can turn a pure athlete into a player. He has signed several players the last two years who don't really fit on offense or defense, but have a place somewhere on the field. There are four "athletes" in this class. All five can play wide receiver, defensive back or running back. Of the five, the one most likely to play this year is **Brian Thomas** (6-1, 195). Thomas had almost 700 yards rushing and he threw for 927 yards while completing over 50 percent of his passes.

Bicknell always wants to have guys who can pull the trigger in this offense, so Tech signed two quarterbacks. One fits the system. The other is something of a mystery acquisition that could end up at another position. McMahon is a New Jersey native and a pure drop back passer. Kubik, from Youngstown, Ohio, threw for 15 touchdowns and 1,470 yards as a senior. But, he had 2,250 yards and 28 touchdowns rushing and was heavily recruited by Navy and Air Force, both of which are option heavy teams.

BLUE RIBBON ANALYSIS

OFFENSE	B-
SPECIAL TEAMS	B-
DEFENSE	C-
INTANGIBLES	C

As long as the offense doesn't turn the ball over as much as it did a year ago and the defense gets better production from what will still be an undersized front seven, Tech can make noise in its first year in the WAC.

The league is as balanced as it has ever been. Fresno State is the only standout team. Almost every other team could finish behind Fresno in second place. WAC teams are going to beat up on each other and the Bulldogs should be right in there with an offense that is going to surprise people in the league.

SMU gets the first look in a Labor Day weekend game in Shreveport. The Mustangs had problems against the pass last year and the wide-open, four-wide receiver look is going to be more passing than even the pass-happy WAC is used to seeing. If Tech can get a win in its opener, the Bulldogs will gain much-needed confidence heading into a three-game road trip and a schedule that has Tech in Ruston only three Saturdays.

There are questions on both sides of the ball and the schedule, beyond the three-game road trip, is tough. Only one receiver is back that caught more than 10 passes last year. McCown and an offense that had more turnovers than any other team in the nation has to take care of the ball.

The defensive line is still undersized and Tech will be relying on a junior college transfer and several young players to make plays behind that line.

The non-conference schedule is loaded with payday games at Oklahoma State, Kansas State and Auburn. If Tech can stay healthy and not let those games crush its confidence, the Bulldogs could surprise some WAC folks.

(C.M.)

2000 STATISTICS

Rushing offense	103.3	97
Passing offense	309.6	7
Total offense	412.9	30
Scoring offense	26.4	56
Net Punting	27.4	112
Punt returns	7.1	99
Kickoff returns	19.0	75
Rushing defense	211.0	106
Passing efficiency defense	125.9	83
Total defense	408.5	91
Scoring defense	32.8	98
Turnover margin	-17	110

Last column is ranking among Division I-A teams.

2000 RESULTS

Mississippi Valley State	W	63-10	1-0
Kansas State	L	10-54	1-1
Penn State	L	7-67	1-2
Stephen F. Austin	L	31-34	1-3
Tulsa	L	10-22	1-4
Middle Tennessee	L	21-49	1-5
Louisiana-Lafayette	W	48-14	2-5
Auburn	L	28-38	2-6
Miami	L	31-42	2-7
Central Florida	L	16-20	2-8
Louisiana-Monroe	W	42-19	3-8
Hawaii	L	10-27	3-9

Nevada

LOCATION	**Reno, NV**
CONFERENCE	**Western Athletic**
LAST SEASON	**2-10 (.167)**

CONFERENCE RECORD 1-7 (9th)
OFFENSIVE STARTERS RETURNING 10
DEFENSIVE STARTERS RETURNING 8
NICKNAME Wolf Pack
COLORS Navy Blue & Silver
HOME FIELD Mackay Stadium (31,545)
HEAD COACH Chris Tormey (Idaho '78)
RECORD AT SCHOOL 2-10 (1 year)
CAREER RECORD 35-33 (6 years)
ASSISTANTS
Jim Mastro (Cal-Poly San Luis Obispo '90)
Assistant Head Coach/Running Backs
Phil Earley (Pacific Lutheran '80)
Offensive Coordinator/Quarterbacks
Jeff Mills (Western Washington '88)
Defensive Coordinator/Linebackers
Steve Morton (Washington State '76)
Offensive Line
Jim House (Wyoming '70)
Tight Ends
D.J. McCarthy (Washington '94)
Wide Receivers
Mike Tuiasosopo (Pacific Lutheran '89)
Defensive Line
Mark Johnson (UC Davis '90)
Linebackers
Kim McCloud (Hawaii '91)
Secondary
TEAM WINS (last 5 yrs.) 9-5-6-3-2
FINAL RANK (last 5 yrs.) 75-86-86-105-105
2000 FINISH Lost to Tulsa in regular-season finale.

COACH AND PROGRAM

Nevada moved from the Big West to the WAC a year ago and knew there were going to be some growing pains. No one really expected them to be this severe. Despite the WAC not being a national, power conference, it was still too much for a Wolf Pack team that had questions in almost every area.

"We weren't really competitive," said coach Chris Tormey, who oversaw Nevada's move to the WAC after leaving his alma mater, Idaho. "We came into the year with concerns everywhere except for quarterback. We were just so inexperienced. We came in without knowing a whole lot or knowing what to expect. I can say this: We are a lot further along at this point than we were a year ago."

Nevada has 18 starters back, 10 on offense. But there are only 15 seniors, meaning Tormey will be dealing with a young team again.

That's how it goes when you're asked to take over a rebuilding project that is moving to a new league. Tormey knew the learning curve was going to be steep a year ago, and it was. Nevada finished last in the conference in total offense and defense. The defense gave up 30 more touchdowns than the offense scored. The lowest point total the Wolf Pack surrendered in a game was 28. They yielded 36 or more 10 times and more than 40 six times. Last year was indeed the lean times.

Times are going to be lean again this year, though not as bad. Quarterback **David Neill** is a senior leader who has been the starter since he was a sophomore. He already holds several school passing records and should hold all the yardage marks when he leaves. The offensive line is still young and the running game needs significant improvement. There is talent on both sides of the ball. But once again, it is in the lower classes.

At this point, that is fine with Tormey. He has significant rope from athletic director Chris Ault, but Nevada does need to show signs of improvement this season. There is no reason for Tormey to be worried. Especially with the recruiting he has done recently and his history of success.

He led Idaho's transition into Division I-A, including a 1998 Humanitarian Bowl win. Before that, he was an 11-year assistant at Washington, where he was part of three straight Rose Bowl teams and the Huskies' 1991 national championship team.

In Seattle, Tormey learned the ropes of recruiting the Pacific Northwest and, especially, California and its fertile junior colleges. This season, Nevada nabbed four junior college transfers and two Division I-A transfers, both originally from California. Of the Wolf Pack's 15 high school signees, all but three are from California.

With the WAC undergoing major renovations with TCU and a host of star players gone, the Wolf Pack can improve this season and eventually be very competitive in this environment. Their high-powered offense and attacking defense mirrors what a lot of teams do in the league. And, the conference has two new members in Louisiana Tech and Boise State that will be going through the same sort of transition that Nevada did a year ago.

The Wolf Pack knows what those pains feel like. More are on the horizon, but the foundation in Reno is slowly beginning to take shape.

2001 SCHEDULE

Sept.	1	@Brigham Young
	8	@Colorado State
	15	Hawaii
	22	@San Jose State
Oct.	6	UNLV
	13	Louisiana Tech
	20	@Rice
	27	@Boise State
Nov.	3	SMU
	17	Fresno State
	24	@UTEP

QUARTERBACKS

Neill (6-5, 200) already holds numerous Nevada passing records and should have almost every yardage mark once he leaves. He might trade all those marks for a better view of the field. Last season, Neill threw for 2,334 yards and 13 touchdowns in the little time he spent standing up. He was sacked a WAC-leading 48 times, including 11 times in the season opener against TCU. The sacks totaled 300 yards, nearly negating a respectable 384 yards rushing.

Neill isn't big, but has shown he can take an incredible amount of punishment. He is a good open field runner who can make plays outside the pocket. He does force passes when he's under pressure, but that has gotten better as he's gotten older. Neill has been the program's heart the last two years. Unfortunately, he may have to fight through another beating this season to help the Wolf Pack improve.

With his totals last year, Neill now holds Nevada's career passing yards (8,983) and total offense (9,427) records. When he is protected, he is effective. And this year, Nevada needs him to be better than he's ever been. The running game is going to struggle early with chemistry, forcing Neill and a receiver corps that returns seven players and two tight ends who caught passes a year ago to be even better than its No. 30 national rating in 2000.

Part of that improvement is being more consistent. Neill had a nice efficiency rating, but his 50.7 percent completion percentage was the worst of any of the league's starting quarterbacks. As a team, Nevada had the worst completion percentage of any team in the WAC with the exception of passing game-challenged Rice.

Neill also needs to throw the ball down field more. Nevada averaged only 6.2 yards per completion. Only SMU and Rice at 5.8 yards per catch were worse.

Neill got hurt last year and played banged up in several games. If that happens again this year, the Wolf Pack has a stable of backups. Junior **Brett Staniger** (6-3, 204) played in 10 games a year ago, completing 49-of-114 passes for 615 yards and three touchdowns. But he was also wild, throwing one interception for every seven completions.

UNLV transfer **Matt Ray** (6-3, 205), a junior, junior **Zack Threadgill** (6-2, 200), who is coming off an injury, and redshirt freshman **Andy Heiser** (6-1, 180) will battle for snaps in the fall.

RUNNING BACKS

In a one-back offense, the running back's job doesn't have to be spectacular. He only needs to be efficient. He needs to provide some kind of production so the defense doesn't sit back with six or seven defensive backs and wait for receivers to come to them. The running game needs to provide some sort of threat so defenses can't be so aggressive with their blitz packages.

Last season, Nevada opponents got as aggressive as they wanted because the running game was almost non-existent. Ten players had carries, but the Wolf Pack was only able to muster 2.2 yards per carry and only 67.7 yards per game, which was 112th in the nation. Considering how many teams now throw the ball almost exclusively, that rating looks even worse.

The yardage total didn't hurt as much as only being able to gain just more than two yards per carry. Not having that threat who could slip under defenses with a draw play or surprise on a quick pitch allowed defenses to tee off on Neill.

"If you can't run, you're going to struggle," Tormey said. "If we can establish a running game it will make our passing game even that much better."

Tormey hopes he has the problem addressed. Sophomore **Marquis Starks** (5-10, 185), who led the team in rushing with 457 yards, and fifth-year senior **Adrien Dugas** (5-10, 190), last year's opening day starter who was lost for the year with a knee injury against Wyoming, are back and will get carries. But the job belongs to transfer **Herman Ho-Ching** (6-1, 220), a bruising runner who played two years at Oregon before taking last year off to attend Long Beach City College.

Ho-Ching played at Oregon as a freshman and has bowl game experience. He had discipline problems with Ducks coach Mike Belotti that led to his eventual dismissal. Nevada is certainly a step down from the Pac-10, but Ho-Ching needs to show early in fall drills that he is in shape and the year off had little effect.

The injuries and lack of offensive spark had a profound impact on sophomore **Josh Griffin** (5-9, 180). He was injured early in the year and appeared headed for a redshirt season. But the Wolf Pack got caught up in a late numbers game and had to burn Griffin's redshirt season. He gained only 40 yards in four games.

Converted tight end **Reggie Kinlaw II** (6-2, 225) adds another big back threat.

"Herman is the one player from [this year's recruiting class] who has a chance to have an immediate impact," Tormey said, "but we're going to give them all a chance to show what they can do."

WIDE RECEIVERS/TIGHT ENDS

Though the running game is full of uncertainty, Nevada has familiar hands at wide receiver. The top seven receivers return in a passing offense that finished 30th in the nation. Neill is the key to the offense, but having young receivers continue to mature may be just as important, especially if the offensive line struggles early.

Because Neill was harassed so much last season the Wolf Pack rarely had a chance to go downfield. Tormey's offense is predicated on having a running game set up short passes that entice defenses to begin thinking short. In 2000, Nevada rarely had a chance to complete anything but short passes because of the pressure Neill was under.

That is going to continue this year, but the receivers are a year older and have a year behind them at playing at a little bit different speed than they were used to seeing. The problem is size. All three starters weigh less than 170 pounds. Only one player in the eight-man rotation is bigger than 185 pounds.

Junior **Nate Burleson** (6-2, 169) is the leader of the three-receiver set. He led the team in receiving and was the Wolf Pack's most versatile player. He had 921 yards and eight touchdowns on 57 catches. He also returned punts and kicks, leading the team with almost 100 all-purpose yards per game.

Junior **Mike Crawford** (5-9, 168) was second on the team with 42 catches. He was the one who made most of the underneath catches, finishing with a 12.1-yard average and no touchdowns. Health is a concern as Crawford missed the final three games a year ago with injuries.

Sophomore **Tim Fleming** (6-1, 165) is the starter in the Z-spot. He started six games as a freshman but will be pushed by junior **Jermaine Brown** (5-11, 175) for the starting job.

Seniors **Mo Jones** (6-1, 185) and **T.W. Cunningham** (5-11, 193) are the size. Neither are big-play threats, but both can go over the middle and make the catches the starters can't. The duo plays behind Crawford in the H-position, but, like most of the receivers, they can and will move around.

Junior **Aaron Carter** (6-2, 185) is another big target who needs to continue to improve. In 10 games last season, he caught 16 passes for 154 yards.

The tight end spot is a three-man rotation that needs more production. Last season, Nevada tight ends caught only 18 passes for 265 yards and one touchdown. Because of the size concerns on the outside, Tormey would like to use his tight ends more in the short passing game. That is a possibility if the offensive line can improve enough to allow the Wolf Pack to not need an additional blocker on every play.

Senior **Scott Asai** (6-3, 235) is the starter, but he does have competition. Junior **Bill Lynch** (6-4, 250) is a junior college transfer who has the size to deal with speedy defensive ends and the hands to make tough catches. Lynch caught 49 passes and scored six touchdowns in his two-year career at Foothill (Calif.) Junior College. He's also a capable blocker.

Junior **Erick Streelman** (6-5, 235) is the most athletic of the bunch. He missed spring practice while playing baseball.

OFFENSIVE LINE

Tormey has his fingers crossed that Herman Ho-Ching can carry the running game. He has his fingers crossed that someone—anyone—will carry an offensive line that struggled mightily last season. In addition to giving up 48 sacks for 300 yards, including 11 in the season opener against TCU, the Wolf Pack was overmatched in almost every game and it showed in the running game and overall production.

Nevada was 98th in the nation in scoring. Only SMU scored fewer touchdowns, and the Mustangs and Wolf Pack were the only teams who didn't score at least 11 rushing touchdowns. Both had nine for the season. The inconsistency was the biggest issue. Nevada averaged only 2.2 yards on 373 carries, putting the offense in second- and third-and-long situations where Neill was forced to make plays while scrambling.

The good news is that all but one starting lineman returns and the team has a new leader in assistant coach Steve Morton. Junior **Cody Johnson** (6-4, 270) is back at center, senior **Kika Kaululaau** (6-0, 305) is at left guard and sophomores **John Tennert** (6-3, 288) and **Alan Parker** (6-6, 290) are the right guard and tackle respectively. Senior **Nice Rae** (6-3, 295) steps in at left tackle, replacing Clark Roosendaal. Freshman **Harvey Dahl** (6-5, 255), who graduated early and went through spring practice, will challenge Rae for playing time.

Tormey's hope is that junior college transfer **David Ah Sue** (6-6, 300) can have a similar transition to Kaululaau's last season and start at left tackle. If that happens, Rae and Dahl will battle for backup spots and possibly contribute elsewhere. Ah Sue, from American Samoa, played two years at Long Beach (Calif.) City College.

Kaululaau is the best of the bunch despite having a lot of size on a small frame. Tennert has the best potential, starting as a freshman, which is rarely done on the Division I-A level. Dahl may match that effort as Morton is going into the fall simply looking for people who can play.

There is depth, and all the reserves learned by fire last season. Redshirt freshman left guard **Nick Schnieder** (6-5, 315), the biggest of Nevada's offensive linemen, and Dahl are the only two among the top 10 linemen who didn't see time a year ago.

The most experienced backup is senior center **Turner Graham** (6-2, 293), who can play elsewhere if needed. Sophomore **Sione Fehoko** (6-3, 285) backs up at right guard and junior **Brian Barnes** (6-6, 302) plays behind Parker at right tackle.

Part of building a program is having seasoned offensive linemen who have had a redshirt year. The Wolf Pack recruited three offensive linemen, but the program isn't to the point where it can redshirt players based on position. Dahl will play, and tackle **Adam Kiefer** (6-5, 280) and **Kyle Gosselin** (6-2, 250) aren't redshirt certainties.

2000 STATISTICS

Rushing offense	67.7	112
Passing offense	244.8	30
Total offense	312.4	98
Scoring offense	17.2	98
Net Punting	31.1	97
Punt returns	3.6	112
Kickoff returns	17.7	99
Rushing defense	232.5	112
Passing efficiency defense	125.5	82
Total defense	434.1	103
Scoring defense	38.7	111
Turnover margin	-2	68

Last column is ranking among Division I-A teams.

KICKERS

Mike Phillips, who made only 8-of-11 attempts last season but ranked second in the league in field goal accuracy, is gone and didn't leave much behind. Either senior **Ray Sanchez** (5-9, 170) or redshirt freshman **Damon Fine** (5-9, 170) will handle the kicking chores, but neither had an attempt last season behind Phillips. Sanchez did handle kickoffs last year and spilt the job with Phillips a year ago. Fine has a strong leg and may be better suited for long range kicks, while Sanchez handles things from 35 yards and closer.

DEFENSIVE LINE

For as many struggles as the offense had, the most difficult part of moving from the Big West to the WAC was on defense. The Wolf Pack had seen high-powered offenses in the WAC, but they never saw the overall talent and depth that some WAC teams had a year ago. The transition was most felt up front, where Nevada had a hard time stopping the run or giving help to a secondary that needed a hand.

The Wolf Pack finished last in the WAC against the run, giving up 232.5 yards per game. That was 112th in the nation. The 41 rushing touchdowns Nevada gave up were 15 more than any other team in the league and four more than any other team in Division I-A. Rutgers was next with 37.

The good news is that the players who went through the mess in 2000 are all back with a very tough year of experience behind them.

At tackle, senior **Horacio Leyva** (6-4, 250) is back after being a co-captain last season. He made 25 tackles but, like a lot of Nevada players, was slowed by injuries. Size is also a concern because Leyva is asked to make plays every week against guards, normally the biggest of the offensive linemen, and centers, most often the most athletic.

Redshirt freshman **Chris Barry** (6-3, 260) will get the first look alongside Leyva, but the likely starter is junior college transfer **Johnnie Thomas** (6-3, 285). Thomas is the only one with true tackle size. He needs to be an impact player immediately.

Thomas earned all-state honors at two different junior colleges. In 1999, he was all state at Chabot (Calif.) Community College, then last fall earned the same honor at Holmes (Miss.) Junior College.

"He is a quick and explosive defensive tackle," Tormey said. "He has excellent power and gets off the ball really well. He has a chance to be an impact player in the WAC this year."

Senior **Pat Estes** (6-2, 275) and freshman **P.J. Hoeper** (6-3, 280), who enrolled early, will challenge for starting spots and will be part of a rotation that didn't have much depth a year ago.

Of the five, Leyva is the only one who made a tackle a year ago, meaning the young players need to learn in a hurry for the Wolf Pack to have a chance of not just being completely manhandled inside.

On the outside, sophomore ends **Derek Kennard, Jr.** (6-1, 235) and **Brant Hill** (6-4, 240) are back after learning their lessons in their freshman seasons. Kennard actually had a decent year, making 37 tackles, seven for loss and registering two sacks and a fumble recovery. He has the most potential of the ends. Hill needs to have a better year than 2000, when he played in 10 games and made only 17 tackles. Two of the 17 were sacks.

The backups both played a year ago but don't have an abundance of Division I-A experience. Senior **Leni Suiaunoa** (6-2, 230) backs up Kennard. He was a junior college transfer a year ago, but didn't have a tackle. Sophomore **Mike Yenick** (6-2, 235) is another small, quick end who will see time.

The concern about Nevada's ends is that they will be pushed around by tackles outweighing them by more than 70 pounds.

LINEBACKERS

The Wolf Pack's 4-4 defense relies on the ends and linebackers being aggressive and having a rover who can play anywhere from defensive end to safety. Like almost every other spot on the Nevada defense, the linebackers are young and inexperienced, but all played impact roles a year ago.

Three of the starting four are sophomores. Backup middle linebacker senior **Jeff Peterson** (6-1, 220) is the only one of the nine players at linebacker or rover who isn't a sophomore or junior. The concern is the inexperience and finding a leader to replace co-captain Josh Smith, who graduated.

Jorge Cordova (6-2, 235) is moving into Smith's spot. He has the size and speed to be a star in the WAC. As a redshirt freshman, he led the team in tackles with 91. He was second with seven tackles for loss and led the team in sacks. Tormey likes to use Cordova to rush the passer, but the fact he led the team in sacks is more of a concern than a positive.

On the inside, sophomores **Daryl Towns** (6-0, 212) and **Jesse Adarme** (6-1, 215) both return after combining for 64 tackles. Towns started four games as a freshman and had six tackles for loss. Once again, size is a concern. On most teams, Towns and Adarme would be safeties, not playing in the middle trying to stuff the run and cover 240-pounds fullbacks in the open field.

On the outside, junior **Paul Jolley** (5-11, 205) is the most experienced of the linebackers. But he missed spring practice with a shoulder injury. He will be fine for fall drills and has proved durable in the past. He is one of only three returning defensive players to play all 12 games a year ago.

With Jolley missing spring practice, sophomores **Carl LaGrone** (6-2, 210) and **Alfred Akinyemi** (6-0, 200) got needed snaps with the first two. The two are expected to be part of the outside linebacker rotation and possibly the rover rotation as well.

Most teams that use the 4-4 have a headhunting former linebacker who has speed like a free safety. Sophomores **Humphrey Grant** (5-9, 185), **Tyrone Rackley** (5-11, 185) and **Breck Dolan** (6-0, 175) all have good speed, but none are the tackling machines that the rover has to be. None of the four have the size to take on tight ends and fullbacks in the flat, which is a large concern.

Junior college transfer **Matt White** (6-2, 235) enrolled early and went through spring practice. He is also a tight end, but could be moved to linebacker full time because of the size questions.

DEFENSIVE BACKS

The Nevada secondary was yet another learning area for the Wolf Pack a year ago. With the defensive front struggling, the defensive backs felt the brunt of the punishment. And, with the rover playing more linebacker than defensive back, Nevada's corners and free safety were left alone most of the time. That's not a good combination when that secondary is littered with underclassmen.

It is still full of underclassmen, but, again, the underclassmen have played significant snaps. Sophomore free safety **Ronnie Hardiman** (6-0, 170), who also returns kicks and could return punts this year as well, is the leader in the secondary.

There could be a transition period for Hardiman, though, after a switch from cornerback. In 2000, he was more of a threat against the run than he needed to be. He led the team in tackles with 94, but only one was for loss, meaning the tackles came on receivers after catches and running backs that were already downfield.

If Hardiman has trouble with the switch, sophomore **Brad Lindstrom** (6-1, 193), who started four games at free safety a year ago and has the size more suited for the position, could slide in.

Junior **Domonic Cruz** (5-9, 180) and sophomore **Leondre Lewis** (5-10, 165) are returning starters on the corner. Neither had standout years last season and both need to be better against the run and in making plays. The two combined for only three interceptions last season.

Because the Wolf Pack will see so much passing and because the defensive line is going to be suspect again, a defensive back rotation is a necessity. Junior **Aaron Dean** (5-10, 170), redshirt freshman **Marlon McLaughlin** (5-10, 180) and true freshman **Carlos Velasquez** (5-10, 180) will all be part of the rotation.

PUNTERS

The Wolf Pack is uncertain at kicker, but the punting job is in good hands. Sophomore **Derek Jones** (6-3, 210) finished fourth in the WAC in 2000 with a 39.5-yard average. Though it was his first year of college football, Jones got in almost two seasons of work. He kicked a league-high 79 times. That was 12 times more than any other WAC punter and 25 more kicks than Rice's Travis Hale or UTEP's Glen Beard, the top punters in the conference, had. Jones put 18 of the 79 kicks inside the 20 and had a long punt of 58 yards.

SPECIAL TEAMS

Things weren't good a year ago on special teams. Nevada finished last in the conference and 112th in the nation with a 3.6-yard punt return average. Burleson returned 14 punts for only a 3.9-yard average. His long run was 20 yards. He will drop back again this season, but he has to be better in order for the offense to be effective. Most of the problems last season on offense came because the sputtering unit stalled deep in its own territory and didn't have the defense to stop teams on a short field.

Putting the offense in improved positions is a must for the kick-returning unit as well. Though better than the punt return team, the Wolf Pack still finished eighth in the league and 99th in the country. Burleson and Holmes are back, but the primary return man is Hardiman, who had the best average (22.8) last season despite returning only six kicks.

Coverage on both units also needs to improve so the defense doesn't have to begin on its heels. A year ago, Nevada, which punted 10 more times than any other WAC team and 35 more times than co-champion TCU, was last in the league in net punting. The Wolf Pack gave up 7.7 yards per return and finished with a net of 31.1 yards per kick.

RECRUITING CLASS

While at Idaho, Tormey laid down roots in the California high schools and junior colleges, a must for any West Coast school, but especially for one that plays in a state that doesn't produce much high school talent.

This year, Tormey signed 25 players, 19 from California. The Wolf Pack signed as many players from Florida (two) as Nevada. The focus was on immediate help in the running game and linemen on both sides. The Wolf Pack signed four linemen on each side of the ball and three running backs, one of which will immediately be a starter. The Nevada basketball team even got better with this class. Wide receiver **Nichiren Flowers** (6-3, 195) will play for Trent Johnson's team after the football season is over.

The class isn't deep and didn't top any analyst's list, but it was effective for the Wolf Pack's purposes.

The jewel is running back Ho-Ching, who spent two years at Oregon before transferring to Long Beach City College last year where he didn't play football. Ho-Ching was considered to be the Ducks next great running back when he signed. In 1998, he played on the 9-3 Oregon team that went to the Sun Bowl. He had 11 carries for 77 yards against Nevada that season.

He left Oregon after several run-ins with coach Mike Belotti. He's getting another chance in Reno, but he had to fit in if he's going to make the contribution Nevada needs and Tormey is expecting.

"Herman is the one player who has the best chance to make a difference next year," Tormey said. "He was the top running back in California in 1998 and had an immediate impact on Oregon's program, playing a lot at the Pac-10 level as a true freshman."

Nevada also signed four junior college transfers and Army tight end Ben Kirish (6-5, 235), who is sitting out 2001 per NCAA transfer rules.

Of the junior college transfers, offensive tackle Ah Sue and wide receiver **Dan Bythwood** (6-5, 185), who may also return kicks, will play large roles this season.

Bythwood needs to shake off some rust. He played at Hutchinson (Kansas) Community College in 1999, but sat out last year while getting his associate's degree.

BLUE RIBBON ANALYSIS

OFFENSE	C-
SPECIAL TEAMS	C-
DEFENSE	D
INTANGIBLES	D

The Wolf Pack will be better than last year's two-win season, but how much better depends on how quickly a team that still has only 15 seniors develops and how it handles a difficult early schedule. Nevada opens with three of its first four on the road, all in consecutive weeks. And the trips are not easy. Up first is BYU, which has a new staff, but is still tough in Provo. The next week is in Fort Collins against Mountain West favorite Colorado State. After a home game against Hawaii, the Wolf Pack is at San Jose State, which has running back Deonce Whitaker, one of the top contenders for WAC Player of the Year. In all, Nevada goes on the road six times, which is actually one less time than the young team did a year ago.

If an offensive line that has only one senior can keep Neill off the ground, the Wolf Pack will put up points. There isn't a lot of depth at any offensive position, so staying healthy is a must. So is establishing a running game. The Wolf Pack's rushing attack was among the nation's worst in 2000.

The offense needs to be more of a ball control unit to keep a defense off the field that was not good a year ago. There is some talent, but it is young, developing talent. The defense is better than the unit that gave up 10 more touchdowns than any other WAC team simply because it is a year older and wiser. But, it is still going to have its problems.

With the balance in the conference, Nevada should win more than the one conference game it did a year ago. Improving on last year's two victories with this non-conference schedule, though, is going to require some major surprises.

(C.M.)

2000 RESULTS

Oregon	L	7-36	0-1
Texas Christian	L	10-41	0-2
Wyoming	W	35-28	1-2
Colorado State	L	14-45	1-3
UNLV	L	7-38	1-4
Fresno State	L	21-58	1-5
San Jose State	L	30-49	1-6
SMU	L	7-21	1-7
UTEP	L	22-45	1-8
Hawaii	L	17-37	1-9
Rice	W	34-28	2-9
Tulsa	L	3-38	2-10

Rice

LOCATION	Houston, TX
CONFERENCE	Western Athletic
LAST SEASON	3-8 (.273)
CONFERENCE RECORD	2-6 (t-6th)
OFFENSIVE STARTERS RETURNING	8
DEFENSIVE STARTERS RETURNING	9
NICKNAME	Owls
COLORS	Blue & Gray
HOME FIELD	Rice Stadium (70,000)
HEAD COACH	Ken Hatfield (Arkansas '65)
RECORD AT SCHOOL	34-42-1 (7 years)
CAREER RECORD	145-104-4 (22 years)
ASSISTANTS	
	Scott Wachenheim (Air Force '84) Offensive Coordinator/Offensive Line
	Roger Hinshaw (Appalachian State '72) Defensive Coordinator/Safeties/Bandits
	John Bland (Arkansas '89) Quarterbacks
	Larry Brinson (Florida '82) Running Backs
	Barney Farrar (Delta State '83) Cornerbacks
	Steve Kidd (Rice '87) Punters/Placekickers/Recruiting Coordinator
	Jeff Sowells (Rice '96) Receivers
	Charlie Rizzo (Auburn '67) Inside Linebackers
	Theo Young (Arkansas '88) Defensive Line
TEAM WINS (last 5 yrs.)	7-7-5-5-3
FINAL RANK (last 5 yrs.)	76-83-76-95-101
2000 FINISH	Lost to Nevada in regular-season finale.

COACH AND PROGRAM

Ken Hatfield has been around. If there's something to see, the Rice head coach, in his eighth year in Houston and 23rd overall, has probably seen it.

Last season, though, Hatfield had to throw his hands in the air and admit he may not have ever experienced a year as strange.

The injury bug was more like the injury monster. The Owls started three different quarterbacks and used four. Offensive lineman **Aaron Sandoval**, expected to be an anchor on an already solid offense line, went down with a knee injury before the year started. Noseguard **B.J. Forguson** missed six games. Even kicker **Derek Crabtree** missed a game with an injury.

Things got so desperate that Hatfield, known for his spread-option attack, had to actually throw the ball. The Owls still averaged less than 82 yards passing per game, but even throwing a few times shows Rice was willing to try almost anything.

"Strange probably sums it up," Hatfield said. "I'd say that's a pretty fair assessment to say the least."

The injuries forced the Owls to go deeper than Hatfield would have liked. It added up to Rice having its worst year since the 1995 team went 2-8-1 in Hatfield's second year, the last in the Southwest Conference. Last year was probably the most disappointing because even though the non-conference schedule was brutal, there were no conference opponents named Texas and Texas A&M.

Hatfield is one of those coaches who believes the lumps pay off the next season, especially when almost the whole team returns. Rice lost only 11 players from the 2000 team. On offense, 18 players return who started at least one game last season. On defense 19 return.

The most important number is 50 total lettermen, all of whom have grown up in a system that gets a lot out of what is mostly limited talent. Scott Wachenheim took over as offensive coordinator, but the offense is Hatfield's baby. It's a system predicated on confusing defenses with multiple blocking schemes and a quarterback who is both smart and experienced running the option.

Hatfield said the Owls will throw more, but don't look for Rice on the passing leader charts. This team is built just like any of Hatfield's other teams. It relies on an offensive line overpowering people and an elusive quarterback running the option to perfection.

The spread-option offense has taken the Owls to several successful seasons under Hatfield. Last season was a bump in the road, but Hatfield has had enough success at the smallest Division I-A school in the country that he will be there as long as he wants.

He has built a program that mirrors the school. It is tough, but stocked with players who know the stock market as well as they know their playbooks. There are more future investment bankers, doctors and lawyers on this team than pro prospects and that's exactly the way the administration wants it. Rice is one of the few schools that understands the Division I-A landscape and knows how to play within the system to make itself money and still stay competitive.

Hatfield's option offense keeps his normally undermanned team in games. And athletic director Bobby May isn't shy about scheduling his Big Ten buddies to get Rice a payday and the Big Ten team a win.

Nebraska is the payday this season. After the Cornhuskers, though, the Owls can win any game. As long as the injuries don't return, Hatfield's program should hover around the seven- to eight win mark like it has seemed to do most of Hatfield's years.

2001 SCHEDULE

Sept.	1	@Houston
	8	Duke
	15	@Nebraska
	29	@Hawaii
Oct.	6	Boise State
	13	@Navy
	20	Nevada
	27	@Louisiana Tech
Nov.	3	@Fresno State
	10	Tulsa
	17	UTEP
	24	@SMU

QUARTERBACKS

There is no other position as important at Rice as quarterback. In every year since Hatfield has been in Houston, the Owls have had a quarterback who was an option quarterback in high school and then flourished in Hatfield's system.

Last season, four quarterbacks got that opportunity because of injuries. This year, Hatfield wants to settle on one. Because of the experience returning, that will be tough. Add in that Rice wants to throw more and the decision may be even more difficult.

Whoever wins the job has the responsibility of being able to read defensive ends, outrun linebackers and make defensive backs miss. The Rice quarterback is the best athlete on the team and sometimes the best athlete on the field.

The starting job is between sophomore **Jeremy Hurd** (5-10, 170) and senior **Corey Evans** (5-11, 170). Hatfield wants Hurd, the better athlete of the two, to start as long as he can avoid the injury bug. Hurd missed half of last season with a broken finger and knee injury. He began the year as the starter and then broke a finger on his passing hand. Just after he returned from that injury, he hurt his knee. Hurd ended up carrying only 63 times for 280 yards and no touchdowns. He completed only 8-of-25 passes and didn't throw a touchdown pass.

When Hurd got hurt, Evans took over. That is until he got hurt. Evans actually started the year banged up with a bad hamstring. He played the first eight games before a knee injury forced him to miss the final three games.

Hurd is the starter if healthy. Evans has the experience, though, and new quarterbacks coach John Bland may have a quick trigger with the Owls expecting to win this season.

Sophomore **Kyle Herm** (5-8, 175) gives Rice yet another choice. He was forced into a starting role a year ago but needs more experience running the offense before he is a true option. Herm is the quick, smart athlete who normally plays quarterback for the Owls. He reminds a lot of fans of former Rice great Chad Nelson.

Herm threw the ball some in high school and is probably the most experienced of the Rice passers. Ben Wulf, the other Rice quarterback last season, is gone after leading the team in passing.

If the Owls are serious about throwing more, both Hurd and Evans need to get better. Despite Hatfield's comments, don't expect an aerial showcase. Hatfield said the Owls will throw because several speed options have developed and they are going to up the reps in practice so the defense can be better prepared for the amount of passing Rice sees during WAC play.

Of note, Rice signed **Thomas Lott III**, (5-7, 165) the son of former Oklahoma quarterback Thomas Lott, one of the most famous option quarterbacks ever. Lott played in an option offense and could be an option down the road if he can put on weight. He is probably headed for a redshirt season.

RUNNING BACKS

Rice normally finishes in the top five in the country in rushing offense and features a couple of players scattered among the national leaders. That didn't happen last season. Part of the reason was injuries on the offensive line. The rest was the development of a stable of running backs who all return this season. Senior **Jamie Tyler** (5-11, 200) and sophomore **Robbie Beck** (5-11, 212) are the 1-2 punch, but as many as four halfbacks will get carries in the spread option offense.

Tyler and Beck are both power backs that have a good understanding of the option offense. Tyler, who is the fullback, led the team in rushing last year with 400 yards on 95 carries. He also scored five touchdowns. The concern with Tyler is injuries. He missed the season opener last year and has been hurt every season except his redshirt freshman year when he was the second-leading rusher on the team.

Beck was a pleasant surprise a year ago, rushing for 348 yards, averaging 4.6 yards per carry and leading the team with seven touchdowns as a freshman. If the quarterback position is stabilized, Beck and Tyler are poised for breakout seasons.

The most experienced of the four halfbacks is **Leroy Bradley** (5-11, 205), who started seven games last season. He played in nine games, carrying 47 times for 220 yards. He isn't as powerful as Tyler or Beck, but he has the outside speed they don't have.

Senior **Derek Gray** (6-0, 204), who missed all of last year with an injury, sophomore **Vincent Hawkins** (5-6, 175) and sophomore **Sean White** (5-6, 175) will all get carries in what is the deepest rotation the Owls have had since Hatfield arrived.

Hawkins is the fastest of the Rice backs. Last season, he had a 41-yard run against SMU, the team's longest of the year.

Sophomore **Jordan Kramer** (6-0, 200) played some as a freshman and will be worked into the rotation. Redshirt freshmen **Ed Bailey** (5-9, 208), **Donald Pinkerton** (5-9, 160) and **Clint Hatfield** (5-9, 184) could see some action, but will mostly be used on special teams.

WIDE RECEIVERS/TIGHT ENDS

Normally, Rice uses a wide receiver as the blocker who springs running backs to the outside or the one who cracks back on linebackers to allow a runner to cut back and make a play in the middle of the field. The tight end is normally another offensive lineman.

Hatfield said throughout the spring that that isn't the case this season. He said the Owls will throw the ball. Hatfield admits reaching double digits in passing attempts might be a stretch, but he maintains that Rice will not be as ground-oriented as it has been in the past.

The reason for Hatfield's change of heart is seeing how much success other WAC teams are having with the pass and because the conference, with the exception of Rice and Fresno State, has few weapons in the secondary. Hatfield also needs help to keep teams from playing as many as nine players close to the line of scrimmage. The Owls' 2000 ranking of 114th in the nation in passing (only six touchdown passes all season) doesn't exactly make defensive backfields shiver, but Rice did spend the majority of spring practice installing more pass plays and several new passing schemes.

The threat at receiver and the main reason for Hatfield's optimism is sophomore **Gavin Boothe** (6-2, 185), a tall, speedy receiver who, as a true freshman, had 18 catches for 313 yards, 110 of which came against WAC co-champion UTEP. Some were surprised when Boothe, who was a high school teammate of Texas big-play receiver B.J. Johnson, signed with Rice because of the kind of ability he showed last season. But Boothe, also a standout student, immediately stepped in, learned how to be a good blocker on the outside and began contributing in the passing game.

Senior **Gilbert Okoronkwo** (6-3, 195) is another tall option and a good run blocker. Seniors **Matt Webber** (5-10, 175) and **Evan Meeks** (5-9, 185) could also see time at split end.

Along with Boothe, senior tight end **Brandon Manning** (6-4, 235) and junior **Travis Thompson** (6-2, 250) will figure more in the passing game. Both started games last season, combining for eight receptions, which is a ton in this offense. Both are good blockers and should catch more balls this year.

OFFENSIVE LINE

As is normally the case under Hatfield, the Owls have good size up front. They also have a starter returning at every position, even though they lost left tackle Rod Beavan, who set the Rice record for career starts with 47.

Despite the experience, there will be movement up front to make room for sixth-year senior Sandoval (6-2, 295), who will move to center after starting two years at tackle. The first sixth-year senior in Rice history, Sandoval was hurt during the last week of fall drills last year. In the three years he played, Sandoval was in 32-of-33 games and started 20. He was part of the 1998 team that ranked fifth in the country in rushing and the 1999 team that finished seventh. Even though Sandoval hasn't played since the end of the '99 season, Rice expects him to be the leader of the offensive line.

With Sandoval's return, sophomore **Ben Stephens** (6-2, 290), who started seven games in 2000, moves into a backup role. The Sandoval-Stephens combination gives Rice the most experienced center tandem in the WAC and two of the bigger centers in the conference.

Senior left guard **Heath Fowler** (6-2, 275) and senior right tackle **Billy Harvin** (6-4, 270) both started every game last year. Senior right guard **Ryan Smith** (6-2, 300) started nine. Senior **Anthony Mowry** (6-4, 260) slides into Beavan's spot, giving the Owls an all-senior starting lineup.

Hatfield hopes the experience up front will alleviate any rust Hurd or Evans may have. The experience is also one of the main reasons Hatfield decided to open the offense a little. He believes the five players, along with the tight ends, both of whom are upperclassmen, will have no problem making the adjustments.

The all-senior offensive line is reminiscent of the way TCU, which ran to a national ranking last year before running to Conference USA, was built. Four of the Horned Frogs' starting linemen where seniors, which helped significantly against teams with younger defensive lines. Add in the size the Owls have and Rice's running game should be back among the national leaders like it normally is every year.

Senior **Brandon Wallace** (6-1, 262), who started four games at center in 2000, leads an experienced corps of backups. Senior **Keith Meyer** (6-3, 260) has starting experience at right guard and can play a variety of positions. Junior tackle **Clint Crisp** (6-3, 285) and redshirt freshmen **Cotey-Joe Cswaykus** (6-4, 265), **Micah Meador** (6-3, 304) and **James Pitman** (6-4, 262) will all play.

2000 STATISTICS

Rushing offense	233.0	11
Passing offense	81.5	114
Total offense	314.5	95
Scoring offense	21.5	83
Net Punting	34.5	58
Punt returns	7.2	98
Kickoff returns	14.9	113
Rushing defense	133.9	40
Passing efficiency defense	131.3	94
Total defense	378.5	67
Scoring defense	29.3	82
Turnover margin	+9	17

Last column is ranking among Division I-A teams.

KICKERS

The injury bug was so bad for the Owls a year ago that it even bit the kickers. Crabtree (6-4, 210), a senior, missed the SMU game, forcing sophomore **Brandon Skeen** (6-1, 185) into action. The luxury this season is that Crabtree is back and Skeen has, at least, played.

Crabtree led Rice in scoring after making 8-of-12 field goals and 26-of-28 extra points. He isn't the most accurate kicker in the league, but he is reliable. His longest field goal was a 42-yarder against Houston in the season opener against Houston.

In the SMU game, Skeen hit a 47-yarder, his only attempt of the season.

DEFENSIVE LINE

The job of the Rice defense is to stop teams quickly and let the offense eat up the clock. That happened some last season, but it normally happened after the Owls gave up a big play. The secondary was picked on early against Oklahoma and Michigan. It got little help from a defensive line that was tied for last in the WAC in sacks.

The front four should be improved simply because, like the offensive line, it is an experienced unit. The best of the bunch are senior tackles **Larry Brown** (6-2, 309) and Forguson (6-3, 290). The two were the reason teams had a hard time running against the Owls in 2000. The unit finished second in the league behind TCU and 40th nationally with a 133.9-yard average. The average is somewhat deceiving because WAC teams don't run much, but it also includes those games against Oklahoma and Michigan.

Forguson and Brown are successful because of their size. The WAC doesn't have overpowering offensive linemen. If a team has a dominating tackle, like Fresno State's Alan Harper, he can be a force both against the run and the pass, which normally isn't the strong suit for a tackle.

The concern, as it is for the rest of team, is injuries. Forguson started the first four games at nose guard before a knee injury against Oklahoma forced him to miss the next three games. He tried to return against TCU, but injured his shoulder and missed the rest of the year.

Brown started the first 10 games before a knee injury that had been bothering him all season forced him to miss the Nevada game.

Brown and Forguson need to have a good year because the ends are of the quick, undersized variety.

Senior **Clint Johnson** (6-2, 240) should take over for Jake Jackson at one end. Junior **Brandon Green** (6-3, 230) is the other end and the only non-senior on the defensive line. Green started five games last year, making 37 tackles, eight for loss. He has to have a better year rushing the passer to take pressure off a secondary that will be looking for an enforcer.

Sophomore **Danny Cestero** (6-2, 238) and junior **Nick Sabula** (6-2, 215), who played running back last year, will get snaps and will push Johnson for his end spot.

The Owls recruited three defensive linemen: **Jeremy Callahan** (6-3, 260), **Pike Pickett** (6-3, 225) and **Rishone Evans** (5-11, 265). Barring injury, all will redshirt.

LINEBACKERS

Rice tries to compensate for a lack of size up front with speedy linebackers and a hard-hitting secondary. The linebacker corps, led by senior **Dan Dawson** (6-2, 200), one of the WAC's top defensive players, returns intact. The outside linebacker, who sat out 1999 with a broken leg, made 88 tackles and picked off a conference-high seven passes, which he returned for a school-record 206 yards. He is small, but he plays much bigger than his frame. He is solid against the run and even better against the pass. If he were on a different team, he would be a free safety. But the Owls need his run support, so he is forced to play out of position.

Senior **Rashard Pittman** (5-11, 237), who started every game a year ago, is back at on the strong side after tying Dawson for the team lead in tackles. If there is an enforcer defensively on this team, it's Pittman. He is almost as big as the Owls' defensive ends and is one of the faster players on the defense. He is solid against the run, but needs to become a bigger part of the pass rush.

Senior **Joe Bob Thompson** (6-0, 224) and sophomore **Jeff Vanover** (5-11, 205) will share the weak-side spot. Once again, size is a concern with Vanover, the better coverage linebacker. But, Vanover does make plays. He had Rice's only punt return for a touchdown last season.

Thompson started seven games last season before getting hurt and missing the last four. He started 11 games in 1999 and played in all 11 as a freshman. He is also very intelligent—he won $3,550 on *Wheel of Fortune* after his freshman year.

Juniors **Justin Engler** (6-2, 214) and **Scott Huffman** (5-10, 225) and sophomore **Julius Mitchell** (6-1, 205) are the only other players who will see time on Rice's deepest unit.

DEFENSIVE BACKS

The secondary is experienced, but will miss enforcer Travis Ortega. Senior free safety **Jason Hebert** (6-0, 192) is an all-conference type. But, there is no head hunter in a secondary that is grossly undersized, with only Hebert weighing more than 190 pounds.

Despite losing Ortega and corner Josh McMillan, the Owls have experience. The secondary just needs to play bigger than its size and get some help up front to help improve on a pass efficiency ranking that was among the worst nationally in 2000.

The problem wasn't that the Owls didn't make plays against the pass (19 interceptions in 12 games). They just gave up a lot of yards and big plays. Only SMU and San Jose State, which featured two of the worst defensive backfields in the nation last year, gave up more yards than Rice.

Teams ran wild because there was no pass rush. That left the secondary on its own to make plays and stop teams. With the schedule the Owls had a year ago, that was a lot to ask. The schedule is lightened somewhat, but Rice will have problems with teams over the middle if no enforcer steps up.

Junior **Antwan Shell** (5-11, 185) steps into Ortega's spot. Shell started once last year when Ortega moved up to outside linebacker.

Junior **Greg Gatlin** (6-0, 175), who started twice a year ago, takes over for McMillan. Senior **Kenny Smith** (5-7, 170) is back at right cornerback after starting every game a year ago. Smith is a decent cover corner, but he needs safety help against faster receivers.

Redshirt freshmen **Raymorris Barnes** (5-9, 170), **Jason Benjamin** (5-7, 155) and **Clifford Sparks** (5-9, 189), a high school teammate of receiver Gavin Boothe, will all be part of the rotation and any of the three could end up starting at left corner.

PUNTERS

Junior **Travis Hale** (6-3, 201) is the WAC's best punter. He was a second-team all-WAC choice as a sophomore after averaging a league-best 41.8 yards per kick. His current 41.6-yard career average is the best in Rice history. Last season, he put 17 kicks inside the 20-yard line and had nine of at least 50 yards. All that and Hale wasn't blocked, either.

Hale is also consistent. He averaged at least 40 yards in eight games and had a 51.7-yard average in the loss to Nevada.

SPECIAL TEAMS

The kicking game is in great shape, but Rice has to find someone to make plays in the return game. The Owls ranked last in the league and 113th in the nation last year in kick returns with a 14.9-yard average. Punt returns weren't much better. Rice was seventh in the WAC and 98th in the country with a 7.2-yard average. That average would have been worse had Vanover not returned one 33 yards for a touchdown in the season opener against Houston.

Five players returned punts in 2000 and six returned kicks. White returned 22 kicks for a 16.3 yard average, but that did little for an offense that was struggling with injuries. Plays have to be made to keep the offense from starting in a large hole. The offense is good enough to go 80 yards for a touchdown. But it isn't good enough to do it on every possession.

White, Webber, Hawkins and Herm will all get a chance to jump start a unit whose longest return of the year was Sadler's 28-yarder against UTEP.

Herm, White or Hebert will return punts. With Hebert being one of the defensive leaders, the duty probably falls on Herm, who was improved during the spring, or White

RECRUITING CLASS

Rice looks for a little bit different player on the recruiting trail. The Owls want to make sure a recruit can play, but it's more important that he can handle the academic load the school requires.

On the field, Rice recruits more to the system rather than just recruiting athletes. Players who have had success with option offenses in high school almost always have a home at Rice. Also, Hatfield is good at taking smaller athletes and turning them into defensive backs or running backs or quarterbacks in the option offense.

This class is full of those kinds of players.

Only four of the 13 weigh more than 200 pounds and none are offensive linemen. Three of the four 200-pounders, Callahan, Pickett and Evans (5-11, 265), are defensive linemen. The other, **Joe Wood** (6-3, 235), is a tight end.

With the experience Rice has returning, none of the freshmen are likely to play. Hatfield may see if running back **Kevin Ford** (6-0, 190), who has 4.5 speed, can make an impact. But producing as a freshman in the Owls' complicated offense is difficult.

The effects of this class will be felt two years down the road after Jeremy Hurd, who played at the same high school as Evans, graduates. The Owls picked up three quarterbacks, all of whom played in run oriented offenses. The biggest name is Lott III, the son of the famed Oklahoma option quarterback.

BLUE RIBBON ANALYSIS

OFFENSE	B
SPECIAL TEAMS	B
DEFENSE	B
INTANGIBLES	B

The Owls play at Nebraska, but don't play three heavyweights like they have in the past. The schedule opens with Houston and Duke, both winnable games, before Rice heads to Lincoln. Rice has two weeks off after the Nebraska shelling to get ready for a trip to Hawaii. Playing at Fresno State will be a tough trip, but there are no games, with the exception of Nebraska, where the Owls will be out-manned.

Experience makes Rice an improved team. If the quarterback situation is settled early and the defense makes the plays it didn't a year ago, Rice could finish among the WAC's top three.

The Owls' scheme will always keep them in games. This season, their experience should help win some of those close ones. Rice's spread option is still one of the toughest offenses to prepare for on short notice. And with 50 returning lettermen, the Owls finally have players who know it well.

The concern is finding out what effect last year's injuries will have. Both of the Owls' top quarterbacks are coming off injuries. Sandoval is moving to center after sitting out a year with an injury. There will be an early season adjusting period.

The kicking game is solid, but Rice has to find ways to make plays in the return game.

If the defense can keep teams from jumping on the Owls early, which forces a time-consuming offensive to play catch up, this team has a chance to reverse its record from last year's injury-plagued nightmare.

(C.M.)

2000 RESULTS

Houston	W	30-27	1-0
Michigan	L	7-38	1-1
Tulsa	L	16-23	1-2
Oklahoma	L	14-42	1-3
San Jose State	L	16-29	1-4
Fresno State	L	24-27	1-5
Hawaii	W	38-13	2-5
TCU	L	0-37	2-6
SMU	W	43-14	3-6
UTEP	L	21-38	3-7
Nevada	L	28-34	3-8

San Jose State

LOCATION	**San Jose, CA**
CONFERENCE	**Western Athletic**
LAST SEASON	**7-5 (.583)**
CONFERENCE RECORD	**5-3 (4th)**
OFFENSIVE STARTERS RETURNING	**9**
DEFENSIVE STARTERS RETURNING	**4**
NICKNAME	**Spartans**
COLORS	**Gold, White & Blue**
HOME FIELD	**Spartan Stadium (30,456)**
HEAD COACH	**Fitz Hill (Ouchita Baptist '87)**
RECORD AT SCHOOL	**First Year**
CAREER RECORD	**First year**

ASSISTANTS

Earl Buckingham (Arkansas '82)
Assistant Head Coach/Defensive Line
Norman Joseph (Mississippi State '77)
Offensive Coordinator/Quarterbacks
Ronnie Lee (Washington State '89)
Defensive Coordinator/Defensive Backs
Carl Dean (San Jose State '97)
Wide Receivers
Charles Nash (Arizona '76)
Running Backs
Kyle O'Quinn (Henderson State '86)
Tight Ends
Tom Quinn (Arizona '90)
Special Teams Coordinator/Defensive Assistant
Charles Roche (Eastern Illinois '97)
Offensive Line

Kenwick Thompson (Harding '92)
Linebackers
TEAM WINS (last 5 yrs.) **3-4-4-3-7**
FINAL RANK (last 5 yrs.) **101-96-99-101-79**
2000 FINISH **Lost to Fresno State in regular-season finale.**

COACH AND PROGRAM

It takes a different kind of person to run the San Jose State football program. The school, for the most part, is a commuter campus and doesn't have a close-knit feel. Its location is beautiful, but it is also in one of the most expensive areas of the country. Assistant coaches have trouble finding affordable housing, often living more than an hour drive from the campus. And even when the Spartans have a good year and pull off an impressive win, the victory isn't often the focus.

Last season, after San Jose handed No. 9 TCU its only loss of the year before a national television audience, students rushed the field and tore down the goal posts. In a local television interview, a San Jose State official told a local news outlet that the win was great and would bring much-needed attention to the school. He then said his biggest concern was how the school was going to find the money to repair the goal posts.

That kind of thinking drove former coach Dave Baldwin out and Fitz Hill in as his replacement. Baldwin complained about not getting his contract renewed late in the season after the Spartans were headed for their best season since 1992. San Jose beat a Top 10 team for only the second time in school history and had an offense that averaged more than 400 yards for the first time in seven years. Baldwin, who had said that he didn't have an ego and could just as easily return to being an assistant, departed to become offensive coordinator for Cincinnati.

Hill comes to San Jose after 12 seasons as an Arkansas assistant. He spent the last nine seasons as the wide receivers coach, adding the recruiting coordinator duties three years ago. He went to six bowl games with the Razorbacks and was part of the 1998 team that won the SEC championship.

Hill is unfamiliar with the WAC's western recruiting grounds, but he does have ties to the league and to the area. Tulsa's Keith Burns was the defensive coordinator at Arkansas from 1998-99. And Hill has spent some time in Northern California with his retired mother now living in Berkeley.

Hill likes a wide-open style and will use a lot of the same formations Arkansas does. The question will be how the changes affect a team that has gotten used to change. Baldwin was an intense, fiery coach. Hill has that in him, but he is a disciplinarian who has surrounded himself with coaches who know the area.

Wide receivers coach Carl Dean and special teams coordinator and defensive assistant Tom Quinn were retained from Baldwin's staff. The two know Northern California and the fertile California junior colleges well.

New running backs coach Charlie Nash gives Hill the statewide knowledge he needed. For the last seven years, Nash, who is in his first college job, was an athletics director and football coach at high schools in Southern California, including the last two at Inglewood High outside Los Angeles. Nash, who coached offensive tackle Jelani Hawkins in high school, is a respected coach in California and gives Hill immediate help and credibility with California coaches and players.

Players will also experience something new with Hill. He is versed in military training, spending eight months in Saudi Arabia during Desert Storm and Desert Shield. He received a Bronze Star Medal, a Kuwait Liberation Medal, an Army Reserve Component Achievement Medal and a Southwest Asia Service Medal for his service. He remains an inactive reserve with a ranking of lieutenant.

2001 SCHEDULE

Sept.	1	@USC
	8	@Colorado
	15	Stanford
	22	Nevada
	29	@Arizona State
Oct.	6	@Louisiana Tech
	13	SMU
	20	@UTEP
	27	Tulsa
Nov.	3	@Hawaii
	17	@Boise State
	24	@Fresno State

QUARTERBACKS

The offense Hill runs doesn't force the quarterback to make spectacular plays. Junior **Marcus Arroyo** (6-1, 197) is capable of scrambling and making plays with his legs, but the Spartans are better off when he makes the safe throws and hands the ball to **Deonce Whitaker**.

Arroyo has started 17 games the last two years. San Jose is 9-8 during that time. Some of those games weren't lost because Arroyo didn't put up enough points to win. The Spartans' defense during Arroyo's tenure has not been, to be kind, very good. Last season, Arroyo threw for 2,334 yards and 15 touchdowns on 166-of-326 passing. He threw only 10 interceptions and added two touchdowns on the ground.

In Hill's offense, he is expected to throw short, quick passes and let the receivers make plays, but Arroyo, who spent most of the year ranked among the national leaders in total offense, can make things happen on his own. He led the Spartans to 31 points per game last season and the best offensive performance (more than 400 yards per game) in seven years.

Seniors **Brennon Crooks** (6-1, 163) and **Clint Carlson** (6-2, 217) both played last season. Crooks, who threw for 388 yards on 23-of-53 passing, is the backup. Carlson threw only two passes.

Redshirt freshman **Lyle Everett** (5-11, 165) made the team as a walk-on last season and is headed back to the scout team for a second straight year.

The intriguing prospect is junior college transfer **Orlando Evans** (6-0, 185), who comes to San Jose as a sophomore. He signed with Oregon after throwing for almost 2,800 yards as a senior in high school. He redshirted as a freshman before transferring to Solano (Calif.) College.

RUNNING BACKS

Hill stepped into a nice offensive situation when he took over the San Jose reins. The Spartans have four returning offensive line starters, all with good size and experience. And Hill has one of the best backs in the country returning in senior Whitaker (5-6, 185), a Doak Walker semifinalist a year ago. Whitaker is explosive and is adept at making people miss. He has the speed to run outside and the moves to get yards in the middle of the field. He isn't tall and has had injury problems his whole career. But when healthy, Whitaker, who also returns kicks, is as big a big-play threat as any back in the country.

Last season, he set a school record with 1,577 yards. He was fourth in the country in rushing and led the nation with a 7.0-yard average. He raised eyebrows with four 200-yard games, including 254 against Stanford. Whitaker really attracted attention after running for 154 yards against Nebraska. Despite missing two September games because of turf toe and a neck injury, Whitaker also finished seventh in the country in all-purpose yards and ninth in scoring. With the Heisman race wide open this season, Whitaker is a serious threat.

Especially if he gets even more involved in the offense. Hill wants to use Whitaker in passing situations, something Baldwin rarely did.

"We think he can be a special, special receiver," Hill said. "We have to take advantage of his skill of making people miss him in the open field and on the perimeter."

Hill also knows about Whitaker's injury history. "We do have to be careful with him," Hill said. "We want to keep him stronger at the end of the year rather than being beat down. We want to utilize him, but be smart how we use him."

If Whitaker does get hurt again, there is help behind him. Senior **Jarmar Julien** (6-0, 225) is a powerful back who will be asked to get the yards inside. He ran for 561 yards and eight touchdowns a year ago.

Redshirt freshmen **David Kemp** (5-9, 167) and **Mike Liranzo** (6-1, 214) may see some time in passing situations. But both are probably going to watch Whitaker work his magic.

Freshmen signees **Clarence Cunningham** (5-10, 168) and **Lamar Ferguson** (5-7, 155) both need to hit the weight room during their redshirt years.

WIDE RECEIVERS/TIGHT ENDS

San Jose returns its top three receivers from last season and welcomes back a junior college transfer. The Spartans also added a new position, but have to replace their top two tight ends from a year ago.

Seniors **Edell Shepherd** (6-1, 170), **Rashied Davis** (5-9, 177) and **Casey Le Blanc** (5-10, 192) accounted for 123 of San Jose's 191 receptions and 10 of the Spartans' 16 receiving touchdowns.

Shepherd and Davis are the deep threats that keep defenses honest and the holes open for Whitaker. The duo combined for 82 catches and both averaged almost 17.0 yards per catch. Shepherd led the team with 42 receptions, including a 72-yarder that was the longest reception of the season for a Spartan receiver.

Davis, the fastest San Jose receiver, led the team in yards (785) touchdowns (six) and average (19.6). Though small, he makes plays after he catches the ball because of his speed and, like Whitaker, he has an innate ability to make people miss in the open field.

Le Blanc is the ultimate possession receiver. He had a 69-yard reception last season and his average for the year was still less than 12 yards per catch on his 41 receptions. He has been a solid contributor for three years, finishing at least second in each of his first three years.

Because of the wide receiver depth, Le Blanc is moving from wide receiver to H-back, the new position in Hill's offense. He will get some carries, but will mainly be used to slip into the middle for the 5-6 yard catches on third down or for the short out patter to pick up short yardage.

Senior **Elonte Vaughn** (5-8, 165) and sophomore **Tuati Wooden** (5-11, 183) are the only other players returning who caught passes a year ago. Junior **Juan Walden** (6-1, 204), who redshirted in 2000 after transferring from junior college, and redshirt freshman **Jared Pimentel** (6-0,

170) will both be a part of the rotation.

Junior **Charles Pauley** (5-9, 162) signed with San Jose in last year's signing period, but spent the year at a junior college. He re-enrolled in the spring and went through spring practice.

San Jose signed two junior college receivers, **Frank Jordan** (6-1, 180) and **Layton Johnson** (6-2, 196), who will both see time in 2001. Freshmen **Larry Kirven** (6-0, 172) and **Rufus Skillern** (5-11, 170) could play on special teams, but are probably headed for redshirt seasons.

The biggest offensive losses were tight ends Sean Brewer, a second-team All-WAC selection, and his backup Jesse Rogers. Junior college signee **Ethan Allen** (6-2, 244) is a good pass catching option and should start. He is already enrolled and went through spring drills. Hill was so concerned with tight end depth, though, that he moved senior **George Campos** (6-4, 266) from center. Allen will make the catches while Campos will play in running situations.

Redshirt junior **Byron Burnett** (6-2, 255) and redshirt freshman **Matt Joyner** (6-4, 226) will also get looks in the fall.

OFFENSIVE LINE

Deonce Whitaker was the nation's fourth-leading rusher a year ago. The Spartans had their best offensive performance since the early '90s and put up the sixth-most points in school history. All of the playmakers return as do four offensive linemen, three of whom earned all-conference recognition, to anchor what could be the best all-around line in school history. It's also a unit that is used to new schemes and new faces as the Spartans are breaking in their third offensive line coach in four years.

The best of the bunch is senior **Chris Fe'easgo** (6-3, 324), a two-time first-team All-WAC selection. He is the school's first Outland Trophy candidate. He is also one of the most versatile linemen in the country. He played left tackle the last two years, but is moving to guard to replace Jeremy Dominguez, the only starter lost up front.

Fe'easgo played guard his freshman year and actually wanted to move to center so he could have played every line position. Hill declined the offer because the Spartans are set with senior **Bruno Contreras** (6-2, 306) back in the middle. Contreras, the biggest center in the WAC, is the first Spartans center in 20 years to finish his career as a three-year starter.

Senior **Jelani Hawkins** (6-4, 302) will slide into Fe'easgo's left tackle spot. Senior **Tim Provost** (6-6, 281) is a two-year starter at right tackle. Sophomore **LeMons Walker** (6-3, 280), who played sparingly last season, is the backup at both tackle spots.

Senior guard **Joel Tautuaa** (6-4, 365), a second-team All-WAC choice in 2000, is opposite Fe'easgo and is the biggest member of the all-senior line.

In addition to providing holes for Whitaker, the line needs to have the same kind of consistency as a year ago. In 2000, the Spartans allowed only 11 sacks and paved the way for 29 rushing touchdowns, the second most in school history. The unit will have to adjust some to a new scheme, but the biggest test will be the big defensive lines it will see in playing USC, Colorado, Stanford and Arizona State in the season's first month.

2000 STATISTICS

Rushing offense	189.1	26
Passing offense	228.3	40
Total offense	417.2	26
Scoring offense	31.2	30
Net Punting	36.5	25
Punt returns	7.8	86
Kickoff returns	20.1	49
Rushing defense	229.9	110
Passing efficiency defense	124.4	78
Total defense	470.5	114
Scoring defense	29.2	81
Turnover margin	+6	30

Last column is ranking among Division I-A teams.

KICKERS

Junior **Nick Gilliam** (5-8, 177) is back, but he can't have the same slow start he did a year ago. He finished strong, making 28 of his last 30 PATs and four of his last field goals, but he was only 2-of-7 from 30 yards and beyond. His 45.5 percentage (5-11) was last among WAC kickers.

If Gilliam struggles early this year, Hill may be inclined to go with redshirt freshman **Jason Shaughnessy** (6-0, 168).

DEFENSIVE LINE

In 2000, San Jose State had one of the strangest years on defense that a team can have. The Spartans finished last in the nation in total defense, giving up 475.9 yards per game. Still, the unit had 31 takeaways and scored six touchdowns on interceptions.

The bad—or possibly good—news is that the Spartans lose all but two players on the front seven. The 4-3 remains, but with a new coach and an influx of junior college signees on the defensive line, the Spartans' defense will look much different than last year's. Whether it's any better depends on how quickly the new players gel and how much confidence they gain against a brutal non-conference schedule.

End **Brandon Miles** (6-0, 252) is the only returning starter. Miles recovered two fumbles a year ago, but he made only 23 tackles. Like every spot on the defense, Miles' end spot is up for grabs.

Senior **Kevin Michaelis** (6-4, 254) was fifth on the team in tackles in 2000 and goes into the fall as the starter opposite Miles. Michaelis is the team's leading returning tackler despite bouncing between offense and defense. Last season, he was the third string tight end.

Seniors **David Coats** (6-0, 252), **David Mauga** (6-2, 238) and **Bill Mateialona** (6-3, 283) all played end last year and will get looks. This staff is going to leave no defensive line stone unturned. The unit had 25 sacks last year, but was inconsistent and left the secondary hanging most of the season.

Junior college transfers **Jason Hall** (6-4, 230) and **Chip Kimmich** (6-4, 240) will push Miles and Michaelis for starting jobs.

The two tackle spots are open after the Spartans lost Bryan Yeager and John Hammer, who combined for 99 tackles and two sacks in 2000. Junior college transfers **Rodney Anderson** (6-3, 298) and **Adonis Forest** (6-2, 305) enrolled early and are the likely starters. The three returning lettermen—**Damurius Richardson** (5-11, 269), **Larry Dawson** (6-0, 284) and **Tim Mathewson** (6-3, 251)—combined for 13 tackles last season.

A couple of more junior college transfers, Dorsey Mitchell (6-4, 327) and **Deon Washington** (6-3, 314), provide much-needed size inside.

LINEBACKERS

There is uncertainty at linebacker after San Jose lost one of its most emotional and best defensive players in school history. Josh Parry was a four-year starter at inside linebacker. He was second in the conference in tackles last year and was a second-team All-WAC selection despite playing on the worst defense in the country.

The Spartans will try to fill Parry's position with junior college transfer **Paul Okumu** (6-0, 239). Though not as tall as the 6-4 Parry, Okumu was a junior college All-American last season. The Spartans need the same leadership and production if they are going to contend for the WAC title.

Seniors **Patrick Battle** (5-11, 228) and **Brandon Lambert** (5-11, 231) and sophomore **Heath Farwell** (6-0, 217) combined for 52 tackles a year ago, but Battle was the only one who saw any significant time at linebacker. Lambert and Farwell played special teams almost exclusively. Lambert and Battle are primarily inside players, but Farwell can also play outside.

On the outside, senior **Alvin Dean** (6-0, 223) returns after a non-productive 2000 in which he made only 27 tackles from a position that should be racking up tackles and harassing quarterbacks. Opposite Dean, Ron Ockimey, who graduated, made 87 tackles and had three sacks despite weighing just more than 200 pounds.

There isn't much help behind Dean. Senior **Luke La Herran** (6-0, 234) and Dean will start, but Hill will have to use as many as seven players in the two outside spots.

Junior **Demtris Starks** (6-1, 228) made 19 tackles last year while backing up Ockimey. **Zack Rance** (5-11, 202) and sophomore **Michael Smith** (5-11, 220) combined for 16 tackles, mostly on special teams.

If freshman **Jamaal Allen** (6-2, 216) comes in and shows signs that he can fill one of the outside spots, he won't be redshirted.

DEFENSIVE BACKS

The San Jose secondary deserved a handshake after last season. The unit didn't perform very well, but it didn't get much help either. The defensive line didn't get a consistent push and the linebackers, with the exception of Josh Parry, were little help. The result was the secondary having to make plays for the defense to stop anyone. The DBs gave it their best shot, intercepting 13 passes and returning six of those for touchdowns.

This season, Hill has to hope for consistency. Last year, only departed strong safety Travis Seaton and senior cornerback **Alex Wallace** (5-10, 169) started at the same position on a regular basis. Wallace began the year as an unknown junior college transfer. He ended the season a second-team All-WAC selection after making 39 tackles and tying for the team lead with three interceptions.

He is the leader of a secondary that will have some new faces. There are three other returning lettermen at cornerback, but the spot opposite Wallace should go to junior college transfer **Shaun Fletcher** (5-10, 175). Juniors **Carlos Koustas** (5-9, 193) and **Kevin Boyer** (5-8, 161), who both have previous starting experience, played sparingly a year ago. They are the only serious threats to Wallace.

At safety, the Spartans are going to miss Seaton's 116 tackles and two interceptions. Senior **Willie Adams** (5-10, 171) returns at free safety. That's where he began last season before finishing the year starting opposite Wallace at corner. Adams had three interceptions in 2000, but Hill wants to play a more aggressive style. That means now that's he back at his natural position, Adams has to become more of a threat against the run and in rushing the passer.

However, Adams is not the primary secondary

concern. Finding someone to become the tackling machine Seaton was a year ago is a priority.

Sophomore **Melvin Cook** (5-9, 199) had one start as a redshirt freshman, but he was mainly a special teams player a year ago. Hill is taking a gamble that Cook or junior **Brian Foreman** (6-1, 202), who moved from outside linebacker, or former cornerback senior **Ricky Lavender** (6-0, 168) can fill the void.

Senior **Larry Thompson** (6-0, 188) finished the year as the starting strong safety after Adams shifted to corner. He will also battle for the strong safety spot.

PUNTERS

Senior **Michael Carr** (5-11, 188) walked on last fall and won the punting job. He may have to fight to keep it. He finished last among WAC punters with a 37.9-yard average. His strength is getting punts away and kicking them high enough that the coverage team can make plays. He didn't have a punt blocked and the Spartans allowed only 1.5 yards per return, which ranked 25th in the nation.

Sophomore **Bryce Partridge** (6-3, 185) and redshirt freshman **Matthew Witcher** (6-1, 186) will battle Carr.

SPECIAL TEAMS

Whitaker is one of the best kick returners in the country, but Hill doesn't want to get him banged up. Instead, Julien, Davis and Le Blanc will handle kick return duties. All three had at least seven attempts a year ago and only Davis didn't average at least 21 yards.

Bailey is gone after returning all but six punts a year ago. Wallace returned five punts and had a nice 16.6-yard average. He will be the full-time returner this year.

Hill won't use Whitaker on special teams, but some regulars will be on what are normally solid coverage teams. Last year, the Spartans were in the top 25 nationally in net punting, allowing only 1.5 yards per return.

RECRUITING CLASS

Hill's first recruiting class reflects San Jose's strength this season. The Spartans figure to have their best offensive line in history. And this year's bunch may be starting a tradition. Hill signed 12 linemen, seven of whom will play on offense.

"We're always going to recruit offensive and defensive linemen first because it all starts up front," Hill said. "You can have people with the ball, but if you don't protect the ball or be successful you will not be successful. Our goal is to always have a minimum 15 scholarship offensive linemen."

The best of the seven is **Kevin Meyers** (6-3, 286) of Grossmont (Calif.) College, a first-team all-state selection in the competitive California junior college scene. There aren't a lot of positions available on the San Jose line, but Meyers could squeeze in at left tackle with Chris Fe'easgo moving inside to guard.

Meyers was one of 18 junior college players San Jose signed. In addition to Meyers, tight end Ethan Allen immediately becomes a big part of the Spartans' plans. San Jose lost its top two tight ends, including Sean Brewer, a second-team All-WAC last year. Frank Jordan, another junior college player, will be part of the wide receiver rotation.

The signees most likely to start are on defense, where San Jose needed an injection of talent. Four junior college linemen will play this year. Rodney Anderson and Adonis Forrest have already shown coaches what they can do. They were two of five San Jose signees who enrolled early and went through spring practice.

With the departure of Josh Parry at linebacker, freshman Jamaal Allen and junior college transfer Paul Okumu need to make an immediate impact. Okumu was a junior college All-American who needs to be the tackling machine that Parry was a year ago.

Junior college transfer Shaun Fletcher, the brother of San Diego Chargers running back Terrell Fletcher, will be one of the starting cornerbacks.

The most intriguing signee is quarterback Orlando Evans, who signed with Oregon two years ago. He red-shirted at Eugene and played only one year of junior college ball.

BLUE RIBBON ANALYSIS

OFFENSE	A-
SPECIAL TEAMS	B-
DEFENSE	D
INTANGIBLES	C

With a first-year coach there are going to be adjustments. Hill isn't changing a whole lot, but he has never been a head coach and there will be an adjustment period. For the Spartans, it would nice if there were room—and some soft games early—for Hill and the team to get to know each other. Instead, because the school needs to play the payday games, San Jose is on the road four of the season's first six weeks. The Spartans play USC, Colorado, Arizona State and Stanford.

If there isn't a large adjustment period, San Jose can play with all of those teams, especially Stanford, which has lost three straight to the Spartans. To contend in the WAC, the Spartans need to be in good position before November. San Jose plays three games that month, all on the road.

The large offensive line will allow San Jose to move the ball as long as Whitaker stays healthy and the outside receivers can provide some big plays so that defenses can't pack the line of scrimmage to stop Whitaker.

The defense needs to erase a very odd 2000 and just get better. The Spartans ranked 114th in the nation in total defense, but has seven interception returns for touchdowns. San Jose settled down in WAC play, but the Spartans had more plays ran against them than any other WAC team and they gave up almost 6.0 yards per play.

The firepower is there to score with any team in the country. If the defense can provide some sort of improvement and the adjustment period doesn't last long, San Jose can surprise any of its non-conference opponents. If Whitaker stays healthy all season, the season-ender at Fresno State Nov. 24 could be for the WAC title.

(C.M.)

2000 RESULTS

Nebraska	L	13-49	0-1
Stanford	W	40-27	1-1
Southern Utah	W	47-7	2-1
USC	L	24-34	2-2
Rice	W	29-16	3-2
SMU	W	35-10	4-2
UTEP	L	30-47	4-3
Nevada	W	49-30	5-3
Hawaii	W	57-48	6-3
TCU	W	27-24	7-3
Tulsa	L	17-28	7-4
Fresno State	L	6-37	7-5

Southern Methodist

LOCATION	Dallas, TX
CONFERENCE	Western Athletic
LAST SEASON	3-9 (.222)
CONFERENCE RECORD	2-6 (t-6th)
OFFENSIVE STARTERS RETURNING	8
DEFENSIVE STARTERS RETURNING	10
NICKNAME	Mustangs
COLORS	Red & Blue
HOME FIELD	Gerald J. Ford Stadium (32,000)
HEAD COACH	Mike Cavan (Georgia '72)
RECORD AT SCHOOL	18-27 (4 years)
CAREER RECORD	85-76-2 (15 years)
ASSISTANTS	Eric Schumann (Alabama '77) Assistant Head Coach/Defensive Coordinator Larry Kueck (Stephen F. Austin '75) Offensive Coordinator/Quarterbacks Daniel Baker (UTEP '96) Offensive Line/Tight Ends Warren Belin (Wake Forest '90) Linebackers Oscar Giles (Texas '91) Defensive Line Pat Henderson (Kansas '75) Defensive Backs Johnny Ringo (Texas '84) Wide Receivers/Recruiting Coordinator Randy Williams (Valdosta State '91) Running Backs
TEAM WINS (last 5 yrs.)	5-6-5-4-3
FINAL RANK (last 5 yrs.)	82-78-82-96-102
2000 FINISH	Lost to TCU in regular-season finale.

COACH AND PROGRAM

The way things are set up in college football's current landscape, a program has to make a choice. It must decide whether it is going to compete on a big-time level.

If the choice is to compete with the big boys, a commitment has to come along with that choice. There has to be a financial commitment. There has to be an administrative commitment. There has to be an academic commitment.

The school has to have all of its cylinders firing as one unit or the gap that the competition will put between you and them is one that is almost too big to overcome.

SMU is seeing how big that gap has become. SMU is a Division I-A football freeloader and has been since the return of football from the death penalty in 1989. The Mustangs don't compete on the field (3-9 in 2000 and only one winning season since 1986). They don't compete on the same level as other schools for talent. They don't compete financially for coaches. The school is the dregs of Division I-A. SMU is at the point where it has to make a choice.

The gap between SMU and the schools that are trying to step up to the big leagues is enormous. Metroplex rival TCU offered former coach Dennis Franchione, now at Alabama, a deal worth more than $1 million per season to stay in Fort Worth. He left, but the school made the offer. SMU coach Mike Cavan earns less than a quarter of that amount.

Of course, Franchione's teams did more. The Frogs won two straight bowl games and made three straight bowl trips. The Frogs are where SMU wants to be. The difference is that TCU made the commitment in all areas a long time ago, a commitment that is required to step up as a player in Division I athletics.

SMU is not a player. Its overbearing academic restrictions hamstring coaches. The Ponies want to compete in the big time but make their coaches recruit as if SMU were an Ivy League school. SMU football gets no exceptions to its regular admissions policy, meaning the talent pool is considerably cut before coaches even begin recruiting. Not even Duke, Vanderbilt, Tulane, Georgia Tech or Northwestern, schools that far exceed SMU academically, have such restrictive policies.

The policies, and the lack of money committed to the program for proper marketing, promotion and personnel, have combined to put SMU in a position where it has to make a decision.

Is it time to step up to the plate or is it time to back down?

Cavan is caught in the middle. His teams haven't performed well and his September starts have become an enigma. This season is a hinge year for the Mustangs. They need to show some sort of improvement or the program, once again, will have to start from scratch.

2001 SCHEDULE

Sept.	1	@Louisiana Tech
	8	TCU
	15	@North Carolina
	22	North Carolina State
Oct.	6	Hawaii
	13	@San Jose State
	27	UTEP
Nov.	3	@Nevada
	10	Fresno State
	17	@Tulsa
	24	Rice

QUARTERBACKS

Ever since Cavan has been at SMU, he hasn't found the kind of quarterback to fit his system. The Mustangs need a steady, accurate passer who doesn't lose games. He doesn't need to make big plays or even be an all-conference type. He just needs to be steady. And he needs to be given a chance to make mistakes and stay in games.

For the fourth straight year, Cavan toyed with his quarterbacks and the result, for the fourth straight year, wasn't a success. Cavan pulled Josh McCown before the Hawaii game and McCown never recovered and eventually transferred after the fall semester.

This season, Cavan has decided to hand the controls to sophomore **Kelan Luker** (6-1, 209), who redshirted last season after playing in five games as a freshman. Luker has the chance to be the quarterback Cavan has so desperately wanted. He is an intelligent, strong-armed quarterback who came from a high school system that threw the ball and gave the quarterback a lot of responsibility.

Cavan believes Luker has matured to the point where he won't try to force throws or make things happen that aren't developing in the natural flow.

"That year sitting out was really good for him," Cavan said. "He understands what you've got to do as far as preparation. He knows that there is more to it than just going out there on Saturday afternoon."

Luker's biggest positive is his quick release and knowledge of the passing game. His tendency to force passes is what Cavan hopes the redshirt season erased.

Even if Luker doesn't stumble, he will have junior **David Page** (6-1, 180) breathing down his neck. Page started three games a year ago and went 1-2. Page is steady, but he doesn't have the physical talents Luker does.

Page, a junior college transfer last year, spent a redshirt year at California before playing a season at Hinds (Miss.) Junior College and then at SMU last year. Cavan has seen Page work with this set of receivers. That could make it easy to have an itchy trigger finger with Luker. If Cavan has learned from the last few years, that finger will stay in his pocket.

There are no real threats behind Luker and Page. The Mustangs signed two freshmen quarterbacks, but **Richard Bartel** (6-4, 190) and **Ashton Nixon** (6-2, 201) will probably be redshirted.

RUNNING BACKS

Cavan was a quarterback at Georgia, but he is steeped in the running game. He believes the offense should be built around a strong running game and then let the rest of the parts fit in somehow. Cavan desperately wants SMU to move away from the en vogue passing attacks and become a grinding team that uses the pass to set up the run.

With the kind of athletes SMU recruits, that may be hard to do. Mammoth offensive linemen who can run and pass block are at a premium. And with the academic restrictions SMU has in place, Cavan has repeatedly said that getting players on both lines has always been his biggest challenge. Still, Cavan and offensive coordinator Larry Kueck will try to run the ball. They do it out of a one-back set, but the Mustangs still want to be a run first team.

Junior **Kris Briggs** (5-11, 224) is the horse for the third straight season. He is a hard runner who is best used between the tackles. He doesn't have the speed to get outside, but given a brief hole in the middle he can get yards. Last season, he was third in the WAC in rushing last season, but had the worst average of anyone in the top 10. Briggs has been hampered by injuries, and SMU has to have him healthy to give young receivers and a rusty quarterback a chance to establish consistency.

Because Briggs, who is a solid receiver, had trouble getting outside last season, Cavan had to play speedy sophomore **Keylon Kincade** (5-11, 200) before he was ready. Kincade made the jump from one of the smallest classifications in Texas high schools to Division I-A. He played in all 11 games, but gained just 58 yards in 17 attempts. The Mustangs also used the now-departed Jason Pipkens and junior **Johnnie Freeman** (5-11, 191), who moved to receiver but is better suited for tailback.

This season, Briggs will again be expected to carry the load. He needs to have a big year to take pressure off the receivers and to give Luker a chance to establish himself. Kincade and Freeman are going to get carries because of Briggs' inability to get outside. Injuries with Briggs have been a factor the last two years, and he was kept out of spring practice. If he doesn't stay healthy, the Mustangs won't have much of an inside attack.

Redshirt freshman **Derron Brown** (5-10, 202) and freshman **ShanDerrick Charles** (5-9, 180), who had almost 4,000 yards in his prep career, will also get carries.

WIDE RECEIVERS/TIGHT ENDS

SMU utilizes positions normally not featured in one-back offenses. The Mustangs like to run the ball, but their best offensive player is junior tight end **John Hampton** (6-2, 245). A year ago, Hampton caught a team-high 46 passes. This season, he's one of the nation's top receiving tight ends. This after not making a catch as a freshman.

Hampton was never spectacular, but he gave the Mustangs the kind of steady production that no one else did. He caught six passes three times and also had four touchdown catches. He isn't the best blocker, but his receiving skills make him indispensable.

When SMU needs a blocking tight end, it turns to senior **Michael Brown** (6-1, 260), who has starting experience and is one of the top academic performers the SMU athletic program has.

If Luker can shake off the rust and Hampton continues his improvement, Luker will have fast, big-play targets on the outside and familiar targets on the inside of the Mustangs' four-wideout look.

Junior **Chris Cunningham** (5-8, 186), also one of the WAC's best kick and punt returners, is SMU's most steady receiver. He has 84 catches in his first two seasons and is healthy after playing last season with a knee injury. He had surgery on the knee after the season and missed spring practice. He shouldn't show any effects.

Cunningham is one of the team's hardest workers and one of its vocal leaders. He probably shouldn't have played last season with the knee injury. The fact he did not only impressed coaches but also showed a lot of his teammates the kind of commitment he expects from them.

Junior Johnnie Freeman is one of the Mustangs' big-play receivers. Last season, he had seven touchdown receptions that averaged 33.0 yards. None was shorter than 19 yards. He is one of the WAC's best deep threats, but he often has trouble holding on to the ball.

Junior **Billy Ford** (6-3, 213), a converted tight end who caught the first touchdown pass in Ford Stadium history, and Luker's high school teammate, junior **Cody Cardwell** (5-10, 177), are the sure-handed, possession receivers on the inside.

Cardwell needs to have a better year. In 2000, his production feel off after a nice freshman season. Cardwell is Luker's security blanket and vice versa. They two have played together since junior high and they set national records together in high school.

Freshmen **Jay Taylor** (6-3, 180) and **Trey Griffin** (5-10, 175) will get a chance early. Taylor was one of the top receivers in Texas last season and Griffin was the best sprinter in Texas' second-largest classification.

OFFENSIVE LINE

SMU has three offensive line starters back, but that doesn't mean a whole lot. Cavan said during the spring, and has continued to stand beside it, that he is going to put his best five offensive linemen on the field regardless of who they may be. The reason is because the Mustangs just need people who can move defensive linemen.

In a six-game losing streak last year, SMU's biggest problem was magnified. The Mustangs don't have enough size on the offensive line to give their backs running room or their quarterback enough time to make good decisions.

In 2000, SMU was last in the WAC in scoring offense (108th in the nation) and tied for last with pass-happy Nevada for the fewest rushing touchdowns. Mustang quarterbacks were often on the run, forcing passes and causing the Ponies to also finish last in the league in turnover margin, a category normally strong under Cavan.

This season, experience up front and a healthy backfield should make those numbers improve somewhat. Senior left tackle **Joey Slaten** (6-6, 309), senior left guard **James McCarthy** (6-3, 294) and junior right guard **Thornton Chandler** (6-2, 277) are returning starters.

Slaten and McCarthy are both solid and experienced, but have trouble with the small, quick defensive end that the WAC offers up. Chandler battled injuries a year ago, but is SMU's best offensive lineman.

The concerns are at center and left guard, where there is little experience. Sophomore **Steve Reindl** (6-3, 274) is the likely starter at center, but redshirt freshman **Eric Neal** (6-3, 279) will push him. This is a position that could require one of the more talented backups to quickly make a transition, especially if Reindl or Neal have trouble picking up defenses and making the calls up front.

At right tackle, redshirt freshman **Townsend Hargis** (6-4, 254) comes in with high praise from coaches. His size is a concern, but he has the quickness to keep up with fast defensive ends.

If Hargis has trouble, senior **Kevin Gober** (6-5, 285), who has starting experience at right guard, could slide over.

Senior **Cory Fross** (6-4, 290), sophomore **Sterling Harris** (6-6, 295), who is more comfortable at guard, or junior **Judson Davis** (6-5, 276) give SMU decent depth, but none are very experienced. Depending on how they make the transition to other positions, if asked, will determine how much they play.

2000 STATISTICS

Rushing offense	115.8	86
Passing offense	209.2	64
Total offense	325.0	85
Scoring offense	15.1	108
Net Punting	32.6	86
Punt returns	9.7	52
Kickoff returns	19.4	66
Rushing defense	138.0	45
Passing efficiency defense	135.5	100
Total defense	379.1	72
Scoring defense	29.3	83
Turnover margin	-13	103

Last column is ranking among Division I-A teams.

KICKERS

Senior **Jacob Crowley** (5-11, 191) was inconsistent all season in 2000, but he improved as the year went along and as the Mustangs figured out his true range. Crowley was 8-11 from 39 yards in, but only 2-10 from 40 and beyond.

The job is Crowley's, but SMU signed **Russ Davis** (6-3, 180) and **Chris McMurtray** (6-0, 170) and aren't expecting the two freshmen to redshirt unless Crowley significantly impresses early in the season.

McMurtray, also a standout soccer player, made all of his extra-point attempts and connected on a 55-yard field goal as a senior.

Davis, the likely punter, was 9-of-10 on field goals as a senior, including a 52-yarder.

DEFENSIVE LINE

The Mustangs return 10 starters on defense, the only loss coming on the defensive line with tackle Chase Schavrda's departure. SMU still has depth up front, but it's not necessarily quality depth. The Ponies have several players who have played the position, but so far they haven't been able to provide the push up front or be the stoppers in the running game SMU has needed to take pressure off a young secondary.

Last season, with three freshmen in the defensive backfield, SMU got pushed around up front and never was able to sustain an effective pass rush. The problems led to defensive coordinator Eric Schumann's unit, normally a bright spot, having to take more chances and bringing linebackers to get a pass rush. The aggression produced some sacks, but it also led to the secondary having to play more one on one than necessary and making more tackles in the running game.

SMU operates from a 4-3 with speedy defensive ends. Seniors **Kevin Aldridge** (6-1, 271) **Markus Pratt** (6-0, 250) and **Johnson Patman** (6-2, 240) combined for 58 tackles and 10 of SMU's 23 sacks a year ago. All three have starting experience. Patman and Pratt will split on the left side while Aldridge, a former linebacker, is on the right side. Aldridge is the best pass rusher, but he needs to be more consistent.

The problem up front comes in the middle, where junior **Warrie Birdwell** (6-4, 272) normally gets pushed around by bigger guards. Junior **Lute Croy** (6-2, 309) and senior **Chris Post** (6-3, 270) also have starting experience at tackle. Croy is the only one of the three with true tackle size. Birdwell, Croy and Post, along with sophomore **John David Blagg** (6-1, 281), provide a nice rotation, but none are stoppers against the run.

Help could arrive in the fall in freshmen **Marcus Dineen** (6-4, 230) and **Marcus Walker** (6-3, 278). Both were heralded recruits who raised eyebrows by signing with SMU. Walker, who runs a 4.9 40-yard dash, will get time in the tackle rotation and could, because of his speed, push Birdwell and Croy.

Dineen comes from the highly successful Bolles School in Jacksonville, Fla. He is the kind of fast, intelligent defensive end the Mustangs need.

LINEBACKERS

For all the problems SMU has up front, the Mustangs can thump their chests when talking about their linebacker corps. Junior middle linebacker **Vic Viloria** (5-10, 237) has started since he was a freshman. He has been the permanent captain since he was a sophomore. He is the heart and soul of the team.

Viloria led the WAC in tackles last year with 130. He had 76 solo tackles and 10 tackles for loss. He had at least 13 tackles four times and 10 or more eight times, including 16 against Fresno State. It's hard to see how he could be even more productive, but he may have to be, especially in helping provide a pass rush.

If Viloria is going to become more involved in rushing the quarterback, outside linebackers **Jarrian James** (6-0, 205), a sophomore, and junior **B.J. Williams** (6-2, 200) are going to have to be better against the run. Both cover backs and receivers well in the flat, but their size hurts against bigger tight ends and pulling linemen. Both are quick but neither are strong enough to fight off blocks from considerably bigger players. Williams still needs to be watched carefully after missing the first eight games a year ago with a broken leg.

This is SMU's deepest position, with five players returning who have starting experience. Just as it is up front, the problem is size. Junior **Khalid Beard** (6-1, 215) and sophomore **Brian Bischoff** (6-0, 214) are solid against the pass, but have to be taken out in running situations. Senior **Corey Riley** (6-0, 234) has good size and has started, but he is woefully inconsistent.

The player to watch is junior **Devonric Johnson** (5-11, 220), a hard-hitting middle linebacker who backs up Viloria and has been making plays on special teams since he was a freshman.

Redshirt freshmen **D.D. Lee** (6-1, 238) and **Derek Swofford** (6-4, 220) will both be in the linebacker rotation and be expected to contribute on special teams. Their size has coaches believing that both could earn significant playing time quickly.

DEFENSIVE BACKS

The first people to get handshakes from Cavan after games a year ago were players in a secondary that got the ultimate baptism by fire. The Mustangs opened the season with a sophomore and three freshmen in the secondary, and they paid for it. With little help coming up front, teams picked the Ponies apart.

As expected with young players, there was often confusion on coverages, which left experienced receivers and quarterbacks having field days. The result was SMU finishing last in the league and 100th in the nation in pass defense efficiency. The Mustangs were the only WAC team that didn't intercept at least 10 passes.

The good news is that the defensive line and linebackers are a year more experienced, and so are the players who were so rudely introduced to college football's realities in 2000.

Junior **Kevin Garrett** (5-10, 196) is the leader of a unit that has no seniors, but five players who started at least one game last year, including four who started as freshmen.

Garrett, a starter since he was a freshman, is one of the fastest defensive backs in the conference. Also on the track team, Garrett is the one SMU player quarterbacks will stay away from. Few receivers can outrun him and his size makes him one of the better cover corners.

Sophomore **Jonas Rutledge** (5-10, 174) starts opposite Garrett. Rutledge started 11 games last year and finished with 50 tackles. He took the brunt of the punishment and often got lost on coverages and allowed receivers to run free in the middle of the field.

Sophomore **Ruben Moodley** (6-0, 186) started four games at free safety as a true freshman. He intercepted two passes against Nevada and is expected to be the playmaker in the backfield now that he completely understands the system. His backup, sophomore **Matt Rushbrook** (5-10, 175) began the year as the starting free safety. He still may start some, but the hard-hitter needs to get better in coverage.

Sophomore **Leroy Price** (6-1, 205) has the most size of anyone in the secondary. He is as big as some of SMU's linebackers and is expected to play a rover-like position where he contributes against the run and pass.

Junior **Brent Briggs** (5-9, 173) is in the cornerback rotation after seeing considerable time a year ago.

The only newcomers who will play are redshirt freshmen **Rico Harris** (6-2, 212) at strong safety and **Wesley Medlock** (6-1, 170) at corner behind Garrett.

PUNTERS

The Mustangs are in search of a punter after Colin Vadheim graduated. SMU needs more consistency from its punter. Vadheim, who had standout sophomore and junior years, struggled as a senior.

Senior **Adam Walterscheid** (5-11, 191), who normally handles kickoffs, punted some in the spring, but the job belongs to Davis, a first-team all-state pick in Texas' highest classification. He averaged almost 42 yards a kick as a senior.

SPECIAL TEAMS

In the season-opening win over Kansas last year, special teams set the tone. The Mustangs forced three errors in the kicking game and took advantage of all three. After that game, there were few signs of life on special teams.

SMU doesn't have the depth some teams do.

As a result, starters play on special teams. That means the best athletes are on the field, but it also means that some of those players are worn out late in games.

The Mustangs make plays in the return game, but they also give them up.

Freeman finished second in the league and in the top 30 nationally with a 23.6 yards kickoff-return average. Cunningham was one of the top punt returners in the WAC as a freshman. He struggled last season (9.5-yards-per-return average) mostly because of injuries.

The concern for SMU is finding ways to stop people. The Ponies had the second-worst net punting average in the league and gave up too many big plays on kickoff returns.

RECRUITING CLASS

Because of its academic reputation, SMU will always pull in players from several states. Though 15 of the 20 signees are from Texas, the two that can most immediately help, defensive tackle Walker and defensive end Dineen, are from out of state.

Defensive back **Matt Terry** (5-10, 190) is also a Bolles School grad.

There is speed with receivers Griffin and Vinson. And fellow receiver Taylor was one of the best at his position in Texas in 2000. Davis is the starting punter while McMurtray will get a chance to take over the kicking duties.

There are no stars, but SMU did get a taste of what it feels like to recruit under some different circumstances.

The administration removed a policy that required players to be officially admitted to school before being allowed an official visit. That helps expand the talent pool that can be brought to campus, but does little for coaches until the university allows the program to admit a certain number of exceptions to the school's highly selective admissions policy.

BLUE RIBBON ANALYSIS

OFFENSE	C-
SPECIAL TEAMS	C-
DEFENSE	C
INTANGIBLES	C-

Cavan knows the spotlight is on him this season. The fifth-year SMU coach knows he needs a team as slick as his year-old Gerald J. Ford Stadium. He knows he needs to reverse a trend that has seen the Mustangs lose one more game than the previous season in each of Cavan's four years on the Hilltop. He knows he needs some breaks at quarterback and on the injury front.

If flipping a switch and making it happen was that easy, Cavan would have done it a long time ago. But things normally don't change that quickly, or easily, at SMU. Though a lot of the Mustangs' misfortunes in 2000 fall directly on him, Cavan operates a program under some of the most restrictive and selective recruiting rules in the country. Late last year, the administration lightened the restrictions that were put in place after the school received the NCAA's "Death Penalty" 14 years ago. But Cavan and staff still don't operate from a budget or talent pool standpoint anywhere close to the schools they recruit against.

The process makes Mustangs coaches be more selective and cross their fingers on more recruits than they would like. The on-field results are a reflection of the antiquated policy.

After an inspiring—and sweltering—win over Kansas to open the on-campus Ford Stadium, the Mustangs lost six in a row and Cavan was up to his old tricks. Four of those losses came in September, making the Ponies 2-14 in that month during Cavan's tenure. That record could get worse this season with the Mustangs playing TCU, North Carolina and North Carolina State in the first four weeks.

(C.M.)

2000 RESULTS

Kansas	W	31-17	1-0
UTEP	L	20-37	1-1
North Carolina State	L	0-41	1-2
Tulane	L	17-29	1-3
Houston	L	15-17	1-4
San Jose State	L	10-35	1-5
Hawaii	L	15-30	1-6
Nevada	W	21-7	2-6
Rice	L	14-43	3-6
Tulsa	W	24-20	4-6
Fresno State	L	7-14	4-7
TCU	L	7-62	4-8

Tulsa

LOCATION Tulsa, OK
CONFERENCE Western Athletic
LAST SEASON 5 7 (.417)
CONFERENCE RECORD 4-4 (5th)
OFFENSIVE STARTERS RETURNING 7
DEFENSIVE STARTERS RETURNING 8
NICKNAME Golden Hurricane
COLORS Old Gold, Royal Blue & Crimson
HOME FIELD Skelly Stadium (40,385)
HEAD COACH Keith Burns (Arkansas '84)
RECORD AT SCHOOL 5-7 (1 year)
CAREER RECORD 5-7 (1 year)
ASSISTANTS
Jeff McInerney (Slippery Rock '82)
Assistant Head Coach/Defensive Coordinator/Defensive Line
Jim Gilstrap (Western Michigan '64)
Offensive Coordinator/Running Backs
Dennis Allen (Texas A&M '95)
Secondary
Brock Berryhill (Boise State '96)
Bandits And Rovers/Recruiting Coordinator
Dan Bitson (Tulsa '91)
Receivers
Kenny Edenfield (Troy State '88)
Tight Ends
Mark Hutson (Oklahoma '90)
Offensive Line
Barry Lunney, Jr. (Arkansas '96)
Quarterbacks
Sam Lawanson (San Diego State '98)
Linebackers
TEAM WINS (last 5 yrs.) 4-2-4-2-5
FINAL RANK (last 5 yrs.) 96-94-88-103-95
2000 FINISH Beat Nevada in regular-season finale.

COACH AND PROGRAM

Keith Burns' task was made clear when he took over the Tulsa program last year. He needed to build a program, but he also needed to win immediately if the Golden Hurricane was going to have a chance of maintaining success as a Division I-A athletic program.

Though Tulsa has more than pulled its weight in basketball, the Golden Hurricane has experienced little success in football the last 10 years, making the school look like one of the classic Division I-A hangers-on. Last year wasn't a breakthrough year, but it did breath some life into a program that has been desperately looking for any kind of hope.

Tulsa still finished below .500, but the strides Burns made and 17 returning starters have Golden Hurricane fans as excited as ever about football.

Despite winning only five games in 2000, the team finished with Tulsa's best record since the 1991 Freedom Bowl season. The Golden Hurricane won two WAC road games for the first time ever and finished the season with two wins for the first time in nine years. And Burns and company did it with a young team that needed 17 freshmen to play a lot.

Tulsa is still young (only four senior starters), but Burns believes this is the year the Golden Hurricane can make a breakthrough. The schedule forces the young team to be mentally prepared for a grueling September. After opening against Indiana State, Tulsa goes to defending national champion Oklahoma and then has WAC favorites Fresno State and UTEP in consecutive weeks. If the Golden Hurricane can win one of those conference games, it will show Burns' team it can compete in a balanced WAC.

The most important part of that stretch is keeping junior quarterback **Josh Blankenship** under control. He has nice talent, but it has to be saddled. If rattled, Blankenship gets wild. Making sure he doesn't do that is quarterbacks coach Barry Lunney, Jr., who has guided Blankenship since he was a freshman starter. Lunney is one example of a coaching staff that is young and has been given a lot of responsibility.

Burns, only 40, has experienced coordinators, but his position coaches and recruiting coordinator are young. Four of Tulsa's nine assistants were in college five years ago. That includes Lunney, who knew how to deal with a tough schedule. He was the quarterback at Arkansas in the SEC and was on the Razorbacks' staff when Burns was the defensive coordinator.

Burns is the kind of coach who lets his assistants do their jobs. He has veteran offensive coordinator Jim Gilstrap handle almost everything on offense so he can be intimately involved with the defense, where his strength and experience lies.

This season could be a breakout one for Tulsa and Burns. He showed last year he could keep the ship righted during tough times when the Golden Hurricane responded by winning its last two games after dropping five straight.

2001 SCHEDULE

Aug.	30	Indiana State
Sept.	15	@Oklahoma
	22	Fresno State
	29	@UTEP
Oct.	6	New Mexico State
	13	@Boise State
	20	Hawaii
	27	@San Jose State
Nov.	3	Louisiana Tech
	10	@Rice
	17	SMU

QUARTERBACKS

Though Tulsa didn't have a hard time scoring points a year ago (20.0 per game, 90th in the country), the Golden Hurricane will be even more explosive now that the offensive line has some stability and Blankenship (6-3, 205) continues to mature.

Blankenship has started since he was a freshman. He was voted the WAC's freshman of the year, but interception problems plagued him. As Blankenship started to throw the ball more last season, he became more comfortable and selective. He began pulling the ball and running rather than forcing passes into coverage like he did as a freshman.

Blankenship's 2,507 yards were the fourth most in school history. He threw for more than 300 yards twice (New Mexico State and Oklahoma State) and is 77 yards short of 4,000 career yards. In his 17 career starts, he has thrown for 200 yards or more nine times and a 212.7-yard average.

The concern has always been that he gets rattled under pressure and forces passes. Lunney has played a large role in Blankenship settling down. Lunney was forced into pressure-packed situations every week when he was the quarterback at Arkansas. Under Lunney, Blankenship's decision-making has improved. As it has, offensive coordinator Jim Gilstrap has grown more confident in Blankenship and allowed the offense to become more wide open.

With several receivers returning, Tulsa expects Blankenship, whose younger brother Caleb is a freshman wide receiver, to be sharp and put up big numbers this season. The running game could struggle with chemistry early, which means Blankenship will have to carry the offense through a tough, early season schedule.

Tulsa needs Blankenship to stay healthy because none of its backups has ever taken a college snap. Redshirt freshman **James Kilian** (6-3, 205) put up massive numbers in high school, but he did so playing eight-man football. He played on the scout team a year ago but has yet to feel what it's like playing the 11-man game on this level.

Redshirt freshman **Zac Lassiter** (6-2, 215) saw time during the spring, but will probably be replaced on the depth chart when freshman **Tyler Gooch** (5-11, 175) arrives.

Gooch was an all-state selection last year and is from the same high school (Tulsa Union) that produced Blankenship.

RUNNING BACKS

In Tulsa' one-back offense, the tailback has to be a receiver who doesn't mind blocking or getting hit. The position gets carries, but they are in short yardage and used to set up the passing game.

A year ago, the running game produced in short yardage, but it didn't give the offense much of a boost. Tulsa finished with a 2.9-yard per carry average, second worst in the conference. That led to defenses being able to use only its down linemen to stop the run and allowing its linebackers and defensive backs to sit back and wait for the pass. Tulsa also struggled with injuries with almost every player who had significant carries being banged up at some point.

The Golden Hurricane ultimately found the right mix, but it was too late for last season. Senior **Ken Bohanon** (6-1, 241), the only upperclassmen is Tulsa's rotation, is a good short yardage back. He was Tulsa's leading rusher a year ago with 802 yards on 202 carries. He scored 10 of the Golden Hurricane's 18 rushing touchdowns. He had more than 100 yards three times, including a career-high 178 against Louisiana Tech. Bohanon is the best blocker of the running backs, meaning he is the most valuable. He is durable, but almost 17 carries a game is too many.

Some of that load needs to fall on sophomore **Eric Richardson** (5-9, 170), who ran for 400 yards in the last two games and became the first Tulsa back since 1952 to go over 190 yards in consecutive games. Before those last two games, Richardson had only eight yards on the year. Against Nevada, he had 206 yards on 35 carries, the 11th-best rushing performance in school history.

The running game can be effective as long as Richardson continues getting outside to get the majority of his yards. He isn't big enough or durable enough to run between the tackles. That is Bohanon's territory, as long as he doesn't have to carry as much as he did last year.

Sophomore **D.J. Barnett** (5-11, 211) is the one back who can block and get yards both outside and inside. However, Barnett hasn't played in more than a year, having sat out last season to concentrate on academics.

Sophomore **Donte Hart** (5-11, 192) was Tulsa's third-leading rusher as a freshman. He scored three times in 11 games, but had only a 2.2-yard average on 78 carries. Redshirt freshman Roswell Kinnard (5-9, 197) will also get carries.

WIDE RECEIVERS/TIGHT ENDS

The key to Tulsa having offensive success is establishing a running game and having Blankenship stay calm the whole year. The way the Golden Hurricane likes to throw the ball, Blankenship is going to make his share of mistakes. A receiver corps that has a superstar but little experience beyond him needs to mature quickly to make sure mistakes are kept to a minimum.

Statistically, senior **Donald Shoals** (5-10, 175), who was a first-team All-WAC selection in 2000, is one of the nation's best returning receivers. He was fourth in the nation in receiving yards (1,195), 10th in yards per game (99.6) and 11th in receptions per game (6.7). If all that wasn't enough, he also finished 10th in the nation in punt return average (15.6).

Shoals isn't exceptionally strong or fast, but he has great hands and runs nice routes. His 11-catch, 271-yard performance—the third-best school and WAC yardage total in history—against New Mexico State a season ago shows he can be explosive. But he normally makes the 10-15 yard catches that take the offense out of precarious positions.

Because Shoals doesn't go deep much, safeties have a hard time double teaming him. He may be asked to run even more underneath routes because sophomore **Darrell Wimberly** (6-0, 195) and junior **Brandon Birks** (5-10, 170) are the only other returning receivers who had a reception last season.

The most experienced receiver besides Shoals is tight end **Jarod Roach** (6-3, 216), who caught 22 passes a year ago. Roach needs to have a big season making catches over the middle so Shoals doesn't have to venture inside. Roach isn't a blocking tight end.

Redshirt freshman **Josh Reed** (6-5, 240) is the only one of four tight ends who may see action who has the prototype tight end size. Roach plays more like a big receiver, though he doesn't have receiver speed.

Burns believes Wimberly has the best chance to play an increased role this season. He will play opposite Shoals be the receiver in coming years expected to put up the same kind of numbers Shoals is right now. Wimberly caught 10 passes a year ago for 148 yards. Birks had only seven catches a year ago. He will be the slot receiver inside Shoals.

Tulsa will be relying on four redshirt freshmen to provide wide receiver depth. **Montiese Culton** (6-0, 170) will play behind Wimberly and could push him for the outside spot opposite Shoals. **Michael Bartel** (6-0, 184) will also get snaps at the position.

Edmond Freeman (6-4, 190), Shoals' backup, has good size and speed. He may have to slide inside to get catches this year. **Cole McNair** (6-5, 200) has the best size of any of the receivers. He is another who needs to make plays inside to keep linebackers and safeties from taking shots at the smaller receivers.

OFFENSIVE LINE

The reason Blankenship was wild his first two seasons was because he was under heavy pressure. He knew little but taking the snap, running outside and firing a pass before he was drilled. Last year, the Golden Hurricane gave up 38 sacks, second worst in the conference. Blankenship was hurried once again and the line didn't exactly pave the way for a successful running game, which averaged less than 3.0 yards per carry.

This season the offensive line is still young, but it does have some experience. How much more seasoned it is will be the difference in the Golden Hurricane contending in the balanced WAC or being just another team.

Tulsa returns three starters, but both guard positions need to be filled. Senior left tackle **Kevin Shaffer** (6-5, 290) is the leader and the only senior among the Golden Hurricane's top 11 lineman. He will be counted on to take control of a young offensive line that needs to keep teams off Blankenship in order for the one-back offense to be successful. Shaffer has started the last 23 games at left tackle and is as much a security blanket for Blankenship as Shoals.

Junior **Anthony Taylor** (6-1, 272), a former walk-on, stated the last 10 games at center a year ago. The other returning starter is junior right tackle **Jake Stoetzner** (6-6, 306), who will have to fight off challenges and a possible position change to keep his starting spot.

Sophomore **Austin Chadwick** (6-3, 270) was impressive in the spring and coaches like his athleticism and pass blocking ability more than that of Stoetzner, who is more of a run blocker. Chadwick doesn't have the size to be a dominant right tackle, but he does have the quickness needed to combat the speedy defensive ends in the WAC.

If Chadwick does develop at right tackle, Stoetzner could be moved inside to one of the open guard spots. Sophomore **Matt Black** (6-2, 304) will get the first shot at right guard, but Stoetzner could slide in if Black doesn't perform well against an early schedule that is going to test the young line.

At the other guard spot, sophomore **Tony Katic** (6-4, 308) is the only one with any experience. Redshirt freshman **Dustin Traynor** (6-5, 375) is the biggest Tulsa linemen, but hasn't played a snap. Sophomore **Earl Ireson** (6-4, 308) is another possibility, but he has been limited to scout team duty in his two seasons.

With Oklahoma, Fresno State and UTEP in consecutive weeks in September, the Golden Hurricane offensive line has to develop quickly. The Oklahoma and UTEP games are on the road and the Fresno State game, with all-American candidate Alan Harper at defensive tackle, will immediately give the young guards a welcome to big time college football.

2000 STATISTICS

Rushing offense	112.2	89
Passing offense	225.5	43
Total offense	337.8	79
Scoring offense	20.0	90
Net Punting	34.4	62
Punt returns	15.3	11
Kickoff returns	17.7	96
Rushing defense	209.8	103
Passing efficiency defense	128.5	91

Total defense	385.8	75
Scoring defense	23.6	49
Turnover margin	+0	59

Last column is ranking among Division I-A teams.

KICKERS

Senior **Chris Earnest** (6-2, 209) tied for the team lead in scoring in 2000. He finished third in the league in field goals per game and is the leading returning kicker in the WAC. He made 80 percent of his kicks inside 40 yards and was 4-7 beyond. He began last year with 10 consecutive successful attempts and twice had three field goals in a game.

Junior **Ricky Tallant** (5-10, 182) and redshirt freshman **Drew Rodgers** (6-0, 224) are the only other kickers on the roster. Neither will play unless Earnest is hurt. Rodgers will probably take over next season after Earnest graduates.

DEFENSIVE LINE

Tulsa's focus is on the offense because the defense could, again, be a problem. Three linemen return, but linebacker Ashon Farley, who averaged almost 10 tackles per game, is gone. Farley's departure, combined with a lack of size up front, will put even more pressure on a secondary that returns intact, but had its share of problems in 2000. A lot of those problems were a result of the defensive line not providing any help. Tulsa tied for last in the WAC in sacks with only 12 in 12 games.

Junior nose guard **Sam Rayburn** (6-3, 290) is the only player with size in the defensive line rotation that returns no one over 260 pounds. That could make for another long season for a run defense that was 103rd in the nation in 2000.

Ends **Drew McLaughlin** (6-3, 225) and **Brad Hawkins** (6-3, 230), the other returning starters, are quick, but they are small and could get pushed around by bigger tackles. Last year, McLaughlin, a senior, was third on the team with 62 tackles. Hawkins, a junior, finished with 53 tackles but didn't move from linebacker to end until late in the year.

The lack of size forces Tulsa to either rush McLaughlin and Hawkins exclusively on the outside or bring linebackers up the middle. There is little the end duo can do inside on stunts or twists. The size simply isn't there.

The Golden Hurricane needs Rayburn, who had 21 tackles last year, to become a better run stopper.

He should get help from junior college transfer **D'Wayne McIntosh** (6-5, 270), who immediately becomes a starter simply because of size. McIntosh, a junior, can also rush the passer—a year ago he racked up 14 sacks (two more than the entire Tulsa team) at Northeastern Oklahoma Junior College. He was ranked No. 63 on *SuperPrep*'s JUCO Top 100 list.

Tulsa will rotate as many as 14 players up front. But once again, the concern is youth and experience. Tackles **Justin Dixon** (6-1, 237) and **Lee Vick** (6-4, 248) and McLaughlin are the only seniors in the 14-player rotation.

Of the young players, redshirt freshman tackle **Josh Walker** (6-4, 260), sophomore tackle **Jeremy Davis** (6-1, 260), who played as a freshman, and sophomore end **Sammy Umobong** (6-3, 240) are the ones expected—and needed—to make large impacts.

LINEBACKERS

The Tulsa linebackers have a different look for the first time in three seasons. Gone is Ashon Farley, who led the team in tackles the last three years, and in are a host of new players, from transfers to those who switched positions to those who are back from injuries.

This season, the linebackers and defensive backs are going to have to make even more big plays to make up for a lack of size up front. Though the linebackers don't have great size, it is the one spot that has a decent amount of experience, even without Farley.

Tulsa coaches are excited about seeing Farley's replacement, junior **Michael Dulaney** (6-2, 218) in action. Dulaney played at Oklahoma for two years before transferring and sitting out last year. He doesn't have great size to play middle linebacker, but he does have good speed and the experience of playing in a major program. In 1998, Dulaney was one of only five true freshmen to suit up for the Sooners. He played in eight games, starting once, and came up with 30 tackles, 19 of them unassisted. Dulaney made a career-high eight stops against Missouri in his only start.

Dulaney's backup, sophomore **Jason Wiltshire** (6-3, 215) is another fast, small linebacker. He played significant time a year ago behind Farley.

Opposite Dulaney are where the questions begin. Sophomore **Jorma Bailey** (6-0, 180) began last season as a running back. He switched to linebacker before the Hawaii game and is now the starter on the outside. His size doesn't allow him to be a true linebacker. He isn't much of a threat against the run, but he is good in coverage, especially against backs out of the backfield.

Sophomore **Chad Smith** (5-11, 189) will get first shot at the bandit position, which is the rover position in most defenses. The Tulsa bandit plays more linebacker than defensive back, but the position still has to do both. Smith is a better run stopper than Bailey is on the other side, but he isn't as good of a coverage man. That could lead to him losing his starting job to junior college transfer **Reginald Reese** (5-11, 185).

Reese, a junior, was a two-year starting strong safety at Southwest Mississippi Community College, where last season he made 90 tackles—52 unassisted and seven for loss. Reese proved a handy guy to have around in his final season at Southwest Mississippi. He also caused five fumbles, intercepted three passes and blocked four kicks.

If Bailey doesn't grasp the position quickly enough, Burns, who takes an intimate role in the defense, will go to two players who have experience, but also substantial injury histories. Senior **Ryan Cook** (6-3, 215) has been hampered the last two years. He made 66 tackles in 10 games in 1998, but has yet to return to that form.

Fellow senior **Philip Abode** (6-1, 190) is back after being granted a fifth year. He played in the season opener a year ago before getting hurt and missing the year.

DEFENSIVE BACKS

The defensive backs are the most experienced unit on the Tulsa team. They are also under the most pressure. Because of the problems in front of them, a unit that returns its entire starting set needs to carry the team through an early transition period and make enough plays to keep Tulsa in games.

The secondary would like to be an attacking one that blitzes and creates havoc. While Burns was the defensive coordinator at Arkansas, the Razorbacks used multiple sets and put players at multiple positions. The result was the defense ranking in the top 10 in the nation in Burns' last year as coordinator. Tulsa isn't at that level because there isn't much size in the secondary and the Golden Hurricane doesn't have the help in front of them that Burns' defenses did at Arkansas.

The leaders are senior free safety **Harold Burgess** (5-11, 188), junior rover **Keithan McCorry** (6-0, 177) and sophomore corner **C.J. Scott** (5-7, 160). Burgess and McCorry are big playmakers against the run. Scott is the best coverage defensive back despite his size.

Last year, McCorry, who has started 22 career games and is the leading returning tackler, made 78 tackles, including 42 solos. He needs to make even more plays against the run to help a defense that gave up 5.1 yards per carry. He will be able to make more plays against the run and possibly be used in pass rushing situations if Burgess continues improving and the cornerbacks don't have to double team as much they did in 2000.

Burgess was fourth on the team in tackles a year ago. He broke up seven passes, but he needs to become a bigger factor. He had just one interception a year ago in a conference that lives on throwing the ball over the middle. For the Golden Hurricane to improve on its 10 interceptions—second worst in the league last season—Burgess needs those numbers to improve.

Scott led the team with 11 passes defended and actually made an impact in the running game despite his lean frame. He had five of the team's 10 interceptions and led Tulsa with three forced fumbles and two recovered. If there is a playmaker, Scott is it.

Opposite Scott, sophomore **Sherman Steptoe** (5-9, 175) is a returning starter. But he will be hard pressed to hold off junior college transfer **Don Gibson** (5-10, 185) for the starting job.

Like Reese, Gibson, a junior, played at Southwest Mississippi, where last season he made 82 tackles—46 solo—while playing cornerback. He earned first-team All-Mississippi Junior College Athletic Association honors, no small feat in a state loaded with quality JC programs.

Redshirt freshman **Courtney Nelms** (5-10, 155) will also see playing time.

Junior **Brett Butler** (6-0, 175) has been a solid contributor at rover the last two years. Sophomore **Lee Young** (5-11, 205) will provide help against the run.

Sophomore free safety **George Delonia** (6-0, 178), who will return kicks, could step in and provide help against the pass. He is a speedy, athletic safety who would be better suited playing corner.

PUNTERS

Senior **Casey Lipscomb** (6-0, 234) is back after averaging 39.3 yards per kick on 64 punts, the third most in the league. Lipscomb is another part of a solid special teams unit. Tulsa gave up only 3.3 yards per return a year ago. A lot of that was because of Lipscomb's ability to place punts. He put 13 of his 64 kicks inside the 20 a year ago.

SPECIAL TEAMS

Before Burns arrived, Tulsa had problems in almost every special teams aspect. Coverage was a disaster and the offense was getting no help from the kick or punt return units.

In one season, Burns changed all of that. He put some of his better athletes on special teams coverage. And, he challenged wide receiver Donald Shoals to improve the punt return team.

Last year, the Golden Hurricane allowed only 3.3 yards per return and Shoals turned into one of the best punt returners in the nation. Finding a consistent kick returner is still a concern, but the rest of the special teams—with both kickers returning—are in good shape.

Last year, Shoals was 10th in the nation and first in the WAC with a 15.6-yard average. He returned two of his 17 attempts for touchdowns, a 71-yarder against Rice and a 41-yarder against Hawaii.

Because Shoals doesn't return kicks, Tulsa may struggle finding someone who can consistently give the Golden Hurricane offense decent field position. Bailey, Delonia and Richardson all had more than 100 yards in kickoff returns last year. But, Bailey is moving to linebacker and Richardson will be shouldering much of the running game load, which could make Delonia the one who needs a breakout year on special teams.

RECRUITING CLASS

This isn't the best class in the league, but it gives Tulsa immediate help in the secondary and on the defensive front with three junior college signees who are likely immediate starters. The class has four wide receivers and 13 defensive players. And they will all get a chance to play.

That doesn't mean no one will redshirt, but Burns showed in his first year on the job that he isn't afraid to give young players a chance. He knows the way to build a young team is by developing players. But Tulsa is in a situation where it doesn't have a ton of depth and young players are forced to play early.

The stars are the three junior college players. Gibson and Reese should step in early and help a pass defense that finished 91st in the nation in pass efficiency defense. McIntosh brings much-needed size at defensive tackle. Tulsa had only 12 sacks (tied for last in the WAC) in 12 games in 2000, which put too much pressure on the secondary and a suspect linebacker corps.

Gibson played cornerback last season, but he also has wide receiver and running back experience. Both he and Reese played for tight ends coach Kenny Edenfield at Southwest Mississippi Community College.

McIntosh had 14 sacks last season, which was two more than the Golden Hurricane team had. Burns is counting on him to be the one who frees the defensive ends and can be the run stopper.

Of the receivers, **Jermaine Landrum** (5-10, 160) could play early. His size is a detriment, but he may already be Tulsa's fastest receiver. As a junior, he won the 400-meter state championship with a 49.2. He was a highly decorated high school player who also led his high school team in rushing and interceptions. The concerns are size and jumping to Division I-A from one of Oklahoma's smaller high school levels.

One of the other receivers Tulsa signed is **Caleb Blankenship** (6-3, 205), the brother of quarterback Josh Blankenship. Caleb is one of four players Tulsa signed from powerhouse Tulsa Union, which is coached by Bill Blankenship, Caleb and Josh's father. Of the four Union players, linebacker **Josh DuPree** (5-11, 215) is the most likely to play as a freshman. He had 11 games of at least 10 tackles as a senior and made 312 tackles his last two seasons.

BLUE RIBBON ANALYSIS

OFFENSE	C
SPECIAL TEAMS	B+
DEFENSE	C-
INTANGIBLES	C

Tulsa has a bevy of returning players, but the Golden Hurricane is still young. Only five of the 17 returning starters are seniors and only one of those is on defense. The firepower is there offensively, but the running game and several spots on the offensive line need to be addressed early for Tulsa to improve on its best season since 1991.

Shoals is one of the top returning receivers, statistically, in the country. Blankenship has started since he was a freshman and Tulsa has two running backs capable of making big plays as long as they are healthy. Last season, Tulsa averaged less than 3.0 yards per carry and teams were able to relax defensively and prepare for nothing but the pass.

The schedule doesn't do the Golden Hurricane any favors, especially early. It features four teams that went to bowl games last year and forces Tulsa to be sharp early with games against defending national champion Oklahoma and WAC favorites Fresno State and UTEP in consecutive weeks in September.

If the schedule doesn't beat down the young team early, a run defense that gave up more than 5.0 yards per carry improves and a wins comes against either Fresno State or UTEP, the Golden Hurricane may have enough confidence to contend in the balanced WAC.

(C.M.)

2000 RESULTS

North Carolina	L	9-30	0-1
Oklahoma State	L	26-36	0-2
Rice	W	23-16	1-2
Louisiana Tech	W	22-10	2-2
Hawaii	W	24-14	3-2
UTEP	L	7-40	3-3
New Mexico State	L	28-42	3-4
Texas Christian	L	3-17	3-5
Fresno State	L	12-34	3-6
SMU	L	20-23	3-7
San Jose State	W	28-17	4-7
Nevada	W	38-3	5-7

UTEP

LOCATION	**El Paso, TX**
CONFERENCE	**Western Athletic**
LAST SEASON	**8-4 (.667)**
CONFERENCE RECORD	**7-1 (t-1st)**
OFFENSIVE STARTERS RETURNING	**5**
DEFENSIVE STARTERS RETURNING	**7**
NICKNAME	**Miners**
COLORS	**Dark Blue, Orange & Silver Accent**
HOME FIELD	**Sun Bowl (52,000)**
HEAD COACH	**Gary Nord (Louisville '79)**
RECORD AT SCHOOL	**8-4 (1 year)**
CAREER RECORD	**8-4 (1 year)**

ASSISTANTS

Patrick Higgins (William Penn '86)
Offensive Coordinator
Bob Wagner (Wittenberg '69)
Defensive Coordinator
Brian Callahan (Eastern Illinois '92)
Offensive Line
Sammy Garza (UTEP '95)
Quarterbacks
Ron Hudson (Muskingum College '87)
Tight Ends
Reggie Johnson (Louisville '96)
Defensive Ends
Troy Reffett (UTEP '90)
Defensive Backs
James Spady (UTEP '95)
Defensive Tackles
Howard Wells (Angelo State '77)
Running Backs

TEAM WINS (last 5 yrs.)	**2-4-3-5-8**
FINAL RANK (last 5 yrs.)	**104-98-93-99-72**
2000 FINISH	**Lost to Boise State in Humanitarian Bowl.**

COACH AND PROGRAM

Gary Nord wasted little time establishing himself. In his first season as a college head coach, Nord produced UTEP's most wins in 12 years and a school-record seven-game winning streak. The Miners shared the WAC title with TCU and went to a bowl game for the first time in 12 years. It was UTEP's first-ever WAC title and first conference title since 1956.

Tight end Brian Natkin was consensus All-America, the school's first. Quarterback Rocky Perez set a school record with 26 touchdown passes and kicker Ricky Bishop finished as the school's second all-time leading scorer.

Even Nord got into the act, winning WAC Coach-of-the-Year honors and receiving a contract extension through 2007.

Now comes the hard part. Gone are 14 seniors, 10 of whom were starters. There is no established quarterback or running back. Senior **Lee Mays** is the only returning receiver who caught a pass last year.

Three new coaches are in the fold, including defensive coordinator Bob Wagner, the former Hawaii coach. Nord, 43, surrounds himself with enthusiastic assistants. A tough, high-energy person himself, Nord expects the same from his staff. Wagner is the oldest coach on a staff that is full of youth and UTEP connections. Three coaches are former UTEP players. Five of the nine graduated from college in the '90s, three in the last six years.

What kind of changes Wagner makes and how quickly the Miners adapt will be crucial, because the offense is likely to struggle early. With seven starters back, including two All-WAC selections, the talent is there to carry the team. Both of the all-conference selections (cornerback **Crance Clemons** and free safety **D.J. Walker**) were in a secondary that ranked 19th in the nation in pass efficiency. And with Wagner expected to add several wrinkles to make UTEP even more aggressive, the Miners should improve on their 30 sacks a year ago, a figure that ranked third in the league.

One of Nord's biggest successes a year ago, and one that is crucial to maintain, was attracting El Paso residents to the Sun Bowl and giving them a reason to come back. The Miners had three home crowds of more than 50,000 and set a school record with 53,304 against Rice. For the year, UTEP averaged 44,715, also a school record.

The fans came because they saw an exciting and successful brand of football. The Miners finished 22nd in the nation in scoring offense and 27th in passing offense, continuing a long line of offensive success under Nord. The offensive coordinator from 1997-99, Nord took UTEP from 97th in the nation in total offense in 1997 to 51st in 1998, 43rd two years ago and 36th last season. UTEP set a school record for first downs and had the best passing output of any Miners team in 14 years.

Those numbers are going to be hard to improve on this year because of the quarterback situation. With three parts of the four running backs rotation returning and Mays, a do-everything receiver, the foundation is there. Nord has a reputation for developing quarterbacks, though. Perez blossomed under Nord, throwing for more than 200 yards 10 times and a school-record 26 touchdown passes in 2000.

With no standout team in the conference, Nord

and the Miners will have time to get their offense going. When it does, UTEP, with six games in the Sun Bowl—where the Miners were undefeated last year for the first time since 1995—will be tough to beat again.

2001 SCHEDULE

Sept.	1	@New Mexico
	8	Texas Southern
	22	@Boise State
	29	Tulsa
Oct.	6	@Alabama
	13	@Hawaii
	20	San Jose State
	27	@SMU
Nov.	10	Louisiana Tech
	17	@Rice
	24	Nevada

QUARTERBACKS

The last two years, the Miners had little to worry about in their backfield. There were several options in the running game and all Perez had to do was be accurate with a bunch of receivers who could go get the ball.

The running game and one major receiving option are still there, but there is no Perez on this team. There is no player who has considerable experience or a young player who has been groomed to take over. The three candidates for the job this year are all green and will test Nord's ability to develop quarterbacks. His project with Perez went as well as he could have imagined. Perez left with several school records and last year directed one of the most successful years in UTEP history.

Senior **Wesley Phillips** (6-4, 220), son of former Buffalo Bills coach Wade Phillips, will get first shot, but Nord is far from committed. Phillips has been in the system a long time, but has thrown only 16 passes. He has good size, but he is still inexperienced. Because he worked on the second team a year ago and got into only five games, Phillips hasn't worked much with the returning offensive linemen or running backs. He has played with some of the receivers who will need to contribute, but in game experience, Phillips is just as limited as some of his competition.

Freshman **Jon Schaper** (6-2, 220) is as close to being groomed as the Miners have. He spent his redshirt year learning Nord's system and watching Perez eat up defenses. But he missed his best opportunity to shine and, more importantly, play with the starters when he slammed his hand in a car door and missed most of the spring.

Sophomore **Gerred Lunnon** (6-5, 210), who has been hampered by injuries, may get the call if Phillips doesn't establish himself early. Lunnon has the best size and the strongest arm, but he has yet to prove that he can stay on the field. He played in three games a year ago but attempted only one pass.

None of the three are going to finish eighth in the nation in passing efficiency or be the heart and soul of the offense like Perez was in 2000. UTEP needs one of the three to step in and be efficient. The Miners have offensive weapons, but one of the three quarterbacks has to be able to aim the gun in the right direction.

"Wesley has been in our system for four years and understands it well," Nord said. "The others are young and have futures. They will all be expected to compete for the job and we expect they will. How it shakes down is going to be interesting."

RUNNING BACKS

When Paul Smith left for the NFL after the 1999 season, the Miners thought their bruising running game was gone. No one back filled Smith's shoes in 2000, but Nord went to a four-back rotation that gave UTEP more options and, ultimately, more success. Senior **Chris Porter** (5-11, 235) and juniors **Sherman Austin** (5-8, 170) and **Rovann Cleveland** (6-1, 220) were all part of a Miners running game that averaged almost 160 yards per game and was ranked in the top 45 in the nation. Porter, Austin and Cleveland each ran for more than 300 yards and each had a 100-yard game.

The best of the bunch is Porter, who could see even more time after rushing for 681 yards and five touchdowns while averaging a team-best 4.8 yards per carry. Porter, a former walk-on, is the same kind of bruising back that Smith was.

In the Humanitarian Bowl loss to now-WAC rival Boise State, Porter ran for 134 yards on 26 carries and scored a touchdown. Unlike most senior backs, Porter has little wear on him. He worked with the scout team his first three years and didn't have a carry going into last year. UTEP doesn't use its backs much in the passing game, but they are vital parts of the blocking scheme and Porter is the best of the three at reading blocks and picking up blitzes. He is also a good student who is involved on campus, holding a spot on the UTEP Student Senate.

Austin gives the Miners a breakaway threat. His size keeps him from getting much inside the tackles, but his speed allows him to get outside. A converted receiver, Austin ran for 410 yards a year ago on 101 carries, including a 69-yarder that showcased the way UTEP coaches want him to run. He got most of the yards after breaking to the outside and cutting back against over-pursuing defenders.

Cleveland is a big back who can wear on defenses as much as Porter. He played in only nine games a year ago after missing two games with a broken foot. He averaged 4.6 yards a carry, giving the Miners three backs with at least a 4.1-yard average.

Sophomore **Josh Wheat** (6-1, 200) and redshirt freshman **John James** (5-11, 195) are the only other players likely to get carries. Wheat had nine carries a year ago and was a standout special teams player. James was one of the most highly regarded signees after rushing for 2,276 yards as a senior in high school.

WIDE RECEIVERS/TIGHT ENDS

Asked about Mays (6-3, 190), Nord shakes his head and starts to talk but can't. Finally, "He's really some kind of athlete isn't he?" is all he can muster.

For UTEP, Mays has been more than just an athlete. He's been the heart of the Miners' run toward the top of the national passing charts. He's a three-year starter who already has his name spread throughout the school record book. This season, Mays needs to be at his best to help a unit that will be relying on younger players and others who are coming back from injuries.

Last season, Mays was 14th in the nation in receptions and eighth in yards at just under 100 per game. He set a school record with 15 touchdown catches, including at least one in UTEP's last 10 games. He led the team and was 26th in the country in scoring with 90 points. He is already the school's career touchdowns leader with 27 and is fourth in yardage. He has nine career 100-yard games and has scored two or more touchdowns in a game seven times. With a repeat of last year's 15 touchdown catch season, Mays will tie Wyoming's Ryan Yarborough for the most career touchdowns in WAC history.

Mays gets open because of his speed. He is a standout on UTEP's All-America 4 x 100-meter relay team and that speed translates to the field. He isn't the strongest receiver, but his height and ability to get position—combined with blazing speed—make him the toughest receiver in the league to cover.

But the Miners have to have someone else emerge on the opposite side to keep the double- and triple-teams off Mays.

No other UTEP receiver caught a pass last year, meaning the duty of taking pressure off Mays falls on senior tight end **Joey Knapp** (6-6, 250). Knapp is in the mold of Natkin, who led the country's tight ends in receptions. A former walk-on who backed up Natkin a year ago in addition to earning six starts in two-tight end sets, Knapp is considered by his coaches to be just as good as his former teammate.

Knapp's four touchdown receptions tied for the second most among the nation's tight ends. He's a good blocker, but because of the lack of experience in the receiver corps, his ability to catch passes and be a security blanket for a new quarterback is his most vital role.

The receiver most likely to emerge and fill the role Allan Ray (27 catches) played a year ago is junior **Terrance Minor** (6-2, 170). Minor caught five balls in 1999 and was expected to be a bigger part of the offense last year until a knee injury sidelined him for the entire season.

Senior **Andre Acree** (6-0, 200) is the only other UTEP receiver who has played, but Acree didn't catch a pass in 2000. Redshirt freshmen **Dirk Dillard** (6-1, 190) and **Will Smith** (6-2, 195) are going to be thrown into the mix and expected to produce, as is another redshirt, **Matt Elwood** (6-1, 175), who Nord said is the best leaper on the team.

The signees who could help this season are freshmen **Howard Jackson** (5-10, 160) and **Aaron Givens** (6-2, 180). Jackson was a running back, receiver, kick returner and defensive back in high school. He will be a receiver and kick returner for the Miners.

Givens had 44 catches for 666 yards as a senior and also played defensive back.

OFFENSIVE LINE

Up front, UTEP has significant experience and a familiar name to help keep pace with what last year's unit was able to do. The Miners kept Perez off his back a year ago and opened enough holes for the running game to pile up almost 160 yards per game. The tackles, both of whom return, were solid enough to contain outside pursuit and let Perez stay in the pocket where he was most comfortable. With Phillips, a pure pocket passer, the likely starter, pushing the WAC's speedy and shifty defensive ends to the inside where they get mauled by bigger guards is a must.

Sophomore right tackle **Trey Darilek** (6-5, 270), junior left tackle **Ariel Famaligi** (6-3, 300) and senior left guard **Lawrence Norman** (6-3, 315) have combined for 59 starts, including every game last year, and give the young Miners offense a nice base to build from. The three helped UTEP drop from 2.3 sacks per game in 1999 to 1.7 last year. Over the last eight games, the line gave up only 12 sacks while helping the offense put up more than 407 yards and 32 points per game.

The replacements are at center and right guard, where Jeff Seeton and Carey Clayton had been mainstays for four seasons. Clayton's brother, sophomore **Robert Clayton** (6-3, 280), moves into the right guard position while sophomore **Chris Kerr** (6-4, 250) takes over at center. The two don't have much experience, but all-conference-type players flank both.

Clayton doesn't have to be outstanding, but Kerr needs to learn quickly with a new quarterback behind him.

Injuries are a concern here because the three starters are the only ones with significant experience.

Senior **Keith Warren** (6-5, 270) is a versatile lineman who prefers to play tackle, but could figure in the mix at center or right guard if Clayton or Kerr falters. Freshman **Robert Espisona** (6-4, 290) is a big right tackle who will spend the year learning behind Darilek.

2000 STATISTICS

Rushing offense	159.3	44
Passing offense	248.2	27
Total offense	407.5	36
Scoring offense	32.3	22
Net Punting	34.2	70
Punt returns	6.1	103
Kickoff returns	15.8	110
Rushing defense	153.8	64
Passing efficiency defense	104.1	19
Total defense	371.8	63
Scoring defense	27.1	74
Turnover margin	+4	39

Last column is ranking among Division I-A teams.

KICKERS

Ricky Bishop is gone after finishing in the top 50 in the country in scoring. He was 13-of-18 on field goals and missed only once in 11 tries inside 40 yards. He was 3-of-7 beyond 40 yards, but he was a consistent threat the team had no problem trotting out in critical situations. Freshmen **Bryce Benekos** (6-5, 195) and **Matt Smith** (5-10, 180) will battle for the kicking and punting jobs.

Benekos is the better punter, but he made 8-of-12 field goals (long of 47) and 41-of-43 PATs as a high school senior.

Smith has a strong leg and is a good athlete. He kicked and punted exclusively his last two years of high school, but he played running back and safety his freshman and sophomore years. He needs to become more consistent on long-range kicks, but his strong leg shows he will eventually be able to do that. He spent last summer working with former Dallas Cowboys kicker Toni Fritsch and improved considerably. Smith will immediately handle kickoffs. As a high school senior, he put 16-of-26 kickoffs last season in the end zone.

Redshirt freshman **Chad Kennedy** (6-4, 250) was the punter throughout the spring and was also listed as the No. 1 kicker. But, his future is in question after being arrested for steroid possession on the Mexican border May 9.

DEFENSIVE LINE

The Miners lost the bulk of their tackles from 2000 after linebacker Trey Merkens graduated. Merkens set the tone for the way the defensive line attacked and how aggressive the defensive backs could be. Merkens has to be replaced, and injuries are a concern in the only linebacker spots. With the middle of the defense that much of a question, UTEP needs production from a defensive line that has six players with starting experience.

The tackle rotation of seniors **Bobby King** (6-4, 265) and **Josh Randolph** (6-3, 250) and sophomores **Samuel Clarke** (6-3, 265) and **Daniel Kerr** (6-4, 250) each started games in 2000. The four need to improve on their four sacks to take pressure off the linebackers and not force the defensive backs to get too aggressive. Like much of the UTEP defense, size is a concern. Most teams have tackles at or near 300 pounds. None of the Miners tackles, or any of the defensive linemen, are anywhere close to 300.

UTEP was still solid against the run last year, finishing in the top half of the conference and country at 153.8 yards a game. The size wasn't a concern because Merkens and Camar Jackson made plays at linebacker and played like two extra linemen. Jackson is back, but the inexperience on the other side will force the defensive line to be better than it was a year ago. And King, who had minor back surgery during the spring, needs to return healthy.

At end, juniors **Rick Fette** (6-4, 245), who started nine games, **Karmul High** (6-4, 235) and **Gabe Williams** (6-5, 225) return after combining for 99 tackles a year ago. Williams had the best 2000 of the group, making 45 tackles and registering five sacks.

The Miners' size is actually decent compared to other ends in the league. High is a good speed rusher, as is Williams, who plays outside of the tackle and is more of a linebacker who plays in a stance. A minor concern is Williams' knee, which kept him out of spring practice.

The Miners have young depth as well with sophomore **Jeremy Castillo** (6-4, 255) and redshirt freshman **Aaron Osborn** (6-6, 250), both of whom came to UTEP as highly recruited players. Coaches are most impressed with redshirt freshman **Ibok Ibok** (6-5, 220), who could sneak into the end rotation.

LINEBACKERS

Even with new defensive coordinator Bob Wagner, UTEP will stay with its two-linebacker set. It worked fine last year when Trey Merkens and junior **Camar Jackson** (6-4, 240) gave the Miners, basically, two more linemen. Jackson is bigger than all but one of UTEP's defensive ends. He is a fast, hard-hitting linebacker who can cover backs in the flats.

This season, Jackson needs to be the defensive leader that Merkens, who made a team-high 112 tackles, was a year ago. Jackson made 51 tackles last year, but his career numbers don't equal Merkens' production of a year ago. Add in shoulder surgery that has kept Jackson away from action since the year ended, and the Miners have cause for concern.

Stepping into Merkens' spot is junior **Bubba Wiseman** (6-0, 260). Wiseman has the size to play defensive tackle and will be used extensively in pass rushing situations. His pass coverage skills need to improve for teams not to take advantage with big tight ends and backs slipping out of the backfield.

Because of the concern, redshirt freshmen **Robert Rodriguez** (6-1, 230), a converted running back, and **Ricky McCutchin** (6-2, 225) and senior **Barry King** (6-3, 250), who had 14 tackles in nine games in 2000, will play.

DEFENSIVE BACKS

The aggression UTEP showed in the secondary last year gave the Miners an attitude. Though not blessed with great size, UTEP's defensive backs developed into one of the WAC's top units by feeding off each other and putting up numbers good enough to finish 19th in the country in pass defense efficiency. UTEP gave up the second-fewest touchdowns in the WAC and averaged more than an interception a game.

With three returning starters, including both corners, the Miners have the bulk of a unit back that allowed less than 188 yards per game passing over the last nine games.

Clemons (5-10, 165) and **Weldon Cooks** (6-2, 185) form the best corner tandem in the league. Clemons was a first-team All-WAC choice last season after making 27 tackles. Though he is small, Clemons, the only senior starter, is fast and one of the best cover corners in the league. He made more tackles as a sophomore, but he became a better coverage player when he wasn't forced to be used as much in the running game.

Cooks has good size and received several All-WAC accolades a year ago. His 12 pass breakups led the league. He is fast enough to keep up with most receivers in the conference and big enough to hit. Cooks and Clemons are in no danger of getting rusty, as Lee Mays provides as good and fast of a receiver every day during practice as either will see all season.

Junior free safety Walker (6-3, 210) was a first-team all-league choice after making 63 tackles and picking off five passes. He is the roaming, hard-hitting center fielder that may have to play closer to the line of scrimmage than he has in the past.

Under Wagner, there is a strong safety, but he plays a rover position that is a hybrid linebacker/defensive back. Junior **Paul Smith** (6-2, 180) has linebacker experience, but may be too small to provide a consistent pass rush. That opens the door for sophomore **Tim Woodard** (5-11, 185) or true freshman **Brandon Yaites** (5-10, 175). Sophomore **Joe Young** (6-1, 205), who has the best size for the position, could also be in the running for playing time pending the outcome of his May steroid arrest.

PUNTERS

Just like the place kicking chores, the punting job will fall to a freshman. Glen Beard is gone after being a consistent weapon in 2000. He averaged 41.3 yards per kick and finished 35th in the nation.

The likely replacement is Bryce Benekos. He averaged 46.3 yards a kick as a senior in high school, including a 62-yarder, and 41.4 as a junior. He is also an accomplished kicker, but will likely concentrate on punting if Smith is able to win the kicking job. Benekos is also a good athlete, having played quarterback and wide receiver in high school.

Redshirt freshman **Chad Kennedy** (6-4, 250) punted in the spring, but a steroid arrest has put his future in doubt.

SPECIAL TEAMS

In addition to replacing its kicker and punter, UTEP needs to find players who can help put its offense in better position. UTEP finished next to last in the league and 103rd in the nation in punt returns with a 6.1-yard average.

Kick returns were even worse. The Miners averaged 15.6 yards, ninth in the WAC and 110th in the nation, and their longest return of the season was 32 yards. Seven players returned kicks last year while the departed Sanchez took care of punts. Singleton and Austin are back on kickoff returns. Austin had an 18.9-yard average and will be joined in the back by Singleton, Clemons, Fenner, James or Woodard. Wheat, Clemons or Austin will return punts.

The Miners were good against the return in 2000, averaging 9.8 yards a punt return and 17.4 on kickoffs. Neither unit gave up a touchdown or a run of more than 38 yards.

Junior deep snapper **Jon Dorenbos** (6-1, 235) is a professional magician in his spare time.

RECRUITING CLASS

With a contract extension through 2007, UTEP

made it clear to Gary Nord that the school wants him around. If this year's recruiting class is an indication, Nord is making plans to stick around a while. Nord signed 25 players, all from the high school ranks. For a school that traditionally recruits junior college players, that step, along with the signing four El Paso players, was a sign of how Nord intends to build his program.

"Our top priority is to get the best players from the El Paso area," Nord said. "That helps feed our walk-on program and gives the team an El Paso feel."

The best of the four signees is Austin (6-0, 185), who ran for 1,600 yards and 24 touchdowns on 143 carries as a senior. He was a standout defensive back and also played basketball and was a regional qualifier in three track events, including the 100 meters. He has an outside chance of playing running back this year, but Nord likely will redshirt him with three of the Miners' top backs returning this season and all of them upperclassmen.

The class filled needs at kicker (Smith) and punter (Benekos) and addressed the defensive line (five signees), linebackers and receivers (four signees each), all areas where UTEP was either hit hard by graduation this year or will be next year.

Of the defensive line, linebacker and receivers signees, Givens or Jackson are most likely to play. Yaites should see time at rover.

Offensive lineman **Jose Garcia** (6-3, 300) may already be the most athletic lineman the Miners have. He won four wrestling gold medals in high school and set a school record for wins and pins. But, linebacker Tevita Fifita may already be the most popular player. His father, Tonga, is the WWF's Haku.

BLUE RIBBON ANALYSIS

OFFENSE	B-
SPECIAL TEAMS	D-
DEFENSE	B+
INTANGIBLES	B+

Last season, the Miners felt what it was like to win. The long-suffering program had its most successful season in 12 years and won its first conference title since 1956. This team is good enough to win the balanced WAC despite an inexperienced quarterback and only one receiver back from last year who caught a pass. The defense is solid. And with three offensive line starters who have combined for 59 starts returning, the Miners have a good base to build from.

Nord is a young, energetic coach who has surrounded himself with a wealth of young, energetic assistants and an experienced one in Wagner, the former Hawaii coach. The Miners are a fun team to watch and the city has rallied around the only game in town in the fall.

El Paso-area recruits are beginning to take notice, as are recruits from Texas' major cities. The Miners are having success fighting Big 12 schools for talent by offering an exciting offense and a chance to play early.

Nord is also demanding discipline from his players. When two players were arrested in May for steroid possession, Nord and athletic director Bob Stull agreed to implement a policy of random, monthly steroid testing, a policy that is far more stringent than most other Division I programs.

Even with the slow development, the Miners can compete for the WAC title. But, the new quarterback needs to show maturity early to keep from losing confidence against a schedule that features Texas Tech's high-powered offense and former TCU coach Dennis Franchione's new Alabama team in Tuscaloosa.

(C.M.)

2000 RESULTS

Oklahoma	L	14-55	0-1
SMU	W	37-20	1-1
Texas A&M	L	17-45	1-2
Hawaii	W	39-7	2-2
New Mexico State	W	41-31	3-2
Tulsa	W	40-7	4-2
San Jose State	W	47-30	5-2
Fresno State	W	23-13	6-2
Nevada	W	45-22	7-2
Rice	W	38-21	8-2
TCU	L	14-47	8-3
Boise St. (Humanitarian)	L	23-38	8-4

Central Florida

LOCATION	**Orlando, FL**
CONFERENCE	**Independent**
LAST SEASON	**7-4 (.636)**
CONFERENCE RECORD	**NA**
OFFENSIVE STARTERS RETURNING	**4**
DEFENSIVE STARTERS RETURNING	**6**
NICKNAME	**Golden Knights**
COLORS	**Black & Gold**
HOME FIELD	**Florida Citrus Bowl (70,188)**
HEAD COACH	**Mike Kruczek (Boston Col. '76)**
RECORD AT SCHOOL	**20-13 (3 years)**
CAREER RECORD	**20-13 (3 years)**
ASSISTANTS	
	Gene Chizik (Florida '85)
	Defensive Coordinator
	Bill D'Ottavio (Millersville '86)
	Linebackers
	Jamie Barresi
	Quarterbacks
	Sean Beckton (UCF '93)
	Wide Receivers
	Scott Fountain (Samford '88)
	Tight Ends/Tackles
	Robert MFarland (McNeese State '85)
	Offensive Line
	Charles Huff (Presbyterian '85)
	Defensive Ends/Special Teams
	Lorenzo Constantini (UTEP '90)
	Defensive Tackles
	Alan Gooch (UCF '83)
	Running Backs
TEAM WINS (last 5 yrs.)	**5-5-9-4-7**
FINAL RANK (last 5 yrs.)	**79-70-55-90-80**
2000 FINISH	**Lost to Virginia Tech in regular-season finale.**

COACH AND PROGRAM

The highly successful 2001 football season served as further proof that the University of Central Florida (UCF) is in desperate need of a football conference it can call home.

With winning records in two of their last three seasons (including a 7-4 mark last season after a 1-2 start), the Golden Knights have made the successful leap from the I-AA ranks to a legitimate independent team. But despite finishing three games above .500 and defeating Alabama from the mighty SEC in what was the biggest win in school history, UCF was unable to get a bowl berth even though it seems that there are 198 different bowl games out there now.

The reason? The bowl bids go to teams from power conferences for the most part, unless you're Notre Dame.

UCF had a chance to take its homeless tag off. But it took a calculated risk last year, when it decided to pass on a chance to join the fledgling Sun Belt Conference. The decision not to join the likes of Louisiana-Lafayette, Louisiana-Monroe and North Texas in the new Sun Belt makes it clear that the Golden Knights have bigger goals, like joining the Big East, ACC or Conference USA. They want national recognition, bowl games and all the bells and whistles that go with being in a big-time conference. The school even hired a sports marketing firm to help spread the word in hopes of getting asked to the table by a major conference.

Thus far, the bigger conferences have shown no interest in the Golden Knights, despite the school's best efforts and the fact that head coach Mike Kruczek plays a wide-open offensive style, that the school is located in the talent-rich Sunshine State, and that the school has started to win games and has produced one of the most exciting, young players in the NFL (Minnesota Vikings quarterback Daunte Culpepper).

So what's it going to take? First of all, time. And second, the Knights must continue to take steps in the right direction. It won't be easy to match last year's 7-4 mark, because UCF must take to the road four of the first five weeks of the year in a murderous September opening stretch. The Golden Knights play at Clemson, at Syracuse, at Tulane and at Virginia Tech before the calendar flips to October. Ouch!

Making matters tougher is the fact that nearly a dozen players, including star-in-the-making quarterback **Ryan Schneider**, were on academic probation in the spring. The no-nonsense Kruczek kept the players out of spring ball, except on Saturdays. Kruczek sees the forward steps that the program has taken and is confident that his team can keep winning, if all of his players hit the books as hard as they hit the weight room over the summer.

"I think we can have a pretty good football team," Kruczek said. "I think we can be very competitive with the people we play and this is not an easy schedule this year."

Danger exists, if UCF posts another 7-4 record and doesn't get into a bowl game or into a new conference. In that case, Kruczek might start looking around for a better coaching gig. And he'd be an attractive candidate. A former backup NFL quarterback who won two Super Bowl rings with the Pittsburgh Steelers, Kruczek has been offered NFL assistant coaching jobs before but has stayed put.

However, if at some point in the not-too-distant future Kruczek doesn't see the UCF program continuing to make progress (read: get an invitation into a high-profile conference), then he might be tempted to move on.

2001 SCHEDULE

Sept.	1	@Clemson
	8	@Syracuse
	15	Louisiana-Lafayette
	22	@Tulane
	29	@Virginia Tech
Oct.	6	UAB
	13	Liberty
	20	Louisiana-Monroe
	27	@Utah State
Nov.	3	Akron
	10	@Arkansas

QUARTERBACKS

One of the brightest spots of the 2000 season was a Wally Pipp moment. When then-senior Vic Penn (who had thrown for 3,078 yards and 16 touchdowns in 1999) went down with a shoulder injury at mid-season, it was actually good news for the long-term future of Golden Knights' football.

That's because then-redshirt freshman Schneider (6-2, 215) took over under center and proved to be an excellent passer and a fearless field leader. Although he wasn't expected to be UCF's quarterback of the future, Schneider completed 176-of-285 throws for 2,334 yards, 21 scores and just 11 interceptions, four of which came in the season's final game, against Virginia Tech.

Schneider's greatest attributes are his toughness and winning ways. He played in nine games, including the last seven as a starter. In those starts, he posted a 5-2 record. He passed for more than 250 yards in all seven starts and finished 17th in the nation in total offense.

His exploits probably don't surprise anyone who follows high school football in Florida. Schneider threw for 6,418 career yards and 98 touchdowns in three seasons at Plantation (Fla.) High School, which went 36-4 under his leadership. Schools like Auburn gave him a look-see, but passed because they didn't think he was mobile enough to play in the SEC.

Schneider sure looked like he could hack it against SEC competition, if his Oct. 28 performance against Alabama is a true indicator of what he can do. Schneider was 27-of-48 for 283 yards and three touchdowns in a 40-38 upset of the Crimson Tide. Now, he must keep his eye on the ball in the classroom or risk being booted off the team by Kruczek, who won't accept any shortcuts.

Schneider's backup is fellow sophomore **Brian Miller** (6-5, 225), who was viewed as UCF's quarterback of the future at this time last year. Miller has a howitzer of a right arm (his fastball was once clocked at 93 miles-per-hour in high school) and was a three-sport star at Science Hill High School in Johnson City, Tenn. That's the same high school that produced University of Florida coach Steve Spurrier.

Miller made some mop-up appearances last fall, completing 3-of-7 passes (42.9 completion percentage) for a mere 26 yards and one touchdown. This spring, Miller solidified his status as Schneider's primary caddy by completing 33-of-58 throws for 467 yards over the course of the Golden Knights' three scrimmages. The bad news? Miller tossed two interceptions and no touchdowns in the three scrimmages. But because Schneider was a Saturday-only player for UCF this spring, Miller got most of the snaps and made tons of progress.

"I think Brian Miller has made massive improvement in his pass development," Kruczek said.

The team's No. 3 quarterback is redshirt freshman **Jon Rivera** (6-3,185) from Perth Amboy, N.J. Like most young quarterbacks, Rivera is still adjusting to the speed and sophistication of Division I-A football. In limited duty in UCF's three spring scrimmages, Rivera was 6-of-11 for 48 yards, one touchdown and no interceptions. He's clearly a work in progress. A three-year starter at Perth Amboy (N.J.) High School, Rivera passed for more than 5,000 yards and 48 touchdowns in his career, including 2,600 yards and 25 touchdowns as a junior and was offered by Auburn and others.

INDEPENDENTS

BLUE RIBBON FORECAST*

1. Notre Dame
2. Utah State
3. Central Florida
4. South Florida
5. Navy

ALL-INDEPENDENT TEAM

OFFENSE

POS. PLAYER SCHOOL HT. WT. CL.

WR Chris Stallworth, Utah State, 6-3, 190, So.
WR David Givens, Notre Dame, 6-3, 214, Sr.
OL Jordan Black, Notre Dame, 6-6, 308, Sr.
OL Kurt Vollers, Notre Dame, 6-7, 307, Sr.
C Jeff Faine, Notre Dame, 6-3, 290, Jr.
OL Willie Comerford, Central Florida, 6-4, 320, Sr.
OL Jim Walker, Utah State, 6-3, 293, Sr.
QB Jose Fuentes, Utah State, 6-3, 188, Jr.
RB Emmett White, Utah State, 5-11, 199, Sr.
RB Julius Jones, Notre Dame, 5-10, 201, Jr.
TE Mario Jackson, Central Florida, 6-2, 230, Jr.

DEFENSE

POS. PLAYER SCHOOL HT. WT. CL.

DL Grant Irons, Notre Dame, 6-5, 275, Sr.
DL Josh McKibben, Central Florida, 6-3, 270, Sr.
DL Anthony Weaver, Notre Dame, 6-3, 276, Sr.
DL Nate Putnam, Utah State, 6-7, 224, So.
LB Jesse Busta, Utah State, 6-2, 235, Jr.
LB Kawika Mitchell South Florida, 6-2, 248, Jr.
LB Tito Rodriguez, Central Florida, 6-2, 235, Sr.
LB Rocky Boiman, Notre Dame, 6-4, 239, Sr.
DB Shane Walton, Notre Dame, 5-11, 186, Sr.
DB Adebola Jimoh, Utah State, 6-1, 185, Jr.
DB Joe Morgan, South Florida, 5-10, 185, Sr.
DB DeJuan Cromer, Navy, 5-9, 187, Sr.

SPECIALISTS

POS. PLAYER SCHOOL HT. WT. CL.

PK Javier Beorlegui, Central Florida, 6-1, 225, Sr.
P Steve Mullins, Utah State, 6-4, 226, Jr.
RS Julius Jones, Notre Dame, 5-10, 201, Jr.

OFFENSIVE PLAYER OF THE YEAR

Emmett White, RB, Utah State

DEFENSIVE PLAYER OF THE YEAR

Anthony Weaver, DL, Notre Dame

NEWCOMER OF THE YEAR

Doug Gabriel, WR, Central Florida

INDEPENDENTS NOTEBOOK

* No official standings for independent schools are kept by the NCAA. *Blue Ribbon*'s preseason rankings seek only to rate the five schools playing as independents. ... How tough is Notre Dame's 2001 schedule? The Fighting Irish will face seven opponents that played in bowl games a year ago: Nebraska (defeated Northwestern in Alamo Bowl), Purdue (lost to Washington in Rose), Texas A&M (lost to Mississippi State in Independence), Pittsburgh (lost to Iowa State in insight.com), West Virginia (defeated Ole Miss in Music City), Boston College (defeated Arizona State in Aloha) and Tennessee (lost to Kansas State in Cotton). Those seven teams combined to finish 54-30 (.643) in 2000. ... Last year, Utah State had a 2,000-yard passer (Jose Fuentes), a 1,000-yard rusher (Emmett White) and a 1,000-yard receiver (Aaron Jones) for the first time since 1995. Fuentes and White both return this year. The senior White shattered the NCAA record for single-game all-purpose yardage by gaining 578 yards against New Mexico State on Nov. 4, 2000. White beat the record by 143 yards as he gained a school-record 322 yards rushing, 134 receiving and 122 in kick returns. White also scored four touchdowns in that game, including the game-winner in the final minute. ... It won't be easy for Central Florida to match last year's 7-4 mark, because it must take to the road four of the first five weeks of the year in a murderous September opening stretch. The Golden Knights play at Clemson, at Syracuse, at Tulane and at Virginia Tech before the calendar flips to October. ... The independent ranks are just a resting place for South Florida as the Bulls will join Conference USA in 2003. ... Speaking of South Florida, the Bulls' defensive line rotation includes a familiar name in Lee Roy Selmon, Jr., the 275-pound son of the former University of Oklahoma and NFL star. ... After a 1-10 season in 2000, Navy coach Charlie Weatherbie hired a new offensive and defensive coordinator. The new offensive coordinator is Mark Hudspeth, whose flexbone offense carried Delta State to the NCAA Division II title last year. Navy's new defensive coordinator is Rick Lantz, who served in the same post at Louisville and Virginia over the last 15 years.

RUNNING BACKS

While passing the ball hasn't been a problem at UCF, a consistent running game has proven difficult to produce. The Knights again struggled to move the ball on the ground in 2000, averaging just 79.2 yards rushing per game. Although the team's pass-first philosophy no doubt contributed to that trouble, UCF's offensive line and backs were rarely able to control the clock and give the Knight defense much help. While that isn't a big deal in games against lesser I-A lights, it is important if UCF wants to operate with the big boys such as Clemson and Syracuse in its first two games of 2001.

While Edward Mack (344 rushing yards, five touchdowns) has exhausted his eligibility and senior Omari Howard transferred to Division I-AA Northeastern, there is reason to believe that the Golden Knights might be better suited to mount a ground assault in 2001. The reason? The squad has a nice deep stable of young runners, led by sophomore **Corey Baker** (417 yards, two touchdowns in 2000), last season's leading rusher.

Howard's transfer says volumes about the talent of the two younger runners, Baker and redshirt freshman **Alex Haynes** (5-11, 205). Howard had 144 carries for 605 yards and nine touchdowns in three seasons as a Golden Knight, but did not want to spend his senior season platooning with Baker, Haynes and fifth-year senior **Terrance Williams** (5-10, 190).

Baker must take care of business in the classroom to remain the team's starting tailback He had four unexplained absences during spring practice, but remained in good standing with the team. Kruczek said Baker was feeling overwhelmed by a heavy academic load and didn't handle the situation as well as he could have. Baker's response was to not show up to practice; Kruczek wishes Baker would have communicated with him better.

"He got himself behind the 8-ball academically during the spring semester," Kruczek said. "It really began last fall. I think he got really worried about not being able to participate this upcoming fall, so he decided to miss the last couple of practices."

While the shifty Baker is a known commodity (if he does his schoolwork), the two wild cards are Haynes and Williams. Haynes was a definite bright spot for the Golden Knight offense this spring.

"He's a very physical runner, has good speed, and is hard to bring down," running backs coach Alan Gooch said. "That's a great combination for a back."

Haynes had few opportunities to stay competitive with sophomore Baker, who has had an impressive spring. Because of academics, Haynes was only allowed to compete on Saturdays during spring ball. Haynes, a graduate of Maynard Evans High School in Orlando, redshirted last season because he was new to the offense and unlikely to see much playing time behind a crowded group of players.

In high school, Haynes was one of the nation's best. He rushed for more than 1,400 yards and had 15 touchdowns his senior year.

Haynes played in both the Florida-Georgia and Florida-California All-Star Games, was selected all-state and all-metro twice, and earned *SuperPrep* All-America honors as a senior. He was also voted to the Florida Super 85, *SuperPrep* Top 35 and Bill Buchalter's Super 27 team.

"He's confirming what we though about him coming out of high school," Gooch said. "We're very happy about that."

Like Haynes, Williams had an impressive resume before his arrival at UCF, but was forced to sit and watch last year. In Williams' case, the reason he was redshirted was ankle surgery that he underwent in the spring of 2000. Kruczek decided last fall to sit Williams, a former JUCO All-American at Hinds (Miss.) Community College, and hope that he would return to his old junior college form. However, Williams, who was UCF's second leading rusher in 1999 with 369 yards, was slowed this past spring with a hip pointer injury.

Junior **Sean Gaudion** (6-2, 240) and redshirt sophomore **Chris Burden** (6-2, 225) are two returning fullbacks, but they'll be pushed by a pair of highly touted newcomers in freshman **Willie "Dee" Brown** (5-11, 238) and jumbo-sized freshman **Andreal Curry** (6-2, 250).

Both Brown and Curry arrive in Orlando with plenty of press clippings and should get some field time.

WIDE RECEIVERS/TIGHT ENDS

With the graduation of wide receivers Tyson Hinshaw and Kenny Clark, UCF lost 39 percent of its offensive production. The duo also accounted for 48 percent of the team's total receptions and receiving yards for the 2000 season.

The record-setting Hinshaw is a big loss. Hinshaw set a school record and finished second in the nation with 89 receptions, despite being slowed by a separated shoulder the final three weeks of the year. He had 1,089 receiving yards and tied for third in the nation with 13 touchdown receptions. He caught eight passes for 102 yards and two touchdowns in UCF's 40-38 win at Alabama despite suffering a separated shoulder in practice the Tuesday before the game.

Despite the departures of Hinshaw and Clark (31 receptions, 474 yards, four touchdowns in 2000), the UCF pass offense should be productive once again, provided battle-tested wideouts like **Jimmy Fryzel** (5-11, 175), **Tavirus Davis** (6-2, 190), and **Mario Jackson** (6-2, 230) step up this fall.

The most experienced receiver on the team is Davis, a fifth-year senior. He was third on the team last season with 34 catches for 445 yards and three touchdowns. Fryzel, a junior, finished the year second on the team with 36 catches for 606 yards and three touchdowns. Jackson, a junior, was the only Golden Knight tight end to catch a psss during the 2000 season. He had eight catches for 101 yards.

Of those returnees, Fryzel appears most ready to take Hinshaw's spot as UCF's featured receiver. Fryzel, who made only four receptions in 1999, came to UCF with a high school pedigree that included 68 catches as a senior at Lakeland (Fla.) High. Speedy (4.42 for 40 yards) and strong (he bench-presses 360 pounds), Fryzel averaged a team-best 16.8 yards per catch last season.

As an insurance policy, Kruczek did sign two tight ends and two wide receivers, one out of high school and the other a junior college transfer. At tight end, the Golden Knights signed **Darcy Johnson** (6-6, 220) from Palatka (Fla.) High School and **Matt Lundy** (6-5, 230) out of Orlando's Cypress Creek High School. With Johnson, UCF gets a versatile athlete who could split out at wide receiver, and with Lundy, the Golden Knights get a player who could beef up and eventually move to the offensive line.

Johnson will join his former teammate at Palatka, UCF tight end Jackson. He runs a 4.6 and has good hands. Rivals.com rated Johnson the No. 81 tight end in the nation. As a senior, he had 30 catches for 611 yards and nine touchdowns.

"(Johnson) can play wideout or tight end in my opinion," Kruczek said. "He's a very successful young guy who was recruited by Clemson, Arizona, South Carolina and opted to come to us."

In Lundy, the Golden Knights will get a late bloomer who has good hands, but expects to make gains through his blocking ability. Lundy caught 23 passes for 330 yards and three touchdowns last season. He will likely redshirt his first year.

"The upside on him is his great verticalness at 6-foot-5," Kruczek said. "He can grow to be quite a large man and if it doesn't work out at tight end, he's tough enough to move down inside. I really feel he's going to be an asset blocking and catching the football in this offense."

Both Johnson and Lundy could redshirt if sophomore **Michael Gaines** (6-3, 265), a top high school recruit two years ago, regains his old form. Gaines caught six catches for 59 yards and a 30-yard touchdown reception in one of UCF's spring scrimmages.

Gaines graduated from Tallahasee (Fla.) High School in 1999 and signed with Alabama. Unable to meet initial eligibility requirements, he did not enroll there. Gaines came to UCF in January of 2000, but was unable to participate last season because of NCAA eligibility requirements.

In high school, Gaines showed the type of versatility that made him a top recruit. He was able to play six positions: tight end, linebacker, kicker, punter, backup quarterback, and offensive tackle. He made 20 receptions for 535 yards and nine touchdowns as a senior and had 110 tackles. He was voted first-team All-Big Bend and all state as a junior and a senior and was chosen to the Florida Super 24 Team as a senior.

Gaines has been out of football for three years, but appears to getting back into the swing of things.

The Golden Knights will have two new wide receivers in **Al Peterson** and **Doug Gabriel** (6-2, 205). Peterson comes from Santa Fe High School in Alachua, Fla. and Gabriel is a junior college transfer who enrolled at UCF in the spring.

Peterson was the last member of the 2001 recruiting class to sign with the Golden Knights, but has the potential to prove he was worth the wait. Although he will probably redshirt this year, this 6-foot-2, 192-pound multi-sport athlete is expected to fit well into UCF's offense. Peterson is a big receiver, reminiscent of Clark, and runs a 4.4. As a senior he made 32 catches for 688 yards and six touchdowns, while grabbing eight interceptions on defense. He was voted all state and all-area.

"How fast he plays depends on how fast he picks up the system," Kruczek said. "This is a very gifted kid. (He) plays tremendous basketball, has great body control, can catch the football and run. We'll have to wait and see. I like big receivers. I want big, tall kids."

If Kruczek does decide to redshirt Peterson, Gabriel will look to be productive amidst a group of young receivers in Fryzel, a pair of redshirt freshmen from Miami in **Tavaris Capers** (5-9, 160) and **Luther Huggins** (5-11, 175), and junior **Britt McGriff** (5-10, 170).

McGriff (two catches in 2000) is the younger brother of former University of Florida flanker Travis McGriff. Huggins, the 2000 Florida State champion in the 100 meters, is an absolute blur—probably the fastest player in UCF's program. Capers, too, is blessed with big-time speed.

Gabriel enrolled early at UCF and participated in spring practice. At Mississippi Gulf Coast Community College, Gabriel set single-season school records for touchdowns (17) and points (104) in 2000. A second-team JUCO All-American pick by JC Gridwire, Gabriel accounted for 1,206 all-purpose yards last year. An Orlando native, Gabriel signed with Miami in 1998 but did not qualify. In 1999, he signed with Oregon State, but ended up going to Gulf Coast Community College instead.

"(Gabriel) will play this season," said Kruczek. "He will be productive in this scheme. How fast he learns this scheme will obviously dictate how successful he is and the amount of touches that he'll get at the football. He's a very motivated young man, studying what we do. So I'm looking forward to really watching him. He can do a lot of things with the ball in his hand on the short game, making people miss, and taking it the distance."

OFFENSIVE LINE

Of the three offensive line starters from the 2000 that need to be replaced, center Chris Lorenti will be missed the most. Lorenti started all 44 games of his career. He graded out better than 80 percent in nine of the 11 games this year, including season highs of 87 percent against Alabama and Virginia Tech. He had 17 knockdowns against Alabama and a total of 106 for the year.

But thanks to the signing of three junior college offensive linemen, the caliber of line play shouldn't slip too far, if at all. One of the JUCO imports, junior **Mike Mabry** (6-2, 277), should beat out mammoth redshirt freshman **Travis Muse** (6-6, 320) for Lorenti's old center spot.

Mabry has a great comfort level with UCF's coaching staff, having known assistants Robert McFarland and Gene Chizik from their days at Stephen F. Austin. A few years back, those coaches used to talk to Mabry about playing for them at Stephen F. Austin. Unhappy with the I-AA offers he was receiving, Mabry elected to play junior college ball. After he completed two successful seasons at Southwest Mississippi Community College, Southern Miss and UCF offered him full rides. Mabry chose UCF because of his relationship with McFarland and Chizik and because he saw a greater need at UCF after the graduation of Chris Lorenti.

"Coach McFarland and coach Chizik have known me since my junior year of high school," said Mabry, who has a 400-pound bench press and a 550-pound squat. "They recruited me (for Stephen F. Austin). I had a better feeling, better vibes about coming to Central Florida than Southern Miss."

Mabry's commitment to UCF allows Kruczek the luxury of keeping his strong-side starting guard from a year ago, senior **Willie Comerford** (6-4, 320) at his old spot rather than shifting him over to center. Comerford is strong (he can squat more than 500 pounds) and experienced (he started 10 games in 2000). He did not surrender a sack in 2000 and graded out at 80 percent or better in seven of his 10 starts.

He'll team with fellow returnee **Steve Edwards** (6-5, 345) on the strong side of UCF's offensive line. Edwards, a senior who transferred to UCF from West Hills Community College in California, made an immediate impact in 2000. He started the first eight games before being sidelined with an ankle sprain. He had a winning grade (80 percent or better) in eight of the nine games he played with his best game coming against Virginia Tech when he graded out at 87 percent.

After a shaky start with three sacks in the opener against Georgia Tech, he was responsible for only a third of a sack the rest of the year. He had a total of 55 knockdowns on the year with a season high 11 against Eastern Michigan. He suffered an ankle sprain against Louisiana-Monroe and missed the Alabama and Louisiana Tech games. He returned to action against Virginia Tech and had his best game of the year. Edwards played his prep ball at Mount Carmel (Ill.) High School, the same high school which produced current NFL players Donovan McNabb and Simeon Rice.

Comerford and Edwards will be backed up by returnees **Garret McCray** (6-4, 300) and **John Wimberly** (6-6, 300). After another year as understudies, McCray and Wimberly—both juniors—should both start as seniors in 2002.

On the other side of the offensive front, a pair of returnees, juniors **Taylor Robertson** (6-6, 280) and **Brian Huff** (6-6, 285), are penciled in as the starters at quick guard and quick tackle, respectively. However, they'll face serious challenges from JUCO imports **Johnovan Morgan** (6-4, 272) and **Alex Mendez** (6-6, 305). Morgan, who chose UCF over Indiana, is the younger brother of the late NFL star Derrick Thomas. He graduated from the noted Sunshine State football factory, Carol City (Fla.) High (the same school where New York Jets' 2001 first round pick Santana Moss played), and originally signed with Alabama back in 1999. But, he was unable to qualify and went the junior college route.

Mendez will push Huff to replace departing senior Kurt Baumann at quick tackle. After starring at Reedley (Calif.) Community College, Mendez had his fair share of D-I offers. He ultimately chose the Golden Knights over West Virginia, Baylor and New Mexico.

2000 STATISTICS

Rushing offense	78.7	107
Passing offense	295.2	12
Total offense	373.9	56
Scoring offense	30.3	34
Net Punting	35.9	36
Punt returns	10.4	43
Kickoff returns	15.4	111
Rushing defense	130.9	37
Passing efficiency defense	110.2	38
Total defense	323.8	28
Scoring defense	20.1	32
Turnover margin	-3	74

Last column is ranking among Division I-A teams.

KICKERS

Kruczek has no worries here. Senior **Javier Beorlegui** made 14-of-18 field goal attempts, including his last 10. He kicked a school-record four field goals, including the game-winning 37-yarder with :03 left in a 40-38 win against Alabama last Oct. 28. His longest field goal of the year was 48 yards. He made 39-of-40 PATs for a total of 81 points.

Beorlegui (6-1, 225) also did stellar work as the team's punter, averaging 40.0 yards per boot on his 45 punts last season.

UCF's place-kicker of the future is redshirt freshman **Will Rhody** (6-2, 185). He'll spend the 2001 season as Beorlegui's backup and then should land the starting job the following fall.

DEFENSIVE LINE

After ranking 28th nationally in total defense last fall, the Golden Knights should once be tough to block. That's because this year's defensive line, led by senior defensive tackle **Josh McKibben** (6-3, 270), might be the best in school history.

McKibben finished with 80 tackles, 14 tackles behind the line of scrimmage (for 64 yards lost) and had five sacks. He also had 10 quarterback hurries, one interception and one blocked field goal. And like most stars, he was able to rise up against UCF's tougher opponents. McKibben had double-digit tackle totals against Alabama, Georgia Tech, and Virginia Tech.

"Josh McKibben steps up his level of play week in and week out," Kruczek said. "He's the catalyst on that defensive line. He's an incredible football player and I just thank the Lord we've got him back this year for his leadership qualities and productivity. I can't say enough about Josh."

McKibben came to UCF in 1997 out of Hardee County High School in Wauchula, Fla., hardly the Sunshine State's most glamorous town. Throughout his first three years as a Golden Knight, his small-town America work ethic has transformed him from a scout team lineman into the anchor of the UCF defense. His blue-collar approach to football has produced results that are anything but blue collar.

In 1998, he earned the team's outstanding defensive rookie award, sharing it with linebacker **Tito Rodriguez**. Last season, he finished second on the team with 70 tackles, including seven for lost yardage and three sacks, and was chosen the Golden Knights' most spirited player and outstanding defensive lineman. And then last year, he was one of seven UCF players to earn a spot on the *Football News* All-Independent team.

Josh McKibben will play next to a familiar face in 2001 as his younger brother, junior **Jake McKibben** (6-1, 285), is slated to be the team's starting nose tackle. Jake was a walk-on in 1999, and, just like his brother, moved quickly up the depth chart because of his hard work and determination. Last season, with then-senior Jeff Mauldin hampered by a knee injury, Jake became the starting nose tackle, allowing for the two brothers to have the unique opportunity of lining up next to each other in a Division I-A football game.

"It's an awesome feeling," said Jake of playing side by side by his older brother. "I really can't describe it, its just there's no better feeling in the world just seeing Josh there beside me on the field. He's a good role model that so many other people can look up to. He's known for being a hard worker and it rubs off on the field. He means a lot to this program."

Backing up the McKibben brothers at the two inside spots will be junior **Thomas Andrews** (6-4, 250) and sophomore **Larry Brown** (6-2, 300). Brown notched 18 tackles and three sacks in 2000, while Andrews had five tackles a year ago.

Junior **Elton Patterson** (6-2, 255) will ably man the starting left end spot again. In 2000, Patterson tallied 88 total tackles, 54 of which were unassisted. He tied a school record with a team-high 19 tackles behind the line of scrimmage. He also had a team-high 10 sacks. He had 25 quarterback hurries and two forced fumbles. His backup will be senior **Boma Ekiyor** (6-3, 225), who appeared in seven games and recorded three tackles last fall.

At right end, sophomore **Brent Bolar** (6-3, 235) and junior **Wanzell Underwood** (6-5, 245) will vie to fill the cleats of the departed Don Page, who recorded 41 tackles, including 10 for loss, last year. Bolar has the upper hand, having notched 34 tackles and three sacks in 2000. Underwood had just one tackle last season.

LINEBACKERS

Even with the loss of UCF's third-leading tackler Tony Hardman, this unit still won't lack for senior leadership. Hardman, who would have been a fifth-year senior, left the team for personal medical reasons. Hardman was third on the team in tackles (96) in 2000 and he led the nation in total fumbles forced and recovered with seven.

Hardman will be missed, but the leader of this

unit will remain senior middle linebacker Rodriguez (6-2, 235). Rodriguez led the team in tackles with 121 (80 unassisted), despite missing the first two games with a knee injury. He had 10 tackles behind the line of scrimmage and two sacks. He had double-digit tackle totals in six of the last seven games, including 18 against Virginia Tech and 14 against Alabama.

Hardman will be flanked by a pair of seniors in weak-side linebacker **Willie Davis** (5-11, 215) and strong-side linebacker **Elliot Shorter** (5-10, 190). On the plus side, Davis and Shorter are experienced guys with the speed to make tackles. Davis finished the 2000 campaign with 83 tackles (fifth best on the team), including nine tackles for loss and four sacks. Shorter had 75 tackles, including 46 solo stops.

On the downside, Davis and Shorter are the size of most major D-I safeties. Davis and Shorter's lack of heft, combined with the fact that UCF's defensive line is somewhat smallish, means that the Golden Knights have trouble stopping opponents with good ground attacks.

Even though UCF should receive some praise for holding four rivals to seven or fewer points last season, it was unable to contain teams like Akron and Northern Illinois when they decided to pound it. Even Alabama was able to run well, and Virginia Tech had 313 rushing yards.

Providing relief for UCF's three starting linebackers will be sophomore **Antoine Poe** (6-0, 205) on the weak side, junior **Chris Pilinko** (6-1, 225) in the middle, and redshirt freshman **Savarris Brown** (6-0, 215) at strong-side linebacker. Poe (18 tackles in 2000) and Brown, who starred at Fort Myers (Fla.) High and chose the Knights over Oklahoma State and Iowa State, have bright futures.

But with Rodriguez, Davis and Shorter in their senior seasons, Kruczek decided to stock up on linebackers. The one the UCF coaches are most excited about is freshman **Andra Hoston** (6-2, 220), the team's top recruit who almost got away.

When Hoston committed to Auburn, the UCF football coaches thought they had lost their top prospect. Two weeks later, they were back on the phone with him and the deal was done, as Hoston de-committed from the Tigers and decided to become a Golden Knight. Hoston, from Tampa's Hillsborough High School, changed his mind because he wanted to stay closer to his family. Hoston is one of six linebackers in UCF's recruiting class.

Hoston was rated as the No. 25 linebacker in the nation by Rivals.com and as the No. 6 linebacker on Max Emfinger's National Nifty 150 Blue Chips. He was the Class 5A Player of the Year in Hillsborough County and was first-team all-state. Hoston was a four-year starter and totaled more than 100 tackles. He also had 12 sacks, four forced fumbles and two interceptions.

"Andra is probably the most visible, most regarded athlete in our signing class," Kruczek said. "He's incredible. He makes plays all over the field. He's tough up inside. He can cover in pass coverage and does a remarkable job and we're very fortunate to have him."

In addition to Hoston, UCF also signed **Lemec Bernard**, **James Cook**, **Stanford Rhule**, **Lamont Stringfield**, and **Kareem (Dee) Williford** at the linebacker position. Bernard is 6-0, weighs 190 pounds and runs a 4.6 in the 40. Bernard comes to UCF from Bishop Verot High School in Fort Myers, Fla. As a senior, he made 72 tackles, seven sacks, had five blocked punts and one touchdown on defense. He doubled as a tailback in high school. On offense, he rushed for 1,000 yards and nine touchdowns.

Cook is a 6-3, 210-pound outside linebacker from Jacksonville's Trinity Christian High School. He was second-team all state. Cook was selected Clay County Offensive and Defensive Player of the Year in both his sophomore and junior years. He had 77 tackles and 10 sacks his senior year. Cook runs the 40-yard dash in 4.6 seconds. Eventually, Cook will probably grow into a defensive lineman for the Golden Knights.

Rhule (5-11, 230) hails from Dillard High School in Ft. Lauderdale, and is an aggressive inside linebacker who loves contact. He was voted MVP of the state championship game, making 12 tackles in the game. In 14 games as a senior, Rhule accumulated 184 tackles, eight sacks, five interceptions, six pass breakups, 12 forced fumbles and five fumble recoveries. He was first-team all-state pick.

Stringfield (6-0, 225) will join former teammates and 2000 UCF signees Capers and Huggins on the Golden Knights. Stringfield, Capers and Huggins played together at Miami's Jackson High School where Stringfield recorded 118 tackles, 14 sacks and five interceptions as a senior. He ran a 4.5 at the Nike Combine and has a 34-inch vertical leap. He chose UCF over Syracuse, N.C. State, Minnesota and Georgia.

"(Stringfield) can play inside, outside athletically and plays the game the way you like it played 100 percent of the time," Kruczek said.

Williford (6-1, 211) is the remaining linebacker UCF added to its roster. Williford bench presses 300 pounds and has 4.5 speed. He was selected second-team all-state, first-team all-county and recorded 157 tackles, four fumble recoveries, three forced fumbles and one blocked punt as a senior at Auburndale (Fla.) High.

DEFENSIVE BACKS

Going into national signing day, UCF had many priorities. Defense was at the forefront of these, in particular landing some linebackers and some additional size on the defensive line. But the Golden Knights also looked to add depth to their defensive backfield. Digging into the junior college and high school ranks, UCF has brought in some potentially talented players to fill in the gaps.

With the graduation of Damian Demps and Tommy Shavers, holes at both safety positions were created. Demps, in particular, will be difficult to replace. He finished second on the team in tackles with 107. He had four tackles for loss, two interceptions and nine pass break ups. He had a game-saving interception on the goal line in the final minute against Louisiana Tech. He also had an interception against Alabama.

The leading suspects to man the safety spots are senior **Ricot Joseph** (6-0, 190) at free safety and JUCO import **James Cody** (6-1, 210) at strong safety. Joseph is a proven commodity, having recorded 74 tackles and a pair of interceptions in 2000. Cody, who has three years of eligibility left after playing last season at Butler (Kansas) Community College. Originally out of Naples (Fla.) High School, Cody recorded 56 tackles and a team-leading four interceptions at Butler last season, helping his team to make the Empire State Bowl in New York.

"(Cody) can play pass," Kruczek said. "He has the athleticism to play two deep and play man. He supports the run very well, a very physical kind of guy that you like in the secondary."

Still, Cody won't be handed the job. He'll have to beat out senior **Albert Snyder** (5-11, 170) and redshirt freshman **Atari Bigby** (5-10, 190) for the No. 1 strong safety spot. But making Cody a pretty safe bet to win the job is the fact that Snyder (three tackles in 2000) and Bigby are both unproven. Joseph's understudy at free safety figures to be junior **Jimmy Grimsley** (6-2, 180).

Senior **Travis Fisher** (5-10, 175) and junior **Asante Samuel** (5-11, 190) are penciled in as the starting cornerbacks. Fisher had 37 tackles and two interceptions last fall, while Samuel finished with 26 tackles and a pair of picks in 2000. The speedy Samuel also made contributions as a return man, bringing back 10 kickoffs for 168 yards (a 16.8 average).

Pushing Fisher and Samuel will be a pair of junior college recruits in juniors **Carlos Thompson** (5-10, 180) and **Terrence Bell** (6-0, 190). Thompson and Bell enrolled at UCF early and participated in spring drills. Both should play significant roles and could eventually become starters.

After a stint in the Marine Corps, Thompson attended Southwest Mississippi Community College, where he had five interceptions and blocked seven punts as a sophomore. Bell is blessed with 4.4 speed and was a former JUCO All-American at Middle Georgia in 1998 when he led the nation in interceptions. After a one-year hiatus, Bell resurfaced at Dodge City (Kansas) Community College and earned second-team All-Jayhawk Conference honors.

UCF also continued to dig into the well of players coming out of Astronaut (Fla.) High School, signing safety **Peter Sands** (6-4, 200). An all-state player and heavily recruited prospect, he chose UCF over Clemson, Southern Cal, Marshall, Kansas State, and Miami. Sands can cover a lot of territory with his big body; evident in the 117 tackles and four interceptions he recorded his senior season. A great athlete, he also participated in basketball and track as a high jumper. If able to learn the UCF defense quickly, Sands has a chance to play this year.

At cornerback, UCF also signed **Omar Laurence** out of Largo (Fla.) High School. Described as a playmaker by Jamie Newberg of Border Wars, he too chose UCF over Clemson. At 5-11, 175, he played a variety of positions in high school and has tremendous speed. Coaches hope for him to be a factor in the secondary in the near future, but he is a candidate to redshirt this year unless injuries strike.

PUNTERS

Senior Javier Beorlegui, who also handles placement duties, remains a one-man kicking show for the Golden Knights. As a punter, Beorlegui averaged 40.0 yards per kick on his 45 punts last season. His understudy is junior **Ryan Flinn** (6-5, 200), who punted twice in 2000 for a 39.5 average.

SPECIAL TEAMS

The Knights continued to be outstanding in this area, blocking five kicks in 2000. If junior college import Carlos Thompson's seven blocked punts last year at Southwest Mississippi Community College are a true indication, then UCF should continue to give opposing punters and kickers the jitters this fall.

UCF's kicking game will rest on the talented toes of senior Javier Beorlegui for a third straight year. Also back in the fold is senior long snapper **Mike Hedge** (6-1, 220). Sure-handed junior wide receiver **Jimmy Fryzel** (5-11, 175) will handle the holding chores on field goals and extra points. JUCO transfer Bell and his 4.4 speed could be put to use in the return game, where junior cornerback Samuel (10 kickoff returns for 168 yards in 2000) is also a possibility.

RECRUITING CLASS

Kruczek and Co. enjoyed a recruiting bonanza even before the national signing day arrived. The reason? Five players, including three junior college transfers, were already enrolled in school and were able to take part in spring practice.

The most promising of the five are former Dr. Phillips (Fla.) High wide receiver Gabriel (6-2, 205), who passed up a chance to play at Florida State coming out of Mississippi Gulf Coast Community College, and cornerbacks Bell from Dodge City Community College and Thompson from Southwest Mississippi Community College.

Former Daytona Beach Mainland (Fla.) High quarterback Brandon Sumner, a transfer from Georgia Tech, also picked UCF, but he'll have to sit out next season before competing for a starting job in 2002.

"We attempted to go out and get the best football players that we could get our hands on, and we think we met that objective," Kruczek said. "Counting the five that we added at the semester break [last December], we added 25 or 26 great football players, far and away the best recruiting class we've had ever."

Perhaps the most highly regarded high school prospect in the class is Tampa Hillsborough (Fla.) High School linebacker Hoston (6-2, 220), who initially committed to Auburn.

UCF coaches also are high on Titusville Astronaut (Fla.) High tight end/defensive end **Marcus Clemons** (6-5, 270), Melbourne Palm Bay (Fla.) High offensive tackle **Jeff Harper** (6-8, 305), St. Petersburg (Fla.) Admiral Farragut Academy center **Adam Butcher** (6-3, 285) and Palatka (Fla.) High tight end Johnson (6-6, 220).

BLUE RIBBON ANALYSIS

OFFENSE	B
SPECIAL TEAMS	C+
DEFENSE	C+
INTANGIBLES	C+

Matching last fall's seven wins could prove difficult for the Golden Knights, even though the overall talent base appears to be better than it was a year ago. The reason for the pessimism? UCF must survive an early schedule that includes trips to Clemson (Sept. 1), Syracuse (Sept. 9), Tulane (Sept. 22) and Virginia Tech (Sept. 29) in the first five weeks in order for 2001 to be successful.

If UCF can beat Louisiana-Lafayette at home in mid-September and can somehow prevail in at least one of the four high-profile September road tests, then another winning season is possible. The key will be avoiding a major injury in the first month. Because the October and early-November slate (UAB, Liberty, Louisiana-Monroe, at Utah State, Akron) is much more manageable before a rugged season-ender at Arkansas.

(B.D.)

2000 RESULTS

Georgia Tech	L	17-21	0-1
Northwestern State	W	19-7	1-1
Akron	L	24-35	1-2
William & Mary	W	52-7	2-2
Eastern Michigan	W	31-10	3-2
Northern Illinois	L	20-40	3-3
Eastern Kentucky	W	34-3	4-3
Louisiana-Monroe	W	55-0	5-3
Alabama	W	40-38	6-3
Louisiana Tech	W	20-16	7-3
Virginia Tech	L	21-44	7-4

Navy

LOCATION	**Annapolis, MD**
CONFERENCE	**Independent**
LAST SEASON	**1-10 (.091)**
CONFERENCE RECORD	**NA**
OFFENSIVE STARTERS RETURNING	**4**
DEFENSIVE STARTERS RETURNING	**7**
NICKNAME	**Midshipmen**
COLORS	**Navy Blue & Gold**
HOME FIELD	**Navy-Marine Corps Memorial Stadium (30,000)**
HEAD COACH	**Charlie Weatherbie (Oklahoma State '77)**
RECORD AT SCHOOL	**30-38 (6 years)**
CAREER RECORD	**45-57 (9 years)**
ASSISTANTS	
	Rick Lantz (Central Connecticut '64) Defensive Coordinator/Linebackers
	Mark Hudspeth (Delta State '92) Offensive Coordinator/Fullbacks
	Sammy Steinmark (Wyoming '79) Assistant Head Coach/Slotbacks
	Todd Spencer (Pacific Lutheran '79) Offensive Line
	Danilo Robinson (Utah State '97) Offensive Line
	Matt Wells (Utah State '96) Wide Receivers
	Mitch Ware (Southwest Missouri State '80) Quarterbacks
	Dale Pehrson (Utah '76) Defensive Line
	Scott Conley (East Texas State '70) Linebackers
	Tim DeRuyter (Air Force '85) Secondary
	Joe Speed (Navy '96) Secondary
	Chad Huff (Delta State '97) Fullbacks
TEAM WINS (last 5 yrs.)	**9-7-3-5-1**
FINAL RANK (last 5 yrs.)	**37-55-85-79-94**
2000 FINISH	**Beat Army in regular-season finale.**

COACH AND PROGRAM

Listen to the enthusiasm in Charlie Weatherbie's voice and you'd think his football team is coming off a 10-1 season rather than the 1-10 debacle it endured last fall.

"It's going great," Weatherbie said shortly after the completion of spring practice in April. "We're excited about the upcoming season."

The Midshipmen do have at least two reasons to be optimistic. One, they did win their finale, beating rival Army for the third time in four years. Two, no matter how trying the upcoming season is, it probably won't come close to matching the difficulty of last season when the Midshipmen battled injuries and had the cloud of a rape scandal—that ultimately led to three players resigning from the Naval Academy—hanging over the program.

Navy's victory celebration didn't last long as Weatherbie fired three assistant coaches, including offensive coordinator Mike Vaught, and reassigned defensive coordinator Tim DeRuyter, now the secondary coach, on Dec. 4, two days after the season ended.

Former Navy assistant Rick Lantz, Virginia's defensive coordinator for the last 10 seasons, was hired in January and charged with retooling a unit that ranked 97th (out of 114 teams) in total defense. Lantz, who will also oversee the linebackers, inherits a group that allowed 188.8 yards per game on the ground (91st) and was second-worst in the country against the pass.

"He may be one of the top five defensive coordinators in the country at the college level," Weatherbie said. "He's a sharp, sharp defensive mind."

The Midshipmen return seven starters on defense, including end **Michael Wagoner** and middle linebacker **Jake Bowen**, and the defensive unit looked strong while defeating the offense, 25-12, in the spring game. Navy got most of the fundamental aspects of its new 4-3 package installed early and will spend the rest of the time leading up to the Aug. 30 season opener at Temple refining things.

Shaka Martin, who started the first seven games at outside linebacker before being suspended from the team after being charged with rape in October, will not be back for his senior season. Martin, defensive back Arion Williams and slotback Cordea Brittingham were charged with raping a female midshipman at an off-campus party June 29, 2000. Prosecutors dropped charges against the three in March and all three resigned from the Academy as part of a settlement.

One of Lantz's biggest challenges will be rebuilding his unit's confidence. Opponents passed for 23 touchdowns and scored 35.5 points per game against the Midshipmen last season. They have scrapped their 5-2 scheme in favor of the 4-3.

"No. 1, they've got to be really confident in the base package and be able to branch out from the base package," Weatherbie said. "They also have to believe in one another and that everyone can get their job done without worrying about trying to do their job and someone else's job. We also have to be able to stop the run and react to the football.

"Every great team that I have ever been associated with has had great defenses. If they can't score on you, they can't beat you."

Offense was also a problem for the Midshipmen last season. Navy ranked 92nd in total offense, including 100th in scoring offense (16.55 points per game) and 108th in passing offense (139.5 yards per game).

Enter new offensive coordinator Mark Hudspeth and his flexbone offense. Hudspeth, the offensive coordinator and quarterbacks coach at Delta State the last two seasons, directed a group that set 21 NCAA Division II records, 12 Gulf Coast records and 21 school records while winning the Division II national championship last season. The Statesmen averaged 40.4 points and 478.5 yards, including 309.6 on the ground.

"He is a great fit for us with his vast experience as a player and coach," Weatherbie said of Hudspeth, a former starting quarterback and free safety at Delta State. "I expect he will come in and install an offense that will be not only exciting to watch, but successful as well."

The Midshipmen will still run their option attack, but will also open up things (as evidenced by the 68 passes thrown in the spring game) with some four- and five-receiver sets. The offense returns just four starters and loses five seniors on the offensive line, but should be bolstered by the return of senior quarterback **Brian Madden**, who tore the ACL in his right knee during the 2000 spring game and missed all of last season.

Madden re-injured the medial meniscus in his right knee during a weight room drill in the off-season and had the knee scoped in March. He was held out of contact in the spring, but is expected to be back at full strength for the fall.

Navy returns the leading rusher **Raheem Lambert** (597 yards) from the nation's 29th-best running attack but will need to take better care of the ball. The Mids fumbled 33 times last season, losing 18 and having four returned for touchdowns.

Contrary to what some say, the Mids did not win the only game that mattered last season. Sure, the Army game has added importance, but the Air Force game also counts in the competition for the Commander-In-Chief's-Trophy and the Notre Dame rivalry is special even though Navy has lost 37 straight to the Fighting Irish dating back to the Roger Staubach days of 1963.

"We always want to win and go to a bowl game," Weatherbie said.

That won't be easy this season with 2000 bowl teams Georgia Tech, Northwestern, Boston College, Air Force and Notre Dame on the schedule. The Mids will also face Toledo, which opened last season with a 24-6 victory at Penn State and finished 10-1.

2001 SCHEDULE

Aug.	30	@Temple
Sept.	8	Georgia Tech
	15	@Northwestern
	22	Boston College
Oct.	6	Air Force
	13	Rice
	20	@Rutgers
	27	@Toledo
Nov.	10	Tulane
	17	@Notre Dame
Dec.	1	Army (Veterans Stadium)

QUARTERBACKS

Although the departed Brian Broadwater and returning senior **Ed Malinowski** did their best, the Navy offense felt the sting of Madden's absence throughout last season.

A punishing runner, the 6-1, 220-pound Madden led the nation's quarterbacks with 897 yards rushing in 1999 even though he did not start until the eighth game. He led Navy to a 3-2 record as a starter and is the first Navy player to rush for more than 100 yards in his first five starts.

"He's very physical, strong-armed, hard-nosed and a good leader," Weatherbie said.

Madden, who was selected a co-captain by his teammates, completed just 45.8 percent of his passes in '99 and will need some real practice time in order to get in sync with Navy's new passing game.

"It is no secret that we are a better football team when he is on the field and we need to keep him healthy and ready for the season," Weatherbie said.

Malinowski (5-10, 202) switched from safety to backing up Broadwater last fall. An unselfish player with a strong arm and good running skills, Malinowski played in all 11 games (starting three) and led the team with five rushing touchdowns. He also threw for 455 yards and three touchdowns and was intercepted twice.

"Probably his best attributes are his leadership and physical strength," Weatherbie said.

Sophomore **Chris Candeto** (5-11, 193) showed promise in limited game action last season, but could be in the mix as a reserve. Candeto, the 6A Player of the Year his senior year at DeLand (Fla.) High School, ran for 36 yards and a touchdown and completed 12-of-27 passes for 128 yards, a touchdown and an interception. The probable quarterback of the future for the Midshipmen, he also hit .245 in 37 games as an outfielder for Navy's baseball team this spring.

"He throws well and has good strength and good speed," Weatherbie said.

RUNNING BACKS

The numbers (178.2 yards per game) seem to indicate a strong running game for Navy last season, but when you consider the 18 fumbles, 3.6 yard-per-carry average and that the team's leading rusher didn't score a touchdown, there is definite room for improvement.

Lambert (5-10, 214) ran for 790 yards and six scores as a sophomore, but was slowed by a separated shoulder for most of last season. A converted tailback, he runs a 4.47 40-yard dash and is not afraid to take a hit. Lambert underwent shoulder surgery in the off-season and had a strong spring. He should flourish in the new offense as the starting fullback and, occasionally, lining up at wide receiver.

Junior **Bryce McDonald** (6-0, 219) and senior **Rashad Jamal** (5-10, 205), a converted slotback, are the leading candidates to back up Lambert.

Speedy slotback **Gene Reese** is one player who should benefit from Hudspeth's arrival. A 5-9, 180-pound junior, Reese runs a 4.42 40 and has good hands. He finished last season with 194 rushing yards and 18 receptions for 183 yards and a score. He could also see time at receiver.

"He had a good spring and he's one of those players that could have a chance to shine in the new offense," Weatherbie said of Reese.

Junior **Brad Tepper** (5-10, 208) played well toward the end of last season and has gained nearly 25 pounds in the off-season. A strong blocker with good hands, he could start at one of the slotback spots. Potential game-breaker **Tony Lane**, a 5-9, 194-pound sophomore, junior **Donnie Fricks** (5-8, 190) and senior **Terrence Coleman** (6-0, 210) also return at slotback.

WIDE RECEIVERS/TIGHT ENDS

Navy is hoping its strength lies in numbers, because Reese is the team's top returning pass catcher. The Midshipmen don't have any returning standouts, but Weatherbie likes this unit's mix of size and speed.

Help could come from converted cornerback **Jeff Gaddy**, winner of the Vice Admiral William P. Mack Award as the most improved player in spring drills. Gaddy, a 5-10, 175-pound senior, moved to receiver at the start of the spring and is listed as a starter heading into the fall. He has run the 40 in 4.35 seconds and owns a 35-inch vertical leap.

"He has good hands and has done an excellent job of learning the new system and then going out and performing in practice," Weatherbie said. "We expect big things out of him this fall."

The same can be said for junior **Chandler Sims** (6-4, 210), a big target who caught five passes last season. Junior **Dominic Bailey** (5-9, 161) logged five starts and made 13 receptions last season. He has good speed and should be productive in the new offense.

Juniors **Mike McIlravey** (5-10, 176) and Garrett Cox (6-0, 205) and sophomores **Martin Huggins** (6-5, 214) and **Mark Tedrow** (6-3, 202) could also contribute to the passing game.

Junior **Steve Mercer** (6-3, 245) will provide a pass-catching threat when Navy goes to a tight-end formation.

Junior **Jim Zakar** (6-5, 265) has moved back to tight end after giving left tackle a try in the spring. He gained 40 pounds in the off-season, but still has a 31-inch vertical leap. Sophomore **Luke Dreyer** (6-6, 242) may also see some time at tight end.

OFFENSIVE LINE

Weatherbie likes this group's quickness and size, but this oft-undersized unit loses five senior starters and must learn a new offense. Their jobs won't be easy.

"They've got a lot to prove and everyone expects a lot out of them," Weatherbie said. "They've got to do a lot and they've got to know a lot because of what we're doing. We're going to have to run the football to be successful."

Senior **Brian Schulz** (6-0, 287) is the only returning starter, but he's playing a new position. Schulz, who bench-presses a team-best 454 pounds, started seven games at left guard last season but is moving to center.

Schulz will be backed up by juniors **Ben Eastburn** (6-3, 265) and **Justin Smith** (6-5, 250).

Junior **David Walsh** (6-6, 288) added 28 pounds in the off-season and showed enough in spring practice to send Zakar, the projected starter at left tackle, back to tight end. Senior **John Jeffery** (6-3, 275) has good mobility and the inside track on the starting right tackle spot. Junior **Grant Moody** (6-4, 265) and sophomore **Tucker Bennett** (6-4, 248), a converted defensive end, are expected to back up Walsh with sophomore **Sean Magee** (6-6, 266) and junior **Derek Jaskowiak** (6-4, 261), another convert from defense, behind Jeffrey.

Junior **Travis Peace** (6-4, 287), who began his Navy career at tight end, is slated to take over for Schulz at left guard and junior **Brett Cochrane** (6-4, 292), who gained 27 pounds in the off-season, is penciled in as the starter at right guard.

Junior **Matt Nye** (6-4, 280) and sophomore **Ryan McKay** (6-2, 259) are behind Peace, and Cochrane has some beef behind him in senior **Dan Venuto** (6-6, 290) and sophomore **Shane Todd** (6-4, 297).

2000 STATISTICS

Rushing offense	178.2	29
Passing offense	139.5	108
Total offense	317.6	92
Scoring offense	16.5	100
Net Punting	33.9	74
Punt returns	5.2	105
Kickoff returns	18.5	79
Rushing defense	188.8	91
Passing efficiency defense	155.5	113
Total defense	418.4	97
Scoring defense	35.5	105
Turnover margin	-5	82

Last column is ranking among Division I-A teams.

KICKERS

Senior **David Hills** (6-1, 172) emerged as a pleasant surprise last season, making 9-of-12 field-goal attempts and 16-of-17 extra points, but he could lose his job to sophomore **Eric Rolfs** (6-2, 161). Rolfs, last year's junior varsity kicker, owns a stronger leg and had a more accurate spring to pass Hills on the depth chart. Sophomore **Josh Dupre** (5-11, 219) hopes to push Hills and Rolfs for the job.

DEFENSIVE LINE

Lantz has been a college football coach for 35 years and certainly knows what it takes to build a winning defense. If the almost-always undersized Midshipmen are truly going to be better, the improvement will need to start up front where Navy got pushed around last season, allowing opponents 418.5 yards per game and generating just 15 sacks.

Wagoner (6-2, 261), a two-year starter with big play ability, led all linemen with 46 tackles, including seven for losses, from his defensive tackle spot. He will play end this year.

"He really has a nose for the football and finds the ball well," Weatherbie said of Wagoner.

Junior **Dan Person** (6-5, 255) had a strong spring and could start opposite Wagoner. Person added 15 pounds in the off-season without losing his quickness.

Senior **Eric Severson** (6-2, 240) has improved his strength and should see time at end along with sophomores **Steve Adair** (6-2, 231) and **Ralph Henry** (6-1, 254) and junior **Glenn Schatz** (6-1, 238).

Juniors **Josh Brindel** (6-2, 264) and **Andy Zetts** (6-1, 265) shared time at nose guard last season and will contribute at tackle. Senior **Matt Berger** (6-2, 245) enters fall practice on an upswing after a strong spring. Juniors **Joey Owmby** (6-3, 262) and **Pete Beuttenmuller** (6-4, 260) will also vie for time at tackle.

LINEBACKERS

The combination of talent and experience could make this unit the strongest on the team.

"I feel like linebacker may be our deepest position," Weatherbie said. "We have five guys there that have started for us and several others that have played. There will be some transition to the new defense, but this group should have no problem adapting."

Senior co-captain Bowen (6-1, 240) certainly won't. Last season Bowen returned from a two-year Mormon mission to Brazil and finished second on the team with 72 tackles. A gutty throwback, he squats 535 pounds, runs a 4.75 40, has a 33-inch vertical leap and turns 24 on Sept. 22. Beyond that, he also makes plays.

"He's a guy with a lot of maturity and savvy," Weatherbie said.

The Mids also welcome back senior **Ryan Hamilton** (6-2, 232), one of the Academy's toughest linebackers in recent memory. Hamilton, who made 101 tackles as a sophomore in 1990, sprained the MCL in his right knee and missed the second half of last season.

Sophomores **Ben Mathews** (6-1, 220) and **Eddie Carthan** (5-11, 221) both gained starting experience as freshmen and will be difficult to keep off the field.

Seniors **Mike Chiesl** (6-1, 238) and **Dan Ryno** (6-1, 225), whose brothers Tom (class of 1997) and David (class of 2000) were standouts at Navy, provide experience.

Sophomores **Donyale West** (6-0, 208), **Andy Sinitere** (5-11, 226) and **Chris Wade** (6-0, 223) could be key contributors in the future.

DEFENSIVE BACKS

The secondary is not to blame for all of Navy's pass defense problems last season, but there is plenty of room for improvement on a unit that ranked second worst in the country and gave up 23 scoring passes. Factor in the fact All-East free safety Chris Lepore (five interceptions) has graduated and it's apparent this group has plenty of work to do.

"I think you will see a big improvement in the secondary this year," Weatherbie said. "We had a lot of young or first-time starters out there last year and they gained a great deal of valuable experience."

Senior **Marcus Jackson** (5-10, 172) started all 11 games at cornerback and finished fourth on the team in tackles. He has the physical tools (4.37 40 time and 37-inch vertical leap) to be an effective player but is being pushed for his starting spot by junior **Clyde Clark** (6-1, 193), a converted safety.

Sophomore **Shalimar Blazier** (5-11, 183) is one of the team's top athletes and started four of the final five games last season. He broke up three passes in the first quarter of his first career start and should be better and more consistent this fall. Sophomores **David Bush** (5-7, 170) and **Sina Ekundayo** (5-11, 180) are competing for the backup spot.

Senior **DeJuan Cromer** (5-9, 187) returns after a solid season at strong safety. Cromer defends the run and pass well and ended last season third on the team with 60 tackles. Junior **Marc Giorgi** (5-10, 193) and sophomore **Ben Michael** (6-0, 203) will back up Cromer.

Matt Brooks (6-0, 185), a senior who played in all 11 games last season, inherits the spot vacated by Lepore. Juniors **Joey Fay** (6-0, 202), **J.P. Blecksmith** (6-3, 221), a converted quarterback, and **Lenter Thomas** (5-11, 190) also hope to play.

PUNTERS

The departure of starting receiver Brian Williams leaves a void at punter, a job he also handled. Williams averaged a fair 39.2 yards per boot, but had three kicks blocked. Sophomore **Bobby Sparks** (6-3, 205) heads the depth chart coming into the fall and is the only contender with game experience—his lone punt last year went for 69 yards. Sophomore **John Skaggs** (6-1, 205), Rolfs, and sophomore **Mason Burk** (5-11, 189), who also doubles as a wide receiver, are also competing for the job.

SPECIAL TEAMS

Navy struggled in these areas here, too, particularly in the punting game where the Midshipmen had three punts blocked and two returned for touchdowns. Opponents averaged almost 10 yards per punt return, compared to 5.4 for Navy.

Jamal averaged 19.1 yards per kickoff return and will get help from Lane. Primary punt returner Billy Hubbard has graduated, leaving the chores to McIlravy and Bailey.

Junior **Heath Sanders** (6-3, 258), a defensive end by trade, returns as the team's long snapper.

RECRUITING CLASS

Navy does not release the names of its incoming freshman class until the student-athletes have completed summer plebe training. Weatherbie expects six to 10 of his newcomers to contribute by the end of the season.

Like other service academies, Navy has stricter qualifying standards that can make recruiting difficult especially at the speed positions and on the defensive line.

"You are trying to recruit the best kind of athlete that you can admit to the Naval Academy," Weatherbie said.

Weatherbie said Navy has landed better skill position players this year, but time will tell. In the meantime look for sophomores Rolfs, Sparks, Lane, Candeto, Tedrow, Magee, Henry, Bush and Ekundayo to move up from the junior varsity ranks and contribute.

BLUE RIBBON ANALYSIS

OFFENSE	D+
SPECIAL TEAMS	C-
DEFENSE	D+
INTANGIBLES	C

Weatherbie hosted an Internet chat session on the Academy's official Web site in February.

While most of the questions were general in nature, one stood out. It went like this: "Excited about next year asks: I am starting to get really excited about next year. Do you expect the new offensive scheme to be mature enough in the first year to produce six or more wins next year?"

Weatherbie's response: "Yes, I do."

The answer wasn't a surprise, but it is difficult to share Weatherbie's optimism.

Injuries aside, Navy struggled last year and new schemes on offense and defense are not going to immediately solve all of the problems. Having Madden back will help, but there are legitimate questions at running back, receiver and on the offensive line. The defense returns seven starters, but that's no sure sign of success.

The bottom line is Navy has to play better. New coordinators Mark Hudspeth and Rick Lantz bring solid schemes for the offense and defense, respectively, but the players have to learn and execute to be successful. Often undersized and facing opponents with more athletic talent, the Midshipmen will also have to play with passion on every down in order to see better results on the scoreboard.

"It was a challenge for everybody, but it was a great challenge because a lot of times you get stagnant and stale with what you are doing," Weatherbie said of all the changes made in the off-season.

There's nothing wrong with a fresh approach and believing in your team, but living up to high expectations can be difficult. The coordinators took the fall for Navy's problems last season and some may grow impatient with Weatherbie if his optimism and changes don't deliver better results this fall.

(S.B.)

2000 RESULTS

Temple	L	6-17	0-1
Georgia Tech	L	13-40	0-2
Boston College	L	7-48	0-3
TCU	L	0-24	0-4
Air Force	L	13-27	0-5
Notre Dame	L	14-45	0-6
Rutgers	L	21-28	0-7
Toledo	L	14-35	0-8
Tulane	L	38-50	0-9
Wake Forest	L	26-49	0-10
Army	W	30-28	1-10

Notre Dame

LOCATION	**South Bend, IN**
CONFERENCE	**Independent**
LAST SEASON	**9-3 (.750)**
CONFERENCE RECORD	**NA**
OFFENSIVE STARTERS RETURNING	**8**
DEFENSIVE STARTERS RETURNING	**7**
NICKNAME	**Fighting Irish**
COLORS	**Blue & Gold**
HOME FIELD	**Notre Dame Stadium (80,012)**
HEAD COACH	**Bob Davie (Youngstown St.'76)**
RECORD AT SCHOOL	**30-19 (4 years)**
CAREER RECORD	**30-19 (4 years)**
ASSISTANTS	

Greg Mattison (Wisconsin-LaCrosse '71)
Defensive Coordinator
Kevin Rogers (William & Mary '74)
Offensive Coordinator/Quarterbacks
Kirk Doll (East Carolina '74)
Inside Linebackers
Joker Phillips (Kentucky '84)
Wide Receivers
Desmond Robinson (Pittsburgh '78)
Running Backs
Steve Addazio (Central Connecticut State '81)
Tackles/Tight Ends/Special Teams
Dave Borbely (DePauw '81)
Centers/Guards
Larry Johnson (Elizabeth City State '73)
Defensive Line
David Lockwood (West Virginia '88)
Secondary
Bill Sheridan (Grand Valley State '82)
Safeties

TEAM WINS (last 5 yrs.)	**8-7-9-5-9**
FINAL RANK (last 5 yrs.)	**20-43-24-45-14**
2000 FINISH	**Lost to Oregon State in Fiesta Bowl.**

COACH AND PROGRAM

All that chatter about the demise of Notre Dame football turned out to be a bit premature.

The Irish improved from a 5-7 record in 1999 to a 9-3 mark that featured a seven-game winning streak to end the 2000 regular season and a first-ever Bowl Championship Series berth, in the Tostitos Fiesta Bowl. Sure, the 41-9 loss to Oregon State in the Fiesta Fiasco was tough for Notre Dame's Subway Alumni to swallow, but the BCS bowl berth added $12-13 million to Notre Dame's coffers and ensured that embattled coach Bob Davie would be around for a while.

Now, Davie firmly believes that his team is ready to take the next step toward national prominence (the Irish were 15th in the final Associated Press poll for 2000 for its best finish since 1995). He thinks that this is his most talented team at Notre Dame, a team that has re-stocked the shelves to the point it can compete every week with the nation's elite.

"When you look at our football team, I certainly think we have enough talent to win every Saturday," said Davie, 30-19 at Notre Dame. "We had enough talent to win the Fiesta Bowl. We would have had to have played perfectly, but I think we have it built back up where we have enough talent to win. I don't see us being outmatched any week."

Another sign that Notre Dame is starting to regain its once-lofty stature is the fact that it had six players selected in last spring's NFL draft. In both 1997 and '99, just one Irish player had been selected.

This spring, guard Mike Gandy, taken by the Bears in the third round, was the first Irish player chosen. He was followed by cornerback Brock Williams (third round, New England), tight end Jabari Holloway (fourth, New England), safety Tony Driver (sixth, Buffalo), tight end Dan O'Leary (sixth, Buffalo) and linebacker Anthony Denman (seventh, Jacksonville).

"Going from one player, a seventh-round pick (Jarious Jackson), to six, I feel good about where we are," Davie said. "We'll have more than that drafted next year. The senior class we have coming back is the best in my eight years at Notre Dame. I think we have a good, strong foundation and everyone's encouraged. I think we've made some progress."

To keep moving forward, Davie must find himself a steady quarterback of the future and re-stock the offensive line and defensive secondary. The quarterback and secondary, in particular, will bear watching. Davie has three sophomores in the mix at quarterback; the most seasoned is **Matt LoVecchio** (who started eight games last year and showed a great deal of maturity in 2000). He will need to be a steady hand on offense. The secondary will be put to the test as the Irish face some of the nation's top quarterbacks (Nebraska's Eric Crouch, Tennessee's Casey Clausen, USC's Carson Palmer) as well as three other teams with pass-happy schemes in Purdue, Pittsburgh and West Virginia.

Despite the unanswered questions, Davis is confident that the Irish have the talent to compete against anyone in the country.

"We have some ingredients to be successful," Davie said. "(But) just having the ingredients is not always the most important thing. It's the dynamics of meshing all those things together that's important. But the bottom line, being dead honest, from a talent standpoint, this is the most talented team we've had."

2001 SCHEDULE

Sept.	8	@Nebraska
	15	@Purdue
	22	Michigan State
	29	@Texas A&M
Oct.	6	Pittsburgh
	13	West Virginia
	20	USC
	27	@Boston College
Nov.	3	Tennessee
	17	Navy
	24	@Stanford

QUARTERBACKS

What a difference a year makes. This time last year, then-junior **Arnaz Battle** (6-1, 220) was the unquestioned No. 1 quarterback and one of the team leaders for the Fighting Irish. But Battle's 2000 season ended because of a broken wrist in the second game against Nebraska and he is now a backup flanker.

The man under center, for now, is sophomore Matt LoVecchio (6-4, 194), who was a bit of a revelation last fall. LoVecchio will start Sept. 8 in Notre Dame's nationally televised opener at Nebraska on ABC, and that's all there is to it.

"When we walk out there in Lincoln, I want to have a guy who's been under the gun," Davie said at the end of spring practice.

LoVecchio, who completed 73-of-125 passing for 980 yards, 11 touchdowns, one interception and helped the Irish rank 17th nationally in passing efficiency last fall, is clearly the most experienced of the three players in the quarterback derby. A year ago, LoVecchio led the Irish to seven consecutive victories before a 9-3 season ended with a lopsided 41-9 loss to Oregon State. He'll start ahead of redshirt freshmen **Carlyle Holiday** (6-3, 203) and **Jared Clark** (6-4, 223), who shared snaps with him in spring drills.

If LoVecchio is to lose his grip on the No. 1 job, it'll probably be Holiday—who showed nifty moves as a runner and completed 7-of-13 passes for 66 yards in the Blue-Gold spring game—who wrestles the job away from him. But for now, Davie says that the decision to go with LoVecchio is solid. But he's also added that all three quarterbacks must get into games this fall—a promise that has gone unfulfilled for previous backups (and resulted in the loss of Zak Kustok to Northwestern)—but dismissed a suggestion that Notre Dame might rotate quarterbacks. LoVecchio's hold on the top job was expected by at least one of his competitors.

"He has eight games under his belt," Holiday said. "He's a smart kid. He knows how to win games."

Most experts think the 6-3 Holiday, whom the Irish somehow wrestled away from Nebraska, will be the long-term, down-the-road answer under center. He's a 21st century quarterback, a guy who can beat opposing defenses with both his arm and his feet—much like Philadelphia Eagles star Donovan McNabb (who thrived under current Notre Dame offensive coordinator Kevin Rogers in Syracuse's freeze-option attack).

"The dimension that Carlyle brings, he's going to make people miss and when he takes off running, it's exciting," Davie said.

After redshirting last year, the 6-4 Clark had a nightmarish first half in the spring game with a fumbled snap and an interception returned for a touchdown by cornerback **Shane Walton** (5-11,

186), but rebounded in the first half to throw a 47-yard touchdown pass.

For now, LoVecchio is the starter and Davie is content to let the quarterback situation play itself out from there.

"We have to get another quarterback ready," Davie said. "At some point, you need to have two quarterbacks, or three quarterbacks. So the other quarterbacks will play. To what percentage, I think it's been made to be a little more dramatic than what we think it's going to be right now. But I think you'll see all three of those quarterbacks play at some time."

RUNNING BACKS

The tailback position is chock-full of experience from junior **Julius Jones** (Notre Dame's leading rusher in 2000 with 162 attempts for 657 yards, seven touchdowns) to seniors **Tony Fisher** (132 for 607, six touchdowns) and **Terrance Howard** (75 for 424 yards, four touchdowns).

Of the bunch, the 5-10, 201-pound Jones strikes the most fear into the enemy, both as a runner and kick returner. Jones' older brother Thomas starred at Virginia in the late '90s. Thomas Jones led the ACC in rushing in 1999 (1,798 yards), made everybody's 1999 All-America team and was the seventh player taken in the 2000 NFL draft by the Arizona Cardinals.

The scary part? Some folks believe Julius Jones is more gifted than his older brother. Jones rushed for 2,564 yards and 36 touchdowns as a senior at Powell Valley High School in Big Stone Gap, Va.

Because of his breakaway speed (4.3 to 4.4 in the 40, depending on how high the grass is), Jones is dangerous—as a return man and a tailback. Davie thinks it will be tough for opposing defenses to keep up with this particular Jones.

"Julius has the ability to make the big play, to take it to the house," Davie said. "There's a super quickness about him that all the great ones have."

While not as flashy as Jones, the 6-2, 225-pound Fisher is a strong between-the-tackles runner. He'll get the most out of each play and then get on the ground. Fisher, like most Notre Dame tailbacks, has an impressive resume. He was Mr. Football in Ohio in 1997, the same award that was won by the likes of current NFLers Andy Katzenmoyer, Charles Woodson and Curtis Enis in recent years. In 2000, Fisher rushed for 607 yards and six scores on 132 carries—that's 4.6 yards per pop against a top-notch schedule.

The other halfback who figures to get plenty of touches is the underrated Howard (6-1, 195), who combines the strength of Fisher and the speed of Jones. After toting the ball a mere 18 times for 100 yards and one score in 1999, Howard was much more productive in 2000, rushing for 424 yards and four touchdowns on 75 carries.

Howard made the most of his opportunity to shine in Tony Fisher and Julius Jones' absence from the spring game, gaining 55 yards on 13 carries. He'll see plenty of time this fall and may even start in the opener against Nebraska.

Another guy who opened some eyes this spring was junior **Chris Yuri** (5-11, 211), something of a tweener (tailback-sized, but can run tough inside like a fullback). He can pick up a key fourth-and-1 every so often, but his main contribution will be as a kamikaze wedge-buster on special teams.

Senior **Mike McNair** (6-0, 237), a former *USA Today* high school All-American in 1997, is the No. 1 man on the depth chart at fullback. But senior bowling bowl **Tom Lopienski** (6-1, 236), the son of a former starting Notre Dame cornerback back in the mid-1970s of the same name, and senior **Jason Murray** (6-1, 256) will also see time at fullback.

Of the three, McNair has the most talent as a runner. But while Lopienski (nine carries, 18 yards in 2000) and Murray (four carries, 14 yards) won't win a 100-meter dash title, both are excellent lead blockers and tough-to-tackle straight-ahead runners.

WIDE RECEIVERS/TIGHT ENDS

The starting wide receivers will once again be the multi-talented senior **David Givens** (25 catches for 310 yards, two touchdowns in 2000) at flanker and senior **Javin Hunter** (13, 256 yards, three touchdowns) at split end. But Davie must come up with a replacement from the pint-sized playmaker Joe Geatherall, who contributed as a clutch third-down receiver and punt returner. And the Irish must find a new starting tight end after their top two guys at the position were drafted: injury-prone, but gifted Jabari Holloway in the fourth round by New England and Dan O'Leary in the sixth round by Buffalo.

But let's start with the good news. Despite being slowed some by a left hamstring pull, the 6-3, 214-pound Givens had a great spring. He was voted the offensive MVP of the spring game after he got behind the Irish defense twice for long touchdown passes (47 and 36 yards). You might recall that Givens arrived with a great deal of fanfare and was one of only six freshmen to letter for the Irish in 1998.

An all-purpose whiz who played quarterback, running back and wide receiver at Humble (Texas) High School (the alma mater of 1999 high first-round NFL pick David Boston), Givens has tons of natural ability. After seeing limited time at slot-back as a freshman, Givens caught 14 balls for 187 yards and one score as a sophomore and then was the team's leading receiver as a junior. He could have a bust-out year as a senior, if his work this spring is any indication.

Givens impressed his teammates, who voted him one of Notre Dame's four team captains. Givens has started 12 games in his career, seven as a junior in 2000, three as a sophomore and two as a freshman. He led Notre Dame in receiving last fall with 25 catches for 310 yards and two touchdowns. He also rushed 24 times for 101 yards and two touchdowns, had 257 yards on kickoff and punt returns and blocked three punts as a special-team standout.

Givens' pass-catching mate will be Hunter, who has been a disappointment during his time in South Bend. Like Givens, Hunter was one of the bluest chips in the high school Class of 1998, but his impact has been minimal on the gridiron his first three years. In 1999, Hunter snared 13 passes for 224 yards. Last year, he caught 15 balls. Hunter has the talent to catch 45-50 passes this season, if he stays healthy and if LoVecchio or Holiday grows into a confident quarterback.

In the spring, Battle, who moved from quarterback, and sophomore **Ronnie Rodamer** (6-4, 210) established themselves as leading contenders to join Hunter and Givens in the regular rotation.

Battle, a senior who is Givens' top backup at flanker, comes from excellent athletic stock. His father played football at North Texas; his cousin Kevin Ollie played college hoops for Jim Calhoun at Connecticut earlier in the 1990s. Battle probably won't run the world's most intricate routes, so the plan will be to hit him with quick passes designed to get him the ball with the opportunity to let his athletic ability take over.

In the Blue-Gold spring game, Battle caught three passes for 38 yards, ran a reverse for 17 yards and reminded onlookers of why he was such an effective option runner.

"The only question I had with Arnaz was whether or not he could catch the ball," Davie said. "After the first couple practices, I knew I didn't have anything to worry about."

Rodamer, the rangy sophomore from Morgantown, W. Va., will see time at split end. He's No. 2 on the depth chart there, behind Hunter. Rodamer is part of a strong sophomore contingent of receivers—the others being No. 3 flanker **Omar Jenkins** (6-1, 187) and third-string split end **Lorenzo Crawford** (5-10, 186).

The biggest question mark among the offensive skill positions comes at tight end, where the top candidates are senior **John Owens** (6-3, 260), sophomore converted quarterback **Gary Godsey** (6-6, 239) and untested sophomore **Billy Palmer** (6-3, 249).

Owens has flip-flopped between the defensive line and tight end during his career. Last year, Owens was No. 2 on the depth chart at left defensive end (behind Anthony Weaver) and No. 3 at tight end.

The 6-6 Godsey was recruited as a tight end, but stepped in at quarterback as a stop-gap measure after the injury to Battle (when LoVecchio wasn't quite ready). Godsey is battle-tested, at least, and has the luxury of having a Division I-A quarterback in his own family (Georgia Tech's starting quarterback George Godsey). That allows him to always have a quarterback to throw him the ball, whether he's on campus or at home. Plus, his 6-6 frame makes him an inviting target down near the goal line.

"Tight end is a bit of a concern, but we've been pleased with John Owens and Gary Godsey," said Davie this spring. "They both made major strides."

OFFENSIVE LINE

Both of last year's starting guards, Mike Gandy and Jim Jones, have graduated. Both will be tough to replace, particularly Gandy. Taken by the Chicago Bears in the third round of last spring's NFL draft, Gandy was the first of six Irish players chosen.

In fact, among the rebuilding, revamping and retooling projects the Irish tackled during the off-season, re-constructing the offensive line is among the most important.

During the 2000 season, Notre Dame's offensive line was the foundation in an evolving offense that utilized three different quarterbacks, three different tailbacks and three different fullbacks. But on the line, left tackle **Jordan Black** (6-6, 308), left guard Jones, center **Jeff Faine** (6-3, 290), right guard Gandy and right tackle **Kurt Vollers** (6-7, 307) started every game.

The unit gave up less than two sacks per game, 20 on the 12-game season. And the line's stability was one of the keys that allowed freshman Matt LoVecchio to settle into the starting quarterback position five games into the season.

This fall, the offensive line is built around

returning senior starting tackles Black (21 career starts) and Vollers (15 career starts), plus returning Faine, a junior, at center. Black is Notre Dame's most talented lineman. He should follow former Notre Dame tackles Luke Pettigout and Mike Rosenthal into the NFL after his final year of eligibility.

Top contenders to fill the guard spots vacated by Gandy and Jones (a free-agent signee with the Super Bowl champion Baltimore Ravens) are seniors and two-time letter winners **Ryan Scarola** (6-5, 310) and **Sean Mahan** (6-3, 290). Another possibility is senior **John Teasdale** (6-5, 305), a 10-game starter at tackle in 1999. Based on his play this spring, Mahan probably has the left guard position sewn up, but he's had nagging shoulder problems.

The right guard spot is still up for grabs, because Teasdale, who had off-season surgery on his left shoulder and missed spring drills, and Scarola, who sprained his knee during spring drills, were unable to take the job.

Vastly improved junior **Sean Milligan** (6-4, 286) is also in the mix at right guard, although a hyper-extended elbow forced him to sidelines near the end of spring practice.

No matter who wins the right guard spot, Vollers is confident.

"I just think that we'll be sound enough as the four that whoever comes in as the fifth, the person will really step it up and give us some support," Vollers said.

Still, there are questions about depth and whether this group is athletic enough to handle ultra-athletic rush ends. Depth will come from other letter winners who are back, including junior left tackle **Brennan Curtin** (6-8, 315), senior right guard/tackle **Casey Robin** (6-7, 312) and senior center **JW Jordan** (6-1, 269).

2000 STATISTICS

Rushing offense	213.5	15
Passing offense	132.2	109
Total offense	345.7	76
Scoring offense	31.3	28
Net Punting	38.4	10
Punt returns	15.1	12
Kickoff returns	24.9	3
Rushing defense	147.6	57
Passing efficiency defense	119.3	61
Total defense	353.8	51
Scoring defense	20.5	35
Turnover margin	+14	5

Last column is ranking among Division I-A teams.

KICKERS

Junior **Nick Setta** (5-11, 169), who made 8-of-14 field goals and all but one of his 45 extra point attempts, will return as the Notre Dame kicker. He was spotty at times in the spring, but Davie gives him the clear edge over senior **David Miller** (5-11, 196), a former two-time Associated Press first-team all-stater at Penn High School in Mishawaka, Ind.

DEFENSIVE LINE

Davie believes his starting front four is as strong as any he's had with the Golden Domers. And it's tough to argue with that opinion, thanks to the return from injury of fifth-year senior captain **Grant Irons** (6-5, 275). Irons, also a captain last season, is the first two-time captain for the Irish since quarterback Ron Powlus in 1996-97. Irons suffered a season-ending separated-shoulder injury against Nebraska in the second game of the year and was granted a fifth year.

Irons has started 20 games in his career, two in 2000, 10 in '99, five in '98 and three in '97. He has 120 career tackles, including 50 as a rookie in '97. He's a management information systems major in the Mendoza College of Business (he earned a 3.00 average in the 2000 spring semester) who also served as president of the Student-Athlete Advisory Council (SAAC) in 2000-01.

Irons comes from a talented gene pool—his brother Jarrett was an All-America linebacker for Michigan, another older brother Gerald played at Nebraska, and his father Gerald Sr. carved our a 10-year pro career (six seasons with Oakland and four with the Cleveland Browns).

The younger Irons arrived at Notre Dame as a 215-pound outside linebacker, but has added 60 pounds of muscle to his frame during his four years in South Bend. How strong is Irons now? As a point of reference, when Irons arrived at Notre Dame, he could squat 320 pounds. Now, he can do 600-plus pounds.

"For a 275-pound defensive end, Grant still runs to the ball like a linebacker," Mattison said. "His return will make a huge impact on this defense."

Irons has adjusted well to the defensive end position.

"I enjoyed running around as a linebacker and making big hits. That was fun," Irons said. "Now I take that same aggressiveness and apply it to the end position, which I actually enjoy more than playing linebacker. The biggest adjustment was changing from the two-point stance and getting into a three-point stance for the first time in my life. Down in the three-point stance, there are a lot of adjustments to your footwork and to a new style of play. The footwork and technique standpoint was all new."

Talented as he is, Irons might Notre Dame's second-best defensive end, behind fellow senior captain **Anthony Weaver** (6-3, 276). Weaver boasts more experience than anyone on the Irish roster, thanks to his 32 previous starting assignments. He led the team in sacks in 2000 with eight and had 49 tackles overall to give him 101 for his career. He developed into the most dominant Irish defensive lineman since Renaldo Wynn (Notre Dame's 1996 MVP and an eventual first-round NFL draft pick).

If that weren't enough talent at defensive end, senior **Ryan Roberts** (6-2, 254) is back after starting all of last year for the Fighting Irish in Irons' absence. Roberts recorded 23 tackles and five sacks last season.

The other name to know at defensive end is sophomore **Kyle Budinscak** (6-4, 246). The emerging Budinscak made his pitch for more playing time this fall with his impressive play in spring practice.

At defensive tackle, junior **Darrell Campbell** (6-4, 285) had an outstanding spring and seems poised to be a pro player, if he keeps working. Notre Dame is lucky to have the gifted Campbell. He originally committed to Northwestern at his mom's request and then changed his mind when coach Gary Barnett left for Colorado.

Campbell got lots of reps with the No. 2 defense as a freshman last year and learned a great deal. He's now moved inside from end to tackle, where his size and quick first step should wreak some havoc. Backing up Campbell will be sophomore **Greg Pauly** (6-6, 271).

Davie will also rotate his nose guards to keep them fresh, giving junior **Cedric Hilliard** (6-2, 294) and fifth-year senior **Andy Wisne** (6-3, 279) a chance to enter the fray. Hilliard arrived at Notre Dame as a puffy 310-pound freshman. He nearly passed out from heat exhaustion after the first team workout. Now he's a more well-toned 294 pounds and has much better mobility. Wisne has battled shoulder problems but is a good bet to be the opening day starter in 2001.

LINEBACKERS

Like the defensive line, the linebacking corps has lots of experienced hands and should be an area of strength, even without Anthony Denman (drafted in the seventh round by the Jacksonville Jaguars). Denman notched a team-high 84 tackles, including 14 for losses in 2000.

The new leader of this pack will be senior captain **Rocky Boiman** (6-4, 239). Boiman, the feisty red-haired throwback, is a modern-day "Rudy" story. He arrived at Notre Dame as a 212-pound safety, but Davie always viewed Boiman as a linebacker because of the young man's speed and ferocity.

During his time at South Bend, Boiman has transformed his body by adding nearly 30 pounds. The additional weight has allowed Boiman to muscle his way up the depth chart in a short amount of time—from a No. 4 outside linebacker in 1998 to a starting role the last two years. He'll start again in 2001 after making 58 tackles and 3-1/2 sacks last fall.

Consistent senior **Tyreo Harrison** (6-2, 240), who missed spring practice with an injury, and either sophomore **Mike Goolsby** (6-1, 223) or junior **Courtney Watson** (6-1, 223), a one-time Notre Dame running back, will win the starting nod at the other spot. The battle between Goolsby and Watson to replace Denman remains too close to call with Goolsby registering six tackles, a sack and a tackle for loss in the spring game and Watson making five stops. A winner won't be announced until August.

With Harrison on the mend in the spring, senior **Carlos Pierre-Antoine** (6-3, 260) finally flashed his enormous potential that folks have been waiting his whole career to see. He had two sacks in the spring game, But overall Pierre-Antoine has been disappointing. He was a *Parade* All-American out of O'Dea High School in Seattle, where he made 105 tackles as a high school senior. Maybe this is the year he finally puts it all together on fall Saturdays.

A pair of sophomores, **Jerome Collins** (6-4, 240) and **Derek Curry** (6-3, 228), also bear watching. They'll see time at drop linebacker when the hard-working Boiman needs a rest.

DEFENSIVE BACKS

The secondary is a primary area of concern for the Irish. The reason: Gone are a pair of guys who ended up being AFC East draft picks, cornerback Brock Williams and safety Tony Driver. Williams was a third round pick of the New England Patriots, while Driver went in the sixth round to Buffalo.

The big question is, who will replace Williams? Will it be senior **Clifford Jefferson** (5-9, 175) or speedy sophomore **Vontez Duff** (5-11, 186)? Jefferson, the undersized second cousin of 1997 Irish captain Allen Rossum, is more battle-tested.

He's started 14 times in his career and has 98 career tackles.

Duff has all the tools to play in the NFL one day. He's probably the fastest player on the roster, but he's as raw as a mid-January day in South Bend. With the steady stream of top-notch teams Notre Dame faces in 2001, can Davie put Duff out on the corner knowing full well that he'll be picked on each week?

"He's got a lot of raw ability," Davie said. "He's probably the fastest player on our team. He's got good ball skills. He's competitive. He's just a baby, though. He's just a baby playing a new position. But he certainly has all the tools."

The other corner will be ably manned by Walton, the defensive MVP of the spring game. In the Blue-Gold game, Walton intercepted a Jared Clark pass and returned it 44 yards for a score. Walton, a senior, showed that same nose for the ball last fall, notching 40 tackles and a pair of interceptions (including one that he returned for a touchdown).

Walton's understudy will be junior **Jason Beckstrom** (5-10, 190). Beckstrom missed spring practice while recuperating from shoulder surgery. His absence allowed a pair of sophomores **Garron Bible** (5-10, 194) and **Preston Jackson** (5-9, 169) to get more reps against live bullets in the spring.

Notre Dame's two most seasoned strong safeties, senior **Ron Israel** (6-0, 208) and junior **Gerome Sapp** (6-0, 213), both missed spring practice. But both are known quantities. Israel registered 47 tackles and three interceptions and figures to be the starter on opening day. Sapp, a 1998 Parade and *USA Today* All-American as a high school senior at Houston's Lamar High School, had 37 tackles last season. Backing them up is sophomore **Abram Elam** (6-0, 202), who impressed coaches in the spring.

The two main contenders for the strong safety spot are senior **Donald Dykes** (5-11, 195) and junior **Glenn Earl** (6-2, 215). Look for Earl to be the opening day starter at strong safety. Both are equally experienced, but Earl is bigger, younger and has a better nose for the football. Last season, Earl recorded 20 tackles and one interception. He also blocked Air Force's potential game-winning field goal as time expired (Notre Dame won the game in overtime).

Dykes appeared in ND's nickel and dime packages in 11 of the Irish's 12 games last season. He finished the 2000 season with 18 tackles.

PUNTERS

Junior **Joey Hildbold** (5-10, 185) is back and will be backed up by classmate Nick Setta. Hildbold punted the ball 60 times last season for a 40.9 average. Hildbold was a valuable field-position weapon for the Fighting Irish, as 22 of his 60 punts ended up inside the 20-yard-line.

If Hilbold is injured or goes into a slump, then the team's live-legged place-kicker Setta is a capable punter, too. Setta averaged 40.0 yards on his four punts in 2000, placing two of them inside the 20.

SPECIAL TEAMS

By season's end, the Irish were one of the nation's top special teams units, and their late-season win over USC proved it. Notre Dame blocked a pair of Trojan punts and turned the sudden changes into touchdowns, providing a springboard for a 38-21 win. It seemed like every game included a big special teams play, whether it was a block, a Joey Getherall return for a score or a big play by kicker Nick Setta, who ran for a touchdown, threw a touchdown pass and kicked the game-winner against Purdue.

The special teams should be strong again in 2001 as the incumbent punter and place-kicker both return.

Davie would like to see a marked improvement in his team's field goal kicking over 40 yards. Last season, the strong-legged Setta was 8 of 14 on field goal attempts and 44-of-45 on extra points for a team-high 74 points, but he was only 1-for-5 between 40 and 49 yards. With Notre Dame's tough schedule. Davie needs more consistency from distance from Setta.

Notre Dame's kickoff and punt return teams should be dangerous with speed balls such as Julius Jones, Vontez Duff, Javin Hunter and Arnaz Battle all willing and able to help in this area. Jones returned 15 kickoffs for 427 yards (a 28.5 yard average) and one touchdown last year, while Givens averaged 20.6 yards per kickoff return. Duff, a promising young corner, is the fastest player on the team and Battle, the former quarterback who has moved to flanker, is a shifty runner.

Seniors **John Crowther** (6-2, 240) and **Adam Tribble** (5-11, 201) will handle the long snapper and holder jobs, respectively.

RECRUITING CLASS

Another year, another impressive recruiting class for the Irish. Despite the school's more stringent admission standards (which scared off future college All-Americans and NFL players such as Michigan wide receiver David Terrell and Michigan State bulldozing runner T.J. Duckett in recent years), the Irish were able to sign a class that includes four of Tom Lemming's top 100 players in the high school class of 2001.

The four bluest of Notre Dame's blue-chip recruits, said Lemming (the Midwest-based publisher of the *Prep Football Report*), are offensive tackle **Mark LeVoir** (No. 27 in the class in Lemming's ratings); linebacker **Corey Mays** (No. 54), wide receiver **Carlos Campbell** (No. 85), and two-way lineman **Zachary Giles** (No. 89).

The 6-7, 300-pound LeVoir was actually a tight end for Eden Prairie (Minn.) High School. He caught 18 balls for 300-plus yards and seven touchdowns, but his forte is run blocking, which is why the Irish will move him to offensive tackle.

The 6-1, 235-pound Mays is nicknamed "The Beast" because of his ferocious style of play. A first-team all-state linebacker from Morgan, Park, Ill., Mays recorded 140 tackles in 2000, including 23 stops for loss.

Campbell might be the most ready to step on the field right away, given Notre Dame's need for speed. The question is, will the Irish play Campbell as a wide receiver or a defensive back? He's from the same fertile town (Hampton, Va.) that has produced Allen Iverson and North Carolina quarterback Ronald Curry in recent years. Blessed with 4.4 in the 40 speed, Campbell caught 75 balls for more than 1,800 yards in his final two prep seasons. When he wasn't playing offense, Campbell was locking up opposing wideouts as an aggressive cover corner. How aggressive? He notched nine interceptions in 1999 and six more in 2000.

The final gem is the 6-4, 280-pound Giles, the No. 1 high school prospect in Massachusetts last fall. Notre Dame coaches project him as an offensive guard because of strength (405-pound bench press) and foot speed (11.9 in the 100 meters). This two-time, first-team all-state selection also excelled on defense in 2000, recording 90 tackles and 10 sacks.

BLUE RIBBON ANALYSIS

OFFENSE	B
SPECIAL TEAMS	B
DEFENSE	B+
INTANGIBLES	B+

Davie believes that this is the most talented Notre Dame team he has coached. If the team is going to reach the level Davie sees for it, the quarterback position must solidify and the secondary must avoid surrendering the big plays to speedy wide receivers like it did in last year's lopsided Fiesta Bowl loss against Oregon State.

Even if LoVecchio proves to be the man under center and the offensive line and secondary gel, matching last year's nine wins won't be easy. The reason: Notre Dame faces a murderous schedule. Overall, Davie's crew meets seven opponents that played in bowl games a year ago: Nebraska (defeated Northwestern in Alamo Bowl), Purdue (lost to Washington in Rose), Texas A&M (lost to Mississippi State in Independence), Pittsburgh (lost to Iowa State in insight.com), West Virginia (defeated Ole Miss in Music City), Boston College (defeated Arizona State in Aloha) and Tennessee (lost to Kansas State in Cotton). Those seven teams combined to finish 54-30 (.643) in 2000.

Winning eight games and ending up in the second half of the top 25 (and in a decent bowl game) against this trying schedule would be quite a reasonable goal with a still-green quarterback. But who said the expectations of most Notre Dame fans were ever reasonable?

Said Davie: "I understand our fans sitting out there and saying, 'Golly, we should be competing for the national championship and he hasn't won enough games.' I don't ask them to lower their expectations at all. That's all fine. But we're going to prove you can do it (compete nationally) the right way."

(B.D.)

2000 RESULTS

Texas A&M	W	24-10	1-0
Nebraska	L	24-27	1-1
Purdue	W	23-21	2-1
Michigan State	L	21-27	2-2
Stanford	W	20-14	3-2
Navy	W	45-14	4-2
West Virginia	W	42-28	5-2
Air Force	W	34-31	6-2
Boston College	W	28-16	7-2
Rutgers	W	45-17	8-2
USC	W	38-21	9-2
Oregon State (Fiesta)	L	9-41	9-3

South Florida

LOCATION	Tampa, FL
CONFERENCE	Independent
LAST SEASON	7-4 (.636 Division I-AA)
CONFERENCE RECORD	NA
OFFENSIVE STARTERS RETURNING	4
DEFENSIVE STARTERS RETURNING	4
NICKNAME	Bulls
COLORS	Green & Gold
HOME FIELD	Raymond James Stadium (41,444)
HEAD COACH	Jim Leavitt (Missouri '78)
RECORD AT SCHOOL	27-17 (4 years)
CAREER RECORD	27-17 (4 years)
ASSISTANTS	Wally Burnham (Samford '63) Co-Defensive Coordinator/Linebackers Mike Hobbie (Murray State '76) Offensive Coordinator Greg Frey (Florida State '96) Offensive Line Rick Kravitz (Troy State '77) Assistant Head Coach/Defensive Coordinator/Secondary Earl Lane South Florida Defensive Line Tom Pajic (Bloomsburg '91) Receivers Rich Rachel (Parsons College '69) Defensive Ends Leroy Ryals (South Florida '96) Running Backs Rodney Smith (Glenville State '97) Pass Game Coordinator/Quarterbacks
TEAM WINS (last 5 yrs.)	NA-5-8-7-7
FINAL RANK (last 5 yrs.)	NA-NA-NA-NA-NA
2000 FINISH	Beat Austin Peay in regular-season finale.

COACH AND PROGRAM

In 10 or 20 years, long after South Florida has established itself as a force in Conference USA and as a possible Top 25 program, researchers will look back and point to April 22, 2001 as the day the Bulls arrived.

Still more than four months away from opening its first season as a Division I-A independent, South Florida burst onto the national scene on the second day of the NFL draft as USF players were selected with the first three picks of the fourth round.

The New England Patriots started it by trading up to take offensive tackle Kenyatta Jones with the 96th overall pick. Cleveland followed by picking defensive back Anthony Henry and the Arizona Cardinals completed the running of the Bulls by choosing kicker Bill Gramatica at No. 98.

And, just like that, five minutes on ESPN had upstaged all of the time and money poured into developing a program that spent four years in Division I-AA before jumping to college football's top level this season.

Count Jim Leavitt, the only coach in South Florida history, among those surprised by the draft developments. He was talking on the phone and watching the draft at home, but couldn't contain himself after Gramatica's name was called.

"I dropped the phone and just started running," Leavitt said.

He didn't slow down much in the following days. Leavitt was a popular guest on several sports radio and television shows, generating gobs of invaluable attention for a young program that has never shied away from pursuing athletes being courted by in-state powerhouses Florida State, Florida and Miami. The Bulls are scheduled to begin play in Conference USA in the 2003 season.

"The publicity was probably as much as Michael Vick had on Day One," Leavitt said. "We are hoping it will be very positive. We certainly got the articles out to all of our recruits."

Those letters also mentioned the fact four other South Florida players signed free-agent contracts with NFL clubs, meaning seven players from last year's squad were in camps this summer. The Bulls also play their home games at Raymond James Stadium, the same place Warren Sapp and Warrick Dunn suit up for the Tampa Bay Buccaneers on Sundays, and practice at the same facilities the Baltimore Ravens used before winning the Super Bowl in January.

All of the above is nice, and indicates South Florida is jumping into the Division I-A pool in much better shape than many young programs, but it is no guarantee for immediate success. The Bulls return only nine starters (four on offense, four on defense and a punter) and have a 1-5 overall record against I-A competition. Their ambitious plan to be competitive in I A includes trying to do something in four years that has taken 10-15 years at other places.

"I think we have laid as good a foundation as possible in a four-year stretch," Leavitt said. "It's absolutely mind-boggling what we're trying to do."

But, he seems to be the man to do it. A former Kansas State assistant, Leavitt admits to borrowing from the model Bill Snyder has used to rebuild the Wildcats into a national power while laying the foundation for his own program. His administration has been so impressed that he was given a three-year contract extension (through January of 2006) in February.

"The stage is set for the future," Leavitt said. "We've just got to do the work and prove we can win at this level."

In addition to the step up in competition (South Florida has eight Division I-A teams on its 2001 schedule) and loss of 15 starters, the Bulls will also be dealing with some staff changes. Mike Hobbie, a member of Leavitt's first staff, returns to coordinate the offense and the promotion of Rick Kravitz to assistant head coach means he will share defensive coordinator duties with Wally Burnham.

The Bulls compiled a 27-17 record their first four seasons and will stick with the same schemes. The offense will primarily use a one-back set behind multi-talented junior quarterback **Marquel Blackwell** and spread the ball to several receivers. South Florida loses its leading rusher and top three pass-catchers from last season, but Leavitt isn't about to turn conservative.

"It's my personality [to throw the ball]," Leavitt said. "I have fun with the ball in the air and I think we can recruit receivers who can make plays for us."

The strength of the defense will be at linebacker, where **Kawika Mitchell** and **Anthony Williams** return. There are questions on the line and in the secondary, both of which were hit hard by graduation.

While many of the components for success are in place, the South Florida program is still in its infancy and there will be growing pains. Leavitt hasn't been able to stockpile scholarship athletes like more established programs and he doesn't have an overrun of talent at many positions.

"We don't have the depth and we don't have the competitive bar in practice," Leavitt said.

But they do have hope. Hope that by continuing to do the right things and recruit the right players, the program will continue to grow at its current rate. Just don't expect too much too fast.

2001 SCHEDULE

Aug.	30	@Northern Illinois
Sept.	8	@Pittsburgh
	15	Southern Utah
	22	@Memphis
	29	North Texas
Oct.	6	@Utah
	13	Connecticut
	27	Liberty
Nov.	3	Houston
	10	Western Illinois
	17	Utah State

QUARTERBACKS

"We want Marquel to be South Florida's Shaun King."

Those were the words of former South Florida offensive coordinator Mike Canales, now the quarterbacks coach at North Carolina State, describing Blackwell in last year's media guide.

If King did as much for the Buccaneers as Blackwell, the team's offensive MVP, did for the Bulls last season, Tampa Bay may have had home-field advantage for the Super Bowl.

Even more (a Donovan McNabb-type season, perhaps) will be expected of Blackwell (6-1, 205), who begins his third season as the starter. The Bulls' top returning rusher (566 yards last season), he has a strong, accurate arm and makes good decisions (13 touchdowns, four interceptions) in 2000. He ranked 24th in total offense in Division I-A last year and is already South Florida's career leader in that category.

"He's a good player who can run and throw, and he's a good athlete," said Leavitt, who, like Blackwell, played quarterback at Dixie Hollins High School in St. Petersburg, Fla.

The biggest challenges for Blackwell this season will be making quicker decisions against improved competition and gaining confidence in his new corps of receivers.

"He's working on stepping it up a notch because of the speed at the Division I level," Leavitt said.

Sophomore **Kevin Patullo** (6-2, 190), last year's backup, and redshirt freshman **Ronnie Banks** (6-3, 220) enter fall practice even in the quest to back up Blackwell. Patullo has good mobility and saw action in five games last season (14-of-22, 173 yards, one touchdown, two interceptions). Banks, who has the strongest arm on the team, improved his footwork while running the scout team last season.

The Bulls signed one quarterback, **David Mullins** (6-2, 200) of Jacksonville, in their 2001 recruiting class.

RUNNING BACKS

The graduation of Rafael Williams (704 yards, four touchdowns), the school's career rushing leader, left this position wide open heading into spring. **Derrick Rackard** (5-1, 210), a natural fullback, made the most of the opportunity and enters the fall as the clear No. 1.

A senior with just 59 career yards to his credit, Rackard isn't a game-breaker but is a hard-working, character player who has impressed the coaching staff with the way he has handled himself throughout his career. He will be a team captain this fall.

"You know what you're going to get with him," Leavitt said. "He's got an unbelievable work ethic and drive. He's real smart, understands the game and doesn't make any mistakes."

Sophomore **Vince Brewer** (5-10, 205) and freshman **Clenton "Boobie" Crossley** (5-10, 210) have more natural talent and could see time as backups. Brewer ran for 105 yards in the 2000 season finale and Crossley is a power back with moves and ran for more than 1,300 yards his senior year in high school.

Sophomores **Courtney Davenport** (6-1, 190) and fullback **Jake Hickson** (6-2, 230) are other returning letter winners. The incoming class includes **Charlie Ross** (6-2, 240), who Leavitt has compared to Eddie George, **Brian Fisher** (5-9, 180) and Georgia transfer DeJuan Green (5-11, 190), who must sit out this season.

Despite a good collection of talent, a lack of experience at this position could be cause for concern.

WIDE RECEIVERS/TIGHT ENDS

Losing last season's top three receivers probably sounds worse than it is. That's no knock on those who have moved on, rather a testament to the new group of Bulls.

Developing the unit will be a priority because, as Leavitt matter-of-factly says, "we'll play as many as we can trust."

Junior **DeAndrew Rubin** (6-0, 180) has that trust. He was well on his way to a solid season before being limited by a severe ankle sprain the second half of the season. He still finished with 17 catches for 189 yards and two scores. A burner (4.45 in the 40) and a high school teammate of Blackwell's, he could emerge as the Bulls' top threat if their old chemistry clicks.

"He's got good speed and good hands," Leavitt said. "We feel like he's going to be pretty good."

South Florida also knows what it has in senior **Hugh Smith** (5-10, 175) and sophomore **Chris Iskra** (6-1, 180). Smith, a converted running back, is the Bulls' fastest receiver and has the ability to run after the catch. Iskra filled in well when Rubin was banged up, starting five of the final six games and making all of his catches during that stretch.

Newcomers **Bruce Gipson**, **Elgin Hicks** and **Huey Whittaker** should also contribute. Gipson (5-10, 170), a freshman who enrolled early, is another speedster who had a strong spring. Like Gipson, Hicks (5-10, 185) attended Charlotte High School in Punta Garden, Fla. He spent one season at Florida before transferring to USF. The 6-foot-5, 225-pound Whittaker is a junior college transfer who gives Blackwell a big target. A sophomore, he also earned the praise of coaches for his efforts during the spring. Junior **Ryan Hearn** (5-9, 185) also had a strong spring and senior **Nasser Qureshi** (6-1, 180) is another returning letter winner.

The incoming class is strong in talent and bloodlines. **Cedric King** (5-11, 170), brother of the aforementioned Shaun, and **Marcus Edwards** (6-0, 185), son of New York Jets coach Herman, combine with Gipson and **C.J. Lewis** (5-11, 175) to give the Bulls more speed. Fellow recruits **Joe Bain** (6-3, 190) and **Eugene Hampton** (6-2, 180) add size to the corps.

Tight end has certainly not been a glory position for the Bulls, who return a trio of sophomores. **Mark Feldman** (6-4, 230) caught five passes as a reserve last season and converted quarterback **Casey Cobb** (6-4, 230) missed the first eight games with a knee injury but has fully recovered and should be a steady contributor. **Tommy Hunter** (6-5, 245) spent some time on the defensive line in the spring before being shifted back to tight end. Leavitt considers recruits **Tim Jones** (6-3, 240) and **Derek Carter** (6-4, 220) to be the two best from Florida and has high hopes for Georgian **Patrick Quinn** (6-4, 220).

OFFENSIVE LINE

Three starters return up front, but the Bulls will miss Jones and fellow four-year starter Joey Sipp along with Anthony McKenzie, a three-year starter at guard. This unit will be built around senior **Jimmy Fitts** (6-3, 318), who moves from right guard to fill Sipp's spot at center.

"He's a draftable player," Leavitt said of Fitts. "He's just a tough, blue-collar type of guy."

Junior **Mike Snellgrove** (6-6, 285) appears to be the heir apparent to Jones at left tackle. He started eight games last season, mainly at right tackle.

"He's got good size and decent feet," Leavitt said.

Senior tackle **Ken Dawson** (6-6, 295) made five starts in 2000 and is expected to be the full-time right tackle this season. Senior **Matt Sparrowhawk** (6-3, 280) saw his reps increase late last season and is penciled in at left guard. Redshirt freshmen **Alex Herron** (6-3, 270) and **Josh Freiselben** (6-3, 275) are the top contenders at right guard. Others providing depth are sophomores **Derrick Sarosi** (6-6, 295), **Chris Robinson** (6-4, 290) and **Mark Sopcik** (6-4, 270).

No unit should benefit more from the move to Division I-A than the offensive line, which lists four redshirt freshmen as reserves on the preseason two-deep. The other backup spot, behind Dawson at right tackle, is vacant. Having more scholarships will help build depth. The incoming class includes two tackles, two guards and a center, and some of those newcomers may be called on right away.

2000 STATISTICS

Rushing offense	152.5	68
Passing offense	203.2	54
Total offense	355.6	62
Scoring offense	25.3	69
Net Punting	36.0	15
Punt returns	12.5	15
Kickoff returns	22.3	14
Rushing defense	122.5	32
Passing efficiency defense	104.6	37
Total defense	297.0	32
Scoring defense	18.3	28
Turnover margin	-2	67

Last column is ranking among Division I-AA teams.

KICKERS

What do you do when you lose your all-time scoring leader to the NFL? Sign his little brother.

Santiago Gramatica, the third in the line of kicking brothers recruited by Leavitt, is Bill's likely successor with the Bulls. Santiago (5-10, 165) kicked seven field goals at LaBelle (Fla.) High School last season and was voted second-team All-America by the *Ft. Myers News Press.*

"I don't know if he's as far along as the other two were, but he's got more upside," said Leavitt, who recruited oldest brother Martin, an All-Pro with the Buccaneers, to Kansas State.

Freshman **Justin Geisler** (6-1, 170) showed promise in spring practice and will have a chance to win the job, but Leavitt says "he'll have to be a whole lot better for us to redshirt Santiago."

DEFENSIVE LINE

This unit could be better than expected, considering three starters need to be replaced. The Bulls don't have a ton of experience, but that could be overcome with talent and depth.

Sophomores **Cedric Battles** (6-4, 255) and **Shurron Pierson** (6-3, 240), two wildcards from Wildwood, Fla., could go a long way toward determining the level of success. Neither qualified academically for the 2000 season, but the pair dominated from opposite sides of the line in high school and could make significant contributions right away.

The versatile Battles can play anywhere on the line and is strong against both the run and pass. Pierson is also a multi-talented athlete who played receiver and defensive back his junior year in high school and has run a 4.4 40.

Junior **Greg Walls** (6-2, 285) and junior **Lee Roy Selmon Jr.** (5-11, 275), son of the college and pro football Hall of Famer, provide an effective tandem at nose tackle. Walls (6-2, 285) led the team with 11 tackles for losses last year.

Junior **Tavares Juineack** (6-3, 290) made 31 tackles last season and appears ready to take over the starting defensive tackle spot vacated by four-year starter Therrimann Edwards. Freshmen **Howard Campbell** (6-2, 250) and **Greg McKay** (6-4, 300) provide depth. McKay, a late bloomer, bench presses 415 pounds and has a 31-inch vertical leap and could contribute right away.

Junior ends **Emerson Morris** (6-2, 235) and **Chris Daley** (6-2, 255) contributed last season. Junior **Tchecoy Blount** (6-2, 252) could boost the pass rush and the Bulls are hoping injury-plagued sophomore **Ian Blackwell** (6-3, 230) can overcome a broken ankle suffered in the spring to contribute.

If a recruiting class of Battles, Pierson and McKay wasn't enough, the Bulls also landed end **Kenny Huebner** (6-3, 225), who totaled 28 sacks as a senior at Gaither High School in Lutz, Fla., last season.

LINEBACKERS

Returning starters **Kawika Mitchell** and **Anthony Williams** make this position the strength of the defense.

Mitchell (6-2, 238) led the team in tackles from his weak-side spot as a sophomore last season, and combines exceptional lateral quickness, strength and speed.

"Kawika Mitchell is probably one of the better linebackers in the country," Leavitt said of the Georgia transfer now in his third season with the Bulls. "He benches 410 and runs a 4.6-flat [40-yard dash]."

Like Mitchell, Williams can play all three linebacker spots, but will probably start in the middle. A senior captain, the 5-11, 220 Williams finished fourth on the team in tackles despite missing two games last season.

Sophomore **Maurice Jones** (6-2, 230), who has shown some ability as a pass rusher, could start on the strong side. Others in the mix for playing time are junior **Julian Johnson** (5-11, 200), sophomores **Mike Minus** (5-11, 225) and **Clay Rebol** (6-0, 210) and freshmen **Jason Allen** (6-2, 220) and **Bryan McKelvy** (6-2, 205).

The incoming class includes three standouts from Florida—**Anthony Caldwell** (6-2, 225), **Elvis Smith** (6-2, 215) and **Terrance Royal** (6-2, 210)—and **Tony Pricor** (6-4, 225) from San Diego.

DEFENSIVE BACKS

The Bulls lose four starters, and the potential loss of another three-year starter dampens the outlook in the defensive backfield.

Senior cornerback **Bernard Brown** (5-10, 180) started 27 games from 1997-99 and redshirted last season to give the team more experience this year. But he suffered a broken leg in the off-season and missed spring practice. Brown's availability for the fall remains in question.

Senior strong safety **Joe Morgan** (5-10, 185), a team captain, can be considered a returning starter. Morgan filled in for the injured Jay Mize last season and finished third on the team with 55 tackles.

The remainder of the backfield is young and relatively untested. Sophomore **Kenny Robinson** (5-10, 180) played in all 11 games last season and is expected to start at one corner while **Ron Hemingway** (5-11, 175), another sophomore, could start at the other corner spot.

Sophomore **J.R. Reed** (5-11, 185) had a great spring and looks to be the man at free safety and classmate **Kevin Verpaele** (6-0, 195) is a capable backup for Morgan.

Redshirt freshman **Sidney Simpson** (5-8, 175) had two interceptions in the spring game and could contend for time at corner while another redshirt freshman, **Javan Camon** (6-0, 170), may work his way into the mix at one of the safety spots.

Senior **Solomon Burgess** (5-8, 165), junior **Maurice Tucker** (6-1, 190), an Indiana transfer, and sophomore **John Miller** (6-1, 185) also hope to get on the field.

Help could be on the way with freshmen **D'Juan Brown** (5-11, 175) and the athletic **Willie Williams** (6-2, 180) coming in at corner and **Johnnie Jones** (6-2, 190) and, possibly, Bain, at safety.

PUNTERS

The job belongs to junior **Devin Sanderson** (6-4, 220), whose 41.1 average was 11th in Division I-AA last season. Sanderson has a strong leg and kicked 10 punts out inside the opponents' 20-yard line, but needs to improve his situational punting as Gramatica handled the "pooch" duties.

SPECIAL TEAMS

The return game is solid with a healthy Rubin bringing back punts and kickoffs. He averaged 27.3 yards on kickoff returns last season and an impressive 23.4 on nine punts, including an 81-yard touchdown against James Madison. Smith and Kenny Robinson may also prove to be effective on returns.

The loss of long snapper Ryan Benjamin, a fixture for four years, could be crucial. Incoming freshman **Justin Daniel** (6-2, 265) may be his replacement.

The Bulls allowed one kickoff return for a touchdown last season (a 90-yarder against Liberty), but will need to be sharper against the improved competition. Experienced Division I-A teams play quality athletes on special teams and the potential for a big play is always there.

RECRUITING CLASS

Leavitt did what he needed to by signing 25 players and having five others enroll early. The Bulls need to develop depth in order to be successful and there are plenty of good football players in Florida to go around.

The group of receivers is particularly impressive and Battles, Huebner, Pierson and McKay will have immediate impact on the defensive line. Ross could be a big contributor at running back and the group of defensive backs has tremendous potential. Bringing in players at every offensive line position was necessary, and the three tight ends are above average. Landing Gramatica (as if there was any doubt where he was going) was also big.

Players in a young program are sometimes called upon before they are ready, but South Florida offers youngsters an immediate chance to play, which is a nice carrot to dangle. Although new players make mistakes, they also gain experience that will help down the road.

BLUE RIBBON ANALYSIS

OFFENSE	C-
SPECIAL TEAMS	C
DEFENSE	C
INTANGIBLES	B+

Although there are a lot of pieces in place, South Florida figures to struggle a bit in its first few seasons of Division I-A.

"It's a real mystery about how things are going to happen," Leavitt said. "None of us are naïve about this. It's a different deal."

Blackwell will make plays for the offense, but the Bulls still figure to struggle a bit without a proven running back, a bunch of new faces at wide receiver and a retooled offensive line. Adjusting to the speed of Division I-A opponents almost every week will be a challenge, and a lack of depth puts an emphasis on staying healthy.

The defense has plenty of potential, but is generally young and inexperienced. Mitchell and Williams are solid at linebacker, but having a young line and secondary could make the Bulls vulnerable to big plays. The same is true in the kicking game, where a freshman kicker and long snapper will be put to the test early. The special teams units will also have to avoid giving up big plays that take inexperienced teams out of games.

The schedule consists of eight Division I-A teams but isn't brutal. Pittsburgh is certainly in a different class, but the Bulls should be able to stay in most games. The support from the community and administration has been outstanding, but the expectation some have for immediate success may be off.

"No [people aren't willing to wait for a winner], it's the state of Florida," Leavitt said. "But, then again, neither am I. If we were doing this the way other people have, it's a 15-year deal, but we're doing it in four."

(S.B.)

2000 RESULTS

Jacksonville State	W	40-0	1-0
Kentucky	L	9-27	1-1
James Madison	W	26-7	2-1
Baylor	L	13-28	2-2
Troy State	W	20-10	3-2
Southern Mississippi	L	7-41	3-3
Liberty	W	44-6	4-3
Connecticut	W	21-13	5-3
Western Kentucky	W	30-24	6-3
Middle Tennessee	L	9-45	6-4
Austin Peay	W	59-0	7-4

Utah State

LOCATION	**Logan, UT**
CONFERENCE	**Independent**
LAST SEASON	**5-6 (.455)**
CONFERENCE RECORD	**4-1 (2nd Big West)**
OFFENSIVE STARTERS RETURNING	**8**
DEFENSIVE STARTERS RETURNING	**7**
NICKNAME	**Aggies**
COLORS	**Blue & White**
HOME FIELD	**Romney Stadium (30,000)**
HEAD COACH	**Mick Dennehy (Montana '73)**
RECORD AT SCHOOL	**5-6 (1 year)**
CAREER RECORD	**54-31 (8 years)**
ASSISTANTS	**Bob Cole (Weidner '82)** **Offensive Coordinator/Quarterbacks** **Kraig Paulson (Montana '87)** **Defensive Coordinator/Secondary** **Carl Franks (Montana '94)** **Linebackers/Special Teams** **Eric Klesau (Portland State '96)** **Wide Receivers** **Derrick Odum (Utah '92)** **Secondary** **Jeff Hoover (UC Davis '91)** **Offensive Line** **Tom McMahon (Carroll '92)** **Defensive Line/Recruiting Coordinator** **Mike Trevathan (Montana '99)** **Running Backs** **David Reeves (Montana '89)** **Assistant Head Coach/Linebackers**
TEAM WINS (last 5 yrs.)	**6-6-3-4-5**
FINAL RANK (last 5 yrs.)	**88-82-90-91-87**
2000 FINISH	**Lost to Idaho State in regular-season finale.**

COACH AND PROGRAM

After arriving in Logan last season after a successful seven-year stint at the University of Montana, Mick Dennehy exceeded everyone's expectations when he won his first four Big West games and had the Aggies playing for the championship at Boise State in mid-November.

Alas, the Aggies were thumped by the powerful Broncos, 66-38, and the following week were upset by a substantially less-powerful Idaho State team of the Big Sky in the season finale. That left Dennehy and the Aggies with a 5-6 overall record and a bad taste in their mouths at season's end, despite that four-game winning streak earlier in the year.

Winning records have been rare for the Aggies over the last two decades. And without the Big West to beat up any more because of the demise of the football-playing portion of the league, it may get tougher to produce a winning season.

Dennehy has brought a winning attitude to Logan and has upgraded the program with better athletes and students, weeding out the less-talented players and those who didn't care to go to class.

Now the Aggies are faced with an independent schedule for the first time since the late 1970s because of the stubbornness of a university president who is no longer there. Instead of following other Big West teams such as New Mexico State, Arkansas State, Idaho and North Texas to the Sun Belt Conference, Utah State decided to wait for an invitation to the Western Athletic Conference, which expanded to only 10 teams instead of 12.

That left the Aggies without a conference to play in this year, although athletic director Rance Pugmire did an admirable job of filling the schedule, getting home games against Oregon and Wyoming as well as road games at LSU and Fresno State and the usual in-state battles against Utah and BYU. If the Aggies can win two of those games, they ought to be doing cartwheels.

The rest of the schedule is winnable with games against Big Sky teams Weber State and Idaho State, Connecticut, South Florida and Central Florida. Unfortunately those games are all in the second half of the season when the Aggies may be too beat up to care.

2001 SCHEDULE

Sept.	1	@Utah
	8	LSU
	15	@Fresno State
	22	Wyoming
	29	Oregon
Oct.	5	@Brigham Young
	20	Idaho State
	27	Central Florida
Nov.	10	@Connecticut
	17	Weber State
	24	@South Florida

QUARTERBACKS

After starting for two seasons, senior **Jeff Crosbie** (6-5, 198) got off to a slow start in Dennehy's new system and lost his job in the second game to junior **Jose Fuentes** (6-2, 188), who threw four second-half touchdown passes against Southern Utah after replacing Crosbie.

Before Crosbie had a chance to win his job back, he was knocked out for the year with a broken thumb in practice the following week. Meanwhile, Fuentes performed exceptionally well for a player who had taken just a handful of snaps the previous season, when he completed 4-of-11 passes for 91 yards.

Heading into the fall, Fuentes is solidly entrenched as the No. 1 quarterback, but the Aggie coaches will feel better than last year, knowing they have a capable backup such as Crosbie ready to step in of needed.

"Jose had a great spring and there's definitely enough separation there between him and Jeff," Dennehy said. "We feel a lot better about (the quarterback position) than a year ago. We need to make sure one or two of our other guys are ready to go."

Fuentes passed for 2,709 yards and 13 touchdowns last year and came up with the second- and fifth-best passing days in USU history with 509 yards against Boise State and 421 against Idaho. Nationally, Fuentes ranked 14th in total offense, 16th in passing and 43rd in passing efficiency.

"Jose picked up right where he left off last year in the spring," Dennehy said. "He's very steady and doesn't make a lot of mistakes."

While he may not be as athletic or mobile as Crosbie, Fuentes displayed an accurate arm (52.7 percent) and strong leadership qualities in leading the Aggies to within a game of the Big West championship.

Crosbie passed for 2,007 yards and 10 touchdowns as a sophomore in 1999, but also had 17 interceptions. The previous year he threw for 1,111 yards and eight touchdowns, starting the final four games.

Travis Cox (6-1, 189), a redshirt freshman who played at the same local high school as Crosbie (Mountain Crest) and **Robert Fockaert** (6-1, 185), another redshirt freshmen, are the Aggie quarterbacks of the future. Those two got the majority of the snaps in the spring as the Aggie coaches looked at a lot of young players, but they'll likely battle for the third-string position this year.

Junior **Steve Mullins** (6-4, 226), who was recruited to USU as a quarterback, is the Aggies' punter and could fill in at QB if a rash of injuries were to strike.

RUNNING BACKS

Junior **Emmett White** (5-11, 199) had big shoes to fill last year, replacing Demario Brown, who had completed his career as the best running back in USU history with 4,053 yards in his career and a season-record 1,536 yards.

It didn't take long for White to change the color of the backfield and make everyone forget about Brown as he rushed for 1,322 yards and 13 touchdowns, while leading the nation in all-purpose yards.

Not only did White lead the nation in all-purpose yards with 238.9 yards per game, he shattered the NCAA single-game record with 578 yards against New Mexico State in early November. The record had been 435 yards by Brian Pruitt of Central Michigan and was set six years earlier.

In that game in New Mexico, White rushed 34 times for 322 yards, caught seven passes for 134 yards, returned four kickoffs for 120 yards and one punt for two yards. The 322 rushing yards was a USU record.

"I am running out of adjectives to describe this kid," Dennehy said. "He does the type of things that amaze you and leave you with your mouth open. He has a great attitude and it carries onto the team. It was really neat to be a part of his breaking the all-purpose yardage record."

White ended up 13th in the nation in rushing (120.2 yards per game), 22nd in kickoff returns (24.1-yard average) and 26th in scoring with 90 points.

As a sophomore White earned first-team All-Big West honors as a returner and finished 10th in the nation in punt returns with a 15.0-yard average and 26th in kickoff returns at 23.9 yards per return.

Senior **John Roberts** (5-9, 195), who gained 99 yards and scored three touchdowns, will be White's backup again and play fullback when the Aggies play a two-back set. His yardage has gone down since gaining 313 yards as a freshman and 141 yards as a sophomore. Even if he doesn't get a lot of carries, Roberts has proven himself to be valuable on the special teams and as a blocker.

David Fiefia (5-8, 189), who was selected Utah's Mr. Football by the *Salt Lake Deseret News* in 1998, excelled as a wide receiver last year, catching 31 passes for 344 yards and a touchdown. However, he played primarily running back in the spring and could see action there this fall when he will be a sophomore.

"We'll utilize David at both spots," Dennehy said. "We want our best players on the field."

Another running back who looked impressive in the spring was redshirt freshman **Roger Fernandez** (5-10, 221), who will give the Aggies some needed depth.

Senior **Joe Solosabal** (5-11, 221), like Roberts, is a valuable special teams player who is utilized mostly as a blocker. He didn't get a single carry last year, but caught a pass for a touchdown against Texas Tech.

WIDE RECEIVERS/TIGHT ENDS

Replacing Aaron Jones, who caught 63 passes for 1,159 yards, won't be easy for the Aggies. However, they should be deeper this year with more targets for Fuentes in the Aggies' pass-happy offense.

Sophomore **Chris Stallworth** (6-3,190), the nephew of former NFL star receiver John Stallworth, should be the go-to guy this year after catching 26 passes for 289 yards and a touchdown in 2000. Although he was fourth on the team in receiving last year, Stallworth is the top returner among the players who strictly play wide receiver.

Fiefia caught 31 passes for 344 yards, but he worked out at his natural running back position in the spring and could play both positions this fall.

Of the other four players expected to see a lot of action at the receiver positions this fall, only one—senior **Marshall Sanders**—has any appreciable experience.

Sanders (5-8, 160), a senior, played in only six games last year because of injuries, but caught 13 passes for 131 yards and a touchdown. In the spring game he caught four passes for 46 yards.

Others expected to fill the Aggie receiver slots are sophomore **Jason Deml** (6-1, 193), who caught one pass last year; junior **Gary Coleman** (5-10, 175), a junior college transfer from Pasadena, Calif.; and junior **Kevin Curtis** (5-11, 183), a walk-on from Snow (Utah) College who sat out as a redshirt last year, but had a great spring camp and caught a 62-yard touchdown pass in the spring game.

Senior **Jeff Berg** (6-3, 185), sophomore **Markus Torian** (6-0, 210) and junior **Derek Jeffery** (5-10, 167) will provide depth at the receiver spots.

"Obviously it's a huge concern to replace Aaron Jones," Dennehy said. "We're better (at receiver), but we still lack depth."

Dennehy is excited about the tight end position, which he calls the "most talented position on the team."

Casey Poppinga (6-5, 247) played well last

year after transferring from Wyoming, ranking fifth on the team in receptions with 15 for 190 yards. The junior has the size to be an effective blocker and has good hands for a big man. Sophomore **Chris Cooley** (6-4, 215) is a local kid who impressed Aggie coaches so much last year they played him on offense, defense and special teams. He didn't catch any passes last year, but is expected to play a lot after having what Dennehy called "an outstanding spring."

Senior **J.R. Suguturaga** (6-3, 220) played both tight end and fullback last year, starting three games and catching five passes for 28 yards. Senior **Scott Collins** (6-6, 243) has battled injuries ever since coming to Utah State and if he stays healthy he could help out at tight end also.

OFFENSIVE LINE

Depth on the lines is a problem at most lower-level Division I-A schools like Utah State, but this year shouldn't be as bad as 2000, when the Aggies were threadbare at the position and kept their fingers crossed all year that the starters wouldn't get injured.

Gone are center Junior Pututau, a three-year starter, and tackle Jeff Long, who were part of a line that allowed just 15 sacks all year and helped open holes for White.

Senior guards **Jim Walker** (6-3, 295) and **Jess Schuck** (6-2, 305) are back along with junior tackle **Jim Newton** (6-10, 294). Walker earned second-team All-Big West honors, while Schuck is a consistent performer whose 22 career starts are second on the team. Newton has improved a lot over the last two years and at his size won't be looking up at any opposing defender that gets in his way.

Senior **Ed Powell** (6-3, 300), who filled in a couple of times for Pututau, will get the starting nod at center, while two junior college transfers, **Grant Calverley** (6-5, 285) and **Aric Galliano** (6-4, 290) will battle it out for the other tackle spot. Galliano can also play center and may push Powell for playing time there.

"I feel really good about our running game with this line and the inside three are solid pass protectors," Dennehy said.

In junior **Luis Trujillo** (6-2, 310) the Aggies have an experienced player who started three of the first five games at the right guard position last year.

Senior **Eric Gwilliam** (6-5, 257), a backup tackle last year after transferring from Ricks (Idaho) Junior College, will back up one of the tackle positions unless he can win a starting spot in the fall.

Other backups on the line include junior **Barry McLaughlin** (6-5, 277), who sat out as a redshirt last year; redshirt junior **Mike Scheper** (5-11, 260); and three redshirt freshman—**Jason Green** (6-5, 260), **Brenan Burningham** (6-7, 256) and **Joshua Newman-Gomez** (6-3, 280). Burningham, a local player from Sky View High School, was selected offensive scout team co-MVP after last season.

2000 STATISTICS

Rushing offense	120.3	85
Passing offense	266.2	21
Total offense	386.5	45
Scoring offense	26.5	54
Net Punting	35.6	39
Punt returns	9.2	62
Kickoff returns	20.1	51
Rushing defense	196.7	96
Passing efficiency defense	133.5	96
Total defense	452.4	100
Scoring defense	32.4	93
Turnover margin	-2	69

Last column is ranking among Division I-A teams.

KICKERS

Since 1997, the Aggies have had little to worry about in their kicking game with diminutive Brad Bohn handling the place-kicking chores. Bohn ended his sterling career with 13 records, including a school-record 59 field goals as well as 107 of 119 PATs. He also finished as the all-time leading scorer at Utah State with 284 points.

With Bohn gone, the Aggies will turn to junior **Dane Kidman** (5-10, 178), who has been the backup for the last two years. He made his only field goal try from 44 yards as a freshman in 1999.

"Dane Kidman had a really good spring and improved a ton," Dennehy said.

The Aggies will also look at **Ben Chaet** (6-1, 175), a freshman from Montana, but he is likely the kicker of the future and could redshirt this year.

DEFENSIVE LINE

A year ago, Utah State faced the daunting prospect of replacing all four starters on the defensive line. Then, when injuries hit some of their only experienced players, the Aggies were forced to go with several newcomers. In a couple of games late in the season, the Aggies had three freshmen and a walk-on playing at the same time on the defensive line.

While it was tough playing a bunch of newcomers last year, all that experience for the Aggie youngsters should pay off in 2000.

Senior **Nick Onaindia** (6-3, 243), began the 2000 season as a starter at defensive end, but went out for the year after just three games with a shoulder injury. He would seem to be an obvious choice to start at one of the defensive end spots this year, but will have to beat out one of two returning starters from last year, sophomore **Nate Putnam** (6-7, 224) or senior **Ryan Duncan** (6-3, 245).

Putnam came back from a church mission and earned raves from Dennehy before the season even started. He moved into a starting spot early, made 59 tackles, including 14 for a loss and ended up earning first-team All-Big West honors. Duncan started every game and made 51 tackles, 10 for loss and came up with four sacks.

Sophomore **Jorge Tapia** (6-2, 277) took over a starting tackle job at mid-season and finished with 36 tackles, including 10 for loss.

"He's played as well at defensive tackle as anybody I've been around," Dennehy said.

Sophomore **Liua Fonua** (6-1, 306), who had eight tackles as a reserve last year, is penciled in for the other tackle position.

Senior **Tyler Olsen** (6-1, 220) is an undersized former walk-on who saw considerable action last year and came up with 26 tackles, including five for loss. Other backups include three red-shirt freshman, **Ty Cahoon** (6-3, 296), **Ronald Tupea** (6-2, 245) and **Jeremy Guenter** (6-4, 260). Dennehy calls Guenter a "high-character guy who's going to have to play somewhere."

LINEBACKERS

On the surface, things look bleak at this position where three starters have graduated, including All-Big West performers Brent Passey and Blake Eagal, along with Cade Smith. However, while there are some holes to fill, the Aggies won't be hurting at the linebacker spot this year.

Though he started only two games, junior **Jesse Busta** (6-2, 232) played starter's minutes most of the year and filled in for Smith when he was injured. He finished second on the team in tackles with 110 and came up with two interceptions and a fumble recovery and also earned All-Big West honors.

"Jesse had as good of a year as anyone at linebacker last year," Dennehy said.

In senior **Tony Newson** (6-1, 221), the Aggies have another returning starter as he started in 1999 when he made 95 tackles and two sacks. Last year Newson sat out with a shoulder injury after earning second-team All-Big West honors the year before.

The other starting spot will likely be filled by junior **Ryan Solomona** (6-0, 229), who left the team before the start of last season for personal reasons, but returned and turned in an impressive spring camp. As a sophomore, Solomona played on special teams and as a backup linebacker.

The backups are young and inexperienced, but Dennehy likes their potential and says several will have to step up this year.

Sophomore **Scott Hunt** (6-4, 217) "is going to be a really good player for us," Dennehy said.

Sophomore **Rodney Wilson** (6-2, 200) had a good spring and **Robert Watts** (6-4, 210) is a redshirt freshman who was chosen the defensive scout team MVP last year.

Others who could see action at linebacker are redshirt freshman **Casey Bingham** (6-0, 212) and junior **Kyle Siever** (6-1, 210), a transfer from Arizona State.

DEFENSIVE BACKS

The Aggies have more experience in the defensive backfield than anywhere else on the team with all four starters returning, along with a player who was a starter before getting injured.

The most experienced player is senior cornerback **Tony Walker** (5-11, 183), who has started 25 games over the last three seasons. Besides starting most of his career in the secondary, Walker has been one of the Aggies' main kick returners.

Walker ranked eighth on the team in tackles in '99 with 51 and broke up eight passes, but Aggie coaches would like to see more interceptions from their talented cornerback. Walker picked off just one pass last year after getting just three the previous two seasons.

The other cornerback slot will be manned by junior **Ade Jimoh** (6-1, 185), who was an All-Big West second-team selection. Jimoh intercepted two passes and broke up 12 more and also registered 46 tackles and blocked a kick.

The safeties are junior **Jamar Glasper** (6-0, 189) and sophomore **Derrek Shank** (5-10, 182). Glasper, who made 60 tackles and broke up six passes, will play strong safety, while Shank will play free safety, where he came up with 39 tackles and five pass break-ups as a true freshman. Shank took over the safety spot midway through the season and never let go.

Senior **Nathan Barber** (6-2, 220) saw a lot of action toward the end of the season at safety and should see a lot of time this year, as could sophomore **Bryan Jackson** (6-0, 185).

While the depth is better at safety, the Aggies must develop some players at the corners, where redshirt freshman **Jerome Dennis** (6-1, 190) is a top candidate. The Aggie coaches have also talked about moving Shank to one of the corners if needed because of the experience at safety.

Aminifu Johnson was slated to be the starter at safety last year, but wrecked his knee the week before the season started and sat out the entire year. Then he came back this spring, only to decide his knee wasn't good enough to play this fall. Scott Goss, who started five games at safety, didn't return to the team this year.

PUNTERS

Mullins has been consistent for two seasons as the Aggie punter, ranking 29th in the nation both seasons. Mullins was recruited to Logan as a quarterback, but latched onto the punting position, where he could have a professional future.

Last year Mullins' average fell a bit to 41.4 yards per kick, but 18 of his 64 punts were inside the 20 and he recorded at least one 50-yard-plus punt in eight games last year. At the end of the year he was selected to the All-Big West second team. As a freshman, Mullins averaged 42.3 yards per kick and was voted to *The Sporting News* Freshman All-America team.

SPECIAL TEAMS

Special teams have been solid for the Aggies the last couple of years thanks to the kicking of Bohn and Mullins and the kick returning talents of White and Walker. The Aggies will miss Bohn and hope that Kidman can fill in adequately.

With 22 kickoff returns for a 24.1-yard average, White ranked 22nd in the nation, while Walker returned 26 kicks for a 17.9-yard average. White handled all but three of the team's 24 punt returns with an 8.7-yard average.

RECRUITING CLASS

After signing 11 junior college transfers his first year, Dennehy concentrated on freshmen with 27 signees last winter, just five of them from junior college.

The junior college players are most likely to see action this year with offensive linemen Calverley and Galliano battling for one of the starting tackle spots.

Another junior college transfer, wide receiver Coleman, who caught 43 passes for 673 yards and seven touchdowns at Pasadena (Calif.) JC, is expected to challenge for one of the wideout starting spots.

The other junior college transfers are defensive lineman **Blake Curci** (6-5, 260) out of Saddleback (Calif.) Junior College and defensive back **Mark Estelle** (5-10, 170) from Southwest (Calif.) Junior College. Both Curci and Estelle will both be sophomores.

Dennehy will try to redshirt as many freshmen as possible, but some will have a chance to play this year. **Steve Tate** (6-1, 180), who was selected Utah's Mr. Football by the *Desert News* after leading Skyline High to the 5A championship game, could see some action at defensive back, although he was a quarterback in high school.

BLUE RIBBON ANALYSIS

OFFENSE	B+
SPECIAL TEAMS	B-
DEFENSE	B-
INTANGIBLES	C+

With no conference title to play for this year because of the demise of the Big West, the Aggies can only try to play for a bowl berth. But unless your name is Notre Dame, the chances of an independent team making a bowl game aren't good.

Still, although the odds are long, the Aggies could gain some national attention with upsets over LSU and Oregon, two teams that should be in the Top 25 this year. But they get no rest in the early season with games against Utah, BYU, Fresno State and Wyoming.

Unfortunately the five most winnable games are the final five, including two games against Division I-AA schools. If the schedule was reversed, the Aggies might be able to gain some confidence as well as experience before taking on the big-name schools.

After coming within one game of a winning season last year, the Aggies should be thrilled if they can get through this year's schedule with a 6-5 record.

(M.S.)

2000 RESULTS

Texas Tech	L	16-38	0-1
Southern Utah	W	30-14	1-1
Arizona State	L	20-44	1-2
Utah	L	14-35	1-3
Brigham Young	L	14-38	1-4
North Texas	W	17-12	2-4
Idaho	W	31-14	3-4
Arkansas State	W	44-31	4-4
New Mexico State	W	44-37	5-4
Boise State	L	38-66	5-5
Idaho State	L	24-27	5-6

2000 Division I-A Conference Standings

(Full-season records do not include postseason play; ties in standings broken by full-season records unless otherwise noted.)

ATLANTIC COAST CONFERENCE

TEAM	Conference W	Conference L	Conference PCT.	Full Season W	Full Season L	Full Season PCT.
Florida St.	8	0	1.000	11	1	.917
Georgia Tech	6	2	.750	9	2	.818
Clemson	6	2	.750	9	2	.818
Virginia	5	3	.625	6	5	.545
North Carolina St.	4	4	.500	7	4	.636
North Carolina	3	5	.375	6	5	.545
Maryland	3	5	.375	5	6	.455
Wake Forest	1	7	.125	2	9	.182
Duke	0	8	.000	0	11	.000

BIG EAST CONFERENCE

TEAM	Conference W	Conference L	Conference PCT.	Full Season W	Full Season L	Full Season PCT.
Miami	7	0	1.000	10	1	.909
Virginia Tech	6	1	.857	10	1	.909
Pittsburgh	4	3	.571	7	4	.636
Syracuse	4	3	.571	6	5	.545
Boston College	3	4	.429	6	5	.545
West Virginia	3	4	.429	6	5	.545
Temple	1	6	.143	4	7	.364
Rutgers	0	7	.000	3	8	.273

BIG TEN CONFERENCE

TEAM	Conference W	Conference L	Conference PCT.	Full Season W	Full Season L	Full Season PCT.
Michigan	6	2	.750	8	3	.727
Northwestern	6	2	.750	8	3	.727
Purdue	6	2	.750	8	3	.727
Ohio St.	5	3	.625	8	3	.727
Wisconsin	4	4	.500	8	4	.667
Minnesota	4	4	.500	6	5	.545
Penn St.	4	4	.500	5	7	.417
Iowa	3	5	.375	3	9	.250
Illinois	2	6	.250	5	6	.455
Michigan St.	2	6	.250	5	6	.455
Indiana	2	6	.250	3	8	.273

BIG 12 CONFERENCE

TEAM	Conference W	Conference L	Conference PCT.	Full Season W	Full Season L	Full Season PCT.
North						
Nebraska	6	2	.750	9	2	.818
Kansas St.	6	2	.750	10	3	.769
Iowa St.	5	3	.625	8	3	.727
Colorado	3	5	.375	3	8	.273
Kansas	2	6	.250	4	7	.364
Missouri	2	6	.250	3	8	.273
South						
Oklahoma	8	0	1.000	12	0	1.000
Texas	7	1	.875	9	2	.818
Texas A&M	5	3	.625	7	4	.636
Texas Tech	3	5	.375	7	5	.583
Oklahoma St.	1	7	.125	3	8	.273
Baylor	0	8	.000	2	9	.182

BIG WEST CONFERENCE

TEAM	Conference W	Conference L	Conference PCT.	Full Season W	Full Season L	Full Season PCT.
Boise St.	5	0	1.000	9	2	.818
Utah St.	4	1	.800	5	6	.455
Idaho	3	2	.600	5	6	.455
New Mexico St.	1	4	.200	3	8	.273
North Texas	1	4	.200	3	8	.273
Arkansas St.	1	4	.200	1	10	.091

CONFERENCE USA

TEAM	Conference W	Conference L	Conference PCT.	Full Season W	Full Season L	Full Season PCT.
Louisville	6	1	.857	9	2	.818
East Caro.	5	2	.714	7	4	.636
Cincinnati	5	2	.714	7	4	.636
Southern Miss.	4	3	.571	7	4	.636
UAB	3	4	.429	7	4	.636
Tulane	3	4	.429	6	5	.545
Memphis	2	5	.286	4	7	.364
Houston	2	5	.286	3	8	.273
Army	1	6	.143	1	10	.091

MID-AMERICAN CONFERENCE

TEAM	Conference W	Conference L	Conference PCT.	Full Season W	Full Season L	Full Season PCT.
East						
Marshall	5	1	.833	7	5	.583
Akron	5	1	.833	6	5	.545
Ohio	4	2	.667	7	4	.636
Miami	4	2	.667	6	5	.545
Buffalo	2	4	.333	2	9	.182
Bowling Green	1	5	.167	2	8	.200
Kent St.	0	6	.000	1	10	.091
West						
Toledo	4	1	.800	10	1	.909
Western Mich.	4	1	.800	9	3	.750
Northern Ill.	2	3	.400	6	5	.545
Ball St.	2	3	.400	5	6	.455
Eastern Mich.	2	3	.400	3	8	.273
Central Mich.	1	4	.200	2	9	.182

MOUNTAIN WEST CONFERENCE

TEAM	Conference W	Conference L	Conference PCT.	Full Season W	Full Season L	Full Season PCT.
Colorado St	6	1	.857	9	2	.818
Air Force	5	2	.714	8	3	.727
UNLV	4	3	.571	7	5	.583
Brigham Young	4	3	.571	6	6	.500
New Mexico	3	4	.429	5	7	.417
Utah	3	4	.429	4	7	.364
San Diego St.	3	4	.429	3	8	.273
Wyoming	0	7	.000	1	10	.091

PACIFIC-10 CONFERENCE

TEAM	Conference W	Conference L	Conference PCT.	Full Season W	Full Season L	Full Season PCT.
Oregon St.	7	1	.875	10	1	.909
Washington	7	1	.875	10	1	.909
Oregon	7	1	.875	9	2	.818
Stanford	4	4	.500	5	6	.455
UCLA	3	5	.375	6	5	.545
Arizona St.	3	5	.375	6	5	.545
Arizona	3	5	.375	5	6	.455
Southern California	2	6	.250	5	7	.417
Washington St.	2	6	.250	4	7	.364
California	2	6	.250	3	8	.273

SOUTHEASTERN CONFERENCE

TEAM	Conference W	Conference L	Conference PCT.	Full Season W	Full Season L	Full Season PCT.
Florida	7	1	.875	10	2	.833
Auburn	6	2	.750	9	3	.750
Georgia	5	3	.625	7	4	.636
South Carolina	5	3	.625	7	4	.636
Tennessee	5	3	.625	8	3	.727
LSU	5	3	.625	7	4	.636
Mississippi	4	4	.500	7	4	.636
Mississippi St.	4	4	.500	7	4	.636
Arkansas	3	5	.375	6	5	.545
Alabama	3	5	.375	3	8	.273
Vanderbilt	1	7	.125	3	8	.273
Kentucky	0	8	.000	2	9	.182

WESTERN ATHLETIC CONFERENCE

TEAM	Conference W	Conference L	Conference PCT.	Full Season W	Full Season L	Full Season PCT.
TCU	7	1	.875	10	1	.909
UTEP	7	1	.875	8	3	.727
Fresno St.	6	2	.750	7	4	.636
San Jose St.	5	3	.625	7	5	.583
Tulsa	4	4	.500	5	7	.417
Hawaii	2	6	.250	3	9	.250
Rice	2	6	.250	3	8	.273
Southern Methodist	2	6	.250	3	9	.250
Nevada	1	7	.125	2	10	.167

DIVISION I-A INDEPENDENTS

TEAM	Full Season W	Full Season L	Full Season PCT.
Notre Dame	9	2	.818
UCF	7	4	.636
Middle Tenn. St.	6	5	.545
Louisiana Tech	3	9	.250
La.-Lafayette	1	10	.091
La.-Monroe	1	10	.091
Navy	1	10	.091

Division I-A 2000-01 Coaching Changes

School	Former Coach	New Coach
Alabama	Mike DuBose	Dennis Franchione
Arizona	Dick Tomey	John Mackovic
Arizona St.	Bruce Snyder	Dirk Koetter
Boise St.	Dirk Koetter	Dan Hawkins
Bowling Green	Gary Blackney	Urban Meyer
BYU	LaVell Edwards	Gary Crowton
Buffalo	Craig Cirbus	Jim Hofher
Georgia	Jim Donnan	Mark Richt
Kentucky	Hal Mumme	Guy Morriss
Maryland	Ron Vanderlinden	Ralph Friedgen
Memphis	Rip Scherer	Tommy West
Miami	Butch Davis	Larry Coker
Missouri	Larry Smith	Gary Pinkel
North Carolina	Carl Torbush	John Bunting
Ohio	Jim Grobe	Brian Knorr
Ohio State	John Cooper	Jim Tressel
Oklahoma State	Bob Simmons	Les Miles
Rutgers	Terry Shea	Greg Schiano
San Jose State	Dave Baldwin	Fitz Hill
Southern Cal	Paul Hackett	Pete Carroll
TCU	Dennis Franchione	Gary Patterson
Toledo	Gary Pinkel	Tom Anstutz
Virginia	George Welsh	Al Groh
Wake Forest	Jim Caldwell	Jim Grobe
West Virginia	Don Nehlen	Rich Rodriguez

2000 Division I-A Individual Statistics

RUSHING

	G	CAR	NET	TD	AVG	YDSPG
1. LaDainian Tomlinson, TCU	11	369	2158	22	5.85	196.18
2. Damien Anderson, Northwestern	11	293	1914	22	6.53	174.00
3. Michael Bennett, Wisconsin	10	294	1598	10	5.44	159.80
4. Deonce Whitaker, San Jose St.	10	224	1577	15	7.04	157.70
5. Anthony Thomas, Michigan	11	287	1551	16	5.40	141.00
6. Ken Simonton, Oregon St.	11	266	1474	18	5.54	134.00
7. Chester Taylor, Toledo	11	250	1470	18	5.88	133.64
8. Robert Sanford, Western Mich.	12	293	1571	18	5.36	130.92
9. Rudi Johnson, Auburn	12	324	1567	13	4.84	130.58
10. Ennis Haywood, Iowa St.	10	230	1237	8	5.38	123.70
11. T.J. Duckett, Michigan St.	11	240	1353	7	5.64	123.00
12. Thomas Hammock, Northern Ill.	9	215	1083	16	5.04	120.33
13. Emmett White, Utah St.	11	242	1322	13	5.46	120.18
14. Travis Henry, Tennessee	11	253	1314	11	5.19	119.45
15. Dwone Hicks, Middle Tenn. St.	11	186	1277	19	6.87	116.09
16. Michael Wallace, Army	10	192	1157	11	6.03	115.70
17. Antwaan Randle El, Indiana	11	218	1270	13	5.83	115.45
18. Lee Suggs, Virginia Tech	11	222	1207	27	5.44	109.73
19. Willie Alderson, Idaho	11	238	1195	12	5.02	108.64
20. William Green, Boston College	11	187	1164	14	6.22	105.82
21. Dan Alexander, Nebraska	11	182	1154	8	6.34	104.91
22. Chris Barnes, New Mexico St.	11	171	1131	5	6.61	102.82
23. Tellis Redmon, Minnesota	11	251	1122	6	4.47	102.00
24. Hodges Mitchell, Texas	11	224	1118	8	4.99	101.64
25. Maurice Morris, Oregon	11	260	1106	8	4.25	100.55
26. Marcus Merriweather, Ball St.	10	225	1004	8	4.46	100.40
27. Avon Cobourne, West Virginia	9	197	893	6	4.53	99.22
28. Steve Little, Miami (Ohio)	10	189	986	8	5.22	98.60
29. Sultan McCullough, So. California	12	227	1163	6	5.12	96.92
30. Derek Watson, South Carolina	11	187	1066	11	5.70	96.91

PASSING EFFICIENCY

(MIN. 15 ATT. PER GAME)	G	ATT	COMP	INT	YDS	TD	RATING
1. Bart Hendricks, Boise St.	11	347	210	8	3364	35	170.6
2. Chris Weinke, Florida St.	12	431	266	11	4167	33	163.1
3. Rex Grossman, Florida	11	212	131	7	1866	21	161.8
4. Casey Printers, TCU	11	176	102	6	1584	16	156.7
5. Ken Dorsey, Miami (Fla.)	11	322	188	5	2737	25	152.3
6. George Godsey, Georgia Tech	11	349	222	6	2906	23	151.9
7. John Turman, Pittsburgh	11	233	128	7	2135	18	151.4
8. Rocky Perez, UTEP	11	338	200	6	2661	26	147.1
9. Mike Thiessen, Air Force	11	195	112	5	1687	13	147.0
10. Ryan Schneider, Central Fla.	9	286	177	11	2334	21	147.0
11. Casey Clausen, Tennessee	9	194	121	6	1473	15	145.5
12. Dave Ragone, Louisville	11	354	216	11	2621	27	142.2
13. John Welsh, Idaho	11	399	251	17	3171	22	139.3
14. Josh Heupel, Oklahoma	12	433	280	14	3392	20	139.2
15. Jason Thomas, UNLV	11	201	106	9	1708	14	138.1
16. Travis Cole, Minnesota	9	223	131	5	1780	11	137.6
17. Matt Newton, Colorado St.	11	336	198	13	2609	21	137.0
18. Major Applewhite, Texas	9	279	152	7	2164	18	135.9
19. Tim Hasselbeck, Boston Coll.	10	229	124	9	1810	16	135.7
20. David Carr, Fresno St.	11	316	194	11	2338	18	135.4
21. Woodrow Dantzler, Clemson	11	212	122	6	1691	10	134.5
22. Byron Leftwich, Marshall	12	457	279	9	3358	21	134.0
23. Patrick Ramsey, Tulane	10	389	229	14	2833	24	133.2
24. Jason Gesser, Washington St.	9	246	128	10	1967	16	132.5
25. Drew Brees, Purdue	11	473	286	12	3393	24	132.4
26. Chris Finlen, Northern Ill.	11	231	131	9	1857	11	132.2
27. Jonathan Beasley, Kansas St.	13	313	156	10	2636	17	132.1
28. Butchie Washington, Akron	11	283	143	11	2319	17	131.4
29. Zak Kustok, Northwestern	11	328	191	7	2251	18	129.7
30. Kurt Kittner, Illinois	10	297	173	8	1982	18	128.9

TOTAL OFFENSE

	G	TOT	YDS/GM
1. Drew Brees, Purdue	11	3939	358.1
2. Jared Lorenzen, Kentucky	11	3827	347.9
3. Chris Weinke, Florida St.	12	4070	339.2
4. Bart Hendricks, Boise St.	11	3633	330.3
5. Timmy Chang, Hawaii	10	2992	299.2
6. Josh Heupel, Oklahoma	12	3536	294.7
7. John Welsh, Idaho	11	3199	290.8
8. Patrick Ramsey, Tulane	10	2886	288.6
9. Byron Leftwich, Marshall	12	3441	286.8
10. Kliff Kingsbury, Texas Tech	12	3431	285.9
11. Antwaan Randle El, Indiana	11	3053	277.5
12. Philip Rivers, North Carolina St.	11	2969	269.9
13. George Godsey, Georgia Tech	11	2945	267.7
14. Jose Fuentes, Utah St.	10	2622	262.2
15. Dave Ragone, Louisville	11	2873	261.2
16. Joey Harrington, Oregon	11	2819	256.3
17. Ryan Schneider, Central Fla.	9	2246	249.6
18. Rocky Perez, UTEP	11	2743	249.4
19. Ken Dorsey, Miami (Fla.)	11	2714	246.7
20. Zak Kustok, Northwestern	11	2701	245.5
21. Mike Bath, Miami (Ohio)	11	2694	244.9
22. David Garrard, East Caro.	11	2690	244.5
23. Ronald Curry, North Carolina	11	2676	243.3
24. Carson Palmer, So. California	12	2919	243.3
25. Sage Rosenfels, Iowa St.	11	2672	242.9
26. Mark Farris, Texas A&M	11	2667	242.5
27. Jonathan Beasley, Kansas St.	13	3135	241.2
28. Mike McMahon, Rutgers	10	2400	240.0
29. Woodrow Dantzler, Clemson	11	2638	239.8
30. Jason McKinley, Houston	11	2565	233.2

RECEPTIONS PER GAME

	G	CT	YDS	CTPG
1. James Jordan, Louisiana Tech	12	109	1003	9.08
2. Tyson Hinshaw, Central Fla.	11	89	1089	8.09
3. Kenny Christian, Eastern Mich.	10	78	808	7.80
4. Robert Kilow, Arkansas St.	10	72	1002	7.20
5. Brian Robinson, Houston	11	79	892	7.18
6. DeRonnie Pitts, Stanford	11	77	882	7.00
7. Kevin Kasper, Iowa	12	82	1010	6.83
8. Antonio Bryant, Pittsburgh	10	68	1302	6.80
9. Adrian Burnette, Tulane	11	74	1075	6.73
9. Kendall Newson, Middle Tenn. St.	11	74	945	6.73
11. Don Shoals, Tulsa	12	80	1195	6.67
12. Vinny Sutherland, Purdue	10	65	926	6.50
13. Deion Branch, Louisville	11	71	1016	6.45
14. Lee Mays, UTEP	11	70	1098	6.36
15. David Bautista, Bowling Green	11	69	915	6.27
16. Freddie Mitchell, UCLA	11	68	1314	6.18
17. Ashley Lelie, Hawaii	12	74	1110	6.17
18. John Simon, Louisiana Tech	12	72	711	6.00
19. Justin McCareins, Northern Ill.	11	66	1168	6.00
20. Jabar Gaffney, Florida	12	71	1184	5.92
21. Josh Reed, LSU	11	65	1127	5.91
22. Nate Poole, Marshall	12	70	818	5.83
23. Brian Natkin, UTEP	11	64	787	5.82
23. Terrell Harris, Tulane	11	64	694	5.82
25. Robert Ferguson, Texas A&M	10	58	885	5.80
26. Aaron Jones, Utah St.	11	63	1159	5.73
26. Ryan McGuffey, Wyoming	11	63	696	5.73
26. Arnold Jackson, Louisville	11	63	609	5.73
26. David Terrell, Michigan	11	63	994	5.73
30. Tim Baker, Texas Tech	12	68	759	5.67

RECEIVING YARDS PER GAME

	G	CT	YDS	YDSPG
1. Antonio Bryant, Pittsburgh	10	68	1302	130.20
2. Freddie Mitchell, UCLA	11	68	1314	119.45
3. Marvin Minnis, Florida St.	12	63	1340	111.67
4. Justin McCareins, Northern Ill.	11	66	1168	106.18
5. Aaron Jones, Utah St.	11	63	1159	105.36
6. Josh Reed, LSU	11	65	1127	102.45
7. Robert Kilow, Arkansas St.	10	72	1002	100.20
8. Lee Mays, UTEP	11	70	1098	99.82
9. Don Shoals, Tulsa	12	80	1195	99.58
10. Tyson Hinshaw, Central Fla.	11	89	1089	99.00
11. Jabar Gaffney, Florida	12	71	1184	98.67
12. Adrian Burnette, Tulane	11	74	1075	97.73
13. Ron Johnson, Minnesota	11	59	1067	97.00
14. Koren Robinson, North Carolina St.	11	62	1061	96.45
15. Vinny Sutherland, Purdue	10	65	926	92.60
16. Ashley Lelie, Hawaii	12	74	1110	92.50
17. Deion Branch, Louisville	11	71	1016	92.36
18. David Terrell, Michigan	11	63	994	90.36
18. Dan Stricker, Vanderbilt	11	61	994	90.36
20. Quincy Morgan, Kansas St.	13	64	1166	89.69
21. Robert Ferguson, Texas A&M	10	58	885	88.50
22. Milton Wynn, Washington St.	11	52	964	87.64
23. Kelly Campbell, Georgia Tech	11	59	963	87.55
24. Rod Gardner, Clemson	11	51	956	86.91
25. Kendall Newson, Middle Tenn. St.	11	74	945	85.91
26. Ryan Fleming, Air Force	11	52	930	84.55
27. Kevin Kasper, Iowa	12	82	1010	84.17
28. James Jordan, Louisiana Tech	12	109	1003	83.58
29. David Bautista, Bowling Green	11	69	915	83.18
30. Brian Robinson, Houston	11	79	892	81.09

INTERCEPTIONS

	G	NO	YDS	TD	IPG
1. Dwight Smith, Akron	11	10	208	2	.91
1. Anthony Floyd, Louisville	11	10	152	1	.91
3. Ed Reed, Miami (Fla.)	11	8	92	2	.73

4. J.T. Thatcher, Oklahoma	12	8	162	1	.67
4. Jamar Fletcher, Wisconsin	9	6	159	0	.67
6. Dan Dawson, Rice	11	7	206	1	.64
7. Nate Jackson, Hawaii	12	7	57	0	.58
8. Walls, Boston College	11	6	29	1	.55
8. Charles Tillman, La.-Lafayette	11	6	15	0	.55
8. Shawn Robinson, Pittsburgh	11	6	-6	0	.55
8. Todd Howard, Michigan	11	6	1	0	.55
8. Rashad Holman, Louisville	11	6	32	0	.55
8. Ardley, Clemson	11	6	61	0	.55
8. Tim Wansley, Georgia	11	6	148	2	.55
8. Willie Pile, Virginia Tech	11	6	22	1	.55
16. Tay Cody, Florida St.	12	6	200	1	.50
16. Lito Sheppard, Florida	12	6	179	1	.50
18. Jerametrius Butler, Kansas St.	13	6	47	0	.46
19. Nijrell Eason, Arizona St.	11	5	39	0	.45
19. Michael Jolivette, Arizona	11	5	50	0	.45
19. Glenn Sumter, Memphis	11	5	76	0	.45
19. Fred Smoot, Mississippi St.	11	5	31	0	.45
19. Watchorn, Nebraska	11	5	64	1	.45
19. Vince Thompson, Northern Ill.	11	5	16	0	.45
19. David Mitchell, Ohio St.	11	5	113	1	.45
19. D.J. Walker, UTEP	11	5	79	0	.45
19. Leo Barnes, Southern Miss.	11	5	123	3	.45
19. Stuart Schweigert, Purdue	11	5	2	0	.45
19. Jake Cookus, Oregon St.	11	5	49	0	.45
19. Harold Blackmon, Northwestern	11	5	18	0	.45
19. Demerist Whitfield, Northern Ill.	11	5	108	1	.45
19. Ken Lucas, Mississippi	11	5	60	0	.45
19. Cedric Henry, Michigan St.	11	5	118	0	.45
19. Hanik Milligan, Houston	11	5	77	0	.45
19. Tedaro France, Central Mich.	11	5	63	0	.45
19. Chris Lepore, Navy	11	5	22	0	.45
19. Ronyell Whitaker, Virginia Tech	11	5	76	0	.45
19. Mike Echols, Wisconsin	11	5	110	1	.45
19. Richard Bryant, West Virginia	11	5	145	1	.45

PUNTING

(MIN 3.6 PUNTS PER GAME)	G	PUNTS	YDS	AVG
1. Preston Gruening, Minnesota	11	46	2080	45.22
2. Brian Morton, Duke	11	77	3478	45.17
3. Kevin Stemke, Wisconsin	12	65	2915	44.85
4. Brooks Barnard, Maryland	11	49	2191	44.71
5. Dave Zastudil, Ohio	11	47	2084	44.34
6. Casey Roussel, Tulane	11	59	2609	44.22
7. Jeff Ferguson, Oklahoma	12	48	2108	43.92
8. Dan Hadenfeldt, Nebraska	9	39	1708	43.79
9. Alan Rhine, Florida	12	47	2035	43.30
10. Aaron Edmonds, Brigham Young	12	67	2898	43.25
11. Damon Duval, Auburn	12	65	2811	43.25
12. Freddie Capshaw, Miami (Fla.)	11	49	2119	43.24
13. Nate Fikse, UCLA	11	72	3109	43.18
14. Brian Simnjamovski, San Diego St.	11	55	2356	42.84
15. Richie Butler, Arkansas	11	65	2784	42.83
16. Mike Abrams, Virginia	11	65	2768	42.58
17. Jason Baker, Iowa	12	74	3145	42.50
18. Tom Waring, Wyoming	11	59	2502	42.41
19. Jonathan Kilgo, Georgia	11	58	2450	42.24
20. Matt Brennie, Wake Forest	11	63	2648	42.03
21. Jeff Edwards, Boise St.	11	47	1975	42.02
22. Kent McCullough, Miami (Ohio)	11	56	2344	41.86
23. Adam Wulfeck, Cincinnati	11	56	2343	41.84
24. Travis Hale, Rice	11	54	2256	41.78
25. Dan Dyke, Georgia Tech	9	34	1420	41.76
26. J.J. Standring, Northwestern	11	64	2667	41.67
27. Nick Avondet, Eastern Mich.	11	71	2954	41.61
28. Nick Harris, California	11	73	3030	41.51
29. Steve Mullins, Utah St.	11	64	2647	41.36
30. Ray Cheetany, UNLV	12	64	2646	41.34

PUNT RETURNS

(MIN 1.2 RETURNS PER GAME)	G	RET	YDS	TD	AVG	RET/GM
1. Aaron Lockett, Kansas St.	13	22	501	3	22.77	1.69
2. Andre Davis, Virginia Tech	9	18	396	3	22.00	2.00
3. Justin McCareins, Northern Ill.	11	19	362	1	19.05	1.73
4. Santana Moss, Miami (Fla.)	11	36	655	4	18.19	3.27
5. Jemeel Powell, California	9	12	218	1	18.17	1.33
6. Pete Rebstock, Colorado St.	11	28	469	1	16.75	2.55
7. Troy Mason, UNLV	12	23	378	1	16.43	1.92
8. Joey Getherall, Notre Dame	11	24	392	2	16.33	2.18
9. J.T. Thatcher, Oklahoma	12	38	599	2	15.76	3.17
10. Don Shoals, Tulsa	12	17	266	2	15.65	1.42
11. Koren Robinson, North Carolina St.	11	14	218	1	15.57	1.27
12. Keith Stokes, East Caro.	10	27	416	1	15.41	2.70
13. Bosley Allen, North Carolina	11	28	421	2	15.04	2.55
14. Joshua Bush, Western Mich.	12	35	526	2	15.03	2.92
15. Bobby Newcombe, Nebraska	11	20	291	1	14.55	1.82
16. Ronyell Whitaker, Virginia Tech	11	17	245	0	14.41	1.55
17. Lito Sheppard, Florida	12	22	307	2	13.95	1.83
18. Johnson, Southern Miss.	11	24	333	0	13.88	2.18
19. Tellis Redmon, Minnesota	11	22	297	1	3.50	2.00
20. Clevan Thomas, Florida St.	12	15	201	0	13.40	1.25
21. Ira Gooch, Central Mich.	11	16	211	0	13.19	1.45
22. Nate Clements, Ohio St.	11	36	470	1	13.06	3.27
23. Wes Welker, Texas Tech	12	28	353	2	12.61	2.33
24. Joe Don Reames, Clemson	11	23	281	1	12.22	2.09
25. Eddie Tillitz, Miami (Ohio)	11	37	450	2	12.16	3.36
26. Maurice Hines, Marshall	12	17	205	1	12.06	1.42
27. Raynald Ray, Ohio	11	33	396	0	12.00	3.00
28. Antonio Bryant, Pittsburgh	10	15	178	0	11.87	1.50
29. Hodges Mitchell, Texas	11	36	427	0	11.86	3.27
30. Ronald Bellamy, Michigan	11	25	293	0	11.72	2.27

KICKOFF RETURNS

(MIN 1.2 RETURNS PER GAME)	G	RET	YDS	TD	AVG	RET/GM
1. LaTarence Dunbar, TCU	11	15	506	2	33.73	1.36
2. Zek Parker, Louisville	11	26	752	0	28.92	2.36
3. David Mikell, Boise St.	11	16	459	1	28.69	1.45
4. Julius Jones, Notre Dame	10	15	427	1	28.47	1.50
5. Ken-Yon Rambo, Ohio St.	11	17	478	0	28.12	1.55
6. Kahlil Hill, Iowa	12	25	680	1	27.20	2.08
7. Robert Kilow, Arkansas St.	10	27	724	0	26.81	2.70
8. Shawn Terry, West Virginia	11	27	720	2	26.67	2.45
9. Kyle Moore, Duke	10	13	335	0	25.77	1.30
10. James Hickenbocham, Arkansas St.	10	17	435	1	25.59	1.70
11. Koren Robinson, North Carolina St.	11	20	506	0	25.30	1.82
12. Victor Ike, Texas	11	20	495	0	24.75	1.82
13. Larry Johnson, Penn St.	12	18	444	0	24.67	1.50
14. John Stone, Wake Forest	11	32	789	1	24.66	2.91
15. Ray Perkins, Vanderbilt	11	14	344	0	24.57	1.27
16. Teddy Johnson, Northwestern	11	16	392	0	24.50	1.45
17. Kelly Campbell, Georgia Tech	11	26	632	0	24.31	2.36
18. Patrick Dyson, Utah	11	14	340	1	24.29	1.27
19. Curtis Jones, Marshall	12	15	364	0	24.27	1.25
20. Tim Carter, Auburn	11	19	461	1	24.26	1.73
21. Derrick Johnson, Washington	11	23	557	0	24.22	2.09
22. Emmett White, Utah St.	11	22	531	0	24.14	2.00
23. Will Allen, Syracuse	11	19	458	0	24.11	1.73
24. Allan Amundson, Oregon	11	22	525	0	23.86	2.00
25. Domanick Davis, LSU	11	24	572	0	23.83	2.18
26. Jermaine Mays, Minnesota	11	21	497	1	23.67	1.91
27. Derin Graham, Indiana	11	38	897	0	23.61	3.45
28. Leonard Scott, Tennessee	10	27	636	0	23.56	2.70
29. Joseph Echema, California	11	22	516	0	23.45	2.00
30. Vinny Sutherland, Purdue	10	20	467	0	23.35	2.00

FIELD GOALS

	G	FGA	FGM	AVG	FG/GM
1. Jonathan Ruffin, Cincinnati	11	29	26	.897	2.36
2. Dan Nystrom, Minnesota	11	34	22	.647	2.00
2. Kris Stockton, Texas	11	26	22	.846	2.00
4. Rhett Gallego, UAB	11	24	19	.792	1.73
4. Dave Adams, Air Force	11	24	19	.792	1.73
4. Dan Stultz, Ohio St.	11	23	19	.826	1.73
7. Alex Walls, Tennessee	11	20	18	.900	1.64
8. Owen Pochman, Brigham Young	12	24	19	.792	1.58
9. Steve Azar, Northern Ill.	9	15	14	.933	1.56
10. Jeff Reed, North Carolina	11	20	16	.800	1.45
10. Chris Kaylakie, TCU	11	18	16	.889	1.45
10. Seth Marler, Tulane	11	21	16	.762	1.45
13. Billy Bennett, Georgia	9	14	13	.929	1.44
14. Jaime Rheem, Kansas St.	12	20	17	.850	1.42
15. Mike Barth, Arizona St.	11	23	15	.652	1.36
15. Todd France, Toledo	11	19	15	.789	1.36
15. Terence Kitchens, Texas A&M	11	18	15	.833	1.36
15. Seth Hanson, Kentucky	11	17	15	.882	1.36
15. Nick Calaycay, Boise St.	11	16	15	.938	1.36
20. Jeff Chandler, Florida	12	19	16	.842	1.33
21. Javier Beorlegui, Central Fla.	11	18	14	.778	1.27
21. Brad Bohn, Utah St.	11	20	14	.700	1.27
21. John Markham, Vanderbilt	11	18	14	.778	1.27
21. Ryan Cesca, Oregon St.	11	17	14	.824	1.27
25. Luke Manget, Georgia Tech	10	16	12	.750	1.20
26. Sean Keel, Arizona	11	17	13	.765	1.18
26. Vitaly Pisetsky, Wisconsin	11	22	13	.591	1.18
26. Ricky Bishop, UTEP	11	18	13	.722	1.18
26. Josh Frankel, Oregon	11	25	13	.520	1.18
26. Kent Passingham, North Carolina St.	11	18	13	.722	1.18
31. Damon Duval, Auburn	12	18	14	.778	1.17
31. Ryan Primanti, Penn St.	12	20	14	.700	1.17
31. J.R. Jenkins, Marshall	12	20	14	.700	1.17
31. Nate Kaeding, Iowa	12	22	14	.636	1.17

SCORING

	G	TD	XPM	XPA	FGM	FGA	PTS	PTPG
1. Lee Suggs, Virginia Tech	11	28	0	0	0	0	168	15.27
2. LaDainian Tomlinson, TCU	11	22	0	0	0	0	132	12.00
2. Damien Anderson, Northwestern	11	22	0	0	0	0	132	12.00

4.	Dwone Hicks, Middle Tenn. St.	11	21	0	0	0	0	126	11.45
5.	Eric Crouch, Nebraska	11	20	0	0	0	0	120	10.91
6.	Thomas Hammock, Northern Ill.	9	16	0	0	0	0	96	10.67
7.	Chester Taylor, Toledo	11	19	0	0	0	0	114	10.36
8.	Ken Simonton, Oregon St.	11	18	0	0	0	0	110	10.00
9.	Deonce Whitaker, San Jose St.	10	16	0	0	0	0	98	9.80
10.	Kris Stockton, Texas	11	0	41	44	22	26	107	9.73
11.	Brock Forsey, Boise St.	10	16	0	0	0	0	6	9.60
12.	Nick Calaycay, Boise St.	11	0	59	61	15	16	104	9.45
12.	Jonathan Ruffin, Cincinnati	11	0	26	27	26	29	104	9.45
14.	Travis Zachery, Clemson	11	17	0	0	0	0	102	9.27
14.	Anthony Thomas, Michigan	11	17	0	0	0	0	102	9.27
14.	Deuce McAllister, Mississippi	11	17	0	0	0	0	102	9.27
17.	Robert Sanford, Western Mich.	12	18	0	0	0	0	108	9.00
18.	Chris Kaylakie, TCU	11	0	50	51	16	18	98	8.91
19.	Steve Azar, Northern Ill.	9	0	38	40	14	15	80	8.89
20.	Dan Nystrom, Minnesota	11	0	31	33	22	34	97	8.82
21.	Brandon Payne, Akron	11	16	0	0	0	0	96	8.73
22.	Todd France, Toledo	11	0	49	49	15	19	94	8.55
22.	Dave Adams, Air Force	11	0	37	39	19	24	94	8.55
24.	Alex Walls, Tennessee	11	0	39	39	18	20	93	8.45
25.	Jaime Rheem, Kansas St.	12	0	49	50	17	20	100	8.33
26.	William Green, Boston College	11	15	0	0	0	0	90	8.18
26.	Willie Alderson, Idaho	11	15	0	0	0	0	90	8.18
26.	Lee Mays, UTEP	11	15	0	0	0	0	90	8.18
26.	Emmett White, Utah St.	11	15	0	0	0	0	90	8.18
26.	Dan Stultz, Ohio St.	11	0	33	36	19	23	90	8.18

ALL-PURPOSE RUNNERS

		G	RUSH	REC	PR	KOR	YDS	YDS/GM
1.	Emmett White, Utah St.	11	132	592	183	531	2628	238.91
2.	LaDainian Tomlinson, TCU	11	215	40	0	0	2198	199.82
3.	Robert Kilow, Arkansas St.	10	42	100	133	724	1901	190.10
4.	Damien Anderson, Northwestern	11	191	120	0	0	2034	184.91
5.	Justin McCareins, Northern Ill.	11	73	116	362	411	2014	183.09
6.	Brock Forsey, Boise St.	10	914	399	0	517	1830	183.00
7.	Deonce Whitaker, San Jose St.	10	157	37	0	151	1765	176.50
8.	Hodges Mitchell, Texas	11	111	386	427	0	1931	175.55
9.	Michael Bennett, Wisconsin	10	159	23	0	94	1715	171.50
10.	Koren Robinson, North Carolina St.	11	95	106	218	506	1880	170.91
11.	Derek Watson, South Carolina	11	106	193	38	537	1834	166.73
12.	Willie Alderson, Idaho	11	119	420	0	200	1815	165.00
13.	Anthony Thomas, Michigan	11	155	239	0	0	1790	162.73
14.	Vinny Sutherland, Purdue	10	52	926	159	467	1604	160.40
15.	Tellis Redmon, Minnesota	11	112	318	297	8	1745	158.64
16.	Kelly Campbell, Georgia Tech	11	87	963	0	632	1682	152.91
17.	Antonio Bryant, Pittsburgh	10	0	130	178	0	1480	148.00
18.	Steve Smith, Utah	10	31	743	365	336	1475	147.50
19.	Santana Moss, Miami (Fla.)	11	201	748	655	0	1604	145.82
20.	Chester Taylor, Toledo	11	147	129	0	0	1599	145.36
21.	Ennis Haywood, Iowa St.	10	123	211	0	0	1448	144.80
22.	Keith Stokes, East Caro.	10	66	449	416	503	1434	143.40
23.	John Simon, Louisiana Tech	12	565	711	74	345	1695	141.25
24.	Tanardo Sharps, Temple	11	103	107	0	397	1542	140.18
25.	Dicenzo Miller, Mississippi St.	11	100	344	102	62	1513	137.55
26.	Rudi Johnson, Auburn	12	156	70	0	0	1637	136.42
27.	Deuce McAllister, Mississippi	11	767	190	191	340	1488	135.27
27.	Ken Simonton, Oregon St.	11	147	14	0	0	1488	135.27
29.	Robert Sanford, Western Mich.	12	157	52	0	0	1623	135.25
30.	Michael Wallace, Army	10	115	187	0	0	1344	34.40

2000 Division I-A Team Statistics

RUSHING OFFENSE

		G	RSH	NET	AVG	YDSPG
1.	Nebraska	11	636	3842	6.04	349.27
2.	Ohio	11	646	3553	5.50	323.00
3.	Air Force	11	647	3244	5.01	294.91
4.	TCU	11	588	3032	5.16	275.64
5.	Virginia Tech	11	570	2975	5.22	270.45
6.	New Mexico St.	11	535	2972	5.56	270.18
7.	Indiana	11	505	2930	5.80	266.36
8.	Northwestern	11	565	2830	5.01	257.27
9.	Toledo	11	514	2792	5.43	253.82
10.	Clemson	11	557	2600	4.67	236.36
11.	Rice	11	626	2563	4.09	233.00
12.	Northern Ill.	11	539	2509	4.65	228.09
13.	UNLV	12	547	2734	5.00	227.83
14.	Michigan	11	500	2422	4.84	220.18
15.	Notre Dame	11	538	2349	4.37	213.55
16.	Washington	11	487	2329	4.78	211.73
17.	Iowa St.	11	447	2288	5.12	208.00
18.	Syracuse	11	509	2279	4.48	207.18
19.	Akron	11	490	2273	4.64	206.64
20.	Boston College	11	461	2211	4.80	201.00
21.	Wisconsin	12	573	2381	4.16	198.42
22.	Kansas St.	13	595	2575	4.33	198.08
23.	Miami (Fla.)	11	434	2143	4.94	194.82
24.	Middle Tenn. St.	11	404	2138	5.29	194.36
25.	Mississippi St.	11	461	2132	4.62	193.82
26.	San Jose St.	12	429	2269	5.29	189.08
27.	Minnesota	11	483	2063	4.27	187.55
28.	Oregon St.	11	497	2047	4.12	186.09
29.	Navy	11	552	1960	3.55	178.18
30.	Boise St.	11	440	1922	4.37	174.73
31.	Michigan St.	11	478	1874	3.92	170.36
32.	Western Mich.	12	492	2022	4.11	168.50
33.	Florida St.	12	455	1980	4.35	165.00
34.	Ball St.	11	537	1813	3.38	164.82
35.	Georgia Tech	11	466	1807	3.88	164.27

PASSING OFFENSE

		G	ATT	COM	YDS	YDPG
1.	Florida St.	12	469	290	4608	384.0
2.	Kentucky	11	564	322	3689	335.4
3.	Tulane	11	506	288	3569	324.5
4.	Hawaii	12	609	309	3875	322.9
5.	Boise St.	11	372	225	3537	321.5
6.	Purdue	11	489	292	3438	312.5
7.	Louisiana Tech	12	546	357	3715	309.6
8.	Florida	12	466	265	3698	308.2
9.	Idaho	11	428	265	3357	305.2
10.	Marshall	12	483	293	3584	298.7
11.	Texas Tech	12	613	372	3548	295.7
12.	Central Fla.	11	415	249	3247	295.2
13.	Oklahoma	12	450	289	3536	294.7
14.	Texas	11	397	220	3225	293.2
15.	North Carolina St.	11	455	242	3218	292.5
16.	Brigham Young	12	487	272	3295	274.6
17.	Georgia Tech	11	374	231	2982	271.1
18.	Pittsburgh	11	339	185	2964	269.5
19.	Houston	11	473	272	2955	268.6
20.	Arizona St.	11	407	191	2935	266.8
21.	Utah St.	11	425	218	2928	266.2
22.	Miami (Fla.)	11	340	198	2926	266.0
23.	UCLA	11	363	196	2904	264.0
24.	Southern California	12	446	245	3148	262.3
25.	Oregon	11	392	202	2835	257.7
26.	Louisville	11	389	234	2822	256.5
27.	UTEP	11	354	207	2730	248.2
28.	Colorado St.	11	356	210	2717	247.0
29.	LSU	11	353	183	2698	245.3
30.	Nevada	12	470	230	2937	244.8
31.	Washington St.	11	341	172	2656	241.5
32.	Colorado	11	368	215	2640	240.0
33.	Middle Tenn. St.	11	366	218	2631	239.2
34.	Stanford	11	385	186	2605	236.8
35.	Texas A&M	11	355	211	2588	235.3

TOTAL OFFENSE

		G	PL	YDS	AVG	TD	YDSPG
1.	Florida St.	12	924	6588	7.13	67	549.00
2.	Boise St.	11	812	5459	6.72	64	496.27
3.	Northwestern	11	911	5232	5.74	56	475.64
4.	Purdue	11	904	5183	5.73	47	471.18
5.	Miami (Fla.)	11	774	5069	6.55	63	460.82
6.	Nebraska	11	808	5059	6.26	63	459.91
7.	Tulane	11	897	4989	5.56	40	453.55
8.	Idaho	11	846	4985	5.89	42	453.18
9.	Air Force	11	852	4971	5.83	47	451.91
10.	Clemson	11	853	4911	5.76	53	446.45
11.	Kentucky	11	869	4900	5.64	30	445.45
11.	Michigan	11	800	4900	6.13	49	445.45
13.	Indiana	11	803	4830	6.01	45	439.09
14.	Texas	11	803	4825	6.01	51	438.64
15.	Georgia Tech	11	840	4789	5.70	48	435.36
16.	Middle Tenn. St.	11	770	4769	6.19	46	433.55
17.	New Mexico St.	11	802	4724	5.89	39	429.45
18.	Oklahoma	12	860	5151	5.99	61	429.25
19.	Northern Ill.	11	813	4706	5.79	51	427.82
20.	Virginia Tech	11	796	4690	5.89	61	426.36
21.	Iowa St.	11	788	4660	5.91	39	423.64
22.	Minnesota	11	805	4647	5.77	40	422.45
23.	TCU	11	772	4632	6.00	52	421.09
24.	Florida	12	827	5024	6.07	58	418.67

25. Ohio	11	780	4599	5.90	44	418.09
26. San Jose St.	12	806	5008	6.21	52	417.33
27. Akron	11	778	4589	5.90	43	417.18
28. Southern California	12	898	4991	5.56	41	415.92
29. Boston College	11	768	4564	5.94	45	414.91
30. Louisiana Tech	12	877	4955	5.65	41	412.92
31. Marshall	12	863	4946	5.73	43	412.17
32. Oregon St.	11	817	4526	5.54	45	411.45
33. Kansas St.	13	933	5330	5.71	66	410.00
34. Oregon	11	828	4498	5.43	40	408.91
35. Washington	11	812	4487	5.53	46	407.91

SCORING OFFENSE

	G	PTS	AVG
1. Boise St.	11	494	44.91
2. Miami (Fla.)	11	469	42.64
3. Florida St.	12	509	42.42
4. Nebraska	11	456	41.45
5. Virginia Tech	11	443	40.27
6. Kansas St.	13	514	39.54
7. Oklahoma	12	468	39.00
8. Texas	11	425	38.64
9. Northwestern	11	424	38.55
10. Florida	12	448	37.33
11. TCU	11	410	37.27
12. Northern Ill.	11	409	37.18
13. Toledo	11	400	36.36
14. Clemson	11	396	36.00
15. Louisville	11	388	35.27
16. Air Force	11	384	34.91
17. Michigan	11	373	33.91
18. Georgia Tech	11	372	33.82
19. Oregon St.	11	359	32.64
19. Tennessee	11	359	32.64
21. Purdue	11	357	32.45
22. UTEP	11	355	32.27
23. Washington	11	353	32.09
24. Middle Tenn. St.	11	350	31.82
25. Boston College	11	347	31.55
25. Mississippi St.	11	347	31.55
27. Minnesota	11	345	31.36
28. Notre Dame	11	344	31.27
29. Ohio	11	343	31.18
30. San Jose St.	12	374	31.17
31. Colorado St.	11	341	31.00
31. North Carolina St.	11	341	31.00
33. Indiana	11	337	30.64
34. Akron	11	333	30.27
34. Central Fla.	11	333	30.27
34. UCLA	11	333	30.27

RUSHING DEFENSE

	G	RSH	NET	AVG	YDSPG
1. Memphis	11	346	800	2.31	72.7
2. Florida St.	12	387	887	2.29	73.9
3. Tennessee	11	338	817	2.42	74.3
4. Louisville	11	395	879	2.23	79.9
5. Toledo	11	365	897	2.46	81.5
6. UAB	11	386	919	2.38	83.5
7. TCU	11	395	928	2.35	84.4
8. Arizona	11	393	973	2.48	88.5
9. Ohio St.	11	396	1008	2.55	91.6
10. Oregon St.	11	385	1024	2.66	93.1
11. Texas	11	387	1034	2.67	94.0
12. Georgia Tech	11	371	1039	2.80	94.5
13. Mississippi St.	11	372	1073	2.88	97.5
14. Kansas St.	13	473	1276	2.70	98.2
15. Auburn	12	356	1180	3.31	98.3
16. Virginia Tech	11	374	1092	2.92	99.3
17. Pittsburgh	11	417	1097	2.63	99.7
18. Clemson	11	397	1120	2.82	101.8
19. North Carolina	11	410	1138	2.78	103.5
20. Western Mich.	12	458	1263	2.76	105.3
21. Southern Miss.	11	414	1162	2.81	105.6
22. Texas A&M	11	389	1169	3.01	106.3
23. Oklahoma	12	412	1298	3.15	108.2
24. California	11	457	1219	2.67	110.8
25. Georgia	11	388	1222	3.15	111.1
26. Miami (Fla.)	11	393	1240	3.16	112.7
27. Nebraska	11	345	1249	3.62	113.5
28. South Carolina	11	386	1266	3.28	115.1
29. New Mexico	12	431	1384	3.21	115.3
30. Brigham Young	12	441	1469	3.33	122.4
31. Oregon	11	386	1364	3.53	124.0
32. Alabama	11	423	1379	3.26	125.4
33. Southern California	12	485	1509	3.11	125.8
34. Oklahoma St.	11	374	1386	3.71	126.0
35. Utah	11	447	1410	3.15	128.2

PASS DEFENSE

	G	ATT	COM	PCT	INT	YDS	TD	YDSPG
1. Central Mich.	11	272	139	51.10	11	1647	12	149.73
2. Arkansas	11	302	143	47.35	10	1683	14	153.00
3. Utah	11	288	137	47.57	7	1761	12	160.09
4. TCU	11	323	143	44.27	15	1767	10	160.64
5. Southern Miss.	11	370	186	50.27	14	1788	9	162.55
6. Texas Tech	12	343	177	51.60	15	1969	7	164.08
7. Michigan St.	11	310	160	51.61	12	1805	11	164.09
8. Boston College	11	289	138	47.75	16	1850	13	168.18
9. Oklahoma	12	397	196	49.37	22	2049	9	170.75
10. Kansas St.	13	399	204	51.13	20	2241	8	172.38
11. Tulsa	12	302	168	55.63	10	2112	19	176.00
12. Syracuse	11	326	148	45.40	7	1937	9	176.09
13. Western Mich.	12	345	179	51.88	9	2136	10	178.00
14. Illinois	11	323	177	54.80	12	1979	8	179.91
15. Marshall	12	340	191	56.18	16	2166	17	180.50
16. Colorado St.	11	311	170	54.66	13	1998	12	181.64
17. Texas	11	379	171	45.12	17	2027	8	184.27
18. North Carolina St.	11	318	176	55.35	10	2030	14	184.55
19. Toledo	11	338	180	53.25	15	2062	5	187.45
20. Mississippi	11	341	160	46.92	18	2064	9	187.64
21. La.-Monroe	11	279	158	56.63	5	2089	23	189.91
22. Miami (Ohio)	11	302	162	53.64	12	2111	15	191.91
23. Central Fla.	11	328	177	53.96	15	2122	11	192.91
24. South Carolina	11	367	201	54.77	18	2123	5	193.00
25. Minnesota	11	336	172	51.19	6	2127	15	193.36
26. New Mexico	12	375	191	50.93	15	2329	12	194.08
27. Hawaii	12	331	184	55.59	12	2333	18	194.42
28. Temple	11	308	169	54.87	10	2162	14	196.55
29. North Texas	11	341	209	61.29	10	2166	9	196.91
30. Louisiana Tech	12	346	196	56.65	11	2370	19	197.50
31. Ball St.	11	315	149	47.30	6	2196	20	199.64
32. Rutgers	11	306	181	59.15	8	2213	14	201.18
33. Purdue	11	327	196	59.94	10	2215	13	201.36
34. Nevada	12	333	188	56.46	13	2419	16	201.58
35. Georgia	11	385	220	57.14	19	2227	10	202.45

TOTAL DEFENSE

	G	PL	YDS	AVG	TD	YDSPG
1. TCU	11	718	2695	3.75	13	245.00
2. Southern Miss.	11	784	2950	3.76	21	268.18
3. Toledo	11	703	2959	4.21	16	269.00
4. Kansas St.	13	872	3517	4.03	29	270.54
5. Memphis	11	755	3028	4.01	20	275.27
6. Florida St.	12	834	3324	3.99	15	277.00
7. Texas	11	766	3061	4.00	26	278.27
8. Oklahoma	12	809	3347	4.14	25	278.92
9. Western Mich.	12	803	3399	4.23	16	283.25
10. Utah	11	735	3171	4.31	24	288.27
11. UAB	11	759	3200	4.22	21	290.91
12. Arkansas	11	714	3213	4.50	34	292.09
13. Tennessee	11	704	3239	4.60	26	294.45
14. Auburn	12	771	3640	4.72	30	303.33
15. Louisville	11	792	3346	4.22	32	304.18
16. South Carolina	11	753	3389	4.50	19	308.09
17. New Mexico	12	806	3713	4.61	31	309.42
18. Syracuse	11	722	3431	4.75	24	311.91
19. Georgia	11	773	3449	4.46	23	313.55
20. Oregon St.	11	753	3458	4.59	23	314.36
21. Arizona	11	769	3492	4.54	27	317.45
22. Michigan St.	11	730	3501	4.80	29	318.27
23. Ohio St.	11	790	3513	4.45	25	319.36
24. Texas Tech	12	838	3848	4.59	30	320.67
25. Texas A&M	11	755	3538	4.69	23	321.64
26. Nebraska	11	738	3540	4.80	26	321.82
27. Virginia Tech	11	728	3560	4.89	36	323.64
28. Central Fla.	11	788	3562	4.52	29	323.82
29. Pittsburgh	11	804	3583	4.46	26	325.73
30. North Carolina	11	746	3602	4.83	38	327.45
31. Colorado St.	11	741	3609	4.87	25	328.09
32. Oregon	11	737	3642	4.94	29	331.09
33. Temple	11	745	3666	4.92	36	333.27
34. Miami (Fla.)	11	821	3667	4.47	23	333.36
35. Alabama	11	767	3707	4.83	29	337.00

SCORING DEFENSE

	G	PTS	PTPG
1. TCU	11	106	9.6
2. Florida St.	12	123	10.3
3. Toledo	11	125	11.4
4. Western Mich.	12	139	11.6
5. Miami (Fla.)	11	170	15.5
6. South Carolina	11	174	15.8
7. Oklahoma	12	192	16.0
8. Southern Miss.	11	182	16.5
9. UAB	11	192	17.5
10. Texas A&M	11	196	17.8
11. Texas	11	197	17.9
12. Georgia	11	198	18.0

12. Ohio St.	11	198	18.0
14. Memphis	11	199	18.1
15. Michigan	11	201	18.3
16. Oregon St.	11	203	18.5
17. Kansas St.	13	240	18.5
18. Utah	11	207	18.8
19. Colorado St.	11	208	18.9
19. Ohio	11	208	18.9
21. Georgia Tech	11	209	19.0
22. Pittsburgh	11	210	19.1
23. Clemson	11	212	19.3
23. Tennessee	11	212	19.3
23. Syracuse	11	212	19.3
26. Nebraska	11	213	19.4
27. Fresno St.	11	214	19.5
28. Auburn	12	235	19.6
29. Florida	12	236	19.7
30. Texas Tech	12	238	19.8
31. Oregon	11	219	19.9
32. Central Fla.	11	221	20.1
32. LSU	11	221	20.1
34. Wisconsin	12	245	20.4
35. Notre Dame	11	226	20.5

NET PUNTING

	G	PUNTS	YDS	AVG	RET	RET YDS	NET AVG
1. Wisconsin	12	65	2915	44.85	25	127	42.89
2. Minnesota	11	47	2080	44.26	22	159	40.87
3. Tulane	11	59	2609	44.22	27	259	39.83
4. Ohio	10	48	2109	43.94	22	204	39.69
5. Virginia	11	65	2768	42.58	17	193	39.62
6. Duke	11	78	3514	45.05	35	429	39.55
7. Georgia	11	58	2450	42.24	26	158	39.52
8. Iowa	12	74	3145	42.50	38	256	39.04
9. Miami (Fla.)	11	50	2119	42.38	23	170	38.98
10. Notre Dame	11	64	2616	40.88	31	156	38.44
11. Alabama	11	61	2443	40.05	19	102	38.38
12. Mississippi St.	11	64	2601	40.64	25	172	37.95
13. Maryland	11	62	2618	42.23	23	271	37.85
14. Oregon	11	68	2647	38.93	21	85	37.68
15. Auburn	12	66	2811	42.59	25	331	37.58
16. TCU	11	47	1872	39.83	18	106	37.57
17. Georgia Tech	10	50	2081	41.62	27	203	37.56
18. UCLA	11	74	3185	43.04	35	407	37.54
19. Tennessee	11	61	2465	40.41	31	176	37.52
20. Brigham Young	12	67	2898	43.25	37	386	37.49
21. Michigan St.	11	63	2528	40.13	24	176	37.33
22. Northwestern	11	64	2667	41.67	24	323	36.63
23. Oklahoma	12	52	2173	41.79	27	274	36.52
24. Arkansas	11	67	2793	41.69	35	349	36.48
25. San Jose St.	12	60	2277	37.95	20	89	36.47
26. Colorado St.	11	52	2035	39.13	22	141	36.42
27. Vanderbilt	11	65	2473	38.05	20	108	36.38
28. Ohio St.	11	56	2156	38.50	20	121	36.34
29. Illinois	11	55	2197	39.95	32	199	36.33
30. Marshall	12	62	2506	40.42	23	257	36.27
31. Arizona St.	11	83	3288	39.61	36	289	36.13
32. Michigan	11	54	2117	39.20	24	168	36.09
33. UNLV	12	67	2646	39.49	27	228	36.09
34. Wake Forest	11	64	2684	41.94	30	377	36.05
35. Oregon St.	11	66	2609	39.53	28	232	36.02

PUNT RETURNS

	G	RET	YDS	TD	AVG
1. Virginia Tech	11	39	711	4	18.23
2. Colorado	10	16	285	2	17.81
3. Miami (Fla.)	11	46	819	5	17.80
4. Kansas St.	12	41	708	4	17.27
5. Army	10	17	290	3	17.06
6. Northern Ill.	10	32	518	1	16.19
7. Colorado St.	10	41	645	1	15.73
8. UNLV	10	27	417	2	15.44
9. Oklahoma	12	42	646	2	15.38
10. Western Mich.	12	37	567	2	15.32
11. Tulsa	8	19	290	2	15.26
12. Notre Dame	11	32	484	2	15.13
13. Florida	12	30	450	2	15.00
14. Clemson	10	35	524	2	14.97
15. East Caro.	11	32	473	2	14.78
16. North Carolina St.	9	19	256	1	13.47
17. Minnesota	11	34	452	1	13.29
18. North Carolina	11	37	485	2	13.11
19. Southern Miss.	11	35	457	0	13.06
20. Arkansas St.	7	14	181	2	12.93
21. Ohio St.	9	37	467	1	12.62
22. Fresno St.	9	25	314	1	12.56
23. Miami (Ohio)	11	40	491	2	12.28
24. North Texas	8	17	208	1	12.24
25. Illinois	10	22	267	1	12.14
26. Alabama	9	16	194	1	12.13
27. Arizona	11	34	408	2	12.00
27. Buffalo	9	17	204	0	12.00
29. Ohio	11	38	454	0	11.95
30. Mississippi	10	19	226	1	11.89
31. Texas A&M	11	30	351	0	11.70
32. Texas	9	39	453	0	11.62
33. Central Mich.	9	23	260	0	11.30
34. Michigan	10	32	361	1	11.28
35. LSU	9	27	298	0	11.04

KICKOFF RETURNS

	G	KRET	YDS	TD	AVG
1. TCU	10	21	605	2	28.81
2. Louisville	10	31	810	0	26.13
3. Notre Dame	11	36	897	1	24.92
4. Ohio St.	11	33	813	0	24.64
5. Arkansas St.	11	52	1256	1	24.15
6. Georgia Tech	11	30	706	0	23.53
7. Tennessee	10	32	751	0	23.47
8. Iowa	12	50	1171	1	23.42
9. North Carolina St.	11	36	826	0	22.94
10. Texas	9	31	711	0	22.94
11. Boise St.	11	44	1007	1	22.89
12. Miami (Fla.)	10	28	636	0	22.71
13. Syracuse	11	35	790	0	22.57
14. Oregon	11	37	834	0	22.54
15. Duke	11	53	1183	0	22.32
16. Colorado St.	11	35	778	1	22.23
17. Vanderbilt	10	34	749	0	22.03
18. Arizona	11	32	701	0	21.91
19. Utah	10	34	743	1	21.85
20. Wake Forest	11	50	1078	1	21.56
21. Mississippi St.	11	41	883	0	21.54
22. Michigan St.	11	37	794	0	21.46
23. Air Force	11	25	534	0	21.36
24. Washington	11	37	783	0	21.16
25. New Mexico	10	26	550	0	21.15
26. Penn St.	12	43	896	0	20.84
27. Purdue	11	37	767	0	20.73
28. UNLV	12	33	684	0	20.73
29. Oregon St.	11	31	641	0	20.68
30. Northern Ill.	11	40	826	0	20.65
31. Oklahoma	11	28	577	0	20.61
32. West Virginia	11	45	923	2	20.51
33. Colorado	10	26	532	0	20.46
34. Tulane	11	48	982	0	20.46
35. Clemson	9	26	531	0	20.42

TURNOVER MARGIN

		TURNOVERS GAINED			TURNOVERS LOST			MARGIN
	G	FUM	INT	TOTAL	FUM	INT	TOTAL	/GAME
1. Toledo	11	16	15	31	5	4	9	2.00
2. Georgia Tech	11	15	15	30	6	6	12	1.64
3. Florida	12	16	24	40	9	12	21	1.58
4. Oregon St.	11	10	22	32	9	7	16	1.45
5. Notre Dame	11	9	13	22	4	4	8	1.27
6. Cincinnati	11	15	19	34	9	13	22	1.09
6. Miami (Fla.)	11	10	23	33	16	5	21	1.09
6. Northwestern	11	13	12	25	6	7	13	1.09
6. Louisville	11	11	27	38	14	12	26	1.09
10. Arizona St.	11	23	13	36	13	12	25	1.00
10. Michigan	11	12	14	26	10	5	15	1.00
10. Boston College	11	10	16	26	3	12	15	1.00
13. Arizona	11	17	16	33	11	12	23	.91
13. Ohio St.	11	10	18	28	6	12	18	.91
13. TCU	11	12	15	27	9	8	17	.91
16. Florida St.	12	13	19	32	8	14	22	.83
17. Mississippi St.	11	14	19	33	15	9	24	.82
17. Rice	11	9	18	27	15	3	18	.82
19. Boise St.	11	10	13	23	7	8	15	.73
19. Northern Ill.	11	15	12	27	8	11	19	.73
19. Texas	11	16	17	33	11	14	25	.73
22. New Mexico	12	12	15	27	9	10	19	.67
23. Air Force	11	12	7	19	6	6	12	.64
23. Akron	11	14	12	26	8	11	19	.64
23. West Virginia	11	10	19	29	12	10	22	.64
23. UCLA	11	17	12	29	11	11	22	.64
23. Mississippi	11	7	18	25	5	13	18	.64
28. Texas A&M	11	5	18	23	8	9	17	.55
28. Virginia Tech	11	6	23	29	16	7	23	.55
30. Oklahoma	12	11	22	33	10	17	27	.50
30. San Jose St.	12	12	15	27	8	13	21	.50
30. Wisconsin	12	6	20	26	11	9	20	.50
30. Texas Tech	12	14	15	29	5	18	23	.50
34. Kansas St.	13	9	20	29	10	13	23	.46
35. Clemson	11	9	14	23	9	9	18	.45
35. Iowa St.	11	13	10	23	5	13	18	.45
35. Colorado	11	14	11	25	11	9	20	.45

2001-02 Bowl Schedule

Date	Bowl	Site	Time*	Matchup
Dec. 19	New Orleans	New Orleans, La.	TBA	Sun Belt champ vs. Mountain West No. 3
Dec. 19	GMAC	Mobile, Ala.	8 p.m.	C-USA No. 2 vs. MAC Nos. 1 or 2
Dec. 20	Las Vegas	Las Vegas	8 p.m.	Mountain West No. 2 vs. at-large
Dec. 27	Independence	Shreveport, La.	8 p.m.	SEC vs. Big 12 No. 6
Dec. 28	galleryfurniture.com	Houston	TBA	Big 12 No. 6 vs. C-USA No. 3
Dec. 28/31	Humanitarian	Boise, Idaho	TBA	WAC Nos. 1 or 2 vs. at-large
Dec. 28	Music City	Nashville	5 p.m.	SEC vs. Big Ten
Dec. 28	Holiday	San Diego	8:30 p.m.	Pac-10 No. 2 vs. Big 12 No. 3
Dec. 29	Motor City	Pontiac, Mich.	Noon	MAC Nos. 1 or 2 vs. C-USA No. 4
Dec. 29	Alamo	San Antonio	TBA	Big 12 No. 4 vs. Big Ten No. 4
Dec. 29	Insight.com	Phoenix	5 p.m.	Big 12 No. 5 vs. Big East No. 3*
Dec. 30	San Francisco Jeep	San Francisco	5 p.m.	Pac-10 Nos. 4 or 5 vs. Big East No. 5*
Dec. 31	Sun	El Paso, Texas	2 p.m.	Big Ten No. 5 vs. Pac-10 No. 3
Dec. 31	Liberty	Memphis	4 p.m.	Mountain West champ vs. C-USA champ
Dec. 31	Peach	Atlanta	7:30 p.m.	SEC No. 4 vs. ACC No. 3
Dec. 31	Silicon Valley	San Jose, Calif.	TBA	WAC Nos. 1 or 2 vs. at-large
Jan. 1	Cotton	Dallas	11 a.m.	Big 12 No. 2 vs. SEC
Jan. 1	Outback	Tampa	11 a.m.	SEC vs. Big Ten No. 3
Jan. 1	Gator	Jacksonville, Fla.	12:30 p.m.	ACC No. 2 vs. Big East No. 2*
Jan. 1	Florida Citrus	Orlando	1 p.m.	Big Ten No. 2 vs. SEC
Jan. 1	Fiesta	Tempe, Ariz.	3 p.m.	BCS vs. BCS
Jan. 1	Sugar	New Orleans	8:30 p.m.	BCS vs. BCS
Jan. 2	Jeep Seattle	Seattle	5 p.m.	Pac-10 Nos. 4 or 5 vs. ACC No. 4
Jan. 2	Orange	Miami	8 p.m.	BCS vs. BCS
Jan. 3	Rose	Pasadena, Calif.	8 p.m.	BCS No. 1 vs. BCS No. 2

Kickoff times EST
* — Bowl can select Notre Dame if eligible

2000-01 Bowl Results

GMAC MOBILE ALABAMA BOWL
Southern Miss 28, TCU 21

EASPORTS LAS VEGAS BOWL
UNLV 31, Arkansas 14

JEEP OAHU BOWL
Georgia 37, Virginia 14

JEEP ALOHA BOWL
Boston College 31, Arizona State 14

MOTOR CITY
Marshall 25, Cincinnati 14

GALLERYFURNITURE.COM BOWL
East Carolina 40, Texas Tech 27

CRUCIAL.COM HUMANITARIAN BOWL
Boise State 38, UTEP 23

INSIGHT.COM BOWL
Iowa State 37, Pittsburgh 29

MICRONPC.COM BOWL
North Carolina State 38, Minnesota 30

MUSIC CITY BOWL
West Virginia 49, Ole Miss 38

WELLS FARGO SUN BOWL
Wisconsin 21, UCLA 20

AXA LIBERTY BOWL
Colorado State 22, Louisville 17

CULLIGAN HOLIDAY BOWL
Oregon 35, Texas 30

CHICK-FIL-A PEACH BOWL
LSU 28, Georgia Tech 14

SYLVANIA ALAMO BOWL
Nebraska 66, Northwestern 17

SILICON VALLEY CLASSIC BOWL
Air Force 37, Fresno State 34

SANFORD INDEPENDENCE BOWL
Mississippi State 43, Texas A&M 41

OUTBACK BOWL
South Carolina 24, Ohio State 7

SBC COTTON BOWL
Kansas State 35, Tennessee 21

TOYOTA GATOR BOWL
Virginia Tech 41, Clemson 20

CAPITALONE FLORIDA CITRUS BOWL
Michigan 31, Auburn 28

ROSE BOWL PRESENTED BY AT&T
Washington 34, Purdue 24

TOSTITOS FIESTA BOWL
Oregon State 41, Notre Dame 9

NOKIA SUGAR BOWL
Miami 37, Florida 20

FEDEX ORANGE BOWL
Oklahoma 13, Florida State 2